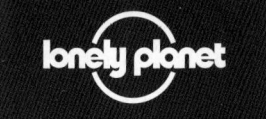

lonely planet

East Coast Australia

Lindsay Brown
Sandra Bao, Simone Egger, Cath Lanigan, Simon Sellars, Ryan ver Berkmoes

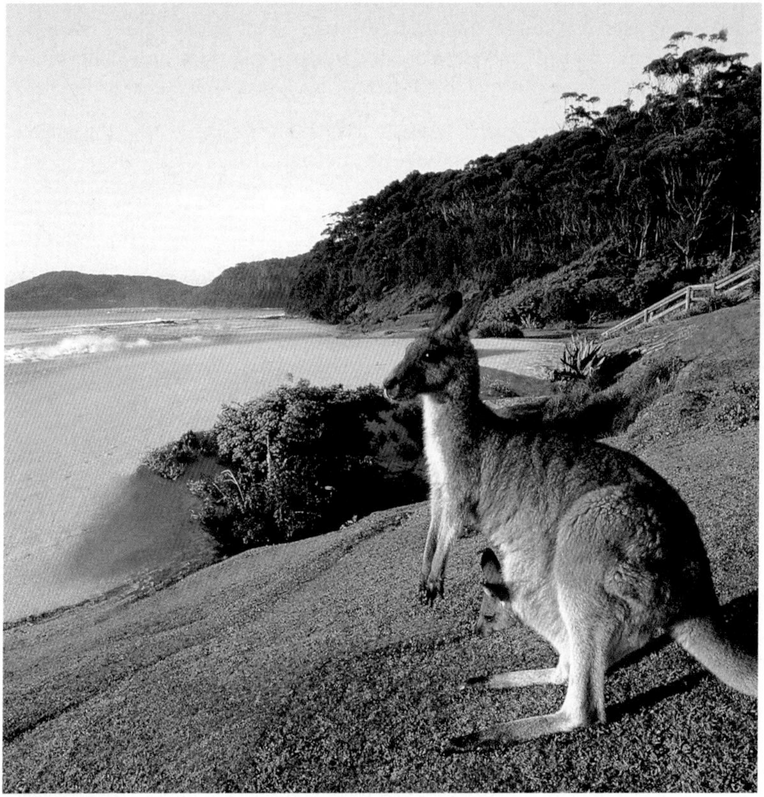

Destination East Coast Australia

Images from the East Coast are among the first things tourists associate with Australia: the Sydney Harbour Bridge; sea and sand; the glitz of the north. The East Coast is an immersive experience, and its highways and byways can whisk you from urban surrounds to beachside towns and tropical climes before you can say 'roadkill'.

Even the major cities are a study in contrasts. There's Melbourne, with its European-inspired café society crossbred with Australia's boldest artistic community. There's Sydney, with a host of natural attractions, including its prominent harbour, and a cockiness that grabs you by the scruff of the neck. Then there's Brisbane, once the ugly duckling, now blooming with sultry vibes and a relaxed attitude.

In among the urban sprawls, it's 'choose your own adventure' time. Want to chase the sun and surf (or perhaps other travellers)? Get a 'Brazilian', pack your wax and boards and hightail it to loose-as-a-goose Byron Bay. Fancy a bit of green? Try the singular Cape Tribulation coast, where the steamy rainforest meets the beach. Got what it takes to sleep with the fishes? Strap on a snorkel and get jiggy with it in the crystal-clear waters of the Great Barrier Reef.

Elsewhere, why don't you watch whales, cultivate your dreadlocks, feed the dolphins, sink a stubby, canoe through the everglades, sail through archipelagos, indulge in top-notch wine and cheese…

Get the picture?

Loads of Aussies travel the East Coast, too, and that's a good sign. You know you're backing the right horse when the locals thank their lucky stars they've got the best backyard around.

OLIVER STREWE

Wilderness & Wildlife

Camp at Tidal River, Wilsons Promontory National Park (p108), Victoria

Enjoy the serenity at Watego's Beach (p262), NSW

Meet a humpback whale, Hervey Bay (p353), Queensland

OTHER HIGHLIGHTS

- A boat tour to Montague Island (p160), on the south coast of NSW, to experience its diverse array of wildlife
- The dunes of enigmatic Fraser Island (p357), Fraser Coast, Queensland
- Rainforests and platypuses at Eungella National Park (p394), Whitsunday Coast, Queensland

4

Beaches & Reefs

DAVID WALL

Put some footprints on a beach at Surfers Paradise (p285), Queensland

Take a running jump at someone's sand castle, Byron Bay (p260), NSW

DALLAS STRIBLEY

Laze on a quiet beach like this one near Cairns (p450) in far north Queensland

PETER HENDRIE

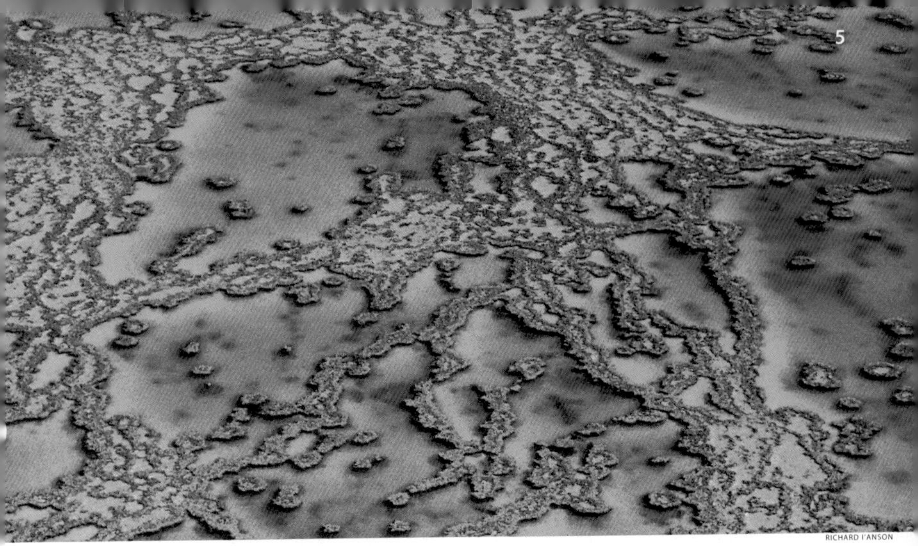

RICHARD I'ANSON

Fly over the Great Barrier Reef (p377), Queensland

MICHAEL AW

Swim among the fish on the Great Barrier Reef (p377), Queensland

OTHER HIGHLIGHTS

- Mission Beach (p430), Queensland, for sunbathing, lunching or strolling in the nearby rainforest
- The tropical beaches of Great Keppel Island (p382), Capricorn Coast, Queensland

Walk to Sealers Cove, Wilsons Promontory National Park (p110), Victoria

WILL SALTER

Outdoor Activities

RICHARD I'ANSON

Cruise around the Whitsunday Islands (p396), Queensland

IAN CONNELLAN

Take a break to absorb the view north from Crescent Head (p239), NSW

Snorkel off Lady Elliot Island (p367), Great Barrier Reef, Queensland

BOB CHARLTON

OTHER HIGHLIGHTS

- Agnes Water (p370), Queensland's most northerly surf beach
- Ku-ring-gai Chase National Park (p212) and the Blue Mountains (p207), NSW
- Cycling a section of the East Coast (p50) – your choice of coast, mountains or café hopping

Country Style

Find your way to quaint Walhalla (p113),
Victoria

CHRISTOPHER GROENHOUT

DALLAS STRIBLEY

Make friends with a pelican on the banks of the
Hastings River, Port Macquarie (p232), NSW

Amble around tiny Tilba (p161), south coast NSW

WAYNE WALTON

City Life

Stroll along South Bank (p301), Brisbane, Queensland

Join the crowds to watch a game of football at the Melbourne Cricket Ground (p76), Victoria

OTHER HIGHLIGHTS

- The atmosphere of sand and surf, continental café scene and stylish nightlife that is St Kilda (p78) in Melbourne, Victoria
- Drinking, partying and staying up late in Sydney's lively Kings Cross (p186), NSW

Check out Sydney's Opera House (p181) and Harbour Bridge (p181), NSW, which are impressive from just about any angle

Contents

Regional Map Contents

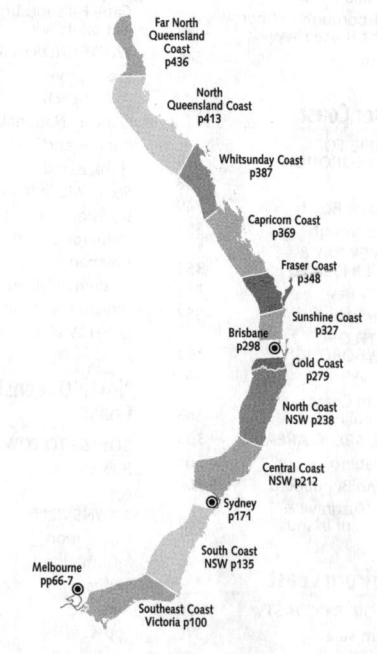

Far North
Queensland
Coast
p436

North
Queensland Coast
p413

Whitsunday Coast
p387

Capricorn Coast
p369

Fraser Coast
p348

Sunshine Coast
p327

Brisbane
p298

Gold Coast
p279

North Coast
NSW p238

Central Coast
NSW p212

Sydney
p171

South Coast
NSW p135

Melbourne
pp66-7

Southeast Coast
Victoria p100

The Authors

LINDSAY BROWN

After completing a PhD on evolutionary genetics, and short stints as a marine scientist and science editor, Lindsay started editing at Lonely Planet. There followed stints as Senior Editor and Series Publishing Manager of Outdoor Activity Guides, responsible for the Walking, Cycling, Diving & Snorkelling and Watching Wildlife series. As a Lonely Planet author Lindsay has contributed to *Queensland*, *Australia*, *South India*, *Nepal* and *Pakistan & the Karakoram Highway*.

My East Coast Australia

I was born in Wollongong (p137), the son of a Bondi lifesaver; the East Coast is in my blood. Growing up, the weekends meant the beach, evening meant holding a fishing line, and school was somewhere in between. Sure, the lights of Sydney (p170) beckoned, but I was more at home discovering the trails of Royal National Park (p136) and the secluded beaches of the south coast. As a biologist prying into the genetics of abalone, I dived the magnificent waters around Montague Island (p160), the bumpy seas off Mallacoota (p130) and the crystal-clear depths off Wilsons Promontory (p108). The southeast corner, with its impressive forests, clean beaches and blue, blue seas, is still a special pilgrimage.

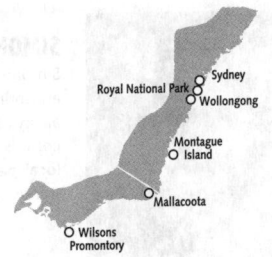

SANDRA BAO

Sandra has been an itinerant traveller since she was eight, when she first left her native Argentina to venture out into the world. Since immigrating to the United States she has travelled in more than 50 countries and earned a psychology degree at UC Santa Cruz. Sydney reigns supreme among her favourite cities and Lonely Planet gigs, and during her research for this book Sandra has learned to appreciate echidnas, the Aussie accent and munching fish and chips at the beach.

LONELY PLANET AUTHORS

Why is our travel information the best in the world? It's simple: our authors are independent, dedicated travellers. They don't research using just the Internet or phone, and they don't take freebies in exchange for positive coverage. They travel widely, to all the popular spots and off the beaten track. They personally visit thousands of hotels, restaurants, cafés, bars, galleries, palaces, museums and more – and they take pride in getting all the details right, and telling it how it is. For more, see the authors section on www.lonelyplanet.com.

RYAN VER BERKMOES

Since before the turn of the millennium, Ryan Ver Berkmoes has thrilled to the feel of New South Wales sand between his toes. An old beach bum who grew up on the Pacific in California, Ryan has done his best to sample the world's shores. A long-time journalist, Ryan's recent watery work for Lonely Planet has included *Bali & Lombok* (beaches and waves beyond compare), *British Columbia* (cold yes, but windswept and atmospheric) and *California* (need we say more). Whether it's fending off faux hippies with attitude in Nimbin or being welcomed by the mellow folk of Eden, he enjoyed every kilometre of the NSW coast.

SIMONE EGGER

Simone Egger works as a freelance photojournalist from Melbourne. Before authoring for Lonely Planet, Simone had a stint as an editor. Travel has always been in her bio, and for Simone, a road trip along Queensland's coast is bliss. Sure, it's about amazing beaches, lush rainforests, history and local people. But it's also about getting a photo in front of as many 'big things' as roadside businesses can build.

CATH LANIGAN

Cath yo-yoed between Melbourne, Gippsland and overseas for a decade or three until she and her partner did the sea-change thing and moved to East Gippsland with their five-year-old daughter. Cath retains a fondness for inner-city Melbourne but is yet to find a nicer place to live than by the lake in East Gippsland.

SIMON SELLARS

Simon Sellars has soft-focus memories of traversing the East Coast as a callow lad, and was thrilled to be able to retrace his steps for this book. Simon wrote the Central Coast New South Wales chapter (up to Port Macquarie) as well as the Destination, Snapshot and Culture sections.

Getting Started

The East Coast is Australia's most populated region, boasting vibrant, cultured cities and some of the country's premier attractions. There's also a well-trodden, traveller-friendly route spanning the region, where all budgets, all interests and all ages can be accommodated. From Australia's largest cities and most popular resorts down to the tiny fishing towns and untamed national parks, you'll generally find first-rate facilities and, by Australian standards, good roads and agreeable distances between stops.

WHEN TO GO

Any time is a good time to be *somewhere* along the East Coast. When it's cold down south, it's magnificent in the north, and when it's too hot and sweaty up north, Victoria is at its finest. In Victoria and along the south coast of NSW, summer (December to February) offers warm weather and longer daylight hours tailor-made for swimming and outdoor activities. From Sydney to Brisbane, summer temperatures hover around a balmy 25°C – perfect for any activity (or inactivity). In the far north of Queensland, summer is the wet season, when the heat and humidity can be pretty uncomfortable. To make things worse, swimming in the sea isn't possible due to the deadly 'stingers' (box jellyfish) frequenting the waters at this time (see the boxed text, p371).

See Climate (p471) for more information.

June through August is winter in the south, with temperatures dropping the further south you travel – not surprisingly it's the time when many travellers head north, where the humidity of the wet season has subsided and the temperature is highly agreeable (the Dry lasts roughly from April to September, and the Wet from October to March, with the heaviest rain falling from January onwards). Autumn (March to May) and spring (September to November) are characterised by a lack of climatic extremes along the entire coast.

The other major consideration is school holidays – the high seasons for domestic travel when prices rise and vacancies plummet in the major destinations. In the south, as with the entire country, the Easter (April) and Christmas (December to January) breaks are considered to be the high season. In Queensland, the main tourist season stretches from April to November, and the official high season is June to September. See p477 for more information on holidays.

COSTS

At the current rate of exchange, Australia is inexpensive if you're from the USA, Britain or continental Europe, making down-under holidays very economical for international visitors, with reasonably priced transport, fuel and accommodation, and excellent-value food and wine.

DON'T LEAVE HOME WITHOUT...

- sunscreen, sunglasses and a hat to deflect ultra-fierce UV rays (p500)
- a travel insurance policy specifically covering you for any planned high-risk activities (p477)
- extra-strength insect repellent to fend off merciless flies and mosquitoes (p472)
- a willingness to call absolutely everyone 'mate', whether you know or like them or not

Of course, your holiday can be as cheap or as expensive as your tastes demand. A midrange traveller who plans to hire a car, see the sights, stay in midrange B&Bs or hotels and indulge in a slap-up restaurant meal in the evening should expect to be out of pocket at least $150 per day ($100 to $130 per person if travelling as part of a pair or a couple).

At the low-cost end, if you camp or stay in hostels, cook your own meals, avoid big nights out in the pub and catch buses everywhere, you could probably manage on $45 per day; for a budget that realistically enables you to have a good time and the occasional splurge, set aside at least $65.

Travellers with a demanding brood in tow will find there are many ways to keep kids inexpensively satisfied, including beach and park visits, camping grounds and motels equipped with pools and games rooms, restaurants with discounted kids' meals and child/family concessions for attractions. Also keep an eye out for the odd 'free' day at museums and galleries. For more information on travelling with children see p470.

LONELY PLANET INDEX

1L petrol (city price) $0.90-1.10

1L bottled water $2-3

Pot/middy of beer (VB/ Toohey's/XXXX) $2.50

Mambo T-shirt $40

Street treat (meat pie) $2.50

PREDEPARTURE READING

Before heading up or down the coast, grab a couple of inspiring, thought-provoking or just plain entertaining books to help put you in the picture.

The Melbourne Book: A History of Now (2003), by Maree Coote, is a stunning pictorial ode to this superb city, with a mix of dramatic photographs and contemporary stories and interviews. Tim Flannery's *The Birth of Melbourne* (2002) contains first-hand accounts of the city from 1802 to 1903.

Author Ruth Park scores with the eponymous *Ruth Park's Sydney* (2003), an account that combines her lyrical prose with obvious affection for and deep knowledge of the city. There's nothing romantic about *Leviathan: The Unauthorised Biography of Sydney* (2002), by John Birmingham. The book looks at every seamy aspect of the town imaginable. Noted novelist Peter Carey gives his own account of his home town in *30 Days in Sydney* (2001). It's quirky, goofy and highly readable.

The Place at the Coast, by Jane Hyde, is a moving novel looking at a woman's aimless life when she returns to her home in a fading coastal NSW town. It was made into the movie *High Tide* (1987) and filmed in Merimbula and Eden. *Salt Rain* (2004), by Sarah Armstrong, is set in the green hills of the north coast of NSW. It deals with the tough life of a teenage girl who must deal with the strange past life of her mother.

Thea Astley's *It's Raining in Mango* (1987) is an almost tangible taste of Queensland's history. It follows a Sydney family's relocation to Cooktown, and its exposure to the tragic and murderous clash of indigenous and European cultures. With poignancy and optimism, *Djabugay Country: An Aboriginal History of Tropical North Queensland,* by Timothy Bottoms, recalls the early days of contact between Europeans and the rainforest tribes of north Queensland.

On a more continental scale, Andrew Bain and wife tackle a circumnavigation by bike with trucks, characters and prevailing headwinds as constant companions in *Headwinds* (2003). Humorist Bill Bryson takes a wry but affectionate look at the southern nation in *Down Under* (2000), while *The Fatal Shore* (1987), by Robert Hughes, endures as a richly detailed and engrossing tale of England's convicts washing ashore in NSW.

INTERNET RESOURCES
Australian Tourist Commission (www.australia.com) Official, federal government–run tourism site with nationwide info for visitors.
LonelyPlanet.com (www.lonelyplanet.com) Great destination summaries, links to related sites and the Thorn Tree.

TOP TENS

Festivals & Events
Aussies love any excuse for a celebration, and flock to the festivals and big sporting events that seem to cram every weekend of the year. These are our top 10 reasons to get festive on the East Coast – other events are listed on p475 and throughout this book.

- Australian Open Tennis Championships, Melbourne (p81) – late January
- Sydney Gay & Lesbian Mardi Gras (p193) – February
- Australia Formula One Grand Prix, Melbourne (p81) – March
- Moomba Festival, Melbourne (p81) – March
- Brisbane Riverfestival (p310) – September
- AFL Grand Final (p81) – September
- Indycar, Gold Coast (p289) – October
- Melbourne Cup (p81) – first Tuesday in November
- Sydney to Hobart Yacht Race (p193) – from 26 December
- Boxing Day International Text Match Cricket, Melbourne (p81) – 26 December

Must-See Movies
One of the best places to do your essential trip preparation (ie daydreaming) is in a comfy lounge with a bowl of popcorn in one hand, a remote in the other and your eyeballs pleasurably glued to a small screen. Head down to your local video store to pick up these Australian flicks, which range from the intelligent and thrilling to the uber-cheesy. See p37 for reviews of some of these and other locally produced films.

- *The Castle* (1997) Director: Rob Sitch
- *Romper Stomper* (1992) Director: Geoffrey Wright
- *Lantana* (2001) Director: Ray Lawrence
- *Rabbit-Proof Fence* (2002) Director: Phillip Noyce
- *Death in Brunswick* (1990) Director: John Ruane
- *Puberty Blues* (1991) Director: Bruce Beresford
- *The Man who Sued God* (2001) Director: Mark Joffe
- *Head On* (1998) Director: Geoffrey Wright
- *Chopper* (2000) Director: Andrew Dominik
- *Ned Kelly* (2003) Director: Gregor Jordan

Top Reads
The following page-turners have won critical acclaim in Australia and abroad, not least because they have something to reveal to the reader about Australia's cultural evolution and contemporary life. See p38 for reviews of some of these and other books.

- *For the Term of His Natural Life* (1874) Marcus Clarke
- *Cloud Street* (1991) Tim Winton
- *True History of the Kelly Gang* (2000) Peter Carey
- *Power Without Glory* (1950) Frank Hardy
- *Monkey Grip* (1977) Helen Garner
- *Loaded* (1995) Christos Tsiolkas
- *Fly Away Peter* (1982) David Malouf
- *The Brush-Off* (1998) Shane Maloney
- *The Harp in the South* (1948) Ruth Park
- *Oscar & Lucinda* (1988) Peter Carey

Queensland Holidays (www.queenslandholidays.com.au) Official tourism site, providing comprehensive information on destinations, accommodation, attractions, tours and more.

Tourism New South Wales (www.visitnsw.com.au) The state's tourism site has vast amounts of information on accommodation, activities and much more.

Tourism Tropical North Queensland (www.tropicalaustralia.com.au) Official tourism site of the far north, with excellent information on the Great Barrier Reef and destinations north of Cairns.

Tourism Victoria (www.visitvictoria.com) Official state tourism site, with excellent sections on festivals and events, accommodation, restaurants, tours and attractions.

Itineraries
CLASSIC ROUTES

EASTCOASTER
One month to a lifetime/Sydney to Cairns

When it's time to clear the head and shed the glam, face north and put **Sydney** (p170) behind you. Enter the **central coast of New South Wales** (p211), where there are more beaches and more evidence that people like to live near beaches. **Newcastle** (p215) has swapped its blue collar for Mambo casual, and the pleasantly inebriated **Hunter Valley** (p221) beckons from upriver. Reclusive types may find themselves searching out the less developed gems such as **Seal Rocks** (p228) and **Myall Lakes** (p228).

That warm tingly feeling is the approaching tropics. Northern NSW basks in subtropical glory. Take in the views at **Hat Head** (p240), go diving at **South West Rocks** (p240) before hitting **Coffs Harbour** (p247), halfway between Sydney and Brisbane. A magnet in **Byron Bay** (p260) is drawing the universe in. Everybody wants a slice of whatever it is that makes it so damn nice. Meditating in Byron's verdant hinterland is the once alternative, still delightful **Nimbin** (p271).

There's a border crossing nearby and, after it's crossed, you'll need to remember how you ordered a beer in Victoria. Gold chains (for both sexes) are the uniform for the **Gold Coast** (p278). The kids can go berserk

You will likely cover at least 3000km by the time you have sampled the best that this route has to offer. Many of the gems are just off the highway, and around every corner is another beach, another food experience, another tempting detour.

at the **theme parks** (p288) while you grab a long board or bungee like you never have before. **Brisbane** (p297) has gone glitzy – it still surprises even the locals – and yet there are wild dolphins to feed at **Tangalooma** (p323) on Moreton Island. Cuisine gets fusion without confusion at style-setting **Noosa** (p336). There are whales to watch in **Hervey Bay** (p353) – they're probably the same fat humpbacks you saw up and down the coast, having made their way north for sex. And don't leave the world's largest sand thing, **Fraser Island** (p357), without taking some of it home between your toes.

You can watch Australia's favourite rum being distilled in **Bundaberg** (p363), and tiny loggerhead turtles hatching at **Mon Repos Beach** (p366). Chill out at **Town of 1770** (p370) before getting a taste of the coral wonders of the big reef at **Lady Musgrave Island** (p367). Wear a big hat, watch someone riding a bull or join them devouring a steak at beef city, **Rockhampton** (p376). Explore the trails and sample the beaches of **Great Keppel Island** (p382), before heading to arty **Mackay** (p389) and spotting a platypus at peaceful **Eungella National Park** (p394).

Your next stop is bustling **Airlie Beach** (p400), gateway to the magical **Whitsunday Islands** (p396), where you can party, dive, sail and snorkel to your heart's content. There are islands and reefs galore up this way, and walkers should not miss the Thorsborne Trail on magnificent **Hinchinbrook Island** (p429). Adrenaline junkies can take to the white water on the mighty Tully River and you may spot a Cassowary at **Mission Beach** (p430) before it spots you. When you reach the tourist town of **Cairns** (p441) you can shout yourself a trip to the reef and a slap-up meal. You've made it!

AROUND THE CORNER   Two to three weeks/Melbourne to Sydney

You've been to the MCG, you've had a beer at Young & Jacksons, and you've nearly been run over by a tram (twice!). It's getting chilly so now's the time to head north from **Melbourne** (p62). But the kids want to see a penguin – it's a kid thing – so you head south. To **Phillip Island** (p102), where penguins, seals and wetsuited surfers frolic in the bracing briny. Next stop, **Wilsons Promontory** (p108). Yes, we are still going south, and yes it is…cool. And clean, and wild and beautiful. And there's nowhere further south to go (sorry Tasmania). So suck in that fresh air and head east and north through the forests, farms and lakes district of **Gippsland** (p112) to Victoria's first and last seaside town, **Mallacoota** (p130). Now turn that corner. Things, you will have noticed, are warming up.

Time constricts on the **NSW south coast** (p134) – distances between towns are noticeably shorter. Each town has a river or an estuary, a golf club and three or four or more golden-sand beaches. People have been known to arrive and never leave – you have been warned. Watch a whale at **Eden** (p167), drop a line at **Narooma** (p159) and take a photo (everybody does) of **Tilba** (p161). Eventually you'll reach blue-collar **Wollongong** (p137) and the sprawling suburbs, followed by the dazzling lights of **Sydney** (p170). How long you need here depends on your love or loathing of heaving metropolises, and your budget. Escapes to the **Blue Mountains** (p207) are *de rigueur* for frazzled Sydneysiders and overwhelmed travellers alike.

This 1500km trip takes you from the multicultural Victorian capital of Melbourne to Australia's biggest showgirl, Sydney. You travel to Wilsons Promontory before heading east and turning the corner into NSW.

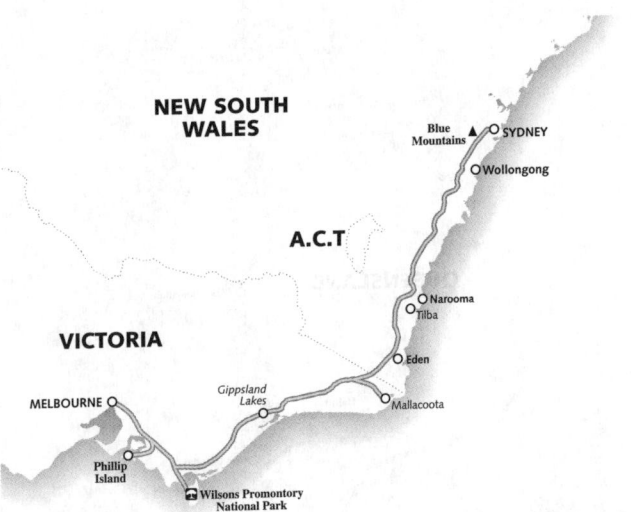

NEW SOUTH WALES

Blue Mountains ▲ ○ SYDNEY

○ Wollongong

A.C.T

○ Narooma
○ Tilba

VICTORIA

Gippsland Lakes

○ Eden

MELBOURNE ○

○ Mallacoota

Phillip Island

Wilsons Promontory National Park

TASMANIA

COOKTOWN OR BUST   One to two weeks/Cairns to Cooktown to Cairns

There are two routes from lively Cairns to languorous Cooktown, so if you can organize a 4WD you can make this excellent loop through tropical rainforest and dry savannah, with perhaps a look at Lizard Island.

Leaving **Cairns** (p441), wend your way north on the Captain Cook Hwy through several pretty beach communities including **Holloways Beach** (p450), **Yorkeys Knob** (p451) and, perhaps the best of all, **Palm Cove** (p451). At **Port Douglas** (p454), just a short drive off the highway, you'll be lured in by good food and reef tours and the lazy local lifestyle. At unassuming **Mossman** (p458) the main attraction is the magnificent gorge and the **Daintree National Park** (p461), which is best seen near **Cape Tribulation** (p459). From Cape Trib the 4WD **Bloomfield Track** (p463) carves its way through dense rainforests and mountains for 80km. It emerges just south of **Cooktown** (p464), a fascinating outpost of civilisation. From here you can organise a tour of **Lizard Island** (p466), the most northerly Barrier Reef resort. Return to Cairns via the inland route, passing the Annan River Gorge to **Lakeland** (p463) – turn right here for the tip of Australia, a mere 700-odd kilometres away. Further along this lonely road there's the Palmer River Roadhouse and the former mining town of Mt Carbine, before you reach the farming hub of Mareeba. Turn east here towards the very popular mountain village of **Kuranda** (p452) before descending to the steamy coast and Cairns.

This loop combines the lovely coast north of Cairns, the salubrious hamlet of Port Douglas and the rainforest of Cape Tribulation with the frontier aspect of Cooktown. The 280km trip north takes several days as you lap up the sights. The 330km return leg takes about five hours' solid driving.

TAILORED TRIPS

INDIGENOUS CULTURE

The East Coast is the most heavily settled and developed region of Australia, so tangible examples of Indigenous culture are not immediately obvious to the traveller. Several cultural centres do, however, welcome visitors and provide guided tours and insights into traditional life. In addition, there are numerous middens, bora rings and other cultural sights protected in national parks and reserves.

Krowathunkoolong Keeping Place (p117) in Bairnsdale is a Gunai Aboriginal space that delivers some truths about the white settlement of southeast Victoria. The NSW south coast, near Bermagui, has the excellent **Umbarra Cultural Centre** (p162), where traditional life including bush tucker can be explored with guides. **Ku-Ring-Gai Chase National Park** (p212), just north of Sydney, protects an extensive array of engravings. The **Yarrawarra Aboriginal Cultural Centre** (p249), north of Coffs Harbour, has a bush-food café and tours. The **Minjungbal Aboriginal Cultural Centre** (p265) in Tweed Heads is also well worth a look.

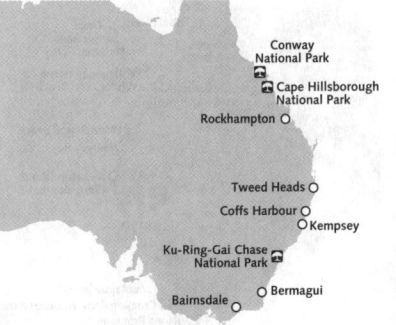

The most accessible place in Queensland is the **Dreamtime Cultural Centre** (p378) in Rockhampton, which offers guided tours and boomerang throwing. There are excellent self-guided walks, made with help from the Indigenous community, at **Cape Hillsborough National Park** (p396) and **Conway National Park** (p405).

FOLLOW THE DREAM

Aussies are sports mad. Sport in all its permutations is big business, with thousands of passionate spectators generating astonishing cash flow and spawning one or two sporting edifices that can makwe the neck hair of a true believer stand on end. To be part of the action, join a queue and buy a ticket.

Every summer the wickets are rolled and the balls shined at the lovely **Sydney Cricket Ground** (SCG; p203), the colossal **Melbourne Cricket Ground** (MCG; p76) and Brisbane's **Gabba** (p318). The year's Grand Slam tennis tournament begins with the **Australian Open** (p90) in January in Melbourne, the self-styled sports capital of Australia, while in March the same city reverberates with the roar of the **Australian Formula One Grand Prix** (p90). Melbourne is also home to **Australian Rules Football** (p89), where stadiums heave with tribal passion between March and September. Sydney and Brisbane are catching the Aussie rules fervour, but **Rugby League** (p203) still dominates the winter psyche. The Gold Coast hosts petrol heads at **Indycar** (p289) in October. In November punters can slip on a hat and wager a bet at the **Melbourne Cup** (p89), while sailors can party –sail – party in December's **Sydney to Hobart Yacht Race** (p193).

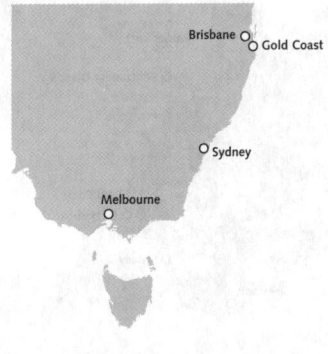

NATURE'S BOUNTY

The East Coast is not the Australia of red sand and big rocks. It's the Australia of long golden beaches and verdant rainforests, of fur seals, migrating whales, nesting turtles and a plethora of colourful bird life.

Jutting out from the Victorian coast is **Wilsons Promontory** (p108), where wildlife, water and squeaky-clean sand converge on mainland Australia's southern extremity. Further along the coast you can take a multiday coastal hike at **Croajingalong National Park** (p132), before entering the realm of the tall eucalypts of the **Erinundra Plateau** (p126). You can dive with seals, watch whales, point at penguins, and drop a line at **Montague Island** (p160). For a breath of mountain air, discover what all the fuss is about in the popular **Blue Mountains** (p207). There are bottlenose dolphins to hand feed

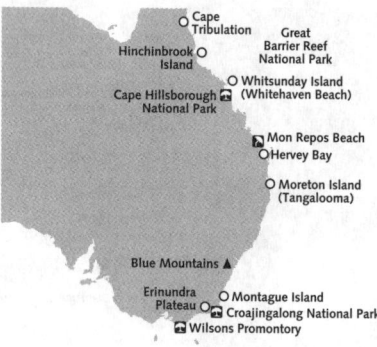

at **Tangalooma** (p323), and migrating whales to gaze upon at **Hervey Bay** (p353). Watch tiny turtles hatch at **Mon Repos Beach** (p366), stroll the metallic beach at **Cape Hillsborough National Park** (p396) with bounding kangaroos, and be astounded by the bright, white arc of **Whitehaven Beach** (p410) on Whitsunday Island. Along the north Queensland coast there are numerous options for getting acquainted with the myriad of colourful denizens of the **Great Barrier Reef National Park** (p377). Take to the classic Thorsborne Trail on mountainous **Hinchinbrook Island** (p429) and be consumed by the dense tropical rainforests of **Cape Tribulation** (p459).

ARE WE THERE YET?

Ahhhh. Kids and travel. The key is to plan ahead.

Along the East Coast there are enough diversions to distract the brightest minds, and activities aplenty to soak up the energy of the most boundless youth.

Feed inquiring minds at Melbourne's **Scienceworks** (p80), Sydney's **Powerhouse Museum** (p185) and Brisbane's **Sciencentre** (p301). These are museums where kids can fiddle and interfere with techno gadgets and learn all about stuff.

Melbourne's **Luna Park** (p80) and Sydney's **Luna Park** (p188) are old-fashioned theme parks of the fairyfloss and laughing clown variety, but for ultimate, screaming, what-brain-would-have-designed-this? type rides

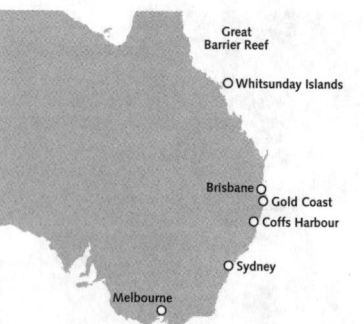

head for the **Gold Coast theme parks** (p288).

Take them snorkelling (but make sure they can swim first) on the **Great Barrier Reef** (p377) or the **Whitsunday Islands** (p396). Instil a deep appreciation of Australia's unique natural heritage by taking them on a **bushwalk** (p48), and reward (or bribe) their gutsy efforts with American-style junk food – the East Coast has oodles of outlets.

And if there's a whimper from the back seat threaten them with the **Big Banana** (p247) at Coffs Harbour, the awfully bloated potato, the truly frightening fibreglass crayfish and the huge...

And if all that fails get a portable DVD player for the car.

Snapshot

It's been a topsy-turvy year for the good old East Coast. For the first time, the population of New South Wales dropped below a third of Australia's total, largely due to Sydney's exorbitant housing prices, now way out of reach of the 'average' family.

This is fairly shocking news. NSW (especially Sydney) has been the leader of the pack for so long (see p33), it's hard to believe it's now lagging behind Victoria and Queensland in some very crucial areas. But the stats don't lie: Victoria is king of the heap in terms of annual output; Queensland provides the highest rate of job growth; Melbourne is the country's fastest-growing city.

As you travel the coast, watch for those canny Sydneysiders. They're the ones with the Cheshire-cat grins, having sold their properties for big bucks to escape Sin City for the northern grail of sun, surf and inexpensive accommodation, or the southern pleasures of affordable art, decent coffee and restaurant meals for under $100.

They might be leaving the state for other reasons. A rampant locust plague continues to torment NSW crops – a recent cookbook (p58) advocates catching the little buggers and turning them into dinner to ease the problem. Meanwhile, in Newcastle's outer suburbs, a spate of frozen chickens falling from the sky had the locals scratching their heads as they repaired smashed roofs, windows and car bonnets. Bizarre theories were put forth. Some say birds plucked the chooks from garbage dumps, dropping them from the heavens when they became too heavy; others say a crazed madman with a grudge fired them from the hills with a homemade bazooka. The mystery was never solved.

In the far north of Queensland, the problems are with thawed-out wildlife. Up there, it seems a crocodile mauls a tourist every year (recently, a granny leapt on a croc that was attacking her son's friend, diverting the killing machine until help arrived). The perennial issue of controlled culling for the beasties is therefore a hot topic once more.

And what of popular culture? It's possibly the hardest time ever to get a home-grown feature film made, although quality facilities mean that Hollywood productions have flocked to the East Coast in recent times (see p37). The situation reflects wider issues: does Australia plump for the Yankee dollar and a watered-down identity, or does it hang on to limited economic appeal and a distinctive cultural voice? In the end, it could be a moot point: the rise in value of the Australian dollar might just prove to be a stumbling block for overseas producers.

In sport (p35), rugby, an East Coast obsession, suffered a cauliflower ear when the Aussies lost the World Cup to the Poms. Even in cricket Australia can't take a trick, despite dominating – the Aussies have been the best for so long, they've run out of top-quality opponents. Home crowds along the coast are simply bored with watching the opposition get spanked day in day out.

Maybe we need a new sporting obsession to take the heat off – anyone for checkers?

FAST FACTS

East Coast population: 15.4 million (75% of Australia's total)

Length of coastline: 17,996km (30% of Australia's total)

World's biggest earthworm: Gippsland (Vic) is home to the *Megascolides australis*

World's first prepaid postal system: introduced in NSW in 1838

World's first Labor party: Queensland

World's longest coral reef: Great Barrier Reef (2000km)

Australia's busiest port: depending on which authority is supplying the facts and figures, either Sydney or Melbourne; let's just agree that they're both *really* busy

Species of dinosaur named after a national airline: Qantassaurus, named by Melbourne's Monash University

History Michael Cathcart

INTRUDERS

By sunrise, the storm had passed. Zachary Hicks was keeping sleepy watch on the British ship *Endeavour* when suddenly he was wide awake. He summoned his captain, James Cook, who climbed into the brisk morning air to a miraculous sight. Ahead of them lay an uncharted country of wooded hills and gentle valleys. It was 19 April 1770. In the coming days, Cook began methodically to draw the first European map of Australia's eastern coast. He was mapping the end of Aboriginal supremacy.

Michael Cathcart presented the ABC TV history series Rewind. He is a lecturer in history at the Australian Centre, the University of Melbourne.

CONVICTS

Eighteen years later, in 1788, the English were back to stay. They numbered 751 ragtag convicts and children, and around 250 soldiers, officials and their wives. This motley 'First Fleet' was under the command of a humane and diligent naval captain, Arthur Phillip. In a small cove, in the idyllic lands of the Eora people, Phillip established a British penal settlement. He renamed the place after the British Home Secretary, Lord Sydney.

Robert Hughes' bestseller, *The Fatal Shore* (1987), depicts convict Australia as a terrifying 'Gulag' where Britain tormented rebels, vagrants and criminals. But other historians point out that powerful men in London saw transportation as a scheme for giving prisoners a new and useful life. Indeed, with Phillip's encouragement, many convicts soon earned their 'ticket of leave', a kind of parole that gave them the freedom of the colony and the right to seek work on their own behalf.

However, the convict system could also be savage. Women (who were outnumbered five to one) lived under constant threat of sexual exploitation. Female convicts who offended their gaolers languished in the depressing 'female factories'. Male re-offenders were cruelly flogged, and could even be hanged for minor crimes such as stealing. In 1803 English officers established a second convict settlement at Hobart in Van Diemen's Land (later called Tasmania). Soon male re-offenders filled the grim prison at Port Arthur on the beautiful and wild coast close by. Others endured the senseless agonies of Norfolk Island in the remote Pacific.

The classic biography of Cook is by JC Beaglehole, The Life of Captain James Cook (1974). Beaglehole also edited Cook's journals.

At first Sydney and these smaller colonies depended on supplies brought in by ship. Anxious to develop productive farms, the government granted land to soldiers, officers, and emancipated convicts. After 30 years of trial and error, their farms began to flourish. The most irascible and ruthless of these landholders was John Macarthur. Along with his spirited wife Elizabeth, Macarthur pioneered the breeding of merino sheep on his verdant property near Sydney.

RUM

John Macarthur was also a leading member of the Rum Corps, a clique of powerful officers, which bullied successive governors (including William Bligh of *Bounty* fame), and grew rich by controlling much of Sydney's

60,000 BC	1770
Aborigines settle in Australia, according to most experts	English captain James Cook maps Australia's eastern coast in the *Endeavour*

trade, notably rum. But its racketeering was ended in 1810 by a tough new governor named Lachlan Macquarie. Under Macquarie's administration the major roads of modern-day Sydney were constructed, some fine public buildings built (many designed by talented convict architect Francis Greenway) and the foundations for a more civil society were laid.

Macquarie also championed the rights of freed convicts, granting them land and appointing several to public office. But this tolerance was not shared by the 'exclusives'. These large landholders, middle-class snobs and senior British officials observed a rigid expatriate class system. They shunned ex-prisoners, and scoffed at the distinctive accent and the easygoing manners of these new Australians.

By now word was reaching England that Australia offered cheap land and plenty of work, and adventurous migrants took to the oceans, in search of their fortunes. At the same time, the British government transported more and more prisoners. In 1825 a party of soldiers and convicts established a penal settlement in the territory of the Yuggera people, close to modern-day Brisbane. Before long this hot, fertile region attracted free settlers, who were soon busy farming, grazing, logging and mining on Aboriginal land.

> The vivid journal of Watkin Tench is widely available as *Watkin Tench 1788* (edited by Tim Flannery). His observations of the settlement are a good read.

SHEEP

In the cooler grasslands of Tasmania, the sheepmen were also thriving, and they too were hungry for new pastures. In 1835 an ambitious young squatter named John Batman sailed to Port Phillip Bay on the mainland. On the banks of the Yarra River, he chose the location for Melbourne, famously announcing that 'This is the place for a village.' Batman then worked a staggering swindle: he persuaded local Aborigines to 'sell' him their traditional lands (a whopping 250,000 hectares – roughly 100 sq miles) for a crate of blankets, knives and knick-knacks. Back in Sydney, Governor Burke declared the contract void, not because it was unfair, but because the land officially belonged to the British Crown. Burke proved his point by granting Batman some prime acreage near Geelong.

LAND

Each year, settlers pushed deeper into the Aboriginal territories in search of pasture and water for their stock. These men became known as squatters (because they 'squatted' on Aboriginal lands), and many held this territory with a gun. In the USA the conflict between settlers and the indigenous people formed the basis for a rich mythology known as 'the wild west'. But in Australia the conflict has largely passed from white memory, so white historians now disagree about the extent of the violence. But Aborigines still recount how their water holes were poisoned and their people massacred. Some of the bitterest struggles occurred in the remote mining districts of central Queensland. In Tasmania the impact of settlement was so devastating that today, no 'full blood' Aborigines survive; all of the island's Aborigines are of mixed heritage.

> Australia was declared 'terra nullius' (empty land) by the British because they did not understand that the Aborigines had their own system of land law. This fanciful legal principle was overturned in the famous Mabo court case (1992).

On the mainland many of the squatters reached a truce with the defeated tribes. In remote regions it became common for Aborigines to take low-paid jobs on farms, working on sheep and cattle stations as drovers, rouseabouts, shearers and domestics. In return, those lucky

1788	1813
The First Fleet settles at Sydney Harbour with its cargo of convicts	Despite chronic diarrhoea, three colonists cross the barrier of the Blue Mountains west of Sydney; the period of inland exploration begins

enough to be working on their traditional lands adapted their cultures to their changing circumstances. This arrangement continued in outback pastoral regions until after WWII.

GOLD & REBELLION

Transportation of convicts to eastern Australia ceased in the 1840s. This was just as well: in 1851 prospectors discovered gold in New South Wales and central Victoria. The news hit the colonies with the force of a cyclone. From every social class, young men and some adventurous women headed for the diggings. Soon they were caught up in a great rush of prospectors, entertainers, publicans, sly-groggers, prostitutes and quacks, from overseas. In Victoria the British governor was alarmed – both by the way the Victorian class system had been thrown into disarray, and by the need to finance law and order on the goldfields. His solution was to compel all miners to buy an expensive monthly licence, in the hope that the lower orders would return to their duties in town.

But the lure of gold was too great. In the reckless excitement of the goldfields, the miners initially endured the thuggish troopers who enforced the government licence. But after three years the easy gold at Ballarat was gone, and miners were toiling in deep, water-sodden shafts. They were now infuriated by a corrupt and brutal system of law that held them in contempt. Under the leadership of a charismatic Irishman named Peter Lalor, they raised the flag of the Southern Cross and swore to defend their rights and liberties. They armed themselves and gathered inside a rough stockade at Eureka, where they waited for the government to make its move.

In the pre-dawn of Sunday 3 December 1854, a force of troopers attacked the stockade. In 15 terrifying minutes, they slaughtered 30 miners and lost five soldiers. The story of the Eureka Stockade is often told as a battle for nationhood and democracy – as if a true nation must be born out of blood. But these killings were tragically unnecessary. The eastern colonies were already in the process of establishing democratic parliaments, with the full support of the British authorities. In the 1880s Lalor himself became Speaker of the Victorian Parliament.

The gold rush also attracted boatloads of prospectors from China. The Chinese prospectors endured constant hostility from whites, and were the victims of ugly race riots on the goldfields at Lambing Flat (now called Young) in NSW in 1860–61. Chinese precincts developed in the back-streets of Sydney and Melbourne and, by the 1880s, popular literature indulged in tales of Chinese opium dens, dingy gambling parlours and oriental brothels. But many Chinese went on to established themselves in business and particularly in market gardening. Today the busy China-towns of Sydney and Melbourne, and the ubiquitous Chinese restaurants in country towns, are reminders of Chinese vigour.

Gold and wool brought immense investment and gusto to Melbourne and Sydney. By the 1880s they were stylish modern cities, with gas-lights in the streets, railways and that great new invention: the telegraph. In fact the southern capital became known as 'Marvellous Melbourne', so opulent were its theatres, hotels, galleries and fashions.

A vivid take on the life of a colonial bushman who grew up with Aborigines is Tom Petrie's *Reminiscences of Early Queensland.*

The Museum of Chinese Australian History (p75) in Melbourne is well worth visiting.

1854	1880s
Gold miners' rebellion brutally put down at the Eureka Stockade; most colonies get self-government soon after	Great boom in the economy of the eastern states

Meanwhile, the huge expanses of Queensland were remote from the southern centres of political and business power. It was a tough, raw frontier colony, in which money was made by hard labour – in mines, in the forests and on cattle stations. In the coastal sugar industry, southern investors grew rich on a plantation economy that exploited tough Pacific Island labourers (known as 'Kanakas'), many of whom had been kidnapped from their islands.

Many white Queenslanders still embody the gritty, independent, egalitarian yet racist attitudes that were the key elements of the so-called 'Australian legend'. The legend reached its classic form at the end of the 19th century, when nationalist writers idealised 'the bush', its people and their code of 'mateship'. The great forum for this bush nationalism was the massively popular *Bulletin* magazine. Its politics were egalitarian, democratic, republican…and white. And its pages were filled with humour and sentiment about daily life, written by a whole swag of writers, most notably Henry Lawson and 'Banjo' Paterson.

But while writers were creating national legends the politicians of Australia were devising the framework for a national constitution.

> Two very different, intelligent accounts of the forces that shaped Australia are Stuart Macintyre's *A Concise History of Australia* and Geoffrey Blainey's *A Shorter History of Australia*.

NATIONHOOD

On 1 January 1901 Australia became a federation. When the bewhiskered members of the new national Parliament met in Melbourne, their first aim was to protect the identity and values of a European Australia from an influx of Asians and Pacific Islanders. Their solution was what became known as the White Australia policy. It became a racial tenet of faith in Australia for the next 70 years. For those who were welcome to live in Australia (ie whites), this was to be a model society, nestled in the skirts of the British Empire.

Just one year later, white women won the right to vote in federal elections. In a series of radical innovations, the government introduced a broad social welfare scheme and protected Australian wage levels with import tariffs. Its mixture of capitalist dynamism and socialist compassion became known as 'the Australian settlement'.

Meanwhile, most Australians lived on the coastal 'edge' of the continent. So forbidding was the arid inland, that they called the great dry Lake Eyre 'the Dead Heart' of the country. It was a grim image. But one prime minister, the dapper Alfred Deakin, was determined to overcome the tyranny of the climate. Back in the 1880s, Deakin championed a scheme by two Canadian engineers to develop irrigated farming on the Murray River at Mildura. The region developed into a prosperous grape and dried-fruit industry. (Today this massively productive region is facing an ecological crisis – as salinity and overuse threaten to kill the Murray River.)

> Nineteenth-century acclimatisation societies tried to replace the 'inferior' Australian plants and animals with superior European ones. Such cute blessings as rabbits and foxes date from this time.

WAR & THE GREAT DEPRESSION

Living on the edge of this forbidding land, and isolated from the rest of the world, most Australians took comfort from the idea that they were still a part of the British Empire. When war broke out in Europe in 1914, thousands of Australian men rallied to the Empire's call. They had their first taste of death on 25 April 1915, when the Australian and New Zealand Army Corps (the 'Anzacs') joined other British and French troops

1901	1915
The Australian colonies federate; federal Parliament meets for the first time in Melbourne	Anzac legend born when Australian troops join allied invasion of Turkey

in an assault on the Gallipoli Peninsula in Turkey. It was eight months before the British commanders acknowledged that the tactic had failed. But by then 8141 young Australians were dead. Soon the Australian Imperial Force was fighting in the killing fields of Europe. When the war ended, 60,000 Australian men had been slaughtered. Ever since, on 25 April, Australians have gathered at war memorials around the country for the sad and solemn services of Anzac Day.

For an accessible version of the Anzac legend, see Peter Weir's Australian epic film *Gallipoli* (1981). The cast includes a young Mel Gibson.

Australia careered wildly through the 1920s, continuing to invest in immigration and growth, until the economy collapsed into the abyss of the Great Depression in 1929. Unemployment brought its shame and misery to one in three houses. For those who were wealthy – or who had jobs – the depression was hardly noticed. In fact, the fall in prices actually meant that the purchasing power of their wages was enhanced.

HEROES

In the midst of the hardship, sport brought escape to a nation in love with games and gambling. The champion racehorse Phar Lap won an effortless and graceful victory in the 1930 Melbourne Cup ('the horse race that stops a nation'). In 1932 the great horse travelled to the racetracks of America where he mysteriously died. In Australia the gossips insisted that the horse had been poisoned by envious Americans. And the legend grew – of a sporting hero cut down in his prime. He was stuffed and is a revered exhibit at the Melbourne Museum (p77).

The year 1932 also saw accusations of treachery on the cricket field. The English team, under its aloof captain Douglas Jardine, employed a violent new bowling tactic known as 'Bodyline'. Jardine's aim was to unnerve Australia's star batsman, the devastating Donald Bradman. The bitterness of the tour became part of the Australian legend. And Bradman batted on – achieving the unsurpassed career average of 99.94 runs.

Don't miss the chance to see Phar Lap himself – this stuffed horse is a seriously odd spectacle. The legend is explored at www.museum.vic.gov .au/pharlap.

That same year, the radical Premier of NSW, Jack Lang, officiated at the opening of the great Sydney Harbour Bridge. Before anyone knew what was happening, a man in military uniform rode forward on a skittish horse. He drew a sabre and cut the ceremonial ribbon in the name of the King. He was Francis de Groot, a member of the fascist New Guard, who accused Lang of being a closet communist. The Bridge survived the controversy to become a great symbol of hope and optimism, uniting a divided city.

WWII

As the economy began to recover, the whirl of daily life was hardly dampened when Australian serviceman sailed off to Europe for a new war, in 1939. Though Japan was menacing, Australians took it for granted that the British navy would keep them safe. In December 1941 Japan bombed the US Fleet at Pearl Harbor. Weeks later the 'impregnable' British naval base in Singapore crumbled, and soon thousands of Australians and other Allied troops were enduring the savagery of Japan's POW camps.

As the Japanese swept through Southeast Asia and into Papua New Guinea, the British announced that they could not spare any resources to defend Australia. But the legendary US commander General Douglas MacArthur saw that Australia was the perfect base for American operations

1927	1949
Federal Parliament moves to the new national capital in Canberra	Robert Menzies' new Liberal Party begins an era of government lasting until 1972

in the Pacific. In a series of savage battles on sea and land, Allied forces gradually turned back the Japanese advance. Importantly, it was the USA, not the British Empire, which came to Australia's aid. The days of the British alliance were numbered.

VISIONARY PEACE

As the war ended, a new slogan rang through the land: 'Populate or Perish!' The Australian government embarked on an ambitious scheme to attract thousands of immigrants. With government assistance, people flocked from Britain and from non-English-speaking countries. They included Greeks, Italians, Slavs, Serbs, Croatians, Dutch, Poles, Turks, Lebanese and so on. These 'new Australians' were expected to assimilate to a suburban stereotype known as 'the Australian way of life'.

This was the great era of the nuclear family in which Australians basked in the prosperity of a 'long boom'. Many migrants found jobs in manufacturing, where companies like General Motors and Ford operated with generous tariff support. At the same time, there was growing world demand for Australia's primary products: metals, wool, meat and wheat. In time, Australia even became a major exporter of rice to Japan.

This era of growth and prosperity was dominated by Robert Menzies, the founder of the modern Liberal Party and Australia's longest-serving prime minister. Menzies had an avuncular charm, but he was also a vigilant opponent of communism. As the Cold War intensified, Australia and New Zealand entered a formal military alliance with the USA – the 1951 Anzus security pact. And when the USA hurled its righteous fury into a civil war in Vietnam, Menzies committed Australian forces to the conflict. The following year Menzies retired, leaving his successors a bitter legacy. The antiwar movement split Australia.

There was a feeling among artists, intellectuals and the young that Menzies' Australia had become a dull, complacent country, more in love with American popular culture and British high arts than with its own talents and stories. Australia, they said, had 'an inferiority complex'. In an atmosphere of youth rebellion, and new-found nationalism, Australians began to embrace their own history and culture. The arts blossomed. Universities flourished. A distinctive Australian film industry made iconic movies, mostly funded by government subsidies.

At the same time, increasing numbers of white Australians saw that the Aborigines had endured a great wrong that needed to be put right – and from 1976 until 1992, Aborigines won major victories in their struggle for land rights. Australia's imports with China and Japan increased – and the White Australia policy became an embarrassment. It was officially abolished in the early 1970s, and Australia became a leader in the campaign against the racist 'apartheid' policies of white South Africa.

By the 1970s, over one million migrants had arrived from non-English-speaking countries, filling Australia with new languages, cultures, foods and ideas. At the same time, China and Japan began to outstrip Europe as Australia's major trading partners. As Asian immigration increased, Vietnamese communities became prominent in Sydney and Melbourne. In both those cities a new spirit of tolerance and diversity known as 'multiculturalism' became a particular source of pride.

Australia's official guardian of war history is the memorial in Canberra – see www.awm.gov.au, or p150.

Read more about Australia's prime ministers, including Menzies, at http://primeministers.naa.gov.au.

1950s	1966
Massive immigration programme from Europe transforms Australian cities; economic boom	Australian troops sent to fight with USA in Vietnam War; protest movement born

A powerful dissenting voice in this time of liberal progress was the irascible Joh Bjelke-Petersen, premier of Queensland for 21 years from 1968. Kept in office by a blatant gerrymander (he never won more than 39% of the vote), he was able to impose his policy of development-at-any-price on the state. Forests were felled. Heritage buildings were demolished. Aborigines were cast aside. Protesters were bashed and jailed. But in the late 1980s a series of investigations revealed that Bjelke-Petersen presided over a system that was rotten. His favoured police commissioner was jailed for graft and it became clear that the police force, which Joh had used as a political hit-squad, was largely racist, violent and corrupt. Yet even today there are voters who insist that 'Joh was good for Queensland'.

A popular, and scathing, commentary on Australia in the 1960s is Donald Horne's *The Lucky Country* (1964).

MATERIALISM

Today Australia faces new challenges. Since the 1970s the country has been dismantling the protectionist scaffolding that allowed its economy to develop. Wages and working conditions, which used to be fixed by an independent authority, are now much more uncertain. And two centuries of development have placed great strains on the environment – on water supplies, forests, soils, air quality and the oceans. The country is closer than ever to the United States. Some say that this alliance protects Australia's independence. Others insist that it reduces Australia to a fawning 'client state'.

Though many Australians pride themselves on their tolerance, under popular conservative Prime Minister John Howard the majority have hardened their hearts to the boatloads of asylum seekers – locking even children in bleak detention camps, and paying neighbouring Pacific Islands to incarcerate other would-be immigrants. At the same time, few Aborigines expect any advance to their cause while Howard remains in power. But since 1996 he has presided over secure economic growth, encouraging an atmosphere in which material self-advancement and self-reliance are the primary measures of what is right.

1967	1992
Popular referendum overwhelmingly gives Aborigines the status of full citizens	High Court rejects terra nullius and rules that some Aborigines have legal title to their traditional lands (Mabo case)

The Culture

REGIONAL IDENTITY

Shrimp-eating, beer-guzzling Paul Hogan has a lot to answer for. The actor's long succession of beloved comedy characters skewered Australian cultural peccadilloes with pinpoint accuracy. Hoges' cultural cachet may be long depleted, but his legacy endures – the worldwide perception of Australians as tanned, outback-dwelling, muscle-bound croc wrestlers. But fair crack of the whip: Aussies are a bit more diverse than that (not that there's anything wrong with a beer or 10 and a bit of bush in your blood).

Take Victoria's capital, Melbourne. The city has a unique, stylish European flavour – almost half of Melbourne's population hails from other shores, importing the best cuisine, fashion and culture from their respective nations. There's a stack of clichés about Melbourne, too: the weather's crap; the locals wear all black; they love to have a go at that big, hedonistic city to the north; coffee and cafés have replaced beer and pubs. But there's a reason why they're clichés – they tend to be true.

Up the coast in New South Wales, we find an identity rooted in the past. NSW was the site of Australia's first permanent European settlement and, as such, the New South Welsh often believe the rest of the country should come to them. That pose has spread from the swish capital, Sydney, to the coastal region, where lively developments are springing up – like Newcastle, once branded an industrial nightmare. Naturally, there's a flipside: residents of coastal havens like Byron Bay fear being priced out, claiming the hordes are taking over.

Speaking of Sydney, her locals are a self-assured lot, and why not? Sydney may be Australia's oldest city, but she's far beyond staid, fizzing and popping instead with sybaritic energy. Sydney loves a party (think Mardi Gras), and any excuse will do (think the Olympics – just kidding). Backed with a stellar economy and lush outdoor attractions (think stretches of sun-drenched beach), there's good reason for that famous confidence (think arrogance – according to other states).

That leaves the Sunshine State – Queensland. Superficially, Queenslanders epitomise the Australian lifestyle of sun, surf and smiles perhaps more than any other state. The classic Aussie drawl is thick and impenetrable north of the state capital, Brisbane, where life is decidedly more languorous. Queenslanders tend to express outright contempt when visitors (mainly Melburnians) talk of brutal winter climes. Easy for them – they have 300 days of sunshine a year, so they can afford to glam it up.

Southerners like to refer to Brisbane as 'BrisVegas' and 'Brisneyland', thumbing their noses at the city's undeniable glitz. As the gateway to the tourist traps up north, perhaps a degree of 'cheese' is unavoidable. But Brisbane, like Newcastle, is no longer the soporific hollow of old – this *is* the 21st century, after all. With its tropical landscape, temperate climate and developing arts scene, Brisbane is coming up as one of Australia's most desirable locations.

LIFESTYLE

Most Victorians live in Melbourne, enjoying a variety of cultural and sporting events, lush green gardens and parks. Melburnians see that as a coveted lifestyle, emboldened by the *Economist*'s Intelligence Unit, which named Melbourne the world's most liveable city in 2002, 2003 and 2004.

Crikey (www.crikey.com .au), a scurrilous, hugely irreverent indie-news service, was started by former Victorian government aide Stephen Mayne. Motto: 'Taking a long spike to bloated egos.'

However, there's a real fear among many locals that the marketing hype generated from such accolades will trap Melbourne in the role of 'lifestyle haven', devoted to shopping, gambling, major events and not much else. As a result, an increasing number of Melburnians are choosing the quieter life instead, plumping for natural beauty and cheap housing in regional towns.

Despite the state's hilariously unpredictable weather, the beach holiday is still a priority for many Vics. Families flock to the coastal regions to follow the sun, or else migrate to Queensland resorts such as Noosa and the Sunshine Coast when the fickle climate plays up.

No such problems in Sydney, where many Sydneysiders see no reason to leave the city limits. There are a lot of ingredients that make Sydney work for its residents: the balmy weather; the long stretches of beach; the well-preserved waterfront; the strong economy and stable local government.

'Despite the state's hilariously unpredictable weather, the beach holiday is still a priority for many Vics.'

Like Melburnians, the identikit image of the 'typical' Sydneysider has become a well-worn cliché: he/she works in real estate; has an ear shaped like a mobile phone; wears designer clothes; lives in a brushed-steel, inner-city apartment; drives a Toyota but dreams of a BMW. Outside work, our identikit citizen loafs on the beach, pumps iron in the gym, jogs around Centennial Park, hits the clubs at night. They could be straight or gay: Sydney, after all, is Australia's gay mecca.

Outside the urban areas, there's a running joke that 'NSW' stands for 'Newcastle, Sydney and Wollongong', based on a suspicion that they're the only three areas of the state that get any government attention or services.

NSW's nonchalant south coast features quiet fishing towns, lonesome wilderness areas and roadside produce stalls. Northern NSW is a different story: many of Australia's hippies have forged a niche there, which means that the farms are organic and alternative philosophies abound – the roadside stalls might sell healing crystals or UFO landing kits.

That leaves Queensland, where, at heart, most citizens are urban types, hugging the coastal suburban sprawl between Coolangatta and Cairns. Inexorable development continues, especially in the densely populated southeast, and, although some Queenslanders might moan about the rising property prices, they're still chuffed that they live in one of the country's fastest-growing regions.

Historically, Queensland has been one of Australia's great bastions of conservatism, and even today that attitude is still hard to shake. Nonetheless, artistic communities dot the Gold Coast and Sunshine Coast hinterlands, and several of Brisbane's inner suburbs have an 'alternative' sheen. The rainforests of far north Queensland are still home to a few 'ferals' (kind of like techno-hippies), as is the hinterland around Noosa and NSW's Byron Bay. Meanwhile, many retirees move to the Gold Coast to chase the casino-driven Grey Dollar and the sun's golden rays.

POPULATION

Australia's population is 20.2 million. NSW, the most populous state, has 6.7 million people, while Victoria has 4.9 million and Queensland 3.8 million. Sydney (4.2 million) and Melbourne (3.5 million) are the largest Australian cities.

The first immigrants were mostly British, Irish and Scottish, but the Chinese came after the discovery of gold in the 1850s, and many Italians migrated here to work in the NSW and Queensland sugar industry, and on southeastern Victorian farms.

After WWII mass-immigration policies brought populations from Italy, New Zealand, the former Yugoslavia, Greece, Germany, the Netherlands, Vietnam, China and other countries. In 2004 Australia accepted 111,000 immigrants, with 40,000 settling in NSW, 28,000 in Victoria and 20,000 in Queensland.

Although most population growth tends to occur on the Melbourne and Sydney fringes, a lot of movement is from NSW northward, making Queensland's east coast the country's fastest-growing region. Development is rampant on the central coast of NSW. In Queensland, there's record annual growth in Cairns, the Sunshine Coast and especially the Gold Coast (even though much of the state's population lives within 150km of Brisbane).

An estimated 459,000 (about 2% of Australia's population) identify themselves as Aboriginal, Torres Strait Islanders or of Indigenous origin. NSW has Australia's largest Indigenous population (around 135,000), with most people residing in and around Sydney. Queensland has the country's second-largest Indigenous population (126,000), focused in Brisbane but also with large populations around Townsville and Cairns. More than half of Australia's 42,000 Torres Strait Islanders, from the islands between Cape York and Papua New Guinea, live in northern Queensland and on the islands of the strait itself.

The Chaser (www.chaser .com.au), like America's Onion, utilises 'mockumentary' to undermine mass culture. Warning: 'Not recommended in places that restrict freedom of speech, or Queensland.'

INDIGENOUS AUSTRALIANS

Around 100,000 Aborigines lived in Victoria before Europeans arrived; by 1860 there were just 2000 left. Now more than half of Victoria's 28,000-strong Indigenous population lives in Melbourne. Victorian Koories (Aborigines from southeastern Australia) lived in 38 dialect groups speaking 10 languages; each group was divided into clans and subclans. 'Dispersion' and 'assimilation' policies eradicated the purely traditional lifestyle, but today some Victorian groups are attempting to revive their cultures, including the Brambuk Aboriginal Cultural Centre, the Krowathunkoolong Keeping Place (p117) and the Dharnya Centre.

When the British first arrived at Sydney Cove, there were approximately 3000 Aborigines, using three main languages encompassing several dialects and subgroups around what is now Sydney. Today more Aboriginal people live in Sydney than in any other Australian city – the region has more than 30,000 Indigenous inhabitants, most descended from migratory inland tribes, including a small number of Torres Strait Islanders. The Sydney suburbs of Redfern and Waterloo have a large Aboriginal population.

Indigenous people of many tribes inhabited the area encompassing Queensland for tens of thousands of years before European settlement. By the turn of the 19th century, the Aborigines who had survived the bloody settlement of Queensland had been run off their lands and the white authorities had set up ever-shrinking reserves to contain the survivors. Today Murri is the term used to refer to the Indigenous people of Queensland.

SPORT

All three East Coast states can stake legitimate claims to the title of Australia's sporting mecca, whether it's in the gladiatorial arena of rugby ('thugby') up north or in the smouldering cauldron of Aussie Rules football ('aerial ping pong') down south. In summer cricket ('watching paint dry') is a nationwide obsession.

Creeping up is soccer, which is gaining a toehold in all states – the game has progressed from when it was strictly for 'sheilas, wogs and poofters' (as memorably articulated by one prominent soccer identity). Confusingly, soccer has just been rebranded as 'football' to match the rest of the world (over a hundred years late, but still…) – see the **National Football League** (www.footballaustralia.com.au) for more details.

Other popular sports on the coast include basketball, netball, motor sports, driving the porcelain bus, hockey, farnarkling, tennis, elbow bending, horse racing, chundering and surfing.

Australian Rules Football

Melbourne is the spiritual home of that weird hybrid, Australian Rules football (like a cross between rugby and Gaelic football), from where the **Australian Football League** (AFL; www.afl.com.au) administers the national competition. Traditionally, most games are played at the Melbourne Cricket Ground (MCG; p89). During season (March to September), Victorians go footy mad, entering tipping competitions, discussing groins and hamstrings and savouring the latest loutish behaviour (on and off the field).

Queensland has one AFL team, the Brisbane Lions, which won premierships in 2001, 2002 and 2003. The Lions play home games at the Brisbane Cricket Ground (the Gabba; p318). Sydney also has one AFL team, the Sydney Swans, which plays at the Sydney Cricket Ground (SCG; p203).

Rugby

In NSW and Queensland, rugby league (the 13-a-side version) is king, and is administered by the **National Rugby League** (NRL; www.nrl.com). Queensland has two teams in the Sydney-dominated competition: the Brisbane Broncos (p318) and the North Queensland Cowboys, which plays in Townsville. There's a Victorian team, too, the Melbourne Storm, which generally underperforms.

Rugby union (the 15-a-side variant) is almost as popular, especially now that it's turned professional; it's run by the **Australian Rugby Union** (www.rugby.com.au). Historically, union was an amateur sport played by posh gits, and its century-long rivalry with rugby league's professional, working-class oiks was a real battle of ideologies. In the end, capitalism was the real winner – and the Poms, who beat the Aussies in the World Cup final.

Sydney to the Max

If ever a footy team channelled the spirit of its city, it was the Sydney Swans outfit from the mid-1980s. Bankrolled by the eccentric doctor/entrepreneur Geoffrey Edelsten, the Swans dominated the competition for a couple of incandescent years, regularly kicking massive scores as spearheaded by its talismanic forward Warwick Capper. With his white boots, bum-hugging shorts and Rod Stewart–style mane, Capper's flamboyance was matched only by the Swanettes, the team's equally scantily clad, equally blonde cheerleading squad – oh, and the good doctor himself, of course. Edelsten and his wife Leanne, a model, had a penchant for conspicuous consumption: pink limos and helicopters, gold-plated bathroom fittings, that kind of thing. The whole circus was 'Sydney' to the max: loud, crass and ultra-confident…until it all went horribly wrong.

Within the space of just three years, Edelsten had succumbed to one of the most telling 'diseases' of the excessive '80s: corporate bankruptcy. Like fellow Aussie high-fliers Christopher Skase and Alan Bond, Edelsten's vapour-thin infrastructure and 'paper' fortune was a flimsy house of cards just waiting to be blown away.

When the doctor couldn't afford to pay the bills, the Sydney Swans haemorrhaged: top players left and the fans deserted in droves. Despite the glitter and the hype, the Swans still hadn't captured the premiership, ostensibly the reason for the team's existence.

The most anticipated event in the union calendar is the State of Origin series every June/July, when Queensland's Maroons (or Cane Toads) take on arch rivals NSW, known as the Blues (or Cockroaches).

Cricket

Although the aggressive, foul-mouthed Australian cricket team has cleaned up its image recently, it continues to dominate the sport, as it has done for the better part of a decade. Australia currently tops the international rankings in both test (five-day) and one-day competitions. The sport is administered by **Cricket Australia** (www.cricket.com.au).

In Melbourne the hordes head to the MCG to catch the drama of international cricket. The SCG is NSW's main cricketing shrine, while Queensland's is the Gabba. There's also a nationwide, interstate competition and numerous local grades.

The first Australian cricket team to tour England was 100% Victorian Aboriginal – in 1868. The subsequent 'whiteness' of the sport in Australia meant that this achievement was unheralded until recently.

ARTS

Aussies are supposed to be sports-mad and arts-shy, yet statistics tell otherwise: attendance figures for galleries or performing arts are almost double that for all football codes. Cinema is the top pastime, with around two-thirds of the population taking in at least one movie annually. Aussie bookworms cough up around $1 billion for books each year, around 25% of Australians attend a music concert annually and 21% visit a gallery.

Cinema

With the recent completion of its Central City Studios, Melbourne is no longer the only East Coast capital without world-class studios. The Hollywood actioner *Ghostrider* was filmed there in 2005, promising a massive boost to Victoria's film and TV industry.

Notable Victorian features include silly-billy comedy *The Castle* (1997), which pokes mild fun at Aussie stereotypes; the gutsy *Head On* (1998), featuring a gay Greek-Australian as the lead character; and *Ned Kelly* (2003).

Melbourne seems to be breeding a crop of nu-skool horror filmmakers (even if they have to find funding elsewhere). There's James Wan and Leigh Whannell, with their super-sadistic *Saw* (2004), and Greg McLean, with the ultra-vicious *Wolf Creek* (2005), which takes a hunting knife to the Crocodile Dundee image.

There's a gritty short-film scene, too, perhaps the country's best, including Adam Elliot and his Oscar-winning claymation, *Harvie Krumpet* (2003).

Benchmark Victorian films from the 1970s include Peter Weir's *Picnic at Hanging Rock* (1975), featuring nubile Anglo schoolgirls mysteriously 'absorbed' into the primitive Aussie landscape; and Dr George Miller's apocalyptic *Mad Max* (1979), starring a raw, pre-fame Mel Gibson as Max, decimating his enemies in a stylised orgy of violence.

In Sydney the construction of Fox Studios cemented NSW's already healthy industry, with many American productions drawn by relatively low costs. Big-budget extravaganzas, financed with overseas money and made for the international market, include *The Matrix* (1999) and *Mission Impossible 2* (2000). Sydneysider Baz Luhrmann's *Moulin Rouge* (2001) was also made there.

Notable Aussie films made in NSW include Ray Lawrence's *Bliss* (1985), a kooky, sexual romp about Sydney advertising exec Harry Joy, and Bruce Beresford's classic *Puberty Blues* (1981), which examines south Sydney's surf culture in all its sordid glory.

Gregor Jordan's *Two Hands* (1999) is a comic look at Sydney's nerdy criminal underworld, while *The Boys* (1998) is a sharply observed, deeply disturbing look at three brothers and the violence that underscores their destiny.

Recently, Queensland has made significant inroads into the Australian film industry. Commercial production is based around the Warner Roadshow studios on the Gold Coast, which has produced successful family-orientated films including *Scooby Doo* (2002) and *Peter Pan* (2003).

Other titles filmed in the state include *The Thin Red Line* (1998), Terence Malick's critically acclaimed tale of WWII soldiers in the Pacific, and *Crocodile Dundee in LA* (2001), the latest instalment in Paul Hogan's record-breaking Aussie series (parts one and two also had Queensland locations).

Local films include *Gettin' Square* (2003), a funny/dark tale of two low-rent crims; *Swimming Upstream* (2002), about Anthony Fingleton, a Queensland swimmer in the 1960s; and *Blurred* (2002), which follows five teenagers during 'schoolies' week.

Then there's *Undead* (2002), made by local boys the Spierig Brothers in southeast Queensland. It's about a town that becomes infected with a zombie virus (southern states might see that as a northern metaphor of sorts, as the brothers slyly hint).

Sydney film *Lantana* (director Ray Lawrence; 2001) examines a small suburban community where action breeds reaction, senses are deadened and paranoia is rife. Yet everyone is dependent on everyone else. An effective metaphor for modern life.

Literature

Victoria has produced a raft of classic works, including *The Getting of Wisdom* (1910), by Henry Handel (Florence Ethel) Richardson, about a girl's coming of age; *The Songs of a Sentimental Bloke* (1915), by CJ Dennis, poetic verse about a good Aussie bloke who likes beer, fighting and the love of a good woman; *For the Term of His Natural Life* (1927), by Marcus Clarke, a powerful account of Australia's convict era; *My Brother Jack* (1964), by George Johnston, the moving story of two brothers between two world wars; and *Picnic at Hanging Rock* (1967), by Joan Lindsay.

Former Victorian Peter Carey is probably the state's best-known contemporary writer; he now lives in New York. He won the Booker Prize in 1988 for *Oscar & Lucinda*, a lush 19th-century tale of a couple who gamble on love and life, culminating in their quest to transport a glass church across the Aussie landscape; and again in 2002 for *True History of the Kelly Gang*, based on the letters of Ned Kelly and controversial for its suggestion that the Kelly gang were transvestites.

Helen Garner's works include *Monkey Grip* (1977; later made into a film), a terrific account of '70s Melbourne bohemia, and *The Children's Bach* (1984). Other significant Melbourne writers include Shane Maloney, Kerry Greenwood, Barry Dickins, Robert Dessaix, Christos Tsiolkas, Fiona Capp, Michelle de Kretser and Andrew Masterson.

Max Barry has largely slipped under the local radar, while garnering a heap of overseas praise for his prophetic anti-corporate novels, including *Jennifer Government* (2003).

Books with NSW settings include *Eucalyptus* (1998), by Murray Bail, a fairy tale set among iconic gum trees; *The Harp in the South* (1948), by Ruth Park, an account of an impoverished family's life in Surry Hills when the suburb was a crowded slum; and Kate Grenville's *The Idea of Perfection* (1999), about the ideological clash when a Sydney museum curator goes to rural NSW to save an old bridge.

Voss (1957), by Patrick White, contrasts the harsh and unforgiving outback with colonial Sydney. In the 1980s David Malouf, a Lebanese-

Australian who is one of Queensland's most recognised writers, transformed it into an opera with a libretto. Malouf is responsible for evocative, often bitter tales of Brisbane boyhood, including *Johnno* (1975). His Gold Coast novel, *Fly Away Peter* (1982), tells the story of a returned soldier struggling to come to terms with ordinary life.

Thea Astley's work includes *Hunting the Wild Pineapple* (1979), set in the rainforests of northern Queensland. More recently, Brissie bad boy John Birmingham has enjoyed success, notably with *He Died with a Felafel in his Hand* (1994), later made into a film by Richard Lowenstein.

Australia's best-known Aboriginal poet and writer is Oodgeroo Noonuccal (Kath Walker), who was born on North Stradbroke Island in 1920. Herb Wharton, an Aboriginal author from Cunnamulla, has written a series of novels and short stories about the lives of the Murri stockmen, including *Unbranded* (1992) and *Cattle Camp* (1994).

Most of the big issues in Aboriginal Australia are covered in contemporary Aboriginal writing. James Miller's *Koori: A Will to Win* (1985), examines the history of European settlement in Australia from a Koori perspective; *My Place* (1987), Sally Morgan's prize-winning autobiography, traces her discovery of her Aboriginal heritage; *The Fringe Dwellers* (1961), by Nene Gare, describes what it's like to be an Aborigine growing up in white society; and Sam Watson's *The Kadaitcha Sung* (1990) combines science fiction, crime fiction, fantasy, social analysis and historical references, enjoying a cult following.

Music

In the East Coast capitals and touristy locales, there are plenty of MCs, DJs and bedroom boffins producing hip-hop, house, techno, drum 'n' bass, breaks, ambient, electro and trance. Melbourne's Avalanches blend hip-hop, sampledelica, breaks, disco, funk and sweaty live performances. The same city also boasts a lineage of experimental 'sound design', with leading practitioners including Philip Brophy, Ollie Olsen and David Thrussell.

Melbourne's pub-rock scene in the late '80s/early '90s was superlative, throwing up such true originals as the scarifying Birthday Party, starring Nick ('the Stripper') Cave as a full-blown madman.

More sedate Melbourne-based artists include troubadours Paul Kelly and Stephen Cummings, South Australian expat Dave Graney (the self-styled King of Pop), grunge godfather Kim Salmon and folksy Lisa Miller. Jet, Melbourne's answer to the Strokes, successfully surf the 'new rock' revival.

The 'Singing Budgie' herself, Kylie Minogue, no longer lives here. Neither does Mr Cave. Nor do gloom-rock merchants, the violin-led Dirty Three.

In the late 1970s Sydney could also claim a ripper pub-rock scene, when incendiary bands like Radio Birdman and the Screaming Tribesmen trod the boards. These days clubs and DJs rule, although there's still some solid rock and pop action to be found. Local performers include long-time faves the Whitlams, whose Sydney-centric tunes have converted into Australia-wide acclaim, and Frenzal Rhomb, popular with moshing teenagers. Other acts include the theatrical Machine Gun Fellatio and the over-hyped Vines.

Avant-jazz trio The Necks were originally based in Sydney, but have since dispersed overseas; their hypnotic, glacial pieces take their sweet time to unfurl and are utterly compelling.

Super-stylised film *Chopper* (director Andrew Dominik; 2000) presents Melbourne celebrity crim Mark 'Chopper' Read as both victim and exploiter of media hype, with black-as-coal humour and action that's hotter than a blowtorch to the soles of the feet.

Queensland has produced some outstanding Indigenous musicians, including Christine Anu, a Torres Strait Islander from Cairns who blends Creole-style rap, Islander chants and traditional languages with English. Other regional artists include Torres Strait Islander Rita Mills and Maroochy Barambah of the Sunshine Coast.

Brisbane's pub-rock scene from the late '70s produced one of Australia's greatest bands, the rowdy Saints, who went on to bigger things in Sydney and London. More recently, Powderfinger has played a dominant role in the music industry. Alternative Queensland bands with loyal followings include Regurgitator and Custard.

Melbourne, Sydney and Brisbane have vibrant classical scenes but most of the state orchestras tour the East Coast's major centres, too. The production company **Musica Viva Australia** (www.musicaviva.com.au) presents around 2500 concerts each year across Australia and the world.

Visual Arts

In the 1880s a group of young artists developed the first distinctively Australian style of watercolour painting, capturing the unique qualities of Australian life and the bush. Their work is generally referred to as the Heidelberg School. In Sydney a contemporary movement worked at Sirius Cove.

Both groups were influenced by the French plein-air painters, whose practice of working outdoors to capture the effects of natural light led directly to Impressionism. The main artists were Tom Roberts, Arthur Streeton, Frederick McCubbin, Louis Abrahams, Charles Conder, Julian Ashton and, later, Walter Withers.

In the 1940s, under the patronage of John and Sunday Reed in suburban Melbourne, a new generation of artists (the Heide movement) redefined the direction of Australian art, including some of Australia's most famous contemporary artists, such as Sir Sidney Nolan and Heide associate Arthur Boyd.

More recently the work of painters such as Fred Williams, John Olsen and Brett Whiteley has made an international impression. Whiteley is certainly Sydney's (and probably Australia's) best-known modern artist; he died in 1992. Other notable Sydney artists include Ian Fairweather, Keith Looby, Ian Grant and Judy Cassab.

Contemporary Melbourne artists like Ricky Swallow, Bill Henson, Nick Mangan, Juan Ford and Christian Capurro explore the relationship between reality and representation across multiple disciplines. Patricia Piccinini takes cues from the technological world, exploring ethical dilemmas with often disturbing results.

Queensland is a rich centre of traditional and contemporary Aboriginal art. Judy Watson and Gordon Bennett have both won the Moët & Chandon Prize for contemporary artists.

The surreal, tragicomic work of photographer and filmmaker Tracey Moffatt seeks to understand Aboriginality via a white media lens, and is well worth seeking out.

Theatre & Dance

Melbourne's main theatre troupe, the **Melbourne Theatre Company** (MTC; www .mtc.com.au), is Australia's oldest, staging around a dozen annual performances at the Victorian Arts Centre (p89). These include works by the leading contemporary Australian playwright, Sydney-based David Williamson, whose dissection of middle-class rituals began in 1971 with *The Removalists* and *Don's Party*.

Andrew McGahan's award-winning novel *Praise* (1991) stuns with its dark take on mismatched love in Brisbane. Sex and drugs attempt to enlighten, but modern life proves exceedingly dull and pointless. Later made into a film.

There's also the **Sydney Theatre Company** (www.sydneytheatre.com.au) and the **Queensland Theatre Company** (www.qldtheatreco.com.au), along with plenty of small-scale progressive theatres.

Australia's national ballet company, the **Australian Ballet** (www.australianballet.com.au), is among the world's finest. It tours locally and internationally and has a diverse repertoire bolstered by renowned guest choreographers.

Australia's innovative modern-dance scene is typified by the **Sydney Dance Company** (www.sydneydance.com) and Melbourne's **Chunky Move** (www.chunkymove.com).

The **Bangarra Dance Theatre** (www.bangarra.com.au) combines 40,000 years of Aboriginal and Torres Strait Islands performance with contemporary, bold choreography.

It's generally agreed that Victoria produced the world's first feature-length fiction film, *The Story of the Kelly Gang* (1906), a hit with Australian and British audiences.

Environment Tim Flannery

Tim Flannery is a
naturalist, explorer and
writer. He is the author
of a number of award-
winning books including
The Future Eaters. Tim
Flannery lives in Adelaide
where he is director of
the South Australian
Museum and a professor
at the University of
Adelaide.

Australia's plants and animals are just about the closest things to alien life
you are likely to encounter on earth. That's because Australia has been
isolated from the other continents for a very long time – at least 45 million
years. The other habitable continents have been able to exchange various
species at different times because they've been linked by land bridges. Just
15,000 years ago it was possible to walk from the southern tip of Africa
right through Asia and the Americas to Terra del Fuego. Not Australia,
however. Its birds, mammals, reptiles and plants have taken their own
separate and very different evolutionary journey, and the result today is
the world's most distinct – and one of its most diverse – natural realms.

The first naturalists to investigate Australia were astonished by what
they found. Here the swans were black – to Europeans this was a metaphor
for the impossible – while mammals such as the platypus and echidna
were discovered to lay eggs. It really was an upside-down world, where
many of the larger animals hopped, where each year the trees shed their
bark rather than their leaves, and where the 'pears' were made of wood.

If you are visiting Australia for a short time, you might need to go
out of your way to experience some of the richness of the environment.
That's because Australia is a subtle place, and some of the natural environment – especially around the cities – has been damaged or replaced
by trees and creatures from Europe. Places like Sydney, however, have
preserved extraordinary fragments of their original environment that are
relatively easy to access. Before you enjoy them though, it's worthwhile
understanding the basics about how nature operates in Australia. This
is important because there's nowhere like Australia, and once you have
an insight into its origins and natural rhythms, you will appreciate the
place so much more.

A UNIQUE ENVIRONMENT

There are two really big factors that go a long way towards explaining nature in Australia: its soils and its climate. Both are unique. Australian soils
are the more subtle and difficult to notice of the two, but they have been
fundamental in shaping life here. On the other continents, processes such
as volcanism, mountain building and glacial activity have been busy creating new soil in recent geological times. Just think of the glacial-derived soils

Pizzey and Knight's *Field
Guide to Birds of Australia*
is an indispensable guide
for bird-watchers, and
anyone peripherally
interested in Australia's
feathered tribes. Knight's
illustrations are both
beautiful and helpful in
identification.

of North America, north Asia and Europe. They feed the world today, and
were made by glaciers grinding up rock of differing chemical composition
over the last two million years. The rich soils of India and parts of South
America were made by rivers eroding mountains, while Java in Indonesia
owes its extraordinary richness to volcanoes.

All of these soil-forming processes have been almost absent from Australia in more recent times. Only volcanoes have made a contribution,
and they cover less than 2% of the continent's land area. In fact, for the
last 90 million years, beginning deep in the age of dinosaurs, Australia
has been geologically comatose. It was too flat, warm and dry to attract
glaciers, its crust too ancient and thick to be punctured by volcanoes or
folded into mountains.

Under such conditions no new soil is created and the old soil is leached
of all its goodness, and is blown and washed away. The leaching is done
by rain. Even if just 30cm of it falls each year, that adds up to a column
of water 30 million kilometres high passing through the soil over 100

million years, and that can do a great deal of leaching! Almost all of Australia's mountain ranges are more than 90 million years old, so you will see a lot of sand here, and a lot of country where the rocky 'bones' of the land are sticking up through the soil. It is an old, infertile landscape, and life in Australia has been adapting to these conditions for aeons.

Australia's misfortune in respect to soils is echoed in its climate. In most parts of the world outside the wet tropics, life responds to the rhythm of the seasons: summer to winter, or wet to dry. Most of Australia experiences seasons – sometimes very severe ones – yet life does not respond solely to them. This can clearly be seen by the fact that although there's plenty of snow and cold country in Australia, there are almost no trees that shed their leaves in winter, nor do any Australian animals hibernate. Instead there is a far more potent climatic force that Australian life must obey: El Niño.

The cycle of flood and drought that El Niño brings to Australia is profound. Its rivers – even the mighty Murray River, the nation's largest, which runs through the southeast – can be miles wide one year, while you can literally step over their flow the next. This is the power of El Niño, and its effect, when combined with Australia's poor soils, manifests itself compellingly. As you might expect from this, relatively few of Australia's birds are seasonal breeders, and few migrate. Instead, they breed when the rain comes, and a large percentage are nomads, following the rain across the breadth of the continent.

So challenging are conditions in Australia that its birds have developed some extraordinary habits. The kookaburras, magpies and blue wrens you are likely to see – to name just a few – have developed a breeding system called 'helpers at the nest'. The helpers are the young adult birds of previous breedings, which stay with their parents to help bring up the new chicks. Just why they should do this was a mystery until it was realised that conditions in Australia can be so harsh that more than two adult birds are needed to feed the nestlings. This pattern of breeding is very rare in places like Asia, Europe and North America, but it is common in a wide array of Australian birds.

Australia is famous as the home of the kangaroo and other marsupials. Unless you visit a wildlife park, such creatures are not easy to see as most are nocturnal. Their lifestyles, however, are exquisitely attuned to Australia's harsh conditions. Have you ever wondered why kangaroos, alone among the world's larger mammals, hop? It turns out that hopping is the most efficient way of getting about at medium speeds. This is because the energy of the bounce is stored in the tendons of the legs – much like in a pogo stick – while the intestines bounce up and down like a piston, emptying and filling the lungs without needing to activate the chest muscles. When you travel long distances to find meagre feed, such efficiency is a must.

Marsupials are so efficient that they need to eat a fifth less food than equivalent-sized placental mammals (everything from bats to rats, whales and ourselves). But some marsupials have taken energy efficiency much further. If you get to visit a wildlife park or zoo, you might notice that faraway look in a koala's eyes. It seems as if nobody is home – and this in fact is near the truth. Several years ago biologists announced that koalas are the only living creatures that have brains that don't fit their skulls. Instead they have a shrivelled walnut of a brain that rattles around in a fluid-filled cranium. Other researchers have contested this finding, however, pointing out that the brains of the koalas examined for the study may have shrunk because these organs are so soft. Whether soft-brained or empty-headed, there is no doubt that the koala is not the Einstein of the animal world,

Despite anything Australians tell you about koalas (AKA dropbears), there's no risk of one falling on your head (deliberately or not) as you walk beneath the trees.

and we now believe that it has sacrificed its brain to energy efficiency. Brains cost a lot to run: our brains typically weigh 2% of our bodyweight, but use 20% of the energy we consume. Koalas eat gum leaves, which are so toxic that they use 20% of their energy just detoxifying this food. This leaves little energy for the brain, and living in the treetops where there are so few predators means that they can get by with few wits at all.

> Of Australia's 155 species of land snakes, 93 are venomous. Australia is home to something like 10 of the world's 15 most venomous snakes.

The peculiar constraints of the Australian environment have not made everything dumb. The koala's nearest relative, the wombat (of which there are three species), have large brains for a marsupial. These creatures live in complex burrows and can weigh up to 35kg, making them the largest herbivorous burrowers on earth. Because their burrows are effectively air-conditioned, they have the neat trick of turning down their metabolic activity when they are in residence. One physiologist who studied their thyroid hormones found that biological activity ceased to such an extent in sleeping wombats that, from a hormonal point of view, they appeared to be dead! Wombats can remain underground for a week at a time, and can get by on just a third of the food needed by a sheep of equivalent size. One day perhaps, efficiency-minded farmers will keep wombats instead of sheep. At the moment, however, that isn't possible, for the largest of the wombat species, the northern hairy-nose, is one of the world's rarest creatures, with only around 100 surviving in a remote nature reserve in central Queensland.

Some of the more common marsupials you might catch a glimpse of in the national parks around Australia's major cities are the species of antechinus. These nocturnal, rat-sized creatures lead an extraordinary life. The males live for just 11 months, the first 10 of which consist of a concentrated burst of eating and growing. And like teenage males, the day comes when their minds turn to sex, and in the antechinus this becomes an obsession. As they embark on their quest for females they forget to eat and sleep. Instead they gather in logs and woo passing females by serenading them with squeaks. Just two weeks after they reach 'puberty' every single male is dead, exhausted by sex and burdened with carrying around swollen testes. This extraordinary life history may also have evolved in response to Australia's trying environmental conditions. It seems likely that if the males survived mating, they would compete with the females as they tried to find enough food to feed their growing young. Basically, antechinus dads are disposable. They do better for antechinus posterity if they go down in a testosterone-fuelled blaze of glory.

> H Cogger's large volume, *Reptiles and Amphibians of Australia*, allows you to identify a goodly assortment of venomous snakes. Alternatively, wield it as a defensive weapon if necessary.

One thing you will see lots of in Australia is reptiles. Snakes are abundant, and they include some of the most venomous species known. Where the opportunities to feed are few and far between, it's best not to give your prey a second chance, hence the potent venom. Around Sydney and other built-up parts of Australia, however, you are far more likely to encounter a harmless python than a dangerously venomous species. Snakes will usually leave you alone if you don't fool with them. Observe, back quietly away and don't panic, and most of the time you'll be OK.

WATCHING WILDLIFE

Some regions of Australia offer unique opportunities to see wildlife. For those intrigued by the diversity of tropical rainforests, Queensland's World Heritage areas are well worth visiting. Birds of paradise, cassowaries and a variety of other birds can be seen by day, while at night you can search for tree-kangaroos (yes, some kinds of kangaroos do live in the treetops). In your nocturnal wanderings you are highly likely to see curious possums, some of which look like skunks, and other marsupials that today are restricted to a small area of northeast Queensland.

GNARLY PODS, SCRIBBLY INSECTS AND TALL STRANGLERS Simon Sellars

Aussies love flora. We even named our favourite brand of margarine 'Flora'. Get the message? And along the East Coast, there's a diverse spread (get it?) of flora. That's because the habitats are rich and the rainfall is reasonably high (by Australian standards): 200mm to 500mm per year.

Estuaries and coastal lakes are surrounded by melaleucas (paperbarks), callistemons (bottle-brushes), leptospermums (tea trees, often shaped by the wind) and avicennia (or 'mangrove' to you, chief). And how about that mangrove? A little Aussie battler, rugged and rough as guts, the mangrove survives saltwater inundation with an arsenal of tricks: it expunges excess salt through its leaves; its tangled root systems allow it to 'breathe' when exposed at low tide; and it stores oxygen in spongy tissues for use during high tide. Now that's tough! Adaptable! Bet you can't store oxygen in spongy tissues.

In the forest areas that back the beaches, you'll do well to avoid the needle-like foliage of casuarinas (she-oaks); xanthorrhoeas (grass trees), with their long, woody flower spikes; acacias (wattles), characterised by clusters of fuzzy, yellow-balled flowers in spring and winter; and the idiosyncratic, gnarled seed pods and furry flowers of the coastal banksia (Banksia integrifolia).

Not far back from the shore is the archetypal Australian 'bush' – forests with a full complement of eucalypt (gum tree) species. Fair dinkum, you thought the mangrove was adaptable? Get a load of the ubiquitous eucalypt. Its unique character is designed to give it a fighting advantage in this harsh land: its leaves have a waxy coating to reduce water loss and they also have a fragrant oil content to discourage herbivores. The oil is what gives the bush its bluish tinge – think 'Blue Mountains' (p207), if you're having trouble.

Eucalyptus maculata (spotted gum), with its conspicuously spotted and dimpled bark, is ever present, but also keep your peepers peeled for E sclerophylla (scribbly gum), with odd, scribbly insect tracks on the bark.

Although forest types change according to geography and other environmental conditions, pockets of warm temperate forests are found everywhere from far-eastern Gippsland (p123) to the subtropical forests at Port Macquarie (p232). Northern Queensland's tropical rainforest covers just 0.3% of the continent, but it contains about half of Australia's plant species. Strike a light – that's really dense.

Some species are found across several rainforest types. Tall strangler figs, with their distinctive lattice-buttressed roots, make an appearance in rainforests from Port Macquarie to the far northern reaches of the Queensland tropical coast.

Fossils from as far afield as western Queensland and southern Victoria indicate that such creatures were once widespread.

The fantastic diversity of Queensland's Great Barrier Reef (see the boxed text, p377) is legendary, and a boat trip out to the reef from Cairns or Port Douglas is unforgettable.

If your visit extends only as far as Sydney, however, don't give up on seeing Australian nature, for the Sydney sandstone – which extends approximately 150km around the city – is one of the most diverse and spectacular regions in Australia. In springtime spectacular red waratahs abound in the region's parks, while the woody pear (a relative of the waratah) that so confounded the early colonists can also be seen, alongside more than 1500 other species of flowering plants. Even in a Sydney backyard you're likely to see more reptile species (mostly skinks) than can be found in all of Great Britain – so keep an eye out!

Some of Australia's most beautiful national parks are on the UN's World Heritage Register (http://whc.unesco.org/heritage.htm), which documents natural and cultural places of world significance.

NATIONAL & STATE PARKS

Australia has more than 500 national parks: nonurban protected wilderness areas of environmental or natural importance. Each state defines and runs its own national parks, but the principle is the same throughout Australia. National parks include rainforests, vast tracts of empty outback, strips of coastal dune land and rugged mountain ranges.

ENVIRONMENTAL CHALLENGES

The European colonisation of Australia, commencing in 1788, heralded a period of catastrophic environmental upheaval, with the result that Australians today are struggling with some of the most severe environmental problems to be found anywhere. It may seem strange that a population of just 20 million, living in a continent the size of the USA minus Alaska, could inflict such damage on its environment, but Australia's long isolation, its fragile soils and difficult climate have made it particularly vulnerable to human-induced change.

Damage to Australia's environment has been inflicted in several ways, the most important being the introduction of pest species, destruction of forests, overstocking rangelands, inappropriate agriculture and interference with water flows. Beginning with the escape of domestic cats into the Australian bush shortly after 1788, a plethora of vermin, from foxes to wild camels and cane toads, have run wild in Australia, causing extinctions in the native fauna. One out of every 10 native mammals living in Australia prior to European colonisation is now extinct, and many more are highly endangered. Extinctions have also affected native plants, birds and amphibians.

The destruction of forests has also had a profound effect. Most of Australia's rainforests have suffered clearing, while conservationists fight with loggers over the last unprotected stands of 'old growth'. Many Australian rangelands have been chronically overstocked for more than a century, resulting in extreme vulnerability of both soils and rural economies to Australia's drought and flood cycle, as well as extinction of many native species. The development of agriculture has involved land clearance and the provision of irrigation, and here again the effect has been profound.

In terms of financial value, just 1.5% of Australia's land surface provides over 95% of agricultural yield, but despite the enormity of the biological crisis engulfing Australia, governments and the community have been slow to respond. It was in the 1980s that coordinated action began to take place, but not until the '90s that major steps were taken. The establishment of **Landcare** (www.landcareaustralia.com.au) – an organisation enabling people to effectively address local environmental issues – and the expenditure of $2.5 billion through the National Heritage Trust Fund have been important national initiatives. Some of the issues the nation faces are so difficult that, as yet, little has been achieved in terms of halting the destructive processes. Individuals are also banding together to help. Groups like the **Australian Bush Heritage Fund** (www.bushheritage.asn.au) and the **Australian Wildlife Conservancy** (AWC; www.australianwildlife.org) allow people to donate funds and time to the conservation of native species. Some such groups have been spectacularly successful; the AWC, for example, already manages many endangered species over its 1.3-million-acre holdings.

Australia's problems are so severe that it will take a revolution before they can be overcome, for sustainable practices need to be implemented in every arena of life, from farms to suburbs and city centres. Renewable energy, sustainable agriculture and water use lie at the heart of these changes, and Australians are only now developing the road-map to sustainability that they so desperately need if they are to have a long-term future on the continent.

Love him or hate him, Steve Irwin – our very own ultraeccentric 'Crocodile Hunter' – is an ambassador for Queensland's north. Wrestle with a croc at www .crocodilehunter.com.

Public access is encouraged as long as safety and conservation regulations are observed. In all parks you're asked to do nothing to damage or alter the natural environment. Camping grounds (often with toilets and showers), walking tracks and information centres are often provided for visitors. In most national parks there are restrictions on bringing in pets.

Some national parks are so isolated, rugged or uninviting that you wouldn't want to go there unless you were an experienced bushwalker or 4WD traveller. Other parks, however, are among Australia's major attractions.

State parks and state forests are other forms of nature reserves, owned by state governments and with fewer regulations than national parks. Although state forests can be logged, they are often recreational areas with camping grounds, walking trails and signposted forest drives. Some permit horses and dogs.

East Coast Australia Outdoors

This vast coastline, spanning cool, temperate and tropical climes, is one of the most picturesque and accessible in the world – a natural playground for the energetic and adventurous. Just about every waterborne or land-based activity you can think of is available. As well as the famous sandy beaches there are idyllic tropical islands, spectacular coral reefs, luscious rainforests and numerous national parks and reserves awaiting discovery.

BOATING

The East Coast is a boatie's paradise throughout the year, though during the southern winter enthusiasts migrate towards the warmer north. There are plenty of opportunities for safe inshore boating and adventurous exploration on the high seas. Always check with the local coast guard and maritime authorities about regional conditions and take note of weather forecasts and warnings broadcast on marine radio.

New South Wales

For its entire length the NSW coastline is kinked and wrinkled with bays, inlets and estuaries; ideal water for motorboats and yachts alike. Sydney Harbour is, of course, the jewel in the crown, and the number of yachts carving its waters on any weekend of the year attest to the popularity of this pastime. The simplest boating activity would have to be a harbour cruise (p190), but this city's greatest natural asset is an ideal setting to learn to sail (p190). Just about every coastal town south and north of Sydney has a small harbour protecting a legion of bobbing yachts, and a boat ramp that bursts with activity on weekends. Some of the more popular boating areas include Pittwater (p189) and the Ku-ring-gai Chase National Park (p212), Port Stephens (p225), Myall Lakes (p228), Jervis Bay (p145), Batemans Bay (p156) and Eden (p167).

Queensland

Queensland's waters are a utopia for seafarers of all skill, with some of the most stunning sailing locations in the world. Topping the bill are the picture-postcard Whitsunday Islands (p396), which can be accessed by charter craft based in Airlie Beach (p400).

You can also explore the Great Barrier Reef and some of the islands off the far north Queensland coast on board a chartered boat or cruise from Cairns (p441), Port Douglas (p454) and Cooktown (p464).

Victoria

Victoria's southeast coast boasts a couple of expansive bays and some pretty estuaries where boating is popular. City-based yachties tend to gravitate to the many sailing clubs around Port Phillip Bay (see p78). Other popular boating areas include the sprawling Gippsland Lakes (see Metung, p119), and the lovely Mallacoota Inlet (p130) near the NSW border. Holiday-makers can get out on the water by hiring yachts and launches, which work out to be quite economical with a group of people.

CANOEING, KAYAKING & WHITE-WATER RAFTING

Canoes and kayaks offer travellers the chance to see parts of the East Coast they might otherwise miss, such as rugged river gorges, secluded island beaches and remote wilderness inlets; they also give another

For detailed descriptions of national park trails and camp sites, see the websites at Parks Victoria (www.parkweb.vic.gov.au), NSW National Parks & Wildlife Service (www.nationalparks.nsw.gov.au) and Queensland Parks & Wildlife Service (www.epa.qld.gov.au), or pick up brochures from park visitor information centres.

100 Magic Miles of the Great Barrier Reef – The Whitsunday Islands, by David Colfelt, is sometimes referred to as the bible of Whitsunday sailing. It contains charts with descriptions of all boat anchorages as well as articles on the islands, resorts, dive sites and marine life.

BUSHWALKING

The East Coast contains Australia's greatest cities and its largest urban sprawls, yet it also boasts an extensive coastline preserved in a network of coastal and hinterland national parks and reserves. Some of these protected areas adjoin major population centres and provide easy access for back-to-nature escapes by city dwellers and travellers alike. Not surprisingly, bushwalking is extremely popular along the East Coast, where it is a year-round pursuit. Summer, however, is the most popular time, particularly in the southeast. It is also the most dangerous period for the major hazard of bushfires (see p473 for more information). Regardless of what time of year it is and no matter how short the walk, you should always take plenty of drinking water. It can get very hot over summer, particularly from the Capricorn Coast north, so if you plan to walk at these times you must take into account the local conditions.

New South Wales

Opportunities for bushwalking abound in coastal NSW, with a variety of standards, lengths and terrains. In Sydney, try the breathtaking, but hardly wilderness, Bondi to Coogee Coastal Walk, which combines coastal panoramas with opportunities for a surf or a coffee, or the numerous popular bushwalks in the Blue Mountains (p207), Ku-ring-gai Chase (p212) and Royal (p136) National Parks. For an extended traverse that encompasses the environment around Sydney, the Great North Walk (p212), from Sydney to Newcastle, can be walked in two weeks, or sampled in sections. For superb coastal vistas, wildflowers and short but rugged hikes, the ascents of Pigeon House Mountain (p147), on the NSW south coast, and Mt Warning (p274), on the NSW north coast, can't be beaten.

Queensland

National parks favoured by bushwalkers include Springbrook (p295) in the Gold Coast Hinterland, and Brisbane Forest Park (p307), which is a popular escape from the city. More good parks for bushwalking include the Cooloola section of Great Sandy National Park (p342), just north of the Sunshine Coast, and Wooroonooran National Park (p439), south of Cairns, which contains Queensland's highest peak, Mt Bartle Frere (1622m).

A recent initiative of the state government is the creation of the Great Walks of Queensland. The six walking tracks are the Whitsundays, Sunshine Coast Hinterland, Mackay Highlands, Fraser Island, Gold Coast Hinterland and the Wet Tropics (tropical north Queensland). The Whitsunday Great Walk (see p401) and Fraser Island Great Walk (see the boxed text, p358) are already completed and the rest should be up and running by mid-2006.

In northern Queensland the 32km Thorsborne Trail on Hinchinbrook Island (p429) is simply spectacular. Walker numbers are limited for this popular trail that traverses remote beaches, lush rainforests and crystal-clear creeks.

Victoria

In Victoria's national parks and state forests, walkers enjoy everything from short walks through cool temperate rainforests to more challenging hikes that climb mountains or trace the wilderness coastline. The infrastructure is usually excellent, with marked trails, campgrounds with fireplaces, toilets and fresh water, and park information centres.

If coastal treks are your scene, head down to Wilsons Promontory National Park (p108) in Gippsland, with marked trails from Tidal River and Telegraph Bay that can take anywhere from a few hours to a couple of days. Expect squeaky white sands and clean aquamarine waters, pristine bushland and stunning coastal vistas. Further east, and almost tipping over into NSW, the Croajingolong National Park (p132), near Mallacoota in East Gippsland, offers rugged inland treks and easier coastal walks past historic lighthouses and over sand dunes.

Resources

There are numerous bushwalking guidebooks that can help you prepare for the bush and choose a trail. Lonely Planet's *Walking in Australia* describes various coastal and hinterland walks, many within easy reach of the major cities. There are full descriptions of walks of different lengths and difficulty, as well as comprehensive information on planning, equipment and how to access the trailheads.

Other resources include Tyrone Thomas' *50 Walks in North Queensland* (for walks on the beach or through the rainforest areas of the World Heritage–listed Wet Tropics), *70 walks in Southern NSW and ACT*, and *50 Walks: Coffs Harbour & Gold Coast Hinterland* (covering Tamborine Mountain, Springbrook and Lamington National Parks). *Take a Walk in Queensland's National Parks Southern Zone*, by John and Lyn Daly, provides a comprehensive guide to walks across the southern stretch of the state.

One of the best ways to find out about bushwalking areas is to contact a local bushwalking club. To find a local bushwalking club check the websites of the **Confederation of Bushwalking Clubs NSW** (www.bushwalking.org.au/code.html), the **Federation of Victorian Walking Clubs** (www.vicnet.net.au/~vicwalk) and the **Queensland Federation of Bushwalking Clubs** (www.geocities.com/qfbwc), or look in the *Yellow Pages* under 'Clubs – Bushwalking'.

Safety Guidelines

Before embarking on a bushwalking trip, consider the following points to ensure a safe and enjoyable experience:

- Be sure you are healthy and feel comfortable walking for a sustained period.
- Obtain reliable information about physical and environmental conditions along your intended route (eg from park authorities).
- Before tackling a long or remote walk, tell someone responsible about your plans and arrange to contact them when you return.
- Walk only in regions, and on tracks, within your realm of experience.
- Boil all water for 10 minutes before drinking it.
- Be aware that weather conditions and terrain vary significantly from one region, or even from one track, to another. Seasonal changes can significantly alter any track. These differences influence the way walkers dress and the equipment they carry.
- Before you set out, ask about the environmental characteristics that can affect your walk and how local, experienced walkers deal with these considerations.

Responsible Bushwalking

To help preserve the ecology and beauty of East Coast Australia please consider the following when bushwalking:

- Stay on established trails, avoid cutting corners and taking short cuts, and stay on hard ground where possible.
- When camping, always use designated campgrounds where provided. When bush camping, look for a natural clearing and avoid camping under large eucalypts, which have a tendency to drop branches without warning.
- Keep your vehicle on existing tracks or roads.
- Pay any fees and possess any permits required by local authorities.
- Do not feed the wildlife as this can lead to animals becoming dependent on hand-outs, to unbalanced populations and to diseases.
- Take all your rubbish out with you – don't burn or bury it.
- Avoid polluting lakes and streams – don't wash yourself or your dishes in them, and keep soap and detergent at least 50m away from waterways.
- Use toilets where provided – otherwise, bury human waste at least 100m away from waterways (taking a hand trowel is a good idea).
- Don't bring dogs or other pets into national parks.
- Take a gas or fuel stove and fuel for cooking.
- Don't light fires unless necessary; if you do need to light a fire, keep the fire small, use only dead fallen wood and ensure you use an existing fireplace. Make sure the fire is completely extinguished before moving on. On total fire ban days, don't (under any circumstances) light a fire.
- Be aware of local laws, regulations and etiquette about wildlife and the environment.

perspective to the coast-hugging metropolitan areas. White-water rafting, on the other hand, may not give you as much time to look around as you negotiate yet another rapid, but the fun factor is cranked up a notch or two.

New South Wales

A good place to have your first sea-kayaking adventure is right in Sydney Harbour (p189); although it is busy and can be challenging for a novice, instruction and guiding is easily arranged. Half-day harbour tours cost about $90 per person. Many of the state's numerous rivers are suitable for canoeing and kayaking, with adventurous swift-flowing runs, and long, lazy paddles. There's good white-water rafting on the Nymboida River (p249) in New England.

For information on events and courses for canoeing and kayaking in NSW, Queensland and Victoria click onto www .nswcanoe.org.au, www .canoeqld.org.au and www.canoevic.org.au, respectively.

Queensland

Not surprisingly, the wet tropical regions boast some renowned white-water rafting locations: the mighty Tully, North Johnstone, Barron and Russell Rivers between Townsville and Cairns top the list. The Tully (p430) is the most popular and has 44 rapids up to grade three to four. Day trips from Cairns (p444) cost about $150 and most of the guides operating tours here have internationally recognised qualifications.

Sea kayaking in the warm Queensland waters is understandably very popular, and there are numerous operations that offer expeditions along the sandy southeast coast, through the calm Barrier Reef lagoon, and among the offshore islands. The protected waterways of the Cooloola section of the Great Sandy National Park (p342) and the inviting beaches of North Stradbroke Island (p321) make for ideal kayaking destinations. Three-hour or half-day tours cost from $60 per person, while kayak hire costs from $30 per person per day. You can rent kayaks and canoes or join tours in several places along the coast, among them Noosa (p336), Magnetic Island (p422), Mission Beach (p432) and around the Whitsunday Islands (p398).

Victoria

Melbourne's Yarra River is popular with paddlers, with its gentle lower reaches suitable for families while more exciting rapids of about grade three can be found in the higher reaches. Keen paddlers hankering for multiday trips can try the classic canoe or raft trip down the Snowy River (p126) from MacKillops Bridge to a pull-out point near Buchan. It takes at least four days and offers superb scenery – rugged gorges, raging rapids – tranquil sections and excellent camping on broad sand bars. Canoe hire costs anywhere from $35 to $75 per day, depending on the operator. Extra expenses may include equipment delivery and pick up.

CYCLING

If you are fit and have the time, you can cycle the entire length of the East Coast. Such long-distance rides are limited only by your endurance and imagination. The East Coast was largely settled on the principle of not having more than a day's horse/coach ride between pubs, so it's possible to tackle lengthy tours and still get a shower and feed at the end of each day. While experienced cyclists can consider a prolonged tour of the coast, those who cycle for fun can sample the great cycling routes for a day or extended weekend. There are helpful bicycle organisations in each of the East Coast states that have lots of maps and useful tips and advice; see the following sections and p487 for details of these organisations and for further information on planning, regulations, and purchasing and hiring bikes.

Other good cycling organisations ready to offer advice include the excellent web resources **Bicycles Network Australia** (www.bicycles.net.au) and also **Bicycling Federation of Australia** (www.bfa.asn.au), with links to cycling clubs and organisations throughout Australia. Alternatively you can look under 'Clubs – Bicycle' in the *Yellow Pages*.

New South Wales & Canberra

Urban bike paths continue to spread through the cities in response to the ever-growing popularity of cycling. Sydney (p189) has an excellent recreational bike-path system and an abundance of bike-hire places. Canberra (p150) is another good place for cycling, with a large network of bike paths.

The NSW coast is an obvious choice for cycle touring, with parks, beaches and little towns constantly providing reasons to dismount. The Hunter Valley (p221) and Blue Mountains (p207) can provide good touring challenges and, again, offer more than just the open road. **Bicycle New South Wales** (☎ 02-9281 4099; www.bicyclensw.org.au; Level 5, 822 George St, Sydney; 🕙 9am-5.30pm Mon-Fri) is an excellent organisation; a stop by the office for advice, maps and books is worthwhile. It publishes *Cycling Around Sydney*, which details routes and cycle paths in Sydney, the Blue Mountains, the Illawarra Coast and the Central Coast, and other booklets on cycling in the state. **Pedal Power ACT** (☎ 02-6248 7995; www.pedalpower.org.au) offers similar information for the nation's capital.

See Lonely Planet's *Cycling Australia* for detailed routes, including a 31-day East Coast Explorer tour, and plenty of useful advice.

Victoria

Melbourne (see the boxed text, p78) has an excellent network of long urban bike trails, and in country areas you'll find thousands of kilometres of diverse cycling terrain, much of it readily accessible by public transport. Highlights include the Great Ocean Rd (p96), one of the world's most spectacular coastal roads (though not strictly on the East Coast); and the popular annual cycling events. The Great Victorian Bike Ride is a 10-day annual ride attracting thousands of cyclists of all ages and fitness levels. Hosted in different parts of the state each year, the ride's entry fees cover meals, mechanical support and access to camping grounds. If time is an issue, the 210km Around the Bay in a Day in mid-October might be more achievable. This annual event attracts thousands of keen cyclists each year, and covers the length of Port Phillip Bay from Melbourne to Sorrento, across on the ferry to Queenscliff and back to Melbourne (or vice versa).

Excellent sources of information include **Bicycle Victoria** (☎ 03-8636 8888; www.bv.com.au) and the **Melbourne Bicycle Touring Club** (☎ 03-9517 4306; www.mbtc .org.au). **Bike Paths Safe Escapes** (www.bikepaths.com.au) is a comprehensive guide to the state's best cycling tracks, both in the city and in country Victoria. Features include colour maps, useful cycling tips and a list of the best café pit stops en route.

Queensland

There are possibilities for some great rides in Queensland. As for bushwalking, the best time for cycling is outside of Queensland's hottest months. Similarly, basic safety precautions like taking plenty of water with you also apply to cycling.

There excellent bike trails around Brisbane (p308) and the chance to join a tour in Cairns (p444). You can also do some excellent mountain biking in and around Noosa (p336).

Click on to the website of **Bicycling Queensland** (www.bq.org.au) for information on bike shops and rentals, cycling events and other useful information. It might also be worth contacting one of the local cycling clubs, like the **Brisbane Bicycle Touring Association** (http://bbta-au.org/index.php). Additionally, the **Queensland Department of Transport** (www.transport.qld.gov.au/cycling) has maps and other resources, including information on road rules. *Pedalling Around Southern Queensland*, by Julia Thorn, has tour notes and mud maps for numerous bike rides in the south of the state.

DIVING & SNORKELLING

There's great scuba diving at a number of places along the East Coast, particularly on the Great Barrier Reef (where there are also many dive schools), but also around the Central Coast of NSW, and the clear cool waters around Wilsons Promontory in Victoria.

'Diving professionals are notoriously fickle and good instructors move around from company to company; ask around to see which ones are currently well regarded.'

Every major town along the coast has one or more diving schools, but standards vary. Diving professionals are notoriously fickle and good instructors move around from company to company; ask around to see which ones are currently well regarded. **Professional Association of Diving Instructors** (PADI; www.padi.com) open-water courses typically cost $300 to $700 for four or five days, depending on how many dives are done from a boat. Note that with all certified PADI courses you'll need to provide a medical certificate, which costs about $60, and usually you will have to show you can tread water for 10 minutes and swim at least 200m.

For certified divers, trips and equipment hire are available just about everywhere. You'll need evidence of your qualifications, and some places may also ask to see your log book. Renting gear or going for a day dive generally costs $60 to $100. You can also hire a mask, snorkel and fins from a dive shop for around $45 and enjoy the underwater marine life without the need for a certificate and all the heavy gear.

New South Wales

There are many good options for shore-based and boat-based dives around Sydney (p189), including the Gordons Bay Underwater Nature Trail, north of Coogee. Elsewhere in NSW, the waters around Byron Bay (p263), the Solitary Islands (p253), Seal Rocks (p228), Jervis Bay (p145), Ulladulla (p147), Narooma (p159) and Merimbula (p166) are among the more popular, with numerous operators providing boats, courses, air fills and equipment hire and sales. Be aware that some of these locations are for experienced divers only.

Queensland

It's no secret that the Queensland coast has the pick of spectacular dive sites. The Great Barrier Reef provides some of the world's best diving and snorkelling and there are dozens of operators vying to teach you or provide you with the ultimate dive experience. There are also some 1600 shipwrecks along the Queensland coast, providing vibrant habitats for marine life. Most cruises to the Great Barrier Reef and through the Whitsunday Islands include free snorkel gear and these are some of the loveliest waters to float in.

During the wet season, usually January to March, floods can wash a lot of mud out into the ocean and visibility for divers and snorkellers is sometimes affected. All water activities, including diving and snorkelling, are affected by the box jellyfish, which line the Queensland coast from the Capricorn Coast up. See the boxed text, p371, for more information.

Learning to dive here is fairly inexpensive and you can usually choose to do a good part of your learning in the warm waters of the Great Barrier Reef itself. If you are choosing a course here, look carefully at how much of your open-water experience will be out on the reef. Many of the budget courses only offer a few boat dives. At the other end of the price scale, the most expensive courses tend to be aboard a boat or yacht for several days, with all meals included.

Cairns (p443) and Port Douglas (p454) have plenty of dive companies that operate in the waters of the Great Barrier Reef. Further south, the SS *Yongala* shipwreck, just off Townsville (p422), has been sitting beneath the water for over 90 years and is now home to a teeming marine community. From Airlie Beach (see p398) you can organise dives in the azure waters surrounding the Whitsundays and the Great Barrier Reef.

The spectacular southern Great Barrier Reef has perhaps the best locations of all: Fitzroy Reef (p371) and Lady Musgrave Island (p367) are accessed by high-speed boats from Bundaberg or Town of 1770. Ultimate diving holidays can be had at the resorts of Lady Elliot Island (p367) and Heron Island (p376). Possibly one of the best and cheapest locations of all in Australia is the hamlet of Bargara where there's superb coral viewing and courses start at $170 (see p365). Wolf Rock (p350) – a group of pinnacles off Double Island Point that teem with turtles, rays and sharks – hosts courses that include several dives at this world-class site.

You can snorkel just about everywhere in the warm waters of this state; it requires minimum effort and anyone can do it. Most of the previously mentioned locations are also relevant and popular snorkelling sites. There are coral reefs off some mainland beaches, and not far from Brisbane are the brilliant Tangalooma Wrecks (p324). Backpacker hostels along the coast provide free use of snorkel gear for their guests.

Whether you're snorkelling or diving on the Great Barrier Reef it's important to remember how vulnerable the ecology is. Most coral damage occurs when divers accidentally cut or break it with their fins. Be aware of where your feet are and never stand on the coral; if you need to rest find sand to stand on or use a rest station.

SAFETY GUIDELINES FOR DIVING

Before embarking on a scuba-diving, skin-diving or snorkelling trip, carefully consider the following points to ensure a safe and enjoyable experience:

- Possess a current diving certification card from a recognised scuba diving instructional agency (if scuba diving).
- Be sure you are healthy and feel comfortable diving.
- Obtain reliable information about physical and environmental conditions at the dive site (eg from a reputable local dive operation).
- Be aware of local laws, regulations and etiquette about marine life and the environment.
- Dive only at sites within your realm of experience; if available, engage the services of a competent, professionally trained dive instructor or dive master.
- Be aware that underwater conditions vary significantly from one region, or even site, to another. Seasonal changes can significantly alter any site and dive conditions. These differences influence the way divers dress for a dive and what diving techniques they use.
- Ask about the environmental characteristics that can affect your diving and how local trained divers deal with these considerations.

Victoria

Despite the often chilly waters, Victoria does possess excellent diving. Most divers opt for 7mm wetsuits or drysuits for year-round activity. Port Phillip Bay, right on Melbourne's doorstep, has several good sites, including pods of dolphins and friendly seals, and most weekends see a legion of beginners learning the ropes at places such as the pier at Portsea on the Mornington Peninsula (p96). Other good bases include Flinders and Sorrento (p97), also on the Mornington Peninsula; Queenscliff on the Bellarine Peninsula; Bunurong Marine Park (p106); Wilsons Promontory (p108); and Mallacoota (p130).

EXTREME SPORTS
Abseiling, Canyoning & Rock Climbing

Climbing Australia (www .climbing.com.au) has excellent info on rock climbing.

The Blue Mountains (p207), especially around Katoomba, are fantastic for abseiling and canyoning, with numerous professionals able to set you up with equipment and training. Believe it or not, Brisbane is a good place to learn rock climbing. A number of operators offer climbing and abseiling instruction on the Cliffs (see p308), a series of 18m rock faces along the southern banks of the Brisbane River.

Bungee Jumping & Skydiving

There are plenty of opportunities for adrenaline-junkies to get a hit on the East Coast. Surfers Paradise (p287) is something of a bungee mecca, offering brave participants a host of creative spins on the original. A jump generally costs around $100.

Tandem skydiving is also big on the East Coast. As well as on the fringe of the big cities, there are popular jump sites at Byron Bay (p260), Caloundra (p330), Airlie Beach (p401), Mission Beach (p432) and Cairns (p444). Prices depend on the height of your jump. Most folk start with a jump of 10,000ft, which provides 35 to 40 seconds of free fall and costs around $200 to $250.

Hang-gliding, Paragliding & Parasailing

Hang-gliding and paragliding are popular at many places along the East Coast, but the best spots include Stanwell Park (p138), south of Sydney, which is also ideal for spectators, and the Carlo Sandblow (p350) at Rainbow Beach. Tandem flights cost $130 to $165 and a two-day lesson costs around $550.

Parasailing (being towed behind a boat) is another exhilarating way to view the coast from above. Rides cost from $55 and outfits operate out of Metung (p119) on the Gippsland Lakes, the Gold Coast (see p292), Airlie Beach (p401) and many other beach and island resorts along the coast.

The Atlas of Australian Surfing, Travellers Edition, by legendary surfer Mark Warren, promises to reveal the biggest waves and the best-kept secret surf in Australia. Features include maps and plenty of practical advice, including warnings about monster waves, sharks and unfriendly locals.

SURFING

The southern half of the East Coast is jam-packed with sandy surf beaches and point breaks. North of Agnes Water in Queensland, the waves disappear thanks to the Great Barrier Reef shielding the coast from the ocean swells. Many travellers who come to the East Coast want to learn to surf, and you'll find plenty of good waves, board hire and lessons available all along the coast. Two-hour lessons cost around $40 to $50 and five-day courses for the really keen go for around $180.

New South Wales

Southern NSW has good breaks at Merimbula (p165), Ulladulla (p147) and Wollongong (p138). Sydney (p191) also has good surf, especially at

Manly, Dee Why and Cronulla. Check out www.realsurf.com for surf reports of Sydney's beaches. Gurus surf Treachery Beach near Seal Rocks (p228), north of Newcastle, which also boasts top surfing beaches.

Queensland

From a surfer's point of view, Queensland's Great Barrier Reef is one of nature's most tragic mistakes – a 2000km-long breakwater! Mercifully, there are some great surf beaches in southern Queensland. Starting right at the border, Coolangatta (p280) is a popular surfing haunt, particularly at Kirra Beach. Nearby Burleigh Heads (p282) has a serious right-hand barrel, which requires some experience, but if you've got it you'll be in seventh heaven.

Further north, the swanky resort of Noosa (p336) is still a popular hang-out for long-boarders, with good wave action at Sunshine Beach and the point breaks around the national park. Near Brisbane, North Stradbroke Island (p321) also has good surf beaches, as does Moreton Island (p323). Queensland's most northern surf beaches are at Agnes Water (p370), just south of Gladstone.

Victoria

With its exposure to the relentless Southern Ocean swell, Victoria's rugged southern coastline provides plenty of quality surf, while the southeast coast is a little more gentle. The usually chilly water (even in summer) has the hardiest surfer reaching for a wetsuit. A full-length 3mm- to 4mm-thick wetsuit is the standard for winter.

Eastern Victoria's best surf is at Phillip Island (p102), especially at Woolami Beach. Other good surfing spots include Inverloch (p106; perfect for beginners), Wilsons Promontory (p108), Lakes Entrance (p120), and Lake Tyers (p123), with good, if inconsistent, surf breaks at Red Bluff and Sandy Point.

For definitive surfing information throughout the East Coast, plus surf cams, events diaries and where to get tuition, click onto www.surfing australia.com or www .coastalwatch.com.

It was summer, 1915, when Hawaiian Duke Kahanamoku introduced the art of surfboard riding before a packed grandstand of Australians. He'd carved a board from local timbers before taking to the ocean at Freshwater, on Sydney's North Shore.

Food & Drink Matthew Evans

Matthew Evans was originally a chef, before becoming a food writer and restaurant critic. He is currently chief restaurant reviewer for the *Sydney Morning Herald* and co-editor of the *Sydney Morning Herald Good Food Guide*.

Born in convict poverty and raised on a diet heavily influenced by Great Britain, Australian cuisine has come a long way. This is now one of the most dynamic places in the world to have a feed, thanks to immigration and a public willing to give anything new and better a go. Sydney and Melbourne can claim to be destinations worthy of touring gourmands from New York to Paris. More importantly, real people, including travellers, feel the effects of a blossoming food culture across the country.

This, however, has only been because of recent history. Australia, despite its world-class dining opportunities, doesn't live to eat. As a nation we're new to the world of good food, of being mesmerised by the latest TV chef, devouring cookbooks and subscribing to foodie magazines in the hundreds of thousands. The eating along the East Coast has never been better, and it's improving by the day.

Yet, despite our fascination with tucker, at heart we're still mostly a nation of simple eaters, with the majority of Australians still novices in anything beyond meat and three veg. This is changing, though, as the influx of immigrants (and their cuisine) has found locals trying (and liking) everything from lassi to laksa. This passionate minority has led to a rise in dining standards, better availability of produce and a frenetic buzz about food in general. It's no wonder Australian chefs, cookbooks and food writers are so sought after overseas.

We've coined our own phrase, Modern Australian, to describe our cuisine. If it's a melange of East and West, it's Modern Australian. If it's not authentically French or Italian, it's Modern Australian – our attempt to classify the unclassifiable. Cuisine doesn't alter between regions, but some influences are obvious, such as the Italian migration to Melbourne.

Dishes aren't usually too fussy, the flavours often bold and interesting. Spicing ranges from gentle to extreme, coffee is great (though it still reaches its greatest heights in the cities), and the meats are tender, full flavoured and usually bargain priced.

STAPLES & SPECIALITIES

The East Coast's best food comes from the sea. Nothing compares to this region's seafood, harnessed from some of the purest waters you'll find anywhere, and usually cooked with care.

Connoisseurs prize Sydney rock oysters (a species living along the New South Wales coast) and sea scallops from Queensland. Rock lobsters are fantastic and fantastically expensive, and mud crabs, despite the name, are a sweet delicacy. Another odd-sounding delicacy is 'bugs' – like shovel-nosed lobsters without a lobster's price tag; try the Balmain and Moreton Bay varieties. Yabbies, the smaller cousins of crayfish, can be found throughout the southeast. Prawns are incredible, particularly sweet school prawns or the eastern king (Yamba) prawns found along northern NSW.

The Cook's Companion, by Stephanie Alexander, is Australia's single-volume answer to Delia Smith. If it's in here, most Australians have probably seen it or eaten it.

Add to that countless wild fish species and we've got one of the greatest bounties on earth. In fact, the Sydney Fish Market (p186) trades in several hundred species of seafood every day, second only to Tokyo.

Despite their greatness, not many actual dishes can truly lay claim to being uniquely Australian. Even the humble 'pav' (pavlova), the meringue dessert with cream and passionfruit, may be from New Zealand. Ditto for lamingtons (large cubes of cake dipped in chocolate and rolled in desiccated coconut).

Anything another country does, Australia does, too. Vietnamese, Indian, Fijian, Italian – doesn't matter where it's from, there's an expat community and interested locals desperate to cook and eat it. Dig deep enough, and you'll find Jamaicans using scotch bonnet peppers and Tunisians making *tagine*. And you'll usually find their houses are the favourite haunts of their locally raised friends. Yum cha (the classic southern Chinese dumpling feast) has found huge popularity with urban locals in recent years, particularly on weekends.

Almost everything we eat from the land (as opposed to the sea) was introduced. The fact that the country is huge (similar in size to continental USA) and varies so much in climate, from the tropical north to the temperate south, means that there's an enormous variety of produce on offer. In summer, mangoes are so plentiful that Queenslanders actually get sick of them. Lamb from Victoria's lush Gippsland is highly prized. And there's a small but brilliant farmhouse cheese movement, hampered by the fact that all the milk must be pasteurised (unlike in Italy and France, home of the world's best cheeses). Despite that, the results can be great.

DRINKS

The closest region to Sydney, the Hunter Valley (p221) first had vines in the 1830s, and does a lively unwooded Semillon that is best aged. Further inland, there's Canberra, Cowra, Orange and Mudgee. Just out of Melbourne are the Mornington (p96) and Bellarine Peninsulas, Mount Macedon and the Yarra Valley. There's even a wine region in Queensland, though not all of it is good.

Plenty of good wine comes from big producers with economies of scale on their side. However, the most interesting wines are usually made by small wineries where you pay a premium; the gamble means the payoff in terms of flavour is often greater. Much of the cost of wine (nearly 42%) is due to a high taxing programme courtesy of the Australian government.

Beer, for years, has been of the bland, chilled-so-you-can-barely-taste-it variety. Now microbrewers and boutique breweries are filtering through. Keep an eye out for James Squire amber ale from Sydney and Mountain Goat from Melbourne. Most beers have an alcohol content between 3.5% and 5%. That's less than many European beers but stronger than most of the stuff in North America. Light beers come in under 3% alcohol and are finding favour with people observing the superstringent drink-driving laws.

In terms of coffee, Australia is leaping ahead, with Italian-style espresso machines in virtually every café, boutique roasters all the rage and, in urban areas, the qualified *barista* (coffee maker) virtually the norm. Expect the best coffee in Melbourne, decent stuff in most other cities, and a chance of good coffee in many rural areas. Melbourne's café scene rivals the most vibrant in the world; the best way to immerse yourself is by wandering the city centre's café-lined lanes.

Fresh fruit juice is extremely popular along the coast and a healthy way to beat the heat. Fresh-fruit-juice bars that specialise in all sorts of yummy concoctions pepper the landscape, but you can also get good versions at cafés and ice-cream stores.

Melbourne has a microbeer called Piss (the lighter strength is 'Piss Weak'; see www.pi55 .com) and Sydney has a pink wine called 'Pansy'.

CELEBRATIONS

Celebrating in the Australian manner often includes equal amounts of food and alcohol. A birthday could well be a barbecue (barbie) of steak (or prawns), washed down with a beverage or two. Weddings are usually a big slap-up dinner, though the food is often far from memorable. Christenings are more sober, mostly offering home-baked biscuits and a cup of tea.

Many regions and cities now hold food festivals. Melbourne, for instance, has a month-long food and wine festival in March (p81). There are harvest festivals in wine regions, and various communities hold annual events.

For many an event, especially in the warmer months, Australians fill the car with an Esky (an insulated ice chest, to keep everything cool), folding tables and chairs, a cricket set or a footy, and head off for a barbie by the lake/river/beach. If there's a total fire ban (which occurs increasingly each summer), the food is precooked and the barbie becomes more of a picnic, but the essence remains the same.

Christmas often finds the more traditional (in a European sense) baked dinner being replaced by a barbecue, full of seafood and quality steak. It's a response to the warm weather. Prawn prices skyrocket, chicken may be eaten with champagne at breakfast, and the main meal is usually in the afternoon, after a swim and before a really good, long siesta.

Various ethnic minorities have their own celebrations. Tongans love an *umu*, where fish and vegetables are buried in an earthen pit and covered with coals; Greeks may hold a spit barbecue; and Chinese go off during their annual Spring Festival (Chinese New Year) every January or February (it changes with the lunar calendar).

> In NSW billions of locusts (sky prawns) plague the land. *Cooking with Sky Prawns* (2005), by Edward Joshua and Chris Carr, aims to ease the problem via consumption, claiming the insects are more nutritious than beef.

WHERE TO EAT & DRINK

The best-value food in most cities is lurking in Chinatown. Melbourne's Little Bourke St (p84) and the lanes nearby boast lots of little joints selling roast duck or wonton soups.

Typically, a restaurant meal along the East Coast is a relaxed affair. It may take 15 minutes to order, another 15 before the first course arrives, and maybe half an hour between entrées and mains. The upside of this is that any table you've booked in a restaurant is yours for the night, unless you're told otherwise. So sit, linger and live life in the slow lane.

Competitively priced places to eat are clubs or pubs with counter meals. Returned Servicemen's League (RSL) clubs are prolific along the coast, and while the décor can be pretty chintzy, the tucker is normally excellent.

The other species of club you're bound to cross is the Surf Life Saving Club. Most coastal towns have at least one, sometimes up to three. They're similar to RSL clubs, but many now compete with finer restaurants, and their bistros stock inventive fare. Additionally, they're almost always perched on the beachfront so the views tend to be worth a visit alone.

Other clubs to keep an eye out for are bowls clubs, Irish clubs and sports clubs.

Solo diners find that cafés and noodle bars are welcoming; good fine-dining restaurants often treat you like a star but, sadly, some midrange places may still make you feel a little ill at ease.

Most restaurants open around noon for lunch and from 6pm or 7pm for dinner. Australians usually eat lunch shortly after noon, and dinner bookings are usually made for 7.30pm or 8pm, though in major cities some restaurants stay open past 10pm.

Quick Eats

There's not a huge culture of street vending, though you may find a pie or coffee cart in some places. Most quick eats traditionally come from a milk bar, which serves old-fashioned hamburgers (with bacon, egg, pineapple and beetroot if you want) and other takeaway foods. Fish and chips is still hugely popular, most often a form of shark (often called flake; don't worry, it can be delicious) dipped in heavy batter, and eaten at the beach on a Friday night.

American-style fast food has taken over recently, though many Aussies still love a meat pie, often from a milk bar, but also from bakeries, kiosks and some cafés. If you're at an Aussie rules football match, a beer, a meat pie and a bag of hot chips are as compulsory as wearing your team's colours.

Pizza has become one of the most popular fast foods; most pizzas that are home-delivered are of the American style (thick and with lots of toppings) rather than Italian style. That said, more and more wood-fired oven, thin Neapolitan-style pizza can be found, even in country towns. In the city, Roman-style pizza (buy it by the slice) is becoming more popular, but you can't usually buy the other pizza in anything but whole rounds.

There are some really dodgy mass-produced takeaway foods, bought mostly by famished teenage boys, including the dim sim (a bastardisation of the dim sum dumplings from China) and the Chiko Roll (p60).

VEGETARIANS & VEGANS

You're in luck. Most cities have substantial numbers of local vegetarians, which means you're well catered for. Cafés seem to always have vegetarian options, and some of our best restaurants have complete vegetarian menus. Take care with risotto and soups, though, as meat stock is often used.

Vegans will find the going much tougher, but local Hare Krishna restaurants or Buddhist temples often provide relief, and there are usually dishes that are vegan-adaptable at restaurants.

The Australian Vegetarian Society's website (www.veg-soc.org) lists a number of vegie-friendly places to eat around the country.

EATING WITH KIDS

Dining with children is relatively easy. Avoid the flashiest places and children are generally welcomed, particularly at Chinese, Greek or Italian restaurants. Kids are usually more than welcome at cafés; bistros and clubs often see families dining early. Many fine-dining restaurants don't welcome small children (assuming they're all ill-behaved).

Most places that do welcome children don't have separate kids' menus, and those that do usually offer everything straight from the deep fryer – crumbed chicken and chips, that kind of thing. Better to find something on the menu (say a pasta or salad) and have the kitchen adapt it slightly to your children's needs.

The best news for travelling families, weather permitting, is that there are plenty of free or coin-operated barbecues in parks. Beware of weekends and public holidays when fierce battles can erupt over who is next in line for the barbecue.

See p470 for more information about travelling with children.

HABITS & CUSTOMS

At the table, it's good manners to use British knife-and-fork skills, keeping the fork in the left hand, tines down, and the knife in the right, though Americans may be forgiven for using their fork like a shovel. Talking with your mouth full is considered uncouth, and fingers should only be used for food that can't be tackled another way.

'Shouting' is a revered custom where people rotate paying for a round of drinks. Just don't leave before it's your turn to buy! At a toast, everyone should touch glasses.

Australians like to linger a bit over coffee. They like to linger a really long time while drinking beer. And they tend to take quite a bit of time if they're out to dinner (as opposed to having takeaway).

Smoking is banned in most eateries in the nation, so sit outside if you love to puff. And never smoke in someone's house unless you ask first. Even then it's usual to smoke outside.

DOS AND DON'TS

Do...

■ show up for restaurant dinner reservations on time. Not only may your table be given to someone else, staggered bookings are designed to make the experience more seamless.

■ take a small gift, and/or a bottle of wine to dinner parties.

■ offer to wash up or help clear the table after a meal at a friend's house.

■ ring or send a note (even an email) the day or so after a dinner party, unless the friends are so close you feel it unnecessary. Even then, thank them the very next time you speak.

■ offer to take meat and/or a salad to a barbecue. At the traditional Aussie barbie for a big group, each family is expected to bring part or all of their own tucker.

■ shout your group to drinks on arrival at the pub.

■ tip (up to 15%) for good service, when in a big group or if your kids have gone crazy and trashed the dining room.

Don't...

■ freak out when the waiter in a restaurant attempts to 'lap' your serviette (napkin) by laying it over your crotch. It's considered to be the height of service. If you don't want them doing this, place your serviette on your lap before they get a chance.

■ ever accept a shout unless you intend to make your shout soon after.

■ expect a date to pay for you. It's quite common among younger people for a woman to pay her own way.

■ expect servile or obsequious service. Professional waiters are intelligent, caring equals whose disdain can perfectly match any diner's attempt at contempt.

■ ever tip bad service.

EAT YOUR WORDS

Australians love to shorten everything, including people's names, so expect many other words to be abbreviated. Some words you might hear:

barbie – a barbecue, where (traditionally) smoke and overcooked meat are matched with lashings of coleslaw, potato salad and beer

Chiko Roll – a fascinating, large spring roll–like pastry for sale in takeaway shops. Best used as an item of self-defence rather than eaten

Esky – an insulated ice chest to hold your tinnies, before you transfer them to your *tinny holder*.

middy – a midsized glass of beer (NSW)

pav – pavlova, the meringue dessert topped with cream, passionfruit and kiwifruit or other fresh fruit

pot – a medium glass of beer (Vic)

rat coffin – a meat pie; the traditional ones are made with minced beef. Compulsory eating (with White Crow tomato sauce) at footy matches.

sanger/sando – a sandwich

schooner – a big glass of beer (NSW), but not as big as a pint

snags – sausages (AKA surprise bags)

snot block – a vanilla slice

Tim Tam – a commercial chocolate biscuit that lies close to the heart of most Australians. Best consumed as a Tim Tam shooter, where two diagonally opposite corners of the rectangular biscuit are nibbled off, and a hot drink (tea is the true aficionado's favourite) is sucked through the fast-melting biscuit. Ugly but good.

tinny – usually refers to a can of beer, but could also be the small boat you go fishing for mud crabs in (and you'd take a few tinnies in your tinny, in that case).

tinny holder – insulating material that you use to keep the *tinny* ice cold, nothing to do with a boat

Try www.australian gourmetpages.com.au for regularly updated, independent reviews of Australian wine, food and restaurants.

Victoria

CHRIS MELLOR

Melbourne

Melbourne is Australia's most liveable and lovable capital. It's comfortable and cosmopolitan, and a melange of the old and new, the bold and the subtle, the indoors and the outdoors, the planned and the impromptu. Tree-lined boulevards and storybook alleys hold countless treasures and commercial endeavours that will feed, shelter and entertain you; character-filled neighbourhoods hum with life; low-key stretches of sand and verdant gardens offer both escape and social outlets. Festivals cram the city's calendar: if you're into films, horse races, food, comedy or just about anything else you care to name, there's an event to celebrate it.

Melbourne offers Australia's richest melting-pot of cultures, with waves of migration over the last several decades from Europe, Asia, the Middle East and Africa resulting in an extraordinarily broad and tantalising array of cuisines in its restaurants. Melburnians love shopping and there's everything from designer boutiques to markets, discount warehouses to unique shopping strips, as well as plenty of quirky little shops. Many residents' lives revolve around sport – it seems to inspire religious commitment.

This city inspires steadfast devotion from citizens and attracts newcomers seeking the latest and greatest – she punches well above her weight for a city of her size. In Melbourne, you can feed your tummy, your imagination and your soul – and all in style.

HIGHLIGHTS

- Visit the world-class **Melbourne Zoo** (p77)
- Sip a latte and watch the eclectic crowd in **Brunswick St** (p77), Fitzroy
- Soak in the **St Kilda Sea Baths** (p78), savour a cake in **Acland St**, then rock up to enjoy the tradition that is the **Espy** (p87)
- Soak up the atmosphere of sand and surf meets continental café scene meets stylish nightlife that is **St Kilda** (p78)
- Explore the gallery or catch a movie at ACMI in **Federation Square** (p64)
- Get caught up in the roar of the crowd at a footy match at the **Melbourne Cricket Ground** (p89)
- Immerse yourself in the **Queen Victoria Market** (p91)
- Shop in fashionable **South Yarra** (p91)
- **Bar hop** (p86) in the city alleyways

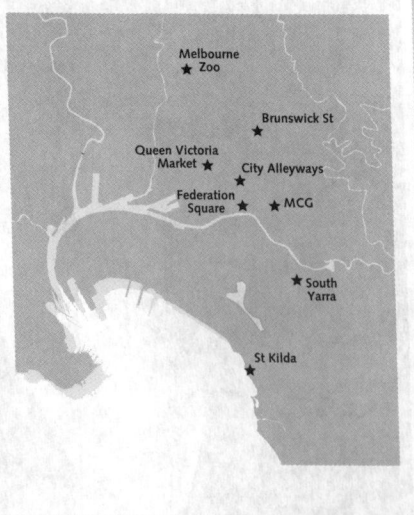

- TELEPHONE CODE: 03   - POPULATION: 3.5 MILLION   - www.melbourne.vic.gov.au/events

MELBOURNE IN...

Two Days
Start at the innovative **Federation Square** (p64) and take our **walking tour** (p79) ending with lunch at **Southgate** (p85). In the afternoon, visit the esteemed **Ian Potter: National Gallery of Victoria Australia** (p65) or catch a film at **ACMI** (p65). Take a stroll through **Chinatown** (p74) and dine there before an evening of **bar hopping** (p86) around the inner city laneways. On the second day visit the bustling **Queen Victoria Market** (p91) and wander around the innovative **Melbourne Museum** (p77) before heading to **Brunswick St** (p85) to sip a latte, have dinner at the **Vegie Bar** (p86) and settle into an evening at a local, such as **Bar Open** (p87).

Four Days
Same first two days. On day three visit the **Melbourne Zoo** (p77). Have lunch in one of the city's arcades and follow it up with a **Melbourne River Cruise** (p81) and see the city from the Yarra. Catch a performance at the **Victorian Arts Centre** (p76) before or after dinner and drinks at some great spot like **Supper Inn** (p85). On your fourth day head to St Kilda and soak in the **Sea Baths** (p78), savour a cake in **Acland St**, stroll along the **pier**, have some fish and chips and then enjoy the tradition that is the **Espy** (p87).

One Week
A full week will allow you to squeeze in the **Ian Potter Centre** (p65) and the **Immigration Museum** (p75), have a monster shop along **Chapel St** (p91) and visit the **Dandenongs** (p94).

ORIENTATION

Melbourne hugs the shores of Port Phillip, with the city centre on the north bank of the Yarra River, about 5km inland from the bay. Most of the attractions covered in this chapter are within the city and inner-suburban areas, and most places are easily accessible by public transport.

The inner suburbs that surround the city centre, known as the central business district (CBD), are like a ring of 'villages', each with its own particular character. Beside the Yarra River, on the corner of Swanston and Flinders Sts, is Flinders St station, the main station for suburban trains. The other major station, for country and interstate services, is Southern Cross station (formerly Spencer St station), at the western end of Bourke St.

Maps

You can pick up a free copy of the *Melbourne Visitors Map*, at the Melbourne Visitor Information Centre (Map pp68–9) at Federation Square or at the information booth (Map pp68–9) on Bourke St Mall. Street directories are detailed and extremely handy if you're driving. They can be purchased from newsagents and bookshops for around $50. Lonely Planet's *Melbourne City Map* provides excellent coverage.

INFORMATION

Bookshops

Borders (Map p71; ☎ 9824 2299; Jam Factory, 500 Chapel St, South Yarra) This vast store has a huge selection and late opening hours – although it lacks warmth.
Hares & Hyenas (Map p71; ☎ 9824 0110; 135 Commercial Rd, Prahran) The place for gay and lesbian titles.
Readings (Map pp72-3; ☎ 9347 6633; 309 Lygon St) This Carlton institution is packed with the best books, DVDs and CDs.

Emergency

In case of a life-threatening emergency, dial ☎ 000 – a free call from any phone. Your call will be diverted to either the police, ambulance service or fire brigade.
Lifeline Counselling (☎ 13 11 14; ☾ 24hr)
Police station (Map pp68-9; ☎ 9247 5347; 228-232 Flinders La, City; ☾ 24hr)
RACV Emergency Roadside Service (☎ 13 11 11; ☾ 24hr)
Royal Women's Hospital Centre Against Sexual Assault (Map pp72-3; ☎ 9344 2201; Royal Women's Hospital, 132 Grattan St, Carlton; ☾ 24hr)

Internet Access

Internet services are available just about anywhere. Most youth hostels and guesthouses have facilities, many of which are free. Almost every hotel will have phone jacks in the

MELBOURNE

room, and many now have broadband access. Internet cafés are also common throughout touristed parts of the city.

E:fiftyfive (Map pp68-9; ☎ 9620 3899; 55 Elizabeth St; ⏰ 9am-1am Mon & Tue, 9am-2am Wed & Thu, 9am-3am Fri, noon-3am Sat, noon-11pm Sun) This buzzing place has coffee, beer and snacks available and DJs playing nightly.

World Wide Wash (Map pp72-3; ☎ 9419 8214; 361 Brunswick St, Fitzroy; ⏰ 9.30am-10pm) Wash your clothes, drink your coffee and check your emails here.

Medical Services

Travellers' Medical & Vaccination Centre (Map pp68-9; ☎ 9602 5788; www.traveldoctor.com.au; Level 2, 393 Little Bourke St) This service dispenses excellent information on vaccinations needed for most countries. Appointments are necessary.

CHEMIST
Mulqueeny Midnight Pharmacy (Map pp66-7; ☎ 9510 3977; cnr Williams Rd & High St, Prahran; ⏰ 9am-midnight)

DENTIST
Dental Emergency Service (Map pp72-3; ☎ 9341 1040; Royal Dental Hospital of Melbourne, 720 Swanston St, Carlton; ⏰ 8.30am-9.15pm)

EMERGENCY ROOMS
Major public hospitals with 24-hour accident and emergency wards that are close to the city centre include:

Alfred Hospital (Map p71; ☎ 9276 2000; Commercial Rd, Prahran)

Royal Melbourne Hospital (Map pp66-7; ☎ 9342 7000; Grattan St, Parkville)

St Vincent's Hospital (Map pp72-3; ☎ 9288 2211; 41 Victoria Pde, Fitzroy)

Money

Changing foreign currency or travellers cheques is no problem at most banks (though they charge a fee). There are foreign-exchange booths at the international terminal at Melbourne Airport, which are open to meet all arriving flights. Most of the large hotels will also change currency or travellers cheques for their guests and the rate will likely be higher.

American Express (☎ 1300 139 060; 233 Collins St) Commission-free service if you're using its travellers cheques.

Post

Branches of Australia Post are everywhere and keep standard business hours.

Melbourne GPO (General Post Office; Map pp68-9; ☎ 13 13 18; cnr Little Bourke & Elizabeth Sts; ⏰ 8.30am-5.30pm Mon-Fri, 9am-4pm Sat, 10am-4pm Sun) Poste restante services are available here.

Tourist Information

Melbourne Visitor Booth (Map pp68-9; ⏰ 9am-5pm Mon-Fri, 10am-5pm Sat & Sun) A small information booth in the Bourke St Mall with helpful staff.

Melbourne Visitor Information Centre (Map pp68-9; ☎ 9658 9658; Federation Square; ⏰ 9am-6pm) An excellent source of information about Melbourne events and attractions. Multilingual assistance is available for booking tours and accommodation, and plenty of printed material is on offer. It's also home to the Melbourne Greeter Service, which pairs visitors with volunteers for a half-day walking orientation of the city (book ahead).

MetShop (Map pp68-9; ☎ 13 16 38; Town Hall, cnr Swanston & Little Collins Sts; ⏰ 8.30am-5.30pm Mon-Fri, 9am-1pm Sat) For information about Melbourne's public transport.

Travellers' Aid Society of Victoria (Map pp68-9; ☎ 9654 2600; Level 2, 169 Swanston St; ⏰ 8am-5pm Mon-Fri) Offers assistance for stranded travellers, as well as information, advice, showers and wheelchair-access toilets. There are also support services for disabled, handicapped and aged people. The service is free.

SIGHTS

Central Melbourne (the CBD), has the greatest concentration of attractions in the Melbourne area. While it's compact enough to cover on foot, it's also possible to navigate it on the many trams that criss-cross the area (see p92 for details). Other neighbourhoods that tend to attract large numbers of visitors include the burgeoning riverfront 'precincts' of Docklands and Southgate, while north of town you'll find Carlton, Fitzroy and Parkville. South-of-the-city attractions can be found in South Yarra, Prahran and St Kilda.

Central Melbourne
FEDERATION SQUARE
The empty rail yards that once stretched along the Yarra River have now been replaced by a riotous explosion of steel, glass and abstract geometry known as **Federation Square** (Map pp68-9; www.fedsq.com), an ambitious move by city planners to create a focal point for Melbourne and to connect the centre of the city with the Yarra River.

Federation Square is centred on its **plaza**, a spacious open courtyard that extends from

THE GRASS IS GREENER

Thankfully Melbourne's early founders had the foresight to dedicate huge swathes of land to gardens smack bang in the heart of the city. Melbourne is incredibly well endowed with parks – the city centre is ringed with a green belt. Melburnians love their parks and they're a favourite of stressed city workers, sweaty joggers, sprawling families, brides and grooms, and ardent sports fans. The parks are astonishingly well used but there's enough that there's always plenty of space unless you're attending a major event.

Many of Melbourne's major sporting venues, such as the MCG (p76), are set in hectares of parkland and occasionally the parks have been battle grounds, too – with the forces of organised sport pitted against the proponents of passive leisure activities. After drawn-out battles, sport usually wins out, and stadiums and car parks are erected, drowning out the protests of local residents.

The somewhat bizarre thing about Melbourne's gorgeous gardens is that they're almost all European, though some remnant eucalypts have been preserved in Royal Park and Yarra Park.

Here are some highlights:

- **Royal Park** – Melbourne's biggest park at a whopping 188 hectares is about the same size as some small suburbs. It's slowly being converted back to an Australian landscape.
- **Carlton Gardens** – These magnificent gardens are home to the World Heritage–listed Royal Exhibition Buildings.
- **Fitzroy Gardens** – One of Australia's best 19th-century landscaped gardens and home to Cooks Cottage.
- **Royal Botanic Gardens** – One of the world's best with a fabulous **children's garden** (p80).

A couple of gems 20 minutes by public transport from the city:

- **Studley Park** (Map pp66–7) – A brilliant spot in Kew to take a punt along the river and have a spot of afternoon tea in the café afterwards.
- **CERES** (☎ 9387 2609; Lee St, East Brunswick) – This lush environment park is a nationally renowned environmental education centre with an alternative energy park, an Indigenous nursery, organic café and farm. It's a great place to take the kids.

Princes Bridge deep into the complex. Next along is the dramatic glass and steel **atrium** and the adjoining 450-seat **amphitheatre**. The atrium functions as an undercover walkway between Flinders St and the Yarra side of the complex, along which visitors can stop for coffee at the cafés and restaurants lining the promenade.

The city's cultural heart also contains the awkwardly named **Ian Potter Centre: NGV Australia** (Map pp68–9; ☎ 8662 1553; www.ngv.vic .gov.au/ngvaustralia; Federation Square; admission free; ☺ 10am-5pm Mon-Thu, 10am-9pm Fri, 10am-6pm Sat & Sun), a dramatic building at the eastern end of Federation Square. The centre houses the National Gallery of Victoria's impressive collection (over 20,000 pieces) of Australian art from the colonial to the modern periods. It has the popular Aboriginal and Torres Strait Islander collection, and temporary exhibitions.

Also at Fed Square you'll find the innovative **Australian Centre for the Moving Image** (ACMI; Map pp68-9; ☎ 9663 2583; www.acmi.net.au; Federation Square; ☺ 10am-6pm), a gallery and cinema space dedicated to film, TV and digital media. The riverside park, **Birrarung Marr**, provides grassy knolls, views upriver and the Federation Bells, which ring out specially commissioned tunes three times a day. The park can be reached from the Federation Square car park, Batman Ave or by walking along the river.

SWANSTON STREET

Swanston St is a pedestrian mall by day, but open to traffic after 7pm. Much of the lower stretch of the street is decidedly low-rent in tone – attempts to elevate the mood of the street are travelling at a pace commensurate with the trams that travel the strip.

(Continued on page 74)

A **B** **C** **D**

Maribyrnong Rd

Highpoint Shopping Centre

Fairbairn Park

Ascot Vale

Ascot Vale

Brunswick

Sydney Rd

1

Epsom Rd

Mt Alexander Rd

CityLink

BRUNSWICK

Jewell

31

Brunswick Rd

Pipemakers Park

Riverside Golf Course

Royal Park Golf Course

Royal Park

Rosamond Rd

Maribyrnong

Showgrounds

Showgrounds

Flemington

Royal Park

9

Princes Park

Gordon

Ballarat Rd

8

Flemington Racecourse

Flemington Racecourse

Newmarket

Racecourse Rd

Flemington Bridge

83

83

Royal Pde

Melbourne General Cemetery

2

Footscray Park

Smithfield Rd

83

Flemington Rd

Royal Rd

Maribyrnong River

Kensington

Macaulay

Royal Childrens Hospital

University of Melbourne

Ballarat Rd

FOOTSCRAY

Geelong Rd

Kensington

Grattan St

Barkly St

West Footscray

83

Kensington Rd

South Kensington

Dynon Rd

50

Curzon St

Erro St

2

Victoria St

Middle Footscray

Footscray

Macaulay Rd

North Melbourne

Queensberry St

15

Seddon

Hyde St

Whitehall St

32

Footscray Rd

North Melbourne

24

13

3

Yarraville St

Coode Island

West Melbourne

Bourke St

Swanston St

Yarraville

Dudley St

New Quay Prm

Telstra Dome

Southern Cross

Flinders Street

Stony Creek

Yarra River

Bolte Bridge

Victoria Harbour

Docklands

M1

Brooker St

Lorimer St

Salmon St

CityLink

See Central Melbourne Map (pp68-9)

4

West Gate Bridge

Westgate Park

Todd Rd

Fishermans Bend

Westgate Fwy

Australian Centre for Contemporary Art (ACCA)

M1

Spotwood

10

South Melbourne

Hall St

Spotswood

Williamstown Rd

Kings Way

Port Melbourne

Sandridge Beach

Beacon Cove

Albert Park

Albert Park Lake

5

Newport Park

Webb Dock

Princes Pier

Lagoon Pier

Victoria Ave

Albert Park

Newport

Greenwich Bay

Station Pier

Hobsons Bay

Canterbury Rd

Douglas Pde

The Strand

33

Pier

Beaconsfield Pde

Middle Park

North Williamstown

Bay Cruises

St Kilda Pier

Ferguson St

Ferries to Tasmania

6

Williamstown Beach

Williamstown

Osborne St

Williamstown

Port Phillip

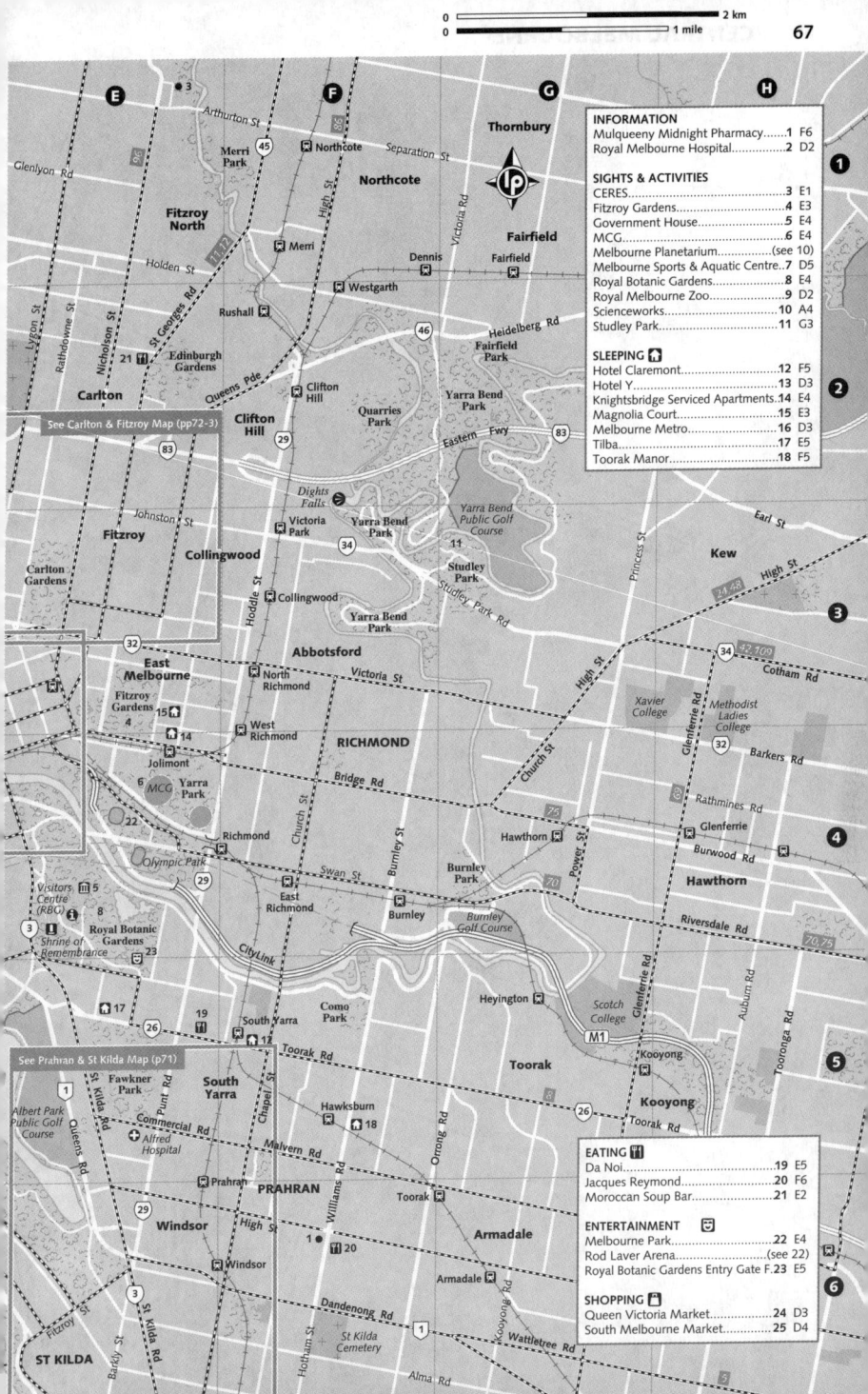

INFORMATION

Mulqueeny Midnight Pharmacy	**1** F6
Royal Melbourne Hospital	**2** D2

SIGHTS & ACTIVITIES

CERES	**3** E1
Fitzroy Gardens	**4** E3
Government House	**5** E4
MCG	**6** E4
Melbourne Planetarium	(see 10)
Melbourne Sports & Aquatic Centre	**7** D5
Royal Botanic Gardens	**8** E4
Royal Melbourne Zoo	**9** D2
Scienceworks	**10** A4
Studley Park	**11** G3

SLEEPING

Hotel Claremont	**12** F5
Hotel Y	**13** D3
Knightsbridge Serviced Apartments	**14** E3
Magnolia Court	**15** E3
Melbourne Metro	**16** D3
Tilba	**17** E5
Toorak Manor	**18** F5

EATING

Da Noi	**19** E5
Jacques Reymond	**20** F6
Moroccan Soup Bar	**21** E2

ENTERTAINMENT

Melbourne Park	**22** E4
Rod Laver Arena	(see 22)
Royal Botanic Gardens Entry Gate F	**23** E5

SHOPPING

Queen Victoria Market	**24** D3
South Melbourne Market	**25** D4

See Carlton & Fitzroy Map (pp72-3)

See Prahran & St Kilda Map (p71)

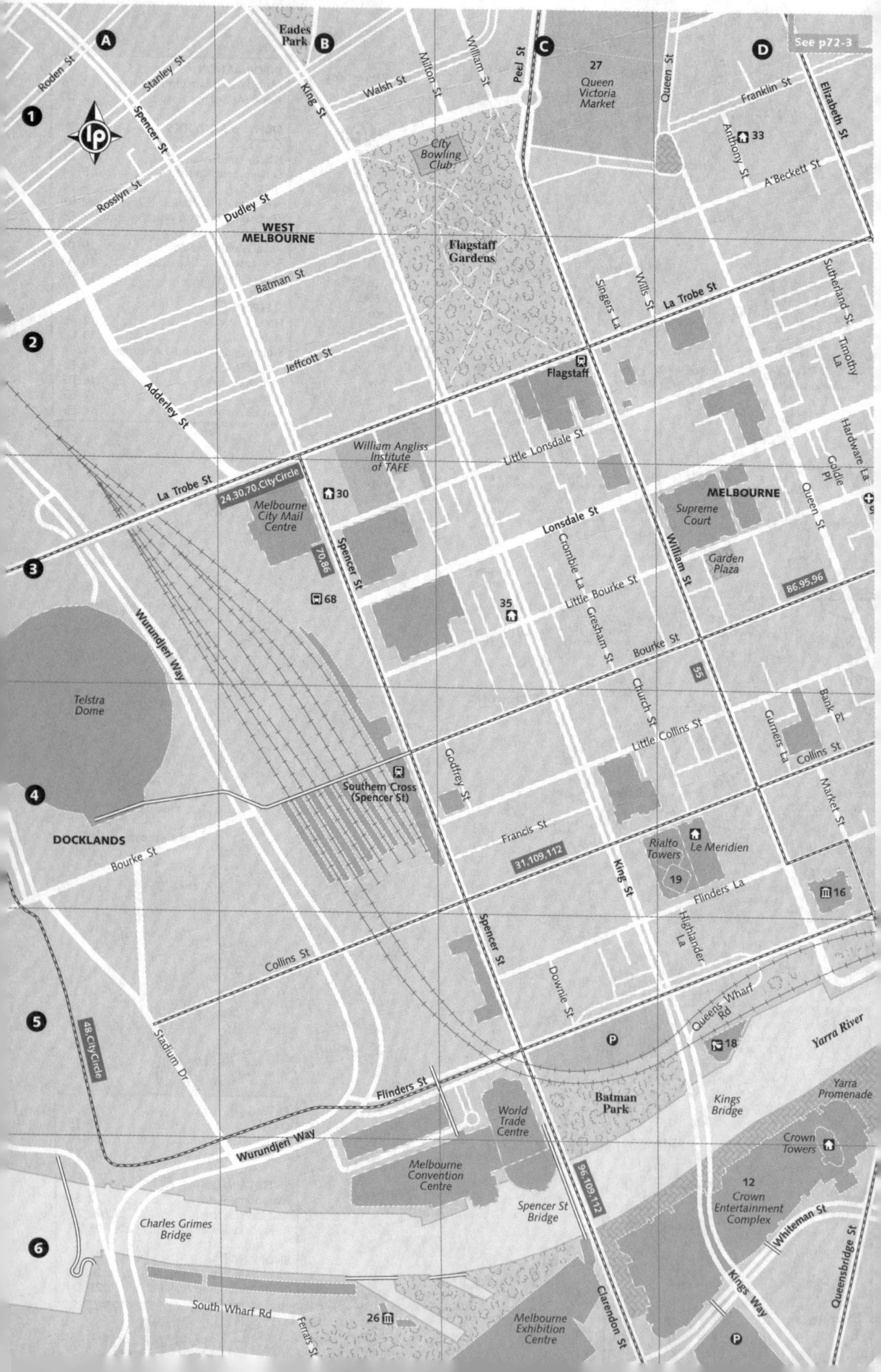

A B Eades Park C D See p72-3

Roden St
Stanley St
Spencer St
Rosslyn St
King St
Walsh St
Milton St
William St
Peel St

27 Queen Victoria Market

Queen St
Franklin St
Elizabeth St
33
Anthony St
A'Beckett St

1

Dudley St
WEST MELBOURNE
City Bowling Club

Flagstaff Gardens

Batman St
Jeffcott St
Adderley St

Singers La
Willis St
La Trobe St
Sutherland St
Timothy La

2

La Trobe St
24,30,70,CityCircle
Melbourne City Mail Centre
William Angliss Institute of TAFE
30
70,86
68
Spencer St

Little Lonsdale St
Lonsdale St
MELBOURNE
Supreme Court
Garden Plaza
Queen St
Hardware La
Goldie Pl
86,95,96

3

Crombie La
Little Bourke St
Gresham St
Bourke St
35
35
William St

Telstra Dome
Wurundjeri Way
DOCKLANDS

Godfrey St
Southern Cross (Spencer St)

Church St
Little Collins St
Currens La
Collins St
Bank Pl
Market St

4

Bourke St
Collins St
Stadium Dr

Francis St
31,109,112
Rialto Towers
19
Le Meridien
Flinders La
Highlander La
16

48,CityCircle

Spencer St
King St
Downie St
Queens Wharf Rd
P
18

5

Yarra River
Yarra Promenade
Crown Towers

Flinders St
Wurundjeri Way
World Trade Centre
Melbourne Convention Centre
Spencer St Bridge
96,109,112
Batman Park
Kings Bridge
12 Crown Entertainment Complex
Whiteman St

6

Charles Grimes Bridge
South Wharf Rd
Ferrars St
26
Melbourne Exhibition Centre
Clarendon St
Kings Way
Queensbridge St
P

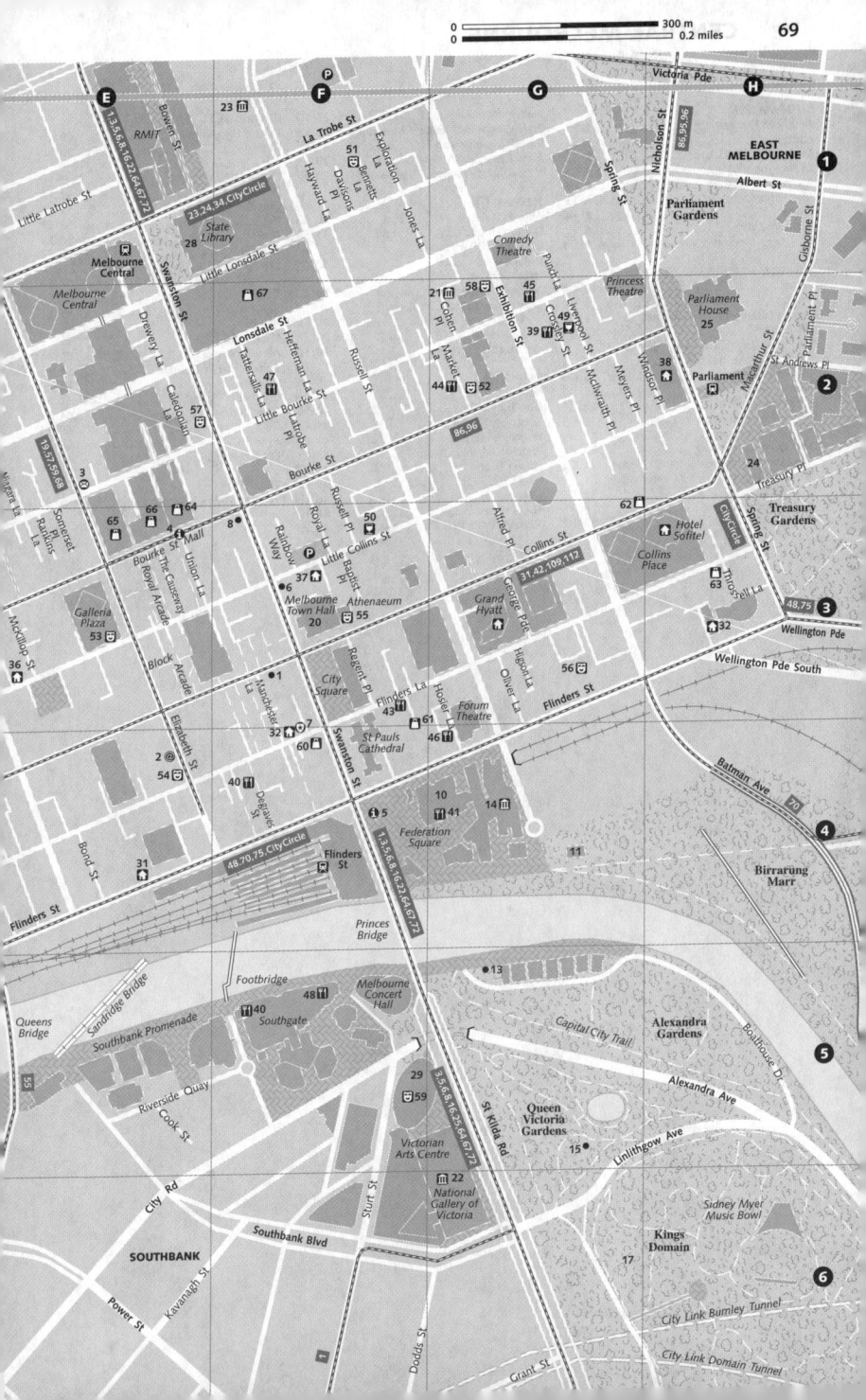

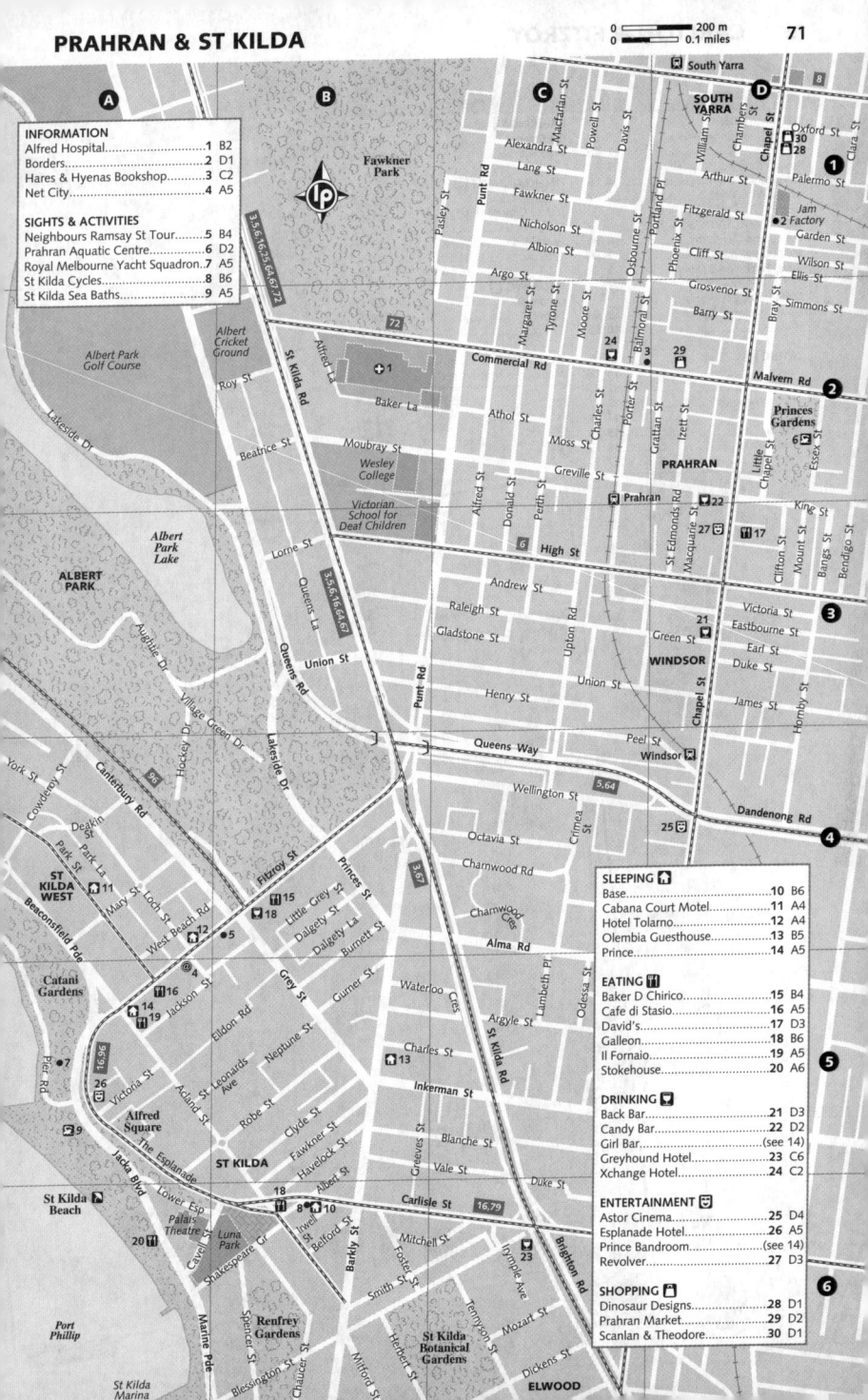

INFORMATION
Alfred Hospital..............................1 B2
Borders..2 D1
Hares & Hyenas Bookshop........3 C2
Net City.......................................4 A5

SIGHTS & ACTIVITIES
Neighbours Ramsay St Tour........5 B4
Prahran Aquatic Centre...............6 D2
Royal Melbourne Yacht Squadron..7 A5
St Kilda Cycles............................8 B6
St Kilda Sea Baths.......................9 A5

SLEEPING
Base...10 B6
Cabana Court Motel....................11 A4
Hotel Tolarno.............................12 A4
Olembia Guesthouse...................13 B5
Prince..14 A5

EATING
Baker D Chirico..........................15 B4
Cafe di Stasio.............................16 A5
David's.......................................17 D3
Galleon......................................18 B6
Il Fornaio...................................19 A5
Stokehouse.................................20 A6

DRINKING
Back Bar.....................................21 D3
Candy Bar...................................22 D2
Girl Bar...................................(see 14)
Greyhound Hotel........................23 C6
Xchange Hotel............................24 C2

ENTERTAINMENT
Astor Cinema.............................25 D4
Esplanade Hotel.........................26 A5
Prince Bandroom....................(see 14)
Revolver....................................27 D3

SHOPPING
Dinosaur Designs........................28 D1
Prahran Market...........................29 D2
Scanlan & Theodore....................30 D1

INFORMATION
Dental Emergency Service.................1 B3
Readings...2 C3
Royal Women's Hospital...................3 B4
St Vincent's Hospital........................4 E6
World Wide Wash.............................5 F2

SIGHTS & ACTIVITIES
Melbourne City Baths.......................6 B6
Melbourne Museum..........................7 D5
Royal Exhibition Building..................8 D5

SLEEPING 🏠
Downtowner on Lygon......................9 B5
Nunnery..10 E5

EATING 🍴
Abla's..11 D3
Brunetti...12 C3
Jimmy Watson's 13 C3
Ladro..14 G6
Marios...15 F3
Pireaus Blues.................................16 F3
Vegie Bar.......................................17 F2

DRINKING 🍷
Bar Open..18 F3
Ume Nomiya...................................19 G6

ENTERTAINMENT 🎭
Alia...20 G6
Dan O'Connell Hotel.......................21 D1
Evelyn Hotel..................................22 F2
Peel Hotel.....................................23 H5
Tote...24 H3

SHOPPING 🛍️
Crumpler.......................................25 G6
Jasper...26 F3
T2...27 F2

TRANSPORT
Melbourne Transit Centre.............28 A6

Melbourne Cemetery

University
of
Melbourne

Elgin St

13 🍴

2 ●

12 🍴

11 🍴

Macarthur Pl North
Macarthur
Square
MacArthur Pl South

Faraday St

University St

Faraday St

Barkly St

Murchison S
Murchison
Square

🏥1
Royal
Womens
Hospital

🏥3

Grattan St

Owen St

Carlton St

CARLTON

Carlton
Gardens
North

Lincoln Sq
North

Lincoln
Square

Pelham St

Argyle Pl North

Argyle
Square

🏛️7
Melbourne
Museum

Lincoln Sq
South

Argyle Pl South

🏛️8

Queensberry St

🏠9

Earl St

Carlton
Gardens
South

Trades
Hall

Victoria St
Therry St

CITY

🏢6

Victoria St

28 ●
Franklin St

23,24,34,CityCircle

RMIT

See Central Melbourne Map (pp68–9)

Davis St

Princes St

21 🎭
Victoria Pl

Neill St

Kay St

Pitt St

Palmerston St

Palmerston St
Cardigan St
Keppel St
Lygon St

1,22,25

Swanston St

Rathdowne St

Canning St

Drummond St

Camning St

Dorrit St

1,3,5,6,8,16,22,64,67,72

Bouverie St

Leicester St

Barry St

Leicester St

Swanston St

Cardigan St

Lygon St

Drummond St

Rathdowne St

Spring St

La Trobe St

Mackenzie St

Russell St

Bowver St

Elizabeth St

19,57,59,68

MELBOURNE

(Continued from page 65)

The **Melbourne Town Hall** (Map pp68-9; ☎ tour bookings 9658 9658; townhalltour@melbourne.vic.gov.au; cnr Swanston & Collins Sts), built between 1870 and 1880, is a fine civic building (don't miss the beautiful wood-panelled Council Chamber). Free guided tours of the building are held at 11am and 1pm from Monday to Friday, and on the first Saturday of each month at 11am, noon and 1pm. The tour includes a wander round the back to view its magnificent 10,000-pipe organ.

The **State Library** (Map pp68-9; ☎ 8664 7000; www.slv.vic.gov.au; 328 Swanston St; admission free; ☉ 10am-9pm Mon-Thu, 10am-6pm Fri-Sun), between Little Lonsdale and Latrobe Sts, was built in various stages from 1854 and boasts a Classical Revival façade. The library collection dates back to a 4000-year-old Mesopotamian tablet and includes the records from the infamous Burke and Wills expedition.

COLLINS STREET

Collins St is Melbourne's most elegant streetscape and has a fashionable end and a financial end: the western end (from Elizabeth St to Spencer St) is home to bankers and stockbrokers, while the eastern or top end, generally known as the 'Paris end', is mostly five-star hotels and exclusive boutiques.

Block Arcade, which runs between Collins and Elizabeth Sts, was built in 1891 and is a beautifully intact 19th-century shopping arcade housing some specialist shops. It features intricate mosaic tiled floors, marble columns, Victorian window surrounds and magnificently detailed plasterwork on the upper walls.

On the 55th floor of the soaring **Rialto Towers**, Melbourne's tallest building, is the justifiably popular **Melbourne Observation Deck** (Map pp68-9; ☎ 9629 8222; www.melbournedeck.com.au; 525 Collins St; adult/child/concession $12.50/7/9; ☉ 10am-10pm), which offers spectacular 360-degree views of Melbourne's surrounds. You can get to the top by stairs (more than 1250 of them) or by an ear-popping lift. For wheelchair access, use the Collins St entrance to the building.

BOURKE STREET

The area around the centre of Bourke St is home to the city's main department stores. The mall section between Swanston and Elizabeth Sts is closed to traffic, and pedestrians share **Bourke St Mall** with an assortment of buskers and trams (beware of the latter!).

The **Royal Arcade** built from 1869 to 1870 is Melbourne's oldest arcade. It's lined with souvenir, travel, food and jewellery shops, and if you look up you'll see the fine detail of the original 19th-century arcade. At the Little Collins St end, the tall figures of **Gog** and **Magog** stand guard. These mythological giants have been striking the hour (with their hammers) on the clock since 1892.

SPRING STREET

Standing at the eastern end of Collins St beside the Treasury Gardens, the **Old Treasury Building** (Map pp68-9; ☎ 9651 2233; www.oldtreasurymuseum.org.au; Spring St; adult/concession $8.50/5; ☉ 9am-5pm Mon-Fri, 10am-4pm Sat & Sun) is considered to be Melbourne's most elegant 19th-century building. It was built in 1862 with huge basement vaults to store much of the $200 million worth of gold that came from the Victorian goldfields. It now houses three permanent exhibitions in the **Gold Treasury Museum**.

Between Bourke and Little Collins Sts, the **Windsor Hotel** (Map pp68-9; ☎ 9633 6000; www.thewindsor.com.au; 103 Spring St) is a marvellous reminder of the 19th century and a time when things were built not only to last but to impress. Constructed in 1883, the hotel was extensively refurbished in the 1980s, allowing it to retain the title of the city's grandest hotel. If you're not staying here, it's still well worth a look.

Opposite the Windsor Hotel, the **Parliament House of Victoria** (Map pp68-9; ☎ 9651 8568; www.parliament.vic.gov.au; Spring St; ☉ Mon-Fri) building was started in 1856, and is still the city's most impressive public building. Australia's first federal Parliament sat here from 1901, before moving to Canberra in 1927. There are free half-hour tours at 10am, 11am, noon, 2pm, 3pm and 3.45pm on weekdays when parliament isn't in session. You can also tour when Parliament is in session; these tours can be arranged by phoning or visiting the website.

CHINATOWN

This is the only area of continuous Chinese settlement in the country, as well as one of Melbourne's most intact 19th-century streetscapes. In the 1850s, the Chinese set up their shops alongside brothels, opium dens, boarding houses and herbalists; these days, the area is much more salubrious and is dominated by restaurants and discount traders.

The interesting **Museum of Chinese Australian History** (Map pp68-9; ☎ 9662 2888; 22 Cohen Pl; adult/concession $6.50/4.50; ☺ 10am-5pm) documents the long history of Chinese people in Australia. The entrance of the museum is guarded by the 218kg Millennium Dragon, which snakes its way through the city streets during Chinese New Year. The museum also conducts walking tours around Chinatown (see above).

QUEEN VICTORIA MARKET
On Victoria St, between Elizabeth and Peel Sts, the **Queen Victoria Market** (Map pp66-7; ☎ 9320 5822; www.qvm.com.au; 513 Elizabeth St; ☺ 6am-2pm Tue & Thu, 6am-6pm Fri, 6am-3pm Sat, 9am-4pm Sun) is the mother of all Melbourne markets. It was saved from demolition in the 1970s and has been around for more than 130 years. Many of the sheds and buildings are registered by the National Trust. See also p91.

OLD MELBOURNE GAOL
This gruesome old gaol, now a **museum** (Map pp72-3; ☎ 9663 7228; Russell St; adult/child $12.50/7.50; ☺ 9.30am-5pm), is at the northern end of Russell St. It was built out of bluestone in 1841 and was used until 1929. In all, 135 prisoners were hanged there. It's a dark, dank and spooky place, and its displays include Ned Kelly's iconic armour and the very gallows from which he was hanged.

IMMIGRATION MUSEUM
The inspiring **Immigration Museum** (Map pp68-9; ☎ 9927 2700; 400 Flinders St; adult/concession & child $6/free; ☺ 10am-5pm) uses multimedia displays to give a moving account of the lives of Melbourne's immigrants from the early 19th century to the present day. The museum is housed in the beautifully restored Old Customs House. Make sure you catch sight of the Long Room, an extraordinary example of Renaissance Revival architecture.

MELBOURNE AQUARIUM
On the river's edge, across from the imposing Crown Casino, you'll find the **Melbourne Aquarium** (Map pp68-9; ☎ 9620 0999; www.melbourneaquarium.com.au; cnr Queenswharf Rd & King St; adult/child/concession $22/12/14; ☺ 9.30am-6pm Feb-Dec, 9.30am-9pm Jan). The highlights of the

aquarium are its floor-to-ceiling coral tank, the 360-degree fishbowl viewing area and the 2.2-million-litre oceanarium.

FITZROY & TREASURY GARDENS
The leafy **Fitzroy Gardens** (Map pp66-7; www.fitzroygardens.com; btwn Wellington Pde, Clarendon, Lansdowne & Albert Sts) divide the city centre from East Melbourne and serve as a verdant retreat from city life. James Sinclair, the first curator, previously landscape gardener to the Russian Tsar Nicholas I, created what is now a rambling blend of elm and cedar avenues, fern gullies, flower beds and lawns. The gardens are a popular spot for wedding photos.

The smaller **Treasury Gardens**, a popular lunchtime and barbecue spot, contain a **memorial to John F Kennedy**, who may not seem the most obvious candidate for a Melbourne memorial, but it's a soothing place to unwind, regardless.

Southbank
On the southern bank of the Yarra River, across from the CBD, the area known as Southbank is a former industrial wasteland that was transformed in the early 1990s by the **Southgate** (Map pp68-9) development. An arched footbridge crosses the Yarra River from behind Flinders St station, linking the city centre to the Victorian Arts Centre, the National Gallery and Southgate itself. Walks flank the river on both sides.

The Southgate complex houses three levels of restaurants, cafés and bars, all of which enjoy a unique outlook over the city skyline and the river. There's also an international food hall, a shopping gallery with upmarket boutiques, and a collection of specially commissioned sculptures and other art works.

NGV INTERNATIONAL
This section of the **NGV** (National Gallery of Victoria; Map pp68-9; ☎ 8620 2222; www.ngv.vic.gov.au; 180 St Kilda Rd; admission free; ☺ 10am-5pm) has arguably the best collection of international art in Australia. The renowned European section has an impressive collection of works by European masters including Rembrandt, Picasso, Turner, Monet, Titian, Pissarro and van Dyck. The **sculpture courtyard** and gallery has some fine sculptures by Auguste Rodin and Henry Moore. The **Great Hall** is a highlight, and the best way to see its stained-glass ceiling is to lie on your back on the floor.

VICTORIAN ARTS CENTRE

The **Victorian Arts Centre** (VAC; Map pp8-9; ☎ 9281 8000; www.vicartscentre.com.au; 100 St Kilda Rd) is made up of two separate buildings – Hamer Hall and the Theatres Building – which are linked to each other and the gallery by a series of landscaped walkways. **Hamer Hall**, the circular building closest to the Yarra, is the main concert hall for major artists and companies. The **Theatres Building** is topped by its distinctive Eiffel-inspired spire (illuminated at night), underneath which are housed the State Theatre, the Playhouse and the George Fairfax Studio. The stylish interiors of both buildings are quite stunning, and are well worth visiting in their own right.

CROWN CASINO & ENTERTAINMENT COMPLEX

The 24-hour, non-stop cavalcade of illuminated excess that is the **Crown Casino & Entertainment Complex** (Map pp8-9; ☎ 9292 8888; www .crowncasino.com.au; Southbank; ☼ 24hr) was for a fleeting moment the world's largest casino (it's still the largest in the southern hemisphere). The complex holds a luxury hotel, a variety of nightclubs, a cinema chain, a 900-seat showroom, speciality and luxury stores, plus dozens of cafés and restaurants, should gambling not appeal. You'll either love it or hate it, like everyone else in Melbourne.

POLLY WOODSIDE MARITIME MUSEUM

The *Polly Woodside*, an old iron-hulled three-masted sailing ship, is the centrepiece of this maritime museum/park (Map pp8-9; ☎ 9699 9760; Lorimer St East; adult/child/concession $10/6/8; ☼ 10am-4pm). She was built in Belfast in 1885, spent the first part of her working life carrying coal and nitrate between Europe and South America, and ended her career as a coal hulk. She was bought by the National Trust in the 1970s and restored by volunteers. Other attractions are the historically listed **cargo sheds**, which house relics, displays and film footage relating to the history of Melbourne's port.

Kings Domain

King's Domain (Map pp68–9) is an area of parkland across from the Melbourne arts precinct that contains the wonderful Royal Botanic Gardens, as well as the Shrine of Remembrance, **Governor La Trobe's Cottage** and the **Sidney Myer Music Bowl**.

Government House (Map pp66-7; ☎ 9656 9800; Government House Dr; adult/child $11/5.50) is home of the Victorian Governor. It's a copy of Queen Victoria's palace on England's Isle of Wight, was built in 1872 and is one of the best examples of the Italianate style in the country. Entry is by guided tours Monday, Wednesday and Friday; bookings essential. The tour price includes entry to La Trobe's Cottage.

Beside St Kilda Rd stands the massive **Shrine of Remembrance** (Map pp66-7; ☎ 9654 8415; ☼ 10am-5pm), built as a memorial to Victorians killed in WWI. The forecourt, with its cenotaph and eternal flame, was built as a memorial to those who died in WWII.

ROYAL BOTANIC GARDENS

Certainly the finest botanic gardens in Australia and among the finest in the world, the **Royal Botanic Gardens** (Map pp66-7; ☎ 9252 2300; www.rbg.vic.gov.au; Birdwood Ave; admission free; ☼ 7.30am-8.30pm Nov-Mar, 7.30am-5.30pm Apr-Oct) are a must-see. With a prime location beside the Yarra River, the beautifully laid out gardens feature plants from around the world, lakes and a surprising amount of wildlife.

Pick up self-guiding leaflets at the entrances; these change with the seasons. There are entrance gates around the gardens, but the visitor information centre is in the National Herbarium inside Gate F on Birdwood Ave. The gardens offer a variety of tours including an **Aboriginal Heritage Walk** (see p81).

MELBOURNE CRICKET GROUND

The **MCG** (or just 'the G'; Map pp66-7; ☎ 9657 8888; www.mcg.org.au; Brunton Ave) is the temple in which sports-mad Melburnians worship their heroes. One of the world's great sporting venues, it's imbued with an indefinable combination of tradition and atmosphere. The first game of Australian Rules football was played here in 1858, and in 1877 the first test cricket match between Australia and England. In 2006 the opening and closing ceremonies of the Commonwealth Games will take place here. If you fancy getting really close to this hallowed hall of recreation, take a **tour** (☎ 9657 8879; adult/concession $10/6). Tours depart every half-hour (on non-match days) from 10am to 3pm, and last for 1¼ hours.

Parkville & Carlton

Up this end of town you'll find a cosmopolitan area that blends the intellectual with the recreational, the multicultural with the mainstream. These two suburbs are divided by the tree-lined Royal Pde and a huge chunk of it is devoted to the enormous Royal Park (see p65).

ROYAL MELBOURNE ZOO

Melbourne's zoo (Map pp66-7; ☎ 9285 9300; www .zoo.org.au; Elliot Ave, Parkville; adult/child/concession $18/9/13.50; ☿ 9am-5pm) is one of the city's most popular attractions, and deservedly so. Established in 1861, this is the oldest zoo in Australia and the third-oldest in the world.

In the summer months, the zoo hosts **twilight concerts** (www.zoo.org.au/melbourne/twilights.htm). Roar 'n' Snore is a programme that allows you to camp at the zoo and join the keepers on their morning rounds of the enclosures.

CARLTON GARDENS

The Carlton Gardens are home to the historic **Royal Exhibition Building** (Map pp72-3; ☎ 9270 5000; www.museum.vic.gov.au/reb; Nicholson St), a wonder of the southern hemisphere when it was built for the Great Exhibition of 1880. Later it was used by the Victorian Parliament for 27 years. It is still used as a major exhibition centre (the oldest surviving example in the world) and in 2004 became Australia's first building to earn Unesco World Heritage status. **Tours** (☎ 1300 130 152; adult/concession $4/2) happen daily at 2pm – phone for bookings.

MELBOURNE MUSEUM

In the middle of the Carlton Gardens is the **Melbourne Museum** (Map pp72-3; ☎ 13 11 02; www .melbourne.museum.vic.gov.au; 11 Nicholson St, Carlton; adult/concession & child $6/free; ☿ 10am-5pm). Billed as 'the southern hemisphere's largest and most innovative museum', the architecturally imposing museum resembles an international air terminal with its open-plan design and use of space. The main attractions include the Aboriginal Centre Bunjilaka; a living forest gallery; and the Australia gallery, with exhibits dedicated to that great Aussie icon Phar Lap (the legendary racehorse), and another dedicated to the TV show *Neighbours* (filmed in Melbourne). Kids will love the interactive Children's Museum. Disabled access is very good.

LYGON STREET

Carlton is Melbourne's Italian quarter, and Lygon St is its backbone. Many of the thousands of Italian immigrants who came to Melbourne after WWII settled in Carlton, and Lygon St became the focal point of their community. Day and night it is filled with people promenading, dining, sipping cappuccinos, shopping and generally soaking up the atmosphere. Each year in late October, Lygon St hosts the lively **Lygon St Festa**, a four-day food-and-fun street party.

Fitzroy & Collingwood

Fitzroy is where Melbourne's bohemian subculture moved when the lights got too bright in Carlton. It's a great mixture of artistic, seedy, alternative and trendy elements, and one of Melbourne's most interesting suburbs to visit, with a vibrant community feel.

Brunswick St is Fitzroy's, and probably Melbourne's, most lively street, and you shouldn't leave the city without going there. This is where you'll find some of the best food, the weirdest shops, the most interesting people and the coolest clothes.

Smith St is the border between Fitzroy and Collingwood, and has an assortment of food shops, bookshops, pubs and restaurants, including some good vegie restaurants and Vietnamese bakeries thrown in. The area has a slightly down-at-heel look and it's also something of an artists' colony – many of the city's most interesting emerging talents have studio spaces on Smith St, or close by.

South Yarra

South Yarra is on the 'right' side of the river – the high-society side of town. It's a bustling, trendy and style-conscious suburb – the kind of place where avid readers of *Vogue Living* will feel at home.

In **Toorak Rd** and **Chapel St** you'll find dozens of exclusive boutiques and specialist shops, cafés and restaurants; see also p91. If you want fashion, this is where you'll see it – in the shop windows, sitting outside the cafés and walking down the street.

Prahran

Prahran has some lively streets, the most notable being **Chapel St** – it's more diverse and a little less fashionable than the South Yarra sector. The highlight of the area is the excellent **Prahran Market** (see p91), established in 1881 and still packing in the crowds.

Commercial Rd is a centre for Melbourne's gay and lesbian communities, and has a small but notable collection of nightclubs, bars, pubs, bookshops and several cafés and **Greville St** has a quirky collection of off-beat retro/grunge clothing shops, record shops, bookshops and some good bars and cafés.

St Kilda

St Kilda is one of Melbourne's liveliest and most cosmopolitan areas, a fact jointly attributable to its seaside location and its chequered history. In Melbourne's early days, St Kilda was a seaside resort, the fashionable spot for those wanting to escape the increasingly grimy and crowded city.

Fitzroy St has been given new life by the opening of a growing number of stylish bars, restaurants and cafés.

Further south, the section of **Acland St** between Carlisle and Barkly Sts, once famed only for its continental cake shops and delicatessens, now also has plenty of stylish bars and eateries, making Acland St another of Melbourne's favourite food strips.

St Kilda pier and breakwater is a favourite spot for strollers. On the foreshore south of the pier, the former St Kilda Baths have been transformed into the **St Kilda Sea Baths**, a Moorish-inspired bathing pavilion that was given a tarting up in the new millennium and holds an indoor pool and gym.

The entrance of **Luna Park** (Map p71; ☎ 9525 5033; www.lunapark.com.au; Lower Esplanade; unlimited ride ticket adult/child $33.95/23.95; ☺ 11am-6pm Sat & Sun), with its laughing face, has been a symbol of St Kilda since 1912. The amusement park is somewhat old-fashioned but that's a big part of its charm. It has some great rides, including the old wooden roller coaster and a beautifully crafted carousel. There are extended hours in summer and school holidays.

ACTIVITIES
Cycling

Melbourne has more than 20 long cycle paths, with many constructed in the green belts along the rivers. All are marked in the Melway *Greater Melbourne Street Directory*. Melbourne also has a growing network of on-road bike lanes, making this a relatively easy way to explore the city via pedal power. You can get maps from the visitor centre at Federation Square (Map pp68–9) or from the website for **VicRoads** (www.vicroads.vic.gov.au).

Most hire places include a helmet and lock in the fee; bring along a credit card or photo ID. Places to hire bikes include **Hire a Bike** (Map pp68-9; ☎ 0412 616 633; Princes Bridge, Southbank), close to the city centre and offering bikes for $35 a day; and **St Kilda Cycles** (Map p71; ☎ 9534 3074; www.stkildacycles.com.au; 11 Carlisle St, St Kilda) offering a helmet and a lock with your bike for $20 a day (add $5 for overnight hire).

Sailing

With about 20 yacht clubs around the shores of Port Phillip, yachting is one of Melbourne's most popular passions. Races and regattas are held most weekends, and the bay is a memorable sight when it's sprinkled with hundreds of colourful sails. However, conditions can change radically and without warning, making sailing on the bay a challenging, and sometimes dangerous, pursuit.

Many yacht clubs welcome visitors to crew on racing boats. Phone the race secretary at one of the major clubs if you're keen. Try the **Royal Melbourne Yacht Squadron** (Map p71; ☎ 9534 0227; Pier Rd, St Kilda), which has a postcard-perfect location and crewing opportunities from Wednesday to Sunday.

Swimming

Swimming is a very popular form of exercise despite all the jokes about Melbourne's weather, and the following pools are all worth trying if you feel the need to lap things up.

Melbourne Sports & Aquatic Centre (Map p71; ☎ 9926 1555; www.msac.com.au; Albert Rd, Albert Park; adult/child $5.70/4.20; ☺ 6am-10pm) has a fantastic indoor 75m 10-lane pool, several smaller pools, water slides, spa/sauna/steam room and spacious common areas. A visit here can easily double as the day's entertainment, plus you can play squash and use the gym. Childcare is also available.

Melbourne City Baths (Map pp72-3; ☎ 9663 5888; cnr Swanston & Victoria Sts; adult/concession $4/3.20) is a stately swimming hall with a 25m indoor pool plus a gym, spas, saunas and squash courts.

Other good pools in Melbourne include **Prahran Aquatic Centre** (Map p71; ☎ 8290 7140; 41 Essex St, Prahran; adult/child $3.80/2; ☺ Oct-Apr), with a good outdoor pool that's very popular with gay men come summer; and **St Kilda Sea Baths** (Map p71; ☎ 9525 4888; 10-18 Jacka Blvd, St Kilda; adult/child $12/6), not the cheapest swim in town, with an indoor 25m sea-water pool that is a miracle worker.

You can also choose from many beaches in the bay and the water temperature is tolerable from mid-November to late March, although the water isn't much to look at.

WALKING TOUR

Start at **Federation Square** (1; p64) and then head south along Flinders St noting the magnificent **Flinders St station (2)**, one of the only Edwardian Baroque buildings in Melbourne. Amble along the **Princes Bridge (3)** over the Yarra, then cross Alexandra Ave and walk into the **Queen Victoria Gardens (4)**. Take the first right fork, follow it through the middle of the park, and detour to the **memorial statue (5)** of the good Queen herself. Back on the trail is a **statue of Edward VII (6)** astride his horse. Follow the path for a short distance until it reaches Linlithgow Ave, cross this and you're on the **Tan (7)**, a 4km running track that is Melbourne joggers' favourite. Follow the Tan to the left (east) until you see the path that will take you into the King's Domain and to the **Sidney Myer Music Bowl (8)** where performances and picnics are a regular feature. With the Bowl on your right, wander through the domain until you sight the imposing

---

WALKING TOUR FACTS

Distance: 5km
Duration: two to four hours

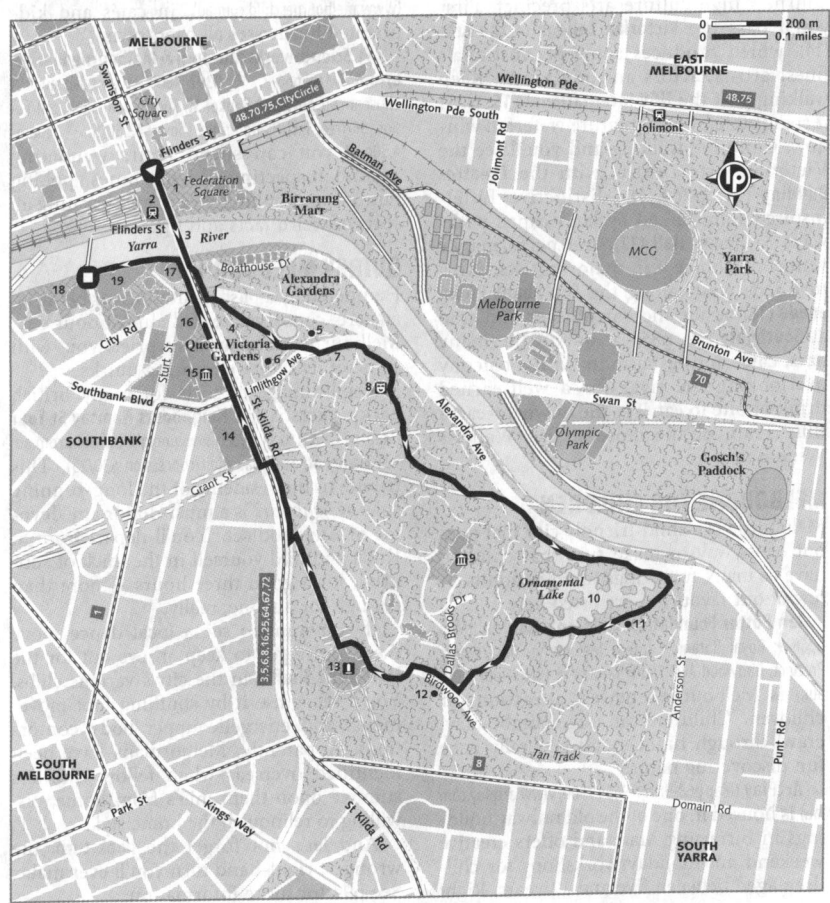

Government House (9; p76) where the Victorian Governor resides. Continue along the path and do a lap of the Royal Botanic Gardens' **ornamental lake (10)**, perhaps stopping at the **kiosk (11)** for a drink, and head for the Gate F exit at Birdwood Ave where you'll rejoin the Tan and see **Governor La Trobe's Cottage (12)**, the original Victorian government house sent from the mother country in prefabricated form in 1840. Walk along the Tan and you can't miss the massive **Shrine of Remembrance (13**; p76), between St Kilda Rd and Birdwood Ave, where you can climb to the top for some great views. Walk down Anzac Ave to St Kilda Rd and stroll along the path by the park until you get to Grant St. Cross and you're in Melbourne's high-culture arts precinct. First you'll pass the **Victorian College of the Arts (14)**, which produces some of Australia's finest artists, actors and musicians. Keep walking past the **NGV International (15**; p75) recognisable by its signature waterfall window. Continue walking and you'll see the Victorian Arts Centre, with the **Theatres Building (16**; p76), its distinctive Eiffel-inspired spire linked by landscaped pathways to **Hamer Hall (17)**, the performance venue of choice for major artists. Now turn left (west) along the **Southbank Promenade (18)** beside the Yarra River and stop at **Southgate (19**; p85) at one of the many bars, cafés and restaurants with a balcony overlooking the river for a well-earned drink or bite to eat. Try the down-to-earth Blue Train or the more stylish Walter's Wine Bar.

MELBOURNE FOR CHILDREN

Melbourne is a child-friendly city that goes out of its way to make sure that children have as many fun things to do as adults. A few of our favourites are listed here.

Ian Potter Foundation Children's Garden (Map pp68-9; Royal Botanic Gardens Melbourne, Observatory Precinct, Birdwood Ave, South Yarra; ☽ 10am-4pm Wed-Sun) is Melbourne's newest attraction for children. Children can dig, climb, play, crawl through tunnels and generally have fun discovering nature.

ArtPlay (Map p68-9; ☎ 9664 7900; www.artplay.com .au) is housed in one of the old railway buildings in Birrarung Marr and offers creative weekend and holiday workshops for children aged between five and 12 years. Right

next to it is a brilliant playground with hammocks, rock climbing, a sandpit and tube slides.

During the Christmas season, from mid-November to 7 January, don't miss the famous **Myer Christmas Windows** (Map pp68-9; ☎ 9661 1111; Myer, Bourke St Mall, City). Each year, the department store chooses a different theme and artists transform the windows along the mall into a magical world that seems to fascinate adults as much as it does children.

Other options include **Luna Park** (p78) and the **Melbourne Museum** (p77). Almost every neighbourhood in every suburb has a park with play equipment. For more information about local attractions and events, look for the free monthly publication **Melbourne's Child** (www.melbourneschild.com.au), in cafés and kid-oriented businesses all over town.

At **Scienceworks Museum & Melbourne Planetarium** (Map p66-7; ☎ 9392 4800; www.scienceworks .museum.vic.gov.au; 2 Booker St, Spotswood; adult/concession $6/free, incl Planetarium show $12.50/5; ☽ 10am-4.30pm) you can spend hours wandering around inspecting old machines, poking buttons and pulling levers, and learning all sorts of weird facts and figures.

QUIRKY MELBOURNE

Hampered by a past reputation for being an austere, conservative and almost dour city, Melbourne may well surprise you with some of its rather endearing quirks.

A pilgrimage of sorts for many British backpackers is the **Neighbours Ramsay St Tour** (Map p71; ☎ 9534 4755; www.neighbourstour.com.au; 121 Fitzroy St, St Kilda; adult/concession $30/25). This tribute to the residents of the long-running soap *Neighbours* is a must-do for any devotee of Aussie kitsch. You'll depart from St Kilda and find yourself in the thick of suburbia for a good three hours – more than enough for anyone, really.

If you want to see a local dance move then you've got to keep an eye out for the **Melbourne Shuffle** in the city's various clubs. You'll recognise it by its shuffling foot movements and energetic upper body contortions. Apparently, Melburnians have been identified overseas when fellow shufflers stumble upon them miles from home, unwilling to relinquish the home style.

And let's not forget the **hook turn**, the wrongest right-hand turn you'll ever make. See p92 for more information.

TOURS

There's a huge array of tours on offer in and around Melbourne. The free *Me!bourne Events* guide, which is updated monthly, is available at visitor information centres, hotels and newsagents and has an extensive section on tours. You can also ask at the visitor information centre in Federation Square.

Aboriginal Heritage Walk (Map pp66-7; ☎ 9252 2300; www.rbg.vic.gov.au; adult/child $15.50/6.60; ☹ 11am Thu & Fri, 10.30am alternate Sun) The Royal Botanic Gardens are on the ancestral lands of the Boonwurrung and Woiworung people, and this tour takes you through their story in 90 fascinating minutes. Departs from the visitor centre in the Royal Botanic Gardens.

Chinatown Heritage Walk (Map pp68-9; ☎ 9662 2888; www.melbournechinatown.com.au/attractions _walk.html; 22 Cohen Pl; adult/concession from $15/12) Be guided through historic Chinatown, with its atmospheric alleys and bustling vibe. You can even be fed on this tour, for a little extra time and money.

City Circle trams (www.metlinkmelbourne.com.au/city _circle) This tram offers a free service and operates from 10am to 6pm. It travels around the city centre, along Flinders, Spring and Nicholson Sts to Victoria Pde and then back along Latrobe and Spencer Sts (there are also trams running in the opposite direction) about every 10 minutes.

City Explorer (Map pp68-9; ☎ 1800 858 687; tickets from 180 Swanston St; adult/child $33/16.50) This service offers double-decker bus tours of Melbourne, with about 20 stops en route.

Melbourne River Cruises (Map pp68-9; ☎ 9681 3284; www.melbcruises.com.au; Vault 11, Banana Alley, Docklands; adult/child from $14/7.50) There's a one-hour cruise upstream or downstream or a 2½-hour return cruise. Regular cruises along the Yarra River depart from a couple of locations – check with the company for details.

FESTIVALS & EVENTS

Melbourne has festivals all year round, and many of these are thematic, bringing out locals and visitors alike to revel in Melbourne life.

The free *Me!bourne Events* guide, available at visitor centres, has listings of all major events going on while you're in town. You can also check it out online at www.melbourne.vic.gov.au/events. Tickets to most major events can be booked through **Ticketmaster7** (☎ 1300 136 166; www .ticketmaster7.com). Some of the highlights are the following:

January

Midsumma Festival (www.midsumma.org.au) Melbourne's annual gay-and-lesbian arts festival is held mid-January to early February, and comprises more than 100 events spread across the city.

February

St Kilda Festival (www.stkildafestival.com.au) A weekend-long celebration of local arts and culture – food, art, music and writing.

March

Australia Formula One Grand Prix (www.grandprix .com.au) Albert Park is invaded by the thoroughbreds of the automotive world, and their party-loving hangers on.

Melbourne Food & Wine Festival (www.melbourne foodwine.com.au) This highly regarded gastronomical event takes place from mid-March to early April.

April

Melbourne International Comedy Festival (www.comedyfestival.com.au) Locals are joined by a wealth of international acts performing at venues all over the city.

July

Melbourne International Film Festival (www .melbournefilmfestival.com.au) Two weeks of the newest and the best in local and international film, plus talks, forums and a lot of drinking.

August

Melbourne Writers' Festival (www.mwf.com.au) Held annually at various venues throughout this most book-loving of Australia's cities in August/September, this 10-day festival covers a wide range of literary genres and issues, with local and international authors.

September

Grand Final (www.afl.com.au) The Australian Football League (AFL) final is played on the last Saturday in September. Join in the spirit of things and pray that it's not contested by two out-of-town teams.

October

Melbourne International Arts Festival (www .melbournefestival.com.au) The city's major arts event has a programme that covers theatre, opera, dance and music.

November

Spring Racing Carnival (www.racingvictoria.net.au) Begins in October and runs into November. There are two feature races: the Caulfield Cup (Caulfield Racecourse) and the Melbourne Cup (Flemington Racecourse).

SLEEPING

Melbourne's sleeping options are broad and generally of a high standard – you can pick from a number of categories in the mid-range to top-end scale, with serviced apartments, motels, boutique guesthouses, B&Bs and five-star hotels concentrated in the city centre and suburbs such as St Kilda, East Melbourne and South Yarra. The city centre is convenient and close to things like theatres, museums and transport terminals, and is also within walking distance of the city's wonderful nightlife. The alternative is to stay in one of the inner suburbs, such as Carlton or Fitzroy, which offer good-quality sleeping, particularly on a budget.

Note that during major festivals and events accommodation in Melbourne is very scarce, so make reservations well in advance.

Budget

There are backpacker hostels in the city centre and most of the inner suburbs. There are usually plenty of rooms to be found in winter, but space gets tight in summer – book well in advance if possible. Several of the larger hostels have courtesy buses that pick up from the bus and train terminals.

The prices listed are per night for the low season; they jump about 10% to 20% in high season (summer). Most places offer discounts for weekly and monthly stays.

CENTRAL MELBOURNE

Greenhouse Backpacker (Map pp68-9; ☎ 9639 6400; www.friendlygroup.com.au; 228 Flinders Lane; dm $25, s/d & tw $55/68; 🖳) A short walk from Flinders St station, this large, well-maintained hostel has very clean rooms, pleasant common

---

areas and staff who are happy to help you make the most of its excellent location. Security is solid.

Melbourne Connection Travellers Hostel (Map pp68-9; ☎ 9642 4464; www.melbourneconnection.com; 205 King St; dm $21-25, d & tw $60; 🖳) Less chaotic than some of the city's larger hostels, this place has a low-key, easy-going appeal. Common areas are in good condition and 24-hour access is available.

Hotel Bakpak (Map pp68-9; ☎ 9329 7525; www.bakpakgroup.com; 167 Franklin St; dm $24-26, s/d $55/70; 🖳) This backpackers' behemoth offers just about everything the budget traveller could ask for, including job-hunting facilities. Its functional and straightforward rooms are sandwiched between the basement bar and rooftop entertainment area with great views over the city. Reception is open 24 hours.

NORTH MELBOURNE & FITZROY

Melbourne Metro (Map pp66-7; ☎ 9329 8599; www.yha.com.au; 78 Howard St; dm $20-28, s/d/f $64/74/82; 🄿 🖳) The YHA showpiece, this huge 348-bed place is well kitted out and managed and has excellent facilities, including modern bathrooms, a good kitchen, a rooftop patio with barbecues, and a secure car park.

Nunnery (Map pp72-3; ☎ 9419 8637; www.nunnery.com.au; 116 Nicholson St; dm $23-27, s $60-75, d & tw $80-110) This is an attractive option, particularly if you're a fan of Victorian-era architecture. Well located on the fringe of the city, opposite the Carlton Gardens and in a converted nunnery, this grand hostel has comfortable furniture, a friendly atmosphere, excellent budget dorms and more upmarket guesthouse and townhouse accommodation.

ST KILDA & SOUTH YARRA

Base (Map p71; ☎ 9536 6109; www.basebackpackers.com; 17 Carlisle St; dm $23-29; d from $75; 🖳) Easily the flashest hostel in St Kilda, this well-run place fronts Carlisle St with a bold red feature wall and shows off inside with sparkling facilities, natty communal areas and enough activities to keep the most revved-up backpackers happy.

Olembia Guesthouse (Map p71; ☎ 9537 1412; www.olembia.com.au; 96 Barkly St; dm/s/d $24/46/78; 🄿) Far more like a boutique hotel than a hostel; the facilities at this excellent place include a cosy guest lounge, dining room, courtyard and off-street parking (and a bike shed for bike tourers). The rooms are quite

---

THE AUTHOR'S CHOICE

Hotel Lindrum (Map pp68-9; ☎ 9668 1111; www.hotellindrum.com.au; 26 Flinders St; d from $300) Every inch of this hotel is simply divine, and it exudes an elegant luxury that is never over the top. The century-old building was the well-known Lindrum's Billiards Centre in the 1980s and still has a full-sized table for guests. The details and features emphasise quality and individual style, and the dark wood furnishings, muted lighting and contemporary touches give it a distinctly stylish feel.

small but are clean and comfortable. It's deservedly popular, so book ahead.

Hotel Claremont (Map pp66-7; ☎ 9826 8000; www .hotelclaremont.com; 189 Toorak Rd; dm/s/d $30/66/76; 🖳) The Claremont, once a grand home, is now a budget hotel. Rooms, while simple and a little spartan, are spotless and freshly painted and communal bathrooms are in excellent condition. Lavish touches such as a grand central staircase and oriental rugs belie the bargain rates.

CAMPING
Ashley Gardens Big 4 Holiday Village (☎ 9318 6866; www.ashleygardens.com.au; cnr Ashley St & Ballarat Rd, Braybrook; powered & unpowered sites $27-33, cabins from $70; P 🖳) Only 9km from the city centre, this is a well-run, spacious camping ground. There are also well-appointed sites that sleep up to six people. You can access the city centre by bus 220, which goes to Flinders St station.

Midrange
Most of the hotels and motels in this section are rated three stars, and they're comfortable but sometimes a little cramped. Doubles usually cost the same as singles.

CENTRAL MELBOURNE
Duxton Hotel (Map pp68-9; ☎ 9250 1888; www.dux ton.com; 328 Flinders St; r from $125; P 🔲 🖳) This heritage-listed hotel was built in 1913 as the Commercial Travellers Club and much of the hotel has been restored to its original splendour. Rich dark timber panelling is a feature throughout the public areas, while modern touches bring it well into the 21st century. Service is ever-helpful.

Atlantis Hotel (Map pp68-9; ☎ 9600 2900; www .atlantishotel.com.au; 300 Spencer St; r from $135; P) A recent addition to the city's sleeping options at this busy end of town. There's good access to transport and city centre sights, and rooms are no-frills but smart.

Hotel Y (Map pp66-7; ☎ 9329 5188; www.hotely .com.au; 489 Elizabeth St; r $80-150) This is an award-winning hotel run by the YWCA. The 'Y' has great facilities, including a café on the premises and a communal kitchen and laundry. You're also within easy reach of the Queen Victoria Market.

Victoria Hotel (Map pp68-9; ☎ 9653 0441; www .victoriahotel.com.au; 215 Little Collins St; s $56-92, d $80-155) The Vic is a Melbourne institution –

it's brilliantly located, surrounded by good shops and some great restaurants and bars.

Quest Fairfax House Serviced Apartments (Map pp68-9; ☎ 9642 1333; www.questapartments.com.au; 392 Little Collins St; apt from $165; P 🔲) These apartments are centrally located at this quiet end of Little Collins St. Apartments, with all the usual amenities, are comfortable and the complex is well run, with baby-sitting and secretarial services on offer.

EAST MELBOURNE & CARLTON
Knightsbridge Apartments (Map pp66-7; ☎ 9419 1333; www.knightsbridgeapartments.com.au; 101 George St; apt from $139; 🔲) This is an excellent choice for those looking for accommodation that's comfortable and well furnished. Complete with thick carpets and four-poster beds, facilities are spotless, modern and stylish.

Magnolia Court (Map pp66-7; ☎ 9419 4222; www .magnolia-court.com.au; 101 Powlett St; r from $140) This bright and friendly boutique hotel has an abundance of lavender bushes and a wing dating back to 1862 with high ceilings and traditional-style furnishings. The best option is the self-contained Victorian cottage, which is ideal for those travelling with children (no under-threes though).

Downtowner on Lygon (Map pp72-3; ☎ 9663 5555; www.downtowner.com.au; 66 Lygon St; r from $149; P 🔲 🖳) With a central courtyard for parking, this is a good option for those with cars, and we love the fact that its rates haven't shifted in years. Business facilities are good and some rooms have modest self-catering options – although you'll not be stumped for places to eat in this location.

ST KILDA & SOUTH YARRA
Hotel Tolarno (Map p71; ☎ 9537 0200; www.tolarno .com.au; 42 Fitzroy St; d from $115; 🔲) The rooms have some of the highest ceilings we've ever seen, and while some may not match those dimensions in width, they're all pretty comfy and have sparkling bathrooms, and original and colourful artworks on the walls. Choose a room at the back if you're a light sleeper.

Cabana Court Motel (Map p71; ☎ 9534 0771; www.cabanacourtapartments.com; 46 Park St; apt from $90; P 🔲) These decent motel-style apartments near pretty, tree-lined Mary St are only a short stroll from the beach and the myriad dining options of busy Fitzroy St. They feature that rarest of midrange aquatic delights: bathtubs.

MELBOURNE

Tilba (Map pp66-7; ☎ 9867 8844; www.thetilba.com .au; cnr Toorak Rd West & Domain St; r from $154) This small and elegant hotel has been lovingly restored in gracious Victorian style. The 15 suites all feature old iron bedsteads, antique lamps, decorative plasterwork and period-style bathrooms. It's highly recommended, with a homey, welcoming feel, although the less-expensive rooms are quite small.

Toorak Manor (Map pp66-7; ☎ 9827 2689; www .toorakmanor.citysearch.com.au; 220 Williams Rd; d from $145) An excellent boutique hotel, this mansion has been impressively converted (every inch seems covered in chintz) and is set in lovely gardens. It has comfortable period-style rooms and cosy sitting rooms.

Top End

Melbourne's top-end hotels and serviced apartments combine excellent location, attractive décor and attentive service. Generally, you'll find a range of packages and deals on offer via the Internet. Parking is often of the 'valet' variety and can incur a charge of between $12 and $25 per day.

Windsor (Map pp68-9; ☎ 9633 6000; www.thewind sor.com.au; 103 Spring St, City; r from $500; P ❷ 💻) Fabulous rooms, a great sense of history and wonderful service (it has accommodated the whims of Sir Laurence Olivier, Vivien Leigh, the Duke of Windsor and even Metallica) make this more than just a hotel – it's on every local's wish list for a romantic weekend. High tea here is justifiably famous, so if you can't get a room, at least get a scone.

Prince (Map p71; ☎ 9536 1111; www.theprince .com.au; 2 Acland St, St Kilda; r from $200; P ❷ 💻) This beautifully furnished boutique hotel seeps minimalist luxury from every surface, crevice and cranny – the fabulous location only adds to its appeal. Service is discreet, smart and considerate. Eating and entertainment options on the premises mean you need never leave its environs.

EATING

Melbourne's ethnic diversity is reflected in the inexhaustible variety of its cuisines and restaurants. Food is a local obsession, and people eat out a lot because Melburnians consider the city to be the country's eating capital (Sydneysiders will disagree just as passionately). Indeed, there are those who believe that Melbourne is one of the world's great eating cities – and they're right.

THE AUTHOR'S CHOICE

Moroccan Soup Bar (Map pp66-7; ☎ 9482 4240; 183 St Georges Rd, North Fitzroy; mains $10-15; ⏱ dinner Tue-Sun) Wander in from the quiet end of Fitzroy to this bustling little soup bar. Nab a table and prick up your ears as the chatelaine of this fabulous down-to-earth restaurant hardly draws breath as she rattles off a list of soups, starters and heavenly North African *tagines* before telling you what you're getting. Surrender to it: the food is divine and authentically Moroccan. Wash it all down with mint tea.

While it's possible to spend well over $100 per person on a meal, you can also eat very well for less than $10, especially at lunch or brunch. Many restaurants are either licensed to sell alcohol or BYO, meaning you can 'Bring Your Own' booze (and usually pay a small corkage fee). Smoking is banned in all places where food is consumed (unless you're having a counter meal at a pub, until 2007).

Central Melbourne

The CBD has some of Melbourne's best and worst restaurants. The bad ones are the most obvious, clogging up the main shopping thoroughfares of the area; the good ones may take a little more effort to find, often hidden down tiny alleyways.

Flinders Lane has plenty of cafés and wonderful little bars in adjacent laneways. Centre Place (*the* classic Melbourne alleyway) is on the opposite side of Flinders Lane from Degraves St. The area in and around Chinatown, which follows Little Bourke St from Spring St to Swanston St, continues to be one of the city's most popular places to eat.

Flower Drum (Map pp68-9; ☎ 9662 3655; 17 Market Lane; mains $35-48; ⏱ lunch Mon-Fri, dinner Mon-Sat) This is Melbourne's best-known Chinese restaurant. Enter via a low-key vestibule and ascend to one of the truly great dining experiences of your life. Exquisite service and an excellent wine list only add to the pleasure. Book well ahead.

Becco (Map pp68-9; ☎ 9663 3000; 11 Crossley St; mains $23-30; ⏱ lunch & dinner Mon-Sat) Part restaurant/bar/produce store, Becco isn't only big on style but has the substance to keep people coming back time and time again. Meat and fish dishes are superbly prepared, service is uniformly excellent, the atmosphere comfortably sexy. Book ahead – it's worth it.

Ezard at Adelphi (Map pp68-9; ☎ 9639 6811; 187 Flinders Lane; mains $35-39; ☺ lunch Mon-Fri, dinner Mon-Sat) Teague Ezard's flawless takes on Asian-inspired cuisine keep this basement restaurant buzzing. It's a smartly designed and staffed spot too, making reservations advisable, particularly if you're one of the many who'd like access to the rooftop bar.

Movida (Map pp68-9; ☎ 9663 3038; 1 Hosier Lane; raciones $8.50-15; ☺ lunch Mon-Fri, dinner daily) Nab a table here and then nibble as much tapas as your heart desires – the *callos a la madrileña* (tripe) will make you swear you're in Madrid.

Supper Inn (Map pp68-9; ☎ 9663 4759; 15 Celestial Ave; mains $15-30; ☺ dinner) If you like to find out where the chefs eat when they finish a shift, then look no further. Open till very late (2.30am) and serving some of the best late-night congee, noodles, dumplings and other yummies to a mixed crowd.

Kuni's (Map pp68-9; ☎ 9663 7243; 56 Little Bourke St; mains $13-27; ☺ lunch & dinner Mon-Fri) This spare, clean-looking space produces some of the best Japanese in town, and even when it gets packed there's something serene about the whole experience of dining here.

Chocolate Buddha (Map pp68-9; ☎ 9654 5688; Federation Square; meals $13-21; ☺ lunch & dinner) Organic noodles and plenty of vegetarian options keep the healthy types flocking to this thriving eatery, where kids will love the chatter, clatter and splatter of Asian treats.

Degraves Espresso Bar (Map pp68-9; ☎ 9654 1245; 23 Degraves St; dishes $8-14; ☺ breakfast & lunch) The perfect antidote to coffee chain stores, Degraves has oodles of character, spilling out on to atmospheric Degraves St. This is a good place for a morning fry-up, a quick sandwich or an eponymous espresso.

Southgate & Crown Casino Entertainment Complex

The Southgate development at Southbank, on the southern side of the Yarra River, has views over the river and city skyline that can't be beaten. There're plenty of bars, cafés and restaurants, and most have outdoor terraces and balconies. Next door, the Crown Casino Entertainment Complex is also chock-a-block with restaurants and cafés.

Walter's Wine Bar (Map pp68-9; ☎ 9690 9211; upper level, Southgate; mains $25-35; ☺ lunch & dinner) Walter's blends culinary flair, professional service and a justifiably famous wine list.

Blue Train (Map pp68-9; ☎ 9696 0111; mid-level, Southgate; mains $6-15; ☺ breakfast, lunch & dinner) This loud and hugely popular place serves all the mainstream staples in a humming environment that satisfies all sorts.

Carlton

Abla's (Map pp72-3; ☎ 9347 0006; 109 Elgin St; mains $12-17; ☺ lunch Thu & Fri, dinner Mon-Sat) We think this is Melbourne's best Lebanese restaurant, and so do a lot of other people, so book a table as the weekend draws near. On Friday and Saturday nights there's a compulsory 13-course banquet wolfed down by appreciative crowds, so put on your elasticised pants and tuck in.

Brunetti (Map pp72-3; ☎ 9347 2801; 198 Faraday St; café dishes $3-7, restaurant mains $12-23; ☺ breakfast, lunch & dinner) A stalwart of Italian culinary obsessions, Brunetti is a haven for those who want excellent coffee, exquisite *dolci*, and mouth-watering Roman-influenced dishes.

Jimmy Watson's (Map pp72-3; ☎ 9347 3985; 333 Lygon St; mains $19-28; ☺ lunch Mon-Sat, dinner Tue-Sat) Wine and talk are the order of the day at this long-running wine bar/restaurant. There's a fabulous garden area for summer days.

Fitzroy

You haven't really eaten out in Melbourne until you've been to Brunswick St. For many, it's the most fascinating street in town, and for a couple of blocks north and south of Johnston St it's lined with dozens of great cafés, bars, pubs and restaurants offering a surprisingly wide range of cuisines. Gertrude St has a few eateries and if you venture across Alexandra Pde to North Fitzroy where Brunswick St joins St Georges Rd, you'll find another little pocket of interesting cafés and restaurants about a kilometre north.

Ladro (Map pp72-3; ☎ 9415 7575; 224 Gertrude St; mains $22-27; ☺ dinner Wed-Sun) Ladro was the winner of the *Age Good Food Guide*'s Best New Restaurant prize in 2005 and, if you can get a table, expect to be served very good pizza and then expect to be rushed if you spend more than about 45 minutes eating. It's a tad overrated, but a quintessential Melbourne pizza experience.

MELBOURNE

Marios (Map pp72-3; ☎ 9417 3343; 303 Brunswick St; mains $17-20; ⊗ breakfast, lunch & dinner) Melbourne has a surfeit of cocky waiters moving at lightning speed between tables and this is where they learnt it. The pasta dishes are uniformly commendable, the atmosphere casual, and the coffee kicks like a mule.

Piraeus Blues (Map pp72-3; ☎ 9417 0222; 310 Brunswick St; mains $10-20; ⊗ lunch Wed-Fri & Sun, dinner daily) Brunswick St may be a long way from Athens, but the excellent food here will transport you to Greece.

Vegie Bar (Map pp72-3; ☎ 9417 6935; 380 Brunswick St; mains under $10; ⊗ lunch & dinner) The Vegie Bar exudes delicious aromas and has a great range of vegetarian meals and snacks.

South Yarra & Prahran
Most of South Yarra's eateries are along Toorak Rd and Chapel St. If you love to shop and eat, you'll be right at home here.

Jacques Reymond (Map pp66-7; ☎ 9525 2178; 78 Williams Rd, Prahran; 2-course menu $68, degustation menu $120; ⊗ lunch Thu & Fri, dinner Tue-Sat) Easily one of Melbourne's greatest restaurants, Jacques Reymond's kitchen presents artful, imaginative cuisine to dressed-up patrons. Service is superb and there are lavish vegetarian dishes. Oh, and this all takes place in a mansion. Book well ahead.

Da Noi (Map pp66-7; ☎ 9866 5975; 95 Toorak Rd, South Yarra; mains $25-35; ⊗ lunch Fri-Sun, dinner daily) The seasonal menu here specialises in Sardinian cuisine, which means you'll find plenty of brilliantly prepared seafood and dishes that seem to have been hunted that very day. Simple, elegant décor, service you can banter with – heaven.

David's (Map p71; ☎ 9529 5199; 4 Cecil Pl, Prahran; mains $17-24; ⊗ lunch daily, dinner Fri & Sat) David's does a roaring trade thanks to its imaginative, healthy spin on yum cha with a Shanghainese influence. Brisk, good value and possessed of a strong wine list, this is a great spot to refuel on a shopping spree.

St Kilda
Fitzroy and Acland Sts are where the majority of cafés and restaurants are to be found, and there are also good places down by the sea.

Baker D Chirico (Map p71; ☎ 9534 3777; Shop 3/4, 149 Fitzroy St; mains $5-8.50; ⊗ breakfast & lunch) With sacks of organic flour piled high and almost toppled by both the heavenly aromas and hungry hordes, carb lovers should make this excellent bakery their first port of call on this strip.

Cafe di Stasio (Map p71; ☎ 9525 3999; 31 Fitzroy St; mains $29-35; ⊗ lunch & dinner) Cafe di Stasio thoroughly deserves its reputation as the best Italian restaurant in Melbourne. Its two-course lunch (which includes a glass of wine or coffee – $25) allows local semi-starving artists to mix it with corporate types. And the food? Sublime.

Il Fornaio (Map p71; ☎ 9534 2922; 2 Acland St; breakfast $2.20-12.50, dinner mains $17-23; ⊗ breakfast, lunch & dinner) Breakfast here is some of the best in Melbourne, with an on-site bakery concocting some of the most melt-in-the-mouth pastries we've ever surrendered to and scrambled eggs so fluffy they could fly off your fork. Lunch and dinner are also great.

Galleon (Map p71; ☎ 9534 8934; 9 Carlisle St; meals $5-14.50; ⊗ breakfast, lunch & dinner) Just off Acland St, Galleon has fuelled the creative juices of St Kilda's arts community for years with simple and inexpensive café-style food and fantastic hot breakfasts.

Stokehouse (Map p71; ☎ 9525 5555; 30 Jacka Blvd; mains $29.50-39.50; ⊗ lunch & dinner) Right on the foreshore, Stokehouse has the location that everyone else dreams about and food that makes it perennially and justifiably popular.

Self-Catering
Supermarkets, often open 24 hours or until midnight, are found in most suburbs – Coles and Safeway are the names to look out for.

Victoria St in Richmond is the place to go for cheap produce and Asian ingredients. Lastly, don't forget the city's fabulous food markets (see p91). Still hungry? Then head to Bourke St Mall, where you'll find food courts in both Myer and David Jones department stores. The one in David Jones is particularly worth a trip.

DRINKING
Melbourne has a famously lively bar scene. You'll find bars hidden down tiny alleys, at the top of darkened staircases and perched atop most of the city's luxury hotels. While the CBD boasts the greatest concentration of bars (and the greatest bars), you may find some of the off-beat bars in the nearby suburbs to your liking. For pubs that offer live music, see opposite.

Gin Palace (Map pp68-9; ☎ 9654 0553; 190 Little Collins St, City) This is the transmutation of a side-alley basement into a sophisticated, dimly lit and beautifully furnished New York–meets–Mittel Europa cocktail bar.

Double Happiness (Map pp68-9; ☎ 9650 4488; 21 Liverpool St, City) An intimate, red-hued space, this Chinese socialist–inspired drinking den has excellent cocktails, plus Tsing Tao beer.

Ume Nomiya (Map pp72-3; ☎ 9415 6101; 197 Gertrude St, Fitzroy) This little charmer offers a range of sake, *shochu*, plum wine and Japanese beer, plus some excellent nibbles to assuage hunger pangs. Art exhibitions take place on a three-week roster.

Bar Open (Map pp72-3; ☎ 9415 9601; 317 Brunswick St, Fitzroy) This is the favourite bar of many a local. Downstairs is a cosy bar/café, with a few couches and a small courtyard, while upstairs is a wide-open space, which occasionally hosts live acts.

Candy Bar (Map p71; ☎ 9529 6566; 162 Greville St, Prahran) The Candy Bar is a grinding Greville St fixture. By day it's a café, by night it's more of a small club where gay-flavoured patrons drink and dance to DJ-played music.

Back Bar (Map p71; ☎ 9529 7899; 67 Green St, Prahran) Take up residence on a well-stuffed couch and enjoy the laid-back atmosphere.

Greyhound Hotel (Map p71; ☎ 9534 4189; 1 Brighton Rd, St Kilda) On Saturday nights, this grotty local boozer with tonnes of rough-round-the-edges charm has drag shows. Other nights you can expect live music and cheap unpretentious drinks.

ENTERTAINMENT

Melbourne has a thriving nightlife, a lively cultural scene, some great nightclubs and a population that gives the distinct impression that if they're not watching sport they're getting into some sort of cultural event.

The best source of information about what's on is the *Entertainment Guide (EG)*, which is published every Friday in the *Age* newspaper. Another good source of information is the Internet. Visit www.melbourne .vic.gov.au/events and www.melbourne.city search.com.au for current listings and recent reviews of venues and performances. *Beat* and *Inpress* are free music and entertainment publications that can be found in cafés, pubs, bars and other venues throughout the city.

> **THE AUTHOR'S CHOICE**
>
> **Esplanade Hotel** (Map p71; ☎ 9534 0211; 11 Upper Esplanade, St Kilda) A Melbourne institution for as long as anyone can remember, the Espy has free live bands almost nightly and on Sunday afternoon. It's also a place to sit back with a beer and watch the sun set over the pier. Make the pilgrimage at least once!

Ticketmaster7 (Map pp68-9; ☎ 1300 136 166; www .ticketmaster7.com; Theatres Bldg, Victorian Arts Centre, 100 St Kilda Rd; ☺ 9am-9pm Mon-Sat) is the main booking agency for theatre, concerts, sport and other events.

Ticketek (Map pp68-9; ☎ 13 28 49; www.ticketek .com.au; 225 Exhibition St, City; ☺ 9am-5pm Mon-Fri, 9am-1pm Sat) covers large sporting events and mainstream entertainment dates.

Half Tix (Map pp68-9; ☎ 9650 9420; Melbourne Town Hall, Swanston St, City; ☺ 10am-2pm Mon & Sat, 11am-6pm Tue-Thu, 11am-6.30pm Fri) sells half-price tickets to shows and concerts on the day of the performance. Cash payments only.

Live Music

Melbourne is widely acknowledged as the country's rock capital, and has long enjoyed a thriving pub-rock scene where internationally successful bands such as AC/DC, Nick Cave & the Bad Seeds and Jet took their first tentative steps towards becoming part of rock's rollercoaster ride. There are a few great jazz joints in Melbourne, and the scene is the best in the country. Expect to pay between zilch and $30 for live performances, but generally you'll get away with about $10 to $15 for a respected local act.

CENTRAL MELBOURNE

The city is more of a bar kind of place, but there are a few pubs and rock lounges scattered about and other venues that cover jazz.

Bennetts Lane (Map pp68-9; ☎ 9663 2856; www .bennettslane.com; 25 Bennetts Lane; ☒) Hidden down a narrow lane off Little Lonsdale St (between Exhibition and Russell Sts), this quintessential dim jazz venue is well worth searching out. It's *the* jazz joint in Melbourne and most big acts that come to town perform here.

MELBOURNE

Ding Dong Lounge (Map pp68-9; ☎ 9662 1020; 18 Market Lane) Smoky, raucous, grotty and everything a classic rock-and-roll bar should be. Great local and international bands play here, and the crowd is usually up for anything.

Green Room (Map pp68-9; ☎ 9620 5100; Basement, 33 Elizabeth St) A curiously shaped space in the basement of the Flinders Station Hotel, this is a good spot to hear live bands from Thursday to Saturday. A little bit grungy, but very relaxed.

FITZROY, COLLINGWOOD & CARLTON
In terms of sheer choice, Fitzroy is the place of choice for a pub crawl in Melbourne. Most venues are along Brunswick St, but there are some gems hidden away from the action on other streets.

Tote (Map pp72-3; ☎ 9419 5320; 71 Johnston St, Collingwood) Where the mosh pit is just that – a pit – and the carpet is as sticky as the tar that must line the lungs of the bands, punters and staff at this stalwart of Melbourne's live music scene. Live music every night except Monday.

Evelyn Hotel (Map pp72-3; ☎ 9419 5500; cnr Brunswick & Kerr Sts, Fitzroy) The Evelyn attracts a mixed bag of local and (occasionally) international acts, and the feel is always warm and welcoming.

Dan O'Connell Hotel (Map pp72-3; ☎ 9347 1502; 225 Canning St, Carlton) This long-running pub is *the* place in town for acoustic music. There are live acts most nights and, yes, you can get a pint of Guinness to go with it.

ST KILDA
Prince Bandroom (Map p71; ☎ 9536 1111; 2 Acland St) The Art Deco Prince has been a fixture of the St Kilda scene for years. The downstairs bar is a good spot for shooting pool and for people-watching. Upstairs, the band room plays host to local and international acts and popular DJ events.

Another seaside (or close) choice is the Espy (see the boxed text, p84).

Nightclubs
Melbourne's club scene is a mixed bag, and what's here today might be gone tomorrow. Clubs range from barn-sized discos, where anyone is welcome, to the smaller and more exclusive places where you stand a good chance of a knock-back at the door. Cover charges range from $5 to $20, although some places don't charge at all. Most places have certain dress standards, but it's generally at the discretion of the door staff to decide whether you are dressed for the occasion.

CENTRAL MELBOURNE
The CBD has the largest concentration of clubs. It's a good place for a club crawl, particularly if you like dancing until dawn. One area we'd recommend avoiding is the concentration of clubs on King St, which tends to attract a yobbish element.

Honkytonks (Map pp68-9; ☎ 9662 4555; Duckboard Pl; ☯ Wed-Sun) Sooner or later, someone's going to tell you that you have to see this place – and you do. The bar is like a shrine to booze, the décor like an acid trip, the music sublime. The turntables are embedded in a white grand piano.

ffour (Map pp68-9 ☎ 9650 4494; Level 2, 322 Little Collins St; ☯ Thu-Sat) Great drinks (perhaps the best in town) and a refreshing antidote to that Melbourne design ethos of 'bung another secondhand couch in the corner'.

Lounge (Map pp68-9; ☎ 9663 2916; 243 Swanston St; ☯ Wed-Sat) Café by day, club by night; this is a good place for a night out in central Melbourne. The crowd is an up-for-it mix of young studenty types and the gainfully employed, and music crosses the genres from electro to hip-hop. Grab a possie on the balcony on a hot summer's night if you can.

OTHER AREAS
Outside the CBD you'll find many of Melbourne's alternative clubs. Check the street press to see which nights suit your tastes.

Revolver (Map p71; ☎ 9521 5985; 229 Chapel St, Prahran) Revolver is a popular venue with Prahran's young, arty crowd. With art-and-stencil covered surfaces and a packed programme featuring DJs, bands, film nights and spoken word, there's a lot to like.

Alia (Map pp72-3; ☎ 9486 0999; 83 Smith St, Fitzroy; ☯ Thu-Sun) Alia is ostensibly a club, but you'll never really feel as though you're in one. It's a mixed, easygoing spot, which has proved popular with lesbians. Decent music may well get you on to the smallish dance floor.

Gay & Lesbian Venues
Most of the newer generation of bars and clubs in Melbourne are gay and lesbian friendly. St Kilda, South Yarra and Prahran are the city's main 'gay precincts', with

Melbourne's Queen Victoria Market (p75), Victoria

DALLAS STRIBLEY

Brunswick Street (p77) in Fitzroy, Victoria

JAMES BRAUND

Nepalese red panda, Melbourne Zoo (p77), Victoria

JASON EDWARDS

Cakes in continental cake shop on Acland St, St Kilda (p78), Victoria

SALLY DILLON

MELBOURNE TRAIN NETWORK

connex

Melbourne Train Network

metlink

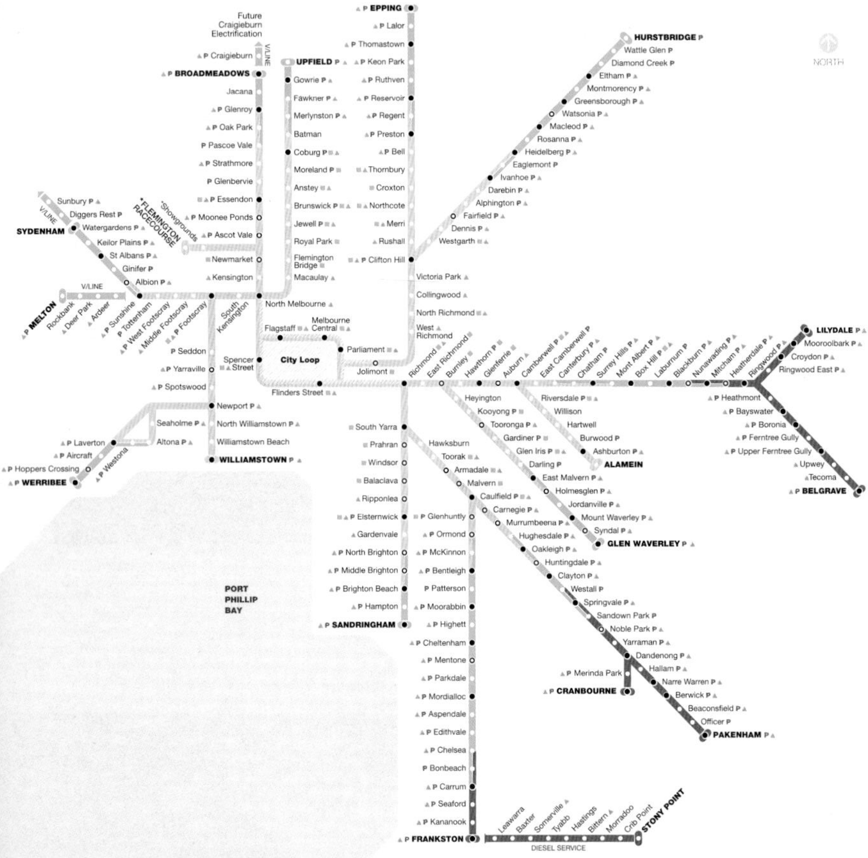

NORTH

Lines and Stations

Future Craigieburn Electrification

P Craigieburn
BROADMEADOWS
Jacana
P Glenroy
P Oak Park
P Pascoe Vale
P Strathmore
P Glenbervie
P Essendon
P Moonee Ponds
P Ascot Vale
Newmarket
Kensington
Flemington Bridge
Macaulay

Sunbury P
Diggers Rest P
Watergardens P
SYDENHAM
Keilor Plains P
St Albans P
Ginifer P
Albion P

MELTON
Rockbank P
Deer Park P
Ardeer P
Sunshine P
Tottenham P
West Footscray P
Middle Footscray P
Footscray P
Seddon P
Yarraville P
Spotswood P

Newport P
Seaholme P
Altona P
North Williamstown P
Williamstown Beach
WILLIAMSTOWN

Laverton P
Aircraft
WERRIBEE
P Hoppers Crossing
P Westona

P EPPING
P Lalor
P Thomastown
UPFIELD
P Keon Park
Gowrie P
P Ruthven
Fawkner P
P Reservoir
Merlynston P
P Regent
Batman
P Preston
Coburg P
P Bell
Moreland
P Thornbury
Anstey
Croxton
Brunswick P
Northcote
Jewell P
Merri
Royal Park
Rushall
Clifton Hill

North Melbourne
Flagstaff
Melbourne Central
Spencer Street
City Loop
Parliament
Flinders Street
Jolimont

HURSTBRIDGE P
Wattle Glen
Diamond Creek P
Eltham P
Montmorency P
Greensborough P
Watsonia P
Macleod P
Rosanna P
Heidelberg P
Eaglemont
Ivanhoe P
Darebin P
Alphington P
Fairfield P
Dennis P
Westgarth

Victoria Park
Collingwood
North Richmond
West Richmond
East Richmond
Richmond
Burnley
Heyington
Kooyong P
Tooronga P
Gardiner P
Glen Iris P
Darling P
East Malvern P
Holmesglen P
Jordanville P
Murrumbeena P
Hughesdale P
Oakleigh P
Huntingdale P
Clayton P
Westall P
Springvale P
Sandown Park P
Noble Park P
Yarraman P
Dandenong P
Hallam P
Narre Warren P
Berwick P
Beaconsfield P
Officer P
PAKENHAM

Hawksburn
Toorak P
Armadale P
Malvern P
Caulfield P
Carnegie P

East Richmond
Camberwell P
East Camberwell
Canterbury P
Chatham P
Surrey Hills P
Mont Albert P
Box Hill P
Laburnum P
Blackburn P
Nunawading P
Mitcham P
Ringwood P
Ringwood East P
LILYDALE P
Mooroolbark P
Croydon P

Riversdale P
Willison
Hartwell
Burwood P
Ashburton P
ALAMEIN

Glenferrie P
Auburn P

Heatherdale P

Heathmont P
P Bayswater
P Boronia
P Ferntree Gully
P Upper Ferntree Gully
Upwey
Tecoma
BELGRAVE P

Glenhuntly P
Ormond P
McKinnon P
Bentleigh P
Patterson P
Moorabbin P
Highett P
Cheltenham P
Mentone P
Parkdale P
Mordialloc P
Aspendale P
Edithvale P
Chelsea P
Bonbeach P
Carrum P
Seaford P
Kananook P
FRANKSTON P

South Yarra
Prahran P
Windsor P
Balaclava P
Ripponlea P
Elsternwick P
Gardenvale P
North Brighton P
Middle Brighton P
Brighton Beach P
Hampton P
SANDRINGHAM

Mount Waverley P
Syndal P
GLEN WAVERLEY

Merinda Park P
CRANBOURNE

PORT PHILLIP BAY

Leawarra
Baxter
Somerville
Tyabb
Hastings
Bittern
Morradoo
Crib Point
STONY POINT
DIESEL SERVICE

Information

Premium Station: Customer service centre staffed from first train to last, seven days a week.
Host Station: Customer service staff at station during morning peak.
*Line to Showgrounds and Flemington Racecourse, only open for special events.

Ticketing Zones

City Saver · Zone 1 · Zone 2 · Zone 3 · Connecting Tram · Connecting Bus · Premium Station · Host Station · Parking

Make Travel more convenient
Your Metcard can be used on train, tram and bus services throughout metropolitan Melbourne. Save time and pre-purchase your Metcard ticket. Remember to validate your Metcard before you start each journey.

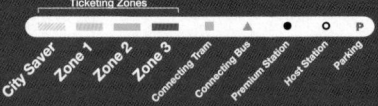

For train, tram and bus information, call **131 638 / (TTY) 9617 2727** or visit **www.metlinkmelbourne.com.au** Metcard Helpline **(TTY) 1800 652 313**

Prahran's Commercial Rd being the traditional centre of Melbourne's gay culture. Other gay-friendly neighbourhoods include Collingwood and Abbotsford, with Northcote being a popular spot for lesbians.

Girl Bar (Map p71; ☎ 9536 1177; www.theprince .com.au; 29 Fitzroy St, St Kilda; admission $15; ☻ 1 Fri a month) This popular ladies night (in the best sense of the phrase) at the Prince will have you partying till the sun comes up. The Prince also has a ground-level gay bar that dates back to the 1940s and is a great spot to start the night – it's open daily and is free.

Peel Hotel (Map pp72-3; ☎ 9419 4762; cnr Peel & Wellington Sts, Collingwood; admission free) The Peel is one of the best-known and most popular gay venues in Melbourne, and it also attracts a lesbian crowd at times.

Xchange Hotel (Map p71; ☎ 9867 5144; 119 Commercial Rd, Prahran; admission free-$10) This is a long-standing fixture on the Prahran scene; the Xchange plays host to a variety of customers and covers all the gay bases.

Also worth checking out are the Greyhound Hotel and Alia.

Cinema

Melbourne has an array of mainstream cinemas playing latest releases, though if you've come from the USA or Europe they might be last season's latest. Tickets cost around $15.

ACMI (Map pp68-9; ☎ 9663 2583; www.acmi.net .au; Federation Square) The fabulously high-tech cinemas here are our fave place to see a mind-blowing range of films, documentaries and animated features – often geared to a central theme.

Astor Cinema (Map p71; ☎ 9510 1414; cnr Chapel St & Dandenong Rd, Prahran) This place contains not-to-be-missed Art Deco nostalgia, with double features every night of old and recent classics (plus great ice cream).

Moonlight Cinema (Map pp66-7; ☎ 1300 136 166; Royal Botanic Gardens, entry gate F, Birdwood Ave, South Yarra; ☻ Dec-Mar) This outdoor cinema has almost nightly outdoor screenings of newish and classic films. Bring along a rug to sit on and a picnic supper, or buy food and drinks.

Theatre

There's no 'theatre district' as such, but the scene is a healthy one, from edgy independent productions on the city's fringe to the biggest, glitziest musicals in the ritziest theatrical premises the city has.

Victorian Arts Centre (Map pp68-9; ☎ 9281 8000; www.vicartscentre.com.au; 100 St Kilda Rd, City) This is Melbourne's major venue for the performing arts. Flanked by the Yarra River on one side and the National Gallery of Victoria on the other, the complex houses the Melbourne Concert Hall (also called Hamer Hall) and three theatres – the State Theatre, the Playhouse, and the George Fairfax Studio.

Sport

Australians in general, and Melburnians in particular, are fanatical supporters of sport. The two biggest events on the sporting calendar (actually, make that the entire city calendar) are a horse race and a game of Australian Rules football!

You can book tickets for various sporting events through Ticketek or Ticketmaster7. A booking fee is charged by both services.

AUSTRALIAN RULES FOOTBALL

Without a doubt, Australian Rules football – otherwise known as 'the footy' – is the city's sporting obsession, and there are games at the **Melbourne Cricket Ground** (MCG; Map p76; ☎ 9657 8888; www.mcg.org.au; Brunton Ave, Jolimont) regularly pulling crowds of 50,000 to 80,000. If you're here between April and September you should try to see a match, as much for the crowds as for the game. Despite the fervour, crowd violence is almost unknown.

CRICKET

During summer, the national cricket competition, international test matches and one-day internationals and are all played at the MCG (p76), one of the world's great sports stadiums. The cricket season in Australia is from October to March. General admission to international matches is around $30 and reserved seats start at around $40, with finals costing more (and generally requiring a booking).

HORSE RACING

Horse racing is on in Melbourne throughout the year – at Flemington, Caulfield, Moonee Valley and Sandown Racecourses – but spring is when the culture of racing is at its most colourful and frenetic.

The Melbourne Cup, one of the world's greatest horse races, is the feature event of Melbourne's Spring Racing Carnival, which runs through October until late November. The two-mile (3.2km) Melbourne Cup is run at **Flemington Racecourse** (Map pp66-7; ☎ 1300 727 575; www.vrc.net.au; 400 Epsom Rd, Flemington) on the first Tuesday in November and brings the whole of Australia to a standstill for three minutes or so.

MOTOR SPORTS
Melbourne hosts both the **Australian Formula One Grand Prix** (☎ 9258 7100; www.grandprix.com.au/cars) and the Australian round of the **World 500cc Motorcycle Grand Prix** (www.grandprix.com.au/bikes) – see p102. The Formula One takes place in Albert Park in March, and the motorcycles race at Phillip Island in October. Tickets for the Formula One Grand Prix start at $39 for a one-day general admission ticket and $599 for a four-day reserved ticket. Tickets can be bought through Ticketmaster7 or check the Grand Prix website.

TENNIS
For two weeks each January **Melbourne Park** (Map pp66-7; ☎ 9286 1244; www.mopt.com.au; Batman Ave) hosts the **Australian Open tennis championships** (www.ausopen.org). Top players from around the world come to compete in the year's first of the big four Grand Slam tournaments. Tickets are available through Ticketek and range from about $25 for early rounds to over $100 for finals.

SHOPPING
Melbourne offers not only the best shopping in Victoria, but in Australia. The widest array of shops is in the CBD, where you can find international heavy-hitters from Paris, London, Tokyo and New York, plus department stores, exclusive shopping centres in renovated buildings and quirky little boutiques lurking in laneways and alleys. The suburbs are home to a growing legion of factory outlets (try Bridge Rd and Swan St in Richmond) and shopping malls, plus some off-beat boutiques and stores that specialise in particular items.

For the ultimate Melbourne souvenir, visit **Crumpler** (Map pp72-3; ☎ 9417 5338; cnr Gertrude & Smith Sts, Fitzroy). This local company started out a few years ago making tough-as-nails bags for cycle couriers. The only trouble was, they looked so good they became a fashion accessory. A great local item you'll drag around the world.

Central Melbourne
In the city centre, there's a cluster of camera shops along Elizabeth St between Bourke and Lonsdale Sts. Little Bourke St, between Elizabeth and Queen Sts, is Melbourne's outdoor-sports mecca. If you're looking for imaginative fashions in the city centre, then linger longer in the lanes around Flinders Lane, Little Collins St and Centre Way.

Alice Euphemia (Map pp68-9; ☎ 9650 4300; shop 6/37 Swanston St, cnr Flinders La) At the more experimental end of Melbourne fashion, with inventive fabrics, cuts and finishes that aim to make you look more interesting than you might actually be. There's a great range of rings, brooches and earrings that's on display, too.

Calibre (Map pp68-9; ☎ 9663 8001; 45 Collins St, Melbourne) Specialises in the sort of suits that make a man look a million bucks. They're classic, yet exude a contemporary sensibility and can be downplayed or updated with the great range of interesting shirts.

GPO Building (Map pp68-9; ☎ 9663 0066; 350 Bourke St, Melbourne) After the GPO burnt down in September 2001, the city's burghers decided that the grand old lady of Bourke St needed a full face-lift and makeover – and voilà! The GPO building is packed with fab boutiques, including Leona Edmiston, Belinda, La Perla and Georg Jensen.

QV (Map pp68-9; ☎ 9658 0100; cnr Swanston & Lonsdale Sts) In an imposing modern skyscraper; features all sorts of populist commercial options, and a few cool international options. In the Red Coates Lane area you'll find surf- and skatewear. It's a monster – taking up the whole block between Russell and Swanston Sts.

Most of the cheap souvenir stores in the city sell poor-quality knock-offs of Aboriginal art. If you want pieces that have a well-established provenance, you'll have to visit an established gallery and pay accordingly. There are several good galleries in the city centre, and Flinders Lane is a good place to start your search:

Anna Schwartz Gallery (Map pp68-9; ☎ 9654 6131; www.annaschwartzgallery.com.au; 185 Flinders Lane) Leader of the pack when it comes to high-profile modern-art exhibitions in a blindingly white, sometimes chilly space.

Counter (Map pp68-9; ☎ 9650 7775; www.craftvic.asn.au; 31 Flinders Lane) The retail wing of Craft Victoria. Stocks wonderful handmade pieces that aren't in the least bit fusty – they're more like wearable works of art.

Fitzroy

Jasper (Map pp72-3; ☎ 9416 0921; 267 Brunswick St, Fitzroy) If trawling back and forth along the caffeinated causeway that is Brunswick St has made you start to think you could do it all yourself, then this is the store for you. All manner of coffee paraphernalia and beans abounds – they don't call themselves 'caffeine dealers' for nothing.

T2 (Map pp72-3; ☎ 9417 3722; 340 Brunswick St, Fitzroy) This stylish tea specialist is a must for the tea lover. The wonderful aroma wafting out the door draws us in every time, and there's a fabulous range of tea cups, pots and strainers to accompany that perfect blend.

Prahran & South Yarra

South Yarra's Chapel St is the most commercially fashionable and popular of Melbourne's fashion zones. The section between Toorak Rd and Commercial Rd is lined with up-to-this-minute boutiques, and it's a fascinating area to visit, whether you come to shop or just to check out all the beautiful people.

Dinosaur Designs (Map p71; ☎ 9827 2600; 562 Chapel St, South Yarra) The fabulous resin *objets d'art* and jewellery moulded in organic shapes and vivid colours are an excellent way to brighten up your home or your body.

Scanlan & Theodore (Map p71; ☎ 9824 1800; 566 Chapel St, South Yarra) Another stalwart of the scene, where whisper-fine evening dresses rub coat-hanger shoulders with luxe suiting, and gorgeous bags and shoes loiter in the hope of attracting your attention. Magic stuff. There's another branch on Little Collins St in the city.

Greville St in Prahran is probably *the* most recognised address for retro-style shops and fashion-forward apparel for young partygoers. Toorak Rd in South Yarra is the ultimate in expensive, visibly labelled style. This street is home to designers and galleries that specialise in big-name Australian art.

GETTING THERE & AWAY
Air

International and interstate flights operate out of **Melbourne airport** (www.melair.com.au) at Tullamarine and some interstate flights operate from **Avalon Airport** (www.avalonairport .com.au). Long-distance trains run there from Southern Cross station. The long-distance bus terminal in the city centre is the Southern Cross coach terminal on Spencer St, and the Skybus airport buses operate from there.

TO MARKET, TO MARKET

Melbourne's world-famous markets allow you to experience the city in all its multicultural glory, as locals shop, socialise, and converse in an array of tongues. The following are some of Melbourne's best markets:

- **Camberwell Market** (Station St, Camberwell; ⏱ 6am-2.30pm Sun) One of the most popular 'trash and treasure' markets, this has hundreds of stalls piled with everything – get there early to fight with the fashionistas for the best retro gear though.

- **Prahran Market** (Map p71; www.prahranmarket.com.au; 163-185 Commercial Rd, Prahran; ⏱ dawn-5pm Tue & Sat, dawn-6pm Thu & Fri, 10am-3pm Sun) This may be the best food market in the city, with several organic-produce stores, a fresh-pasta store, great delis, and a whole wing devoted to meat (including an organic butcher).

- **Queen Victoria Market** (Map pp66-7; ☎ 9320 5822; www.qvm.com.au; cnr Victoria & Elizabeth Sts, City; ⏱ 6am-2pm Tue & Thu, 6am-6pm Fri, 6am-3pm Sat, 9am-4pm Sun) There are more than 500 stalls selling everything under the sun, including fruit and vegetables (organic produce can be found here), meat and fish, jeans, furniture, budgies and sheepskin products.

- **South Melbourne Market** (Map pp66-7; ☎ 9209 6295; cnr Cecil & Coventry Sts, South Melbourne; ⏱ 8am-4pm Wed, Sat & Sun, 8am-6pm Fri) This general market covers most bases, with delis, food stuffs and the addiction-inspiring dim-sim stall that attracts a permanent queue.

Bus

Long-distance bus services for **V/Line** (☎ 13 61 96; www.vlinepassenger.com.au) and **Firefly** (☎ 1300 730 740; www.fireflyexpress.com.au) operate from the Southern Cross coach terminal in Spencer St. **Greyhound** (☎ 13 20 30; www.mccaffertys.com.au) services operate from the **Melbourne Transit Centre** (Map pp72-3; Franklin St). Basic one-way fares from Melbourne to Sydney cost between $65 and $200 (12 hours) to Brisbane from $165 to $190 (24 hours). There are at least six departures per day to these cities.

Car & Motorcycle

The quickest and easiest way in and out of Melbourne heading for the East Coast is via CityLink – follow the blue signs. If you wish to avoid the tolls, join at Toorak Rd. CityLink becomes the Princes Hwy, the road you need to be on to explore all the places in the following chapter.

Train

Long-distance trains depart from Southern Cross station in Spencer St. **V/Line** (☎ 13 61 96; www.vlinepassenger.com.au) has daily services from Melbourne to Bairnsdale stopping at all major towns along the Princes Hwy in west Gippsland.

Countrylink (☎ 13 22 32; www.countrylink.info) runs XPT trains between Melbourne and Sydney (economy/1st class/1st-class sleeper $115/162/243, 11 hours, two daily), with one morning and one evening departure daily in each direction. There are discounts of up to 50% for booking seven or 14 days in advance.

GETTING AROUND
To/From the Airport

Melbourne airport is at Tullamarine, 22km northwest of the city centre. There are two information desks at the airport: one on the ground floor in the international departure area and another upstairs next to the duty-free shops.

If you're driving, take the Tullamarine Fwy from the airport to the CityLink toll road, which will take you into town. A 24-hour Tulla Pass costs $3.40.

A taxi between the airport and the city centre costs around $40 (including the cost of the tollway). **Skybus** (☎ 9335 2811; www.skybus.com.au) operates a 24-hour shuttle-bus service (one way $13, 20 minutes) between

the airport and the city. Skybus has departures approximately every 30 minutes between 6am and midnight, and every hour between midnight and 6am, in either direction. Buy your ticket from the driver or online; bookings are not usually necessary. You can take your bicycle on the Skybus and the service is also wheelchair-accessible.

Car & Motorcycle

If you're lucky enough to find on-street parking in the city centre you'll pay from $2 an hour. Check parking signs for restrictions and times, and watch out for clearway zones that operate during peak hour. There are more than 70 car parks in the city.

Car drivers should treat trams with caution – you can only overtake a tram on the left and you must *always* stop behind a tram when it halts to drop off or collect passengers (except where there are central 'islands' for passengers). Melbourne has a notoriously confusing road rule, known as the 'hook turn', for getting trams through the city centre without being blocked by turning cars. To turn right at many major intersections in the city, you have to pull to the left of the actual intersection, wait until the light of the street you're turning into changes from red to green, then complete the turn. These intersections are identified by a black-and-white hook sign that reads 'Right Turn from Left Only' and hangs from the overhead cables.

All the big car-rental firms are represented in Melbourne and have desks at the airport. For disabled travellers Avis rents hand-controlled vehicles. The **Yellow Pages** (www.yellowpages.com.au) lists lots of other firms, including some cheaper operators.

TOLL ROADS

CityLink (☎ 13 26 29; www.transurban.com.au) consists of two main sections: the western link that runs from the Calder Hwy intersection of the Tullamarine Fwy down the western side of the city to join with the Westgate Fwy; and the southern link that runs from Kings Way, on the southern edge of the CBD, to the Malvern section of the Monash Fwy. Both sections are tollways.

Tolls are 'collected' electronically by overhead readers from a transponder card displayed in the car (an e-Tag). If you want to use any section of CityLink and don't have an e-Tag, you can purchase a day pass, which is valid for 24 hours from your first trip on any CityLink section, or a weekend pass, which is valid from noon Friday to midnight Sunday. Either pass costs $9.65. If you only intend to use the western link to go from the airport to Flemington Rd, you can purchase a Tullapass for $3.40. Day and weekend passes can be purchased at any Australian post office, Shell service stations, CityLink customer service centres, over the Internet or by phone. If you blunder on to CityLink without a pass, you have until midnight the following day to call CityLink and arrange payment for your sins.

Motorcycles can use CityLink for free.

Public Transport

Melbourne's public transport system, known as the Met, incorporates buses, trains and the famous trams. There are about 750 trams and they operate as far as 20km out from the centre. Buses take routes where the trams don't go, and replace them at quiet weekend periods. Trains radiate from the city centre to the outer suburbs. Services usually cease around midnight. On Friday and Saturday night (ie Saturday and Sunday morning), NightRider buses depart from the City Square hourly from 12.30am to dawn for many suburban destinations. The Night-Rider fare is a flat $6.

For information on public transport including maps, timetables, fares and zones, contact the **Metlink Information Centre** (☎ 13 16 38; www.metlinkmelbourne.com.au). **MetShop** (Map pp68-9; ☎ 13 16 38; Town Hall, cnr Swanston & Little Collins Sts; ☽ 8.30am-5.30pm Mon-Fri, 9am-1pm Sat) has transport information and sells tickets. It sells the excellent *Melbourne's Public Transport Map* for $2.20.

TICKETING

Metcards allow you to travel on any and all Melbourne bus, train and tram services, even if you transfer from one to another. They're available from Metcard vending machines and service counters at train stations, on board trams (coins only), from retailers displaying the Metlink flag (usually newsagents and milk bars) and from the MetShop. You can purchase tickets directly from the driver on bus services.

The metropolitan area is divided into three zones, and the price of the ticket depends on which zone(s) you will be travelling in and across. Zone 1 covers the city and inner-suburban area (including St Kilda), and most travellers don't venture beyond, unless they're going right out of town.

The adult fares are as follows:

Zones	Two Hours	All day	Weekly
1	$3.10	$5.80	$25
2 or 3	$2.20	$4	$17.20
1 & 2	$5	$9.40	$42.60
1, 2 & 3	$7	$12.30	$52

BUS

Melbourne's privatised bus network generally continues from where the trains finish. Buses also go to places not reached by other services, such as hospitals, universities, suburban shopping centres and the outer suburbs.

TRAIN

An extensive train network covers the city centre and suburban areas. Trains are generally faster than trams or buses, but they don't go to many inner suburbs.

Flinders St station is the main suburban terminal, and each suburban line has a separate platform. The famous row of clocks above the entrance on the corner of Swanston and Flinders Sts indicates when the next train will be departing from each line.

During the week, trains on most lines start at 5am and finish at midnight and run about every 10 minutes during peak hour, every 15 to 20 minutes at most other times, and every 30 minutes after 7pm on weekdays. On Saturday they run every half-hour from 5am to midnight, while on Sunday it's every 40 minutes from 7am to 11.30pm. The city service includes an underground City Loop, which is a quick way to get from one side of the city centre to the other. The stations on the loop are Parliament, Melbourne Central, Flagstaff, Southern Cross and Flinders St.

Bicycles can be carried free on trains during off-peak times and weekends. During peak hour you'll need to buy a concession ticket for the bike.

TRAM

Melbourne's trundling trams are one of the city's most distinctive features and cover the city and inner suburbs quite extensively. In theory, trams run along most routes about every six to eight minutes during peak hour and every 12 minutes at other times. Unfortunately, trams have to share the roads with cars and trucks, so they are often delayed. Services are less frequent on weekends and late at night.

Be extremely careful when getting on and off a tram; by law, cars are supposed to stop when a tram stops to pick up and drop off passengers, but that doesn't always happen.

See p81 for details on the free City Circle tram service.

Taxi

There are plenty of taxi ranks in and around the city and you'll spot taxis quite easily as they're all yellow. The main ones in the town centre are outside the major hotels and outside Flinders St and Southern Cross train stations. Finding an empty taxi in the city on Friday or Saturday night can be difficult.

Flagfall is $2.80, and the rate is $1.33 per kilometre thereafter. There is a $1 surcharge for rides between midnight and 6am, if you place any luggage in the boot and for telephone bookings.

Yellow Cabs and Silver Top Taxis have cars with wheelchair access, or phone ☎ 1300 364 050. To book a taxi, phone any of the following companies:

Black Cabs Combined (☎ 13 22 27)
Embassy Taxis (☎ 13 17 55)
Silver Top Taxis (☎ 13 10 08)
Yellow Cabs (☎ 13 19 24)

AROUND MELBOURNE

Two of the best day trips out of town are the lovely Dandenong Ranges and the Mornington Peninsula. They're both accessible by public transport and are a perfect day-trip distance.

DANDENONGS

On a clear day, you can see the Dandenong Ranges from Melbourne. The 633m summit of Mt Dandenong is the highest peak – watch the sun set over the city from the lookout. The lush hills are about 35km or an hour's drive east of the city.

Information

Dandenong Ranges & Knox Visitor Information Centre (☎ 9758 7522; www.yarrarangestourism.com; 1211 Burwood Hwy, Upper Ferntree Gully; ☼ 9am-5pm) Outside the Upper Ferntree Gully train station.
Parks Victoria (☎ 131 963; www.parkweb.vic.gov.au; Ferntree Gully Picnic Ground, Mt Dandenong Tourist Rd; ☼ 8am-4.30pm Mon-Fri) Maps and advice on walking routes.

Sights & Activities
PUFFING BILLY

A restored steam train, usually full of excited kids, **Puffing Billy** (☎ 9754 6800; www.puffingbilly .com.au; Old Monbulk Rd, Belgrave; Belgrave-Gembrook return adult/child/family $40/20/81) toots and puffs its way through the hills and gullies of the Dandenongs. There are up to six departures on holidays, three or four on other days (none on Total Fire Ban days). The Puffing Billy station is a stroll from Belgrave train station.

DANDENONG RANGES NATIONAL PARK

Dandenong Ranges National Park is made up of the four largest areas of remaining forest in the Dandenongs. The Ferntree Gully and Sherbrooke Forest sections are of the most interest to day-trippers.

Ferntree Gully, named for its abundance of tree ferns, has several short walks, including the popular **1000 Steps Track** up to **One Tree Hill picnic ground** (about two hours return). This route is part of the **Kokoda Memorial Track**, which memorialises Australian servicemen who fought and died along New Guinea's Kokoda Trail in WWII.

Sherbrooke Forest has a towering cover of mountain ash trees and a lower level of silver wattles, blackwoods, sassafras, as well as springy tree ferns. You can reach the start of the **eastern loop walk** (three hours), about 1km from Belgrave station, by walking to the end of Old Monbulk Rd past Puffing Billy's station. Combining this walk with a ride on Puffing Billy makes a great day out.

GARDENS

In spring, gardens and nurseries overflow with visitors who come to see the colourful displays of tulips, daffodils, azaleas and rhododendrons.

Giant eucalypts tower over shady lawns and brilliant flower beds at the **National Rhododendron Gardens** (☎ 9751 1980; the Georgian Rd, Olinda; adult/child/family Sep-Nov $7.50/2.50/17, Dec-Aug

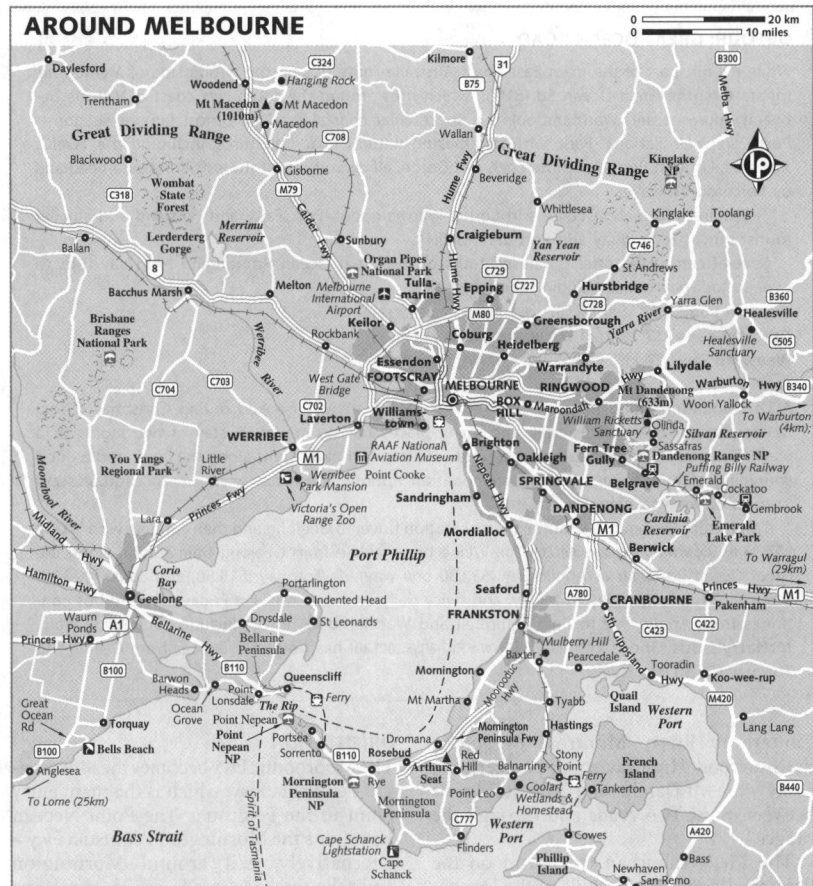

AROUND MELBOURNE

$6/2.50/15; 10am-5pm), with superb views and chirruping birds. There are groves of cherry blossoms, oaks, maples and beeches, and over 15,000 rhododendrons and 12,000 azaleas.

The **Alfred Nicholas Memorial Gardens** (9755 2912; Sherbrooke Rd, Sherbrooke; adult/child/family $6/2.50/15; 10am-5pm) were originally part of the grounds of the country mansion of Alfred Nicholas, co-founder of Aspro and the Nicholas pharmaceutical company. At their peak in the late 1930s these were the best private gardens in the country. A downhill walk leads to the very pretty ornamental lake.

Eating

Ripe (9755 2100; 376-78 Mt Dandenong Tourist Rd, Sassafras; mains $8-16; breakfast & lunch) Lovers of gourmet produce should make a beeline for Ripe, which is a café–produce store in a cute weatherboard cottage with outdoor decking.

Pie in the Sky (9751 2128; 43 Olinda-Monbulk Rd, Olinda; pies $3.50-5.50, lunch $8-12; 9.30am-5pm) Stop in for traditional favourites and more adventurous combos such as tomato and basil, korma chicken, and spinach, rice and feta.

Getting There & Around

You really need your own transport to explore the Dandenongs properly. Cyclists should note that a lot of traffic travels along its otherwise pleasantly narrow, winding roads. From the city, you can take either

MELBOURNE

DETOUR: GREAT OCEAN ROAD

While it's not part of the main East Coast Australia route (it's on the wrong side of Melbourne, for starters) the Great Ocean Rd (B100), which runs around the southwest coast of Victoria between Anglesea and Warrnambool, is a spectacular coastal road. The most famous section is Port Campbell National Park, with its amazing natural rock sculptures, including the Twelve Apostles, London Bridge and the Loch Ard Gorge, all carved out of the soft limestone headland by fierce ocean waves.

There are information centres in Lorne, Warrnambool, Port Fairy and Portland and smaller tourist offices in Torquay and Port Campbell.

Several companies offer organised tours of the Great Ocean Rd, ranging from day trips to two- to four-day tours, including the following:

Autopia Tours (☎ 1800 000 507; www.autopiatours.com.au)
Groovy Grape (☎ 1800 661 177; www.groovygrape.com.au)
Wayward Bus (☎ 1300 653 510; www.waywardbus.com.au)

Accommodation along this coastal stretch is always heavily booked during Christmas school holidays and Easter, prices peak and many places have a minimum stay of two nights or a week. There are plenty of camping grounds and caravan parks right along the coast and a good sprinkling of hotels. For other accommodation options check out www.greatoceanroad.stays .com.au or www.takeabreak.com.au.

Trains from Melbourne's Southern Cross station travel to Geelong and then connect with **V/Line** (☎ 13 61 96; www.vlinepassenger.com.au). V/Line buses cruise from Geelong train station along the Great Ocean Rd as far as Apollo Bay ($32.30 one way) via Torquay ($15.50) and Lorne ($26.20) three times daily Monday to Friday, and twice daily on weekends. On Friday a V/Line bus continues from Apollo Bay to Port Campbell and Warrnambool. Prices include connecting train. **McHarry's Bus Lines** (☎ 5223 2111; www.mcharrys.com.au) has frequent services from Geelong to Torquay ($5.30 one way).

Canterbury Rd to Montrose or go via the Burwood Highway to Upper Ferntree Gully – the Mt Dandenong Tourist Rd runs between these two roads and through the ranges.

The Met's suburban trains run on the Belgrave line to the foothills of the Dandenongs (Zones 1, 2 and 3 Met ticket). From Upper Ferntree Gully train station it's a 10-minute walk to the start of the Ferntree Gully section of the national park.

MORNINGTON PENINSULA

Mornington Peninsula is a boot-shaped peninsula between Port Phillip and Western Port Bays. It's been a favourite summer destination since the 1870s, when paddle steamers carried droves of holidaying Melburnians to Portsea and Sorrento.

The calm 'front beaches' are on the Port Phillip and Western Port sides. The rugged ocean 'back beaches' face Bass Strait – there are stunning walks along this coastal strip, which is protected as part of Mornington Peninsula National Park.

ORIENTATION

The Moorooduc Fwy becomes the Mornington Peninsula Fwy, which is the main entry point to the Peninsula. The Point Nepean Hwy joins the Mornington Peninsula Fwy – alternatively, exit around Mornington and take the coast roads, which run along Port Phillip Bay, via Dromana, Rosebud, Blairgowrie and Sorrento to Portsea. The back beaches between Rye, Cape Schanck and Flinders are mostly national park and largely undeveloped.

INFORMATION

Peninsula Visitor Information Centre (☎ 5987 3078, 1800 804 009; www.visitmorningtonpeninsula.org; Nepean Hwy, Dromana; ⏰ 9am-5pm) Has a free accommodation booking service.

GETTING THERE & AROUND
Bus & Train

Met trains (Zones 1, 2 and 3 ticket, one hour, at least one hourly) run from Flinders St station to Frankston. From Frankston train station, the **Portsea Passenger Service** (☎ 5986

5666; www.portseapas.com.au) bus 788 runs to/from Portsea (one way $8.20, 90 minutes, every half-hour Monday to Friday, hourly Saturday, every two hours Sunday), via Mornington, Dromana and Sorrento.

Car & Motorcycle
On the freeway, the trip from Melbourne takes just over an hour; via the scenic route, around 1½ to 1¾ hours.

Ferry
Inter Island Ferries (☎ 9585 5730; www.interisland ferries.com.au; return adult/child/bike $18/8/8; ☙ every 30min 8.30am-5pm plus 7pm Fri) runs daily to/from Stony Point to Cowes (on Phillip Island) via French Island. There are at least two trips daily year-round.

Sorrento
pop 1200
Sorrento has the best range of accommodation, cafés and restaurants on the Peninsula, and dolphin swims and cruises are incredibly popular.

ACTIVITIES
There are plenty of **swimming** and **walking** opportunities at Sorrento's wide, sandy beaches and bluffs. At low tide, the **rock pool** at the back beach is a safe spot for adults and children to swim and **snorkel**. The 10-minute climb up to **Coppins Lookout** for peninsula and bay views is worthwhile.

TOURS
Moonraker Charters (☎ 5984 4211; www.moonraker charters.com.au; adult/child sightseeing $40/35, swimming $80/65; ☙ tours 8am, noon & 4pm Oct-May, 9am & 1pm Jun-Sep) offers dolphin swims and sightseeing cruises. Cruises depart from Sorrento Pier and run for three to four hours; bookings essential.

EATING, DRINKING & ENTERTAINMENT
Sorrento's many eateries consist mainly of relaxed cafés and delis. You'll find most of them on Ocean Beach Rd and by the water. Like most seasonal resorts, the peninsula comes alive in summer and buzzes for three months before going into hibernation for the rest of the year.

Stringer's (☎ 5984 2010; 2 Ocean Beach Rd; sandwiches & snacks $4-8; ☙ breakfast & lunch) Long-running Stringer's is a Sorrento staple. All

the food is homemade and Mornington Peninsula wines are for sale.

The Baths (☎ 5984 1500; 3278 Point Nepean Rd; mains $17-30; ☙ breakfast, lunch & dinner) A sunny café-restaurant with big breakfasts and premium waterfront views – this site used to be the sea baths. At lunch and dinner the menu edges into more sophisticated fare.

Mornington Peninsula National Park
POINT NEPEAN
Full of super-helpful staff, the well-run **visitors information centre** (☎ 5984 4276; Point Nepean; ☙ 9am-6pm Jan, 9am-5pm Feb-Apr & Oct-Dec, 10am-5pm May-Sep) is your first port of call in this **national park** (adult/child/family $7.20/3.20/18). From here, you can walk or cycle (bike hire per three hours $15) to the point (12km return), or take the **Point Explorer** (adult/child/family incl admission one way $11/6/26, return $13/8/34), a hop-on, hop-off bus service that stops at walks along the way. There are plenty of **trails** throughout the park – the visitors centre has all the maps you'll need.

Cheviot Beach is famous as the spot where former prime minister Harold Holt is thought to have drowned in 1967. There's a memorial stone and original, slightly decayed chairs overlooking the wild surf.

OCEAN BEACHES
The southwestern coastline of the peninsula faces Bass Strait. Along here are the beautiful and rugged **ocean beaches** of Blairgowrie, Rye, St Andrews, Gunnamatta and Cape Schanck. There are a series of points and bays backdropped by cliffs, sand dunes, spectacular scenery and tidal rock pools – this is the fragile natural habitat of coastal bird life, surfers and rock-fishing people. Swimming or surfing is dangerous at these beaches: the undertow and rips can be severe and drownings have occurred.

CAPE SCHANCK
Cape Schanck Lightstation (☎ 5988 6184, 0500 527 891; adult/child/family museum $8/6/22, museum & lighthouse $10/8/28, daily adult/child $50/25; ☙ 10am-4pm), built in 1859, is a spick-and-span operational lighthouse, which has a kiosk, museum and information centre; parking is $4. Guided tours are held half-hourly in summer, less often at other times. From the lightstation, wander along the **boardwalk** that leads to the Cape – the views are phenomenal.

Western Port Bay

Western Port Bay's mainly residential towns are less developed and crowded than their Port Phillip equivalents, though populations gently swell at weekends and in summer when Melburnians escape to their beach houses.

Flinders has a fishing fleet, rugged beaches with rocky point breaks for surfers and an oceanside **golf course**. From the point at West Head there are views to Phillip Island and, on one side, a sheltered harbour with a jetty. **Flinders Village Cafe** (☎ 5989 0700; 49 Cook St; dinner mains $10-25; ☼ breakfast & lunch daily, dinner Sat & Sun) is a serene and popular spot for quality food.

Coolart Wetlands & Homestead (☎ 5931 4000; www.visitor.com.au/coolart.html; Lord Somers Rd, Somers; adult/child $7/3.50; ☼ 10am-5pm) is a graceful historic mansion with some interesting old photos, beautiful landscaped gardens, nature displays, a series of walking trails and a great wetlands sanctuary with a wide variety of bird life – it has seven distinct habitats and 150 bird species.

Mulberry Hill (☎ 5971 4138; Golf Links Rd, Baxter; admission by donation; ☼ tours 1.30pm, 2.15pm & 3pm Sun) is the former home of Joan and Sir Daryl Lindsay. Joan wrote *Picnic at Hanging Rock*, published in 1967; Sir Daryl was a noted Australian painter.

Southeast Coast Victoria

This is gorgeous Gippsland, home to some of Australia's most diverse wilderness, scenery and wildlife. There are the star attractions, such as Wilsons Promontory National Park and the insanely popular Phillip Island penguins, but venture further into the sparsely populated corner pocket of this region and discover national parks with stunning mountains, rainforests, rivers and beaches, and few other travellers.

Expect to be impressed along the way with off-the-radar south Gippsland with its lush, green rolling hills and rural back roads, and some of the best scuba diving and snorkelling in Australia along its rugged and spectacular coastline. You can get a glimpse of its former appearance at Tarra Bulga National Park, which is even more impressive, covered in towering mountain ash and valleys of giant tree ferns.

There are loads of small hamlets where the locals are hospitable and the dogs wait outside the pubs for their owners, as well as the occasional larger town with contemporary galleries, cafés and restaurants, and a sprinkling of attractions.

The Lakes District is Australia's largest inland waterway system, a rich haven for birds, and a favourite water sports spot. It's separated by coastal dunes from the long and lonely stretch of Ninety Mile Beach, which has some superb isolated beaches and both sophisticated and sleepy little towns dotted along its length.

HIGHLIGHTS

- Bushwalking through isolated wilderness areas at **Wilsons Promontory** (p110)
- Eating fresh seafood and drinking fine wine at a floating restaurant in **Lakes Entrance** (p122)
- Bar hopping in **Sale** (p115)
- Rock hopping and snorkelling at **Bunurong Marine Park** (p106)
- Walking, swimming, camping and communing with nature at beautiful **Cape Conran Coastal Park** (p127)
- Detouring to explore the ancient rainforests of **Errinundra National Park** (p126)
- Discovering the idyllic tiny former gold-mining town of **Walhalla** (p113) and staying at a stylish hotel
- Chartering a boat in peaceful **Mallacoota** (p130)

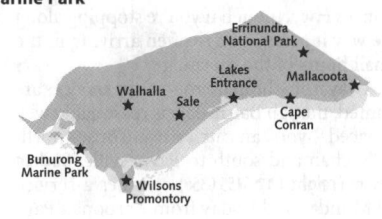

- TELEPHONE CODE: 03
- www.gippslandinfo.com.au

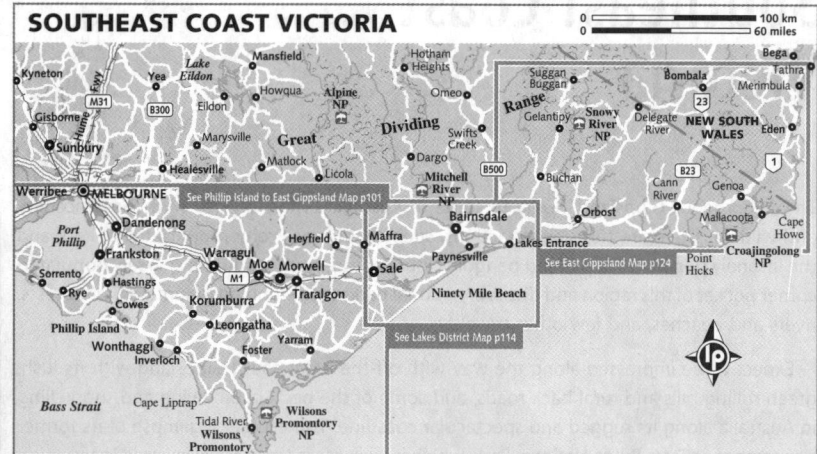

SOUTHEAST COAST VICTORIA

Getting There & Around

There's a good supply of public transport to take you as far as Bairnsdale, after that you're limited to a few bus options. You'll get the most out of this region if you have a car, preferably a 4WD, so you can check out the national parks and small towns.

BUS

There are services every day from Melbourne heading up the east coast.

V/Line (☎ 13 61 96; www.vlinepassenger.com.au) buses pick up where the train leaves off. V/Line has bus services along the Princes Hwy (A1) from Bairnsdale to Bateman's Bay during the day. Another twice-weekly service follows the Princes Hwy as far as Cann River, then veers north to Canberra. **Premier** (☎ 13 34 10; www.premierms.com.au) has a daily overnight service from Melbourne to Sydney along the Princes Hwy, though if you're stopping along the way it means you're often arriving in the small hours of the morning.

Away from the main routes bus services are limited, though Bairnsdale is reasonably well serviced – you can catch private buses north to Buchan and south to Paynesville. **Buchan Bus 'n' Freight** (☎ 5155 0356) operates a service on Monday and Friday from Karoonda Park to Bairnsdale (one way/return $16/25) via W Tree, Buchan, Nowa Nowa, Lakes Entrance and Lake Tyers. **Paynesville Bus Lines** (☎ 0418 516 405) runs daily (except Sunday) services between Bairnsdale train station and Paynesville (one way $6.10).

V/Line has the other major routes in Gippsland covered with buses running from Traralgon to Sale via Maffra; Melbourne to Yarram, stopping along the Sth Gippsland Hwy; and Melbourne to Inverloch, stopping along the Bass Hwy.

Oz Experience (☎ 1300 300 128; www.ozexperience .com) backpackers' bus line is a hop-on hop-off bus with a party atmosphere. It stops at Foster, Bairnsdale, Lakes Entrance and W Tree (near Buchan).

CAR & MOTORCYCLE

Two major routes through Gippsland are the Princes Hwy (joins the M1 in Melbourne), which runs through the centre of the region, and the Sth Gippsland Hwy, which rejoins the Princes Hwy at Sale.

Some of the national parks and other off-the-beaten-track spots in Gippsland require a 4WD (although 2WD access is often possible during the summer months) as many roads are unsealed. Check road conditions with visitor information centres and Parks Victoria before heading on to unsealed roads. Some of the roads are closed during the wetter winter months. And keep an eye out for logging trucks and wildlife; they're both prolific.

TRAIN

The efficient **V/Line** (☎ 13 61 96; www.vlinepassenger .com.au) service from Melbourne to Bairnsdale stops at all major towns along the Princes Hwy. There are three daily services during the week and two daily on the weekend.

PHILLIP ISLAND TO EAST GIPPSLAND

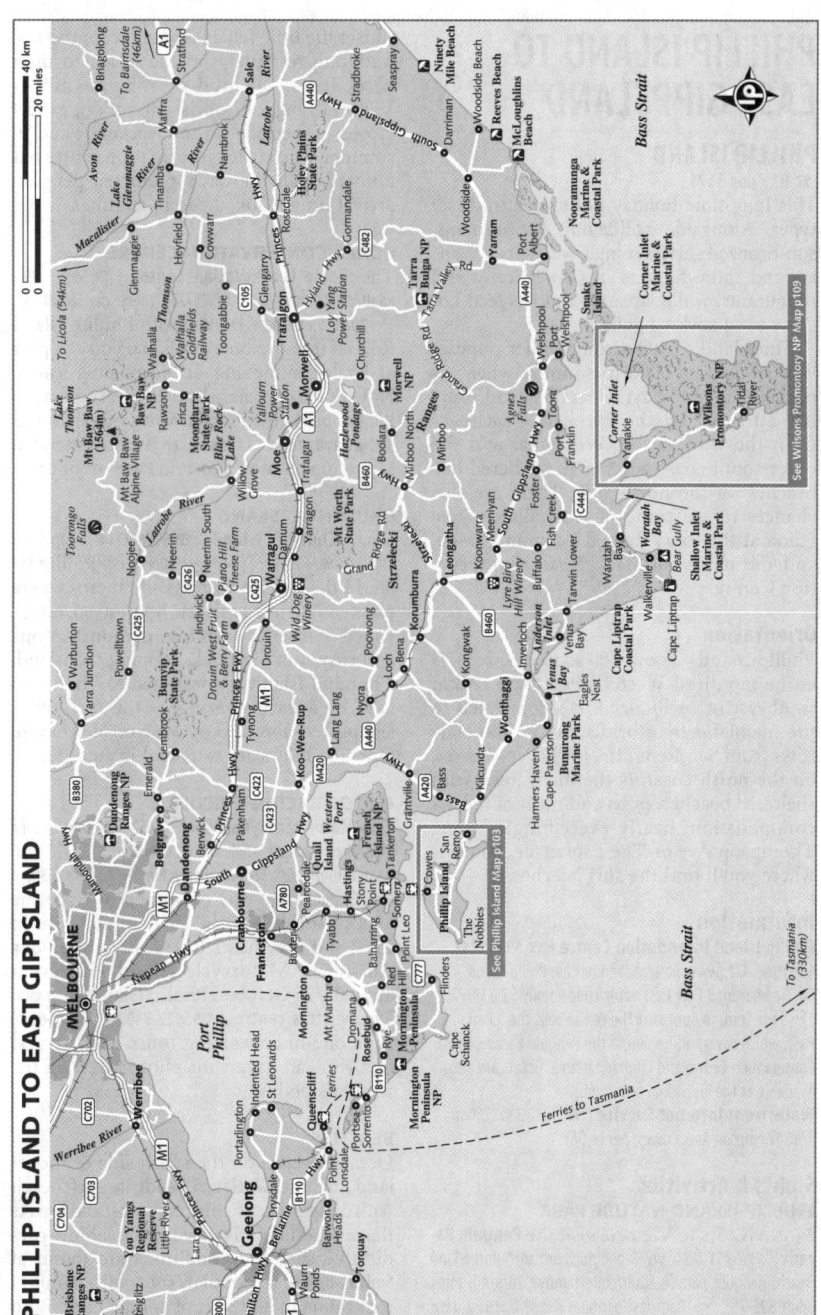

PHILLIP ISLAND TO EAST GIPPSLAND

PHILLIP ISLAND

☎ 03 / pop 3571

This long-time holiday hot spot attracts all types. Alongside holidaying Melburnians, sun-bronzed surfers mingle with sheep farmers and cattle farmers in Cowes' cafés and restaurants, while Japanese tourists feed hot chips to squawking gulls.

The island's 6700-strong winter population swells to 40,000 in summer when it's packed with holidaying families and tourists attracted by the excellent beaches – from the wild surf at Woolamai and the other south coast beaches to sheltered bay beaches on the north side. There are also chances to see some of Australia's native fauna at the much-hyped Penguin Parade, and the more laid-back Koala Conservation Centre.

Orientation

Phillip Island – about 100 sq km in area – is at the mouth of Western Port Bay, 125km southeast of Melbourne. It's connected to the mainland by a bridge across the Narrows from San Remo to Newhaven. Cowes, on the north coast, is the main town with sheltered beaches, pubs and most of the accommodation; nearly everything is along Thompson Ave or The Esplanade. South is where you'll find the surf beaches.

Information

Phillip Island Information Centre (☎ 5956 7447, 1300 366 422; www.phillipisland.net.au; Phillip Island Rd, Newhaven; 3 Park Pass adult/child/family $28/14/72; ☽ 9am-5pm, to 6pm Jan) The centre sells the 3 Parks Pass, which covers admission to the Penguin Parade, Koala Conservation Centre and Churchill Island. Tickets are also available at the individual attractions.
Waterfront Internet Service (☎ 5952 3312; Shop 1/30 Thompson Ave, Cowes; per hr $6)

Sights & Activities

PHILLIP ISLAND NATURE PARK

Most visitors to Victoria visit the **Penguin Parade** (☎ 5951 2800; www.penguins.org.au; Summerland Beach; penguin parade adult/child/family $16/8/40, tours adult $25-75; ☽ 10am-last penguin show) to see the smallest penguin species in the world. After sunset the little fellers emerge from the sea, waddling resolutely up the beach to their nests. It's a delightful sight but, as this is Victoria's biggest tourist attraction, expect crowds, especially on the weekends and in summer. The visitor information centre has a board with the day's predicted penguin arrival time; book ahead in summer.

KOALA CONSERVATION CENTRE

The **Koala Conservation Centre** (☎ 5952 1307; adult/child/family $8.50/4.25/23, tours per adult $6; ☽ 10am-5pm, tours 11.30am), off Phillip Island Rd, has tree-top boardwalks so you can peer at koalas munching on eucalyptus leaves. Note that the koalas sleep 20 hours a day, so it's probable they'll be dozing but sightings are guaranteed. The centre is open extended hours in summer. Eco tours are on offer.

CHURCHILL ISLAND

Small **Churchill Island** (☎ 5956 7214; adult/child/family $8.50/4.25/23; ☽ 10am-4.30pm), off Phillip Island Rd, is where Victoria's first crops were planted. There's a historic homestead, established gardens, farming demonstrations and easy walking tracks looping the island. Churchill Island is connected to Phillip Island by a narrow bridge – the turn-off is signposted about 1km west of Newhaven. Opening hours are extended in summer.

MOTOR RACING CIRCUIT

The **Motor Racing Circuit** (☎ 5952 2710; www.phillip islandcircuit.com.au; adult/child/family tour $12/6/28, museum & tour $16/8/38; Back Beach Rd; ☽ 8.30am-5.30pm Mon-Fri, tour 11am) was revamped to stage the 500cc World Motorbike Championships in 1989 and now hosts the massive three-day Australian Motorcycle Grand Prix event annually in October. Phillip Island goes off! The **visitors centre** (☎ 5952 9400; ☽ 9am-5pm) runs one-hour walking tours of the track, and you can have your photo taken on the winner's podium.

BEACHES

Ocean beaches on the south side of the island include **Woolamai Beach**, a surf beach with dangerous rips and currents, and breaks that are best for advanced surfers. More predictable surf and conditions are found at **Smiths Beach**, a popular spot with families that caters to all levels of competence. Both beaches are patrolled in summer.

SOUTHEAST COAST VICTORIA

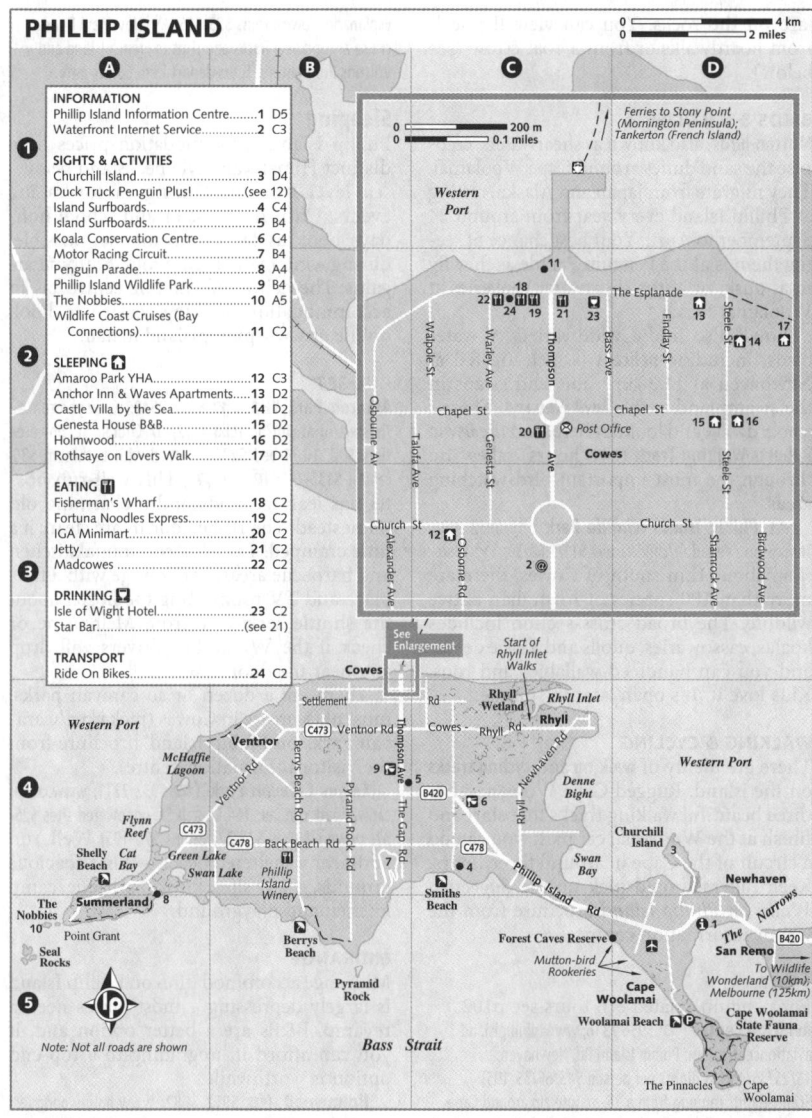

PHILLIP ISLAND

0   4 km
0   2 miles

Note: Not all roads are shown

If you're not a strong swimmer or you worry about your kids in the surf, head to the quieter, sheltered northern beaches.

Island Surfboards (☎ 5952 3443; www.island surfboards.com.au; 65 Smiths Beach & 147 Thompson Ave, Cowes; surfing lesson $40, surfboard hire per hr/day $10/35) gives surfing lessons and hires out boards and wetsuits.

SEAL ROCKS & THE NOBBIES

Off Point Grant, the extreme southwestern tip of the island, a group of rocks called the Nobbies rise from the sea. Beyond these are the Seal Rocks, inhabited by Australia's largest colony of fur seals. The rocks are most crowded during the October-to-December breeding season when up to 6000 seals laze on the rocks. You can view the seals from boardwalks or from a boat cruise (see below).

BIRDS & WILDLIFE

Mutton-birds, also known as shearwaters, colonise the sand dunes around Cape Woolamai. They migrate from Japan and Alaska, resting at Phillip Island every year from around 24 September to April. Your best chance of seeing them is at the Penguin Parade as they fly in at dusk, or at the shearwater rookeries at Woolamai Beach.

You'll also find a wide variety of water birds, including **pelicans** (which are fed at Newhaven at 11.30am), ibis and swans in the swampland at the **Rhyll Wetland**. There's a boardwalk and lookout here, and the **Oswin Roberts Walking Track** (two hours) takes you through the most important bird-watching areas.

At **Phillip Island Wildlife Park** (☎ 5952 2038; Thompson Ave; adult/child/family $11/5.50/30; ☻ 10am-5pm), about 1km south of Cowes, there are more than 100 species of Australian native wildlife. The broad cross-section includes koalas, cassowaries, quolls and Tassie devils, and you can handfeed wallabies and roos. Kids love it. It's open later in summer.

WALKING & CYCLING

There are plenty of **walking** and **cycling tracks** on the island. Rugged Cape Woolamai has three beautiful walking tracks that start and finish at the Woolamai car park; you can do a circuit of the Cape in around three hours. Keen hikers should pick up the *Suggested Walks on Phillip Island* brochure from the visitor information centre.

Tours

For penguin-related eco tours see p102.
Aviation Centre (☎ 5956 7316; www.phillipisland aviationcentre.com; Phillip Island Rd, Newhaven; 15/25/35/45min flights per person $45/65/85/105) Scenic flights ranging from a 15-minute zip around Cape Woolamai to a 45-minute loop around Western Port Bay. Minimum of two people.
Duck Truck Penguins Plus! (☎ 5952 2548; tours $145) Run by Amaroo Park YHA, the Penguins Plus package includes three nights' dorm accommodation, a picnic lunch, penguin parade admission, an island tour, bike hire and transport to/from Melbourne.
Wildlife Coast Cruises (☎ 5952 3501; www.bay connections.com.au; Rotunda Bldg, jetty car park, The

Esplanade, Cowes; tours $25-135; ☻ Nov-May) Runs a cruise around Seal Rocks and trips to French Island and Wilsons Promontory. Tours depart from Cowes jetty.

Sleeping

Phillip Island accommodation prices have distinct Himalayan-style peaks and below–sea level troughs. During motor racing events, Christmas, Easter and school holidays book as far in advance as possible; during winter you'll score rock-bottom bargains. The visitor information centre has an accommodation booking service or book online at www.phillipisland.net.au.

BUDGET

Amaroo Park YHA (☎ 5952 2548; www.yha.com.au /hostels/print.cfm?hostelid=102; 97 Church St; powered sites $30, 10-/4-bed $23/25, 4-bed with bathroom $30, cabin f $135-145; P ☐ ☻) This well-run hostel has leafy grounds and a charming old homestead. The 10-bed dorms are clean, if a little cramped. There's a communal kitchen and barbecue areas, bar, lounge with a fireplace and TV room. Ring the hostel about the shuttle service to/from Melbourne or check if the V/Line bus drivers will drop you near the door.

There are a dozen or so caravan parks; most of them are in Cowes (pick up a 'Caravan Parks on Phillip Island' brochure from the visitor information centre).

Cowes Caravan Park (☎ 5952 2211; www.cowes caravanpark.com.au; 164 Church St; unpowered sites $25-37, powered sites $27-37, cabins $70-105) Well run and near a sheltered beach – it has spacious grounds, shady sites, kiosk, barbecue, camp kitchen and playground.

MIDRANGE

Midrange accommodation on Phillip Island is largely depressing – most places need a revamp. B&Bs are a better option and, if you can afford it, upgrading to a top-end option is worthwhile.

Holmwood (☎ 5952 3082; www.holmwoodguest house.com.au; 37 Chapel St, Cowes; B&B s/tw & d $140/170, 2-r townhouse $215; ☻) This delightful and well-kept boutique accommodation, with a leafy, colourful garden, offers cosy B&B guesthouse rooms; self-contained modern cottages with wood fires, spas and private courtyards; and a family townhouse. Extra pillows are plumped on quality linen, while bathrobes wait in the cupboards. Breakfast

Exterior detail of Federation Square (p64), Victoria

JOHN BANAGAN

DAVID HANNAH

Shopping on Melbourne's Chapel St (p91), South Yarra, Victoria

The undercover walkway between Melbourne Park tennis centre (p90) and the Melbourne Cricket Ground (p76), Victoria

PHIL M WEYMOUTH

PAUL SINCLAIR

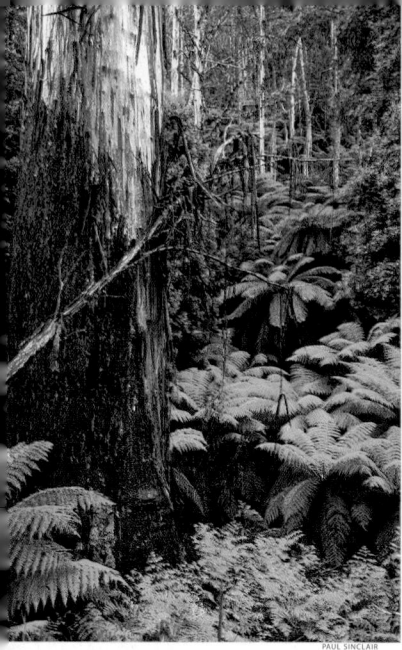

Errinundra National Park (p126), Victoria

Cape Conran (p127), Victoria

JOHN HAY

Boat moored at Gipsy Point (p129) jetty, Victoria

GREG ELM

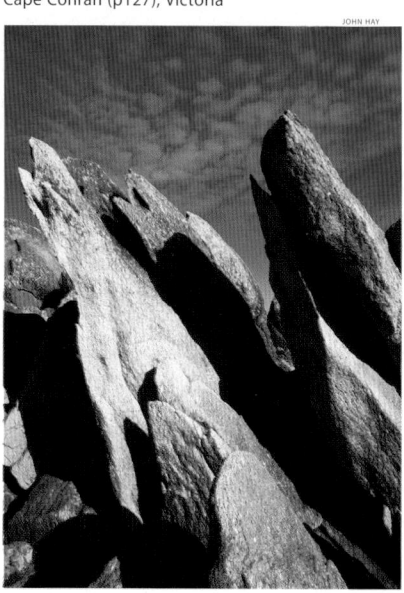

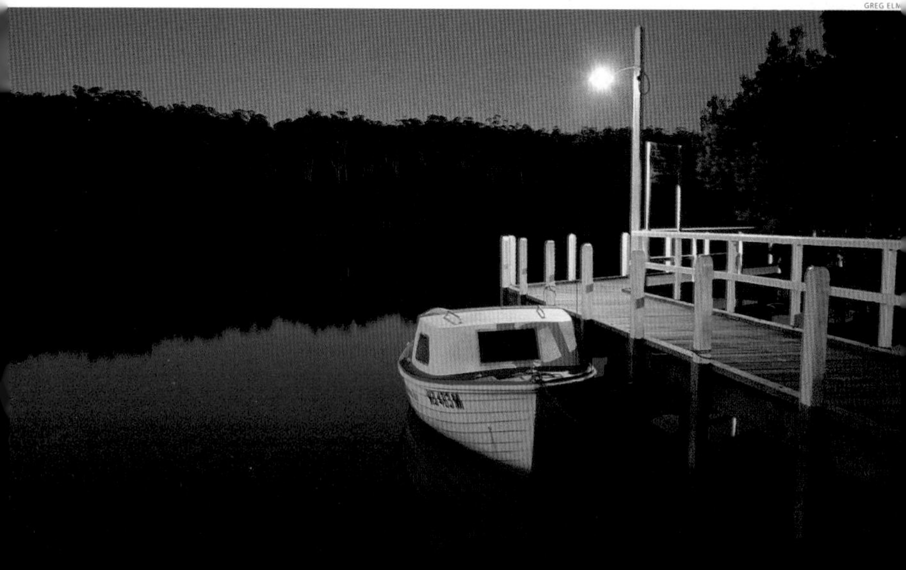

and afternoon tea are included and it even has an espresso machine. Three-course dinner is available for $50.

Genesta House B&B (☎ 5952 3616; www.genesta .com.au; 18 Steele St, Cowes; B&B $120-150) A cosy and luxurious B&B with four guest rooms in a beautiful old house surrounded by leafy garden. The peaceful garden has a barbecue area and a heated saltwater spa to soak away those walking aches. Leave the kids at home.

Anchor Inn & Waves Apartments (☎ 5952 1351; www.thewaves.com.au; 1 The Esplanade; Anchor Inn r $115-170, Waves apt $160-250; P ⊠) The Anchor Inn offers beachside, standard three-star motel accommodation popular with families. The beachside, four-star apartments offer generic, but snazzy, self-contained accommodation. Each has a balcony (many overlook the beach), spa and kitchenette. Rates include breakfast.

TOP END

Castle Villa by the Sea (☎ 5952 1228; www.thecastle .com.au; 7 Steele St, Cowes; ste $125-165, apt $225-330) If you're after a romantic getaway with healthy doses of splurging and pampering, stay at the immaculate, Mediterranean-style Castle Villa. Boutique self-contained apartments and suites are furnished individually with modern, artistic opulence – you feel like you're renting a house rather than a room. Artworks by Jeni Doyle grace the walls and the outdoor Jacuzzi in the Castle Suite is a winner. Downstairs, Boyle's restaurant is available exclusively to guests.

Rothsaye on Lovers Walk (☎ 5952 2057; www .rothsaye.com.au; 2 Roy Ct, Cowes; B&B d from $140, cottages $150-180) This place has beautiful self-contained cottages close to the beach.

Eating

Cowes is the best place on the island for food. There's the standard collection of takeaway and pizza places, plus a couple of upmarket restaurants.

Madcowes (☎ 5952 2560; 17 The Esplanade; meals $4-12; ⊗ breakfast & lunch) This is a stylish, breezy café-foodstore cooking big brekkies and quality lunches. Go for thick and fluffy ricotta hotcakes with caramelised banana, yogurt and maple syrup. At lunch wash down a roast beef and brie sandwich with some Victorian wine, sold by the glass.

Fortuna Noodles Express (☎ 5952 3888; Shop 1, 15-16 The Esplanade; mains $9-12; ⊗ lunch & dinner) A

noodle bar with spicy wok-fried Hokkein noodles, soupy coconut laksa and red and green Thai-style curries. Yum.

Jetty (☎ 5952 2060; cnr The Esplanade & Thompson Ave; mains $18-25; ⊗ dinner, closed Tue & Wed Apr-Sep) A spacious, modern restaurant with a big open kitchen, lots of tables inside and out, and a long wall banquette. Busy chefs barbecue kangaroo fillet and whip up nasi goreng. Meals are hearty and draw on European and Asian cuisines for inspiration.

Fisherman's Wharf (☎ 5952 6077; Shop 4, 15-16 The Esplanade; meals $2-10; ⊗ lunch & dinner) This is the place for fish 'n' chips, burgers and souvlakis. Depending on the season, you can feast on fresh sea perch, barramundi and flounder, calamari, scallops and NZ mussels.

Phillip Island Vineyard & Winery (☎ 5956 8465; Berrys Beach Rd; platters $14-17; ⊗ 11am-6pm Nov-Mar, 11am-5pm Apr-Oct) Drive out of town and sample the velvety wines made by renowned Diamond Valley winemakers and share platters with delectable morsels such as cheeses, terrine, smoked salmon, trout fillets and pâté. With views of Bass Strait and Western Port Bay from the cellar door, this is a worthy stop.

For self-catering, head to the **IGA minimart** (☎ 5952 1363; cnr Settlement St & Thompson Ave; ⊗ 7am-10pm) and bottle shop.

Drinking & Entertainment

During the high season the island is festive and full, with live bands playing at several of the pubs; in winter it's dead. During racing events, the island's nightspots heave with a drunken mass of excited flag-waving revellers – either join 'em or stay at home, you're certainly not going to beat 'em.

Isle of Wight Hotel (☎ 5952 2301; The Esplanade; admission $5-8; ⊗ lunch & dinner, Splash 10pm-2am) Isle of Wight is a rambling pub with a front bar, fantastic beer garden and meals on offer (mains $16 to $24). It also has Splash – the upstairs cocktail bar, which has live bands, jam sessions and DJs spinning commercial dance and hip-hop.

Star Bar (☎ 5952 2060; cnr The Esplanade & Thompson Ave; admission $10; ⊗ 7pm-2am Fri & Sat) At the back of the Jetty, Star Bar is Phillip Island's nightclub. It's a mixed bag of clientele, which the music reflects with a grab-bag of commercial techno, dance, hip-hop and R&B.

Getting There & Away

Travelling by car from Melbourne, take the Monash Fwy (M1) and get off at the Phillip Island exit on to the South Gippsland Hwy (M420) near Cranbourne.

The only direct service from Melbourne to Cowes is a **V/Line** (☎ 136 196; www.vlinepassenger.com.au) bus (one way $17, 3¼ hours) departing at 3.50pm from Southern Cross station (formerly Spencer St station) Monday to Friday. Other services run daily but require taking a Metlink train to Dandenong station and then two different coaches. Another option is to take a Met train from Melbourne to Stony Point ($7, 1¾ hours, six daily), then catch the ferry.

Inter Island Ferries (☎ 9585 5730; www.interislandferries.com.au; return adult/child/bike $18/8/8; ☺ every half-hr 9.10am-5.25pm, plus 7.45pm Fri) runs daily to/from Cowes to Stony Point (on the Mornington Peninsula) via French Island. There are at least two trips daily year-round.

Getting Around

There's no public transport around Phillip Island. You can hire bicycles from **Ride On Bikes** (☎ 5952 2533; www.rideonbike.com.au; 2-17 The Esplanade, Cowes; bike hire per half-/full day $15/25) and **Amaroo Park YHA** (☎ 5952 2548; www.yha.com.au/hostels/print.cfm?hostelid=102; 97 Church St).

Cowes/San Remo taxis (☎ 5952 2200) services Phillip Island.

KILCUNDA

☎ 03 / pop 300

Overlooking the ocean on the Bass Hwy is Kilcunda with its rugged cliffs and pounding surf. Gawk too long at the ocean views and you'll miss the town centre, which consists of a pub, general store and café (with Internet facilities). The **George Bass Coastal Walk**, a 7km one-way walk from Kilcunda Caravan Park west to San Remo is a popular trek, though you should resist the temptation to dive into the water here as there are dangerous undertows and rips. The mouth of the **Powlett River**, 3km east of Kilcunda, enclosed by high sand dunes, is also worth exploring.

Kilcunda Caravan Park (☎ 5678 7260; Bass Hwy; unpowered/powered sites $14/17.50, cabins from $55), perched on the cliff top, has sensational views from faded cabins. There are grassy camp sites, and some overlook the ocean.

Ocean Walk B&B (☎ 5678 7419; oceanwalk@waterfront.net.au; 8-14 Gilbert St; s/d from $120, cottages $170;

☒) is a friendly B&B with superb views over Bass Strait. Antiques adorn the rooms, and there's the option of a home-cooked three-course meal ($35).

The Ocean View Hotel houses the friendly Killy Pub and has highly recommended meals in **Mario's Ocean View Bistro** (☎ 5678 7011; mains $15-32; ☺ lunch & dinner), as well as a deck to watch the sunset.

V/Line (☎ 13 61 96; www.vlinepassenger.com.au) coaches operate daily from Melbourne (one way $15.60, 2½ hours) and continue to Inverloch.

BUNURONG MARINE PARK

This unassuming little stretch of marine park offers some of Australia's best snorkelling and diving. Head down from the car parks dotted along the Cape Paterson–Inverloch Rd and explore some of the 17km coastal strip of Bunurong Marine Park, which starts at Harmers Haven, just south of Wonthaggi, and goes east to Inverloch. Eagles Nest, Shack Bay and Twin Reefs are great for snorkelling and Eagles Nest, Shack Bay, Cape Paterson and Flat Rocks are also popular **scuba diving** sites.

SEAL Diving Services (☎ 5174 3434; www.sealdivingservices.com.au; 27 Princes Hwy, Traralgon; PADI 4-day course $495, introductory dive $99) offers PADI training as well as full hire facilities, and shore and boat diving tours for certified divers to Wilsons Prom and Bunurong Marine Park.

INVERLOCH

☎ 03 / pop 2450

Burgeoning Inverloch gets ritzier each year and the population explodes in summer. Beach goers flock to the ocean **beaches** along the road to Cape Paterson, and families swamp the inlet beaches close to town. Inverloch hosts a lively **jazz festival** (☎ 5674 3141) each March.

The **Inverloch Information Centre** (☎ 5671 2233; invyinfo@basscoast.vic.gov.au; 6 A'Beckett St) and the **Bunurong Environment Centre** (☎ 5674 3738; Ramsey Blvd; ☺ 10am-4pm Thu-Sun, daily peak season) have plenty of local knowledge.

Screw Creek Nature Walk is an easy 40-minute return walk with great views from the bluff and plenty of bird life.

You can take lessons with **Learn to Surf Offshore Surf School** (☎ 5674 3374; 45 Beach Ave; 2hr lesson $40). Everything is provided, you just need to book and turn up at the beach.

There's an assortment of tourist town shops, including the new **Inverloch Antique Centre** (☎ 5674 3003; 36 Bear St; ☒ 10am-5pm Wed-Sun), a warehouse and gallery full of old and exotic furniture and bric-a-brac, which also has a museum section with 19th-century dresses.

Inverloch Foreshore Reserve (☎ 5674 1236; cnr Esplanade & Ramsay Blvd; unpowered/powered sites $17/19) is as close to the beach as you can stay and the sites are protected from the wind by coastal scrub. It's a 10-minute walk to shops and cafés. The reserve is managed by the neighbouring Inverloch Holiday Park. Prices increase 50% during the Christmas school holidays.

Lofts (☎ 5674 3656; www.stockdaleleggo.com.au/ Inverloch; Ramsay Blvd; apt $150; ☒) will make you feel very Zen in its classy Japanese-influenced self-contained apartments in the town centre. Some have water views and there's a spa to soak in.

Moilong Express (☎ 0439 842 334; fax 5674 3710; 405 Inverloch-Venus Bay Rd; d $80) will put train lovers in heaven in two converted guards' vans. Sleeping on a train has never been so comfortable with a palatial queen-sized bed and all the mod cons. The carriages accommodate up to five people and have views over Anderson's Inlet. No credit cards.

Kiosk Cafe by the Sea (☎ 5674 3611; meals $3-14.50; ☒ breakfast & lunch), opposite the beach, is the perfect breakfast spot. Grab your newspaper and plonk down out the front of this little red shack for a generous breakfast and delicious juices and smoothies.

Cafe Pajez (☎ 5674 1516; 27 A'Beckett St; mains $5-10; ☒ lunch & dinner Wed-Sun) The wafting aroma of its speciality, curries, will entice you into this comfortable café with Asian-inspired décor.

V/Line (☎ 13 61 96; www.vlinepassenger.com.au) coaches to/from Melbourne stop on Beach Rd (one way $21.60, 3¼ hours).

VENUS BAY

☎ 03 / pop 441

This small holiday settlement by Cape Liptrap Coastal Park is popular for its excellent walking tracks and fine swimming beaches, although watch out for rips (Venus Bay No 1 Beach is patrolled during summer). **Anderson Inlet Walk**, 4km return, starts at the car park at Doyles Rd (6km from the shops) and passes along mudflats and mangroves teeming with crabs and bird life.

Venus Bay Caravan Park (☎ 5663 7723; venbay cp@tpgi.com.au; 113A Jupiter Blvd; powered sites from $23, cabins from $55; ☒) is one of the friendliest and best-run caravan parks in Gippsland. An 800m walk to the beach and a children's playground make it a winner with families.

Sundowner Lodge Guesthouse (☎ 5663 7099; www.sundownerlodge.com; 128 Inlet Rd; d $130), an award-winning boutique guesthouse, is the place for a romantic weekend away. There's a large spa, it has its own fully licensed restaurant and your privacy is guaranteed.

Venus Bites (☎ 5663 7887; 114A Jupiter Blvd; dishes $4.50-20; ☒ breakfast, lunch & dinner Thu-Mon, daily summer) is a sleek grey-and-maroon-toned café and wine bar that serves good coffee and has a seafood and Italian-inspired menu. For something different, try the chicken laksa ($17.50).

WARATAH BAY, WALKERVILLE & BEAR GULLY

West of the Prom is the half-moon shaped Waratah Bay, with a couple of quiet and remote holiday townships and some wonderful long stretches of white-sand beach. The leafy **Waratah Bay Caravan Park** (☎ 5684 1339; Freycinet St; unpowered/powered sites from $17/20, cabins from $50) is right by the beach. Prices double during the Christmas school holiday period. There are no shops, although the park office sells supplies. Waratah Bay is a 30km drive from Foster. There's no public transport to Waratah Bay.

Overlooking Waratah Bay, and part of **Cape Liptrap Coastal Park**, Walkerville is a pretty spot with holiday houses scattered across the hills. There are some great beach walks in this area, and you can drive the 14km down to the lighthouse at **Cape Liptrap**. Right on the foreshore, is the simple **Walkerville Camping Reserve** (☎ 5663 2224; unpowered/powered sites $14/17, caravans $60). Free bush camping is also possible at the pleasant and well-maintained Bear Gully camp site (BYO water), south of Walkerville. **Bear Gully Coastal Cottages** (☎ 5663 2364; www.beargully cottages.com.au; 33 Maitland Court; d from $230), with expansive water views, are stylish, modern self-contained cottages, with sliding glass doors opening from bedrooms on to the decking. There's a delicious feeling of isolation. Bear Gully is 7km southwest of Walkerville.

DETOUR: KOONWARRA

This tiny township has a fantastic general store with its own café, a shop selling organic produce and a winery down the road. It's roughly 25km from Venus Bay, via Tarwin Lower and Tarwin.

Koonwarra Store (☎ 5664 2285; Sth Gippsland Hwy; lunch $10.50-15.50, dinner $19.50-32; ☺ break-fast & lunch daily, dinner Fri & Sat) is a destination in its own right. Local produce and wines are on sale in the renovated timber building, and it houses a renowned café that serves simple food with flair. Try the roasted vegetable pie with orange salad ($10) for lunch, served in relaxed surroundings, which include a garden with a children's cubbyhouse.

Prom Country Slow Food Festival (☎ 5674 2094), an innovative two-week festival held in August, celebrates food that is neither processed nor mass-produced and brings together all the local food, wine and beer producers. Events are held at vineyards, riverbanks and farms.

Lyre Bird Hill Winery & Guest House (☎ 5664 3204; www.lyrebirdhill.com.au; 370 Inverloch Rd; guest-house s/d $100/150, cottage d $110; ☺ 10am-5pm Thu-Mon) is a popular winery with an old-fashioned B&B with light-filled rooms overlooking the garden. There are also rooms in a faded country cottage. A three-course dinner can be arranged ($60) accompanied by the house wines.

WILSONS PROMONTORY NATIONAL PARK

One of the most loved national parks in Australia, 'the Prom' as it's affectionately known by locals, covers the southernmost tip of the mainland. Surrounded on three sides by sea, the Prom offers a superb variety of activities including more than 80km of walking tracks, abundant wildlife and a wonderful selection of beaches suitable for surfing, swimming or seclusion. Wood fires are not permitted anywhere in the park.

Information

The helpful **Parks Victoria Information Office** (☎ 5680 9555, 1800 350 552; www.parkweb.vic.gov.au ☺ 8am-4.30pm) in Tidal River books all accommodation in the park and issues permits for camping away from Tidal River. From gentle strolls to overnight hikes, you can find all the details here.

Day entry to the park is $9.30 per car (included in the overnight charge if you're camping). There's one access road into the park which leads to Tidal River, where there's a park office, education centre, general store, café (with Internet facilities) and an open-air cinema (in summer only) with latest releases. Petrol is also available and a medical centre operates for limited hours in high season.

Bushwalking

You don't have to go far from the car parks to get away from it all. The walking tracks take you through swamps, forests, marshes, valleys of tree ferns and long beaches lined with sand dunes. If you're staying more than a couple of days, it's worth buying a copy of *Discovering the Prom* ($15) from the park office.

The northern area of the park is much less visited, mostly because all facilities are at Tidal River. Most walks in this 'wilderness zone' are overnight or longer, and mainly for experienced bushwalkers.

Tours

Bunyip Tours (☎ 9531 0840; www.bunyiptours.com; 2-/3-/4-day tour $225/345/425) An eco-friendly company offering hiking tours of the Prom. There's a discount for ISIC and IYHA members.

Hiking Plus (☎ 1300 13 83 12; www.hikingplus.com; 2-6 day hikes $675-1410) This tour company organises hikes to the Prom from nearby Foster where it has comfortable guesthouse accommodation (including spa) for the start and end of each trip. Packages include meals; some also include massages. Ask about its specials.

Sleeping

There aren't any hostels in the park, but in nearby Foster is **Prom Coast Backpackers** (☎ 56822171;www.gippsland.com/web/WarraweeHoliday Apartments/; 40 Station Rd; 4-bed dm/d/f $25/60/75), a cosy place in a small renovated cottage with polished floorboards. It has a small kitchen and a lounge and sleeps 10. The friendly owners can usually organise a lift to the Prom for about $10.

HUTS & UNITS

There are a number of Parks Victoria self-contained cabins and units at Tidal River that can accommodate four to six people.

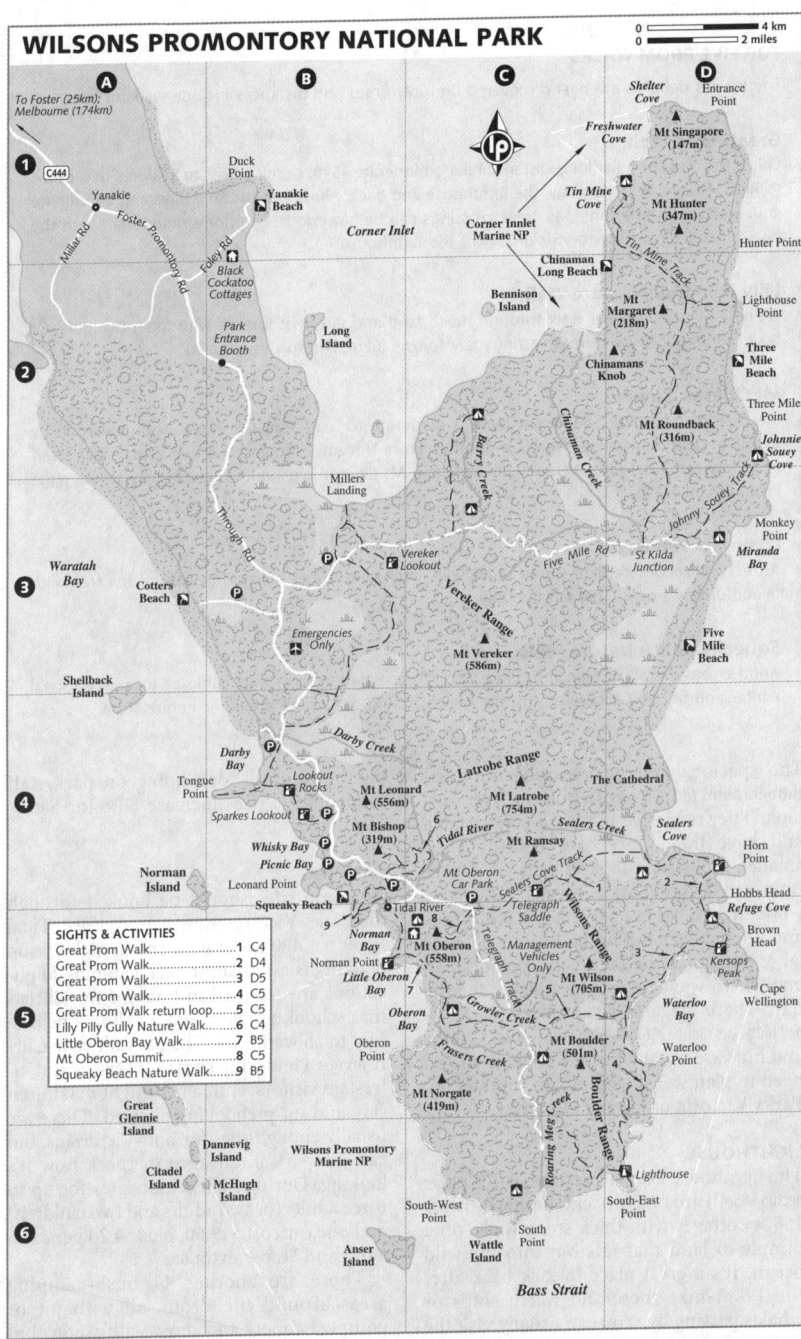

WILSONS PROMONTORY NATIONAL PARK

0 ————— 4 km
0 ————— 2 miles

A   **B**   **C**   **D**

To Foster (25km);
Melbourne (174km)

1

C444

Yanakie

Foster–Promontory Rd

Millar Rd

Duck
Point

Yanakie
Beach

Foley Rd

Black
Cockatoo
Cottages

Park
Entrance
Booth

Corner Inlet

Long
Island

**Shelter
Cove**   Entrance
Point

*Freshwater
Cove*

Mt Singapore
(147m)

*Tin Mine
Cove*

Corner Innlet
Marine NP

Chinaman
Long Beach

Bennison
Island

Mt Hunter
(347m)

Hunter Point

Tin Mine Track

Mt
Margaret
(218m)

Lighthouse
Point

Chinamans
Knob

**Three
Mile
Beach**

Three Mile
Point

Mt Roundback
(316m)

*Johnnie
Souey
Cove*

2

Corner Inlet

Millers
Landing

Barry Creek

Chinaman Creek

Johnny Souey Track

Monkey
Point

*Miranda
Bay*

3

*Waratah
Bay*

Through Rd

Cotters
Beach

Vereker
Lookout

Five Mile Rd

St Kilda
Junction

**Five
Mile
Beach**

Emergencies
Only

Vereker Range

Mt Vereker
(586m)

Shellback
Island

Darby Creek

Latrobe Range

The Cathedral

4

*Darby
Bay*

Tongue
Point

Lookout
Rocks

Sparkes Lookout

Mt Leonard
(556m)

Mt Latrobe
(754m)

Sealers Creek

*Sealers
Cove*

Horn
Point

Mt Bishop
(319m)

Tidal River

Mt Ramsay

Sealers Cove Track

1

2

Whisky Bay
Picnic Bay

Leonard Point

Mt Oberon
Car Park

Hobbs Head

Refuge Cove

Brown
Head

**Norman
Island**

Squeaky Beach

Tidal River

Telegraph
Saddle

Wilsons Range

Kersops
Peak

Cape
Wellington

9

8

3

**Norman
Bay**

Norman Point

Mt Oberon
(558m)

Management
Vehicles
Only

5

Mt Wilson
(705m)

*Waterloo
Bay*

*Little Oberon
Bay*

7

Telegraph Track

Growler Creek

Waterloo
Point

*Oberon
Bay*

Oberon
Point

Mt Boulder
(501m)

4

Mt Norgate
(419m)

Frasers Creek

Roaring Meg Creek

Boulder Range

Lighthouse

**Great
Glennie
Island**

Dannevig
Island

**Wilsons Promontory
Marine NP**

Citadel
Island

McHugh
Island

South-West
Point

South
Point

South-East
Point

Anser
Island

Wattle
Island

Bass Strait

SIGHTS & ACTIVITIES

Great Prom Walk..........................1	C4
Great Prom Walk..........................2	D4
Great Prom Walk..........................3	D5
Great Prom Walk..........................4	C5
Great Prom Walk return loop......5	C5
Lilly Pilly Gully Nature Walk.......6	C4
Little Oberon Bay Walk..............7	B5
Mt Oberon Summit.....................8	C5
Squeaky Beach Nature Walk.......9	B5

5

6

**SOUTHEAST COAST
VICTORIA**

TOP FIVE PROM WALKS

The Prom's delights are best discovered on foot. Times and distances include walking back.

Great Prom Walk

This is the most popular long-distance hike, a moderate 45km circuit across to Sealers Cove, down to Refuge Cove, Waterloo Bay, the lighthouse and back. Allow two to three days and coordinate your walks with tide times, as creek crossings can be hazardous. By prior arrangement with the park office it's possible to visit or stay at the lighthouse.

Lilly Pilly Gully Nature Walk

An easy 5km (two-hour) walk through heath land and eucalypt forests, with lots of wildlife. Or take the longer route through stringybark forests (6km, two to three hours).

Mt Oberon Summit

Starts from Telegraph Saddle car park. A moderate to hard 7km (2½-hour) walk rewarded by excellent panoramic views from the summit. From November to Easter a free shuttle bus operates between Tidal River visitors car park and Mt Oberon car park (a gentle way to start the Prom Circuit Walk).

Little Oberon Bay

An easy to moderate 8km (three-hour) walk over sand dunes covered in coastal tea tree with beautiful views over Little Oberon Bay.

Squeaky Beach Nature Walk

Another easy stroll of 5km returning through coastal tea trees and banksias to a sensational white-sand beach. Go barefoot on the beach to find out where the name comes from.

The spacious and private self-contained **timber cabins** (d $144) have a bush or river outlook. They're simple but ultra-comfortable and have the luxury of a bathtub. The smaller 1960s-style **Lorikeet Units** (d $104) are uninspired motel-style rooms. The cosy wooden **huts** (up to 4 people $55) have bunks and kitchenettes but no bathroom. They're large enough to be comfortable and small enough to want to get you outside for the day. There are also **group lodges** (12-/24-/30-bed lodge per night $256/516/644) available. Cabins and huts are usually heavily booked, so you need to plan well ahead. Again, contact the Parks Victoria office at Tidal River.

LIGHTHOUSE

The lighthouse keepers' **cottages** (8-/12-bed per person $65/41) are magnificent, heritage-listed, 1850s cottages with thick stone walls, on a pimple of land that juts out into the wild ocean. It's a great place to kick back after the 19km hike there and watch ships or whales passing by. You can usually visit the lighthouse itself, depending on park staff availability. Prices increase 50% for Saturday nights.

CAMPING

All camp sites should be booked through the Parks Victoria information office. Tidal River has 480 camp sites, and in high season booking is essential. In fact, camping applications are accepted in June for the Christmas school holidays, and a ballot is held in July to allocate sites. The park office usually reserves a few camp sites for overseas and interstate visitors, with a two-night maximum stay and no prebooking allowed. There are usually enough sites for non-Victorians, but call the park in advance to check how it's looking. During high season sites for up to three adults (or two adults and two children) and one car cost $19.60, plus $4.20 per extra adult and $6 per extra car.

There are another 11 bush-camping areas around the Prom, all with pit or compost toilets and most with water, but nothing else in the way of facilities. Overnight hikers need camping permits (adult/child $6.50/3.25), which should be booked ahead through the park office.

Getting There & Away

There isn't any direct public transport between Melbourne and the Prom, though there are day trips and organised tours. Prom Coast Backpackers can usually organise a lift to the Prom for its guests.

YANAKIE

The nearest settlement to the Prom, Yanakie – an Aboriginal word meaning 'between waters' – is a tiny place with many gorgeous sleeping options. At **Black Cockatoo Cottages** (☎ 5687 1306; www.blackcockatoo.com; 60 Foley Rd; d $120) you can take in glorious views of the Prom without leaving your very comfortable bed in these private, stylish, black timber self-contained cottages.

Yanakie Caravan Park (☎ /fax 5687 1295; yanakiecaravanpark@hotmail.com; 390 Foley Rd; powered sites $19, cabins from $55) has a few light and bright deluxe cabins ($90) with a deck overlooking the Prom; linen is provided with these.

You need a car to get to Yanakie, which is 25km from Foster.

PORT ALBERT

☎ 03 / pop 250

Don't come here looking for action. But if you want to potter around a quaint old fishing village, learn something about its maritime history from the museum and the friendly locals, and eat some of the best fish and chips in the state then stop by. Port Albert was Victoria's first established port and was the

---

arrival point for those trying their luck on the gold fields of Dargo and Omeo. It has an assortment of historic timber buildings dating from its busy 1850s port days, each with a brass plaque outlining its history.

The **Maritime Museum** (☎ 5183 2520; Tarraville Rd; adult/child $4/1; ☽ 10.30am-4pm daily Sep-May, Sat & Sun Jun-Aug) is Port Albert's star act (well, its only act, really) and covers the town's whaling and sealing days as well as having boats and the top of a lighthouse to tinker with.

Port Albert Hotel/Motel (☎ 5183 2212; Wharf St; s/d $55/67) is crowded on weekends with hardy fishing types. The bistro has decent pub fare (mains $12 to $17). The hotel is the oldest continually licensed pub in Victoria, and has clean rooms with faded bedcovers.

Boathouse (☎ 5183 2434; ☽ lunch & dinner) doesn't advertise, staff don't wear a uniform and the place doesn't even have a business card, but the crowds are queuing out the door in summer for the renowned fish and chips – don't miss out, they're delicious.

V/Line (☎ 13 61 96; www.vlinepassenger.com.au) drop-off is possible at the turn-off to Port Albert on the Sth Gippsland Hwy, but it's another 7km to Port Albert.

MCLOUGHLIN'S BEACH

The small holiday-shack settlement of McLoughlin's Beach is part of Nooramunga Marine & Coastal Park. This quite beautiful place with salt marshes, mangroves and low-lying scrub is preserving its character well with not a shop or accommodation option to be seen.

There's a lovely one-hour **walk** you can do here. From the jetty a boardwalk crosses an area of salt marsh, coastal saw edge and swamp weed, fringed with pigface (a pink flower); expect to see orange-bellied parrots flying through the air. Cross the wide arm of the inlet at the old wooden bridge to meet a sandy track. The jetty by the bridge is a popular fishing spot; pelicans wait patiently nearby for any fishy leftovers. The sandy track passes through banksia forest to the ocean and another popular fishing spot on Ninety Mile Beach (the slope down to the sand is steep). The banksia track intersects with a walk east to **Reeve's Beach** (12.5km, four hours return) on Ninety Mile Beach (where bush camping is possible), or west to **McLoughlin's Entrance** (6km, two hours return).

> **THE AUTHOR'S CHOICE**
>
> **Port Albert Bed & Breakfast** (☎ 5183 2525; www.portalbertbedandbreakfast.com; 27 Wharf St; d from $200) The house looks out of place in historic Port Albert, but once inside this boutique accommodation you won't give a toss. It's like stepping into a *Gone with the Wind* film set except for the sweeping views of the Prom and the port. Each tastefully furnished room has a king-sized bed and spa. For a romantic weekend away ask for the sublime Lovers Suite ($230). It's worth coming to Port Albert just to stay here.

WEST GIPPSLAND – TYNONG TO YARRAGON

From Melbourne, the Princes Hwy follows the power lines back to their source, past the dairy country northwest of Warragul, to the industrial heartland of the Latrobe Valley – the region between Moe and Traralgon – before heading on to Sale. The power stations built on the coalfields at Yallourn, Morwell and Loy Yang provide the majority of Victoria's power requirements. The immense Loy Yang power station that you'll spot on the drive through is the largest in the southern hemisphere.

An hour's drive from Melbourne at Tynong, the wildlife park **Gumbayah Park** (☎ 5629 2613; 2705 Princes Hwy; adult/child/family $8.50/4.60/25; ☽ 10am-6pm) is a large bushy park with emus, kangaroos, wallabies, one lone caged dingo, and bird life in walk-through aviaries, including flamboyant peacocks. You can't miss the massive peacock statue out the front. Picnic tables abound and there's a children's playground; avoid the park on the weekends unless you love crowds. The amusement rides will be a winner with older children ($4 per ride).

The excellent **Wild Dog Winery** (☎ 5623 1117; South Rd; ☽ 9am-5pm) is 3km off the Princes Hwy on the Warragul–Korumburra Rd. This winery was one of Gippsland's first and produces a range of stellar reds and whites, all grown and bottled on its 12 hectares.

YARRAGON

☎ 03 / pop 707

Yarragon has successfully reinvented itself over the years into a Gippsland mecca for quality art, gifts and gourmet produce. The **Town & Country Gallery** (☎ 5634 2229; Princes Hwy) has a beautiful range of art works, with a quality display of Australian paintings, hand-blown glassware, ceramics and metalwork for sale. **Gippsland Food & Wine** (☎ 5634 2451; www.yarragonvillage.com/yv-gippsfoodwine.htm; 123 Princes Hwy) is a large deli and café, showcasing gourmet produce and wine from Gippsland's 25 wineries. It also triples as a visitor information centre with a reasonable selection of brochures.

With Yarragon's shiny new image has come some quality cafés and accommodation. The star among the eating places is **Sticcado** (☎ 5634 2101; The Village Walk; breakfast $4.50-9, lunch mains $9.50-17.50; ☽ breakfast & lunch Wed-Mon), specialising in beef dishes from its own cattle farm, but also providing a classy space to have a cuppa.

A short stroll from the centre of town is **Yarragon Villas** (☎ 5634 2623; www.yarragonvillas.com.au; 16 Campbell St; s/d Mon-Thu from $125/140, s & d incl breakfast Fri-Sun $170-250; ✄). Decked out with spas and wood fires, and with country French, modern Asian and completely over the top pink-and-green chintzy floral themes, these villas are all luxuriously stylish. For a complete bliss-out, next door there's **Santoshi Bodyworks** (☎ 5634 2314; 18 Campbell St; ☽ by appointment only) offering massage, private yoga classes, body balance, all $50 per hour.

The area around Yarragon is dubbed **Gippsland Gourmet Deli Country** (www.gourmetgippsland.com) and there are a few places close together that make a fun country jaunt; all are signposted from the highway. **Drouin West Fruit & Berry Farm** (☎ 5628 7627; 315 Fisher Rd; ☽ 10am-5pm, to 3pm winter, closed Jul–mid-Aug) is a pick-your-own berry and fruit orchard and has a great little café, the **Berry Good Cafe** (lunch mains $10.50) where you can tuck into focaccias, pies and platters, and some delicious desserts. A few kilometres away is **Piano Hill Cheese Farm** (☎ 5628 5377; Main Neerim Rd; ☽ 11am-4pm Fri-Tue, Fri-Sun winter) for, er, cheese tastings. **Sunny Creek Fruit and Berry Farm** (☎ 5634 7526; 69 Tudor Rd, Chiltern; ☽ Sat-Sun & school holidays Dec-Apr) has certified organic berries and it's a beautiful 7km drive from the highway through some remnant rainforest to pick a bucketful of organic raspberries, strawberries or gooseberries.

LAKES DISTRICT

Gippsland's Lakes District is the largest inland waterway system in Australia. There are three main lakes that interconnect, Lake King, Lake Victoria and Lake Wellington, which are actually shallow coastal lagoons that were once part of a large bay. Over thousands of years, sand has built up in deposits along the coastline, and the lakes are now separated from the ocean by a narrow strip of coastal sand dunes known as Ninety Mile Beach. Most of Ninety Mile Beach, from Woodside Beach to Lakes Entrance, is part of the 17,200-hectare **Gippsland Lakes Coastal Park**. Within this area is the Lakes National Park (p116).

DETOUR: WALHALLA

☎ 03 / pop 23

Tiny Walhalla, 46km northeast of Moe, is one of Victoria's most historic and charming towns (so authentic that it was only connected to the electricity grid at the close of the 20th century!). Gold was discovered here in 1862 by Ned Stringer and the population exploded. However, by the time the railway from Moe came into service in 1910, the gold supplies and population were (and still are) in decline. There's still plenty to see in Walhalla, and the drive up to the town is beautiful (mind the hairpin bends). Stringers Creek runs through the centre of the town, which is in an idyllic valley encircled by a cluster of historic buildings set into the hillsides.

Sights & Activities

Many of Walhalla's attractions are open year-round but there's more happening on weekends and during high season. The best way to see the town is on foot – take the **circuit walk** that leads from the car park by the information shelter as you enter the town. It passes the main sights before climbing up the hill to follow the old timber tramway back to the car park. There are many mine shafts in the area so keep to the marked tracks, and allow a couple of hours.

Guided tours of the **Long Tunnel Extended Gold Mine** (☎ 5165 6259; adult/child/family $9/6.50/27; ✆ tours 1.30pm Mon-Fri, noon, 2pm & 3pm Sat & Sun), off Walhalla-Beardmore Rd, give you a look at Cohens Reef, once one of Australia's top reef gold producers.

You can take a very scenic 25-minute ride between Thomson Station and Walhalla on the **Walhalla Goldfields Railway** (☎ 9513 3969, 5126 4201; adult/child/family return $15/10/35; ✆ from Thomson Station 11.30am, 1.20pm & 3.10pm Wed, Sat & Sun, public & school holidays; from Walhalla station 12.10pm, 2pm & 3.50pm). The train snakes along Stringers Creek Gorge, passing lovely forested gorge country and crosses a number of trestle bridges.

Back in town, steps lead up a steep hillside to **Walhalla Cricket Ground**, a spectacular place to hit a six.

Walhalla Cemetery gives a more sombre insight into the history of the area and the terrain is so steep that some souls were buried sideways.

There's a group of restored shops on the main street, including **Walhalla Corner Store & Gold Era Museum** (☎ 5165 6250; ✆ 10am-4pm), which offers ghost tours ($15, 1¼ hours) on the first Saturday of each month and shares some of the local legends.

The southern trail head of the **Australian Alps Walking Track** – which goes all the way to Canberra and takes six weeks to hike – is in Walhalla. There are some good day trips along it too.

For some rugged mountain adventuring, **Copper Mine Adventure** (☎ 5134 6875; www.mountaintopexperience.com; adult & child $15, family $50) operates a 1½-hour 4WD trip most weekends and Wednesdays along old coach roads to a disused mine. **Wheels to Walhalla** (☎ 5165 3212; 2hr tour $20, bike hire per day $10) runs tailor-made small-group mountain-bike trips in the bush tracks around Walhalla during the warmer months.

Sleeping & Eating

Walhalla Star Hotel (☎ 5165 6262; www.starhotel.com.au; Main Rd; d from $169) The rebuilt historic Star offers stylish boutique-hotel accommodation with sophisticated designer décor and king-sized beds. The hotel's restaurant, Parker's, is open for dinner only. Mains range from $19 to $23 and nonguests should reserve a table.

Windsor House (☎ 9882 5985, 5165 6237; www.windsorhouse.com.au; d from $150) The clock turns back more than a century when you step into this B&B with four-poster beds, fires and a library of old books. This building was a guesthouse during Walhalla's heyday and has been restored to its former glory.

Camping in Walhalla is free and there are good bush camping areas along Stringer's Creek and a designated camping area at the top of the town with toilets.

Walhalla Lodge Family Hotel (☎ 5165 6226; mains $12-15; ✆ lunch daily, dinner Wed-Mon) A cosy one-room pub decked out with prints of old Walhalla and serving reasonable pub grub.

Miner's Cafe (☎ 5165 6227; dishes $4.50-10.50; ✆ lunch) A tiny café next to the general store with a limited menu and some takeaway options.

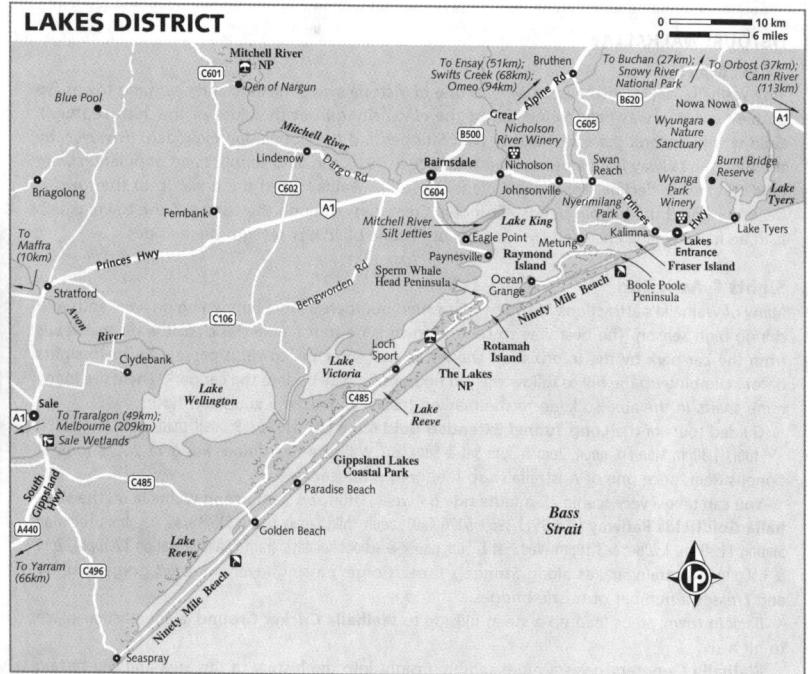

LAKES DISTRICT

SALE
☎ 03 / pop 12,850

Sale is the gateway to the Lakes District and is getting more contemporary by the month with the opening of its striking entertainment centre, classy restaurants and bars, and the development of the old port area.

Information
Central Gippsland Information Centre (☎ /fax 5144 1108; www.gippslandinfo.com.au; 8 Foster St) Has Internet facilities and an online accommodation booking service.
Parks Victoria (☎ 5144 3048; 1 Lacey St; ☽ Mon & Fri) Turn right at Foster St into Guthridge St.

Sights & Activities
Sale Wetlands Walk is signposted from Lake Guthridge. The 4km walking trail skirts around the lake via **Sale Common**, a 330-hectare wildlife refuge with bird hides, an observatory, boardwalks and other walking tracks and is part of an internationally recognised wetlands system. The best time to go is early morning or late evening (wear some mosquito repellent, they're vicious).

The **Gippsland Art Gallery** (☎ 5142 3372; 68 Foster St, Civic Centre; adult/child $3/1.50; ☽ 10am-5pm Tue-Fri, 1-5pm Sat & Sun) is a small gallery always worth a look exhibiting work by locally and nationally renowned artists and also hosting touring exhibitions.

Sale's old **port** has been given a face-lift with new timber walkways and picnic tables. There are grand plans to have a marina and upmarket accommodation and eateries overlooking the port, once a busy place during the paddle-steamer heyday.

Sleeping & Eating
Free camping is permitted (no facilities) in the Sale wetlands area, as long as you're at least 20m away from the water.

Bon Accord (☎ 5144 5555; www.bonaccordb-b.com.au; 153-155 Dawson St; s/d from $135/170) Sleeping in the ironing room becomes an incredibly attractive proposition at this 1860s homestead where the school room and the stables have also been restored as luxury accommodation. The stables with a loft upstairs and a claw bath is more spacious and the best option. A full breakfast is served in the homestead.

Cambrai Backpackers (☎ 5147 1600; www.south easthostel.com; 117 Johnson St, Maffra; dm/d incl breakfast $25/55; ▣) There's no backpackers in Sale but in nearby Maffra this place is a haven for backpackers and one of Gippsland's best. It's in a 120-year-old building that was once a doctor's residence and is now a re-laxed hostel with licensed bar, open fire and pool table in the cosy lounge, small self-catering kitchen and clean, cheerful rooms. It's family-friendly with a set of bunks in the double rooms, and there's wheelchair access.

Relish@the Gallery (☎ 5144 5044; 68-70 Foster St, Gippsland Art Gallery; dishes $6-19; ☺ breakfast & lunch daily, dinner Wed-Sat) Relaxed but stylish design with great views of the old port of Sale make Relish a top choice. Breakfast is available all day. Foccacias are good, as are the Thai sea-food cakes with Malibu sweet chilli sauce ($14). There's disabled access, and baby change facilities are available.

Drinking & Entertainment

Phoenix (☎ 5144 4989; 118-24 Raymond St; ☺ 5pm-1am) With the rising of the Phoenix, Sale has a very cool new bar and lounge in the Art Deco AMP building – check out those Grecian pillars. This is one classy place to hang out. There's usually entertainment Thursday to Sunday.

Redd Catt (☎ 5143 1911; Raymond St) A velvet ceiling, bold paintings, a friendly vibe and music from Wednesday to Saturday make this place another good drinking option.

Wellington Entertainment Centre (☎ 5143 3200; www.wellington.vic.gov.au/entertainment; 100 Fos-ter St; tickets $25-45) Top-class state and national

---

THE AUTHOR'S CHOICE

Bis (☎ 5144 3388; 100 Foster St, Wellington En-tertainment Centre; breakfast & lunch $8-17, dinner mains $23-31; ☺ breakfast Sat & Sun, lunch daily, dinner Tue-Sat) This is one of Gippsland's best restaurants. The service is relaxed but atten-tive, the Italian-influenced food is superb. Try the grilled goats cheese with pear, balsamic and rocket entree ($13) for an exquisite blend of tastes, or the pistachio-stuffed chicken with pancetta, parmesan, polenta and jus ($25). The staff are friendly but you'll probably feel uncomfortable here with children.

---

theatre productions, comedy shows and music performances make brief appear-ances at the centre. There's disabled access and a baby change room.

Getting There & Away

Sale's train station is in Petit Dr on the western side of town. Trains run twice daily between Melbourne and Sale (one way $32.20).

NINETY MILE BEACH

Isolated Ninety Mile Beach is a long, narrow strip of beach backed by dunes, swamplands and lagoons, and stretches from McLough-lin's Beach to Marlo. Beaches are great for surf-fishing and walking, though they can be dangerous for swimming, except where patrolled at Seaspray, Woodside and Lakes Entrance.

From Seaspray to Lakes Entrance is the Gippsland Lakes Coastal Park with oodles of low-lying coastal shrubs, banksias and tea tree, and bursts of native wildflowers in spring. It's also home to plenty of kanga-roos and black wallabies, so take it easy when driving, especially at night.

The main access roads are from Yar-ram to Woodside Beach and from Sale to Seaspray, Golden Beach and Loch Sport. Come prepared, the townships along here are small and facilities are limited.

If you're keen, and interested in the chal-lenge of hiking the length of the Ninety Mile Beach, permission for remote camping can be obtained from **Parks Victoria** (☎ 13 19 63).

At the western end of Ninety Mile Beach, **Reeves Beach** has a camping ground with pit toilets. **Seaspray** has somehow escaped the rampant development along the coast and is packed full of old holiday shacks. There's a licensed general store with ATM facilities, a takeaway shop and the **Seaspray Caravan Park** (☎ 5146 4364; powered sites $16, cabins $48), which is sardine-like, but only a short stroll over the dune to the patrolled beach. **Ronnie's Tea Rooms** (☎ 5146 4420; 13 Trood St; coffee & cake $5.50; ☺ Sat-Sun & holidays) seems a touch surreal in Seaspray but adds a bit of class with a sunny tea room overlooking Ron-nie's immaculate garden. On the road be-tween Seaspray and Golden Beach, there are Parks Victoria camp sites, nestled in on the beach side and shaded by tea tree – they're hugely popular over summer. No camping fees or permits apply, it's first in,

TIME FOR A SEA CHANGE

What's going on? There's an extraordinary number of Australians who are chucking in their well-paid, high-stress jobs and 'downshifting'. The Australia Institute reports that over the past decade, 25% of Australians aged in their career prime between 30 and 59 years of age have decided to work less hours, many wanting to spend more time with their families and all wanting to 'live a more simple and sustainable lifestyle'. You'll likely meet an enormous number of them along the East Coast because that's where a lot of them have headed, wanting not just a simpler and sustainable lifestyle but also to live in beautiful place. You'll also hear the shift from city to coast called a 'sea change' a concept popularised by a TV programme of the same name set in a Victorian coastal town.

How do all these sea changers survive? Travellers will see a good number of them in the flourishing contemporary arts scene along the south East Coast. Ask at tourist information Centres for the 'Creative Gippsland' brochures, which highlight the area's thriving scene of artists making a living from their work. Many galleries are included in this chapter, but a couple of our favourites that are not covered are listed here.

Cowwarr Art Space (☎ 5148 9321; www.cowwarr.com; Main Rd, Cowwarr; ☼ 11am-5pm Fri-Mon or by appointment), rising out of dairy country in the tiny town of Cowwarr, is a magnificent heritage-listed butter factory that has been creatively converted into an exhibition space of changing art and is the studio of sea changer and leading Australian marble sculptor Clive Murray-White, who gave up work at a university to pursue his art, which is now exhibited at the National Gallery of Victoria. Detour off the highway at Traralgon and head towards Maffra.

Gallery owner Sharon is a local but she exhibits the work of many a downshifter at her gallery **Green Gates Gallery** (☎ 5156 8788, Princes Hwy, Nicholson; ☼ 10.30am-4pm Thu-Mon, public & school holidays), in an historical former church featuring ceramic, art, sculpture and wood and serves a good espresso. The gallery is on the highway in the small town of Nicholson, 10 minutes east of Bairnsdale.

first served. Some sites have barbecues and pit toilets, but there's no water or firewood. Dogs are permitted at camp sites 1–6 at Golden Beach.

Kangaroos graze on front lawns (really) at **Loch Sport**, a small sprawling town without a centre surrounded by lake, ocean and bush, with some good swimming areas for children. The bright and friendly **Marina Hotel** (☎ 5146 0666; mains $15-23.50 ☼ lunch & dinner) is only metres from the lake, does great sunset views and decent Tuscan-style seafood. A Loch Sport real estate agent has more than 30 **holiday houses** (☎ 5146 0411; www.garypowers realestate.com; Lot 217, Lake St; houses per night $85-250), from the mundane to the classy, available for nightly or weekly rental.

90 Mile Beach Holiday Retreat (☎ 5146 0320, www .90milebeachholidayretreat.com; Track 10; unpowered/powered sites $22/24, caravans $60, lodge & cottage d $100), is on a huge chunk of land with 2.4km of beach frontage, and is separated from the rest of the world by 7km of dirt track off Loch Sport-Seaspray Rd. There are plenty of grassy areas for camping, the two ex–Sydney Olympic 2000 lodges are ultra-

stylish and the self-contained cottage is like being at your granny's but only a short toddle to the beach.

Lakes National Park

A spit of land surrounded by lakes and ocean, Lakes National Park covers 2400 hectares of coastal bushland. It's a quiet little spot to set up camp, except over summer. You can reach it by road from adjoining Loch Sport or by boat from Paynesville (5km).

Banksia and eucalypt woodland abound with areas of low-lying heath land and some swampy salt-marsh scrub. In spring the park is carpeted with native wildflowers and has one of Australia's best displays of native orchids. You're likely to spot kangaroos, as well as wallabies, possums, emus and possibly koalas. There's plenty of bird life, with more than 190 species sighted including the rare white bellied sea eagle and the endangered little tern.

There is a **Parks Victoria rangers' office** (☎ 5146 0278) at the park entrance near Loch Sport; opening hours vary. A loop road provides good car access, and there are well-marked

walking trails, including some short walks, and several picnic areas (BYO water). **Point Wilson**, at the eastern tip of the mainland section of the park (20-minute drive) is the best picnic area and a popular gathering spot for kangaroos (don't even think about feeding them!). The only camping is at **Emu Bight** (sites up to 6 people $14), which has pit toilets and fireplaces; BYO water. Sites can be booked and paid for through the park office.

STRATFORD
☎ 03 / pop 1330

Stratford is a pretty little blip on the Princes Hwy, a 15-minute drive from Sale, and has retained its authenticity and appeal without going tourist-kitsch. There's a vibrant arts community here, with the **Eye 2 Eye Theatre Company** (☎ 5145 7088; Tyers St; ☿ Fri & Sat) presenting regular high-calibre productions and the contemporary **Red River Designs Gallery** (☎ /fax 5145 6769; Tyers St; ☿ 10am-4.30pm Wed-Fri & Sun) both on Tyers St (Princes Hwy). The **Shakespeare on the River Festival** is held here annually in April/May.

At **Overland Gold Adventures** (☎ /fax 5145 6701; Tyers St; day trip per person incl lunch $100) Graham, a friendly third-generation gold miner, operates 4WD tours exploring the gold-mining areas of Gippsland, tailor-made to suit the needs of the group. Visit old mines and prospect for gold. Overnight trips in the Dargo area are also possible.

Sleeping & Eating
Stratford Motel (☎ 5145 6500; stratfordmotel@ozemail .com.au; 26 Tyers St; s/d/f $55/60/90, spa r $100; ☒) This friendly motel has some of the most home-like motel rooms around with well-chosen fluffed up doonas. The spa room is spacious and air-conditioned.

Stratford Top Tourist Park (☎ 5145 6588; www .toptouristparks.com.au/vic/sttp.html; McMillan St; tent/powered sites $15/17, dm from $18, cabins with en suite from $53) On the banks of the Avon, this leafy park has a bunk room for backpackers with a separate kitchen as well as standard sites and cabins.

Wa-de-Lock (☎ 5145 7050; 76 Tyers St; dishes $3-11.50; ☿ breakfast & lunch Sat-Thu) In this smart café you can try local produce such as smoked trout and Gippsland cheese, and drink wine by the glass. The breads in the gourmet pizzas, foccacias and sandwiches are all made on site.

Stratford Bakehouse (☎ 5145 6003; 35 Tyers St; items $2-4.50) Justifiably popular for its pies and cakes and is a nice no-frills spot for a quick bite or espresso.

BAIRNSDALE
☎ 03 / pop 10,670

On the banks of the Mitchell River, Bairnsdale is East Gippsland's commercial hub with a bustling main street, a sprinkling of attractions and the last stop for a 24-hour petrol station. The shopping strip along the highway demands your attention but it's worth going beyond the main drag for an absorbing insight into Aboriginal history, gourmet cafés and the quite astonishing contrast to the hubbub of the main street that is the Macleod Morass wetlands.

Information
Bairnsdale Visitor Information Centre (☎ 5152 3444, 1800 637 060; www.egipps.vic.gov.au; 240 Main St)
East Gippsland Shire Library (☎ 5152 4225; Service St) Free Internet access is available.
Parks Victoria (☎ 5152 0600; 73 Calvert St)

Sights & Activities
The **Krowathunkoolong Keeping Place** (☎ 5152 1891; 37-53 Dalmahoy St; adult/child $3.50/2.50; ☿ 9am-5pm Mon-Fri) is a Koorie cultural exhibition space that explores Gunai (or Kurnai) life before and after white settlement. The Aborigines of Gippsland, collectively known as the Gunai (Kurnai), are estimated to have inhabited Gippsland for more than 65,000 years. Descended from their Dreamtime ancestors, Borun the Pelican and his relative Tuk the Musk Duck, the five Kurnai clans lived together in relative harmony. The exhibition covers life at Lake Tyers Mission, east of Lakes Entrance, which is now a trust privately owned by Aboriginal shareholders. Items such as an impressive 2.5m bark canoe and a trumpet-like eel-and-fish basket reveal the Kurnai's skill in fishing the waterways of the area. The unmitigated massacres of the Kurnai during 1839–49 are also detailed. The Keeping Place is behind the train station.

The grand red-brick **St Mary's Catholic Church**, beside the visitor information centre, is notable for its opulent ceiling murals of rosy-cheeked cherubs. After some serious neck-craning, think of Italian-Australian Frank Floreani who painted the murals over four years in the 1930s.

On the edge of town (signposted from the highway at Forge Creek Rd) the **MacLeod Morass Boardwalk** is a stunning internationally recognised wetland reserve with walking tracks and bird hides.

East Gippsland Art Gallery (☎ 5153 1988; 222 Nicholson St; ⊗ 10am-4pm Tue-Fri, 10am-2pm Sat) is a bright, open space that has regular exhibitions, mostly the work of East Gippsland artists.

Howitt Park is a popular playground stop on the highway and also the starting point for the popular bike and walking track, the **East Gippsland Rail Trail** leading northeast to Bruthen, 30km away. A new extension, the **Discovery Trail**, extends the trail through state forest to Lakes Entrance.

A few kilometres east of town is **Bairnsdale Archery, Mini Golf & Games Park** (☎ 5156 8655; www.bairnsdalefunpark.com.au; 459 Princes Hwy) boasting Australia's only bungee trampoline.

About 4km northeast of the town of Nicholson and signposted from the highway, **Nicholson River Winery** (☎ 5156 8241; 57 Liddells Rd, Nicholson; ⊗ 10am-4pm), best known for its award-winning whites, has tastings in a garden overlooking the river ($2 refundable with purchase).

Sleeping & Eating

There are numerous motel options on the highway (Main St).

Riversleigh Country Hotel (☎ 5152 6966; fax 5152 4413; 1 Nicholson St; s/d incl breakfast from $114/159; dinner mains $21-25, lunch $12-19; ⊗ lunch Thu-Fri, dinner Mon-Sat; ⊠) This Victorian-era boutique hotel has elegant rooms with crisp linen, brass beds and antique furnishings that transport you back in the most comfortable way possible to a bygone era. Breakfast is served in the sunny conservatory. There's a formal restaurant here as well, maximising the use of local ingredients in inventive modern cuisine. Disabled facilities are available.

Mitchell Gardens Holiday Park (☎ 5152 4654; www.gippsland.com/web/MGHP; unpowered/powered sites $17/20, cabins from $44) East of the town centre on the banks of the Mitchell River, this is a friendly park with shade for cabins and full sun for tents. The holiday units ($74), actually deluxe cabins, have river views.

Larrikin's Cafe Deli (☎ 5153 1421; 2 Wood St; breakfast $6-14, meals $9-16; ⊗ breakfast & lunch Mon-Sat) This smart little café, in converted 1880s stables, has stunning farmland views and is a local favourite. The food options are typical city café–fare with salads, foccacias, bagels and gourmet offerings, all available with wine by the glass or a good coffee.

Drinking

The casual G Bar has a sunny beer garden and live music from Thursday to Saturday nights.

Getting There & Away

Bairnsdale's **V/Line** (☎ 13 61 96; www.vlinepassenger.com.au) station is on McLeod St, one block south of the town centre. There are two daily train services between Melbourne and Bairnsdale (one way $41). From Bairnsdale, **V/Line buses** (☎ 5152 1711) operate daily to Lakes Entrance ($8.70) and Orbost ($15.50).

EAGLE POINT

☎ 03 / pop 394

Eagle Point is humbly home to the natural wonder of the 8km-long **Mitchell River Silt Jetties**, the second longest silt jetties in the world (after the Mississippi). There's an information board explaining how they're created and you can drive out onto them. **Eagle Point Lookout**, just before the jetties, provides extensive views across the jetty, Lake King and Lake Victoria. The area is a prime fishing, bird-watching and walking spot and has the six-hectare **Eagle Point Reserve**, which is great bushland for walks and spotting wildlife.

Eagle Point Caravan Park (☎ /fax 5156 6232; Bay Rd; unpowered/powered sites $13/17, cabins from $58; ⊠) is a friendly park that has camp sites and deluxe cabins by the lake and a fully equipped camp kitchen

PAYNESVILLE & RAYMOND ISLAND

On the edge of Lake Victoria, Paynesville, a relaxed little town that proudly claims the title of boating capital of Victoria. It also hosts a popular **jazz festival** each February. The most reliable ATM is at the petrol station on the way into town. You can take a **boat cruise** (☎ 0417 137 590; Fisherman's Wharf jetty; adult/child cruise $25/12.50, 3hr trip $15/7.50; ⊗ trips Wed, Sat & Sun or by arrangement) around Paynesville's canals or for a three-hour trip on the lake to Ocean Grange on Ninety Mile Beach.

Raymond Island, a skip away across McMillan Strait, is famous for its large colony of koalas, which were relocated from Phillip Island in the 1950s. The koalas have become so rampant and the eucalypts they feed on so denuded that many of the koalas have been relocated elsewhere but you should still be able to spot some. **Clydesdale Carriage Tours** (☎ 0413 028 084; Ferry Park; adult/child $8.50/5; ♡ tours 10.30am-3pm Sat & Sun, public & school holidays) offers a Koala-spotting drive by horse and cart.

The small island has large areas of bush, with some good **walking tracks**.

Sleeping & Eating

Lake Gallery B&B (☎ 5156 0448; www.lakegallerybed andbreakfast.com; 2A Backwater Ct; r incl breakfast $205; ♡ gallery noon-5pm Thu-Sun) This stylish B&B is perched on the water's edge and each room has its own original art work, king-sized bed and en suite spa, as well as dreamy views and private balconies. The B&B also has a small art gallery.

Gippsland Lakes Escapes (☎ 5156 0432; www .gippslandlakesescapes.com.au; The Esplanade; d per 2 nights from $280) This business offers a booking service for midrange and classy holiday homes in Paynesville, Raymond Island and beyond.

Paynesville Hotel (☎ 5156 6442; 75 The Esplanade; s/d with en suite $55/70) The rooms will give you '70s flashbacks but two have brilliant views overlooking the water; there's one room suitable for families.

Fisherman's Wharf Pavilion (☎ 5156 0366; 70 The Esplanade; mains $22; ♡ breakfast, lunch & dinner Wed-Sun) This light-filled restaurant is as close to the water as you get. Try the free-range eggs with spinach, mushroom and Gippsland Cheddar ($14.50) for breakfast or the grilled Japanese spiced flathead tails ($19.50) for dinner and dine contentedly knowing that you're eating non–genetically modified, fresh, local produce. It serves the best coffee in town and is food allergy– and vegan friendly, though service varies.

Paynesville Seafoods (☎ 5156 6080; 67A The Esplanade, ♡ lunch & dinner) On a fine day, it's hard to beat sitting on the foreshore with these ultra-fresh fish and chips.

Getting There & Away

A car and passenger ferry runs a constant shuttle service between Paynesville and Raymond Island (return per car $7, pedestrians free) from 8am to 10.30pm or longer.

Paynesville Bus Lines (☎ 0418-516 405) runs daily (except Sunday) services between Bairnsdale train station and Paynesville, and will drop off at Eagle Point Caravan Park (one way $6.10).

METUNG

☎ 03 / pop 520

On the shores of the Gippsland Lakes, Metung is a small, unhurried village, and its shoreline is dotted with jetties and small wooden craft. The town is perched on a narrow spit of land and surrounded by the waters of Lake King to the west and Bancroft Bay to the east. Opposite Metung Yacht Club on the edge of Bancroft Bay is **Legend Rock**, a sacred Aboriginal site. According to Aboriginal oral histories, the rock represents a hunter who was turned to stone for not sharing the food he had caught. There were originally three rocks; the other two were destroyed during road-construction work, and the remaining one was saved when an injunction was issued, under community pressure. The road into town shaves past the rock.

Metung is an upmarket base for all sorts of water-based activities – sailing, cruising and fishing. Diagonally opposite the post office **Metung Village Store** (☎ 5156 2201; www .metung.com; Metung Rd) is the informal visitor information office, and also sells petrol and bait. There's an ATM at the pub. **Metung Yacht Club** (☎ 5156 2315) welcomes visiting yachties and non-members. It has a bar with great views open from Wednesday to Sunday, and serves dinners from Thursday to Saturday.

Sights & Activities

Pelicans crash land in the lake outside the Metung Hotel at noon each day for a feed of fish. For a dip, head to the safe **swimming beach** by Lake King Jetty.

The historic ketch **Spray** (☎ 0428 516 055; adult/child/family $32/10/74) runs 4½-hour picnic cruises (BYO lunch) to various lake destinations; cruises depart at 11am from the jetty at the Metung Hotel. Book tickets at Metung Village Store.

Boats and yachts for cruising, fishing and sailing on the Gippsland Lakes are available from **Riviera Nautic** (☎ 5156 2243; www.riviera nautic.com.au; 185 Metung Rd; motor boat per day $110, 4-berth yacht per week from $1945). The lake floor is sand and mud, so it's ideal for boating – there are no reefs, rocks or sharks!

If the pace is too slow, there are thrillseeking opportunities with **Parasailing Victoria** (☎ 5155 3032; single/tandem rides per person $70/60), which has rides over the lakes.

Sleeping

There's little in the way of budget accommodation here. Holiday homes and other accommodation are available through **Metung Accommodation** (Slipway Villas; ☎ 5156 2861; www.metungaccommodation.com).

Anchorage B&B (☎ /fax 5156 2569; www.beautiful accommodation.com/anchorage.html; 11 The Anchorage; d $130) On Chinaman's Creek, the Anchorage is built around views, views, views, and the rooms match up in quality. It's a cosy spot in winter, especially the sunny glasshouse-like breakfast room and Trish cooks up a delicious full breakfast.

McMillans of Metung (☎ 5156 2283; www.mc millansofmetung.com.au; 155 Metung Rd; d from $130; ✖ ⬢) This lake-side resort has won stacks of tourism awards for its complex of country-style cottages, set in three hectares of manicured gardens. Massages, tennis, a games room, and a lagoon with resident bird life are also on offer here. There's a two-night minimum and rates increase by 10% to 50% in peak periods.

Moorings At Metung (☎ 5156 2750; www.themoor ings.com.au; d/f from $125/170; ✖ ⬢) Overlooking Bancroft Bay, this large, contemporary apartment complex has rooms and units all with water views. It's a luxuriously comfortable option with modern rooms, a tennis court and spa, and promises to pander to your every whim. Minimum stays apply during Christmas and Easter school holidays when prices increase by about 20%.

Arendell Holiday Units (☎ /fax 5156 2507; 30 Mairburn Rd; d/f $66/77; ⬢) The units are very '70s and don't have water views but they're comfortable timber cottages, a few hundred metres from the beach and a couple of kilometres from the town centre. They are the cheapest accommodation option in Metung, although prices double during Christmas school holidays.

Eating

Marillee (☎ 5156 2121; 50 Metung Rd; mains $16-46; ✖ breakfast, lunch & dinner Wed-Mon) If you get in early or crane your neck you'll get a water view at this restaurant, offering food that is elegantly presented and usually delicious.

It's the best restaurant in town. Seafood is the theme; the Atlantic salmon in white wine and caper sauce ($22) is a good choice. Children get their own menu. On Thursday and Friday nights, hang out at the bar or the lounge for the half-price cocktails.

Metung Hotel (☎ 5156 2206; Kurnai Ave; meals $15.50-26; ✖ lunch & dinner) Perched on the edge of the lake, with an outdoor deck and garden area, Metung Hotel offers slightly upmarket pub food; the scallops and calamari in beer batter with lemon aïoli dipping sauce ($19) are worth trying. The children's meals ($4.50) are the cheapest in Gippsland.

Gourmet Appetite (☎ 5156 2877; Shop 3, 51 Metung Rd; dishes $3-12; ✖ breakfast & lunch Tue-Sun) Some of Metung's best food comes out of this tiny café serving up gourmet offerings made from local produce. Don't miss Jan's spinach pie ($7).

Getting There & Away

V/Line (☎ 13 61 96; www.vlinepassenger.com.au) services from Melbourne can drop people off in Swan Reach (one way $44), from where you can call **Tambo Taxis** (☎ 5156 2222) for the 5km trip to Metung ($18).

AROUND METUNG

Tricia Allen Glass (☎ 5156 3211; 105 Jetty Rd, Nungurner; ✖ glassblowing 11am-4pm Sun Nov-Apr) is the studio of this renowned Australian glass blower, a few kilometres from Metung.

Ten kilometres east of Metung, the homestead at **Nyerimilang Park** (☎ 5156 3253; Metung-Kalimna West Rd; adult $4; ✖ 9am-4pm) was originally built in 1892 as a gentleman's holiday retreat. Managed by Parks Victoria and staffed by volunteers, the property has an East Gippsland Garden, showcasing varieties of indigenous vegetation, and a picnic area. There are easy **walking tracks** and some exceptional views of Fraser Island and Boole Poole Peninsula.

LAKES ENTRANCE

☎ 03 / pop 5500

Lakes Entrance is a brash seaside resort that's home to one of Australia's largest fishing fleets. The town sprawls along The Esplanade (Princes Hwy) with way too many crass developments – in stark contrast to the other side of the highway where the gentle waters of Cunninghame Arm are backed by sand dunes and small fishing boats. Just be-

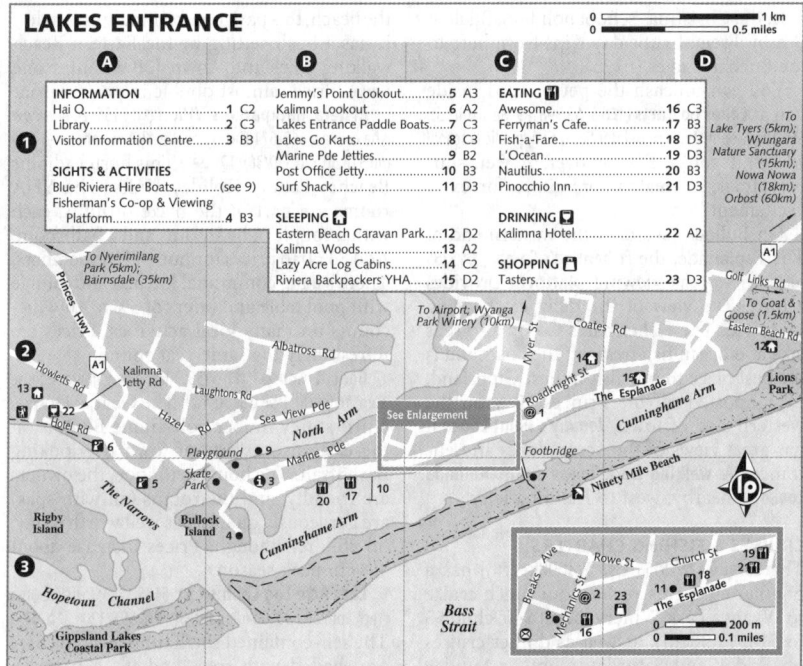

LAKES ENTRANCE

INFORMATION	
Hai Q................................**1** C2
Library...............................**2** C3
Visitor Information Centre........**3** B3

SIGHTS & ACTIVITIES	
Blue Riviera Hire Boats.............(see 9)
Fisherman's Co-op & Viewing
Platform..........................**4** B3

Jemmy's Point Lookout............**5** A3
Kalimna Lookout....................**6** A2
Lakes Entrance Paddle Boats....**7** C3
Lakes Go Karts.....................**8** C3
Marine Pde Jetties................**9** B2
Post Office Jetty..................**10** B3
Surf Shack.........................**11** D3

SLEEPING	
Eastern Beach Caravan Park.....**12** D2
Kalimna Woods.....................**13** A2
Lazy Acre Log Cabins............**14** C2
Riviera Backpackers YHA.........**15** D2

EATING	
Awesome............................**16** C3
Ferryman's Cafe....................**17** B3
Fish-a-Fare........................**18** D3
L'Ocean............................**19** D3
Nautilus............................**20** B3
Pinocchio Inn......................**21** D3

DRINKING	
Kalimna Hotel......................**22** A2

SHOPPING	
Tasters.............................**23** D3

To
Lake Tyers (5km);
Wyungara
Nature Sanctuary
(15km);
Nowa Nowa
(18km);
Orbost (60km)

To Nyerimilang
Park (5km);
Bairnsdale (35km)

To Airport; Wyanga
Park Winery (10km)

To Goat &
Goose (1.5km)

**Bass
Strait**

**Gippsland Lakes
Coastal Park**

yond them is a magnificent stretch of ocean beach. Lakes, as the locals call it, is primed to cater for almost every water-related whim you may have.

Information

Hai Q (☎ 5155 4247; cnr Myer St & The Esplanade; per hr $8) Internet access is available. A computer business with a quirky gift shop.

Lakes Entrance Visitor Information Centre (☎ 5155 1966, 1800 637 060; www.lakesandwilderness .com.au; Princes Hwy) Eternally busy.

Library (☎ 5153 9500; 18 Mechanics St) Free Internet access.

Sights & Activities

A footbridge crosses the Cunninghame Arm inlet from the centre of town to the ocean and the magnificent **Ninety Mile Beach**. From there, you can walk along a 2.3km **walking track** to the 'entrance' to the lakes; the current entrance is actually artificial, the original was near the footbridge. Return via the **Eastern Beach Walking Track**. There is a town map with the track marked, available from the visitor information centre.

Surfing lessons are offered at the **Surf Shack** (☎ /fax 5155 4933; 507 The Esplanade; 2hr lesson $40). Qualified instructors lead the surf lessons at Lake Tyers Beach and surf gear is provided.

If you want to explore the lakes independently, three motorboat hire companies along Marine Parade offer boats at the same price, including **Blue Riviera Hire Boats** (☎ 5155 3113; Marine Pde jetties; 1/4hr hire $30/80). Ask about its off-peak season specials.

There's a vast array of watery activities offered by **Lakes Entrance Paddle Boats** (☎ 0419 552 753; paddleboats/canoes per 30min $15/10, catamarans per hr $40, body boards per hr $5; ☯ Nov-Apr). It's located at the ocean end of the footbridge.

Wildlife at Night (☎ 5156 5863; Wyungara Nature Sanctuary; adult/child/family $22/13/55) is a great chance to get up close to Australian wildlife. Armed with a torch, you can spot gliders, possums, koalas, wallabies, wombats and owls in the wild while comfortingly in the company of an experienced naturalist at the Wyungara Nature Sanctuary, 15km from town.

In the Christmas school holidays, Buchan Bus 'n' Freight runs day trips from here to the Buchan Caves (p125).

You can unleash the petrol head inside you at **Lakes Go Karts** (☎ 5155 3981; 9 Mechanics St; ✆ 10am-6pm Mon-Fri, to later Sat & Sun, public & school holidays) if you're five or over. A wet, slippery track is created sometimes for extra excitement.

On Bullock Island, at the western end of The Esplanade, the **Fisherman's Co-op** (☎ 5155 1688; ✆ 9am-5pm) viewing platform provides a bird's-eye view of the daily catch being unloaded. The Fisherman's Co-op also sells lake and ocean fish fresh off the boats and is the best place to buy fish in East Gippsland.

Signposted off the Princes Hwy on the western side of town, **Jemmy's Point Lookout** has great views of the ocean, lakes and entrance. A **walking track** leads from **Kalimna Lookout**, nearby, west to Kalimna Jetty.

CRUISES & FISHING CHARTERS

The **Corque** (☎ 5155 1508; Post Office Jetty) has a popular all-inclusive 4½-hour lunch cruise to Wyanga Park Winery (adult $40, child $5 to $18, 11.30am), as well as dinner cruises on Friday and Saturday nights, a Sunday brunch trip (except in winter) and a lunch trip to Metung on Thursdays.

Mulloway Fishing Charters (☎ 5155 3304, 0421 943 154; 3hr trip per adult $40), at the jetty opposite 66 Marine Pde, has regular fishing cruises in the lake. In a novel pricing system, children are charged by their age, if they're eight years old, its $8. Rods, tackle, bait and morning or afternoon tea are provided.

Peels Tourist & Ferry Services (☎ 5155 1246; Post Office Jetty; adult/child $25.30/12.65) has several daily two-hour cruises exploring Reeves Channel, Bancroft Bay and Lake King, and a daily cruise also runs to Metung (including lunch $38.50, 11am, four hours).

Sleeping

Kalimna Woods (☎ 5155 1957; www.kalimnawoods.com.au; Kalimna Jetty Rd; d $95-140; ✖) Rainforest, gardens, possums, birds, wood fires and spas – this is a very comfortable retreat from the hustle and bustle of Lakes Entrance town centre 2km away. The log cottages, which have quality timber furnishings and fluffy towels, are spacious and very comfortable.

Eastern Beach Caravan Park (☎ 5155 1581; Eastern Beach Rd; unpowered/powered sites $15/18) Close to

the beach, this park is refreshingly old-style – it has a bush setting by the Eastern Beach walking track into town (30 minutes one way). Prices almost double in peak season.

Riviera Backpackers YHA (☎ 5155 2444; www.yha.com.au; 660-671 The Esplanade; YHA members 4-6-bed dm $18.50, s/d $30/38; ☐ ☒) This hostel adjoins Beaches Family Holiday Units. The YHA rooms are part of the maze of units, each with a couple of bedrooms and a bathroom. Add $3.50 to prices for non–YHA members. There's a big communal kitchen and lounge with pool table and offers of 5% to 10% discounts on many local activities. Prices are refreshingly the same year round.

Goat & Goose (☎ 5155 3079; www.goatandgoose.com; 16 Gay St; B&B d $130-160) The Goat & Goose, a two-storey timber pole-frame B&B, is on the eastern outskirts of town overlooking Bass Strait. The house is unique, the owners are friendly, and the rooms (all with spas) are gorgeously quaint. It's well worth a stay, no children though. Prices increase about 40% in peak season.

Lazy Acre Log Cabins (☎ 5155 1323; lazyacre@net-tech.com.au; 35 Roadknight St; d/f $95/120; ✖ ☒) The self-contained small timber cabins here are shaded with trees and it's a friendly, relaxed place to stay. There's bicycle hire and a babysitting service. Disabled access is available. Prices increase by 50% in peak season.

Eating & Drinking

Nautilus (☎ 5155 1400; mains $23-47; ✆ dinner Tue-Sat) *Nautilus*, a glass-sided barge, moored on the water offers fine food and an exclusively Gippsland wine list. Unsurprisingly, seafood is the feature act on the menu, which includes Eden blue mussels in broth and six variations on the oyster theme.

Pinocchio Inn (☎ 5155 2565; 569 The Esplanade; dishes $13-25; ✆ lunch & dinner) This friendly little home-style Italian eatery is a long-time local favourite offering traditional pizza, pasta and seafood dishes. Children will love the collection of Pinocchio dolls and puppets.

Ferryman's Cafe (☎ 5155 3000; The Esplanade; mains $8-17; ✆ lunch & dinner daily, breakfast Sat & Sun) The latest waterside dining option in Lakes is in a converted Raymond Island ferry on the western side of the clock tower. It's not as classy as the *Nautilus* but it offers a good selection of seafood dishes including bouillabaisse ($21).

There's a few excellent fish-and-chip shops in Lakes including the traditional **Awesome** (☎ 5155 3166; 337 The Esplanade), the bright and efficient **Fish-a-Fare** (☎ 5155 4535; 509 The Esplanade) and the award-winning **L'Ocean** (☎ 5155 2253; 19 Myer St) catering for the gluten-free crowds.

Kalimna Hotel (☎ 5155 1202) For a drink with views, you can't beat this hotel, off the highway on the Melbourne side of Lakes Entrance.

Shopping

Tasters (☎ 5155 3955; 357 The Esplanade; ☺ Wed-Sun) This new business is the place to stock up on delicious gourmet dips, deli produce and discounted wine.

Getting There & Away

There are daily **V/Line** (☎ 13 61 96; www.vline passenger.com.au) services between Lakes Entrance and Bairnsdale, connecting with trains to/from Melbourne (Melbourne to Lakes Entrance one way $49.60). V/Line and **Premier** (☎ 13 34 10; www.premierms.com .au) have daily buses continuing along the Princes Hwy into NSW, and V/Line also has a bus service to Lake Tyers ($2.50).

LAKE TYERS

☎ 03 / pop 517

This small and peaceful settlement is popular with surfers and there are good **surf breaks** at Red Bluff.

On bush land with beach frontage the **Lakes Beachfront Holiday Retreat** (☎ 5156 5582; www.holidayretreats.com.au; 430 Lake Tyers Beach Rd; unpowered/powered sites $20/22, cabins $55-90, beach cottage $120; ☒) is a brilliant camp park with space for tents in shady bush sites. It has a new rock swimming pool and is a minute's walk from the ocean. Prices go up 50% to 100% in peak season.

Lake Tyers Beach House (☎ 5156 5995; www .laketyersbeachhouse.com.au; 3 Larkins Pl; d $150) is an artistically inspired four-bedroom cliff-top house with stunning ocean views and a hot pink retro-chic look. There's a yoga studio next door where visitors can join in a class or have private tuition.

Airdrie (☎ 5156 5640; 19 Cross St; d from $140) is a comfortable, modern B&B that has rooms with garden or lake views.

Waterwheel Tavern (☎ 5156 5530; 557 Lake Tyers Beach Rd; mains $18.50-35) has an inspired bistro menu with offerings such as its famous Big

Arse Seafood Platter ($35 or $60 for two) and marinated kangaroo fillets with juniper berries and tomato *confit* ($19.50). This is not your average pub bistro – there's quality food, stylish presentation and the accompanying views over the lake are fantastic.

V/Line (☎ 13 61 96; www.vlinepassenger.com.au) buses go to Lake Tyers passing via Lakes Entrance ($4).

NOWA NOWA

Tiny Nowa Nowa, on the north arm of Lake Tyers, hosts the stirring **Nowa Nowa Nudes** art exhibition annually in November.

Mingling Waters (☎ 5155 7247; Princes Hwy; un-powered/powered sites $15/18, 22-bed dm $20, cottages d $60) is a gem not to be missed. There's a great little café/gallery here with eclectic furnishings and rustic farm-style accommodation by the lakeside with amazing wooden furnishings. Children will love the swing.

A few kilometres east of Nowa Nowa, **Yelens Studio Gallery** (☎ 5155 7277; Nelsons Rd), down a dirt road and overlooking Lake Tyers, is home to painter Gary Yelen and is worth a visit to see his vibrant oil paintings, sensuous sculpture, and to have an espresso stop. It's open most days; call to check.

EAST GIPPSLAND

This section of Gippsland contains some of the most remote and spectacular national parks in the state. Unlike the rest of Victoria, much of this region has never been cleared for agriculture. So, instead of the vast and barren sheep pastures that characterise the Western District on the opposite side of the state, or the denuded hills of the Strzeleckis, which were once rich with towering mountain ash and giant tree ferns, this area is a wonderland of dense forests ranging from the coastal wilderness areas of Croajingolong to the lush rainforests of the Errinundra Plateau.

The Princes Hwy (A1) carves its way through the centre of the region. Happily, the magnificent coastal areas of Cape Conran, Mallacoota and Croajingolong are all uncrowded, unspoiled and undeveloped.

Orbost is the only sizeable town and has a useful visitor information office. There are excellent Parks Victoria visitor information centres at Cann River and Mallacoota.

www.lonelyplanet.com

EAST GIPPSLAND

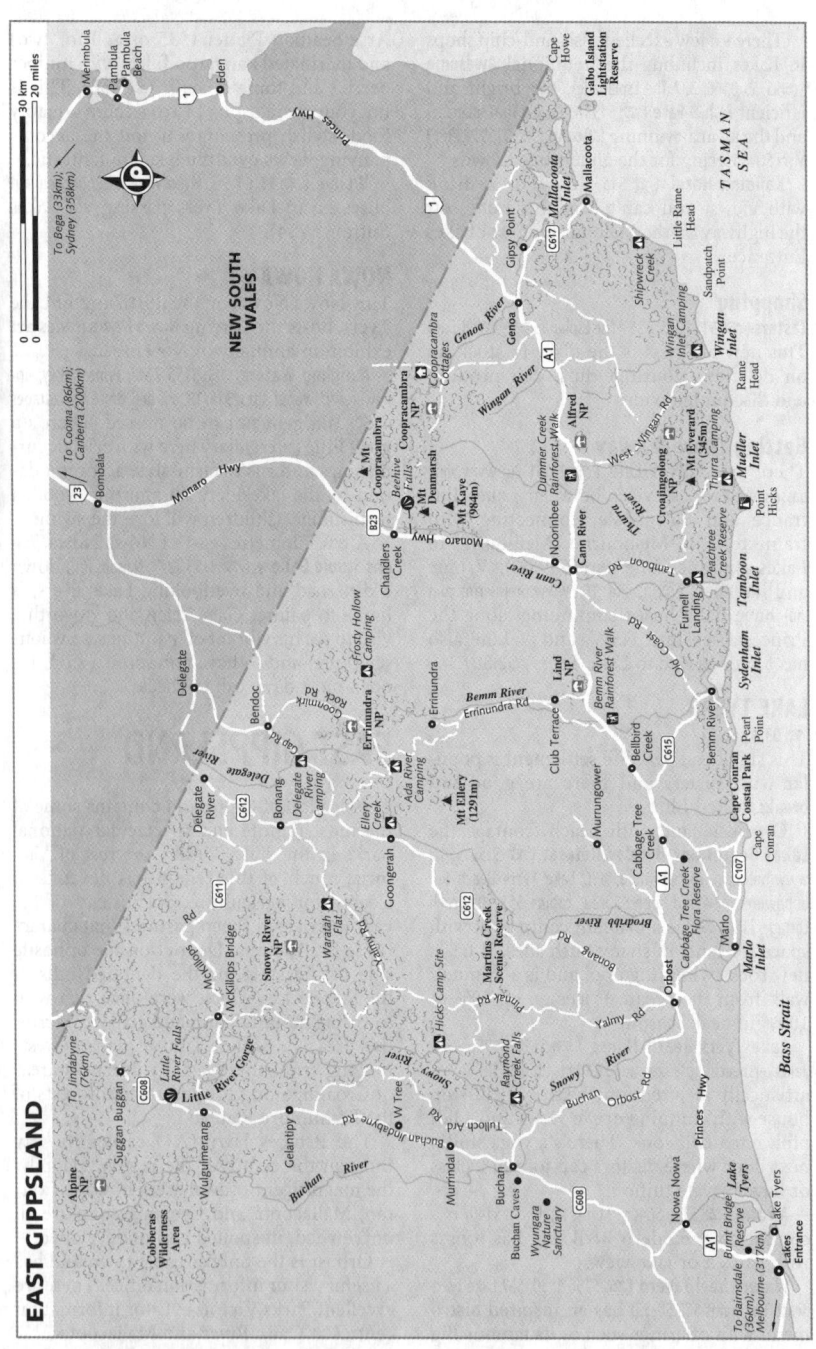

OFF THE BEATEN TRACK

You can't explore most of the Snowy River or Errinundra National Parks with a 2WD and there are only a few companies providing organised trips into this beautiful wilderness area.

Snowy River Expeditions (☎ 5155 9353; Karoonda Park, Gelantipy) runs adventure tours, including one-, two- or four-day rafting trips on the Snowy costing $130 per day; half-day or full-day abseiling or caving trips are also available. Costs include transport, meals and camping gear.

Buchan Bus 'n' Freight (☎ 5155 0356; buchanbusnfreight@hotmail.com; 4-day tour $540) offers an East Gippsland Wilderness Tour visiting Buchan Caves as well as Snowy River and Errinundra National Parks, camping and staying at Ontos (see below). The tour starts at Bairnsdale or Lakes Entrance and operates between November and April.

Echidna Walkabout (☎ 9646 8249; www.echidnawalkabout.com.au; 4 days incl air transfer $1325, 5 days incl bus transfer $1190) has upmarket treks starting from Melbourne and focusing on national parks and wildlife in East Gippsland. All you need to carry is a day pack – backpacks are delivered to the night's luxury camping spot or B&B.

BUCHAN

☎ 03 / pop 400

Buchan, a beautiful town in the foothills of the Snowy Mountains, is chiefly known for its spectacular limestone cave system. Less attention is given to its black marble, which was used in notable public buildings, such as the Shrine of Remembrance in Melbourne.

Buchan Valley Roadhouse sells petrol and the general store/post office has Eftpos and local tourist information.

Sights & Activities

Small pieces of black marble are on display at **Buchan Black Marble Hut** (☎ 5155 9296; Main St).

Just over a kilometre from the tiny township is the **Buchan Caves Reserve**. Underground rivers cutting through limestone rock that formed about 300 to 400 million years ago carved the caves and caverns. The underground wonderland developed over time. The Royal and Fairy are the main caves, and are worth visiting. The reserve itself is also a pretty spot with shaded picnic areas, **walking tracks**, grazing kangaroos and a rock pool.

Parks Victoria (☎ 5162 1900), at Caves Reserve, runs regular guided caves tours (adult/child/family $12/6/30.50). The rangers also offer hard-hat guided tours to Federal Cave during the high season (the Federal is equally as impressive as Fairy or Royal, but has no artificial lighting).

Buchan Bus 'n' Freight (☎ 5155 0356) runs a day trip from Lakes Entrance (adult/child/family $50/30/110) to the Buchan Caves during the Christmas school holidays. The price includes admission to the caves and lunch at the Caves Hotel.

Sleeping & Eating

Natural Healing & Spiritual Centre (☎ 5155 0245; 2337 Gelantipy Rd, W Tree; s/d incl all meals $125/250) This is the place for a de-stress. Overlooking bush and mountains, you can stay in Carol and Hans' lovely timber home, be fed vegetarian meals, taken on bushwalks, and given kinesiology natural healing treatments in the adjoining centre – it's all part of the package.

Ontos (☎ 5155 0275; www.ontos.com.au; Gelantipy Rd, W Tree; cabins s/d $40/50, units s/d $50/80) People used to let out sighs when you mentioned Ontos, a health retreat that drew people back time and again until its main building was destroyed by fire. Ontos is rebuilding and has rustic wooden cabins with pot belly stoves, sleeping up to six, and some simple units. A full healthy breakfast including home-made bread is provided. A café using organic and local produce serving lunch and dinner should be open by the time you read this.

Buchan Caves Caravan Park (☎ 5162 1900; Buchan Caves Reserve; unpowered/powered sites $12/16, cabins $55; 🖭) This picturesque camping ground has a camp kitchen, open fireplaces and a couple of cabins.

Buchan Lodge Backpackers (☎ 5155 9421; www.buchanlodge.com; Saleyard Rd; 12-bed dm per person $20) A short walk from the caves and the town centre, and just by the river, this friendly, rough-and-ready, timber-lined building is great for lounging about and taking in the country views. Children under 14 only by arrangement. Rates include breakfast.

Caves Hotel (☎ 5155 9203; mains $13.50-18.50; 🍽 lunch Tue-Sun, dinner daily) A pretty timber pub that does a well-recommended steak ($16.50).

Getting There & Away

Buchan Bus 'n' Freight operates a service on Monday and Friday from Karoonda Park to Bairnsdale (one way/return $16/25) via W Tree, Buchan, Nowa Nowa, Lakes Entrance and Lake Tyers.

SNOWY RIVER NATIONAL PARK

This area is one of Victoria's most isolated and spectacular national parks, dominated by deep gorges carved through limestone and sandstone by the mighty Snowy River. The entire park is a smorgasbord of unspoiled and superb bush and mountain scenery. It covers more than 95,000 hectares and includes a huge diversity of vegetation, ranging from alpine woodlands and eucalypt forests to rainforests and even areas of mallee-type scrub.

The two main access roads to the park are the Buchan–Jindabyne Rd from Buchan and the Bonang Rd from Orbost. These roads are joined by MacKillops Rd (also known as Deddick River Rd), which runs across the northern border of the park from Bonang to just south of Wulgulmerang. Various access roads and scenic routes run into and alongside the park from these three main roads. The Deddick Trail, which runs through the middle of the park, is only suitable for 4WDs.

Along MacKillops Rd you'll come across MacKillops Bridge, which crosses the Snowy River, a spectacular and beautiful area. Near the bridge are the park's main camp sites (sites for up to 5 people $12.50) toilets and fireplaces, as well as some sandy river beaches and swimming spots. There are several good short walks around here, and the 15km Silver Mine Walking Track starts at the eastern end of the bridge. The views from the lookouts over Little River Falls and Little River Gorge, the deepest in Victoria, signposted about 20km to the west of MacKillops Bridge, are spectacular.

There are various other free bush camping areas and picnic grounds in the park. Walking and canoeing are the most popular activities, but you need to be well prepared for both as conditions can be harsh and subject to sudden change. The classic canoe or raft trip down the Snowy River from MacKillops Bridge to a pull-out point near Buchan takes at least four days and offers superb scenery: rugged gorges, raging rapids, tranquil sections and excellent camping spots on broad sand bars.

Good scenic drives in and around the park include MacKillops Rd, Rising Sun Rd from Bonang, Tullock Ard Rd from just south of Gelantipy, and Yalmy Rd, which is the main access road to the southern and central areas and places like Waratah Flat, Hicks Camp Site and Raymond Creek Falls. These roads are unsealed and usually closed during winter.

For information about camping, road conditions and other details contact the park offices (Bairnsdale ☎ 03-5152 0600; Buchan ☎ 03-5162 1900; Deddick ☎ 02-6458 0290) at Deddick, Buchan or Bairnsdale.

Sleeping

Karoonda Park (☎ 5155 0220; Gelantipy Rd; 7-12 bed dm $24, d $58, cabins for 6-10 people $95;) At Gelantipy, 40km north of Buchan, is this cattle and sheep property and horse-riding ranch, home to Snowy River Expeditions, which also has backpacker and cabin accommodation. The backpacker accommodation is in a newish timber lodge. The cabins are older and more faded but comfortable. You'll receive a relaxed friendly country welcome here. Rates include breakfast, and a three-course home-cooked meal in the large camp kitchen costs $14; fully catered packages are also available. Activities available include abseiling (per hour $20) and horseriding (per hour $30), wild caving (per 1½ hours $30) as well as white-water rafting (see p125).

Getting There & Away

Buchan Bus 'n' Freight (☎ 5155 0356) operates a twice weekly bus service to Bairnsdale from Karoonda Park and during Christmas school holidays runs a day trip from Lakes Entrance to MacKillops Bridge (adult/child/family $70/35/150).

ERRINUNDRA NATIONAL PARK

The Errinundra Plateau is a misty and verdant wonderland that also happens to contain Victoria's largest remaining areas of cool-temperate rainforest. It's one of East Gippsland's most outstanding natural areas and a battleground between environmentalists and loggers (see the boxed text, p128) and also one of the least visited parts of East Gippsland.

The national park coves an area of 25,000 to 30,000 hectares and has three granite outcrops that extend into the clouds resulting in high rainfall, deep, fertile soils and a network of creeks and rivers that flow north, south and east. The park has several climatic zones and areas of the park are quite dry, while its peaks regularly receive snow. This is a rich habitat for native birds and animals, which include many rare and endangered species such as the potoroo.

Errinundra is one of the best examples in the world of 'mixed forest' vegetation – it's dominated by southern sassafras and black oliveberry, with tall eucalypt forests providing a canopy for the lower rainforests. Some of the giant trees are many hundreds of years old.

The main access roads to the park are Bonang Rd from Orbost and Errinundra Rd from Club Terrace. Bonang Rd passes on the western side of the park, while Errinundra Rd passes through the centre. Road conditions are variable and the roads are often closed or impassable during the winter months or after floods – check with the park offices in Orbost or Bendoc first. Watch out for logging trucks. Roads within the park are all unsealed but are 2WD accessible for seven to eight months of the year, though they can deteriorate quickly at any time of the year after rain.

You can explore the park by a combination of scenic drives, and short and medium-length walks. **Mt Ellery** has spectacular views; **Errinundra Saddle** has a rainforest boardwalk; and from **Ocean View Lookout** there are stunning views down the Goolengook River where you can see as far as Bemm River. The park also has **mountain plum pines**, some of which are more than 400 years old, which are easily accessible from Goonmirk Rocks Rd.

The only camping area is at Frosty Hollow on the eastern side of the park, and there are a few basic picnic and camping areas on the park's edges – at Ellery Camp on Green's Rd, Ada River and Delegate River. A new camp site has opened in Goongerah featuring a fancy compost toilet. Camping is free at all of these sites. **Jacarri** (☎ 5154 0145; www.eastgippsland.net.au/jacarri; Bonang Hwy, Goongerah; s/d/f $85/85/95) is a gorgeous little cottage, made from recycled and plantation timber, on Jill Redwood's organic farm. It's solar-powered, has a slow

combustion stove for heating and cooking, and sleeps four. There's a petrol station and general store at Bonang, a pub at Bendoc and another pub and cabins at Delegate River (see opposite).

For more information contact **Parks Victoria** (Bendoc ☎ 02-6458 1456; Orbost ☎ 03-5161 1222) at Bendoc or Orbost.

MARLO
☎ 03 / pop 350

Sleepy little Marlo sits at the mouth of the Snowy River, 15km south of Orbost. The river flows into a large lagoon before entering the sea, and the area has excellent fishing and abundant bird life around the inland waterways. **French's Narrows Walking Track** follows the river to the beach from a starting point about 2km out of the town on the Marine Pde–Cape Conran Rd.

Marlo's general store has an ATM and some tourist information. **Marlo Bush Races** are a major event on New Years Day. The racetrack is just out of town on the Marlo–Cape Conran Rd.

Marlo Hotel & Country Retreat (☎ 5154 8201; fax 5154 8493; Argyle Pde; s/d $120; mains $16; ☺ lunch & dinner) has adults-only suites in a historic white timber pub; they come with spas and a choice of a jaw-dropping ocean view or an open fireplace. King-sized beds, comfy sofas and antique furniture make this an indulgently comfortable option. Prices go up 25% in peak periods. In the bistro the tasty garlic prawns with rice ($14) are worth trying.

Tabbara Lodge (☎ 5154 8231; fax 5154 8430; 1 Marlo Rd; s/d $50; ☒) offers wood-lined rooms decorated with country crafts that give these family-friendly self-contained units a homely ambience. They're set in a shady garden with a barbecue and playground. The lodge is on the right as you enter town from Orbost. Prices go up 30% in peak periods.

CAPE CONRAN COASTAL PARK

This is a blissfully undeveloped part of the coast. The pretty 19km coastal route from Marlo to Cape Conran is bordered by banksia trees, grass plains, sand dunes and the ocean.

There are some simply beautiful, remote white-sand beaches along this coast. The cape is excellent for snorkelling and scuba diving, boating and fishing, and in the warmer weather, swimming and surfing.

IF YOU GO DOWN TO THE WOODS TODAY...

You'll be in for a big surprise all right – East Gippsland's mighty old-growth forests are being logged at a rapid rate – every day the equivalent of an astounding 13 football fields are lost. East Gippsland contains Victoria's last and largest area of ancient forest and while 35% of the forests are protected by national park, the remainder, under state government control, continue to be clear felled. It's a controversial issue that has divided many communities that live, work and play among the forest giants.

Nestled in the very heart of East Gippsland's forest is tiny **Goongerah**. A school, a CFA building and a phone box are the only visible signs of the settlement (population 50) – but there's a thriving community with its own organic food co-op, probably the only totally 'greenie'-run CFA in Victoria and two active community environmental organisations: **Goongerah Environment Centre** (GECO; ☎ 5154 0156), which organises ongoing protests and blockades in the forest; and **Environment East Gippsland** (EEG; ☎ 5154 0145; www.eastgippsland.net.au).

Goongerah is home to Jill Redwood, who spearheads EEG. Jill's name has been synonymous with the fight to save East Gippsland's forest since she moved here more than 20 years ago. She's a gentle, quietly spoken woman, steadfast in her beliefs.

Redwood and EEG have pointed out to the government that people come to East Gippsland to see the old-growth forests, yet there's not a single walk where they can do that. In a move that confounds all the stereotypes that portray 'greenies' and loggers as having no common ground, the Orbost & District Community Forum, comprised of environmentalists, loggers, farmers, businesspeople and Aboriginal interests, is working on a grand vision to build a 300km world-class walk through East Gippsland's forests, taking in and linking up Errinundra, Snowy River, Croajngolong and Cape Conran National Parks. To date, it's received funding for a feasibility study into shorter walks.

Public education is one of the aims of EEG and each year it provides people with the chance to explore the forests under the guidance of environmental experts at the **Forests Forever Ecology Camp** (☎ 5154 0145; www.eastgippsland.net.au; adult/teenager/child per day $40/20/free) held each Easter at the back of Jill Redwood's property. BYO camping gear and food. Ecologists guide you through the forest and hope that you'll be awed by their beauty and complexity, outraged by their destruction and will spread the word.

There are several good picnic areas and loads of short nature walks, Parks Victoria can provide a brochure. Bring everything you need; there aren't any shops at Cape Conran, in fact there's nothing except the accommodation mentioned following.

Parks Victoria (☎ 5154 8438; www.conran.net .au) manages the accommodation at Cape Conran.

Banksia Bluff Camping Area (camp sites for up to 4 people $15) is right on the foreshore and surrounded by banksia woodlands. The camping ground has toilets, cold showers and a few fireplaces, but you'll need to take drinking water if you don't like the taste of bore water.

Cape Conran Cabins & Lodge (☎ 5154 8438; www .parkweb.vic.gov.au; Cape Conran Coastal Park; cabins for up to 4 people $100) has self-contained cabins, which sleep up to eight people, are surrounded by bush, far enough apart to offer some privacy, and are just 200m from the beach. Built from local timbers, the cabins are like oversized cubby houses with cosy nooks for sleeping. The Hideaway cabin, for two people only, is popular with couples wanting to get away from it all; Oliveberry Lodge sleeps up to 17 for group bookings (BYO linen). The cabins have rain water on tap.

BEMM RIVER

Edged by Cape Conran Coastal Park, Bemm River is a small and friendly holiday hamlet favoured by fisherfolk, 23km off the Princes Hwy on the shores of Sydenham Inlet. The general store has Eftpos, basic food supplies and bait. Fuel is not available. Facilities include a pub, a general store, Internet facilities, a couple of caravan parks and a few holiday flats. Sydenham Inlet is rich with bird life, including black swans and wading birds, and good bream and perch fishing is possible. There's also access to coastal beaches a few kilometres from town.

Bemm River Hotel (☎ /fax 5158 4241; bemmriver hotel@hotmail.com; 3-5 Sydenham Pde; d/f $80/100) offers new timber cabins that are well designed with a double room with en suite, and three or four bunks in a separate room. The pub has a timber deck with views of the inlet. Generous meals are available for lunch and dinner ($5 to $19).

Bemm River Holiday Lodge (☎ 5158 4233; bemm riverholidaylodge@net-tech.com.au; 37-41 Sydenham Pde; s/d/f $50/60/100) has old-fashioned units and friendly owners. Hire boats are available ($60 per day).

LIND NATIONAL PARK

Signposted just east of the turn-off from the Princes Hwy to Club Terrace, this small park (1365 hectares) was declared in 1926 as a scenic stopover spot for travellers along the highway. A number of creeks run through the park, and the vegetation ranges from warm-temperate rainforests and wet-gully plants alongside the creeks to open eucalypt forests in the drier areas. There are several **walking tracks**, a picnic area in the centre of the park and a **nature drive** that follows the Euchre Creek through the park from Club Terrace back to the Princes Hwy.

CANN RIVER

☎ 03 / pop 250

Cann River is a small saw-milling centre with a massive crossroad at the junction of the Princes and Monaro Hwys. The **Parks Victoria office** (☎ 5158 6351) in the centre of town is the main information centre for Croajingolong National Park. Road access information, overnight hiking and camping permits and walking-trail park notes are available. A range of topographic maps and walking guides are available for purchase.

The town itself has a small supermarket, a caravan park and several motels. Meals are available from the pub or cafés. The Mobil petrol station has an ATM. From Cann River, the Monaro Hwy heads north to the Cooptracambra National Park, and the unsealed Tamboon Rd heads south to Tamboon Inlet and Croajingolong National Park.

Eleven kilometres east of Cann River, on the northern side of the Princes Hwy, **Drummer Creek Rainforest Walk** is an easy half-hour walk that starts at the picnic area and takes you through warm-temperate rainforest.

COOPRACAMBRA NATIONAL PARK

Cooptracambra is one of the most remote and least developed of the state's national parks. It was declared a national park in 1979 and now covers an area of more than 35,000 hectares. It's bordered in the north by the NSW border and on the west by the Monaro Hwy. The landscape is rugged and spectacular, with the dramatic deep gorges of the Genoa River and a series of smaller creeks running through it. The vegetation is mainly open eucalypt forest, with a few areas of sheltered rainforest, and there are various difficult climbs to high peaks, such as Mt Denmarsh, Mt Kaye and Mt Cooptracambra.

One 4WD track passes through the centre of the park from the Monaro Hwy to the Princes Hwy west of Genoa. Apart from this route, there are no other access tracks, camping grounds or walking trails through Cooptracambra, which makes it a great spot for experienced bushwalkers who want to escape the madding crowds. On the Monaro Hwy side, the **Beehive Creek Falls** (signposted) is an idyllic and scenic spot, with small cascades falling into rock pools shaded by the surrounding bush – there are some great swimming holes for the warmer weather.

It's a fascinating journey from Cann River to Bombala in NSW. The Victorian sector of the highway is very pretty, winding through national parks and thick forests, but as soon as you cross the border the landscape changes dramatically into dry, denuded sheep pastures, and a landscape that is stripped of its natural vegetation.

Cooptracambra Cottages (☎ 5158 8277; www.malla coota.com; d $60) is a wonderfully remote get away set on a scenic farm bordering Coopracambra National Park. The octagonal timber cottages, which sleep six, are built of local timbers, with solar power and log-fire heating. Bird-watching and 4WD tours of the area are available, and walking trails are close at hand. The turn-off to the cottage is just outside Genoa, and from there it's 16km on an unsealed road.

The **V/Line** (☎ 13 61 96; www.vlinepassenger.com .au) bus service from Sale to Canberra travels up the Monaro Hwy.

GIPSY POINT

Named after the schooner *Gypsy* that tied up here in the 19th century, Gipsy Point is an idyllic settlement at the head of Mallacoota

SOUTHEAST COAST VICTORIA

Inlet. Although it's only 10km off the Princes Hwy, it has a deliciously remote atmosphere – once you're sitting on the jetty looking out over the inlets, you'll feel like you're a million miles from anywhere (unless, of course, you're here during the Christmas holidays). A resident mob of Eastern grey kangaroos lives in the area and you'll often see them, especially at dusk, as they graze by the water.

Friendly **Gipsy Point Lodge** (☎ 5158 8205, 1800 063 556; www.gipsypoint.com; self-contained cottages per person $105, guesthouse r per person $145; ⊠) is in a peaceful setting surrounded by bush and water, the guesthouse rooms have glorious water views. Rates include all meals. Facilities include a tennis court, use of canoe and rowboats, and motorboat hire ($75 per day). Non-guests are welcome for the well-recommended dinner (a three-course set meal for $55 per person) but be sure to book ahead.

Gipsy Point Luxury Lakeside Apartments (☎ 1800 688 200; www.gipsy.com.au; r from $195; ⊠ ⊠) is one of only two five-star accommodation options in Gippsland and it's indulgently luxurious. There can be so many decisions in a place where there's seemingly nothing to do – a boat cruise, a dip in your private spa or the free-form pebble sheen pool, or watching the kangaroos graze on the grass from your deck. The modern, spacious, split-level apartments with king-sized beds are in a prime location on the edge of the lake. No children under eight.

MALLACOOTA
☎ 03 / pop 1040

Completely surrounded by the internationally acclaimed Croajingolong National Park, Mallacoota is a one-road-in, one-road-out town populated by alternative lifestylers, retirees, abalone fishers and surfers. Everything is fairly low-key and relaxed, and life revolves around the ocean, the inlet, the bush and the pub. It's been a haven for travellers since the early 20th century when a camp set up by the poet EJ Brady on the shores of the inlet attracted notable Australian literary figures, such as Henry Lawson and Katherine Susannah Pritchard.

Mallacoota's attractions are unique: there is access to remote ocean beaches, an extensive estuarine waterway system, the fabulous Croajingolong National Park, an abundance of bird life, great fishing, bushwalks, surf-

ing and swimming. Mallacoota's character changes in the Christmas school holidays and at Easter when everyone wants to share its delights, even then you can still find a quietish bit of bush or beach.

Information
Mallacoota Information Shed (☎ 5158 0800; main wharf, cnr Allan & Buckland Dr; ☉ 10am-4pm) Operated by friendly volunteers.

Mallacoota Telecentre (☎ 5158 0603; Mallacoota Community House, cnr Genoa Rd & Mattson St; per hr $5; ☉ 9am-5pm Mon-Fri) Offers Internet access.

Parks Victoria (☎ 5161 9500; cnr Buckland & Allan Drs; ☉ 9.30am-noon & 1-3.30pm Mon-Fri) Has an information centre opposite the main wharf with excellent outdoor displays and information on Croajingolong and Mallacoota.

Sights & Activities
CRUISES & BOAT HIRE
One of the best ways to experience Mallacoota is by boat. The estuarine waters of Mallacoota Inlet are completely surrounded by national park and have more than 300km of shoreline. Fewer cruises operate in the winter months, so call ahead to check.

Porkie Bess (☎ 5158 0109, 0408 408 094; 2hr cruise per person $25), is a 1940s wooden boat offering fishing trips and cruises around the lakes. It also acts as a ferry for hikers (per person $10, minimum four).

Wilderness Coast Ocean Charters (☎ 0418 553 809; Gabo Island $60, Skerries $100) runs trips to Gabo Island (accommodation drop-off is possible) from Bastion Point, leaving early in the morning and with pick up in the afternoon. The Skerries seal colony trip views these delightful creatures off Wingan Inlet. Whales are sometimes spotted on trips from September to November.

Mallacoota Hire Boats (☎ 0438 447 558; Main Wharf, cnr Allan & Buckland Drs; motor boats per half-/full day $70/110, canoes per hr $15) is centrally located and hires out canoes and boats; no licence is required.

GABO ISLAND LIGHTSTATION RESERVE
The windswept 154-hectare island, 14km from Mallacoota, is home to sea birds and one of the world's largest colonies of Little Penguins. Whales, dolphins and fur seals are regularly sighted off shore. The island has an operating **lighthouse**, built in 1862, which is the tallest in the southern hemisphere; tours are available for $8 per per-

son, and accommodation is also available (right). Access to the island is possible by boat (see opposite) or by air with **Mallacoota Air Services** (☎ 0408 580 806). It costs $176 return for up to three adults, or two adults and two children.

WALKING
There's plenty of great short walks around the town, the inlet, and in the bush, ranging from a half-hour stroll to a four-hour walk. The easy 5km one-way **Bucklands Jetty to Captain Creek Jetty walk**, starts about 4km north of the town and follows the shoreline of the inlet past the Narrows (and past many patient anglers). The walk can be extended from Captains Creek via eucalypt forests to either Double Creek (3km) or the Mallacoota–Genoa Rd (3km). The 7km **Mallacoota Town Walk**, which loops round Bastion Point, and combines five different walks, is also popular. Walking notes with maps are available from Parks Victoria and the Information Shed.

BEACHES
For good surf, head to Bastion Point or Tip Beach. There's swimmable surf and some sheltered waters at Betka beach and it's patrolled during Christmas school holidays. There are also good swimming spots along the beaches of the foreshore reserve, at Bastion Point and Quarry Beach.

OTHER ATTRACTIONS
Mallacoota Air Services (☎ 0408 580 806; flights for 3 adults $35-250) offers scenic flights over the inlet, to Gabo Island, and as far afield as Eden in NSW.

The **Mallacoota Arts Festival** (☎ 5158 0890) and is held biannually at Easter and has a different theme each year. It focuses on creative arts, writing, theatre and music workshops, which may lead you to be in a performance during the course of the festival. Contact the organisers to find out whether it's a festival year.

Sleeping
There are plenty of options, though during Easter and Christmas school holidays you'll need to book well ahead and expect prices to be about 20% up on those included here (peak prices are mentioned here where they're a whole lot more).

Karbeethong Lodge (☎ 5158 0411; www.karbee thonglodge.com.au; 16 Schnapper Point Dr; d/f with bathroom from $85/95, without bathroom $65/75) It's hard not to be overcome by a sense of serenity as you rest on the broad verandas of this early 1900s timber guesthouse overlooking Mallacoota Inlet. The large guest lounge and dining room are equally comfortable with an open fire and period furnishings, and there's a mammoth kitchen if you want to prepare meals. The bedrooms are pastel toned and small.

Mallacoota Foreshore Caravan Park (☎ 5158 0300; camppark@vicnet.net.au; Allan Dr; unpowered/powered sites $14/17.50, caravan d $50) Hundreds of grassy sites extend along the foreshore and have sublime views of the lake with its resident population of black swans and pelicans. Prices go up 50% at Christmas and Easter.

Adobe Mudbrick Flats (☎ 5158 0329; www.adobe holidayflats.com.au; 17 Karbeethong Ave; d/f flats $65/80) These eco-friendly, comfortable mud-brick flats are about 5km from the town centre and are particularly fun for families, with birds to feed, a farmyard of ducks and kangaroos and a lyrebird to look out for. Check out the gorgeous inlet views from the comfort of your hammock. Linen costs extra.

Mallacoota Houseboats (☎ 5158 0775; 3-night minimum low/high season $750/1250, then per night $100/200) These houseboats are a divine way to explore Mallacoota's waterways. The clean and cosy boats sleep up to six and have kitchen, toilet and shower. There's a barbecue on the deck for a bit of alfresco dining.

Gabo Island Lighthouse (self-contained residence from $156) Accommodation is available in the Assistant Lighthouse Keeper's residence. The self-contained residence sleeps up to eight people; book through **Parks Victoria** (☎ 5161 9500).

Mallacoota Hotel Motel & Backpackers (☎ 5158 0455; inncoota@speedlink.com.au; 51-55 Maurice Ave; 2-4 bed dm $22, motel s/d/f from $55/66/75; ☒ ☲) The backpackers rooms are a bit shabby but there's a good shared kitchen, use of the motel pool and it's conveniently next door to the pub. Simple motel and family units overlook the lawn and pool.

Eating
Croajingolong Cafe (☎ 5158 0098; Allan Dr; mains $6.50-11; ☺ breakfast & lunch Tue-Sun) Overlooking the inlet, this café is a perfect place to linger over a latte, and watch the world as it moves by. The menu has some inspired offerings

and it does great fruit smoothies. Try the Vegie Brekky – tomatoes, mushrooms, beans and eggs on avocado toast ($10) or the chicken with sage and mushroom on a bed of noodles ($8). No credit cards.

Mallacoota Hotel Motel & Backpackers (☎ 5158 0455; 51-55 Maurice Ave; mains $14-26; ☺ lunch & dinner) For hearty meals try the pub bistro, where you can sample porterhouse in seafood sauce ($26) and the rich profiterole mousse cake ($7.50). Bands play at the pub regularly in the summer.

Tide Restaurant (☎ 5158 0100; 70 Maurice Ave; mains $15-25; ☺ dinner) In a prime lakeside location; serves quality food and wine. Its sunny outdoor deck is deservedly popular.

Getting There & Away

Mallacoota is 23km off the Princes Hwy, and, while buses stop at Genoa (from Melbourne $48), there is no public transport from Genoa to Mallacoota. At the time of writing, the **Mallacoota Information Shed** (☎ 5158 0800) was planning to change all that with a shuttle bus service. **Mallacoota Taxis** (☎ 5158 0192) does the Genoa–Mallacoota run for $30.

CROAJINGOLONG NATIONAL PARK

Croajingolong is one of Australia's finest national parks and was designated a World Biosphere Reserve by Unesco in 1977. This coastal wilderness park covers 87,500 hectares and stretches for about 100km along the easternmost tip of Victoria from Bemm River to the NSW border. Magnificent unspoiled beaches, inlets, estuaries and forests make this an ideal park for camping, walking, swimming and surfing. The five inlets, Sydenham, Tamboon, Mueller, Wingan and Mallacoota, are popular canoeing and fishing spots. Mallacoota Inlet is the largest and most accessible (see p130).

Contact **Parks Victoria** (Cann River ☎ 5158 6351; Mallacoota ☎ 5161 9500) offices in Cann River or Mallacoota for information, road conditions, overnight hiking and camping permits, and track notes. Lonely Planet's *Walking in Australia* has an excellent detailed description of the walk from Thurra River to Mallacoota.

Two sections of the park have been declared wilderness areas (which means no vehicles, access to a limited number of walkers only and permits required): the Cape Howe Wilderness area, between Mallacoota Inlet and NSW border, and the Sandpatch Wilderness area, between Wingan Inlet and Shipwreck Creek. The **Wilderness Coast Walk**, only for the well-prepared and intrepid, starts at Sydenham Inlet, by Bemm River and heads along the coast to Mallacoota. You can start anywhere in between. Thurra River is a good starting point, making the walk an easy-to-medium 59km (five-day) hike to Mallacoota. **Tony Gray** (☎ 5158 0472, 0408 516 482) runs a car shuttle (leave your car at Mallacoota airport; five people Thurra/Wingan $190/150) to Thurra River from Mallacoota.

Croajingolong is a bird-watcher's paradise, with more than 300 recorded species, including glossy black cockatoos and the rare ground parrot, while the inland waterways are home to a myriad of water birds such as the delicate azure kingfisher and the magnificent sea eagle. There are many small mammals, including possums, bandicoots and gliders, and the reptile population includes a colony of huge goannas at Goanna Bay, on the Top Lake of Mallacoota Inlet. The vegetation ranges from typical coastal landscapes to thick eucalypt forests, with areas of warm-temperate rainforest. The heath land areas are filled with impressive displays of orchids and wild flowers in the spring.

Access roads of varying quality lead into the park from the Princes Hwy. Apart from Mallacoota Rd, all roads are unsealed and can be very rough in winter, so check with Parks Victoria on road conditions before venturing on, especially during or after rain.

The main camping areas are at Wingan Inlet, Shipwreck Creek, Thurra River and Mueller Inlet. The serene and secluded Wingan Inlet has the best facilities, with pit toilets, fireplaces, picnic tables and fresh water. Other bush camping areas (permits required) lie along the Wilderness Coast Walk but you may need to bring drinking water.

Point Hicks was the first part of Australia to be spotted by Captain Cook and the *Endeavour* crew in 1770 and was named after his first Lieutenant, Zachary Hicks. The remote **Point Hicks Lighthouse** (☎ 5158 4268; www .pointhicks.com.au/cottages; up to 8 people per night from $210) has two comfortable heritage-listed cottages that originally housed the assistant lighthouse keepers. The cottages have ocean views and wood fires. Thurra River and Mueller Inlet camping grounds are less than 5km from here, with pit toilets, running water and fireplaces; tent sites are $13.50.

New South Wales

GILLIANNE TEDDER

South Coast
New South Wales

For many the south coast of New South Wales marks a respite from the clatter and chaos of the popular coastal towns north of Sydney. Part of this is simply a matter of access; where the north coast is on the main highway between Sydney, Brisbane and the north, the south coast is served by the meandering Princes Hwy, the secondary road from Sydney to Melbourne. For people who want their coastal time to combine untrammelled nature with a dash of charm, this is a very good thing.

And these aren't chic retreats of the wealthy either (although a phalanx of well-heeled Sydneysiders has started mining for weekend gems); rather you'll find an interesting mix of old-timers, fishers, labourers and others who have simply escaped the bustle of life elsewhere in NSW. Most of the towns owe their existence to the ocean, which remains a focus. The often chilly waters lure people to the myriad of activities above and below the waves. Sea creatures of all sorts are also lured to the area, and activities from whale watching to fishing are popular with locals and visitors alike.

Beach towns like Wollongong, Kiama and Ulladulla enjoy their fine beaches almost as an afterthought. Other places shelter from the shore along the many rivers and inlets that break up the coast. Nowra, Batemens Bay and Merimbula are laid-back bases for enjoying the ocean and many national parks. Further inland are little towns like Berry and Bega, steeped in history and set among the green rolling hills.

SOUTH COAST
NEW SOUTH WALES

HIGHLIGHTS

- Wandering the historic main drag of **Berry** (p142)
- Hitting the untouched trails of **Booderee National Park** (p146)
- Enjoying the verdant rolling hills and history around **Tilba** (p161)
- Taking a boat tour to see the wildlife on **Montague Island** (p160) near Narooma
- Diving or snorkelling in the coastal waters off **Jervis Bay** (p145) and **Merimbula** (p166)
- Taking a Koori cultural tour of **Wallaga Lake** (p162)
- Exploring the rugged coastal scenery around **Bermagui** (p162)
- Whale-watching at Twofold Bay in **Eden** (p169)

Berry ★
Jervis Bay ★
★ Booderee National Park
Tilba ★ ★ Montague Island
★ Bermagui & Wallaga Lake
★ Merimbula
★ Eden

■ TELEPHONE CODE: 02   ■ www.southcoast.com.au

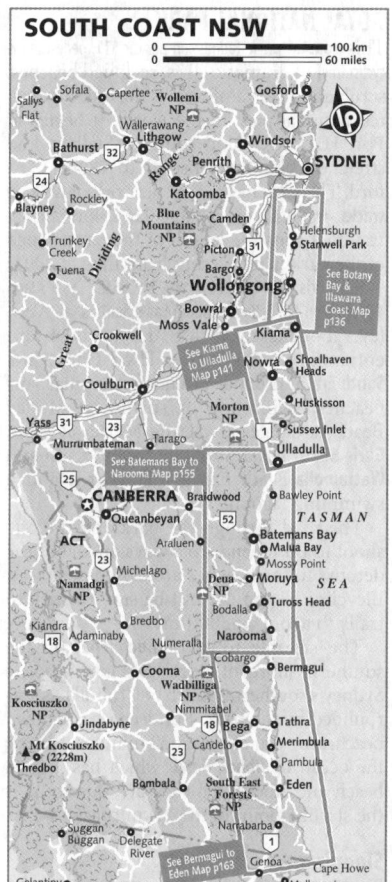

SOUTH COAST NSW

turn-offs to interesting places, both on the coast and up in the Great Dividing Range, where there's an almost unbroken chain of superb national parks and state forests. It's a longer, slower route between Sydney and Melbourne than the Hume Hwy, but it's infinitely more interesting.

TRAIN

CityRail (☎ 13 15 00; www.cityrail.info) has commuter services from Sydney as far south as Bomaderry, 3km north of Nowra.

BOTANY BAY & ILLAWARRA COAST

Botany Bay forms the southern border to metropolitan Sydney. The Illawarra Coast is a strip of coastal towns at the base of the spectacular sandstone escarpment that runs from Royal National Park south past the cities of Wollongong and Port Kembla.

The region was explored by Europeans in the early 19th century, but apart from timber cutting and dairy farming there was little development until the escarpment's coalfields attracted miners. By the turn of the 20th century Wollongong was a major coal port. Steelworks were developed in the 1920s and today the region is one of the country's major industrial centres. Botany Bay is home to many chemical plants.

Despite the industry in the area, there is also spectacular natural scenery and some great beaches, especially at Royal National Park. This beauty can be visually exploited from **Bulli Lookout**, high on the escarpment off the Princes Hwy, with enormous views down to the coastal strip and out to sea. Nearby, **Sublime Point Lookout**, and **Bald Hill Lookout** in Stanwell Tops are similarly breathtaking. **Mt Keira Summit Park** (Queen Elizabeth Dr, Mt Keira) offers an even higher viewpoint.

BOTANY BAY

Botany Bay is 15km to 30km south of Sydney, on the fringe of the city. This was Captain Cook's first landing point in Australia, and it was named by Joseph Banks, the expedition's naturalist, for the many botanical specimens he found here.

Getting There & Around

BUS

Bus access along the coast is good. **Greyhound** (☎ 13 14 99; www.greyhound.com.au) and Nowra-based **Premier Motor Service** (☎ 13 34 10; www.premierms.com.au) have services all along the Princes Hwy between Sydney and Melbourne.

CAR & MOTORCYCLE

The Princes Hwy starts at Sydney's George St and continues all the way to Adelaide via Melbourne. It's known as the coastal route, but don't expect too many ocean views (although there are some beauties). Most of the way the highway runs a little way inland. All along this route there are

This area is a major industrial centre so don't expect too many unspoilt vistas. If you're still keen to visit, the **Botany Bay National Park** has bushland and coastal walking tracks, picnic areas and an 8km cycle track. Drop into the park's **Discovery Centre** (☎ 9668 9111; Cape Solander Dr, Kurnell; admission per car $7; ☙ 11am-3pm Mon-Fri, 10am-4.30pm Sat & Sun) for more information.

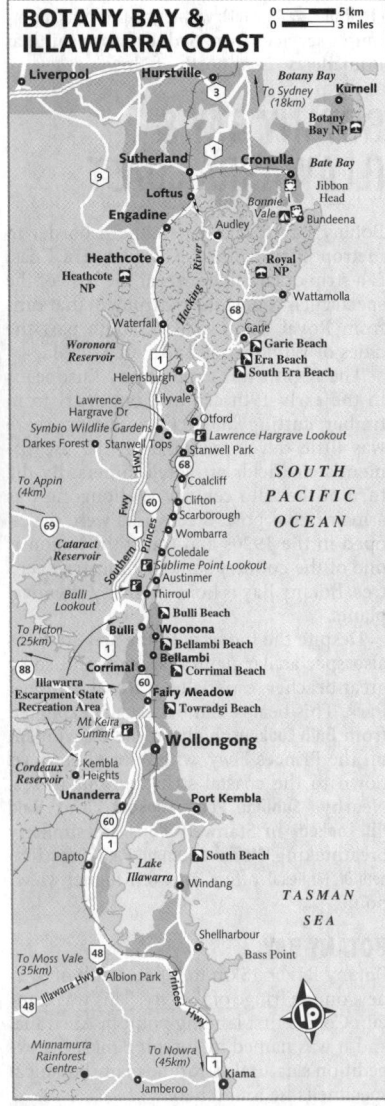

ROYAL NATIONAL PARK

This **coastal park** (admission per car $11, pedestrian & cyclist free) of dramatic cliffs, secluded beaches, scrub and lush rainforest is the oldest gazetted national park in the world. It begins at Port Hacking, 30km south of Sydney, and stretches 20km further south to just near Otford. The park has a large network of **walking tracks**, including a spectacular 29km coastal trail that runs the length of the park. Much of the park is recovering from fires in 2001.

The **visitors centre** (☎ 9542 0648; ☙ 9.30am-4.30pm Mon-Fri, 8.30am-4.30pm Sat & Sun) is at Audley, about 2km inside the northeastern entrance, off the Princes Hwy. Garie, Era, **South Era** and **Burning Palms** are popular surf beaches; swimming or surfing at Marley Beach is dangerous (Little Marley is safe). **Garie Beach** has a Surf Life Saving Club and **Wattamolla Beach** has a picnic area and a swimming lagoon.

The road through the park and the offshoot to Bundeena are always open, but the detours to the beaches are closed at sunset. Bicycling is popular but be sure to stick to trails to avoid a $300 fine.

The sizeable town of **Bundeena**, on the southern shore of Port Hacking opposite Sydney's southern suburb of Cronulla, is surrounded by the park. Bundeena has its own beaches, or you can walk 30 minutes towards the ocean to **Jibbon Head**, which has a good beach and Aboriginal rock art. Bundeena is the starting point of the 29km coastal walk.

Sleeping

Beachhaven Bed & Breakfast (☎ 9544 1333; www .beachhavenbnb.com.au; 13 Bundeena Dr, Bundeena; d $200-50; ℗ ☙ ☐) Shaded by palms and overlooking gorgeous Hordens Beach, there are two swank suites here. Amenities include DVD players, antiques and deck chairs overlooking the sand. Options include silk sheets and champagne.

Garie Beach YHA Hostel (☎ 9692 8418; www.yha .com.au; Garie Beach, Royal National Park; dm $13) Secluded behind the dunes, this hostel is near great surf breaks and has no phone, power, showers or other amenities to spoil the rustic mood. You need to book, collect a key and get detailed directions from the YHA Membership & Travel Centre (p181) in Sydney.

The only park camping ground accessible by car is at **Bonnie Vale** (adult/child per night $8/4), near Bundeena. Bush camping is allowed in several other areas, but you must obtain a permit (adult/child $3/2) from the visitors centre, where you can get information about current usable camp sites. Book well ahead during the summer months.

Getting There & Away

From Sydney, take the Princes Hwy and then a turn-off south of Loftus to reach the north end of the park. From Wollongong the coast road north offers spectacular views of the Illawarra escarpment.

Cronulla National Park Ferries (☎ 9523 2990; www.cronullaandnationalparkferrycruises.com; adult/child $4.50/2.25; ☼ hourly 8.30am-5.30pm) travels from Cronulla, which you can reach by train from Sydney, to the northeastern corner of the park. Call for schedules; hours are longer weekends and in summer.

The Sydney to Wollongong **CityRail** (☎ 13 15 00; www.cityrail.info) service forms the western boundary of the park. The closest station to the visitors centre is Loftus, 6km west. Engadine, Heathcote, Waterfall and Otford stations are on the park boundary and have walking trails leading into the park.

WOLLONGONG & AROUND

☎ 02 / pop 228,846

Wollongong, 80km south of Sydney, is NSW's third-largest city and sprawls south to the biggest steelworks in Australia at Port Kembla. It has some excellent surf beaches, especially north of the centre where the Illawarra Escarpment draws closer to the coast. The hills behind provide a fine backdrop, good walks and great views over the city and coast – just don't look south.

Wollongong's surf ethos is a happy contrast to its blue-collar grit, and the result is genuine locals and a laid-back lifestyle. The city's culture and cuisine measure up to that of any major city, and Wollongong is an excellent base to explore the area.

Orientation

Crown St is the main commercial street, and between Kembla and Keira Sts is a two-block somewhat sterile pedestrian mall. West of this the town is in the throes of regeneration; east are some lovely cafés. Keira St is part of the Princes Hwy, but through traffic bypasses the city on the Southern Fwy.

Information

There's a post office and banks with ATMs on Crown St Mall.

Network Café (☎ 4228 8686; Upstairs, Shops 4 & 5, 157 Crown St; per hr $3.50; ☼ 10am-6pm Mon-Wed, to 9pm Thu-Sat, to 5pm Sun) You can jump online here.

NPWS office (☎ 4225 1455; 4/55 Kembla St; ☼ 8.30am-4.30pm Mon-Fri) Has maps.

Wollongong visitors centre (☎ 4227 5545, 1800 240 737; www.tourismwollongong.com; 93 Crown St; ☼ 9am-5pm Mon-Fri, 10am-4pm Sat & Sun) Will book accommodation for you.

Sights & Activities

Wollongong's fishing fleet is based at the southern end of the harbour, **Belmore Basin**, which was cut from solid rock in 1868. There's a fishing cooperative and an 1872 lighthouse on the point. Nearby, on the headland, is the newer **Breakwater Lighthouse**.

North Beach generally has better surf than the south **Wollongong City Beach** and you can't see the mill. The harbour itself has beaches that are good for children. Other beaches run north up the coast.

The excellent **Wollongong City Gallery** (☎ 4228 7500; www.wollongongcitygallery.com; cnr Kembla & Burelli Sts; admission free; ☼ 10am-5pm Tue-Fri, noon-4pm Sat & Sun) displays a permanent collection of modern Australian, Indigenous and Asian art, and diverse temporary exhibits, ranging from contemporary photography to political histories and jewellery.

Quizzical kids of all ages can indulge their senses at the **Science Centre & Planetarium** (☎ 4283 6665; www.uow.edu.au/science_centre; Squires Way, Fairy Meadow; adult/child $10/6; ☼ 10am-4pm). Operated by the University of Wollongong, this interactive science extravaganza covers everything from the dinosaur to the electrical age. There are planetarium shows and a Friday night laser show (8pm to 10pm).

The utterly serene **Wollongong Botanic Gardens** (☎ 4225 2636; 61 Northfields Ave, Keiraville; admission free; ☼ 7am-4.45pm Mon-Fri, 10am-4pm Sat & Sun Apr-Sep, to 6.45pm Oct-Mar) is a beautiful spot to wind down with a picnic lunch. The gardens represent a range of habitats including tropical, temporal and woodland. During summer, outdoor movies are often played.

Just south of the city the Buddhist **Nan Tien Buddhist Temple** (☎ 4272 0600; www.nantien .org.au; Berkeley Rd, Berkeley; admission free; ☼ 9am-5pm Tue-Sun) is the largest temple in the southern hemisphere. The custodians of this stunning

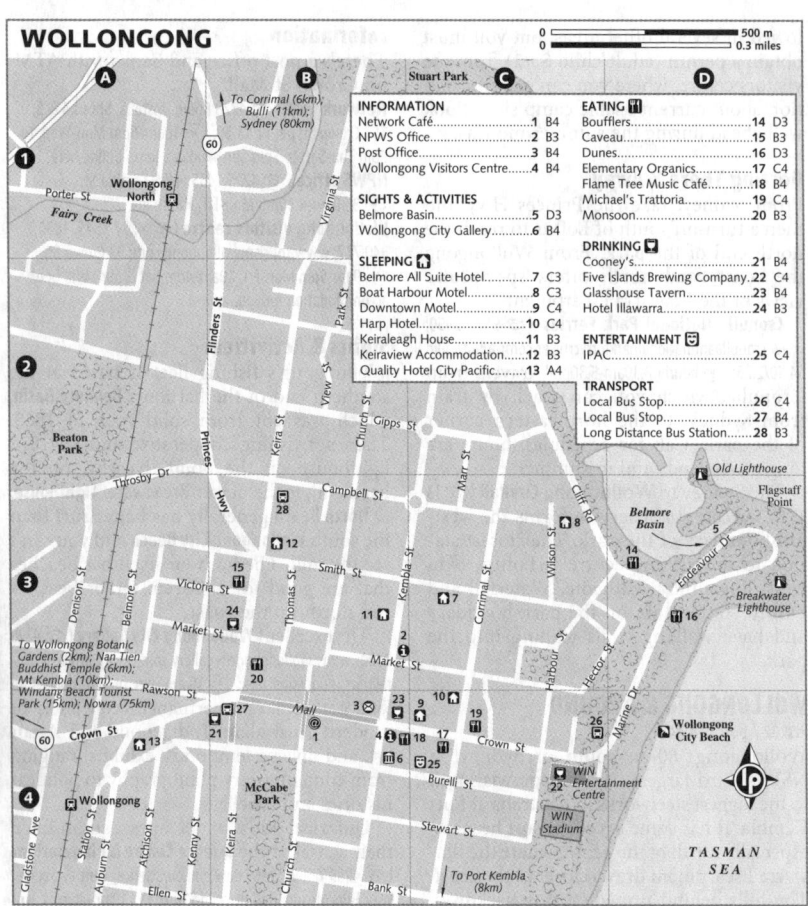

WOLLONGONG

0 ——————— 500 m
0 ——————— 0.3 miles

INFORMATION
Network Café.................................1 B4
NPWS Office...............................2 B3
Post Office..................................3 B4
Wollongong Visitors Centre......4 B4

SIGHTS & ACTIVITIES
Belmore Basin..............................5 D3
Wollongong City Gallery..........6 B4

SLEEPING
Belmore All Suite Hotel..............7 C3
Boat Harbour Motel....................8 C3
Downtown Motel.........................9 C4
Harp Hotel.................................10 C4
Keiraleagh House.......................11 B3
Keiraview Accommodation......12 B3
Quality Hotel City Pacific........13 A4

EATING
Boufflers...................................14 D3
Caveau.....................................15 B3
Dunes.......................................16 D3
Elementary Organics................17 C4
Flame Tree Music Café...........18 B4
Michael's Trattoria..................19 C4
Monsoon..................................20 B3

DRINKING
Cooney's....................................21 B4
Five Islands Brewing Company.22 C4
Glasshouse Tavern....................23 B4
Hotel Illawarra.........................24 B3

ENTERTAINMENT
IPAC..25 C4

TRANSPORT
Local Bus Stop..........................26 C4
Local Bus Stop..........................27 B4
Long Distance Bus Station.......28 B3

South Coast New South Wales (side tab)

and ornate complex encourage visitors to contemplate the 10,000 buddhas and participate in meditations and cultural activities.

NORTH OF THE CITY

Wollongong sprawls north nearly to the edge of Royal National Park, but the beachside suburbs are almost individual towns. **Bulli** and **Thirroul** (where DH Lawrence lived during his time in Australia; the cottage where he wrote *Kangaroo* still stands) are both popular. At **Coalcliff** (appropriately named – coal was mined near this cliff for most of the 19th century), the road heads up the escarpment. A short way along, near **Stanwell Park**, it enters thick forest and you drive through the Royal National Park.

Up the coast there are several excellent beaches. Those with good surf include **Austinmer** and the nearby **Sandon Point**, **Headlands** (only for experienced surfers) and **Sharkies**.

On the road to the village of **Otford** and Royal National Park, the **Lawrence Hargrave Lookout** at Bald Hill above Stanwell Park is a superb cliff-top viewing point. Hargrave, a pioneer aviator, made his first attempts at flying in the area early in the 20th century. His art has since been picked up by avid hang-gliders. To join in, **HangglideOz** (☎ 0417 939 200; www.hangglideoz.com.au) and **Sydney Hang Gliding Centre** (☎ 4294 4294; www.hanggliding.com.au) offer tandem flights from $180.

Symbio Wildlife Gardens (☎ 4294 1244; www .symbiowildlife.com; 7-11 Lawrence Hargrave Dr, Stanwell

Tops; adult/child $17/9; 9.30am-5pm) has more than 1000 cute and furry critters. Some are native, some are exotic and some are farm animals, but all are popular with families.

You can hit the trails on the back of a horse at **Darkes Forest Riding Ranch** (☎ 4294 3441; www.horseriding.au.com; 84 Darkes Forest Rd, Darkes Forest; per hr from $35).

SOUTH OF THE CITY
Southwest of Wollongong, the **Illawarra Escarpment** is a state recreation area (SRA), which takes in land donated by the Broken Hill Proprietary (BHP) company. There's no vehicle access but it's good for bushwalking. The park is a number of separate sections from Bulli Pass to Bong Bong; it isn't very large but the country is spectacular. Contact the Wollongong National Parks & Wildlife Service (NPWS) office (p137) for information on the park and about bush camping.

Just south of Wollongong, **Lake Illawarra** is popular for water sports including windsurfing. Further south is **Shellharbour**, a popular holiday resort, and one of the oldest towns along the coast. Its name comes from the number of shell middens (remnants of Aboriginal feasts) that the early Europeans found here. There are good beaches on the Windang Peninsula north of the town.

Sleeping
BUDGET
Keiraleagh House (☎ 4228 6765; backpack@primus.com .au; 60 Kembla St; dm/s/tw $18/30/50) This rambling heritage house is clogged with atmosphere and as scruffy as the veteran Bird of Paradise plant out front. Inside are slightly faded but comfortable rooms and a large kitchen. The basic dorms are out the back, along with a sizable patio, bench seating and a BBQ.

Keiraview Accommodation (☎ 4229 1132; bookings @keiraviewacco.com.au; 75-79 Keira St; dm/d/f $24/72/77; P) Modern and clinically clean, this complex contains the YHA hostel, which caters to students and backpackers in tidy four-bed dorms. The double and family rooms are a bargain and a step up in style, with verandas and kitchenettes.

There are several beachside caravan parks outside of Wollongong city:
Wollongong Surf Leisure Resort (☎ 4283 6999; www.wslr.com.au; Pioneer Rd, Fairy Meadow; unpowered/ powered sites from $17/20, cabins from $75)

Corrimal Beach Tourist Park (☎ 4285 5688; http://touristparks.wollongong.nsw.gov.au/corrimal; Lake Pde, Corrimal; unpowered/powered sites from $18/21, cabins $66-164)

MIDRANGE
Boat Harbour Motel (☎ 4228 9166; www.boatharbour -motel.com.au; cnr Campbell & Wilson Sts; s/d $120/140; P) The name says it all about the views at this comfortable motel overlooking, well, you guessed it. Actually, some of the rooms would qualify for the name City View Motel, but those facing the water have nice balconies and comfortable if unmemorable décor.

Downtown Motel (☎ 4229 8344; info@downtown motel.net; 76 Crown St; s/d from $100/110; P) Straight out of the 1960s, this friendly option has clean, functional rooms in a very convenient spot.

Belmore All Suite Hotel (☎ 4224 6500; www .belmore.net; 39 Smith St; d $130, ste $149-175; P) All the units are spacious in this gracious, conservatively decorated building near the beaches. There are kitchenettes and attractive patios on the lush grounds.

Harp Hotel (☎ 4229 1333; theglasshouse@optusnet .com.au; 124 Corrimal St; d $95-110; P) Close to the hum of Crown St, this hotel is good for an overnighter, with small modern rooms, bright and busy décor and compact bathrooms. It gets loud on weekends.

TOP END
Quality Hotel City Pacific (☎ 4229 7444; www.city pacifichotel.com.au; 112 Burelli St; d $175-200, f $200; P) Catering to a largely corporate clientele, this hotel is in an older, well-maintained building. Some rooms have city and water views as well as broadband Internet. If you can't make it to the beach, there's a small saltwater pool.

Eating
For three blocks north of the mall, Keira St is jammed with eateries of all types and budgets. Other places are spread out across town.

Caveau (☎ 4226 4855; 122-124 Keira St; 3 courses $55; dinner Tue-Sat;) Inside this double shopfront in a vintage building, Peter and Nicola Sheppard serve inventive food in a spare setting of warm beige. The Mod Oz menu changes often and makes use of the produce from many nearby speciality farms.

Service from the young staff is smooth and relaxed.

Michael's Trattoria (☎ 4225 9542; 50 Crown St; mains $30; ☺ lunch Tue-Fri, dinner Tue-Sat; ✖) Not far from the beach is a slice of old Italy; its main bow to modernity is fantastic food. Super popular with locals, Michael's skimps on pasta in favour of a range of creative meat dishes with Italian flavours; try the steak with rosemary.

Dunes (☎ 4228 7111; Marine Dr; mains from $25; ☺ breakfast Sat & Sun, lunch & dinner daily; ✖) Resplendent in modern trappings, this flashy place soars above City Beach. The views are tremendous, especially from the outside tables. Action in the open kitchen centres on meat and fish dishes prepared simply.

Monsoon (☎ 4229 4588; 193 Kiera St; mains $12-20; ☺ lunch Tue-Sat, dinner Tue-Sun; ✖) The old wooden floors in this shopfront have weathered to a golden brown in contrast to the trendy yet simple trappings. Vietnamese cuisine gets a healthy dose of Mod Oz reality on the long menu of inventive dishes. It hums with festive groups every night of the week.

Other recommendations:

Boufflers (☎ 4227 2989; cnr Harbour St & Cliff Rd; mains $5-15; ☺ lunch & dinner) Takeaway seafood at its best, but not open late.

Flame Tree Music Café (☎ 4225 7409; 89 Crown St; mains $10; ☺ breakfast & lunch) A café with hippy-cum-bohemian-cum-affable vibes.

Elementary Organics (☎ 4226 6300; 2/47 Crown St; mains $5-15; ☺ breakfast & lunch) Delectable smells and fresh organic food.

Drinking

Five Islands Brewing Company (☎ 4220 2854; www.fiveislandsbrewery.com; WIN Entertainment Centre, cnr Crown & Harbour Sts; ✖) Nine draughts brewed on the premises lube up the crowd, which bursts the seams on weekends. There's a great patio overlooking the sea.

Glasshouse Tavern (☎ 4226 4305; 90 Crown St; 10am-late Mon-Sat) All blonde wood and chrome, this bar-cum-nightclub gets a young crowd. During the week it's mellow, on Saturday night it jams till 5am.

Cooney's (☎ 4229 1911; 234 Keira St) This vast, dark bar has dim lighting, cosy nooks, pool tables and constant tunes. There's also a beer garden out the back if you need to clear your head. There's often live music here, including Irish bands on Thursday.

Hotel Illawarra (☎ 4229 5411; cnr Keira & Market Sts; ☺ 11am-late) A modernised old pub; the purple pool tables prove popular most nights.

Entertainment

Illawarra Performing Arts Centre (IPAC; ☎ 4226 3366; www.ipac.org.au; 32 Burelli St) This busy venue presents an excellent and continuous stream of theatre, dance and music. Many performances staged at the Sydney Opera House head there on tour, and, between big gigs, the impressive local contingent struts its stuff.

Getting There & Away

BUS

All long-distance buses leave from the **bus station** (☎ 4226 1022; cnr Keira & Campbell Sts). The helpful staff will make all necessary bookings for you. **Premier Motor Service** (☎ 13 34 10; www.premierms.com.au) operates buses to and from Sydney ($14, two hours, three weekdays, twice weekends) and to Eden (adult/child $60/38, 7½ hours, twice daily). **Murrays** (☎ 13 22 51; www.murrays.com.au) travels to Canberra (adult/child $31/19, three hours, one daily).

TRAIN

CityRail (☎ 13 15 00; www.cityrail.info) trains run from Sydney's Central station to Wollongong (adult/child $9.80/4.90, 1¾ hours, frequent), continuing south to Kiama, Gerringong and Bomaderry (Nowra).

The **Cockatoo Run** (☎ 1300 653 801; www.3801limited.com.au; adult/child/family $40/35/100; ☺ Wed & Sun) is a heritage tourist train that travels inland across the Southern Highlands, from Port Kembla to Robertson. The route traverses the escarpment, coursing through dense rainforest along the way.

Getting Around

The main local bus stops are on Marine Dr, and the corner of Crown and Keira Sts. **Dion's Bus Service** (☎ 13 34 10; www.dions.com.au) is one of several local operators.

You can reach most beaches by rail and trains are fairly frequent. Bringing a bike on the train from Sydney is a great way to get around; a cycle path runs from the city centre north to Bulli and south to Port Kembla.

To get a taxi, call ☎ 4229 9311.

KIAMA TO ULLADULLA

Just south of Wollongong is where the real charm and beauty of the south coast kicks in. The region has some great beaches, state forests and, in the ranges to the west, the big Morton National Park.

This area is a popular family holiday destination but, apart from weekenders from Sydney, it rarely feels too busy. If you've been driving for a bit, take a breather when you get there and start decompressing to the sounds of the sea.

KIAMA & AROUND
☎ 02 / pop 12,284

Kiama is a pretty town with some fine old buildings, good beaches and a moody ocean setting. The **Kiama Area visitors centre** (☎ 4232 3322; www.kiama.com.au; ☼ 9am-5pm) is on Blowhole Point. Nearby is the town's major attraction, the **blowhole**, which has drawn visitors for a century and is now floodlit at night. Beside the visitors centre is the small **Pilot's Cottage Museum** (adult/child $3/2; ☼ 11am-3pm Fri-Mon).

The **Terrace** (Collins St) is a neat strip of restored houses that date back to 1886 and are now mostly occupied by craft shops and restaurants.

There's a good **lookout** from the top of Saddleback Mountain, just behind the town. From Manning St, turn right on to Saddleback Mountain Rd. There's a small enclosed **surf beach** right in town and the broad **Werri Beach**, 10km south in Gerringong. **Bombo Beach**, 3km north of the centre has a great beach and a CityRail stop right near the sand. The visitors centre has a lot of good hiking info.

Minnamurra Rainforest Centre (☎ 4236 0469; car $10; ☼ 10am-5pm) is in **Budderoo National Park**. It's on the eastern edge of the park, about 14km inland from Kiama. There's a NPWS visitor centre from where you can take a 1.6km loop walk on a boardwalk through the rainforest; the boardwalk circuit takes you past several small waterfalls. There's a secondary 2.6km walk on a paved track to the Minnamurra Falls. The visitor centre has a café.

On the way to Minnamurra you'll pass through the old village of **Jamberoo**, which has a nice pub.

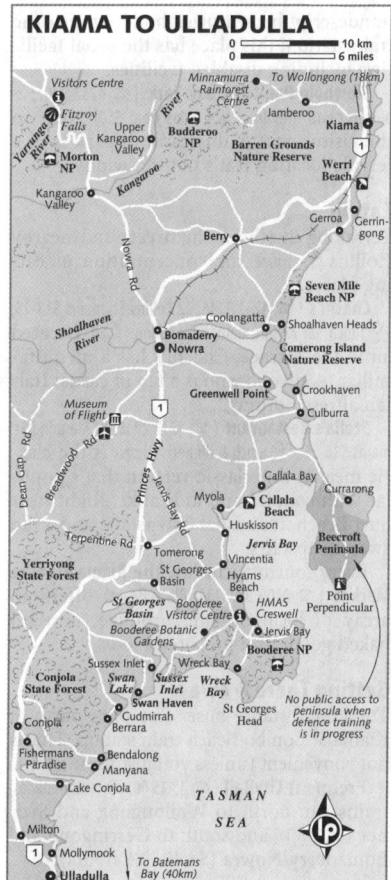

KIAMA TO ULLADULLA

Sleeping

Bellevue Accommodation (☎ 4232 4000; www.bellevueaccommodation.com.au; 21 Minnamurra St; units $140-250; P X) Six large units are set in a traditionally designed building with wide porches and good town views. The décor is plush and units have DVD players and kitchen facilities.

Kiama Terrace Motor Lodge (☎ 4233 1100; www.kiama.com.au/kiamaterrace; 45-51 Collins St; r from $125; P X R) A motel classic right in the heart of town and near the beach, shops and pubs. The 50 units are comfortable and if you wake up groggy you might think it is 1967.

Kiama Backpackers (☎ 4233 1881; tomtom@1earth .net; 31 Bong Bong St; dm $21, d $50; ☐) In the nondescript brown-brick building near the train station, this place has the usual facilities, including disabled facilities.

Blowhole Point Holiday Park (☎ 4232 2707; 2-person camp sites from $24, vans from $50) Next to the visitor centre, this caravan park is in a terrific location if it's not too windy.

Eating

Terralong St (the main street) and nearby Collins St have the concentration of eating places.

Chachi's (☎ 4233 1144; 32 Collins St; mains $18-25; ☾ lunch Sat & Sun, dinner Wed-Mon; ☒) Located amid the Terrace, Chachi's has a menu familiar to anyone who is a fan of casual Italian alfresco dining.

Stella's Restaurant (☎ 4232 2936; 78 Manning St; mains $16-26; ☾ lunch & dinner) Pizza is the classic meal at this classic veteran that's popular with couples and kids alike. Right near Surf Beach, it's casual downstairs and a tad swanky upstairs.

Every fourth Saturday, the **Kiama Produce Market** (☎ 0409 377 132; Black Beach) offers an array of local organic produce, unusual baked goods and prepared foods.

Getting There & Away

The long-distance buses stop 3km north of Kiama at Bombo Beach train station. This is not convenient (unless you just want a tan).

Frequent **CityRail** (☎ 13 15 00; www.cityrail.info) trains run north to Wollongong and Sydney ($12.80), and south to Gerringong and Bomaderry/Nowra ($4.40, 2½ hours).

BERRY

☎ 02 / pop 1597

Inland of Kiama and about 20km north of Nowra is Berry, a nearly mandatory place to stop and stroll. Founded in the 1820s, it remained a private town on the Coolangatta Estate (see p145 for more information) until 1912. **Queen St**, Berry's short main street, is worth a stroll for its National Trust–classified buildings and a multitude of shops and cafés.

Pottering Around (☎ 4464 2177; Berry Stores complex, 99 Queen St; ☾ 10am-5pm) is both the best and only place for tourist information. The town's website (www.berry.org.au) is also useful.

The **museum** (135 Queen St; admission free; ☾ 11am-2pm Sat, to 3pm Sun), near the post office, is in an interesting 1884 bank building and the curators are more than happy to talk you through every exhibit in the place. Among the oodles of antique shops, **Berry Antiques** (☎ 4464 1552; 83 Queen Street; ☾ 9am-5pm) stands out.

A recommended tour operator is **Mild to Wild** (☎ 4464 2211; www.m2w.com.au; 84 Queen St; trips from $40), which organises adventure trips (rock-climbing, kayaking, abseiling etc) of varying adventurousness.

The popular **Berry Country Fair** is held on the first Sunday of the month at the showgrounds. There are several wineries in the area and the Hotel Berry runs a short but exceptionally good-value wine tour ($15, 10.30am Saturday).

Jasper Valley Winery (☎ 4464 1596; www.jaspervalleywines.com.au; 152 Croziers Rd; ☾ 10am-4pm) is only 5km south of Berry, and is open for tastings and lunches. Try the Lambrusco on a hot day.

Sleeping

For a small town, Berry has some wonderful accommodation options, and wandering weekenders take full advantage. Prices are higher on weekends and you'll need to book ahead.

Bunyip Inn Guesthouse (☎ 4464 2064; 122 Queen St; s/d with breakfast $60/120; ☒) Next to the Hotel Berry, this is an excellent place in one of the town's more impressive buildings: an old bank. There's a variety of spacious, beautiful rooms, some with spas and all with loads of character.

Great Southern Hotel (☎ 4464 1009; 95 Queen St; r $44) Eccentric embellishments in the bar, such as the hubcap collection, set the tone for the rooms, which have various themes. After a long night, waking up to see a 2m-tall statue of a devious-looking Santa can be a shock. There's great seats outside where you can ponder Queen St – and get that image of Santa out of your head.

Hotel Berry (☎ 4464 1011; berrypub@shoal.net .au; 120 Queen St; s/d from $30/40) This country pub is a rarity – it caters to weekending city slickers without totally losing its status as a local watering hole. The rooms are standard pub bedrooms, but large and well presented.

Eating & Drinking

Twenty Three (☎ 4464 2323; 85 Queen St; lunch $10-14; ☾ breakfast Sun, lunch Wed-Sun, dinner Thu-Sun)

There's a small but upmarket and stylish dining room inside as well as a courtyard and a garden. The menu is adventurous with various bruschettas and salads gracing the changing lunch menu. At night there are more adventurous Mod Oz mains. Tea's a speciality.

Berrylicious (☎ 4464 3880; 89 Queen St; lunch $7-10; ☺ breakfast & lunch) Seize a seat under the huge tree out front and enjoy the Mediterranean treats. There are salads, burgers, wraps and more, all made fresh daily.

Hotel Berry (☎ 4464 1011; 120 Queen St; meals $10-18) A nice courtyard dining area and meals a cut above the usual pub standard. Check out the Kylie shrine behind the front bar.

Getting There & Away
Premier Motor Service (☎ 13 34 10; www.premierms .com.au) buses between Kiama and Nowra stop here on request. The main road to Kangaroo Valley and Mittagong leaves the Princes Hwy south of Berry, but there's also a scenic route to Kangaroo Valley from Berry via Woodhill and Wattamolla.

NOWRA
☎ 02 / pop 24,765
The largest town in the Shoalhaven area, Nowra is a centre for the area's dairy farms, and for increasing tourism and retirement development. It's a workmanlike town and is not, as many people expect, on the coast – the nearest beach is at Shoalhaven Heads, about 17km east. It is, however, a handy base for excursions to beaches and villages around Jervis Bay, north to Berry and inland to Kangaroo Valley and Morton National Park. And if you've been travelling for a while, there's no shortage of places to stock up.

Information
NPWS office (☎ 4423 2170; 55 Graham St; ☺ 8.30am-4.30pm Mon-Fri)
Post office (cnr Junction & Berry Sts) In central Nowra.
Shoalnet Internet Cafe (☎ 4422 5014; 46A Berry St; per hr $5; ☺ 9am-4.30 Mon-Fri, 9-11am Sat) In central Nowra.
Shoalhaven visitors centre (☎ 4421 0778; www .shoalhaven.nsw.gov.au; cnr Princes Hwy & Pleasant Way; ☺ 9am-4.30pm) Just south of the bridge over the Shoalhaven River and has lots of information and a stern attitude.

Sights & Activities
The 6.5-hectare **Nowra Wildlife Park** (☎ 4421 3949; adult/child $10/5; ☺ 9am-5pm), on the north bank of the Shoalhaven River, is where you can kiss a cockatoo and meet other native animals. Head north from Nowra, cross the bridge and immediately turn left, then branch left on to McMahons Rd at the roundabout; turn left again at Rockhill Rd.

Nowra Museum (☎ 4421 2021; cnr Kinghorne & Plunkett Sts; $1; ☺ 1-4pm Sat & Sun) has heaps of local history, tools and other old stuff. **Meroogal** (☎ 4421 8150; cnr West & Worrigee Sts; adult/child $7/3; ☺ 1-5pm Sat, 10am-5pm Sun Feb-Dec, 10am-5pm Thu-Sun Jan) is a historic 1885 house containing the artefacts accumulated by four generations of women who lived there.

If you're at all interested in planes and helicopters, **Australia's Museum of Flight** (☎ 4421 1920; www.museum-of-flight.org.au; 489A Albatross Rd; adult/child $10/5; ☺ 10am-4pm), 10km south of Nowra at an operational airfield, has an excellent display, including a Sopwith Camel WWI biplane and a Douglas Dakota, which you can climb aboard.

The visitors centre produces a handy compilation of walks in the area. The relaxing **Ben's Walk** starts at the bridge near Scenic Dr and follows the south bank of the Shoalhaven River (6km return). North of the river, the circular 5.5km **Bomaderry Creek Walking Track** runs through sandstone gorges from a trailhead at the end of Narang Rd.

Shoalhaven River Cruises (☎ 4447 1978; tickets $23; ☺ 10.30am & 1.30pm Wed & Sun) has two tours up the beautiful river, leaving from the wharf just east of the bridge near the visitors centre.

Sleeping
White House Heritage Guest House (☎ 4421 2084; www.whitehouseguesthouse.com; 30 Junction St; s/d from $55/77; P ☒) A friendly family operates this beautifully restored guesthouse. The light breakfast out on the wide veranda is a great way to start the day. The lounge has a fireplace.

George Bass Motor Inn (☎ 4421 6388; www .georgebass.com.au; 65 Bridge Rd; s/d $93/99; P ☒ ☐) An unpretentious but well-appointed single-storey motor inn, the George Bass is part of the Golden Chain. Some of the 21 rooms have broadband Internet.

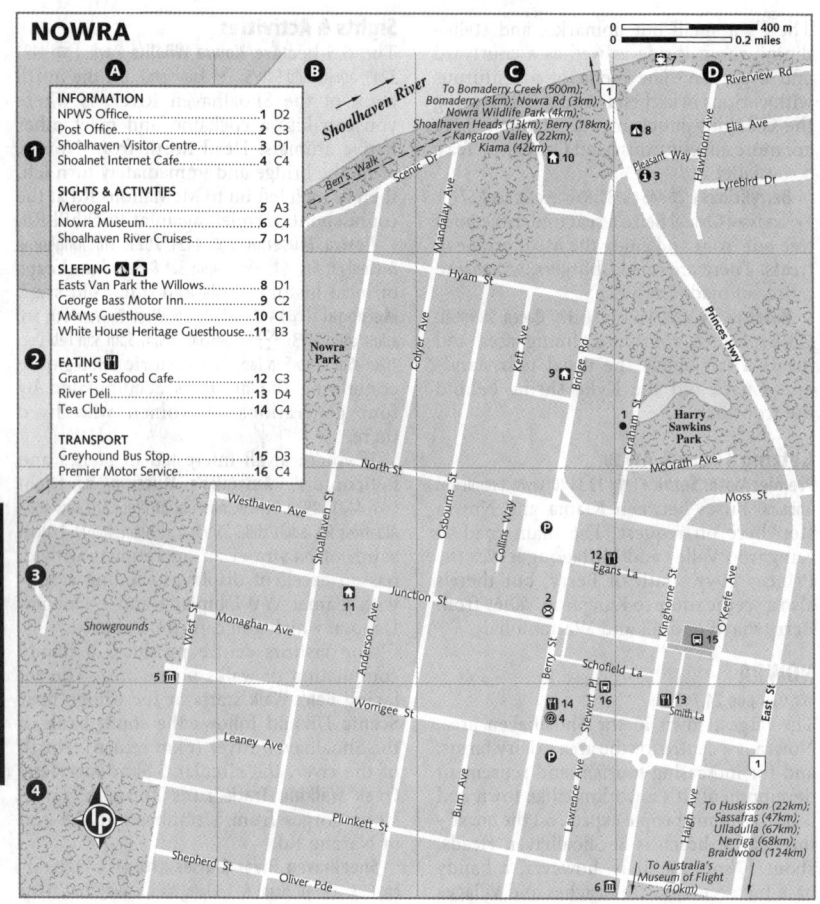

NOWRA

M&Ms Guesthouse (☎ 4422 8006; www.nowra backpackers.com; 1A Scenic Dr; dm/d $25/60) This is a wonderfully rustic place in a good location near the river. There are common rooms, including a games room with jukebox and pool table, large porches and an outdoor barbecue area. Call for pick-up from the train or bus.

Easts Van Park the Willows (☎ 4421 2977; Pleasant Way; camp sites $19, cabins $51) This place is off the highway close to the bridge (and thus noisy), but on the upside it's also right on the river.

Eating

Grant's Seafood Cafe (☎ 4421 2742; 9 Egans La; mains $10-15; ☽ lunch daily, dinner Thu-Sat; ☒) This casual indoor/outdoor eatery serves superb fish and chips in several iterations. There's also pasta, salads and ribs, but, really, have the fish.

River Deli (☎ 4423 1344; Kinghorne St; meals $8-15; ☽ breakfast & lunch Mon-Sat) The smart set gathers at this trendy spot to pour over the stacks of newspapers and savour the array of deli items including unusual filled baguettes, and salads such as grilled olive and polenta.

Tea Club (☎ 4422 0900; 46 Berry St; mains $10; ☽ breakfast & lunch Mon-Sat) Nowra's Bohemian set hangs out at this comfortable little café with a vast back garden. There are informal jam sessions here on Friday and Saturday nights.

DETOUR: FITZROY FALLS

Water falling 81m makes a big roar and that's what you hear as you enter the car park at this stunning spot in **Morton National Park** (admission per vehicle $3). As if the rainforest at the base had enough water, the falls fill the air with perpetual mist. This is a blessed stop on a hot day and an atmospheric and slightly mysterious stop on a cool one. The **visitor centre** (☎ 4887 7270; ☺ 9am-5.30pm) has a small café and good displays. From Nowra, take Nowra Rd (turn off the Princes Hwy 3km north of the river) 35km northwest. The road itself is a delight as it climbs the rugged and often misty Budawang Range.

Getting There & Around

Premier Motor Service (☎ 13 34 10; www.premierms .com.au; Stewart Pl) runs bus services to Sydney ($21, three hours) and Melbourne.

The train never made it across the Shoalhaven River, so the **train station** (☎ 4421 2022) is 3km north of town at Bomaderry. Frequent **CityRail** (☎ 13 15 00; www.cityrail.info) trains go to Sydney ($15, 2¾ hours). **North Nowra Bus Lines** (☎ 44235244; www.nowracoaches.com.au) links Nowra to the Bomaderry train station every one to two hours on weekdays and only three times on Saturday. Or take a **taxi** (☎ 4421 0333).

The Princes Hwy runs north to Kiama (42km) and south to Ulladulla (67km), with several turn-offs to Jervis Bay. An interesting and mainly unsealed road runs from Nowra to Braidwood, through Morton National Park and the hamlets of Sassafras and Nerriga. At the south end of Kinghorne St take Albatross Rd, which veers off to the right.

AROUND NOWRA

East of Nowra, the Shoalhaven River meanders through dairy country in a system of estuaries and wetlands, finally reaching the sea at Crookhaven Heads.

On the north side of the estuary is **Shoalhaven Heads**, where the river once reached the sea but is now blocked by sandbars. Just north of the beach here is the **Seven Mile Beach National Park** (admission free) stretching up to Gerroa.

Just before Shoalhaven Heads you pass through **Coolangatta**, the site of the earliest

European settlement on the South Coast. **Coolangatta Estate** (☎ 4448 7131; www.coolangatta estate.com.au; r per person $45-160; ☺ winery 10am-5pm) is a slick winery with a golf course, a good restaurant and accommodation in convict-built buildings. You shouldn't have to guess too hard at what's in the minibars.

JERVIS BAY

Despite extensive housing development, this large, sheltered bay retains its clean, white beaches and crystal-clear water (no large rivers flow into it). Dolphins are regularly seen, and whales sometimes drop in when swimming past on their annual migrations from June to October.

In 1995 the Aboriginal community won a land claim in the Wreck Bay area and now jointly administers the Booderee National Park (Booderee means 'plenty of fish') at the southern end of the bay.

Most development in Jervis Bay is on the southwestern shore, around the towns of Huskisson and Vincentia. The northern shore is much less developed and state forest backs on to the beaches at **Callala Bay**. There are caravan parks nearby. Despite the close proximity of Callala Beach, south of Callala Bay, to Huskisson, there's no way of crossing Currambene Creek – you have to drive back out to the highway and head south (which is just the way the locals like it). **Beecroft Peninsula** forms the northeastern side of Jervis Bay. Most of the peninsula is navy land, and is off limits to civilians

Huskisson
☎ 02 / pop 3309
With much of this area turning into a sprawl of holiday homes, it's surprising that Huskisson, the oldest town on Jervis Bay, still has the feel of a small fishing port although it's right on the beach.

SIGHTS & ACTIVITIES
The recommended **Lady Denman Heritage Complex** (☎ 4441 5675; www.ladydenman.asn.au; Dent St; adult/child $8/4; ☺ 10am-4pm), by the bay on the Nowra side of Huskisson, includes an interesting maritime museum and the *Lady Denman*, a ferry dating from 1912. Also here, **Timbey's Aboriginal Arts & Crafts** displays and sells work produced on site by the local Koori community. A boardwalk runs through wetlands.

South of Huskisson, **Hyams Beach** is a spectacularly white stretch of reasonably secluded sand.

Dolphin Watch Cruises (☎ 1800 246 010; www.dolphinwatch.com.au; Owen St; adult/child $20/10) has several dolphin and whale-watching trips on its custom catamaran. June to November is prime whale time.

Jervis Bay is popular with divers and a few places in Huskisson offer diving and courses. **Deep 6 Diving** (☎ 4441 5255; www.deep6 divingjervisbay.com.au; 64 Owen St) charges $90 for two boat dives, plus equipment hire (from $35 for a full set). There are also numerous courses available. There are some good wreck dives in the bay.

Wrecks will likely be far from your mind if you rent a luxury catamaran from **Jervis Bay Sailing Charters** (☎ 4441 8777; www.jervisbay sailingcharters.com.au; 9 Hawke St). You call the shots during a two- or three-hour cruise or something much longer. The boat holds up to 12 passengers and rates vary widely.

SLEEPING & EATING

There's quite a lot of guesthouse and motel accommodation in Huskisson and Vincentia (which more or less merge into one), but book ahead on weekends. Prices can be quite reasonable during the week and at off-peak times, but prices rocket on weekends and holidays.

Jervis Bay Guesthouse (☎ 4441 7658; www.jervis bayguesthouse.com.au; 1 Beach St; r $115-235; 🔀) This beautifully restored wooden guesthouse is opposite the beach. Most rooms have a beach view and wide verandas and breakfast is included. Kids are discouraged.

Husky Pub (☎ 4441 5001; www.thehuskypub.com.au; Owen St; s/d $40/60) The funnest place in town has reasonable pub rooms, and fabulous bay views from indoors and outside at the many picnic tables. Live music on weekends may be an inducement or a reason to flee.

Huskisson Beach Tourist Resort (☎ 4441 5142; Beach St; powered/unpowered sites from $26/24, cabins from $68; 🖭) Run by the Shoalhaven Council, this camping ground has a great location right on the beach. It's a little way out of Huskisson on the road to Vincentia. There are many other caravan parks in the area.

Seagrass Brasserie (☎ 4441 6124; 13 Currumbene St; dinner mains $26-28; 🕑 lunch Fri-Sun, dinner Tue-Sun) The changing menu always features fresh

seafood in many forms along with a bit of beef and fowl. The front deck is a great place to while away a balmy evening in high, convivial style.

Booderee National Park

This national park occupies Jervis Bay's southeastern spit. It's a vast and unspoiled park offering good swimming, surfing and diving on bay and ocean beaches. Much of it is heath land, with some forest, including small pockets of rainforest. It's administered jointly by the federal government and the Wreck Bay Aboriginal Community, and it's home to the naval training base HMAS *Creswell*, which is off limits to the public.

There's a good **visitors centre** (☎ 4443 0977; www.deh.gov.au/parks/booderee; 🕑 9am-4pm) at the park entrance with walking-trail maps and information on camping. Inside the park is the **Booderee Botanic Gardens** (☎ 4442 1122; 🕑 8.30am-4pm), which is a branch of the National Botanic Gardens and includes some enormous rhododendrons.

There are many walking trails around the park and some good secluded beaches. Keep an eye out for the 206 species of birds, 27 species of land mammals and 23 species of reptiles among others. Amphibian enthusiasts can thrill to the 15 species of frogs.

Although Wreck Bay is a closed community, tours are sometimes offered by **Wreck Bay Enterprises** (☎ 4442 1029). Call for details.

Entry to the park costs $10 per vehicle per day or you can buy an unlimited annual pass for $30 (NPWS passes are not valid). There are camping grounds at **Green Patch** (camp sites $14-17) and **Bristol Point** (camp sites $14-17). For a more secluded experience try the basic camping area at **Caves Beach** (camp sites $8-11), which is 300m from a car park. You have to book through the visitors centre or via the Web up to four months in advance; sites might not be available at peak times. There is a 24-hour self-registration system at the entrance to the park.

JERVIS BAY TO ULLADULLA

The southern peninsula of Jervis Bay encircles **St Georges Basin**, a large body of water that has access to the sea through narrow Sussex Inlet. The north shore of the basin has succumbed to housing developments reminiscent of the suburban sprawl on the central coast.

Milton, on the highway 6km north of Ulladulla, is this area's original town, built to serve the nearby farming communities. In a sign of how values have changed, note that Milton, like so many early towns in this coastal region, was built several kilometres inland, away from the cold and stormy coast. The **Settlers Fair** is held on the first holiday Monday in early October.

There are several cafés and a few antique shops on the main street (Princes Hwy) and it gets pretty busy here on weekends. **Pilgrim's Café** (meals $8-11; breakfast & lunch Mon-Sat) has interesting vegetarian lunches and coffee.

ULLADULLA

☎ 02 / pop 9609

That one of Ulladulla's great claims to fame is that it's the largest town on the highway between Nowra and Batemans Bay speaks volumes. It's by no means a bad place, just dull despite excellent beaches nearby. The bright lights of Sydney are clearly on another planet.

Ulladulla is on rocky Warden Head, but a short walk north of Ulladulla harbour is Mollymook, on a lovely surf beach.

Information

Library (per hr $3; 10am-6pm Mon-Fri, 9am-2pm Sat) In the same building as the visitors centre; has Internet access.

Visitors centre (☎ 4455 1269; www.ulladulla.info; 10am-5pm Mon-Fri, 9am-5pm Sat & Sun) In the Civic Centre opposite the harbour along the Princes Hwy.

Sights & Activities

The **Coomee Nulunga Cultural Trail** is a 700m walking trail in town, established by the local Aboriginal Land Council. It begins near the Lighthouse Oval (take Deering St east of the highway) and follows the headland through native bush to the beach.

Climbing **Pigeon House Mountain** (720m) in the far south of Morton National Park (Map p155) is an enjoyable challenge. A road runs close to the summit, from where it's a walk of three to four hours and 5km to the top and back. The first hour's walk from the car park is a steady climb, but after that it levels out a little. Challenges return for the last stretch, which features steep steps and ladders. The main access road to Pigeon House Mountain leaves the highway about

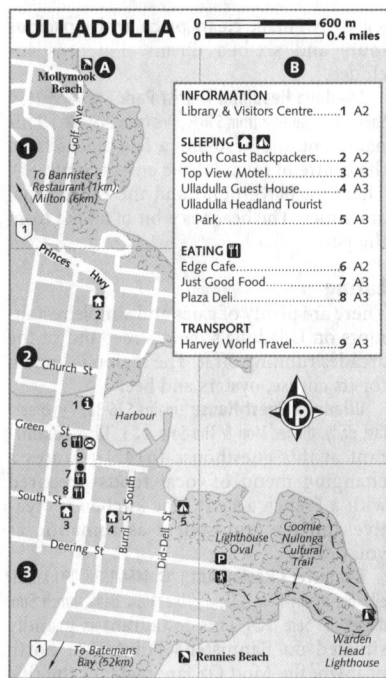

5km north of Ulladulla just before Milton, then it's 28km to the car park.

Festivals & Events

At Easter there is a **Blessing of the Fleet** ceremony and local celebrations. In late August there's a **Food & Wine Fair**.

Sleeping

Being a large town, Ulladulla has plenty of accommodation options.

Ulladulla Guest House (☎ 4455 1796; www.guesthouse.com.au; 39 Burrill St; r from $180; P X 📶 📶) An award-winning, luxury guesthouse, set in beautiful gardens. The on-site gallery features work by various artists and the seven rooms nearly groan with amenities. The restaurant (p148) serves the most interesting food in town.

Top View Motel (☎ 4455 1514; www.topviewmotel .com; 72 South St; s/d from $60/66; P X) Possibly one of the friendliest motels on the south coast, and in a good location overlooking the town. The rooms have DVD players.

South Coast Backpackers (☎ 4454 0500; www .southcoastbackpackers.com.au; 63 Princes Hwy; dm/d

$20/45) A small, clean place with spacious four- and six-bed dorms. Linen is included.

Ulladulla Headland Tourist Park (☎ 4455 2457; South St; camp sites from $16, cabins from $45; ☒) This park is on the headland a few blocks from the centre of town (at the end of South St). There's a playground and the other usual amenities. The beach is a bit of a hike from the park.

Eating
There are plenty of cafés and simple restaurants on Ulladulla's main street and in the arcades running off it. The region is known for its cheese, oysters and beef.

Ulladulla Guest House (mains $26-30; ☺ breakfast daily, dinner Mon & Thu-Sat; ☒) The restaurant at this guesthouse (p147) features a changing menu of local foods prepared with a French accent. The kitchen is creative and the atmosphere as romantic as you desire.

Bannister's Restaurant (☎ 4454 1933; 191 Mitchell Pde; mains from $35; ☺ breakfast daily, lunch Sun, dinner Tue-Sun; ☒) This restaurant is grandly situated on Bannister's Point 1km north of town; the Mod Oz fare matches the fine views. Look for local ingredients in the creative menu.

Edge Cafe (☎ 4454 3565; cnr Green & Boree Sts; lunch $7-12; ☺ lunch Mon-Sat, dinner Fri & Sat; ☒) Part licensed café, part gallery and part bakery, Edge Cafe has an enticing menu of foccacia sandwiches, curries and salads. Settle into one of the pavement tables.

Good choices if you want picnic supplies for jaunts in the local parks or beaches:

Just Good Food (☎ 4455 1156; Bellbrook Arcade; ☺ breakfast & lunch Mon-Fri) Excellent coffee, sandwiches and fresh juices.

Plaza Deli (☎ 4455 4590; Princes Hwy; ☺ lunch Mon-Sat) A deli known for its ham and numerous vegetarian specialities.

Getting There & Away
Long-distance buses stop on the highway outside the Marlin Hotel (northbound) or Traveland (southbound). Get tickets from **Harvey World Travel** (☎ 4455 5122; Rowen's Arcade).

Ulladulla Bus Lines (☎ 4455 1674) services the local area, mainly between Milton, Mollymook, Ulladulla and Burrill Lake. There are two services each weekday.

CANBERRA

☎ 02 / pop 297,000

The first things you'll notice about Canberra are the space and how green it is – the orderly layout and the millions of trees are thanks to the fact that the city was planned from the ground up.

When the separate colonies of Australia were federated in 1901, a decision to build a national capital was included in the constitution. American architect Walter Burley Griffin won the competition to design the city and in 1908 this site, diplomatically situated between rivals Sydney and Melbourne, was selected. In 1911 the Commonwealth government bought land for the Australian Capital Territory (ACT) and in 1913 decided to call the capital Canberra, a name derived from an Aboriginal term for 'meeting place'.

An exploration of Canberra will unearth some of the best examples of modern Australian architecture and some of the grandest public edifices and cultural attractions that taxes can buy.

ORIENTATION
The city is arranged around Lake Burley Griffin. Approaching the lake from the north, the main arterial road, Northbourne Ave, intersects compact Canberra City (AKA Civic). The pedestrian malls that are to the east comprise Canberra's main shopping areas.

South of the city, Northbourne Ave becomes Commonwealth Ave, which spans Lake Burley Griffin and also intersects Capital Circle. This road encircles Parliament House on Capital Hill, the apex of Walter Burley Griffin's parliamentary triangle. Located within and near the triangle are several noteworthy buildings; the group includes the High Court of Australia, National Gallery of Australia and Old Parliament House.

The rest of the city is made up of suburban clusters, each with their own 'town centres'. These comprise Gungahlin and Belconnen to the north of Civic, and Weston Creek, Woden Valley and Tuggeranong to the south.

Canberra International Airport is 7km southeast of the city; see p154.

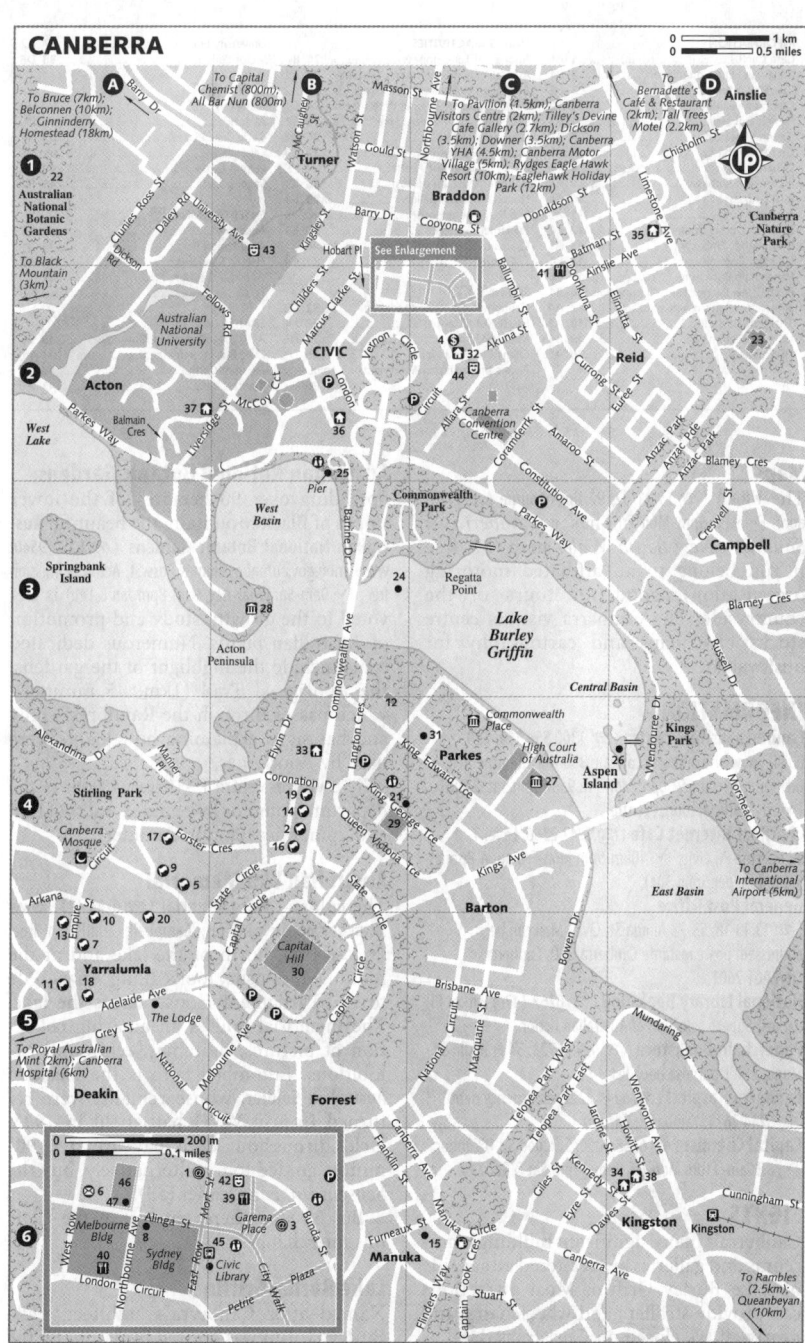

Maps

The **NRMA** (☎ 13 21 32; 92 Northbourne Ave, Braddon; ☼ 9am-5pm Mon-Fri) has a *Canberra & Southeast New South Wales* map ($7; free if you belong to an affiliated motoring organisation), good for tours of the countryside. The Canberra visitors centre stocks city maps and cartography for bushwalks.

INFORMATION

Canberra visitors centre (☎ 1300 554 114, 6205 0044; www.visitcanberra.com.au; 330 Northbourne Ave, Dickson; ☼ 9am-5.30pm Mon-Fri, 9am-4pm Sat & Sun) The city's official tourist centre.

CivicPort Internet Cafe (☎ 6247 2366; Level 1, 16 Garema Pl, Civic; ☼ 10am-9pm Mon-Fri, noon-8pm Sat & Sun; per 5min 30¢)

General Post Office
(☎ 13 13 18; 53-73 Alinga St, Civic) Mail can be addressed: poste restante Canberra GPO, Canberra City, ACT 2601.

National Library Bookshop (☎ 6262 1424; Parkes Pl, Parkes) Superb selection of Australian fiction.

Paperchain Bookstore (☎ 6295 6723; 34 Franklin St, Manuka) All-purpose book list.

Canberra Hospital (☎ 6244 2222, emergency dept ☎ 6244 2611; Yamba Dr, Garran)

Capital Chemist (☎ 6248 7050; Sargood St, O'Connor; ☼ 8.30am-11pm Mon-Fri, 9am-11pm Sat & Sun)

SIGHTS

Canberra's many significant buildings, museums and galleries are scattered either side of Lake Burley Griffin. Most attractions can provide strollers and wheelchairs, and nearly all are closed on Christmas day.

Australian National Botanic Gardens

Spreading over 90 hectares of the lower slopes of Black Mountain, the beautiful **Australian National Botanic Gardens** (☎ 6250 9540; www.anbg.gov.au/anbg; Clunies Ross St, Acton; admission free; ☼ 9am-5pm Mar-Dec, 9am-8pm Jan & Feb) is devoted to the growth, study and promotion of Australian plants. Numerous dedicated trails include the highlight of the gardens, the Aboriginal Trail (1km, 45 minutes), which passes through the Rainforest Gully and has signs explaining how plants were used by Aborigines.

The **visitors centre** (☼ 9.30am-4.30pm) is the departure point for free guided walks (11am and 2pm, plus 10am in summer).

Australian War Memorial

The colossal **war memorial** (☎ 6243 4211; www.awm.gov.au; Treloar Cres, Campbell; admission free; ☼ 10am-5pm), north of the lake and at the foot of Mt Ainslie, looks along Anzac Pde to Old Parliament House across the lake. The memorial houses an amazing collection of pictures, dioramas, relics and exhibitions. Entombed here is the **Unknown Australian Soldier**, whose remains were returned from a WWI battlefield in 1993. Held throughout each day are free 90-minute guided tours; alternatively, buy the *Self-guided Tour* leaflet ($3).

Bus 33 stops here; catch it at the Civic bus interchange.

Lake Burley Griffin

Named after Canberra's architect, Lake Burley Griffin was created by damming the

Molonglo River in 1963. Swimming is not recommended, but the lake is suitable for boating and great to cycle around. Boats, bikes and in-line skates are available for hire at Acton Park ferry terminal, on the northern shore.

Around the lake's 35km shoreline are many places of interest. The most visible is the **Captain Cook Memorial Water Jet**, built in 1970 for the bicentenary of Captain Cook's landfall.

National Gallery of Australia

This excellent **National Gallery** (☎ 6240 6502; www.nga.gov.au; Parkes Pl, Parkes; permanent collection free; ✆ 10am-5pm) showcases Australian art, ranging from traditional Aboriginal art to 20th-century works by Arthur Boyd, Sidney Nolan and Albert Tucker. Aboriginal works include bark paintings from Arnhem Land and *pukumani* burial poles from the Tiwi people of Melville and Bathurst Islands. The Sculpture Garden has a variety of striking pieces.

There are all-inclusive guided tours (11am and 2pm), plus a tour (11am Thursday and Sunday) focusing on Aboriginal and Torres Strait Islander art. The gallery often has free lectures and film screenings; phone for details. Visually impaired visitors should ask about the *Braille Guide*.

National Library of Australia

On Parkes Place beside the lake is the **National Library of Australia** (☎ 6262 1111; www.nla .gov.au; Parkes Pl, Parkes; admission free; ✆ main reading room 9am-9pm Mon-Thu, 9am-5pm Fri & Sat, 1.30-5pm Sun), one of the most elegant buildings in Canberra.

The library has more than six million items. Among its displays are collections of rare books, paintings, early manuscripts, photographs, oral histories and maps. Bookings are required for the free, 45-minute **Behind-the-Scenes Tour** (☎ 6262 1271; ✆ tour 12.30pm Thu). The **Exhibition Gallery** (admission free; ✆ 9am-5pm) presents thematic displays collated mainly from the library's diverse collections.

National Museum of Australia

This **museum** (☎ 6208 5000; www.nma.gov.au; Lawson Cres, Acton Peninsula; admission free; ✆ 9am-5pm), on the northern shore of the lake, showcases the land, nation and people of Australia through Australian eyes and with the aid of inter-active gizmos. There are lots of attendants on hand to help you navigate exhibitions on environmental change, indigenous culture, national icons and more, and you can take one-hour guided tours (adult/child/family $7.50/5/20).

Bus 34 from the Civic bus interchange runs here.

National Zoo & Aquarium

This impressive **zoo** (☎ 6287 8400; www.zooquar ium.com.au; Lady Denman Dr, Yarralumla; adult/child/concession/family $19/10.50/16/55; ✆ 9am-5pm) is near Scrivener Dam at the western end of Lake Burley Griffin.

Old Parliament House

Sitting between Parliament House and Lake Burley Griffin is **Old Parliament House** (☎ 6270 8222; www.oph.gov.au; King George Tce, Parkes; adult/concession/family $2/1/5; ✆ 9am-5pm). Smaller than the new Parliament House, it was the seat of government from 1927 to 1988. There's a free, 40-minute guided tour (9.30am, 10.15am, 11am, 11.45am, 12.45pm, 1.30pm, 2.30pm and 3.15pm), or guide yourself via a free leaflet. Old Parliament House incorporates the **National Portrait Gallery** (☎ 6270 8236; www.portrait.gov.au), which often stages special exhibitions.

Opposite the main entrance is the **Aboriginal Tent Embassy**, established in 1972 in response to governmental refusal to recognise land rights.

Parliament House

The four-legged, 81m flagpole atop Capital Hill marks the location of **Parliament House** (☎ 6277 5399; www.aph.gov.au; admission free; ✆ 9am-5pm).

Excellent free 45-minute guided tours on non-sitting days and 20-minute tours on sitting days are held every half-hour from 9am to 4pm. You're welcome to find your own way around but you may have to queue to watch parliamentary proceedings from the public galleries, especially in the House of Representatives. Note that tickets for question time (2pm on sitting days) in the House of Representatives are free but must first be booked through the **Sergeant at Arms** (☎ 6277 4889); tickets aren't required for the Senate Chambers.

Bus 39 runs to Parliament House; catch it at the Civic bus interchange.

Questacon – National Science & Technology Centre

Right near the library, this 'hands-on' **museum** (☎ 1800 020 603; www.questacon.edu.au; adult/child/concession/family $14/8/9.50/42; ☼ 9am-5pm) is educational and great fun. The 200-plus interactive exhibits show how science and technology work in everyday life.

FESTIVALS & EVENTS

National Multicultural Festival (www.multicultural festival.com.au) Celebrated over 10 days in February.
Royal Canberra Show (www.rncas.org.au/showweb site/main.html) The country meets the city at the end of February.
Celebrate Canberra (www.celebratecanberra.com) The city's extended birthday party in mid-March.
National Folk Festival (www.folkfestival.asn.au) One of the country's largest, held every March/April.
Floriade (www.floriadeaustralia.com) Held in September/October and dedicated to Canberra's spectacular spring flowers.

SLEEPING

There are only a handful of accommodation choices in the centre of Canberra. Most hotels and motels are either strung out along Northbourne Ave or ensconced in northern suburbs and around Capital Hill.

Budget

Canberra City Accommodation (☎ 6257 3999, 1800 300 488; www.canberracityaccommodation.com.au; 7 Akuna St, Civic; dm/s/d from $24/55/70; ✄ ▯ ▣) This bright complex incorporates Canberra Backpackers and, judging by its impressive roll call of services, it's mighty eager to please. Rates include an indoor pool, gym, 24-hour reception, bar, Internet café, and pay TV. Continental breakfasts ($4.50) and bike hire ($16 per day) are also available.

Victor Lodge (☎ 6295 7777; www.victorlodge.com.au; 29 Dawes St, Kingston; dm/s/d $25/55/70; ℗ ▯) This high-standard budget B&B is excellent value, offering lodgers an all-you-can-eat breakfast, spotless rooms (with linen) and reliable facilities. Guests can hire bikes ($15 per day) or simply stroll to the nearby Kingston cafés and shops. There's a pick-up/drop-off service, or catch buses 38, 39 or 80.

Canberra YHA (☎ 6248 9155; canberra@yhansw .org.au; 191 Dryandra St, O'Connor; dm/d/f from $20/55/85; ℗ ▯) This appealing purpose-built hostel is set in bushland beneath O'Connor Ridge, 6km northwest of Civic. It's a peaceful place

with an open-plan kitchen-lounge and pleasant outside decks. Bus 35 takes you there.

Canberra Motor Village (☎ 6247 5466; canmotor village@ozemail.com.au; Kunzea St, O'Connor; unpowered sites $15, powered sites $21-28, d $60-125; ℗) Dozing in a peaceful bush setting 6km northwest of the centre, this place has good amenities and an orderly arrangement of motel rooms and self-contained cabins.

Midrange & Top End

Hyatt Hotel Canberra (☎ 6270 1234; www.canberra .park.hyatt.com; Commonwealth Ave, Yarralumla; r from $250; ℗ ✄ ▣) Luxurious Art Deco hotel. Lavish facilities and round-the-clock room service make it Canberra's only five-star accommodation. Try for a room with a view of the lake, and ask about the various B&B packages.

Pacific International Apartments – Capital Tower (☎ 6276 3444, 1800 676 241; www.pacificint hotels.com; 2 Marcus Clarke St, Civic; apt from $185; ℗ ✄ ▣) Rooms on the southern side of this apartment complex's curving façade face Lake Burley Griffin's wind-rippled waters. The facilities are excellent and apartments have up to three bedrooms.

University House (☎ 6125 5211; www.anu.edu .au/unihouse; 1 Balmain Cres, Acton; s $80-130, d $115-185; ℗) This 1950s building, with furniture to match, is soothingly positioned in the midst of the rambling university grounds. Many of the spacious rooms have small balconies, and there's a good selection of wine in the cellar bottleshop.

Olims Hotel Canberra (☎ 6248 5511, 1800 020 016; www.olimshotel.com; cnr Ainslie & Limestone Aves, Braddon; r $100-155; ℗ ✄) This 1927 heritage-listed building and its later refurbishments surround a lovely terraced courtyard. The ground-floor 'superior' rooms are quite comfortable, but the 1st-floor, self-contained 'loft' rooms are more spacious and have balconies overlooking the garden.

Tall Trees Motel (☎ 6247 9200, 13 17 79; www .bestwestern.com.au/talltrees; 21 Stephen St, Ainslie; s/d from $100/120; ℗ ✄) The green grounds of this motel and its location in leafy Ainslie lend it a relaxed air. It's a good place to base yourself if you want to be near but not in the centre.

Motel Monaro (☎ 6295 2111; www.bestwestern .com.au/motelmonaro; 27 Dawes St, Kingston; r $125; ℗ ✄ ▯) Offers compact, well-maintained rooms on a quiet street near the Kingston shops. It has several large, multi-bed rooms that are ideal for groups, and does good walk-in rates when business is slow.

EATING

Most restaurants are in Civic, Kingston, Manuka and Griffith. There's also a fantastic Asian strip in Dickson and many other possibilities scattered throughout the suburbs.

Sage (☎ 6249 6050; Gorman House Arts Centre, Ainslie Ave, Braddon; lunch $10-18, mains $26; ☺ lunch & dinner Tue-Sat) A classy, intimate restaurant of warm tones, which serves delicious, beautifully presented dishes like marlin steak, and rabbit, leek and mushroom pie. A sturdy wine list complements the mains.

Caffe della Piazza (☎ 6248 9711; 19 Garema Pl, Civic; mains $12-24; ☺ lunch & dinner) The outdoor tables of this well-established favourite are usually crammed at lunchtime, and often at dinnertime too. Its tasty trademark pastas come in big portions and there's an excellent wine list.

Alanya (☎ 6295 9678; Upstairs, Style Arcade, Franklin St, Manuka; mains $18-26; ☺ lunch & dinner Mon-Fri, dinner Sat) The recipient of several industry accolades during its 20 years in the business, Alanya is an excellent Turkish eatery with a vaguely formal air and some curious ceiling decorations. Sample the *köfte* (meatballs) or some skewered chicken or lamb.

Dickson Asian Noodle House (☎ 6247 6380; 29 Woolley St, Dickson; mains $10-15; ☺ lunch & dinner) Perennially popular Laotian and Thai café, overflowing with customers all week long. Renovations have modernised the décor, but there are still no credit card facilities and there's a $30 minimum charge for Eftpos.

Lemon Grass (☎ 6247 2779; 65 London Circuit, Civic; mains $9-17; ☺ lunch & dinner Mon-Fri, dinner Sat) This small, informal Thai restaurant has garnered culinary awards for its dependable cuisine with a sizeable vegetarian selection. The spicy scents of stir fries and curries pull you in by the nostrils from the front door.

Legends (☎ 6295 3966; Franklin St, Manuka; mains $16-23; ☺ lunch & dinner Mon-Fri, dinner Sat) Upstairs Spanish restaurant suffused with a cheerful atmosphere and the strains of a flamenco guitarist most evenings. Nibble your way through the tapas menu ($7.50 to $9.50) or hoe into specialities like *bacalao* (salted cod), or Valencia paella.

THE AUTHOR'S CHOICE

Atlantic (☎ 6232 7888; 20 Palmerston La, Manuka; mains $28-31; ☺ lunch & dinner Mon-Fri, dinner Sat) A sea of white tablecloths is adrift in Atlantic's quiet, intimate interior and up on the breezy rooftop terrace. Dine on Atlantic salmon, lobster and other fresh, expertly prepared catches, or keep your tastebuds on dry land with slow-braised Wagyu beef.

ENTERTAINMENT

For entertainment listings, see the 'Fly' section of Thursday's *Canberra Times* and the free monthly street mag *bma*. **Ticketek** (☎ 6219 6666; www.ticketek.com.au; Akuna St, Civic) sells tickets to major events, including big-name gigs at the Royal Theatre in the Canberra Convention Centre.

Electric Shadows (☎ 6247 5060; www.electricshadows.com.au; Akuna St, Civic; adult/child/concession $14/8/9) A venerable art-house cinema with weekday matinees (pre-5pm, adults $9) and $8 Wednesday sessions.

Toast (☎ 6230 0003; City Walk, Civic; admission $3-10) Many pubs have free live music. Diversity reigns supreme in this place, where fans of goth, industrial, salsa and folk mingle. It's located upstairs behind Electric Shadows.

ANU Union Bar (☎ 6125 2446; www.anuunion.com.au; Union Court, Acton; admission $5-20; ☺ gigs 8pm) Has energetic live music up to three times a week during semester.

Academy (☎ 6257 3355; www.academyclub.com.au; Bunda St, Civic; admission $5-15; ☺ 10pm-late Thu-Sun) A striking nightclub – the original movie screen of this former cinema dominates the crowded main dance space with frenetic, larger-than-life visuals.

GETTING THERE & AWAY
Air

Canberra International Airport (☎ 6275 2236) is serviced by **Qantas** (☎ 13 13 13; www.qantas.com.au; Jolimont Centre, Northbourne Ave, Civic) and **Virgin Blue** (☎ 13 67 89; www.virginblue.com.au), with direct flights to Brisbane (from $180), Melbourne (from $140) and Sydney (from $120).

Bus

The interstate bus terminal is at the **Jolimont Centre** (Northbourne Ave, Civic), which has left-luggage lockers, showers, Internet access and free phone lines to the visitors centre.

SOUTH COAST NEW SOUTH WALES

Inside is the **CountryLink travel centre** (☎ 13 22 32, 6257 1576; www.countrylink.com.au; ⏱ 9am-5pm Mon-Fri), which books seats on most services. Travellers headed to the south coast can board a CountryLink coach that travels via Cooma to Eden (adult/concession $45/25, 4¼ hours).

Greyhound (☎ 13 14 99; www.greyhound.com.au; ⏱ Jolimont Centre office 6am-9.30pm) has frequent services to Sydney (adult/concession $35/32, five hours) and Melbourne ($70/65, nine hours).

Murrays (☎ 13 22 51; www.murrays.com.au; ⏱ Jolimont Centre counter 7am-7pm) has daily services to Sydney (adult/concession $35/24, 3¼ hours), Batemans Bay ($24/22, 2½ hours), Narooma ($36/32, 4½ hours) and Wollongong ($31/24, 3½ hours).

Car & Motorcycle
The Hume Hwy connects Sydney and Melbourne, passing 50km north of Canberra. The Federal Hwy runs north to connect with the Hume near Goulburn and the Barton Hwy meets the Hume near Yass. To the south, the Monaro Hwy connects Canberra with Cooma.

Train
Kingston train station (☎ 6295 1198; Burke Cres), off Wentworth Ave, is the city's rail terminus. Buses 39 and 80 run between here and Civic. You can book trains and connecting buses inside the station at the **CountryLink travel centre** (☎ 13 22 32, 6239 7053; www.countrylink.com .au; ⏱ 6.15am-5.30pm Mon-Sat, 10.30am-5.30pm Sun).

CountryLink trains run to/from Sydney (adult/child $50/25, 4¼ hours, two daily). There's no direct train to Melbourne, but a CountryLink coach to Cootamundra links with the XPT train to Melbourne ($95/50, nine hours, one daily). A longer but more scenic bus/train service to Melbourne is the V/Line Capital Link ($60/38, 10½ hours) running every Tuesday and Friday via Cooma and the East Gippsland forests to Sale, where you board the Melbourne-bound train.

GETTING AROUND
To/From the Airport
Canberra International Airport is 7km southeast of the city. A taxi to the city costs $20. **Deane's Buslines** (☎ 6299 3722) operates the AirLiner bus ($5, 20 minutes, 11 times daily Monday to Friday) between the airport and the city.

Bus & Taxi
Canberra's public transport provider is the **ACT Internal Omnibus Network** (Action; ☎ 13 17 10; www.action.act.gov.au). Visit the **information kiosk** (East Row, Civic; ⏱ 7.15am-5pm) for free route maps and timetables, or buy the all-routes *Canberra Bus Map* ($2.20) from newsagents.

You can purchase single-trip tickets (adult/concession $2.40/1.30), but a better deal is a daily ticket (adult/concession $6/3). Pre-purchase tickets from Action agents (including the visitors centre and some newsagents) or buy them from the driver.

Canberra Cabs (☎ 13 22 27) has wheelchair-accessible vehicles. There's a convenient taxi rank on Bunda St, outside the Greater Union cinema.

BATEMANS BAY TO NAROOMA

The far south coast of NSW is the least developed stretch in the state and it has some of the best beaches and forests. In between population centres such as Batemans Bay and Narooma are regions just begging to be explored. (And calling those two 'population centres' is a bit rich, given that they slumber much of the year, only stirring during school holidays).

The visitors centres in Batemans Bay (p156) and Narooma (p159) sell topographic maps and copies of Graham Barrow's book *Walking on the South Coast*, which details many short walks between Nowra and Eden. Information on national parks is available from the NPWS office in Narooma (p159).

Montague Island exemplifies the closeness of nature that typifies the region: some 10km off-shore, it is home to scores of penguins who blithely ignore the iconic lighthouse.

MURRAMARANG NATIONAL PARK
This beautiful **coastal park** (admission per car $7) begins about 20km south of Ulladulla and extends almost all the way south to Batemans Bay.

Merry, **Pebbly** and **Depot Beaches** are all popular with surfers, as is **Wasp Head** south of Durras. There are numerous walking trails snaking off from these beach areas

SOUTH COAST NEW SOUTH WALES

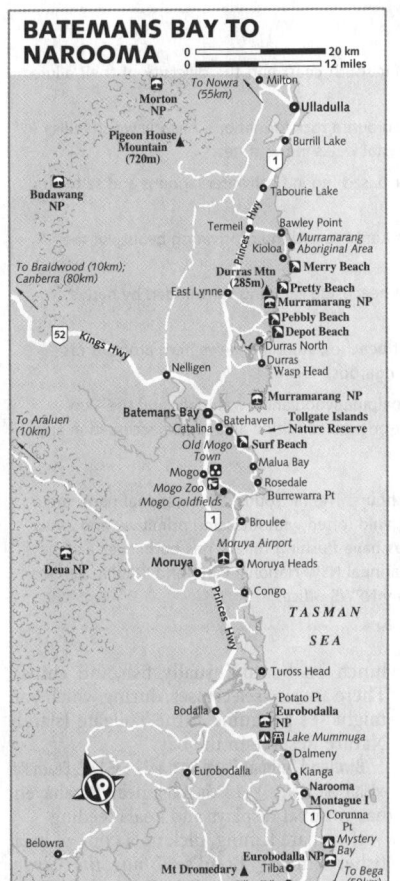

BATEMANS BAY TO NAROOMA

Depot Beach camping area (☎ 4478 6582; camp sites per person $5) Another beachside NPWS camping ground, with basic amenities.

NEARBY SETTLEMENTS

There are small towns on the borders of the park and one or two on old leases within the park itself. If camp sites in the park are booked out you could try these places.

Turn off the highway at Termeil to get to Bawley Point and Kioloa, near the north end of the park. There are caravan parks in these small towns, and just south of Kioloa are the excellent Merry Beach and Pretty Beach, both with privately run caravan parks. However this area lacks the steep and forested slopes behind the beaches that you'll find further south.

Take the East Lynne turn-off from the highway to get to North Durras, on the inlet to Durras Lake. There's not much here except a lovely beach and swarms of caravans squeezed into three abutting caravan parks.

Durras Lake North Holiday Park (☎ 4478 6072; 57 Durras North Rd; camp sites from $7-30, dm $12, cabins $45-150) has just over 100 camp sites and eight cabins that comprise this friendly place. It is popular during holidays.

In the south of the park (turn off the highway at Benandarah), Durras is a quiet village of substantial holiday houses. At the south end of the town is **Murramarang Resort** (☎ 4478 6355; www.murramarangresort.com.au; camp sites $14, cabins from $62). It's a big, modern place with a row of Norfolk pines between it and the beach. Posh extras like camp sites with their own bathrooms and cabins with full kitchens and spas are the norm.

Getting There & Away

The Princes Hwy runs parallel to Murramarang, but it's 10km from the highway to the beaches or the small settlements in and near the park. There's no public transport into the park and many of the roads are unsealed.

BATEMANS BAY

☎ 02 / pop 10,219

Batemans Bay is a fishing port that has boomed to become one of the south coast's largest holiday centres, partly because of its good beaches and beautiful estuary, and partly because it's the closest coastal town to landlocked Canberra. Either way it's easily the most attractive large town in the region.

and a steep but enjoyable walk up **Durras Mountain** (283m). Kangaroos abound in the gum- and rainforests and around lovely Durras Lake. Camping fees apply if you stay overnight.

Sleeping

IN THE PARK

Pebbly Beach camping ground (☎ 4478 6006; camp sites per person per night $5) This camping ground, run by the NPWS, is in a lovely spot. Sites are scarce during school holidays, so you should book. To get to Pebbly Beach, turn off the highway on to North Durras Rd south of East Lynne – avoid Pebbly Beach Rd, which is very rough. Caravans can't be taken on the last section of the road to Pebbly Beach.

THE SOUTH COAST'S BEST PARKS

Some of NSW's best parks are found along the far south coast and the diversity of their allure is surprising. Choices include:

- **Ben Boyd National Park** (p169) Surreal, multicoloured rock formations, historic wood mills and whaling stations, and some of the best coastal walks in the state.
- **Bournda National Park** (p165) Plenty of water-based fun in freshwater lagoons and saltwater lakes.
- **Eurobodalla National Park** (p158) Indigenous heritage and the captivating beauty of the rock formations at Bingie Bingie Point.
- **Mimosa Rocks National Park** (p163) Secluded beachside camping surrounded by native forests, caves and pounding surf.
- **Murramarang National Park** (p154) Good surf beaches, stunning views from atop Durras Mountain (283m) and almost overly friendly kangaroos.
- **Wadbilliga National Park** (p162) Dramatic subalpine woodlands, waterfalls and the 5km Tuross River Gorge. Much of this park is in near-pristine condition and can be accessed in any type of car.

And your visit need not be limited to just a few hours. The far south coast national parks are a camper's dream: uncrowded for most of the year, wild (often without being primitive) and easily accessed in most cars. Most of the camping areas have flushing toilets, gas barbecues and hot showers. For more details, pick up a copy of the annual NSW National Parks and Wildlife Service (NPWS) *Guide to NSW National Parks*, free from any NPWS office.

Information

Bay Bookshop (☎ 4472 6338; Blandford Centre, Orient St; ⊗ 9am-5.30pm Mon-Fri, 9am-4pm Sat, 10am-2pm Sun) Excellent independent store with a good selection of local titles.

DragNet (☎ 4472 7009; Shop B3, Stocklands Mall, Perry St; per hr $6) Top-notch Internet shop with Wi-Fi, CD burning and more.

Visitors centre (☎ 4472 6900, 1800 802 528; cnr Beach Rd & Princes Hwy; ⊗ 9am-5pm) Large centre; has a gallery with local works.

Sights & Activities

The **Old Courthouse Museum** (☎ 4472 8993; Museum Place; adult/child $5/1; ⊗ 1-4pm Tue-Thu), just off Orient St, has displays relating to local history. Just behind the museum is the small **Water Garden Town Park** and a **boardwalk** through wetlands. The **Mara Mia** is a nice waterside walkway.

On the north side of the Clyde River estuary just across the bridge are a couple of boat-hire places. **Oyster Shed Boat Hire** (☎ 4472 6771; Last Shed, Wray St) hires out runabouts from $50 for two hours.

Several boats offer **cruises** up the estuary from the ferry wharf just east of the bridge. The standard three-hour cruise stops at Nelligen (adult/child $26/13) and you can have lunch on board (usually fish and chips). There are also sea cruises, during which you might see penguins at the Tollgate Islands Nature Reserve in the bay.

Birdland Animal Park (☎ 4472 5364; 55 Beach Rd; adult/child $14/7; ⊗ 9.30am-4pm), near Batehaven, has wombat displays and koala feeding.

If you are fishing, pick up a copy of local fisher Lindsay Bond's *Fishing the Clyde, Tips and Secrets* at Bay Bookshop. Even non-anglers will enjoy his wit.

BEACHES

The closest beach to the town centre is **Corrigans Beach**. South of Corrigans Beach is a series of small beaches dotting the rocky shore. There are longer beaches along the coast north of the bridge, leading into Murramarang National Park.

Surfers flock to **Surf Beach**, **Malua Bay**, the small **McKenzies Beach** (just south of Malua Bay) and **Broulee**, which has a small wave when everywhere else is flat. For the experienced, the best surfing is at **Pink Rocks** (near Broulee) when a north swell is running. Locals say the waves are sometimes 6m high. Broulee itself has a wide crescent of sand, but there's a strong rip at the northern end.

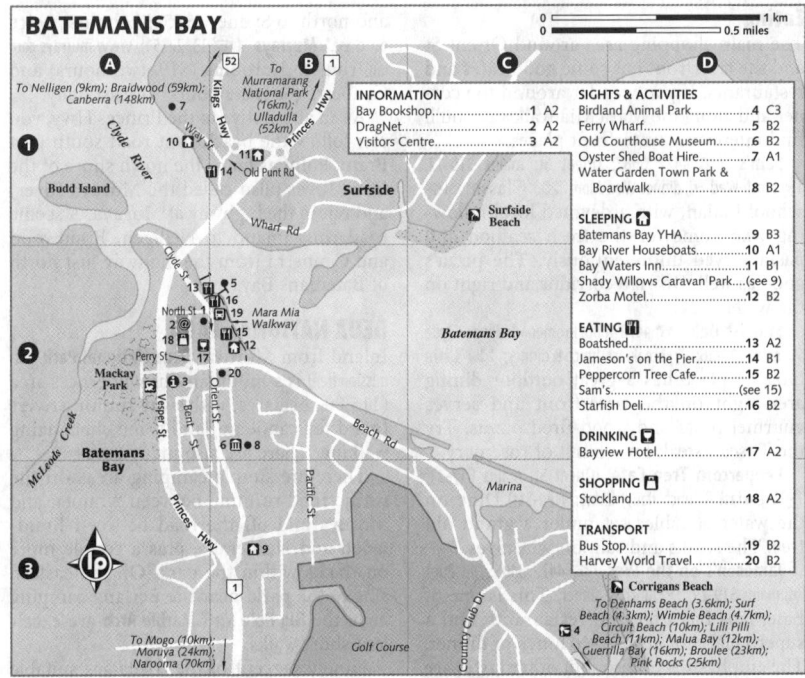

BATEMANS BAY

INFORMATION
Bay Bookshop............................1 A2
DragNet...................................2 A2
Visitors Centre.........................3 A2

SIGHTS & ACTIVITIES
Birdland Animal Park..................4 C3
Ferry Wharf.............................5 B2
Old Courthouse Museum............6 B2
Oyster Shed Boat Hire...............7 A1
Water Garden Town Park &
   Boardwalk............................8 B2

SLEEPING
Batemans Bay YHA....................9 B3
Bay River Houseboats..............10 A1
Bay Waters Inn........................11 B1
Shady Willows Caravan Park....(see 9)
Zorba Motel...........................12 B2

EATING
Boatshed................................13 A2
Jameson's on the Pier.............14 B1
Peppercorn Tree Cafe.............15 B2
Sam's...................................(see 15)
Starfish Deli...........................16 B2

DRINKING
Bayview Hotel.........................17 A2

SHOPPING
Stockland...............................18 A2

TRANSPORT
Bus Stop................................19 B2
Harvey World Travel...............20 B2

To Nelligen (9km); Braidwood (59km); Canberra (148km)
To Murramarang National Park (16km); Ulladulla (52km)
Clyde River
Budd Island
Surfside
Surfside Beach
Old Punt Rd
Wharf Rd
Batemans Bay
Clyde St
North St
Mara Mia Walkway
Perry St
Mackay Park
Orient St
Batemans Bay
McLeods Creek
Vesper St
Bent St
Beach Rd
Marina
Princes Hwy
Pacific St
To Mogo (10km); Moruya (24km); Narooma (70km)
Golf Course
Country Club Dr
Corrigans Beach
To Denhams Beach (3.6km); Surf Beach (4.3km); Wimbie Beach (4.7km); Circuit Beach (10km); Lilli Pilli Beach (11km); Malua Bay (12km); Guerilla Bay (16km); Broulee (23km); Pink Rocks (25km)

0 ———— 1 km
0 ———— 0.5 miles

Festivals & Events

There are **game-fishing tournaments** in January and March. Up in Nelligen, a **Country Music Festival** (☎ 4478 6368) twangs along on various Sundays.

Sleeping

There are many holiday apartments that do good business in summer. Out of season you might be able to rent one for less than a week. Letting agents include **Advantage Byron Bay** (☎ 4472 4444; www.professionalsbb.com.au).

Zorba Motel (☎ 4472 4804; Orient St; s/d $75/85; P ⊠) You can't beat the views from Zorba, which has a great spot in the middle of town. The motel is little changed in decades but continues to offer comfort and a friendly welcome. If full, there are others nearby.

Bay Waters Inn (☎ 4472 6344; cnr Princes & Kings Hwys; r from $90; P ⊠ ⊠) The rather long list of amenities make up for this motel's north-of-the-river location. There's mini golf, a playground, a spa, tennis courts and more. Rooms are nondescript but comfortable.

Batemans Bay YHA (☎ 4472 4972; www.yha.com.au; cnr Old Princes Hwy & South St; dm $22-28, d $48-56; ⊠) The youth hostel is in the Shady Willows Holiday Park just south of the centre. The location is verdant and besides the pool there is a playground, which is popular with kids of all ages.

There are several caravan parks along the coast road south of town.

Shady Willows Caravan Park (☎ 4472 4972; Old Princes Hwy; site $18-30, cabins from $46; ⊠) A well-equipped park that shares the site with the Bateman's Bay YHA. The site is shady and everything in town is a short walk.

HOUSEBOATS

Bay River Houseboats (☎ 4471 2253; www.bayriverhouseboats.com.au; Wray St) You can hire eight- and 10-berth houseboats from this operation on the north side of the river. From May to August (low season) an eight-berth boat costs $510 for four nights (Monday to Friday) or a weekend, or $820 for a full week. Prices almost double in December and January. Shared between a few people these boats can become your own party barge.

Eating

The main shopping area around Orient St and the riverfront has some good cafés and restaurants. If you wander around the corner and along the Mara Mia walkway you'll find interesting waterfront places.

Sam's (☎ 4472 6687; Orient St; mains $10-12; ☺ lunch Wed-Fri, dinner Wed-Mon; ☻) Classic old-school Italian, with a devoted local following who come for the fresh seafood and pasta served unpretentiously. The pizza's good as well. Down a corridor and right on the water. BYO.

Starfish Deli (☎ 4472 4880; Promenade Plaza, Clyde St; mains $13-26; ☺ breakfast, lunch & dinner; ☻) This buzzing place has a great outdoor dining area right on the waterfront and serves gourmet pasta and wood-fired pizzas. Try the Tuscan steak for a burst of rosemary.

Peppercorn Tree Café (Orient St; mains $17-21; ☺ breakfast & lunch daily, dinner Wed-Sat) Dine on the water at tables set under a grand old tree. The steaks and salmon win raves.

Jameson's on the Pier (☎ 4472 6405; Old Punt Rd; mains $19-29; ☺ lunch & dinner) This is one of Batemans Bay's fanciest restaurants, and a superb place for an alfresco lunch or dinner. The emphasis is on fish, but other tastes are likely to find something from the short but exquisite menu.

Boatshed (☎ 4421 2419; Clyde St fishing wharf; lunch $5-15; ☺ lunch) You can buy seafood straight off the boats at this dockside place as well as fish and chips.

Drinking

Bayview Hotel (☎ 4472 4522; 20 Orient St; ☺ 10am-midnight) The only real pub in town, the Bay-view attracts everyone from tourists chilling to yobbos yelling. There's a DJ and dancing on Fridays and cover bands on Saturdays.

Shopping

Stockland (☎ 4472 1466; 1 Perry St) The centre itself is undergoing a bit of a commercial boom, with the opening of this huge new mall with 30 stores and supermarkets.

Getting There & Away

Harvey World Travel (☎ 4472 9990; cnr Beach Rd & Orient St) handles bus bookings and has timetables in the window. The bus stop is outside the newsagent on Clyde St.

Premier Motor Service (☎ 13 34 10; www.premierms.com.au) runs south to Eden ($30, 3½ hours)

and north to Sydney ($35, 5½ hours) twice a day. **Murrays** (☎ 13 22 51; www.murrays.com.au) runs to Narooma ($19, two hours) and Canberra ($24, 2½ hours) at least daily.

As an alternative to the Princes Hwy, you can follow the beachfront road south past Pretty Point as far as the north shore of the Deua River (also called the Moruya River) and rejoin the highway at Moruya. A scenic road runs inland to Nelligen, Braidwood and Canberra from the highway just north of Batemans Bay.

DEUA NATIONAL PARK

Inland from Moruya, **Deua National Park** (admission free) is a mountainous wilderness area (115,000 hectares) with swift-running rivers (good for canoeing) and some challenging walking. There are also many caves.

There are simple camping areas off the scenic road running between Araluen and Moruya and off the road between Braidwood and Numeralla, plus a couple more on tracks within the park. On the eastern side of the park, near the Berlang camping area, the **Big Hole** and **Marble Arch** are excellent short walks.

Ninety percent of the roads are suitable for 4WD. Contact the Narooma NPWS (opposite) for more information.

EUROBODALLA NATIONAL PARK

The stretch of coast that features the segmented **Eurobodalla National Park** (admission free) is an area of many lakes, bays and inlets backed by spotted-gum forests. Eurobodalla is an Aboriginal word meaning 'place of many waters' and there are Aboriginal middens (the remains of shellfish feasts) here, as well as native wildlife such as potoroos, hooded plovers and white-footed dunnarts. Don't miss the incredible rock formations at Bingie Bingie Point. Contact the Narooma NPWS (opposite) for more information.

MOGO
☎ 02 / pop 223

Mogo is a quaint strip of old wooden shops and houses almost entirely devoted to Devonshire teas, crafts and antiques. Just off the highway is **Old Mogo Town** (☎ 4474 2123; www.oldmogotown.com.au; James St; adult/child $14/6; cabins per person $22-105; ☺ 10am-5pm), a rambling re-creation of a pioneer village. You can stay in cabins inside the complex, giving you a good opportunity to play pioneer after the day-trippers are gone.

Mogo Zoo (☎ 4474 4930; 222 Tomakin Rd; adult/child $16/8; ☺ 9am-5pm), 2km east off the highway, is a small but interesting zoo with exotic wildlife such as Bengal and Sumatran tigers and the ever-playful lemurs. Feeding time for the tigers is 11am and 2pm.

Willow Cafe (☎ 4474 5445; Princes Hwy; meals $7-14; ☺ brunch Sat & Sun, lunch Wed-Mon) is a perfect spot for a break from everything twee. This gem of a café has creative sandwiches, salads and baked goods. Kids, vegans and more will find items just for them on the changing menu.

MORUYA
☎ 02 / pop 2549

Moruya, 25km south of Batemans Bay and about 5km inland, is on the estuary of the Deua (Moruya) River. The river's banks turn into wetlands as it sprawls down to the sea at **Moruya Heads**, the hamlet on the south head, where there's a good **surf beach** and views from Taragy Point.

The **Bush Orchestra** (☎ 4474 3554; cnr Cheetham St & Ted Hunt Tce; adult/family $4/8; ☺ 8am-6pm), about 2km west of the highway, is a guided forest walk with music by the abundant bird life. With advance notice, you can listen to prose spoken by the resident philosopher.

There's a popular country **market** (☎ 4474 4106) every Saturday morning, on the south side of Moruya Bridge.

The best place to stay in town is the **Post & Telegraph B&B** (☎ 4474 5475; www.southcoast.com .au/postandtel; cnr Page & Campbell Sts; s/d from $90/110), the beautifully restored old post office, which features polished floorboards, iron beds and verandas overlooking gardens. Rooms come with full breakfast.

The River (☎ 4474 5505; 16B Church St; mains $12-22; ☺ lunch & dinner Wed-Sun; ☒) is right on the…you guessed it. The views outside are complemented by the sleek country design inside. The food is proof that rural doesn't mean bumpkin: Mod Oz mixes liberally with international flavours on the ever-changing menu. There's a long wine list and you can walk things off in the herb garden.

Priors Scenic Express (☎ 1800 816 234) buses run from Batemans Bay to Moruya and you might be able to get a lift to Moruya Heads on a school bus.

CONGO

South of Moruya Heads, Congo, in Euro-bodalla National Park, is a small cluster of houses on an estuary and a long surf beach. It's very pretty and peaceful. Volunteers are helping to repair damage to the dunes here and they welcome assistance. There's a basic camping area ($5). You'll need to bring in all your food and bring or boil drinking water.

A dirt road to Congo turns off the road between Moruya and Moruya Heads; another partly sealed road leaves the highway about 10km south of Moruya.

NAROOMA
☎ 02 / pop 3412

Narooma is a seaside holiday town that isn't as developed as Batemans Bay to the north or Merimbula to the south. The natural beauty of the waterfront fades as you head up to the commercial centre on the hill.

Information

Visitors centre (☎ 4476 2881; Princes Hwy; ☺ 9am-5pm) Just south of the bridge.

NPWS information office (☎ 4476 2888; cnr Princes Hwy & Field St; ☺ 8.30am-4.30pm Mon-Fri) Narooma is an access point for both Deua and Wadbilliga National Parks, and this is a very helpful office.

Library (☎ 4476 1164; Field St; ☺ 10am-5pm Mon-Fri, 9.30am-2pm Sat) There's free Internet access at the popular new library.

Sights & Activities

You can cruise inland up the Wagonga River on the **Wagonga Princess** (☎ 4476 2665; Riverside Dr; adult/child $20/14). Call for schedules of the three-hour cruises, which include a stop for a walk through the bush and some billy tea. Book directly or through the visitors centre.

There are several boat-hire places along Riverside Dr, so you can go **boating** on Wagonga Inlet under your own steam. There's a nice **walk** along the inlet and around to the ocean, and safe swimming just inside the heads.

A good rainy-day weekend activity is to see a film at the **Narooma Cinema** (☎ 4476 2352; 94 Campbell St), a picture palace that began showing flicks in 1926 and hasn't changed much since.

For **surfing**, Mystery Bay, between Cape Dromedary and Corunna Point, is rocky but good, as is Handkerchief Beach, especially at the north end. Narooma's Bar Beach is

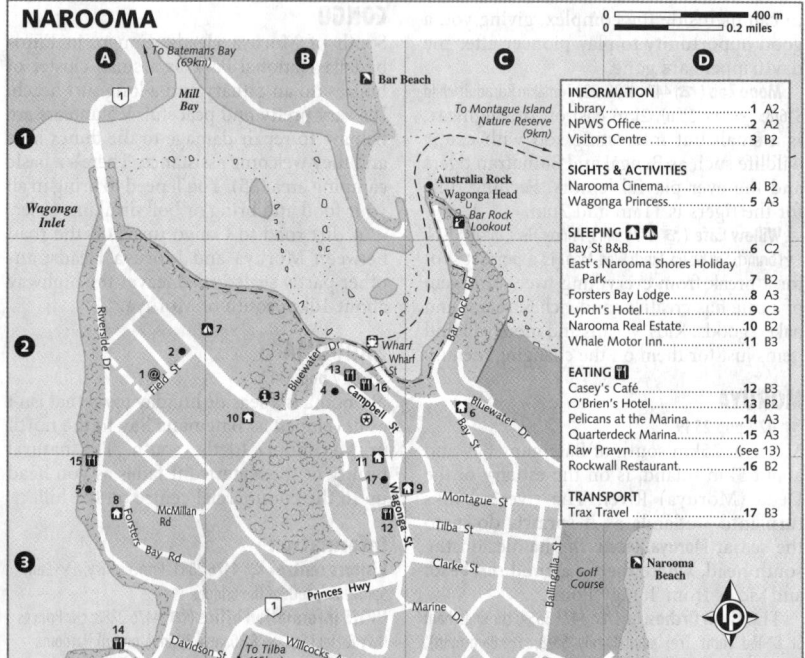

NAROOMA

INFORMATION	
Library...1 A2	
NPWS Office.....................................2 A2	
Visitors Centre 3 B2	

SIGHTS & ACTIVITIES	
Narooma Cinema.............................4 B2	
Wagonga Princess..........................5 A3	

SLEEPING	
Bay St B&B..6 C2	
East's Narooma Shores Holiday	
Park...7 B2	
Forsters Bay Lodge.........................8 A3	
Lynch's Hotel....................................9 C3	
Narooma Real Estate.....................10 B2	
Whale Motor Inn............................11 B3	

EATING	
Casey's Café...................................12 B3	
O'Brien's Hotel...............................13 B3	
Pelicans at the Marina...................14 A3	
Quarterdeck Marina.......................15 A3	
Raw Prawn...................................(see 13)	
Rockwall Restaurant......................16 B2	

TRANSPORT	
Trax Travel.....................................17 B3	

best when a southeasterly is blowing. Potato Point is another popular hang-out.

Fishing charters are popular and cost around $80 for four hours including all equipment. The visitors centre has a list of operators.

The small **Lighthouse Museum** is in the visitors centre and features an old Fresnel light.

MONTAGUE ISLAND

About 10km offshore from Narooma, this small island was once an important source of food for local Aborigines (who called it Barunguba) and is now a nature reserve. **Fairy penguins** nest here and, although you'll see some all year round, there are more than 10,000 in late winter and spring. Many other sea birds and hundreds of sea lions make their homes on the island. There's also a historic **lighthouse**.

The only way to see the island is via a 30-minute **boat trip** (☎ 4476 2881; adult/child $89/69), and three-hour tours are conducted by a NPWS guide. Trips usually leave daily in summer, but are dependent on numbers and weather conditions at other times, so book ahead through the visitors centre.

Take the afternoon trip if you want to see the fairy penguins.

The clear waters around the island are good for **diving**, especially from February to June; you can snorkel with the sea lions. **Island Charters Narooma** (☎ 4476 1047; www.island chartersnarooma.com; 16 Old Princes Hwy; tours per person from $65) offers diving, snorkelling, whale-watching and other tours. Attractions in the area include grey nurse sharks, sea lions and the wreck of the SS *Lady Darling*. Meet at the wharf.

Festivals & Events

The **Narooma Festival** is held in February and the **Surfboat Marathon** is in November.

Sleeping

Narooma Real Estate (☎ 4476 2169; www.narooma realestate.com.au; Princes Hwy) deals in the myriad of holiday accommodation.

Forsters Bay Lodge (☎ 4476 2319; 55 Forsters Bay Rd; d $68-85) In a quiet spot near pretty Wagonga Inlet, Forsters has six simple but comfortable rooms. There are laundry facilities and full kitchens.

Bay St B&B (☎ 4476 3336; 5 Bay St; d $140-90) A central place, with modern rooms and wide sunny verandas, this home is up on the hill.

Whale Motor Inn (☎ 4476 2411; www.whalemotor inn.com; Wagonga St; s/d from $100/115; P ⊠ ▣) This motel offers large, clean rooms and a restaurant that provides room service to guests. Amenities include DVD players and kitchenettes.

Lynch's Hotel (☎ 4476 2001; 135 Wagonga St; s/d $40/60) Serving the sleepy and the thirsty for more than 100 years, Lynch's offers basic pub accommodation and cheap beers late at night.

East's Narooma Shores Holiday Park (☎ 4476 2046; www.easts.com.au; Princes Hwy; camp sites from $19, cabin d from $50) East's is a large place that has more than 260 camp sites and 43 cabins. There are many extras including camp sites with bathrooms, and cabins with full kitchens.

Eating

Quarterdeck Marina (☎ 4476 2763; 13 Riverside Dr; lunch $6-8, dinner from $12; ☙ lunch daily, dinner Sat) Pull up a chair on the great deck overhanging the river and watch the pelicans while you tuck into the good portions of fresh seafood. The takeaway window is busy all day.

Pelicans at the Marina (☎ 4476 2403; 31 Riverside Dr; meals $10-17; ☙ breakfast & lunch Tue-Sun) The simple, elegant interior yields enticing views of the harbour. The menu is also simple and elegant and features such luxuries as oysters five ways and specials such as prawns in kumquat glaze. Go ahead, have a pesto roll.

Casey's Café (☎ 4476 1241; 120 Wagonga St; meals $6-12; ☙ breakfast & lunch) Casual Casey's Café has not only the best coffee in town, it also serves up great smoothies, burgers, salads and sandwiches.

Raw Prawn (☎ 4476 3691; 101 Campbell St; meals $7-16; ☙ breakfast, lunch & dinner) This bistro, inside O'Brien's Hotel, serves good solid pub meals with an awesome view out to the ocean off the rear deck.

Rockwall Restaurant (☎ 4476 2040; 107 Campbell St; mains $18-22; ☙ dinner Wed-Sun) The long wine list has many a choice to complement the fresh seafood, steaks and salads. Both the vino and many of the ingredients are sourced locally.

Getting There & Away

Bus bookings are handled by **Trax Travel** (☎ 4476 2688; 108 Wagonga St), near the post office on the hill. Buses stop nearby.

Premier Motor Service (☎ 13 34 10; www.premier ms.com.au) buses stop in Narooma on the run between Sydney and Melbourne. **Murrays** (☎ 13 22 51; www.murrays.com.au) stops on its daily run between Narooma and Canberra via Batemans Bay.

AROUND NAROOMA
Tilba & Around

Tilba is a tiny town that's set in a nook of a valley that has remained almost unchanged since the 19th century – except that now the main street is jammed with visitors' cars, especially during the weekends in summer. Still, the detour off Princes Hwy is worth the effort, even if just for the scenery, which is postcard perfect. And if you can't get enough cute, visit **Tilba Tilba**, a nearby town smaller than its singularly named neighbour.

There's information, including a handy town guide, at the **Bates Emporium** (☎ 4473 7290; ☙ 8am-5pm) at the start of the main street. It also serves as community centre and post office.

You can visit several working craft shops and the **ABC Cheese Factory** (☎ 4473 7387; ☙ 9am-5pm), the producer of fine cheeses, especially the smoked ones. The honey is good too.

The **Tilba Festival**, with lots of music, entertainment and several thousand visitors is held at Easter.

Central Tilba is perched on the side of **Mt Dromedary** (797m), one of the highest mountains along the south coast. There's lush forest on the mountain, which is part of the **Gulaga Flora Reserve**, and there are great views from the top. Beginning at Pam's Store in Tilba Tilba you can walk up along an old **pack-horse trail**. The return walk of 11km takes about five hours, but don't miss the loop walk at the summit. There is often rain and mist on the mountain, so come prepared.

SLEEPING & EATING

Two Storey B&B (☎ 4473 7290; www.babs.com.au /twostory; r $105-135) This 1894 place, next to the Tilba store, has plenty of atmosphere and charm with great views and a cosy log fire. Some rooms have bathrooms.

DETOUR: WADBILLIGA NATIONAL PARK

A rugged, subalpine wilderness area of 77,000 hectares, Wadbilliga covers much of the rugged hills away from the coast and Narooma. It offers good walking for experienced bushwalkers. One popular trail is along the 5km **Tuross River Gorge** to the **Tuross Falls**. There's a camping area on the northwestern side of the park, near the walk to the falls. Another camping area, in the centre of the park on the Wadbilliga River, is reached via Bourkes Rd from the east. About 85% of the roads in the park are suitable for 4WD only. At Brogo Dam, **Brogo Wilderness Canoes** (☎ 6492 7328) offers canoe hire in the park for $20 per person for four hours. Call to reserve. Access is via unsealed Warrigal Range Rd, 11km north of Bega off the Princes Hwy. For more information, contact the Narooma NPWS (p159).

Wirrina (☎ 4473 7279; www.naturecoast-tourism.com.au/goodnite; Blacksmiths Lane; s/d with breakfast $90/110) The veranda overlooks a cute valley and the three rooms are surrounded by a prolific garden.

Dromedary Hotel (☎ 4473 7223; 5 Bate St; d with breakfast $60) This is a nice old pub in Central Tilba with basic rooms. The pub throws locals and tourists together in a tight mix.

There are plenty of frilly cafés and teashops on Bate St in Central Tilba.

Rose & Sparrow (☎ 4473 7229; 2-5 Bate St; lunch $10; ☺ breakfast & lunch) Serves generous portions of healthy food, like lentil burgers ($10).

Tilba Dromadelly (☎ 4473 7857; 31 Bate St; ☺ 10am-5pm) This idiosyncratic market is run by thespians who set the stage for a good picnic with a range of local epicurean delights.

GETTING THERE & AWAY

Premier Motor Service (☎ 13 34 10; www.premierms.com.au) buses serve Tilba daily on the route between Sydney and Melbourne.

If you're heading for Bermagui or if you just want an interesting drive, leave the highway at Tilba Tilba and take the sealed road that follows the coast through Wallaga Lake National Park to Bermagui.

BERMAGUI TO MERIMBULA

Driving along the Princes Hwy, you should feel confident that taking about any road east will yield a bit of mostly unblemished coast set in rugged surrounds. The coastal road north and south of Tathra is a good example. Information on national parks in the area is available from the NPWS office in Merimbula (p165).

BERMAGUI

☎ 02 / pop 1320

Bermagui is a small fishing community centred on pretty Horseshoe Bay. Many visitors come here, mainly to fish, and there are six big-game tournaments a year. April to May is the busiest season.

Pulp novelist Zane Grey (1872–1939), author of more than 80 books and considered the father of the American West literary genre, was a game-fishing enthusiast. He visited Bermagui and included his experiences in *An American Angler in Australia*.

The **visitors information centre** (☎ 6493 3054; info@bigfoot.com.au; 18 Lamont St; ☺ 10am-4pm) is on the main street.

The town marks the north end of an extended 90km detour along the coast to Merimbula in the south. In some places banal and others sublime (such as just south of Bermagui), the road should be the preferred route for anyone not in a hurry. Access the route from the north at a turn off the Princes Hwy just south of the Tilba Tilba road.

North of Bermagui, you'll pass beautiful **Wallaga Lake**. Just 3km off the main road, is the **Umbarra Cultural Centre** (☎ 4473 7232; ☺ 9am-5pm Mon-Fri, 9am-4pm Sat & Sun), which is run by the Yuin people from the Wallaga Lake Koori community. Various tours of the lake and cultural sites are offered.

There are several **walks** around Bermagui. You can wander 6km along the coast north to **Camel Rock Beach** (a good surfing spot) and a further 2km around to Wallaga Lake. The route follows **Haywards Beach**.

Sleeping & Eating

There are many holiday houses and apartments. Letting agents include **Fisk & Nagle** (☎ 6493 4255; www.fisknagle.com.au; 14 Lamont St).

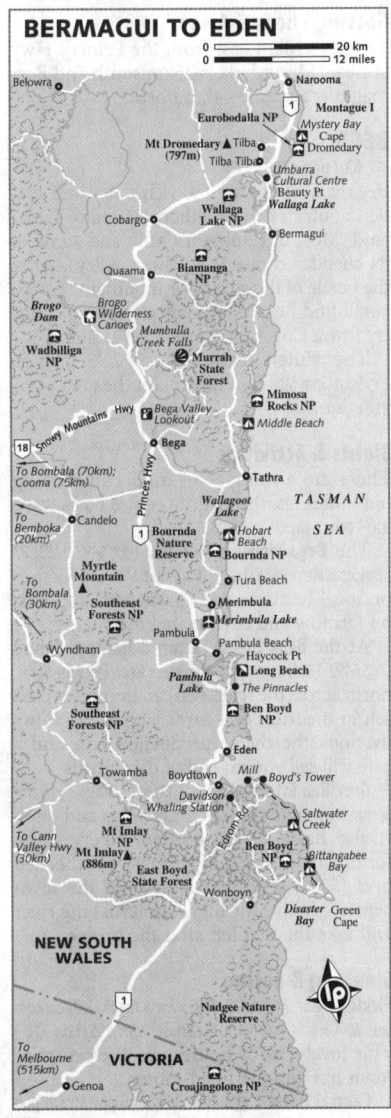

BERMAGUI TO EDEN

rooms. Splash out for the rooms with balconies and spas overlooking the bay.

Zane Grey Park (☎ 6493 4382; Lamont St; camp sites from $18, cabins $57-79) Overlooking Horseshoe Bay, this park has almost 200 sites and is both central and close to the beach.

Saltwater (☎ 6493 4328; mains $15-25; ☺ lunch Wed-Sun, dinner Thu-Sat, takeaway noon-8pm Tue-Sun) Reason enough to come to town, Saltwater has the freshest seafood on the coast. The restaurant overlooks the marina, and the clean lines of the interior complement a changing menu of fresh catches. The platter for two is amazing value for $48; so is the takeaway fish and chips for $6.

That Italian Mob (☎ 6493 3165; Lamont St; mains $12-18; ☺ lunch & dinner) The flashy interior here can best be described as modern mobster. The menu is best described as long, the food tasty. Try the calzones.

Cool O Cream Gelati (☎ 6493 3555; 1/6 Bunga St; cones $3; ☺ 1-9pm) The Italians who run this place have brought along the sensuous taste of authentic gelato. There's 15 to 30 flavours made fresh daily.

Getting There & Away

Bermagui is 21km off the Princes Hwy, so not all long-distance buses call in here. **Premier Motor Service** (☎ 13 34 10; www.premierms .com.au) stops here once a day on the Sydney–Melbourne run.

MIMOSA ROCKS NATIONAL PARK

Running along 17km of beautiful coastline, Mimosa Rocks (5802 hectares) is a wonderful coastal park with dense and varied bush, caves, lagoons and great beaches. There are basic camp sites (per person $5) at Aragunnu Beach, Picnic Point and Middle Beach, and a camping area with no facilities at Gillards Beach. These camping areas and the picnic areas are accessible from the coastal road running between Bermagui and Tathra.

Contact the NPWS in Narooma (p159) or Merimbula (p165) for more information. **Sapphire Coast Ecotours** (☎ 6494 0283; www.sapp hirecoastecotours.com.au; tours from $60) runs highly regarded walks for two to four people through the park. Led by a naturalist, the routes explore the varied ecosystems and can include an Aboriginal guide who will explain how people lived here for thousands of years.

Bermagui Motor Inn (☎ 6493 4311; singos@ozemail .com.au; 38 Lamont St; s/d $79/89; **P**) Right in town, this classic motel has 17 rooms and very friendly owners.

Horseshoe Bay Hotel/Motel (☎ 6493 4206; 10 Lamont St; dm $10-20, motel r $49, pub r $60-135; **P** **X**) This sprawling place has basic motel rooms, dorm rooms and recently renovated pub

TATHRA

☎ 02 / pop 1646

This small town starts on a headland, where you'll find a market and a pub as well as access to the historic wharf. Down a steep hill and to the north, the coastal road follows a long beach towards Mimosa Rocks National Park. There are one-lane bridges, rugged scenery and wild beaches.

Dating from 1862, **Tathra Wharf** (☎ 6494 4062) is the last remaining coastal steamship wharf in the state and a popular place for fishing. The wharf storehouse houses a small **Maritime Museum** (adult/child $2/1; 10am-6pm), a good **seafood café** (meals $8-15) and a bait shop.

Cliff Place, a narrow street that runs off the headland road next to the road down to the wharf, has great views. You can take a path that begins near the surf club. **Tathra Beach** is 3km long and has a remote and windy appeal.

Sleeping & Eating

Tathra Beach Accommodation Service (☎ 6494 1306) is one of many agents handling holiday letting.

Tathra Beach House Apartments (☎ 6499 9900; www.tathrabeachhouse.com.au; 57 Andy Pool Dr; r $85-290; P) Right across from the beach, choice is the theme at this popular property: choose from motel rooms or apartments, choose between three pools, and choose a balcony with an ocean view or something more private. The bistro has good views.

Tathra Hotel-Motel (☎ 6494 1101; Bega St; s/d from $50/80) This is a popular eating, drinking and dancing place on the headland. Some of the decent motel-style rooms have excellent sea views. The pub has entertainment on weekends and in summer it hosts big touring acts and small cover bands.

Tathra Beach Tourist Park (☎ 6494 1302; camp sites from $17, cabins from $50) This caravan park in the centre of town is a bit run down, but you can't beat the seaside location.

Across from the beach:

Mimosa Rocks Pizza (☎ 6494 1483; 61 Andy Poole Dr; mains $14-20; dinner Wed-Sun) Excellent wood-fired pizza, including a fine garlic and prawn number, are the main draw. Kids get their own menu.

Tathra Bakehaus Swiss (☎ 6494 1822; Andy Poole Dr; snacks $3-6; 8am-5pm) Passing Europeans give this place the thumbs up for its delicious fresh-baked pastries and savouries. There are tables inside and out.

Getting There & Away

Tathra is 18km east from the Princes Hwy at Bega. Merimbula is 25km south and Bermagui is a scenic 44km north.

BEGA

☎ 02 / pop 4389

Bega is a centre for the rich dairy and cattle country of the southern Monaro Tableland. Most of Canberra's milk and some of its cheddar comes from these valleys. After the bustle of the coastal or mountain resorts, you'll find Bega very much a working country town. Cow fanciers will feel at home.

The **visitors centre** (☎ 6492 2045; Gipps St; 9am-5pm Mon-Fri) can explain the area's bovine heritage.

Sights & Activities

There are a number of mildly interesting old buildings; the visitors centre has a **walking-tour** map.

The **Bega Pioneers Museum** (☎ 6492 1453; 87 Bega St; adult/child $5/1; 10am-4pm Mon-Sat) focuses on local heritage, with particular emphasis on farming and cow-related machinery.

At the **Bega Cheese Factory & Heritage Centre** (☎ 6492 1714; Lagoon St; admission free; 9am-5pm), north across the river, you can immerse yourself in the fruits of a cow's labour. Windows overlook the cheese production area and a café will sell you no end of dairy treats.

Grevillea Estate Winery (☎ 6492 3006; 9am-5pm) is open to visitors for tastings and sales. It also has a decent outdoor eatery, open for lunch, featuring big hunks of barbecued beef ($13). It's about 2km from the town centre – follow the highway across the river and take the first left after the bridge.

Sleeping & Eating

Pickled Pear (☎ 6492 1393; www.thepickledpear.com.au; 60 Carp St; s/d with breakfast from $95/110;) This lovely 1870s house near the centre of town has antique-filled rooms.

Central Hotel (☎ 6492 1263; 90 Gipps St; s/d pub $46/56, motel $66/72; P) This big, converted pub has a bit of character and some permanent residents. The large pub rooms are clean and light, and the motel rooms are set in a leafy garden out the back.

Bega Caravan Park (☎ 6492 2303; camp sites from $16, cabins from $36) This park is on the highway south of the centre near a good place to spot cows. Prices climb in summer.

DETOUR: CANDELO & BEMBOKA

If you'd like a change from all the magnificent coastal scenery, maybe you should head for the hills. About 8km south of Bega on the Princes Hwy is the turn-off for Candelo, a tiny village that packs out on the first Sunday of the month for market day. The drive there is on a beautiful sealed road, which swoops through undulating dairy country past quaint homesteads and tranquil cows.

Candelo itself is cute, built on both sides of a steep valley, and if it's not market day you could spend an hour or so wandering the streets checking out the ramshackle houses before stopping at the pub to marvel at its memorabilia collection. From Candelo it's another 20km on a similarly gorgeous road to Bemboka, a town perched on the crest in a valley and famed for its pie shop.

From Candelo you can return to the Princes Hwy via Toothdale or continue south to the Bombala road. This route takes you over **Myrtle Mountain** where there's a picnic area with good views, and drives in the state forest. Some 2km west on the Bombala road is the cute village of **Wyndham**, or you can head east to Pambula and Merimbula.

Getting There & Away

Buses leave from near the tourist office. **Greyhound** (☎ 13 14 99; www.greyhound.com.au) buses stop here on the run between Sydney and Melbourne. **Premier Motor Service** (☎ 13 34 10; www.premierms.com.au) also stops here. **CountryLink** (☎ 13 22 32; www.countrylink.com.au) has an Eden to Canberra service that passes through Bega.

BOURNDA NATIONAL PARK

Taking in most of the coast from Merimbula north to Tathra, **Bournda National Park** (admission per car $6) is a 2590-hectare park with some good beaches and several walking trails, as well as tea-tree forests, heaths, abundant bird life and the chance to swim in freshwater lagoons and saltwater lakes. The various headlands offer good views. Birds include Little Terns and the intriguing Pied Oystercatcher.

Camping is permitted at **Hobart Beach** (camping per person $8), on the southern shore of the big **Wallagoot Lagoon**, where there are toilets and hot showers. During the holidays, sites are usually booked out. Contact the Merimbula NPWS (right) for more information.

MERIMBULA

☎ 02 / pop 4883

Merimbula is a holiday and retirement haven, and motels and apartments have mushroomed on the hillsides surrounding the appealing inlet (which locals insist on calling a lake). This is one of the few places on the far south coast that really heaves during summer school holidays. Nearby Pambula Beach is a fair bit quieter. Outside the busy holiday periods the entire region slumbers peacefully.

Information

DragNet (☎ 1300 662 344; Shop 3, 11 Merimbula Dr; per hr $8; ☯ 9am-5pm Mon-Sat) Has Internet access and offers services such as Wi-Fi and CD burning.

NPWS office & Discovery Centre (☎ 6495 5000; cnr Merimbula & Sapphire Coast Drs; ☯ 8.30am-4.30pm Mon-Fri) Useful; you can book park tours and walks as well as camp sites.

Tourist information centre (☎ 6497 4900; www .sapphirecoast.com.au; Beach St; ☯ 9am-5pm Mon-Sat, 9am-4pm Sun) Covered in advertisements outside; cramped and on the waterfront. It has a **booking office** (☎ 1800 150 457, 6497 4901) for accommodation, tours and activities.

Sights & Activities

At the wharf on the eastern point is the small **Wharf Aquarium** (☎ 6495 4446; adult/child $9/5; ☯ 10am-5pm). There are good views across the lake from near here and the jetty is a popular fishing spot. The **Old School Museum** (☎ 6495 2114; Main St; adult/child $2/free; ☯ 2-4pm Tue, Thu & Sun) isn't dedicated to ageing rappers, but it *is* one of those delightful volunteer-run museums featuring knick-knackery from over the years and displays on local history.

A **nature boardwalk** follows the estuary southwest of the causeway. A plethora of birds and mammals are visible. Pick up the useful brochure at the tourist information centre.

Diving is popular, with plenty of fish and several wrecks in the area, including the large *Empire Gladstone*, which sunk in 1950. **Merimbula Divers Lodge** (☎ 1800 651 861; 15 Park St) offers basic instruction and one shallow dive from $40. Four-day PADI (Professional Association of Diving Instructors)-certificate courses cost $400. It also does snorkelling trips.

There are cruises from the **Merimbula Marina** (☎ 6495 1686), opposite the Lakeview Hotel, including fishing charters by various operators that cost about $30 per person.

There are boat-hire places – at the Merimbula Marina jetty and at Top Lake, on the north shore west of the bridge (follow Lakewood Dr). They have power boats (first hour $35), small yachts, canoes and rowing boats. **Cycle 'n' Surf** (☎ 6495 2171; 18 Marine Pde), south of the lake, hires out bikes (per hour $16), boogie boards and surf-skis as well as fishing tackle.

Sleeping

There are hundreds of motels and holiday apartments scattered around Merimbula.

Self-contained apartments are usually let on a weekly basis, particularly in summer. Many are on the isthmus across the causeway from the centre. Letting agents for the area include **Fisk & Nagle** (☎ 6495 3222; 31 Market St).

Crown Apartments (☎ 6495 2400; www.crown apartments.com.au; 23 Beach St; d $125-225; P 🐕 🖭) Eschewing the grim dark brick of so many holiday units, Crown has an attractive, airy design. One- and two-bedroom units come with full kitchens, balconies and great views. Satellite TV fills in when you can't bear another second looking at the beach.

Town Centre Motor Inn (☎ 6495 1163; 8-10 Princes Hwy; s/d $60/70; P 🐕 🖭) This 20-room three-level motel is typical of scores of other nearby places. Rooms are large and there are good views from the walkways on the top level. There is a nice little area to lounge by the pool.

Seachange B&B (☎ 6495 3133; www.sapphirecoast .com.au/seachange; 49 Imlay St; s/d from $100/125; P) This comfortable and modern B&B is 2km out of town. It has fantastic water views and well-appointed units.

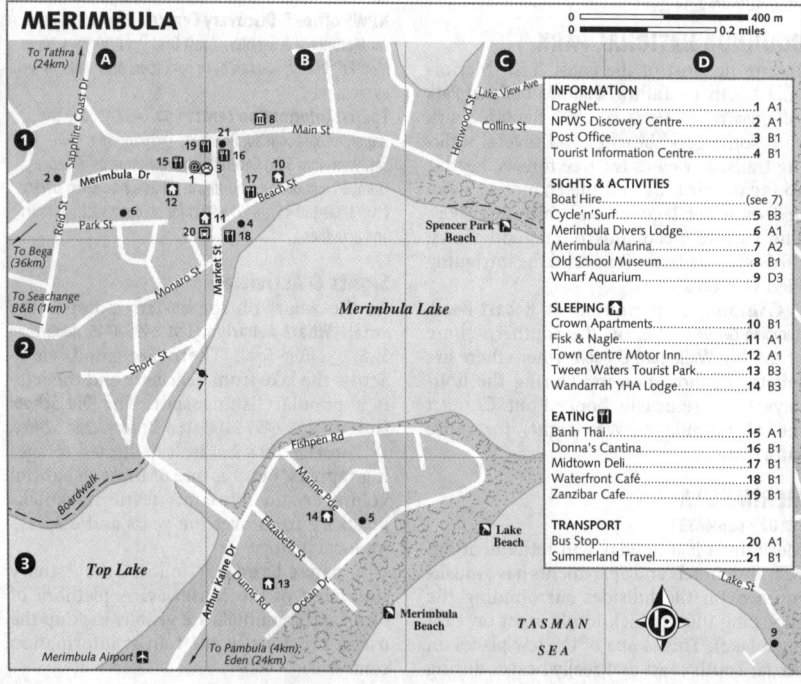

MERIMBULA

0 — 400 m
0 — 0.2 miles

INFORMATION
DragNet..1 A1
NPWS Discovery Centre...................2 A1
Post Office..3 B1
Tourist Information Centre..............4 B1

SIGHTS & ACTIVITIES
Boat Hire.......................................(see 7)
Cycle'n'Surf....................................5 B3
Merimbula Divers Lodge..................6 A1
Merimbula Marina...........................7 A2
Old School Museum.........................8 B1
Wharf Aquarium..............................9 D3

SLEEPING
Crown Apartments..........................10 B1
Fisk & Nagle....................................11 A1
Town Centre Motor Inn....................12 A1
Tween Waters Tourist Park..............13 B3
Wandarrah YHA Lodge.....................14 B3

EATING
Banh Thai..15 A1
Donna's Cantina..............................16 B1
Midtown Deli...................................17 B1
Waterfront Café...............................18 B1
Zanzibar Cafe..................................19 B1

TRANSPORT
Bus Stop..20 A1
Summerland Travel..........................21 B1

Wandarrah YHA Lodge (☎ 6495 3503; www.yha
.com.au; 8 Marine Pde; dm $22-27, d $48-58; P 🖥)
This is a clean place, with a good kitchen,
barbecue and common areas. It's near the
surf beach, hires out bikes and canoes, and
offers tours.

Tween Waters Tourist Park (☎ /fax 6495 1530;
Dunns Rd; powered sites from $26, cabins from $65; 🐾)
Located over the causeway; has access to
surf and lake beaches. There are 96 sites
and 26 cabins.

Eating & Drinking

Merimbula offers a fair range of eateries,
most of them concentrated in the busy
shopping area.

Zanzibar Cafe (☎ 6495 4038; cnr Main & Market Sts;
mains $22-30; 🕑 dinner Tue-Sat) As toney as dining
gets in Merimbula; Zanzibar features a short
but varied menu of Mod Oz cuisine that
leans towards the sea. But go ahead, have the
eye fillet. See and be seen behind the huge
plate glass windows or out on the patio.

Donna's Cantina (☎ 6495 1085; 56 Market St; tapas
$11, mains $22; 🕑 lunch & dinner) Always busy, the
changing menu features imaginative seafood dishes and Spanish and Mediterranean
dishes. Get a plate of tapas and join the
throngs outside with a glass of red wine.
Note that success comes at a price: service
can be curt.

Banh Thai (☎ 6495 3800; 17 Merimbula Dr; mains
$13-17; 🕑 dinner) This Thai restaurant serves
authentic food in attractive surrounds.
Book for weekends.

Midtown Deli (☎ 6495 1876; Market St; meals $4-5;
🕑 7am-4pm Mon-Sat, plus Sun summer) This swell-
smelling spot has organic breads, soups,
sandwiches and alluring prepared foods.
The coffee is fine.

Waterfront Café (☎ 6495 7684; cnr Beach & Market Sts; mains $12-16; 🕑 breakfast, lunch & dinner) Try
this place for coffee or a snack while looking out over Merimbula Lake (Inlet!).

Getting There & Away

Travel bookings can be made at **Summerland
Travel** (☎ 6495 1008; 16 Market St).

There are several daily flights to Mel-
bourne and Sydney with **Regional Express
Airlines** (Rex; ☎ 13 17 13). Merimbula's airport
(MIM) is 1km out of town on the road to
Pambula.

Buses stop outside the Centrepoint Mall
on Market St.

Greyhound (☎ 13 14 99; www.greyhound.com.au)
and **Premier Motor Service** (☎ 13 34 10; www
.premierms.com.au) buses stop in Merimbula on
their numerous daily Sydney–Melbourne
services. **CountryLink** (☎ 13 22 32; www.countrylink
.com.au) stops here on the four-times-weekly
Eden–Canberra run.

Deane's (☎ 6496 1422; www.deanesbuslines.com
.au) is a local bus company that runs between Bega and Eden.

PAMBULA
☎ 02 / pop 1109

Just south of Merimbula, Pambula is a
small town that has largely avoided the
development of its glitzy neighbour. On
your way you will see numerous farmed
oyster beds.

No longer a mere kiosk, **Wheeler's** (☎ 6495
6089; Arthur Kaine Dr; mains $18-30; 🕑 takeaway 9am-
5pm daily, lunch daily, dinner Tue-Sat) is in a flashy
new complex 1.5km north of town. The
restaurant serves up all manner of seafood,
but those in the know opt for the takeaway
and its myriad of options (if only there were
more tables outside!). Long an oyster producer, Wheeler's offers tours (adult child
$7/3.50, 11am) of its farm.

EDEN
☎ 02 / pop 3157

Eden is still very much a fishing port, with
one of the largest fleets in the state and a
busy enclosed harbour. It's a good place to
base yourself, with easy access to the surrounding national parks and a more laid-
back feel than Merimbula. One of the most
popular activities here is whale watching.

For an engaging insight into the life of
the many fishing and whaling families that
have been at the heart of the community,
get a copy of *Down to the Sea* by John
Little; the fishing port will take on a new
meaning.

The **Eden visitor centre** (☎ 6496 1953; cnr Princes
Hwy & Mitchell St; 🕑 9am-5pm) can answer most
questions. In the same building, the **library**
(☎ 6496 1687; per hr $6; 🕑 9am-5pm Mon-Fri, 9am-
noon Sat) has Internet access.

Sights & Activities

The interesting **Killer Whale Museum** (☎ 6496
2094; 94 Imlay St; adult/child $6/2; 🕑 9.15am-3.45pm
Mon-Sat, 11.15am-3.45pm Sun) was established in
1931, mainly to preserve the skeleton of Old

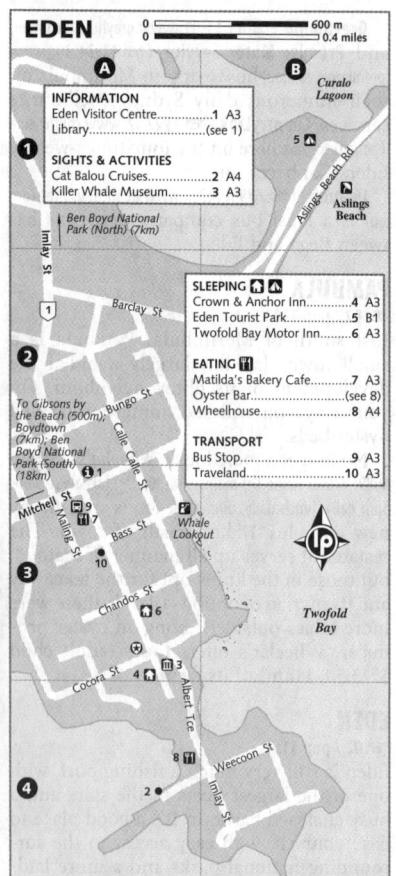

EDEN

INFORMATION	
Eden Visitor Centre	1 A3
Library	(see 1)

SIGHTS & ACTIVITIES	
Cat Balou Cruises	2 A4
Killer Whale Museum	3 A3

SLEEPING	
Crown & Anchor Inn	4 A3
Eden Tourist Park	5 B1
Twofold Bay Motor Inn	6 A3

EATING	
Matilda's Bakery Cafe	7 A3
Oyster Bar	(see 8)
Wheelhouse	8 A4

TRANSPORT	
Bus Stop	9 A3
Traveland	10 A3

Tom, a killer whale and local legend who was reputed to help whalers herd whales to their deaths.

Cat Balou Cruises (☎ 6496 2027) has whale-spotting cruises (adult/child $60/55) in October and November. At other times of the year, dolphins, sea lions, sea birds can usually be seen during the shorter bay cruise (adult/child $28/17).

Among the many whale lookouts, there is a good one at the base of Bass St.

Festivals & Events

Eden comes alive in early October for the **Whale Festival**, with the typical carnival, street parade and stalls plus some innovative local events such as the Slimy Mackerel Throw.

Sleeping

Twofold Bay Motor Inn (☎ 6496 3111; 164-166 Imlay St; r $77-165; P ☒ ☒) Located centrally this typical motel has 24 units and a tiny indoor pool. Rooms are well equipped and some have nice views down to the water.

Crown & Anchor Inn (☎ 6496 1017; www.crownan danchoreden.com.au; 239 Imlay St; s/d from $110/130; P) This historic house (1845) has been beautifully restored and has a lovely view over Twofold Bay from the back patio. Each of the five rooms is different, but all have stylish period furniture (such as four-post beds and claw-foot baths).

Gibsons by the Beach (☎ 6496 1414; www.babs .com.au/gibsons; 10 Bay St; s/d with breakfast from $95/120; P) This B&B has two large rooms. The beach is five minutes' walk away, through lush bushland and the owner's garden.

Eden Tourist Park (☎ 6496 1139; Aslings Beach Rd; powered/unpowered sites $20/17, cabins from $55) This park with 160 sites is serenely situated on a spit separating Aslings Beach from Lake Curalo.

Eating

Down by the wharf are some excellent cafés and restaurants.

Wheelhouse (☎ 6496 3392; 253 Imlay St; mains $25-30; ☽ lunch & dinner) Local seafood in all its variations is served simply here. Oysters and mussels are specialities. Gaze from upper-floor tables inside and out at the harbour's tugs and fishing boats. Ignore the shabby entrance.

Oyster Bar (☎ 6496 1304; 253 Imlay St; mains $15; ☽ breakfast & lunch daily, dinner Thu-Sat) An atmospheric, tiny seafood café where the chef, Giancarlo, serves up an array of fresh and often garlicky treats – many caught locally. Coffee at one of the outside tables is a good way to start the day.

Matilda's Bakery Cafe (☎ 6496 0800; 161 Imlay St; snacks $3-6; ☽ 8am-5pm) This large and newish place almost borders on posh. The baked goods are popular with locals and you can enjoy various treats and sandwiches at the many airy tables.

Getting There & Away

Bus bookings can be made at **Traveland** (☎ 6496 1314; cnr Bass & Imlay Sts).

Greyhound (☎ 13 14 99; www.greyhound.com.au) and **Premier Motor Service** (☎ 13 34 10; www .premierms.com.au) buses stop in Eden on their

MARK ANDREW KIRBY

Jervis Bay National Park (p145), NSW

Little penguin chick at Montague Island (p160), NSW

MITCH REARDON

Bermagui coastline (p162), NSW

ROSS BARNETT

Wagonga Inlet, Narooma (p159), NSW

WAYNE WALTON

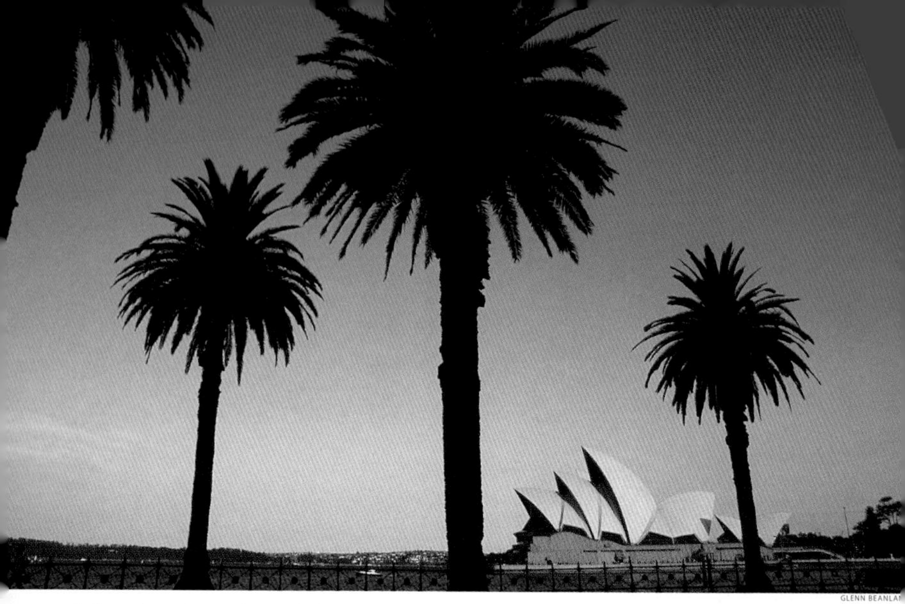

GLENN BEANLAN

Sydney Opera House (p181), Sydney, NSW

Manly (p189), Sydney, NSW

SIMON BRACKEN

NEIL SETCHFIELD

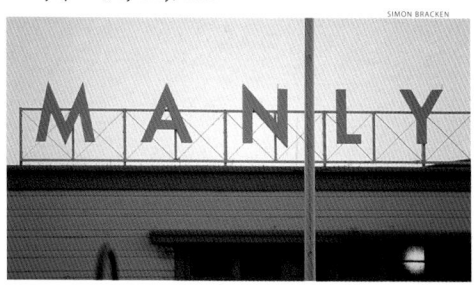

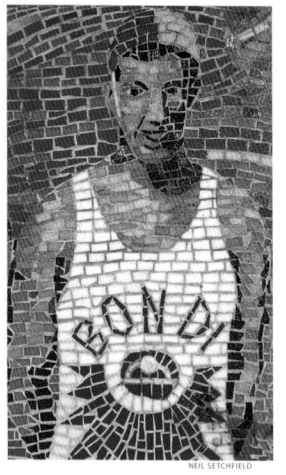

Bondi Beach (p187) mosaic detail, Sydney, NSW

The Three Sisters, Katoomba (p208), NSW

MIKE COTTEE

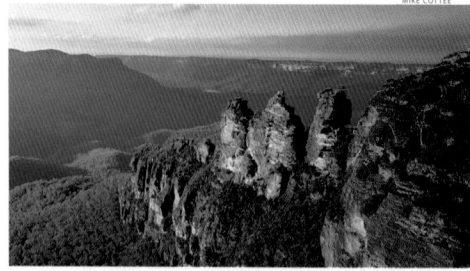

A TALE OF TWO WHALES

Migrating humpback and southern right whales pass so close to the coast near Eden that whale-watching experts consider this one of the best places in Australia to observe these magnificent creatures. Often they can be seen feeding or resting in Twofold Bay during their southern migration back to Antarctic waters.

Hunted to near extinction by 1930, the whales have been making a slow comeback over the last 50 years. Whales can be seen migrating north in May and June and returning south from September to November. Once you know what to look for, you can easily spot tell the two species apart.

Humpback whales got their name because they arch or hump their backs when diving. Some 16m at their longest, humpbacks have somewhat ragged tails that are light on the underside. They blow out a single cloud of mist when they surface to breathe. To the thrill of whale watchers, they like to leap out of the water or 'breach'.

In contrast to humpbacks, southern right whales earned their name for more sinister reasons – they were deemed the 'right' whale to hunt. They reach 17m in length, their body colour is mostly dark and their tails smooth. When expelling air it is usually in the shape of a V.

various daily Sydney–Melbourne services. **CountryLink** (☎ 13 22 32; www.countrylink.com.au) runs four times weekly to Canberra.

BEN BOYD NATIONAL PARK

Ben Boyd was an entrepreneur who failed spectacularly in his efforts to build an empire in and around Eden in 1850. Protecting some of his relics, the national park (10,407 hectares) has dramatic coastline and isolated beaches. The main access road to the park is the sealed Edrom Rd, which leaves the Princes Hwy about 25km south of Eden.

Before the mill at the end of the road there's a turn-off to the left that leads to the old **Davidson Whaling Station** on Twofold Bay, now a historic site. There's not much left, but interpretive signs tell the story. Further along Edrom Rd is the turn-off for **Boyd's Tower**, an impressive structure built with sandstone brought from Sydney. It was intended to be a lighthouse but the government wouldn't give Boyd permission to operate it.

Off Edrom Rd closer to the highway is Green Cape Rd, which runs right down to Green Cape, from where there are some good views and a **lighthouse** (☎ 6495 5000; cottages $165-250). There are tours (1pm and 3pm) or if you really like the isolation, you can spend the night. Two cottages that belonged to the keepers have been lavishly restored and each sleep six. For more information see the website of the **NSW NPWS** (www.nationalparks.nsw.gov.au).

Running off Green Cape Rd are smaller roads which lead to **Saltwater Creek** and **Bittangabee Bay**. There are camp sites at both places and a 9km walk between the two. You should book sites well in advance for Christmas and Easter through the Merimbula NPWS (p165).

The northern section of Ben Boyd National Park runs up the coast from Eden; access is from the Princes Hwy north of the town. From Haycock Point, where there are good views, a walking trail leads to a headland overlooking the Pambula River. Another good walk is to the **Pinnacles**, an eroded formation of layered rock; access is from the car park not too far in from the Princes Hwy.

NADGEE NATURE RESERVE

Continuing down the coast from Ben Boyd National Park, but much less accessible, is **Nadgee Nature Reserve** (admission free). Much of it is official Wilderness Area, but vehicle access is allowed as far as the ranger station near the Merrica River, 7km from Newton's Beach.

On Wonboyn Lake at the north end of the reserve, the small settlement of **Wonboyn** has a store selling petrol and basic supplies. Wonboyn is near access roads into Nadgee, including one down to Wonboyn Beach.

Wonboyn Cabins & Caravan Park (☎ 6496 9131; camp sites $18-30, cabins $50-115; ▣) is spacious and has some friendly rainbow lorikeets.

Sydney

As one of the world's greatest and most vibrant cities, beautiful Sydney tosses off style like there's no tomorrow. This spectacular city boasts multicultural energy and offers almost everything you could ask for in a travel destination. Its stunning harbour is spanned by an equally striking bridge; the famous Opera House is as gorgeous as you've imagined; there are heavenly beaches and surf ridiculously close by; plenty of great restaurants, hip bars and nightlife are everywhere; and, finally, a heaping handful of distinctly flavoured neighbourhoods will add flavour to your visit. While the East Coast's other capital cities, Melbourne and Brisbane, lay claim to being uniquely Australian cities, Sydney is Australia's international darling, and many travellers who have come for a week end up staying a year or more. Sydney is just the place for you to combine relaxed hedonism, stylish decadence and look-at-me antics.

Australia's first European settlement was established in 1788 at Sydney Cove, where the ferries run from Circular Quay, so it's not surprising Sydney has a strong sense of history. But that doesn't stop the city from being far brasher and livelier than many of its younger Australian counterparts. The city is built on land once occupied by the Eora tribe, whose presence lingers in the place names of some suburbs and whose artistic legacy can be seen at many Aboriginal engraving sites around the city. Many ascribe Sydney's raffish spirit to the fact that the military were essentially in charge of things in the late 18th century and early 19th century.

HIGHLIGHTS

- Strolling around the **Opera House** (p181), **the Rocks** (p182) and across the **Harbour Bridge** (p181)
- Visiting the **Royal Botanical Gardens** (p185), and the chittering flying fox colony
- Walking through pedestrian-friendly **Darling Harbour** (p185) and its many attractions
- Ferrying to the world-class **Taronga Zoo** (p188) and taking in the stunning views
- Checking out the beach and grabbing some fish 'n' chips in **Bondi** (p187) or **Coogee** (p188)
- Taking the ferry to **Manly** (p189), and doing the Manly Scenic Walkway
- Drinking, partying and staying up late in lively **Kings Cross** (p186)
- Taking the train to Katoomba and the **Blue Mountains** (p207)

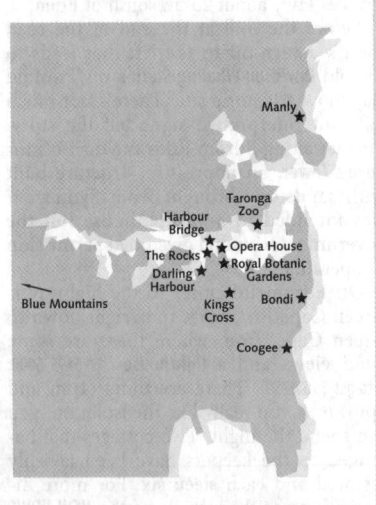

■ TELEPHONE CODE: 02   ■ POPULATION: 4 MILLION   ■ www.sydney.citysearch.com.au

GREATER SYDNEY & BLUE MOUNTAINS

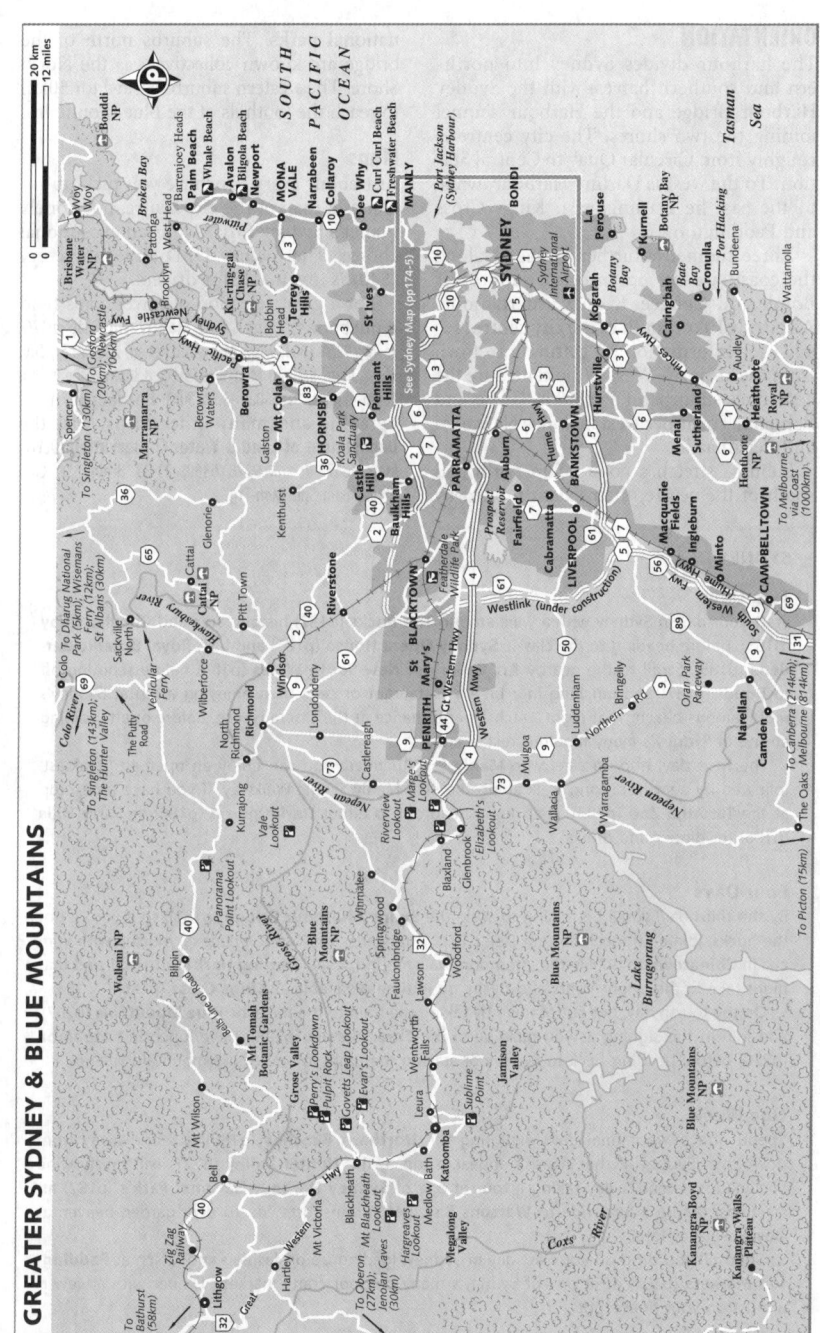

See Sydney Map (pp174–5)

SYDNEY

ORIENTATION

The harbour divides Sydney into northern and southern halves, with the Sydney Harbour Bridge and the Harbour Tunnel joining the two shores. The city centre is roughly from Circular Quay to Central Station. To the west is Darling Harbour, while to the east lie Darlinghurst, Kings Cross and Paddington.

Three kilometres further southeast, along the coast, are the ocean-beach suburbs of Bondi and Coogee. Sydney International Airport is 10km south of the city centre (see p204 for information on getting into town from the airport). West of the centre are the gentrified suburbs of Pyrmont, Glebe and Balmain. The inner west includes Newtown and Leichhardt.

Suburbs stretch a good 20km north and south of the centre, their extent limited by national parks. The suburbs north of the bridge are known collectively as the North Shore. The western suburbs sprawl for 50km to reach the foothills of the Blue Mountains.

Maps

Just about every brochure you pick up includes a map of the city centre, but Lonely Planet's *Sydney City Map* is an exceptional choice. The *Sydney* UBD street directory ($40) is invaluable for drivers.

For a great selection of travel maps (and guidebooks) check out **Map World** (Map pp176-7; ☎ 9261 3601; www.mapworld.net.au; 280 Pitt St, City; ☻ 8.30am-5.30pm Mon-Wed & Fri, 8.30am-6.30pm Thu, 10am-4.30pm Sat, 10am-3pm Sun). For aerial, topographic and many other maps, visit the **Department of Land & Water Conservation** (DLWC; Map pp176-7; ☎ 9228 6360; 23-33 Bridge St, City; ☻ 8.30am-5pm Mon-Fri).

SYDNEY IN...

Two Days

Start your day in Sydney with a walk around **The Rocks** (p182) historic area and **Circular Quay** (p183), before heading to the classic **Sydney Opera House** (p181) and lush **Royal Botanic Gardens** (p185). Stroll to the nearby **Art Gallery of New South Wales** (p184) before scooting off to **Bondi** (p187) and lunching in a breezy restaurant or café, then enjoying a dip at Sydney's most famous beach. That night, catch a performance at the Opera House, before or after dining at one of Sydney's many fabulous restaurants.

The next day, hop on a ferry to **Manly** (p189), where you can enjoy an open-air breakfast, followed by a swim or long walk along the 9km Manly Scenic Walkway. If you have time, stop at the **Taronga Zoo** (p188). That night, head out to either **Darlinghurst** (p186) or **Surry Hills** (p186) for dinner and drinks.

Four Days

By the third day, you'll be itching to scale the **Sydney Harbour Bridge** (p181), so if you've got the bucks, join a Bridgeclimb tour (see p192). Afterwards you can re-energise yourself with yum cha in **Chinatown** (p197). In the afternoon, walk around scenic **Darling Harbour** (p185), and that night take in the bright lights and trashy good times available at **Kings Cross** (p186).

On the fourth day, get out of town by taking the train to the majestic **Blue Mountains** (p207), and join in the sighing as you gaze upon the **Three Sisters** (p208). Have lunch in **Katoomba** (p210) before heading back to Sydney or staying the night in one of the mountain villages.

One Week

Spend one of your final days exploring the **Northern Beaches** (p188), a world away from downtown Sydney. If that doesn't appeal, a trip to the **Hunter Valley** (p221) will satisfy wine aficionados. Spend a day taking a tour of one of **Sydney Harbour National Park's** (p182) attractions, before a ferry ride to **Watsons Bay** (p187) transports you to beer-garden heaven at Doyles Palace Hotel.

Shop till you drop on your last day in Sydney, loading up on fashion and kitsch at **Paddington Markets** (p203) or at one of Sydney's many outdoor crafts markets. Dinner with a view is a must on your final night.

INFORMATION

Bookshops

Desire Books (Map p180; ☎ 9977 0888; 3/3 Whistler St, Manly; ☺ 10am-6pm Mon-Wed, 10am-10pm Thu, 9.30am-6pm Sat, 11am-5pm Sun) Chess on Thursday nights, sofas and a small collection of new and used books (will take trades).

Dymocks Books (Map pp176-7; ☎ 9235 0155; 424 George St, City; ☺ 9am-6.30pm Mon-Wed, Fri & Sat, 9am-9pm Thu, 10am-5.30pm Sun) In excess of 250,000 titles spread over three floors; includes a Lonely Planet aisle! Several branches in town.

Gleebooks (Map pp174-5; ☎ 9660 2333; 49 Glebe Point Rd, Glebe; ☺ 9am-9pm) Frequent winner of 'bookshop of the year' awards. Also have children's books and used books at their annex at 191 Glebe Point Rd.

Travel Bookshop (Map pp176-7; ☎ 9261 8200; Shop 3, 175 Liverpool St, City; ☺ 9am-6pm Mon-Fri, 10am-5pm Sat) Crammed with, you guessed it, travel books. Also has used books (trade 'em in).

Emergency

In case of a life-threatening emergency, dial ☎ 000 – a free call from any phone. Your call will be diverted to either the police, ambulance service or fire brigade.

Lifeline (☎ 13 11 14) Twenty-four hour phone counselling services.

National Roads & Motorists' Association (NRMA; Map pp176-7; ☎ 13 21 32; www.nrma.com.au; 388 George St, City) For auto insurance and roadside service.

Police City (Map pp176-7; 570 George St, City); The Rocks (Map pp176-7; 132 George St, The Rocks)

Rape Crisis Centre (☎ 1800 424 017, 9819 6565)

Wayside Chapel (Map p179; ☎ 9358 6577; 29 Hughes St, Potts Point; ☺ 7am-10pm) Crisis centre in the heart of Kings Cross.

Internet Access

Internet cafés are common, especially in Kings Cross, Chinatown and Bondi. Rates are around $3 an hour. Plenty of hostels and hotels offer Internet access to their guests.

Global Gossip (Map p179; ☎ 9326 9777; 61 Darlinghurst Rd, Kings Cross; ☺ 9am-1am) Also in Bondi, near Central Station and in the city.

Travellers Contact Point (Map pp176-7; ☎ 9221 8744; www.travellers.com.au; Level 7, 428 George St, City; first 30min email free; ☺ 9am-6pm Mon-Fri, 10am-4pm Sat)

Internet Resources

www.cityofsydney.nsw.gov.au City news and politics.

www.sydney.citysearch.com.au What's happening in Sydney.

www.visitnsw.com.au Info on Sydney and NSW, including events.

www.viewsydney.com.au The official visitor website for the Rocks precinct.

www.whitepages.com.au Find a business or service anywhere in Australia.

Medical Services

Kings Cross Travellers Clinic (Map p179; ☎ 9358 3066; 13 Springfield Ave, Kings Cross; ☺ 9am-1pm & 2-6pm Mon-Fri, 10am-noon Sat) Bookings advised for morning-after pill scripts and dive medicals.

Sydney Hospital (Map pp176-7; ☎ 9382 7009; 8 Macquarie St, City) Has a 24-hour emergency ward.

Travellers Medical & Vaccination Centre (Map pp176-7; ☎ 9221 7133; www.traveldoctor.com.au; Level 7, 428 George St, City; ☺ 9am-5.30pm Mon, Wed & Fri, to 7.30pm Thu, to 1pm Sat, 8am-5.30pm Tue) The best place to get your shots and medical advice related to travel.

Money

There are plenty of banks and ATMs throughout Sydney. Change bureaus include the two at Central Station (open approximately 8am to 5pm Monday to Friday, 9am to 6pm Saturday and Sunday) and one opposite Wharf 6 at Circular Quay (open 8am to 8.30pm). There are several in the city centre, Kings Cross and at the airport (where they're open until the last flight comes in; rates aren't quite as good as in the centre, however).

American Express (Map pp176-7; ☎ 1300 139 060; 105 Pitt St, City; ☺ 9am-5pm Mon-Fri, 10am-1pm Sat) Helps with travel arrangements; has other branches throughout town, including an exchange booth inside the Travel Bookshop (left).

Post

There are many post-office branches throughout the city centre. See Map pp176–7 for locations.

General Post Office (Map pp176-7; 1 Martin Pl, City; ☺ 8.15am-5.30pm Mon-Fri, 10am-2pm Sat)

Poste Restante Service (Map pp176-7; Level 2A, Hunter Connection Bldg, 310 George St, City; ☺ 8.15am-5.30pm Mon-Fri) You'll need identification.

Tourist Information

All hours vary with the seasons; summer hours (listed here) are longer.

City Host Information Kiosks (Map pp176-7); Circular Quay (cnr Pitt & Alfred Sts; ☺ 9am-5pm); Martin Pl (btwn Elizabeth & Castlereagh Sts); Town Hall (cnr George & Bathurst Sts) Hours and days vary at the Martin Pl and Town Hall kiosks.

(Continued on page 181)

SYDNEY

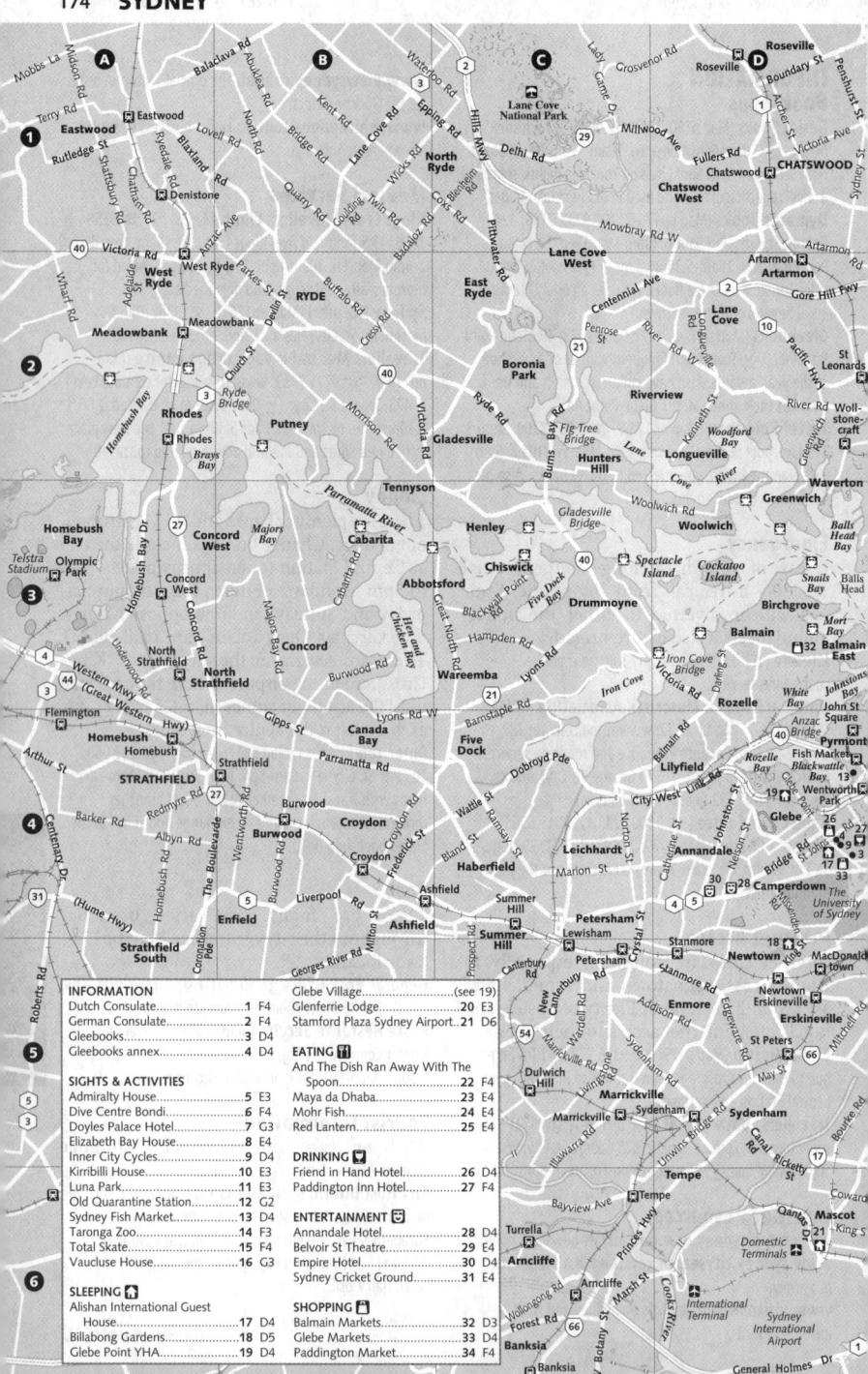

SOUTH
PACIFIC
OCEAN

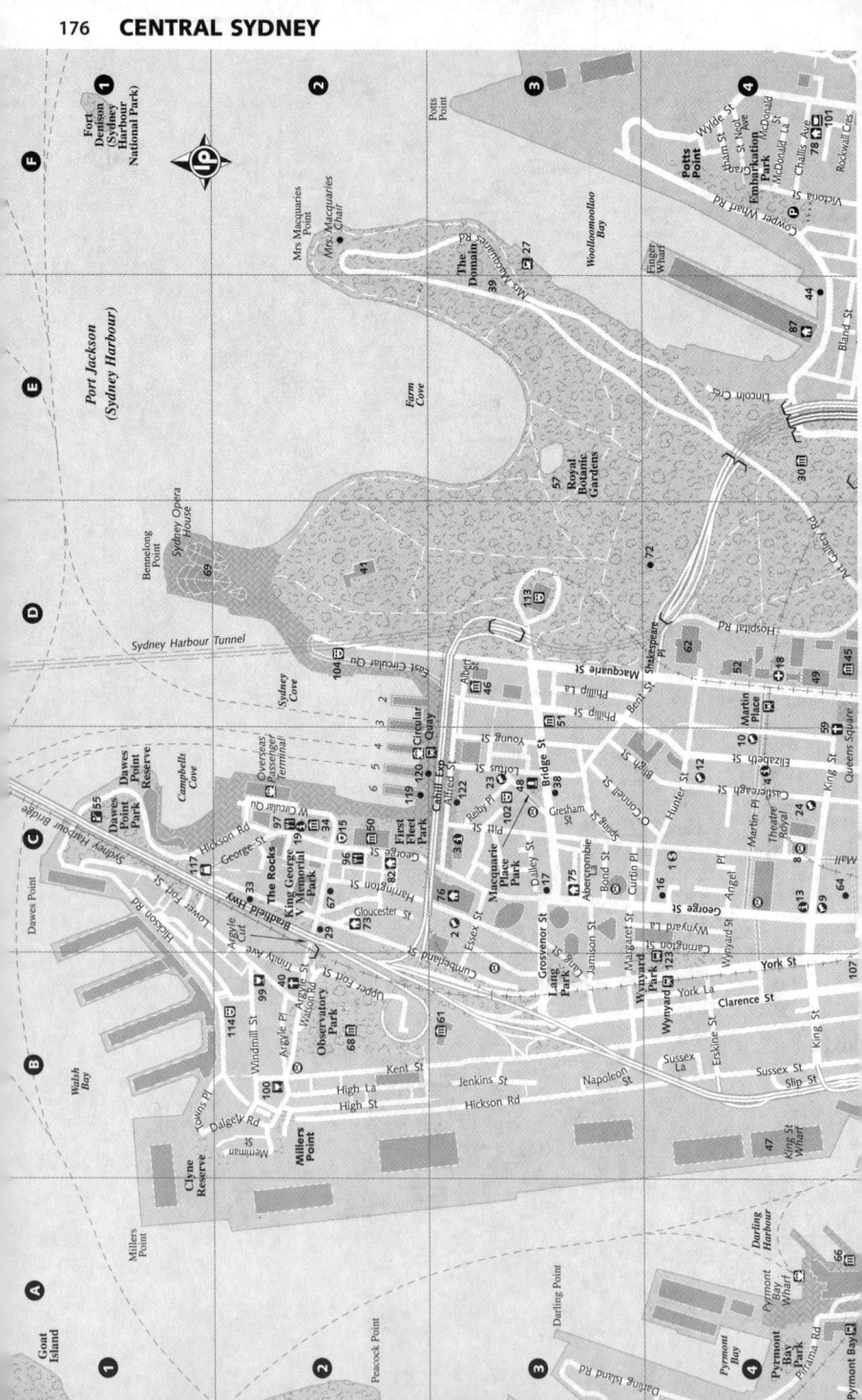

0   500 m
0   0.3 miles

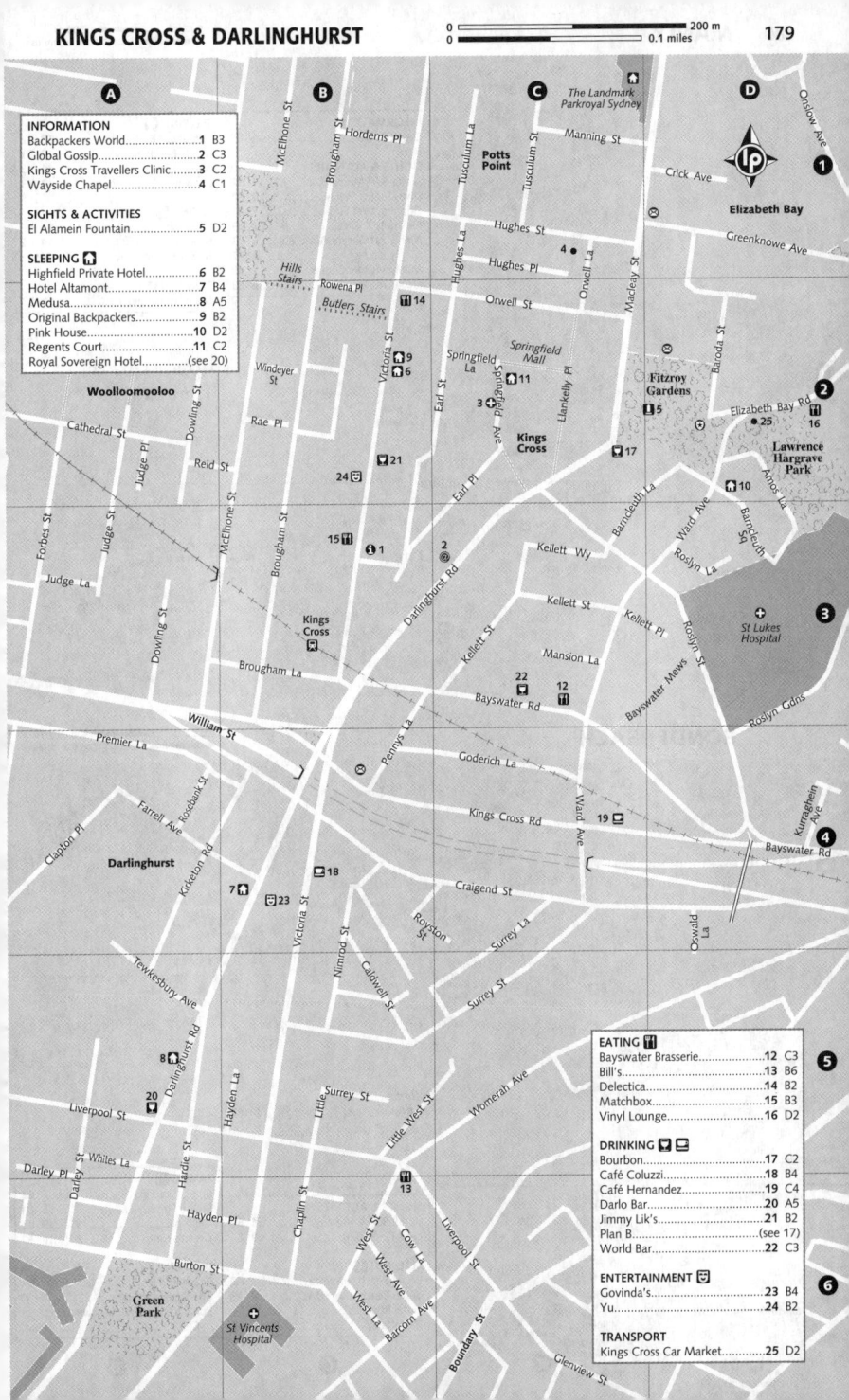

INFORMATION
Backpackers World	**1** B3
Global Gossip	**2** C3
Kings Cross Travellers Clinic	**3** C2
Wayside Chapel	**4** C1

SIGHTS & ACTIVITIES
El Alamein Fountain	**5** D2

SLEEPING
Highfield Private Hotel	**6** B2
Hotel Altamont	**7** B4
Medusa	**8** A5
Original Backpackers	**9** B2
Pink House	**10** D2
Regents Court	**11** C2
Royal Sovereign Hotel	(see 20)

EATING
Bayswater Brasserie	**12** C3
Bill's	**13** B6
Delectica	**14** B2
Matchbox	**15** B3
Vinyl Lounge	**16** D2

DRINKING
Bourbon	**17** C2
Café Coluzzi	**18** B4
Café Hernandez	**19** C4
Darlo Bar	**20** A5
Jimmy Lik's	**21** B2
Plan B	(see 17)
World Bar	**22** C3

ENTERTAINMENT
Govinda's	**23** B4
Yu	**24** B2

TRANSPORT
Kings Cross Car Market	**25** D2

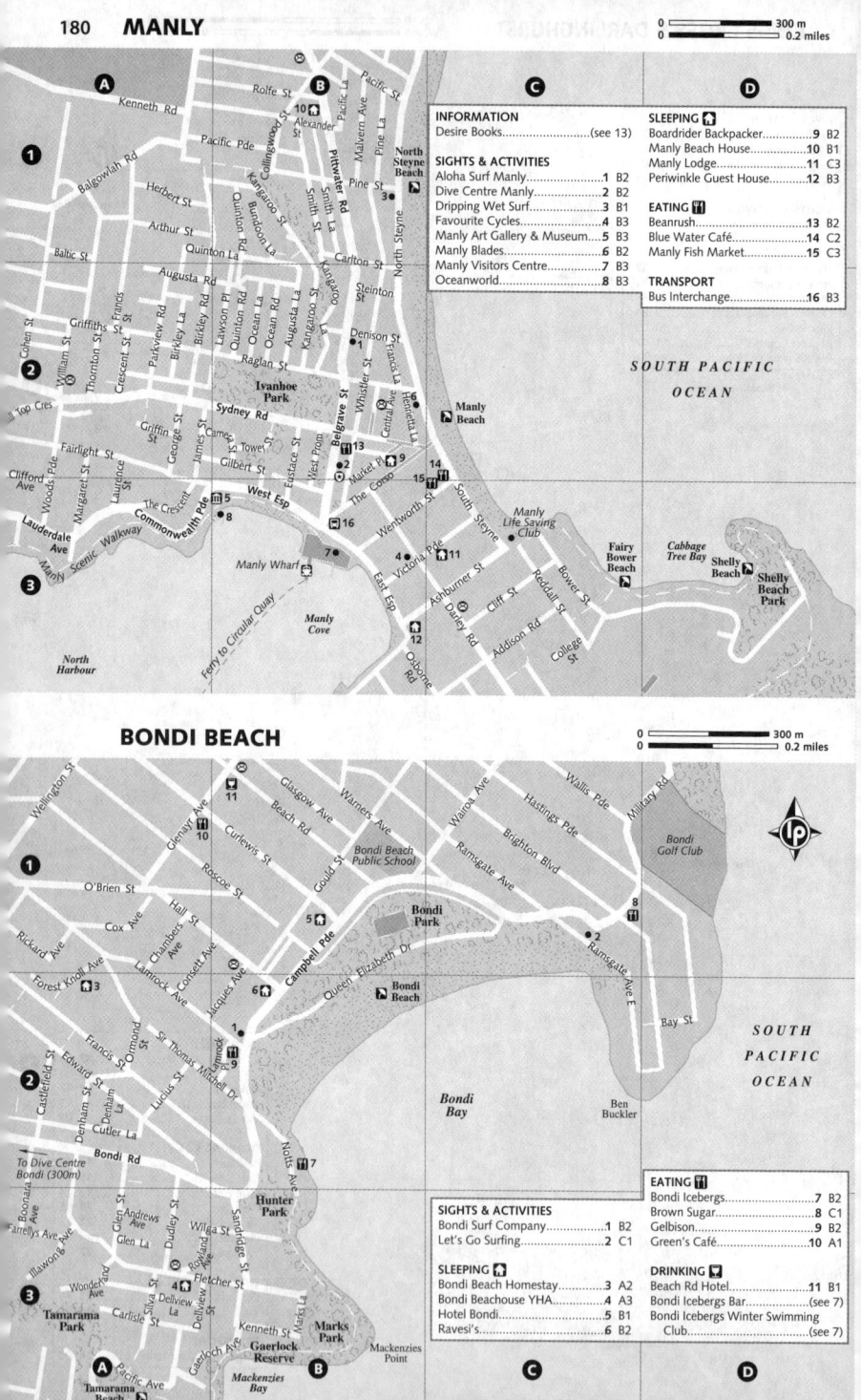

MANLY

INFORMATION	
Desire Books......................(see 13)	
SIGHTS & ACTIVITIES	
Aloha Surf Manly............................1 B2	
Dive Centre Manly.........................2 B2	
Dripping Wet Surf..........................3 B1	
Favourite Cycles............................4 B3	
Manly Art Gallery & Museum.....5 B3	
Manly Blades..................................6 B2	
Manly Visitors Centre....................7 B3	
Oceanworld....................................8 B3	

SLEEPING	
Boardrider Backpacker..................9 B2	
Manly Beach House.....................10 B1	
Manly Lodge.................................11 C3	
Periwinkle Guest House...............12 B3	
EATING	
Beanrush......................................13 B2	
Blue Water Café...........................14 C2	
Manly Fish Market.......................15 C3	
TRANSPORT	
Bus Interchange...........................16 B3	

BONDI BEACH

SIGHTS & ACTIVITIES	
Bondi Surf Company.....................1 B2	
Let's Go Surfing..............................2 C1	
SLEEPING	
Bondi Beach Homestay..................3 A2	
Bondi Beachouse YHA....................4 A3	
Hotel Bondi.....................................5 B1	
Ravesi's...6 B2	

EATING	
Bondi Icebergs...............................7 B2	
Brown Sugar..................................8 C1	
Gelbison...9 B2	
Green's Café.................................10 A1	
DRINKING	
Beach Rd Hotel............................11 B1	
Bondi Icebergs Bar....................(see 7)	
Bondi Icebergs Winter Swimming	
Club...(see 7)	

To Dive Centre Bondi (300m)

(Continued from page 173)

Global Gossip (Map p179; ☎ 9326 9777; 61 Darlinghurst Rd, Kings Cross; ☒ 9am-1am) Offers discount long-distance and international calls.

NSW Visitors Centre (☎ 9667 6053; www.visitnsw .com.au; Sydney International Airport; ☒ 6am-11pm) Book discounted hotel rooms and onward travel here.

Sydney Visitors Centre (Map pp176-7; ☎ 9240 8788; www.sydneyvisitorcentre.com; 106 George St, The Rocks; ☒ 9.30am-5.30pm) Very helpful and stuffed full of brochures.

Visitors Centre (Map pp176-7; ☎ 9240 8788; Darling Harbour; ☒ 10am-6pm) Behind the Imax Theatre.

Travel Agencies

Backpackers World (Map p179; ☎ 9380 2700, 1800 676 763; www.backpackersworld.com.au; 212 Victoria St, Kings Cross; ☒ 9am-7pm Mon-Fri, 10am-6pm Sat, 11am-5pm Sun) Five Sydney locations.

STA Travel (Map pp176-7; ☎ 9252 8022; www.sta travel.com.au; Shop 1, 2 Bridge St, City; ☒ 9.30am-5.30pm Mon-Sat) Twenty Sydney branches.

Travellers Aid Society (☎ 9211 2469; Platform 1, Central Station; ☒ 8am-2.30pm Mon-Sat) Provides general information, travel assistance, phone recharge and hot showers.

Travellers Contact Point (Map pp176-7; ☎ 9221 8744; www.travellers.com.au; Level 7, 428 George St, City; ☒ 9am-6pm Mon-Fri, 10am-4pm Sat) Full-blown backpacker agency. Also holds mail and has a good bulletin board.

YHA Membership & Travel Centre (Map pp176-7; ☎ 9261 1111; www.yha.com.au/yhainfo/membership _travel.cfm; 422 Kent St, City; ☒ 9am-5pm Mon-Wed & Fri, 9am-6pm Thu, 9am-2pm Sat) Offers travel packages and YHA bookings worldwide; also try the travel agent in the Sydney Central YHA (p193).

SIGHTS

Sydney's chock-full of things to see and do. Much of it doesn't cost a cent. Many of Sydney's attractions are within walking distance of the city centre, with surrounding suburbs and beaches easily reachable by bus, train or ferry. If you plan on seeing an exceptional number of museums, attractions and tours, check out the **Smartvisit card** (☎ 1300 661 711; www.seesydneycard.com).

Practically all sights and museums in Sydney have good disabled access.

Sydney Harbour

Sydney's stunning harbour (Port Jackson) is both a major port and the city's playground. It stretches some 20km inland to join the mouth of the Parramatta River. The headlands at the entrance are known as North Head and South Head. The most scenic part of the harbour is between the heads and the Harbour Bridge, 8km inland. Middle Harbour is a large inlet that heads northwest a couple of kilometres inside the Heads.

SYDNEY HARBOUR BRIDGE

The much-loved 'old coat hanger' crosses the harbour at one of its narrowest points, joining central Sydney with the satellite business district in North Sydney. The bridge was completed in 1932 at a cost of $20 million and has always been a favourite icon, partly because of its sheer size, partly because of its function in uniting the city and partly because it boosted employment during the Depression.

You can climb up almost 200 stairs inside the southeastern stone pylon, which houses a small (free) museum and the **Pylon Lookout** (Map pp176-7; ☎ 9240-1100; www.pylonlookout.com.au; admission $8.50; ☒ 10am-5pm), or you can join a climbing group and scale the bridge itself (see p192).

Cars, trains, cyclists, joggers and pedestrians use the bridge. The cycleway is on the western side and the pedestrian walkway is on the eastern; pedestrian access is from the **Argyle Stairs**, near Cumberland St, in The Rocks. The best way to experience the bridge is on foot, so put on your walking shoes and get going.

SYDNEY OPERA HOUSE

The postcard-perfect **Sydney Opera House** (Map pp176-7; www.sydneyoperahouse.com) is dramatically situated on the eastern headland of Circular Quay. Its soaring shell-like exterior is one of *the* must-see sights in the world, and brings tingles the first time you clap eyes on it. Its construction was an operatic blend of personal vision, long delays, bitter feuding, budget blowouts and righteous politicking. Construction began in 1959 after Danish architect Jørn Utzon won an international design competition with plans for a $7-million building. After political interference, Utzon quit in disgust in 1966, leaving a consortium of Australian architects to design a compromised interior – at a cost of $102 million. Utzon hasn't personally seen the Opera House since. Finally completed in 1973, it was lumbered with an impractical internal design for staging operas. The first public performance here was, ironically, Prokofiev's *War and Peace*. Today some 3000 events are staged here annually.

A worthwhile, hour-long **tour** (☎ 9250 7250; adult/concession $23/16; 9am-5pm) of the Opera House buildings is almost compulsory and very informative. Not all tours can visit all theatres because of rehearsals, but you're more likely to see everything if you take an early tour. Tours run every half-hour and include a free drink. Phone or email beforehand if you need wheelchair access.

SYDNEY HARBOUR NATIONAL PARK

This park protects the scattered pockets of bushland around the harbour and includes several small islands. It offers some great walking tracks, scenic lookouts, Aboriginal carvings and a handful of historic sites. Pick up information at **Sydney Harbour National Park Information Centre** (Map pp176-7; ☎ 9247 5033; 110 George St, The Rocks; 9.30am-4.30pm Mon-Fri, 10am-4.30pm Sat & Sun), which is housed inside historic Cadman's Cottage.

Fort Denison is a small, fortified island off Mrs Macquaries Point, originally used to isolate troublesome convicts. The fort was built during the Crimean War amid fears of a Russian invasion (seriously!). Two tours are available: The heritage tour (adult/child/family $22/18/72) or the brunch tour (adult/child $47/43). There are also tours of **Goat Island**, just west of the Harbour Bridge, which has been a shipyard, quarantine station and gunpowder depot. Pick the heritage tour (adult/child/family $20/16/62) or a Gruesome Tales tour ($25). All of these tours can be booked at the Sydney Harbour National Park Information Centre in Cadman's Cottage.

THE ROCKS

Sydney's first European settlement was established on the rocky spur of land on the western side of Sydney Cove, from where the Harbour Bridge now crosses the harbour to the North Shore. It was a squalid, raucous and notoriously dangerous place full of convicts, whalers, prostitutes and street gangs, though in the 1820s the nouveaux riches built three-storey houses on the ridges overlooking the slums, starting the city's obsession with prime real estate (which continues today).

The Rocks later became an area of warehouses and maritime commerce, and then slumped into decline as modern shipping and storage facilities moved away from Circular Quay. An outbreak of bubonic plague in the early 20th century led to whole streets being razed, and the construction of the Harbour Bridge resulted in further demolition.

Since the 1970s, redevelopment has turned much of The Rocks into a sanitised, historic tourist precinct, full of narrow cobbled lanes, fine colonial buildings, old pubs, fancy restaurants and Australiana shops. Despite the kitsch it's delightful to spend an afternoon strolling the poky backstreets and soaking up the atmosphere, especially on weekends when the Rocks Market (p203) is in full swing.

The oldest house in Sydney is the 1816 **Cadman's Cottage** (Map pp176-7; ☎ 9247 5033; 110 George St, The Rocks; 9.30am-4.30pm Mon-Fri, 10am-4.30pm Sat & Sun). It's also the former home of the last government coxswain, John Cadman; it now houses the Sydney Harbour National Park Information Centre.

A short walk west along Argyle Street, through the awe-inspiring **Argyle Cut** (excavated by convicts) takes you to the other side of the peninsula and **Millers Point**, a delightful district of early colonial homes with an English-village feel. Nearby lies the 1848 **Garrison Church** and the more secular delights of the Lord Nelson Brewery Hotel (p200) and the Hero of Waterloo (p200), which tussle over the title of Sydney's oldest pub.

Sydney Observatory (Map pp176-7; ☎ 9217 0485; www.sydneyobservatory.com.au; Watson Rd, Observatory Hill; admission free; 10am-5pm), off Argyle St, has a commanding position atop Observatory Park overlooking Millers Point and the harbour. There's a pleasant garden and an excellent free astronomy museum. Nightly visits for sky-watching (adult/child/family $15/12/40) must be paid in advance, and run two times a night; there's also a 3-D theatre with daily shows (adult/child/family $6/4/16). Daytime tours ($6) run twice daily Monday to Friday and four times a day on weekends.

Close by, in the National Trust Centre, is the **SH Ervin Gallery** (Map pp176-7; ☎ 9258 0173; www.nsw.nationaltrust.org.au/ervin.html; Watson Rd, Observatory Hill; adult/concession $6/4; 11am-5pm Tue-Fri, noon-5pm Sat & Sun). It shows temporary exhibitions on Australian art and is also the home of the annual Salon des Refuses show, for rejected Archibald Prize contenders; see the Art Gallery of NSW (p184) for an explanation of this art award. The café here serves good food.

CIRCULAR QUAY

Circular Quay, built around Sydney Cove, is one of the city's major focal points. The first European settlement grew around the Tank Stream, which now runs underground into the harbour near Wharf 6. For many years this was the shipping centre of Sydney, but it's now both a commuting hub and a recreational space. It combines ferry quays, a train station and the Overseas Passenger Terminal (read: huge cruise ships) with harbour walkways, parks, restaurants, buskers and lots of tourists.

The **Museum of Contemporary Art** (MCA; Map pp176-7; ☎ 9250 8467; www.mca.com.au; 140 George St, The Rocks; admission free; ☼ 10am-5pm) is set in a stately Art Deco building. It has a fine collection of modern art (sculpture, painting, installations and the moving image) from Australia and around the world, and temporary exhibitions (price varies) on a variety of themes. Its classy café is worth a stop.

City Centre

Central Sydney stretches from Circular Quay in the north to Central Station in the south. The business hub is towards the northern end, but most redevelopment is occurring at the southern end and this is gradually shifting the focus of the city.

Sydney lacks a true civic centre; **Martin Pl** lays claim to the honour by default. This grand, revamped pedestrian mall extends from Macquarie St to George St and is impressively lined by the monumental buildings of financial institutions and the colonnaded Victorian General Post Office (p173). There's plenty of public seating, a cenotaph commemorating Australia's war dead and an amphitheatre where lunchtime entertainment is staged occasionally.

The **Sydney Town Hall** (Map pp176-7; cnr George & Druitt Sts), a few blocks south of Martin Pl, was built in 1874. The elaborate chamber room and concert hall inside match the outrageously ornate exterior. Next door, the Anglican **St Andrew's Cathedral**, built around the same time, is the oldest cathedral in Australia.

The city's most sumptuous shopping complex, the Byzantine-style **Queen Victoria Building** (QVB), is next to the town hall and takes up an entire city block. Another lovingly restored shopping centre is the much smaller **Strand Arcade**, which connects Pitt and George Sts.

For the best view in town, whoosh to the top of **Sydney Tower** (AMP Tower; Map pp176-7; ☎ 8251 7800; www.sydneyskytour.com.au; cnr Market & Castlereagh Sts; adult/concession $22/15.85; ☼ 9am-10.30pm, to 11.30pm Sat), a needle-like column with an observation deck and revolving restaurants set 250m above the ground. The views extend west to the Blue Mountains and east to the ocean. A virtual-reality tour is included.

The splendidly over-the-top **State Theatre** (☎ 9376 6861; 49 Market St; tours $15) was built in 1929; tours are for groups of 10 or more, by appointment only. To the southwest are the tiny **Spanish Quarter** and larger **Chinatown**, dynamic areas breathing life into the city's southeastern zone, which includes the busy hub of Central Station.

On the eastern edge of the city centre is the formal **Hyde Park**, once the colony's first racetrack and cricket pitch. It has a grand avenue of trees, delightful fountains and a giant public chessboard. It contains the dignified **Anzac Memorial** (Map pp176-7; ☼ 9am-4.30pm), which has a free exhibition on the ground floor covering the 10 overseas conflicts in which Australians have fought. **St Mary's Cathedral** (Map pp176-7), with its new copper spires, overlooks the park from the east, while the 1878 **Great Synagogue** (Map pp176-7; ☎ 9267 2477; www.greatsynagogue.org.au; 187A Elizabeth St) stands on the west. Tours of the synagogue take place at noon Tuesday and Thursday (adult/child $5/3; entry at 166 Castlereagh St).

MACQUARIE PLACE & SURROUNDS

Narrow lanes lead south from Circular Quay towards the centre of the city. At the corner of Loftus and Bridge Sts, under the shady Moreton Bay figs in Macquarie Place Park, are a cannon and anchor from the First Fleet flagship, HMS *Sirius*. Also here is the **Macquarie Place Obelisk**, erected in 1818, indicating road distances to various points in the nascent colony. Nearby is the rear façade of the imposing 19th-century **Department of Land & Water Conservation (DLWC) Building** (Bridge St).

Two blocks east, the excellent **Museum of Sydney** (Map pp176-7; ☎ 9251 5988; www.hht.net.au; 37 Phillip St, City; adult/concession $7/3; 9.30am-5pm) is on the site of the first – and infamously fetid – government house, built in 1788. Sydney's early history (including pre-1788) comes to life here in whisper, argument, gossip and artefacts. There's also a worthy café on the premises and a damn fine gift shop.

The 1856 **Justice & Police Museum** (Map pp176-7; ☎ 9252 1144; www.hht.net.au; 8 Phillip St, City; adult/concession $7/3; 10am-5pm Sat & Sun, daily Jan), in the old water-police court and station on the corner of Phillip and Albert Sts, has fascinating exhibitions on crime and policing, with a Sydney focus. The drug and addiction exhibition (with its creative bongs) is especially interesting. Wheelchair access is to the ground floor only. Braille and audio guides are available.

MACQUARIE STREET

Sydney's greatest concentration of early public buildings grace Macquarie St, which runs along the eastern edge of the city from Hyde Park to the Opera House. Many of the buildings were commissioned by Lachlan Macquarie, the first governor to have a vision of the city beyond its being a convict colony. He enlisted convicted forger Francis Greenway as an architect to realise his plans.

Two Greenway gems on Queens Sq, at the northern end of Hyde Park, are **St James Church** (1819–24) and the 1819 Georgian-style **Hyde Park Barracks Museum** (Map pp176-7; ☎ 8239 2311; www.hht.net.au; Queens Sq, Macquarie St, City; adult/concession $7/3; 9.30am-5pm). The barracks were built originally as convict quarters, then became an immigration depot, and later a court. The museum details the history of the building and provides an interesting perspective on Sydney's social history, with the best use of rats you'll ever see in a display. Next door is the lovely **Mint Building** (Map pp176-7; ☎ 8239 2288; 10 Macquarie St, City), which was originally the southern wing of the infamous Rum Hospital, built by two Sydney merchants in 1816 in return for a monopoly on the rum trade (see p26). It became a branch of the Royal Mint in 1854. There's a fancy café on the premises, but nothing else is open to the public.

The Mint's twin is **Parliament House** (Map pp176-7; ☎ 9230 2047; Macquarie St, City; admission free; 9am-4pm Mon-Fri), which was originally the northern wing of the Rum Hospital. This simple, proud building has been home to the NSW Parliament since 1829. The public gallery is open on days when parliament is sitting.

Next to Parliament House is the **State Library of NSW** (Map pp176-7; ☎ 9273 1414; www .sl.nsw.gov.au; Macquarie St, City; 9am-9pm Mon-Fri, 11am-5pm Sat & Sun), which is more of a cultural centre than a traditional library. It holds over five million tomes, and hosts innovative temporary exhibitions in its galleries. The library's modern wing also has a great bookshop filled with Australian titles. Free one-hour tours are available.

The **Sydney Conservatorium of Music** (☎ 9351 1222; www.usyd.edu.au/su/conmusic; Macquarie St, City) was built by Greenway as the stables and servants' quarters of Macquarie's planned government house. Macquarie was replaced as governor before the house could be finished, partly because of the project's extravagance. See p202 for more information about the music recitals held here.

Built between 1837 and 1845, **Government House** (Map pp176-7; ☎ 9931 5222; www.hht.net.au; Macquarie St, City; admission free; grounds 10am-4pm, house 10am-3pm Fri-Sun) dominates the western headland of Farm Cove and, until early 1996, was the official residence of the governor of NSW. It's a marvellous example of the Gothic Revival style. Tours of the house begin every half-hour from 10.30am (unless a special event cancels).

The **Domain** is a pleasant grassy area east of Macquarie St that was set aside by Governor Phillip for public recreation. Today it's used by city workers as a place to escape the city hubbub, and on Sunday afternoon it's the gathering place for soapbox speakers who do their best to engage or enrage their listeners.

ART GALLERY OF NSW

The **art gallery** (AGNSW; Map pp176-7; ☎ 9225 1744; www.artgallery.nsw.gov.au; Art Gallery Rd, City; admission free; 10am-5pm daily, to 9pm Wed) has an excellent permanent display of 19th- and 20th-century Australian art, Aboriginal and Torres Strait Islander art, 15th- to 19th-century European and Asian art, and some inspired temporary exhibits. It's in the Domain, east of Macquarie St. The frequently controversial, much-discussed Archibald Prize exhibition is held here annually, with portraits of the famous and not-so-famous bringing out the art critic in almost every Sydneysider. There's usually a charge for temporary exhibitions; free tours are available (call for times).

AUSTRALIAN MUSEUM

This natural-history **museum** (Map pp176-7; ☎ 9320 6000; www.amonline.net.au; 6 College St, City; adult/concession $10/5; ❧ 9.30am-5pm) has an excellent Australian wildlife collection (including skeletons) and a gallery tracing Aboriginal history and the Dreamtime. It's on the eastern flank of Hyde Park, on the corner of College and William Sts. There's an Indigenous performance at noon and 2pm every Sunday, and a range of kids' exhibits.

ROYAL BOTANIC GARDENS

The city's favourite picnic spot, jogging route and place to stroll is the enchanting **Royal Botanic Gardens** (Map pp176-7; ☎ 9231 8125; www.rbgsyd.nsw.gov.au; Mrs Macquaries Rd, City; admission free; ❧ 7am-sunset, gardens shop 10am-4pm), which borders Farm Cove, east of the Opera House. The gardens were established in 1816 and feature plant life from the South Pacific. They include the site of the colony's first paltry vegetable patch, which has been preserved as the First Farm exhibit.

The fabulous, leech-free **Sydney Tropical Centre** (Map pp176-7; adult/child $2.20/1.10; ❧ 10am-4pm) is housed in the interconnecting Arc and Pyramid glasshouses. The multistorey Arc has a collection of rampant climbers and trailers from the world's rainforests, while the Pyramid houses the Australian collection, including monsoonal, woodland and tropical rainforest plants.

Free tours depart at 10.30am daily (and at 1pm Monday to Friday) from the information booth at the Gardens Shop. As far as wildlife goes, you can't fail to notice the gardens' resident colony of grey-headed **flying foxes** (*Pteropus poliocephalus,* or fruit bats), who spend their days chittering loudly and hanging around upside down until it's time to commute south across the city at dusk. Cockatoos, small reptiles and large orb spiders can also be seen. The park's paths are for the most part wheelchair accessible, although there are some flights of stairs scattered about.

Darling Harbour

This huge waterfront leisure park on the city centre's western edge, once a thriving dockland area, was reinvigorated in the 1980s by a combination of vision, politicking and big money. The supposed centrepiece is the **Harbourside Shopping Centre** (Map pp176-7), which houses shops and restaurants. More interesting attractions are the aquarium, excellent museums and the Chinese Garden.

The snazzy wining and dining precincts of **Cockle Bay Wharf**, opposite Harbourside, and **King St Wharf** have lent the area more kudos with Sydneysiders and visitors alike. Stretching across the water is the unmissable **Pyrmont Bridge**, a pedestrian-and-monorail-only route once famous as the world's first electrically operated swingspan bridge.

The monorail and Metro Light Rail link Darling Harbour to the city centre. Ferries leaving from Circular Quay's Wharf 5 stop at Darling Harbour's Aquarium and Pyrmont Bay wharves ($4.80). If you're confused, there's a visitors centre (p173) under the highway and behind the Imax theatre.

SYDNEY AQUARIUM

Near the eastern end of Pyrmont Bridge, this good **aquarium** (Map pp176-7; ☎ 8251 7800; www.sydneyaquarium.com.au; Aquarium Pier, Darling Harbour; adult/concession $25/16; ❧ 9am-10pm) displays the richness of Australian marine life. Three 'oceanariums' are moored in the harbour with sharks, rays and big fish in one, and Sydney Harbour marine life and seals in the others. There are also informative and well-presented exhibits of freshwater fish and coral gardens. The transparent underwater tunnels are mesmerising.

AUSTRALIAN NATIONAL MARITIME MUSEUM

This wonderful thematic **museum** (Map pp176-7; ☎ 9298 3777; www.anmm.gov.au; 2 Murray St, City; admission free; ❧ 9.30am-5pm) tells the story of Australia's relationship with the sea, from Aboriginal canoes and whaling history to the First Fleet and surf culture. Keep an eye out for the beer-can boat. Admission to the nearby ships and submarine costs extra (adult/concession $20/10).

POWERHOUSE MUSEUM

Sydney's hippest **museum** (Map pp176-7; ☎ 9217 0100; www.powerhousemuseum.com; 500 Harris St, Ul-

SYDNEY

timo; adult/concession $10/6; ☺ 10am-5pm) covers the decorative arts, social history, and science and technology, with eclectic exhibits ranging from costume jewellery and musical instruments to steam locomotives and space capsules. The collections are well displayed and the emphasis is on hands-on interaction. Find it behind the Sydney Exhibition Centre; it's in a former power station for Sydney's now-defunct trams.

CHINESE GARDEN OF FRIENDSHIP

The tranquil **Chinese Garden** (☎ 9281 6863; www.chinesegarden.com.au; adult/child/family $6/3/15; ☺ 9.30am-5.30pm), in the southeastern corner of Darling Harbour, was designed by landscape architects from Guangdong, and is an oasis of lush serenity. Enter through the Courtyard of Welcoming Fragrance, circle the Lake of Brightness and finish with tea and cake in the **Chinese teahouse** (☺ 10am-4.30pm), or by having your photo taken in a Chinese opera costume ($10).

SYDNEY FISH MARKET

Selling more than 15 million kilograms of seafood annually, this large **fish market** (Map pp174-5; ☎ 9552 2180; www.sydneyfishmarket.com.au; cnr Pyrmont Bridge Rd & Bank St, Pyrmont; ☺ 7am-4pm) is the place to get on first-name terms with a bewildering array of scaly critters. You can see fish auctions (early mornings), eat sushi or fish and chips, buy super-fresh seafood and attend seafood cooking classes (call for details). It's west of Darling Harbour, on Blackwattle Bay. The Metro Light Rail (the stop's called Fish Market) is the best way to get here.

Kings Cross

The Cross is a lovably raffish, fairly tame cocktail of restaurants, cafés, backpacker hostels, traveller services and pubs, though at night you can add the elements of strip joints, prostitution and drugs. It attracts an odd mix of highlife, lowlife, tourists and suburbanites looking for cheap services and an adrenaline-charged party scene. On Sunday a few stalls set up around **El Alamein Fountain** (Map p179) in Fitzroy Gardens, for a small flea market.

The Cross was a centre of Bohemianism during the Vietnam War era, when it gained its reputation as the centre of vice in Australia. It appeals to the free-wheelin'

spirit and to those with devil-may-care attitudes seeking 24-hour drinking. Many budget travellers begin and end their Australian adventures in the Cross – lots of Sydney's hostels are here – and it's a good place to swap information, meet up with friends, find work, browse notice boards and buy or sell a car.

In the dip between the Cross and the city is **Woolloomooloo**, one of Sydney's oldest areas and an interesting place to stroll around. The **Finger Wharf** houses apartments, restaurants and an ultrafancy hotel. **Harry's Café de Wheels** (Map pp176-7), next to the wharf, must be one of the few pie carts in the world to be a tourist attraction. It opened in 1945, stays open 18 hours a day (till way after midnight on weekends) and offers the cheapest meals with water views in town (you'll be sitting on a concrete bench with the seagulls, though).

Inner East

The backbone of Darlinghurst, Surry Hills and Paddington, **Oxford St** is one of the more happening places for late-night action. It's a strip of shops, cafés, bars and nightclubs whose flamboyance and spirit can be largely attributed to the vibrant and vocal gay community. The route of the Sydney Gay & Lesbian Mardi Gras parade (see p193) passes this way.

The main drag of Oxford St runs from the southeastern corner of Hyde Park to the northwestern corner of Centennial Park, though it continues in name to Bondi Junction. Taylor Sq is the main hub. (An orientation warning: Oxford St's street numbers restart on the Darlinghurst–Paddington border, west of the junction with South Dowling and Victoria Sts.) Buses 380 and 382 from Circular Quay, and 378 from Railway Sq (near Central Station), run the length of the street.

Darlinghurst is a vital area of urban cool, full of bright young things. There's no better way to soak up its studied ambience than to loiter in a few outdoor cafés and do as others do. Darlinghurst is wedged between Oxford and William Sts, and encompasses the vibrant 'Little Italy' of Stanley St in East Sydney.

South of Darlinghurst is **Surry Hills**, home to a mishmash of inner-city residents, heaps of cheap and tasty ethnic eateries (especially on Crown St) and a swag of good pubs. Once the undisputed centre of Sydney's rag trade and print-media industry, many of its warehouses have been converted to flash apartments.

Next door to Surry Hills, **Paddington** is an attractive residential area of leafy streets that are tightly packed Victorian terrace houses and numerous small art galleries. It was built for aspiring artisans, but during the lemming-like rush to the outer suburbs after WWII, the area became a slum. A renewed interest in Victorian architecture and the pleasures of inner-city life led to its restoration during the 1960s, and today many terraces swap hands for a million dollars. The best time to visit is on Saturday when the Paddington Market (p203) is in full swing.

Sydney's biggest park is **Centennial Park**, which has running, cycling, skating and horse-riding tracks, duck ponds, barbecue sites and sports pitches. It's 5km from the centre, just southeast of Paddington. **Moore Park** abuts the western flank of Centennial Park and contains sports pitches, a golf course, an equestrian centre, the Fox Studios, the Aussie Stadium and the Sydney Cricket Ground (SCG; p203).

Eastern Suburbs

A short walk northeast of the Cross is the harbourside suburb of **Elizabeth Bay**. One of Sydney's finest colonial homes is **Elizabeth Bay House** (Map pp174–5; ☎ 9356 3022; www.hht .net.au; 7 Onslow Ave; adult/concession $7/3; ☺ 10am-4.30pm Tue-Sun), by architect John Verge, dating from 1839. It's open on Mondays if it's a public holiday.

Beautiful **Rushcutters Bay** is the next bay east. Its handsome harbourside park is just a five-minute walk from the Cross and a great spot for cooped-up travellers to stretch their legs.

Further east is the ritzy suburb of **Double Bay**, which is endowed with old-fashioned cafés and exclusive stores. The views are stupendous from the harbour-hugging New South Head Rd as it leaves Double Bay, passes **Rose Bay** and climbs east towards wealthy **Vaucluse**. In Vaucluse Park, **Vaucluse House** (Map pp174–5; ☎ 9388 7922; www.hht.net.au; Wentworth Rd, Vaucluse; adult/concession $7/3; ☺ 10am-4.30pm Tue-Sun) is a beautifully preserved colonial mansion dating from 1827.

At the entrance to the harbour is **Watsons Bay**, a snug community with restored fisherman's cottages, a palm-lined park and a couple of nautical churches. If you want to forget you're in the middle of a large city, have a beer at the famous **Doyles Palace Hotel**. Nearby **Camp Cove** is one of Sydney's best harbour beaches, and there's a nude beach (mostly male) near South Head at **Lady Bay**. South Head has great views across the harbour entrance to North Head and Middle Head. The **Gap** is a dramatic cliff-top lookout on the ocean side; it has a reputation for suicides.

Buses 324 and 325 from Circular Quay service the eastern suburbs via Kings Cross. Sit on the left side heading east to make the most of the views.

Southern Beaches

Bondi lords it over every other beach in the city, despite not being the best one for a swim, surf or, damn it, a place to park. Still, the crashing waves, flashy cafés, rocky scenic points, grassy picnic lawns and strutting boardwalks aren't shabby at all. The suburb itself has a unique atmosphere due to its mix of old Jewish and other European communities, dyed-in-the-wool Aussies, New Zealanders who never went home, working travellers and the good-looking beach bums.

The ocean road is Campbell Pde, home to most of the commerce. There are **Aboriginal rock engravings** on the golf course in North Bondi. Catch bus 380, 382, L82 or 389 from the city to get to the beach or, if you're in a hurry, catch a train to Bondi Junction and pick up one of these buses as they pass through the Bondi Junction bus station.

Just south of Bondi is **Tamarama**, a lovely cove with strong rips. It's about a 15-minute (gorgeous) walk from Bondi. Another 10 minutes further south is **Bronte**, a nice beach hemmed in by a bowl-shaped park and sandstone headlands. The cafés with outdoor tables on the edge of the park make it a great chill-out destination. Further south again is **Clovelly Bay**, a narrow, scooped-out beach with little surf that's good for swimming (especially for children). As well as the saltwater baths here, there's a wheelchair-access boardwalk so the chairbound can take a sea dip.

SYDNEY

Something of a poor cousin to Bondi, **Coogee** has a relaxed air, a good sweep of sand and plenty of places to stay and eat. You can reach Coogee by catching bus 372 from Railway Sq or 373 from Circular Quay. Alternatively, take a train to Bondi Junction and pick up bus 314 or 315 from there. From Bondi, it's a beautiful two-hour walk.

Inner West

West of the centre is the higgledy-piggledy peninsula suburb of **Balmain**. It was once a notoriously rough neighbourhood of dockyard workers but has been transformed into an artsy, middle-class area of restored Victoriana flush with pubs, cafés and trendy shops. It's a great place for a stroll, and cars will actually stop when you cross the street. Catch a ferry from Circular Quay or bus 442 from the QVB.

Cosy, bohemian **Glebe** lies southwest of the centre, boasting a large student population, a café-lined main street, a tranquil Buddhist temple, yuppies galore, and several decent places to stay. A market is held at Glebe Public School, on Glebe Point Rd, on Saturday (see p203). Buses 431 to 434 from Millers Point run via George St along Glebe Point Rd. The Metro Light Rail also travels through Glebe.

Bordering the southern flank of the University of Sydney is **Newtown**, a melting pot of social and sexual subcultures, students and home renovators. King St, its relentlessly urban main drag, is full of funky recycled-clothing stores, bookshops, cheap cafés, pubs and Thai eateries. While it's definitely moving upmarket, Newtown comes with a healthy dose of youthful grunge, and harbours a decent live-music scene. The best way to get there is by train, but buses 422, 423, 426 and 428 from the city all run along King St.

Predominantly Italian **Leichhardt**, southwest of Glebe, is becoming increasingly popular with students, lesbians and young professionals. Its Italian eateries have a city-wide reputation, but main drag Norton St also offers cafés, bookstores and boutiques without an elitist sneer. Buses 436 to 438 run from Railway Sq to Leichhardt.

North Shore

On the northern side of the Harbour Bridge is **North Sydney**, a high-rise office centre with

little to tempt the traveller. **McMahons Point** is a lovely, forgotten suburb wedged between the two business districts, on the western side of the bridge. There's a line of pleasant alfresco cafés on Blues Point Rd, which runs down to Blues Point Reserve on the western headland of Lavender Bay. The reserve has fine city views.

Luna Park (Map pp174-5; ☎ 9922 6644; www.luna parksydney.au; Milson's Point; admission free), on the eastern shore of Lavender Bay, is an amusement park and a highly visible landmark. Rides cost extra and hours vary widely. At the end of Kirribilli Point, just east of the bridge, stand **Admiralty House** and **Kirribilli House**, the Sydney residences of the governor general and the prime minister respectively (Admiralty House is the one nearer the bridge; both are closed to the public). East of here are the upmarket suburbs of **Neutral Bay**, **Cremorne** and **Mosman**, all with pleasant coves and harbourside parks perfect for picnics. Ferries go to all these suburbs from Circular Quay.

On the northern side of Mosman is the pretty beach suburb of **Balmoral**, which faces Manly across Middle Harbour. There are picnic areas, a promenade and three beaches.

TARONGA ZOO

In a superb harbourside setting, **Taronga Zoo** (Map pp174-5; ☎ 9969 2777; www.zoo.nsw.gov.au; Bradleys Head Rd, Mosman; adult/child/family $27/14/70; ☻ 9am-5pm) has some 3000 critters (from seals to tigers, koalas to giraffes, echidnas to platypuses), all in decent habitats and well cared for. Ferries to the zoo depart from Circular Quay's Wharf 2 half-hourly from 7.15am on weekdays, 8.45am Saturday and Sunday. Bus 247 gets you there from the QVB building ($3.50). A ZooPass ($33.50), sold at Circular Quay and elsewhere, includes return ferry rides and zoo admission. Bring a picnic lunch if you want to avoid expensive zoo food.

Northern Beaches

A string of ocean-front suburbs sweep 30km north along the coast from Manly, ending at beautiful, well-heeled **Palm Beach** and the spectacular Barrenjoey Heads at the entrance to Broken Bay. Beaches along the way include Freshwater, Curl Curl, Dee Why, Collaroy and Narrabeen. The most spectacular are **Whale Beach** and **Bilgola** (near Palm

Beach), both with dramatic, steep headlands. Several of the northernmost beach suburbs also back on to **Pittwater**, a lovely inlet off Broken Bay and a favoured sailing spot.

Buses 136 and 139 run from Manly (near the wharf) to Curl Curl and Freshwater respectively. Bus L90 from Wynyard Park bus interchange in the city runs to Newport and then north to Palm Beach.

MANLY

The jewel of the North Shore, Manly is on a narrow peninsula that ends at the dramatic cliffs of North Head. It boasts harbour and ocean beaches, a ferry wharf, all the trappings of a touristy beach destination and a great sense of community. It's a sun-soaked place not afraid to show a bit of tack and brashness to attract visitors, and makes a refreshing change from the prim upper-middle-class harbour enclaves nearby.

The **Manly Visitors Centre** (Map p180; ☎ 9977 1088; Manly Wharf; 9am-5pm Mon-Fri, 10am-4pm Sat & Sun), just outside the ferry wharf, has free pamphlets along with information on the 10km Manly Scenic Walkway. From Circular Quay JetCats traverse the harbour in a mere 15 minutes, while the ferries do the trip in a cool 30 minutes – and offer great views.

A short walk from the Manly wharf brings you to the Corso, Manly's lively pedestrian mall, and trendy Manly Beach. A footpath follows the shoreline from South Steyne around the small headland to tiny **Fairy Bower Beach** and the picturesque cove of **Shelly Beach**.

Oceanworld (Map p180; ☎ 9949 2644; West Esplanade; adult/child/family $17.50/9/30; 10am-5.30pm), near Manly wharf, is a tacky aquarium whose big draw is divers feeding sharks and stingrays. After 3.30pm the admission price drops 15%. Nearby is the small **Manly Art Gallery & Museum** (Map p180; ☎ 9949 1776; West Esplanade Reserve; adult/concession $3.60/1.20, free Wed; 10am-5pm Tue-Sun), which focuses on the suburb's special relationship with the beach. Behind the gallery is the wonderful 10km-long **Manly Scenic Walkway**, which has a 2km-long wheelchair-accessible path. Bring water as there are no shops along the way.

North Head, at the entrance to Sydney Harbour, is about 3km south of Manly. Most of the dramatic headland is in Sydney Harbour National Park. The **Old Quarantine Station** (Map pp174-5; tours ☎ 9247 5033; adult/child

$11/7.70; 1.15pm Tue & Thu, 1.15pm & 3.30pm Sat & Sun) represents an interesting slice of Sydney's social history; it housed suspected disease carriers from 1832 right up until 1984. To visit the station, book a guided tour. The station is reputedly haunted and there are spooky three-hour ghost tours ($22 Wednesday, $28 Friday to Sunday; over 12 years only) at night. Kids' ghost tours are also available.

ACTIVITIES

Sydney's most popular activities include surfing, swimming and cruising the harbour on a tour, but the more adventurous can rent in-line skates, bicycles, kayaks and even sailing boats.

Canoeing & Kayaking

Contact the **New South Wales Canoeing Association** (☎ 9660 4597; www.nswcanoe.org.au) for information on canoeing.

Exhilarating bridge and island paddles with **Natural Wanders** (☎ 9899 1001; www.kayaksydney.com) cost $90 for a half-day tour.

Sydney Harbour Kayaks (☎ 9960 4389; www.sydneyharbourkayaks.com.au) offers lessons, sales and rentals, along with half-day ecotours for $99 per person.

Cycling

Sydney is a big city and thus full of bike-unfriendly traffic; the best spot to get some spoke action is Centennial Park, southeast of Paddington. Many cycle-hire shops require a hefty deposit on a credit card. Try the following:

Favorite Cycles (Map p180; ☎ 9977 4590; 22 Darley Rd, Manly; per hr/day $9/22; 9am-6pm Mon-Wed & Fri, to 7pm Thu, to 5pm Sat, 10am-4pm Sun)

Cheeky Monkey (Map pp176-7; ☎ 9212 4460; 456 Pitt St, City; per day/week from $25/100; 8.45am-5.30pm Mon-Fri, 10am-4pm Sat)

Inner City Cycles (Map pp174-5; ☎ 9660 6605; 151 Glebe Point Rd, Glebe; per day/week $33/90; 9.30am-6pm Mon-Wed & Fri, to 8pm Thu, to 4pm Sat, 11am-3pm Sun)

Diving

The best shore dives in Sydney are Gordons Bay Underwater Nature Trail, north of Coogee; Shark Point, Clovelly; and Ship Rock, Cronulla. Popular boat dives are Wedding Cake Island, off Coogee; around Sydney Heads; and off the Royal National Park.

A TALE OF TWO CITIES

Athens and Sparta, Paris and Milan, Springfield and Shelbyville – their struggles pale beside the epic 150-year rivalry between Sydney and Melbourne. Australia's biggest city, Sydney is also its oldest, having begun in 1788 as a convict colony. Melbourne, currently in the number-two slot, was founded in 1835. Sixteen years later, prospectors struck gold in Victoria, and the ensuing rush rocketed Melbourne ahead of Sydney in both wealth and population. The Sydney–Melbourne Rivalry (SMR) had begun.

Competition flared when Melbourne became Australia's temporary capital following nationhood in 1901. Purpose-built Canberra didn't replace Melbourne until 1927, by which time a driven Sydney had begun catching up financially, having already retaken the lead in human numbers.

These days, the SMR plays out for the most part as friendly chaffing, though discussions can get heated. Melburnians will point to Sydney's convict origins, its high housing prices and what they see as a lack of culture, while talking up their own city's multi-ethnicity, great restaurants and lively arts scene. Sydneysiders will often either feign ignorance of any rivalry, or maintain that it's one-sided, an invention of envious Melburnians deluded enough to compare their boring burgh with the obviously superior Sydney. And each side accuses the other of being unfriendly and snobbish.

A few unhappy souls seem dead earnest in their enmity towards the opposing city, convinced that no friendship or even meaningful dialogue can take place between the two groups.

If you should get caught in the middle between such types, don't try to pour oil on the waters by saying the two cities are nearing parity in their cultural diversity and culinary sophistication, or claiming that Sydney's scenery is balanced by Melbourne being Lonely Planet HQ and the birthplace of footy.

No, just put on your most innocent face and ask, 'Hey, does Canberra really suck as much as they say?'

Pro Dive (Map pp176-7; ☎ 9264 6177; www.prodive online.com.au; 478 George St, City; shore dives with gear $85, boat dives with/without gear $169/109, diving courses $295-495) has several outlets around Sydney.

Dive Centre (www.divesydney.com; Bondi Map pp174-5; ☎ 9369 3855; 192 Bondi Rd, Bondi; Manly Map p180; ☎ 9977 4355; 10 Belgrave St, Manly) has shore dives with gear starting at $100; boat dives at $130. An open-water PADI (Professional Association of Diving Instructors) course costs $345.

Harbour Cruises

There's an endless range of cruises on the harbour, from paddle steamers to sailing yachts. Smart penny-pinchers just take the $5.80 ferry to Manly and call it a night.

Harboursights Cruises (☎ 13 15 00; adult/child/family from $18/9/45) are run by the STA. These excellent short cruises let you take in the sights, sounds and smells of the harbour. Choose from morning (one hour), afternoon (2½ hours) or evening (1½ hours) cruises. Tickets can be bought at ferry ticket offices in Circular Quay.

Other popular cruises run hourly and include a drink:

Magistic Cruises (☎ 8296 7222; www.magisticcruises .com.au; adult/child/family $22/16.50/60) Pick-up points are King St Wharf 5, Darling Harbour or Wharf 6, Circular Quay.

Captain Cook Cruises (☎ 9206 1111; www.captaincook .com.au; adult/child/family $25/12/55) Pick-up points are Aquarium Wharf, Darling Harbour or Wharf 6, Circular Quay.

Matilda Rocket Express (☎ 9264 7377; www .matilda.com.au; adult/child/family $22/14/50) Picks up passengers at Aquarium Wharf, Darling Harbour.

In-line Skating

The beach promenades at Bondi and Manly and the paths of Centennial Park are the most favoured spots for skating.

Manly Blades (Map p180; ☎ 9976 3833; 49 North Steyne, Manly; ☺ 9am-6pm) rents blades (from $15), scooters (from $7) and skateboards (from $10).

Total Skate (Map pp174-5; ☎ 9380 6356; 36 Oxford St, Woollahra; 1st hr $10, per hr thereafter $5) is near Centennial Park; fee includes safety equipment.

Sailing

There are plenty of sailing schools in Sydney and, even if you're not serious about learning the ropes, an introductory lesson can be a fun way of getting out on the harbour.

EastSail Sailing School (☎ 9327 1166; www.east sail.com.au) has courses, charters, cruises, corporate events and overnight packages. Plenty of boats, but you'll need big bucks.

Sydney by Sail (☎ 9280 1110; 2 Murry St; www .sydneybysail.com) offers lots of courses, including a weekend introductory sail course for $425.

Swimming

Sydney's harbour beaches offer sheltered swimming spots. Just remember that after heavy rains excess water gets washed into the harbour from city streets.

If you want to frolic in real ocean waves, stay within the flagged areas patrolled by lifeguards. There are some notorious but clearly signposted rips, even at Sydney's most popular beaches, so don't underestimate the surf just because it looks safe.

Andrew 'Boy' Charlton Pool (Map pp176-7; ☎ 9358 6686; Mrs Macquaries Rd, The Domain; adult/child $5/3.50; ⏲ 6am-8pm Oct-Apr) Saltwater, smack bang on the harbour and popular with the gay crowd; Sydney's best pool and for serious swimmers only.

Wylie's Baths (☎ 9665 2838; Neptune St, Coogee; admission $3; ⏲ 7am-6pm) The waves wash in, but the sharks don't. It's like swimming in the ocean, but you're in a saltwater pool.

Surfing

South of the Heads, the best spots are Bondi, Tamarama, Bronte and Maroubra. Cronulla, south of Botany Bay, is also good. On the North Shore the best beaches are Manly, Curl Curl, Dee Why, North Narrabeen, Mona Vale, Newport Reef, North Avalon and Palm Beach itself. For current wave activity check www.wavecam.com.au.

Aloha Surf (Map p180; ☎ 9977 3777; www.aloha .com.au; 44 Pittwater Rd, Manly) has half-/full-day board hire for $20/40; also sells and trades equipment.

Dripping Wet Surf (Map p180; ☎ 9977 3549; www .drippingwetsurf.com; Shop 2, 93 North Steyne, Manly) has board rentals for $13/45 per hour/day and wet suits $5/20 per hour/day.

Bondi Surf Company (Map p180; ☎ 9365 0870; 72-76 Campbell Pde, Bondi) rents board and wet suit for $15 per hour, bodyboards and flippers for $10 per hour.

Let's Go Surfing (Map p180; ☎ 9365 1800; www.lets gosurfing.com.au; 128 Ramsgate Ave, Bondi) offers private lessons from $95; it also rents boards and wet suits ($20 per hour).

WALKING TOUR

Setting out on foot is the best way to really experience Sydney's nooks and crannies.

Start in Hyde Park at the **Anzac Memorial** (**1**; p183). Walking north, on your right you'll see the **Australian Museum** (**2**; p185) and, a bit further on, the impressive **St Mary's Cathedral** (**3**; p183).

Keep going north to reach **Macquarie St** (**4**; p184), with its collection of early colonial

---

WALK FACTS

- Distance: 5km
- Duration: two to three hours

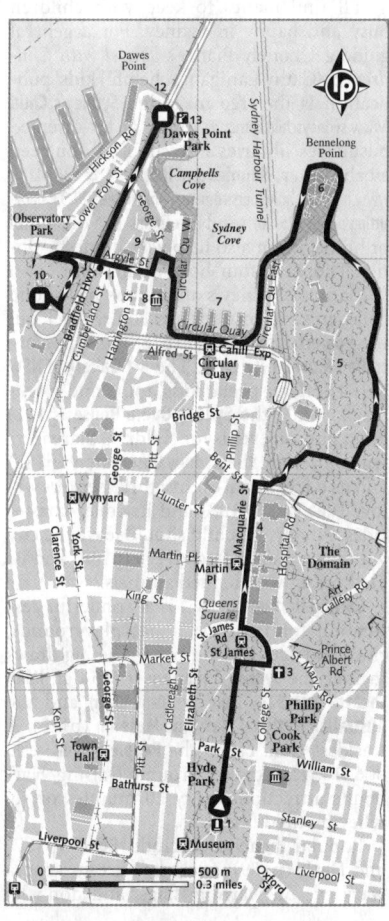

SYDNEY

buildings. If you love gardens, head east and wander through the **Royal Botanic Gardens** (5; p185). Follow the waterfront path to the spectacular **Sydney Opera House** (6; p181) and **Circular Quay** (7; p183). On the west side of Circular Quay, behind the **Museum of Contemporary Art** (8; p183), is **The Rocks** (9; p182) – very much worth exploring.

Work your way up to the **Sydney Observatory** (10; p182). If you want to cross the **Harbour Bridge** (12; p181), find the **Argyle Stairs** (11; p181) and head up; the views from the bridge are worth every step, especially from the **Pylon Lookout** (13; p181). Head back to The Rocks for a refreshing drink (see p200).

SYDNEY FOR CHILDREN

You'll find plenty to keep your children busy and happy in Sydney. For a general guide get Lonely Planet's *Travel with Children*, by Cathy Lanigan. A helpful kids' publication is the free magazine **Sydney's Child** (www.sydneyschild.com.au), found at tot-oriented businesses, libraries and schools. If you need a baby-sitter, **Nannies and Helpers** (☎ 9363 4221; www.nanniesandhelpers.com.au; booking fee $20-33; baby-sitting per hr $15-20) sends helpers to your hotel or home; it can also help with domestic duties. There is a four-hour minimum.

Many of Sydney's attractions have good children's exhibits; for museums, check out the **Powerhouse Museum** (p185) and the **Australian Museum** (p185). The **Art Gallery of NSW** (p184) offers special kids' tours and workshops, while the **Sydney Opera House** (p181) often puts on events for children. Stargazers will appreciate the **Sydney Observatory** (p182) and its educational events; thrill-seekers will love **Luna Park** (p188) and its roller-coaster rides. Finally, no child should leave the city without a visit to **Taronga Zoo** (p188) and its plethora of well-tended animals.

Darling Harbour (p185) is a wonderful destination for families; it has playgrounds, rides and activities on offer. The big draws include the **Sydney Aquarium** (p185), an **IMAX theatre** (☎ 9281 3300; ☺ 10am-10pm) and the **Australian National Maritime Museum** (p185). A trackless train called the **People Mover** (adult/child $3.50/2.50) snakes around Darling Harbour's attractions every 20 minutes or so, relieving tired little legs.

Popular beaches include **Bondi** (p187) and **Manly** (p189) – just be sure to keep a wary eye on warning flags, and don't let your children wander too far into the water by themselves. Glorious, grassy parks include the **Royal Botanic Gardens** (p185), with its riveting flying-fox population; **Centennial Park** (p187), which offers activities along with picnic areas; and **Moore Park** (p187), which includes the Fox Studios complex.

Whichever way you look at it, your kids will have a ball in Sydney – just make sure you've got the energy to keep up with them!

QUIRKY SYDNEY

Sydney has so much of everything that a few oddities pop up here and there. If you're looking for something offbeat check these things out.

There's nowhere to run on Goat Island's **Gruesome Tales Tours** (p182) – you're on an island!

The **Justice & Police Museum** (p184) has all you ever wanted to know about Sydney's criminal past. Great drug bust exhibitions.

Harry's Café de Wheels (p186) is Sydney's famous whimsy pie cart.

Mardi Gras (opposite) is Sydney's wildest festival, gay and lesbian–style. Folks come from all corners of the globe to partake.

The Royal Botanical Gardens' **flying-fox colony** (p185) is, in our opinion, a stand-out oddity. Seeing these bats chittering during the day and commuting over the city at night is quite a sight.

Other recommendations:

Destiny Tours (☎ 9943 0167; www.destinytours.com .au) Shake up the skeletons in Sydney's closet as you tour the city at night, cruising in a haunted hearse. Ghosts and intrigue abound (tours from $49).

Friend in Hand Hotel (☎ 9660 2326; 58 Cowper St, Glebe) Drink up while taking in poetry slams on Tuesdays, hermit-crab races on Wednesdays and comedy gigs on Thursdays. Bric-a-brac rules the walls.

TOURS

There are countless tours available in Sydney, and you can book some at the visitor centres. Here are just a few:

Bridgeclimb (Map pp176-7; ☎ 8274 7777; tour www .bridgeclimb.com.au; 5 Cumberland St, The Rocks; $160-225) Once-in-a-lifetime, unforgettable views from the peak of the Sydney Harbour Bridge. This 3½-hour tour includes thorough safety checks, your own climbing suit and an enthusiastic guide.

Maureen Fry (☎ 9660 7157; www.ozemail.com .au/~mpfry) Two-hour guided walks around Sydney cost $18 per person (minimum 10 people, or $180 per tour).

Sydney Architecture Walks (☎ 9518 6866; www
.sydneyarchitecture.org; adult/concession $20/15) An
introduction to Sydney's architecture, both old and new.
Strolls start at the Museum of Sydney and last two hours.
Sydney Day Tours (☎ 9251 6101; www.sdtours.com;
Shop 122, Clocktower Centre, cnr Argyle & Harrington
Sts, The Rocks) More tours than you can shake a stick at,
including cuddling koalas and wine tasting.

FESTIVALS & EVENTS
Sydney loves any excuse for a party. Some
of the highlights:
Sydney Festival (www.sydneyfestival.org.au) In January;
it's massive.
Gay & Lesbian Mardi Gras (www.mardigras.org.au)
Features an outrageous parade along Oxford St in late
February.
City to Surf Run Fourteen kilometres; second Sunday
in August.
Sculpture by the Sea (www.sculpturebythesea.com)
Transforms the Bondi to Bronte walk into an outdoor
sculpture gallery during mid-November.
Christmas Day Thousands of backpackers descend on
Bondi Beach.
Sydney to Hobart Yacht Race Boxing Day sees
hundreds of boats in the harbour bidding farewell to the
competitors in this gruelling race.
New Year's Eve Sydney's famed fireworks attract
thousands of spectators around the harbour.

SLEEPING
Sydney has a huge variety of accommodation: you can grab some shuteye at a cheap
hostel, cosy B&B, seedy motel, authentic
Aussie pub or five-star luxury behemoth
with breathtaking harbour views.

Exactly where you stay in Sydney will
depend on your budget and holiday needs.
For example, those travellers seeking hostels and party atmosphere should think
about heading to Kings Cross or the beach
destinations of Bondi or Manly, while those
willing to spend more and wanting to be
closer to tourist sights might wish to stay
in The Rocks or the city centre. Areas like
Chinatown and Surry Hills are still close to
the centre while offering distinctive atmosphere and more culinary and transport options. So decide what you want and read up
a little on Sydney's many neighbourhoods
before deciding where to settle in.

If you're travelling the East Coast by car,
Sydney will present a parking challenge.
Many hotels offer a place for your car, but
some charge dearly ($15 to $20 per day) for

it. When you make your hotel reservation
ask if they offer parking, how much it costs
and if you need to reserve a spot.

Budget
CITY CENTRE
Railway Square YHA (Map pp176-7; ☎ 9281 9666;
www.yha.com.au; 8-10 Lee St; dm $27-33, d $78-88;
▢ ✖) This tastefully renovated, railroad-
themed hostel is housed in a former parcels
shed. Original cargo doors, exposed ceilings, and dorms in reproduction train cars
add flavour, while the spa, bathroom-floor
warmers, comfortable rooms and trendy
common areas make your budget stay almost luxurious. It's right next to Central
Station (look for it behind the Medina
building) and much more intimate than its
sister YHA just down the street.

Sydney Central YHA (Map pp176-7; ☎ 9281 9111;
www.yha.com.au; 11 Rawson Pl; dm $28-33, d $82-94;
▣ ✖ ▢ ▨) The Cadillac of Sydney hostels,
this huge heritage-listed building offers 500-
plus beds, swank artsy spaces, a games room,
nightly movies, all the services you'd expect
(including a full-on travel agency) and even
an ATM in the lobby. And don't forget the
rooftop swimming pool! It's within spitting
distance of Central Station and very popular so reserve ahead (especially for private
rooms). Wheelchair accessible.

Big Hostel (Map pp176-7; ☎ 9281 6030, 1800
212 244; www.bighostel.com; 212 Elizabeth St; dm $25-
34, d $72-93; ✖) This 'boutique' hostel is a
new concept in accommodation. It works,
though, so you can expect good dorms with
lockers, a very hip TV lounge/kitchen area,
great rooftop patio and light breakfast included. Most doubles come with private
bathroom, and all rooms have TV and air-
con. It's *not* a party hostel.

KINGS CROSS
Pink House (Map p179; ☎ 9358 1689, 1800 806 385;
www.pinkhouse.com.au; 6-8 Barncleuth Sq; dm $23-25, d
$65; ▢) Yes, it's pink, but it's also a beautiful
historical mansion with charming personal-
ity and relaxing leafy patios. There's good
atmosphere, a communal kitchen and light
breakfast (with vegemite!) included. Doubles
share baths.

Original Backpackers (Map p179; ☎ 9356 3232, 1800
807 130; www.originalbackpackers.com.au; 160-162 Victoria
St; dm $25-28, d $70; ▢) Smack bang in the centre of Kings Cross and set in a wonderful

historic mansion, this long-running hostel offers 176 beds, friendly staff, two small kitchens and great outdoor spaces. It's a mazelike place where rooms have high ceilings and fridges, and all (including the doubles) share baths. Free pick-up from the airport.

Highfield Private Hotel (Map p179; ☎ 9326 9539; www.highfieldhotel.com; 166 Victoria St; s $50-65, d $65-80) A clean and welcoming hotel owned by a Swedish family (and therefore a Swede magnet), this well-run place offers good security, simple bright rooms (shared bathrooms), 24-hour access and a spot-on location. A common lounge sports fridge and microwave.

BONDI & COOGEE
Bondi Beachouse YHA (Map p180; ☎ 9365 2088; www.yha.com.au; 63 Fletcher St, Bondi; dm $27, s/d from $60/$70; 🖳) Bondi's best hostel, offering clean rooms (some boasting water views), two TV lounges and an unsurpassable rooftop terrace with spa. Cheap meals, free sports-equipment rentals and nightly activities also on tap. Catch bus 380 from the city or Bondi Junction and alight at the Fletcher St stop.

Coogee Beachside Accommodation (☎ 9315 8511, 1800 013 460; www.sydneybeachside.com.au; 178 Coogee Bay Rd, Coogee; d $75) Here's a very good option for those seeking simple but clean rooms with fridge, TV and shared bathrooms. There's a small kitchen with counter seating, and a garden patio below. Family rooms are available ($95); check the website for current rates.

MANLY & NORTH SHORE
Manly Beach House (Map p180; ☎ 9977 7050; www.manlybeachhouse.com; 179 Pittwater St, Manly; s/d/tr $50/70/80; P 🖳) Nine private rooms (that share baths) welcome couples and families looking for a more intimate and quiet Manly stay. There's a homey front living room, small kitchen and sunny patio. Rooms are basic but good-sized.

Boardrider Backpacker (Map p180; ☎ 9977 6077; www.boardrider.com.au; Rear, 63 The Corso, Manly; dm $28, d $75-85; 🖳) Smack in the middle of the Corso, Manly's happenin' pedestrian mall, this hostel caters to the young and surfing. It has a large TV room and rents out watersports equipment. The rooftop patio's pretty cool, and there's a balcony to check on the waves.

Sydney Beachouse YHA (☎ 9981 1177; www.yha.com.au; 4 Collaroy St, Collaroy; dm/d/f $26/64/104; P ✂ 🖳 🏊) This clean, airy hostel comes with great outdoor spaces, including a solar-heated pool! It's also wheelchair- and child-friendly and lies close to some of Sydney's best beaches (free surfboard rental). To get here, catch bus L90 or L88 from Railway Sq (the bus interchange next to Central Station), Town Hall or Wynyard train stations. From Manly, take bus 155 or 156.

GLEBE & NEWTOWN
Glebe Point YHA (Map pp174-5; ☎ 9692 8418; www.yha.com.au; 262-264 Glebe Point Rd, Glebe; dm $24-28, d $68; 🖳) Well run and pleasant, this large, friendly hostel offers good facilities, lots of activities and simple but clean rooms with sinks. There's a covered rooftop area with picnic tables and BBQ, which feels airier than the basement common rooms.

Glebe Village (Map pp174-5; ☎ 1800 801 983; www.glebevillage.com; 256 Glebe Point Rd; dm $26-28, d $75; 🖳) Those seeking more of a party atmosphere should head next door to this place.

Billabong Gardens (Map pp174-5; ☎ 9550 3236, 1800 806 419; www.billabonggardens.com.au; 5-11 Egan St, Newtown; dm $19-25, s $49, d $66-88; 🖳) This brick-and-tile hostel has some pleasant common spaces along with a kitchen, cosy TV room and tiny murky pool. Most importantly, however, it's located close to hoppin' King St. From Railway Sq catch bus 422, 423, 426 or 428 up King St and get off at Missenden Rd. By train, go to Newtown Station and turn right; Egan St is four blocks up on the left.

CAMPING
Sydney's caravan parks, most of which also have sites for tents, are a fair way out of town. The following are up to 26km from the city centre. Note that peak seasons (like Christmas) see rate hikes.

Lane Cove River Tourist Park (☎ 9888 9133; www.lanecoverivertouristpark.com.au; Plassey Rd, North Ryde; unpowered sites $28-30, powered sites $32-36; 🖳) This cheery place lies 14km north of the city and has good facilities (including over 150 caravan sites, plus cabins). You can chill out in the pool when temperatures swelter.

Sydney Lakeside Caravan Park (☎ 9913 7845; www.sydneylakeside.com.au; Lake Park Rd, Narrabeen; unpowered sites $28-33, powered sites $33-40) Located 26km north of Sydney, this nifty place occupies prime real estate around the northern beaches. If roughing it doesn't appeal, there are good cabins and lakeside 'villas' ($150 to $240).

Grand Pines Tourist Park (☎ 9529 7329; www.thegrandpines.com.au; 289 The Grand Parade, Sans Souci; powered sites $35-45; 💻) This friendly, good-quality caravan park is 17km south of Sydney on beautiful Botany Bay. Take your pick from sites, vans and cabins ($66 to $154); high standards are maintained.

Midrange

CITY CENTRE & THE ROCKS

Stellar Suites (Map pp176-7; ☎ 9264 9754, 1800 025 575; www.stellarsuites.com.au; 4 Wentworth Ave, City; r $135-360; 🅿 🍴 💻) Gorgeous, luxurious rooms in dark rich colours heal well-travelled bones at this hip boutique hotel, primly located right near Hyde Park. All 38 modern rooms have kitchenette, telephone, safe and Internet connection, and a three-bedroom apartment is available (along with free movies for all).

Russell (Map pp176-7; ☎ 9241 3543; www.therussell.com.au; 143A George St, The Rocks; d $140-280; 🍴) Located smack in the middle of The Rocks' main tourist drag, this charming 29-room hotel offers creaky floors, modest flowery rooms, pleasant lounge areas and a sunny roof garden. There's an intimate feel and narrow staircase (no elevator), with the cheapest rooms sharing baths.

Australian Hotel (Map pp176-7; ☎ 9247 2229; www.australianheritagehotel.com; 100 Cumberland St, The Rocks; d incl breakfast $125) Ten sweet rooms are on offer here, some with shared bathrooms. There's a rooftop terrace (great views) and cosy communal lounge with tea- and coffee-making facilities. The highlight might just be the cool pub downstairs, however.

CHINATOWN & DARLING HARBOUR AREA

Pensione Hotel (Map pp176-7; ☎ 9265 8888, 1800 885 886; www.pensione.com.au; 631 George St; d $125; 🍸) A great contemporary choice in Chinatown, this hip new boutique hotel offers stylish and tasteful rooms with minimalist décor and basic services like fridge and cable TV. Friday and Saturday nights see rate hikes to $140, however.

Vulcan Hotel (Map pp176-7; ☎ 9211 3283; www.vulcanhotel.com.au; 500 Wattle St; d $99-150; 🅿 🍴 💻) The location of this boutique hotel is just a bit off-centre, but the rooms are stunning in their simple design and décor. There's also abundant charm in this heritage-listed building, and a courtyard garden is in the works.

Hyde Park Inn (Map pp176-7; ☎ 9264 6001; www.hydeparkinn.com.au; 271 Elizabeth St; s/d from $155/170; 🅿 🍴 💻) Nicely located across from Hyde Park (the higher floors have awesome leafy views), this pleasant hotel offers good spacious rooms with kitchenettes. Deluxe rooms come with balcony and offer the best views (and cost more). Two-bedroom apartments are available.

KINGS CROSS

Royal Sovereign Hotel (Map p179; ☎ 9331 3672; www.royalsov.com.au; cnr Liverpool St & Darlinghurst Rd; d $77-88; 🍴) Perched above one of Sydney's favourite drinking dens (the Darlo Bar; p200), these 19 small but sharply decorated rooms all come with TV and clean shared bathrooms. Upper rooms are quieter but more expensive, and come with fridge and coffeepot. Even the halls are nice.

Maisonette Hotel (Map p179; ☎ 9357 3878; maisonettehotel@bigpond.com; 31 Challis Ave; s/d $60/95) Not a bad deal for this clean, friendly hotel, and the price gets better if you stay longer than one night. The small, bright doubles come with bath, kitchenette and TV, but singles share bathrooms.

DARLINGHURST

Sullivans Hotel (Map pp176-7; ☎ 9361 0211; www.sullivans.com.au; 21 Oxford St; d $135-150; 🅿 🍴 🍸) Situated in an area often referred to as 'Paddinghurst', this well-managed 64-room motel has good simple rooms and a charming pool courtyard. The pricier rooms face inside, and those in front come with balcony. Bookings are essential during Mardi Gras.

BONDI & COOGEE

Ravesi's (Map p180; ☎ 9365 4422; www.ravesis.com.au; cnr Campbell Pde & Hall St, Bondi; d $125-275, ste $275-450; ⊠) Gorgeous and sleek describes the 16 contemporary rooms and two-level suites at this posh place. Luxurious balconies offer five-star peeps at the ocean, and the modern baths are spotless. It's a fabulous place to stay, and the trendy bar downstairs attracts beautiful crowds.

Bondi Beach Homestay (Map p180; ☎ 9300 0800; 10 Forest Knoll Ave, Bondi; www.bondibeachhomestay.com .au; s $80, d $125-135; P ⊡) In a charmingly decorated home with friendly owners, this is one of Bondi's hidden gems. Immaculate bathrooms are shared among the four homey rooms, and comfortable common areas include a lounge and sunny deck. Breakfast included; kitchen access.

Hotel Bondi (Map p180; ☎ 9130 3271; www.hotel bondi.com.au; 178 Campbell Pde, Bondi; s $75, d $110-120, ste $160-220; ⊠) The beachfront peach-coloured Hotel Bondi resembles a tasty layered cake and offers small, tidy rooms a cut above the usual pub standard. Choice front rooms have views, but note that the hotel is also home to three bars and a nightclub. Prices drop April to September.

Dive Hotel (☎ 9665 5538; www.divehotel.com.au; 234 Arden St, Coogee; d from $150; P ⊡) The 14 rooms at this delightful boutique hotel are wonderfully luxurious, and come with kitchenette, small groovy bathroom and breakfast; those in front sport ocean views. There's an elegant kitchen for all and a relaxing, Asian-flavoured back patio.

MANLY & NORTH SHORE

Periwinkle Guest House (Map p180; ☎ 9977 4668; www.periwinkle.citysearch.com.au; 18-19 East Esplanade, Manly; s/d from $110/135; P) This beautifully restored Victorian house offers 18 pleasant and well-appointed rooms, all with fridge and TV (and some with stunning water views). There's a family atmosphere and a relaxing shady courtyard. Cook up dinner in the nifty kitchen, but remember that a light breakfast is on the house.

Manly Lodge (Map p180; ☎ 9977 8655; www.manly lodge.com.au; 22 Victoria Pde, Manly; d $135-200; ⊠) Vaguely Spanish in appearance, Manly Lodge is a labyrinthine guesthouse with 28 rooms and suites, all with kitchenette and some with private patio. It's a comfortable, though not luxurious, setup and sports a

spa, sauna and small, leafy patio. Family rooms available (from $150).

Glenferrie Lodge (Map pp174-5; ☎ 9955 1685; www.glenferrielodge.com; 12A Carabella St, Kirribilli; s/ d from $60/105; ⊡) This large, beautiful old house lies on a quiet residential street and has a wonderfully grassy back garden. Rooms come with fridge and shared bathrooms are clean; dorm beds are available. Cheap dinners are available and rates include breakfast, but there's no kitchen access. Arrive here via the Milsons Point train station or by ferry from Kirribilli wharf.

GLEBE

Alishan International Guest House (Map pp174-5; ☎ 9566 4048; www.alishan.com.au; 100 Glebe Point Rd; dm $22-33, s $88-99, d $99-115; ⊡) This well-run gem is housed in an old building, offering clean rooms with character and a communal kitchen. There's also a beautiful airy balcony and a nice garden in which to hang out, along with a bright dining area.

Top End

CITY CENTRE

Establishment Hotel (Map pp176-7; ☎ 9240 3100; www.establishmenthotel.com; 5 Bridge Lane, City; d from $340; ⊠ ⊡) These ultraslick digs are hidden off a dark, alley, but inside the premises you'll find 33 silky rooms tricked out in simple modern lines and two-colour design schemes. Beds are lined with fine cotton linen, baths are encircled in marble or limestone and two equally extravagant bars (p200) help slake your thirst.

Four Seasons (Map pp176-7; ☎ 9238 0000; www .fourseasons.com; 199 George St; d from $440; P ⊠ ⊡) Easily one of the main contenders for the title of 'best hotel in Sydney', the Four Seasons offers an unbeatable location, luxurious rooms, professional staff and knockout views (city, Opera House, or harbour – take your pick) from more than half its rooms. Those seeking spa services will find them here.

KINGS CROSS & WOOLLOOMOOLOO

Regents Court (Map p179; ☎ 9358 1533; www.regents court.com.au; 18 Springfield Ave, Kings Cross; d $187-255; P ⊠) Loyal followers keep coming back to the spacious, luxurious rooms at this family-owned place. All are bright and boast fully stocked kitchens and pleasant dining areas. The highlight, however, has to be the lush and lovely rooftop garden – it's a wonderfully relaxing spot in Kings Cross.

W Hotel Sydney (Map pp176-7; ☎ 9331 9000; www .whotels.com; 6 Cowper Wharf Rd, Woolloomooloo; d from $335; P ❷ 🖳 ⚑) With what must be the most impressive lobby in Sydney, this lavishly contemporary boutique hotel – housed in an old wool-processing warehouse – offers ultrachic loft suites with stunning water views. Even standard rooms sport slick minimalist design, and surround an open central space fitted with airy bar and café. The elegant underground pool is a plus.

DARLINGHURST & SURRY HILLS

Medusa (Map p179; ☎ 9331 1000; www.medusa.com .au; 267 Darlinghurst Rd, Darlinghurst; d $270-385; ❷ 🖳) This sultry 18-room boutique hotel is pure Sydney – glamorous, flashy, sexy and decadent. Lose yourself in the colourful, curvaceous furniture, and enjoy the chocolates on your pillow, soft linens on your bed and Aveda toiletries in your bath. A lovely, sunny fountain courtyard offers dreamy lounging; gay travellers and design buffs will be in heaven.

Medina on Crown (Map pp174-5; ☎ 9360 6666, 1300 300 232; www.medinaapartments.com.au; 359 Crown St, Surry Hills; apt from $218; P ❷ 🖳 ⚑) The comfortable one- and two-bedroom apartments on offer here are all spacious and come with well-stocked kitchens, so they're great for families. Plenty of services and a peaceful courtyard pool area might turn Crown St into a holiday spot for you, especially if you consider the rooftop grass tennis court.

THE AUTHOR'S CHOICE

Hotel Altamont (Map p179; ☎ 9360 6000; www.altamont.com.au; 207 Darlinghurst Rd; dm $20, d $89-130; ❷) Flashy in that rustic sort of way, this modern boutique hotel offers lovely rooms – some with patio – and a smart, intimate lobby strewn with leather chairs. There's a great terrace to hang out in, and cheap but tasteful dorm rooms are available for those pinching pennies. Continental breakfast is included (though those in dorms pay $2). This is a great deal, considering the surroundings, services and location. Reception is open only from 8am to 8pm.

EATING

With great local produce, innovative chefs and BYO licensing laws, it's no surprise that eating out is one of the great delights of a visit to Sydney.

City Centre

There's no shortage of places for a snack or quick meal in the city, especially on weekdays when most restaurants cater to the business crowds. Lots of cheap grub is hidden away in food courts, however, so snoop around.

Rockpool (Map pp176-7; ☎ 9252 1888; 107 George St, The Rocks; mains $54-60; ☽ dinner Tue-Sat) It's one of the best eateries in Sydney, with good reason. Chef Neil Perry churns out beautiful (in all senses) dishes, and the seafood especially shines. Go for the southern rock lobster *tagine* with roast apricots and couscous for two, while enjoying the cool, slick and modern atmosphere – you'll thank us later.

Bodhi (Map pp176-7; ☎ 9360 2523; cnr College St & Phillip Park; yum cha $5-8, mains $6-8; ☽ lunch & dinner Tue-Sun, lunch Mon) Vegans need look no further than this flashy spot, located below the plaza in front of the cathedral. Lunch means tasty yum cha, though the outdoor seating can be windy. There's another (much smaller) branch at Central Station.

Casa Asturiana (Map pp176-7; ☎ 9264 1010; 77 Liverpool St; tapas $8-14, mains from $22; ☽ lunch & dinner) Located in Sydney's tiny 'Spanish Quarter', this joint reputedly serves the best tapas in town. Try small platefuls of seafood, meat and vegetarian tidbits, and order a fine Spanish white (or red) to help wash it all down. If you're in the mood for a *cazuela* (Spanish stew), paella or weekend flamenco you're also in luck.

Chinatown

Much of Sydney's cheapest (and tastiest) food can be found in bustling Chinatown.

BBQ King (Map pp176-7; ☎ 9267 2586; 18-20 Goulburn St; mains $12-24; ☽ lunch & dinner) Vegetarians should give this place a wide berth, 'cause the roast duck and barbecued pork are the main attractions. It's an old-school Chinese eatery, with bustling service, generous pots of tea and a lack of fancy décor. Open till 2am.

Xic Lo (Map pp176-7; ☎ 9280 1678; 215A Thomas St; mains $9-12; ☽ lunch & dinner) Sleek lines, stainless-steel counters and muted colours

---

THE AUTHOR'S CHOICE

Sailor's Thai and **Sailor's Thai Canteen** (Map pp176-7; ☎ 9251 2466; 106 George St; mains $25-36; ⊗ lunch Mon-Fri, dinner Mon-Sat) This is actually two restaurants in one, but both are famous for some of the best Thai food this side of Bangkok. Upstairs is casual: sit at the long, communal stainless-steel table and chat with your neighbours, who could be artists, politicians or tourists. For something more special, put on your fancy wear and head on downstairs, where you'll be surrounded by white tablecloths and romantic atmosphere. Either way, consultant chef David Thompson whips up complex dishes that will joyously tingle your tastebuds.

---

translate into hip Vietnamese food, and the crowds drop in en masse during lunchtime. The crispy chicken with rice ($9) is a winner, but the *pho* (noodle soup) and rice rolls are also popular.

Emperor's Garden BBQ & Noodles (Map pp176-7; ☎ 9281 9899; 213-215 Thomas St; mains $9-16; ⊗ lunch & dinner) This is a busy eatery specialising in meat and poultry dishes. The little takeaway section out front has many goodies, including some crimson-hued offerings hanging in the window; give the duck and rice (takeaway $9) a try – it's simply decadent.

Darling Harbour

The areas around Darling Harbour have dining options as far as the eye can see – some hit, many miss. Most have nice views, though they don't usually come cheap.

Blackbird Café (Map pp176-7; ☎ 9283 7385; Level 2, Cockle Bay Wharf; mains $8-19; ⊗ breakfast, lunch & dinner) Here's a good budget option with something for everyone: hot stone pizzas, plenty of salads, a vegetarian list and staples like pasta and meat selections. There's even wok stir-fries. The shady outdoor balcony is pleasant, as are the harbour views. Open late.

Chinta Ria...Temple of Love (Map pp176-7; ☎ 9264 3211; Level 2, Cockle Bay Wharf, 201 Sussex St; mains $10-26; ⊗ lunch & dinner) It ain't really cheap Malaysian food but the atmosphere sure is fun. An enormous Buddha greets you at the door, while the spicy chicken laksa ($16) is worth getting excited about. Jazzy music, colourful décor, clanging dishes and efficient service abound.

Darlinghurst & Paddington

Victoria St sports the most eateries in Darlinghurst. There's a second cluster of (mostly Italian) restaurants on Stanley St, just south of William St between Crown and Riley Sts.

Bill's (Map p179; ☎ 9360 9631; 433 Liverpool St; mains $18-23; ⊗ breakfast & lunch daily, dinner Mon-Sat) Beautifully presented gourmet food. Gleaming open kitchen. Fresh flowers and fashion magazines. Large communal table for conversations about your sweet-corn frittata with bacon ($18.50) and his grilled Hiramasa kingfish with chickpea salad ($22.50) Unbearable weekend brunch crowds. No sign outside. Bill Granger.

Bill & Toni's (Map pp176-7; ☎ 9360 4702; 74 Stanley St; mains $13-15; ⊗ lunch & dinner) Folks come here because it's a stalwart for basic Italian cuisine, a cheap and cheerful tradition, and – in our opinion – a national treasure. The service is lightning fast, you get your orange cordial for free and everyone leaves with a smile. The café downstairs has good coffee.

Foodgame (Map pp176-7; ☎ 9380 8585; 185 Campbell St; mains $7-15; ⊗ lunch & dinner) The steel deli counters work well with the plush lounge area, communal table and pavement seating. Whichever way you sit, you'll enjoy the salads (Thai to Caesar), burgers (satay to steak) and pasta (ravioli to fettuccine). And don't even think about leaving without dessert (lemon tart, sticky date pudding, lime-infused coconut panna cotta...)

And the Dish Ran Away with the Spoon (Map pp176-7; ☎ 9361 6131; 226 Glenmore Rd, Paddington; mains $5-10; ⊗ breakfast, lunch & dinner) Local yuppies cram this charming little Paddington deli to lunch on great pasta anxd burgers, and it's a primo spot to pick up picnic fixings or takeaway lunches and dinners. Try the low-fat 'skinny burger' ($8) – it tastes too good to be true.

Surry Hills

Crown St is the main thoroughfare through Surry Hills, but it's a long street and the restaurants occur in fits and starts. It's worth a wander along, though, as it has good shops and eateries.

Red Lantern (Map pp174-5; ☎ 9698-4355; 545 Crown St; mains $12-20; ⊗ lunch Tue-Fri, dinner Tue-Sun) Before anything else, call to make reservations – and ask for a front patio table. This hot new Vietnamese joint serves up some

SYDNEY

great shrimp rolls in rice paper ($9) and an exotic *muc rang muoi* (chilli salted squid, $14), all the while softly glowing in atmospheric lighting.

Mohr Fish (Map pp174-5; ☎ 9318 1326; 202 Devonshire St; mains $7-18; ☒ lunch & dinner) Don't expect a fancy eatery – this place takes up a space the size of your living room. It's very casual and has only a short, simple menu of fried seafood – can you say fish and chips ($7.50)? Expect the locals to join you at the crowded counter.

Maya Da Dhaba (Map pp174-5; ☎ 8399 3785; 431 Cleveland St; mains $8-15; ☒ dinner) Better-than-average Indian fare is served among natty surroundings covered in wall hangings at this popular restaurant. The Andrakhi lamb chops ($14.50) arrive sizzling and juicy, while the chicken Makhani ($13) is also quite tasty, but there are plenty of vegetarian choices as well.

Kings Cross

The Cross has a good mixture of tiny cafés, swanky eateries and fast-food joints serving greasy fare designed mainly to soak up beer.

Bayswater Brasserie (Map p179; ☎ 9357 2177; 32 Bayswater Rd; mains $22-31; ☒ lunch Tue-Fri, dinner Mon-Sat) This classy restaurant has good service and a relaxing back-room bar for predinner aperitifs. The menu is short and simple and offers delicious things like roast lamb rump, prosciutto-wrapped chicken, and barramundi with anchovy butter.

Delectica (Map p179; ☎ 9368 1390; 130 Victoria St; mains $7-14; ☒ breakfast & lunch daily, dinner occasionally) Breakfast is served all day, so get your blueberry pancakes with yoghurt and honey for dinner if you like. Or try the burger with beetroot or pumpkin salad with hummus dressing.

Matchbox (Map p179; ☎ 9326 9860; 197 Victoria St; mains $10-12; ☒ breakfast & lunch) Tiny as a matchbox indeed; there are just four small pavement tables and a wraparound counter. And this trendy breakfast (served all day) place gets packed on weekends, so come early.

Vinyl Lounge (Map p179; ☎ 9326 9224; 17 Elizabeth Bay Rd; mains $8-13; ☒ breakfast & lunch) More a locals' café than restaurant, this hip, white hole in the wall has shots of coffee guaranteed to kick. Enjoy your semolina with apples, currants and yoghurt ($7.50) on the classic '60s yellow plastic tables.

Bondi

The touristy eateries stretch along the Campbell Pde promenade, while fancy bistros can be found on side streets. You'll generally have to forgo a table with sea view if you're seriously pinching pennies, but a bag of takeaway and patch of sand works just as easily.

Bondi Icebergs (Map p180; ☎ 9365 9000; 1 Notts Ave; mains $32-44; ☒ lunch & dinner) So damn hot we get scorch marks just walking past, this supremely upscale restaurant (and bar) epitomises the flash of Sydney's best restaurants. Not only are the food and wine fantastic, but the views over Bondi come unmatched. Reservations are crucial – as is decent dress.

Brown Sugar (Map p180; ☎ 9365 6262; 100 Brighton Blvd; mains $8-14; ☒ breakfast & lunch) This cramped space really churns out brekkie to the smooth set on weekends – and one bite of their black-stone eggs ($13) will tell you why. Weekdays are much less frantic, but the linguine with asparagus and rocket tastes just as good.

Green's Café (Map p180; ☎ 9130 6181; 140 Glenayr Ave; mains $8-14; ☒ breakfast & lunch Wed-Mon) A green-hued, laid-back and homey experience awaits those seeking tasty and healthy salads, sandwiches and scrambles. The teas and peach lassis are special too. (It's not strictly vegetarian, despite the name.)

Gelbison (Map p180; ☎ 9130 4042; 10 Lamrock Ave; mains $11-16; ☒ dinner) An old favourite with many beach bums, celebrities and assorted gluttons looking for great Italian staples. There are pizzas galore (27 kinds), even more pastas and a few veal and risotto dishes.

Manly

The ocean end of the Corso (Manly's pedestrian mall) is jam-packed with takeaway places and outside tables. Manly Wharf and South Steyne have plenty of airy eateries that catch the sea breeze and bustle on sunny days. Note that weekends see restaurant surcharges of 10%.

Manly Fish Market (Map p180; ☎ 9976 3777; Shop 1, Wentworth St; mains $9-13; ☒ breakfast, lunch & dinner) A small fish shop with just two tables, though with the beach so near most folks grab the delicious fish-and-chips bag and head to the water.

Blue Water Café (Map p180; ☎ 9976 2051; 28 South Steyne; mains $16-27; ☒ breakfast, lunch & dinner) The huge portions are a major draw

SYDNEY

at this bustling, popular beach café. The whopping lemon chicken burger ($14) will really satisfy a post-surf hunger, although the boards on the wall will remind you to get back into the foam.

Beanrush (Map p180; ☎ 9977 2236; 7 Whistler St; coffees $2.50-4, mains $7-10; ☺ breakfast & lunch Mon-Sat) A small hole-in-the-wall café with truly great coffee, and the snacks are mighty fine, too. Worth a visit if your engine needs revving, but keep in mind it closes at 5.30pm.

DRINKING
Bars & Pubs

There's no shortage of drinking holes in Sydney. The Rocks and Kings Cross are popular magnets, but attractive, low-key places can be found in inner-city suburbs such as Surry Hills and Darlinghurst. The beaches have their share, obviously, plus ocean breezes to boot.

CITY CENTRE

Establishment Bar (Map pp176-7; ☎ 9240 3000; 252 George St) Slicker than greased lightning, this upscale, yuppy-ish bar brings white columns, leather sofas and dressed-up crowds together. The patio garden out the back is fine.

THE ROCKS

Lord Nelson Brewery Hotel (Map pp176-7; ☎ 9251 4044; 19 Kent St, The Rocks) The Lord Nelson is an atmospheric old pub that claims to be the 'oldest pub' in town (although others do, too!) and brews its own beers (Quayle Ale, Trafalgar Pale Ale, Victory Bitter, Three Sheets, Old Admiral and Nelsons Blood). Go ahead and try them all.

THE AUTHOR'S CHOICE

Paddington Inn Hotel (Map pp174-5; ☎ 9380 5913; 338 Oxford St) Large, popular and pretty, this pub doesn't look like much from the outside – but it's surprisingly swanky on the inside. The airy window seats are gold, especially on weekend afternoons when the nearby Paddington Market is in full swing. The music was once described as 'funky shit' by one staff member; come and decide for yourself. And if you need a change of pace, Oxford Street's more rowdy (read: gay) bars are a stone's throw west.

Hero of Waterloo (Map pp176-7; ☎ 9252 4553; 81 Lower Fort St, Millers Point) Enter into the wonderful stone interior, meet the boisterous locals and enjoy the nightly music (piano, folk, jazz or Irish tunes). Downstairs is an original dungeon, where drinkers would sleep off a heavy night before being shanghaied to the high seas.

Australian Hotel (☎ 9247 2229; 100 Cumberland St, The Rocks) Grab a pleasant pavement table at this classic pub and order a Scharer's lager on draft – it's got a cult following here in Sydney. Exotic gourmet pizzas (try the crocodile, emu and 'roo toppings) help fill the time between drinks. It's located in the hotel of the same name (see p195).

KINGS CROSS & DARLINGHURST

Jimmy Lik's (Map p179; ☎ 8354 1400; 188 Victoria St, Kings Cross) Long benches and a long cocktail list (try the Japanese pear with lemon juice, sake and vodka) fit well into the highfalutin atmosphere. It's a great place to wait for a table at their restaurant next door.

Bourbon (Map p179; ☎ 9358 1144; 24 Darlinghurst Rd, Kings Cross; ☺ to 6am) Flash to the max and attracting young, hip and upper-crust crowds that come to lounge in booths, sit back on sofas or overlook the park and bustling sidewalk. Hip music, mod lighting and swanky service are included.

World Bar (Map p179; ☎ 9357 7700; 24 Bayswater Rd, Kings Cross) Three floors of cool spaces attract the backpacking crowd, and two-for-one cocktails during happy hour keep 'em happy (Tuesday's a big night). DJs spin nightly and there's an airy tropical terrace out front.

Darlo Bar (Map p179; ☎ 9331 3672; 306 Liverpool St, Darlinghurst) Service is friendly, the furniture is retro mix 'n' match, and there's a boisterous crowd scene on weekends. Darlo's got a great vibe, comfortable atmosphere and hip music, all wrapped up in an interesting neighbourhood.

BONDI

Beach Road Hotel (Map p180; ☎ 9130 7247; 71 Beach Rd) Reputedly 'the' pub in Bondi, though it's well inland. This huge but beautiful place offers a snazzy atmosphere, a large and pleasant beer garden, and a swanky cocktail bar upstairs with live music. Wednesday nights are especially popular with backpackers.

CITYRAIL'S SYDNEY SUBURBAN NETWORK

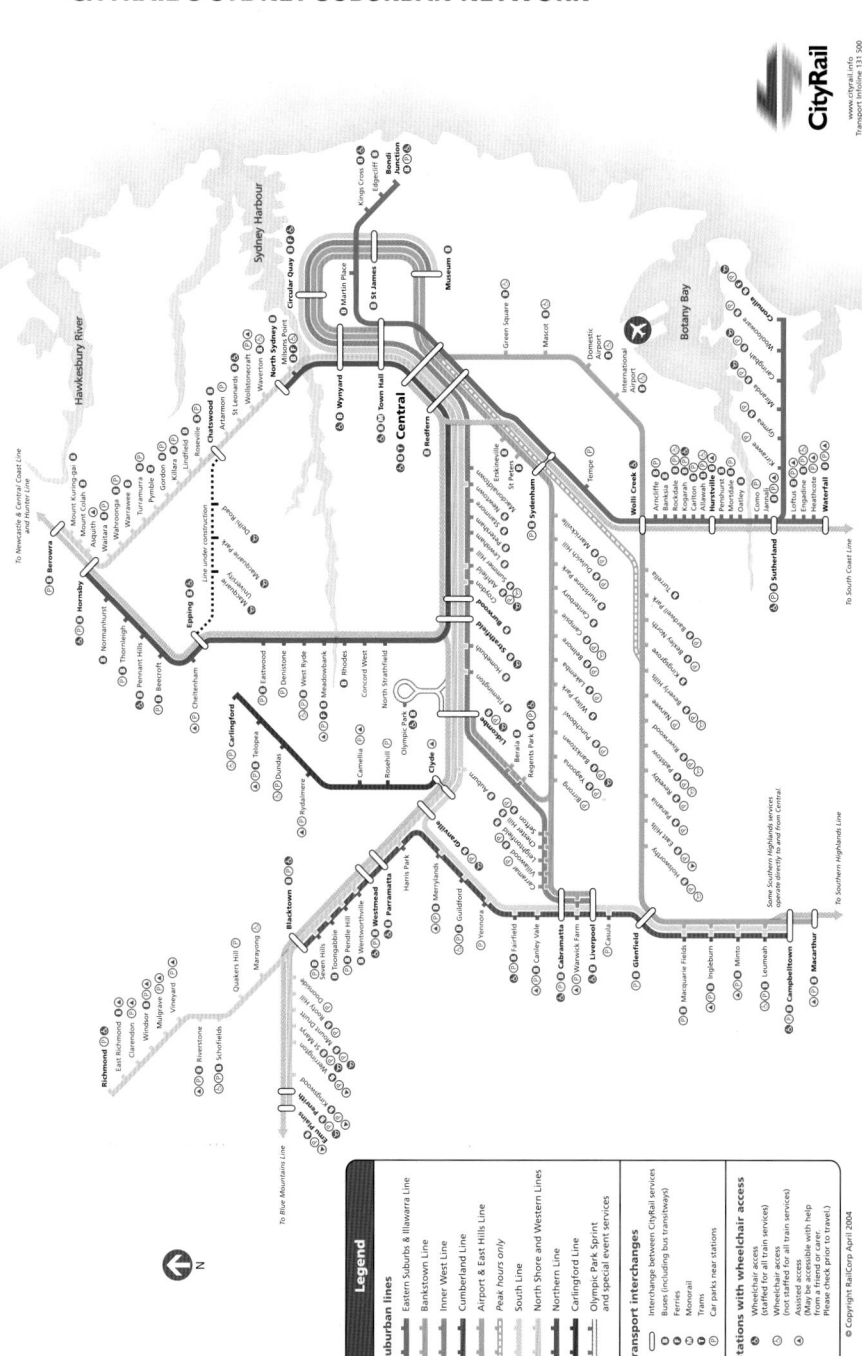

CityRail
www.cityrail.info
Transport Infoline 131 500

© Copyright RailCorp April 2004

TRANSPORT MAP

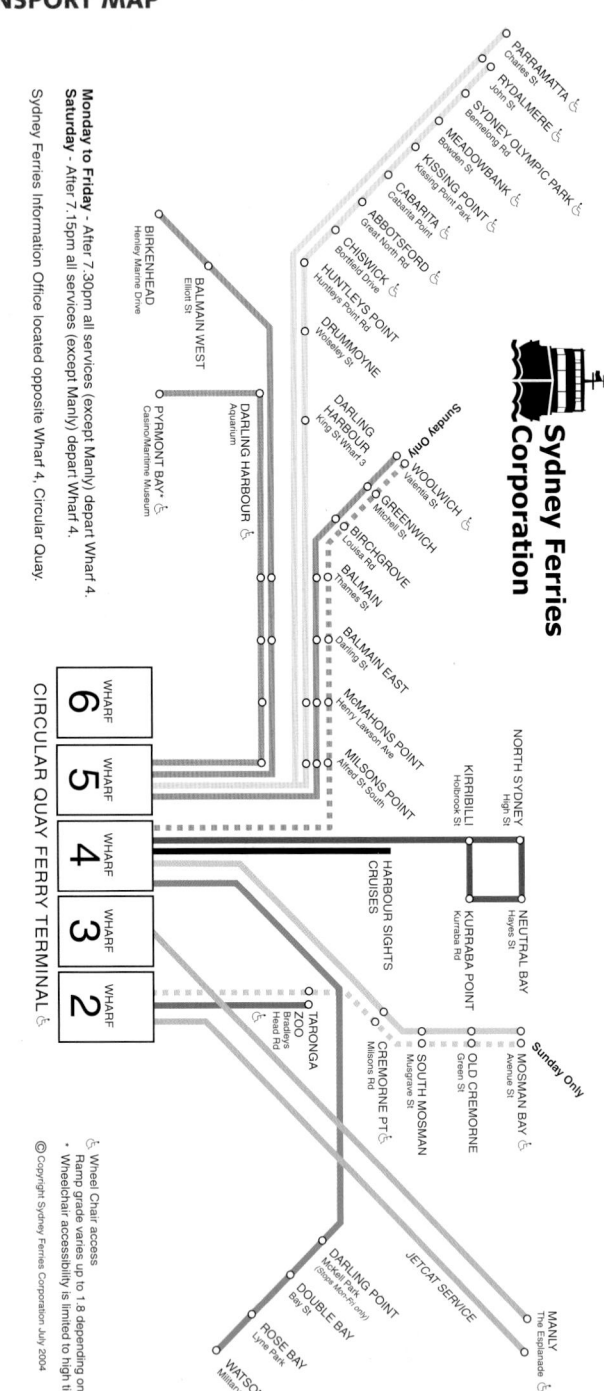

Sydney Ferries Corporation

CIRCULAR QUAY FERRY TERMINAL ⚬

WHARF 6
WHARF 5
WHARF 4
WHARF 3
WHARF 2

PARRAMATTA ⚬
Charles St

RYDALMERE ⚬
John St

SYDNEY OLYMPIC PARK ⚬
Bennelong St

MEADOWBANK ⚬
Bowden St

KISSING POINT ⚬
Kissing Point Park

CABARITA ⚬
Cabarita Point

ABBOTSFORD ⚬
Great North Rd

CHISWICK ⚬
Bortfield Drive

HUNTLEYS POINT ⚬
Huntley's Point Rd

DRUMMOYNE ⚬
Wolseley St

BIRKENHEAD
Henley Marine Drive

BALMAIN WEST
Elliot St

DARLING HARBOUR
Aquarium

PYRMONT BAY ⚬
Casino/Maritime Museum

DARLING
HARBOUR
King St Wharf 3

WOOLWICH ⚬
Valentia St

GREENWICH ⚬
Mitchell St

BIRCHGROVE ⚬
Louisa Rd

BALMAIN ⚬
Thames St

BALMAIN EAST
Darling St

McMAHONS POINT
Henry Lawson Ave

MILSONS POINT
Alfred St South

Sunday Only

NORTH SYDNEY
High St

KIRRIBILLI
Holbrook St

NEUTRAL BAY
Hayes St

KURRABA POINT
Kurraba Rd

HARBOUR SIGHTS
CRUISES

TARONGA
ZOO
Bradleys
Head Rd

CREMORNE PT ⚬
Milsons Rd

SOUTH MOSMAN ⚬
Musgrave St

OLD CREMORNE ⚬
Green St

MOSMAN BAY ⚬
Avenue St

Sunday Only

MANLY ⚬
The Esplanade

JETCAT SERVICE

DARLING POINT ⚬
McKell Park
(Social Mon-Fri only)

DOUBLE BAY ⚬
Bay St

ROSE BAY ⚬
Lyne Park

WATSONS BAY
Military Rd

Monday to Friday - After 7.30pm all services (except Manly) depart Wharf 4.
Saturday - After 7.15pm all services (except Manly) depart Wharf 4.

Sydney Ferries Information Office located opposite Wharf 4, Circular Quay.

⚬ Wheel Chair access
- Ramp grade varies up to 1:8 depending on tide.
- Wheelchair accessibility is limited to high tide only

© Copyright Sydney Ferries Corporation July 2004

Bondi Icebergs Bar (Map p180; ☎ 9365 9000; 1 Notts Ave) You can't get more modern and trendy than this classy spot. The hanging chairs, colourful sofas and elegant cocktails are just fine, but the view's the killer. Make sure your bank account's up to snuff.

Bondi Icebergs Winter Swimming Club (Map p180; ☎ 9130 3120; 1 Notts Ave) Located just below the Bondi Icebergs Bar, this is a more affordable and laid-back place with practically the same views. Order café food (pizzas and burgers) and $3.50 beers. Bring ID, since if you're not a member you need to prove you live at least 5km away.

Cafés

Sydney's most classic and atmospheric cafés are clustered around the casual Kings Cross area, but you'll find shiny modern joints (with decent brews) in every neighbourhood and suburb.

Café Coluzzi (Map p179; ☎ 9380 5420; 322 Victoria St, Darlinghurst; ⏱ 5am-7pm) The traditional Italian coffee attracts the city's java addicts; early on weekend mornings cyclists pedal in for their fix. They've achieved legendary status by making coffee for over 50 years, and claim to be the heart and soul of Sydney's coffee world.

Spring Espresso (Map pp176-7; ☎ 9331 0190; cnr Macleay St & Challis Ave, Potts Point; mains $8-12; ⏱ 6.30am-6.30pm) For good coffee and good snacks try this small and bustling café. Pavement tables are hot spots during the morning rush, but the wait is worth it.

Café Hernandez (Map p179; ☎ 9331 2343; 60 Kings Cross Rd, Kings Cross; snacks $5-9; ⏱ 24hr) This tiny place has classic atmosphere and grinds up exotic Kenyan, Honduran and Columbian beans into great coffee. Everyone from taxi drivers to arty students come to sip, and at 3am you'll think you're in Valencia, Spain.

ENTERTAINMENT

The *Sydney Morning Herald* 'Metro' lift-out (published on Friday) and the *Daily Telegraph* 'SLM' lift-out (published on Wednesday) list events in town for the coming week. Free newspapers, such as *Drum Media, Revolver, 3D World* and *Sydney Star Observer* (this last one is gay), also have useful listings and are available from bookshops, bars, cafés and record stores.

Ticketek (Map pp176-7; ☎ 9266 4800; www.ticketek .com.au; 195 Elizabeth St, City; ⏱ 9am-7pm Mon-Fri, 9am-

4pm Sat) is the city's main booking agency for theatre, concerts, sports and other events. Book by phone, Internet or agencies around town.

Halftix (Map pp176-7; ☎ 1300 668 413; 91 York St, City; ⏱ 9.30am-5.30pm Tue-Fri, 10am-3.30pm Sat) sells discount tickets, though choices are limited. Phone and Internet bookings are available.

Cinemas

Generally, cinema tickets cost between $12 and $16 for adults (less for concessions). Tuesday is often discount day, with movies going for about $11.

Dendy (Map pp176-7; ☎ 9247 3800; www.dendy .com.au; Shop 9, 2 East Circular Quay; general/concession $14/10.50) Lavish cinema within spitting distance of the Opera House. Great bar for ticketholders only. On Mondays movies cost $9 for everyone.

Greater Union Hoyts Cinemas (Map pp176-7; ☎ 9273 7431; 505 George St, City) A monster-sized movie palace with 17 screens and plenty of eateries. An orgy of popcorn-fuelled mainstream entertainment.

Govinda's (Map p179; ☎ 9380 5155; www.govindas .com.au; 112 Darlinghurst Rd; dinner & movie $20, movie only $11; ⏱ 6-10.30pm) The Hare-Krishna Govinda's is an all-you-can-gobble vegetarian smorgasbord; the cinema is floor cushions with incense and yoga in the atmosphere.

Nightclubs

Sydney's dance club scene is alive and kicking, and the discos are spread out all over.

Home (Map pp176-7; ☎ 9266 0600; Cockle Bay Wharf, 101 Wheat Rd, Darling Harbour; admission $20-25) With gorgeous views of Darling Harbour, this huge club offers stupendous sound systems and speciality nights like 'Together' on Saturdays (funky house music) or 'Queer Nation' on the Sundays of three-day weekends. Also check out the Mobo Bar, in a separate section.

Yu (Map p179; ☎ 9326 0333; 171 Victoria St, Potts Point; admission $10-20) Yu wants you to get down to the best of house and funk, played by some of Sydney's most venerable DJs. We love After Ours, which solves the dilemma of what to do on a Sunday night. The club itself is slick-looking and attached to a fancy Soho bar.

GoodBar (Map pp176-7; ☎ 9360 6759; 11A Oxford St, Paddington; admission $10) Two-level and trendy, this popular hanky-sized club is

---

GAY NIGHTS ON OXFORD

Colombian (Map pp176-7; ☎ 9360 2151; cnr Oxford & Crown Sts, Darlinghurst; ☼ 10am-4am Sun-Thu, 9am-6am Fri & Sat) Insanely popular, this swanky drinking spot offers up an intoxicating mix of cute guys, thumping music and heady drinks. The décor is to die for and a street-facing counter makes it oh so easy to check out the boisterous street scene. Women and handlebar moustaches welcome.

Oxford Hotel (Map pp176-7; ☎ 9331 3871; 134 Oxford St, Darlinghurst; ☼ downstairs 24hr, upstairs 5pm-1am Mon-Wed, 5pm-9am Thu-Sun) The bustling corner locale can't be beat – especially if you land a patio table. Downstairs it's the hardcore gay crowd, while on the 2nd floor Gilligan's cocktail bar attracts a fancy mixed bunch. The top floor is open weekends only, and definitely worth a stop.

Stonewall (Map pp176-7; ☎ 9360 1963; 175 Oxford St, Darlinghurst; ☼ 10.30am-4am Mon-Thu, 10.30am-7am Fri & Sat) The nightly shows and good vibe make this friendly spot one of the most popular on the strip, and the open airy location also helps. The recent ceiling collapse here caused the DJ to proclaim, 'I finally brought the house down!'

---

still attracting crowds of the pretty people. It boasts R&B, hip-hop and a chance at celebrity-spotting. Best nights are Wednesdays and Saturdays.

Plan B (Map p179; ☎ 9358 1144; 24 Darlinghurst Rd, Kings Cross; admission $5-20) So hot and new the bouncers are working overtime, this classy disco sports a glowing pink bar, lounge area for wallflowers and of course the hoppin' dance floor. Wear your best and get ready for slammin' house and funk music.

Live Music

Sydney doesn't have as dynamic a music scene as Melbourne, but you can still find live music most nights of the week. For detailed listings of venues and acts, see the listings in the papers mentioned on p201.

CLASSICAL

Sydney Opera House (☎ 9250 7777; www.sydney operahouse.com; Bennelong Point, East Circular Quay) The heart of performance in Australia, with the Concert Hall and Opera Hall holding about 2600 and 1500 people respectively. Witness theatre, comedy, music, dance and ballet, but it's opera that really shines. Box office hours are 9am to 8.30pm Monday to Saturday and two hours before a Sunday performance. See also p181.

Sydney Conservatorium of Music (Map pp176-7; ☎ 9351 1222; www.usyd.edu.au/su/conmusic; Macquarie St, City) This historic music venue showcases the talents of its students and their teachers. Choral, jazz, operatic and chamber concerts are held here from March to September, along with a range of free lunchtime recitals Wednesdays at 1pm (March to November).

JAZZ & BLUES

Sydney has a healthy and innovative jazz and blues circuit, with quite a few venues worth a swing.

Basement (Map pp176-7; ☎ 9251 2797; www.global network.com.au; 29 Reiby Pl, Circular Quay; admission $12-50) This subterranean place has decent food, good music (plus the odd spoken-word and comedy gig) and some big international names occasionally dropping by – making cover charges skyrocket. Exotic notes come with the monthly Indian and African gigs.

Empire Hotel (Map pp174-5; ☎ 9557 1701; www .sydneyblues.com; 103A Parramatta Rd, Annandale; admission Fri & Sat $5-15) Blues (along with ska, pop and rockabilly) buffs should investigate the Empire for live acts, aided by a very good sound system. It's trying to diversify, with Tuesday nights seeing free swing-dance lessons.

ROCK & POP

There's sometimes no charge to see young local bands, while between $5 and $20 is charged for well-known local acts, and up to $60 for international performers.

Annandale Hotel (Map pp174-5; ☎ 9550 1078; www.annandalehotel.com; 17 Parramatta Rd, Annandale) This venue plays host to a sometimes eclectic assortment of local and international alternative music acts. Loud rock, heavy metal, dance and acoustic gigs jam nightly from Tuesday to Sunday (tickets $8 to $30), while cult movies (!) play Monday nights.

Metro Theatre (Map pp176-7; ☎ 9287 2000; www .metrotheatre.com.au; 624 George St, City; tickets $10-75) Easily the best place to see local and alternative international acts (plus the odd DJ) in well-ventilated comfort. Other offerings include comedy, cabaret, music and theatre.

Hopetoun Hotel (Map pp176-7; ☎ 9361 5257; 416 Bourke St, Surry Hills; admission $6-12) This great little venue offers flexibility for artists and patrons alike, featuring an array of modern musical styles from folk to rap to DJs. Both local bands and the occasional international group plays; think Spiderbait, Tex Perkins and You Am I.

Sport
Sydney's sunshine, parks, beaches and love of showing off all conspire to make this a delightful city for staying fit or watching sport.

Sydney Cricket Ground (SCG; Map pp174-5; Moore Park) The venue for sparsely attended state cricket matches, well-attended five-day Test matches and sell-out one-day World Series cricket matches.

Sydney is one of rugby league's world capitals. **National Rugby League** (NRL; www.nrl .com.au) games are played from March to October at a variety of venues, including Aussie Stadium in Moore Park and Telstra Stadium in Homebush Bay.

The (sometimes) high-flying Sydney Swans (see p36) are NSW's contribution to the **Australian Football League** (AFL; www.afl.com .au), play matches between March and September. Their home ground is the SCG.

Theatre
Sydney Theatre (Map pp176-7; ☎ 9250 1999; www .sydneytheatre.org.au; 22 Hickson Rd, Walsh Bay) Opened in January 2004, this stylish venue seats 850 and is managed by Australia's largest theatre company, Sydney Theatre Company. It works with national and international companies to bring theatre-goers the best in ambitious and artistic drama and dance.

Belvoir St Theatre (Map pp174-5; ☎ 9699 3444; www.belvoir.com.au; 25 Belvoir St, Surry Hills; tickets adult $27-45, concession $21-30) Located in a residential neighbourhood and sporting a cute café, this intimate venue hosts experimental Australian theatre and twists on original productions with big names like Geoffrey Rush and Cate Blanchett.

SHOPPING
The hub of city shopping is Pitt St Mall (running north–south through Sydney's city centre), with department stores, shopping centres and numerous shops all within arm's reach. It's much more relaxing to shop for fashion on popular inner-city strips such as Oxford St, Paddington; for furnishings and antiques on Queen St, Woollahra (an exclusive eastern suburb); for CDs around Crown St, Surry Hills; for outdoor gear around the corner of Kent and Bathurst Sts in town; or at Sydney's popular markets. The Rocks is where you'll generally find what's known as 'Australiana' (ie souvenirs), though it won't be cheap. Try Paddy's Markets instead.

Late-night shopping is on Thursday night, when many stores stay open until 9pm.

Markets
Paddington Market (Map pp174-5; ☎ 9331 2923; www.paddingtonmarket.com.au; St John's Church, 395 Oxford St, Paddington; ⊗ Sat) Very popular, upscale and pricey, with vintage clothing, creative crafts, beautiful jewellery, tasty food and holistic treatments.

Paddy's Markets (Map pp176-7; ☎ 1300 361 589; www.paddysmarkets.com.au; cnr Hay & Thomas Sts, Haymarket; ⊗ 9am-5pm Thu-Sun) In the heart of Chinatown, this Sydney institution is a great place to find cheap souvenirs, clothing, cheap electronics, sheepskin rugs and plenty of knick-knacks.

Rocks Market (Map pp176-7; ☎ 9240 8717; www .therocksmarket.com; George St, The Rocks; ⊗ Sat & Sun) Held at the top end of George St, this touristy market offers wonderful crafts made of metal, ceramic, stone, leather and glass. Souvenirs (including 'roo balls) also available.

Balmain Markets (Map pp174-5; ☎ 0418 765 736; St Andrew's Church, 223 Darling St, Balmain; ⊗ Sat) This small but good local market offers crafty stuff like handmade candles and soaps, jewellery, exotic textiles, artwork and used clothing and books.

Glebe Markets (Map pp176-7; Glebe Public School, cnr Glebe Point Rd & Derby Pl; ⊗ Sat) A large, popular and slightly grungy market selling the usual books, vintage clothing, leather goods, hippie crafts and curios.

GETTING THERE & AWAY
Air
Sydney International Airport is Australia's busiest and has flights from all over the country and the world. **Qantas** (☎ 13 13 13; www.qantas.com.au) and **Virgin** (☎ 13 67 89; www .virginblue.com.au) offer frequent flights from other capital cities. Smaller airlines, linked to Qantas, fly within NSW.

Boat

Heading to Tasmania? Check out the huge freighter **TT Lines** (☎ 1800 634 906; www.spiritof tasmania.com.au).

Bus & Train

All long-distance train and bus services operate from Central Station (the Sydney Coach Terminal is also here); book tickets in advance. **CountryLink** (☎ 9379 9606, after hr call ☎ 13 22 32; www.countrylink.com.au; Platform 1 Central Station; ☺ 6.15am-8.45pm), the government's network of trains and buses, offers discounts of up to 50% with two weeks' notice. They also have an office at **Circular Quay** (☎ 9224 3400; ☺ 9.45am-5.30pm Mon-Fri). Sample train fares (without discount) include Brisbane ($115, 14 hours), Byron Bay ($102, 13 hours), Canberra ($50, 4½ hours) and Melbourne ($115, 11 hours).

Major bus operators include **Greyhound** (☎ 13 14 99; www.greyhound.com.au), **Premier** (☎ 13 34 10; www.premierms.com.au) and **Murrays** (☎ 13 22 51; www.murrays.com.au). An example of costs and durations are the following destinations: Brisbane ($90, 16 hours), Byron Bay ($85, 13 hours), Canberra ($35, 3½ hours) and Melbourne ($60, 13 hours).

GETTING AROUND

For information on buses, ferries and trains phone **Transport Infoline** (☎ 13 15 00; www.131500 .com.au) between 6am and 10pm daily; the operators can tell you exactly how to get from one point to another.

Bus

Sydney's bus network extends to most suburbs. Fares depend upon the number of 'sections' you pass through. As a rough guide, short jaunts cost $1.60 and most other fares in the inner suburbs are $2.70. If you plan on taking many buses, it's cheaper to buy passes (see p206). Regular buses run between 5am and midnight.

Some major starting points for bus routes are Circular Quay, Argyle St in Millers Point (just west of the Rocks), Wynyard Park (Map pp176-7), the QVB on York St and Railway Sq. Most buses head out of the city on George or Castlereagh St and take George or Elizabeth St coming in. Pay the driver as you enter, or dunk your prepaid pass in the green ticket machines by the door.

At Circular Quay there's a **Transit Shop** (Map pp176-7; ☺ 7am-7pm Mon-Fri, 8.30am-5.30pm Sat & Sun) that sells bus passes and dispenses bus route information. Look for this kiosk right in front of the McDonald's on the corner of Alfred and Loftus Sts. Other bus Transit Shops also sell passes. For more bus information you can call ☎ 9244 1991 or ☎ 13 15 00 or check www.sydneybuses.info.

Car & Motorcycle

Cars are good for out-of-the-way day trips out of town, but driving one in the city is like wearing an anchor around your neck. Heavy traffic, elusive parking (even at hotels) and the extra costs just aren't worth the stress.

GETTING INTO TOWN FROM SYDNEY'S AIRPORT

Sydney International Airport (☎ 9667 9111; www.sydneyairport.com.au) is 10km south of the city centre. The international and domestic terminals are a 4km bus trip apart on either side of the runway.

One of the easiest ways to get from the airport into the centre is with one of the shuttle companies. These service providers take you straight to your hostel/hotel and cost $9 to $12 one way. All go into the city centre; some reach surrounding suburbs and beach destinations. Companies include **Kingsford Smith Transport** (KST; ☎ 9666 9988; www.kst.com.au), **Super Shuttle** (☎ 0500 513 789, 9311 3789; www.supershuttle.com.au) and **Shuttle Bus Services** (SBS; ☎ 0500 503 220; www .shuttlebusservices.com).

If you want the cheapest route to Bondi, take bus 400 or 400 express ($4.30) to Bondi Junction, then the L82, 380, 381 or 382.

Airport Link (☎ 8337 8417; www.airportlink.com.au) is a train line that runs between city train stations and the domestic ($11) and international ($11.80) airport terminals every 10 to 15 minutes. Trains run from approximately 5am to midnight daily.

Taxi fares from the airport are approximately $25 to Circular Quay, $35 to North Sydney and Bondi, and $50 to Manly.

PURCHASE

Sydney is the capital of car sales for most travellers. The **Kings Cross Car Market** (Map p179; ☎ 9358 5000, 1800 808 188; www.carmarket.com.au; cnr Ward Ave & Elizabeth Bay Rd, Kings Cross; ⊙ 9am-5pm) gets mixed reports, but it seems popular with travellers. Always read the fine print on anything you sign with regards to buying or selling a car. Several dealers will sell you a car with an undertaking to buy it back at an agreed price. Do not accept any verbal guarantees – get it in writing.

The *Trading Post*, a weekly rag available from all newsagents, is also a good place to look for secondhand vehicles. You can also check the *Sydney Morning Herald*'s classified section (www.smh.com.au). Car prices will probably be a bit cheaper if you buy from a private party.

Yet another option is going to a car auction. One place is **Auto Auctions** (☎ 9724 9111; www.auto-auctions.com.au; 682 Woodville Rd, Guildford).

Before you buy any vehicle, regardless of the seller, we strongly recommend that you have it thoroughly checked by a competent mechanic. The **NRMA** (Map pp176-7; ☎ 13 21 32; www.nrma.com.au; 388 George St, City; ⊙ 9am-5pm Mon-Fri) charges $240 for nonmembers ($200 for members). We've heard some real horror stories from readers who've failed to get their vehicles checked.

The **Register of Encumbered Vehicles** (REVS; ☎ 9633 6333; www.revs.nsw.gov.au) is a government organisation that checks the car you're buying is fully paid-up and owned by the seller. Other helpful websites, especially if you have problems with your vehicle, are www.fairtrading.nsw.gov.au and www.accc.gov.au.

RENTAL

Car-rental contracts sometimes include insurance and unlimited kilometres, and some require you to be over 25 years old. Rates depend on time of year, so call ahead. **Avis** (☎ 13 63 33; www.avis.com.au), **Budget** (☎ 13 27 27; www.budget.com.au), **Europcar** (☎ 1300 131 390; www.europcar.com.au), **Hertz** (☎ 13 30 39; www.hertz.com.au) and **Thrifty** (☎ 1300 367 227; www.thrifty.com.au) all have desks at the airport, and some have offices in the centre (most on William St).

TOLL ROADS

The Harbour Tunnel and Harbour Bridge both impose a southbound toll of $3; if you're heading from the North Shore to the eastern suburbs, it's much easier to use the tunnel. The Eastern Distributor imposes a northbound toll of $4.

The new Cross City tunnel should soon be finished, with the hope that it will ease traffic congestion and slash travel times across the city. Tolls will be $1.10 or $2.50, depending on distance travelled.

Ferry

Sydney's **ferries** (☎ 9207 3166; www.sydneyferries.info) provide the most enjoyable way to get around the harbour. Many people use ferries to commute so there are frequent connecting bus services. Some ferries operate between 6am and midnight, although ferries servicing tourist attractions operate much shorter hours.

There are three kinds of ferry: regular STA ferries, fast JetCats that go to Manly ($7.90) and RiverCats that traverse the Parramatta River to Parramatta ($7.40). All ferries depart from Circular Quay. At Wharf 4 you'll find the **ferry information office** (☎ 9207 3170; ⊙ 7am-5.45pm Mon-Sat, 8am-5.45pm Sun), near the ticket booths. Most regular harbour ferries cost $4.80, although the longer trip to Manly costs $6. A few fare deals are available; see earlier.

Metro Light Rail & Monorail

The **Monorail** (☎ 9285 5600; www.metromonorail.com.au) and **Metro Light Rail** (MLR; ☎ 9285 5600; www.metrolightrail.com.au) are other good means of transport within the centre.

The Monorail circles Darling Harbour and links it to the city centre. There's a monorail every three to five minutes, and the full loop takes about 14 minutes. A single trip costs $4.20, but for $8 you can have unlimited rides for the day. The monorail operates from 7am to 10pm Monday to Thursday, to midnight on Friday and Saturday and from 8am to 10pm Sunday.

The MLR operates 24 hours a day between Central Station and Pyrmont via Darling Harbour and Chinatown. The service runs to Lilyfield via the Fish Market, Wentworth Park, Glebe, Jubilee Park and Rozelle Bay from 6am to 11pm Sunday to Thursday (to midnight Friday and Saturday). Tickets cost $2.80 to $5.20, but for $8.40 you can have unlimited rides for the day.

SYDNEY

FARE DEALS

There's a confusing number of transport deal passes to be had in Sydney. Decide your preferences and do some research to save money. Most passes are sold at train stations, bus Transit Shops and major newsagents.

The **SydneyPass** (adult/child/family 3 days $100/50/250, 5 days $130/65/325, 7 days $150/75/375) is tourist-oriented, offering three, five or seven days' unlimited travel over a seven-day period on all buses, trains (within the city centre and surrounding suburbs) and ferries as well as Airport Link, the Explorer hop-on/off buses, the JetCats, RiverCats and three STA-operated harbour cruises.

TravelPasses (most tourist destinations $32, plus Manly ferry $40) are more commuter-oriented (but great for tourists who don't need frills) and offer cheaper weekly travel on the regular buses, trains and ferries. There are several colour-coded grades.

The **Daytripper** (adult/child $15/7.50) is good for one day only, and covers all buses, ferries and trains you're likely to need for sightseeing in central Sydney. It also offers discounts to some popular tourist destinations, like the zoo and aquarium.

If you're just catching buses, get a **TravelTen** (5 sections $19.70) ticket, which gives a big discount on 10 bus trips. There are various colour codes for distances so check which is the most appropriate for you. A brown TravelTen costs should get you to most tourist destinations, but ask at a Transit Shop to make sure.

FerryTen (10 inner-harbour ferry trips $30.30, plus Manly ferry $45.10) tickets are similar. They can be purchased at Circular Quay.

Several transport-plus-entry tickets are available, which work out cheaper than catching a ferry and paying entry separately. They include the **ZooPass** (adult/child $33.50/16.50) and the **Aquarium-Pass** (adult/child $29.10/14.50). Buy them at Circular Quay.

Taxi

There are heaps of metered taxis in Sydney. Flag fall is $2.75, and the metered fair is $1.56 per kilometre. There is a 20% surcharge between 10pm and 6am and for heavy luggage and Harbour Bridge and Tunnel tolls. The radio booking fee is $1.15. The four big taxi companies offer a reliable service:

Legion (☎ 13 14 51)
Premier Cabs (☎ 13 10 17)
RSL Cabs (☎ 13 22 11)
Taxis Combined (☎ 8332 8888)

Train

Sydney has a vast suburban rail network and frequent services, making trains much quicker than buses. The underground City Circle comprises seven city-centre stations. Lines radiate from the City Circle, but do not extend to the northern and southern beaches, Balmain or Glebe. All city-bound suburban trains stop at Central Station, and usually one or more of the other City Circle stations as well (a ticket to the city will take you to any station on the City Circle). Trains run from around 5am to midnight.

After 9am on weekdays and at any time on weekends, you can buy an off-peak return ticket for not much more than a standard one-way fare.

Staffed ticket booths are supplemented by automatic ticket machines at stations. If you have to change trains, it's cheaper to buy a ticket to your ultimate destination – but don't depart from an intermediary station en route to your destination or your ticket will be invalid.

Every station has train information. Central Station has a good **information kiosk** (☒ 6am-10pm) near platforms 4 and 5. The **transport information booth** (☎ 9224 2649; ☒ 9am-5pm) at Circular Quay also hands out advice; it's right next to CountryLink. You can also check www.cityrail.info.

AROUND SYDNEY

There are superb national parks to the north and south of Sydney, and historic small towns to the west. There is also the Hunter Valley, and many organisations run day trips from Sydney. It's easier to visit the Hunter from Newcastle, however; see the Central Coast New South Wales chapter (p221) for details.

BLUE MOUNTAINS

The Blue Mountains, part of the Great Dividing Range, were initially an impenetrable barrier to white expansion from Sydney. Despite attempts to find a route through the mountains – and a bizarre belief among many convicts that China, and freedom, was just on the other side – it took 25 years before a successful crossing was made by Europeans. A road was built soon afterwards that opened the western plains to settlement.

The foothills begin 65km inland from Sydney and the mountains rise up to 1100m. Be prepared for the climatic difference between the Blue Mountains and the coast – you can swelter in Sydney but shiver in Katoomba. It usually snows sometime between June and August, when the region has a Yuletide Festival complete with Christmas decorations and dinners.

There are several national parks in the area. The Blue Mountains National Park has some truly fantastic scenery, excellent bushwalks, Aboriginal engravings and all the canyons and cliffs you could ask for. It's a favourite with adrenaline junkies, and is the most popular and accessible of the three national parks in the area. Great lookouts include Evans Lookout and Govetts Leap Lookout near Blackheath – both are more spectacular than the Echo Point Lookout in Katoomba.

Wollemi National Park, north of the Bells Line of Road, is NSW's largest forested wilderness area and stretches all the way to Denman in the Hunter Valley. It has limited access and the park's centre is so isolated that a species of tree, the Wollemi pine, was only discovered here in 1994.

Kanangra-Boyd National Park is southwest of the southern section of the Blue Mountains National Park. It has bushwalking opportunities, limestone caves, including the famous Jenolan Caves, and grand scenery. It includes the spectacular Kanangra Walls Plateau, which is surrounded by sheer cliffs and can be reached by unsealed road from Oberon or from Jenolan Caves.

For more information on these parks (including camping) contact the **NPWS (National Parks & Wildlife Service) Visitor Centre** (☎ 4787 8877; www.nationalparks.nsw.gov.au; Govetts Leap Rd, Blackheath; ◷ 9am-4.30pm), about 2.5km off the Great Western Hwy and 10km north of Katoomba.

> **WHAT'S IN A NAME?**
> The blue haze, which gave the mountains their name, is a result of the ultrafine oily mist given off by eucalypts. This haze, seen from a distance, makes the ranges look serenely blue.

Activities
BUSHWALKING

The roads across the mountains offer tantalising glimpses of the majesty of the area, but the only way to really experience the Blue Mountains is on foot. There are walks lasting from a few minutes to several days. The two most popular areas are Jamison Valley, south of Katoomba, and Grose Valley, northeast of Katoomba and east of Blackheath. The area south of Glenbrook is also good.

The NPWS centre can help you pick a hike or, for shorter walks, ask at the Katoomba visitors centre (p208). It's rugged country and walkers sometimes get lost, so it's highly advisable to get reliable information, not to go alone, and to tell someone where you're going. Many Blue Mountains watercourses are polluted, so you must sterilise water or take your own. Be prepared for rapid weather changes.

Good walking books on the area include *Exploring the Blue Mountains* (Key Guide, $30) and *Walks in the Blue Mountains* (Neil Paton, $11).

ADVENTURE ACTIVITIES & TOURS

Most operators have offices in Katoomba – competition is steep, so shop around for the best deal. If you have a YHA card, ask if you're eligible for a discount.

Australian School of Mountaineering (ASM; Map p209; ☎ 4782 2014; www.asmguides.com; 166 Katoomba St, Katoomba) Rock climbing from $165, abseiling from $125 and canyoning from $135.

Blue Mountains Adventure Company (Map p209; ☎ 4782 1271; www.bmac.com.au; 84A Bathurst Rd, Katoomba) A bit more expensive than ASM; also has bushwalking (from $135) and mountain biking (from $125).

Blue Mountains Walkabout (☎ 0408 443 822; www.bluemountainswalkabout.com) Eight-hour, at times strenuous, bushwalks with Aboriginal themes and spirituality ($95 cash only; 25% donated to Aboriginal causes). Its meeting point is the railway station.

Katoomba Adventure Centre (☎ 1800 824 009; www.kacadventures.com.au; 1 Katoomba St, Katoomba) Canyoning and waterfall abseiling, among other things.

Tread Lightly Eco Tours (☎ 4788 1229; www.tread lightly.com.au; 100 Great Western Highway, Medlow Bath) Eco-bushwalks and 4WD tours from two to eight hours ($30 to $165). Most tours run out of Katoomba and Blackheath.

Katoomba

Katoomba and adjacent Wentworth Falls and Leura form the tourist heart of the Blue Mountains. Despite the number of visitors and its proximity to Sydney, Katoomba retains a friendly and otherworldly ambience, which is accentuated by its Art Deco and Art Nouveau guesthouses and cafés, its thick mists and occasional snowfalls.

INFORMATION

For information on local walks head to the **visitors centre** (☎ 1300 653 408; Echo Point; ☽ 9am-5pm), right near Echo Point.

SIGHTS

The major scenic attraction is **Echo Point**, which is about 2km down Katoomba St from the train station. From here are some of the best views of the Jamison Valley and the magnificent **Three Sisters** rock formation.

To the west of Echo Point, at the junction of Cliff Dr and Violet St, is **Scenic World** (☎ 4782 2699; www.scenicworld.com.au; ☽ 9am-5pm), which includes a railway (steep inclinator), skyway and flyway (both cable cars). All offer breathtaking views from breathtaking heights; each costs adult/child/family $14/7/35 roundtrip. Nearby eateries offer excellent views.

SLEEPING

There are heaps of places to stay in Katoomba; unless noted, all but budget offerings include breakfast. For more options ring the visitors centre or check www.bluemts.com.au.

Budget

Flying Fox (☎ 4782 4226, 1800 624 226; www.theflying fox.com.au; 190 Bathurst Rd; dm/d $21/58; P ☐) This small, homey hostel is a few blocks from the centre and offers colourful spaces, laidback atmosphere and a small deck out back. Spacious dorms and three private rooms share baths, and grassy camping sites are available for $12 per person. Your VIP card earns a dollar off.

Blue Mountains YHA (☎ 4782 1416; www.yha.com .au; 207 Katoomba St; dm $26-32, d $72-80; P ☐) This is an excellent hostel in a heritage-listed building; it comes complete with hip lounge areas in an old dance hall. The sunny terrace with fountain is a major plus. Plenty of services are available, including area tours and activities; possession of a YHA card earns a $3.50 discount.

Katoomba Falls Caravan Park (☎ 4782 1835; www.bmcc.nsw.gov.au under recreational services; Katoomba Falls Rd; unpowered/powered sites $13/17; cabins $86-100) About 2km south of the highway, this green spot offers good camping facilities but sniffy management. Outside January and February rates drop 20%.

Midrange

Balmoral Guesthouse (☎ 4782 2264; www.balmoral house.com.au; 196 Bathurst Rd; d Sun-Thu from $110, Fri & Sat from $125) This historic guesthouse has attractive period details, charming rooms (some with wraparound veranda) and lushly overgrown gardens. In winter it's kept cosy with a log fire, and you'll find an electric blanket on your bed.

Avonleigh Guesthouse (☎ 4782 1534; www.blue mts.com.au/avonleigh; 174 Lurline St; d Sun-Thu from $120, Fri & Sat from $130) Twelve flowery rooms are waiting for the romantic in you at this quaint cottage-style guesthouse – teddy bears adorn your pillow. The large common room is great for getting to know your fellow guests, and the free tea, coffee and port help.

Kurrara Guesthouse (☎ 4782 6058; www.kurrara .com; 17 Coomonderry St; d Sun-Thu $100-140, Fri & Sat $130-170; P) This guesthouse, located in a historic building, is a little shabby around the edges, but in a charming sort of way. Rooms that may remind you of Grandma's house come cluttered with antiques, and some sport spa baths. Afternoon tea is served on the veranda, which overlooks the rampant garden.

Belgravia Guesthouse (☎ 4782 2998; www.blue mts.com.au/belgravia; 179 Lurline St; d $86-96; P) Just seven decent but no-nonsense rooms are available at this simple guesthouse, along with a small living room area. It's no-frills and cheap, and not too far from Echo Point.

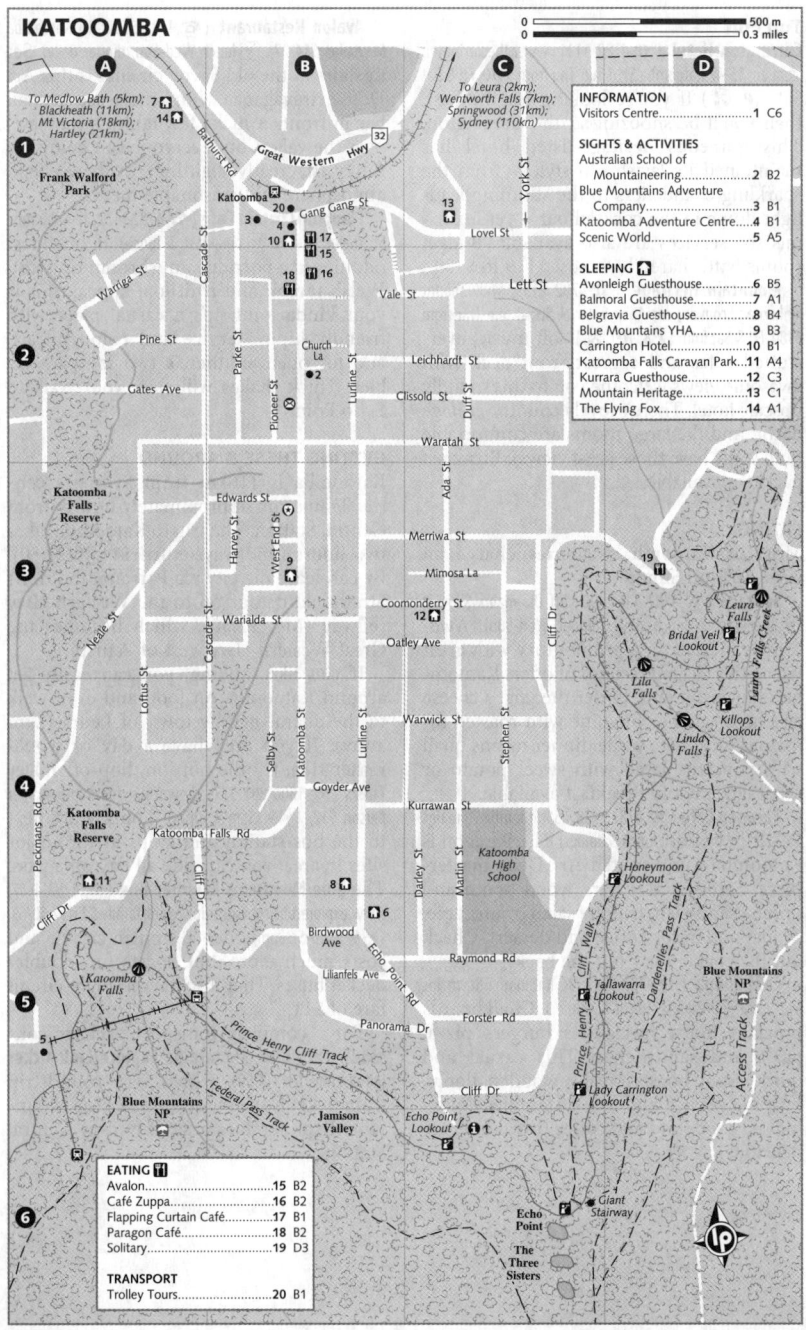

KATOOMBA

0 — 500 m
0 — 0.3 miles

To Medlow Bath (5km); 7
Blackheath (11km);
Mt Victoria (18km);
Hartley (21km)

14

To Leura (2km);
Wentworth Falls (7km);
Springwood (31km);
Sydney (110km)

Great Western Hwy

32

INFORMATION
Visitors Centre..........................1 C6

SIGHTS & ACTIVITIES
Australian School of
  Mountaineering...................2 B2
Blue Mountains Adventure
  Company..............................3 B1
Katoomba Adventure Centre....4 B1
Scenic World.............................5 A5

SLEEPING
Avonleigh Guesthouse..............6 B5
Balmoral Guesthouse................7 A1
Belgravia Guesthouse...............8 B4
Blue Mountains YHA.................9 B3
Carrington Hotel.....................10 B1
Katoomba Falls Caravan Park...11 A4
Kurrara Guesthouse.................12 C3
Mountain Heritage..................13 C1
The Flying Fox.........................14 A1

Frank Walford
Park

Katoomba
Falls
Reserve

Katoomba
Falls
Reserve

Katoomba

Gang Gang St

Lovel St

Vale St

Lett St

Leichhardt St

Clissold St

Waratah St

Edwards St

Merriwa St

Mimosa La

Coomonderry St

Oatley Ave

Warwick St

Goyder Ave

Kurrawan St

Katoomba Falls Rd

Birdwood
Ave

Lilianfels Ave

Panorama Dr

Raymond Rd

Forster Rd

Katoomba
High
School

Leura
Falls

Bridal Veil
Lookout

Lila
Falls

Linda
Falls

Killops
Lookout

Honeymoon
Lookout

Tallawarra
Lookout

Lady Carrington
Lookout

Blue Mountains
NP

Prince Henry Cliff Track

Federal Pass Track

Blue Mountains
NP

Jamison
Valley

Echo Point
Lookout

Echo
Point

Giant
Stairway

The
Three
Sisters

Katoomba
Falls

Prince Henry Cliff Walk

Dardenelles Pass Track

Access Track

EATING
Avalon...................................15 B2
Café Zuppa.............................16 B2
Flapping Curtain Café...............17 B1
Paragon Café...........................18 B2
Solitary...................................19 D3

TRANSPORT
Trolley Tours...........................20 B1

SYDNEY

Top End

Carrington Hotel (☎ 4782 1111; www.thecarrington
.com.au; 15-47 Katoomba St; d Sun-Thu from $170, Fri & Sat
$190; **P** **✗**) If you're looking for the best,
then you'll be snoozing at the Carrington.
This gorgeous heritage-listed hotel has
maintained its lavish old style – from the
sparkling chandeliers to the stunning lead-
light dome in the cocktail bar – yet luxurious spa services are also available. Budget
rooms with shared bath cost $119 to $139.

Mountain Heritage (☎ 4782 2155; www.mount
ainheritage.com.au; cnr Apex & Lovel Sts; d Sun-Thu from
$180, Fri & Sat from $238; **P** **✗**) Soft music, over-
stuffed sofas and a great front deck with
awesome views welcome you to this friendly
upscale hotel. There's lovely country-cottage
décor, and the large rooms are comfortable
(and some have those great views). Breakfast
packages available.

EATING

Most of Katoomba's eateries charge an
extra 10% on Sundays.

Solitary (☎ 4782 1164; 90 Cliff Dr; mains $26-32;
⊙ breakfast & lunch daily, dinner Wed-Sun) Awe-
somely located on a promontory with great
views, this elegant restaurant offers Katoomba's fanciest menu. Order the goat's cheese
and herb salad or linguine with roasted tomatoes for lunch, while dinner means quail
with pancetta, lamb with sweet potato or
asparagus ravioli. Breakfast available.

Paragon Cafe (☎ 4782 2928; 65 Katoomba St; mains
$15-22; ⊙ breakfast, lunch & dinner) The Paragon is
Katoomba's undisputed Art Deco master-
piece. Settle in at a dark wood booth and
order a sandwich, frittata, salad or meat pie,
or just pop in for coffee and dessert. Check
out the cocktail bar out the back.

Café Zuppa (☎ 4782 9247; 36 Katoomba St; mains
$12-20; ⊙ breakfast, lunch & dinner) Chalkboards
proclaim house specialities: burgers, pizza,
pasta and sandwiches. This casual and
quirky spot boasts creaky wooden floors,
bustling service and lots of families enjoying the good food and coffee (breakfasts are
delicious).

Avalon Restaurant (☎ 4782 5532; 18 Katoomba
St; mains $14-27; ⊙ lunch Wed-Sun, dinner daily) Set
upstairs in the old Savoy cinema is this Art
Deco extravaganza, with a must-see cocktail
bar in front. A lucky few tables have views
over the valley, but everyone can enjoy the
funky art, creative lighting, rowdy weekend
atmosphere and reasonable menu.

Flapping Curtain Café (☎ 4782 1622; 10 Katoomba
St; mains $7-11; ⊙ breakfast & lunch) If breakfast
oddities like porridge, mushroom on toast,
Welsh rarebit and fruit loaf appeal, this is
your kinda joint. It's a casual place with
friendly hippy service and colourful art,
and for open air there's two footpath tables. Thick shakes will slow your walk to
Echo Point.

GETTING THERE & AROUND

Katoomba is 110km from Sydney's cen-
tre. Trains run approximately hourly from
Central Station. The trip to Katoomba takes
two hours (one way/return $11.40/22.80).
By car, leave the city via Parramatta Rd. At
Strathfield detour on to the Western Hwy
tollway (M4; $2.30), which becomes the
Great Western Hwy west of Penrith.

If you like walking, you can easily get
around Katoomba on foot, and even walk
to the quaint nearby town of Leura (2km
away). If you only have a day or would
rather ride, try the hop-on, hop-off **Trolley
Tours** (☎ 1800 801 577; www.trolleytours.com.au; per
person $12; ⊙ 9.15am-4.50pm). Tours start next
to the bus station and stops at the major
sites in area; you can ride all day on a pass.
The **Blue Mountains Explorer Bus** (☎ 4782 4807;
www.explorerbus.com.au; adult/child/family $25/12.50/63;
⊙ 9.30am-5.30pm) does a similar circuit and
costs much more, but boasts fun double-
decker buses. They also have a single-circuit
fare of $11.

For a complete transport package consider the **Blue Mountains ExplorerLink ticket**
(adult/child $36/14.50), which is a round-trip
train ticket from Sydney plus a Blue Mountains Explorer Bus pass. Buy it at Central
Station.

Central Coast New South Wales

Although the NSW Central Coast might not be as popular as the North Coast, it's not quite as subdued as the South Coast – culturally (and geographically), it's somewhere in between. Extending from Gosford to Port Macquarie, it's got utopian beaches, lakes that shimmer, sumptuous national parks – all of it balm for stressed city slickers, jaded workers and jealous internationals. But it's also got secluded inlets and dainty historical towns…along with a dollop of overdevelopment.

Newcastle is the big noise here, a former steel town that's now concentrating on promoting other assets, like its beaches, its harbour and its de facto status as capital of the region. From here, you can explore the spectacular Hunter Valley, with its collection of quality vineyards.

Beyond the Hunter is a series of inlets and bays that will make grandma swoon and junior squeal. Fresh seafood, azure water and sand in your joints – these are timeless pleasures that cut across generations and Port Stephens is the exemplar, with its collection of sheltered coves: Anna Bay, Nelson Bay and Shoal Bay.

The Pacific Highway bifurcates the region, a mainline blacktop cable plugged in to the electric climes up north. Many of the sights mentioned are off the highway, though, and there's more besides. Maybe just throw the map away every now and then, make a few random right-hand turns, and stop and smell the wax flowers.

HIGHLIGHTS

- Watching party-hearty **Newcastle** (p215) head-butting the future with new-found vim
- Savouring the gentle delicacy dancing on your tongue at the **Hunter Valley wineries** (p221)
- Wondering where the seals are at gorgeous **Seal Rocks** (p228)
- Getting so mellow you're sideways amid the wondrous sheltered bays of **Port Stephens** (p225)
- Squeezing in for flicks at the world's second-smallest cinema in **Tinonnee** (p230)
- Conspiring with colonial atmospherics at **Port Macquarie** (p232)
- Wondering if that camel is real or a mirage amid mighty sand dunes at **Stockton Bight** (p225)

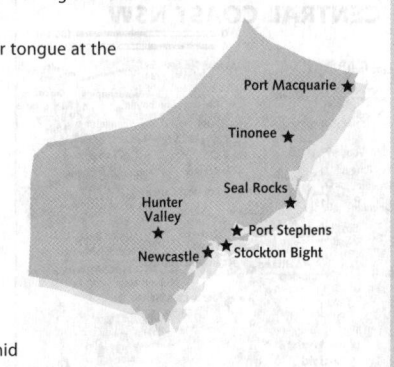

- TELEPHONE CODE: 02
- www.visitnsw.com.au

SYDNEY TO NEWCASTLE

Once you relieve yourself of Sydney's urban zone, the terrain becomes remarkably spectacular, with the Pacific Hwy blazing a trail through the rocky hills of Ku-ring-gai Chase National Park, crossing the wide Hawkesbury River and passing by lush Brisbane Water National Park.

KU-RING-GAI CHASE NATIONAL PARK

The exhilarating, 150-sq-km **Ku-ring-gai Chase National Park** (admission per car $11) lies 24km north of Sydney, bordering the southern edge of Broken Bay and the western shore of Pittwater.

The area's history is the usual colonial mix of tragedy, desperation and compulsion: Ku-ring-gai was once inhabited by the Guringai and Garrigal Aboriginal people, who – in that same old, bitter refrain – were wiped out just after colonisation through violence or introduced disease. Soon after, Pittwater became a dumping ground for human flotsam: fugitives from the law, smugglers, even shipwrecked sailors. In the 1800s, the rich got their mitts on it, using the park as a virtual retirement village. In 1894 the national park itself was created by a chap named Eccleston du Faur, who wasn't too enamoured of the concept of flower power: du Faur, appalled at the way flower sellers in Sydney contributed to the elimination of native flora, lobbied hard for a public reserve here and got it.

Thankfully, the Aboriginal cultural heritage is visible today, with the ongoing preservation of more than 800 sites: rock paintings, middens, cave art and more can be found in this classic mix of sandstone, bushland and water vistas. Also deep within are walking tracks, picnic areas and spectacular views of Broken Bay, particularly from West Head. There are several roads through the park and four entrances.

Turn off the Pacific Hwy at Mt Colah to get to the **Kalkari visitor information centre** (☎ 9472 9300, 9472 9301; ⏰ 9am-5pm), 3km into the park. The road descends from the visitor information centre to the picnic area at **Bobbin Head** on Cowan Creek.

The America Bay Trail and the Gibberagong and Sphinx Tracks are particularly good, but if you want to see **Aboriginal engravings**, head for the Basin Trail and the Garigal Aboriginal Heritage Walk at West Head. There's a mangrove boardwalk at Bobbin Head.

The **Great North Walk**, a two-week hike from Sydney to Newcastle, passes through Ku-ring-gai. This 14-day odyssey begins from the centre of Sydney and, after a short ferry ride, follows natural bushland almost the entire way to Newcastle.

It's unwise to swim in Broken Bay due to sharks, but there is a netted swimming area at the Basin.

Boat hire is available from the marinas at Akuna Bay and Bobbin Head.

Sleeping

Pittwater YHA Hostel (☎ 9999 5748; pittwater@yha nsw.org.au; Towlers Bay; dm/d $23/60) The idyllic location is noted for its teeming wildlife – wallabies, lizards and so on – and the views from the hostel's balcony are majestic. There are canoes for hire, but the palpable sense of peace is free. The hostel is a 15-minute walk uphill from Halls Wharf.

Basin camp sites (☎ 9974 1011; basin.campground @npws.nsw.gov.au; camping per person $10) Near West Head, on Pittwater. Walk about 2.5km from West Head Rd, or take a ferry or water-taxi from Palm Beach. You need to book a site before arrival.

Getting There & Around

The Pacific Hwy turns off at Mt Colah on to Ku-ring-gai Chase Rd in the west of the park; in the south, turn off from the

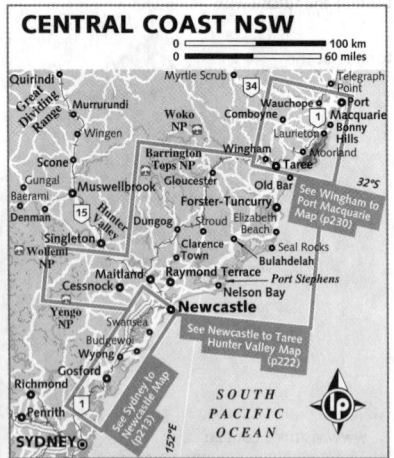

CENTRAL COAST NSW

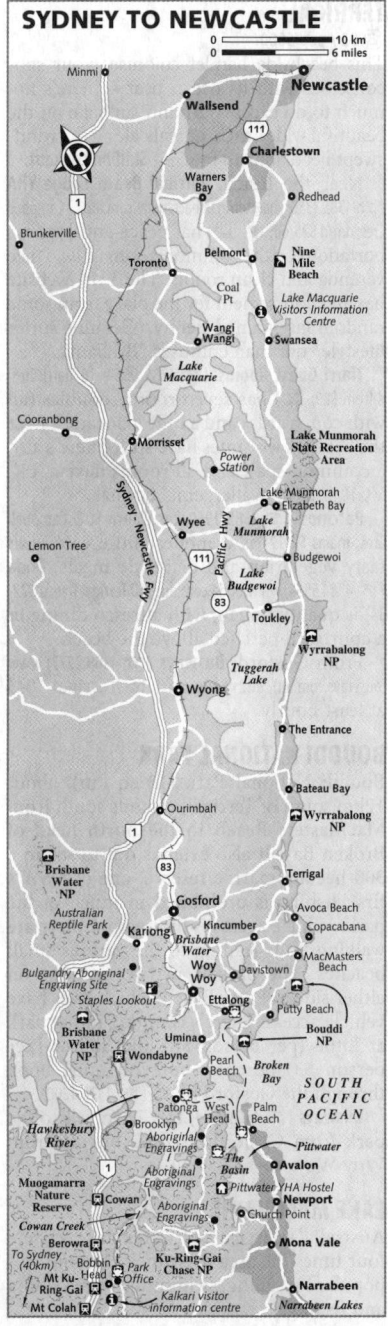

SYDNEY TO NEWCASTLE

Sydney–Newcastle Fwy into Bobbin Head Rd. Both roads will take you to the Kalkari visitor information centre and Bobbin Head.

Sydney Buses (☎ 13 15 00; www.sydneybuses.nsw .gov.au) runs a service (bus 190, $5.20) to Palm Beach.

Shorelink (☎ 9457 888; www.shorelink.com.au) buses (bus 577, $2.70) depart from Turramurra train station (on the CityRail Sydney–Newcastle line) and arrive at the park gates at North Turramurra.

The **Palm Beach Ferry** (☎ 9974 2411; www.palm beachferry.com.au; adult/child one way $10/5; ☼ 9am–5pm Mon-Thu, to 8pm Fri, to 6pm Sat & Sun) runs hourly from Palm Beach to Mackerel, via the Basin. **Water taxis** (☎ 0415 408 831) are also available from Palm Beach.

Palm Beach & Hawkesbury River Cruises (☎ 9997 4815; adult/child return $32/16) departs Palm Beach for Bobbin Head (via Patonga) at 11am daily, returning at 3.30pm.

There's no car access. From Sydney, take bus 156 from Manly to Church Point. From Sydney's centre, bus E86 is a direct peak-hour service to Church Point. From Church Point, take **Church Point Ferries** (☎ 9999 3492) to Halls Wharf.

BRISBANE WATER NATIONAL PARK

The Brisbane Water National Park (120 sq km) is on the northern side of the Hawkesbury River, across from Ku-ring-gai Chase, extending from the Pacific Hwy in the west to Brisbane Water in the east (the park has only a tiny frontage on to that body of water).

For around 11,000 years, a portion of the area was occupied by the Dharruk and the Darkinjung Aboriginal people. Their distinctive art survives, engraved in Hawkesbury sandstone, and the **Bulgandry Aboriginal Site** features examples, like engravings of people and animals that are life sized (and sometimes larger). Fish are the most common subjects, probably as a result of their economic importance at the time. If you want to photograph the engravings, go in the early morning or late afternoon, when the light is best, otherwise results can be rather disappointing. The site is 2km along Woy Woy Rd from Kariong. A few kilometres further south, **Staples Lookout** has epic views over the park.

The park is also known for its wildflowers (especially waratahs), in bloom from July to October. There are many walking trails, including a leg of the Great North Walk (p212).

There are no camping facilities, but you can stay at the well-appointed **Patonga Caravan & Camping Area** (☎ 4365 6709; powered/unpowered sites from $16.50/11.50) at Patonga, a small fishing village on Broken Bay, south of the park.

Not far away, on the eastern edge of the park, is **Pearl Beach**, a sweet National Trust–listed hamlet. Try www.pearlbeachrealestate .com.au for accommodation options.

The main road access to Brisbane Water National Park is via Woy Woy Rd at Kariong, along the Pacific Hwy. **CityRail** (☎ 13 15 00; www.cityrail.info) trains stop at Wondabyne train station inside the park upon request.

Palm Beach & Hawkesbury River Cruises (☎ 9997 4815; adult one way $7) runs a daily ferry leaving Palm Beach at 11am, arriving half an hour later at Patonga, at the edge of the park. The **Palm Beach Ferry** (☎ 9974 2411; www.palmbeachferry.com.au; adult/child one way $16/8; ☺ 9am-6.15pm Mon-Fri, to 5pm Sat & Sun) runs from Palm Beach to Ettalong, east of the park.

AROUND BRISBANE WATER

The **Australian Reptile Park** (☎ 4340 1146; www .reptilepark.com.au; adult/child $16/8; ☺ 9am-5pm), east of Kariong, is home to Eric, a celebrity saltwater crocodile. Eric used to live at a breeding farm in Darwin, where he was accused of the disappearance of two children (but was later acquitted). He then got into a stoush with a fellow croc (possibly defending his innocence, and losing a leg in the process) and was deported to the Reptile Park for his own protection. There, he rebuilt his life and appeared on TV variety shows. Only in Australia, eh? Arachnophobes will loathe the Funnel Web Milking Show.

Hilly **Gosford** (population 55,000) is about 85km north of Sydney, in a valley-bed setting on the shores of Brisbane Water. The **Gosford Visitor information centre** (☎ 4325 2835; 200 Mann St; ☺ 9am-5pm Mon-Fri, 9am-2pm Sat) is near the train station, and there's a **NPWS office** (National Parks & Wildlife Service; ☎ 4320 4200; central.coast@npws.nsw.gov.au; Suite 36-38, 207 Albany Street North, Gosford; ☺ 8.30am-4.30pm Mon-Fri).

There are frequent **CityRail** (☎ 13 15 00; www.cityrail.info) trains to Sydney ($7.80) and Newcastle ($9.60). From Gosford station, **Busways** (☎ 4368 2277) runs frequently to Terrigal and towns around the Brisbane Water National Park, less often on weekends.

TERRIGAL
☎ 02 / pop 5000

This beachside hamlet colonises your subconscious with its ocean beat – there's not much to do except surf and sunbake on the beautiful wide beach, or walk along the windswept headlands to bracing **Skillion Lookout**.

Near the beach, **Terrigal Beach Lodge YHA** (☎ 4385 3330; yha@terrigalbeachlodge.com.au; 12 Campbell Cres; dm/d $25/60; Ⓟ ☐) has peace-and-love exhortations on the common-room walls, a nice veranda and clean rooms. The YHA website has an endorsement for the place from some random guy named Benny. 'Genuine surfer lifestyle,' our man enthuses. 'Brilliant!'

Tiarri Guest Rooms (☎ 4385 9564; 16 Tiarri Cres; d from $89; ✗) has seven roomy doubles (all with courtyards) and a hilltop location near the beach. Two suites have spas (there's also a common spa), and all rooms have a TV, VCR and 'non-allergenic' doonas.

Patcinos (☎ 4385 1960; cnr Church St & Campbell Cres; mains $7-12) is a modest little café with tasty vegetarian and deli-style meals. **Onda** (☎ 4384 5554; www.onda.com.au; 150 Terrigal Dve; d $22-34) is quality Italian, with alfresco dining in a courtyard perched above the beach.

From Gosford, **Busways** (☎ 4368 2277; www .busways.com.au) services run to Terrigal ($4) at least hourly.

BOUDDI NATIONAL PARK

Bouddi National Park (12 sq km), about 12km south of Terrigal, extends south from MacMasters Beach to the north head of Broken Bay. It also extends out to sea in a 300-hectare marine reserve, one of NSW's first; fishing is prohibited in much of the park. Vehicle access is limited but there are walking trails leading to the various small beaches. The park is in two sections on either side of Putty Beach, which does have vehicle access. There's camping in the park at Little (per person $8) and Tallow (per person $3) beaches, but you must book through the Gosford **NPWS** (☎ 4320 4200).

Busways (☎ 4368 2277) bus 77 travels to the park from Gosford, as does bus 86 from Woy Woy.

LAKE MACQUARIE

Australia's largest saltwater lake covers four times the area of Sydney Harbour. It's popular for sailing, swimming, water-skiing and fishing.

The main centres around Lake Macquarie are **Charlestown** and **Belmont**, both outer suburbs of Newcastle, and **Swansea**, a long-time holiday resort for Newie holidaymakers. If you feel like a dip, there's plenty of room to spread your towel at **Nine Mile Beach**.

The **Lake Macquarie visitor information centre** (☎ 1800 802 044, 4972 1172; 72 Pacific Hwy; ☿ 9am-5pm Mon-Fri, 9am-4pm Sat & Sun) is just north of the bridge in Swansea.

NEWCASTLE

☎ 02 / pop 137,000

Newcastle has had some unflattering press over the years, due to its status as a former steel town, but it's quite an appealing place, with outstanding architecture, a beautiful foreshore and some classy eateries.

In 1989 Newcastle suffered Australia's most destructive recorded earthquake; 12 people died. However, the shakeup also enabled Newcastle to slough off its old identity and start again – in the midst of all this tourist-fuelled rebranding, it's in serious danger of becoming 'cosmopolitan'. But despite the money that's being spent on attracting hi-tech business, cleaning up the air and greening the foreshore, that famous Hunter larrikin spirit is, thankfully, still present – Newcastle's steely past is not the albatross you might expect.

Like other industrial towns worldwide, Newcastle has spawned an innovative, often confrontational arts scene that has, all at once, reacted against and been inspired by the sights and sounds of heavy industry. Newcastle also has a good reputation for live music; it was the stomping ground of silverchair, super-successful Nirvana clones, and there are loads of local bands hoping to surf similar sound waves today.

Finally, Newcastle is ideal for exploring the sumptuous Hunter Valley, with its collection of quality vineyards.

ORIENTATION

The central business district (CBD) is bordered by the Hunter River and the sea. The train station, post office and banks stand at the northeastern edge. The shopping centre is Hunter St, a pedestrian mall between Newcomen and Perkins Sts. The lively suburb of Hamilton is adjacent to Newcastle West.

INFORMATION

Bookshops

Angus & Robertson (☎ 4929 4601; Shop 2, 147 Hunter St Mall)
Cook's Hill Books & Records (☎ 4929 5079; 72 Darby St) Mostly secondhand books and records.
Rice's Bookshop (☎ 4929 2752; 699 Hunter St) Exclusively secondhand tunes and tomes.

Internet Access

Alternatively, try the hostels – Nomads (p218) is cheapest.
Battle Ground (☎ 4926 3898; Shop 2, 169/173 King St; per hr $6) Also offers multiplayer gaming.
Newcastle Regional Library (☎ 4974 5300; Laman St; per hr $5.50)

Medical Services

John Hunter Hospital (☎ 4921 3000; Lookout Rd, New Lambton) With emergency care.
Royal Newcastle Hospital (☎ 4923 6000; Pacific St) No emergency department.

Money

Banks are in Hunter St Mall. Most have foreign exchange and Westpac will change Amex travellers cheques for free.

Tourist Information

Newcastle visitor information centre (☎ 4974 2999; www.newcastletourism.com; 361 Hunter St; ☿ 9am-5pm Mon-Fri, 10am-3.30pm Sat & Sun) Books accommodation and tours and has extensive Hunter Valley information.

SIGHTS

Queens Wharf Tower on the waterfront and the **obelisk** above King Edward Park provide commanding views of the city and the water. Across the river (about five minutes by ferry) is **Stockton**, a modest settlement with striking views back towards Newcastle and the exposed shipwrecks lurking in its waters.

Nobby's Head

Nobby's used to be an island until it was joined to the mainland in 1846 to create a singularly pretty (and long) sand spit; it was twice its current height, too, before being reduced to 28m above sea level in 1855. The walk along the spit towards the lighthouse and meteorological station is exhilarating, as waves crash about your ears and joggers jostle your elbows.

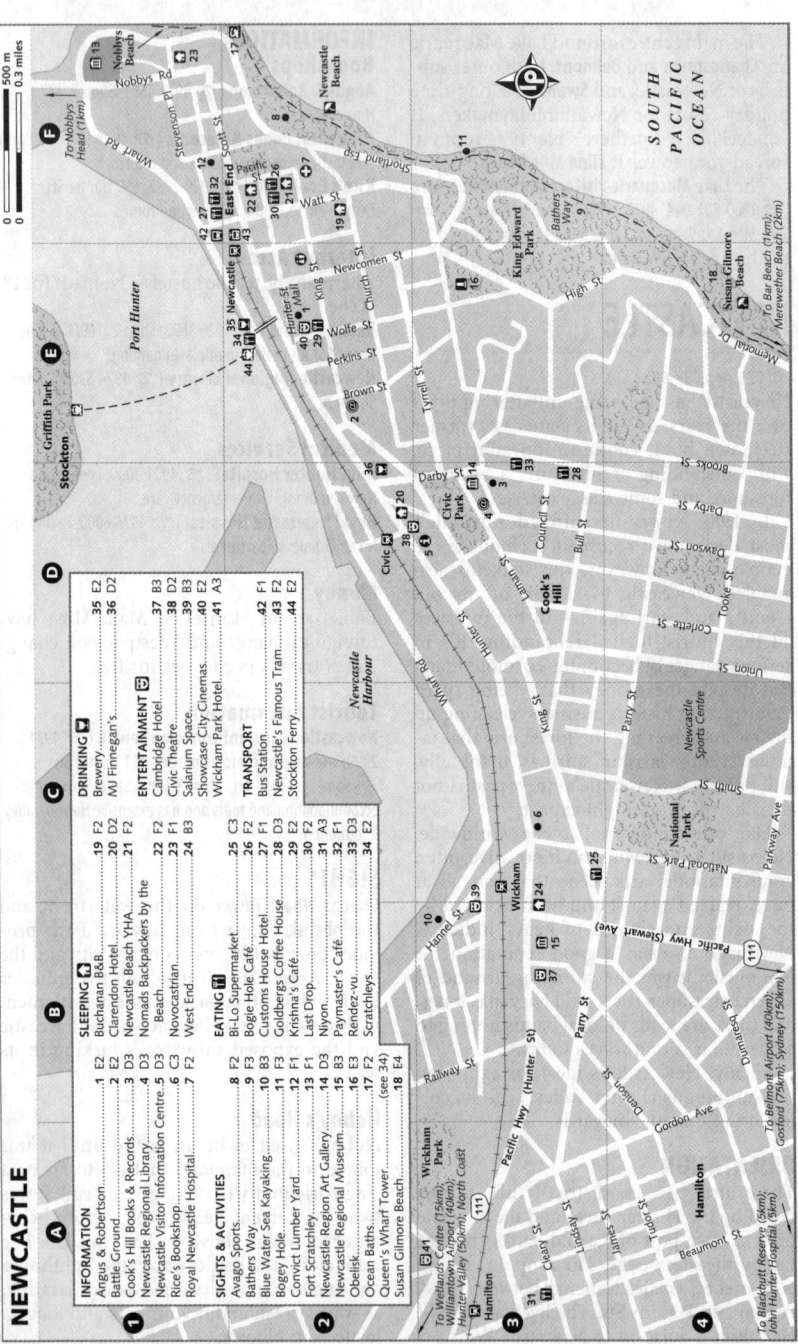

CENTRAL COAST NEW SOUTH WALES

NEWCASTLE

INFORMATION
Angus & Robertson.............1 E2
Battle Ground.....................2 E2
Cook's Hill Books & Records..3 D3
Newcastle Regional Library....4 D3
Newcastle Visitor Information Centre..5 D3
Rice's Bookshop..................6 C3
Royal Newcastle Hospital......7 F2

SIGHTS & ACTIVITIES
Avago Sports.....................8 F2
Bathers Way......................9 F3
Blue Water Sea Kayaking.....10 B3
Bogey Hole.......................11 F1
Convict Lumber Yard...........12 F1
Fort Scratchley..................13 F1
Newcastle Region Art Gallery..14 D3
Newcastle Regional Museum...15 B3
Obelisk...........................16 E3
Ocean Baths......................17 F2
Queen's Wharf Tower.........(see 34)
Susan Gilmore Beach...........18 E4

SLEEPING
Buchanan B&B...................19 F2
Clarendon Hotel..................20 D2
Newcastle Beach YHA..........21 F2
Nomads Backpackers by the Beach..22 F2
Newcastle Regional Library.....23 F1
Novocastrian.....................23 D2
West End.........................24 B3

EATING
Bi-Lo Supermarket...............25 C3
Bogie Hole Café..................26 F2
Customs House Hotel...........27 F1
Goldbergs Coffee House........28 D3
Krishna's Café....................29 E2
Last Drop.........................30 F2
Niyon.............................31 A3
Paymaster's Café................32 F1
Rendez-vu........................33 D3
Scratchleys......................34 E2

DRINKING
Brewery...........................35 E2
MJ Finnegan's....................36 D2

ENTERTAINMENT
Cambridge Hotel.................37 B3
Civic Theatre.....................38 D2
Salarium Space..................39 B3
Showcase City Cinemas.........40 E2
Wickham Park Hotel.............41 A3

TRANSPORT
Bus Station.......................42 F1
Newcastle's Famous Tram.....43 E2
Stockton Ferry...................44 E2

Fort Scratchley

This was one of the few gun installations in Australia to fire a gun in anger during WWII. On 8 June 1942, a large Japanese submarine suddenly surfaced, raining shells on the city. Fort Scratchley returned fire, negating the threat after just four rounds. According to local mythmaking, the only casualty of the attack was Bombardier Stan Newton, who was returning to the fort in a taxi when the shelling began. The clearly spooked driver dropped Stan off at Customs House with the kiss-off, 'You're on your own from here, mate.'

The complex houses the Military Museum, the Maritime Museum and underground defensive tunnels, but the site is closed to the public for renovations until late 2005/early 2006. It's still worth visiting the grounds, though, for a glimpse of the big guns and I-can-see-for-miles views of the city and coastline.

Museums & Galleries

The **Newcastle Region Museum** (☎ 4974 1400; www.ncc.nsw.gov.au/services/culture/museum; cnr Wood & Hunter Sts; admission free; ⊗ 10am-5pm Tue-Sun, 10am-5pm Mon school holidays; ▣), in a restored brewery, has a variety of exhibits including interactive science gadgets, an indigenous section and a shrine to local sports legends. The section on the 1989 earthquake is perhaps the most engaging; those who put on airs when confronted with Newcastle's industrial past might be interested to know that the coal mines in the area actually prevented the damage from escalating, as the terrain was strengthened by the mining infrastructure.

The excellent **Newcastle Region Art Gallery** (☎ 4974 5100; www.ncc.nsw.gov.au/services/culture/art gallery; 1 Laman St; admission free; ⊗ 10am-5pm Tue-Sun) collects works by revered Australian artists (Drysdale, Nolan, Whiteley) and hosts hip exhibitions by international stars and young local artists. Recent showings include hyper-real photographs of Australian celebrities and a treatise on automobile fetishism.

For art of a different kind, take a look at the numerous graffiti splattering the CBD; a lot of it is crap, but some of it is pretty good. When the council recently tried to clamp down on 'the people's art', a posse of writers 'bombed' virtually the entire CBD overnight.

ACTIVITIES
Swimming & Surfing

Newcastle's favourite surfing son is still four-time world champ Mark Richards, and many surfers rip and gouge the breaks where he cut his teeth.

Right by the East End, the needs of surfers and swimmers are sated at **Newcastle Beach**, but if you're paranoid about sharks, the **ocean baths** are a mellow alternative, encased as they are in wonderful multicoloured 1922 architecture – there's a shallow pool for toddlers and a compelling backdrop of heaving ocean and chugging cargo ships. Surfers should goofy-foot it to **Nobby's Beach**, just north of the baths – the fast left-hander known as the **Wedge** is at its north end.

South of Newcastle Beach, below King Edward Park, is Australia's oldest ocean bath, the convict-carved **Bogey Hole**. If your swimsuit is chafing you, scramble around the rocks and under the headland to the (unofficial) nude beach, **Susan Gilmour Beach**.

The most popular surfing break is at **Bar Beach**, 1km south. At nearby **Merewether Beach**, home of grommet Richards, the opening of the winter swimming season is heralded at its **ocean baths**, where blocks of ice are dumped into the water so that the cold-blooded freaks from the Merewether Mackerels Winter Swimming Club can strut their stuff. Frequent local buses from the CBD run as far south as Bar Beach, but only bus 207 continues to Merewether.

Avago Sports (☎ 0404 278 072; www.avago.com.au; Newcastle Beach; equipment per 3hr/day/week $30/40/95; ⊗ 7am-7pm) will deliver surfboards, body-boards, sand boards and mountain bikes, including maps and local tips, to your Newcastle accommodation. Sailboards and windsurfers are also available for hire.

Watching Wildlife

Walking trails meander through grey gums and native wildlife enclosures at **Blackbutt Reserve** (☎ 4952 1449; www.ncc.nsw.gov.au/services /environment/naturewatch/blackbutt.cfm; Carnley Ave, New Lambton Heights; admission free; ⊗ 9am-5pm); get up and close with koalas, wombats, emus, kangaroos, wallabies and quolls (fascinating cat-shaped marsupials from Tasmania). The fastest bus from the CBD is 363 ($2.40, 35 minutes), but it stops at the Lookout Rd entrance, which is a fair hike from the creatures.

The **Wetlands Centre** (☎ 4951 6466; www.wetlands.org.au; Sandgate Rd, Shortland; adult/concession $5/3; ⊙ 9am-3pm Mon-Fri, 9am-5pm Sat & Sun) is a swampy wonderland, home to 200 bird and animal species. You can hire a canoe ($7.50 for two hours) here. Take the Pacific Hwy toward Maitland and turn left at the cemetery, or catch bus 106 from the railway station.

Walking

Newcastle has two self-guided walks. The **Bathers Way** takes you from Nobby's Beach to Merewether Beach; signposts teach you about indigenous, convict and natural history in between swims.

The **Newcastle East Heritage Walk** takes you past many of the highlights of Newcastle's colonial history (throwing in some quite breathtaking beach scenery), like the **Convict Lumber Yard**, opposite the Newcastle train station – excavations have shown this was once a convict industrial workplace. Surrounding historic buildings have been put to good commercial use, including the old paymaster's cottage (see opposite) and Customs House (see opposite).

Brochures for both walks are available at the visitor centre, or just follow the signs.

Sea Kayaking

Blue Water Sea Kayaking (☎ 4961 1233; www.seakayaking.com.au; Shop 4, Newcastle Cruising Yacht Club Commercial Centre, Hannell St, Wickham) rents kayaks (from $20) and leads tours.

Flights

Air Sports (☎ 0412 607 815; www.air-sports.com.au; King Edward Park) offers tandem hang-gliding flights (from $165).

TOURS

Newcastle's Famous Tram (☎ 4963 7954; tram@idl.net.au; adult/child $10/6) trundles around the East End for 45 minutes, taking in major historical sites. It leaves the railway station on the hour between 10am and 2pm (last tram at 1.45pm Monday to Friday).

FESTIVALS & EVENTS

Newcastle Regional Show (☎ 4961 2085) This country fair–type show gits on down in early March.
Surfest (www.surfest.com) Hangs-ten late March.
Newcastle Jazz Festival (www.newcastlejazz.com.au) Jammin' late August.

National Young Writers' Festival (www.youngwritersfestival.org) Cracking mix of established and emerging writers giving talks, workshops, panels; late September.
Electrofringe (www.electrofringe.org) Explores bleeding-edge electronic and digital realms: sound, video, online etc; late September.
Mattara Festival (www.mattarafestival.org.au) Celebrating Newcastle early October.

SLEEPING
Budget

Newcastle Beach YHA (☎ 4925 3544; mail@newcastleyha.com.au; 30 Pacific St; dm/s/d from $24/42/60; ☐) This heritage-listed building is a bikini strap away from Newcastle Beach. Inside, it's a bit like an English public school (without the humiliating hazing rituals): grand and ostentatious, high ceilings, huge dorms, plush-leather common room. Unlike most hostels, you'll stand a good chance of getting some privacy with all that room. There's also free surfboard hire, pub meals, quizzes, pizza nights etc, and a palm-tree courtyard with a BBQ.

Nomads Backpackers by the Beach (☎ 1800 008 972, 4926 3472; www.backpackersbythebeach.com.au; 34 Hunter St; dm/d $25/55; Ⓟ ☐) This one's also in a terrific location, right near the beach and Hunter St eateries. It's bright, clean, modern and relaxed and the staff dispense knowledge on Newcastle nightlife and surfing.

West End (☎ 4961 4446; accommodationwestend@bigpond.com; cnr Hunter St & Stewart Ave; dm/s/d $30/60/65; Ⓟ) Nice old place, newly renovated, with clean bathrooms, a good balcony, a garden-and-barbecue area and a dorm with a large en suite. It's still got that new-paint smell.

Midrange

Clarendon Hotel (☎ 4927 0966; www.clarendonhotel.com.au; 347 Hunter St; s/d/ste $121/132/143; ✷ ☐) In an old Art Deco building, the Clarendon is thickly atmospheric with mod furniture and lighting, and lavishly painted walls and stylish furniture; David Lynch (or James Ellroy) would feel right at home. There's a bar, a brasserie and lashings of conviviality downstairs.

Buchanan B&B (☎ 4926 5828; www.buchanan-bb.com.au; 20 Church St; s/d from $75/120; ☐) This restored heritage house offers beautiful high French beds and a tasty home-made breakfast. The outside is done up in those delightful pastel hues that characterise

Australian coastal architecture, and the interior is 19th-century glam.

Novocastrian (☎ 4926 3688, 1800 005 944; www .novocastrian.bestwestern.com.au; 21 Parnell Pl; d $110-185, f $165; ❄) It's yet another cog in the world's largest hotel chain, but at least its location is individual: right above Nobby's Beach.

EATING

Darby and Beaumont are the main eat streets, rammed to the gills with culinary establishments of all perversions.

For self-catering head to **Bi-Lo Supermarket** (☎ 4926 4494; cnr King & National Park Sts).

Restaurants

Customs House Hotel (☎ 4925 2585; www.customs house.net.au; 1 Bond St; mains $12-27; ❧ lunch & dinner) Once HQ for confiscating contraband, this lovely old building, with scenic alfresco patio, is now part pub, part classy bistro. The fusion menu might include Atlantic salmon (a Newcastle culinary staple) or roast supreme of duck.

Brewery (☎ 4929 6333; www.qwb.com.au; Queens Wharf, 150 Wharf Rd; mains $24-26; ❧ lunch & dinner) Perched on Queen's Wharf; the views and outdoor tables are naturally sought after. The food is good, hearty marine-type fare: chargrilled rumps, fisherman's baskets, grilled fish. Features a NSW-centric wine list. Wear your boat shoes for best results.

Niyon (☎ 4961 0825; 49 Beaumont St; mains $12-18; ❧ dinner) This upstairs Thai restaurant has a prime balcony overlooking epicurean Beaumont. Great green curries (some without coconut milk, in a surprising non-traditional gambit) and laconic service.

Rendez-vu (☎ 4929 2244; 115 Darby St; mains $10-25; ❧ lunch & dinner) Although good sandwiches and a large cocktail list draw crowds to the sidewalk tables, the staff's phone manner may mean others never make it. Take your chances.

Scratchleys (☎ 4929 1111; www.scratchleys.com.au; 200 Wharf Rd; mains $13-28; ❧ lunch & dinner) Claims to be Australia's most 'environmentally friendly restaurant', but can the food cut it? Latest foodie awards say 'yes'. Prawns were a recent feature at this seafood palace, and the variants on show – chilli prawns, prawn salads, king prawn spaghetti – indeed indicate that some thought goes into the menu.

Cafés

Last Drop (☎ 4926 3470; 37 Hunter St; dishes $7-10) A gem of a café, packing on the charm with terrific smoothies and gourmet wraps, radiant staff and the comfy couch in back.

Paymaster's Café (☎ 4925 2600; 18 Bond St; mains $20-28; ❧ lunch & dinner) Wicker chairs, sea breezes, heritage surrounds and an Asian-influenced menu. If they have it, promise you'll try the Char Sui Pork, with bok choy and udon noodles.

Bogie Hole Café (☎ 4926 1790; cnr Hunter & Pacific Sts; mains $11-21; ❧ breakfast, lunch & dinner) This café is always packed. It's metres from the beach, has masses of sidewalk tables and serves huge helpings of nicely prepared standards: pastas, salads, burgers, steaks, lamb, chicken.

Goldbergs Coffee House (☎ 4929 3122; 137 Darby St; meals $7-18; ❧ breakfast & dinner) A smooth café, European style with open frontage, but featuring a typically earthy Novocastrian twist: a wrought-iron chandelier descending like an oversize arachnid. Attracts chatty crowds of all persuasions.

Krishna's Café (☎ 492 6900; cnr King & Wolfe Sts; lunch/dinner $7.50/9.50) This airy, skylighted café serves the usual Krishna fare (*pakoras*, rice fancies etc) but it's unusually tasty.

DRINKING

Brewery (☎ 4929 6333; 150 Wharf Rd) Right on the harbour. Share the jetty with Novocastrian office workers and uni students. It's just as well it has got that jetty and that view, as the upstairs bar is poorly designed, with pillars in the way of the bands on the stage.

MJ Finnegan's (☎ 4926 4777; www.irishpub.com .au; 21-23 Darby St) A comfy establishment, with Irish stylings that aren't as contrived as the typical Celtic chains.

Also recommended:
Customs House Hotel (☎ 4925 2585; 1 Bond St) Foreshore atmosphere.
Clarendon (☎ 4927 0966; www.clarendonhotel.com.au; 347 Hunter St) Art Deco décor.

ENTERTAINMENT

Ever seen the film *The Cars that Ate Paris*? Similarly, Newcastle's CBD can seem like it's been handed over to rampaging youth at night; in the morning, it's somehow returned to the town burghers with (mostly) everything intact. This swaggering frontier atmosphere is harmless really; depending on one's disposition, it can either be exhilarating or off-putting. The rest of Newie is sedate by comparison.

Octapod (www.octapod.org) is the mob behind the Newcastle Young Writers' Festival and Electrofringe (p218). Creative and committed, it puts on loads of events around town, including workshops, screenings and gigs.

Live Music

Staff at the hostels, music-store employees and Thursday's paper are your best bets for inside goss. Most pubs feature bands Wednesday to Sunday.

Salarium Space (☎ 4961 5191; www.angelfire.com /oz/salariumspace; Morrow Park Bowling Club, Station St, Wickham) Dripping with good vibes, Salarium is hosted in an old, converted bowling club. Dig it: cushions, candles, fairy lights…it's certainly a change from Newie beer pits. Diverse acts play here: jazz, world music, funk, noise. It's open 'when we feel like it'.

Live Sites (www.livesites.org.au) This councilled initiative has proved very popular. In malls, squares and public spaces around town, expect a varied lineup of acts: Latin jazz, professional street performers, Indian raga music. Takes place January to April.

Cambridge Hotel (☎ 4962 2459; www.yourcam bridge.com; 789 Hunter St) Cambridge launched silverchair and the tourist brochures won't let them forget it – but Newie's House of Rock has moved on, showcasing touring national bands and local acts.

Wickham Park Hotel (☎ 4962 3501; www.wph .com .au; 61 Maitland Rd) Features a very welcoming, neighbourhood-pub feel, with acoustic shows in the beer garden and suchlike. It has a wacky website in bright colours which should give you an sense of its business.

Cinemas

Showcase City Cinemas (☎ 4929 5019; 31 Wolfe St; tickets $9-10.50) Specialises in foreign and independent flicks.

Greater Union (☎ 4926 2233; 183-185 King St) Has mainstream releases.

Theatre

Civic Theatre (☎ 4926 1289; www.civictheatrenew castle.com.au; 375 Hunter St) The Civic hosts theatre, musicals, concerts and dance in an evocative Newcastle building. It was designed by 'picture palace' architect Henry White, a man responsible for around 180 theatres in Australia, North America and New Zealand.

GETTING THERE & AWAY
Air

Newcastle's main **airport** (☎ 4928 9800; www .newcastleairport.com.au) is at Williamtown, about 15km north of the city. **Virgin Blue** (www.virgin blue.com.au) and **Jetstar** (www.jetstar.com.au) fly to Brisbane and Melbourne, while **Qantas** (www .qantas.com.au) goes one better by flying to Sydney, as well. **Belmont Airport** (☎ 6884 3120) is located to the south of the city.

Bus

Nearly all long-distance buses stop behind the station in Newcastle. **Port Stephens Coaches** (☎ 4982 2940; www.pscoaches.com.au) has services from Nelson Bay to Newcastle ($10.40, 1¼ hours), and Newcastle to Sydney ($24, 2¼ hours, once daily). **Rover Coaches** (☎ 4990 1699; www.rovercoaches.com.au) travels to Cessnock ($11.60, 1¼ hours, four times daily).

Car

ARA (☎ 4962 2488, 1800 243 122,; www.ararental.com .au; 86 Belford St, Broadmeadow) offers rental from $29 a day. Alternatively, Tudor St in Hamilton has the big rental agencies.

Train

CityRail (☎ 13 15 00; www.cityrail.info) has frequent trains to Sydney ($17, three hours).

GETTING AROUND
To/From the Airport

Port Stephens Coaches (☎ 4982 2940; www.ps coaches.com.au) goes to and from Williamtown airport frequently ($5.90, 35 minutes) en route to Nelson Bay. Local buses 310, 311, 322 and 363 go to Belmont Airport from Newcastle train station ($2.50, 1½ hours).

Taxis (☎ 4979 3000) cost around $45 to Williamtown or Belmont airport.

Bus

Most **local buses** (☎ 13 15 00; www.newcastlebuses .info) operate every half-hour on weekdays, less frequently on weekends. Fares are time-based, with one-hour ($2.70), four-hour ($5.30) and all-day ($8.10) passes available. The main depot is near the train station.

Ferry

The Stockton ferry ($2) goes every half-hour from Queens Wharf, 5.15am till midnight on Friday and Saturday, till 11pm Monday to Thursday and 10pm on Sunday.

NEWCASTLE TO TAREE & HUNTER VALLEY

LOWER HUNTER VALLEY

The Hunter Valley is the oldest wine region in Australia, best known for its Semillon and Shiraz varieties, but sometimes it just can't get respect. Those loyal to South Australia's Barossa and Victoria's Yarra valleys tend to look down their noses at the Hunter, and a recent newspaper article quoted a Melbourne restaurateur as saying the valley was only good for 'growing bananas'. That's their misfortune, because there are some quality establishments. All up, there are more than 90 wineries in the Lower Hunter (mainly around Cessnock and Pokolbin, both about 40km west of Newcastle) and half a dozen or so in the Upper Hunter.

Vines were first planted here in the 1820s; by the 1860s there were 20 sq km under cultivation. A Hunter sparkling wine made its way to Paris in 1855 and was favourably compared with the French product. However most Hunter wineries gradually declined, and it wasn't until the 1960s that wine making again became an important industry. Perhaps that's the root of all this tribal loyalty – old perceptions die hard in Australia.

The Hunter has an important ace up its sleeve: these wineries are refreshingly attitude-free and welcoming of viticulturists and novices alike. Staff will rarely give you the evil eye if you leadenly twirl your glass once too often, or don't take the proper time to inhale the fumes. With all the good will in the world, they'll correct your technique. You can learn a lot from a comprehensive tour of the region and tastings are free. Even those with only a casual interest in wine should tour around – it's a lovely area.

Orientation

Most of the Lower Hunter's attractions lie in an area bordered to the north by the New England Hwy and to the south by the Wollombi/Maitland Rd. The main town serving the area is Cessnock, close to the southern edge of the vineyards. Most of the action happens along Broke Rd; the town of Pokolbin is at the intersection of Broke and McDonald Rds.

The former coal-mining centre of Maitland is the northern gateway into the Hunter.

Information

Hunter Valley visitor information centre (☎ 4990 4477; www.winecountry.com.au; Allandale Rd; ☻ 9am-5pm Mon-Sat, 9am-4pm Sun) In a large complex with a café, and is very well organised. Make sure you pick up a copy of the comprehensive *Hunter Valley Wine Country Visitors Guide*, featuring summaries of all the vineyards and an excellent map. Information is posted outside for those who arrive out of hours.

Muswellbrook visitor information centre (☎ 6541 4050; www.muswellbrook.org.au; 87 Hill St; ☻ 9am-5pm) For information about the Upper Hunter.

Sights & Activities

WINERIES

The **Hungerford Hill** (☎ 4998 7666; www.hungerford hill.com.au; 1 Broke Rd; ☻ 9am-5pm Mon-Fri, 10am-5pm Sat & Sun) winery is shaped like a big barrel, with its 'lid' permanently propped open; this commanding spectacle stands sentinel over the lakes and valleys below, and makes an excellent introduction to your winery tour. Features an on-site restaurant.

Pepper Tree Wines (☎ 4998 7539; www.pepper treewines.com.au; Halls Rd; ☻ 9am-5pm Mon-Fri, 9.30am-5pm Sat & Sun) is set in gorgeous, New England–style gardens. And the wine? It's won around 60 trophies and 500 medals (see the boxed text, p223). The fabulous Robert's Restaurant (p224) is on the property.

Self-deprecating and informal, **Piggs Peake Winery** (☎ 6574 7000; www.piggspeake.com; 697 Hermitage Rd; ☻ 10am-5pm) produces limited-edition, unwooded wines (see the boxed text, p223) to impress your mates back home. In 2004 lucky swines were able to sample wines including the Sows Ear Semillon and the Wiggly Tail Marsanne. Post-2004, the porcine theme continues unabated.

If the previously mentioned wineries are 'major labels', the **Small Winemakers Centre** (☎ 4998 7668; www.smallwinemakerscentre.com.au; McDonalds Rd; ☻ 10am-5pm) is indie and proud, acting as a cellar door for 10 wine makers who don't have their own vineyards. Organic wines are among the booty on offer.

OTHER ATTRACTIONS

The **Bluetongue Brewery** (☎ 4998 7945; www.blue tonguebrewery.com.au; Hunter Resort, Hermitage Rd; ☻ breakfast, lunch & dinner; tours 11am & 2pm) is a new kid on the block as far as beer is

NEWCASTLE TO TAREE & HUNTER VALLEY

CENTRAL COAST
NEW SOUTH WALES

SLEEPING
Belford Country Cabins...........11 A1
Big 4 Valley Tourist Park........12 B3
Cessnock Hotel.........................13 B3
Hill Top Country Guest House...14 B2
Hunter Valley Accommodation
Centre.............................(see 1)
Wentworth Hotel.....................15 B3

EATING
Australian Regional Food Store &
Café................................(see 10)
Hunter Valley Cheese Company...16 A2
Robert's Restaurant.............(see 7)

TRANSPORT
Grapemobile...........................17 A2
Pokolbin Horse Coaches.........18 A2

INFORMATION
Hunter Valley Visitor Information
Centre..................................1 B2

SIGHTS & ACTIVITIES
Balloon Aloft...........................2 B1
Bluetongue Brewery..................3 A1
Hungerford Hill........................4 B2
Hunter Olive Centre..................5 A2
Hunter Valley Chocolate
Company...........................(see 8)
Hunter Valley Wine School........6 A2
Pepper Tree Wines....................7 A2
Peterson's Champagne House.....8 B2
Piggs Peake Winery...................9 A2
Small Winemakers Centre........10 A2

30 km
20 miles

0
0

SOUTH
PACIFIC
OCEAN

Manning
Point
Old Bar
Diamond Beach
Hallidays Point
Forster
Cape Hawke
(224m)
Green Point
Booti Booti
NP
Pacific Palms
Smiths Lake
Seal Rocks
Treachery Beach
Tuncurry
Wallis
Lake
Bodi Booti
NP
Bungwahl
Coomba
Park
Taree
Nabiac
The Lakes Way
Myall Lake
Mungo Brush
Manns River
Pacific Hwy
The
Grandis
Myall
Lakes
NP
Bulahdelah
Myall River
Nerong
Bombah
Point
Tea Gardens
Hawks Nest
Tomaree
Peninsula
Tomaree
NP
Tomaree
Nelson
Bay
One
Mile
Beach
Shoal Bay
Port
Stephens
Anna
Bay
Stockton Bight
Lemon Tree
Passage
Salt Ash
Williamtown
Stockton
The Rock
Roadhouse
Stroud Rd
Stroud
Booral
Dungog
Clarence
Town
Paterson
Morpeth
Raymond
Terrace
Hexham
Newcastle
Minmi
Maitland
Kurri
Kurri
Pelaw
Main
Sydney
Newcastle
Fwy
Gresford
Hunter
River
Grahamstown
Lake
Barrington
Tops NP
Gloucester
Gloucester River
Camping Area
Gloucester Tops
Gloucester Falls
Williams River
Day Use Area
Upper
Chichester
Chichester
Dam
Upper
Allyn
The Buckets Way
Gloucester
River

Hunter Valley enlargement:
Hunter River
Branxton
Greta
Allandale
Camp Rd
Nulkaba
Rd
Tuckers La
Talga Rd
Wilderness Rd
Lovedale Rd
Majors Rd
Neath
Maitland Rd
Aberdare
Rd
Vincent St
Branxton
Aberman
Neath
Cessnock
Kurri
Kurri
Wine Country Dr
Wine Country Dr
McDonalds Rd
Palmers La
Hall Rd
Deaseys Rd
Broke Rd
Oakey Creek Rd
Marrowbone Rd
Mt Bright
Lookout
Bimbadeen
Lookout
Bellbird
Mt View Rd
Wollombi Rd
Pokolbin
Broke
Bulga
Wollombi
NP
Yengo
NP
See Enlargement
New England Hwy
To Muswellbrook (65km);
Scone (91km)
Hermitage Rd
Old North Rd
To Gosford (78km)
To Windsor (100km)
Putty Rd

5 km
3 miles
0
0

TOP FIVE HUNTER VALLEY TIPPLES

Before embarking on your Odyssey of the Senses, keep in mind that drink-driving laws are heavily enforced in New South Wales. If you are driving, remember that to stay under the blood-alcohol limit of 0.05, men can have two standard drinks in the first hour and one every hour after. Women can have one standard drink per hour. Wineries offer 20ml tastes of wine – five of these equals one standard drink.

Other ways to minimise the damage: choose a designated driver; buy a bottle to take with you; use the spittoons provided; take a tour if you can; give up the demon drink.

And now, to the drinks…

- **2003 House of Bricks Shiraz** 'One very big wine: 15% alcohol, deeply coloured, perfumed, big fruit, big tannin, big wood. Not for the inexperienced or the faint hearted, it will stain your glassware and turn your teeth black. The ideal food for this style of wine would be an ox roasted over an open fire.' *Piggs Peake Winery* (p221)

- **Spring Cream Ale** 'Ten-per-cent crystal malt in the brewing grist imparts the copper colour and adds soft caramel flavours. Clean on the palate, yet complex, with an accent on creamy fruitiness. It begins assertively, then mellows out to a long, slightly sweet finish.' *Bluetongue Brewery* (p221)

- **2003 Hunter Valley Shiraz** 'The 2003 vintage had superb ripening conditions, and coupled with extremely low yields, resulted in the most intense Shiraz wine since 1991. The masses of fruit are balanced with new French oak. The aroma is a blend of ripe berries and spice, while the palate is intense and lasting. This wine will age for many years.' *Pepper Tree Wines* (p221)

- **2002 Sparkling Merlot** 'Vibrant crimson in colour, with strawberries and rhubarb on the nose and loads of sweet berries filling the palate. This vintage wine shows good length with a hint of white pepper spice showing the regional influence. Soft, subtle, dry finish, which is very rare for a merlot.' *Peterson's Champagne House* (below)

- **1828 Merlot** 'A distinctly Australian style of Merlot with luscious plummy fruit characters balanced by spicy fruit and oak aromas. Soft, round and generous representing a perfect example of The Big Australian Taste.' *Wyndham Estate* (www.wyndhamestate.com/winery)

concerned, but one that's attracting attention for creative, refreshing and exquisitely addictive brews. Try alcoholic ginger beer (great idea); its Premium Lager, malty and crisp; Hunter Bitter, with a caramel finish; Spring Cream Ale, creamy with more caramel; and Framboise, with raspberries added during fermentation (see the boxed text, above). Sample them all using the brewery's patented Tasting Paddle.

Also recommended:

Peterson's Champagne House (☎ 4998 7881; www.petersonhouse.com.au; cnr Broke & Branxton Rds; ✹ breakfast & lunch) Lovely jubbly bubbly (see the boxed text, above) and an on-site restaurant.

Hunter Valley Chocolate Company (☎ 4998 7301; Peterson's Champagne House, cnr Broke & Branxton Rds) All manner of cacao derivatives.

Hunter Olive Centre (☎ 4998 7524; Pokolbin Estate Vineyard, McDonalds Rd) Wine – *check*; cheese (p224) – *check*; beer – *check*; champagne – *check*; olive oil? Now you can go home.

Tours

Visitors centres and places to stay in Sydney and Newcastle can help you organise a tour of the wineries any which way you please: from above, from below, sideways. Some pubs in the area conduct informal tours for a low price, a bit like the classic 'pub crawl' with all of the good-time atmosphere that implies.

Balloon Aloft (☎ 1800 028 568, 4938 1955; www .balloonaloft.com; 1443 Wine Country Dr, North Rothbury; flights $280) Airborne tours of the vineyards.

Hunter Valley Day Tours (☎ 4938 5031; www.hunter tourism.com/daytours) Wine-and-cheese-tasting tours; prices vary according to how many people in a group.

Hunter Valley Skydiving Centre (☎ 4322 9884)

Pokolbin Horse Coaches (☎ 4998 7305; www.hunter web.com.au/pokolbinhorsecoaches; McDonalds Rd) Day tours in a quaint, open-air carriage (from $45), including pick-up, picnic lunch and tastings.

Tumbleweed Trike Tours (☎ 4938 1245) Motor around on extravagant, customised trikes – one seat in front, two in back. Rates start at $100 per couple for the first hour, decreasing in $50-dollar increments each subsequent hour.

Vineyard Shuttle Service (☎ 4998 7779; www .vineyardshuttle.com.au; per person from $33) Bus tours.

Festivals & Events

Harvest Festival February to May.

Lovedale Long Lunch Seven wineries and chefs produce gut-bursting lunches, served with music and art; May.

Budfest Held in Cessnock; September.

Jazz in the Vines (www.jazzinthevines.com.au) October.

Opera in the Vineyards (www.4-d.com.au) October.

Sleeping

As always, ask staff at the visitor information centre to match accommodation to your budget and standards. Prices at motels adjust to whatever the market will bear, and are higher on weekends; there's usually a minimum two-night stay. Maitland and Singleton are good alternatives to basing yourself in the vineyards or in Cessnock; they're further from the vineyards but prices tend to be cheaper.

VINEYARDS

Belford Country Cabins (☎ 6574 7100; www.belford cabins.com.au; 659 Hermitage Rd; d from $100; P 🔀 🖳) Choice accommodation in bushland, among kangaroos, possums and ironbark trees. The sense of space and the great outdoors on your doorstep is almost worth the price alone; added to that are the roomy and cosy cabins. Children are welcome (cots, high chairs and so forth are available) and there's a pool, barbecues and a games room.

Hill Top Country Guest House (☎ 4930 7111; www.hilltopguesthouse.com.au; 81 Talga Rd; d from $88; P 🔀 🖳) Off Lovedale Rd, Hill Top offers great views, horse riding, in-house massage, canoeing, a pool, self-drive buggies, wildlife safaris, double spas, a grand piano, cattle mustering, a billiard room. And you thought you were here for the wine.

Hunter Valley Accommodation Centre (☎ 4991 4222; www.huntervalleyaccommodation.com; Lot 210 Main Rd; s/d from $60/80; P 🔀 🖳) Well located, right by the visitor information centre. There's a pool and tennis courts.

CESSNOCK

Cessnock Hotel (☎ 4990 1002; 234 Wollombi Rd; s/d from $35/60) This classic restored pub has cottage-type rooms – a bit more cosy than your standard pub accommodation.

Downstairs is a lively bar, with a bistro and expansive courtyard.

Wentworth Hotel (☎ 4990 1364; murphys@went worthhotelcessnock.com.au; 32 Vincent St; s/d from $50/70) The Wenty, dating from the 1920s, is another old pub that's tarted up its décor. Breakfast is included, there's a restaurant and live music features some nights.

Big 4 Valley Vineyard Tourist Park (☎ 4990 2573; Mt View Rd; powered sites $24, deluxe cabins $60; 🔀 🖳) A spacious, orderly park with a pool and on-site Thai restaurant. It's ideally placed for the wineries.

Eating

Many wineries have picnic tables and barbecues, and a goodly proportion also have restaurants.

Robert's Restaurant (☎ 4998 7330; www.roberts restaurant.com; Halls Rd; mains $36-40) Book ahead, as Robert's has quite the reputation – it's extraordinarily atmospheric, located in a settler's cottage in the Pepper Tree grounds (p221). The gourmet menu induces rapture, combining the best of French and Italian traditions with Aussie country produce.

Australian Regional Food Store & Café (☎ 4998 6800; www.australianregionalfoods.com.au; Small Winemakers Centre, McDonalds Rd; 🕑 breakfast, lunch & dinner) Like the centre in which it's located, this food store champions 'indie', often organic, produce ('lean and green', they say). Stock up – you won't get the likes of its extraordinarily tangy dill-and-lemon mustard, salmon sauce or chilli olive oil in your standard supermarkets. Free tastings are available and the café makes good use of the store's products (mains $17 to $19).

The **Hunter Valley Cheese Company** (☎ 4998 7744; McGuigans Complex, McDonalds Rd, Pokolbin; www .huntervalleycheese.com.au; 🕑 9am-5.30pm) anoints Monty Python as its patron saint: 'Blessed are the cheesemakers' quotes the staff T-shirts, and the people inside those shirts will chew your ear about cheesy comestibles all day long. Using vegetarian rennet and no preservatives, there's a bewildering, sinful variety of styles, including 'washed rinds to remember'. There are free tastings and more structured ones for $6. Watch your girth.

Getting There & Around

There's no public transport around the vineyards. Hire a car in Sydney or Newcastle, or join a tour (p223).

Grapemobile (☎ 0500 804 039; www.grapemobile .com.au; cnr McDonalds Rd & Palmers Lane) hires bikes (per hour/day $5/30), while the **Vineyard Shuttle Service** (☎ 4998 7779; www.vineyardshuttle .com.au) takes you from your accommodation to anywhere in the valley and back ($10).

Kean's (☎ 6543 1322) goes to Cessnock ($30, 2¼ hours, once daily), Muswellbrook ($39, 3½ hours) and Scone ($47, 3¾ hours) from Sydney, and from Port Macquarie to Scone ($84, 11 hours).

Rover Coaches (☎ 4990 1699; www.rovercoaches .com.au) goes to Cessnock ($10.60, 1¼ hours) from Newcastle.

Sid Fogg's (☎ 4928 1088; www.sidfoggs.com.au) travels up the valley to Dubbo ($59, six hours) via Maitland.

TRAIN
CityRail (☎ 13 15 00; www.cityrail.info) has services from Newcastle to Maitland ($4.40, 30 minutes), and Sydney to Maitland via Newcastle ($21, 3½ hours).

CountryLink (☎ 13 22 32; www.countrylink.com.au) travels from Sydney to Scone ($49.50, 2¼ hours) and Muswellbrook ($44, 3¾ hours).

PORT STEPHENS
This stunning sheltered bay is about an hour's drive north of Newcastle, occupying a submerged valley that stretches more than 20km inland. It's a popular boating and fishing spot and takes in friendly **Nelson Bay** (population 7000) – the 'dolphin capital of Australia' – along with all kinds of adventure activities and several near-deserted beaches fringed with bungalows.

At the mouth of the Myall River, opposite Nelson Bay, are the small, pretty towns of **Tea Gardens**, on the river, and **Hawks Nest**, on the beach. **Jimmy's Beach** at Hawks Nest fronts a glass-like stretch of water, while **Bennett's Beach** has great views of Broughton Island.

On the southern side of the Tomaree Peninsula, **One Mile Beach** is a gorgeous semicircle of softest sand and bluest water, favoured by those in the know: surfers, beachcombers, idle romantics. Nearby **Samurai Beach** is popular with folks from the local nudist resort and has great surf.

Back on the highway, a few kilometres before the turn-off to Tea Gardens and Hawks Nest, is the **Rock roadhouse** – a replica of Uluru (Ayers Rock). This place is a mar-vel of…something. Inside, there are shops, a café and a Big Foot. It's Australiana at its finest and is highly recommended even if your tank is full and your cynicism is in the red.

Getting There & Around
To drive from Nelson Bay to Tea Gardens, you have to backtrack to Raymond Terrace.

Port Stephens Coaches (☎ 4982 2940; www.ps coaches.com.au) goes from Nelson Bay via Anna Bay to Newcastle ($10.40, 1¼ hours, 13 times daily). The 9am bus from Nelson Bay continues to Sydney ($35, 3½ hours).

Port Stephens Ferry Service (☎ 4984 1262; cruisein@nelsonbay.com) chugs from Nelson Bay to Tea Gardens and back three times a day ($18 return, one hour).

Anna Bay & Around
The surfside village of **Anna Bay** is certainly pleasant enough, but wait till you see what it's backed by – the incredible **Stockton Bight**, the longest moving sand dunes in the southern hemisphere, stretching 35km to Newcastle. The tourist board claims the dunes are *Mad Max* style, but if you want to talk films, think *Lawrence of Arabia* – more Sahara than outback. In the heart of it, it's possible to get so surrounded by shimmering sand, you'll lose sight of the ocean and the townships. Other cultural reference points to help you paint a visual picture: an early Tintin book; a well-known Salvador Dalí painting; one Pink Floyd album in particular – it's incredibly evocative, in short. At the far west end of the beach the wreck of the *Sygna* founders in the water.

SLEEPING
Melaleuca Surfside Backpackers (☎ 4981 9422; www.melaleucabackpackers.com.au; 33 Eucalyptus Dr, One Mile Beach; unpowered sites/dm/d $14/25/70) A gorgeous site: the wooden cabins, custom-built from red cedar, are set amid peaceful scrub right across from the beach. There's a huge, comfortable communal lounge area and kitchen, and the campsites are 'free range'– you pick your own and cars are not allowed near tents, which equates to purest bliss. The grounds are also inhabited by koalas, land mullets, sugar gliders and possums.

Samurai Beach Resort (☎ 4916 3400, 1800 822 200; www.samuraibeachresort.com.au; 288 Gan Gan Rd, Anna

Bay; d from $99; (P) (bed) (wheelchair)) This new resort features luxury units, self-contained villas and studios. The décor is nothing to shout about, but once again the woodland surroundings are a treat and the beach is close to hand.

Samurai Beach Bungalows (☎ 4982 1921; www .portstephens.org.au/samurai; cnr Frost Rd & Robert Connell Cl, Anna Bay; dm/d from $20/62) Rustically furnished wooden-floored cabins, separated by pleasant bushland and lawns, with an outdoor camp kitchen, surfboards and bikes.

O'Carrollyn's (☎ 4982 2801; www.ocarrollyns.com .au; 36 Eucalyptus Dr, One Mile Beach; d from $119) Wheelchair accessible, self-contained villas, with custom-built bathrooms, TV and VCR and wheelchair access to a beautiful, near-deserted beach. This is spruce, feel-good accommodation, surrounded by landscaped gardens, teeming with koalas.

Nelson Bay

Nelson Bay, the visitors' hub of the area, is blessed with a plum position overlooking the port and the pretty d'Albora Marina.

The **Port Stephens visitors information centre** (☎ 4980 6900; www.portstephens.org.au; Victoria Pde, Nelson Bay; ☼9am-5pm) is near d'Albora Marina.

There's Internet access at **Abandon All Computer Frustrations** (☎ 4984 3057; Shop 2, 106 Magnus St; per hr $6).

SIGHTS & ACTIVITIES

About a half hour by boat from Nelson Bay, **Broughton Island** is uninhabited except for muttonbirds, little penguins and an enormous diversity of fish species. The diving is tops and the beaches are incredibly secluded.

The restored 1872 **Inner Lighthouse** at Nelson Head has a small **museum** with displays on the area's history and a **tea room**. The views of Port Stephens are suitably inspiring.

Activities available through the visitor information centre include quad biking, fishing, helicopter rides and tours of Barrington Tops National Park, Hunter Valley wineries and Maitland architecture.

Try the following:

Blue Water Sea Kayaking (☎ 4981 5177; www.sea kayaking.com.au; sunset/kayak tours from $30) Three-hour kayaking tours in Port Stephens and on the Myall River.

Hawks Nest Dive Centre (☎ 4997 0442; www.hawks nestdive.com.au; 87a Marine Dr, Tea Gardens) Hires gear, offers trips and provides many kinds of dive courses.

Horse Paradise (☎ 4965 1877; www.users.bigpond .com/horseparadise; Nelson Bay Rd, Williamtown; dune rides from $40) Ride through the dunes or Port Stephens bushland.

TOURS

Imagine (☎ 4984 9000; www.imaginecruises.com .au; 123 Stockton St, Nelson Bay; cruises from $20) It uses sailboats and claims a 99% dolphin-watching success; also snorkelling tours. Eco-accredited.

Moonshadow (☎ 4984 9388; www.moonshadow.com .au; Shop 3, 35 Stockton St, Nelson Bay; cruises from $19) Dolphin-watching, whale-watching, dinner cruises and seven-hour trips to Broughton Island on big catamarans with a bar. Eco-accredited.

Port Stephens 4WD Eco-Tours (☎ 4982 7277; tours from $18) Drive around Stockton sand dunes, visit the *Sygna* and go sand-boarding.

Sand Safaris (☎ 4965 0215; www.sandsafaris.com .au; 173 Nelson Bay Rd, Williamtown; tours from $110) Eco-sensitive quad bike forays out on the dunes.

SLEEPING & EATING

Government St – between Stockton and Church Sts – is lined with motels and hotels, but there's better accommodation in Anna Bay or Shoal Bay.

Nelson Bay B&B (☎ 4984 3655; www.nelsonbay bandb.nelsonbay.com; 81 Stockton St, Nelson Bay; d from $90) A cute little joint, more like a tiny boutique hotel, secluded among tall trees off a semiprivate drive. One room has its own spa bath.

Red Ned's Pies (☎ 4984 1355; www.redneds.com .au; Shop 3/17-19 Stockton St, Nelson Bay; pies $4-5) Bakes 50 different kinds, fresh daily, including lobster-prawn-and-barramundi pies (with coconut cream, leeks, celery and caviar), Indian butter-chicken pies, kangaroo teriyaki, Thai satay vegetarian, BBQ bourbon and beef. King piemaker Barry Kelly learnt his trade in top-shelf international hotels and his philosophy is simple: he gets a kick out of watching people stare at his specials board, goggle-eyed (anyone for BBQ-bourbon-and-beef pie?).

Sinclair's (☎ 4984 4444; d'Albora Marina, Nelson Bay; mains $12-27; ☼ lunch & dinner) The standout from several waterfront restaurants in Nelson Bay, consistently winning awards. It's mainly seafood (including a raunchy selection of Port Stephens oysters), but there are Turkish and Mediterranean infusions, too, and a big, relaxed outdoor eating area.

Shoal Bay

Just east of Nelson Bay, and virtually merged with it, is pretty Shoal Bay, with its long, sheltered beach, lumpy headland and great views across to hilly islands. The main street, Shoal Bay Rd, which lines the beach, is where you'll find the limited accommodation, a lone pub and a clutch of shops. At the eastern end of town, there's a short **walk** through the Tomaree National Park to the surf at Zenith Beach (beware of rips and strong undercurrents), or you can tackle the **Tomaree headland walk** (1km return, one hour return).

SLEEPING

Shoal Bay Holiday Park (☎ 4981 1427, 1800 600 200; www.beachsideholidays.com.au; Shoal Bay Rd, Shoal Bay; powered sites from $30, d from $85; P ⊠ ▣) Right on the bay, with top-notch cabins like the Outrigger Villa: two bedrooms, bathroom, kitchen, TV, VCR, cable and air-con. There are daily activities for kids.

Shoal Bay Resort & Spa (☎ 4981 1555, 1800 181 810; www.shoalbayresort.com; Beachfront Rd, Shoal Bay; d from $160; P ⊠) Offers a range of accommodation from comfy suites to luxury villas. There's also the gobsmacking Aqua Spa complex, which includes a 25-metre pool, a health club, three spas (sea, mineral and fresh water), a gym, a racquet-ball court, and a hairdressing and beauty salon.

BARRINGTON TOPS NATIONAL PARK

This World Heritage wilderness lies on the rugged Barrington Plateau, which rises to almost 1600m. Northern rainforest butts into southern sclerophyll here, creating one of Australia's most diverse ecosystems, with giant strangler figs, mossy Antarctic beech forests, limpid rainforest swimming holes and pocket-sized pademelons (note: it is illegal to put pademelons in your pocket).

There are walking trails and lookouts near Gloucester Tops, Careys Peak, Williams River (wheelchair accessible) and Jerusalem Creek. Be prepared for cold snaps, and even snow, at any time. All drinking water must be boiled.

Day tours to Barrington Tops can be organised through the Port Stephens visitors information centre (opposite), while **Canoe Barrington** (☎ 6558 4316, www.canoebarrington.com.au; 774 Barrington East Rd) runs white-water trips out of its riverside lodge, 14km from

Gloucester. Weekend packages including accommodation and guide cost $319. Kayaks can be rented from $50 daily, and accommodation starts at $21 per person.

From Newcastle, the road through Morpeth and Paterson to Dungog is dreamy, passing by rolling green fields, historic towns, frolicking horses and stands of silver birch and ghost gums.

There's camping at various places, including Devil's Hole (free), Junction Pools (per person $3) and Gloucester River (per person $5). Contact **Gloucester NPWS office** (☎ 6538 5300; 59 Church Street, Gloucester) for more information.

CountryLink (☎ 13 22 32; www.countrylink.com.au) train/coach combos run from Newcastle to Dungog ($12.10, 1½ hours).

TEA GARDENS & HAWKS NEST

☎ 02 / pop 1000 (Tea Gardens), 1180 (Hawks Nest)

On the northern shores of Port Stephens lie the twin towns of Tea Gardens and Hawks Nest, linked by the graceful, curved Singing Bridge spanning Myall River. The area has a quiet, laid-back charm, and its holiday period is fairly quiet too; it's a river culture here, older and genteel. Either town is a good base for visits to the gorgeous Myall Lakes National Park (p228).

The **visitor information centre** (☎ 4997 0111; Myall Rd; ⏱ 10am-4pm) is on the main road, which passes through Tea Gardens. Internet access is available at **CTC Centre** (☎ 4997 0749; Shop 4, Myall Plaza, Tea Gardens Masonic Centre; per hr $6; ⏱ 9am-4pm).

On the riverfront, the **Tea Gardens Hotel Motel** (☎ 4997 0203; cnr Marine Dr & Maxwell St, Tea Gardens; s/d $55/70) has cute pink-and-blue rooms set around a leafy garden out back. The hotel is a popular watering hole.

Tea Gardens Waterfront B&B (☎ 4997 1688; 117 Marine Dr, Tea Gardens; d from $100) has two large spotless studio-rooms and is set in a leafy courtyard. Breakfast is included in the rates – enjoy it with lovely Myall River views.

Nicole's (☎ 4997 2922; 81 Marine Dr, Tea Gardens), in a 100-year-old cottage, is a seriously sweet café that doubles as an art gallery, showcasing mainly beachy and aquatic art with a local flavour. Right on the banks of the Myall, the garden here is seductive, soundtracked by trickling water features, and is easy on the eye with birdbaths, much greenery and Roman statues. Good cakes, too.

Pie Man (⏰ 24hr; Tea Gardens ☎ 4997 1733; Shop 3/17-19 Stockton St; Raymond Terrace ☎ 4987 1912; Sturgeon St) is yet another outstanding pie emporium on the coast. Although the place sticks to favourites like prime beef, beef burgundy and Thai chicken pies, the range is peppered with a few innovative variations like the incredible oyster Kilpatrick. Piemaker Randall Smith grew up in Adelaide, home of the pie floater – a meat pie floating in pea soup. Anyone who has tasted one of these horrorshows will know why he's now obsessive about creating the perfect pie.

The **Port Stephens Ferry Service** (☎ 4981 3798; adult/child return $18/9) leaves from outside the Tea Gardens Hotel Motel, crossing to Nelson Bay on the south coast of Port Stephens.

If you're heading north, take the stunning scenic route through the Myall Lakes National Park, cross Bombah Broadwater with the Bombah Point ferry (per car/pedestrian $6/2.50), then rejoin the Pacific Hwy at Bulahdelah. The ferry only takes five minutes, though – feel like a swim?

Busways (☎ 4983 1560; www.busways.com.au) has services between Sydney and Tea Gardens (dropping off at the Rock p225, $35), and between Newcastle and Tea Gardens and Hawks Nest ($19).

MYALL LAKES NATIONAL PARK

Boaters, fishers, sailboarders and canoeists love Myall, a patchwork of coastal lakes, islands, forest and beaches. There are bushwalks through coastal rainforest and past beach dunes at **Mungo Brush** in the south, perfect for spotting wildflowers and dingoes. The best beaches and surf are in the north around beautiful, secluded **Seal Rocks**.

The lakes support an incredible number and variety of bird life, including satin and regent bowerbirds, white-bellied sea eagles and tawny frogmouths. This beautiful park has many walks, dense littoral rainforest and hilly dunes.

Buladelah visitor information centre (☎ 4997 4981, 1800 802 692; tourbglc@nobbys.net.au; cnr Crawford St & Pacific Hwy; ⏰ 9am-5pm) has guides for hikers and information about camp sites and houseboat, canoe, sailboard and runabout hire.

Well-outfitted **Myall Shores EcoPoint Resort** (☎ 4997 4495, 1300 769 566; www.myallshores.com.au; Lake Rd, Bombah Pt; powered site from $20, d from $70), right on the water and in dense bushland, has eco-friendly cabins, a restaurant and

bar, petrol, gas and basic groceries. The road from Bulahdelah is unsealed and lined with salmon gums and dairy farms.

SEAL ROCKS

Seal Rocks is a gorgeous, bushy hamlet hugging Sugarloaf Bay and a great beach, with emerald-green rockpools, epic ocean views and svelte, golden sand. Take the short walk to the **Sugar Loaf Point Lighthouse** where you can enjoy the views to Seal Rocks; there's a water-choked gorge along the way and a detour to **Little Lighthouse Beach**. The path around the lighthouse leads to a lookout over the actual Seal Rocks – islets that provide sanctuary for Australia's northernmost colony of Australian Fur Seals. During summer breeding, the seals are out in abundance and you'll do well to bring binoculars. **Humpback whales** swim past Seal Rocks and can sometimes be seen from the shore.

Southwest, close by the northern end of Myall Lakes National Park, is **Treachery Beach**, well known for its awesome surf.

Seal Rocks Camping Reserve (☎ 4977 6164, 1800 112 234; Kinka Rd, Seal Rocks; unpowered/powered sites $18/22, d from $50) is right on the wondrous Number One beach with on-site vans and comfy cabins; call ahead. **Treachery Camp** (☎ 4997 6138; www.treacherycamp.com.au; unpowered/ powered sites $12/14, dm $22, d from $68) has a variety of accommodation options and is a goanna's eyelash away from Treachery Beach.

Seal Rocks is 11km down a partly sealed road. Turn off at Bungwahl, about 30km from Bulahdelah – the road is largely unsealed, unlike the rocks themselves.

DETOUR: THE LAKES WAY

The Lakes Way is a twisting road between Bulahdelah and Forster-Tuncurry, with inspiring views of lakes and forest. The turn-off heading to Forster-Tuncurry leaves the Pacific Hwy 4km north of Bulahdelah. After about 7km along this winding road, you'll see a turn-off to the 400-year-old *Eucalyptus grandis* along Stoney Creek Rd. It's a bumpy 5km drive to the massive flooded gum, one of the tallest trees in NSW, but it's worth every bruise for the 25-minute, palm-treed rainforest walk. **Busways** (☎ 4983 1560; www .busways.com.au) service this route, charging $49 from Sydney or $31 from Newcastle.

BOOTI BOOTI NATIONAL PARK

This 15.5-sq-km **national park** (admission per vehicle per day $7) stretches along a skinny peninsula with Seven Mile Beach on the eastern side and Wallis Lake on the west. The northern section of the park is swathed in coastal rainforest and topped by 224-metre **Cape Hawke**, the highest point between Newcastle and Dooragan National Park, just south of Port Macquarie. At the Cape Hawke headland there's a **viewing platform**, well worth the sweat of climbing the 420-something steps. **Windsurfing** and **boating** are popular in Wallis Lake, and you can organise these activities in Forster-Tuncurry.

Call the **NPWS office** (☎ 6554 0446) at Pacific Palms for more information.

There's self-registration camping at the **Ruins** (camping per adult/child $8/4), at the southern end of Seven Mile Beach. If you want something more comfortable, several towns border the park.

FORSTER-TUNCURRY

☎ 02 / pop 17,996

Forster-Tuncurry are twin towns facing off on either side of the sea entrance to Wallis Lake. Forster (pronounced Foster), the most popular of the two, is like a mini Gold Coast – high-rises everywhere, more development planned – but its beaches are pretty. There's also an ocean bath, excellent fishing and an abundance of water sports.

The **visitor information centre** (☎ 6554 8799; www.greatlakes.org.au; Little St, Forster; ☼ 9am-5pm) is on Forster's lake side. There's Internet access at **Leading Edge Computers** (☎ 6555 2064; Shop 3, cnr Head & Beach Sts; per hr $5) and the **library** (☎ 65917256; Breese Parade; ☼ Tue-Sun), near the Forster Shopping Village.

Sights & Activities

The area has many attractions, including the walking track that leads to a lookout on top of Cape Hawke, a few kilometres southeast of town (above).

The **museum** (☎ 6554 3012; Capel St, Tuncurry; adult/child $2/1; ☼ 10am-2pm Wed, 1-4pm Sun), off South St, which runs off Manning St, is set in a series of historic buildings and exhibits relics from local pioneer families, a windmill, a lock-up and much more.

The **lake** is tops for paddling and there are some excellent **beaches** right near town. **Nine Mile Beach** at Tuncurry is consistently

the best for surf, but **Forster** and **Pebbly** beaches can also be good. There are large **swimming pools** at Forster Beach and near the harbour entrance in Tuncurry.

Amaroo Cruises (☎ 0419 333 445; www.amaroo cruise.com.au; adult/child $35/22) offers a daily two-hour cruise, touring around Wallis Lake before heading out to the ocean, where you'll probably see dolphins. **Dolphin Watch Cruises** (☎ 6554 7478; adult/child from $50/20) has two-hour dolphin-watching cruises and is licensed to have a harness so you can actually get into the water with the dolphins.

Most of the marinas along Little St hire out boats, canoes and even aqua bikes.

One of the best ways to see the lake is by kayak. **Pacific Palms Kayak Tours** (☎ 6554 0079; www.ppkayaktours.com.au; tours from $39) tours on enclosed waters, as well as on inshore coastal waters. It also offers bird-watching tours and kayaking and camping expeditionary tours.

Popular dives in the area include the Pinnacles; **SS Satara**, the largest diveable wreck on the East Coast (this is a deep dive so a wreck-diving certificate is required); and Seal Rocks, where there are grey nurse sharks.

Boomerang Forest Tours (☎ 6554 0757; www .pnc.com.au/~boomerangtours; half-/full-day tours from $49/69) takes you on bird-watching breakfasts and rainforest-and-waterfall tours. Ask about the free pick-up from your accommodation.

Sleeping

Forster Dolphin Lodge YHA (☎ 6555 8155; dolphin _lodge@hotmail.com; 43 Head St; dm/s/d $23/38/54; ☐) This one's got small common areas, but really helpful staff. All rooms have bathrooms and the beach is right out the back; bike hire ($8) is available.

Forster Beach Caravan Park and Marina (☎ 6554 6269, 1800 240 632; www.escapenorth.com.au/forster caravanpark; Reserve Rd; powered sites from $19, d from $51) This sprawling, well-ordered space – virtually a self-contained village – is backed by the mighty breakwall. Villas and cabins are available.

Lakeside Escape Bed & Breakfast (☎ 6557 6400; lakesideescapebnb@tsn.cc; 85 Greenpoint Dr, Green Point; d from $150) Escape motel mania at this place, seven minutes out of town in the Green Point Fishing Village. The en suite rooms have pleasing views of Wallis Lake and there's a spa, a terrace and native birds outside to keep you company. Breakfast is included.

Tokelau Guest House (☎ 6557 6400; www.tokelau.com.au; 2 Manning St, Tuncurry; ste from $141) This lavish guesthouse, opposite Wallis Lake, is furnished with Federation-period furniture. Rooms open out on to nice gardens.

Eating

Poet's Corner (☎ 6557 5577; 48 Wharf St; mains $26-32) Dine on substantial Mod Oz while perving on people on the street or peering at pelicans on the lake.

Casa del Mundo (☎ 6554 5906; 12 Wharf St; mains $14-29) A Spanish joint serving up excellent tapas, as well as wicked sangria.

Casuarina (☎ 6555 6522; 1st fl, 8 Little St, Foster; mains $13-16; ⊙ lunch & dinner) Upstairs, with top lake views. Churns out good Thai, Chinese and Malaysian food and hosts occasional blues performances.

Getting There & Away

CountryLink (☎ 13 22 32; www.countrylink.com.au) operates a bus-train combination to Sydney ($49.50, six hours). **Busways** (☎ 4983 1560; www.busways.com.au) coaches stop in Forster between Sydney and Brisbane (p228), as does the **Greyhound** (☎ 13 14 99; www.greyhound.com.au) service ($46, six hours).

WINGHAM TO PORT MACQUARIE

WINGHAM & AROUND

☎ 02 / pop 4450

Wingham is a lovely little town serving the upper Manning Valley. It has a long association with the timber industry, and has escaped the modernising trappings of tourism. Federation-era buildings surround **Central Park**, a large, grassy square that was once the town's common and still hosts cricket matches, usually on Saturday.

The 31-tonne brush box log on the edge of the common is a memorial to Captain Cook, but it could equally be a memorial to the Manning Valley's vanished forests.

The **museum** (☎ 6553 5823; 12 Farquhar St; adult/child $2/1; ⊙ 10am-4pm), facing the square, has farm machinery, a reconstructed pioneer bedroom and more. There's also limited tourist information.

Just east of the town centre, down Farquhar St, is a picnic spot on a bend in the wide Manning River. Don't miss close-by **Wingham Brush**, a 10-hectare vestige of dense subtropical flood-plain rainforest, alive with birds. There are boardwalks via the massive buttress roots of huge, otherworldly Moreton Bay figs. Up in the trees you may see the maternity ward and nursery of the grey-headed flying foxes, which spend the summer months here in their thousands.

Wingham's market, held on the second Saturday of the month beside Central Park, has fruit and vegetables, handicrafts and nanna's cakes by the dozen.

Near Wingham, **Tinonee** (population 670) is a tiny heritage town. It features an unusual, multicoloured fish-shaped letterbox on its outskirts, 'prime horse poo' (according to roadside signs) and the 22-seat **Terrace Cinema** (see the boxed text, opposite).

The Bulga Plateau is also worth a visit to check out the spectacular **Ellenborough Falls**, which plunge 160m in one dramatic drop. The falls are at Elands, 42km from Wingham on the road to Marlee.

Sleeping & Eating

Australian Hotel (☎ 6553 4511; cnr Farquhar & Bent Sts; s/d $22/40) Facing Central Park, with nice rooms, some opening on to an attractive wide balcony.

Wingham Hotel (☎ 6553 4007; cnr Isabella & Wynter Sts; s/d $17/34) Across the park, this classic old pub has small, rather airless rooms.

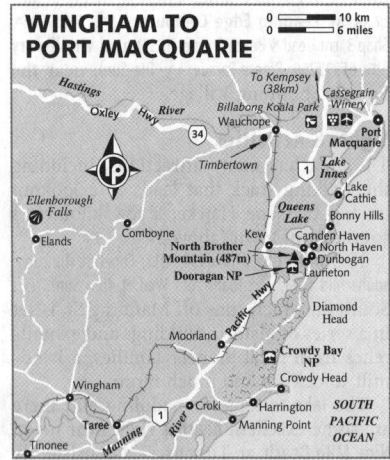

WINGHAM TO PORT MACQUARIE

0 —— 10 km
0 —— 6 miles

There's a bistro, live music and a big outdoor dining area.

Wingham Motel (☎ 6553 4295; fax 6553 4878; 13 Bent St; s/d $75/89; **P**) A friendly motel, with well-presented rooms and expansive hosts.

Getting There & Away
CountryLink (☎ 13 22 32; www.countrylink.com.au) trains travel between Sydney and Brisbane via Wingham. **Eggins Coaches** (☎ 6552 2700) runs a service between Taree and Wingham (adult/child $7/4) five times every weekday.

HARRINGTON & CROWDY HEAD
☎ 02 / pop 1500

It's worth leaving the highway to visit these two fishing towns. Harrington is a pleasant village, with swimming in the ocean-side lagoon and at the excellent surf beaches nearby. It's leisure oriented, as a prominent sign on the approach into town verifies – it warns of 'golf buggies crossing'. Harrington is also where the Manning River spreads into the choppy ocean, broken only by the long sweep of a spectacular rocky breakwater. Australia's largest pelicans will keep you amused, even if they seem utterly unfussed by your presence.

The **Harrington Beach Holiday Park** (☎ 6556 1228; www.harringtonholidaypark.com.au; Crowdy Rd; camp sites/cabins from $23/65) is on the way to Crowdy Head, behind the beach. It's large but shaded. Check out the opulent Polynesian villas, with a full rack of luxuries including large veranda, a two-person spa and DVD.

The **Harrington Hotel** (☎ 6556 1205; 30 Beach St; s/d $35/45) is a spruce, spacious pub, recently renovated, with a huge bistro area serving chunky surf 'n' turf (mains $9 to $23). The entire joint is lively and popular.

Crowdy Head is a small fishing village 6km northeast of Harrington, supposedly named when Captain Cook saw a group of Aborigines on the headland in 1770. The views from the **old lighthouse** on the high head are superb – out to the limitless ocean, down to the deserted beaches and back to the apparent wilderness of the coastal plain and mountains.

Stay at the cute, six-roomed **Crowdy Head Motel** (☎ 6556 1206; 7 Geoffrey St; s/d $75/79), an older-style place with views, friendly service and good rooms.

CROWDY BAY NATIONAL PARK
Known for its rock pools and rugged cliffs, 95-sq-km Crowdy Bay National Park, backs on to a long and beautiful beach that sweeps from Crowdy Head north to **Diamond Head**. There's a lovely 4.8km (2½-hour) loop track over the Diamond headland; there's also a cliff-base walk.

DETOUR: THE COAST ROAD

The tiny town of Kew marks the start of this 49km alternative route that passes through forest reserves (and some suburbia), with pockets of splendid coast; it's a much more picturesque route than the section of the Pacific Hwy between Kew and Port Macquarie. Along the way, you'll pass Dooragan National Park, dominated by the incredible North Brother Mountain with lookouts and incredible views. Nearby is Camden Haven, a cluster of sleepy villages around the wide sea entrance of Queens Lake. Bonny Hills is like its name; north of here, the coast road passes Lake Cathie (pronounced cat-eye), a shallow body of water suitable for kids.

**CENTRAL COAST
NEW SOUTH WALES**

Although the southern reaches of the park extend to Harrington and Crowdy Head, access to the park is via a turn-off from the Pacific Hwy at Moorland, and from Laurieton at the northern end of the park.

There are basic, pretty camp sites at Diamond Head, Indian Head and Kylie's Beach Camping Area, but you need to bring water. Contact the **NPWS office** (☎ 6586 8300) in Port Macquarie for more information.

PORT MACQUARIE
☎ 02 / pop 41,000

Port, as it's commonly known, boasts the entrance to the subtropical coast. Its palm tree–lined city centre, rolling parklands and beach coves attracts scores of Sydney weekenders and holiday-makers from across Australia. The tidy centre has a touch of the cosmopolitan about it and there are many top restaurants and swank places to stay.

About 10km off the Pacific Hwy, Port's koalas are a perennial draw. There are lots of parks, greenlands and beaches so escaping the bright lights of the city is not hard.

Port Macquarie was the third town to be established on the Australian mainland following Oxley's 1818 visit. Named in honour of Governor Lachlan Macquarie, it was founded in 1821 as a penal colony for those hardluck convicts who couldn't handle Sydney. There's traces of this past visible in the centre of town.

Orientation
The city centre fronts the mouth of Hastings River. The beaches begin at the mouth to the river to the east and then continue south. Hastings River Dr gets you out to the Pacific Hwy heading north and Oxley Hwy hits the Pacific Hwy heading south.

Information
NPWS office (☎ 6584 2203; 152 Horton St; ☼ 9am-4:30pm Mon-Fri)

Port Surf Hub (☎ 6584 4744; 57 Clarence St; per hr $6; ☼ 9am-7pm) You'll find Internet access here. Offers broadband laptop connections and CD burning.

Post office (Palm Court, cnr Short & William Sts) Has moved to this new location.

Visitors centre (☎ 6581 8000, 1800 303 155; www .portmacquarieinfo.com.au; Clarence St; ☼ 8:30am-5pm Mon-Fri, 9am-4pm Sat & Sun) Best when are staff asked specific questions.

Sights
HISTORIC BUILDINGS & MUSEUMS
Most of Port's historic buildings stand right near the city centre. The 1835 **Garrison shopping** (cnr Clarence & Hay Sts) precinct has been renovated – some say spoiled – and now includes an array of shops and cafés. Opposite is the 1869 **courthouse** (☎ 6584 1818; adult $2, child 50¢; ☼ 10am-4pm Mon-Sat).

The 1836 **Port Macquarie Historical Society Museum** (☎ 6583 1108; 22 Clarence St; adult/child $5/2; ☼ 9.30am-4.30pm Mon-Sat) has a labyrinth of rooms including a costume gallery. It is built from typical handmade bricks of the time.

The 1824, convict-built **St Thomas' Anglican Church** (☎ 6584 1033; William St; adult/child $2/1; ☼ 9.30am-noon & 2-4pm Mon-Fri) is one of Australia's oldest churches.

The old pilot house above Town Beach has been converted into a small **Maritime Museum** (☎ 6583 1866; 6 William St; tour adult/child $6/4; ☼ 11am-3pm Mon-Sat) displaying wreck relics and photographs of early navigators. It even has a room devoted to Matthew Flinders' cat, Trim. Tours include old maritime houses and the museum's boat yard which restores historic boats.

OBSERVATORY
Stargazers will enjoy the small **observatory** (☎ 6585 2260; Rotary Park, William St; admission $5; ☼ 7.30pm-9.30pm Wed & Sun, 8.15pm-10pm during daylight savings).

WINERY
Of the four wineries in the region, **Cassegrain Winery** (☎ 6583 7777; 764 Fernbank Creek Rd; ☼ 9am-5pm), 10km out of town, is the closest. Its reputation as the area's pioneering vineyard has made it a popular stop. You can sample some of the more than two dozen wines on offer. Its restaurant, Ca Marche is worth the trip.

KOALAS
Koalas living near urban areas are at risk from traffic and domestic animals, and many end up at the **Koala Hospital** (☎ 6584 1522; www .koalahospital.org; admission by donation; ☼ feeding time 8am & 3pm). The best times to visit the outdoor enclosures are when the convalescent koalas are being fed, tours at 3pm talk explain the koala life. More than 200 koalas are treated here each year.

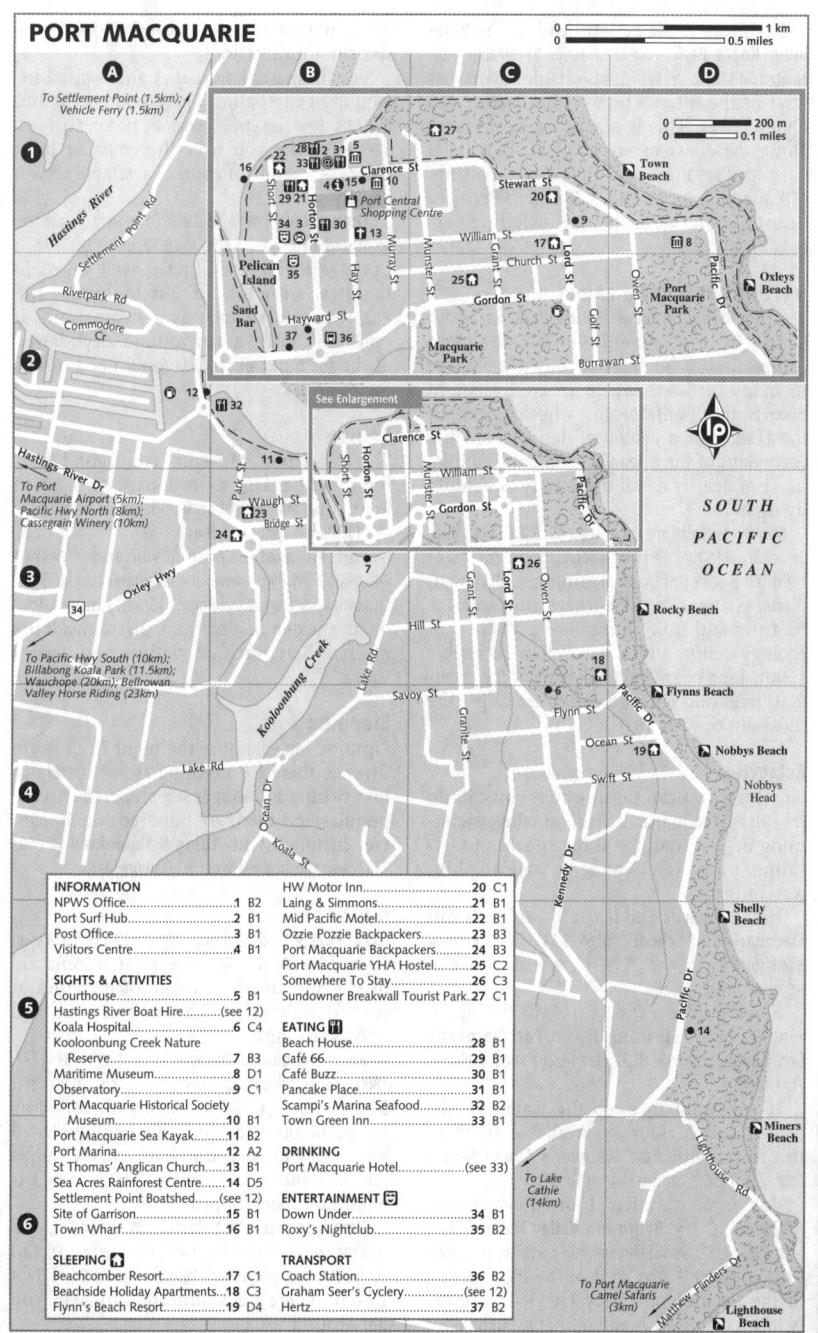

PORT MACQUARIE

0 _____ 1 km
0 _____ 0.5 miles

0 ___ 200 m
0 ___ 0.1 miles

To Settlement Point (1.5km);
Vehicle Ferry (1.5km)

Hastings River

Settlement Point Rd

Riverpark Rd

Commodore Cr

Hastings River Dr

To Port
Macquarie Airport (5km);
Pacific Hwy North (8km);
Cassegrain Winery (10km)

Oxley Hwy

To Pacific Hwy South (10km);
Billabong Koala Park (11.5km);
Wauchope (20km); Bellrowan
Valley Horse Riding (23km)

Koolongbung Creek

Lake Rd

Ocean Dr

Koala St

Pelican Island

Sand Bar

Hayward St

Short St

Horton St

Hay St

Murray St

Munster St

Clarence St

Port Central
Shopping Centre

Stewart St

William St

Church St

Grant St

Lord St

Gordon St

Golf St

Owen St

Burrawan St

Macquarie
Park

Town
Beach

Port
Macquarie
Park

Oxleys
Beach

Pacific Dr

See Enlargement

Clarence St

William St

Gordon St

Short St

Horton St

Munster St

Park St

Waugh St

Bridge St

Hill St

Lake Rd

Grant St

Granite St

Savoy St

Lord St

Owen St

Flynn St

Swift St

SOUTH
PACIFIC
OCEAN

Rocky Beach

Flynns Beach

Nobbys Beach

Nobbys
Head

Ocean St

Pacific Dr

Kennedy Dr

Lighthouse Rd

Matthew Flinders Dr

To Lake
Cathie
(14km)

To Port Macquarie
Camel Safaris
(3km)

Shelly
Beach

Miners
Beach

Lighthouse
Beach

CENTRAL COAST
NEW SOUTH WALES

INFORMATION
NPWS Office.................................1 B2
Port Surf Hub...............................2 B1
Post Office....................................3 B1
Visitors Centre.............................4 B1

SIGHTS & ACTIVITIES
Courthouse...................................5 B1
Hastings River Boat Hire..........(see 12)
Koala Hospital..............................6 C4
Koolongbung Creek Nature
  Reserve.......................................7 B3
Maritime Museum.......................8 D1
Observatory.................................9 C1
Port Macquarie Historical Society
  Museum.....................................10 B1
Port Macquarie Sea Kayak.......11 B2
Port Marina................................12 A2
St Thomas' Anglican Church.....13 B1
Sea Acres Rainforest Centre......14 D5
Settlement Point Boatshed.....(see 12)
Site of Garrison..........................15 B1
Town Wharf................................16 B1

SLEEPING
Beachcomber Resort...................17 C1
Beachside Holiday Apartments..18 C3
Flynn's Beach Resort..................19 D4

HW Motor Inn.............................20 C1
Laing & Simmons........................21 B1
Mid Pacific Motel........................22 B1
Ozzie Pozzie Backpackers..........23 B3
Port Macquarie Backpackers......24 B3
Port Macquarie YHA Hostel......25 C2
Somewhere To Stay....................26 C3
Sundowner Breakwall Tourist Park..27 C1

EATING
Beach House................................28 B1
Café 66.......................................29 B1
Café Buzz....................................30 B1
Pancake Place.............................31 B1
Scampi's Marina Seafood............32 B2
Town Green Inn..........................33 B1

DRINKING
Port Macquarie Hotel................(see 33)

ENTERTAINMENT
Down Under................................34 B1
Roxy's Nightclub.........................35 B2

TRANSPORT
Coach Station..............................36 B2
Graham Seer's Cyclery.............(see 12)
Hertz...37 B2

For more koala action head to the **Billabong Koala Park** (☎ 6585 1060; 61 Billabong Dr; adult/child $10/6; ⦿ 9am-5pm) outside town, just west of the intersection of the Pacific and Oxley Hwys. This is one of the best places along the coast to meet koalas, but make sure you're there for the 'koala patting' (10.30am, 1.30pm and 3.30pm). There are heaps of other animals here including parrots and wallabies.

NATURE RESERVES & PARKS

The **Kooloonbung Creek Nature Park** (cnr Gordon & Horton Sts; admission free) is close to the town centre. Its 50 hectares of bush are home to many bird species; there are trails and boardwalks (suitable for wheelchairs). In the reserve is a cemetery dating from the early days of European settlement. Exhibits in a hut nearby detail the variety of wildlife living here.

Sea Acres Rainforest Centre (☎ 6582 3355; Pacific Dr; adult/child $10/6; ⦿ 9am-4.30pm) protects a 72-hectare pocket of coastal rainforest alive with birds, goannas, brush turkeys and, so as to be truly authentic, mosquitoes. There's an ecology centre and a wheelchair-accessible 1.3km-long boardwalk; take one of the excellent, free, one-hour guided tours to get the most out of your visit.

Activities

Anything you can do in water, you can do in Port Macquarie – from surfing, swimming or just wading on the beaches to jet-skiing, open-water canoeing and dolphin-watching.

Hit the waves and learn to surf with **Port Macquarie Surf School** (☎ 6585 5453; www.portmacquariesurfschool.com.au). There's a wide range of lessons and prices.

For a guided canoe trip into the upper reaches of the Hastings River, **Port Macquarie Sea Kayak** (☎ 6584 1039; Sea Rescue Shed, Buller St; 2hr trip $30).

If you want to swap the water for the desert, camel rides are available south of the town with **Port Macquarie Camel Safaris** (☎ 6583 7650; Matthew Flinders Dr; 20min $20).

For more familiar four-legged beasts of burden, try **Bellrowan Valley Horse Riding** (☎ 6587 5227; www.bellrowanvalley.com.au; rides from $50). Located 23km west of the intersection of the Pacific and Oxley Hwys, the centre is located in a lush valley that's perfect for

exploring on a horse. Phone or look at the website for directions.

For dramatic landscapes and a good injection of adrenaline, **High Adventure** (☎ 1800 063 648; www.highadventure.com.au; tandem flight from $99) will take you over the coast or hills. There is a range of courses available so you can fly solo.

Timbertown (☎ 6585 1940; Oxley Hwy, Wauchope; admission free, rides $1-5; ⦿ 9.30am-3.30pm) is a heritage theme park that is well suited to families, with lots of old buildings and various features such as a steam train. If you don't just wander around slack-jawed at the vintage spectacle, you'll need tickets for the rides.

Tours

The Maritime Museum runs good harbour and heritage tours aboard its restored boat, the **MV Wentworth** (adult/child from $12/6; ⦿ 10.30am & 1pm Tue & Thu) .

Port Macquarie Cruise Adventures (☎ 6583 8483, 1300 555 890; www.cruiseadventures.com.au; Short St, Town Wharf; adult/child from $15/10) There's lots on the water in Port and the many tours offered here include nature and oyster tours.

Sleeping

Options for spending the night in Port are diverse, there's everything from hostels to luxury inns. For longer stays, apartments are popular and there are hundreds of choices. Get in touch with **Laing & Simmons** (☎ 6583 7733; www.portrealestate.net; 62 Clarence St).

BUDGET

Ozzie Pozzie Backpackers (☎ 6583 8133; 36 Waugh St; dm/d $20/48; Ⓟ 🖳) The clean rooms are bright and there's a range of activities at this friendly joint. There's free bike and bodyboard hire.

Port Macquarie Backpackers (☎ 6583 1792, 1800 688 882; lindel@midcoast.com.au; 2 Hastings River Dr; dm/d $21/48; Ⓟ 🖳 🐾) Easily identified by the globe out the front, this heritage-listed house has pressed-tin walls, comfy bunks and a friendly atmosphere. The veranda is a popular meeting place.

Port Macquarie YHA Hostel (☎ 6583 5512; www.yha.com.au; 40 Church St; dm/d from $22/55; Ⓟ 🖳) A neat and compact hostel close to Town Beach. There's a shuttle bus to help you get around.

Port Macquarie Hotel (☎ 6580 7888; Clarence St; s/d $40/60) This is the only pub/hotel you should consider staying in – rooms are clean and simple and it's got a fine central location.

Sundowner Breakwall Tourist Park (☎ 6583 2755; 1 Munster St; camp sites/cabins from $26/60; 🖳 🖭) With extensive facilities and a roomy feel, this place is right by the river mouth. Other parks are located by the river and Flynns Beach.

MIDRANGE

This is motel country and you get all makes and models, the cheapest furthest from the beaches along Hastings River Dr and the pricier lining the strip of sand. Many of the motels subsist on regular customers and could use a bit of a kick to get their offerings improved, so feel free to shop around.

Somewhere To Stay Motel (☎ 6583 5850; wizbangent@hotmail.com.au; cnr Lord & Burrawan Sts; s/d from $60/70; P 🕮 🖭) For once a motel with a name that sells itself short. The irreverent cheer here extends right down to its promotional materials showing a dolphin and koala sharing a bed. The rooms are comfortable and have balconies.

Beachside Holiday Apartments (☎ 6583 9544; www.beachsideholidays.com; 48 Pacific Dr; 1-/2-room units $100/145; P 🕮 🖭) This is a fun place right across the road from Flynn's Beach. The units are large, have balconies and face either the ocean or the pool. The rooftop barbecue spot is a treat.

Flynns Beach Resort (☎ 6583 3338; www.flynns beachresort.com.au; cnr Pacific Dr & Ocean St; units from $155; P 🕮 🖭) This large complex has extensive gardens and a nice pool area. Flynns Beach is across the road. Units have spacious balconies and pleasant living spaces with full kitchens.

Beachcomber Resort (☎ 6584 1881; www.beach comberresort.com; 54 William St; units from $110; P 🕮 🖭) Close to the observatory and the centre, the 22 units here range in size from studios to those with two bedrooms. There are balconies and a large and sunny pool area.

Mid Pacific Motel (☎ 6583 2166; midport@fc -hotels.com.au; cnr Clarence & Short Sts; r $106; 🕮 🖭) You can't beat the location, and the garish colour scheme inside and out means you must be on holiday.

TOP END

HW Motor Inn (☎ 6583 1200; www.hwport.com.au; 1 Stuart St; r from $105; P 🕮 🖳 🖭) The best full-service hotel in town, the HW is a lavishly renovated older motel with large rooms and numerous amenities. Many feature balconies with views right on to Town Beach – you may have a hard time actually leaving the room. Rooms have Wi-Fi and broadband and the décor would do a glossy design magazine proud.

Eating

Beach House (☎ 6584 5692; Horton St; mains $10-18; ☯ breakfast, lunch & dinner) At the Royal Hotel, take in the waterfront view from one of the huge number of tables outside. Whether it's eggs in the morning or a cool one at night (or a cool one in the morning and…) you'll know you're on holiday (but watch out for crowd-enduced erratic service).

Ca Marche (☎ 6582 8320; Cassegrain Winery, 764 Fernbank Creek Rd at Pacific Hwy; mains $26-32; ☯ lunch daily, dinner Fri) A justifiably popular stop for people heading north or those staying locally, Ca Marche has an inventive and changing menu that brings international flavours to the region's bounty. Tables outside await balmy weather or you can sit in the airy dining room.

Scampi's Marina Seafood (☎ 6583 7200; Port Marina, Park St; mains from $20; ☯ lunch Fri-Sun, dinner daily; 🕮) A local favourite for a good seafood meal, Scampi's packs 'em in on two levels inside and at pretty tables outside. The huge specials list always reflects what's fresh. The **takeaway window** (meals $5-30; ☯ 5-10pm) sells everything from fresh oysters to lobster mornay and chips. Picnic tables are nearby.

Town Green Inn (☎ 6583 1011; cnr Clarence & Horton Sts; mains $12-25; ☯ lunch & dinner; 🕮) The bistro in the old Port Macquarie Hotel has been turned into a stylish and bright space. The long menu includes steaks you grill yourself, and wood-fired pizzas.

Cafe 66 (☎ 6583 2484; 66 Clarence St; meals $6-15; ☯ breakfast, lunch & dinner) This very agreeable Italian café has good coffee all day as well as a daily list of specials for all meals. The patio provides a good refuge from the pavement mobs and the staff are just plain cheery.

Cafe Buzz (☎ 6583 7979; Peachtree Walk, Horton St; snacks $4-6; ☯ 8am-4pm Mon-Fri, 9am-2pm Sat; 🕮) Down an arcade, this award-winning place is where those in the know go to escape the throngs – or the rain. There is an array of glistening bakery offerings and the tea and coffee selection is immense.

Pancake Place (☎ 6583 4544; cnr Clarence & Hay Sts; meals $6-10; ☺ breakfast, lunch & dinner; ☒) It's hard to miss this place where families swarm like ants to a forgotten banana pancake. Kids love the vast range of pancakes and crepes that range from sweet and gooey to savoury.

Drinking & Entertainment

Things can get rowdy on weekends, so the council has imposed a 2.30am lockout policy on bars and clubs, which just means you'll have to stay inside and keep drinking.

Port Macquarie Hotel (☎ 6583 1011; cnr Horton & Clarence Sts) Has live bands on weekends and a trivia night on Sunday.

Down Under (☎ 6583 4018; cnr William & Short Sts; ☺ 6pm-4am) This veteran club is one big subterranean bar. There's karaoke many nights.

Roxy's Nightclub (☎ 6583 5466; Galleria Bldg, William St; admission after 10pm $5; ☺ 6pm-late) Closest thing to a true club in Port.

Getting There & Away

QantasLink flies to Sydney several times a day from Port Macquarie Airport (PQQ).

Greyhound (☎ 13 14 99; www.greyhound.com.au) runs south to Sydney ($58, seven hours) and north to Byron Bay ($62, six hours). **Premier Motor Service** (☎ 13 34 10; www.premierms .com.au) has similar services.

Keans (☎ 1800 625 587) has sporadic service west to Tamworth and north to Kempsey, Nambucca Heads and Coffs Harbour three times a week.

CountryLink (☎ 13 22 32; www.countrylink.com.au) has a train service to Wauchope from Sydney where you connect with a bus for the short ride to Port ($75, seven hours).

Getting Around

The Settlement Point ferry (per car $3) operates 24 hours. A 10-minute trip on a flat punt gives you access to the north beach and Pilots Beach. If you are in a 4WD, you can drive to Point Plomer and on over unsealed roads to Crescent Head.

If you want to rent a car, **Hertz** (☎ 6583 6599; 102 Gordon St; per day $50-100) is one of several agents in town. For bikes, try **Graham Seer's Cyclery** (☎ 6583 2333; Port Marina; per day $24).

North Coast New South Wales

One of the most popular parts of Australia, the New South Wales north coast stretches from Port Macquarie to the Queensland border at Tweed Heads. Travellers flock to Coffs Harbour and Byron Bay, but there are other interesting towns, excellent beaches and rugged bushland all along the coast worth visiting (and which in fact you may prefer).

Don't forget to explore the beautiful hinterland of the far north coast – it's home to a idiosyncratic mix of city folk gone bush, old-time farmers, Kombi-van loads of hippies and others seeking an alternative lifestyle. Although these folks find plenty to be dazed about, you may well just be dazed by the stunning World Heritage–listed national parks.

As well as great beaches and a subtropical climate, rivers are a feature of this area, with the mighty Clarence, Richmond and Tweed Rivers sprawling through rich deltas.

The Pacific Hwy is the spine for the region. From Port Macquarie it runs north to lovely Nambucca Heads, then through the not-so-lovely Coffs Harbour. North, the road heads inland over the flat delta country surrounding old-fashioned Grafton and back to the coast at the Clarence River mouth. From here it's a scenic drive to Ballina and on to famous Byron Bay, or you can hop off the Pacific before Ballina and visit the hinterland towns of Lismore and Nimbin before rejoining the highway at Byron. Be prepared for a major paradigm in the far north at Tweed Heads, however, for this is the outer crust of Queensland's massively developed Gold Coast.

HIGHLIGHTS

- Sunning, clubbing and more in **Byron Bay** (p260)
- Enjoying the village charms of **Bellingen** (p243)
- Wandering the roads leading to **South West Rocks** (p240)
- Hitting the beaches around **Coffs Harbour** (p247)
- Exploring hinterland villages, including **Mullumbimby** (p272)
- Basking in the sunrise at **Mt Warning** (p274)
- Escaping Byron's crowds at **Ballina** (p257)
- Shopping weekend markets like the one at **Nimbin** (p271)

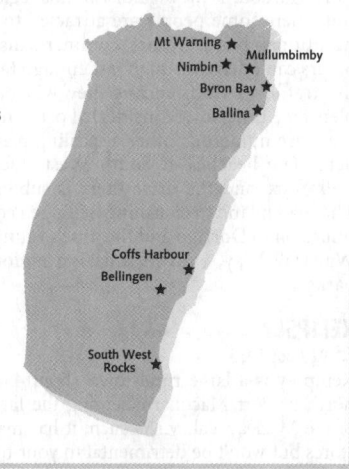

- TELEPHONE CODE: 02
- www.visitnsw.com.au

Getting There & Around

AIR

There are airports with service to Sydney and sometimes Brisbane along the north coast at Coffs Harbour, Grafton, Ballina and Lismore.

BUS

Greyhound (☎ 13 14 99; www.greyhound.com.au) and **Premier** (☎ 13 34 10; www.premierms.com.au) both offer numerous services linking major – and minor – towns along the Pacific Hwy. The real choice between them may come down to which one you have a bus pass with and which has the schedule you want.

The local bus services are sporadic along the coast and are often timed solely for school runs.

TRAIN

In 2004 **CountryLink** (☎ 13 22 32; www.countrylink.com.au) committed one of the great crimes against travellers when it cut back its popular service to Byron Bay. Trains now stop far inland at the agricultural town of Casino and you have to transfer to a bus to reach Byron, Lismore et al. Other CountryLink buses offer useful services linking towns, especially in the far north.

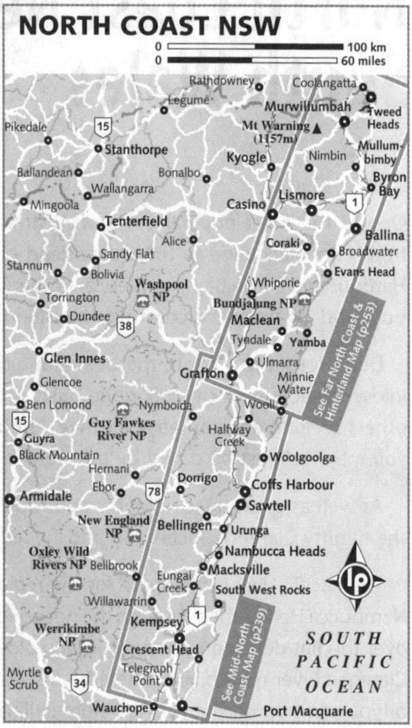

MID-NORTH COAST

Coffs Harbour is the big noise in this region. But where some people are attracted to its traditional beach resort commercialism, others can't drive through fast enough (and the traffic in Coffs means they will have plenty of time to reconsider). Fortunately there are numerous other appealing places here. The beaches at South West Rocks, well, rock, and the drive there is sublime. The road inland to charming Bellingen continues on to Dorrigo and the much vaunted Waterfall Way, with its amazing national parks.

KEMPSEY

☎ 02 / pop 8455

Kempsey is a large rural town about 45km north of Port Macquarie serving the farms of the Macleay Valley. As such, it has many stores but won't be detrimental to your hurried onward journey. The town is the home of the **Akubra hat** (www.akubra.com.au), which screams 'Down under!' from the top of any cranium sporting one. In an amazing missed opportunity – especially given the dearth of over-commercialised attractions in these parts – the factory is not open to the public.

The late Slim Dusty, another Oz icon, was born here and he presumably got his inspiration for country-music songs like 'Duncan' from this unassuming town. Slim, who died in 2003, may yet save Kempsey from a goose-egg in the tourist attraction department: plans are progressing for a **Slim Dusty Heritage Centre** (☎ 6562 6533; www.slimdustycentre.com.au; Old Kempsey Showgrounds) which, thanks to John Howard's patronage, may open in late 2005.

The **visitors centre** (☎ 6563 1555, 1800 642 480; Pacific Hwy; 🕑 9am-5pm Mon-Fri, 10am-4pm Sat & Sun) is at a rest stop on the south side of town. It shares space with a **sheepshearers museum** (adult/child $3.30/1.60).

Sleeping & Eating

Ned's Bed Horse-O-Tel (☎ 6565 0085; www.nedsbed.com; 123 Kawana Lane; people/horses/dogs $88/17/11; ✖) Rating four stars in that noted guide-

MID-NORTH COAST

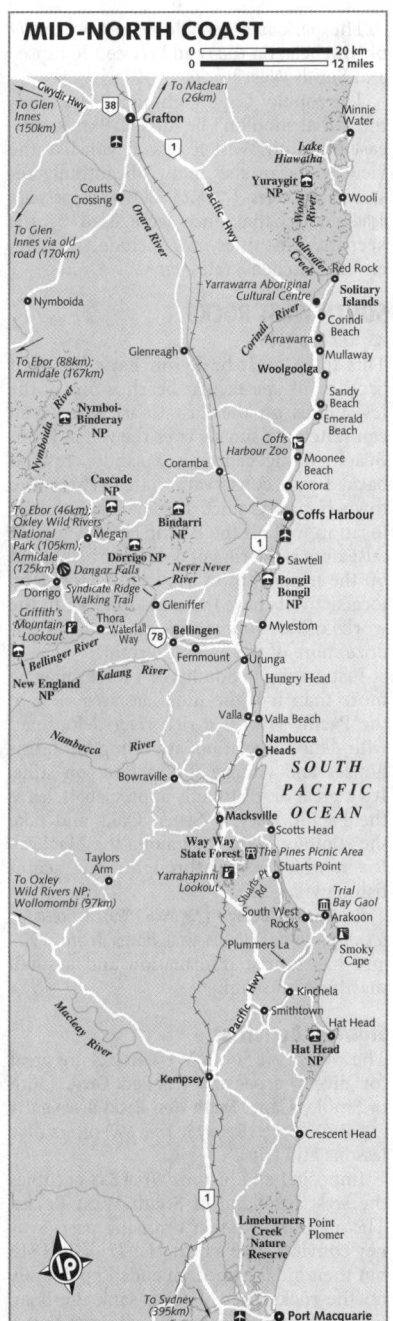

book for dogs *Lonely Pooch*, Ned's welcomes all critters be they large or small and standing on two legs or four.

Moon River (☎ 6562 8077; 157 Pacific Hwy; s/d from $55/69; P ✗ ⚑) A mere shrub of a place in a thicket of motels on the north side of town, Moon River may not be as Andy Williams sang, but it does have 33 comfortable, good-sized rooms.

Of the five caravan parks, **Sundowner Caravan Park** (☎ 6562 1361; 161 Pacific Hwy; camp sites $25) has the best and quietest position.

Fredo Pies (☎ 6566 8226; 75 Macleay St, Frederickton; pies $3; ☼7am-7pm) Just 6km north of Kempsey is an Australian icon that will give Akubra and Slim a run for their money: Fredo Pies is legendary for its scrumptious meat pies that come in 56 varieties, from kangaroo to beef. Few cars manage to get past this place – and for good reason.

Getting There & Around

Greyhound (☎ 13 14 99; www.greyhound.com.au) and **Premier** (☎ 13 34 10; www.premierms.com.au) passed through several times a day on their Pacific Hwy runs.

What's left of the **CountryLink** (☎ 13 22 32; www.countrylink.com.au) north coast train service goes north to Coffs Harbour ($17, 1½ hours) and Grafton ($32, three hours) and south to Sydney ($75, seven hours).

See the Crescent Head (p240) and South West Rocks (p241) sections for local bus services.

CRESCENT HEAD
☎ 02 / pop 1186

In surfing circles, this is where the Malibu surfboard gained prominence in Australia during the '60s. Now a third generation continues the surfing legacy this town cherishes. Many come just to watch the longboard riders surf the epic waves of **Little Nobby's Junction** when the swell's up. Crescent Head itself is an intimate town that caters mainly for family getaways, surfers and the odd backpacker who has ventured off the beaten track.

For holiday rentals, try the **Crescent Head Accommodation Bureau** (☎ 1800 352 272; www.pointbreakrealty.com.au).

Mediterranean Motel (☎ 6566 0303; 35 Pacific St; r $80-120; meals $10-25; ☼ breakfast, lunch & dinner; P ✗ ⚑) is the best motel in town. The rooms in the main building are comfortable.

LOCAL LAND RIGHTS

Crescent Head is the first town on mainland Australia to experience the effects of the Mabo decision, the High Court ruling that recognised that Aboriginal people could have historic title to land. In 1996 the government recognised that the Dunghutti people have native-title rights to 12.4 hectares of Crescent Head, which now is home to a subdivision. The ruling meant that the Dunghutti received compensation. So while it may be hard to spot this historic piece of land on a drive through the town, it is part of a larger issue that is much discussed in Australia today.

Groups of up to eight may enjoy the 'surf shacks' out back ($90 to $200). The food here (Mediterranean influenced, of course) is a cut above the usual standard.

Right at the mouth of the river, **Crescent Head Holiday Park** (☎ 6566 0261; Pacific St; camp sites from $19, cabins from $65) has a great location.

If you're driving, the road to Crescent Head is near the visitors centre in Kempsey. Alternatively, from the north you can take the very scenic Belmore Rd, which leaves the Pacific Hwy at Seven Oaks and follows the Belmore River.

Busways (☎ 1300 555 611; www.busways.com.au) runs two or three times daily Monday to Saturday to and from Kempsey (Belgrave St).

HAT HEAD NATIONAL PARK

This coastal park of 6500 hectares runs north from near Crescent Head to almost South West Rocks. It protects scrubland, swamps and some excellent beaches backed by one of NSW's largest sand dunes. Bird life is prolific on the wetlands. Rising up from the generally flat landscape is Hungry Hill, near Hat Head, and sloping Hat Head itself, where there's a walking track.

Surrounded by the national park, the village of **Hat Head** is much smaller and quieter than Crescent Head. **Hat Head Holiday Park** (☎ 6567 7501; camp sites from $16, cabins from $60) is large and close to a beautiful sheltered bay. You can camp ($3 per person) in the park at Hungry Head, 5km south of Hat Head. There are pit toilets and no showers, and you'll need to take your own water.

The park is accessible from the hamlet of Kinchela, on the road between Kempsey and South West Rocks.

The Smoky Cape Lighthouse is a landmark that shouldn't be missed, 9km southeast of South West Rocks. If you like the view, you can stay in two beautifully restored **cottages** (☎ 6566 6301; www.smokycape lighthouse.com) that once were used by the keepers. Amenities now include CD players and kitchens; rates vary.

SOUTH WEST ROCKS
☎ 02 / pop 4116

This town must be Byron Bay's long-lost brother; its spectacular beach is one of the few places on the East Coast where you can watch the sun set over the water. Front Beach in the centre is a sandy crescent backed by a conservation area. The entire town is pretty quiet, largely thanks to its location well off the Pacific Hwy. The only false note is the ring of dull suburban blight on the fringe; however, recent victories by local activists have thrown a spanner in the works of developers who planned to bulldoze more of the natural terrain.

Just getting to South West Rocks may be more than half the fun. The area west of the Pacific Hwy is a rich river delta lined with dense vegetation, appealing old farmhouses and vintage shacks built on stilts. It's a great drive; to fully appreciate it, leave the Pacific Hwy at Seven Oaks and take the sinuous 22km road along the MacLeay River, which passes through a few quaint fishing villages.

Boatman's Cottage (☎ 6566 7099; cnr Ocean Ave & Livingstone St; ✆ 10am-4pm) dates from 1902 and has tourist information and a small maritime museum.

Sights & Activities

The waters off South West Rocks are great for divers, especially **Fish Rock Cave**, south of Smoky Cape. **South West Rocks Dive Centre** (☎ 6566 6474; 5/98 Gregory St; 1 dive $90) offers dive lessons and trips.

Imposing and historic, **Trial Bay** occupies the west headland of South West Rocks. The area has a rather dramatic past: Sydney convicts stole a boat, the *Trial*, in 1816 but their bid for freedom ended up literally on the rocks after a storm sank the boat. Eventually the government decided that a breakwater was needed to protect boats – stolen or otherwise – taking shelter in the now-named Trial Bay. As a result, the **Trial Bay Gaol** (☎ 6566 6168; admission $3; ◉ 9am-5pm) was built to house convicts charged with the breakwater's construction. However, plans fizzled and except for a brief interlude in WWI when it housed Germans, the gaol has been unoccupied for more than 100 years. It's now a museum.

The **Arakoon State Conservation Area** is behind the gaol and has camp sites which are primitive but picturesque. From South West Rocks it's a pleasant walk to Trial Bay along the beach; look out for the **love shack**, formerly a fisherman's abode, about halfway between South West Rocks and Trial Bay.

Sleeping & Eating

Seabreeze Hotel (☎ 6566 6909; www.macleaycbd.com.au/seabreeze.html; Livingstone St; r from $80; meals $8-18; ◉ bistro lunch & dinner; ✴) More than a pub, the Seabreeze is an empire that has 28 basic rooms in a great spot at the front of town. The large bar and bistro have tables inside and out and are great for soaking up the sun while chilling to the, ahem, sea breezes.

Rock Pool Motor Inn (☎ 1800 180 133; www.rockpoolmotorinn.com.au; 45 Mcintyre St; r $82-160; P ✴ ✦) This neat and tidy place has 28 large rooms with plenty of amenities and a good restaurant.

Heritage (☎ 6566 6625, café 6566 9557; 21-23 Livingstone St; meals $5-10; ◉ café 8am-5pm) An 1885 guesthouse that's set to be reborn as an upscale boutique hotel. Some of the nine rooms have great views and all have amenities like DVD players, fridges and antiques. The building is a gem. Out front, the café serves up interesting and creative fare. The tables outside have glimpses of the sea.

Horseshoe Bay Beach Park (☎ 6566 6370; Livingstone St; camp sites from $18, cabins from $55) Superb position right in town and right on the sheltered Town Beach. The 82 sites and 12 cabins are usually booked out over the summer holidays.

Trial Bay Tourist Park (☎ 6566 6142; www.trialbay.com.au; 161-171 Phillip Dr; camp sites from $19, cabins from $80; ✦) This well-run place has a great family feel and good activities for the youngsters. The on-site takeaway makes 'dirty burgers' (with chips and gravy in the bun) and deep-fried Mars Bars. Together think of it as a coronary special.

Kiosk (☎ 6566 7100; Trial Bay; mains $16; ◉ lunch) Great food is on offer here, and rewards the walk from South West Rocks.

Getting There & Away

Cavanaghs (☎ 6562 7800) has two runs daily to and from Kempsey.

NAMBUCCA HEADS
☎ 02 / pop 6146

Nambucca Heads (nam-*buk*-a) has a dull centre atop a hill, but wander towards the water and you'll be rewarded by stunning vistas. Get closer and you'll discover walks through untrammelled bits of coastline as well as perfect beaches surrounded by azure waters. This is a low-key place that will give you plenty of time to catch up on several novels.

The Nambucca Valley (which means 'many bends') was occupied by the Gumbainggir people until European timber-cutters arrived in the 1840s. There are still strong Aboriginal communities in Nambucca Heads and up the valley in Bowraville.

Orientation

The town is just off the Pacific Hwy. Riverside Dr runs alongside the estuary of the Nambucca River, then climbs a steep hill to Bowra St, the main shopping street. A right turn onto Ridge St at the top of the hill leads through the old part of town to the beaches.

Information

Bookshop Cafe (☎ 6568 5855; cnr Ridge & Bowra Sts; meals $6-10; ◉ 8am-5pm) You'll find plenty of novels to catch up on here. The fruit smoothies are excellent and there are used books and Internet access.

Visitors centre (☎ 6568 6954; cnr Riverside Dr & Pacific Hwy; ◉ 9am-5pm) Very helpful (they may follow you out to your car with recommendations); doubles as the main bus terminal. It has a nice spot on the estuary.

Sights & Activities

The only patrolled beach in town is **Main Beach**; **Beilby's** and **Shelly** beaches are just to the south, closer to the river mouth – where the best surf is – which can be reached by going past the Captain Cook Lookout (a prime place for spotting the tidal topography).

Wellington Dr leads downhill off Bowra St to the waterfront and the V-Wall breakwall with its gentle graffiti by locals and

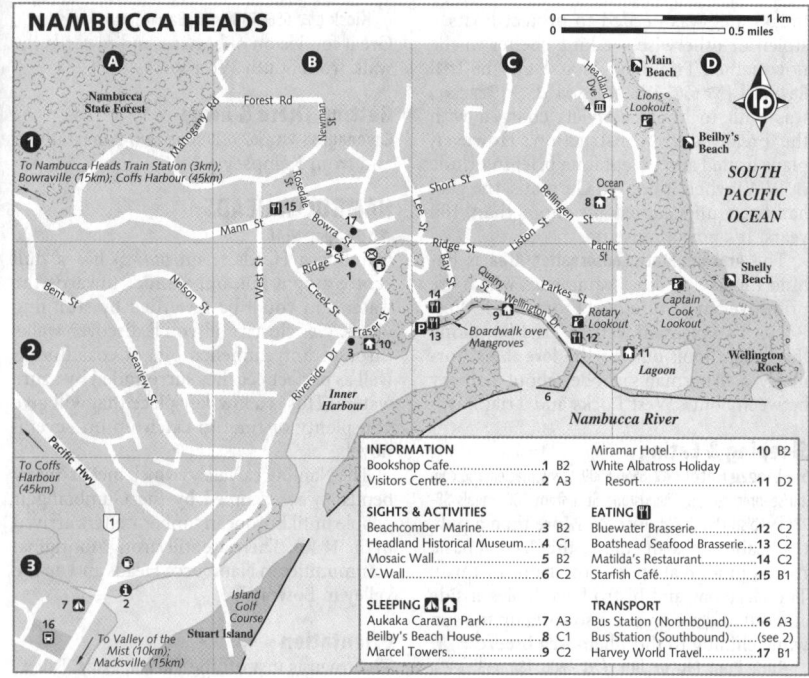

NAMBUCCA HEADS

INFORMATION		Miramar Hotel	10 B2
Bookshop Cafe	1 B2	White Albatross Holiday	
Visitors Centre	2 A3	Resort	11 D2

SIGHTS & ACTIVITIES		EATING	
Beachcomber Marine	3 B2	Bluewater Brasserie	12 C2
Headland Historical Museum	4 C1	Boatshead Seafood Brasserie	13 C2
Mosaic Wall	5 B2	Matilda's Restaurant	14 C2
V-Wall	6 C2	Starfish Café	15 B1

SLEEPING		TRANSPORT	
Aukaka Caravan Park	7 A3	Bus Station (Northbound)	16 A3
Beilby's Beach House	8 C1	Bus Station (Southbound)	(see 2)
Marcel Towers	9 C2	Harvey World Travel	17 B1

travellers: the messages are like those in pub toilets, but in prettier colours. For art of a similar genre, the **Mosaic Wall** in the town centre was created by a local artist using materials such as tiles and broken crockery. Look for Elvis – he hasn't left the wall.

Worth a visit is the **Headland Historical Museum** (☎ 6568 6380; Main Beach; adult/child $2/50¢; ♥ 2-4pm Wed, Sat & Sun), with local history exhibits, including a collection of over 1000 photos and displays of maritime equipment.

For boating enthusiasts, **Beachcomber Marine** (☎ 6568 6432; Riverside Dr) has various boats for rent by the hour or day.

Valley of the Mist (☎ 6568 3268; Macksville; tours $8-50) is a traditional farm set 10km south of Nambucca Heads and west of the village of Macksville. A variety of tours are offered, from learning the bush tucker possibilities of living off the land to exploring the rich wetlands by canoe. Call for times and directions.

Pub With No Beer (☎ 6564 2100; Taylors Arm Rd; ♥ noon-late) is 25km west of Macksville; see p426 for more details.

Sleeping

Typical of the coast, you'll find high prices and no-vacancy signs during summer, so book ahead.

Beilby's Beach House (☎ 6568 6466; www.beilbys .com.au; 1 Ocean St; s/d from $45/60; ✖ ⬜ ☒) The owners here speak English, French and German. The rooms are very comfortable and the location is right near the beach. There's also an all-you-can-eat breakfast, and children are welcome.

Marcel Towers (☎ 6568 7041; 12 Wellington Dr; r $70-130; Ⓟ) The bland architecture won't clash with the dreamy location overlooking the Inner Harbour. The foreshore walk is right across the street.

Miramar Motel (☎ 6568 7899; 1 Nelson St; s/d from $72/77; Ⓟ ☒) Right on the headland; the views here are worth the premium. The basic rooms have useful amenities like fridges.

White Albatross Holiday Resort (☎ 6568 6468; www.white-albatross.com.au; Wellington Dr; camp sites from $22, cabins from $55) Located near the river mouth with an adjacent lagoon to swim in, this is a tourism award–winner with a view. A deluxe waterfront villa is $135.

Aukaka Caravan Park (☎ 6568 6647; 2 Pacific Hwy; camp sites from $16, cabins from $33) Close to the bus stop, Aukaka is convenient to shopping and good if you just need a place for the night. It arranges shared cabins for backpackers.

Eating & Drinking

Matilda's Restaurant (☎ 6568 6024; Wellington Dr; mains $15-25; ☉ lunch & dinner Mon-Sat) Steaks and freshly caught seafood are the highlights at this unassuming wooden building that literally creaks with character. BYO.

Bluewater Brasserie (☎ 6568 6394; V-Wall Tavern, Wellington Dr; mains $18; ☉ lunch & dinner) Out of keeping with the rough-and-tumble pub it lives in, this brasserie is slightly fancy and has Mod Oz aspirations.

Starfish Café (☎ 6569 4422; 5 Mann St; mains $14-28; ☉ breakfast, lunch & dinner) There's a great view from the back veranda, and a modern menu that offers local seafood, steaks and various fusion specials. Live music some nights.

Boatshed Seafood Brasserie (☎ 6568 9292; 1 Wellington Dr; 3-course set menu $30; ☉ lunch & dinner Wed-Sun) Whether it's fried calamari and chips to takeaway or sumptuous barramundi fillets, this is the place. And you can't beat the waterfront location.

Getting There & Around

Harvey World Travel (☎ 6568 6455; 16 Bowra St) handles bookings.

Nearly all southbound buses stop outside the visitors centre. Northbound buses stop at the shopping centre nearby. **Keans** (☎ 1800 625 587) runs three times a week to Tamworth. **Premier** (☎ 13 34 10; www.premier ms.com.au) charges $59 to either Sydney or Brisbane (both eight to nine hours) on the Pacific Hwy. **Greyhound** (☎ 13 14 99; www.grey hound.com.au) is slightly more.

The train station is about 3km out of town: follow Bowra St then Mann St. **CountryLink** (☎ 13 22 32; www.countrylink.com.au) has trains north to Coffs Harbour ($5.50, 40 minutes) and beyond, and south to Sydney ($84, eight hours).

URUNGA

☎ 02 / pop 2704

Urunga is a good family retreat, with safe river beaches, good fishing and an innocent atmosphere, about 20km north of Nam-

bucca Heads. Hungry Head, just down the coast, is a popular surf spot.

The **Bellingen Shire visitors centre** (☎ 6655 5711; ☉ 9am-5pm Mon-Sat, 10am-2pm Sun) is on the Pacific Hwy, just before you reach the river, and services the whole area. It has a model that will help you finally make sense of the region's chaotic topography.

The most prominent building in town, the **Ocean View Hotel** (☎ 6655 6221; 15 Morgo St; s/d $35/55; mains $10-15; ☉ breakfast, lunch & dinner) is good for a meal, fine views and simple accommodation. **Urunga Heads Holiday Park** (☎ 6655 6355; Morgo St; camp sites from $18, cabins from $44; ☉) is next to the Urunga Lagoon in the centre of town.

MYLESTOM

☎ 02 / pop 382

Mylestom is just north of Urunga and is another attractive, unassuming place. It has nice beaches on one side and a wide river on the other.

Just south of the Raleigh Bridge is **Raleigh Winery** (☎ 6655 4388; www.raleighwines.com; 36 Queen St; ☉ 10am-5pm Wed-Sun), the most easterly vineyard in the land. It produces a well-regarded Semillon Chardonnay.

Next to the waves, the council-run **North Beach Caravan Park** (☎ 6655 4250; Beach Pde; camp sites from $20, cabins from $36) has clean facilities and 120 sites.

BELLINGEN

☎ 02 / pop 2731

Bellingen is a charming hill town that succeeds by not trying too hard. It is definitely worth the 12km drive off the Pacific Hwy to sample the community's laid-back vibe, spiced with a dose of art and alternative lifestyles. Spend a couple of hours wandering the streets and lazing away down by the Bellingen River.

The valley was part of the extensive territory of the Gumbainggir people until European timber-cutters arrived in the 1840s. The first settlement here was at Fernmount, about 5km east of Bellingen, but later the administrative centre of the region was moved to Bellingen. River craft were able to come up here until the 1940s, when dredging was discontinued. Until tourism boomed at Coffs Harbour in the 1960s, Bellingen was the most important town in this area.

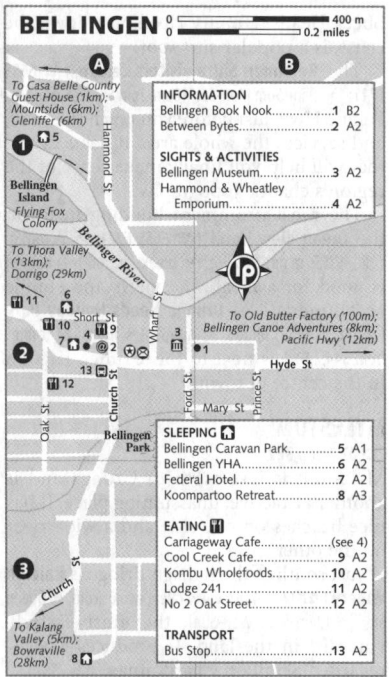

BELLINGEN

INFORMATION
Bellingen Book Nook...............1 B2
Between Bytes.....................2 A2

SIGHTS & ACTIVITIES
Bellingen Museum..................3 A2
Hammond & Wheatley
Emporium........................4 A2

SLEEPING
Bellingen Caravan Park............5 A1
Bellingen YHA.....................6 A2
Federal Hotel.....................7 A2
Koompartoo Retreat................8 A3

EATING
Carriageway Cafe................(see 4)
Cool Creek Cafe...................9 A2
Kombu Wholefoods.................10 A2
Lodge 241........................11 A2
No 2 Oak Street..................12 A2

TRANSPORT
Bus Stop.........................13 A2

Orientation

The main road from the Pacific Hwy to Dorrigo and the Waterfall Way becomes Hyde St in town. Next to the post office, Wharf St leads across the river to North Bellingen and Gleniffer. There isn't a visitors centre, so stop at the regional centre in Urunga (p243).

Information

Bellingen Book Nook (☎ 6655 9372; 25 Hyde St; 10am-4pm Mon-Fri, 9am-3pm Sat market) In a real nook. An amazing amount of books are crammed into this small space. There's always a few itinerant readers lounging around while others gossip.
Between Bytes (☎ 6655 9821; Shop 7D, Church St; per hr $6; 9am-4.30pm Mon-Fri) Has Internet access.
www.bellingen.com The community website is an excellent resource.

Sights & Activities

To get a feel for the place, head to the magnificent **Hammond & Wheatley Emporium** (Hyde St), which looks like a musty old department store until you see the range of stylish goods for sale in the restored surrounds. There's also an art gallery and a café.

The historic **Old Butter Factory** (☎ 6655 2150; 1 Doepel Lane; 9.30am-5pm) houses craft shops, a local art gallery, opal dealers, a masseur and a good café.

Bellingen Museum (☎ 6655 0289; adult/child $2/free; 10am-3pm Tue, 10am-noon Wed & Fri) is one of those places run by enthusiastic volunteers who you suspect hang out there even when it's closed. It has a range of booklets on local walks and history.

For a nature fix, from December to March there's a huge colony of flying foxes on **Bellingen Island**. It's an impressive sight when thousands head off at dusk to feed (best seen from the bridge). There's also an interesting walk to **rope swings** into the river, near the YHA hostel.

About 8km east of town in Fernmount, **Bellingen Canoe Adventures** (☎ 6655 9955; www.bellingen.com/canoe; 4 Tyson St) rents out canoes (from $10) and organises ecofriendly river tours ($45 to $90). The sunset tour is a corker.

On the third Saturday of the month the community **market** takes to the streets and it is quite an event, with over 250 stalls. On the second and fourth Saturday of the month there's an **organic market**. Both markets are good reasons for a visit.

Festivals & Events

Stamping Ground (☎ 6655 2472; www.stampingground.com.au) A festival of international dance performances in January.
Bellingen Jazz & Blues Festival (www.bellingenjazzfestival.com.au) Features a strong line-up of jazz names in late August.
Global Carnival (www.globalcarnival.com) A multicultural mix of music and performances held annually in early October.

Sleeping

Koompartoo Retreat (☎ 6655 2326; www.midcoast.com.au/~koompart; cnr Lawon & Dudley Sts; chalets $135;) A delightful experience: four stylish, cosy timber chalets with private balconies. The champagne glasses in each room are suggestive in the extreme.

Rivendell Guest House (☎ 6655 0060; www.rivendellguesthouse.com.au; 12 Hyde St; r $85-135;) Right in town. Escape civilization on the flower-bedecked veranda and in the lush gardens. Everything is comfortable without being fussy.

Mountside (☎ 6655 2206; www.midcoast.com.au/~mountside; 309 Roses Rd; s/d $70/99;) Some

6km out of town towards Gleniffer, this B&B offers an escape with country hospitality. The pool is very secluded – enjoy.

Casa Belle Country Guest House (☎ 6655 0155; www.casabelle.com; 90 Gleniffer Rd; r $135-220; 🖭) Mediterranean in design, Casa Belle is a haven in the hills where pampering is the norm. Lavish breakfasts and teas are served on the pretty veranda. There are fireplaces and spas.

Bellingen YHA (☎ 6655 1116; www.yha.com.au; 2 Short St; dm/d from $23/56; 🅿 🖳) Backpackers flock here in droves and it's not hard to figure out why. A tranquil, engaging atmosphere pervades this renovated weatherboard house. There's a free shuttle to the bus stop and train station in Urunga.

Federal Hotel (☎ 6655 1003; Hyde St; s/d $25/40) There's a high degree of character at this place in the heart of town.

Bellingen Caravan Park (☎ 6655 1338; www .bellingen.com/caravanpark; Dowle St; camp sites $20) Perched next to Bellingen Island and the flying foxes, the 32 sites here have a tranquil and green setting.

Eating & Drinking

There are plenty of excellent options to choose from in this hedonistic town.

No 2 Oak St (☎ 6655 9000; 2 Oak St; mains $28) No 2 is renowned in the region for modern Australian cuisine with a continental accent. Host Toni Urquart keeps the wine list as intriguing as the changing menu. As a bonus, it's housed in a 1910 heritage cottage with a verdant veranda.

Lodge 241 (☎ 6655 2470; 117-121 Hyde St; mains $16; 🕑 breakfast & lunch) Cool jazz plays inside and there's valley views outside at this upmarket café set in an old Masonic Lodge. Much of the food is organic and there are extra touches such as wood-fired sourdough bread.

Cool Creek Cafe (☎ 6655 1886; 5 Church St; mains $16-20; 🕑 dinner Thu-Mon) A first and only in Bellingen! A place where you can expect to see a Joni Mitchell cover band. This upmarket hippy joint is BYO and has live music (blues, folk, Mitchell) many nights. The food is organic and there is a kids' menu.

Carriageway Café (☎ 6655 1672; Hyde St; mains $15; 🕑 10am-9pm Wed-Mon) In the Hammond & Wheatley Emporium, this café matches the exquisite mood of the place.

Federal Hotel (☎ 6655 1003; 77 Hyde St; meals $8-15; 🕑 11am-late) A classic bar in the hotel of the same name, filled with character *and* characters.

Kombu Wholefoods (☎ 6655 9299; 105 Hyde St) Bellingen is the kind if place that can easily support this place, which is organic grocery-cum-community centre.

Getting There & Away

Keans (☎ 1800 625 587) has buses east to Coffs Harbour ($15) and west to Dorrigo and Tamworth a measly three times a week.

From Bellingen the Waterfall Way climbs steeply to Dorrigo – it's a spectacular drive. From Dorrigo you can continue west to the Armidale–Grafton road. A network of unsealed roads leads south to Bowraville and some tiny mountain settlements.

WAITING FOR RUSSELL CROWE

Since 2003 the good people of Bellingen have been waiting for Hollywood's fortune to smile upon them in the form of Russell Crowe, Nicole Kidman and the rest of the cast and crew of *Eucalyptus*. A lavish film-version of the bestselling novel by Murray Bail has been in the works for several years and residents were thrilled when not only was Belligen picked as a location but a lavish farmhouse set and studio were constructed just outside town. So excited were the locals that they busily rented out their homes to the crew and wondered aloud if Nicole might just turn up to do a turn crooning Joni Mitchell at the Cool Creek Cafe.

Sadly – and appropriately melodramatically – their hopes were continually dashed. First there was a mysterious delay in 2004. Then in early 2005 just as rehearsals started, the plug was pulled on the film. Flurries of press releases followed but the oft-quoted reason was 'script problems' and media reports said that trying to rewrite the plot to have the central character (19 in the book) more closely match Kidman (37 in real life) was proving a challenge. Crowe was reported to be angry (surprise!) and everybody went home to Sydney and Hollywood except for the locals who sadly returned to their now unrented local homes.

Reports indicated that production might resume late in 2005, but few are optimistic.

AROUND BELLINGEN

There are some beautiful spots waiting to be discovered in Belligen's surrounding valleys. The most accessible is the tiny hamlet of **Gleniffer**, 10km to the north and clearly signposted from North Bellingen. There's a good swimming hole in the **Never Never River**, behind the small Gleniffer School of Arts at the crossroads. Then you can drive around Loop Rd, which takes you to the foot of the New England tableland – a great drive that words don't do justice to.

If you want to sweat, tackle the **Syndicate Ridge Walking Trail**, a strenuous 15km walk from Gleniffer to the Dorrigo Plateau following the route of a tramline once used by timber-cutters. There's a very steep 1km climb on the way up. To get to the start of the trail, take the Gordonville Rd from Bellingen, turning into Adams Lane soon after crossing the Never Never River. The walking track commences at the first gate.

The **Kalang Valley**, southwest of town, and the **Thora Valley**, about 10km west of town, are also well worth exploring. People who pursue alternative lifestyles represent the majority around here.

DORRIGO

☎ 02 / pop 969

Beautiful wide streets, lush green forests and a sleepy feel – that's Dorrigo in a nutshell. This is densely forested mountain country, bordering the eastern escarpment of the **Great Dividing Range** and, not surprisingly, one of the last places to be settled by Europeans in the eastward push across the New England tableland.

The **visitors centre** (☎ 6657 2486; 36 Hickory St; ☽ 10am-4pm) is run by volunteers who share a passion for the area. The town's main attraction is **Dangar Falls**, which pound down into a swimming hole – think of it as aquatic massage.

The proposed **Steam Railway Museum** is still not open, but it's well worth visiting the site: there's a long line of steam engines and lots of old railway paraphernalia scattered about.

Sleeping & Eating

Dorrigo Hotel/Motel (☎ 6657 2017; www.hotelmotel dorrigo.com.au; cnr Cudgery & Hickory Sts; r $46-85) This classic country pub is a stately example of 1920s architecture. The hotel rooms have been restored to their original charm – no cheesy modernisation here (and the bathrooms are still shared). The pub serves good food.

Bridgewater Country Homestead (☎ 6657 2477; www.midcoast.com.au/~bridgewater; Everinghams Rd; s/d $65/110) The cosy rooms look out to glorious country views.

Commercial Hotel (☎ 6657 2003; 15 Cudgery St; s/d $35/45) The basic rooms at this pub will inspire you to sleep it off even if you don't need to.

Dorrigo Mountain Resort (☎ 6657 2564; www .dorrigomountainresort.com.au; Waterfall Way; camp sites from $18, cabins from $48) Just north of the Dome Rd turn-off, this resort has 16 basic, self-contained wooden cabins, 49 camp sites and sweeping views.

Art Place (☎ 6657 2622; 18-20 Cudgery St; meals $7-14; ☽ lunch) Right in the centre, the Art Place has a gallery where you can ponder local works while you sip your excellent coffee.

Misty's (☎ 6657 2855; 33 Hickory St; mains $14-20; ☽ lunch Sun, dinner Wed-Sat) This charming little restaurant has a changing regional menu and is in a renovated weatherboard house.

Dorrigo Bakery (☎ 6657 2159; 39 Hickory St; snacks $3; ☽ 8am-4pm Mon-Sat) Come here for a snack or lunch.

Getting There & Away

Three times a week **Keans** (☎ 1800 625 587) heads to Port Macquarie and Tamworth.

DORRIGO NATIONAL PARK

This is the most accessible of Australia's World Heritage rainforests. This 11,732-hectare park is home to a huge diversity of vegetation owing to its rich soil and subtropical conditions. All those trees mean there's plenty of places for birds to perch and at last count there were over 120 species present.

The turn-off to the park is just south of Dorrigo. The **Rainforest Centre** (☎ 6657 2309; Dome Rd; ☽ 9am-5pm), at the park entrance, has information about the park's many walks as well as a café. There's also the elevated **Skywalk** walkway over the rainforest canopy. You can see right down to the ocean on a fine day. The **Wonga Walk** is three-hour return walk on a sealed track through the heart of the rainforest. It's well worth making the drive down to the **Never Never rest area** in the middle of the national

DETOUR: THE WATERFALL WAY

Once you've travelled the 41km from the Pacific Hwy through Bellingen to Dorrigo, you've gone pretty far from the coast, although there's still another 124km of the Waterfall Way to go before you reach Armidale. Should you press on these are the highlights:

■ Forty-eight kilometres past Dorrigo (2km west of Ebor) there's a turn for Ebor Falls, where the Guy Fawkes River takes a big plunge.

■ A further 7km on is Point Lookout Rd, which leads to New England National Park, another World Heritage site. There are numerous walks into this misty rainforest.

■ After another 30km, look for Wollo-mombi Falls, a highlight of the World Heritage–listed Oxly Wild Rivers National Park. Here the water plunges down 260m.

park, from where you can walk to waterfalls or begin longer walks. Bush camping is permitted in some areas; call the Rainforest Centre for more details.

COFFS HARBOUR

☎ 02 / pop 26,083

Prepare to be bemused by a big banana – a ridiculously popular holiday destination and an icon for Coffs Harbour. The town has been working hard to burnish its image and it's generally a clean, family-friendly place. Of course 'family friendly' can also mean 'dull and predictable' and it seems that some people feel that way about it. Either way Coffs Harbour is the biggest town between Newcastle and the Gold Coast and hence an important regional centre.

Originally called Korff's Harbour, the town was settled in the 1860s. The jetty was built in 1892 to load cedar and other logs; it fell into disrepair some years ago but is now restored to its former glory. Bananas were first grown in the area in the 1880s, but no-one made much money from them until the railway came to town in 1918.

Banana growing is still big business – you'll see trees everywhere – but these days tourism is the mainstay of the local economy.

Orientation

The town is split into three areas: the jetty, town centre and beaches. The Pacific Hwy becomes Grafton St and then Woolgoolga Rd on its run through town. The city centre is around the Grafton St and Harbour Dr junction. Note that High St and Harbour Dr are one and the same, with both names used interchangeably by adjoining businesses.

The Pacific Hwy is the best way to access the beaches and resorts to the north. South of Coffs is Sawtell, a sprawl of housing developments fronting some fabulous surf beaches, which merge into Coffs Harbour.

Information

Jetty Village Internet Shop (☎ 6651 9155; Jetty Village, Harbour Dr; per 15min $2; ☺ 10am-8pm Mon-Sat, 10am-4pm Sun) Down by the marina; offers broadband laptop connections and CD burning.

Main post office (Ground fl, Palms Centre Shopping Complex) In a mall. There's another outlet at the jetty, opposite the Pier Hotel, and a third at Park Beach Plaza (the large mall off the Pacific Hwy).

Pages (☎ 6652 2588; Park Beach Plaza) For books.

Planet Games (☎ 6652 5188; 7/20 Gordon St; per 20min $2; ☺ 10am-7pm) Internet access a short walk from the bus stop.

Visitors centre (☎ 6652 1522, 1300 369 070; www .coffscoast.com.au; cnr Pacific Hwy & McLean St; ☺ 8am-5pm) Has a complete rundown on accommodation, activities and tours, although some of the friendly volunteers are more enthusiastic than knowledgeable.

Sights

The **Big Banana** (☎ 6652 4355; www.bigbanana.com; Pacific Hwy; ☺ 9am-4.30pm) is hailed by some as a national icon, ridiculed by others as preposterous. The park offers ice-skating ($12), a snow slope (adult/child $15/10) and other attractions. It's great for kids, not so great for the cynical visitor or those easily bored. However, banana fanatics will find that the overloaded gift store has much appeal.

Strolling through **North Coast Botanic Gardens** (☎ 6648 4188; Hardacre St; admission by donation; ☺ 9am-5pm) you can immerse yourself in the subtropical surrounds. Lush rainforest and numerous endangered species are some of the features, which also include sections devoted to places as faraway and foreign as Africa, China and Queensland. The 6km Coffs Creek Habitat Walk passes by, starting opposite the council chambers on Coff St and finishing near the ocean.

COFFS HARBOUR

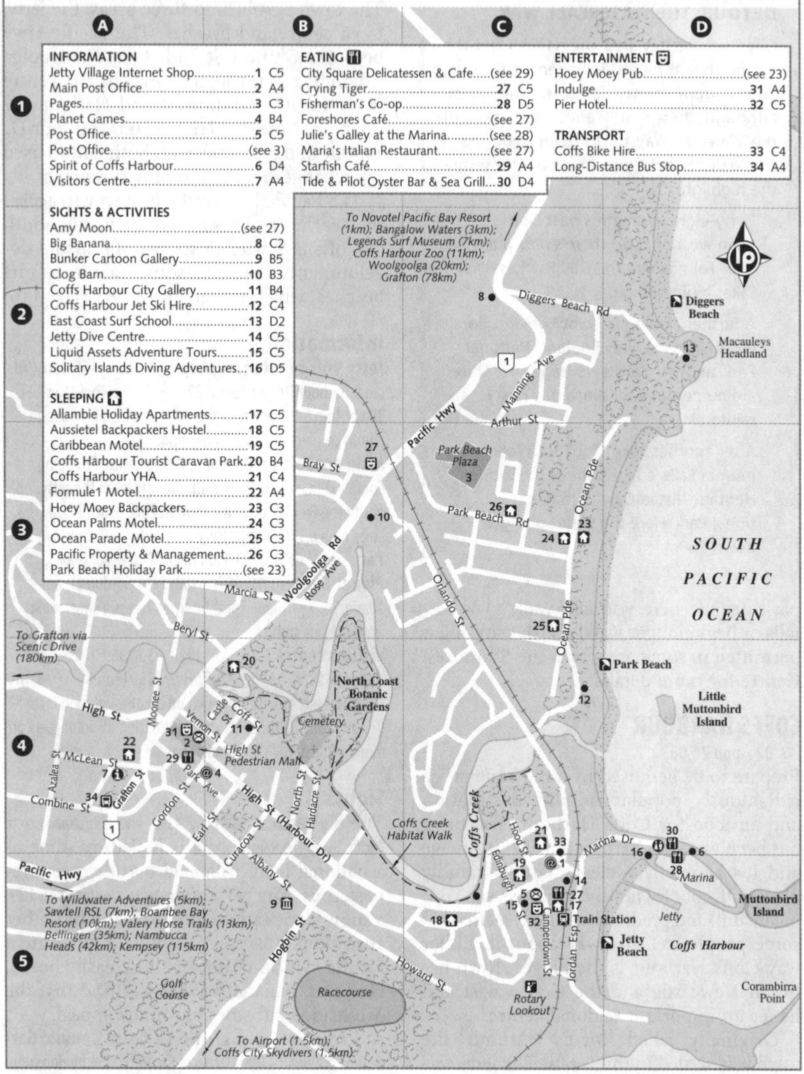
0 1 km
0 0.5 miles
A
B
C
D
1
2
3
4
5
INFORMATION
Jetty Village Internet Shop....1 C5
Main Post Office....2 A4
Pages....3 C3
Planet Games....4 B4
Post Office....5 C5
Post Office....(see 3)
Spirit of Coffs Harbour....6 D4
Visitors Centre....7 A4
SIGHTS & ACTIVITIES
Amy Moon....(see 27)
Big Banana....8 C2
Bunker Cartoon Gallery....9 B5
Clog Barn....10 B3
Coffs Harbour City Gallery....11 B4
Coffs Harbour Jet Ski Hire....12 C4
East Coast Surf School....13 D2
Jetty Dive Centre....14 C5
Liquid Assets Adventure Tours....15 C5
Solitary Islands Diving Adventures....16 D5
SLEEPING
Allambie Holiday Apartments....17 C5
Aussietel Backpackers Hostel....18 C5
Caribbean Motel....19 C5
Coffs Harbour Tourist Caravan Park....20 B4
Coffs Harbour YHA....21 C4
Formule1 Motel....22 A4
Hoey Moey Backpackers....23 C3
Ocean Palms Motel....24 C3
Ocean Parade Motel....25 C3
Pacific Property & Management....26 C3
Park Beach Holiday Park....(see 23)
EATING
City Square Delicatessen & Cafe....(see 29)
Crying Tiger....27 C5
Fisherman's Co-op....28 D5
Foreshores Café....(see 27)
Julie's Galley at the Marina....(see 28)
Maria's Italian Restaurant....(see 27)
Starfish Café....29 A4
Tide & Pilot Oyster Bar & Sea Grill....30 D4
ENTERTAINMENT
Hoey Moey Pub....(see 23)
Indulge....31 A4
Pier Hotel....32 C5
TRANSPORT
Coffs Bike Hire....33 C4
Long-Distance Bus Stop....34 A4
To Novotel Pacific Bay Resort (1km); Bangalow Waters (3km); Legends Surf Museum (7km); Coffs Harbour Zoo (11km); Woolgoolga (20km); Grafton (78km)
Diggers Beach Rd
Diggers Beach
Macauleys Headland
Manning Ave
Pacific Hwy
Arthur St
Park Beach Plaza
Bray St
Park Beach Rd
Ocean Pde
SOUTH PACIFIC OCEAN
Woolgoolga Rd
Rose Ave
Marcia St
Orlando St
Beryl St
To Grafton via Scenic Drive (180km)
Park Beach
Little Muttonbird Island
North Coast Botanic Gardens
Cemetery
High St
Moonee St
Castle St
Coff St
Vernon St
High St Pedestrian Mall
McLean St
Azalea St
Grafton St
Park Ave
Combine St
Gordon St
Earl St
North St
Hardacre St
High St (Harbour Dr)
Coffs Creek Habitat Walk
Coffs Creek
Hood St
Edinburgh St
Marina Dr
Marina
Muttonbird Island
Curacoa St
Albany St
Pacific Hwy
To Wildwater Adventures (5km); Sawtell RSL (7km); Boambee Bay Resort (10km); Valery Horse Trails (13km); Bellingen (35km); Nambucca Heads (42km); Kempsey (115km)
Camperdown St
Train Station
Jetty
Jetty Beach
Coffs Harbour
Jordan Esp
Hogbin St
Howard St
Golf Course
Racecourse
Rotary Lookout
Corambirra Point
To Airport (1.5km); Coffs City Skydivers (1.5km)

Muttonbird Island, at the end of the northern breakwater, is occupied by some 12,000 pairs of muttonbirds from late August to early April, with cute offspring visible in December and January. This marks the southern boundary of Solitary Islands Marine Park (p253), a meeting place of tropical waters and southern currents.

Legends Surf Museum (☎ 6653 6536; Pacific Hwy; adult/child $5/2; 10am-4pm) lets you smell the wax. Over 160 boards are on display, including ancient ones from, like, 50 years ago, man. Hundreds of photos show people catching waves worldwide. The museum is 100m off the Pacific Hwy 10km north of Coffs; look for signs.

Coffs Harbour Zoo (☎ 6656 1330; Pacific Hwy; adult/child $16/8; ☒ 8.30am-4pm) has lots of local fauna on display. If you've only seen kangaroos lying by the side of the road, here you can see them behind a fence. The zoo is 14km north of Coffs.

Clog Barn (☎ 6652 4633; www.clogbiz.com; 215 Pacific Hwy; adult/child $4.50/3.50; ☒ 7.30am-5pm) is a bizarre miniature Dutch village with windmills and a clog barn with a ridiculously large range of collectable spoons and plenty of clogs. There's also a bunch of non-Dutch lizards.

The **Yarrawarra Aboriginal Cultural Centre** (☎ 6649 2669; 170 Red Rock Rd; ☒ 8am-4pm Mon-Fri), north of Coffs Harbour, has a bush food café and tours.

BEACHES
The main beach is **Park Beach**, which has a picnic ground and is patrolled at weekends and school holidays: be careful of rips. **Jetty Beach** is more sheltered. **Diggers Beach**, reached by turning off the highway near the Big Banana, has a nude section and is quite a sensational place in its own right. Surfers enjoy Diggers and **Macauleys Headland**.

GALLERIES
Coffs Harbour City Gallery (☎ 6648 4861; Rigby House, cnr Coff & Duke Sts; ☒ 10am-4pm Wed-Sat) has exhibits of regional art and travelling shows.

Bunker Cartoon Gallery (☎ 6651 7343; City Hall Dr; admission $2; ☒ 10am-4pm) has lots of original works in an old WWII bunker.

Activities
Jetty Dive Centre (☎ 6651 1611; www.jettydive.com.au; 398 Harbour Dr; open-water courses from $200) offers great-value PADI (Professional Association of Diving Instructors) certification; the diving is pretty spectacular as you explore the Solitary Islands Marine Park.

Marine National Park kayaking can be arranged at **Liquid Assets Adventure Tours** (☎ 6658 0850; www.surfrafting.com; 328 Harbour Dr; half-day surf rafting $40), which offers a variety of thrilling watery trips.

Coffs Harbour Jet Ski Hire (☎ 0418 665 656; 263 Shepards Lane, Park Beach; per 15min $78) rents just what the name implies at the south end of Park Beach.

East Coast Surf School (☎ 6651 5515; Diggers Beach; lessons from $50) is particularly female-friendly as it is run by noted East Coast surfer Helene Enevoldson.

If you ever get that urge to throw yourself out of a plane, call **Coffs City Skydivers** (☎ 6651 1167; www.coffscentral.dnet.tv/CoffsCitySkyDivers; airport; tandem jump $320). Instead of strapping on a parachute, you strap on an instructor.

Valery Horse Trails (☎ 6653 4301; Gleniffer Rd; 2hr rides from $40) has a stable of 60 horses and plenty of acreage to explore in the hills behind town.

Once you are out of the water or off the trail, you might just want to lay down for a massage. **Amy Moon** (☎ 6651 6558; 4/364A Harbour Dr; per hr $50; ☒ 10am-6pm) offers a range healing massages and natural beauty treatments. Anyone for an exfoliation?

Tours
Mountain Trails (☎ 6658 3333; tours from $60) Award-winning ecofriendly 4WD rainforest, waterfall and bush tucker tours.
Solitary Islands Diving Adventures (☎ 6651 2401; Marina Dr; 4 boat dives $129) Runs diving and snorkelling trips to the amazing park.
Spirit of Coffs Harbour Cruises (☎ 6651 4612; International Marina; whale-watching $35) Runs June to November, watch for price wars among operators.
Wildwater Adventures (☎ 6653 3500; www.wildwateradventures.com.au; 754 Pacific Hwy; 1-day trip $153) Traverses the thrilling rapids of the Nymboida River in one- or multiday trips.

Festivals & Events
Gold Cup (☎ 6652 1488) Coffs Harbour's premier horse race, run in early August at the racetrack on Howard St.
Coffs Harbour Food & Wine Festival (☎ 6651 6888) On the last weekend of each October.
Pittwater to Coffs Yacht Race Starts in Sydney and finishes here, coinciding with New Year celebrations.

Sleeping
Motels cluster in two spots: out on the Pacific Hwy by the visitors centre where they can nab road-trippers, and down by Park Beach where they can nab beachgoers.

One of many holiday-apartment agents is **Pacific Property & Management** (☎ 6652 1466; www.pacificpropertysales.com.au; Park Beach Rd). The range of offerings is numbing. The visitors centre has an accommodation booking service.

BUDGET
If you're visiting during peak times, it's good to note that most hostel prices remain consistent all year, but book ahead.

Coffs Harbour YHA (☎ 6652 6462; www.yha.com
.au; 51 Collingwood St; dm/d from $25/70; ☐ ☎) New
in 2005, this purpose-built hostel rents all
manner of activity equipment. As you'd expect, rooms are clean and sparkling.

Aussitel Backpackers Hostel (☎ 6651 1871;
www.aussitel.com; 312 Harbour St; dm/d $22/55;
☐ ☎) Right next to the jetty; you can
take the canoes for a paddle on the river
or jump off the jetty as part of the experience. The Internet café offers a range of
services.

Hoey-Moey Backpackers (☎ 6651 7966; Ocean
Pde; dm/d $22/50; ☐) Right on the beach, Hoey
Moey is the party hostel (they give you a
beer when you arrive). There's a pub (opposite) and bottleshop and clean four-bed
dorm rooms.

Formule1 Motel (☎ 6650 9101; www.formule1
.com.au; 1A McLean St; r from $49; P ☒) One of
the French chain of budget motels sweeping across Australia; the small rooms here
have a small bathroom and a small TV. If
you want a truly anonymous experience,
this is good value.

Park Beach Holiday Park (☎ 6648 4888; Ocean
Pde; camp sites from $21, cabins from $52; ☐) Massive with 445 sites and 52 cabins; beautifully
located at the beach.

MIDRANGE
Although repeated often, the rates listed
here will be much higher during holidays.

Premier Motor Inn (☎ 6652 2044; www.premier
motorinn.com; Pacific Hwy; s/d from $70/78; P ☒ ☎)
One of the better choices among the thicket
of motels lining the Pacific Hwy near the
centre. It's back from the road and spacious
grounds help muffle the burble of truck ex-
hausts. Rooms are large and well appointed;
some have kitchenettes.

Caribbean Motel (☎ 6652 1500; www.stayincoffs
.com.au; 353 High St; r $75-115; P ☒ ☎) Close to
Coffs Creek, this 22-unit motel has a bit of
style as shown by the water-shooting statuary along the pool. The best rooms have
balconies, views and spas.

Ocean Palms Motel (☎ 6651 5594; www.ocean
palmsmotel.com.au; cnr Park Beach Rd & Ocean Pde; s/d from
$69/79; P ☎) The mature palms at this ma-
ture motel give it a South Seas feel. There's
a nice pool surrounded by lush gardens
and the rooms have been kept updated. A
charming choice of the many motels near
the beach.

Bangalow Waters (☎ 6653 7999; www.bangalow
waters.com.au; 95 James Small Dr, Korora; d from $90;
P ☒ ☎) These 12 cottages have a nice garden setting you can enjoy from the porches.
The units have an atmospheric tropical
décor and amenities include full kitchens.
Close to the beach at Korora, 5km north
of Coffs.

Ocean Parade Motel (☎ 6652 6733; 41 Ocean Pde;
s/d $60/70; P ☒ ☎) A solid option along the
beach. Rooms offer numerous diversions,
including cable TV and movies.

Allambie Holiday Apartments (☎ 6652 6690;
www.stayincoffs.com.au; 22 Camperdown St; r $110-160;
P ☒ ☎) The one- and two-bedroom apartments have great views of the harbour and
there's a pretty pool area and spa to keep
you from straying. All six units have full
kitchens.

TOP END
Novotel Pacific Bay Resort (☎ 6659 7000; www
.pacificbayresort.com.au; cnr Pacific Hwy & Bay Dr; r $162-
236; P ☒ ☎) Has all the features of a large
resort: tennis courts, cocktail bars, volleyball
courts, walking trails and a fitness centre.
The grounds are large and the 180 rooms
have balconies, many with kitchens.

Boambee Bay Resort (☎ 6653 2700; www.boam
beebay.com; 8 Barber Cl; villas $120-220; ☒ ☎) Set in
tropical gardens, the resort has a vast pool,
spas and full menu of resort activities. Large
villas have kitchens and can sleep six.

Eating
Coffs has a good selection of places to eat,
with all price levels and most types of cuisine on offer somewhere. There's no places
run by chefs who have their own TV shows
but you should find something you like.

JETTY
The Jetty on Harbour Dr is the main restaurant strip, and there's really no point eating
elsewhere; most of the CBD closes down
around 6pm. As well as the listings here,
you'll find budget Italian, Vietnamese, Thai,
Indian, and fish and chips. Kitchens start
closing around 8.30pm, so come early and
make a reservation if you have your heart
set on a particular place. Most places here
have pavement tables.

Foreshores Café (☎ 6652 3127; 394 Harbour
Dr; mains $6-20; ☼ breakfast & lunch) Quick and
friendly service, huge breakfasts (including

snazzy French toast) and ocean breezes on the terrace make this a great spot to start the day.

Crying Tiger (☎ 6650 0195; 386 Harbour Dr; mains $8-16; ☷ dinner; ☷) Thai food is served in this stylish gem of a restaurant with colour and flair. It's not all satay either (although it does a good one); there are more unusual Thai items such *choo choo talay* (red curry seafood).

Maria's Italian Restaurant (☎ 6651 3000; 368 Harbour Dr; mains $9-15; ☷ dinner) Who can go wrong with a name like Maria? This is the kind of old-fashioned Italian place (pizza and spag bol) that never goes out of style. And thank goodness. Families love it for the long, satisfying and cheap menu.

MARINA
Second to the Jetty in popularity; there is some good seafood here.

Fisherman's Co-op (☎ 6652 2811; 69 Marina Dr; meals $7; ☷ 9am-6pm winter, 9am-8pm summer) Fresh fish right off the boats. There are lots of specials depending on what's been caught, but you'll never go wrong with the fish and chips. Homemade gelato and a nice picnic area complete the joy.

Tide & Pilot Oyster Bar & Sea Grill (☎ 6651 6888; Marina Dr; mains restaurant $20-30, café $6-12; ☷ café breakfast, lunch & dinner) Right on the ocean (if you're lucky, you might spot a whale through the north-facing glass wall), this elegant seafood restaurant has truly great food. The downstairs café has tables in and out and serves everything from classic eggs and bacon to fresh fish.

Julie's Galley at the Marina (☎ 6650 0188; Marina Dr; meals $4-7; ☷ 8am-6.30pm) Have your egg-and-bacon roll with the blokes off the boats. Burgers (including several vegie options) are served by the cheery chef.

CBD
The downtown area is good for lunch, or for coffee all day, but most places are closed in the evening. The pedestrian area opposite Palm Mall (part of High St Pedestrian Mall) has lots of pavement cafés.

Starfish Café (☎ 6651 5005; City Sq; mains $5-12; ☷ 8am-4pm Mon-Fri, 8am-noon Sat) The most up-scale of the cafés on the pedestrian zone off High St. Good coffee and meals presented with artistic touches. The eggs Bennedict is superb, as are the sandwiches and salads.

City Square Delicatessen & Cafe (☎ 6652 5855; City Sq; sandwiches $6-8; ☷ 8am-4pm Mon-Fri, 8am-noon Sat) Create your own sandwich from the array of delicacies in the counter-display cases or sip a tasty coffee while you decide what prepared foods and cheeses you want to take home to your holiday unit.

Entertainment
See Thursday's edition of the *Coffs Harbour Advocate* for listings. Clubs change names with the seasons.

Hoey Moey Pub (☎ 6852 3833; Ocean Pde) In the same building as the Hoey Moey Backpackers, this party pub caters to the demanding backpacker market and is your best bet for local acts and AC/DC cover bands. It also has pool comps and trivia nights. Now if you can just keep those other three bunkies away while you slip back to the room…

Coffs Hotel (☎ 6652 3817; cnr Pacific Hwy & West High St) This pub complex has bands, bars, DJs and more. It rocks on Friday nights.

Pier Hotel (☎ 6652 2110; cnr Hood & High Sts) The cover bands that aren't at Hoey Moey can often be found here. It's a classic 1930s local corner pub.

Indulge (☎ 6658 6426; 15 City Blvd Mall) Upstairs in an older part of the mall, you'll find foam parties, travelling acts and general mayhem until very late. Cover charge varies.

Getting There & Away
AIR
Coffs Harbour Airport (CFS) is just south of town. **Virgin Blue** (☎ 13 67 89) has flights to Sydney and Melbourne. **QantasLink** (☎ 13 13 13) flies to Sydney. **Sunshine Express** (☎ 13 13 13) goes to Brisbane.

BUS
Long-distance and regional buses leave from a shelter adjacent to the information centre.

Greyhound (☎ 13 14 99; www.greyhound.com.au) has several services a day north, including Byron Bay ($43, four hours) and south to Sydney ($62, nine hours). **Premier** (☎ 13 34 10; www.premierms.com.au) offers similar services in both directions.

Busways (☎ 6652 2744) has local school runs to Bellingen ($7, one hour, three times daily Monday to Friday).

Keans (☎ 1800 625 587) has services that include Tamworth ($59), Armidale ($32) and Bellingen ($15) three times a week.

TRAIN

CountryLink (☎ 13 22 32; www.countrylink.com.au) goes all the way north to the non-thriving town of Casino (where the train used to branch off to Byron Bay) and Brisbane ($75, 5½ hours), and south to Sydney ($84, nine hours).

Getting Around

Hostel shuttles meet all long-distance buses and trains.

Coffs Bike Hire (☎ 6652 5102; cnr Orlando & Collingwood Sts; per day from $25; ☼ 8.30am-5.30pm Mon-Fri, 9am-2pm Sat & Sun) rents cruisers, mountain bikes and more.

Ryan's Buses (☎ 6652 3201) runs to Grafton ($19) twice a day and also goes to the beaches ($8 to $9) north of Coffs several times a day.

Major car-rental companies are at the airport.

For a cab, **Coffs District Taxi Network** (☎ 13 10 08, 6658 5922) operates a 24-hour service.

COFFS HARBOUR TO GRAFTON
Woolgoolga
☎ 02 / pop 3800

With a nice beach in a deep cove, Woolgoolga is a less-developed coastal town just north of Coffs that is renowned for its surf and sizable Sikh community. As you drive by on the highway you will notice the impressive **Guru Nanak Temple**, the *gurdwara* (place of worship). Don't confuse it with the **Raj Mahal**, an Indian-influenced decrepit concrete extravagance that has two giant elephant statues out the front. Its origins are a mystery, but it's possible it was once a temple. If you drive straight through town up to the point, you'll get a magnificent view of the Solitary Marine Reserve.

The **Woolgoolga Beach Caravan Park** (☎ 6654 1373; Beach St; camp sites $20, cabins $50) is right on the beach and has a fine position.

The location of the **Beach Motel** (☎ 6654 1333; 78 Beach St; r $85-175; P ✗ ☎) lives up to the name, and 10 rooms provide good comfort. Good value out of high season.

Opposite the temple, **Maharaja Tandoori Indian Restaurant** (☎ 6654 1122; 10-12 River St; mains $26) produces a suitably authentic curry.

On the beachfront, **Bluebottles Brasserie** (☎ 6654 1962; cnr Wharf & Beach Sts; mains $10-30; ☼ breakfast & lunch daily, dinner Thu-Sat) has live

music (mostly jazz) Thursday nights in summer. There's a changing and creative menu served throughout the day and the many tables on the plaza are good for lazing away a few hours.

Red Rock
☎ 02 / pop 290

Red Rock, a site that's sacred to the Gunawarri tribe, is a sleepy village with a beautiful inlet and gorgeous surrounds. Soak up the sun or catch a fish while camping at **Red Rock Caravan Park** (☎ 6649 2730; 1 Lawson St; camp sites from $12, cabins from $65).

Yuraygir National Park

Yuraygir (20,000 hectares) is the southernmost in a chain of coastal national parks and nature reserves that runs almost all the way north to Ballina. The beaches are outstanding and there are some bushwalking paths where you can view endangered coastal emus. The park is in three sections, from **Red Rock** to the Wooli River (turn off the highway just north of Red Rock); from the township of **Wooli** to the Sandon River (turn off the highway 12km south of Grafton); and from near **Brooms Head** to **Angourie Point** (accessible from those towns). Together the areas comprise 60km of coast but there is no vehicle access between the sections; on foot you'd have to cross the challenging Wooli and Sandon Rivers.

Walkers can bush camp and there are basic camping areas ($5 per person) at Station Creek in the southern section; at the Boorkoom and Illaroo rest areas in the central section; and on the north bank of the Sandon River, and at Red Cliff at the Brooms Head end of the northern section. These are accessible by car; there are also walk-in camp sites in the northern section: Plumbago Headland, Shelly Head and Shelly Beach. Self-service kiosks collect the park's $7 day-use fee.

Wooli
☎ 02 / pop 561

The beauty of this town is that it is surrounded by the Yuraygir National Park on land and the Solitary Islands Marine Park by sea. This means you are encircled by wildlife and crisp waters. The long beach is backed by bush-covered dunes.

On the Queen's Birthday long weekend in June, the locals hold their big event, the **Goanna Pulling Championships**. It's not all it claims to be, as contestants wrap a leather strap around their head for a good old-fashioned tug-of-war.

The **Wooli Hotel/Motel** (☎ 6649 7532; Wooli Rd; s/d $55/66) does stock-standard pub accommodation, but is far from the beach. There are two camping grounds, with the **Wooli Camping & Caravan Park** (☎ 6649 7519; North St; camp sites from $18, cabins from $55) a fairly peaceful option.

Solitary Islands Marine Park

This group of five islands is the meeting point of warm tropical currents and cooler southern currents, making for a wonderful combination of corals, reef fish and seaweeds. Dubbed the 'rivers of life', this is the best area in North Coast NSW in which to dive or snorkel (look out for extremely rough conditions). The **park** (☎ 6652 0900) protects some 280 species of fish and 90 species of coral. Check at tourism information centres and dive shops for a handy booklet outlining the many rules and regulations designed to preserve the park. There are many tours – above and below the waters – that run from Coffs Harbour (see p249).

FAR NORTH COAST

This is where the coast heats up in activity, hype and temperature. Byron Bay is the centre of all the attention, with its nightlife, stunning location and beach. But there are places with equal beauty that are much quieter. Lennox Head and its surrounds are much more serene than the tourist Babylon to the north, and Yamba sits serenely on its estuary.

Coupled with the beaches and ideal subtropical climate are rivers rich in colour. The Clarence River vies to be the most beautiful river down under, such is its striking blueness. The Richmond and Tweed Rivers sprawl out into rich deltas and provide classic visuals. The land is used to produce sugar cane and you will smell it burning as you drive through. The weather is why many come: warm winters and long, hot summers.

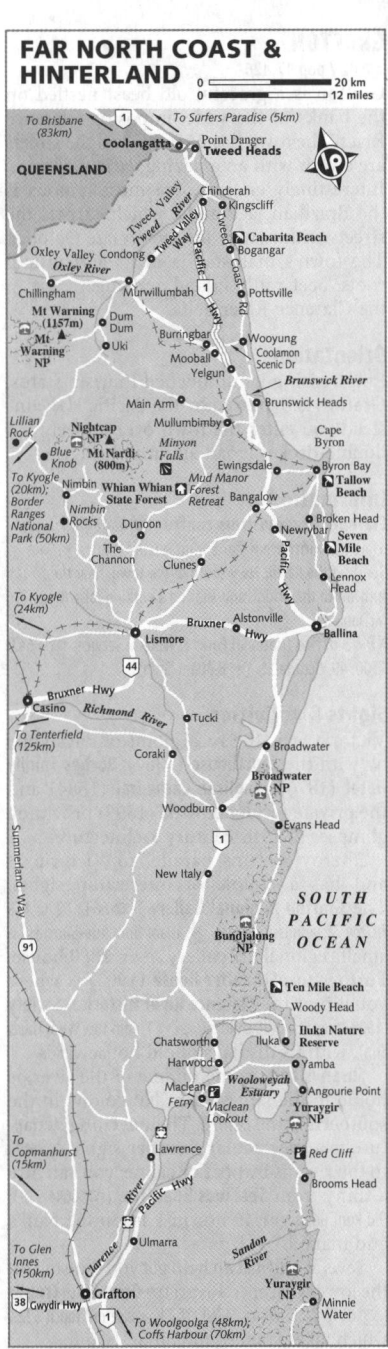

FAR NORTH COAST & HINTERLAND

GRAFTON

☎ 02 / pop 17,426

Grafton is a graceful old beast nestled on the banks of the wide, imposing Clarence River. The town has 24 parks and the streets are awash with an amazing variety of trees. Interestingly enough, the most famous is the Brazilian jacaranda, which carpets the streets with mauve flowers in late October. The town's mainstay is in its agricultural roots: beef cattle inland and sugar cane in the Clarence River delta.

Orientation

Emphasising its untouched tourism status, Grafton is bypassed by the Pacific Hwy; instead you enter the town over a lovely old double-decker (road and rail) bridge.

Information

Clarence River visitors centre (☎ 6642 4677; www .clarencetourism.com; cnr Spring & Charles Sts; ☼ 9am-5pm) On the Pacific Hwy south of the town, near the turn-off to the bridge and sharing a parking lot with a McDonald's.
NPWS office (National Parks & Wildlife Service; ☎ 6641 1500; 49 Victoria St; ☼ 8.30am-5pm)

Sights & Activities

Victoria St is the focal point of days gone by with the **courthouse** (1862), **Roches Family Hotel** (1870), **Anglican Cathedral** (1884) and the private residence **Istria** (1899) providing glimpses of 19th-century architecture.

Fitzroy St runs parallel to Victoria St and has a couple of interesting sights. The **Grafton Regional Gallery** (☎ 6642 6996; 158 Fitzroy St; admission free; ☼ 10am-4pm Tue-Sun) is a small regional art gallery in an 1880 house. Further up, **Schaeffer House** (1903) is where you'll find the **Clarence River Historical Society** (190 Fitzroy St; adult/child $3/1; ☼ 1-4pm Tue, Wed, Thu & Sun), with its displays of old housewares.

Susan Island, in the middle of the river, is home to the largest fruit-bat colony in the southern hemisphere. Their evening departure is a spectacular summer sight. Access to the river is by boat or canoe; you can hire a tinny from **Seelands Boat Hire** (☎ 6644 9381; Old Punt Rd; per day $60) or just sit on the banks and marvel.

Several outfits can help get you cruising on the lower Clarence River; try **Great Time Cruises** (☎ 6642 3456; Prince St Wharf; 2hr cruise incl lunch $22), which takes you around Susan Island.

Festivals & Events

Horse Racing Carnival Every July; this is the richest in country Australia.
Jacaranda Festival In the week joining October and November, Australia's longest-running floral festival sees Grafton come alive in an ocean of mauve.

Sleeping

There are a number of interesting options here.

Crown Hotel/Motel (☎ 6642 4000; 1 Prince St; hotel s/d $35/45, motel s/d $70/80; ☒) Attractively located on the Clarence River, this place has old beds and clean rooms, some overlooking the river and all opening on to an inviting veranda.

Rosary (☎ 6642 2292; johnmelenhorst@bigpond .com; 41 Bacon St; s/d $75/90; ☒ ☒) A 1905 Federation-style home only two blocks from the main shopping area. The hosts have an intimate knowledge of the area and the rooms are comfortable.

Grafton Meadow B&B (☎ 6643 2331; www .graftonmeadow.com; 95 Crown St; s/d $70/85) Has classic jacarandas out the front and a pastoral setting, just three minutes from town. Rates include a healthy continental breakfast.

There are a number of motels along Fitzroy St that vary in quality and price.

Jacaranda Motor Lodge (☎ 6642 2833; welcome@ jacarandamotorlodge.com.au; Pacific Hwy; r $77-115; ☐ ☒ ☒) This place is quiet, and suitably purple in season. Rooms are large and it has a fine view of the Clarence River valley.

Gateway Village (☎ 6642 4225; 598 Sumerland Way; camp sites/cabins from $18/69; ☒ ☒) A central, scenic tourist park, which has the usual playground and barbecue facilities.

Eating

There are a number of delightful options.

Crown Hotel/Motel (☎ 6642 4000; 1 Prince St; mains $10-20) A favourite of many, this strong Mod Oz bistro in the historic pub has a stunning view.

Georgie's at the Gallery (☎ 6642 6996; 158 Fitzroy St; mains $20; ☼ lunch Tue-Sun, dinner Tue-Sat) Rises above the modest expectations of its slogan 'satisfies your taste', with surprisingly inventive and tasty food that ranges from snacks to full meals. Order at the counter and sit outside in the lovely courtyard.

Left Bank Cafe (☎ 6643 4535; 50 Skinner St; meals $5-10; ☼ breakfast & lunch) On the south side of the Clarence, this charming old storefront has delectable deli items and good sandwiches and coffee.

Courtyard Cafe (☎ 6642 6644; cnr Prince & Fitzroy Sts; meals $5-10; ☼ lunch Mon-Fri) Unassuming everywhere but the food department: home-made breads and muffins lead off a line-up of excellent sandwiches and salads.

Getting There & Away

Busways (☎ 6642 2954) runs to Yamba ($10, 75 minutes, six times daily). **Ryan's Buses** (☎ 6652 3201) goes to Coffs Harbour ($18).

Greyhound (☎ 13 14 99; www.greyhound.com.au) and **Premier** (☎ 13 34 10; www.premierms.com.au) stop at the train station on the daily East Coast runs.

CountryLink (☎ 13 22 32; www.countrylink.com.au) stops here on its north coast route. Sydney is served three times daily ($90, 10 hours).

Near Grafton there are several scenic routes that parallel the Pacific Hwy. Try the north bank of the Clarence route between Grafton and Maclean, which involves a ferry crossing at Lawrence.

Getting Around

Grafton Radio Taxis (☎ 6642 3622) runs 24 hours.

CLARENCE RIVER VALLEY

The Clarence River rises in Queensland's McPherson Ranges and runs south through the mountains before thundering down a gorge in the Gibraltar Range west of Grafton. It then meanders northeast to the sea at Yamba, giving life to a beautiful and fertile valley along the way.

The delta between Grafton and the coast is a patchwork of farmland in which the now sinuous and spreading Clarence River forms over 100 islands, some very large. If you're driving, the profusion of small bridges and waterways makes it hard to keep track of whether you're on an island or the mainland.

This is the start of sugar-cane country and also the beginning of Queensland-style domestic architecture: wooden houses with high-pitched roofs perched on stilts to allow air circulation in the hot summers. The burning of the cane fields (May to December) adds a smoky tang to the air.

Clarence Riverboats (☎ 6647 6232; Brushgrove; per week $1200) has reliable equipment for a break with a difference.

DETOUR: INLAND FROM GRAFTON

The Clarence River is navigable as far upstream as the village of **Copmanhurst**, about 35km northwest of Grafton. Further upstream the Clarence River descends rapidly from the Gibraltar Range through the rugged **Clarence River Gorge**, a popular and challenging site for white-water canoeing.

Private property flanks the gorge. On the south side the land is owned by the Winters family, who allow day visitors and have cabin accommodation at **Winters' Shack** (☎ 6647 2173). Access is via Copmanhurst. It's best to ring first to get permission and to arrange for the gates to be unlocked. On the north side, **Wave Hill Station** (☎ 6647 2145) has homestead or inexpensive cottage accommodation, and 4WD or horse-riding trips to the gorge. These trips cost $200 for the day.

MACLEAN

☎ 02 / pop 3254

Some might say that, given the tartan power poles, Maclean takes its Scottish heritage a little too seriously. That said, the town is set in charming surrounds with the imposing Clarence River beginning its lazy sprawl over the delta. Prawn fishing is popular.

The **Lower Clarence visitors centre** (☎ 6645 4121; Pacific Hwy; ☼ 9am-5pm) is on the southern entry to town in a large building with a café. Pick up a copy of *Maclean Heritage Trail*, which gives great detail on this largely preserved river town.

To take in the beautiful surrounds, head up the hill to **Maclean Lookout**. The **Maclean Historical Society** (☎ 6645 3416; www.macleanhistory .org.au; cnr Wharf & Grafton Sts; adult/child $3/1; ☼ 1-4pm Wed & Sat, 10am-4pm Fri) gives a good insight into the town's Scottish roots. It's in an 1879 stone cottage.

The 1867 **Historic Gables B&B** (☎ 6645 2452; 2B Howard St; d $95) is a great place to enjoy the technicolour sunsets over the Clarence. It has four rooms. There are also motels nearby.

To get an elegant view of the river, look no further than **Historic Gables B&B** (☎ 6645 2452; http://users.northnet.com.au/~gables; s/d $80/100). This charming Federation house has six bedrooms, an extensive upstairs lounge area, open fireplace and wide veranda.

YAMBA

☎ 02 / pop 5660

Beaches on three fronts, a relaxed pace and interesting diversions such as a burgeoning café culture mean that Yamba's popularity will just keep growing.

Sights & Activities

The centre sits behind a head, which is indented with small cove beaches. The **Port of Yamba Historical Society Story House Museum** (☎ 6646 2316; River St; adult/child $3/50c; ⏰ 2-5pm Wed, Thu, Sat & Sun) has hundreds of photos telling the story of the once pervasive local maritime culture. Check out details of the dozens of shipwrecks in the seemingly serene Clarence.

If you're interested in a kayak tour, **Yamba Kayak** (☎ 6646 1137; from $40) operates on demand. Pick up is at Gorman's Restaurant at Yamba Bay. To use the motorised version, **Yamba Boat Hire** (☎ 6645 8525; Boat Harbour Marina; full-day, up to 8 people $120) has simple, square boats. It's near Blue Dolphin Caravan Park.

There's a **community market** held at the Yamba Oval on the fourth weekend of each month.

Sleeping

Pacific Hotel (☎ 6646 2466; www.pacifichotelyamba .com.au; 1 Pilot St; dm $18-20, d $50-130; 🖥) Gorgeously situated overlooking the ocean, this place has a plethora of varying rooms so feel free to compare – despite management's weariness at the prospect. The views are superb, as is the bistro.

Angourie Rainforest Resort (☎ 6646 8600; www.angourieresort.com.au; 166 Angourie Rd; 1-bedroom ste $140-200; 🅿 ⊠ 🖥 🏊) This impressive resort is located, as the name implies, in rainforest, 1km west of town. Management take an ecological approach to running the place and the architecture blends in with the surroundings. Rooms reach posh-sized in large villas. There are pools and a lavish spa.

Aston Villa Motor Inn (☎ 6646 2785; 3 Mulgi St; r $74-115; 🅿 ⊠ 🏊) With wide verandas and attractive gardens, this is a good choice among the nearly dozen motels.

Calypso Holiday Park (☎ 6646 2468; Harbour St; camp sites from $19, cabins from $70; 🏊) This place is close to everything, and has a good spot on the river.

Eating

Pacific Hotel (☎ 6646 2466; 1 Pilot St; mains $15-24; ⏰ lunch & dinner) It's not just the view but the food that has people flocking to this cliffside bistro. Joining the steaks and sandwiches are numerous specials such as king prawns in chickpea flour batter. There's a kids' menu.

Restaurant Castalia (☎ 6646 1155; 15 Clarence St; mains $20-30; ⏰ breakfast Fri & Sat, lunch Wed-Sun, dinner Tue-Sat) Relaxed yet stylish. Fresh local seafood and locally grown produce are the focus of the innovative and changing menu.

There are a couple of other good choices on this little strip on the headland.

Two excellent cafés vie for your affection in the centre.

Caught Snacking at the Corner Store (☎ 6646 2322; cnr Coldstream & Yamba Sts; meals $6-8; ⏰ breakfast & lunch Mon-Sat) The food is as fun as the name with homemade treats such as banana bread and spinach quiche on offer. Enjoy a good sandwich at the pavement tables.

Yamba Trading Co (☎ 6646 3909; cnr Coldstream & Yamba Sts; meals $8-12; ⏰ breakfast & lunch) There's a long tapas menu and good baked goods at this café, which has a gift store sure to make any ageing hippy nostalgic.

Getting There & Away

Yamba is 15km east of the Pacific Hwy; turn off at the Yamba Rd intersection just south of the Clarence River. A passenger-only **ferry** (☎ 6646 6423; adult/child $5/2.50) runs to Iluka, on the north bank of the Clarence River, four times daily.

Busways (☎ 6642 2954) runs across to Grafton ($10, 75 minutes, six times daily).

CountryLink (☎ 13 22 32; www.countrylink.com.au) buses go to Grafton ($12) where you can connect to Byron Bay ($19).

AROUND YAMBA

A surf haven where epic breaks beckon, **Angourie Point** lies 5km south of Yamba. There are good views from the small cliffs at the end of the road above the rocky shore.

Iluka is a carbon copy of Yamba but less developed due to its distance from the Pacific Hwy (17km). Fishermen love this area as much as nature enthusiasts; the town acts as a gateway to the World Heritage–listed **Iluka Nature Reserve**.

To reach this quaint village from Yamba by foot, take the ferry or it's a long – albeit scenic – drive around (38km).

BUNDJALUNG NATIONAL PARK

Created in 1980, this park comprises almost 4000 hectares of coastal land. There are 30km of unspoilt beaches for surfing and swimming. The entrance is 60km north of Grafton or 50km south of Ballina and there are four main areas.

The first is the **Gumma Garra** picnic area, with creeks, islands, rainforests and a midden that can be seen by the river. You can get there via Evans Head on the Bundjalung Rd. The second is **Black Rocks** (☎ 6646 6134; camping per person $3) picnic area and camping, which is tucked in behind the sand dunes of Ten Mile Beach. You can sit in the shade of a Tuckeroo tree.

The third area is the **Woody Head** (☎ 6646 6134; camping per person $8) picnic and camping area, which has rock pools and is 6km north of Iluka. The fourth is **Shark Bay**, where you can bushwalk and swim.

The day-use fee is $7 per vehicle.

EVANS HEAD

☎ 02 / pop 2614

Evans Head is a low-key little place that eschews charm and instead concentrates on its intense prawn and fishing industry.

The **Silver Sands Caravan Park & Camping Reserve** (☎ 6682 4212; Park St; camp sites from $17, cabins from $40) is green, spacious and well kept. For a

---

NEW ITALY MUSEUM

This will prove to be one of your more bizarre highway stops. Here, there's an unusual exhibition that follows the Marquis de Ray's ambitious plan to colonise the Papua New Guinean island of New Ireland. It is a tale of one man's scheme to exploit over 300 Italians in his pursuit to colonise the islands (a plan that ended when Marquis de Ray was sent to a lunatic asylum). Many of the sailors who survived settled around this area, making it 'New Italy'. An adjoining building has a folk museum devoted to Italy. A copy of Michaelangelo's David suffers from serial fondling.

If nothing else, think of this place as an entertaining rest stop. There's an Aboriginal art and craft shop as well as a **café** (☎ 6682 2622; ☺ 9am-5pm). It's right on the Pacific Hwy, 16km south of Woodburn and 19km north of the turn-off for Iluka.

---

pub room, try the classic 1930s **Hotel Illawong** (☎ 6682 4222; Evans Head; r $25-50). **Pacific Motor Inn** (☎ 6682 4318; 38 Woodburn St; r $57-75; P 🅧 🅡) has inviting rooms and a family feel.

Evans Head is 10km east of the Pacific Hwy; turn off at Woodburn.

Broadwater National Park

Extending from north of Evans Head to Broadwater, this small coastal park (3750 hectares) protects an 8km stretch of beach backed by coastal heath. You can drive all the way through the park on the roads between Evans Head and Broadwater. Camping is not allowed in the park.

BALLINA

☎ 02 / pop 16,599

The crossing of the Richmond River marks the end of the fishing villages and the beginning of the tourist-driven economy. Ballina is a sign of the times, basing its appeal around family holidays and nature activities. Although it likes to tout itself as a quiet alternative to Byron, Ballina is booming along the riverfront.

The Pacific Hwy approaches from the south and turns into River St, the main drag.

The **visitors centre** (☎ 6686 3484; www.discover ballina.com; cnr Lasbalsas Plaza & River St; ☺ 9am-5pm) has detailed information on surrounding attractions. Pick up the excellent brochure on local birds.

Sights

Behind the information centre is the **Naval & Maritime Museum** (☎ 6681 1002; Regatta Ave; admission by donation; ☺ 9am-4pm). Here you will find the amazing remains of a balsawood raft that drifted across the Pacific from Ecuador as part of the Las Balsas expedition in 1973.

White and sandy, like all good beaches, **Shelley Beach** is patrolled. Calm **Shaws Bay Lagoon** is popular with families.

Cruises up the Richmond River are a good way to get away from it all; **Richmond River Cruises** (☎ 6687 5688; Regatta Ave; 2hr trip adult/ child $20/10) is the most established.

Just north of Ballina, the **Thursday Plantation** (☎ 1800 029 000; Pacific Hwy; ☺ 9am-5pm) is a café and collection of shops selling therapeutic products. It lures visitors with a tea-tree maze and has a sculpture show in summer.

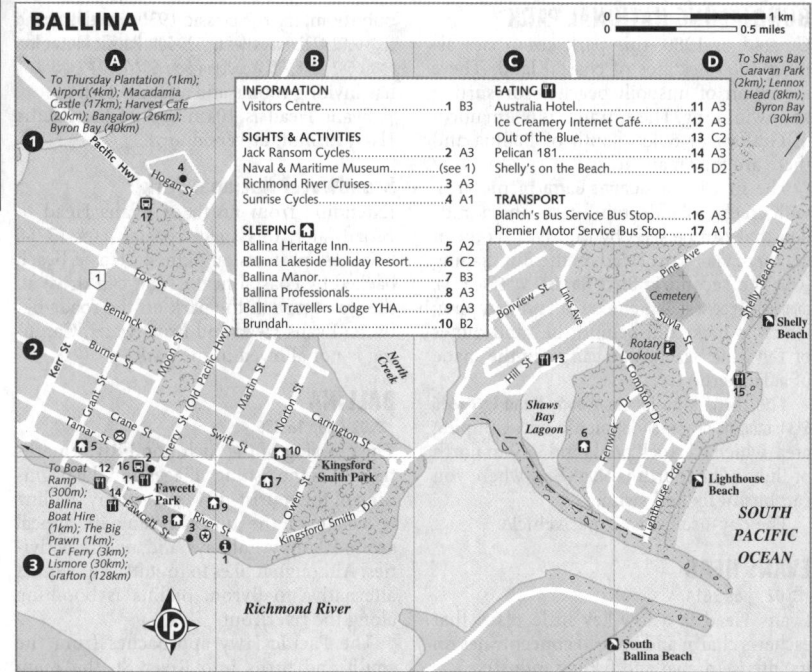

BALLINA

Activities

Ballina is renowned for its great walking and bike tracks, so hiring a bike can be rewarding. **Sunrise Cycles** (☎ 6686 6322; 3 Hogan St; per day from $10) is one of several rental shops. Also good is **Jack Ransom Cycles** (☎ 6686 3485; Cherry St; ☼ 8am-5pm Mon-Fri, 8am-noon Sat), with similar rates.

Ballina Boat Hire (☎ 0403 810 277; cnr Brunswick St & Winton Lane; per half-hr/half-day $50/75) has tinnies for fishing and catamarans for the more adventurous. It's 1km northwest of the centre.

Ballina Ocean Tours (☎ 0408 863 999; www .ballinaoceantours.com) has whale- and dolphin-watching tours, parasailing and various other exciting aquatic diversions.

Sleeping

River St in the centre and the northern approach from the Pacific Hwy both have many motels to choose from. Among the local holiday-rental agents is **Ballina Professionals** (☎ 6686 3511; www.professionalsballina.com .au; cnr Martin & River Sts). Ballina has two excellent restored inns.

Ballina Manor (☎ 6681 5888; www.ballinamanor .com.au; 25 Norton St; r $150-210; P ✕ ▯) One of the best places to stay in the region, this beautiful hotel began in the 1920s as an Edwardian-style girls' school. It's been beautifully restored and the rooms boast many antiques. The small restaurant is good.

Brundah (☎ 6686 8166; 37 Norton St; s/d $165/130; P ✕) Another gem, this restored Federation home is completely surrounded by lovely gardens.

Ballina Heritage Inn (☎ 6686 0505; 229 River St; s/d from $80/90; P ✕ ▭) Proof that motels don't all have to be built from bland bricks, this modern place is right in the centre and has 26 very comfortable units.

Ballina Travellers Lodge YHA (☎ 6686 6737; 36-38 Tamar St; dm/s/d $25/64/74; P ✕ ▯ ▭) Part hostel, part motel, this place has friendly owners, modern dorms, and bikes and body boards available for hire if you want to leave the pool. The setting is central and peaceful.

Ballina Lakeside Holiday Resort (☎ 6686 8755; Fenwick Dr; camp sites $25, cabins $45; ▭) Close to Shelley's Beach, with access to fresh and saltwater swimming holes, this resort has many amenities including spas.

Shaws Bay Caravan Park (☎ 6681 1413; 1 Brighton St; camp sites from $22, cabins from $50) Right on the lagoon and low-key. It's about 2km northeast of town.

Eating & Drinking

Ballina Manor (☎ 6681 5888; 25 Norton St; mains $24-30; ☽ dinner) The restaurant in the fine hotel of the same name has an atmospheric dining room or, even better, a fine veranda. The emphasis is on fresh seafood prepared creatively.

Out of the Blue (☎ 6686 6602; 3 Compton Dr; mains $15-25; ☽ lunch Sun, dinner Wed-Sat) The good views of Shaw's Bay complement the huge variety of fresh seafood at this popular restaurant. Lots of daily specials.

Pelican 181 (☎ 6686 9181; 12-24 Fawcett St; meals $6-20; ☽ breakfast, lunch & dinner) A breezy restaurant and takeaway right on the river; the ebullient staff here serve up seafood that's a cut above the norm.

Shelly's on the Beach (☎ 6686 9844; Shelley Beach Rd; meals $7-15; ☽ breakfast & lunch) Great casual food and superb views.

Australia Hotel (☎ 6686 2015; cnr Cherry & River Sts; meals $10-20; ☽ lunch & dinner) This big old pub gracefully keeps the pokies in a separate place. The bistro has a huge menu of steaks, seafood and pasta and there's a sizable beer garden. The bar is open until 3am Saturdays.

Ice Creamery Internet Cafe (☎ 6686 5783; 178 River St; meals $6-8; ☽ 8.30am-9pm) Sip a good banana smoothie while you surf the Internet at this very simple café.

Getting There & Away

Regional Express (☎ 13 17 13) and **QantasLink** (☎ 13 13 13) fly to Sydney from the airport (BNK) near town; this is also the closest service to Byron Bay.

Greyhound (☎ 13 14 99; www.greyhound.com.au) stops at the Big Prawn, 1km northeast of town. **Premier** (☎ 13 34 10; www.premierms.com.au) stops at the Ampol station (on the corner of Kerr St and Pacific Hwy) on the Pacific Hwy run.

Blanch's Bus Service (☎ 6686 2144; http://tropical nsw.com.au/blanchs) operates several daily services to Lennox Head, Byron Bay, Bangalow and Mullumbimby from the Tamar St bus stop.

CountryLink (☎ 13 22 32; www.countrylink.com.au) has buses connecting to trains at the Casino train station.

If you're heading to Byron Bay, take the coast road through Lennox Head. It's much prettier than the highway and shorter as well.

AROUND BALLINA

Inland from Ballina, the closely settled country of the north-coast hinterland begins, with winding, hilly roads running past tropical fruit farms, tiny villages and the occasional towering rainforest tree that has somehow escaped the wholesale clearing of the forest.

The name **Macadamia Castle** (☎ 6684 8432; Pacific Hwy; ☽ 8.30am-5pm) alone should tell you that you've found a classic roadside attraction, some 17km north of Ballina. There's a gift store (surprise!) and a café.

Harvest Cafe (☎ 6687 2644; 18 Old Pacific Hwy, Newrybar; mains $10-22; ☽ breakfast & lunch Tue-Sun) is in an old bakery that has been scrubbed up into a gem of a restaurant where Mod Oz principles are applied to the bounteous local produce. The changing choices range from sandwiches to complex mains. It's 20km north of Ballina.

LENNOX HEAD

☎ 02 / pop 5843

Just a few kilometres south but light years away in terms of crowds, Lennox Head shares the great beaches and waters of Byron to the north but without the hullabaloo. Best of all, you can always pop up to Byron for some excitement and then head back for a rest.

Lake Ainsworth is a freshwater lake that is conducive to pleasant swimming and windsurfing. Swimming there can be somewhat beneficial to the skin as the water has a trace of tea-tree oil.

Lennox Head Visitor & Tourism Centre (☎ 6687 5728; 90 Ballina St; ☽ 8am-5.30pm Mon-Fri, 8am-3.30pm Sat & Sun), a privately run information place, is also a great Internet café and is where serious computer-users in Byron come to do work. Sit outside sipping a banana smoothie while enjoying the surf and Wi-Fi access.

Wind & Water Action Sports (☎ 0419 686 188; www.windnwater.net; sailboard or long board per day $60) rents all forms of active gear to help you get everything possible out of the surf. Kitesurfing lessons are $250. Its van looks like something out of *Scooby-Doo*.

Sleeping & Eating

The **Professionals** (☎ 6687 7209; www.professionals
.com.au/lennoxhead; 66 Ballina St) is a good agent
for holiday rentals.

Lennox Head Beach House (☎ 6687 7636; www
.yha.com.au; 3 Ross St; dm/d $24/60; 🖳) This YHA-
affiliated place has immaculate rooms and
a great vibe. For $5 you can use the boards,
sailboards and bikes.

Lake Ainsworth Caravan Park (☎ 6687 7249;
Pacific Pde; camp sites $20, cabins $50) Has a nice sea
breeze flowing through it.

Ruby's by the Sea (☎ 6687 5769; 17-19 Pacific Pde;
pub meals $9-16, bistro meals $12-24; 🕑 lunch & dinner)
Part of the Lennox Point Hotel. Downstairs
in the pub it's sandwiches and burgers with
a twist, upstairs in the scenic bistro it's Mod
Oz chow with a twist. All of it is very well
prepared.

7 Mile Café (☎ 6687 6210; 41 Pacific Pde; mains $12-
24; 🕑 lunch & dinner) Right on the beach strip,
this unadorned place offers airy and shady
seating for that surf respite or something
more committed, like a major meal.

Two cafés add to Lennox Head's laid-
back cred:

Café de Mer (☎ 6687 7132; Ballina St; mains $7-14;
🕑 breakfast, lunch & dinner) Funky and stylish.

Red Rock Cafe (☎ 6687 4744; 3/60 Ballina St; mains
$10; 🕑 breakfast, lunch & dinner) Hip Mod Oz.

Getting There & Away

Premier (☎ 13 34 10; www.premierms.com.au) stops
three times a day (on request) heading
both north and south; pick up is from the
CountryLink Coach Stop. **Blanch's Bus Service** (☎ 6686 2144; tropicalnsw.com.au/blanchs) has
services to Ballina, Byron Bay as well as to
Mullumbimby.

BYRON BAY

☎ 02 / pop 7032

When Byron Bay is good, it's very, very
good. Long days, balmy weather, endless
beaches, delightful accommodation, delec-
table food, rapturous nightlife – you get the
picture. But when Byron Bay is bad, well
let's just say it's crowded. Very crowded.
But let's focus on those periods when the
traffic isn't so thick on Jonson St that driving to the chaotic mess of Woolworths
takes forever; let's instead think about the
qualities that make Byron the most desirable beach town in NSW. Let's think about
the opportunities for endless walks on the

endless shore, the fact that backpackers and
swells can still coexist and that nearby are
delightful little towns that make the whole
region greater than its parts.

The thing to remember about Byron is
that under all the glitz it is still at heart a
small town. The whole place is set up for
the several thousand who live there year-
round. So if the roads were widened and
new shopping centres built, the essential
charm would be gone.

Byron was a quiet, unassuming little village until 1963. That year surfers discovered 'The Pass' and over the following years
the town became a cauldron of artistically
minded people. Surfers adore the seven different beachfronts that surround the point,
knowing that at least one will always have a
break. Meanwhile the town's popularity is
the cause of much debate. Property prices
have soared, long-time residents are being
priced out and developers see the high-
rise horrors of the Gold Coast as a way to
satisfy demand. Residents have responded
by electing the first Green Party council in
Australia.

Information

In addition to the resources listed here,
the website www.byron-bay.com is helpful.
The *Pink Guide* is a local publication aimed
at gay and lesbian tourists; have a look at
its very useful website (http://pinkguide.ozi
gay.com).

BOOKSHOPS

Book City (☎ 6685 7820; 3/9 Lawson St) Limited selection, more a book hamlet.

Icon Books (☎ 6680 9455; 109 Jonson St) Good and
interesting selection of used books.

INTERNET ACCESS

Byron is packed with Internet-access places
that cram customers together in tight,
sweaty little pods to stare at tiny screens.
If you want to use your own laptop, or use
Wi-Fi easily, you are out of luck – it's an
embarrassment. You'll have to go down to
Lennox Head (p259). Many of the places
listed under Tourist Information (p262)
offer cheap, low-quality access as well.

Global Gossip (☎ 6680 9140) Internet outlet at the
Byron Bus & Backpackers Centre.

Internet Outpost (☎ 6685 6762; 58 Jonson St; per min
$1; 🕑 9am-8pm Mon-Fri, 9am-6pm Sat & Sun)

BYRON BAY

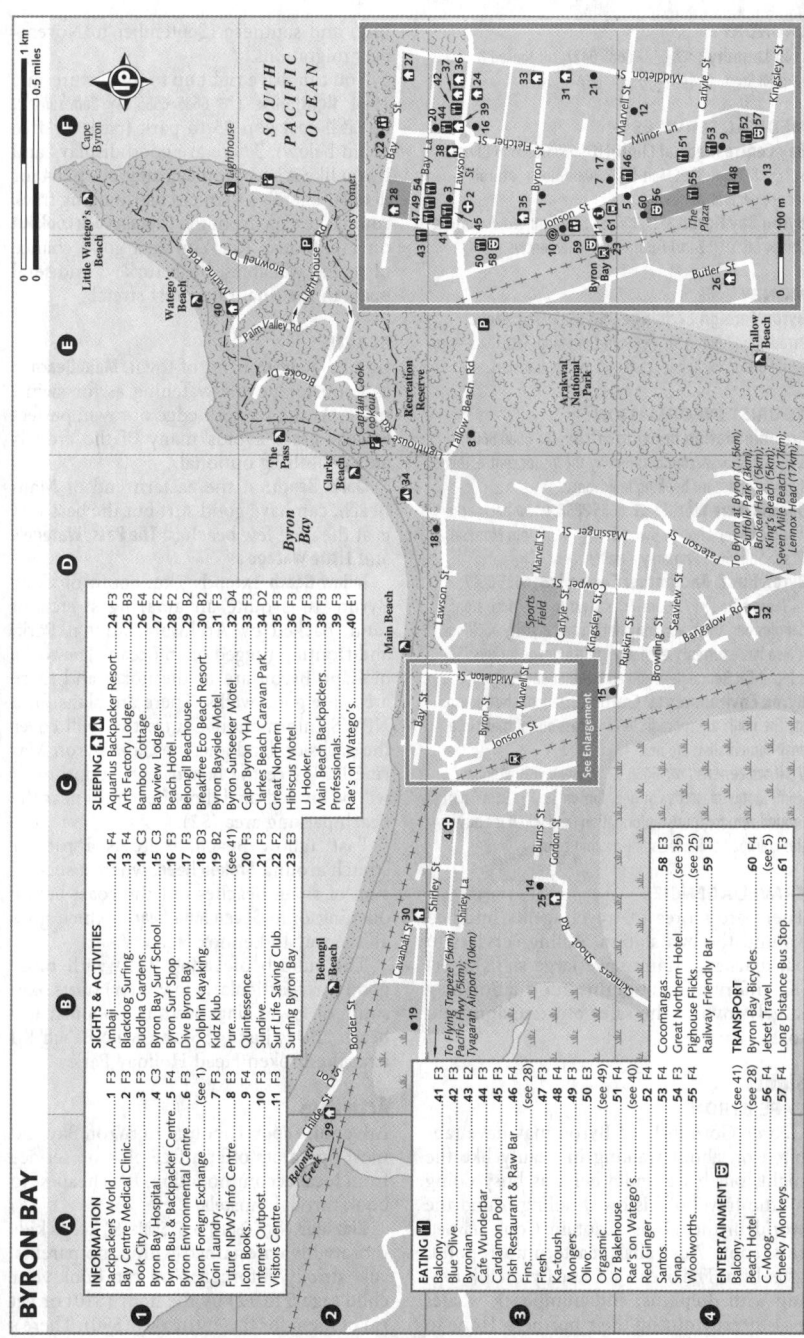

To Flying Trapeze (5km);
Pacific Hwy (5km);
Tyagarah Airport (10km)

To Byron at Byron (1.5km);
Suffolk Park (3km);
Broken Head (5km);
King's Beach (5km);
Seven Mile Beach (17km);
Lennox Head (17km)

SOUTH PACIFIC OCEAN

Cape Byron

LAUNDRY
Coin Laundry (☎ 0427 6685 0427; cnr Jonson & Marvell Sts; load $4; ☼ 7am-7pm)

MEDICAL SERVICES
Bay Centre Medical Clinic (☎ 6685 6206; 6 Lawson St; ☼ 8.30am-5pm Mon-Fri, 8.30am-noon Sat) Full-service general surgery.

Byron Bay Hospital (☎ 6685 6200; cnr Wordsworth & Shirley Sts; ☼ 24hr) For medical emergencies.

MONEY
Byron Foreign Exchange (☎ 6685 7787; Central Arcade, 4/47 Byron St; ☼ 9am-5pm Mon-Sat, 10am-4pm Sun) Foreign exchange, cash and money transfers.

TOURIST INFORMATION
Accommodation booking office (☎ 6680 8666; www.byronbayaccom.net) Run by the visitor centre, this is a great service for booking in advance.

Backpackers World (☎ 6685 8858; www.backpackers world.com.au; Shop 6, Byron St; ☼ 9am-7pm Mon-Sat, 11am-5pm Sun) Primarily a travel agent.

Byron Bus & Backpacker Centre (☎ 6685 5517; 84 Jonson St; ☼ 7.30am-7pm) Next to the coach stop; handles bus, train, accommodation and activity bookings. It also has a currency exchange, left-luggage lockers ($5), a Jetset Car Rental desk and an Internet outlet.

Byron Environmental Centre (Octagonal hut, Jonson St) The hours are sporadic but the passions of these local environmentalists are not.

Visitors centre (☎ 6680 9279; www.visitbyronbay .com; Stationmaster's Cottage, Jonson St; ☼ 9am-5pm) Ground zero for tourist information (and when it's busy this cramped office feels like ground zero).

TRAVEL AGENCIES
There are scores of travel agents huddled around the bus station, selling services to backpackers. Many have large signs offering 'information', but this information may largely involve the sales of excursions and tours.

Sights
CAPE BYRON
George Gordon Lord Byron may have rabbited on about walking in beauty like the night, but his grandfather was busy doing a little travel of his own, sailing round the world in the 1760s. Captain Cook named this spot, Australia's easternmost point, after him. The ocean at Cape Byron is jumping with dolphins, and humpback whales pass nearby during their northern (June to

July) and southern (September to November) migrations.

You can drive right up to the picturesque 1901 **lighthouse** (☎ 6685 6585; ☼ 8am-sunset), but it'll cost you $5 to park (park for free 300m below). There are good displays and if you like it here, you can stay; see p264 for details. There's a 4km circular walking track round the cape from the **Captain Cook Lookout** on Lighthouse Rd. You've a good chance of seeing wallabies, bush turkeys and feral goats in the final rainforest stretch.

BEACHES
Immediately in front of town, **Main Beach** is as good for people-watching as for swimming. At the western edge of town, perfect **Belongil Beach** avoids many of the crowds and is clothing optional.

Clarks Beach, at the eastern end of Main Beach, can have good surf but the best surf is at the next few beaches: **The Pass**, **Watego's** and **Little Watego's**.

Tallow Beach extends 7km south of Cape Byron. It is quite an amazing stretch of sand, backed by Arakwal National Park, and fronting rugged open ocean. The rocks of Cape Byron are to the north and there are some good walks. There are plans for a NPWS Information Centre that will cover the parks on land and the Cape Byron Marine Park (see the boxed text, opposite). It will be located on Tallow Beach Rd near the beach parking area ($2).

Past Tallow Beach, there is a rockier stretch around **Broken Head**, where a succession of small beaches dot the coast before opening onto **Seven Mile Beach**, which goes all the way to Lennox Head.

The suburb of **Suffolk Park** (with more good surf, particularly in winter) starts 5km south of town. **Kings Beach** is a popular gay beach and is just off Seven Mile Beach Rd near the Broken Head Holiday Park.

Activities
Adventure sports abound in Byron Bay and most operators offer a free pick-up service from local accommodation. It's cheapest to book through hostels.

Kidz Klub (☎ 6680 8585; 67 Shirley St) keeps kids thoroughly entertained with a 'no parents' rule strictly enforced. You can book your child (age 5 to 12) by the hour ($10) or get rid of them for the entire day ($90). There's

---

CAPE BYRON MARINE PARK

Created in 2002, the **Cape Byron Marine Park** (☎ 6639 6200) is a work in progress. It covers 22,700 hectares of coastal waters from Brunswick Heads south past Byron to Lennox Head. At the moment there is little to show for the park but plans are progressing rapidly on the bureaucratic front. Although the devil is in the details, ongoing consultations are designed to produce regulations that will protect the park while balancing the needs of nature, recreational users, commercial fishers and others.

Once protections are in place, the Marine Parks Authority of NSW will expand knowledge of the park and its vast marine habitat. An information centre shared with NPWS is planned for near Tallow Beach (opposite).

---

all sorts of fun activities that may make you jealous, including sand-castle making and bushwalking.

Time for a career change? You can get circus lessons at **Flying Trapeze** (☎ 0417 073 668; www.flyingtrapeze.com.au; Byron Bay Beach Club, Bayshore Dr; from $40). It's 5km west of the centre.

ALTERNATIVE THERAPIES
The *Body & Soul* guide, available from the visitors centre, is a handy guide to the many alternative therapies Byron has to offer.

Ambaji (☎ 6685 6620; www.ambaji.com.au; 6 Marvell St; massage from $60; ☽ 9am-5pm Mon-Sat, 11am-3pm Sun) Treats include blueprint healing, craniosacral balancing, crystal singing bowls and life coaching.

Buddha Gardens (☎ 6680 7844; www.buddhagardens .com; 21 Gordon St; ☽ 10am-6pm) Balinese-style day spa in a secluded spot behind walls.

Pure (☎ 6685 5988; cnr Lawson & Jonson Sts; massage from $40; ☽ 9am-7pm) There's a long list of therapies and treatments at this day spa.

Quintessence (☎ 6685 5533; 8/11 Fletcher St; massage from $45; ☽ 10am-5pm) A sign at the entrance says, 'Please enter our tranquillity zone'; you'll be whispering in no time.

Surf Life Saving Club (Main Beach; massage from $55; ☽ 8am-6pm Mon-Sat) Escape the heat of the sand with a therapeutic treat or a yoga class ($12).

DIVING
About 3km offshore, **Julian Rocks** is a meeting point for cold southerly and warm northerly currents, attracting a profusion

of marine species and divers alike. PADI open-water certification costs about $300 locally; dive trips are about $80.

Dive Byron Bay (☎ 1800 243 483, 6685 8333; www .byronbaydivecentre.com.au; 9 Marvell St) Large selection of rental equipment.

Sundive (☎ 6685 7755; www.sundive.com.au; 8 Middleton St) Long-running and respected.

FLYING
Byron Airwaves (☎ 6629 0354, 0427 615 950; www .byronair.cjb.net) Has tandem hang-gliding ($145) and courses (from $1500).

Byron Bay Skydivers (☎ 6684 1323; www.skydive byronbay.com; Tyagarah Airport) Has tandem dives from $239.

Byron Gliding Club (☎ 6684 7627; www.byrongliding .com; Tyagarah Airport) Does joy rides in gliders from $80. Love it? Lessons are offered.

KAYAKING
You can paddle within 30m of dolphins with **Dolphin Kayaking** (☎ 6685 8044; www.dolphinkayaking .com.au; half-day tour $60; ☽ 9am-2pm) It's on the beach across from 56 Lawson St.

SURFING
Byron Bay waves are often quite mellow. Most hostels provide free boards to guests, or you can rent equipment. Classes typically start at $60.

Blackdog Surfing (☎ 6680 9828; Shop 8, The Plaza, Jonson St) Intimate group lessons and a special course for women.

Byron Bay Surf School (☎ 1800 707 274; www.byron baysurfschool.com; 127 Jonson St; classes from $60) Vast curriculum offered.

Byron Surf Shop (☎ 6685 7536; cnr Lawson & Fletcher Sts) Shop selling gear and renting boards (from $20) and wetsuits.

Surfing Byron Bay (☎ 6685 7099; 84 Jonson St) An emphasis on having fun and, not surprisingly, getting wet.

Tours
Numerous operators run tours to Nimbin and other interesting places in the hinterland. See p271 for details. Most tour companies will pick you up from where you're staying.

Byron Bay Eco Tours (☎ 6685 4030; www.byron bayecotours.com; $85) Small tours to the World Heritage national parks.

Mountain Bike Tours (☎ 0429 122 504; www .mountainbiketours.com.au; from $90) Ride through the rainforest, lunch included.

Festivals & Events

East Coast International Blues & Roots Music Festival (☎ 6685 8310; www.bluesfest.com.au) At Easter, this is a major event. Book early.

Byron Bay Writers Festival (☎ 6685 5115; www .byronbaywritersfestival.com.au) Late July/early August. Draws writers and fans from across Australia.

Sleeping

There's every kind of accommodation you could hope for in and around Byron. Just don't be a duffus and turn up in January without a reservation or you'll join the hordes of backpackers and jet-set models milling around the visitors centre with hangdog looks on their faces because they thought there would be just one more room.

Motels are clustered in town and south along Bangalow Rd. There are scores of B&Bs and apartments all along Belongil Beach.

Holiday houses during low/peak season cost from $400/600 per week and go much, much higher. Rental agents:

LJ Hooker (☎ 6685 7300; www.ljhooker.com; Shop 1, Byron Arcade, 13 Lawson St)

Professionals (☎ 6685 6552; www.byronbaypro.com .au; cnr Lawson & Fletcher Sts)

BUDGET

Byron has more than 10 hostels; here is a selection.

Main Beach Backpackers (☎ 6685 8695; www .mainbeachbackpackers.com; cnr Lawson & Fletcher Sts; dm/d from $18/50; P X ⛶ ⛶) A modern and very good quality place near the beach. There's a good deck for sunsets.

Arts Factory Lodge (☎ 6685 7709; www.artsfactory .com.au; Skinners Shoot Rd; camp sites from $15, dm/d $24/60; ⛶) If you dig the alternative lifestyle, this huge place is for you. Accommodation choice ranges from teepees to funky tents. Amusements here include yoga classes, live music and Pighouse Flicks (p266). There are free minibuses around town.

Cape Byron YHA (☎ 6685 8788, 1800 652 627; www .yha.com.au; cnr Middleton & Byron Sts; dm/d from $24/80; X ⛶ ⛶) This excellent complex is situated close to the town centre and has its own shops and heated pool. It's very clean and orderly.

Belongil Beachouse (☎ 6685 7868; www.belongil beachouse.com; Childe St; dm/d from $26/65, self-contained cottages from $150; ⛶) Across from Belongil

Beach, this is a fantastic place to stay, and great value for money. Polished floorboards, stained glass in the dorm doors, and mosaics add to the atmosphere. It's all aimed at a slightly more mature crowd.

Aquarius Backpacker Resort (☎ 6685 7663, 1800 028 909; www.aquarius-backpack.com.au; 16 Lawson St; dm $18-35, d $55-200; ⛶ ⛶) Close to Main Beach. Has a bar, café, pool and garden. Rooms have bathroom, TV and fridge. There's cheap beer when *The Simpsons* is on TV.

Clarkes Beach Caravan Park (☎ 6685 6496; camp sites from $22, cabins from $85) Off Lighthouse Rd. The 109 small sites can be jammed up here, but it's quiet and you're right on the beach.

MIDRANGE

Byron Bayside Motel (☎ 6685 6004; www.byronbay sidemotel.com.au; 14 Middleton St; r from $75; P X) Right across from lush forest, this new 20-unit motel is close to the beach. Rooms are large and have good balconies.

Byron Sunseeker Motel (☎ 6685 7369; www.byron sun.com.au; 100 Bangalow Rd; r $85-210; P X ⛶ ⛶) This compact motel has spacious rooms and balconies. It's quiet and away from the action. Small cottages are also available.

BreakFree Eco Beach Resort (☎ 6639 5700; www.breakfree.com.au; 35 Shirley St; ste from $125; P X ⛶ ⛶) This is a new addition to the many holiday apartment complexes and B&Bs on this stretch of Belongil Beach, and this 30-unit resort is designed to blend in with the surroundings. The rooms have a slightly chic feel and it's a good place for couples.

Bamboo Cottage (☎ 6685 5509; www.byron-bay .com/bamboocottage; 76 Butler St; r $75-200; ⛶) The three bedrooms in this pretty 1930s house are luxurious and great value. French, English, sign language and some Japanese are spoken.

Bayview Lodge (☎ 6685 7073; www.byron-bay.com /bayview; 22 Bay St; 1-/2-bedroom units from $155/200; P) Right across from the beach, some units here have excellent views from their balconies, others don't. Units are large and have full kitchens. Some are decorated with clown art.

Hibiscus Motel (☎ 6685 6195; www.byronbay resorts.com/hibiscus; 33 Lawson St; d $135-295; X) Excellent location, right in town and right near Main Beach. The seven clean rooms at this cheery place have cable TV.

The lighthouse at Port Macquarie (p232), NSW

DALLAS STRIBLEY

OLIVER STREWE

Hunter Valley wineries (p221), NSW

The Wharf, Newcastle (p215), NSW

JOHN BORTHWICK

SIMON SELLARS

Seal Rocks (p228), NSW

JOHN BORTHW

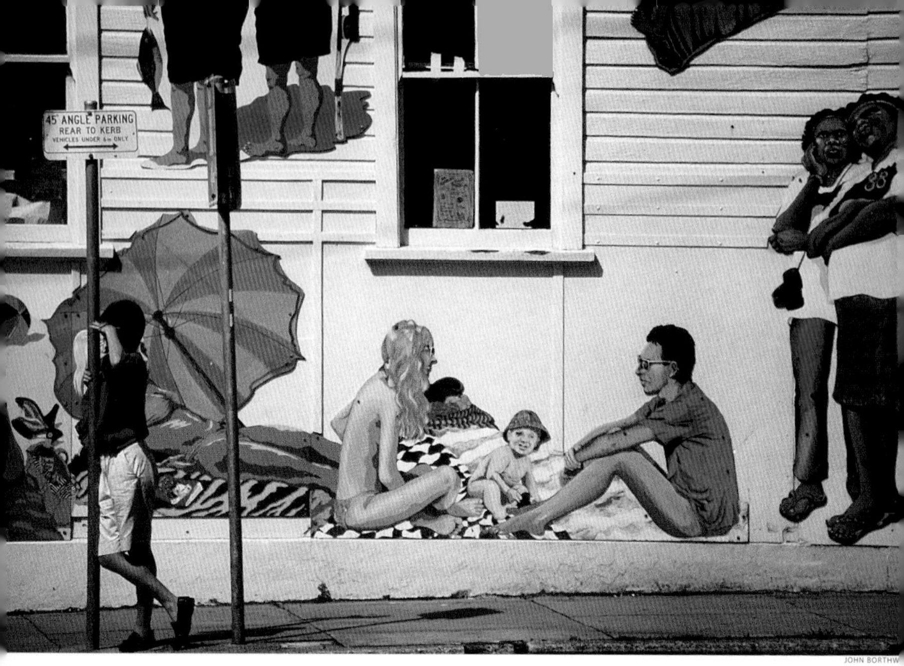

Community Centre, Byron Bay (p260), NSW

DAVID BRYANT

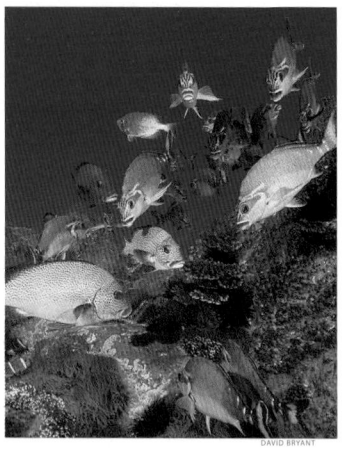

Trumpeter and red morwong near Coffs Harbour (p247), NSW

Mural in Nimbin (p271), NSW

MARK ANDREW KI

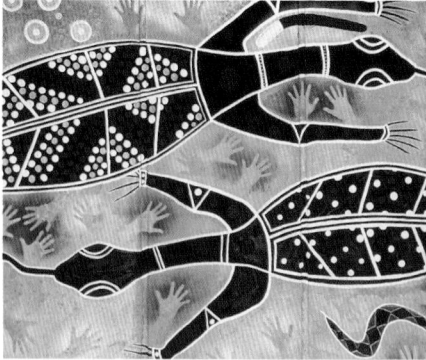

Great Northern (☎ 6685 6454; Jonson St; s/d $45/55) Basic pub rooms; the perfect place to crash after you've been listening to the great tunes and bands playing downstairs.

Lighthouse Keeper Cottages (3-day rentals from $550) Located right at the Byron Bay Lighthouse (p262), these two historic 1901 cottages have fabulous views, and you have the place to yourself after dusk. The cottages are comfy. Book through the **Professionals** (☎ 6685 6552; www.byronbaypro.com.au).

TOP END

Beach Hotel (☎ 6685 6402; www.beachhotel.com.au; cnr Jonson & Bay Sts; r $220-700; P 🍴 🖳) Nothing is more central than this icon of the Byron beachfront. Ground-floor rooms open onto lush gardens and a heated pool; rooms in the upper storeys have ocean views.

Rae's on Watego's (☎ 6685 5366; www.raes.com .au; Marine Pde; d $370-1150; P 🍴 🖳 🖳) This dazzlingly white Mediterranean villa was rated by *Condé Nast Traveller* as one of the world's top 25 hotels. The rooms here are seriously gorgeous and breathtakingly luxurious. The restaurant (right) is worth the trip alone.

Byron at Byron (☎ 1300 554 362; www.thebyron atbyron.com.au; 77-97 Broken Head Rd; ste from $270; P 🍴 🖳 🖳) New in 2005, this swanky resort is a vision in white. South of Byron proper, the 60 suites are set among the rainforest and are a 15-minute walk from the beach. Rooms have broadband, DVD players and many more luxuries. However, if your sleep is disturbed by open warfare it will be between owner Gerry Harvey (of the Harvey Norman retailing empire) and the local council. The council has been critical of Harvey and tried to fine him for permit violations; he has responded by calling them 'idiots, nitwits and ratbags'. So there.

Eating
CAFÉS

Cafe Wunderbar (☎ 6685 5909; 2 Fletcher St; treats $4; 🕑 7.30am-5pm) Beguiling baked goods are the big draw for locals, who wash their joy down with Byron's best coffee.

Fresh (☎ 6685 7810; 7 Jonson St; meals $7-22; 🕑 breakfast, lunch & dinner) Top spot for breakfast with excellent pancakes. Mod Oz at night is great at the beachy, open-air tables.

Orgasmic (☎ 6680 7778; 11 Bay Lane; mains $6-9; 🕑 10am-10pm) A simple Middle Eastern place

off the alley that is a perfect spot to escape the hordes.

Byronian (☎ 6685 6754; 58A Jonson St; mains $7-14; 🕑 breakfast & lunch) A relaxing café that's good for people-watching on busy Jonson St.

Snap (☎ 6680 9300; 13 Bay Lane; meals $6-16; 🕑 breakfast & lunch) Once you settle into the amazing wicker chairs here you may never want to get up. Fusion café specials make this a prime retreat to catch up on the newspaper or gossip.

RESTAURANT

Fins (☎ 6685 5029; Beach Hotel, cnr Jonson & Bay Sts; mains $25-35; 🕑 dinner) Let the sounds of the sea and the buzz of the bar next door float over your table to create the perfect vacation indulgence. The fresh seafood here is rightfully considered the best on the coast and the preparations are delightfully artistic.

Red Ginger (☎ 6680 9779; 109 Jonson St; mains $12-20; 🕑 breakfast, lunch & dinner) The fragrance of fresh flowers that greets you as you enter this open-air place sets the mood for perfectly prepared food. The menu is fusion, from the organic bagels at breakfast to the soba-noodle salad at lunch to the prawn linguini at dinner.

Rae's on Watego's (☎ 6685 5366; Marine Pde; mains $36-46; 🕑 lunch & dinner) Exquisite Mod Oz cuisine on a terrace with the sound of surf providing background noise to your witticisms. The common picnickers in the park below may even be eating cake.

Balcony (☎ 6680 9666; cnr Lawson & Jonson Sts; dinner $18-28; 🕑 breakfast, lunch & dinner) Finally, the food in this location matches its commanding location. The eponymous architectural feature wraps around the building and gives you tremendous views of the town. The food is Mediterranean fusion, with global influences.

Olivo (☎ 6685 7950; 34 Jonson St; mains $22-28; 🕑 dinner) The long and narrow brick-walled space here is complemented by beige leather seating. On arrival you're served garlic-and-thyme olives. This sets the mood for a Mod Oz menu that runs rampant from Europe to Asia. It may be fancy, but they treat kids well.

Dish (☎ 6685 7320; cnr Jonson & Marvell Sts; mains $27-35; 🕑 dinner) This opulent place has a Mod Oz menu and impressive wine list. The mains tend to be hearty; look for substantial seafood specials. Hit the adjoining

Dish Raw Bar – with stylish black-and-white leather furnishings with red accents – for a half-dozen oysters and a drink.

Ka-toush (☎ 6680 7718; The Plaza, Jonson St; mains $8-15; ☺ dinner) Pull up a pillow at the traditional low tables outside or be conventional and use a chair; either way the Middle Eastern food here is excellent. Go for the mixed entrée plate.

QUICK EATS

Mongers (☎ 6680 8080; 1 Bay Lane; meals $9-15; ☺ lunch & dinner) Tucked behind the Beach Hotel, the smooth jazz playing tells you that this isn't your drunken uncle's fish and chips. The standards here are so high even the tartar sauce is gourmet. Enjoy some of the best fish or calamari you've ever had at the open-air tables.

Oz Bakehouse (☎ 6685 7717; 20 Jonson St; mains $8-12; ☺ 24hr) Ideal for those who get the munchies at all times, this bakery never closes. The pies and sandwiches are pretty good.

Cardamom Pod (Shop 8, Pier Arcade, 7 Lawson St; meals $10-15; ☺ lunch & dinner) A very unassuming place with a few tables and a case full of fantastic vegetarian Indian fare.

SELF-CATERING

Byron Farmers' Market (☎ 6685 9792; Butler St; ☺ 8-11am Thu) This is a great place to sample some of the amazing food produced in the region.

Red Ginger (p265) sells a fine array of prepared Asian foods and ingredients. Other good sources of food to fill your holiday kitchen (or picnic basket) include:

Blue Olive (☎ 6680 8700; 27 Lawson St; ☺ 9am-5.30pm Mon-Fri, 9.30am-4.30pm Sat, 9.30am-3.30pm Sun) Fine cheeses and deli items, prepared foods, fantastic pesto.

Santos (☎ 6685 7071; 105 Jonson St; ☺ 8.30am-6pm Mon-Fri, 9.30am-5pm Sat, 10am-4pm Sun) Bright organic foods grocery.

Woolworths (☎ 6685 7202; The Plaza, Jonson St; ☺ 8am-9pm Mon-Fri, 8am-8pm Sat & Sun) The legend! The horror! At peak times watch holiday-makers battle for the last boneless chicken breast.

Entertainment

Byron Bay's nightlife has something over all the other towns on the north coast. Check the gig guide in Thursday's *Byron Shire News* or tune into Bay 99.9 FM.

CINEMAS

Pighouse Flicks (☎ 6685 5828; Gordon St; admission $10) The cinema at the Arts Factory Lodge (p264) shows second-run and arthouse flicks nightly.

CLUBS

Cheeky Monkeys (☎ 6685 5886; 115 Johnson St; ☺ 6pm-late) Cheap food, cheap meals, cheap drinks, cheap…well, even if you're not a backpacker the table-top-dancing mayhem may tempt you to strap one on.

Cocomangas (☎ 6685 8493; 32 Jonson St; ☺ 9pm-very late Tue-Sat) You can dance the night away at this nightclub, with fusion, funk and techno nights.

C-Moog (☎ 6680 7022; 9-10 The Plaza, Jonson St; ☺ 8pm-3am Tue-Sat) A late-night club, C-Moog spins funk and beats and has occasional gay-themed nights.

PUBS

Beach Hotel (☎ 6685 6402; cnr Jonson & Bay Sts; ☺ 11am-late) This enormous beachfront beer garden at the hotel of the same name (see p265) draws everyone from pensioners on bus tours to fire twirlers on acid. All of Byron is happening around you.

Balcony (☎ 6680 9666; cnr Lawson & Jonson Sts; ☺ until late) The good restaurant (see p265) is also a fine bar. Sit and soak up the view from stools, chairs or sofas while working through the long wine list.

Railway Friendly Bar (☎ 6685 7662; Jonson St; ☺ 11am-late) The railway may have deserted Byron but this bar stays true. It's a great indoor/outdoor pub with mighty fine food that may exceed your expectations: smoked trout and linguini etc. There's live music (rock) many nights.

Great Northern Hotel (☎ 6685 6454; Jonson St) This enormous, boisterous pub has live music many nights.

Getting There & Away

AIR

The closest airport is at Ballina (p259) but most people use the larger Coolangatta airport on the Gold Coast (see p279).

BUS

Long-distance buses for **Greyhound** (☎ 13 14 99; www.greyhound.com.au) and **Premier** (☎ 13 34 10; www.premierms.com.au) stop on Jonson St. Approximate times and fares for both are as follows: Brisbane ($30, three hours), Coffs Harbour ($43, four hours) and Sydney ($86, 12 to 14 hours).

Kirklands (☎ 6622 1499; www.kirklands.com.au) goes to Lismore ($13.20, 70 minutes), Murwillumbah (two hours) and Coolangatta Airport (two hours).

Blanch's (☎ 6686 2144; www.tropicalnsw.com.au/blanchs) goes to Ballina, Lennox Head, Bangalow and Mullumbimby.

Byron Bay Airbus (☎ 6684 3232; www.airlinkairbus.com) goes to/from Coolangatta (from $35, 50 minutes) and Ballina (from $30, 30 minutes) airports to Byron. Call to arrange pick up.

TRAIN
In case you haven't heard, the NSW government killed the popular train to Byron from Sydney. Service now sputters to a halt at Casino, over an hour by bus to the west – when the traffic is good. And often it is not; in fact the same minister also admitted a few months after he killed the train service that full improvements to the many horrid parts of the Pacific Hwy may take at least 20 years. In contrast, the highway is complete in Queensland.

Getting Around
Byron Bay Bicycles (☎ 6685 6067; The Plaza, 85 Jonson St) hires mountain bikes for $25 per day.
Jetset Travel (☎ 6685 6554; Byron Bus & Backpacker Centre, 84 Jonson St) rents new, small cars from $49. For a taxi call ☎ 6685 5008.

DETOUR: THE HINTERLANDS
You can have a pretty amazing day out from Byron Bay going on a circuit through the hinterlands. Head north on the Pacific Hwy to the river town of **Murwillumbah** (p274). Enjoy a coffee at a café in the centre before continuing on the verdant backroads 52km to **Nimbin** (p271). If the drive doesn't get you back to nature, some aggressive hippy in Nimbin will surely order you to. Grab lunch and partake of the alternative lifestyle theme-park atmosphere. From here it's more lush backroads 46km south to **Lismore** (p268). Here the conventional shopping is better than in Byron, so stock up. Some 32km east and close to Byron is **Bangalow** (p272), a quaint little one-street town good for a wander or a meal.

BRUNSWICK HEADS
☎ 02 / pop 1862
Fresh oysters and mud crabs call the Brunswick River home, as do retirees and families, who love this place as a quiet getaway with good beaches and great fishing. It is somewhat of a minnow on this coastline, wedged between the Gold Coast and Byron.

Brunswick Sails Motor Inn (☎ 6685 1353; Tweed St; r $58-110; P ⊠ ⬚) is one of several motels in town and like the rest is low-key and centrally located. Rooms have kitchenettes.

Hotel Brunswick (☎ 6685 1233; Mullumbimby St; r from $70) offers refurbished rooms at an affordable rate. The bistro, **Bruns** (mains $14; ☙ lunch & dinner), serves typical pub food in the shade of poinciana trees.

The **Terrace Reserve Caravan Park** (☎ 6685 0071; Fingal St; camp sites from $18, cabins from $70), right on the Simpson River and right in town, has 182 sites 500m from the beach. The cabins are posh by cabin standards – they even have cable TV.

You'll flip over the **Dolphin Cafe** (☎ 6685 1355; 8 The Terrace; meals $8-12; ☙ breakfast & lunch). One of several excellent places that give the town its own little café culture, the Dolphin has a gallery, a deli and good meals such as creative salads and sandwiches.

CountryLink (☎ 13 22 32; www.countrylink.com.au) has buses to Byron Bay ($5.50, 30 minutes) and Casino ($17, 90 minutes) for the train connection.

TWEED HEADS
Tweed Heads is the butt end of the Gold Coast – and that's not a good place to be. The mirrored-glass high-rises have nothing to do with the cool vibe of the beach towns to the south. But the showy lack of taste at the water pales in comparison to the nightmare of strip malls littering the Pacific Hwy. Either way, you might just want to keep driving on the new stretch of the Pacific Hwy which bypasses much of this.

Tweed Heads represents the beginning of the Gold Coast strip, the 18m monument at **Point Danger** a testament to the ghastly designs that are apparent along this belt. The border between NSW and Queensland can pass by unnoticed, as there is no river or landmark, but rather an imaginary line. It's not pretty on either side.

Coming from the south, after the bypass road branches off, the old Pacific Hwy crosses the river at Boyds Bay Bridge and becomes Wharf St, the long main street. You then meet Boundary St, which will veer to the right to take you up to Point Danger for great views and ghastly monuments.

Most of the cafés, surfers' bars and motels are just over the border in Coolangatta (Tweed Heads having cornered the market on discount auto-parts stores). See p280 for places to sleep and eat locally.

It's only fitting that the **Tweed & Coolangatta tourist centre** (☎ 5536 4244; Tweed Mall, Tweed Wharf St; ☺ 9am-5pm Mon-Sat) is buried in the heart of an enclosed mall.

There are sweeping views back down the Tweed Coast and up to the glittering high rises of the Gold Coast from the **Mt Toonbarabah Lookout** (Mt Razorback).

The **Minjungbal Aboriginal Cultural Centre** (☎ 5524 2109; cnr Kirkwood & Duffy Sts; adult/child $15/7.50; ☺ 9am-4pm Mon-Fri, 10am-2pm Sat) is set in bushland on the Tweed River. Displays detail how the Minjungbal people were able to live in harmony with the land.

Tweed Heritage Maritime Museum (☎ 5536 8625; Kennedy Dr; adult/child $4/50c; ☺ 11am-4pm Tue, Thu & Fri, 1-4pm Sun) has an array of photos documenting the time when locals fished for fish and not tourists.

For beaches, **Kirra Point** is a big favourite with surfers. Further around, **Kirra Beach** is patrolled year-round.

FAR NORTH COAST HINTERLAND

Part of the incredible allure of places like Byron Bay is actually its proximity to the nonbeach places of the hinterland. It's really the stunning lush scenery, organic markets, wilderness B&Bs and alternative lifestyles inland that make the far north coast region complete, and make it easily one of the most desirable areas in Australia – for locals and visitors alike.

Twenty-two million years ago, an eruption of lava from Mt Warning created the northern half of the hinterland, flattening the valley and enclosing it with dramatic mountain ranges. The southern end is a maze of steep hills and beautiful valleys, some still harbouring magnificent stands of rainforest while others have been cleared

for cattle grazing as well as macadamia-nut, avocado and coffee plantations. The area's three national parks – Border Ranges, Mt Warning and Nightcap – are all World Heritage rainforest.

LISMORE

☎ 02 / pop 27,358

A great base for visiting the hinterland, or even Byron, Lismore is close to rainforest, beaches and the river, has some interesting cafés and places to stay and has a thriving arts scene. It's definitely shaking its old pejorative moniker: Dis-more. The campus of Southern Cross University gives the town a young vibe and there are numerous cool cafés serving the locally grown coffee.

The **visitors centre** (☎ 6622 0122; Ballina St; Internet access per 20min $3; ☺ 9am-5pm Mon-Fri, 10am-4pm Sat & Sun) has a rainforest display ($1). Little kids dig the **Heritage Park** playground, next to the centre, with its skate park and **train rides** ($1.80; ☺ 10am-2pm Thu, 10am-4pm Sat).

The **Lismore Regional Art Gallery** (☎ 6622 2209; www.lismore.nsw.gov.au/gallery; 131 Molesworth St; admission by donation; ☺ 10am-4pm Tue-Fri, 10.30am-2.30pm Sat & Sun) displays the works of many local artists.

The **Koala Care & Research Centre** (☎ 6622 1233; Rifle Range Rd; admission free; ☺ 9.30-10.30am Sat) is home to recovering koalas and well worth a visit (you can view animals from outside anytime). To get a glimpse of a platypus, head up the northern end of Kadina St and walk up to **Tucki Tucki Creek**; your best bet to witness these animals in the wild is at dawn or dusk.

Tucki Tucki Nature Reserve (☎ 6628 1177; Wyrallah Rd), 16km south of town, protects koala habitat. Initiation ceremonies were once held at the Aboriginal **bora ring** nearby.

Sleeping

One thing Lismore could use is some new motels; the string of ones along Molesworth St are pretty much all awful.

Karinga Motel (☎ 6621 2787; 258 Molesworth St; r $62-100; ☒) Clean, affordable and central, Karinga and its 31 comfortable rooms is the best motel option and it's close to the centre and art gallery.

Tulloona House (☎ 6624 2897; 106 Ballina Rd, Goonellabah; s/d $80/100) This National Trust–classified Victorian mansion is packed to bursting with antique bric-a-brac. Outside

MARKETS OF THE HINTERLAND

You can get a real insight to the far north Hinterlands at one of the myriad of markets, which bring together hippies, yuppies and just about anyone else you can imagine. The food offerings are exquisite and diverse and you get a chance to experience the region first-hand.

Expect to find oodles of seasonal organic produce along with other foodstuffs such as farmhouse cheeses, honey and baked goods. There are often vendors selling crafts and its common to hear some live folk music, especially at the weekend markets. Hours can be erratic, but you're safest aiming to arrive in the morning.

Weekly Markets
Bangalow Farmer's Market (Byron St; 🕙 8-11am Sat) Organic produce.
Lismore Farmers Market (Lismore Showground; 🕙 8am-noon Sat)
Rainbow Region Organic Markets (Lismore Showground; 🕙 8-11am Tue)

First Weekend of the Month
Brunswick Heads (Memorial Park; 🕙 Sat)
Lismore Car Boot Market (Lismore Shopping Centre; 🕙 Sun)

Second Weekend of the Month
Alstonville Market (Apex Pavilion, Alstonville Showground; 🕙 Sun)
Channon Craft Market (Coronation Park; 🕙 Sun)
Lennox Head Lakeside Market (Lake Ainsworth Foreshore; 🕙 Sun)

Third Weekend of the Month
Aquarius Fair Markets (Nimbin Community Centre; 🕙 Sun) Produce and art. Live music.
Ballina Markets (Circus Ground; 🕙 Sun)
Lismore Car Boot Market (Lismore Shopping Centre; 🕙 Sun)
Mullumbimby Museum Market (Stuart St, 🕙 Sat)
Uki Buttery Bazaar (Uki Village Buttery; 🕙 Sun)

Fourth Weekend of the Month
Bangalow Village Market (Bangalow Showground; 🕙 Sun)
Evans Head Riverside Market (Recreation Reserve; 🕙 Sat)

Fifth Weekend of the Month
Aquarius Fair Markets (Nimbin Community Centre; 🕙 Sun) Produce and art. Live music.
Lennox Head Lakeside Market (Lake Ainsworth Showground; 🕙 Sun)

---

are clutter-free gardens. It's 5km towards Ballina; pick ups can be arranged. Rates include breakfast.

Lismore Palms Caravan Park (☎ 6621 7067; 42-48 Brunswick St; camp sites from $15, cabins from $50; 🖳) The best of Lismore's caravan parks, this one has pleasant staff and atmosphere. It's right on the river and has 13 self-contained cabins.

Eating
Unlike many other places nearby, Lismore stages its farmers market every Saturday at the Showground, off Nimbin Rd. It's a feast for the senses.

Paupiettes (☎ 6621 6135; 56 Ballina St; mains $10-17; 🕙 dinner Tue-Sat; 🕎) With little fuss, this small bistro has been providing locals with superb Mod Oz cuisine that's a showpiece of local produce. The décor is simple (think brown) but that just means there's little to compete with what's on the plate.

Left Bank Café (☎ 6622 2338; 133 Molesworth St; mains $8-16; 🕙 breakfast & lunch Mon-Sat; 🖳) Like all gallery cafés worth their sea salt, the Left Bank – which is on the left bank by the art gallery and transit centre – is delightfully pretentious and makes a very good cup of coffee. Surf with Wi-Fi while sitting in the shade.

Mega Pizza (☎ 6622 2900; 120 Ballina St; meals $8-12; ☻ dinner) Chef Barry is a pizza magician and cooks up some of the most tasty and innovative pizzas on or near the north coast. This tiny place is takeaway so you'll have to find someplace to eat the amazing meatball pizza or the unique and fabulous Mega Chicken Workz pizza.

Cross the river on the road to Nimbin and you'll find a funky little strip of cafés.

20,000 Cows Café (☎ 6622 2517; 58 Bridge St; mains $6-10; ☻ dinner Wed-Sun) This vegan café has décor as eclectic as the menu of Indian and Middle Eastern delights.

Blue Tongue (☎ 6622 0750; 43 Bridge St; meals $8-20; ☻ breakfast & lunch daily, dinner Fri) A groovy little place with '50s kitsch and a big 'back-to-nature' garden out back. Food includes good sandwiches and baked goods. Live jazz on Friday nights.

Drinking

Mecca Café (☎ 6621 3901; 80 Magellan St) On Friday and Saturday nights they close the kitchen at this splendid café and open the bar. Cosy booths make it a pleasant place for a drink or three.

Northern Rivers Hotel (☎ 6621 5797; Bridge St) What a socially conscious place this pub is: while you're meeting the Lismore locals over a schooner, the in-house crèche (Thursday to Saturday nights) will mind your kids.

Entertainment

Lismore is a diverse community and one notable local group is the **Tropical Fruits** (www.tropicalfruits.org.au), a lesbian and gay group that stages parties through the year climaxing in big New Year's revelry.

Canberra Hotel (☎ 6622 4736; 77 Molesworth St) This classic hotel has a nightclub that claims to be the 'only true nightspot in Lismore'. There are live bands Thursday to Saturday.

Winsome Hotel (☎ 6621 2283; 11 Bridge St) Enjoy live bands, DJs, pool competitions and other entertainment under the benevolent eye of the Big Regina (one of Australia's least-known 'big things': a huge portrait of HM Queen Elizabeth II). The bar is both family- *and* gay- and lesbian-friendly.

Getting There & Away

Rex (☎ 13 17 13; www.regionalexpress.com.au) has flights to Sydney (75 minutes) from Lismore's airport (LSY).

Lismore may well have the most helpful transit centre in NSW. It's right on Molesworth St by the gallery.

Greyhound (☎ 13 14 99; www.greyhound.com.au) travels to Byron Bay ($36, two hours) where you can connect for buses up and down the coast.

Kirklands (☎ 6622 1499; www.kirklands.com.au) runs to Ballina ($11, 50 minutes) and to Byron Bay ($13.20, 1¼ hours). **Waller's** (☎ 6687 8550) school buses run to Nimbin ($9, 45 minutes).

CountryLink (☎ 13 22 32; www.countrylink.com.au) now only runs buses from the sad, disused train station. Enjoy traffic while you ride a bus to the train at Casino, where you can connect to Sydney.

THE CHANNON

The Channon is an intimate village off the beaten track between Nimbin and Lismore. If you can, time your visit for the second Sunday of each month. No, it's not a religious outing; it's the 'mother of all markets', according to local pundits. Other times you'll find a café or two where you can chill out and find out about the many idiosyncratic B&Bs hidden in the hills.

Havan's (☎ 6688 6108; www.rainbowregion.com/havan; Lot 1, Lawler Rd; s/d $75/115) is an ecotourist retreat set in the heart of a rainforest. There are numerous walks near the property, including ones where you can see platypus and other exotic creatures.

NIGHTCAP NATIONAL PARK

South of Murwillumbah, north of Lismore and bordering the small towns of Nimbin and the Channon is the Nightcap National Park, encompassing 8080 hectares. It was given World Heritage status in 1989.

The park is home to diverse subtropical rainforests and many species of wildlife, notably the bent-winged bat, the wompoo fruit-dove, the masked owl and the red-legged pademelon (a relative of the wallaby). With the highest annual rainfall in NSW, the park has spectacular waterfalls, gorgeous green gullies and sheer cliff walls. The exposed rock pinnacles of the **Sphinx** can be seen from Lismore.

You can choose from walks, lookouts and picnic spots to enjoy, and **Mt Nardi** (800m) offers a challenging climb. However most of the access is on unsealed roads and the park is – rightfully – undeveloped. The NPWS office in Murwillumbah visitors centre (see p274) can supply complete details.

NIMBIN

☎ 02 / pop 400

A true product of the 1970s and the legendary Aquarius Festival, Nimbin works so hard at being alternative it's almost mainstream. But not too mainstream. The air is redolent with whiffs of incense, pot, and body odour from ecofriendly armpits. Hippies young and old prowl the streets and there are numerous businesses and community centres that attest to the unique culture found locally.

Still, Nimbin is a study in contrasts. At noon when the hordes of bussed-in daytrippers from Byron are prowling the streets in gaggles while being hectored by pot dealers it can all seem like a theme park on an acid trip. But at other times when the true locals are dominant, you get a sense of the real Nimbin, where anyone searching for their own perfect place can find it.

Orientation & Information

Despite the size of its reputation, Nimbin is a tiny village. Most businesses are on Cullen St – and horror of environmental horrors – there's lots of parking in back.

Given that some locals would have a hard time answering the question: 'Which came first, Nimbin or the organic farms?', it shouldn't surprise that there are nearly 100 local farms more than happy to host volunteers willing to yank weeds and perform other chores. The international **Willing Workers on Organic Farms** (www.wwoof.org) coordinates many such programs.

The **Nimbin Connexion** (☎ 6689 1764; www .nimbinconnexion.com; 80 Cullen St; ☺ 10am-6pm) is at the northern end of town and has accommodation options, bus tickets and a wealth of knowledge. Local literature on offer should give you a gauge of the town's issues; *Nimbin Magazine* ($3.30) is an absorbing read. Nimbin Connexion also rents bikes ($20 per day) and has Internet terminals and Wi-Fi. Ask about tours of Nimbin and the surrounds.

Sights & Activities

Despite the reticence of many locals to be pinned down on exact opening times, for fear of ruining Nimbin's image, generally everything is open 10am to 6pm.

Nimbin Museum (☎ 6689 1123; 62 Cullen St; admission $2; ☺ 'Nimbin time, man') is an interpretive and expressionistic museum, far more a work of art than of history. Across the street, the **Hemp Embassy** (☎ 6689 1842; www .hempembassy.net; 51 Cullen St; ☺ 'whenever') raises consciousness about marijuana legalisation, as well as providing all the tools and fashion items you'll need to get high. The embassy leads the **Mardi Grass** festival each May. Smokers are welcome at the coffee shop next door.

There's even more artists than pot dealers and you can find their work on display at the **Nimbin Artists Gallery** (☎ 6689 1444; 47 Cullen St; ☺ 10am-4pm).

Every third and fifth Sunday, Nimbin has its own **market**, a spectacular affair of produce and art where locals revel in their culture. There's live music.

Djanbung Gardens (☎ 6689 1755; www.earthwise .org.au; 74 Cecil St; admission free; ☺ 10am-4pm Tue-Sat) is a permaculture education centre, café and bookshop.

The town's biggest employer is the **Rainbow Power Company** (☎ 6689 1430; www.rpc.com .au; 1 Alternative Way; admission free; ☺ Mon-Fri 9am-5pm, 9am-noon Sat), designers of home-energy systems using sun, wind and water.

Sleeping

Nimbin Rox Hostel (☎ 6689 0022; www.nimbinrox .com; 74 Thornburn St; camp sites $10, dm/d $24/60; ☺) Rox has hammocks, permaculture gardens, craft workshops, live bands, Thai massage and a pool. Everything is clean and the atmosphere is relaxed and friendly.

Rainbow Retreat Backpackers (☎ 6689 1262; 75 Thornburn St; camp sites $8, dm/d $15/40) Very basic, but totally in the age-of-Aquarius spirit; you'll feel like you've fallen through a timewarp at Rainbow Retreat. Relax, chill out, play the didjeridu or camp out in the gypsy vans. There's a free courtesy bus from Byron Bay.

Nimbin Backpackers at Granny's Farm (☎ 6689 1333; 110 Cullen St; camp sites $10, dm/d $20/48; ☺) There are two pools, as well as train-carriage accommodation that's off the rails, and cabins.

Nimbin Hotel (☎ 6689 1246; Cullen St; dm $25) The two- and four-bed rooms are tidy and the veranda is great.

Grey Gum Lodge (☎ 6689 1713; www.nimbinaustralia.com/greygumlodge; 2 High St; r $40-60; 🐾) All rooms in this 1927 weatherboard house have bathroom, TV and fridge. There's a great veranda.

Nimbin Caravan & Tourist Park (☎ 6689 1402; 29 Sibley St; camp sites from $19) A simple place next to the local swimming pool, down Cullen St past the Nimbin Hotel.

Eating & Drinking

Rainbow Café (☎ 6689 1997; 64A Cullen St; mains $4-8; ⏲ breakfast & lunch) The original Nimbin institution makes delicious cakes, breakfast, burgers and vegetarian fare, and has a big backyard.

Aquarius Bakery/Cafe (☎ 6689 1566; 45 Cullen St; meals $4-8; ⏲ 6am-5pm) An excellent mainstream bakery where you can have a tasty sandwich on fresh bread and a delicious coffee out on the patio.

Nimbin Trattoria & Pizzeria (☎ 6689 1427; 70 Cullen St; mains $7-16, pizzas $4-23; ⏲ dinner daily, lunch Thu-Sun) You'll have to choose between gorging on the tasty pizza, pasta and salads and saving room for one of the groovy desserts.

Nimbin Hotel (☎ 6689 1246; Cullen St) The classic local boozer. A vast new porch out back overlooks a verdant valley. Inside artistic photos of regulars grace the walls.

Getting There & Around

Several outfits run shuttles and tours for day-trippers from Byron Bay; some include many stops in the region. For the latest details, check with the Byron Bay visitors centre (p262). The tours charge $25 to $35 depending on the itinerary and time of year, but most offer a lower rate if you just want to get to or from Nimbin.

Operators include:

Grass Hoppers (☎ 0500 881 881; www.grasshoppers .com.au) Offers tours daily and makes special itineraries around the markets.

Jim's Alternative Tours (☎ 6685 7720; www.byron -bay.com/jimstours) A long-running Byron outfit with a definite party bent.

Nimbin Shuttle (☎ 6680 9189) Operates to and from Byron Bay ($12 one way, except Sunday).

For a traditional trip (as it were), **Waller's** (☎ 6687 8550) school buses run to Lismore ($9, 45 minutes).

AROUND NIMBIN

The country around Nimbin is superb. Nimbin Rocks, an Aboriginal sacred site, lies about 6km south of town, well signposted off Stony Chute (Kyogle) Rd. It's not open to visitors, however. **Hanging Rock Creek** has falls and a good swimming hole. Take the road through Stony Chute for 14km, turn right at the Barkers Vale sign, then left onto Williams Rd; the falls are nearby on the right.

See Nightcap National Park (p270) for information on Mt Nardi.

BANGALOW

☎ 02 / pop 1230

Bangalow's appeal lies in the character of its main street, Byron St, where a collection of old buildings is occupied by galleries, delis and yoga practitioners. There's a good weekly **farmer's market** (Byron St; ⏲ 8-11am Sat) with a lot of top local organic produce on hand. Just 14km out of Byron Bay, Bangalow is a nice easy day trip.

Riverview B&B (☎ 6687 1317; 99 Byron St; r $75-195) has lavish gardens near the eponymous waterway, and bubbling waters in the hydrospa. The bright, cheery yet traditional interior may make you want to stay.

Urban Café (☎ 6687 2678; 33 Byron St; meals $12-16; ⏲ breakfast & lunch daily, dinner Thu-Sat) has the classic rocket-salad-burger-bruschetta café menu and you can enjoy your meal on the vast terrace. There's live jazz, blues or country on weekend nights. BYO.

At the Bangalow Hotel, **Fresca** (☎ 6687 1711; 1 Byron St; mains $16-25; ⏲ lunch & dinner) is a new bistro that has already won raves for its changing menu of fresh seafood and Mod Oz cuisine. Book a table on the deck. The same kitchen sends some mighty fine burgers and the like to punters in the pub.

Blanch's Bus Company (☎ 6686 2144; tropicalnsw .com.au/blanchs) has services to Byron Bay, Ballina and Mullumbimby.

MULLUMBIMBY

☎ 02 / pop 3000

The hip and happening are spilling over from Byron and this atmospheric former centre for fertiliser sales is now on the cusp of becoming the next big thing. Trendy cafés and bistros are sprouting up and you'll see no shortage of beautiful people darting about town snapping up pricey organic treats. It's definitely worth a break from a drive on the Pacific Hwy, or a day trip from the coast.

Burringbar St is the main shopping street and runs off Dalley St, which is the main road through town. There isn't a visitors centre, but **Tassa** (☎ 6684 6555; Tincogan St; ☺ 9am-7pm) keeps an array of local information brochures and pamphlets out on its porch. It also has Internet access.

Sights & Activities

The best thing to do in Mullumbimby is simply walk around. Besides the interesting commercial streets, there is a trail along the Brunswick River in town that passes through tropical forest and is lined with signs relating Aboriginal stories.

The **Brunswick Valley Historical Society Museum** (☎ 6684 1149; Stuart St; ☺ 10am-3pm Sat) offers a comprehensive insight into the many grand old buildings around town. Call to confirm opening hours.

Crystal Castle (☎ 6684 3111; Monet Dr; admission free; ☺ 10am-5pm) has labyrinthine gardens and an impressive collection of crystals. You may just draw enough energy from these things to unburden your wallet in the gift shop.

Sleeping

Mullumbimby Motel (☎ 6684 2387; 121 Dalley St; r $52-100; ℗ ✺) The 10 rooms here are lushly shaded by gardens. A good choice.

Commercial Hotel (☎ 6684 3229; cnr Burringbar & Stuart Sts; s/d $30/45) Standing since 1907; the rooms here are good value.

Maca's Camping Ground (☎ 6684 5211; Main Arm Rd, Main Arm; camp sites $18) Camping under a macadamia-nut plantation is what Maca's offers and delivers. This otherwise basic place is 12km north of town.

Eating & Drinking

Milk & Honey (☎ 6684 1422; 59A Station St; mains $15-20; ☺ dinner Mon-Sat) Chef Chris Pellen has created this delightful little spot on a quiet little street, and serves up sublime thin-crust wood-fired pizza. There's always at least a dozen on offer. Specials are also impressive; if you see something with the amazing aïoli, order it.

Lulu's Café (☎ 6684 2415; Dalley St Plaza; mains $8; ☺ breakfast & lunch Mon-Sat) Lulu's is a great vegetarian place to enjoy, say, a pesto and avocado sandwich out on the patio.

Commercial Hotel (☎ 6684 3229; cnr Burringbar & Stuart Sts; meals $7-16; ☺ breakfast, lunch & dinner) The options here are bewildering: simple bistro, formal dining area serving huge steaks, wine bar and traditional sports bar.

Getting There & Away

Blanch's Bus Service (☎ 6686 2144) runs several times daily to Byron Bay, Lennox Head and Ballina.

CountryLink (☎ 13 22 32; www.countrylink.com.au) now serves the train station in town with buses to the train at Casino ($15, 1½ to two hours).

WHIAN WHIAN STATE FOREST

Timber is still produced in this **state forest** (☎ 6627 0200), which leads to certain tensions given the beauty of the area. The forest adjoins the southeast side of Nightcap National Park and is home to the Albert's lyrebird. There are plans to develop camping areas.

The spectacular **Minyon Falls** are found here, plunging 100m into a rainforest gorge and surrounded by a flora reserve with several walking tracks. Take a dip under the falls for an unforgettable experience.

The **Nightcap Track** (16km long) passes through state forest and Nightcap National Park, and was the original track used by postal workers and others in the late 19th and early 20th centuries. **Rummery Park** is not far off the road down from the falls and has a picnic spot with barbecues and cold showers. **Peate's Mountain Lookout**, just on from Rummery Park, gives you a great panoramic view from Jerusalem Mountain in the north to Byron Bay in the east.

Mud Manor Forest Retreat (☎ 6688 2205; www .mudmanor.com; Fox Rd, Rosebank; r from $120; 🖳 🖳), southeast of the state forest, is a perfect haven for those who just want to get away from the crowds. The rooms have hand-crafted luxuries and large decks. There are spa bathrooms and lush gardens.

UKI
☎ 02 / pop 211

Uki (uke-i) is a cute spot of a town that is overshadowed by the dominating peak of Mt Warning. The alternative feel of the town is typical of the region. The **visitor information centre** (☎ 6679 5399; 🕒 10am-4pm) has Internet access and details of the nearby national parks.

The **Uki Dreaming Guesthouse** (☎ 6679 5777; Mitchell St; s/d $40/60) is in an old weatherboard house overlooking the crossroads. **Uki Dreaming Café** (☎ 6679 5351; Main St; mains $6-12; 🕒 lunch daily, dinner Fri & Sat) serves creative sandwiches and salads. The town also has a bead shop and leathergoods store.

There are a number of other places to stay in the area, including the **Midginbil Hill Country Resort** (☎ 6679 7158; 252 Midginbil Rd; r with dinner $128), where you can go horse riding, as well as canoeing on the Clarrie Hall dam. It also has dorm bunkhouses (per person $16).

MT WARNING NATIONAL PARK

Relatively small in size (2380 hectares), this park is the most dramatic feature of the hinterland, with Mt Warning (1156m) towering over the valley. The peak is the first part of mainland Australia to be touched by sunlight each day. Over 60,000 people a year make the 4.4km, five-hour round-trip trek to the top from Breakfast Creek. If you'd like a guide and a chance to learn much more about the local ecology, try **Mt Warning Eco Tours** (☎ 1800 097 587; www.myaussieadventures .com; tours from $60), which offers a range of climbs and tours.

Captain Cook aptly named this mountain in 1770 to warn seafarers of the offshore reefs. The Aboriginal people called it Wollumbin, meaning all of these: 'cloud catcher', 'fighting chief of the mountain' and 'weather maker'.

You can't camp at Mt Warning, but the **Mt Warning Caravan Park & Tourist Retreat** (☎ 6679 5120; Mt Warning Rd; camp sites from $18, cabins from $50), on the Mt Warning approach road,

is a viable option, with good kitchen facilities and a well-stocked kiosk.

Wallers (☎ 6687 8550) runs from Lismore ($20) to Dum Dum, the town at the turn-off for Mt Warning. Call for departure times.

MURWILLUMBAH
☎ 02 / pop 7596

This relaxed town may well take its cues from the Tweed River, which it straddles. The waters flow wide and slow here, and views of the river are simply soothing. Murwillumbah is a focal point of the hinterland's agriculture; tourism is not the focus but it does have stunning views of Mt Warning (including spectacular sunsets).

The **visitors centre** (☎ 6672 1340; www.tweed -coolangatta.com.au; 13 Commercial Way; 🕒 9am-4.30pm) has national-park info and passes, a great rainforest display and prime position on the Tweed River. It's off Old Pacific Hwy.

Sights

The **Tweed River Art Gallery** (☎ 6670 2790; www .tweed.nsw.gov.au/artgallery; cnr Mistral Rd & Tweed Valley Way; admission free) is a great regional institution. The gallery administers Australia's richest prize for traditional art, the $100,000 Doug Moran Prize. Works of past winners are on display. Check out the always popular and enigmatic portrait of Jonathan Aatty by Hui Hai Xie. The gallery is 3km south of town.

The **Murwillumbah Museum** (☎ 6672 1865; 2 Queensland Rd; adult/child $2/1; 🕒 11am-4pm Wed & Fri) has a solid account of local history and an interesting radio room.

Tropical Fruit World (☎ 6677 7222; www.tropicalfruit world.com.au; Duranbah Rd; adult/child $30/15; 🕒 10am-4.30pm) is a much-hyped family attraction 12km northeast of Murwillumbah, which, despite being home to the Big Avocado, is really a bit of a lemon. There's some rides and various displays of fruit but it never quite justifies the melon-sized price of admission.

Tours

Northern Breeze (☎ 07-5524 2264; northernbreeze@ omcs.com.au; tours per person $20-45) runs tours that pick you up at your door and take you through the local national parks, Nimbin and attractions of the Tweed Valley.

Sleeping

Murwillumbah YHA (☎ 6672 3763; www.yha.com .au; 1 Tumbulgum Rd; dm/d $25/54) Beautifully located

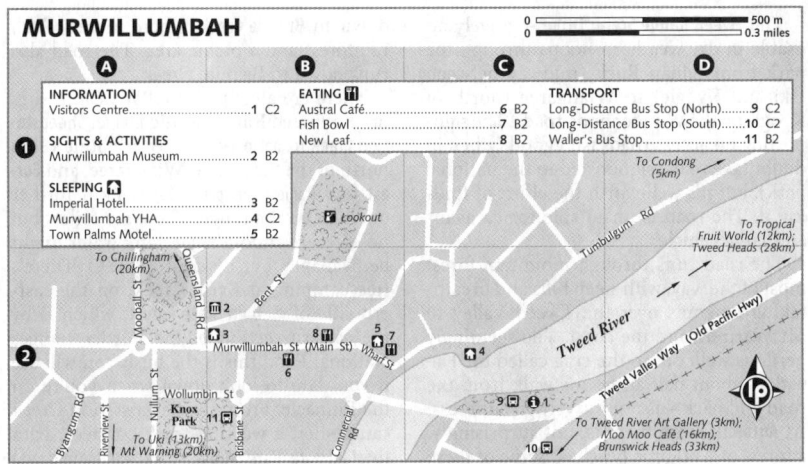

MURWILLUMBAH

0 _____ 500 m
0 _____ 0.3 miles

INFORMATION		
Visitors Centre	1	C2

SIGHTS & ACTIVITIES		
Murwillumbah Museum	2	B2

SLEEPING		
Imperial Hotel	3	B2
Murwillumbah YHA	4	C2
Town Palms Motel	5	B2

EATING		
Austral Café	6	B2
Fish Bowl	7	B2
New Leaf	8	B2

TRANSPORT		
Long-Distance Bus Stop (North)	9	C2
Long-Distance Bus Stop (South)	10	C2
Waller's Bus Stop	11	B2

on the edge of the Tweed River, this friendly hostel cements its reputation by giving out free ice cream every night at 9pm. Canoes and bikes are available to hire, and there's free transport to the base of the Mt Warning climb if you stay more than two nights.

Town Palms Motel (☎ 6672 8600; 3 Wharf St; r $55-60;) The pick of the motels, with position, facilities and 10 rooms.

Imperial Hotel (☎ 6672 2777; 115 Main St; s/d $25/40) Big and pink, this hotel has standard but pink rooms. However, renovations are planned so confirm prices – and room colours.

Eating

Austral Café (☎ 6672 2624; 88 Main St; mains $6; breakfast & lunch Mon-Sat;) The motto at this 1950s icon is 'a great place to meet and eat', which says it all.

Fish Bowl (☎ 6672 2667; 3 Wharf St; meals $5-10; 9am-7.30pm Mon-Sat, 9am-5pm Sun) Fresh fish in many forms is on offer at this café and takeaway. The dory fillets are justifiably popular.

New Leaf (☎ 6672 4073; Shop 10, Murwillumbah Plaza; meals $5-10; 7.30am-5pm Mon-Fri;) The food here is creative and vegetarian. There's many Middle Eastern dishes and a long list of salads. Enjoy inside, out on the courtyard or take away.

Moo Moo Café (☎ 6677 1230; Tweed Valley Way, Mooball; mains $8; breakfast & lunch) Halfway between Murwillumbah and Brunswick Heads, this famous café takes the cow kitsch to udder extremes.

Getting There & Away

Greyhound (☎ 13 14 99; www.greyhound.com.au) stops here on its Pacific Hwy runs north to Brisbane ($24, three hours) and south to Sydney ($100, 13 hours). **Premier** (☎ 13 34 10; www.premierms.com.au) runs a similar service in both directions.

Waller's (☎ 6687 8550) has school-day buses to Nimbin and Lismore.

BORDER RANGES NATIONAL PARK

The Border Ranges National Park, a World Heritage area of 31,729 hectares, covers the NSW side of the McPherson Range, which runs along the NSW–Queensland border, and some of its outlying spurs. The park's wetter areas protect large tracts of superb rainforest and it has been estimated that a quarter of all bird species in Australia can be found in the park.

There park is made up of three main sections. The eastern section – which includes the escarpments of the massive Mt Warning caldera – is the most easily accessible area. Access it via the Tweed Range Scenic Drive, which begins at Barkers Vale, 40km southwest of Murwillumbah. It's possible to access the smaller central section from the Lions Rd, which turns off the Kyogle–Woodenbong road 22km north of Kyogle. The large and rugged western section is almost inaccessible except to well-equipped bushwalkers, but it's possible to get good views of the peaks in the area from the Kyogle–Woodenbong road.

The **Tweed Range Scenic Drive** – gravel and usable in dry weather – loops through the park from Lillian Rock (midway between Uki and Kyogle) to Wiangaree (north of Kyogle on the Woodenbong road). The signposting on access roads isn't good (when in doubt take roads signposted to the national park), but it's well worth the effort of finding it. The road is unsuitable for caravans and large vehicles.

The road runs through mountain forest most of the way, with steep hills and breathtaking lookouts over the Tweed Valley to Mt Warning and the coast. The seemingly perilous walk out to the crag called the **Pinnacle** – about half an hour's walk from the road and back – is not for vertigo sufferers! At **Antarctic Beech** there is, not surprisingly, a forest of Antarctic beeches. Some of these trees are more than 2000 years old. From here, a walking track (about 5km) leads

down to **Brindle Creek**, where there is lush rainforest and a picnic area. The road also runs down to Brindle Creek.

There are a couple of NPWS camp sites on the Tweed Range Scenic Drive: **Sheepstation Creek** (camping per person $3) is about 15km north of the turn-off at Wiangaree, and **Forest Tops** (camping per person $3) is 6km further on, high on the range. There are toilets but no showers at both sites. Tank water might be available, but it's best to BYO. There's free camping at Byrill Creek, on the eastern side of **Mebbin State Forest**, which is by the eastern section of the Border Ranges National Park; this is the bush you will see if you dare to look down when you're on the Pinnacle. From the Sheepstation Creek camp sites, a walking track connects with the Caldera Rim Walk (three or four days) in Lamington National Park, over the border in Queensland.

Queensland

OLIVER STREWE

Gold Coast

The Gold Coast is a shimmering ribbon of intensive tourist development – a showpiece of Queensland's much touted free and easy lifestyle stretching for 35km between Southport and the NSW border. It's glitzy and crowded, and offers a host of ways to spend your recreational time and superfluous money. The theme parks, shopping malls and casinos, all on a grand scale, don't appeal to everyone, but the brash commercialism, enviable climate and family-friendly attractions draw more than two million visitors a year.

The nerve centre is Surfers Paradise, which, depending on your viewpoint, is either the heart of the action or place you'll most want to avoid. Ultimately, the only real way to enjoy it is to plunge in and visit a theme park, cuddle a koala, bungee jump and dance until dawn. For respite, however, you won't need to head far. Mermaid Beach, Broadbeach, and Southport are part of the urban sprawl, but the hype diminishes away from the epicentre. At the southern end of the Gold Coast, Coolangatta is the quietest (and cheapest) of the resorts. Unexpected peace can be found at the northern end of the strip on South Stradbroke Island.

The Gold Coast has excellent surfing at Burleigh Heads, Kirra and Duranbah Beach and, while many are drawn by the surf, sun and fun, there's a stunning hinterland less than 30km from the beaches and high-rises. This densely forested region embraces two of Queensland's best national parks, Lamington and Springbrook, and the cool mountain retreat of Mt Tamborine.

HIGHLIGHTS

- Accelerate the exhilaration factor on rides at the **Gold Coast theme parks** (p288)
- Cuddle the furred and feathered at the **wildlife sanctuaries** (p283) near Burleigh Heads
- Wax it up and barrel down the huge right-hander at **Burleigh Heads** (p284)
- Party hard and overdose on glitz during Queensland's biggest party – **IndyCar** (p289) at Surfers Paradise
- Catch a wave or three at the pleasant **Kirra** and **Coolangatta Beaches** (p280)
- Cool off and slow down among the tumbling waterfalls, rich green rainforest and spectacular views of **Springbrook plateau** (p295)
- Relax in style or simplicity far from the crowds on the sandy expanse of **South Stradbroke Island** (p294)

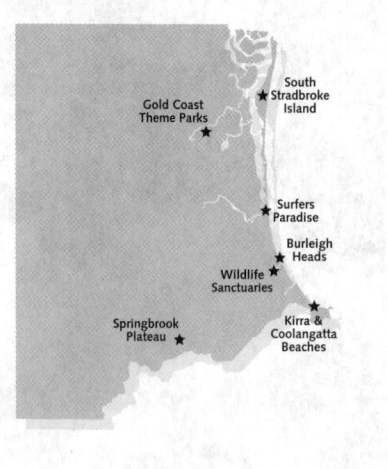

- TELEPHONE CODE: 07
- www.goldcoastguide.com

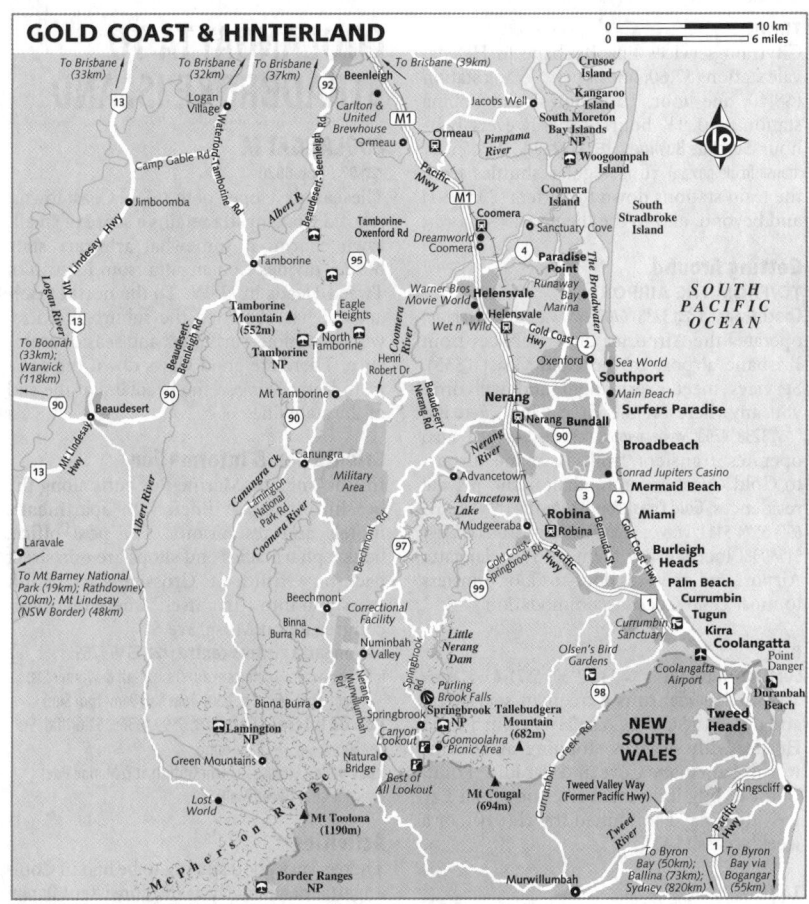

GOLD COAST & HINTERLAND

GOLD COAST

Getting There & Away

AIR

The Gold Coast airport is based at Coolangatta, about 25km south of Surfers Paradise. **Qantas** (☎ 13 13 13; www.qantas.com.au) flies direct to Coolangatta Airport from Sydney ($110, 1½ hours) and Melbourne ($165, two hours). **Jetstar** (☎ 13 15 38; www.jetstar.com.au) also operates flights between Coolangatta and Sydney ($80) or Melbourne ($120).

BUS

Long-distance buses stop at the bus transit centres in Southport, Surfers Paradise and Coolangatta. Most companies will let you stop off on the Gold Coast if you have a through ticket.

Greyhound (☎ 13 14 99; www.greyhound.com.au) has frequent services that run between Surfers Paradise and Brisbane ($15, 1½ hours), also to Byron Bay ($25, two hours) and to Sydney ($100, 15 hours). **Premier** (☎ 13 34 10; www.premierms.com.au) covers the same routes as Greyhound but for slightly less. **Kirklands** (☎ 1300 367 077) travels to Surfers Paradise from Byron Bay ($27) and Brisbane ($15), stopping at most Gold Coast settlements along the way.

Coachtrans (☎ 13 12 30, 3238 4700; www.coachtrans .com.au) offers shuttle services that run from Brisbane to Surfers ($23, 1½ hours) as well as Coolangatta/Tweed Heads ($23, two hours) and to many of the theme parks in the area.

GOLD COAST

TRAIN

Citytrain services link Brisbane to Helensvale station ($7.60, one hour), Nerang station ($8.40, one hour, 10 minutes) and Robina station ($10, 1¼ hours) roughly every half-hour. **Surfside Buslines** (☎ 13 12 30, 5571 6555; www .transinfo.qld.au) runs regular shuttles from the train stations down to Surfers ($3 to $4) and beyond, and to the theme parks.

Getting Around

TO/FROM THE AIRPORT

Coachtrans (☎ 3238 4700; www.coachtrans.com.au) operates the Airporter direct services from Brisbane airport to the Gold Coast ($35). Services meet every flight and will drop you anywhere on the Gold Coast. **Aero Bus** (☎ 3238 4700; www.aerobus.net; one way $25) also operates transfers from Brisbane airport to Gold Coast accommodation and private residences. **Gold Coast Tourist Shuttle** (☎ 1300 655 655, 5574 5111; www.gcshuttle.com.au; adult/child/family $15/8/38) meets every flight into Coolangatta Airport and operates door-to-door transfers to most Gold Coast accommodation.

BUS

Surfside Buslines (☎ 13 12 30, 5571 6555; www .transinfo.qld.gov.au) runs a frequent service up and down the Gold Coast Hwy from Tweed Heads, with services stopping at Dreamworld, Sanctuary Cove and Paradise Point. You can buy individual fares or get an Ezy Pass for a day's unlimited travel ($10), or a weekly pass ($43).

TAXI

The recommended statewide taxi number, ☎ 13 10 08, will get you a taxi anywhere along the Gold Coast.

COOLANGATTA TO STRADBROKE ISLAND

COOLANGATTA

☎ 07 / pop 6820

The least developed of the Gold Coast towns, relaxed Coolangatta retains a sense of small-town charm. A somewhat arbitrary state border divides Coolangatta from its twin of Tweed Heads in NSW. To the north, Coolangatta has absorbed the suburb of Kirra, with its famous surf break and seaside ambience. There are good views down the coast from Point Danger, the headland at the end of the state line.

Orientation & Information

In Coolangatta, Marine Pde runs along the beachfront and is lined with apartments, motels and restaurants. The post office, banks, pharmacies and shops are one street back on Griffith St. Crossing Kirra Point takes you into Kirra itself, where the shops congregate on Musgrave St.

Coolangatta visitors centre (☎ 5536 7765; infocoolangatta@gctb.com.au; cnr Griffith & Warner Sts; ✆ 8am-5pm Mon-Fri, 8am-4pm Sat, 9am-1pm Sun)

PB's OZ Internet Cafe (☎ 5599 4536; 152 Griffith St; per 30min $4; ✆ 9am-6pm)

Post office Coolangatta (cnr Griffith St & Marine Pde); Tweed Heads (**Tweed Mall**)

Activities

There's very good surfing to be had in Coolangatta, particularly at the consistent **Duranbah Beach** by Point Danger and **Kirra Point**. Gentler breaks can be found at **Greenmount Beach** and **Rainbow Bay**.

SCHOOLIES ON THE LOOSE

Every year in November, hundreds of teenagers flock to Surfers Paradise to celebrate the end of their high-school education in a month-long party that's become known as 'schoolies week'.

Schoolies week started in the early '90s and quickly gained popularity – and notoriety – as an anything-goes party, with drunk and drug-addled teens a common sight in the streets and pubs of Surfers. However, the local authorities have stepped in and these days schoolies week is a highly organised affair with plenty of free entertainment, sections of the beach devoted to drug- and alcohol-free parties, and accessible emergency and counselling services to temper the inevitable excesses.

Such is the success of schoolies week that it's taken off at other tourist towns up and down the east coast, notably Byron Bay, Noosa, Airlie Beach and Magnetic Island and has its own website, www.schoolies.com.

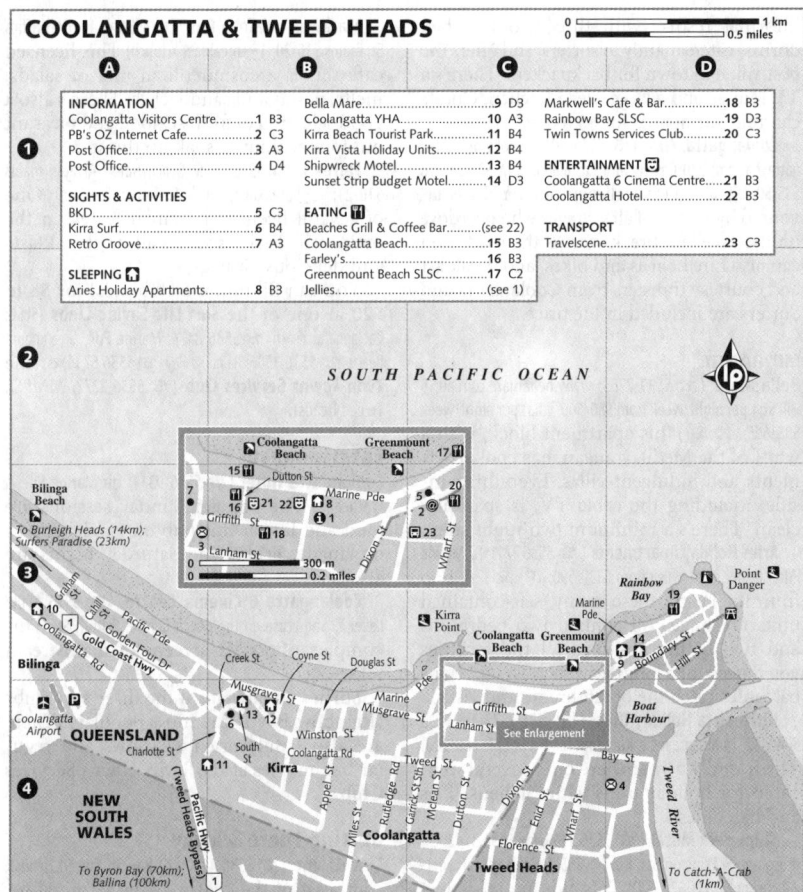

COOLANGATTA & TWEED HEADS

INFORMATION
Coolangatta Visitors Centre............	1	B3
PB's OZ Internet Cafe....................	2	C3
Post Office....................................	3	A3
Post Office....................................	4	D4

SIGHTS & ACTIVITIES
BKD..	5	C3
Kirra Surf.....................................	6	B4
Retro Groove................................	7	A3

SLEEPING
Aries Holiday Apartments..............	8	B3
Bella Mare....................................	9	D3
Coolangatta YHA...........................	10	A3
Kirra Beach Tourist Park...............	11	B4
Kirra Vista Holiday Units...............	12	B4
Shipwreck Motel...........................	13	B4
Sunset Strip Budget Motel............	14	D3

EATING
Beaches Grill & Coffee Bar..........	(see 22)	
Coolangatta Beach........................	15	B3
Farley's..	16	B3
Greenmount Beach SLSC...............	17	C2
Jellies..	(see 1)	

Markwell's Cafe & Bar..................	18	B3
Rainbow Bay SLSC........................	19	D3
Twin Towns Services Club.............	20	C3

ENTERTAINMENT
Coolangatta 6 Cinema Centre.....	21	B3
Coolangatta Hotel........................	22	B3

TRANSPORT
Travelscene..................................	23	C3

GOLD COAST

Kirra Surf (☎ 5536 3922; 6 Creek St) has an excellent range of boards and gear, and you can rent boards for $30 per day from **Retro Groove** (☎ 5599 3952; 3 McLean St) or **BKD** (backdoorsurfwear@yahoo.com; Boundary St).

Tours

There are various operators running 2½- to 4½-hour cruises along the Tweed River; the tours usually visit oyster farms, bird-watching haunts and crabbing areas. **Catch-A-Crab** (☎ 5599 9972; www.catchacrab. au; adult/child incl lunch $90/54) operates half-day tours along the Terranora Inlet of the Tweed River. On these trips you can try your hand at crabbing as well as fishing, pelican feeding and yabbie hunting.

Sleeping

Over the Easter, Christmas and school-holiday periods tariffs can rise by up to 50%; at other times you can sometimes bargain the price down.

BUDGET

Kirra Beach Tourist Park (☎ 5581 7744; www.gctp .com.au/kirra; Charlotte St, Kirra; tent sites $21-24, caravan sites $23-26, cabins from $70; ☒ ☒) This large park is spread out and has plenty of grassy sites, modern self-contained cabins and good-value doubles. Facilities include a TV room, camp kitchen and wheelchair access.

Sunset Strip Budget Resort (☎ 5599 5517; www .sunsetstrip.com.au; 199 Boundary St, Coolangatta; dm/s/d $28/39/60, ste per 3-night stay $225-330; ☒) This informal resort (with three- to four-bed dorms) caters mainly to surfers, and offers the best value in town for backpackers. There's a TV lounge and a large, clean kitchen. Guests can rent surfboards for $5 a day.

Coolangatta YHA (☎ 5536 7644; booking@coolangattayha.com; 230 Coolangatta Rd, Bilinga; dm $22-24, s/d $35/50; ▢ ☎) This well-equipped YHA is favoured by surfies of all vintages who overdose on the excellent breaks across the road. You can also hire boards and bikes, and breakfast and courtesy transfers from Coolangatta and Surfers are included in the price.

MIDRANGE

Bella Mare (☎ 5599 2755; www.bellamare.com.au; 5 Hill St; r per night/week from $80/560, villas per night/week $95/665; ▨ ☎) This apartment block, with a whiff of the Mediterranean, has cool apartments and indulgent villas. Everything inside, including the cable TV, is sparkling clean. There's a minimum two-night stay.

Aries Holiday Apartments (☎ 5536 2711; 82 Marine Pde; ste per night/week from $130/590; ℗ ☎) A hop from the beach, these sunny, self-contained units are huge. All contain two bedrooms and two bathrooms plus all the facilities you'd need for a long-term stay. The spacious balconies catch the ocean breeze and vista.

Kirra Vista Holiday Units (☎ 5536 7375; fax 5536 5640; 12-14 Musgrave St, Kirra; apt for 2-4 people $80-100) The friendly owners here offer several well-cared-for holiday units with kitchens, TVs and balconies.

Shipwreck Motel (☎ 5536 3599; fax 5536 3742; cnr Musgrave & Winston Sts, Kirra; r $55-60, self-contained 1- 2-bedroom units $80-120) This tidy motel is just across from the beach.

Eating

Beaches Grill & Coffee Bar (☎ 5536 9311; Coolangatta Hotel, cnr Marine Pde & Warner St; mains $12-18; ☒ breakfast, lunch & dinner) The menu exceeds any pub bistro expectations with dishes like salt-and-pepper seared chicken or New York sirloin dusted with pepper and rosemary. There's plenty of room, it's good value and it's kid-friendly.

Jellies (☎ 5536 1741; 91 Griffith St; mains $20-30; ☒ breakfast, lunch & dinner) The menu in this sun-flooded restaurant is the most inventive in town; their fish of the day is topped with a chilli, mango, macadamia and coriander salsa. Pizzas, snacks and kids' meals are also served.

Markwell's Cafe & Bar (☎ 5536 4544; 64 Griffith St; mains $10-20; ☒ breakfast & lunch) This licensed café serves a cosmopolitan mix of salads, melts, pastas and sandwiches. There's also a good selection of fresh seafood and pleasant outdoor seating to soak up the sun.

Farley's (☎ 5536 7615; Beach House Arcade; mains $10-21; ☒ breakfast, lunch & dinner Tue-Sun) One of several licensed pavement cafés on the main strip, Farley's serves all-day breakfasts and delicious pastas.

You can fill up on a club meal for $8 to $20 at one of the **Surf Life Saving Clubs** (SLSC; Coolangatta Beach ☎ 5536 8474; Marine Pde; Greenmount Beach ☎ 5536 1506; Rainbow Bay ☎ 5536 6736) or the **Twin Towns Services Club** (☎ 5536 2277; Wharf St, Tweed Heads).

Entertainment

Coolangatta Hotel (☎ 5536 9311; cnr Marine Pde & Warner St) The popular Sunday sessions are loud and live at this pub on Coolangatta's esplanade. Friday and Saturday nights are also busy.

Coolangatta 6 Cinema Centre (☎ 5536 8900; Level 2, Showcase on the Beach Centre, Griffith St) This complex offers six screens of mainstream releases.

Surfies congregate at the three surf clubs (Rainbow Bay is the most popular). There are also family-oriented shows and regular free movies at the Twin Towns Services Club.

Getting There & Away

Travelscene (☎ 5536 1700; 29 Bay St, Tweed Heads), southeast of the centre, is the terminal for Greyhound, Kirklands and Coachtrans bus services. Take a look at p279 if you need further information.

BURLEIGH HEADS

☎ 07 / pop 8430

An altogether busier and more compact place than Coolangatta, Burleigh Heads tends to fill up with families, although it's also legendary among surfers for the spectacular barrel of its right-hand break off the headland. The strong rip and jagged rocks make this one for experienced surfers only.

The town's other notable attraction is Burleigh Heads National Park, a tiny, steep park that covers the bulk of the headland. From the park's highest point, you can see the beach stretching far into the distance.

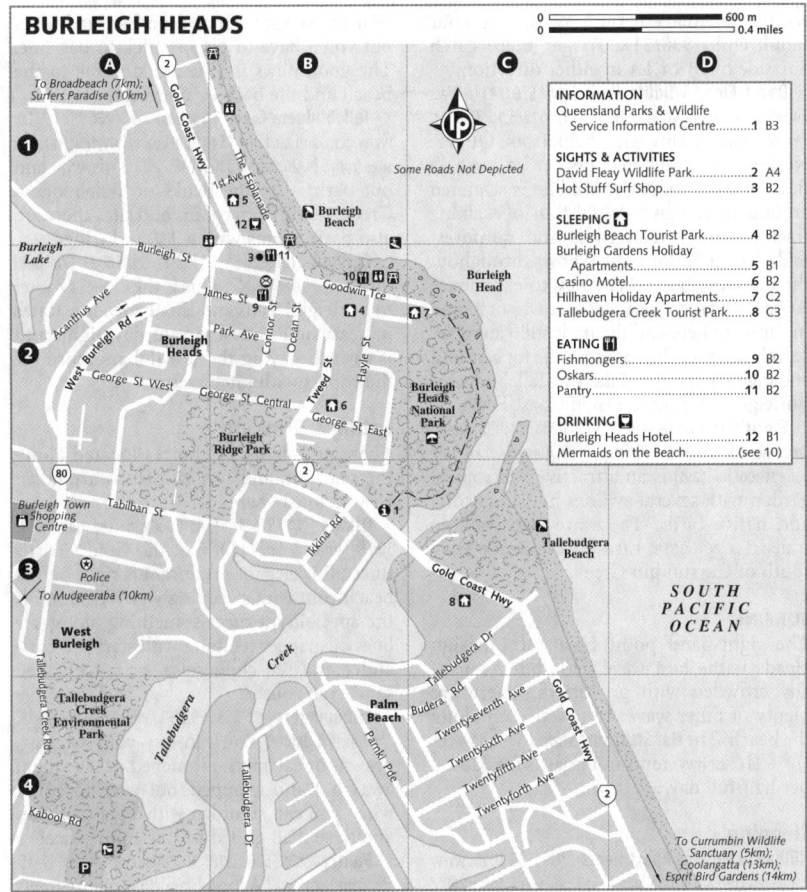

BURLEIGH HEADS

0 ———————— 600 m
0 ———————— 0.4 miles

Some Roads Not Depicted

INFORMATION
Queensland Parks & Wildlife
   Service Information Centre..........**1** B3

SIGHTS & ACTIVITIES
David Fleay Wildlife Park.................**2** A4
Hot Stuff Surf Shop......................**3** B2

SLEEPING 🏠
Burleigh Beach Tourist Park............**4** B2
Burleigh Gardens Holiday
   Apartments.................................**5** B1
Casino Motel.................................**6** B2
Hillhaven Holiday Apartments.........**7** C2
Tallebudgera Creek Tourist Park.....**8** C3

EATING 🍴
Fishmongers..................................**9** B2
Oskars...**10** B2
Pantry...**11** B2

DRINKING 🍸
Burleigh Heads Hotel.....................**12** B1
Mermaids on the Beach.............(see 10)

GOLD COAST

Information

You can get information on the natural aspects of the area from the **Queensland Parks & Wildlife Service Information Centre** (QPWS; ☎ 5535 3032; 3032 Gold Coast Hwy; ☙ 9am-4pm) at the northern end of Tallebudgera Creek.

Sights & Activities
BURLEIGH HEADS NATIONAL PARK (JELLURGAL)

The last remnant of native bush along the entire Gold Coast, this tiny park is crisscrossed with **walking trails** and is popular with locals for morning constitutionals. Home to a sizable population of brush turkeys, its main feature is the large basalt columns poking through the temperate forest, which hold

considerable cultural significance to the local Kombumerri people.

WILDLIFE SANCTUARIES

There are three wildlife sanctuaries in the vicinity of Burleigh Heads.

   Currumbin Wildlife Sanctuary (☎ 5534 1266; www.currumbin-sanctuary.org.au; Gold Coast Hwy, Currumbin; adult/child $22/15; ☙ 8am-5pm) provides an easy way to see Australian native animals. Tree kangaroos, koalas, emus, wombats and other cute and furries are joined daily by flocks of brilliantly coloured rainbow lorikeets. Throughout the day you can catch a number of informative and sometimes interactive shows, and there is also an Aboriginal Dance Show. One of the best ways to see the sanctuary is on a Wildnight Tour (adult/child $38/21). To get there catch Surfside bus 1 or 1A in either direction.

David Fleay Wildlife Park (☎ 5576 2411; West Burleigh Rd; adult/child/senior/family $13/6.50/8.50/33; ☽ 9am-5pm) is run with help from QPWS. Nestled in a sheltered pocket of bush, a fine collection of native wildlife is scattered around three dams. With 4km of walking tracks through mangroves and rainforest and plenty of informative shows throughout the day, it's an excellent way to experience Australian fauna. The platypus was first bred in captivity here and the park still runs a research and breeding programme for rare and endangered species. Take the Tallebudgera-Burleigh exit from the Gold Coast Hwy.

Esprit Bird Gardens (☎ 5533 0208; 746 Currumbin Creek Rd; adult/child $2.50/free; ☽ 9.30am-5pm Fri-Sun, daily school holidays) is an attractive subtropical garden with several aviaries housing exotic and native birds. There are also walking trails. To get here, turn off the Bruce Hwy south of Currumbin Creek.

SURFING

The right-hand point break at Burleigh Heads is the best wave here, but it's usually crowded with prosurfers. There are plenty of other waves to practise on along the beach. The **Hot Stuff Surf Shop** (☎ 5535 6899; 1706 Gold Coast Hwy) rents out boards for $20/30 per half/full day.

Sleeping

Hillhaven Holiday Apartments (☎ 5535 1055; www .hillhaven.com.au; 2 Goodwin Tce; r per week from $605; ☒ 🖳 🖾) These opulent apartments are perched high on the headland overlooking Burleigh Heads with the best views in town. The apartments are fully self-contained and staff can arrange baby-sitting. Call for shorter stays.

Burleigh Gardens Holiday Apartments (☎ 5576 3955; www.burleighgardens.com; 1849 Gold Coast Hwy; 1-bedroom ste per night/week from $90/460, 2-bedroom ste from $100/550; 🖾) These comfortable, self-contained units are solid value and their proximity to the beach and their balcony views make them popular. Interiors vary but they all have plenty of room and all amenities are included.

Burleigh Beach Tourist Park (☎ 5581 7755; www .gctp.com.au/burly; Goodwin Tce; tent/caravan sites from $21/23, cabins $115; ☒) This council-run park

is in a great spot. There are a few shady sites but you'll have to get in quick to bag one. The good news is you can stumble to the beach and the barbies are free.

Tallebudgera Creek Tourist Park (☎ 5581 7700; www.gctp.com.au/tally; 1544 Gold Coast Hwy; tent/caravan sites from $24/26, cabins $105-140; ☒) This well laid out park is on the banks of Tallebudgera Creek. Aside from cabins and sites there are also basic rooms with a TV and fridge.

Casino Motel (☎ 5535 7133; fax 5576 8099; 1761 Gold Coast Hwy; d $70-90; ☒) This is the closest motel to Burleigh Heads and isn't bad value. Rates increase on Friday and Saturday nights and it's worth paying the few dollars more for the rooms with kitchenettes.

Eating & Drinking

There are plenty of choices located along the seafront, and fish and chips are taken very seriously here.

Oskars (☎ 5576 3722; 43 Goodwin Tce; mains $19-30; ☽ lunch & dinner) One of the Gold Coast's finest, this elegant restaurant is right on the beachfront with sweeping views. Seafood is the speciality; expect something along the lines of snapper tempura with starfruit, coriander and red-chilli salsa, or twice-baked sand-crab soufflé.

Fishmongers (☎ 5535 2927; 9 James St; mains $7-15; ☽ lunch & dinner) You can buy your whiting, prawns or calamari untouched or take them away hot and wrapped, but why do either when you can sit down with a glass of vino and have it all grilled for the same price?

Pantry (☎ 5576 2818; 15 Connor St; mains $7-15; ☽ 6am-5pm; ☒) A long breakfast menu greets the cappuccino set at this cheery café with umbrellas alfresco. For lunch you can tuck into tasty burgers, wraps, melts and salads.

Burleigh Beach Club (☎ 5520 2972; cnr Goodwin Tce & Gold Coast Hwy; mains $10-18; ☽ lunch Mon-Sat, dinner Sun-Thu) For family-friendly surrounds, this club is hard to beat. The ubiquitous burgers, steak, fish and chicken dishes are on offer but it's all tasty and portions are huge.

Mermaids on the Beach (☎ 5520 1177; 31 Goodwin Tce) The best spot for a drink. Outside meal hours the bistro environment makes way for a snappy beach bar with views.

Burleigh Heads Hotel (☎ 5535 1000; 12 The Esplanade) Alternatively, this place is not bad for a drink if you don't mind the pokies in the background. There are live bands on Friday and Saturday evenings.

BROADBEACH

☎ 07 / pop 5180

Broadbeach is an unassuming place with a nice beach, large foreshore reserve, countless holiday apartments and that temple to mammon, Conrad Jupiters Casino. A few kilometres south of Surfers Paradise, Broadbeach marks the southern gateway of the Gold Coast's giddy core, and is a good alternative to Surfers if you want a peaceful night's sleep.

There's an **American Express** (Amex; ☎ 1300 139 060; Pacific Fair Shopping Centre, Hooker Blvd, Broadbeach) in the Pacific Fair Shopping Centre.

Sights & Activities

Queensland's first (legal) casino, **Conrad Jupiters Casino** (☎ 5592 8100; www.conrad.com.au; Gold Coast Hwy; admission free; ⏰ 24hr) has the usual wallet-lightening exercises for the optimistic or hopelessly addicted, plus a collection of eateries and bars. Also here is **Jupiters Theatre** (☎ 1800 074 144), with live music and glamorous dinner shows. The casino complex is connected to the Oasis Shopping Centre by a short monorail.

Sleeping

Conrad Jupiters (☎ 5592 8130, 1800 074 344; www .conrad.com.au; Gold Coast Hwy; r $280-880, penthouse ste $2100; P ⌧ ☒) The penthouse suite at this spectacular hotel is the place to stay if you hit the jackpot, otherwise the standard rooms are still very comfortable. Facilities include six restaurants, four tennis courts, three pools, two spas and a gym.

Mermaid Beach Motel (☎ 5575 5688; www.mer maidbeachmotel.com.au; 2395 Gold Coast Hwy; apt Sun-Thu from $60, Fri & Sat from $70; P ☒) This small and personable motel has spotless units that are a mark above the surrounding budget options.

Eating

Broadbeach has several good restaurants, but breakfast is the thing to do here, and the place to do it is Victoria Sq on Broadbeach Mall, where several very good outdoor cafés compete for your custom.

Sonatas (☎ 5526 9904; cnr Surf Pde & Queensland Ave; mains $15-25; ⏰ breakfast, lunch & dinner) Locals flock to this sunny, cosmopolitan café on weekend mornings to get their lattes and indulgent breakfasts. At lunch and dinner you can indulge in goodies like wok-tossed prawns and Moreton bay bugs, Cajun barramundi or brie and almond salad. Vegetarians get their slice of the pie too.

Champagne Brasserie (☎ 5538 3877; 2 Queensland Ave; mains $20-28; ⏰ lunch Tue-Fri, dinner Tue-Sun) This lively and unassuming restaurant could have been plucked from a French village. Favourites such as beef bourguignon or snails are on the menu but some fancy combinations like homemade ravioli with chicken, goats cheese, pine nuts and a tomato-and-basil dressing make the choice difficult.

Three Beans Espresso (☎ 5538 8744; Phoenician Bldg, 90 Surf Pde; mains $5-12; ⏰ 24hr) It's all very casual in this groovy little neck of the woods, but they take their coffee very seriously here and their meals aren't bad either.

Entertainment

There are two cinemas in the area, **Mermaid 5 Cinemas** (☎ 5575 3355; 2514 Gold Coast Hwy) and **Pacific Square 12 Cinemas** (☎ 5572 2666; cnr Hooker Blvd & Gold Coast Hwy), buried in the huge Pacific Fair Shopping Centre. The casino also regularly offers live Vegas-style dinner-shows at **Jupiters Theatre** (☎ 1800 074 144).

SURFERS PARADISE

☎ 07 / pop 24,090

In 1965 local entrepreneur Bernie Elsey had the brainwave of employing 'meter maids' in gold lamé bikinis to feed the parking meters on the main strip, and Surfers Paradise has never looked back.

The popularity of Surfers these days rests not so much on the sand and surf, (which is better down the coast), but on the shopping, nightlife and its proximity to the major theme parks. Surfers is also the acknowledged party hub of southern Queensland, happily catering for all demographics, from 40-somethings getting squiffy on martinis, to Gen Xers dropping pills on the dance floor and schoolies cutting loose on the beach. The backpacker places particularly go all out to ensure that the town goes off every night of the week. The partying reaches its peak during the IndyCar races in October and is topped up by a massive influx of celebrating high-school students during 'schoolies week' in November (see the boxed text, p280).

Even if you're not here to inflict damage on your major organs, there's an outrageous number of activities to keep you

GOLD COAST

(and any kids) occupied, as well as some fine day tours to the hinterland, a good art gallery and the best restaurants and fashion boutiques on the coast.

Orientation

Downtown Surfers consists of just a few main streets. Cavill Ave is the main strip and becomes a pedestrian mall as it runs down to the seafront. Orchid Ave, one block back from The Esplanade, is the nightclub and bar strip. The Gold Coast Hwy runs through Surfers one block back from Orchid Ave. It takes the southbound traffic while Ferny Ave, the next road inland, takes the northbound traffic.

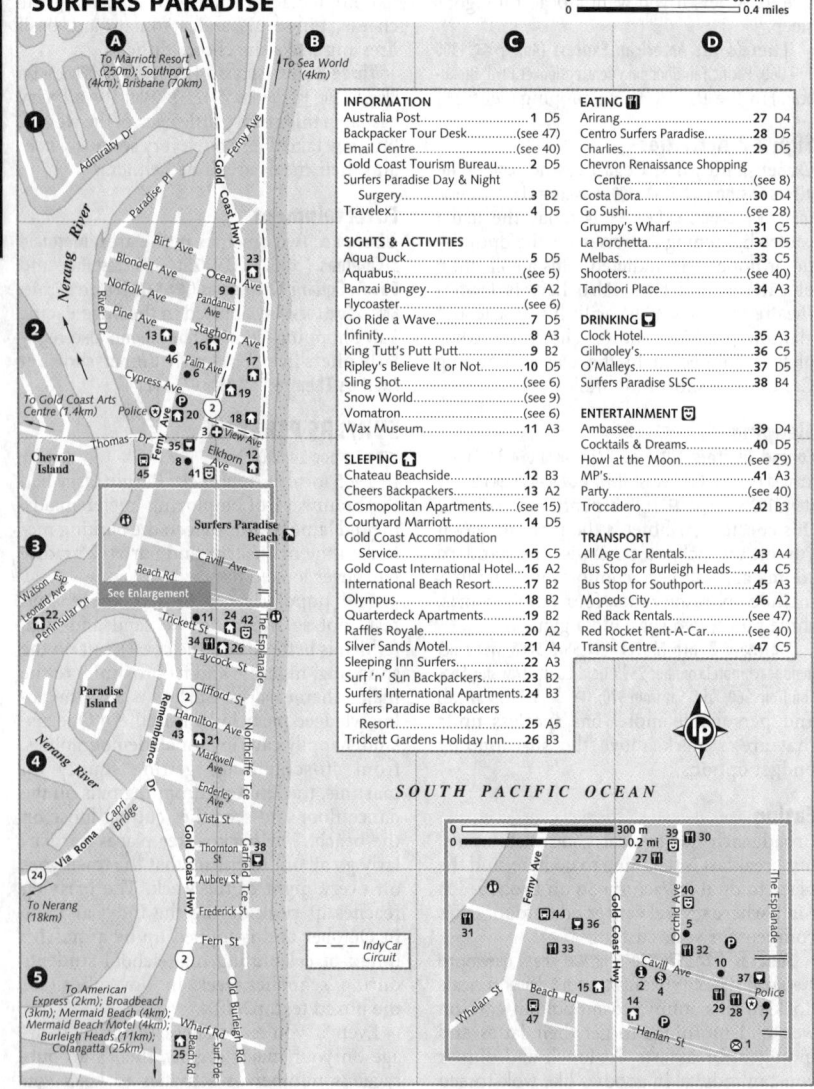

SURFERS PARADISE

0 ——————— 600 m
0 ——————— 0.4 miles

GOLD COAST

INFORMATION
Australia Post	**1** D5
Backpacker Tour Desk	(see 47)
Email Centre	(see 40)
Gold Coast Tourism Bureau	**2** D5
Surfers Paradise Day & Night Surgery	**3** B2
Travelex	**4** D5

SIGHTS & ACTIVITIES
Aqua Duck	**5** D5
Aquabus	(see 5)
Banzai Bungey	**6** A2
Flycoaster	(see 6)
Go Ride a Wave	**7** D5
Infinity	**8** A3
King Tutt's Putt Putt	**9** B2
Ripley's Believe It or Not	**10** D5
Sling Shot	(see 6)
Snow World	(see 9)
Vomatron	(see 6)
Wax Museum	**11** A3

SLEEPING
Chateau Beachside	**12** B3
Cheers Backpackers	**13** A2
Cosmopolitan Apartments	(see 15)
Courtyard Marriott	**14** D5
Gold Coast Accommodation Service	**15** C5
Gold Coast International Hotel	**16** A2
International Beach Resort	**17** B2
Olympus	**18** B2
Quarterdeck Apartments	**19** B2
Raffles Royale	**20** A2
Silver Sands Motel	**21** A4
Sleeping Inn Surfers	**22** A3
Surf 'n' Sun Backpackers	**23** B2
Surfers International Apartments	**24** B3
Surfers Paradise Backpackers Resort	**25** A5
Trickett Gardens Holiday Inn	**26** B3

EATING
Arirang	**27** D4
Centro Surfers Paradise	**28** D5
Charlies	**29** D5
Chevron Renaissance Shopping Centre	(see 8)
Costa Dora	**30** D4
Go Sushi	(see 28)
Grumpy's Wharf	**31** C5
La Porchetta	**32** D5
Melbas	**33** C5
Shooters	(see 40)
Tandoori Place	**34** A3

DRINKING
Clock Hotel	**35** A3
Gilhooley's	**36** C5
O'Malleys	**37** D5
Surfers Paradise SLSC	**38** B4

ENTERTAINMENT
Ambassee	**39** D4
Cocktails & Dreams	**40** D5
Howl at the Moon	(see 29)
MP's	**41** A3
Party	(see 40)
Troccadero	**42** B3

TRANSPORT
All Age Car Rentals	**43** A4
Bus Stop for Burleigh Heads	**44** C5
Bus Stop for Southport	**45** A3
Mopeds City	**46** A2
Red Back Rentals	(see 47)
Red Rocket Rent-A-Car	(see 40)
Transit Centre	**47** C5

SOUTH PACIFIC OCEAN

0 ——————— 300 m
0 ——————— 0.2 mi

– – – IndyCar Circuit

SURFERS PARADISE FOR CHILDREN

Apart from the theme parks there are plenty of other options to keep inquisitive minds happy and bundles of energy contained.

Infinity (☎ 5538 2988; www.infinity.com.au; Chevron Renaissance, cnr Surfers Paradise Blvd & Elkhorn Ave; adult/child/family $20/12/53; ⏲ 10am-10pm) promises to 'ignite your imagination' by transporting you into the future. Essentially the future is a walk through a maze cleverly disguised by an elaborate sound and light show.

At **Ripley's Believe It or Not** (☎ 5592 0040; Raptis Plaza, Cavill Mall; adult/child $13.50/8; ⏲ 9am-11pm) you can feast your eyes on all manner of freaky sights, including the world's tallest and heaviest humans, 'genuine' shrunken heads and musical instruments that play themselves. Many of the exhibits are in the form of reproductions or photos, however, and chances are you probably will believe it.

You can play a startling round of minigolf at **King Tutt's Putt Putt** (☎ 5570 2277; cnr Gold Coast Hwy & Pandanus Ave; adult/child/family $12/7/30), which features moving crocodile and sarcophagus props from Movie World. Next door, you can freeze your buns looking at the gigantic ice sculptures at **Snow World** (☎ 5570 3633; cnr Gold Coast Hwy & Ocean Ave; adult/child $18/12).

For the bloodthirsty, the **Wax Museum** (☎ 5538 3975; cnr Gold Coast Hwy & Trickett St; adult/child $15/11) gleefully depicts the depths of human depravity with its Chamber of Horrors.

Other ways to keep kids happy include a visit to a **TimeZone** (Centro Surfers Paradise) and **Surfers Paradise Ten Pin Bowling** (☎ 5538 5222; Level 1, Centro Surfers Paradise; per game $12).

Information

There are plenty of free glossy booklets available, including *Wot's On*, *Destination Surfers Paradise*, *Today Tonight on the Gold Coast* and *Point Out*. Some have street plans and discount vouchers among all the advertising.

Australia Post (☎ 13 13 18; Shop 165, Centro Surfers Paradise; ⏲ 9am-5.30pm Mon-Fri, 9am-12.30pm Sat)

Backpacker Tour Desk (☎ 5592 2911, 1800 359 830; Transit Centre, cnr Beach & Cambridge Rds) For help with finding somewhere to stay try the helpful backpackers' accommodation booking desk.

Email Centre (☎ 5538 7500; Shop 51, 315 Orchid Ave, Surfers Paradise; ⏲ 9am-11pm)

Gold Coast Tourism Bureau (☎ 5538 4419; www.goldcoasttourism.com.au; Cavill Ave Mall; ⏲ 8.30am-5.30pm Mon-Fri, 8.30am-5pm Sat, 9am-4pm Sun)

Surfers Paradise Day & Night Surgery (☎ 5592 2299; 3221 Gold Coast Hwy; ⏲ 7am-10pm) Chemist attached.

Sights

Housed in the **Gold Coast Arts Centre** (☎ 5588 4008; 135 Bundall Rd), the **Art Gallery** (☎ 5581 6567; admission free; ⏲ 10am-5pm Mon-Fri, 11am-5pm Sat & Sun) has an excellent permanent collection featuring many of Australia's finest artists, plus a substantial number of local works. A busy programme of exhibitions fills its three display spaces, while the Evandale Sculpture Walk on the Nerang River

foreshore is well worth a wander. The arts centre also has a 1200-seat theatre that hosts live national and international productions, an art-house movie theatre (all shows $8 on Tuesday) and a restaurant. It's about 1.5km inland.

Activities

There are an absurd number of ways to spend your cash in and around Surfers. Here's just a taste.

Balloon Down Under (☎ 5593 8400; www.balloondownunder.com; 1hr flights per adult/child $255/210) offers early morning flights over the Gold Coast hinterland, including transfers and ending with a hot breakfast. **Tandem Skydive** (☎ 5599 1920; Hanger 22, Coolangatta Airport) offers exactly that every day for around $250. If the jumping-out-of-a-plane thing isn't quite your style, **Surfers Paradise Parasail** (☎ 5591 5100; Mariner's Cove; rides $55) gives you a pretty good rush without the same altitude.

Betting your life on the strength of a giant rubber band at **Banzai Bungey** (☎ 5526 7611; cnr Cypress & Ferny Aves; jumps from $100) is a rite of passage in Surfers. On the same block there are new and inventive ways to revisit your breakfast. **Flycoaster** (☎ 5539 0474; www.flycoaster.com; per person $39) swings you like a pendulum after you've been released from a hoist 20m up. **Sling Shot** (☎ 5570 2700; per person $30) catapults you into the air at around 160km, and

GOLD COAST

GOLD COAST THEME PARKS

Immediately northwest of Surfers Paradise, four American-style theme parks summon you with thrilling rides and entertaining shows. Discount tickets are sold in most of the tourist offices on the Gold Coast; the **3 Park Super Pass** (adult/child $160/100), available at Sea World, Movie World and Wet 'n' Wild, covers entry to all three parks.

Sea World (☎ 5588 2222, show times ☎ 5588 2205; www.seaworld.com.au; Sea World Dr, Main Beach; adult/child $60/38; ☺ 10am-5.30pm) started out in 1971 as a water-ski show in the Nerang River and has grown into a huge aquatic theme park. The main draws are the animal performances, including twice-daily dolphin and sea-lion shows, and shark feeding. There are also waterslides and rollercoasters, and a zoo with two celebrity resident polar bears.

Dreamworld (☎ 5588 1111; www.dreamworld.com.au; Pacific Hwy, Coomera; adult/child $60/38; ☺ 10am-5pm), on the Pacific Hwy 17km north of Surfers, is thrill-ride central. Squeals and shrieks are mandatory on such delights as the Tower of Terror, where you accelerate to 161km/h in seven seconds; Wipeout, a twisting, tumbling roller coaster; or The Giant Drop, a terminal-velocity machine where you free fall from 38 storeys. There are also plenty of attractions to keep the kids entertained, including the Nickelodeon Park and a bunch of wildlife shows, the highlight of which is the interactive tiger show.

Warner Bros Movie World (☎ 5573 8485; www.movieworld.com.au; Pacific Hwy, Oxenford; adult/child $60/38; ☺ 10am-5.30pm), otherwise known as 'Hollywood on the Gold Coast', claims to be Australia's number-one tourist attraction. You can mingle with your favourite Loony Tunes characters here, all of whom leap at photo opportunities with the kids. There's a constantly changing 'ride of the moment' as well as stunt shows and movie-themed rides.

Wet 'n' Wild (☎ 5573 2255; www.wetnwild.com.au; Pacific Hwy, Oxenford; adult/child $38/24; ☺ 10am-5pm Feb-Apr & Sep-Dec, to 9pm 27 Dec-26 Jan, to 4pm May-Aug) is loads of fun. If the beach is too sedate, this colossal water-sports park offers plenty of creative ways to get wet. You can slippery-slide down inventive water slides; dip into colossal pools; or zoom down the mighty Mammoth Falls at 70km/h, a white-water rapids ride on a giant rubber ring. If all that sounds too energetic, you can always just float around on a big rubber ring.

Vomatron (☎ 5570 200; per person $30) whisks you around in a giant arc at about 120km/h.

Numinbah Valley Adventure Trails (☎ 5533 4137; www.numinbahtrails.com), 30km south of Nerang, and **Gum Nuts Horse Riding Resort** (☎ 5543 0191; Biddaddaba Creek Rd, Canungra) offer half-day rides from around $60, including pick-ups from the coast.

Surfers is a great place to get wet, and behind the seemingly impenetrable wall of high-rises, Surfers Paradise Beach has enough swell to give beginners a feel for the craft of surfing. Surf schools are abundant and charge between $40 and $50 for a two-hour lesson. Try the following:

Cheyne Horan School of Surf (☎ 1800 227 873, 0403 080 484; www.cheynehoran.com.au) World-champion surfer offers excellent tuition as well as three lessons for $100.

Go Ride a Wave (☎ 5526 7077, 1800 787 337; www .gorideawave.com.au; Cavill Ave Mall; ☺ 9am-5pm) Also rents out short boards and Malibu boards for $15/25/40 per hour/three hours/day.

Splash Safaris Sea Kayaking (☎ 0407 741 748; www.seakayakingtours.com; tours per person $45-65)

Kayak tours ranging from introductory courses to five-hour safaris including snorkelling, dolphin searching, bushwalking and lunch.

Tours

Semi-aquatic bus tours are all the rage in Surfers, and several operators explore Surfers by road and river in a boat on wheels (around $27), including **Aquabus** (☎ 5539 0222; 7 Orchid Ave) and **Aqua Duck** (☎ 5538 3825; 7 Orchid Ave). Both charge around $35/25/90 per adult/child/family and it's certainly an unusual way to explore Surfers Paradise.

Several boat companies operate cruises between Main Beach and Surfers Paradise; see p293 for more information.

You can also access the Gold Coast hinterland with a number of tour operators from Surfers Paradise. See p294 for more information.

Festivals & Events

Big Day Out (www.bigdayout.com) Huge international music festival in late January.

Quicksilver Pro-Surfing Competition Mid-March; sees some of the world's best surfers out on the waves.
Surf Lifesaving Championships Also in mid-March.
Gold Coast International Marathon Run in July.
IndyCar See the boxed text, below.
Schoolies Week Month-long party by school-leavers from mid-November to mid-December; see the boxed text, p280.

Sleeping

The helpful **Gold Coast Accommodation Service** (☎ 5592 0067; www.goldcoastaccommodationservice .com; Shop 1, 1 Beach Rd) can arrange and book accommodation for you. Many properties increase their tariffs by 20% to 50% during school holidays. The most expensive time of year is during Indy (late October) and Christmas Eve to late January, when most properties demand a three-night minimum stay. These increases are adhered to most in Surfers Paradise, though you may encounter more flexibility the further away from the action you get. All prices in this section are based on 'normal' season or any time other than the aforementioned.

BUDGET

Surfers has several decent hostel options, all of which offer vouchers for the nightclubs in town.

   Sleeping Inn Surfers (☎ 5592 4455, 1800 817 832; www.sleepinginn.com.au; 26 Peninsular Dr; dm $21, d with/without bath $65/55; 🖵) A bit flashier than your average hostel, this converted motel has modern facilities and a choice of rooms

from basic dorms to classier doubles with TVs. It's also large enough to cater to party punters as well as those in dire need of sleep.

   Cheers Backpackers (☎ 5531 6539, 1800 636 539; 8 Pine Ave, Surfers Paradise; dm/d $23/60; 🖵 🏊) Amid the friendly blur of theme nights, karaoke, pool comps, pub crawls, happy hours and barbecues here, you'll also stumble across adequate rooms and good facilities. Only a short walk from the clubs, it's a flat-out party place.

   Surf 'n' Sun Backpackers (☎ 5592 2363, 1800 678 194, ; www.surfnsun-goldcoast.com; 3323 Gold Coast Hwy, Surfers Paradise; dm/d $23/60; 🏊) Another party central, this hostel is the best option for Surfers' beach and bars. There are surfboards for hire and pool tables, and the beach is a hop, skip and a jump away.

   Other recommendations:

Mermaid Beach Motel (☎ 5575 5688; www.mermaid beachmotel.com.au; 2395 Gold Coast Hwy, Mermaid Beach; r $55-65; 🐾 🏊) Small motel with clean, self-contained rooms. It's about 4km south of the centre.
Surfers Paradise Backpackers Resort (☎ 5592 4677, 1800 282 800; www.surfersparadisebackpackers.com.au; Gold Coast Hwy, Surfers Paradise; dm/d/tr $22/55/80; 🖵 🏊) Motel-style hostel with sauna, tennis court, pool room and bar.

MIDRANGE

Self-contained units, many with high-rise views, are prolific in Surfers, and these tend to offer better value than the few remaining hotels.

GOLD COAST

INDYCAR FEVER

Since 1991 Surfers Paradise has been host to what has been dubbed Queensland's biggest party – the Australian leg of the IndyCar series (the US equivalent of Formula One motor racing). Each October, the main streets of central Surfers are transformed into a temporary race circuit, around which hurtle some of the world's fastest cars, with drivers who push them up to speeds of more than 300km/h. The champ cars are the main attraction, but plenty of folk come to see Ford and Holden battle out their famous rivalry in the V8 Supercars.

Over the entire four days, when the tracks aren't screeching with races or practice sessions, you can catch motorcycle stunt shows and spectacular airshows. There are also plenty of opportunities to meet the masters for autograph sessions, and revheads can shell out $22 and take a tour through either the Champ Car Pit Lanes or a V8 Supercar Pit Lane.

On a good year, around a quarter of a million spectators descend for the festival. Surfers is fairly over the top at the best of times, but IndyCar gives the town a chance to *really* let its hair down.

General admission charges to the races ranges from $30 to $75 per day at the gate, cheaper if you book. Four-day grandstand seating is between $210 and $530. For more information call ☎ 1800 300 055 or check www.indy.com.au.

Gold Coast International Hotel (☎ 5584 1200, 1800 074 020; www.gci.com.au; cnr Staghorn Ave & Gold Coast Hwy; d $135-235; ✷ ✷) The colour-coordinated rooms at this hotel have plenty of space to stretch out, and come with a balcony view of either the hinterland or ocean.

Surfers International Apartments (☎ 5579 1299, 1800 891 299; www.surfers-international.com.au; 7-9 Trickett St; r per 3-night stay $420-510; ✷ ✷) This high-rise, just off the beach, has plush apartments containing modern kitchens, sizable bedrooms, cable TV and modem ports. Balconies with spectacular beach views are standard and the complex has a small gym and poolside barbecue.

Chateau Beachside (☎ 5538 1022; www.strand .com.au; cnr Elkhorn Ave & The Esplanade; r $110-140, ste $120-150; ✷ ✷) Right in the heart of Surfers, this seaside complex has comfortable and spacious units with excellent views. There's an inexpensive restaurant attached.

Cosmopolitan Apartments (☎ 5570 2311; cnr Gold Coast Hwy & Beach Rd; apt from $85; ✷ ✷) Set back from the beach but still very central, this complex of privately owned, self-contained apartments also has a barbecue area, spa and sauna. Each unit has been furnished by the owners but standards include dishwashers, balconies, laundries and phones. Most also have cable TV.

Trickett Gardens Holiday Inn (☎ 5539 0988; www.trickettgardens.com.au; 24-30 Trickett St; d/f $85/150; ✷ ✷) This friendly low-rise block is great for families, with a central location and well-equipped self-contained units.

Raffles Royale (☎ 5538 0099; www.rafflesroyale .com.au; 69 Ferny Ave; r from $85; P ✷ ✷) This unintrusive low-rise block has bright and cheerful self-contained units that are blessed with a healthy dose of sunlight. It's incredibly secure and a popular choice with families.

International Beach Resort (☎ 1800 657 471, 5539 0099; www.internationalresort.com.au; 84 The Esplanade, Surfers Paradise; r from $80, with sea view $105; ✷) Another seafront high rise, this place is just across from the beach and has good studios and one- and two-bedroom units.

Other recommendations:

Olympus (☎ 5538 7288; bookings@olympusapartments .com.au; 62 The Esplanade, Surfers Paradise; d $130) Opposite the beach with spacious one- or two-bedroom units.

Quarterdeck Apartments (☎ 5592 2200, 1800 635 235; fax 5538 0282; 3263 Gold Coast Hwy; r $90; ✷) Comfortable one-bedroom apartments, some with great views.

Silver Sands Motel (☎ 5538 6041; www.silversands motel.com.au; 2985 Gold Coast Hwy; d Sun-Thu $7, Fri & Sat $90; ✷ ✷) Reasonable motel rooms just out of the centre.

TOP END

Courtyard Marriott (☎ 1800 074 317, 5579 3499; www.marriott.com; cnr Gold Coast Hwy & Hanlan St; d/ste from $155/165; ✷) Right in the centre of Surfers, this plush top-end hotel is attached to the Paradise Centre Mall and offers all the luxury you would expect in this price range, including sea views, and spa baths in the top-price suites.

Marriott Resort (☎ 5592 9800; fax 5592 9888; 158 Ferny Ave; d/ste from $350/415; ✷ ✷) Just north of the centre, this resort is ridiculously sumptuous, from the sandstone-floored foyer with punka-style fans to the lagoonlike pool complete with artificial white-sand beach and waterfall.

Eating

Surfers Paradise is brimming with cafés and restaurants reflecting its multicultural palate, and while it boasts some of the Gold Coast's best restaurants, the emphasis here tends towards quantity over quality.

Grumpy's Wharf (☎ 5531 6177; Tiki Village, Cavill Ave; mains $25-35; ✷ lunch & dinner; ✷) Right on the water, Grumpy's is a secluded and tranquil retreat serving fine seafood with Asian and Mediterranean touches.

Tandoori Place (☎ 5592 1004; cnr Gold Coast Hwy & Trickett St; mains $15-20; ✷ lunch & dinner; ✷) On the extensive menu here you'll find seafood, chicken, lamb, beef and even kangaroo done with subcontinent flair. Vegetarians are also spoiled for choice and the service is friendly and efficient.

Melbas (☎ 5592 6922; 46 Cavill Ave; mains $25-35; ✷ lunch & dinner; ✷) Melba's menu is revolutionary amid Surfers' churned out fare; think Thai baked lamb rack with Tom Yum broth, or oven-baked, butter-curried snapper with cashews. The lunch menu (mains $12) is cheaper. Melbas is also a popular drinking hole.

Costa Dora (☎ 5538 5203; 27 Orchid Ave; dishes $12-22; ✷ lunch & dinner; ✷) The menu of this popular restaurant is authentic and good value, if predictable – pastas, pizzas, salads and mains. A splash of shellfish graces the menu as does a kids' selection; and the $10 pasta and cappuccino lunch deal is a bargain.

Charlies (☎ 5538 5285; Cavill Mall; meals $10-20; ☺ breakfast, lunch & dinner) With décor devoted to Charlie Chaplin, who undoubtedly never ate here, this sprawling café has a hint of American diner and serves hearty burgers, pizzas, pastas, sandwiches and breakfasts.

Other recommendations:

Arirang (☎ 5539 8008; Shop 8, Centre Arcade; mains $8-16; ☺ lunch & dinner) Authentic Korean noodle dishes.

Go Sushi (☎ 5526 8766; Centro Surfers Paradise, Cavill Ave Mall; sushi $2-4; ☺ lunch & dinner)

Two kid pleasers serving cheap and tasty pizzas are **La Porchetta** (☎ 5527 5273; 3 Orchid Ave; meals $10-15; ☺ breakfast, lunch & dinner; ☷) and **Chateau Beachside** (☺ breakfast, lunch & dinner), which also dishes up good burgers and an all-you-can-gobble $10 breakfast. Supermarkets can be found in **Centro Surfers Paradise** (Cavill Mall) and **Chevron Renaissance Shopping Centre** (cnr Elkhorn & Gold Coast Hwy).

Drinking

Melbas (☎ 5592 6922; 46 Cavill Ave) This excellent restaurant hangs on to its glitzy edge once the dinner plates are cleared and primes a well-heeled crowd with cocktails, dim lighting and pumping music. The recipe is popular and it heaves most nights.

Gilhooley's (☎ 5538 9122; cnr Gold Coast Hwy & Cavill Ave) An Irish pub nestled into a convenient spot on the main drag, Gilhooley's hosts live music, DJs and big-screen TV sports…or you can just people-watch on the terrace out the front.

O'Malleys (☎ 5570 4075; Level 1, 1 Cavill Ave; ☷) By day this is a respite from the hectic heat of Cavill Ave. The network of booths and stools overlooking the ocean fill up at night when the atmosphere is happy and rowdy.

Clock Hotel (☎ 5539 0344; 3282 Gold Coast Hwy) By day this Surfers institution is a favourite with the older crowd, which dominates the bar like an episode from Cheers. Each night of the week, however, it's the 20- and 30-somethings who dig the 'Latin Fire' Tuesdays, 'Champers' Thursdays, karaoke Sundays and consistent big-screen sports.

Surfers Paradise SLSC (☎ 5531 5966; The Esplanade) This sprawling club is a great place for unpretentious drinking and socialising. Don't expect the Ritz – the unadorned expanse is Surfers' best joint for cheap beer and beach views. Start early if you want a table.

Entertainment

Orchid Ave is Surfers' main bar and night-club strip. Many places offer vouchers for backpackers and cover charges are usually between $5 and $10.

NIGHTCLUBS

Ambassee (☎ 5592 0088, 26 Orchid Ave) This chic venue is the closest Surfers has to a serious club, but wear your fancy threads – even the bouncers look polished. Doors open around 10pm and resident DJs spin edgy house, techno and funk from Thursdays to Sundays.

Cocktails & Dreams (☎ 5592 1955; Level 1, The Mark, Orchid Ave) Drink deals, dancing and general debauchery pulls the crowds in.

Party (☎ 5538 2848) Linked by a stairway to Cocktails & Dreams, the Party offers more of the same with $2 drink deals from Thursday to Sunday nights.

Shooters (☎ 5592 1144; 15 Orchid Ave) This is an American-style saloon with pool tables and big-screen videos. It has occasional live entertainment.

MP's (☎ 5526 2337; Forum Arcade, 26 Orchid Ave) This popular gay club has cheap drinks and drag shows Tuesdays, Thursdays and Sundays.

LIVE MUSIC

Howl at the Moon (☎ 5527 5522; Shop 7, Upper Level, Centro Surfers Paradise) Talented musos belt out everything from rap to blues on the pianos. Howl-alongs are encouraged.

Basement (☎ 5588 4000; Gold Coast Arts Centre, 135 Bundall Rd) Beneath the Arts Centre, this funky bar hosts touring performers excelling in jazz, blues and folk. Regular Sunday sessions specialise in blues and world music courtesy of the resident band. Tickets cost around $16.

Troccadero (☎ 5536 4200; 9 Trickett St) When the big guns are in town they strut their stuff at Troccadero. If it's not high profile Aussie and international acts playing you'll catch live rock in all its genres.

Getting There & Away

The transit centre is on the corner of Beach and Cambridge Rds. Surfers is a major stop on the East Coast route and all the major bus companies have desks here. For more information on buses and trains, see p279.

Regular Surfside buses for Gold Coast towns north and south stop at the corner of Ferny Ave and Cavill Ave.

Getting Around

There are plenty of car-rental firms around with fliers in every hostel, motel and hotel. Local outfits that offer good deals include **All Age Car Rentals** (☎ 1800 671 361; 3024 Gold Coast Hwy; used cars per day from $19), **Red Back Rentals** (☎ 5592 1655; Transit Centre; per day from $25) and **Red Rocket Rent-A-Car** (☎ 5538 9074, 1800 673 682; Shop 9, The Mark, Orchid Ave; per day from $15), which also rents scooters and bicycles. Insurance costs extra.

Mopeds City (☎ 5592 5878; 102 Ferny Ave) hires out brand-new mopeds (per hour/day $35/70) and bicycles (per hour/day $10/20).

SOUTHPORT & MAIN BEACH

☎ 07 / pop 24,830

Sheltered from the ocean by a long sandbar, known as the Spit, and the Broadwater estuary, Southport is a relatively quiet residential enclave. It's a pleasant alternative to Surfers for a good night's sleep or place to chill out for a couple of days. Just to the south, Main Beach is more developed and is the gateway to the Spit, where Sea World (see the boxed text, p288) and a string of upmarket hotels, restaurants and shopping malls can be found.

The eastern side of the Spit has been preserved as Philip Park, a long strip of natural bushland that fronts the last stretch of untouched beach on the Gold Coast. The surfing is often good and it's a place where you can lose the crowd.

Activities

You can indulge in just about any water activity from numerous operators based at Mariner's Cove. The easiest way to sift through them is to book at the **Mariner's Cove Booking Office** (☎ 5591 8883; Mariner's Cove). The following are recommended.

Australian Kayaking Adventures (☎ 0412 940 135; www.australiankayakingadventures.com.au; 2-3hr/half-day tours to South Stradbroke Island per person $45/65) Guided tours include breakfast.

Queensland Scuba Diving Company (☎ 5526 7722; Mariners Cove Marina; dives per person from $100) Single dives including fish feeding.

Seabreeze Sports (☎ 5527 1099; jet ski & parasailing package per person $80, Aquanaut per person $100) These

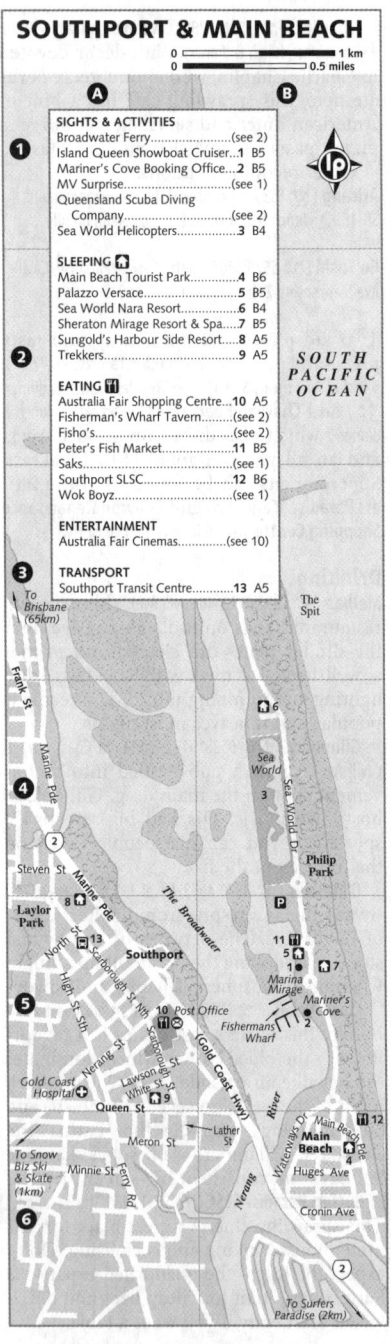

SOUTHPORT & MAIN BEACH

SIGHTS & ACTIVITIES
Broadwater Ferry.........................(see 2)
Island Queen Showboat Cruiser...**1** B5
Mariner's Cove Booking Office...**2** B5
MV Surprise..............................(see 1)
Queensland Scuba Diving
   Company..............................(see 2)
Sea World Helicopters................**3** B4

SLEEPING
Main Beach Tourist Park...............**4** B6
Palazzo Versace..........................**5** B5
Sea World Nara Resort.................**6** B4
Sheraton Mirage Resort & Spa....**7** B5
Sungold's Harbour Side Resort....**8** A5
Trekkers....................................**9** A5

EATING
Australia Fair Shopping Centre....**10** A5
Fisherman's Wharf Tavern.........(see 2)
Fisho's.....................................(see 2)
Peter's Fish Market....................**11** B5
Saks..(see 1)
Southport SLSC.........................**12** B6
Wok Boyz.................................(see 1)

ENTERTAINMENT
Australia Fair Cinemas..............(see 10)

TRANSPORT
Southport Transit Centre...........**13** A5

guys do everything but best of all is the underwater scuba cruise 'Aquanaut'.

Snorkelling Adventures (☎ 0405 427 174; snorkelling adventures@bigpond.com; 2-3hr tours per person $35) Snorkelling and fish feeding off Wavebreak Island.

Snow Biz Ski & Skate (☎ 5531 3035; 7 Nerang St Southport) Hires out in-line skates with pads and all the gear from $12.50/20 for two hours/overnight.

Tours

Sea World Helicopters (☎ 5588 2224; Sea World) offers flights starting from $50/40 per adult/child for five minutes up to $150/115 for 30-minute flights. The longer flights take in Burleigh Heads, Coolangatta and the Gold Coast hinterland.

Island Queen Showboat Cruises (☎ 5557 8800; www.islandqueen.com.au; Marina Mirage, Seaworld Dr, Main Beach) offers dinner and cabaret cruises (from $55/35 per adult/child), day cruises to South Stradbroke Island (from $75/45), including morning tea, lunch and boom netting, and a 1½-hour morning-tea cruise (adult/child/family $38/23/100) to Sanctuary Cove, which includes theme-park transfers.

Several companies cruise between Main Beach and Tiki Village Wharf in Surfers Paradise:

Broadwater Ferry (☎ 0412 179 582; per person $14) Hop-on-hop-off cruise between Mariner's Cove and Surfers Paradise.

MV Surprise (☎ 0418 768 801; www.mv-surprise.com; Marina Mirage; 2hr cruise per adult/child/senior/family $37/20/30/100) Heads north from Marina Mirage, touring the Broadwater before cruising south to Surfers Paradise. Includes morning or afternoon tea.

Sleeping

BUDGET & MIDRANGE

Harbour Side Resort (☎ 5591 6666; www.harbourside resort.com.au; 132 Marine Pde; studio & 1-bedroom units in low/high season $80/100, 2-bedroom units $120/140; ☒ ☒) Disregard the overwhelming brick façade; within this sprawling property you'll find pastel-hued self-contained units with oodles of room and charm. High-season rates apply on weekends.

Trekkers (☎ 5591 5616, 1800 100 004; www.trekkers backpackers.com.au; 22 White St, Southport; dm $23, d & tw $60; ☐ ☒) A beautiful renovated Queenslander, Trekkers' garden is a mini oasis. Some of the themed doubles are en suite and come with TV; the communal areas are spotless. Rates also include breakfast.

Main Beach Tourist Park (☎ 5581 7722; www .gctp.com.au/main; Main Beach Pde; tent/caravan sites from $26/27, cabins from $120; ☒ ☒) Just across the road from the beach, this caravan park is a favourite with families. It's a tight fit between sites, but the facilities are good and the colourful cabins are comfortable.

Sea World Nara Resort (☎ 5591 0000, 1800 074 448; www.seaworldnara.com.au; Sea World Dr; d from $169; ☒ ☒) Aimed squarely at the family market; the standard rooms here are adequate without being anything special. There's a large central pool, playground, gym, spa and sauna, and you also get discounted entry into Sea World via a short monorail.

TOP END

Palazzo Versace (☎ 1800 098 000, 5509 8000; www .palazzoversace.com; Sea World Dr, Main Beach; d $380-725, condominiums from $1200; ☒ ☒) The Palazzo is extravagance defined. Everything from the pool furniture to the buttons on the staff uniforms has the Versace mark on it. If you can draw yourself from the sumptuous rooms, you can venture to resort's equally indulgent restaurants and bars.

Sheraton Mirage Resort & Spa (☎ 1800 073 525, 5591 1488; www.sheraton.com/goldcoast; Sea World Dr, Main Beach; d from $320, ste $500-650; ☒ ☒) It may not have designer furnishings, but the exquisite rooms do have stereos, cable TV, views and all the five-star touches. The lagoon-style pool takes you right onto the beach and there are three restaurants and three bars to explore.

Eating

Saks (☎ 5591 2755; Marina Mirage, 74 Seaworld Dr, Main Beach; mains $15-25; ☯ lunch daily, dinner Wed-Sun; ☒) This smart bar and restaurant lures cultured palettes with a brief but sophisticated menu that boasts delights such as roast duck and macadamia nut salad as well as gourmet wood-fired pizzas. Its tall glass windows offer uninterrupted views of the marina.

The cheapest place to eat is the food court in the Australia Fair Shopping Centre on Scarborough St. Counters here serve up pizza, noodles, roasts, kebabs and more.

Also recommended:

Southport SLSC (☎ 5591 5083; MacArthur Pde; dishes $9-17; ☯ lunch & dinner) Great bistro serving pasta, roasts, sangers and burgers.

GOLD COAST

Fisherman's Wharf Tavern (☎ 5571 0566; 60-70 Mariner's Cove, Main Beach; mains $14-25; 🕑 lunch & dinner; 🔀) The menu at this stylish tavern is an impressive combo of fresh fish (prawn rolls with 'really hot chilli' or Atlantic salmon with coconut, chilli and lime butter) and multicultural fusions including a mean jungle curry. There's an atmospheric deck and it's a social haunt as much as a restaurant. Attached is Fisho's, where you can munch on barramundi and chips for around $12 in less fancy surrounds.

Peter's Fish Market (☎ 5591 7747; Sea World Dr, Main Beach; meals $10; 🕑 lunch & dinner) A no-nonsense fish and chippery and fish market with fresh seafood at reasonable prices.

Wok Boyz (☎ 5591 6808; Marina Mirage, 74 Seaworld Dr, Main Beach; dishes $12; 🕑 lunch & dinner) Towering, tasty bowls of noodles.

Entertainment

Australia Fair Cinemas (☎ 5531 2200), Southport's huge Australia Fair Shopping Centre conceals Australia Fair Cinemas, which shows new-release movies on 10 screens.

Getting There & Away

The Southport Transit Centre is on Scarborough St, between North and Railway Sts. Premier, Coachtrans, Kirklands and Greyhound buses all stop here. Surfside buses 1 and 1A run to Surfers day and night from outside the Australia Fair Shopping Centre on Scarborough St.

SOUTH STRADBROKE ISLAND

This narrow, 20km-long sand island was separated from North Stradbroke Island by a savage storm in 1896. These days, most people cross to the Southport end of the island, which is just 200m away from the northern end of the Spit. Most of the island is undeveloped, and there are some peaceful camping grounds where you can almost forget how close you are to the Gold Coast. In fact, this is the island's best feature – the main activities here include swimming, surfing, bushwalking and fishing. More adventurous types can also get stuck into canoeing, bike riding and jet-skiing through Couran Cove Island Resort.

The **Couran Island Resort** (☎ 5597 9000, 1800 268 726; www.couran.com; d from $310; 🔀 🖭) is a luxury resort with four restaurants, a day spa and a private marina. All rooms have spectacular water views. For something less extravagant, you can head to the **Couran Point Island Beach Resort** (☎ 5501 3533; www.couranpoint .com.au; d from $130; 🖭), which has comfortable hotel rooms, and slightly larger units with kitchenettes; rates include breakfast. Ferry transfers are extra (return per adult/child/ family $20/10/50). Nonguests can access the resort as day visitors for $60/24/155 per adult/child/family, which includes a barbecue lunch.

The South Stradbroke Island Resort ferry (return adult/child $25/12.50, 20 minutes each way) leaves from Runaway Bay Marina at the northern end of the Gold Coast every day at 10.30am and 4pm, returning at 2.30pm and 5pm.

GOLD COAST HINTERLAND

Inland from Coolangatta, the mountains of the McPherson Range stretch back 60km to the NSW border. The charming settlements and the dense green forest seem a million miles from the surf and concrete high-rises down on the coast. The climate is cooler and the national parks are a paradise for walkers, and it's all easily accessible by car or on organised tours from the Gold Coast.

Tours

The only way to access the Gold Coast hinterland without your own wheels is on a tour. All of the following offer pick ups from points along the Gold Coast.

Bushwacker Ecotours (☎ 5520 7238; www.bush wacker-ecotours.com.au; adult/child from $90/50) An ecofriendly tour group; has quite an extensive array of ecotours into the Gold Coast hinterland.

4X4 Hinterland Tours (☎ 1800 604 425, 0429 604 425; sales@hinterlandtours.com.au; day tours adult/child $130/80) Specialising in small group 4WD ecotours to either Springbrook or Lamington National Park and Mt Tambourine.

Mountain Trek Adventures (☎ 5536 1700; half-day tours adult/child $85/50) Offers tours that include Springbrook National Park and Tamborine Mountain.

SPRINGBROOK PLATEAU

The forested, 900m-high Springbrook Plateau is the remnant northern edge of a huge ancient volcano centred on Mt Warning in NSW, which last erupted 22 million years ago. It's an excellent winding drive up from the Gold Coast via Mudgeeraba, with great views over the surrounding countryside.

Much of the area is protected as **Springbrook National Park**, with three sections: Springbrook, Mt Cougal and Natural Bridge. Famed for its high waterfalls, rugged cliffs and panoramic views, the park has an extensive network of walking tracks and picnic areas. The main section of the park is Springbrook, where the majority of the lookouts and walking tracks are found, along with the park's information centre and the bulk of the accommodation. The Natural Bridge section is home to a large rock archway and glow-worm cave, while Mt Cougal is a rarely visited place with a single walking track and picnic area.

Coming from Nerang, take the Springbrook to Nerang road for the Springbrook section and the Murwillumbah to Nerang road for the Natural Bridge section. Mt Cougal is reached via Currumbin Creek Rd from Currumbin.

Springbrook

The village of Springbrook is balanced right on the edge of the plateau, with numerous waterfalls that tumble over 100m down to the coastal plain. There is a QPWS ranger's office and **information centre** (☎ 5533 5147; 2873 Springbrook Rd) here, where you can pick up a copy of the National Parks walking tracks leaflet for all three park sections; opening hours for the centre vary. Understandably, lookouts are the big attraction here, and there are several places where you can get the giddy thrill of leaning out over the edge.

At Gwongorella Picnic Area, just off Springbrook Rd, the lovely **Purling Brook Falls** drop 109m into the rainforest. There are two easily accessed lookouts so views of the falls can be seen from either side. There are coin-operated barbecues at the picnic area, a pleasant camping ground and a number of walking trails, including a 6km-return walk to **Waringa Pool**, a beautiful swimming hole. Just south is the national park information centre, and **Canyon Lookout**, which affords jagged views through the valley all the

way to the coast. The starting point for a 4km circuit walk to **Twin Falls** and the 17km **Warrie Circuit** is here.

At the end of Springbrook Rd, the **Goomoolahra Picnic Area** is another pleasant picnic area that has barbecues beside a small creek. A little further on, there's a great lookout point beside the falls, which offers views across the plateau and all the way back to the coast.

True to its name, the **Best of All Lookout**, which is reached via Lyrebird Ridge Rd, offers spectacular views from the southern edge of the plateau to the plains below. There's a 350m trail from the car park to the lookout that takes you past a clump of mighty Antarctic beech trees.

SLEEPING & EATING

Most guesthouses are along or signposted off Springbrook Rd.

Springbrook Mountain Lodge (☎ /fax 5533 5366; 317 Repeater Station Rd; s/d Mon-Thu $44/70, Fri-Sun $65/90, per extra person $22, cabin d $135) You can bask in the millionaire views at this YHA-affiliated lodge, which claims the highest perch on the plateau. All the rooms within are split-level en suites with a private section of balcony affording jaw-dropping views of the hinterland and coastline. The communal areas are huge and there are also two self-contained lodges for families or groups.

Springbrook Mountain Chalets (☎ 5533 5205; http://smchalets.com.au; 2058 Springbrook Rd; d $140-170) These stylish wooden chalets are scattered throughout a plot of bush providing plenty of privacy. All are split-level and spacious. The newer, more expensive chalets are pure style, with walls of glass, pot-belly stoves, spas and views.

English Gardens (☎ 5533 5244; 2832 Springbrook Rd; r $120-$140; mains $4-11; ☺ breakfast & lunch) This place has two self-contained cottages set amid a sprawling garden. Both are spacious, laden with character and the en suites have spas. The hosts are friendly and there's also a small café, which sells cakes, toasted sandwiches and pies.

Rosellas at Canyon Lookout (☎ 5533 5120; 8 Canyon Pde; s/d $85/95; dishes $10-20; ☺ 10am-4pm Wed-Fri, 9am-5pm Sat & Sun, dinner Fri & Sun) With Canyon Lookout at your doorstep, this guesthouse has comfortable en-suite rooms with TVs and bar fridges. The restaurant serves up great homemade soups and grills.

GOLD COAST

DETOUR: TAMBORINE MOUNTAIN

This pleasant side trip takes you around 20km inland of the Bruce Hwy through some pleasant farming and gourmet food-producing areas, before climbing steeply to the Tamborine Mountain area with its heritage towns and multiple national parks.

From Oxenford, the Tamborine-Oxenford Rd takes you through pleasant farmland and past **Thumm Estate Wines** (☎ 5573 6990; 87 Kriedeman Rd, Upper Coomera; ☒ 9am-5pm), a winery with a small museum and a restaurant. Further up the road is the **Nut Shed** (☎ 5545 1799; 1459 Tamborine Rd; ☒ 10am-5.30pm), a working macadamia farm that sells a huge range of nut-based products.

After a tortuous climb you reach the Mt Tamborine area, which sits on a 600m-high plateau in the northern spur of the McPherson Range. Despite the area including Queensland's first national park, Witches Falls (proclaimed in 1908), only tiny patches of the area's original forests remain in nine small parks.

All the areas in between the park sections are filled with the excessively cute heritage communities of Mt Tamborine, North Tamborine and Eagle Heights, which were established in the late 19th century. Made up of art and craft shops, B&Bs, wineries, Devonshire teahouses, cafés and nurseries, the towns receive busloads of visitors every day.

Some of the best spots are **Witches Falls National Park**, southwest of North Tamborine, and **Cedar Creek Falls** and **Cameron Falls**, northwest of North Tamborine. **Macrozamia Grove National Park** has some extremely old macrozamia palms.

In the town of North Tamborine, the **visitor information centre** (☎ 5545 3200; Doughty Park; ☒ 10.30am-3.30pm Sun-Fri, 9.30am-3.30pm Sat) has plenty of brochures, a small display on the area's ecology, and information on the well-established wineries scattered around the mountain.

The fabulous **Tamborine Mountain Distillery** (☎ 5545 3452; 87-91 Beacon Rd, North Tamborine; ☒ 10am-3pm Wed-Sun) is a boutique distiller that manufactures its own schnapps, liqueurs and other spirits from organically grown fruits. A great place for a meal and a relaxing drink is the **St Bernards Hotel** (☎ 5545 1177; fax 5545 2733; 101 Alpine Tce, Tamborine; mains $10-18; ☒ lunch daily, dinner Mon-Sat), a rustic old mountain pub with a large deck that captures commanding views of the gorge.

Purling Brook Falls Campground (www.epa.qld .gov.au; per person $4) This small national park camping ground is near Gwongorella Picnic Ground. Its has no showers or bins. You need to book in advance through **QPWS** (☎ 13 13 04).

Springbrook Homestead (☎ 5533 5200; 2319 Springbrook Rd; mains $8-18; ☒ lunch) This tavern serves ploughman's lunches and steaks, and is a pleasant spot for a beer after a long walk.

Natural Bridge

The Natural Bridge section of the national park is just a couple of kilometres west of Springbrook as the crow flies, but you'll have to drive back up to Numinbah from

Springbrook and then down the Murwillumbah road to get here – a total trip of about 35km. A steep 1km walking circuit leads to a rock arch spanning a water-formed cave, which is home to a huge colony of glow-worms, and a small waterfall tumbling into a swimming hole.

Mt Cougal

The Mt Cougal section is also linked to Springbrook, but to get here, you'll have to go all the way back to the Pacific Hwy and pick up Currumbin Creek Rd at Currumbin. There's a nice picnic area, plus a walking trail that passes several cascades and cooling swimming holes on Currumbin Creek.

Coolum Beach (p335), Queensland

LAWRIE WILLIAMS

Fine dining in Noosa (p340), Queensland

JOHN HAY

RICHARD I'ANSON

A mystical sunset over Noosa National
Park (p336), Queensland

Tobacco plants and the Glass House Mountains (p329), Queensland

JOHN BANAGA

Brisbane

Australia's third-largest city, Brisbane has had a rapid rise from rural town to tinseltown over recent decades, earning it tags such as BrisVegas and Brisneyland, and the enviable climate and legendary lifestyle have established it as one of the most desirable places to live in Australia. It wasn't always so. The first European settlement was a penal colony at Redcliffe on Moreton Bay in 1824, but after struggling with inadequate water supplies and hostile Aborigines, the colony was relocated to safer territory on the banks of the Brisbane River.

Warm to hot summers and blissfully mild winters make Brisbane a year-round destination, and the city's heart beats with a multitude of festivals. Brisbane enjoys dozens of theatres, art-house cinemas, concert halls, galleries and museums. A prosperous, cosmopolitan atmosphere nurtures a great café scene, world-class restaurants and a vibrant nightlife.

Matching the urban dynamism are the city's natural attractions, the leafy parks hugging the banks of the meandering river, and the proximity of some of the state's major tourist destinations, including the Gold and Sunshine Coasts and the islands of Moreton Bay.

Moreton Bay is reckoned to have some 365 islands, around which whales, dolphins and dugongs frolic. Moreton Island is a rugged wilderness where you can go bushwalking and four-wheel driving, and a pod of wild but friendly dolphins have put Tangalooma on the tourist map. North Stradbroke is the most developed island, with glorious beaches and swimming holes, where the surfing, swimming and fishing are excellent.

HIGHLIGHTS

- Explore **Mt Coot-tha's** (p307) bush tracks, gardens, planetarium and city lookout
- Bathe in Sunshine State sophistication at the museum and art galleries of the **Queensland Cultural Centre** (p301)
- Discover what's behind every bend of the Brisbane River on a **scenic river cruise** (p310)
- **Cycle** (p308) beside the meandering Brisbane River through Brisbane's leafy parks and gardens
- Savour a lazy latte with a large late breakfast in cosmopolitan **Fortitude Valley** (p315)
- Dive with dolphins and snorkel in the wrecks at **Tangalooma** (p324)
- Bushwalk, cool off in a freshwater lake or sea kayak the fine breaks on the coastline of **North Stradbroke Island** (p321)

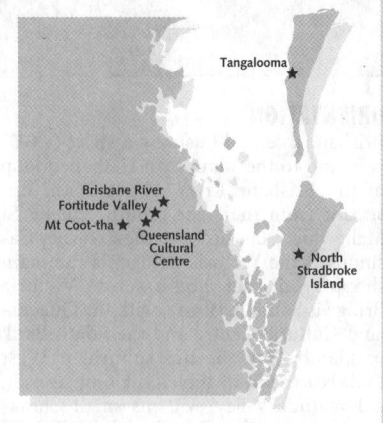

| TELEPHONE CODE: 07 | POPULATION: 1.6 MILLION | www.ourbrisbane.com |

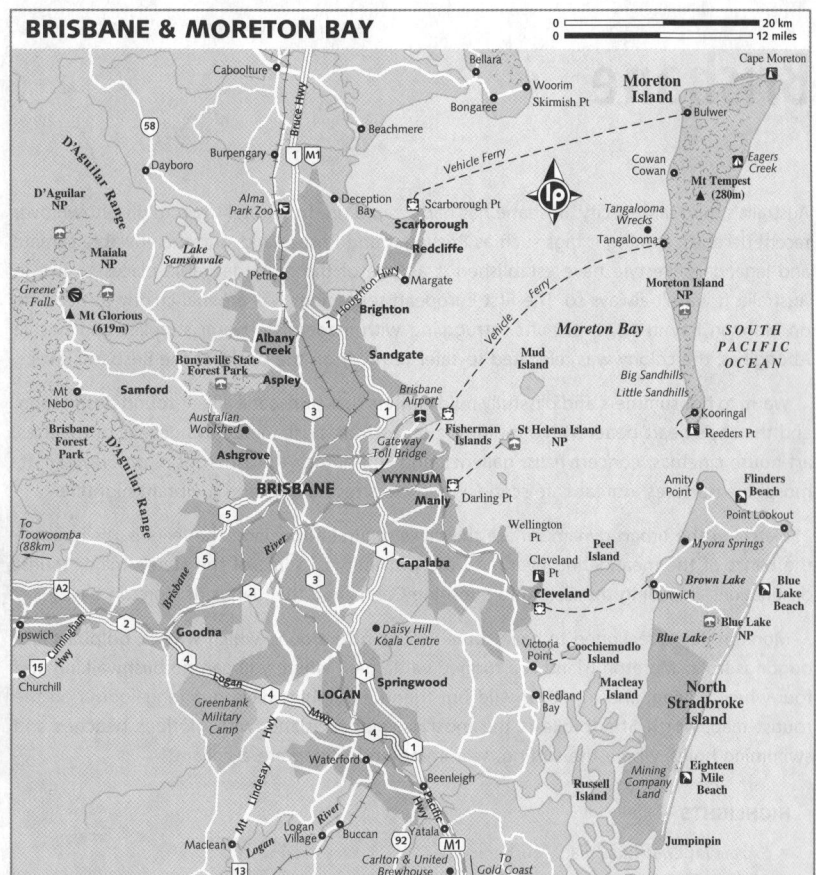

BRISBANE & MORETON BAY

Brisbane (p297) from Kangaroo Point, Queensland
ROSS BARNETT

Amusement park at Surfers Paradise (p288), Queensland
DAVID WALL

Surf life saving club activities at Burleigh Heads (p282), Queensland
RICHARD I'ANSON

South Stradbroke Island (p294), Queensland
RUSSELL MOUNTFORD

ORIENTATION

Brisbane's central business district (CBD) is bound to the south by a U-shaped loop of the Brisbane River, about 25km upstream from the river mouth. Queen St Mall, which runs down to the Treasury Casino and the Victoria Bridge, is the main shopping district. South across Victoria Bridge is South Brisbane, with the Queensland Cultural Centre and the South Bank parklands, and the hip suburb of West End. Northeast of the city, along Ann St, is Fortitude Valley, with its small Chinatown, alternative scene and lots of cafés and restaurants.

The Roma St Transit Centre, where you'll arrive if you're coming by bus, train or air-

port shuttle, is about 500m northwest of the Queen St Mall. Just west of the Transit Centre is Petrie Terrace, with several hostels, and the upmarket dining districts of Paddington and Milton.

Brisbane airport is about 15km northeast of the city; see p320 for information about getting to/from the airport.

Maps

For a comprehensive and handy map pick up a copy of Lonely Planet's *Brisbane and Gold Coast City Map*. The visitors centre can provide you with free copies of *The Brisbane Map*, *i on Brisbane* and *Brisbane Map – a Backpackers Guide*. All include detailed maps of the CBD.

INFORMATION

Bookshops

Angus & Robertson Post Office Sq (Map pp304-5; ☎ 3229 0717; Shop 1-4, Post Office Sq, Adelaide St); Queen St Mall (Map pp304-5; ☎ 3229 8899; City Arcade, 52 Queen St Mall) Generic chain selling books of all genres.

Borders Bookstore (Map pp304-5; ☎ 3210 1220; 162 Albert Street)

World Wide Maps & Guides (Map pp304-5; ☎ 3221 4330; Shop 30, Anzac Sq Arcade, 267 Edward St) Comprehensive range of travel guides and maps.

Emergency

In case of a life-threatening emergency, dial ☎ 000 – it's a free call from any phone. Calls will be diverted to the police, ambulance service or to the fire brigade, as appropriate to the situation.

Ambulance (☎ 1300 369 003)

Fire (☎ 3247 5539)

Police City (Map pp304-5; ☎ 3224 4444; 67 Adelaide St); Fortitude Valley (Map pp304-5; ☎ 3131 1200; Brunswick St Mall); Headquarters (Map pp304-5; ☎ 3364 6464; 100 Roma St)

Royal Automobile Club of Queensland (RACQ; ☎ 131 905, breakdown 13 11 11) City (Map pp304-5; GPO Bldg, 261 Queen St); St Pauls Tce (Map pp304-5; 300 St Pauls Tce)

Internet Access

Internet cafés are prolific in Brisbane. Rates range from $3 to $6.

Central City Library (Map pp304-5; ☎ 3403 8888; Lower ground fl, City Plaza complex, 69 Ann St; ⌚ 9am-6pm Mon-Fri, 10am-3pm Sat & Sun) Free but there's a two-hour limit and bookings are essential.

Global Gossip City (Map pp304-5; ☎ 3229 4033; 290 Edward St; ⌚ 8am-midnight) Fortitude Valley (Map pp304-5; ☎ 3666 0900; 312 Brunswick St; ⌚ 8am-midnight)

Internet City (Map pp304-5; ☎ 3003 1221; Level 4, 132 Albert St; ⌚ 24hr).

State Library of Queensland (Map pp304-5; ☎ 3840 7666; South Bank; ⌚ 10am-8pm Mon-Thu, to 5pm Fri-Sun) Free but advance booking required.

Medical Services

Brisbane Sexual Health Clinic (Map pp302-3; ☎ 3227 8666; 270 Roma St)

Royal Brisbane Hospital (Map pp302-3; ☎ 3253 8111; Hertson Rd, Hertson; ⌚ 24hr casualty ward)

Travel Clinic (Map pp304-5; ☎ 1300 369 359, 3211 3611; 1st fl, 245 Albert St; ⌚ 7.30am-7pm Mon-Thu, to 6pm Fri, 8.30am-5pm Sat, 9.30am-5pm Sun)

Travellers' Medical & Vaccination Centre (TMVC; Map pp304-5; ☎ 3221 9066; 5th fl, 247 Adelaide St; ⌚ 8am-5pm Mon & Fri, 10am-7pm Tue, 8am-9pm Wed, 8am-2am Thu, 8.30am-2pm Sat)

BRISBANE IN...

Two days

Greet the day with an unhurried breakfast in trendy **West End** (p315) before strolling to the **South Bank Parklands** (p306) to get acquainted with offerings at the **Queensland Cultural Centre** (p301). Already hungry? Then slip into one of the riverside cafés (p314) and watch the city's morning routine. As the day warms up, cool those heels, and everything else, at **Streets Beach** (p308). If it's summer, stick around for an alfresco movie in the park. Looking for dinner? Why not jump on a ferry and head to the Riverside Pier, then walk up to **C** (p314) for a sublime feast.

On day two stroll downtown through the city's mix of old and new architecture. Explore Brisbane's history at **City Hall** (p301) and enjoy the beautiful old **Treasury Building** (p301), before heading south to the **City Botanic Gardens** (p301). The massive Moreton Bay Figs shade the perfect spot for a lazy picnic. Finish the day with a brew at the **Belgian Beer Cafe** (p316) and a banquet in **Fortitude Valley** (p315).

Four Days

On day three check out the cafés in **Fortitude Valley** (p315) and delve into the trendy shops and **galleries** (p307). Spend the afternoon at the lookout at **Mt Coot-tha Reserve** (p307). Take in a short bushwalk, visit the beautiful **Brisbane Botanic Gardens** (p307) and stargaze at the **Sir Thomas Brisbane Planetarium** (p307) before heading back to the Valley for dinner.

On day four you'll need to give the feet a rest, so take a cruise up the Brisbane River to **Lone Pine Koala Sanctuary** (p307). As you cruise back, watch the city glide past, before re-educating your palate at the Belgian Beer Cafe (p316) and gravitating to **Paddington** (p314) for a feast.

BRISBANE RIVER & INNER SUBURBS

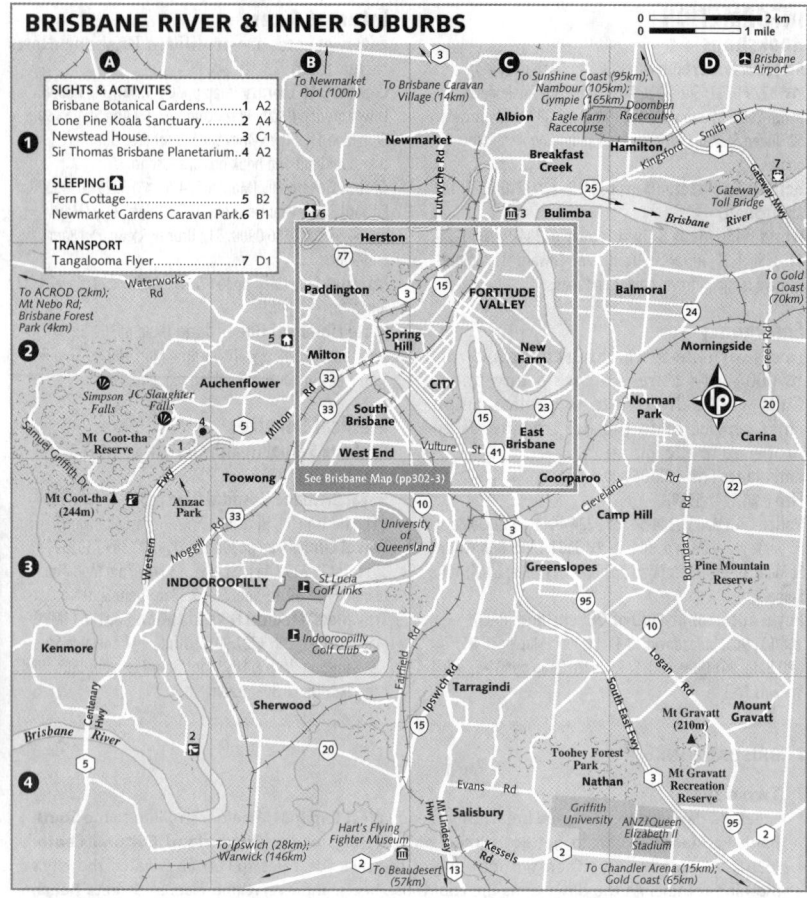

SIGHTS & ACTIVITIES
Brisbane Botanical Gardens..........1 A2
Lone Pine Koala Sanctuary..........2 A4
Newstead House.......................3 C1
Sir Thomas Brisbane Planetarium..4 A2

SLEEPING
Fern Cottage...........................5 B2
Newmarket Gardens Caravan Park.6 B1

TRANSPORT
Tangalooma Flyer.....................7 D1

See Brisbane Map (pp302-3)

Money

There are plenty of foreign-exchange bureaus at Brisbane airport's domestic and international terminals, as well as ATMs that accept most international credit cards. If you're in need of after-hours foreign exchange, the tellers in the casino in the Treasury Building are open for business 24 hours a day. ATMs are prolific throughout Brisbane.

American Express (Map pp304-5; ☎ 1300 139 060; 131 Elizabeth St)

Interforex Brisbane (Map pp304-5; ☎ 3221 3562; Shop Q 255, Wintergarden, 171-209 Queen St)

Travelex Edward St (Map pp304-5; ☎ 3221 9422; 276 Edward St); Queen St Mall (Map pp304-5; ☎ 3210 6325; Shop 149F, Queen St Mall)

Post

Australia Post (☎ 13 13 18) Queen St (Map pp304-5; 261 Queen St; ⏰ 7am-6pm Mon-Fri); Wintergarden (Map pp304-5; Post Shop; 2nd fl, Wintergarden Centre, Queen St; ⏰ 8.30am-5.30pm Mon-Fri, 9am-4pm Sat) The General Post Office at 261 Queen St has poste restante.

Tourist Information

Brisbane Visitor Information Centre (Map pp304-5; ☎ 3006 6290; cnr Albert & Queen Sts; ⏰ 9am-5.30pm Mon-Thu, to 7pm Fri, to 5pm Sat, 9.30am-4.30pm Sun) Great one-stop information counter for all things Brisbane.

Brisbane Visitors Accommodation Service (Map pp304-5; ☎ 3236 2020; 3rd fl, Roma St Transit Centre, Roma St; ⏰ 7am-6pm Mon-Fri, 8am-5pm Sat & Sun) Privately run outfit specialising in backpacker travel, tours and accommodation in Brisbane and elsewhere in Queensland.

Naturally Queensland (Map pp304-5; ☎ 3227 7111; 160 Ann St; ⏰ 8.30am-5pm Mon-Fri) The Queensland Parks & Wildlife Service (QPWS) runs an excellent information centre. You can get maps, brochures and books on national parks and state forests, as well as camping information and Fraser Island permits.

South Bank visitors centre (Map pp304-5; ☎ 3867 2051; Stanley Street Plaza, South Bank Parklands; ⏰ 9am-6pm, to 9pm Fri)

SIGHTS

A walk through the city will reveal Brisbane's colonial history and architecture, and a ferry ride across the river takes you to the attractions and activities of South Bank. Chinatown and Brunswick St, both in Fortitude Valley, are vibrant shopping and dining precincts. A little further afield is Mt Coot-tha Reserve; its lookout has spectacular views and is easily accessed by bus. The free *Brisbane's Living Heritage* brochure, available from the visitor centre, highlights many of these sights.

City Centre

Brisbane's **City Hall** (Map pp304-5; ☎ 3403 6586; btwn Ann & Adelaide Sts; admission free; ⏰ lift & viewing tower 10am-3pm Mon-Fri, to 2.30pm Sat) is a historic sandstone building overlooking the sculptures and fountains of King George Sq, and offers one of the best views across the city. On the ground floor is the **Museum of Brisbane** (Map pp304-5; admission free; ⏰ 10am-5pm), which describes the city's historical journey with interactive exhibits, as well as showcasing art and crafts. There are free guided tours of the museum on Tuesdays, Thursdays and Saturdays at 11am.

At the western end of the Queen St Mall is the magnificent Italian Renaissance–style **Treasury Building**. Behind the lavish façade you won't find pin-striped bureaucrats and tax collectors, but rather spruikers and an entirely different kind of money spinner: Conrad's 24-hour casino. In the block southeast of the casino, the equally gorgeous former **Land Administration Building** has been converted to a five-star hotel (see the boxed text, p313).

Further south along George St is **Parliament House** (Map pp304-5; ☎ 3406 7562; cnr Alice & George Sts; admission free), dating from 1868, where you're free to watch Queensland's law-makers in action on sitting days. Free guided tours are available on demand be-

tween 9am and 4pm Monday to Friday, and 10am to 2pm weekends, unless parliament is sitting, in which case you can hang out in the public gallery and watch.

Brisbane's **City Botanic Gardens** (Map pp304-5; ☎ 3403 0666; Albert St; ⏰ 24hr) is right on the river and its lawns are popular with lunching office workers, joggers and picnickers. There is a free guided tour at 11am and 1pm Monday to Saturday. See p317 for details of the Moonlight Cinemas held here.

In the grounds of Queensland University of Technology (QUT) is the **QUT Art Museum** (Map pp304-5; ☎ 3864 2797; 2 George St; admission free; ⏰ 10am-4pm Tue-Fri, noon-4pm Sat & Sun), which has regularly changing exhibits of contemporary Australian art and work by Brisbane art students. Next door is the former **Old Government House**, a beautiful colonnaded building dating from 1860 and now the home of the National Trust.

Built by convicts in 1829, the **Commissariat Stores Building** (Map pp304-5; ☎ 3221 4198; 115 William St; adult/child $4/2; ⏰ 10am-4pm Tue-Fri & Sun) is one of Brisbane's oldest buildings. Today it houses a museum devoted to Brisbane's convict and colonial history.

South Bank

QUEENSLAND CULTURAL CENTRE

In South Bank, just over the Victoria Bridge from the CBD, is the extensive Queensland Cultural Centre, which takes in the Queensland Museum, Queensland Art Gallery and Performing Arts Centre (p317).

The austere exterior of the **Queensland Art Gallery** (Map pp304-5; ☎ 3840 7303; www.qag.qld.gov.au; Melbourne St, South Brisbane; admission free; ⏰ 10am-5pm Mon-Fri, 9am-5pm Sat & Sun) reveals little of the fine collection of works by European and Australian artists, including Sidney Nolan, Brett Whitely, Charles Blackman and Fred Williams. There are free guided tours 11am, 1pm and 2pm Monday to Friday, and 11.30am, 1pm and 2.30pm Saturday and Sunday.

At the back of the complex, the **Queensland Museum** (Map pp304-5; ☎ 3840 7555; www.qmuseum.qld.gov.au; Grey St, South Brisbane; admission free; ⏰ 9am-5pm) has an eclectic collection of exhibits relating to Queensland's history, including a skeleton of Queensland's own dinosaur *Muttaburrasaurus*, and the *Avian Cirrus*, the tiny plane in which Queensland's Bert Hinkler made the first England to Australia solo flight in 1928. It also has a very good

BRISBANE

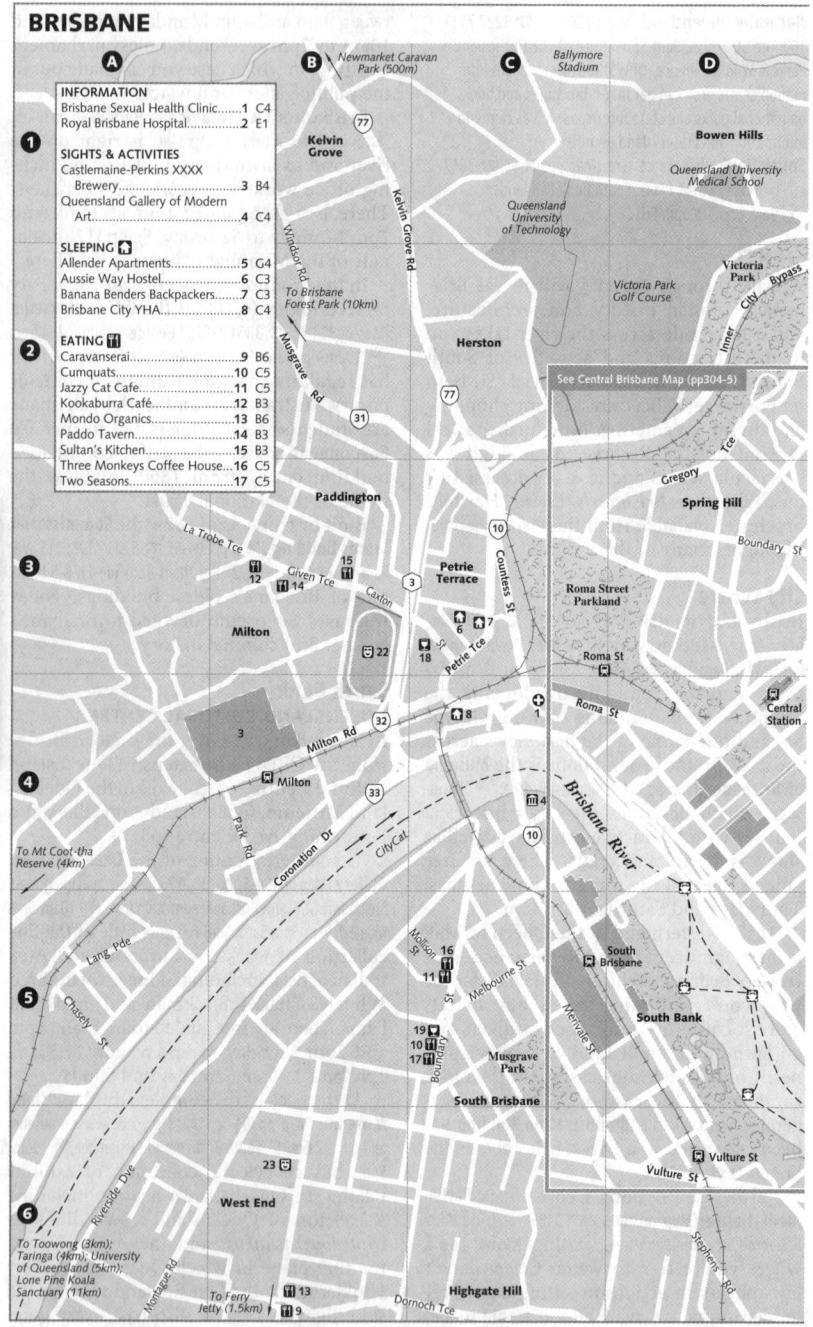

INFORMATION
Brisbane Sexual Health Clinic......**1** C4
Royal Brisbane Hospital..............**2** E1

SIGHTS & ACTIVITIES
Castlemaine-Perkins XXXX
   Brewery..............................**3** B4
Queensland Gallery of Modern
   Art.....................................**4** C4

SLEEPING 🏠
Allender Apartments................**5** G4
Aussie Way Hostel....................**6** C3
Banana Benders Backpackers.......**7** C3
Brisbane City YHA....................**8** C4

EATING 🍴
Caravanserai.............................**9** B6
Cumquats................................**10** C5
Jazzy Cat Cafe.........................**11** C5
Kookaburra Café.......................**12** B3
Mondo Organics.......................**13** B6
Paddo Tavern...........................**14** B3
Sultan's Kitchen.......................**15** B3
Three Monkeys Coffee House...**16** C5
Two Seasons............................**17** C5

See Central Brisbane Map (pp304-5)

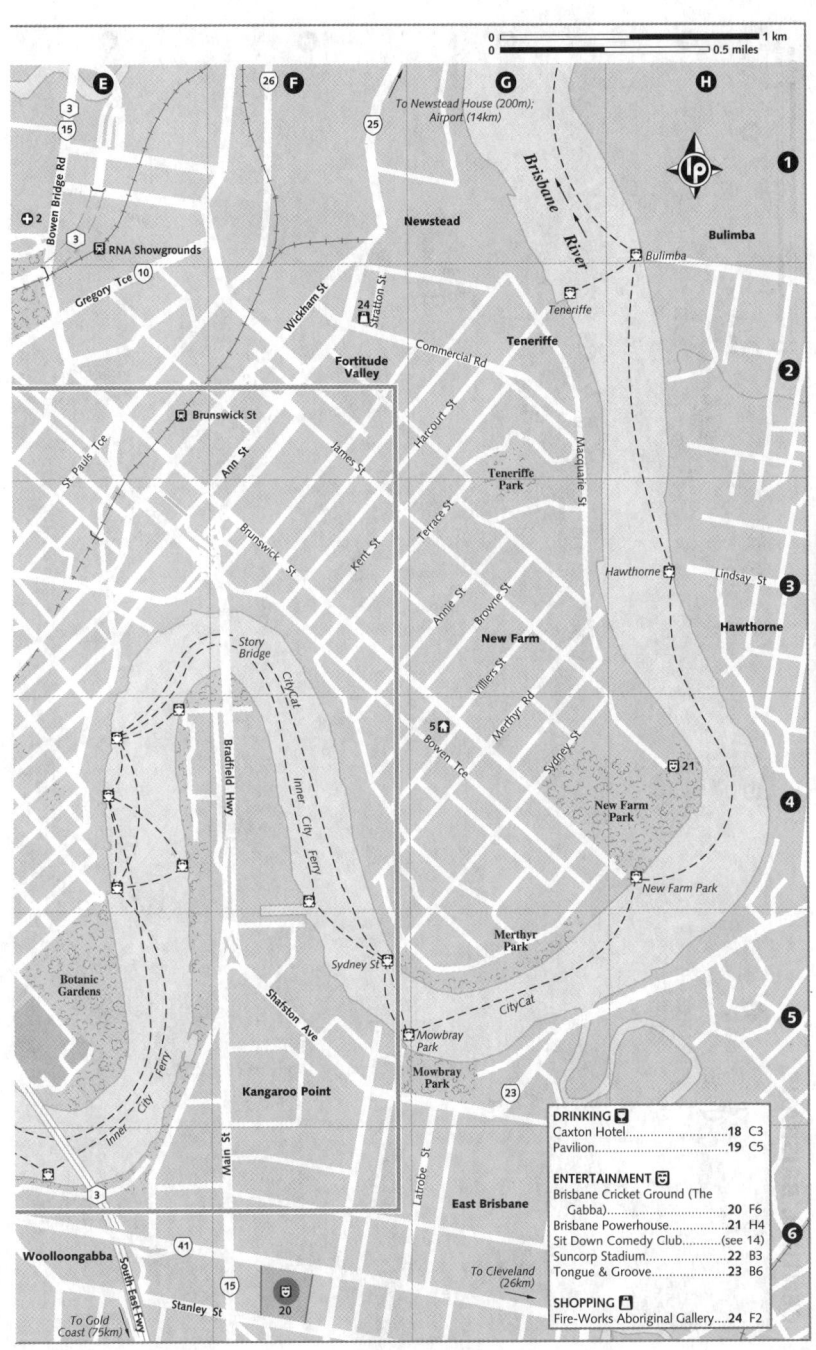

BRISBANE

DRINKING 🍺
Caxton Hotel..............................18 C3
Pavilion....................................19 C5

ENTERTAINMENT 🎭
Brisbane Cricket Ground (The
 Gabba)..................................20 F6
Brisbane Powerhouse..................21 H4
Sit Down Comedy Club..........(see 14)
Suncorp Stadium.......................22 B3
Tongue & Groove.......................23 B6

SHOPPING 🛍️
Fire-Works Aboriginal Gallery....24 F2

CENTRAL BRISBANE

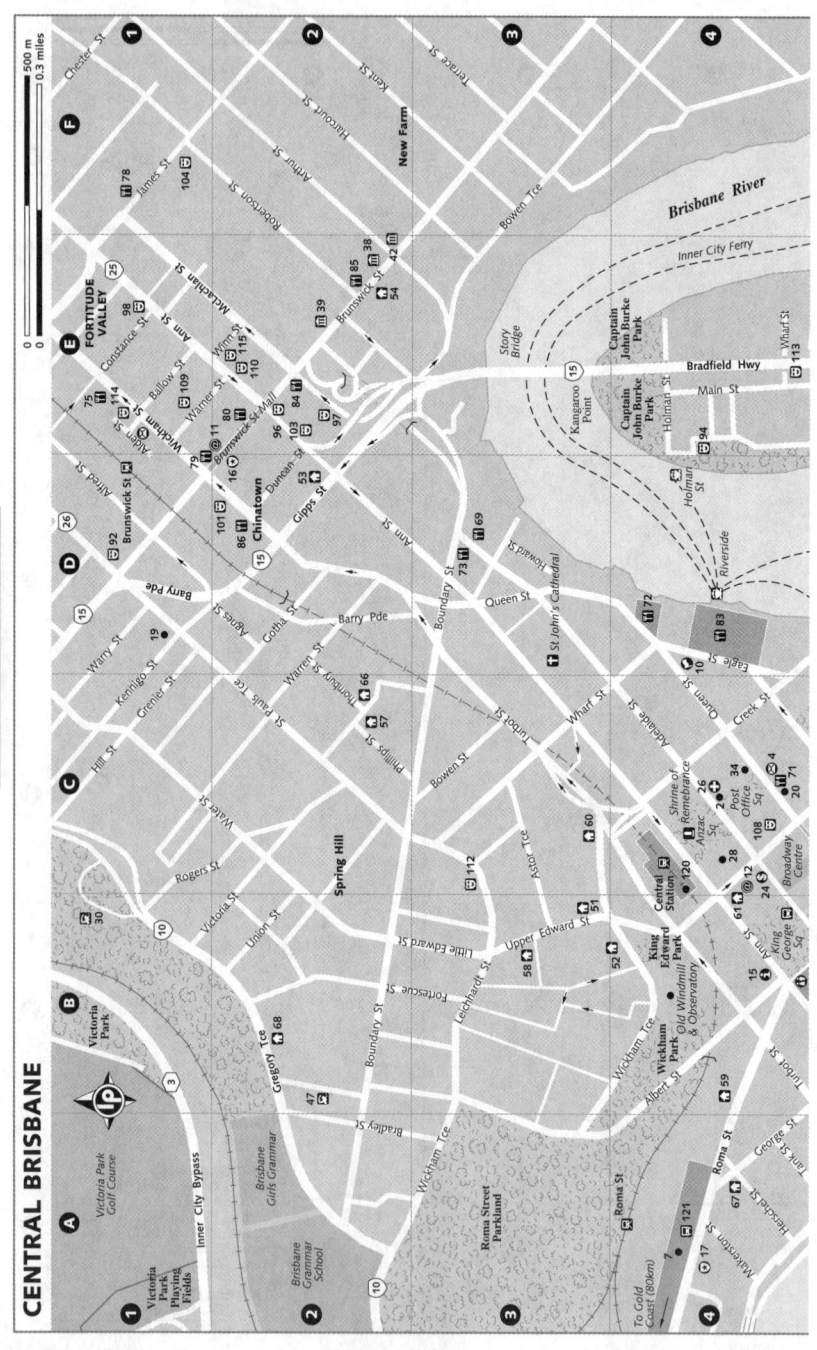

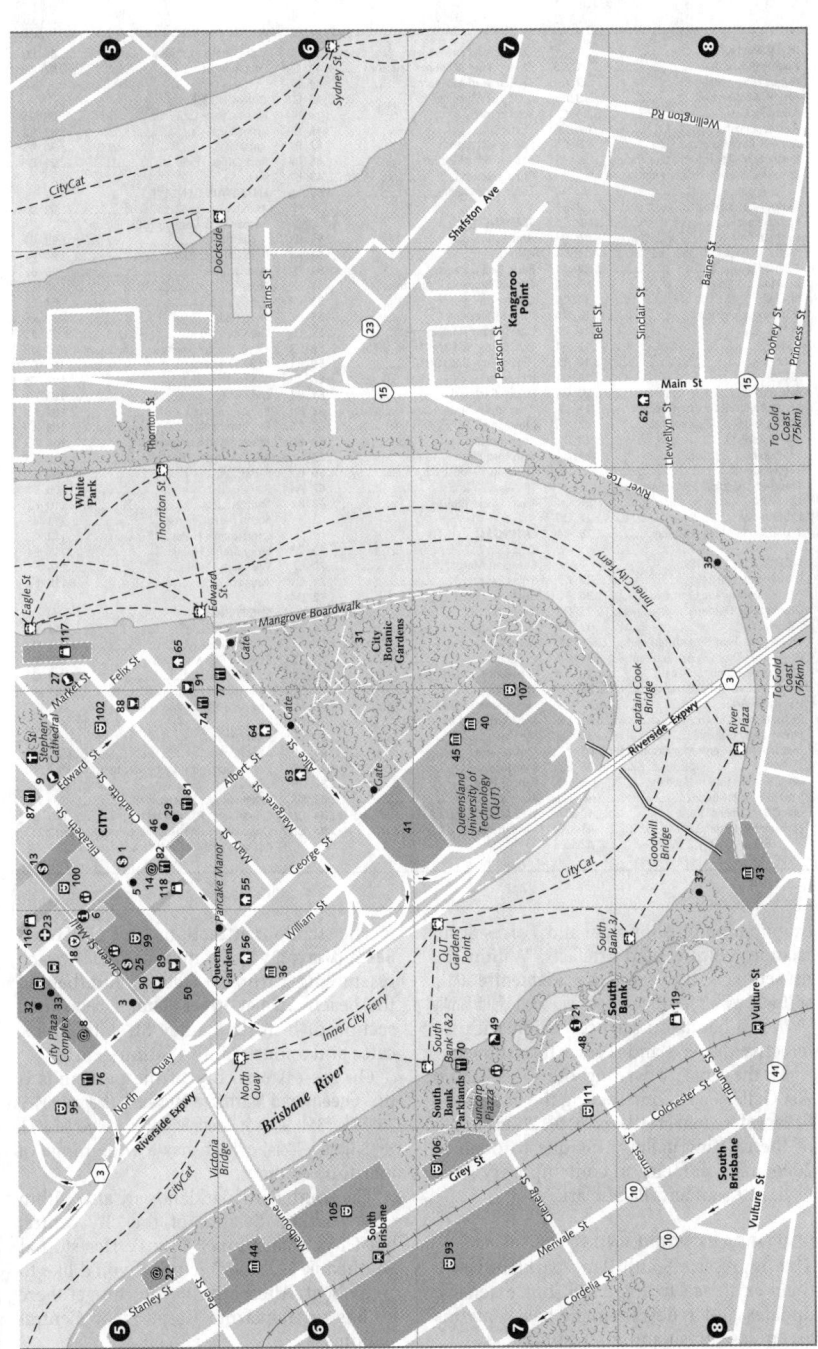

examination of Aboriginal and Torres Strait Islander cultures and artefacts. Within the museum is the excellent **Sciencentre** (Map pp304-5; www.sciencentre.qld.gov.au; adult/child/family $9/7/28), a hands-on science exhibit with interactive displays and regular film shows.

At the time of writing the Queensland Art Gallery was constructing the **Queensland Gallery of Modern Art** (Map pp302-3), 200m north of the existing gallery. It's due to open in 2006 and will focus on contemporary Australian, Asian and Pacific art.

SOUTH BANK PARKLANDS

The impressive South Bank parklands owe their existence to Expo '88, but extensive updates and redevelopment has kept this green oasis fresh and interesting.

The standout attractions here are **Streets Beach** (Map pp304-5), a funky artificial beach resembling a tropical lagoon, and, behind the beach, **Stanley Street Plaza**, a renovated section of historic Stanley St, with shops, cafés and a tourist information centre.

On the eastern edge of the parklands is the **Queensland Maritime Museum** (Map pp304-5; ☎ 3844 5361; Sidon St, South Brisbane; adult/child $6/3; ☺ 9.30am-4.30pm), which has a wide range of maritime displays.

The South Bank parklands are also within easy walking distance of the city centre, but CityCat and Inner City Ferries stop at Southbank 1, 2 and 3 jetties if you'd like to go by boat. Alternatively, you can get there by bus or train from Roma St or Central station.

Fortitude Valley

INSTITUTE OF MODERN ART

The **Institute of Modern Art** (Map pp304-5; ☎ 3252 5750; www.ima.org.au; ⊙ 11am-5pm Tue-Fri, to 4pm Sat) is a noncommercial gallery with showings by local names, housed inside the **Judith Wright Centre for Contemporary Arts** (Map pp305-5; ☎ 3872 9000; www.judithwrightcentre.com; 420 Brunswick St).

OTHER GALLERIES

Other private galleries include **Jan Murphy Gallery** (Map pp304-5; ☎ 3254 1855; 486 Brunswick St; ⊙ 10am-5pm Tue-Sat) and **Philip Bacon Gallery** (☎ 3358 3555; 2 Arthur St; ⊙ 10am-5pm Tue-Sat).

Newstead

North of the centre on the Brisbane River is Brisbane's best-known heritage site, the lovely, old **Newstead House** (Map p300; ☎ 3216 1846; Breakfast Creek Rd; adult/child/family $4.40/2.20/11; ⊙ 10am-4pm Mon-Fri, 2-4pm Sun). Set in attractive, forested grounds, the homestead dates from 1846 and is beautifully fitted out with Victorian furnishings. You can get here by bus from Adelaide St in the CBD, or Wickham St in the Valley; look for bus 322, 306 or 300.

Mt Coot-tha Reserve

A short drive or bus ride from the city, this huge bush reserve and parkland has an excellent botanic garden, a planetarium, eateries and a superb lookout over the city. On a clear day you can see the Moreton Bay islands. The lookout is accessed via Samuel Griffith Dr and has wheelchair access.

Just north of the road to the lookout, on Samuel Griffith Dr, is the turn-off to **JC Slaughter Falls**, reached by a short walking track, plus a 1.5km **Aboriginal Art Trail**, which takes you past eight art sites with work by local Aboriginal artists.

The pleasant **Brisbane Botanic Gardens** (Map p300; ☎ 3403 8888; admission free; ⊙ 8.30am-5.30pm Sep-Mar, 8am-5pm Apr-Aug) cover 0.5 sq km and include over 20,000 species of plants, an enclosed tropical dome, an arid zone, rainforests and a Japanese garden, plus a restaurant. There are free guided walks at 11am and 1pm Monday to Saturday.

Within the gardens is the **Sir Thomas Brisbane Planetarium** (Map p300; ☎ 3403 2578; adult/child/family $2/1/5; ⊙ 2.30-4.30pm Tue-Fri, 10am-4.30pm Tue-Fri during school holidays, 11am-8.30pm Sat, 11am-4.30pm Sun), Australia's largest planetarium with a series of astronomical displays. The shows inside the **Cosmic Skydome** (Map p300; adult/child/family $11.50/6.80/31) will make you feel like you've stepped on board the *Enterprise*.

To get here take bus 471 from Adelaide St, opposite King George Sq ($2.60, 30 minutes). The bus drops you off in the lookout car park and stops outside the Brisbane Botanic Gardens en route. The last trip to the city leaves at around 4pm on weekdays and 5pm at weekends.

Brisbane Forest Park

This 285-sq-km natural bushland reserve in the D'Aguilar Range, just 10km from the city centre, is a popular recreation area for city dwellers. At the park entrance, the **Brisbane Forest Park information centre** (☎ 3300 4855; 60 Mt Nebo Rd; ⊙ 8.30am-4.30pm Mon-Fri, from 9am Sat & Sun) has information about bush **camping** (per person/family $4/16) in the park and maps of walking trails. Beside the information centre is **Walk-About Creek** (adult/child/family $5/2.50/12.50; ⊙ 9am-4.30pm), a freshwater study centre where you can see a resident platypus up close, as well as fish, lizards, pythons and turtles.

To get to the park from the city, take any bus for the Gap from the corner of Albert and Adelaide Sts (bus 385 is an express service).

Lone Pine Koala Sanctuary

Just a 35-minute bus ride south of the city centre, **Lone Pine Koala Sanctuary** (Map p300; ☎ 3378 1366; Jesmond Rd, Fig Tree; adult/child/family $16/11/39; ⊙ 8.30am-5pm) is set in attractive parklands beside the river. It is home to 130 or so koalas, as well as kangaroos, possums and wombats. The koalas are undeniably cute and most visitors readily cough up the $15 to have their picture taken hugging one.

To get here catch the 430 express bus ($3.40, 35 minutes), which leaves hourly from the Queen St Mall bus station. Alternatively, **Mirimar Cruises** (☎ 1300 729 742; adult/child/family incl park entry $44/25/120) cruises to the sanctuary along the Brisbane River from North Quay, next to Victoria Bridge. It departs daily at 10am, returning from Lone Pine at 1.30pm.

BRISBANE

ACTIVITIES

The **Cliffs** (pp304-5) at Kangaroo Point, opposite the Botanic Gardens on the south bank of the Brisbane River, is a rock-climbing venue that's flood-lit at night. Several operators offer climbing and abseiling instruction here, including **Worth Wild Rock Climbing** (☎ 3395 6450; www.worthwild.com.au; group instruction per person $75) and **K2 Extreme** (☎ 3257 3310; k2extreme@k2basecamp.com.au; per person $30).

Skatebiz (Map pp304-5; ☎ 3220 0157; 101 Albert St; per 2/24hr $13/20; ☺ 9am-5.30pm Mon-Thu, to 4pm Sat, 10am-4pm Sun) rents out in-line skates and the necessary protective equipment. Some of the best skating areas are the South Bank Parklands, the City Botanic Gardens and the bike paths that follow the Brisbane River.

Brisbane has some 500km of bike trails, all of which are detailed in the *Brisbane Bicycle Experience Guide*, available from visitors centres. The most scenic routes follow the Brisbane River. Bicycles are allowed on Citytrains, except on weekdays during peak hours. You can also take bikes on CityCats and ferries for free. You can rent a bike from **Brisbane Bicycle Sales** (Map pp304-5; ☎ 3229 2433; www.brizbike.com; 87 Albert St; per hr/day $12/20; ☺ 8.30am-5.30pm Mon-Fri, to 4pm Sat, 10am-4pm Sun).

There are several good swimming pools in Brisbane, including **Centenary Aquatic** (Map pp304-5; ☎ 3831 7665; 400 Gregory Tce, Spring Hill; adult/child $4.30/3.30; ☺ 5.30am-7.30pm Mon-Fri, 6am-6pm Sat & Sun), **Newmarket Pool** (Map p300; ☎ 3356 8434; 71 Alderson St, Newmarket; adult/child $3.50/2; ☺ 6am-7pm Mon-Fri, 8am-7pm Sat, 9am-7pm Sun mid-Apr-Oct), **Spring Hill Baths** (Map pp304-5; ☎ 3831 7881; 14 Torrington St, Spring Hill; ☺ morning & evening in summer) and the **Streets Beach** lagoon at the South Bank parklands.

You can tandem skydive with the **Brisbane Skydiving Centre** (☎ 5464 6111; www.brisbaneskydive.com.au; tandem skydive from $250), or go ballooning with **Fly Me to the Moon** (☎ 3423 0400; www.flymetothemoon.com.au; Mon-Fri $250, Sat & Sun $290).

WALKING TOUR

With its downtown parks, riverside paths, historic buildings and gentle landscape, Brisbane is a great place to explore on foot. The city council produces the free *Experience Guide*, which suggests good itineraries. Alternatively, the following walk covers about 5km and takes at least a couple of hours.

Starting at Central Station, head south, crossing Anzac St before you descend the steps into **Anzac Sq** (**1**), where city workers and ibises enjoy the grass and shady trees on weekdays. Scattered throughout the square are touch-and-tell displays where you can learn more about the significance of the park. At the northwestern end of the park, the **Shrine of Remembrance** (**2**) is a Greek Revivalist cenotaph where a flame burns in remembrance of Australians who died in WWI.

Take the pedestrian bridge over the road at the southeastern corner of the square, which leads into **Post Office Sq** (**3**). Heading in the same direction, cross Queen St to Brisbane's historic **General Post Office** (**4**). Walk down the small alley that skirts the eastern side of the post office through to Elizabeth St. Cross the road and explore the beautiful 1874 **St Stephen's Cathedral** (**5**) and the adjoining **St Stephen's Chapel**. Built in 1850, the chapel is Brisbane's oldest church.

Back on Elizabeth St, head northeast on to Eagle St. Pass the **Riverside Centre** (**6**) and enter the gracious **Customs House** (**7**). From the back of the building you can access a riverfront boardwalk, head south again and take in the city and river views.

When you get to Edward St Pier take the **Mangrove Boardwalk** (**8**), which cuts southwest into the **City Botanic Gardens** (**9**; p301). Follow the boardwalk along the riverbank and then take the signposted walking track through the gardens to the Queensland University of Technology (QUT). Check out the columned foyer of the **Old Government House** (**10**; p301), built in 1860, and pop into the **QUT Art Museum** (**11**; p301).

By now you'll be heading northwest; continue past the museum and pause to take in the splendour of Queensland's regal **Parliament House** (**12**; p301). Turn left at Parliament House and head down to the QUT Gardens Point ferry terminal. Catch a southbound ferry to South Bank 3 terminal.

Meander north through the pleasant **South Bank Parklands** (**13**; p306), past **Stanley St Plaza** (**14**; p306) and **Streets Beach** (**15**; left). Continue past the Queensland Cultural Centre and be sure to pop into the **Queensland Art Gallery** (**16**; p301) and the **Queensland Museum** (**17**; p301).

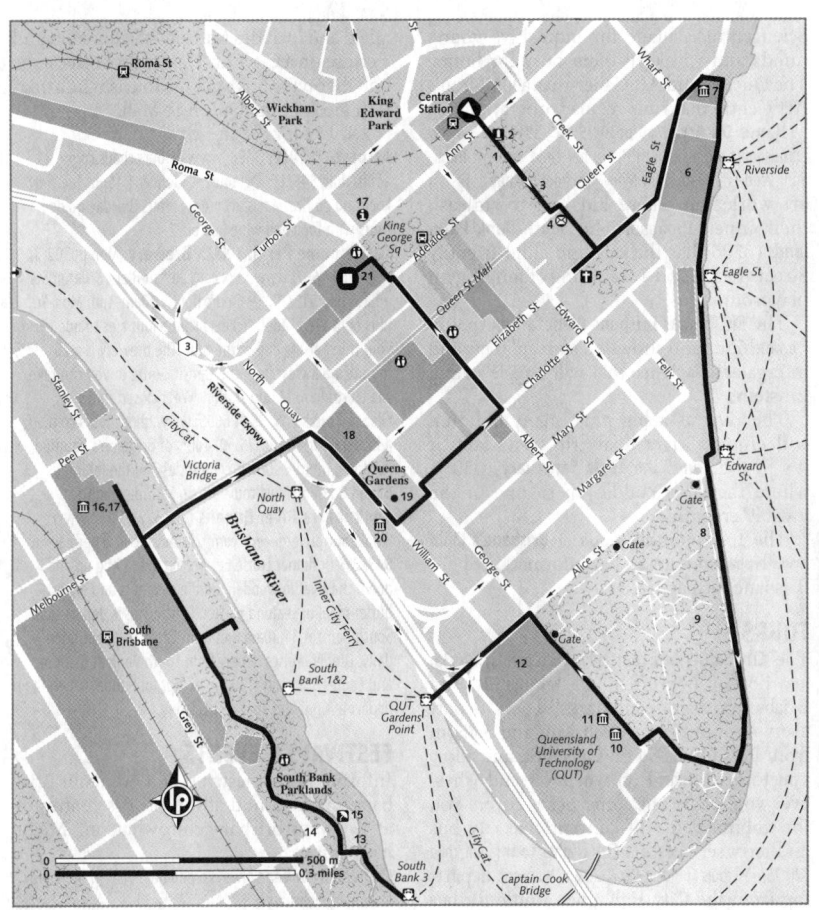

BRISBANE

Once you've exhausted these, head back towards the CBD on Victoria Bridge, which will take you to the Italian Renaissance–style **Treasury Building** (18; p301). Turn right on William St and you'll pass another spectacular building, the **Land Administration Building** (19; p301). Cross William St and delve into Brisbane's history at the **Commissariat Stores Building** (20; p301).

Just south of the stores a small alley (Stephens Lane) cuts through to George St. Turn left on George St and then immediately right onto Charlotte St. Continue along Charlotte and then turn left onto Albert to explore Brisbane's modern CBD.

At the top of Albert St cross Adelaide St into King George Sq. On your left is **City Hall** (21; p301). Wrap your tour up here by taking the lift up to the top of the bell tower and soaking up the views over the CBD.

BRISBANE FOR CHILDREN

One of the best attractions for children is the **Queensland Cultural Centre** (p301), where the Queensland Museum runs a range of fantastic hands-on programmes. The incorporated

Sciencentre is made for inquisitive young minds and will keep them busy for hours. The Queensland Art Gallery has a Children's Art Centre that runs regular programmes.

Hands On Art (Map pp304-5; ☎ 3844 4589; www.handsonart.org.au; South Bank; per child $6; ☒ 10am-5pm Wed-Fri, 10am-5pm Mon-Fri school holidays) is an art workshop where kids get to unleash their inner Picasso. The **South Bank Parklands** (p306) has the safe and child-friendly Streets Beach and a scattering of jungle gym playgrounds.

The **Sir Thomas Brisbane Planetarium** (p307) has exhibits and shows on stars, planets and intergalactic science that will boggle young Einsteins.

The river is a big plus; many children will enjoy a river-boat trip, especially if it's to the **Lone Pine Koala Sanctuary** (p307), where they can cuddle up to one of the lovable creatures.

The free monthly booklet **Brisbane's Child** (www.brisbaneschild.com.au) has information about Brisbane for parents.

TOURS

The **City Sights bus tour** (adult/child per day $20/15) is a hop-on-hop-off shuttle taking in 19 of Brisbane's major landmarks. Tours depart every 45 minutes between 9am and 3.45pm from Post Office Sq on Queen St. and allow you to get off and on whenever and wherever you want. The same ticket covers you for unlimited use of conventional city bus and ferry services. Its **City Nights tour** (adult/child $20/15; ☒ tours 6pm Mar-Oct & 6.30pm Nov-Feb), departing from the City Hall, goes a little further

afield and includes Mt Coot-tha Lookout and a cruise on a CityCat. Tickets for both can be bought on the bus or at the tourism information kiosk in the Queen St Mall.

Other tours of the city:

Artours (☎ 3899 3686; www.artours.coaus.com; adult/child $45/15; ☒ tours 9.15am & 1.15pm Tue-Sat) Focusing on Brisbane's art scene; offers full-day guided tours with food and wine laid on.

Castlemaine Perkins XXXX Brewery (Map pp302-3; ☎ 3361 7597; www.xxxx.com.au; cnr Black & Paton Sts; adult/child $18/10; ☒ tours hourly 10am-4pm Mon-Fri, plus 6pm Wed) Adult tickets include four ales to quench your thirst at the end of the tour. The brewery is a 20-minute walk west from the transit centre or you can take the Citytrain to Milton station. Wear closed shoes.

Ghost Tours (☎ 3844 6606; www.ghost-tours.com.au; adult/child from $30/15.50) Tours of Brisbane's haunted heritage, murder scenes, cemeteries and the infamous Boggo Rd Gaol. Most tours are on Saturday nights.

Kookaburra River Queens (☎ 3221 1300; www.kookaburrariverqueens.com; 2hr lunch cruise per person $45, 2½-hr dinner cruise per person $60) Chug up and down the river in wooden paddle steamers and enjoy a buffet meal or seafood platter. Lunch cruises depart from South Bank at 11.30am and from Eagle St Pier at noon daily. Dinner cruises depart from South Bank at 6.30pm and Eagles St Pier at 7.30pm, except for Sunday when they depart at 6pm and 7pm respectively.

FESTIVALS & EVENTS

Information on festivals and events in Brisbane can be found at the visitors centres or at www.ourbrisbane.com/whatson. Major happenings:

Chinese New Year Always a popular event in the Valley in January/February.

QUIRKY BRISBANE

It may not be the Melbourne Cup, but Brisbane is mighty proud of the annual **Australia Day Cockroach Races**, held at the Story Bridge Hotel (p316) every January 26. If racing keeps you on the edge of your seat, then you'll also be in the front row for the annual **Great Brisbane Duck Race**. This is a *rubber* duckie race, an annual event on the Brisbane Riverfestival calendar (see above). You get to 'adopt a duck' for $5 and spur it down the river (strictly a vocal affair), willing it to defeat its competitors and become the first to cross the line. The competition is fierce – an estimated 20,000 ducks fight for the winner's crown each year. If you happen to be the lucky caretaker of the victor you'll be rewarded for your efforts with a new car! If your duck performed at a substandard level you get to go home knowing you helped raise funds for the Surf Life Saving Foundation.

Perhaps not so much quirky as quintessential is the **National Festival of Beers** (www.nfb.com.au; RNA Showgrounds, Gregory Tce, Bowen Hills; per person $20), held over three days in mid-September. Beer-lovers gather to pay homage to the amber ale and are indulged with brews from around 45 Australian breweries. There's also a fairly impressive entertainment line-up to enhance the mood, and the *University of Beer* – for invaluable tuition from expert brewers

A CITY CELEBRATES ITS RIVER

Running over 10 days from late August to early September, **Riverfestival** (www.riverfestival.com .au), the city's biggest arts event of the year, celebrates Brisbane's relationship with its river. The common thread between the performances, artistic displays, mini food festivals and cultural celebrations is that they are as intrinsic to Brisbane as its meandering river; continuously shaping and developing with the city's evolving character.

The following events are constants and highlights.

The festival is opened each year with a bang – literally. Staged over the Brisbane River, with vantage points from South Bank, the city and the West End, **Riverfire** is a massive fireworks show with dazzling visual choreography, Royal Australian Air Force (RAAF) jets and a synchronised soundtrack. Also a staple is the **Riversymposium**; an international conference on best practice for water management. Over the years it has attracted some of the world's foremost scientists on the topic, and been the confluence of invaluable innovation. Other events combine Indigenous culture with contemporary performance to pay homage to the river and celebrate cultural collaboration.

Leading restaurants converge to engage in outstanding culinary events, such as the **Seafood Festival**, where you can chow down on your favourite dish from the deep or try your hand at prawn peeling and oyster shucking.

Music plays the role of a constant backdrop throughout the festival, either as an accompaniment to a main event, or an event on its own. The **Riverconcert**, held in the City Botanic Gardens, features live acts performing everything from jazz to hip hop to electronic soundscapes. The city's live-music venues also fill their playlist nightly.

Most of the events are free and family-friendly and there's a smorgasbord of activities for the kids. For more information click on to the Riverfestival website.

Tropfest (www.tropfest.com) This nationwide short film festival is telecast live from South Bank during late February.

Brisbane Pride Festival (www.pridebrisbane.org.au) Brisbane's fabulously flamboyant gay and lesbian celebration, held in June.

Queensland Music Festival Outstanding celebration of the world of music, held over 15 days in July on odd-numbered years.

Brisbane International Film Festival (www.biff.com .au) Ten days of quality films in July.

Ekka Royal National Agricultural Show (www .ekka.com.au) The country comes to town in early August.

Brisbane Riverfestival (www.riverfestival.com.au) Brisbane's major festival of the arts, with buskers, performances, music and concerts. Held in September.

Livid (www.livid.com.au) Annual one-day alternative rock festival in October.

SLEEPING

Brisbane has plenty of hostels, motels, apartments, B&Bs and boutique hotels within easy reach of the city centre. The Brisbane Visitors Accommodation Service (p300) has a free booking service, and brochures and information on budget accommodation options.

Budget

Most of Brisbane's hostels are concentrated in the inner suburbs of Petrie Terrace, Spring Hill and Fortitude Valley.

CITY & FORTITUDE VALLEY

Annie's Inn (Map pp304-5; ☎ 3831 8684; 405 Upper Edward St, City; s/d $50/60, d with bathroom $70; P) In a central location, walking distance to the CBD, this modest B&B is awash with lace and frills and the owners are helpful and friendly.

Tinbilly (Map pp304-5; ☎ 3238 5888, 1800 446 646; www.tinbilly.com; 462 George St, City; 13-/7-/4-bed dm $22/25/27, tw & d $85; ☒ ▣) This hostel flaunts a modern interior, excellent facilities and clinical cleanliness. Each room has a bathroom and individual lockers, and it's wheelchair-accessible. Downstairs is a helpful job centre, travel agency and a popular bar.

Palace Backpackers (Map pp304-5; ☎ 1800 676 340, 3211 2433; www.palacebackpackers.com.au; cnr Ann & Edward Sts, City; dm/s/d $22/36/60; ☒ ▣) This colossal backpackers is the only hostel in the city centre and is the choice for party animals. Rooms are a little cramped but there are comfy TV rooms, a kitchen, a tour-information desk, job club and great rooftop sundeck.

Bunk Backpackers (Map pp304-5; ☎ 1800 682 865; www.bunkbrisbane.com.au; cnr Ann & Gipps St, Fortitude Valley; dm $23-26, s/d & tw $40/70; P ⊠ ☐ ⛑) More like a snazzy hotel, this excellent hostel has en-suite dorms, gleaming kitchens and bathrooms and a fabulous bar and swimming pool. It's secure, the beds are comfortable and it's wheelchair-friendly.

PETRIE TERRACE

Brisbane City YHA (Map pp302-3; ☎ 3236 1004; brisbanecity@yhaqld.org; 392 Upper Roma St; dm $23, tw & d $55-70; P ⊠ ☐) You can't miss the Legoland exterior of this hostel, but inside it's classy, spacious and comfortable. There's a great café here as well as a tour desk and provisions for the disabled. It's very popular, attracting all ages and groups.

Banana Benders Backpackers (Map pp302-3; ☎ 1800 241 157, 3367 1157; www.bananabenders.com; 118 Petrie Tce; dm $21-23, tw & d $50; ☐) This small and comfy hostel is a great spot if you're planning to hang your hat for awhile. Rooms are spacious and functional and there's also an outdoor patio and BBQ area. The friendly owners can also help you find work.

Aussie Way Hostel (Map pp302-3; ☎ /fax 3367 0083; 34 Cricket St; dm/s/d $22/36/50; ⊠) A small hostel housed in a picturesque Queenslander that feels more like a guesthouse than a hostel. Dorms are a tad more spacious than most and come with fridges and televisions. The friendly hosts are knowledgeable and can organise just about anything for you.

SPRING HILL

Tourist Guesthouse (Map pp304-5; ☎ 3252 4171, 1800 800 589; 555 Gregory Tce; dm $20, s/d/tr $60/75/85; P ⊠ ☐) A short way from Brunswick St, this hotel/hostel is scrubbed-up rustic; plenty of faded pine but mod cons, too. Rooms have TVs and fridges; doubles are excellent value.

CAMPING

As all the camping grounds are far from the centre of town, hostels are generally a better bet for budget travellers.

Newmarket Gardens Caravan Park (Map p300; ☎ 3356 1458; www.newmarketgardens.com.au; 199 Ashgrove Ave, Ashgrove; tent sites $20-21, caravan sites $21-23, caravans $38, cabins $70-90; P ⊠ ☐) This clean site is just 4km north of the city centre and is well connected to town by bus routes and Citytrain (Newmarket station). Some cabins are wheelchair-friendly.

Brisbane Caravan Village (Map p300; ☎ 3263 4040, 1800 060797; www.caravanvillage.com.au; 763 Zillmere Rd, Aspley; tent/caravan sites $21/25, cabins $80-90; P ⊠ ☐ ⛑) Tidy and excellent facilities.

Midrange

Brisbane has a good range of midrange city hotels. Most cater to the business trade and offer discount rates on the weekend.

CITY & FORTITUDE VALLEY

Inchcolm Hotel (Map pp304-5; ☎ 3226 8888; www.inchcolmhotel.com.au; 73 Wickham Tce, City; r $140; P ⊠ ⛑) This small and personable hotel is inside a converted block of medical offices. Much of the heritage structure and charm remains, but the rooms have been renovated extensively and are supercomfortable. All come with kitchenettes and cable TV. There are good standby deals during slow periods.

Central Brunswick Apartments (Map pp304-5; ☎ 3852 1411; www.centralbrunswickhotel.com.au; 455 Brunswick St, Fortitude Valley; r $120-140; P ⊠) The studios and apartments in this modern complex have a fairly generic, business-traveller manner about them but are still very comfortable. Some have balconies and spas and week-long stays attract excellent discounts. All guests have access to the sauna and gym and baby-sitting can be arranged.

Holiday Inn Brisbane (Map pp304-5; ☎ 3238 2222; reserve@holidayinnbrisbane.com.au; Transit Centre, Roma St, City; r from $120; P ⊠ ⛑) Right beside the Transit Centre, this four-star hotel offers all the services and comforts you would expect of the chain: foreign exchange, babysitting, tour desk and laundry facilities. Rooms are unremarkable but spacious and clean. Look out for Internet and weekend deals.

Royal on the Park (Map pp304-5; ☎ 3221 3411, 1800 773 337; www.royalonthepark.com.au; cnr Alice & Albert Sts, City; r $140-175; P ⊠ ⛑) With wonderful views of the City Botanic Gardens, this four-star hotel has stylish rooms, a spa, gym and two restaurants. It's very popular with business travellers, so the cheaper rates are for Friday to Sunday nights.

Astor Metropole (Map pp304-5; ☎ 3144 4000; www.astorhotel.com.au; 193 Wickham Tce, City; d $100-110, ste from $120; P ⊠) This central complex has a good range of rooms. The standard rooms feel like small apartments and it's worth paying a few dollars more to get one with a balcony and a view. The suites are self-contained but they're a little dated.

Chifley on George (Map pp304–5; ☎ 3221 6044; reservations.george@chifleyhotels.com; 103 George St, City; r from $150; P ☒ ☒) The Chifley has pleasant, straightforward hotel rooms, a spa and a restaurant. Most of the rooms are standard doubles and suites, though there are also several commodious and swanky spa suites.

NEW FARM & KANGAROO POINT

Allender Apartments (Map pp302–3; ☎ 3358 5832; www.allenderapartments.com.au; 3 Moreton St, New Farm; r $100–135; ☒) The yellow-brick façade may not grab you but Allender's studios and one-bedroom apartments are tasteful and immaculate. The cool and shaded interiors are a fusion of funky décor and homely amenities and there's plenty of room to spread out.

Paramount Motel (Map pp304–5; ☎ 1800 636 772, 3393 1444; www.paramountmotel.com.au; 649 Main St, Kangaroo Point; s/d/f $70/75/105; P ☒ ☒) This complex has cheery and impeccably clean rooms. Facilities include TVs, fully equipped kitchens and hairdryers. There's also a BBQ by the pool and the staff are friendly and helpful.

PADDINGTON

Fern Cottage (Map p300; ☎ 3541 6685; 89 Fernberg Rd, Paddington; s/d $90/120; ☒) This beautifully renovated Queenslander with a splash of Mediterranean ambience has comfortable rooms with shady balconies and there's a lush garden retreat out the back.

SPRING HILL

Thornbury House B&B (Map pp304–5; ☎ 3839 5334; thorn-b@bigpond.net.au; 1 Thornbury St; d $90–100) Behind a trellised wall lies this beautifully maintained two-storey Queenslander built in 1886, with cool, crisp rooms and warm hosts. The polished timber throughout is spotless but there's nothing clinical about the ambience here. Little extras like televisions in each room and bathrobes come free of charge and breakfast is served in a lovely courtyard.

Dahrl Court Apartments (Map pp304–5; ☎ 3830 3400; www.dahrlcourt.com.au; 45 Phillips St; r per night/week $90/560; P ☒) Tucked into a quiet and leafy pocket of Spring Hill, this boutique complex offers self-contained apartments with heritage flavour. Timber furnishings grace the bedrooms and there are plump

couches in the living rooms from where you can watch cable TV. The commodious townhouses are a step up in style and go for $120/770 per night/week.

Dorchester Self-Contained Units (Map pp304–5; ☎ 3831 2967; www.dorchesterinn.com.au; 484 Upper Edward St; unit s/d/tr $70/80/90; P ☒) The self-contained units in this renovated two-storey block may be a little dated in the décor department but they're spotless, and for space, amenities and service the Dorchester is virtually unbeatable. There are also laundry facilities and if the hosts were any friendlier you'd take them home.

Top End

Brisbane has several fabulous top-end places, and they often give discounts to walk-in guests, particularly on weekends.

CITY

Quay West Suites Brisbane (Map pp304–5; ☎ 1800 672 726, 3853 6000; reservations@qwsb.mirvac.com.au; 132 Alice St; ste $250–320; P ☒ ☒) This sophisticated hotel has opulent self-contained rooms with modern kitchens, laundries, numerous televisions, stereos, modem ports and spectacular views. Recently refurbished, the refined interiors are worth the price tag. The price range is for suites with one or two bedrooms.

Stamford Plaza Brisbane (Map pp304–5; ☎ 3221 1999; sales@spb.stamford.com.au; cnr Edward & Margaret Sts; r from $280; P ☒ ☒) At the southern end of the city, the Stamford has a historic façade in front of a modern tower. The indulgent rooms have antique touches, large beds and plenty of atmosphere. On site is a gym, sauna, spa and several restaurants.

THE AUTHOR'S CHOICE

Conrad Treasury (Map pp304–5; ☎ 3306 8888; www.conradtreasury.com.au; 130 William St; r $230–350, ste $330–1075; P ☒) Brisbane's classiest hotel is in the beautifully preserved former Land Administration Building. Every room is unique and awash with heritage features, marble and polished wood, and elegant furnishings. Rates start with standard rooms but a step up takes you to the voluminous Parlour Rooms; those on the 4th floor have balcony access. The suites will make you giddy.

BRISBANE

EATING

Brisbane has a sophisticated and varied dining scene, with the best places to be found in Fortitude Valley, New Farm, West End, Petrie Terrace and the CBD. Many eateries take advantage of Brisbane's climate with open-air courtyards or tables out on the pavement. For cheap eats, there are breezy outdoor food courts at the Riverside Centre and Eagle St Pier on the riverfront northeast of the city and the South Bank Parklands.

City Centre & South Bank

C (Map pp304-5; ☎ 3832 4722; 483 Adelaide St, City; mains around $35; ☺ lunch Mon-Fri, dinner Mon-Sat; ☒) The menu at C has earned more than a couple of awards and you can expect to see meals along the lines of lamb rump with a warm salad of artichoke and beans served with grilled goats cheese, or a warm croustade of sand crab with sweet-corn puree. Seating is arranged to exploit the extensive views of the river, and the service is excellent.

F.I.X. (Map pp304-5; ☎ 3210 6016; cnr Edward & Margaret Sts, City; mains $15-25; ☺ lunch Mon-Fri, dinner Mon-Sat; ☒) This bustling brasserie delights with a varied menu. You don't have to splurge to enjoy prawns with *wakame* (Asian seaweed) and ginger in crisp wontons or sticky duck shanks, and although vegie options are limited to pastas and salads, they're all good.

II (Map pp304-5; ☎ 3210 0600; cnr Edward & Alice Sts, City; mains $33-40; ☺ lunch Mon-Fri, dinner Mon-Sat; ☒) This classy restaurant attracts refined foodies and the business crowd. Dishes include seared scallops with seaweed and lemon risotto or veal with porcini risotto and artichoke chips.

Pané e Vino (Map pp304-5; ☎ 3220 0044; cnr Albert & Charlotte Sts, City; mains $15-20; ☺ breakfast, lunch & dinner) Here you'll find authentic Italian fare, simple and refined, including pasta, risotto and focaccia, and lashings of olive oil.

Cafe San Marco (Map pp304-5; ☎ 3846 4334; South Bank Parklands; mains $16-25; ☺ breakfast, lunch & dinner) This waterfront bistro is the perfect spot for a relaxed feed of char-grilled steaks, Asian curries, salads and good seafood dishes. Good for families.

Grosvenor on George (Map pp304-5; ☎ 3236 2288; 320 George St, City; mains $17-25; ☺ lunch & dinner; ☒) Sassy suits love this classy bar during the week, when they tumble in for creative fu-

sions like *hoi sin* duck pizza or vanilla-bean and sweet-pea risotto. The menu is in a constant state of flux and the walls carry work by local artists.

Customs House Brasserie (Map pp304-5; ☎ 3365 8921; 399 Queen St, City; mains $20-27; ☺ lunch daily, dinner Tue-Sat) Wedged at the base of Customs House with views of the river, this refined brasserie has an impressive menu including gems such as prawn and green papaya salad or beef mignons wrapped in pancetta.

Metro Cafe (Map pp304-5; ☎ 3221 3181; cnr Albert & Mary Sts, City; dishes $4-8; ☺ breakfast & lunch Mon-Fri) This petite diner dishes up mountainous breakfasts, sizzling burgers and kebabs and dozens of fresh and tasty sandwiches.

Petrie Terrace & Paddington

Sultans Kitchen (Map pp302-3; ☎ 3368 2194; 163 Given Tce, Paddington; dishes $15-20; ☺ dinner; ☒) If Indian food is your weakness, then this award winner is worth trekking to. The service is impeccable and flavours from all corners of the subcontinent are represented. It's BYO and you can grab your beer and wine from Paddo's bottleshop down the road.

Kookaburra Café (Map pp302-3; ☎ 3369 2400; 280 Given Tce, Paddington; meals $10-25; ☺ lunch & dinner) Dressed down in timber and tin, this popular eatery serves good grills with a distinctly Aussie twist. Tourists and locals alike savour the perfect steaks, fancy fish and chips and pizzas.

The bistros at both the **Caxton Hotel** (Map pp302-3; ☎ 3369 5544; 38 Caxton St, Petrie Tce; mains $10-25; ☺ lunch & dinner; ☒), a popular pub (opposite), and the **Paddo Tavern** (Map pp302-3; ☎ 3369 0044; 186 Given Tce, Paddington; mains $8-15; ☺ lunch & dinner; ☒) serve good pub food.

Fortitude Valley & New Farm

Garuva Hidden Tranquillity Restaurant & Bar (Map pp304-5; ☎ 3216 0124; 324 Wickham St; mains around $20; ⊗ dinner; ⌘) Garuva's rainforested foyer leads to stylish, private tables concealed by walls of fluttering white silk. Choices like Turkish shark and Chinese roast beef along with dim lighting, smooth soundtracks and lulled voices create a unique atmosphere.

Vietnamese Restaurant (Map pp304-5; ☎ 3252 4112; 194 Wickham St; mains $10-13; ⊗ lunch & dinner; ⌘) This bustling restaurant serves exquisite food in no-nonsense surrounds. Dishes come in every carnivorous, seafood and vegetarian version imaginable.

Monsoon (Map pp304-5; ☎ 3852 6988; 455 Brunswick St; mains $20-30; ⊗ lunch & dinner Tue-Sat; ⌘) This trendy eatery serves a fusion of modern Asian and Australian cuisine. Mains include baked kangaroo rump with mint and turnip pudding or Moreton Bay bugs in a red curry. The staff are knowledgeable and professional but the vegie options are limited.

Sunbar Restaurant & Lounge (Map pp304-5; ☎ 3257 4999; 367 Brunswick St; mains $28; ⊗ lunch Tue-Fri, dinner Tue-Sat; ⌘) Superslick and chic, Sunbar dazzles with a sophisticated menu, including vanilla and sea salt–encrusted reef fish, carpacio of tuna, scallops, foie gras and sea-urchin roe emulsion.

Also recommended:

Mellino's (Map pp304-5; ☎ 3252 3551; 330 Brunswick St Mall; mains $7.50-17.50; ⊗ 24hr) Good pizza and pasta.

Tibetan Kitchen (Map pp304-5; ☎ 3358 5906; 454 Brunswick St; mains $8-16; ⊗ dinner) Tasty Tibetan fare.

West End

Jazzy Cat Cafe (Map pp302-3; ☎ 3864 2544; 56 Mollison St; mains $15-20; ⊗ breakfast, lunch & dinner) Set in a beautifully restored Queenslander, this restaurant-cum-café is a warren of dining nooks with bohemian vibes and friendly staff. The menu is imaginative and amid the risottos, Asian salads and pastas are tofu steaks as well as the cow sort.

Cumquats (Map pp302-3; ☎ 3846 6333; 145 Boundary St; mains $15-25; ⊗ lunch & dinner Tue-Sat; ⌘) The menu at this multi-award-winning restaurant reads like a who's who of Australian game: seared wallaby, braised Tasmanian possum and emu fillets to name a few. There are also vegie dishes for the timid.

Mondo Organics (Map pp302-3; ☎ 3844 1132; 166 Hardgrave Rd; mains $16-30; ⊗ breakfast Sat & Sun, lunch daily, dinner Tue-Sat) Blow your tastebuds,

not your arteries, at this exquisite organic restaurant, with dishes like roast vegetable, pine nut and lemon terrine or crispy squid stuffed with seafood, pistachios and rice.

Three Monkeys Coffee House (Map pp302-3; ☎ 3844 6045; 58 Mollison St; mains $8-18; ⊗ breakfast, lunch & dinner) This laid-back café is steeped in pseudo-Moroccan décor and ambience. You can munch away on focaccias, *panini*, pizzas and salads, or indulge in wicked cakes and strong coffee.

Also recommended:

Caravanserai (Map pp302-3; ☎ 3217 2617; 1-3 Dornoch Tce; mains $10-18; ⊗ lunch Thu-Sun, dinner Tue-Sun) Lovely Turkish restaurant with an open kitchen in the centre.

Two Seasons (Map pp302-3; ☎ 3217 2622; 151 Boundary St; mains $14-20; ⊗ lunch & dinner Tue-Sun) North Chinese cuisine in a cool and crisp setting.

Self-Catering

James Street Market (Map pp304-5; James St, Fortitude Valley) The produce is pricey but the quality is excellent and there's a good fishmonger here.

There's a great produce market inside **McWhirters Marketplace** (Map pp304-5; cnr Brunswick & Wickham Sts) in Fortitude Valley. The Asian supermarkets in Chinatown mall also have an excellent range of fresh vegies, Asian groceries and exotic fruit.

There's a **Coles Express** (Map pp304-5; Queen St) just west of the mall, and a **Woolworths** (Map pp304-5; Edward St) in the city.

DRINKING

Port Office Hotel (Map pp304-5; ☎ 3221 0072; 40 Edward St, City; ⌘) The industrial edge of this renovated city pub is spruced up with swathes of dark wood and jungle prints. Pull up a stool, find a bench early and settle in for the evening. When things get hectic (Thursday to Saturday nights) the crowd fills the upstairs balcony and seating.

Jorge (Map pp304-5; ☎ 3012 9121; 183 George St, City; ⌘) After sunset from Wednesday to Sunday, the permanent decks at this city café-cum-bar get a good workout when DJs spin funk into the wee hours. More lounge bar than dance venue, the funky punters sip boutique beers and cocktails in between conversations.

Caxton Hotel (Map pp302-3; ☎ 3369 5544; 38 Caxton St, Petrie Tce; ⌘) This unpretentious but stylish pub is hugely popular on Friday and

THE AUTHOR'S CHOICE

Belgian Beer Cafe (Map pp304-5; ☎ 3221 0199; Cnr Edward & Mary Sts, City; ✗) With no less than 26 Belgian nectars and local boutique brews, connoisseurs of the art of imbibing will surely find their holy grail of ale. It's not all about the beer though; convivial socialising is a mainstay in the sunny courtyard and inside the big brassy bar good wine is also served. Any night of the week you could be entertained by mariachi musos or acoustic folk, and regardless of the hour, the city outside feels miles away.

Saturday nights, when the buzz of the heaving crowd wafts out the wide open bay windows on to the street. Expect mainstream music in the background and sports on the telly.

Pavilion (Map pp302-3; ☎ 3844 6172; cnr Boundary & Wilson Sts, West End; ✗) The Pavilion contains a café and bistro but the bar dominates. Drink specials are on offer most week nights and there's live entertainment on Friday and Saturday nights. The crowd of 20- to 30-somethings come for frenzied socialising and fierce pool.

Story Bridge Hotel (Map pp304-5; ☎ 3391 2266; 196 Main St, Kangaroo Point; ✗) This beautiful old pub beneath the bridge at Kangaroo Point is a perfect place for a pint after a long day sightseeing. You can mingle with the fashionable in the back bar with its floor to ceiling glass or hunker down in the casual beer garden.

Irish Murphy's (Map pp304-5; ☎ 3221 4377; cnr George & Elizabeth Sts, City; ✗) An old-fashioned public house that's a popular choice for an after-work drink. A warren of booths, open street-side windows and a fair selection of ales on tap add to the atmosphere.

ENTERTAINMENT

Brisbane has an excellent nightlife, as well as a lively and stimulating array of cultural attractions. The *Courier-Mail* has daily arts and entertainment listings and a comprehensive 'What's On In Town' section each Thursday.

Pick up copies of the free entertainment papers **Time Off** (www.timeoff.com.au), **Rave** (www.ravemag.com.au) and **Scene** (www.sceneonline.com.au)

from any café in the Valley. Another good source of information is www.brisbane247.com. Other useful papers include *Brisbane News* and *This Week in Brisbane*.

Ticketek (☎ 13 19 31; http://premier.ticketek.com.au) is a centralised phone-booking agency that handles bookings for many major events, sports and performances. You can pick up tickets from the Ticketek booth on Elizabeth St, at the back of the Myer Centre.

Nightclubs

Brisbane has a lively nightclub scene centred on the Valley, which attracts a mixed straight and gay crowd. Most clubs are open Thursday to Sunday nights, are adamant about ID and charge between $5 and $15 entry. Carry proof of age and avoid wearing tank-tops, shorts or thongs (flip-flops).

Family (Map pp304-5; ☎ 3852 5000; 8 McLachlan St; ✗) Voted Australia's best nightclub two years in a row, Family exhilarates dance junkies every weekend on four levels with two dance floors, four bars, and four funky themed booths. Elite DJs from home and away frequently grace the decks.

Monastery (Map pp304-5; ☎ 3257 7081; 621 Ann St) From the outside this club resembles a generic office block but there's nothing suit-and-tie about the dim interior with soft suede couches and lucid soundscapes.

Empire (Map pp304-5; ☎ 3852 1216; 339 Brunswick St; ✗) Things get going at this huge, converted hotel after 9pm on weekends when DJs upstairs in the Moon Bar serve drum 'n' bass.

Other nightclubs:

Fringe Bar (Map pp304-5; ☎ 3252 9833; cnr Ann & Constance Sts, Fortitude Valley; ✗) Live DJs get their groove on from Wednesday to Sunday nights.

R-Bar (Map pp304-5; ☎ 3220 1477; 235 Edward St, City) Dance tunes get a workout from Wednesday to Sunday but Satellite Saturdays are the main event.

Source (Map pp304-5; 697 Ann St, Fortitude Valley; ✗) Live DJs from Thursday to Saturday nights playing R&B, hip-hop and drum 'n' bass. On Sundays there's an open-mic session.

Live Music

In recent years successful acts including Powderfinger, Regurgitator and Pete Murray have illustrated Brisbane's musical cred. You can get in early to see history in the making at any number of venues. Cover charges start at around $6.

Zoo (Map pp304-5; ☎ 3854 1381; 711 Ann St, Fortitude Valley; ☒) The long queues here start early for a good reason and whether you're into hard rock or electronic soundscapes, Zoo has a gig for you. Musos rate this as an excellent venue and this is one of your best chances to hear some raw, local talent.

Indie Temple (Map pp304-5; ☎ 3852 2851; 210 Wickham St, Fortitude Valley; ☒) Good and grungy, the emphasis is on alternative music and rock at this student stomping ground. Metal nights and live music alternate with theme nights.

Tongue & Groove (Map pp302-3; ☎ 3846 0334; 63 Hardgrave Rd, West End; ☒) This funky little venue in the West End hosts everything from reggae and blues to dance beats from Tuesday to Sunday. Jazz is another common theme on the line-up and all the action takes place in the subterranean bar.

Rev (Map pp304-5; 25 Warner St, Fortitude Valley; ☒) Another promoter of home-grown talent, this smallish venue presents live rock, punk and electronic music from around Brisbane.

Other live venues:

Arena (Map pp304-5; ☎ 3252 5690; 210 Brunswick St, Fortitude Valley) Another industrial-sized venue that attracts local and international rock acts.

Brisbane Convention & Exhibition Centre (Map pp304-5; ☎ 3308 3000; Glenelg St, South Bank; ☒) When the big acts are in town they perform at this multifunctional entertainment complex.

Brisbane Jazz Club (Map pp304-5; ☎ 3391 2006; 1 Annie St, Kangaroo Point; ☒ Fri-Sun; ☒) A Brissy institution for jazz purists on Saturday and Sunday nights.

Cinema

There are several mainstream cinemas along the Queen St Mall, and Brisbane has excellent art-house cinemas. For details of what's showing see the daily *Courier-Mail* or the free *Scene*.

South Bank Cinema (Map pp304-5; ☎ 3846 5188; cnr Grey & Ernest Sts, South Bank; P ☒) Has the cheapest tickets.

Greater Union (Map pp304-5; ☎ 3027 9999; Level A, Myer Centre, Queen St Mall; P ☒) Mainstream blockbusters.

Hoyts Regent Theatre (Map pp304-5; ☎ 3027 9999; 107 Queen St Mall; P ☒) A lovely old cinema worth visiting for the building alone.

Both the **Dendy Cinema** (Map pp304-5; ☎ 3211 3244; 346 George St, City; ☒) and **Palace Centro** (Map pp304-5; ☎ 3852 4488; 39 James St, Fortitude Valley; P ☒) play art-house films.

There's also the alfresco **Moonlight Cinemas** (☎ 1300 551 908; www.moonlight.com.au; adult/child $12.50/8; ☒ 6pm Tue-Sun Oct-Mar) in the City Botanic Gardens (p301).

Theatre

Brisbane is well stocked with theatre venues, most of them located in the South Bank Parklands. The **Queensland Cultural Centre** (☎ 13 62 46) handles bookings for all the South Bank theatres and publishes *Centre Stage*, the events diary for the complex.

Performing Arts Centre (Map pp304-5; ☎ 3840 7444; www.qpat.com.au; Queensland Cultural Centre, Stanley St, South Bank; P ☒) This centre consists of three venues and features concerts, plays, dance and performances of all genres.

GAY & LESBIAN BRISBANE

Most action, centred in Fortitude Valley, is covered by the fortnightly **Q News** (www.qnews.com.au). *Queensland Pride*, another gay publication, takes in the whole of the state. **Dykes on Mykes** (www.queerradio.org), a radio show on Wednesday from 9pm to 11pm on FM102.1, is another source of information on the city.

Major events on the year's calendar include the **Queer Film Festival**, held in late March, which showcases gay, lesbian, bisexual and transgender films, and Brisbane Pride Festival in June (see p310). Pride attracts up to 25,000 people every year, and peaks during the parade held mid-festival.

Brisbane's most popular gay and lesbian venue is the **Wickham Hotel** (Map pp304-5; ☎ 3852 1301; cnr Wickham & Alden Sts), a classic old Victorian pub with dance music, drag shows and dancers. The Wickham celebrates the Sydney Mardi Gras and the Pride Festival in style. The **Sportsman's Hotel** (Map pp304-5; ☎ 3831 2892; 130 Leichhardt St) is another fantastically popular gay venue, with a different theme or show for each night of the week.

The **Gay & Lesbian Welfare Association of Brisbane** (GLWA; ☎ 1800 184 527; www.glwa.org.au) can offer information on groups and venues and also counselling.

Queensland Conservatorium (Map pp304-5; ☎ 3875 6375; 16 Russell St, South Bank) South of the Performing Arts Centre, the Conservatorium showcases the talent of attending students.

Brisbane Powerhouse (Map pp302-3; ☎ 3358 8622, box office 3358 8600; 119 Lamington St, New Farm; P ⚅) Stages a contemporary programme of drama, music, dance and workshops.

Metro Arts Centre (Map pp304-5; ☎ 3221 1527; 109 Edward St, City; ⚅) This progressive venue hosts community theatre, dance and art shows.

QUT Gardens Theatre (Map pp304-5; ☎ 3864 4213; Queensland University of Technology, George St, City; P) This university theatre hosts touring national and international productions as well as student performances.

Sit Down Comedy Club (Map pp302-3; ☎ 3369 4466; Paddo Tavern, Given Tce, Paddington; P ⚅) The most prominent comedy venue in town, with a good programme of touring acts. Thursday is stand-up night, and Wednesday is given over to improvisation.

Sport
Brisbane is sports-mad (in case you haven't noticed already) and fields teams in every national competition. Tickets for the cricket, rugby union, Australian Rules football and soccer are available from **Ticketmaster7** (☎ 13 61 00; www.ticketmaster7.com). For rugby league and basketball tickets, contact **Ticketek** (☎ 3404 6700; http://premier.ticketek.com.au).

CRICKET
You can see interstate cricket matches and international test cricket at the **Brisbane Cricket Ground** (The Gabba; Map pp302-3; ☎ 3008 6166; www.thegabba.org.au) in Woolloongabba, just south of Kangaroo Point. The cricket season runs from October to March, with the first international test match of the season in November.

FOOTBALL
During the other half of the year, rugby league is the big spectator sport. The Brisbane Broncos National Rugby League (NRL) team plays its home games at **Suncorp Stadium** (Map pp302-3; ☎ 3331 5000; Castlemaine St, Milton).

Once dominated by Victorian teams, the Australian Football League (AFL) has been mastered by the Brisbane Lions, after they won the flag in 2001, 2002 and 2003 (and were runners up in 2004). You can watch them kick the ball and some south-

ern butt at a home game at the Gabba between March and September.

The Queensland Reds rugby union team plays against provincial New Zealand and South African teams in the Super 12 competition (soon to be Super 14). These games, plus international test matches, are played at Ballymore Stadium in Herston.

The Queensland Lions compete in the eight-team, A-League soccer competition and play their home games at Suncorp Stadium in Milton.

BASKETBALL & NETBALL
Brisbane's National Basketball League (NBL) side, the Brisbane Bullets, is based at the **Brisbane Convention & Exhibition Centre** (Map pp304-5; ☎ 3308 3000; www.bcec.com.au; cnr Merivale & Glenelg Sts, South Brisbane).

Queensland also has a side in the National Netball League – the Queensland Firebirds. Their home stadium is the **Chandler Arena** (Map p300; Old Cleveland & Tiley Rd, Chandler). You can book tickets through Ticketek, or online at http://firebirds.netballq.org.au.

SHOPPING
Aboriginal Art
Queensland Aboriginal Creations (Map pp304-5; ☎ 3224 5730; Little Stanley St, South Bank) This is probably Brisbane's best Indigenous arts store, stocking a good range of authentic art, crafts and souvenirs, including paintings and prints, didjeridus, boomerangs, jewellery, bullroarers and clothing.

Fire-Works Aboriginal Gallery (Map pp302-3; ☎ 3216 1250; 11 Stratton St, Newstead) Worth a look for contemporary and often quite political Aboriginal art.

Clothing
For something fashionable, there are plenty of Australian and international boutiques in the upmarket **Elizabeth Arcade** (Map pp304-5), between Elizabeth and Charlotte Sts, and **Brisbane Arcade** (Map pp304-5), between Queen St Mall and Adelaide St. For club fashions, head to Fortitude Valley around Brunswick, Wickham and Ann Sts.

Markets
Every Sunday, the carnival-style Riverside Centre and Eagle St Pier markets have over 150 stalls, including glassware, weaving, leather work and children's activities.

Crafts Village Markets (Stanley St Plaza, South Bank; ⏰ 5-10.30pm Fri, 10am-6pm Sat, 9am-5pm Sun) Popular markets with a great range of clothing, crafts and souvenirs.

Brunswick St Markets (Brunswick St, Fortitude Valley; ⏰ 8am-4pm Sat & Sun) These colourful markets fill the mall in Fortitude Valley with diverse crafts, clothes and budding designerware and the inevitable junk.

King George Square Contemporary Craft & Art Market (King George Sq, City; ⏰ 8am-4pm Sunday) These markets transform a pocket of the city centre into a bustling arts and crafts fair on the weekends.

GETTING THERE & AWAY
Air
Brisbane's main airport is about 16km northeast of the city centre at Eagle Farm and has separate international and domestic terminals about 2km apart, linked by the Airtrain ($3 per person).

Qantas (Map pp304-5; ☎ 13 13 13; www.qantas.com.au; 247 Adelaide St; ⏰ 8.30am-5pm Mon-Fri, 9am-1pm Sat) has an extensive network, connecting Brisbane with Sydney ($100, 1½ hours), Melbourne ($150, 2½ hours), Adelaide ($170, 2½ hours), Canberra ($140, two hours), Hobart ($210, four hours), Perth ($300, five hours) and Darwin ($180, four hours).

Virgin Blue (☎ 13 67 89; www.virginblue.com.au) also flies from Brisbane to Sydney ($105), Melbourne ($120), Adelaide ($140), Canberra ($110), Hobart ($150), Perth ($250) and Darwin ($180).

Jetstar (☎ 13 15 38; www.jetstar.com.au) connects Brisbane with Melbourne ($120) and Cairns ($120) and Hobart ($150).

Within Queensland, Qantas, Jetstar or Qantaslink connect Brisbane to Proserpine (one-way adult fare $110, 1¾ hours), Townsville ($120, two hours), Rockhampton ($80, 1¼ hours) and Cairns ($140, 2½ hours).

Sunshine Express (☎ 13 13 13; www.sunshineexpress.com.au) connects Brisbane with the Sunshine Coast ($95), Hervey Bay and Maryborough ($165).

Bus
Brisbane's Roma St Transit Centre (Map pp304-5), about 500m west of the city centre, is the main terminus and booking office for long-distance buses and trains. The centre has shops, food places, a post office and an accommodation booking serv-

ice. Bus companies have booking desks on the 3rd level. **Greyhound** (☎ 13 14 99; www.greyhound.com.au) is the main company on the Sydney to Brisbane run; you can either go via the New England Hwy (17 hours) or the quicker Pacific Hwy (16 hours) for $100. **Premier** (☎ 13 34 10; www.premierms.com.au) does the same route and often has slightly cheaper deals.

North to Cairns, Premier Motor Service runs two services daily and Greyhound runs five. The approximate fares and journey times to places along the coast are as follows:

Destination	Duration	One-way fare
Cairns	29hr	$200 (3 free stops)
Hervey Bay	5½hr	$50
Mackay	16½hr	$140
Noosa Heads	2½hr	$4
Rockhampton	11½hr	$70
Townsville	23hr	$180

Car
There are five major routes into and out of the Brisbane metropolitan area, numbered from M1 to M5. The major north–south route, the M1, connects the Pacific Hwy to the south with the Bruce Hwy to the north, but things get a bit confusing as you enter the city.

Coming from the Gold Coast, the Pacific Hwy splits into two at Eight Mile Plains. From here, the South East Freeway (M3) runs right into the centre, skirting along the riverfront on the western side of the CBD, before emerging on the far side as the Gympie Arterial Rd.

All of the major companies – **Hertz** (☎ 13 30 39), **Avis** (☎ 13 63 33), **Budget** (☎ 13 27 27), **Europcar** (☎ 13 13 90) and **Thrifty** (☎ 1300 367 227) – have offices at the Brisbane airport terminals and throughout the city.

There are also several smaller companies in Brisbane that advertise slightly cheaper deals, including **Abel Rent A Car** (Map pp304-5; ☎ 1800 131 429, 3236 1225; www.abel.com.au; Ground fl, Roma St Transit Centre).

Train
Brisbane's main station for long-distance trains is the Roma St Transit Centre. For train reservations and information call into the **Queensland Rail Travel Centre** (Map pp304-5;

BRISBANE

☎ 13 22 32; www.qr.com.au; Central Station ☎ 3235 1323; Ground fl, Central Station, 305 Edward St City; ☺ 7am-5pm Mon-Fri; Roma St ☎ 3235 1331; Roma St Transit Centre, Roma St, City; ☺ 7am-5pm Mon-Fri). You can also make reservations online or over the phone.

CountryLink (☎ 13 22 32; www.countrylink.nsw.gov .au) has a daily XPT service between Brisbane and Sydney (economy/1st class $115/165, 14 hours). The northbound service runs overnight, and the southbound service runs during the day. A sleeper ($245) is available in the northbound service only.

Coastal services within Queensland:

Spirit of the Outback (seat/economy sleeper/1st-class sleeper $165/215/340, 24hr) Brisbane–Longreach via Rockhampton ($95/$145/$230) twice weekly.

Sunlander ($187/240/380, 32hr) Departs Tuesday, Thursday and Saturday for Cairns via Townsville.

Tilt Train (economy $280, 25hr) Brisbane–Cairns train leaves Brisbane at 6.25pm Monday, Wednesday and Friday, returning from Cairns at 8.15am Sunday, Wednesday and Friday.

Concessions are available to children under 16 years, students with a valid International Student Identity Card (ISIC), and senior citizens. For details contact **Queensland Rail** (☎ 13 22 32; www.traveltrain.qr.com.au).

GETTING AROUND
To/From the Airport
The easiest way to get to and from the airport is the **Airtrain** (☎ 3215 5000; www.airtrain .com.au; adult/child $10/5; ☺ 5am-8pm), which runs every 15 minutes between the airport and the Roma St Transit Centre and Central Station. There are also half-hourly services to the airport from Gold Coast Citytrain stops.

Coachtrans (☎ 3238 4700; www.coachtrans.com.au) runs the half-hourly Skytrans (adult/child to city $9/6, to city accommodation $11/7; services 5.45am to 10pm) shuttle bus between the Roma St Transit Centre and the airport. A taxi into the centre from the airport will cost around $30.

Bicycle
See p308 for information on cycling.

Car
Be warned that Brisbane's peak hour(s) traffic is notorious. There is free two-hour parking on many streets in the CBD and in the inner suburbs, but the major thoroughfares

become clearways (ie parking is prohibited) during the morning and afternoon rush hours.

Queensland's motoring association is the RACQ (p299). You can obtain insurance and maps at the city branch.

Public Transport
Information on bus, train and ferry routes and connections can be obtained from the **Trans-Info Service** (☎ 13 12 30; www.transinfo.qld .gov.au; ☺ 6am-10pm). Bus and ferry information is also available at the Brisbane Visitor Information Centre (p300), the **bus station information centre** (Map pp304-5; Queen St Mall), and the Queensland Rail Travel Centres.

Fares on buses, trains and ferries operate on a zone system. The city centre and most of the inner-city suburbs fall within zone one, which translates to a single fare of $2/1 per adult/child.

If you're going to be using public transport more than once on any single day, it's worth getting a daily ticket. These allow you unlimited transport on all buses, trains and ferries and are priced according to the number of zones you'll be travelling in:
Zone 1 (adult/child $4/2)
Zone 2 (adult/child $4.80/2.40)
Zone 3 (adult/child $5.60/2.80)

You can also buy cheaper off-peak daily tickets that allow you to do the same thing between 9am and 3.30pm and after 7pm from Monday to Friday and all weekend.

BOAT
Brisbane's CityCat catamarans run every 20 to 30 minutes, between 5.50am and 10.30pm, from the University of Queensland in the west to Bretts Wharf in the east, and back. Stops along the way include North Quay (for the Queen St Mall), South Bank, Riverside (for the CBD) and New Farm Park. City-Cats are wheelchair accessible at all stops except for West End, QUT Gardens Point, Riverside, Bulimba and Brett's Wharf.

Also useful are the Inner City Ferries, which zigzag back and forth across the river between North Quay, near the Victoria Bridge, and Mowbray Park. Services start at 6am from Monday to Saturday and from 7am on Sunday, and run till 9pm from Sunday to Thursday and until 11pm on Friday and Saturday.

BUS

The Loop is a free bus that circles the city, stopping at QUT, Queen St Mall, City Hall, Central Station and Riverside; it runs every 10 minutes on weekdays from 7am to 6pm.

The main stop for local buses is in the basement of the Myer Centre, where there's a small information centre. You can also pick up most of the useful buses from the colour-coded stops along Adelaide St, between George and Edward Sts.

Red City Circle bus 333 does a clockwise loop round the area, stopping at City Plaza, Anzac Sq, Riverside, QUT and the Queen St Mall. Buses run every 10 to 20 minutes Monday to Friday, from 5am till about 6pm, and with the same frequency on Saturday morning (starting at 6am). Services are less frequent at other times, and cease at 7pm Sunday, and midnight on other days.

Useful buses from the city centre include 190 and 191 to Fortitude Valley and New Farm, which leave from Adelaide St between King George Sq and Edward St. You can pick up Bardon bus 375 to Paddington from opposite the transit centre or on Adelaide St.

Taxi

There are usually plenty of taxis around the city centre, and there are taxi ranks at the transit centre and at the top end of Edward St, by the junction with Adelaide St. The major taxi company here is **Black & White** (☎ 13 10 08). Rivals include **Yellow Cab Co** (☎ 13 19 24) and **Brisbane Cabs** (☎ 13 22 11).

Train

The Citytrain network has seven lines that run as far as Nambour, Cooroy and Gympie in the north (for the Sunshine Coast) and Nerang and Robina in the south (for the Gold Coast). Other useful routes include Rosewood (for Ipswich) and Cleveland (for the North Stradbroke Island ferry). The lines to Pinkenba, Shorncliffe and Ferny Grove are mainly for suburban commuters.

The Airtrain service integrates with the Citytrain network in the CBD and along the Gold Coast line. All trains go through Roma St and Central stations in the city, and Brunswick St station in Fortitude Valley.

Trains run from around 4.30am, with the last train to each line leaving Central station between 11.30pm and midnight. On Sunday the last trains run at around 10pm.

AROUND BRISBANE

MORETON BAY ISLANDS

Moreton Bay, at the mouth of the Brisbane River, is reckoned to have some 365 islands. The two most popular are North Stradbroke Island, which is an uncomplicated place renowned for its beaches and surf, and Moreton Island, which is famous for its population of wild (or wildish) dolphins at Tangalooma.

North Stradbroke Island

Affectionately known as 'Straddie', this lovely sand island is just a 30-minute ferry ride from Cleveland, 30km south of Brisbane. Traditionally a cheap holiday destination for Brisbane families, Straddie's surf beaches and swimming are excellent and there are some good places to stay and eat.

ORIENTATION & INFORMATION

Straddie has three small settlements, Dunwich, Amity Point and Point Lookout, all grouped around the northern end of the island. In the hilly central area is the beautiful Blue Lake National Park, and, while the wild southern half of the island is inaccessible due to mining, Eighteen Mile Beach, which runs clear down the eastern edge of the island, is accessible to 4WDs.

Stradbroke Island visitor information centre (☎ 1800 099 049, 3409 9555; www.stradbroketourism .com; 🕒 8.30am-5pm Mon-Fri, 8.30am-5pm Sat & Sun) is near the ferry terminal in Dunwich.

SIGHTS & ACTIVITIES

Straddie's best beaches for both **surfing** and **swimming** are around Point Lookout, where there's a series of points and bays around the headland and long stretches of white sand.

If you're not so keen on the surf, there are a couple of inland lakes worth exploring. If you don't have your own vehicle, you can take a tour or hire a bike, but be warned that there are some punishing hills to be negotiated. Both Brown Lake and Blue Lake are accessed via the sealed Mining Company Rd from Dunwich. The turn-off to **Brown Lake** is reached first after about 3km; the lake is a short distance down a dirt track. The water is indeed brown, and shallow to boot, but it's a decent spot for a picnic and popular with young families.

Blue Lake, accessed from a car park a further 5km along the road, is a different proposition altogether. The centrepiece of Blue Lake National Park, it's reached via a beautiful and winding 2.1km walking track (there's also a sandy 4WD track, but you'd be doing yourself a disservice). The lake itself is small, crystal clear and very deep – the bottom drops away quickly and a little alarmingly right by the shore – but it's a serene and very beautiful spot. If you're lucky you'll have it all to yourself, and if you're even luckier you'll spot a rare and shy golden wallaby. There's no camping or drinking water in the park, so come prepared.

The eastern beach, known as **Eighteen Mile Beach**, is open to 4WD vehicles and campers and finishes up at the popular fishing spot of **Jumpinpin** on the island's southern tip. You can hire fishing gear from **Dunwich Sports & Hobbies** (☎ 3409 9252; Bingle Rd; ⏲ 7.30am-5pm Mon-Fri, to 4pm Sat, to 3pm Sun), as well as bicycles. You can hire surfboards and bodyboards from various places; kayak hire is around $20/50 per hour/day, surfboards $15/40 and bodyboards $10/30.

Straddie Adventures (☎ 3409 8414; Point Lookout) offers sea-kayaking trips (including snorkelling stops $35) around Straddie, and sandboarding ($25), which is like snowboarding, except on sand.

TOURS

A number of tour companies offer tours of the island. Generally the 4WD tours take in a strip of the eastern beach and several freshwater lakes.

Awesome Wicked Wild (☎ 3409 8045; half-/full day $35/50) Offers tours of Amity Point and the lakes in 20ft glass-bottom canoes.

Coastal Island Safaris (☎ 5547 4120; www.coastal islandsafaris.com; adult/child $175/125) Offers full-day tours, picking up in either Brisbane or on Straddie. Prices include morning tea, a BBQ lunch, fishing and swimming.

Straddie Kingfisher Tours (☎ 3409 9502; www.straddiekingfishertours.com.au; adult/child from $70/40) Operates six-hour tours.

SLEEPING

Most accommodation is at Point Lookout, which is strung along 3km of coastline on the northern shore of the island.

If you're thinking of staying awhile, a holiday flat or house can be good value, especially outside the holiday seasons. There are numerous real estate agents on the island including **Ray White** (☎ 3409 8255; Mintee St).

Budget

Stradbroke Island YHA (☎ 3409 8888; www.stradbroke islandscuba.com.au; 1 East Coast Rd; dm $22, tw & d $50) A large beachside hostel with clean dorms, friendly staff and good facilities, including a dive school, bikes and surfing gear. The hostel runs a shuttle bus from opposite the transit centre in Brisbane, but you need to book.

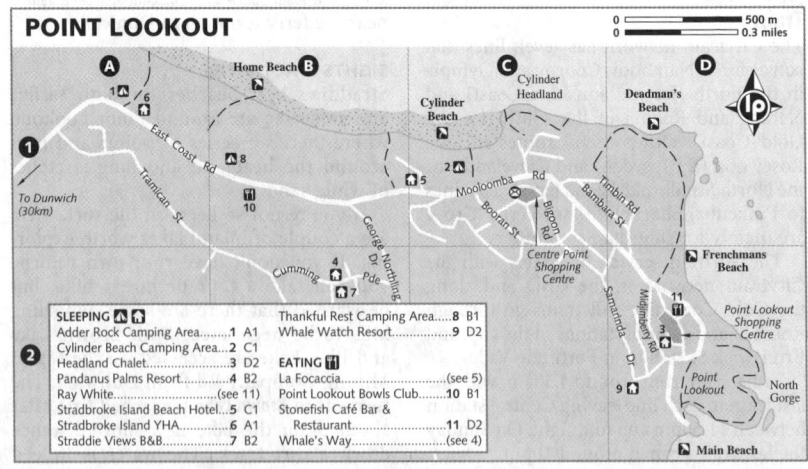

POINT LOOKOUT

SLEEPING		
Adder Rock Camping Area	1	A1
Cylinder Beach Camping Area	2	C1
Headland Chalet	3	D2
Pandanus Palms Resort	4	B2
Ray White	(see 11)	
Stradbroke Island Beach Hotel	5	C1
Stradbroke Island YHA	6	A1
Straddie Views B&B	7	B2
Thankful Rest Camping Area	8	B1
Whale Watch Resort	9	D2

EATING		
La Focaccia	(see 5)	
Point Lookout Bowls Club	10	B1
Stonefish Café Bar & Restaurant	11	D2
Whale's Way	(see 4)	

Headland Chalet (☎ 3409 8252; 213 Midjimberry Rd; cabin d & tw per person Sun-Thu $25, Fri & Sat $30; ⟨☀⟩) A cluster of cabins on the hillside overlooking Main Beach with good views, TV room and a small kitchen.

Stradbroke Island Beach Hotel (☎ 3409 8188; straddie@itxpress.com.au; East Coast Rd; s/d Sun-Thu $55/80, r Fri & Sat $100; ⟨☀⟩) Straddie's only pub sits on a headland above Cylinder Beach and offers comfortable, unexceptional motel-style rooms.

There are six camping grounds on the island operated by **Stradbroke Camping** (☎ 1300 551 253; tent/caravan sites per adult $9/12, per child $4.20/5.30, foreshore camping adult/child $5.30/3.20), but the most attractive are the places grouped around Point Lookout. The Adder Rock Camping Area and Thankful Rest Camping Area both overlook lovely Home Beach, while the Cylinder Beach Camping Area sits right on Cylinder Beach, one of the most popular beaches on the island.

Midrange & Top End
Whale Watch Resort (☎ 1800 450 004, 3409 8555; www.whalewatchresort.com.au; Samarinda Dr; r per 2/5 nights from $326/720; ⟨✦ ▯ ☀⟩) This complex of secluded apartments boasts a spa, gym and games room. The cavernous units are filled with stylish furniture and appointments, which open on to large decks, many with ocean views.

Straddie Views B&B (☎ 3409 8875; www.north stradbrokeisland.com/straddiebb; 26 Cumming Pde; r Sun-Thu $100, Fri & Sat $120) The en-suite rooms at this friendly B&B are spacious and classy. The hosts have made a real effort to provide little comforts and breakfast is served with views on the upstairs deck.

Pandanus Palms Resort (☎ 3409 8106; fax 3409 8339; 21 Cumming Pde; r $200-250; ⟨☀⟩) Perched high above the beach, this resort has comfortable self-contained units, a tennis court and a pool. The best units are the (pricier) two-bedroom ones with private courtyards, BBQs and outdoor dining settings.

EATING
There are a couple of general stores selling groceries in Point Lookout, but it's worth bringing basic supplies.

Whale's Way (☎ 3409 8106; Pandanus Palms Resort, 21 Cumming Pde; mains $20-30; ⟨☾⟩ dinner Tue-Sat) This elegant restaurant serves delicate concoc-

tions like Moreton Bay bugs and ocean king prawns layered between filo pastry with a light curry sauce. The elevated views are just as special.

Stonefish Cafe Bar & Restaurant (☎ 3409 8549; cnr Mooloomba Rd & Mintee St; ⟨☾⟩ breakfast & lunch) No boring bacon and eggs here; instead you'll be filling up on vanilla-bean French toast or an Israeli breakfast with coriander toast. The eclectic menu represents Middle Eastern, Thai and Aussie flavours and most of the seating is outdoors.

La Focaccia (☎ 3409 8778; Meegera Pl; mains $15-22; ⟨☾⟩ dinner) This casual pizzeria cooks up fresh pastas and excellent pizzas.

Point Lookout Bowls Club (☎ 3409 8182; East Coast Rd; mains $7-18; ⟨☾⟩ dinner) The bistro at the bowls club isn't exactly exciting, but you can fuel up on a roast, steak or chicken parma fairly cheaply.

GETTING THERE & AWAY
The gateway to North Stradbroke Island is the seaside town of Cleveland. Regular **City-train** (☎ 13 12 30; www.transinfo.qld.gov.au) services run from Central or Roma St station to Cleveland station ($4, one hour) and buses to the ferry terminals meet the trains at Cleveland station ($1).

Stradbroke Ferries (☎ 3286 2666) runs a water taxi to Dunwich almost every hour from about 6am to 6pm ($13 return, 30 minutes). It also has a slightly less frequent vehicle ferry (per vehicle including passengers return $95, 45 minutes) from 5.30am to 6.30pm (later at weekends). The **Stradbroke Flyer** (☎ 3821 3821; www.flyer.com.au) also runs an almost-hourly catamaran service from Cleveland to One Mile Jetty ($13 return, 45 minutes), 1.5km north of central Dunwich.

GETTING AROUND
Local **buses** (☎ 3409 7151) meet the ferries at Dunwich and One Mile Jetty and run across to Point Lookout ($10.50 return). The last bus to Dunwich leaves Point Lookout at about 6pm. There's also the **Stradbroke Cab Service** (☎ 0408 193 685), which charges $30 from Dunwich to Point Lookout.

Moreton Island
North of Stradbroke, Moreton Island comes a close second to Fraser Island for excellent sand-driving and wilderness, and sees

far fewer visitors. Apart from a few rocky headlands, it's all sand. Sand-mining leases on the island have been cancelled and 96% of the island is now a national park. The island's bird life is prolific. Off the west coast are a number of shipwrecks, the Tangalooma Wrecks, which provide good snorkelling and diving.

ORIENTATION & INFORMATION

Moreton Island doesn't have any paved roads, but 4WD vehicles can travel along beaches and a few cross-island tracks; seek local advice about tides and creek crossings. You can get QPWS maps from the vehicle-ferry offices or the **rangers** (☎ 3408 2710) at Tangalooma. Vehicle permits for the island cost $31 and are available through the ferry operators or from the Naturally Queensland office in Brisbane (p300). Note that ferry bookings are *mandatory* if you want to take a vehicle across, see right for operators.

Apart from the Tangalooma resort, the only other settlements are **Bulwer** near the northwestern tip, **Cowan Cowan** between Bulwer and Tangalooma, and **Kooringal** near the southern tip. The shops at Kooringal and Bulwer are expensive, so bring what you can from the mainland.

SIGHTS & ACTIVITIES

Tangalooma, halfway down the western side of the island, is a popular tourist resort sited at an old whaling station. The main attraction is the **dolphin feeding**, which takes place each evening around sunset. Usually about eight or nine dolphins swim in from the ocean and take fish from the hands of volunteer feeders. Although you have to be a guest of the resort to participate, onlookers are welcome.

Without your own vehicle, walking is the only way to get around the island, and you'll need several days to explore it. Fortunately, there are loads of good walking trails and decommissioned 4WD roads. It's worth making the strenuous trek to the summit of 280m **Mt Tempest** – the highest coastal sand hill in the world – about 3km inland from Eagers Creek.

About 3km south and inland from Tangalooma is an area of bare sand known as the **Desert**, while the **Big Sandhills** and the **Little Sandhills** are towards the narrow south-

ern end of the island. The biggest lakes and some swamps are in the northeast.

At the island's northern tip is a **lighthouse** built in 1857.

You can hire snorkelling gear from **Get Wet Sports** (☎ 3410 6927; Tangalooma Wild Dolphin Resort; 4hr per person $12) and immerse yourself amid the colourful coral and marine life of the **Tangalooma Wrecks**.

TOURS

Gibren Expeditions (☎ 1300 559 355; 2-/3-day tours from $210/320) Offers tours of the island with heaps of activities thrown in, including snorkelling, sandboarding, sea kayaking and scuba diving. The guides are locals and really know the island.

Sunrover Expeditions (☎ 3880 0719, 1800 353 717; www.sunrover.com.au; adult/child $120/90) A reliable 4WD tour operator with good day tours, which include lunch. Tours depart Roma St Transit Centre on Friday, Sunday and Monday. They also operate two-day camping tours (adult/child $195/150) and three-day national park safaris (adult/child camping $300/250, in cabins $400/350). Both of these include meals.

SLEEPING

Tangalooma Wild Dolphin Resort (☎ 1300 652 250, 3410 6000; www.tangalooma.com; packages $230-330; ❄ ✆) If price is no obstacle, this modern resort is the most desirable locale. It has plush rooms, nice beaches and tame dolphins. Package rates include transfers, overnight accommodation and dolphin feeding.

Bulwer Cabins (☎ 3203 6399; www.moreton-island .com/accommodation.html; cabins from $90) These spacious self-contained units, 200m from the beach at Bulwer, sleep up to six.

There are nine national park **camping grounds** (per person/family $4/16), all with water, toilets and cold showers. For information and camping permits, contact the Naturally Queensland office in Brisbane (p300) or the **ranger** (☎ 3408 2710). Camping permits are also available from the ferry operators.

GETTING THERE & AROUND

A number of ferries operate from the mainland. The **Tangalooma Flyer** (☎ 3268 6333; www .tangalooma.com/tangalooma/transport; adult/child return $60/30; ⊙ departs 6am, 10am & 5pm Mon; 8am, 10am & 5pm Tue-Fri; 8am, 10am, noon & 5pm Sat & Sun), a fast catamaran operated by the resort, sails from a dock at Holt St, off Kingsford Smith Dr (in Eagle Farm). A bus ($5) departs the Brisbane Transit Centre at 9am. You can use it for a day trip (it returns at 9am and 4pm, plus 2pm weekends) or for camping drop-offs. The trip takes 1¼ hours.

The **Moreton Venture** (☎ 3895 1000; www.more tonventure.com.au; return adult/child $20/30, vehicle plus 2 passengers $135; ◷ departs 8.30am daily, plus 6.30pm Fri & 2.30pm Sun) is a vehicle ferry that runs from Howard-Smith Dr, Lyton, at the Port of Brisbane, to Tangalooma. It leaves the island at 3.30pm daily plus 8pm on Friday and 4.30pm on Sunday.

The **Combie Trader** (☎ 3203 6399; www.morton -island.com/how.html; return adult/child $35/20, vehicle plus 4 passengers $150; ◷ departs 8am & 1pm Mon; 8am Wed & Thu; 8am, 1pm & 7pm Fri; 6am & 11am Sat; 8am, 1pm & 5.30pm Sun) sails between Scarborough and Bulwer, the trip taking about two and a half hours.

You can hire 4WDs to explore the island from **Moreton Island 4WD hire** (☎ 3410 1338; www.moretonisland.com.au/4wd_page.htm) in Bulwer. Rates start at $145 per day.

BRISBANE

Sunshine Coast

The string of low-key resort towns along the Sunshine Coast has the odd regiment of high-rises, but mostly you can look forward to days spent on long stretches of golden beach with laid-back locals.

The Sunshine Coast reaches from the top of family-friendly Bribie Island to just north of Noosa. The ethereal Glass House Mountains are made up of one spectacular volcanic plug after another – forming a dramatic curtain above the coastal plain. The mountains give way to the first place on this strip, Caloundra – an idling beach resort. Further along the coast is the laconic suburban swell of Maroochy, which is the most developed quarter in the Sunshine neighbourhood. The Maroochy shire encompasses a number of suburban pockets including: Maroochydore, Cotton Tree, Alexandra Geadlands and Mooloolaba.

North of Maroochy, there's a paramount patch of coastline at Coolum and Peregian Beaches. The squeaky white sand and sparkling blue waters may seduce you to strip down and dive right in. You then arrive in Noosa: an exclusive, low-rise and leafy resort where you can mix with high-end holidaymakers, dine in fine restaurants and party until you're ready to stop. Temper your indulgences by going natural in the area's national parks. The Noosa and Great Sandy National Parks each have a network of walking trails and picnic spots.

Filling the space between beaches drenched in sunshine and the vast emptiness of Queensland's interior is the Sunshine Coast's undulating hinterland, where charming villages linger on the outskirts of some beautiful national parks.

HIGHLIGHTS

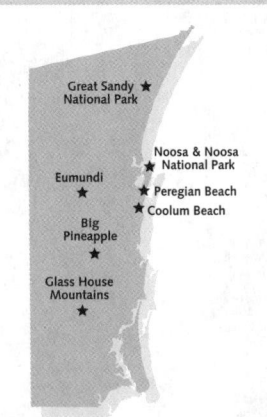

- Pondering the legend and stunning looks of the **Glass House Mountains** (p329)
- Patting the sand into a pillow on a lonely patch of beach at **Coolum** and **Peregian Beaches** (p335)
- Making eating into an event at one of Noosa's renowned **restaurants** (p340)
- Treading through heath land before reaching sand at a secluded bay at **Noosa National Park** (p336)
- Hopping in a canoe to explore the Cooloola Section of the **Great Sandy National Park** (p342)
- Sift through the 200-plus stalls for goodies at the **Eumundi market** (p344)
- Get your fix of kitsch at the **Big Pineapple** (p344)

Great Sandy ★
National Park

Noosa & Noosa
★ National Park

Eumundi
★

★ Peregian Beach

★ Coolum Beach

Big
Pineapple
★

Glass House
Mountains
★

■ TELEPHONE CODE: 07   ■ www.tourismsunshinecoast.com.au

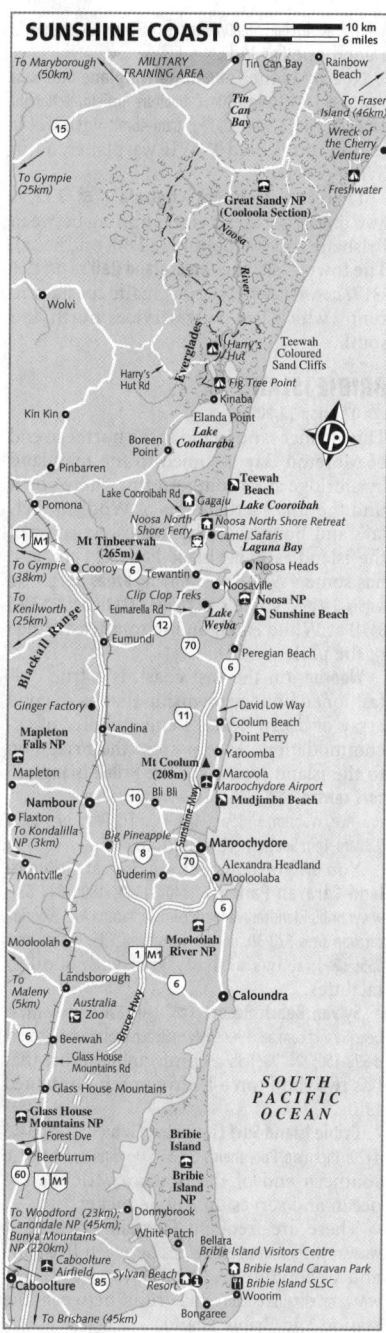

SUNSHINE COAST

Getting There & Away

AIR

The Sunshine Coast Airport is on the coast road at Mudjimba, 10km north of Maroochydore and 26km south of Noosa, although it's referred to as Maroochydore airport. **Sunshine Express** (www.sunshineexpress.com.au) flies there daily from Brisbane ($95, 30 minutes). **Jetstar** (☎ 13 15 38; www.jetstar.com.au) and **Virgin Blue** (☎ 13 67 89; www.virginblue.com.au) have daily connections to Sydney ($90) as well as Melbourne ($130). Virgin Blue also flies to the Sunshine Coast from other state capitals.

BUS

Greyhound (☎ 13 14 99; www.greyhound.com.au) and **Premier** (☎ 13 34 10; www.premierms.com.au) both stop at Maroochydore and Noosa en route from Brisbane to destinations further north; see those sections for further details.

Suncoast Pacific (www.suncoastpacific.com.au; Brisbane ☎ 3236 1901; Caloundra ☎ 5491 2555; Maroochydore ☎ 5443 1011) runs between Brisbane's Roma St Transit Centre and airport, to points along the Sunshine Coast. There are around seven services every weekday, and six on Saturday and Sunday. One-way trips from Brisbane include to Caloundra ($24, two hours), Maroochydore ($21, two hours) and Noosa ($24, three hours). It also offers standby fares to the aforementioned places for $15.

Getting Around

Several private companies offer transfers from Maroochydore airport and Brisbane to points along the Sunshine Coast. Fares from Brisbane cost around $40 for adults and $25 for children. Fares from Maroochydore airport are around $15/11 per adult/child.

Col's Airport Shuttle (☎ 5473 9966; www.airshuttle .com.au)

Sun-Air Bus Service (☎ 5478 2811, 1800 804 340; www.sunair.com.au)

Suncoast Link (☎ 3236 1901; www.suncoastpacific .com.au)

The blue minibuses operated by **Sunbus** (☎ 5492 8700; www.sunbus.com.au) run frequently between Caloundra and Noosa, stopping along the way; see those sections for further details. Sunbus also has regular buses across from Noosa to the train station at Nambour, on the Bruce Hwy ($4.40, one hour), via Eumundi and Yandina.

FESTIVALS & EVENTS

Abbey Medieval Tournament (www.abbey
tournament.com) Frocked-up lords, ladies and
squires converge on Caboolture in July for jousting,
faux combats, markets and parades.

Noosa Jazz Festival (www.noosajazz.com.au)
Highly regarded four-day music festival from late
August to early September.

Noosa Triathlon (www.usmevents.com.au)
Held in November; includes a week's worth of
sporting events.

Woodford Folk Festival (www.woodford
folkfestival.com) This extraordinary music festival,
which runs from 27 December to 1 January, is held
about 25km northwest of Caboolture.

BRISBANE TO LANDSBOROUGH

Once you clear the small town of Caboolture, 44km north of Brisbane, you begin to feel you've evaded the city's urban sprawl. Caboolture is also the turn-off point for Bribie Island.

About 10km north of Caboolture, the Glass House Mountains Rd leaves the Bruce Hwy and passes through an area of rich fruit production at the base of the beautiful Glass House Mountains, before rejoining the highway just past Landsborough at the Caloundra turn-off 30km later. It's definitely the go; you're not missing anything on the highway.

CABOOLTURE
☎ 07 / pop 40,400

The prosperous rural commuter town of Caboolture is studded with museums. The **Abbey Museum** (☎ 5495 1652; www.abbeymuseum .asn.au; 1 Abbey Place; adult/child $8/4.50; ☒ 10am-4pm Mon-Sat) keeps an impressive art and archaeology collection that spans the globe and includes items such as bronze foot armour and an alchemist's flask. The museum is about 7km east of Caboolture, on the far side of the Bruce Hwy, just off Toorbul Point Rd.

More than 60 structures – including buildings belonging to the council , a courthouse and general stores – have been recreated for **Caboolture Historical Village** (☎ 5495 4581; Beerbur-

rum Rd; adult/child $8.80/6.60; ☒ 9.30am-3.30pm); it's a good one for kids.

Nearby is the **Caboolture Warplane Museum** (☎ 5499 1144; Hangar 104, Caboolture Airfield, McNaught Rd; adult/child $6.50/3.50; ☒ 10am-4pm), with a collection of restored WWII warplanes, all in flying order.

There are frequent **Citytrain** (☎ 13 12 30; www.citytrain.com.au) services running between Brisbane and Caboolture ($4.80, one hour). The town is also on **Queensland Rail's** (☎ 1300 131 722; www.traveltrain.com.au) main coastal rail route, which has daily services north and south.

BRIBIE ISLAND
☎ 07 / pop 12,900

This slender sand island at the northern end of Moreton Bay is joined to the mainland by a bridge at its southern tip, where you'll find the small settlements of Woorim, Bellara and Bongaree. The northwest coast of the island is **Bribie Island National Park**, and has some 4WD-only **camping areas** (per person/ family $4/16). There's a **ranger station** (☎ 3408 8451) at White Patch on the southeast fringe of the park.

Woorim, on the east coast, is a true old-fashioned holiday township that has a good array of ocean beaches and a choice of accommodation. As you cross the bridge on to the island, you'll see the **Bribie Island visitors centre** (☎ 3408 9026; www.bribie.com.au; Benabrow Ave, Woorim; ☒ 9am-4pm Mon-Fri, 9am-3pm Sat & 9.30am-1pm Sun) on the median strip.

You might consider staying at **Bribie Island Caravan Park** (☎ 3408 1134, 1800 649 831; www.bribieislandcaravanpark.com.au; Jacana Ave, Woorim; caravan sites $20-30, on-site vans from $35, cabins from $55; ☒); it has a shady area with spotless facilities.

Sylvan Beach Resort (☎ 3408 8300; www.sylvan beachresort.com.au; 19-23 Sylvan Beach Esplanade, Woorim; d $90-150; ☒ ☒) is a comfortable resort that has two- and three-bedroom self-contained units.

Bribie Island Surf Lifesaving Club (SLSC; ☎ 3408 4420; Rickman Pde; mains $8-15; ☒ dinner), at the southern end of the beach, overlooks the ocean and serves up Aussie tucker.

There are frequent **Citytrain** (☎ 13 12 30; www.citytrain.com.au) services between Brisbane and Caboolture. A **Trainlink** (☎ 1300 131 722; www.traveltrain.com.au) bus runs between the station and Bribie Island.

CABOOLTURE TO LANDSBOROUGH

The Glass House Mountains Rd leaves the Bruce Hwy about 10km north of Caboolture, passing the Glass House Mountains National Park and the tiny towns of Glass House Mountains, Beerwah and Landsborough, rejoining the highway at the Caloundra turn-off.

While the Glass House Mountains are the indisputable attraction, you could also stop at the **Australia Zoo** (☎ 5494 1134; www.crocodile hunter.com; Glass House Mountains Rd, Beerwah; adult/child $29/19; ☺ 9am-4.30pm), known as much for its owner – Steve 'Crikey' Irwin – as for its animals. This highly commercialised zoo has crocodile, snake and birds-of-prey demonstrations every day, as well as an extensive collection of native and exotic animals. The zoo is included in tours offered by many operators out of Brisbane and the Sunshine Coast (see p344), and the zoo operates a free courtesy bus from Beerwah train station.

Glass House Mountains National Park

About 20km north of Caboolture, the Glass House Mountains are a curious group of volcanic crags rising up from the coastal plain. Indigenous legend talks of these rocky peaks belonging to a family of mountain spirits; see the boxed text, below.

The Glass House Mountains National Park is broken into several sections and surrounds Mts Tibrogargan, Cooee, Beerwah, Coonowrin (Crookneck), Ngungun, Miketeebumulgrai, Elimbah and Coochin with picnic grounds and lookouts, but no camping grounds. The peaks are reached by a series of sealed and unsealed roads known as Forest Dr, which head inland from Glass House Mountains Rd. You need a permit to access Mt Coonowrin, which you can get from **Queensland Parks & Wildlife Service** (QPWS; ☎ 5494 0150; www.epa.qld .gov.au; Bells Creek Rd, Beerwah; ☺ 7am-3.30pm).

There are low-grade mountain climbs on several of the peaks, from where the views are spectacular. Tibrogargan is probably the best climb, with a steep rock-cut trail and several amazing lookouts from the flat summit. Reaching the summit requires a reasonable level of fitness and you should allow three to four hours for the return trip. Mt Beerwah and Mt Ngungun can also be climbed via steep trails.

THE WEEPING MOUNTAIN & HIS WAYWARD SON

According to Aboriginal legend, the Glass House Mountains are a family of mountain spirits, presided over by Tibrogargan (364m), the father of all tribes, and his wife Beerwah (556m). They had several offspring, of whom Coonowrin (377m) was the eldest. His siblings include Tunbubudla (the twins; 293m and 312m), Coochin (235m), Ngungun (253m), Tibberoowuccum (200m), Miketeebumulgrai (199m) and Elimbah (129m).

One day Tibrogargan was looking out towards the coast when he noticed the sea level rising. Anticipating a flood, he became fearful for Beerwah, who was close to the water. But he was also concerned about his children, and would not be able to save them all. So Tibrogargan called to his eldest son Coonowrin to assist his mother.

As Tibrogargan gathered his younger children he looked behind him to see if Coonowrin and Beerwah were safe, but to his dismay Coonowrin had fled and left his mother unassisted. In a blinding rage, Tibrogargan picked up his *nulla nulla* (club) and struck Coonowrin, dislocating his neck.

Once the waters subsided the family were able to return to their home. Upon seeing his crooked neck, Coonowrin's siblings began to tease him. This made him feel ashamed and he went to his father for forgiveness. Tibrogargan wept huge tears of despair and asked his son how he could abandon his mother. Coonowrin answered that she was so much bigger than any of them, he thought she should be able to take care of herself. What he did not realise however was that Beerwah was not just big, but heavily pregnant. Coonowrin's siblings began to weep too; their tears formed many streams, some reaching all the way out to sea.

According to the law of the tribe, Tibrogargan could not forgive his son who had disgraced him, so he turned his back on Coonowrin forever. To this day Tibrogargan faces out to sea while his son hangs his crooked neck in shame and cries. As for Beerwah, well she is still pregnant – it takes a long time to give birth to a mountain.

SUNSHINE COAST

Sleeping & Eating

Glasshouse Mountains Holiday Village (☎ /fax 5496 9338; Glass House Mountains Rd, Glass House Mountains; tent/ caravan sites $16/19, cabins from $65; 🕲 🕲) Comfy self-contained cabins and well-spaced sites are often sprinkled with flowers from the overhanging jacaranda trees here. Facilities include barbecues, a tennis court and a small takeaway shop.

Glasshouse Mountains Tourist Park (☎ 5496 0151; www.glasshousetouristpk.com.au; Glass House Mountains Rd, Beerburrum; tent/caravan sites $16/19, cabins from $50; 🕲) Caravans crowd tightly together at this ageing park with a stunning mountain backdrop – making for a reasonable overnight option.

Glasshouse Mountains Tavern (☎ 5493 0933; 10 Reed St, Glass House Mountains; mains $12-23; 🕲 lunch & dinner) This welcoming pub serves up hearty steaks, curries and chicken parma. Its dark-wood interior and open fire keeps things cosy when it's cold and the smattering of outdoor seating is great for a midday middy on sunny days.

NORTH OF LANDSBOROUGH

Leaving the Bruce Hwy at the Caloundra turn-off, about 35km north of Caboolture, this stretch takes in the resort towns of Caloundra, Mooloolaba, Maroochy and Noosa. Noosa is also the gateway to the Great Sandy National Park, a 4WD haven that runs north to Rainbow Beach and Fraser Island. The main road along the coast is David Low Way, which links Caloundra with Noosa, but inland is the much faster Sunshine Mwy. From Noosa, the road swings back inland to Cooroy and the Bruce Hwy.

The alternative route for this section is straight up the Bruce Hwy through Nambour and Eumundi (see p344).

CALOUNDRA

☎ 07 / pop 50,150

Caloundra's curvaceous coast proffers pleasant surf beaches that are favoured by families and fisherfolk. The town's humble spread of weatherboard and brick bungalows are interrupted by a clutch of medium-rise condos, and interspersed with pockets of pine and scrubby coastal scenery.

Bulcock St is the main thoroughfare, with a post office, banks, a cinema and a few takeaway cafés.

The Caloundra **visitors centre** (☎ 5491 0202; 7 Caloundra Rd; 🕲 9am-5.30pm) is near the roundabout at the entrance to town.

Sights & Activities

The beaches are the major attraction. Bulcock Beach, just down from the main street and pinched by the northern tip of Bribie Island, captures a wind tunnel, which is popular with kitesurfers. For conventional surfing, head north to Moffat's Beach or Dicky Beach. **North Caloundra Surf School** (☎ 0411 221 730; 2hr lesson from $55) is highly regarded. You can rent boards from **Beach Beat** (Caloundra ☎ 5491 4711; 119 Bulcock St; 🕲 9am-5pm; Dicky Beach ☎ 5491 8215; 4-6 Beerburrum St; 🕲 9am-5pm), surfboards/bodyboards cost $35/25 per day.

Sunshine Coast Skydivers (☎ 5437 0211; www .jumpSCS.com; Caloundra Aerodrome; from $180) will have you whooping for joy while you plummet to earth on one of its popular tandem jumps.

The **Queensland Air Museum** (☎ 5492 5930; 7 Pathfinder Dr, Caloundra Aerodrome; adult/child $8/4; 🕲 10am-4pm) is best for budding aviators. Plenty of photos, displays and old machinery parts provide an insight into Queensland's aviation history.

The **Sunshine Coast Turf Club** (☎ 5491 6788; www.sctc.com.au; Pierce Ave), west of town, has popular race meetings every Sunday.

An increasingly popular way to see the water around Caloundra is to cruise Pumicestone Channel, along the water separating Bribie Island from the mainland. **Caloundra Cruise** (☎ 5492 8280; www.caloundracruise.com; adult/ child/concession $14.50/5/13.50) operates 1½-hour ecocruises (departing from Majova Ave Jetty at 11am and 1pm), taking in the channel and coursing around Bribie Island.

Sleeping

Belaire Place (☎ 5491 8688, www.belaireplace.com; 34 Minchinton St; r $105-75; 🅿 🕲 🕲) These spacious and light-filled apartments overlooking Bulcock Beach are great value. The modern interiors all contain sparkling kitchens, cable TV and big balconies. You can pay a premium for a room with a view.

Dicky Beach Family Holiday Park (☎ /fax 5491 3342; 4 Beerburrum St; tent/caravan sites from $20/24, cabins from $60; 🕲 🕲) This well-ordered park right

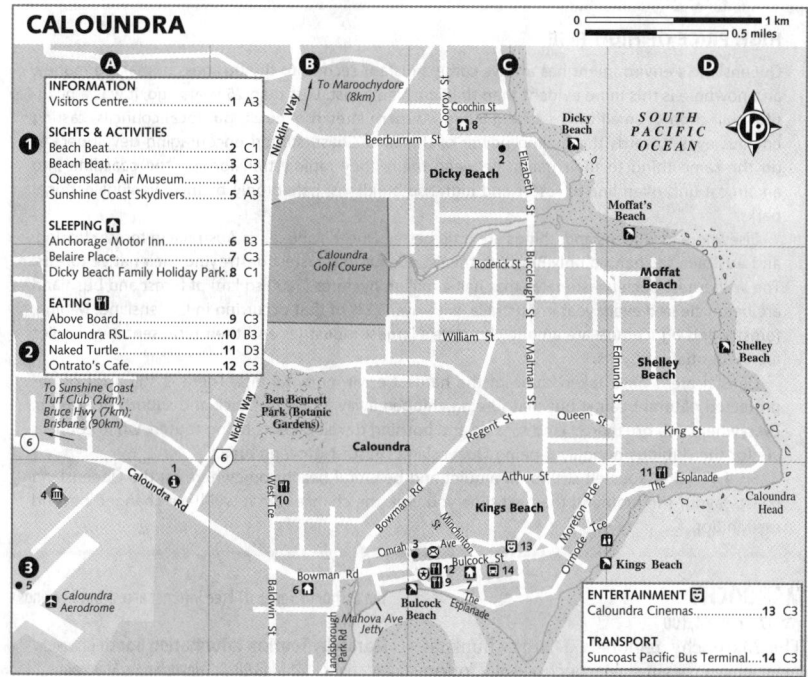

CALOUNDRA

INFORMATION	
Visitors Centre.................................**1** A3	

SIGHTS & ACTIVITIES	
Beach Beat..**2** C1	
Beach Beat..**3** C3	
Queensland Air Museum................**4** A3	
Sunshine Coast Skydivers.............**5** A3	

SLEEPING	
Anchorage Motor Inn....................**6** B3	
Belaire Place...................................**7** C3	
Dicky Beach Family Holiday Park.**8** C1	

EATING	
Above Board.....................................**9** C3	
Caloundra RSL.................................**10** B3	
Naked Turtle...................................**11** D3	
Ontrato's Cafe.................................**12** C3	

ENTERTAINMENT	
Caloundra Cinemas.........................**13** C3	

TRANSPORT	
Suncoast Pacific Bus Terminal....**14** C3	

on the beach front would win over even the most finicky of families; absolutely everything is in its place. The immaculate grounds feature plenty of green grass and tree cover.

Anchorage Motor Inn (☎ 5491 1499; fax 5491 7279; 18 Bowman Rd; s/d $80/85; P ✗ ☎) This friendly motel has simple and clean rooms. There's also a pleasant pool set in a mini oasis to offset the concrete.

Eating
Above Board (☎ 5491 6388; Shop 8, The Esplanade; mains $10-24; ☼ breakfast, lunch & dinner) The menu at this casual haunt is a cut above regular offerings. Dinner highlights include mahi mahi fillets with macadamia pesto dressing, or pistachio-stuffed pork fillets sitting on a wine-glazed mash. Brekkie and lunch are simpler affairs.

Naked Turtle (☎ 5491 7565; Shop 2, Shearwater Resort, The Esplanade, Kings Beach; mains $15-25; ☼ breakfast, lunch & dinner) A big glass-domed dining room is the setting for this spunky eatery. It's a great spot to watch people tucking into lentil samosas, tandoori chicken, spring rolls, tapas or salt-and-vinegar dory fillets.

Caloundra Returned Serviceman's League (RSL; ☎ 5491 1544; 19 West Tce; dishes $10-25; ☼ breakfast, lunch & dinner) Caloundra's award-winning RSL is flamboyant and glitzy enough to rival Liberace. Its two enormous restaurants and café cater to a range of tastes and budgets, and the food is excellent.

Ontrato's Cafe (☎ 5437 0944; cnr Bulcock St & Ontrato Ave; dishes $5-11; ☼ breakfast, lunch & dinner) This quaint café serves up sweet and savoury crepes, focaccias and fresh wraps. Families gather for cake and scrummy breakfasts.

Entertainment
Caloundra Cinemas (☎ 1902 240 508; cnr Knox & Bulcock Sts) Located on the upper floor of an arcade, this multiscreen complex has budget days on Tuesdays and Thursdays ($7.50).

Getting There & Away
Long-distance buses stop at the **Suncoast Pacific bus terminal** (☎ 5491 2555; Cooma Tce); see p327 for more information. **Sunbus** (☎ 13 12 30; www.sunbus.com.au) connects Caloundra to Noosa ($5.20, 1½ hours) via Maroochydore ($2.80, 50 minutes) frequently.

SUNSHINE COAST

HIGH PRICE OF HIGH-RISE

Queensland's environment has always come a distant second to the business of making money, and nowhere is this more evident than the Sunshine Coast. Less than 25 years ago, it was a beautiful collection of small towns strung along a superb stretch of coast, but local councils, casting envious eyes towards the pulling power of the Gold Coast, started encouraging developers to do the same thing to their patch. Between them, they rapidly transformed the coastline into an almost-unbroken line of resort and high-rise buildings, halted only by inconvenient national parks.

Elsewhere in Queensland, things are little better. Queensland leads Australia in forest clearing, and Australia sits behind only Brazil on the list of countries fastest destroying their native forests. The Wilderness Society estimates that half a million hectares (5000 sq km) of forest and bushland are being cleared every year in Australia, with over 75% of that occurring in Queensland. Mining, forestry and agriculture are among the state's largest industries and their representative bodies are influential lobbyists.

Coastal areas have taken some of the hardest environmental hits. There is still a lot of unprotected natural beauty, but that's being chipped away, block by block and suburb by suburb. Everywhere you go, there's land for sale and housing developments being touted, while councils vie for the dubious honour of being Queensland's fastest-growing area.

So if you find yourself sitting on a quiet and beautiful beach somewhere on the Queensland coast, savour the moment; the next time you visit, the chances are it will have changed beyond recognition.

MAROOCHY

☎ 07 / pop 44,100

The Maroochy region is a large chunk of coast encompassing Maroochydore, Cotton Tree, Alexandra Headland and Mooloolaba. It's a happily developed suburban spread, where the surf culture has been supplanted by shopping plazas, and the shoreline sports vistas of high-rise apartments. But the affable and relaxed ethos of the beach is dominant except for bursts in summer, when loads of families converge to indulge in good fishing and surf beaches.

Mooloolaba is the most pleasant, and most developed, of the suburbs, with a good beach, good surf and some excellent restaurants and nightspots.

Orientation

The main thoroughfare in Maroochydore is Aerodrome Rd, which becomes Alexandra Pde along the seafront at Alexandra Headland, before turning into Mooloolaba Esplanade at Mooloolaba.

Information

Computer Rescue (☎ 5451 0750; cnr Ocean Ave & Duporth Ave, Maroochydore; per hr $6; ☻ 8am-5pm Mon-Fri, to noon Sat) Internet access.

Maroochydore Library (☎ 5475 8900; Sixth Ave, Cotton Tree; ☻ 9am-5.30pm Mon, Wed & Fri, to 8pm Tue & Thu, to 5pm Sat) Free Internet access but bookings essential.

Maroochy Tourism Information Booth (Maroochydore airport ☎ 5448 9088; Friendship Dr, Marcoola; ☻ 9.30am-3pm; Mooloolaba ☎ 5478 2233; cnr Brisbane Rd & First Ave, Mooloolaba; ☻ 9am-5pm)

Maroochy Visitors Centre (☎ 5479 1566, 1800 882 032; www.maroochytourism.com; cnr Sixth Ave & Melrose St, Maroochydore; ☻ 9am-5pm Mon-Fri, to 4pm Sat & Sun) Main office with plenty of information, helpful staff and a free accommodation booking service.

QPWS Office (☎ 5443 8940; 29 The Esplanade, Cotton Tree; ☻ varying)

Sights & Activities

Underwater World (☎ 5444 8488; www.underwaterworld.com.au; The Wharf; adult/child/family $23/13/60; ☻ 9am-6pm) is the largest oceanarium in the southern hemisphere. Its transparent tunnel allows you to relax even though sharks and giant stingrays surround you. There are also billabong environments, jellyfish, seal shows and a touch tank. If you have the gumption you can dive with the sharks here, organised by **Scuba World** (☎ 5444 8595; www.scubaworld.com.au; The Wharf, Mooloolaba), which takes certified divers on coral dives off the coast (from $55); newbies can do a PADI (Professional Association of Diving Instructors) course ($450).

There are a number of good surf breaks along this strip, the best being Pin Cushion near the mouth of the Maroochy River, which is particularly good in winter. In summer, it's relatively quiet; most visitors head to the more easily accessed Maroochy and Memorial Avenue. If you're new to the surfing game, consider taking a one-hour lesson with **Robbie Sherwell's XL Surfing Academy** (☎ 5478 1337; 63 Oloway Cres, Alexandra Headland; per person $20; ☼ 9.30am Mon-Fri, 7.30am Sat). The experienced can rent boards from **Beach Beat** (☎ 5443 2777; 164 Alexandra Pde, Alexandra Headland; surfboards/bodyboards per day $35/25; ☼ 9am-5pm).

FunSail (☎ 5446 6410; www.funsail.com.au; The Wharf, Mooloolaba; per person $100) spends three hours teaching you the finer points of sailing a 37ft yacht.

Tours

Aussie Sea Kayak Company (☎ 5477 5335; www.ausseakayak.com.au; The Wharf, Mooloolaba; 1-/2-day tours per person $135/250) offers a variety of sea-kayaking adventures on the Sunshine Coast, with tours out to North Stradbroke Island or Moreton Island.

Several outfits cruise along the Mooloolah River and its canals, departing from the wharf in Mooloolaba. **Cruiz Away River Tours** (☎ 0419 704 797; www.cruizaway.com; ecotour per adult/child $35/25, sunset cruise $25/15) operates two-hour ecotours into the Mooloolah River National Park as well as sunset cruises (one hour); call for departure times. **Harbour River Canal Cruise** (☎ 5444 7477; www.sunshinecoast.au.nu/canalcruise.htm; adult/child $13.50/5) operates

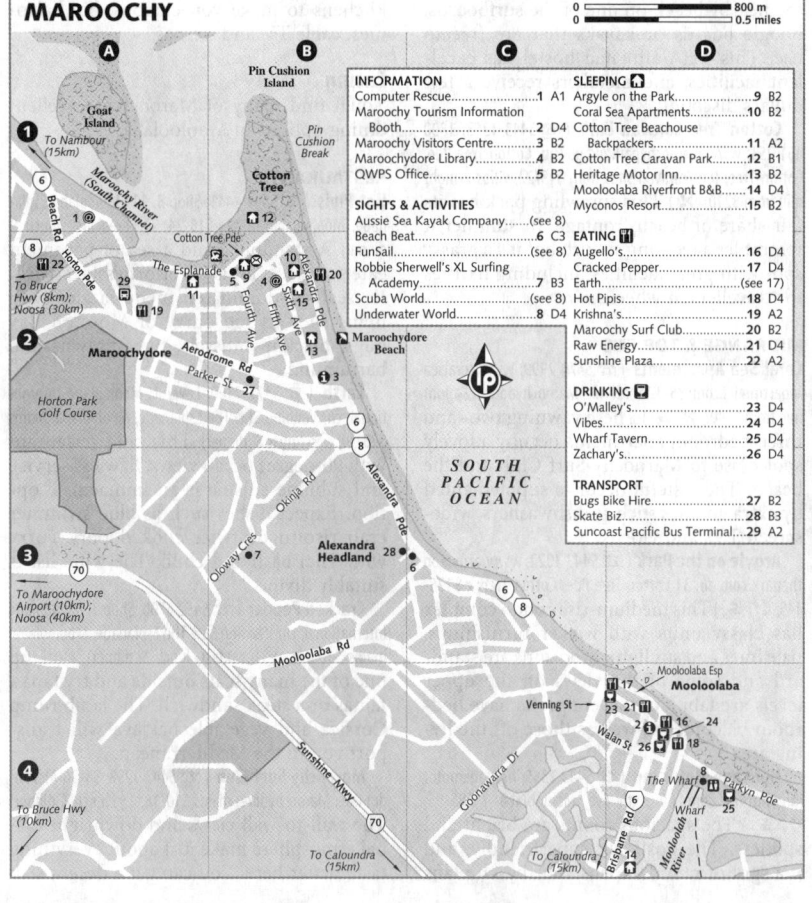

MAROOCHY

0   800 m
0   0.5 miles

INFORMATION
Computer Rescue...........................1 A1
Maroochy Tourism Information
  Booth.......................................2 D4
Maroochy Visitors Centre...........3 B2
Maroochydore Library.................4 B2
QWPS Office................................5 B2

SIGHTS & ACTIVITIES
Aussie Sea Kayak Company.......(see 8)
Beach Beat.................................6 C3
FunSail.....................................(see 8)
Robbie Sherwell's XL Surfing
  Academy..................................7 B3
Scuba World.............................(see 8)
Underwater World......................8 D4

SLEEPING 🏠
Argyle on the Park......................9 B2
Coral Sea Apartments................10 B2
Cotton Tree Beachouse
  Backpackers............................11 A2
Cotton Tree Caravan Park..........12 B1
Heritage Motor Inn....................13 B2
Mooloolaba Riverfront B&B.......14 D4
Myconos Resort.........................15 B2

EATING 🍴
Augello's..................................16 D4
Cracked Pepper........................17 D4
Earth.....................................(see 17)
Hot Pipis..................................18 D4
Krishna's..................................19 A2
Maroochy Surf Club...................20 B2
Raw Energy...............................21 D4
Sunshine Plaza.........................22 A2

DRINKING 🍷
O'Malley's.................................23 D4
Vibes......................................24 D4
Wharf Tavern............................25 D4
Zachary's.................................26 D4

TRANSPORT
Bugs Bike Hire..........................27 B2
Skate Biz..................................28 B3
Suncoast Pacific Bus Terminal....29 A2

SUNSHINE COAST

cruises (one hour, departing from the wharf in Maloolooba at 11am, 1pm and 2pm) with plenty of historical commentary aboard the MV *Mudjimba*.

Sleeping

Decent stand-by rates are usually available during the week at Maroochy's many self-contained units; most have a two-night minimum stay. Over school holidays and Christmas, rates for anything other than hostels hit the roof.

BUDGET

Cotton Tree Beachouse Backpackers (☎ 5443 1755; www.cottontreebackpackers.com; 15 The Esplanade, Cotton Tree; dm/d $21/46; ☐) Relax in the spa at this homey timber Queenslander, or hit the nearby beach on one of the surfboards, boogie boards or kayaks that are free to use. This YHA-affiliated hostel has excellent facilities, and members receive a few dollars discount.

Cotton Tree Caravan Park (☎ 5443 1253, 1800 461 253; www.maroochypark.qld.gov.au; Cotton Tree Pde, Cotton Tree; tent/caravan sites from $19/22, villas 2-night min from $210; ☒) This sprawling park has its fair share of beach frontage. In summer it resembles a teeming suburb but it's a grassy spot with great facilities, including fixtures for travellers in wheelchairs.

MIDRANGE & TOP END

Coral Sea Apartments (☎ 5479 2999; www.coralsea-apartments.com; 35-37 Sixth Ave, Maroochydore; r 2-night min from $240; ☒ ☒) These yawning two- and three-bedroom apartments occupy a lovely spot close to Maroochy Surf Club and the beach. The tasteful décor is supplemented by extra goodies such as dishwashers, wide-screen TVs and videos.

Argyle on the Park (☎ 5443 3022; www.argyleon thepark.com; 31 Cotton Tree Pde, Cotton Tree; r $125-145; ☒ ☒) This medium-rise condo complex has classy units with wicker furnishings, pale hues and sunlight. Mod cons are standard and some of the views on the upper levels are fabulous. Several units have bedroom balconies as well as those off the living area.

Heritage Motor Inn (☎ 5443 7355; heritagemotor inn@hotmail.com; 69 Sixth Ave, Mooloolaba; r $85-95; ☒ ☒) The spacious rooms are bright and spotless. The hosts are superfriendly, and if a spot of rain dampens your beach plans

there are free in-house movies. It's also wheelchair-friendly.

Mooloolaba Riverfront B&B (☎ 5452 5400, 0418 989 099; pm@rpdata.com.au; 7 Bindaree Cres, Mooloolaba; s/d $100/125; ☒) The sweet self-contained bedrooms at this B&B are nestled in a small riverfront residence tucked away from the main drag, but still within easy walking distance of the CBD. Each has its own balcony, and there's also a huge three-bedroom apartment.

Myconos Resort (☎ 5451 1711, 1800 041 166; www .myconosresort.com; 45 Sixth Ave, Maroochydore; r 2-night min $265-85; ☒ ☒) At a glance this loud tower looks like every other high-rise, but inside are a multitude of stylish themed rooms with overtones of Africa, the Middle East or the Mediterranean. All come with spas, kitchens to make you envious, big balconies, cable TV and stereos.

Eating

You'll find many of Maroochy's excellent dining options in Mooloolaba.

RESTAURANTS

Hot Pipis (☎ 5444 4441; Shop 3, 11 Mooloolaba Esplanade, Mooloolaba; dishes $15-24; ☒ breakfast, lunch & dinner) A standout amid a sea of pavement eateries, Hot Pipis is effortlessly stylish. Its seafood-dominated menu sizzles with items such as red curry of Moreton Bay bugs, blacklip mussels, tiger prawns and barramundi.

Earth (☎ 5477 7100; Level 1, Mooloolaba International, cnr Venning St & The Esplanade, Mooloolaba; mains $26-30; ☒ lunch & dinner) This chic restaurant with 90-degree ocean views, flawless service and sublime cuisine is an immaculate option. Expect dishes such as blue swimmer crab risotto or twice-cooked pork curry with Thai basil and chilli. The wine list is suitably divine.

Cracked Pepper (☎ 5452 6700; Shop 1, Mooloolaba International, cnr Venning St & The Esplanade, Mooloolaba; mains $10-20; ☒ breakfast, lunch & dinner) Pull up one of the many seats outside and try tapas, fajitas or a steak sandwich. The lamb rump Corsica and vegetable baklava will transport you to the Mediterranean.

Maroochy Surf Club (☎ 5443 1298; 34-36 Alexandra Pde, Maroochydore; mains $10-18; ☒ lunch & dinner) The wall-to-wall views and downright casual atmosphere make just about everything taste better here. You can get a decent slab of lasagne, but try the grilled prawn tails with egg noodles and tomato-chilli broth or marmalade pork salad, these are the real heroes.

Augello's (☎ 5478 3199; cnr The Esplanade & Brisbane Rd, Mooloolaba; mains $15-25; ✆ lunch & dinner) This Mooloolaba institution spoils diners of all ages with outstanding Italian food. Authentic pizzas including the hefty Milanese appear alongside nouveau concoctions such as Moroccan chicken with sun-dried tomatoes and lime yoghurt dressing. The mains are a step up again and you also get ocean views from upstairs.

CAFÉS & QUICK EATS

Raw Energy (☎ 5446 1444; Shop 3, The Esplanade, Mooloolaba; dishes $6-13; ✆ breakfast & lunch) This fresh fuel stop is devoted to health food but it's not all alfalfa wraps and mung beans. Marinated tofu or macadamia and lentil burgers, savoury tartlets and toppling vegetable stacks are the order of the day, plus there's a smorgasbord of fresh juices and smoothies.

Krishna's (Shop 2, 7 First Ave, Maroochydore; lunch $7, dinner $8; ✆ lunch Mon-Fri, dinner Fri & Sun) Krishna's may not have extended its ambience budget too far but the Indian veggie buffet here is excellent value and the food is hot and healthy.

Sunshine Plaza (Horton Pde, Maroochydore; meals $5-8) This plaza has a whole host of quick eat options in its large food court, as well as supermarkets for self-caterers.

Drinking

Vibes (☎ 5478 3222; Ground fl, Peninsula Bldg, Brisbane Rd, Mooloolaba) Vibes pulls in a mixed and happy crowd with busy Sunday sessions, cheap cocktails on Tuesday night and live music most nights.

Zachary's (☎ 5477 6877; 17 Brisbane Rd, Mooloolaba) Trendy things sporting plenty of hair products and rips in the right places come for the avid socialising amid dim lighting, black leather block couches and widescreen TVs.

If you're just looking to take the edge off the heat with a cool beer, head to **O'Malley's** (☎ 5452 6344; Ground fl, Mooloolaba International, The Esplanade, Mooloolaba) or the **Wharf Tavern** (☎ 5444 8383; The Wharf, Parkyn Pde, Mooloolaba). Both have live music most nights, sports on the telly, cold beer and no pretensions.

Getting There & Away

The long-distance buses stop at the **Suncoast Pacific bus terminal** (☎ 5443 1011; First Ave, Maroochydore). Both **Greyhound** (☎ 13 14 99; www.greyhound.com.au) and **Premier** (☎ 13 34 10; www.premierms.com.au) have two connections to Brisbane daily ($19, 1½ hours). Suncoast Pacific has the same connections on offer; see p327 for more information.

Sunbus (☎ 13 12 30; www.sunbus.com.au) has frequent services between Maroochydore and Noosa ($4.40, one hour). En route north from Brisbane, **Greyhound** (www.greyhound.com.au) and **Premier** (www.premierms.com.au) both stop in Maroochydore (from $25, two hours), Greyhound also stops in Coolum (from $25, one hour 20 minutes).

Getting Around

Bugs Bike Hire (☎ 5443 7555; 42 Aerodrome Rd, Maroochydore; per day $12) hires out good bicycles. **Skate Biz** (☎ 5443 6111; 150 Alexandra Pde, Alexandra Headland; 1hr/2hr $8.50/12) hires out in-line skates with all the safety gear, as well as bicycles.

COOLUM & PEREGIAN

☎ 07 / pop 7000

You can soak up the sunshine and frolic in the sea without the crowds by heading to the peaceful beach towns of Coolum and Peregian. There's a small **visitors centre** (David Low Way; ✆ 9am-1pm Mon-Sat). The southern section of the Noosa National Park buffers the beach between Coolum and Peregian with coastal heath land and several walking trails.

Sleeping & Eating

Coolum Beach Resort (☎ 5471 7744; www.coolumbeachresort.com; 7-13 Beach Rd, Coolum Beach; r $135-95; ✆ ✆) The sunny, self-contained units at this complex in the heart of Coolum Beach reflect its trendy urban edge. All come with balconies and cable TV, and there's a spa and sauna on site where you can soak sun-kissed limbs.

Pacific Blue Apartments (☎ 5448 3611; www.sun.big.net.au/~pacificblue; 236 David Low Way, Peregian Beach; r $80-$85; ✆ ✆) This sapphire-coloured gem is close to the pub *and* the beach. Pacific Blue has cheerful studios and one-bedroom units, all self-contained with a healthy dose of space.

Villa Coolum (☎ 5446 1286; www.villacoolum.com; 102 Coolum Tce, Coolum; r $80; ✆) This modest row of bungalows is hidden behind a cool and leafy veranda. Each spacious and spotless bungalow is fitted out simply, and a great option for families. There's also a communal barbecue by the pool.

Coolum Beach Caravan Park (☎ 5446 1474, 1800 461 474; www.maroochypark.qld.gov.au; David Low Way, Coolum; tent sites $18-26, caravan sites $21-30) This wee council-run park is rudimentary but it's on a grassy plot in front of the beach and just across the road from Coolum's main strip.

Castro's Bar & Restaurant (☎ 5471 7555; cnr Frank St & Beach Rd, Coolum; mains $15-25; ✆ dinner) There's a definite zeal to the menu at this convivial restaurant. Delicious wood-fired pizzas are the speciality, or you could opt for a duck-wonton salad or risotto with corn, smoked chicken and macadamia.

There's a bakery and takeaway shops on David Low Way in Coolum Beach.

NOOSA
☎ 07 / pop 36,400

The vogue and vivacious of the Sunshine Coast have been marinating in Noosa's tropical vegetation, crystalline beaches and towering gum trees for more than 40 years. Its exclusive quality makes it popular with wealthy holiday-makers. Yet, despite the glut of stylish condominiums and swish restaurants, the beach and bush are still free, so the well heeled share the beat with flip-flops, board shorts and bronzed bikini bodies.

Noosa is undeniably developed, but the chichi landscape has been cultivated without losing sight of simple seaside pleasures. From the eastern 'Paris end' of bustling Hastings St, it's only a short walk to the beachfront Noosa National Park, thick with stunning views, bird life and native flora. The area north of the Noosa River is preserved as the Cooloola Section of the Great Sandy National Park, and offers great opportunities for four-wheel driving, hiking and kayaking.

Orientation

Noosa consists of three areas around the mouth of the Noosa River: Noosa Junction, Noosaville and Noosa Heads. The latter is the fanciest sibling with trendy Hastings St. Heading west along the river, you'll find Tewantin, the departure point for the Noosa River ferry. Around the headland from Noosa Heads on the eastern coast is the peaceful and ambient resort of Sunshine Beach, with some good surf breaks.

Information

There are ATMs and banks in the Noosa Junction area.

Adventure Travel Bugs (☎ 5474 8530, 1800 666 720; 9 Sunshine Beach Rd, Noosa Junction; per hr $1; ✆ 8am-8pm Mon-Fri, 9am-7pm Sat & Sun) Internet access.

Australia Post (☎ 5473 8591; 91 Noosa Dr)

Noosa visitors centre (☎ 5447 9088; www.tourism noosa.com.au; Hastings St, Noosa Heads; ✆ 9am-5pm) Extremely helpful and professional setup. Free tour- and accommodation-booking service.

Urban Mailbox (☎ 5473 5151; Shop 3, Ocean Breeze, Noosa Dr, Noosa Heads; per hr $6; ✆ 9am-9pm Mon-Fri, till 7pm Sat, 10am-7pm Sun) Superfast Internet access.

Sights

One of Noosa's best features, the small but lovely **Noosa National Park** extends 2km southwest from the headland that marks the end of the Sunshine Coast. It has fine walks, great coastal scenery and a string of bays on the north side with waves that draw surfers from all over the country. Alexandria Bay on the east side has the best beach, and is also an unofficial nudist beach.

The most scenic way to access it is to follow the boardwalk along the coast from town. This continues all the way to the park's main entrance at the end of Park Rd (the eastern continuation of Hastings St). Here you'll find a car park, picnic areas and the **QPWS centre** (☎ 5447 3243; ✆ 9am-3pm), where you can obtain a walking track map. Sleepy koalas are often spotted in the trees in the afternoon and dolphins are commonly seen from the rocky headlands around Alexandria Bay.

For a panoramic view of the park, you can walk or drive up to the **Laguna Lookout** from Viewland Dr in Noosa Junction. From Sunshine Beach, access to the park is via McAnally Dr or Parkedge Rd.

Activities
CANOEING & KAYAKING

The Noosa River is excellent for canoeing; it's possible to follow it up through Lakes Cooroibah and Cootharaba, and through the Cooloola Section of the Great Sandy National Park to just south of Rainbow Beach Rd. The Elanda Point Canoe Company (p343) rents canoes and kayaks from Elanda Point and can collect and return you from the bus stop at Sidoni St in Tewantin. See the full listing, p339 for tour options.

SUNSHINE COAST

NOOSA

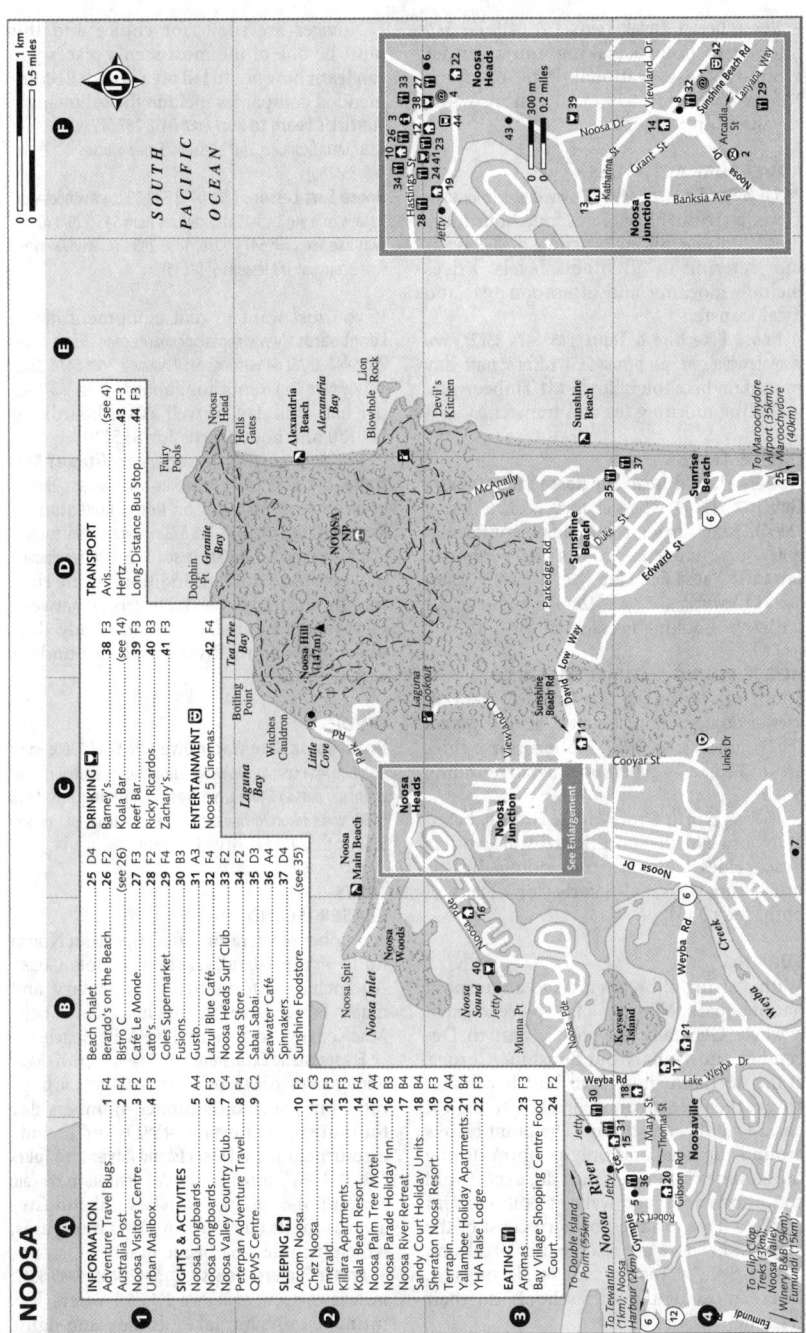

SUNSHINE COAST

Noosa Ocean Kayak Tours (☎ 0418 787 577) offers two-hour kayaking tours, either around Noosa National Park or along Noosa River, for $50. You can also hire kayaks from $40 a day.

ADVENTURE ACTIVITIES

Pedal & Paddle (☎ 5449 2671; www.pedalandpaddle .com.au; per person $70) operates four-hour tours that combine hiking, cycling and kayaking, catering to all fitness levels. Prices include morning and afternoon tea, and local transfers.

Noosa Bike Hire & Tours (☎ 5474 3322; www .noosabikehire.com; per person $55) offers half-day mountain bike tours down Mt Tinbeerwah, including morning tea and transfers.

GOLF & TENNIS

Golfers should head for **Noosa Valley Country Club** (☎ 5449 1411; Links Dr, Noosa Heads; 9/18 holes $20/35), which has an 18-hole championship golf course and tennis courts ($15 per hour). **Tewantin Noosa Golf Club** (☎ 5447 1407; Cooroy-Noosa Rd, Tewantin; 9/18 holes $22/35) is a quieter alternative. Booking is essential for both.

HORSE RIDING & CAMEL SAFARIS

South of Noosa **Clip Clop Treks** (☎ 5449 1254; info@clipcloptreks.com.au; Eumarella Rd, Lake Weyba; 2hr/day rides per person $60/145) offers horse rides around Lake Weyba and the surrounding bush.

Noosa North Shore Horse Riding, based at Noosa North Shore Retreat also offers beach rides and bush trail riding. Just as much fun is Camel Safaris (for details of both, see p343).

SURFING

With a string of breaks around an unspoilt national park, Noosa is a fine place to catch a wave. Generally the surf is best in December and January but Sunshine Corner, at the northern end of Sunshine Beach, has an excellent year-round break, although it has a brutal beach dump. The point breaks around the headland only perform during the summer but, when they do, expect wild conditions and good walls at Boiling Point and Tea Tree, on the northern coast of the headland. There are also gentler breaks on Noosa Spit, at the far end of Hastings St, where most of the surf schools do their training.

Novices are spoilt for choice and this must be one of the most scenic places you can learn how not to fall off a board. Recommended companies include the following. **Merrick's Learn to Surf** (☎ 0418 787 577; www .learntosurf.com.au; 2hr/2 lessons/5-day courses $45/85/180)

Noosa Surf Lessons (☎ 0412 330 850; www.noosasurf lessons.com.au; 1-/3-/5-day courses from $45/120/170) **Wavesense** (☎ 5474 9076, 1800 249 076; www.wave sense.com.au; 1/3 lessons $50/135)

If you just want to rent equipment, **Noosa Longboards** (www.noosalongboards.com; Noosa Heads ☎ 5447 2828; 64 Hastings St; Noosaville ☎ 5474 2722; 187 Gympie Tce) rents longboards for $30/45 per half-/full day, as well as surfboards for $20/30 and bodyboards for $15/20.

For kite-surfing lessons, try **Kitesurf Australia** (☎ 5455 6677; www.kite-surf.com.au; 2hr/4hr lesson per person $140/260) or **Noosa Adventures & Kite-Surfing** (☎ 0438 788 573; www.noosakitesurfing .com.au; per person 2hr/8hr lesson $120/380, equipment rental per hr/day $30/100). Conditions at the river mouth and Lake Weyba are best between October and January, but on windy days the choppy Noosa River is a playground for serious funsters.

DIVING

Both **Noosa Blue Water Dive** (☎ 5447 1300; www .fishingnoosa.com.au/DiveNoosa.htm; Noosa Harbour, Tewantin; per person $400) and **Resort 2 Diving** (☎ 5455 6488; www.resort2diving.com, Noosa Harbour; per person $350) offer PADI dive courses.

Tours
FRASER ISLAND

A number of operators offer trips from Noosa up to Fraser Island via the Cooloola Coast. All include informative commentary and major Fraser Island highlights such as Lake MacKenzie and Seventy Five Mile Beach.

Fraser Island Excursions (☎ 5449 0393; www.fraser islandexcursions.com.au; per person $160) gets a huge rap from readers. Its limited-numbers day tours are in comfortable 4WDs and include a gourmet lunch. **Fraser Island Adventure Tours** (☎ 5444 6957; www.fraserislandadventuretours.com.au; adult/child $145/105) has won several industry awards for its day tours in 4WD minibuses, which include a barbecue lunch.

Fraser Explorer Tours (☎ 5447 3845, 5449 8647; www.fraser-is.com; adult/child $115/65) offers less intimate tours but takes in the same sights and stops for lunch. **Trailblazer Tours** (☎ 4125 2343, 1800 626 673; 3-day safari adult/child $295/225) operates small-group tours and can pick up and drop off at either Noosa or Rainbow Beach. For more information about tours to Fraser Island see the boxed text, p360).

If you want to do it in style, several companies offer fly-drive packages including flights to Fraser Island and 4WD hire for self-guided day trips. Tours cost $250 to $300 per person:

Air Fraser Island (☎ 1800 247 992; www.airfraser island.com.au)

Fraser Island Heli-Drive (☎ 4125 3933, 1800 063 933; www.fraserislandco.com.au/helidrive.html)

Sunshine Coast Scenic Flights (☎ 5450 0516; www .noosaaviation.com)

EVERGLADES

Several companies run boats from the Noosa Harbour at Tewantin up the Noosa River into the 'Everglades' area – essentially the passage of the Noosa River that cuts into the Great Sandy National Park. Companies include the following:

Beyond Noosa (☎ 5449 9177, 1800 657 666; www .beyondnoosa.com.au) Morning tours adult/child $28/15. Day tours including lunch adult/child $70/30. All tours include Noosa transfers.

Everglades Water Bus Co (☎ 5447 1838, 1800 688 045) Four-hour tour adult/child $55/40. Six-hour tour including lunch adult/child $65/45. Tours include Noosa transfers.

MV Noosa Queen (☎ 5455 6661; adult/child incl lunch $38/19; ☯ tours 12.30pm) Lunchtime cruises up the river.

For the active among us, **Peterpan Adventure Travel** (☎ 1800 777 115; www.peterpans.com; Shop 3, 75 Noosa Dr, Noosa Junction; per person $130) offers three-day canoe tours into the park including all equipment. Alternatively, the **Elanda Point Canoe Company** (☎ 5485 3165, 1800 226 637; www .elanda.com.au/noosa; Elanda Point; per adult/child $60/50; ☯ tours 9.30am) offers three-hour canoe tours including transfers.

Sleeping

There are several budget hostels and caravan parks in among the glitzy resort hotels and apartments. With the exception of hostels, accommodation prices may rise by 50% in busy times and 100% in the December to January peak season. All prices quoted below are for the low season.

BUDGET

Sandy Court Holiday Units (☎ 5449 7225; fax 5473 0397; 30 James St, Noosaville; d $55-70; ☒) These self-contained units offer unbeatable value. The décor is a tad weary, with mix-and-match furnishings and crockery, but they're clean, comfortable and well managed. Multinight stays attract bargain rates.

YHA Halse Lodge (☎ 5447 3377, 1800 242 567; backpackers@halselodge.com.au; 2 Halse Lane, Noosa Heads; dm/d $27/70; ☐) This splendid timber Queenslander is a legend on the backpacker route for its colonial charm, good looks and lofty position. The dorms and kitchen are a little cramped, but the bar is a mix-and-meet bonanza and serves great meals ($6 to $11).

Koala Beach Resort (☎ 5447 3355, 1800 357 457; www.koala-backpackers.com; 44 Noosa Dr, Noosa Junction; dm $22, tw & d $55; ☐ ☒) One of the Koala chain, this hostel has the usual trademarks: popular bar, central location and party atmosphere. Your buck buys huge dorms, good facilities, professional staff and great grassy grounds to rest surf-weary bones.

Bougainvillia Holiday Park (☎ 5447 1712, 1800 041 444; jsjs@optusnet.com.au; 141 Cooroy-Noosa Rd, Tewantin; tent/caravan sites from $24/26, cabins $55-95; ☒ ☒) Neat as a pin and meticulously landscaped, this is the best camping option in the area. The facilities are spotless, and include an on-site café and petrol station; travellers in wheelchairs are well catered for. The park is about 2km west of Noosa.

MIDRANGE

Accommodation on Hastings St can be ridiculously expensive, but there are a few bargains in town. One of the best areas is along Gympie Tce, the riverside main road through Noosaville. **Accom Noosa** (☎ 1800 072 078; www.accomnoosa.com.au; Shop 5, Fairshore Apartments, Hastings St, Noosa Heads) has an extensive list of private holiday rentals, which are good for stays of a week or more.

Noosa Parade Holiday Inn (☎ 5447 4177; www .noosaparadeholidayinn.com; 51 Noosa Pde, Noosa Heads; r $110; ☒ ☒) These tiled and spotless apartments resemble an Ikea showroom, with cool interiors in bold colours. They face away from the street and passing traffic. Multinight stays attract discounts.

Noosa Valley Winery B&B (☎ 5449 1675; fax 5449 1679; 855 Eumundi Rd, Doonan; r $120; ☒) This pretty B&B is away from the bustle and incorporated into a boutique winery.

SUNSHINE COAST

Surrounded by thin pockets of bush and with a hint of the Mediterranean, the elegant rooms are swimming in sunlight and have private alcoves where breakfast is served. Is wheelchair-friendly.

Terrapin (☎ 5449 8770; www.terrapin.com.au; 15 The Cockleshell, Noosaville; r per night/week $140/580; ☒) If you're hanging about for a week or so, these two-storey townhouses are a good option. Bold furnishings and balconies or gardens lift the earthy interiors. All contain every mod con you need to sustain your stay.

Noosa River Retreat (☎ 5474 2811; pauline@esc apesresorts.com.au; cnr Weyba Rd & Reef St, Noosaville; r $75-85; ☒ ☒) This orderly complex houses spick, span and spacious units. On site are a central barbecue and laundry, and the corner units are almost entirely protected by small native gardens. It's a popular spot, so bookings are advised.

Killara Apartments (☎ 5447 2800; www.killara noosa.com; 42 Grant St, Noosa Junction; r per 3 nights/week from $280/630; ☒ ☒) These functional and modern units have plenty of space and colour. They're in a picturesque street, close to the river and Hastings St, and some come with private barbecues and courtyards. There's a three-night minimum stay.

Noosa Palm Tree Motel (☎ 5449 7311; fax 5474 3246; 233 Gympie Tce, Noosaville; r $80-95; ☒ ☒) Close to the water, this complex has sound motel rooms with kitchenettes and larger, fully equipped units with cheery furnishings. This is a practical option for beach-addicted kiddies.

Also recommended are the following:

Chez Noosa (☎ 5447 2027; www.cheznoosa.com.au; 263 David Low Way, Sunshine Beach; d $75-85; ☒) Modern, self-contained units low on flair but heavy on value and facilities.

Yallambee Holiday Apartments (☎ 5449 8632; 29 Weyba Rd, Noosaville; r from $65) Older-style building with individually owned units; spotless and shady.

TOP END

Sheraton Noosa Resort (☎ 5449 4888; www.starwood hotels.com/sheraton; 14-16 Hastings St, Noosa Heads; r from $280-400; ☒ ☒) Tastefully coordinated rooms contain sueded fabrics, fabulous beds, balconies, kitchenettes and spas. This five-star hotel has four bars, three restaurants, and a gym, sauna and spa. There are some great deals if you book online. Wheelchair-friendly.

Emerald (☎ 5449 6100, 1800 803 899; www.emerald noosa.com.au; 42 Hastings St, Noosa Heads; r $230-450; ☒ ☒) The stylish Emerald has indulgent rooms bathed in white and sunlight. Expect clean, crisp edges and exquisite furnishings. All rooms are self-contained and the mod cons are so lovely you'll miss them when you leave.

Eating

RESTAURANTS

Sabai Sabai (☎ 5473 5177; 46 Duke St; mains $22-28; ☒ lunch & dinner) Like the chilled village it resides in, inconspicuous Sabai Sabai is class without the brass. The Asian-infused menu shows moments of genius with items such as silken fried tofu with green pawpaw salad and kaffir limes or grilled cuttlefish with cashews, coconut and chilli.

Café Le Monde (☎ 5449 2366; Hastings St, Noosa Heads; mains $17-28; ☒ breakfast, lunch & dinner) Café Le Monde's enormous menu has fusspots and those with specific dietary requirements covered. The large, open-air patio buzzes with diners digging into burgers, seared tuna steaks, curries, pastas, salads and plenty more. Great for families and groups.

Cato's (☎ 5449 4888; 12-14 Hastings St, Noosa Heads; mains $18-26; ☒ breakfast, lunch & dinner) Cato's voluptuous bar beckons thirsty style cats with a dazzling array of alcoholic wares and an impressive wine list. Once they've soaked up the scene, refined punters savour European-inspired cuisine or hover over the spectacular seafood buffet ($60).

Spinnakers (☎ 5474 5177; Sunshine Beach SLSC, The Esplanade, Sunshine Beach; mains $15-25; ☒ lunch & dinner) This club bistro treats the taste buds with dinner dishes like braised lamb shanks with winter veggies and a tomato-celery sauce, or Indian bean and eggplant curry. The T-bones and fish dishes are enormous, while lunch is a tamer affair.

Seawater Café (☎ 5449 7215; 197 Gympie Tce, Noosaville; meals $8-20; ☒ breakfast, lunch & dinner) Mermaids, portholes and sea paraphernalia adorn the walls of this colourfully kitsch restaurant that serves excellent seafood. If you prefer something nonfishy, the nightly roast and daily sandwiches are also good.

Bistro C (☎ 5447 2855; On the Beach Arcade, Hastings St, Noosa Heads; mains $18-26; ☒ breakfast, lunch & dinner) This boisterous bistro is famous for its quirky people sculptures. The egg-fried

THE AUTHOR'S CHOICE

Gusto (☎ 5449 7144; 257 Gympie Tce, Noosaville; mains $17-30; ⏰ lunch & dinner) This outstanding restaurant must be the very definition of Modern Australian dining. The flawless menu will dazzle your taste buds with offerings such as Mooloolaba prawn and garlic ravioli with leek confit and lemon *beurre* (butter), or melt-in-your-mouth crisp-fried cuttlefish salad with Persian fetta, roasted roma tomatoes and olives. The extensive wine list is discerning and the atmosphere epitomises coastal chic: large open bay windows flush the crisp, white interior with a balmy sea breeze and sunlight. The service is utterly perfect.

calamari with chilli lime coriander dip is legendary and you get to wine and dine in a wonderful location overlooking the beach.

Also recommended are the following:

Berardo's on the Beach (☎ 5448 0888; 49 Hastings St, Noosa Heads; dishes $10-26; ⏰ lunch & dinner) Excellent Asian, Italian and Middle Eastern flavours served with stunning beachside views.

Noosa Heads Surf Club (☎ 5474 5688; Hastings St; mains $10-20; ⏰ breakfast Sat & Sun, lunch & dinner daily) Popular surf club serving good club grub.

CAFÉS & QUICK EATS

Sunshine Foodstore (☎ 5474 5611; 46 Duke St, Sunshine Beach; dishes $6-14; ⏰ breakfast & lunch) This ambient outdoor café has long wooden benches attended by many a local ploughing through newspapers and conquering crosswords. Brekkies include plenty of egg options with fresh pesto and veggies. For lunch you can savour gargantuan ciabattas, and the cakes are exhausting.

Aromas (☎ 5474 9788; 32 Hastings St, Noosa Heads; mains $16-25; ⏰ breakfast, lunch & dinner) Aromas' Parisian-style seating confronts the street with outward-facing tables. You might choose Victorian lamb for main followed by panna cotta with strawberry-rhubarb soup from the brief menu. Most come for the coffee and atmosphere.

Fusions (☎ 5474 1699; 271 Gympie Tce, Noosaville; mains $15-20; ⏰ breakfast, lunch & dinner) The wide-open doorways usher in beach breezes enjoyed by patrons propped on high-backed Balinese chairs inside, or slouching at the oversized tables outside. Gourmet sand-

wiches, woodfired pizzas and spruced-up café fare graces the menu. It's also an ideal breakfast spot.

Beach Chalet (☎ 5447 3944; 3 Tingira Cres, Sunrise Beach; dishes $5-8; ⏰ breakfast & lunch) A sneeze south of Sunshine Beach, this small café in Sunrise Beach is just a small extension of a general store. The brekkies, burgers and sandwiches border on legendary, as do the views of the breakers.

Lazuli Blue Café (☎ 5448 0055; 9 Sunshine Beach Rd, Noosa Junction; meals $7-12; ⏰ breakfast & lunch) Celebrating slow living, this relaxed café specialises in colossal fresh juices and smoothies. The breakfasts, Turkish toasties, salads and meatier dishes such as Cajun chicken are pretty special too.

You can eat well for around $8 at the **Bay Village Shopping Centre food court** (Hastings St, Noosa Heads). Self-caterers can head to the **Noosa Store** (33 Hastings St, Noosa Heads), **Action supermarket** (Plaza Shopping Centre, Sunshine Beach Rd, Noosa Junction) or **Coles Supermarket** (Noosa Fair Shopping Centre, Lanyana Way, Noosa Junction).

Drinking

Zachary's (☎ 5447 3211; 30 Hastings St, Noosa Heads) Set back and above Hastings St, this slinky bar imbues a splash of urban cool into Noosa's coastal milieu. Dark colours, dim lighting and ambient beats swirl about trendy young things getting down to the business of being cool.

Ricky Ricardos (☎ 5447 2455; The Wharf, Quamby Pl, Noosa Heads) This genial bar is a great spot for cocktails, sultry Latin music and partaking in some meet-and-greet action. The snappy bar staff and waterfront location add to the sophisticated air.

Barney's (☎ 5447 4800; Noosa Dr, Noosa Heads) A bit of an all-day drinking bonanza, this outdoor bar plays a relentless soundtrack of loud music to an appreciative crowd. Threads shift from board shorts to strappy heels and shirts as the sun goes down.

Koala Bar (☎ 5447 3355; 44 Noosa Dr, Noosa Junction) Noosa's backpackers and other free spirits start their nightly revelry at this popular hostel bar. Live rock music fills every crevice several nights a week and, when it doesn't, the place hums to the harmony of beery chatter and beer tunes.

Reef Bar (☎ 5447 4477; 9 Noosa Dr, Noosaville) A little bit country, a little bit coastal and a whole lot Oz, the Reef Bar is a cruisy watering hole with a strong local feel. You've every chance of grasping the secrets of Australian football while listening to Australian rock or dancing to doof doof.

Entertainment

Noosa 5 Cinemas (☎ 1300 366 339; 29 Sunshine Beach Rd, Noosa Junction) This plush, comfortable cinema screens the latest blockbusters.

Getting There & Away

Long-distance buses stop at the bus stop near the corner of Noosa Dr and Noosa Pde. All of Noosa's hostels have courtesy buses that will pick up from the bus stop (except YHA Halse Lodge – it's only 100m away).

Both **Greyhound** (☎ 13 14 99; www.greyhound .com.au) and **Premier** (☎ 13 34 10; www.premierms .com.au) have two connections to Brisbane daily ($24, 2½ hours), as well as destinations north including Hervey Bay ($27, 3½ hours). Suncoast Pacific also connects Noosa and Brisbane; see p327 for more information.

Sunbus (☎ 13 12 30; www.sunbus.com.au) has frequent services between Maroochydore and Noosa ($4.40, one hour) and between Noosa and Nambour train station ($4.40, one hour). It also connects Noosa with Caloundra ($5.20, 1½ hours).

Getting Around

BICYCLE

Noosa Bike Hire & Tours (☎ 5474 3322; www.noosa bikehire.com; 4hr/full day $15/20) hires bicycles out from several locations in Noosa including Halse Lodge. Alternatively, it'll deliver and collect the bikes to/from your door for free.

BOAT

Riverlight Ferry (☎ 5449 8442) operates ferries between Noosa Heads and Tewantin (adult/child/family $9.50/4/25, all-day pass $13.50/5/35; 30 minutes; six to 10 daily). Tickets include on-board commentary, so it's something of a tour as well as a people mover.

BUS

During peak holiday seasons – 26 December to 10 January and over Easter – there are free shuttle buses every 10 to 15 minutes between Weyba Rd, just outside Noosa Junction, travelling all the way to Tewantin, and stopping just about everywhere

between. **Sunbus** (☎ 13 12 30; www.sunbus.com .au) has local services linking Noosa Heads, Noosaville and Noosa Junction.

CAR

The **Other Car Rental Company** (☎ 5447 2831; www.noosacarrental.com; per day from $45) delivers cars and 4WDs to your door. The big guns are also in town and rent cars from around $35 per day. They include **Avis** (☎ 5447 4933; Shop 1, Ocean Breeze Resort, cnr Hastings St & Noosa Dr, Noosa Heads) and **Hertz** (☎ 5447 2253; Noosa Blue Resort, 16 Noosa Drive, Noosa Heads).

COOLOOLA COAST

The Cooloola Coast is a 50km stretch of sandy beach between Noosa and Rainbow Beach, backed by the Cooloola Section of the Great Sandy National Park. Although this area is relatively undeveloped, it teems with 4WDs and tinnies, which can disturb the peace. If you head off on foot or by canoe along the many inlets and waterways, you'll soon escape the crowds.

From the end of Moorindil St in Tewantin, the **Noosa North Shore Ferry** (☎ 5447 1321; pedestrians/cars $1/5; ☺ 5am-12.30am Fri & Sat, 6am-10.30pm Sun-Thu) shuttles across the river to Noosa North Shore taking a few minutes. If you have a 4WD you can drive up the beach from Noosa North Shore to Rainbow Beach (and on up to Inskip Point, where you can take a ferry across to Fraser Island), but check the tide times before setting out.

On the way up the beach you'll pass the Teewah coloured sand cliffs, estimated to be about 40,000 years old, and the rusting *Cherry Venture*, a 3000-tonne freighter swept ashore by a cyclone in 1973.

Great Sandy National Park

The Cooloola Section of the Great Sandy National Park covers more than 54,000 hectares from Lake Cootharaba north to Rainbow Beach. It's a varied wilderness area with long sandy beaches, mangrove-lined waterways, forest, heath and lakes, all with plentiful bird life and lots of wild flowers in spring.

The Cooloola Way, which runs from Tewantin up to Rainbow Beach, is open to 4WD vehicles unless there's been heavy rain; check with the rangers before setting out. Most people prefer to barrel up the beach, though you're restricted to a few hours either side of low tide.

Although there are many 4WD tracks running to lookout points and picnic grounds, the best way to see Cooloola is by boat or canoe, along the numerous tributaries of the Noosa River. Boats can be hired from Tewantin and Noosa (along Gympie Terrace), Boreen Point and Elanda Point.

There are some fantastic walking trails starting from Elanda Point on the shore of Lake Cootharaba, including the 46km Cooloola Wilderness Trail that goes to Rainbow Beach and a 7km trail to the **QPWS information centre** (☎ 5449 7364; ☷ 7am-4pm) at Kinaba Island.

Before you go, pop into the **QPWS Great Sandy Information Centre** (☎ 5449 7792; 240 Moorindil St, Tewantin; ☷ 7am-4pm), which can provide information on park access, tide times and fire bans within the park, as well as issuing camping permits for the Great Sandy National Park, and car and camping permits for Fraser Island.

There are around 15 camping grounds in the park, many of them along the river. The most popular (and best equipped) camp sites are Fig Tree Point, at the northern end of Lake Cootharaba, Harry's Hut about 4km upstream, and Freshwater, about 6km south of Double Island Point on the coast. You can also camp on the beach if you're driving up to Rainbow Beach. Standard national park rates (per person/family $4/16) apply and you must purchase permits for all camping grounds along the river at Elanda ranger's station. You can purchase permits for Harry's Hut, Fig Tree Point, Freshwater and all beach camping at the QPWS Great Sandy Information Centre. Apart from Harry's Hut and Freshwater, all sites are accessible by hiking or river only.

Lake Cooroibah

A couple of kilometres north of Tewantin, the Noosa River widens into Lake Cooroibah. If you take the ferry across the Noosa River, you can drive up to the lake in a conventional vehicle and camp along sections of the beach.

Camel Safaris (☎ 5442 4402; www.camelcompany .com.au; Beach Rd, Noosa North Shore; 1hr adult/child $40/30, 2hr adult/child $55/45) operates glorious camel treks along the beach. Die-hards will also love the six-day Fraser Island safari (adult/child $1400/850).

Noosa North Shore Horse Riding (☎ 5447 1369; 1hr/2hr rides per person $40/70), based at Noosa North Shore Retreat (following), operates great rides along Teewah Beach and through the surrounding bush.

Noosa North Shore Retreat (☎ 5447 1706; www .noosanorthshore.com.au; Beach Rd; tent/caravan sites from $14/19.50, r from $70, cabins from $90; ⊠ ☒) is a sprawling park with an accommodation option for everyone, from camping to cottages. There's also a **pub** (mains $8-15; ☷ lunch & dinner) and small shop. Activities on offer include bushwalking, canoeing, fishing, tennis and horse riding.

Gagaju (☎ 5474 3522, 1300 302 271; www.travo holic.com/gagaju/; 118 Johns Dr, Tewantin; tent sites $11, dm $17) is a riverside ecowilderness camp with basic dorms constructed entirely out of recycled timber. The folk who head here love the rustic digs. Activities include canoeing, mountain biking and bushwalking. You need to bring your own food, and the Gagaju minibus shuttles to and from Noosa three times a day.

Lake Cootharaba & Boreen Point

Cootharaba is the biggest lake in the Cooloola Section, measuring about 5km across and 10km in length. On the western shores of the lake and at the southern edge of the national park, Boreen Point is a relaxed little community with several places to stay and eat. The lake is the gateway to the Noosa Everglades, offering bushwalking, canoeing and bush camping.

From Boreen Point, an unsealed road leads another 5km up to **Elanda Point**, where there's a **ranger station** (☎ 5485 3245; ☷ 7am-4pm) and the headquarters of the **Elanda Point Canoe Company** (☎ 5485 3165, 1800 226 637; www.elanda.com.au/noosa; Elanda Point; per day for 1 or 2 people $25), which rents canoes and kayaks. If you want to do a self-guided safari up the river, this company also rents camping equipment, arranges permits and organises transfers from Noosa. If it's just the transport you're after, they'll shuttle you up to Kinaba or Fig Tree Point (one way $25) and Harry's Hut ($45) camping grounds. Rates are much cheaper if you rent a canoe. **Everglades Waterfront Holidays** (☎ 5485 3164; Boreen Point Pde, Boreen Point) also rents kayaks, charging $45 per day ($15 for subsequent days); see p338 for more information on guided tours to the area.

The gorgeous old **Apollonian Hotel** (☎ 5485 3100; fax 5485 3499; Laguna St, Boreen Point; dm/d with shared bathroom $25/45; mains $12; ☻ lunch & dinner) has sturdy timber walls, shady verandas and a beautifully preserved interior. Rooms are in the Queenslander out the back and the pub grub is tasty and popular.

The two self-contained units at **Lake Cootharaba Gallery Units** (☎ 5485 3153; 64 Laguna St, Boreen Point; r per night/week from $80/400) are both homey and practical. The gallery they're attached to is a tad out there, and the hosts are lovely.

On a serene strip by the river, the quiet and simple **Boreen Point Caravan & Camping Area** (☎ 5485 3244; Dun's Beach, Teewah St, Boreen Point; tent sites $12) is dominated by large gums and native bush. Take a right turn off Laguna St on to Vista St and bear right at the lake.

LANDSBOROUGH TO COOROY VIA THE BRUCE HWY

The Blackall Range rises a short distance inland from the coast, with spectacular countryside, some appealing national parks, and numerous (rather chintzy) rustic villages, full of Devonshire tearooms, antique shops and craft emporiums. There are plenty of tours, but it's worth coming up here with your own transport as the landscape between villages is the real attraction.

Tours

Plenty of tour companies operate through the hinterland. Most combine a trip through the Blackall Range with other attractions like the Glass House Mountains, the Big Pineapple, the Ginger Factory or Australia Zoo, and will pick up from anywhere along the Sunshine Coast.

Mystic Mountain Tours (☎ 5445 7874; www.mystic mountaintours.com.au; adult/child $40/30) Operates excellent small-group tours. It has set itineraries but can tailor a trip to your preference.

Off Beat Rainforest Tours (☎ 5473 5135; www.off beattours.com.au; adult/child $125/80) In a similar vein to Mystic Mountain Tours, Off Beat offers excellent 4WD ecotours to Canondale National Park, including morning tea, lunch and transfers.

Storyline Tours (☎ 5474 1500; adult/child $65/30) Another good operator, with small-group tours to Montville and nearby rainforests and wineries, and to the Glass House Mountains.

Henry's Tours (☎ 5474 0199; adult/child $55/20) Offers the same as Storyline Tours.

Nambour & Yandina

Nambour is the main commercial centre in the hinterland, but there's little to wow travellers.

The **Big Pineapple** (☎ 5442 1333; www.bigpine apple.com.au; Nambour Connection Rd, Nambour; ☻ 9am-5pm) is one of Queensland's kitschy big things. You can walk through the 15m-high fibreglass 'fruit' itself for free but the main attractions lie beyond. A plantation train tour (adult/child $11.50/9.50) takes you through the pineapple fields with informative commentary on everything you wanted to know about growing a lot of pineapples. There are also tours through macadamia orchards and rainforests ($9.70/8) and a harvest boat ride ($9.70/8) through hydroponic waterways. If you want to do the lot you can buy a combined ticket ($26/21). Don't forget to spend more money at the souvenir shop.

On the Bruce Hwy about 7km north of the Big Pineapple is Yandina, where you'll find the **Ginger Factory** (☎ 5446 7096; 50 Pioneer Rd; admission free; ☻ 9am-5pm), a tacky souvenir store-cum-attraction. There are train rides, factory and plantation tours and, of course, a huge range of ginger products and souvenirs on sale.

Spirit House Restaurant (☎ 5446 8994, 4 Ninderry Rd, Yandina; mains $23-33; ☻ lunch daily, dinner Wed-Sat) is a legendary stop on this route. The subtropical surrounds create an authentic Southeast Asian setting, while the kitchen creates Thai-infused innovations such as whole crispy reef fish with tamarind and chilli or salmon spring rolls with sambal dressing.

Nambour is on the main coastal train line, and is well connected to Brisbane by frequent **Citytrain** (☎ 13 12 30; www.citytrain.com .au) services ($11.60, 1¾ hours). **Sunbus** (☎ 13 12 30; www.sunbus.com.au) runs regular buses from the train station to Noosa ($4.40, one hour) via Eumundi and Yandina.

Eumundi

☎ 07 / pop 463

Sweet little Eumundi has the quaint ambience of a highland village thawed generously by the coast, only a whiff away. There's a pervading new-age vibe running through the main street, amplified greatly during its famous Saturday **market** when thousands of visitors descend to potter through the

---

DETOUR: MAPLETON FALLS NATIONAL PARK

From Mapleton, instead of heading east and back to the Bruce Hwy, head west on to Obi Obi Rd. A few kilometres out of town is the wee but pretty Mapleton Falls National Park, where Pencil Creek plunges 120m down into Obi Obi Valley. There's a lookout point just a couple of hundred metres from the car park and several walking tracks with loads of colourful bird life.

If you head further west for around 18km you'll come to Kenilworth, where you should take a breather at **Kenilworth Country Foods** (☎ 5446 0144; 45 Charles St; ☺ 9am-4pm Mon-Fri, 10.30am-3.30pm Sat & Sun), which sells wickedly good cheeses and ice creams.

Heading north, the Kenilworth–Brooloo Rd snakes its way past the Imbil State Forest on the left-hand side. Traditional old farmhouses dot the scenic route, in between the occasional mountain and floods of jacarandas.

After 23km turn right (east) on to the Tuchekoi Rd, which travels for 5km before a T-junction at Kenilworth-Skyring Creek Rd. Turn left (north) for 6km and you'll be back on the Bruce Hwy near Eumundi.

200-plus stalls. You'll find everything here, from home-made cheese graters to aromatic sneeze abators, and then there's the clothing, food and music. The market is open from 6.30am to 2pm every Saturday, and a smaller version is held on Wednesdays from 8am to 1.30pm.

The town's other claim to fame is **Eumundi Lager**, originally brewed in the Imperial Hotel. Nowadays it's made down at Yatala on the Gold Coast, but you can still sample it on tap in the Imperial Hotel. The former brewing room is now an art gallery with glass-blowing displays.

The fairly small **Eumundi Historical Museum** (☎ 5442 8762; Memorial Dr; admission free; ☺ 9am-4.30pm Wed & Fri, till 3pm Sat) offers an insight to the town's history.

About 10km northwest of Eumundi, the little village of **Pomona** sits in the shadow of looming Mt Cooroora (440m), and is home to the wonderful **Majestic Theatre** (☎ 5485 2330), one of the only places in the world where you can see a silent movie accompanied by the original Wurlitzer organ soundtrack. The Majestic only plays one film, Rudolph Valentino's last screen performance, *The Son of the Sheik*, every Thursday at 8.30pm (which it's done every Thursday for 13 years); seats cost $6.

SLEEPING & EATING

Taylor's Damn Fine B&B (☎ 5442 8685; www.taylors bandb.com.au; 1502 Eumundi-Noosa Rd; d incl breakfast $120-75) The damn fine rooms in this pleasant B&B are a well-designed combination of antique Oz and contemporary class. All have private balconies and bar fridges or there are simpler rooms in the converted railcar in the garden. It's about 1km from Eumundi on the Noosa road.

Eumundi Rise B&B (☎ 5442 8855; www.eumundi risebandb.com.au; 37-39 Crescent Rd; s/d from $90/125) Behind a sweeping veranda, this attractive Queenslander is home to neat and pleasant rooms. There are tea- and coffee-making facilities and it's wheelchair-friendly.

Eumundi Caravan Park (☎ 5442 8411; fax 5442 7414; 141 Memorial Dr; tent/caravan sites $16/19; ☒) About 1km north of the centre of town, this pretty caravan park has plenty of flat grass and tree clusters. Outside school holidays you should get plenty of space to yourself.

Treefellers Cafe (☎ 5442 7766; 69 Memorial Dr; mains $13-22; ☺ breakfast & lunch Wed-Sun, dinner Fri & Sat) Eumundi's most cosmopolitan eatery extends itself under a beautiful timber shelter, and treats your palate to global dishes such as Moroccan spiced chicken salad, almond and ricotta gnocchi or grilled Atlantic salmon.

Imperial Hotel (☎ 5442 8303; Memorial Dr; ☺ breakfast Wed & Sat, lunch Tue-Sun, dinner Tue-Sat) The Queensland drawl is thick behind the bar at this big old timber pub. There's a breezy, shady beer garden where you can dig into hearty pub nosh, and live music or comedy on the weekend.

GETTING THERE & AWAY

Sunbus (☎ 13 12 30; www.sunbus.com.au) buses 631 and 630 ($4, one hour, roughly hourly) head to Eumundi from Noosa Heads, stopping in the centre of town. Alternatively, both **Storeyline Tours** (☎ 5474 1500; www.sunshine coastdaytours.com.au) and **Henry's** (☎ 5474 0199)

SUNSHINE COAST

offer door-to-door transfers from Noosa accommodation (adult/child $15/10, 30 minutes, Wednesday and Saturday), allowing around two hours at the markets. **Everglades Water Bus Co** (☎ 5447 1838, 1800 688 045; adult/child $65/50) does a Eumundi Markets tour every Saturday, which also includes a cruise on the Everglades.

MALENY
☎ 07 / pop 1108

Beautiful Maleny nestles on a rolling patch of hinterland and complements the wealth of greenery surrounding it with a quirky bohemian edge. There's a refreshing lack of tacky heritage developments and ye olde tourist-trap shoppes. Maple St – the main drag – offers pleasant street cafés and craft shops selling work by local artists.

There's a small **visitors centre** (☎ 5499 9033; www.tourmaleny.com.au; Maple St; �ও 9am-5pm) at the Maleny Community Centre. Maleny has a craft market on Sunday morning.

Mary Cairncross Scenic Reserve (☎ 5499 9907; Mountain View Rd; admission free; �ও 8am-6pm) is a pristine rainforest shelter spread over 52 hectares southeast of town. A plethora of Queensland plants, including spectacular strangler fig trees, inhabits the area, as does a healthy range of bird life and cute pademelons. Wheelchair-friendly tracks enable visitors to traverse the park without damaging the ecosystem. The best time to visit is early morning or late afternoon, when the birds are most active.

Sleeping

Maleny Lodge Guest House (☎ 5494 2370; www .malenylodge.com; 58 Maple St; s incl breakfast $95-140, d incl breakfast $130-85; ☒) This rambling B&B boasts a myriad of gorgeous rooms with four-poster beds and lashings of stained wood and antiques. There's an open fire for cold winter days and an open pool house for warm summer ones.

Maleny Palms Tourist Park (☎ 5494 2933; bookings@malenypalms.com.au; 23 Macadamia Dr; tent sites $22, cabins $70-80, villas $95-120; ☒) Northwest of the centre, this tidy park has villas the size of small houses and simpler self-contained cabins. The grounds are beautifully landscaped with native flora but the camp sites aren't much to write home about.

Also recommended are the following:

Maleny Hills Motel (☎ 5494 2551; www.malenyhills .com.au; 932 Montville Rd; s/d from $60/70; ℗ ☒) Comfortable and clean motel option.

Maleny Hotel (☎ 5494 2013; fax 5494 3108; 6 Bunya St; s/d $55/70) Basic rooms with shared bath upstairs in this convivial pub.

Eating

Maleny is known for its fine dining, with several very posh restaurants just south of the centre. There are several good cafés along Maple St.

Terrace (☎ 5494 3700; Mary Cairncross Corner; mains $25-30; �ও lunch & dinner) One of Queensland's best, this award winner serves delectable seafood and spectacular views of the Glass House Mountains. If you're ravenous, try the Moreton Bay bugs, king prawns, salmon and mahi mahi served on a sizzling granite tile with vegetable skewers, wild rice and garlic aïoli.

Up Front Club (☎ 5494 2592; 31 Maple St; dishes $6-9; �ও breakfast Mon-Sat, lunch Mon-Fri, dinner daily) This cosy little café injects funk by the bucketful into Maleny's main strip, with organic breads, and tofu and tempeh salads. Live music takes to the stage Friday to Sunday nights (cover charges $5 to $8) and you'll catch anything from reggae to a bout of folk. Musicians are welcome to the blackboard sessions on Monday evenings. Food is limited to snacks so don't pack your appetite.

Perry's (☎ 5494 2822; 76 Maple St; mains $14-26; �ও dinner) The chef at this intimate restaurant fills the menu with goodies like prawn and calamari curry with lime leaves, and the drunken chocolate sponge with Belgian chocolate sauce and macadamias will leave you with that choco-intoxicated slur. Perry's also does Thai takeaway ($12 to $18).

Monicaz Cafe & Deli (☎ 5494 2670; 11/43 Maple St; mains $7-15; �ও breakfast & lunch) Snazzy Monicaz dishes up excellent lamb and asparagus stacks, grilled tofu salad, Sicilian risotto balls and spicy Mexican tortillas. There are no packets to be found: it's all home-made in this kitchen and the coffee is excellent.

Fraser Coast

For a relatively small stretch, the Fraser Coast embraces a lot: it's a sparsely populated patch where the horizon is always visible over plantations or parkland, and is home to the undisputedly beautiful and unique Fraser Island.

The world's largest sand island, Fraser Island is a magnet for outdoorsy types. Its long forest-backed beach draws thrill-seeking four-wheel drivers, and its thick forests and luminous lakes are favoured by bushwalkers. Walking trails lead hikers through the sand, under the rainforest canopy, around lakes and over sandblows. You can take the whole lot in whether you're travelling five star or camping out under the stars.

On either side of the island are contrasting gateways. Tiny Rainbow Beach hooks avid fisher folk with its deserted beaches, but you don't need to cast a line to enjoy the views of the vivid coloured cliffs. At the other end is Hervey Bay, a coastal community with a suburban hum. From July to October whales stream into the bay to chill out before continuing their trek south to the Antarctica – a humbling sight.

Bundaberg, the largest city in the area, is the home of Queensland's favourite spirit, Bundaberg rum, made from local cane sugar. It's also the gateway to numerous natural attractions in the area. The two ladies of the Southern Reef Islands, Lady Musgrave and Lady Elliot Islands, graciously give themselves over to nature lovers, offering snorkelling and hiking opportunities. Between November and March the beach at Mon Repos becomes a nursery – from which teeny turtles emerge and make a dash to the sea.

HIGHLIGHTS

- Discovering the dunes of enigmatic **Fraser Island** (p357)
- Being on the water with the gentle giants of **Hervey Bay** (p353)
- Copping an eyeful of colour at Rainbow Beach's coloured cliffs at the **Carlo Sandblow** (p350)
- Appreciating the past in the gracious architecture of **Maryborough** (p351)
- Witnessing turtles make their first stumble down the beach at **Mon Repos** (p366)
- Getting acquainted with the ladies of the Southern Reef Islands: **Lady Musgrave** and **Lady Elliot Islands** (p367)

Lady ★ Musgrave Island   Lady Elliot ★ Island

Mon Repos ★   Hervey Bay ★

Maryborough ★   ★ Fraser Island

Carlo Sandblow ★

- TELEPHONE CODE: 07
- www.frasercoastholidays.info

FRASER COAST

GYMPIE TO MARYBOROUGH

GYMPIE

☎ 07 / pop 10,600

Gympie sprang up virtually overnight after gold was discovered here in 1867, but the excitement of the gold rush ended long ago. It's now a peaceful little town that ambles along, and it makes a perfect place to stretch the legs and nibble on a snippet of rural Queensland. The town was named Gympie after *gimpi gimpi*, the Aboriginal name for a local tree (see the boxed text, p440).

Orientation

The Bruce Hwy forms the western border of town, and changes its name several times to River Rd, Wickham St, Rove St, Violet St and Chatsworth St as it heads north, before reverting back to the Bruce Hwy. Most activity hums along Mary, Nash and O'Connell Sts, which run more or less parallel to the highway.

Information

Cooloola Regional Development Bureau (www .cooloola.org.au; Gympie ☎ 5483 6656; 224 Mary St, Gympie; ⏰ 9am-5pm; Lake Alford ☎ 5483 6411; Bruce Hwy, Gympie; ⏰ 8.30am-4pm; Matilda ☎ 5483 5554; Matilda Service Centre, Bruce Hwy; ⏰ 9am-5pm) There are three offices, all of which can provide information for the whole of the Fraser Coast. They also stock the (free) *Heritage Walking Tour Map*, which details Gympie's relics of the gold-mining days.

Queensland Parks & Wildlife Service (QPWS) office (☎ 1300 130 372, 5482 4189; O'Connell St; ⏰ 8.15am-5pm Mon-Fri) Can provide general information but no permits for Fraser Island or Great Sandy National Park. For these you'll need to head to the office at Rainbow Beach (p350) or Tewantin (p343).

Sights & Activities

The **Cooloola Shire Public Gallery** (☎ 5482 0733; 39 Nash St; admission free; ⏰ 10am-4pm Wed-Fri, 11am-4pm Sat & Sun) displays temporary exhibits of Australian art, with a third of the gallery devoted to local works. There are sporadic talks and lectures by visiting artists.

The **Gympie Gold Mining & Historical Museum** (☎ 5482 3995; 215 Brisbane Rd; adult/child $8.80/4.40;

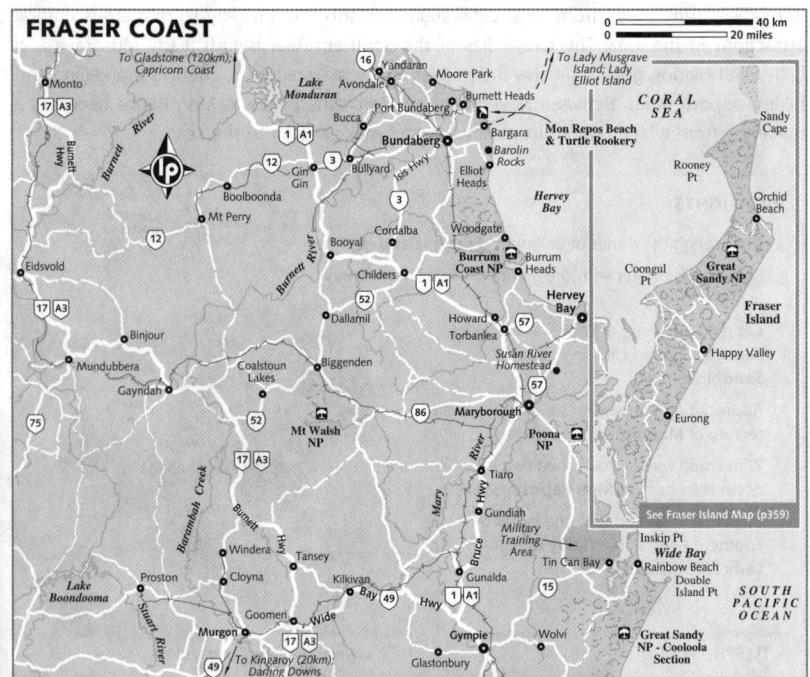

⊙ 9am-4.30pm) has a large collection of mining equipment and functioning steam-driven engines. It also offers the more traditional exhibits of a historical museum.

The lucrative forestry industry, which has been intrinsic to the region's character, is well depicted at the **Woodworks Forestry & Timber Museum** (☎ 5483 7691; cnr Fraser Rd & Bruce Hwy; adult/student $4/2; ⊙ 9am-4pm Mon-Fri, 1-4pm Sun). Machines, trucks and wagons from all stages of the industry's history are on display with informative documentation.

The **Valley Rattler steam train** (☎ 5482 2750; www.thevalleyrattler.com; adult/child half-day tour $24/12, full-day tour $30/15) runs the 40km from the old Gympie train station on Tozer St to the tiny township of Imbil and back, departing Gympie on Wednesday and Sunday morning at 10am. At 10am on Saturday there are half-day tours that go to Amamoor, 20km away.

Sleeping & Eating

Gympie Muster Inn (☎ 5482 8666; fax 5482 8601; 21 Wickham St; d $100; ⊠) This popular motel is centrally located and has a summery décor. Spotless rooms have free cable TV, telephones, mini bars, and facilities for tea- and coffee making.

Great Eastern Motor Inn (☎ 5482 7288, 1800 072 093; gteasternmi@bigpond.com; 27-29 Geordie Rd; d from $95; ⊠ ⊠) The rooms at this pretty spot just south of town are on the larger side and well equipped. For a few bucks more you can have a room with a view, and there's a wheelchair-friendly room.

Gympie Caravan Park (☎ 5483 6800; gympark @tpg.com.au; 1 Jane St; camp sites $15, caravan sites $18.50, cabins $40-55; ⊠ ⊠) Gympie's camping option is central but a little on the cramped side. There are plenty of trees on the grounds and there's a good mix of accommodation:

from good-value self-contained cabins to the smattering of camp sites.

Kingston House Impressions (☎ 5483 6733; 11 Channon St; mains $16-28; ⊙ lunch & dinner Tue-Sat) This classy restaurant, situated in a beautiful sprawling Queenslander (that's the type of house), serves mostly seafood with international flavours. There's also red meat and tapas on the menu. The wine list is excellent and you could spend way too long on the veranda or on a suede couch inside.

Imperial Hotel (☎ 5482 1506; 170 Mary St; mains $8-15; ⊙ breakfast, lunch & dinner) The striking Imperial is Gympie's most attractive pub but the setup inside is no-nonsense. The bar is made for downing cold beers and the functional bistro serves hot and simple pub grub.

Getting There & Away

Greyhound Australia (☎ 13 14 99; www.greyhound .com.au) services Gympie from Noosa ($15, two hours, three daily) and Hervey Bay ($20, 1½ to two hours, frequently). **Premier** (☎ 13 34 10; www.premierms.com.au) operates the same routes (once daily). All long-distance coaches stop at the Gympie Transit Centre, which is also the head office for **Polley's Coaches** (☎ 5482 2700; 28 Duke St). Polley's has buses to Rainbow Beach ($13.50, 1¾ hours), departing from the Transit Centre at 6am, 1.30pm and 3pm Monday to Friday. See p351 for return journey details.

Traveltrain (☎ 1300 131 722; www.traveltrain.com .au) operates *Tilt Train* (adult/child $36/18, 2½ hours, one to three daily) and *Sunlander* (adult/child $36/18, 2½ hours, four times weekly), which travel from Brisbane to Gympie on the way to Rocky and Cairns. The **train station** (Tozer St) is 1km east of the centre.

RAINBOW BEACH

☎ 07 / pop 1050

The tiny township of Rainbow Beach is at the base of the Inskip Peninsula. Rainbow Beach's coloured cliffs arc their way around stunning Wide Bay, offering a sweeping panorama from the lighthouse at Double Island Point in the south to Fraser Island in the north. Beyond Double Island Point is the Cooloola Section of **Great Sandy National Park**, with the rusting hulk of the *Cherry Venture*, a Singaporean freighter blown ashore by heavy winds in 1973. With a 4WD it's possible to drive all the way to Noosa. See p342 for more information.

FRASER COAST

Information

QPWS office (☎ 5486 3160; Rainbow Beach Rd; ⏱ 7am-4pm) Permits for Fraser Island.

Rainbow Beach visitors centre (☎ 5486 3227; 8 Rainbow Beach Rd; ⏱ 7am-6pm) Privately run and moderately helpful.

Rainbow Photographics (☎ 5486 8777; 12 Rainbow Beach Rd; per hr $4; ⏱ 9am-5pm Mon-Fri, to 3pm Sat, to noon Sun) Internet access.

Sights & Activities

The **Carlo Sandblow** is a 120m-high dune that sits atop a hill overlooking town; the views from here have been known to make even the most cynical sightseer gasp. A 600m track along the cliffs at the southern end of Cooloola Dr will take you here. A 2km walk along the beach accesses the coloured sand cliffs after which the town is named.

Double Island Point has a decent surf break, but fishing is the most popular activity. The vast shoreline provides abundant beach fishing and the really serious can access Tin Can Bay (see the boxed text, p345) inlet from either Carlo Point Boat Ramp or Bullock Point Boat Ramp. Both are just north of town.

Rainbow Paragliding (☎ 5486 3048, 0418 754 157; per person $130) offers tandem glides above the Carlo Sandblow, where the national championships are held every January. If you've got the gumption, this must be one of the most remarkable ways to take in the surrounding views.

A pod of dolphins drops in regularly to Rainbow Beach. **Rainbow Beach Dolphin View Sea Kayaking** (☎ 0408 738 192; 4hr tour per person $65) operates kayak safaris and guarantees sightings or offers a part refund. **Carlo Canoes** (☎ 5486 3610; per half-/full day $30/45) hires canoes if you want to explore for yourself.

Teeming with gropers, turtles, manta rays and harmless grey nurse sharks, Wolf Rock – a collection of four volcanic pinnacles off Double Island Point – is widely regarded as one of Queensland's best scuba-diving sites. The **Wolf Rock Dive Centre** (☎ 5486 8004; wolfrockdive@bigpond.com) offers four-day PADI (Professional Association of Diving Instructors) courses ($360) that include four dives at Wolf Rock.

Tours

Surf & Sand Safaris (☎ 5486 3131; www.surfandsand safaris.com.au) runs half-day 4WD tours south down the beach, taking in the lighthouse at Double Island Point, the *Cherry Venture* wreck and the coloured sands (adult/child $55/28). It also offers half-day tours on an amphibious vehicle (adult/child $65/35).

Sun Safari Tours (☎ 5486 3154) offers day trips to Fraser Island (adult/child $90/50), which take in all the southern highlights and include morning tea and lunch. It also offers two- and three-day tours (from $195/250 per person respectively), which include accommodation.

Sleeping & Eating

Rainbow Sands Holiday Units (☎ 5486 3400; fax 5486 3492; 42-46 Rainbow Beach Rd; d $80, 1-bedroom units $100; 🅿 🛏) This low-rise, palm-fronted complex has neat and appealing motel rooms with poolside glass doors and bar fridges, as well as self-contained units with full laundries for comfortable longer stays.

Rainbow Shores Resort (☎ 5486 3999; www .rainbowshores.com.au; 12 Rainbow Shores Dr; r from $115; 🅿 🛏) This sprawling resort has loads of accommodation options including standard holiday units, funky three-bedroom beach houses and polished split-level villas. The latter two have a two-night minimum stay and rates for everything leap in high season. On site is a nine-hole golf course, barbecues, children's playground, restaurant and plenty of bush.

Rainbow Beach Holiday Village (☎ 5486 3222, 1300 366 596; www.beach-village.com; 3 Rainbow Beach Rd; tent/caravan sites from $20/22, cabins from $90; 🅿 🛏) This excellent park has decent camp sites and a range of self-contained cabins. There's enough foliage to create a small jungle and it's extremely popular.

Frasers on Rainbow YHA (☎ 5486 8885, 1800 100 170; bookings@frasersonrainbow.com; 18 Spectrum St; dm/ d from $20/55; 🅿 🖳) Located in a converted motel, this hostel has roomy dorms with fabulously comfy beds and en-suite bathrooms. Locals join guests at the sprawling outdoor bar, and there are enough nooks and crannies for a quiet night.

Rainbow Beach Hotel (☎ 5486 3125; 1 Rainbow Beach Rd; mains $15-25; ⏱ breakfast Sat & Sun, lunch & dinner daily) This pub's smoky public bar is a great spot to linger with the locals, but if you want to keep to yourself the front beer garden and bistro are quiet and classy. The menu typically offers fresh fish alongside juicy steaks, calamari and chicken dishes.

Archie's (☎ 5486 3277; 12 Rainbow Beach Rd; mains $5.50-15; ☺ breakfast, lunch & dinner) This popular café encapsulates Rainbow's laid-back surfer chic, with its menu including classy smoothies, vegie burgers, nachos and more.

There's also a supermarket and bakery on Rainbow Beach Rd for quick eats and self-catering.

Getting There & Around

Both **Greyhound** (☎ 13 14 99; www.greyhound.com .au) and **Premier** (☎ 13 34 10; www.premierms.com.au) have daily services to Rainbow Beach from Brisbane ($35, 5½ hours, daily), via Noosa ($20, 2½ hours), which continue to Hervey Bay ($19, 1½ hours). **Polley's Coaches** (☎ 5482 2700) has buses from Rainbow Beach to Gympie ($13.50, 1¾ hours) departing at 7.30am and 3.45pm Monday to Friday. See p349 for return journey details.

Rainbow Beach is a good spot to hire a 4WD for Fraser Island, and several companies oblige.

Aussie Adventure 4WD Hire (☎ 5486 3599; fax 5486 3388; Shop 2, 26 Goondi St)

Aussie All Terrain Vehicle Hire (☎ 5486 8000; Shop 1, 54 Rainbow Beach Rd)

Rainbow Beach Adventure Centre 4WD Hire (☎ /fax 5486 3288; 66 Rainbow Beach Rd)

Safari 4WD (☎ 5486 8188, 1800 689 819; 3 Karoonda Ct)

If you need more information on rental specifics see the boxed text, p360. **Cooloola Coast & Country Realty** (☎ 5486 3411; Shop 2, 6 Rainbow Beach Rd; per night $90) rents lock-up garages if you need a place to leave your own car in town.

MARYBOROUGH
☎ 07 / pop 21,200

Once a mere borough on the River Mary, Maryborough is a beautifully preserved town that has broad sweeping streets lined with handsome heritage buildings. Many have stood there since 1860, when Maryborough came to prominence as the port of entry to Australia for some 21,000 European immigrants. The town also distinguishes itself with possibly the friendliest population in Queensland.

Orientation & Information

Kent St is the main strip but you'll find most of Maryborough's residents at the modern Railway Sq Shopping Centre (Ferry St) near the intersection of Kent St and the Bruce Hwy.

The excellent **Maryborough visitors centre** (☎ 4121 4111; City Hall, Kent St; ☺ 9am-5pm Mon-Fri) is staffed by knowledgeable locals and stocks plenty of brochures on this region.

Sights & Activities

The **Brennan & Geraghty's Store** (☎ 4121 2250; 64 Lennox St; adult/child $5/3.5; ☺ 10am-3pm) opened in 1871 and traded for 100 years before becoming a museum. Hundreds of tins and bottles cram onto the ceiling-high shelves, including ancient Vegemite jars. Correspondence from poverty-stricken customers unable to pay their accounts affords a personal insight into the difficulties of life at the turn of the 20th century.

Housed inside the original Bond Store, construction of which began in 1864, is the **Heritage Gateway & Bond Store Museum** (☎ 4190

DETOUR: TIN CAN BAY

En route from Rainbow Beach to Maryborough, turn north off Rainbow Beach Rd on to Tin Can Bay Rd, which journeys for about 10km before reaching the idyllic and quiet settlement of Tin Can Bay. Sitting at the southern tip of the Great Sand Strait, it's a fabulous veer from the beaten track.

Mystique, the resident dolphin, makes regular breakfast visits to the Tin Can Bay marina boat ramp and monitored feeding takes place from 8am to 10am.

On the main road into town, the **Sandcastle Motel** (☎ 5486 4555; sandcastle@spiderweb.com.au; Tin Can Bay Rd; d $65; ☷ ☲) has large rooms with small kitchenettes, or you could style it up at **Dolphin Waters** (☎ 5486 2600; admin@dolphinwaters.com.au; 40-41 The Esplanade; d per 2 nights/week from $185/470; ☷ ☲), which has spotless self-contained units with balconies.

You can fuel up on pub nosh at the boisterous **Sleepy Lagoon Hotel** (☎ 5486 4124; 18 Bream St; mains $10-20; ☺ lunch & dinner) or the more sedate **Yacht Club** (☎ 5486 4308; The Esplanade; mains $15-25; ☺ lunch Sat & Sun, dinner Wed-Sun).

FRASER COAST

5730; 101 Wharf St; adult/child $3/1; 🕙 10am-4pm Mon-Fri, 10am-1pm Sat & Sun). This complex has informative and well-assembled displays on Maryborough's immigration, Kanakas and industrial history in the traditional Bond Store Museum, as well as an interactive wing in the Heritage Gateway.

There are many fine old buildings in the historic port district along Wharf St. The 1866 Italianate **post office**, on the corner of Bazaar and Wharf Sts, is Queensland's oldest. Over on Richmond St is the revival-style **Woodstock House** and the neoclassical **former Union Bank**, where PL Travers, the author of *Mary Poppins*, was born.

Maryborough is well worth visiting on Thursday for the **heritage market**, which is held between 8am and 2pm along Adelaide and Elena Sts.

Sleeping

Royal Centrepoint Motel (☎ 4121 2241; ron_beryl@bigpond.com; 326 Kent St; s/d $55/60; 🐕) The very lovely Centrepoint has 1920's style that dwells mostly in the hallways – not quite reaching into the rooms. But perks include VCRs, views of the street and friendly hosts.

McNevin's Parkway Motel (☎ 4122 2888, 1800 072 000; fax 4122 2546; 188 John St; r/ste from $95/130; 🐕) This well-run complex is popular with business folk but the fresh and light motel rooms are comfortable regardless of your agenda. A step up in style and price are the smart executive suites with separate bedrooms and spas. All rooms come with kitchenettes but no utensils.

Blue Shades Motor Inn (☎ 4122 2777; www.blueshades.au00.com; cnr Ferry & Queen Sts; r/ste from $80/130; 🐕) This large motel complex has a range of accommodation from generic and simple motel rooms to modern executive rooms that could lodge a small tribe. All rooms have cable TV and minibars.

Wallace Caravan Park & Units (☎ 4121 3970; www.wallacemotel.4mg.com; 22 Ferry St; tent/caravan sites $16/19, cabins $40-60; 🐕 🐾) This pleasant park spreads itself across a gentle slope underneath a canopy of trees. The cabins are newish and there are also good self-contained motel units.

Eating & Drinking

Muddy Waters Cafe (☎ 4121 5011; 71 Wharf St; mains $15-25; 🕙 10am-3.30pm Sun & Tue, 10am-10pm Wed-

Sat) The shady riverfront deck at this classy café is perfect for long, languid lunches of perhaps tuna steak or pink peppercorn–poached chicken. The extensive wine list complements the excellent food and murders any pretences you may have entertained of having a schedule.

Black Cat Cafe (☎ 4121 2870; 222 Adelaide St; dishes $5-10; 🕙 breakfast & lunch Mon-Sat) This industrious café is extremely popular with locals grabbing their lunch fix in the form of superfresh hot and cold wraps, rolls, sandwiches, pies and cakes. Just about everything is made up in front of you and there's oodles of seating.

Royal Hotel (☎ 4121 6225; 340 Kent St; mains $16; 🕙 lunch & dinner) This friendly and affable pub serves an unbeatable $7 buffet daily, plus fancier à-la-carte pub grub. The renovated section of the bistro provides a pleasant greenery-drenched environment in which to dine.

For a cold beer with a warm greeting head to the **White Lion Pub** (☎ 4121 3374; 37 Walker St), where you're likely to make new mates at the bar, or the historic **Red Roo Hotel** (☎ 4121 3586; 100 Adelaide St), with a gorgeous beer garden out the back.

Getting There & Away

Sunshine Express (www.sunshineexpress.com.au) flies from Brisbane to Maryborough daily ($140, 50 minutes).

Queensland Rail (☎ 1300 131 722; www.traveltrain.com.au) operates *Sunlander* ($55, five hours, four weekly) and *TiltTrain* ($55, 3½ hours, Sunday to Friday), which connect Brisbane with Maryborough West, 7km west of the centre. There's a shuttle bus from the main bus terminal (beside the Maryborough train station on Lennox St). This is also the stop for long-haul buses north and south.

Greyhound (☎ 13 14 99; www.greyhound.com.au) and **Premier** (☎ 13 34 10; www.premierms.com.au) bus services both connect Maryborough with Gympie ($15, one hour), Bundaberg ($27, three hours) and Brisbane ($44, 4½ hours).

Wide Bay Transit (☎ 4121 3719) has hourly services between Maryborough and Hervey Bay Marina every weekday, five on Saturday and three on Sunday ($5.90, 1½ hours). Buses depart Maryborough from outside the city hall in Kent St.

HERVEY BAY & FRASER ISLAND

HERVEY BAY

☎ 07 / pop 36,100

Hervey Bay is coastal Queensland in a seashell: headlined by a 10km stretch of sand that connects the five suburbs of Point Vernon, Pialba, Scarness, Torquay and Urangan. The pockets of sedate suburbia rubbing shoulders with flawless beach dissolve into an industrial jungle on the outskirts of town. It's this infrastructure that makes Hervey Bay the most popular launching pad to Fraser Island, and its proximity to this marvel is intrinsic to the town's culture. Fortunately, the genuine affability of the locals perks up Hervey Bay's otherwise dull string of souvenir shops and overpriced motels.

Hervey Bay's other celebrated drawcard is the opportunity to see the whales that visit the town's sheltered waters each spring. This spectacular sight, complemented by sublime swimming, fishing and other water-related activities, seduces Queensland families by the campervan-load. It seems many have been coming for so long they've not bothered to leave, and the town has a healthy percentage of retirees among its permanent population.

Information

There is only one official tourist office, but numerous booking agents in town also provide tourist information.

Adventure Travel Centre (☎ 4125 9288, 1800 554 400; 410 The Esplanade, Torquay; per hr $4; ☼ 7am-10pm) Internet access and tour booking agent.

Hervey Bay Tourism & Development Bureau (☎ 1800 811 728; www.herveybaytourism.com.au; cnr Urraween & Maryborough Rds, Hervey Bay; ☼ 8.30am-5pm Mon-Fri, 10am-4pm Sat & Sun) Helpful and official visitors centre about 1.5km southwest of town.

Hervey Bay Visitor & Tourist Information Centre (☎ 4124 4050, 1800 649 926; 401 The Esplanade, Torquay; per hr $4; ☼ 8.30am-8.30pm Mon-Fri, 9am-5pm Sat & Sun) Privately run booking office with Internet access.

Post office (☎ 4125 1101; 414 The Esplanade, Torquay)

Whale Watch Tourist Centre (☎ 1800 358 595; Urangan Marina, Urangan; ☼ 9am-5pm) Privately run but good information.

Sights

Reef World (☎ 4128 9828; Pulgul St, Urangan; adult/child $14/8; ☼ 9.30am-5pm) is a small aquarium well stocked with colourful characters. You can get nose to nose with fish through the glass, but the resident turtles reputedly love a good pat on the back – there's ample opportunity to test the theory.

Run by the Korrawinga Aboriginal Community, the **Scrub Hill Community Farm** (☎ 4124 6908; Scrub Hill Rd; tours adult/child $16.50/5.50), about 2km southwest of town, produces organic vegetables, tea-tree oil and excellent art works. Guided tours (call to arrange) detail how the farm operates and the slightly more expensive option (adult/child $25/10) includes bush tucker and a traditional dancing display.

The **Hervey Bay Historical Museum** (☎ 4128 1064; 13 Zephyr St, Scarness; adult/child $2.50/50c; ☼ 1-5pm Fri-Sun) has over 3000 items on display. Gems include a list of rules for female teachers from 1915 (such as 'You may not loiter in ice-cream parlours') and several artefacts from the *Maheno* shipwreck on Fraser Island (see p358).

A WHALE OF A TIME

Every year, from August to early November, thousands of humpback whales (*Megaptera novaeangliae*) hang out in the sheltered waters of Hervey Bay to escape predators and rest before continuing their arduous migration south to the Antarctic. Having mated and given birth in the warmer waters off northeast Australia, they arrive in Hervey Bay in groups of about a dozen (known as pulses), before splitting into smaller groups of two or three (pods). The new calves utilise the time to develop the thick layers of blubber necessary for survival in icy southern waters, by consuming around 600L of milk daily.

Viewing these majestic creatures is simply awe-inspiring. Their annual trek has endowed the whales, which can measure up to 15m in length and weigh 40 tonnes, with a surprising tolerance for spectators. Some roll up beside the numerous boats with one eye clear of the water, making those on board wonder who's actually watching whom.

FRASER COAST

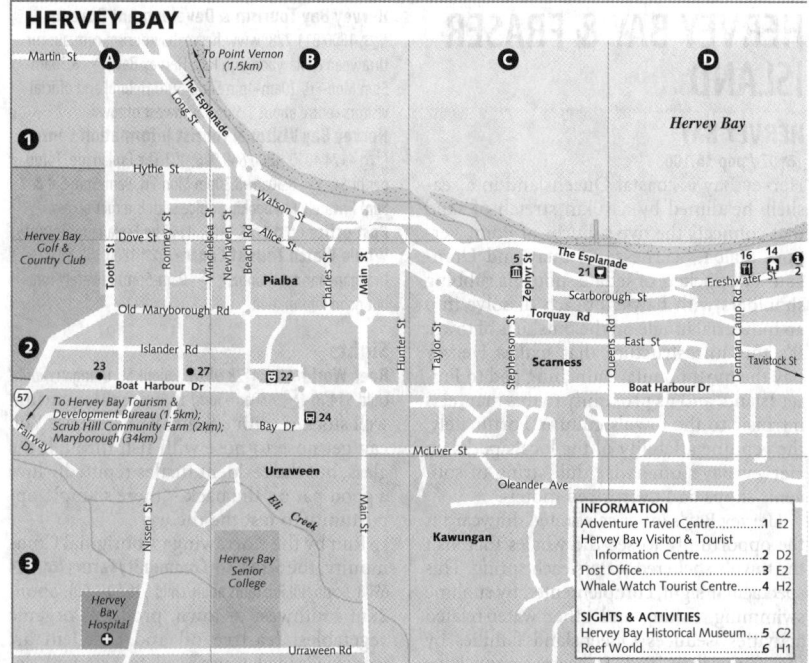

HERVEY BAY

INFORMATION

Adventure Travel Centre	1 E2
Hervey Bay Visitor & Tourist Information Centre	2 D2
Post Office	3 E2
Whale Watch Tourist Centre	4 H2

SIGHTS & ACTIVITIES

Hervey Bay Historical Museum	5 C2
Reef World	6 H1

Hervey Bay's pretty **Botanic Gardens** (Elizabeth St, Urangan) are a lush mix of small lagoons, dense foliage and walking tracks. It's a beautiful spot that attracts around 80 bird species. There's also a small orchid house and an Aboriginal bush-tucker garden.

Activities & Tours
WHALE WATCHING

Whale-watching tours operate out of Hervey Bay every day, weather permitting, from mid-July to November. Sightings are guaranteed from August to the end of October, with a free trip if the whales don't show. Out of season many boats offer dolphin-spotting tours, with the same free-trip guarantee.

The boats cruise from the Urangan Harbour out to Platypus Bay and then zip around to find the most active whales. Most vessels offer half-day (four hour) tours that cost around $90 for adults and $60 for children, and generally include breakfast or lunch.

Bookings for boats can be made with your accommodation or the information centres. Take a hat, sunglasses and sunscreen, and don't forget your camera.

Tours include:

MV Tasman Venture (☎ 1800 620 322; www.tasman venture.com.au; ☼ tours 8.30am & 1.30pm) Maximum of 80 passengers; underwater microphones and viewing windows.

Quick Cat II (☎ 4128 9611, 1800 671 977; www .herveybaywhalewatch.com.au; ☼ tours 8am & 1pm) Underwater cameras, maximum of 80 passengers and wheelchair accessible.

Spirit of Hervey Bay (☎ 4125 5131, 1800 642 544; www.spiritofherveybay.com; ☼ tours 8.30am & 1.30pm) Large vessel with underwater viewing rooms, carrying up to 150 passengers.

Tasman Venture II (☎ 1800 099 636; www.tasman venture.com.au; ☼ tours 9.30am) Five-hour tour; maximum of 50 passengers.

Whale Planet (☎ 1800 800 862; ☼ tours 5.30am, 7.30am & 10.30am)

Whalesong (☎ 4125 6222, 1800 689 610; whalesong@bigpond.com; ☼ tours 7.30am & 1pm) Maximum of 70 passengers. Caters to disabled travellers.

FISHING

SilverStar Fishing Charters (☎ 4128 9778; silver star_fishing@bigpond.com; per person $150), **MV Fighting Whiting** (☎ 4124 6599; per adult/child $55/30) and **MV Princess II** (☎ 4124 0400; per person $90)

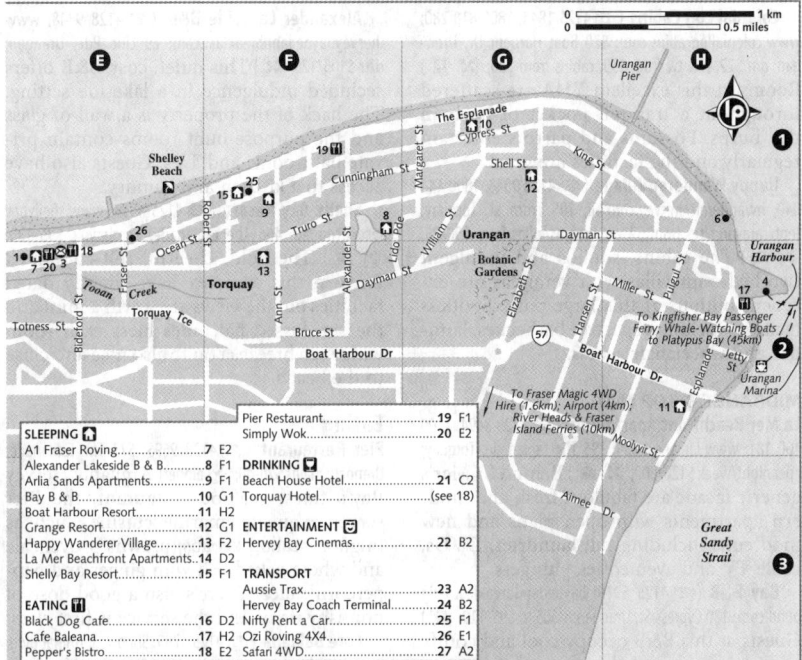

SLEEPING
A1 Fraser Roving.........................**7** E2
Alexander Lakeside B & B.........**8** F1
Arlia Sands Apartments............**9** F1
Bay B & B................................**10** G1
Boat Harbour Resort................**11** H2
Grange Resort..........................**12** G1
Happy Wanderer Village..........**13** F2
La Mer Beachfront Apartments.**14** D2
Shelly Bay Resort.....................**15** F1

EATING
Black Dog Cafe.........................**16** D2
Cafe Baleana...........................**17** H2
Pepper's Bistro.........................**18** E2

Pier Restaurant........................**19** F1
Simply Wok.............................**20** E2

DRINKING
Beach House Hotel...................**21** C2
Torquay Hotel.......................(see **18**)

ENTERTAINMENT
Hervey Bay Cinemas................**22** B2

TRANSPORT
Aussie Trax..............................**23** A2
Hervey Bay Coach Terminal.....**24** B2
Nifty Rent a Car.......................**25** F1
Ozi Roving 4X4.........................**26** E1
Safari 4WD..............................**27** A2

all offer calm-water fishing trips that run
for around eight hours and include lunch,
departing Urangan Harbour.

RIDING

The **Susan River Homestead** (☎ 4121 6846; www
.susanriver.com; Hervey Bay Rd), about halfway between Maryborough and Hervey Bay, gets
a rap from readers. Horse-riding packages
(all inclusive) cost $155/120 per adult/child.
Casual two-hour horse rides through bush
land cost $60 and you need to book.

Alternatively, try **Humpback Camel Safaris**
(☎ 0419 648 629; per person $55), which operates
relaxing camel rides through the bush and
beach, and can arrange courtesy transfers
to/from your accommodation.

SCENIC FLIGHTS

Air Fraser Island (☎ 4125 3600, 1800 247 992) operates aerial whale-watching tours ($40)
and scenic flights over Fraser Island and
the southern fringes of the Great Barrier
Reef ($135). **Suncoast Helicopters** (☎ 4125 6799;
per person $155-360) operates a range of scenic
flights, from 25 minutes to one hour.

OTHER ACTIVITIES

Skydive Hervey Bay (☎ 4124 9249; www.skydive
fraser.com) offers tandem skydives over the
beach. Rates start at $180 for 8000ft and
increase with the height and freefall up to
$360 for 14,000ft.

Torquay Jet Ski & Beach Hire (☎ 4125 5528), a
beach shed on the foreshore, hires canoes
(per half-hour/hour $12/18) and windsurf-
ers (per half-hour/hour $12/20) among other
water-related equipment.

Sleeping

BUDGET

Hervey Bay is inundated with caravan parks
and hostels; most hostels organise pick-ups
from the bus station and trips to Fraser
Island.

A1 Fraser Roving (☎ 4125 6386, 1800 989 811; www
.fraserroving.com.au; 412 The Esplanade, Torquay; dm $20-25,
d with/without bathroom $55/50; ☐ ☒) Fraser Rov-
ing's atmospheric bar guarantees new mates,
but there's plenty of space to buffer the
noise. The rooms are spartan but spacious
and there are spotless bathrooms, a decent
kitchen and good wheelchair facilities.

Colonial Log Cabins (☎ 4125 1844, 1800 818 280; www.coloniallogcabins.com; 820 Boat Harbour Dr, Urangan; dm $22, d & tw from $55, cabins from $80; ✖ ▢) Rooms at this excellent YHA are scattered throughout a tranquil pocket of bush in the 'burbs. Possums and parrots entertain regularly and the facilities are great.

Happy Wanderer Village (☎ 4128 9048, 1800 444 040; hwanderer@hervey.com.au; 105 Truro St, Torquay; tent/caravan sites from $21/25, cabins/villas from $50/85; ✖ ▣) The cabins, studios and indulgent two-bedroom villas with verandas are excellent options at this large park. Spotless facilities include a spa, free barbecues, laundry and wheelchair access.

MIDRANGE & TOP END

La Mer Beachfront Apartments (☎ 4128 3494, 1800 100 181; www.lamer.com.au; 396 The Esplanade, Torquay; r per night/week $120/600; ✖ ▣) Behind La Mer's generic façade are fabulous fresh and modern apartments with open plans and new mod cons including full laundries, DVDs, cable TV and even coffee plungers.

Bay B&B (☎ 4125 6919; baybedandbreakfast@big pond.com; 180 Cypress St, Urangan; s $65, d $95-110; ▣) Guests at this B&B occupy cool and comfy rooms in a secluded annex. The interior blends modernity with comfort: there's a stylish lounge area and kitchenette, plus a lagoon-style saltwater pool outside.

Grange Resort (☎ 4125 2002; www.thegrange -herveybay.com.au; cnr Elizabeth & Shell Sts, Urangan; r $160-185; ✖ ▣) This stylish complex houses fancy split-level condos filled with life's little luxuries. Glossy bathrooms and kitchens with stainless-steel appliances, plump couches, spacious boudoirs and commodious decks are the norm; bookings are advised.

Boat Harbour Resort (☎ 4125 5079; www.boat harbourresort.com; 650 The Esplanade, Urangan; r $80-95; ✖ ▣) These timber studios and two-bedroom villas have mountain-flavoured exteriors but they're bright and summery inside. The studios have sizable decks out the front and the roomy villas are great for families.

Arlia Sands Apartments (☎ 4125 3778; www .arliasands.com.au; 13 Ann St, Torquay; r $120; ✖ ▣) These refurbished units contain plush furniture, wide-screen TVs, stereos and beautiful kitchens. They're the self-contained unit for the style cat, and each has an ample balcony.

Alexander Lakeside B&B (☎ 4128 9448; www .herveybaybedandbreakfast.com; 29 Lido Pde, Urangan; d/tr $105/120; ✖) This quiet, cosy B&B offers secluded indulgence in a lakeside setting. The back of the property is a wall of glass and the purpose-built rooms contain private bathrooms and TVs. Guests also have access to a kitchen and laundry.

Shelly Bay Resort (☎ 4125 4533; www.shellybay resort.com.au; 466 The Esplanade, Torquay; r $95-130; ✖ ▣) The bold, cheerful self-contained units at this complex have slightly dated facilities but the views are worth a mint and the sun-kissed balconies bless each room with a sea breeze. You're also nice and close to the beach.

Eating

Pier Restaurant (☎ 4128 9695; 573 The Esplanade, Urangan; mains $20-40; ⌚ dinner) Arguably Hervey Bay's finest seafood restaurant, the Pier serves exquisite 'marine cuisine' such as mignon scallop kebabs, prawns provençale and whole baked fish with ginger and peppercorn sauce. There's also a good dose of nonfishy items and the service is first class.

Cafe Balaena (☎ 4125 4799; Shop 7, Terminal Bldg, Buccaneer Ave, Urangan; mains $10-25; ⌚ breakfast, lunch & dinner) This waterfront café provides atmospheric views with a laid-back twist and wallet-friendly prices. The menu is hip-café fare – mountainous *paninis* and salads – with a fair share of seafood.

Pepper's Bistro (☎ 4125 2266; 421 The Esplanade, Torquay; mains $10-20; ⌚ lunch & dinner) Perennially popular Pepper's at the Torquay Hotel (opposite) dishes out huge servings of steak, pasta, salad, seafood and curries. The street-side dining adds a dash of people-watching panache and the atmosphere is relaxed and friendly.

Simply Wok (☎ 4125 2077; 417 The Esplanade, Torquay; mains $7-15; ⌚ breakfast, lunch & dinner; ✖) Actually there's nothing simple about the variety here, which includes gourmet sandwiches, divine salads, seafood and inventive Asian cuisine. The food is positively grown-up but you get to be 10 again with the markers and paper at every table.

Black Dog Cafe (☎ 4124 3177; 381 The Esplanade, Torquay; mains $10-20; ⌚ lunch & dinner) You'll find East-meets-West inventions on your fork at this funky café. Sushi, Japanese soups, fresh burgers, club sambos and seafood salads are on offer; good for families.

Self-caterers can stock up at the supermarkets inside Urangan Central and Bay Central shopping centres. There are plenty of takeaways and fish-and-chip shops on The Esplanade in Torquay and Urangan.

Drinking

Beach House Hotel (☎ 4128 1233; 344 The Esplanade, Scarness) Cable sports and pool tables entertain loyal locals here, while ample tables accommodate those looking to indulge in conversation. It's all seasoned with sea breezes from the beach across the road.

Torquay Hotel (☎ 4125 2266; 421 The Esplanade, Torquay) Torquay Hotel settles for décor with an RSL flavour, but the vibes are convivial and social. International sports get a workout on the big TV, and once the diners have had their fill the outside tables get back to being a beer garden.

Entertainment

For movies, check out **Hervey Bay Cinemas** (☎ 4124 8200; 128 Boatharbour Dr). This six-screen cinema shows Hollywood flicks and offers $8 seats all day Tuesday and all 9.30am sessions.

Getting There & Away

AIR

Sunshine Express (www.sunshineexpress.com.au) has a daily service between Brisbane and Hervey Bay ($140, one hour). Hervey Bay airport is off Booral Rd, Urangan, on the way to River Heads.

BOAT

Boats to Fraser Island leave from River Heads, about 10km south of town and Urangan Marina (see p362). Most tours leave from Urangan Harbour.

BUS

Buses depart **Hervey Bay Coach Terminal** (☎ 4124 4000; Central Ave, Pialba); hostels run minibuses to meet the coaches. **Greyhound** (☎ 13 14 99; www.greyhound.com.au) and **Premier** (☎ 13 34 10; www.premierms.com.au) run several times daily between Hervey Bay and Brisbane ($50, 5½ hours), as well as Noosa ($27, 3½ hours), Bundaberg ($17, 1½ hours) and Rockhampton ($55, 5½ hours).

Wide Bay Transit (☎ 4121 3719) has hourly services between Maryborough and the Urangan Marina in Hervey Bay every week-

day, five on Saturday and three on Sunday ($5.90, 1½ hours), but it isn't much use for local transport; most places to stay will pick you up from the bus station.

There are **Trainlink** (www.traveltrain.com.au) buses between Maryborough West and Hervey Bay Couch Terminal ($5.50, 45 minutes).

Getting Around

BICYCLE

Bay Bicycle Hire (☎ 0417 644 814; per half-/full day $15/20) rents bicycles from various outlets along The Esplanade or it can deliver bikes to your door.

CAR

Nifty Rent a Car (☎ 4125 4833; 463 The Esplanade, Torquay) has small cars from $30 a day (based on several days' hire).

Plenty of choice makes Hervey Bay the best place to hire a 4WD for Fraser Island:

Aussie Trax (☎ 4124 4433, 1800 062 275; 56 Boat Harbour Dr, Hervey Bay)

Bay 4WD Hire (☎ 4128 2981, 1800 687 178; www .bay4wd.com.au; 52-54 Boat Harbour Dr, Pialba)

Fraser Magic 4WD Hire (☎ 4125 6612; www.fraser -magic-4wdhire.com.au; Lot 11, Kruger Court, Urangan) About 1.5km south of town.

Ozi Roving 4X4 (☎ 4125 6355; 10 Fraser St, Torquay)

Safari 4WD (☎ 4124 4244, 1800 689 819; www.safari 4wdhire.com.au; 102 Boat Harbour Dr, Pialba)

FRASER ISLAND

It is said that all the sand from the east coast of Australia eventually ends up at Fraser Island, a gigantic sandbar measuring 120km by 15km, created by thousands of years of longshore drift. Seen from the coast this beautiful enigma appears too lush and green to be the world's biggest sand island, but the island's diverse ecology is just one of the many wonders of the place.

The fringe of pounding surf contains an interior of tropical rainforests, gorges and freshwater lakes. There are some 40 different mammal species and a profusion of birds and reptiles, and from towering dunes and headlands you can often spot whales, dolphins, sharks and turtles offshore. It's an amazing environment, but as 350,000 people arrive annually to delight in its beauty, Fraser can also feel like a giant sandpit with its own peak hour and congested beach highway.

Fraser was inscribed on the World Heritage List in 1993 and since 1990 the island

FRASER COAST

FRASER ISLAND GREAT WALK

The Fraser Island Great Walk is a stunning way to experience this enigmatic island. The trail undulates through the island's interior for almost 87km from Dilli Village to Happy Valley. Broken up into seven sections of around six to eight kilometres each, it follows the pathways of Fraser Island's original inhabitants, the Butchulla people. En route, the walk passes underneath the rainforest canopies, circles around some of the island's vivid lakes and courses through shifting dunes.

Pick up the 'Fraser Island Great Walk' brochure from a QPWS office (or download it from www.epa.qld.gov.au under the Parks and Forests heading) and seek updates on the track's conditions.

---

has been protected as the Great Sandy National Park. For anyone with a yearning for camping, fishing, walking, off-road driving or simply the exhilaration of the great outdoors, it's pure utopia.

Four-wheel-drive vehicles are essential here (see the boxed text, p360). The lakes are lovely to swim in, but the sea's lethal: undertows and sharks make it a no-go area. The native dingoes are one of Fraser's highlights, and thought to be the most genetically pure population.

Yet none of this detracts from the enjoyment of a location unlike any other on earth. If the dunes, forests, lakes and wildlife aren't enough, gaze up at the night sky: with little light pollution, the Milky Way blazes bright.

Orientation & Information

General supplies and rather expensive fuel are available from the stores at Cathedral Beach, Eurong, Kingfisher Bay, Happy Valley and Orchid Beach. Most stores stock some camping and fishing gear, and those at Kingfisher Bay, Eurong and Happy Valley sell alcohol. There are public telephones at all these locations and at most camping grounds.

There are several ranger stations on the island with information leaflets, tide times, and free drinking water:

Central Station (☎ 4127 9191; ⏱ 10am–noon)
Dundubara (☎ 4127 9138; ⏱ 8–9am)

Eurong (☎ 4127 9128; ⏱ 10.30am–3.30pm Mon, 8am–3.30pm Tue–Thu, 8am–1pm Fri)
Waddy Point (☎ 4127 9190; ⏱ 7–8am & 4–4.30pm)

There are tow-truck services at **Eurong** (☎ 4127 9188) and **Yidney Rocks** (☎ 4127 9167). See below for information on the main settlements on the island.

MAPS

When you get your vehicle permit, you'll receive a Fraser Pack with a basic map and leaflets about camping, natural features and walking trails on the island. The Queensland Government publishes the excellent *Sunmap Tourist Fraser Island Map*, and Hema and other companies produce decent, detailed maps of around a 1:130,000 scale (about $8).

PERMITS

You'll need a permit to take a vehicle on to the island and to camp, and these must be purchased before you arrive from **QPWS** (☎ 13 13 04; www.epa.qld.gov.au). If you're heading over from Hervey Bay, there's a **kiosk** (☎ 4125 8485; ⏱ 6.15–11.15am & 2–3.30pm) at the River Heads ferry terminal, or you can get your permits from the QPWS office at Rainbow Beach (p350). Vehicle permits cost $33 and camping permits cost $4 per person per night. Permits aren't required for the private camping grounds or resorts.

Other issuing offices are Bundaberg QPWS (p363), Great Sandy Information Centre (p343) and Naturally Queensland (p300).

Sights & Activities

Starting at the island's southern tip, where the ferry leaves for Inskip Point on the mainland, a high-tide access track cuts inland, avoiding dangerous Hook Point, and leads you to the entrance of the Eastern Beach's main thoroughfare. The first settlement you reach is **Dilli Village**, the former sand-mining centre; **Eurong**, with shops, fuel and places to eat, is another 9km north. From here, an inland track crosses to Central Station and Wanggoolba Creek (for the ferry to River Heads).

Right in the middle of the island is the ranger centre at **Central Station**, the starting point for numerous walking trails. From here you can walk or drive to the beautiful

BOAT

Several large vehicle ferries (known as barges) connect Fraser Island to the mainland. Most visitors use the two services that leave from River Heads, about 10km south of Hervey Bay, or from Inskip Point, near Rainbow Beach.

Fraser Venture (☎ 4125 4444; return per pedestrian $18, vehicle incl 4 passengers $115, additional passengers $6) makes the 30-minute crossing from River Heads to Wanggoolba Creek on the west coast of Fraser Island. It departs daily from River Heads at 9am, 10.15am and 3.30pm, and returns from the island at 9.30am, 2.30pm and 4pm. On Saturday there is also a 7am service from River Heads that returns at 7.30am from the island. This company also operates the **Fraser Dawn Vehicular Ferry** (☎ 4125 4444; return per pedestrian $18, vehicle incl 4 passengers $115, additional passengers $6) from the Urangan marina to Moon Point on Fraser Island, but car-hire companies won't allow you to drive their cars here so it's limited to car-owners and hikers.

Kingfisher Vehicular Ferry (☎ 4120 3333, 1800 072 555; return per pedestrian $18, vehicle incl 4 passengers $115, additional passengers $6) operates two boats. Its vehicle ferry does the 45-minute crossing from River Heads to Kingfisher Bay daily, departing at 7.15am, 11am and 2.30pm, and returning at 8.30am, 1.30pm and 4pm. The **Kingfisher Fast Cat Passenger Ferry** (return adult/child $45/22) makes the 30-minute crossing between Urangan marina and Kingfisher Bay at 8.45am, noon and 4pm daily, returning at 7.40am, 10.30am, 2pm, 5pm and 8pm daily. There are additional services from Thursday to Sunday.

Coming from Rainbow Beach, **Rainbow Venture** (☎ 5486 3227; return per pedestrian $10, vehicle incl 4 passengers $60) and **Manta Ray** (☎ 0418 872 599; return per pedestrian $10, vehicle incl 4 passengers $60) both make the 15-minute crossing from Inskip Point to Hook Point on Fraser Island continuously from about 7am to 5.30pm daily.

Getting Around

See the boxed text, p360, for information on getting around Fraser Island. If you've somehow landed on Fraser without transport you can hire a 4WD through **Kingfisher Bay 4WD Hire** (☎ 4120 3366) but expect to pay $200 per day and upwards.

NORTH OF MARYBOROUGH

It's mostly farming country north of Maryborough, with fruit orchards and fields of vegetables disappearing into the distance, interrupted by a few small towns. The turn-off to Bundaberg, along the Isis Hwy, is 6km north of Childers.

CHILDERS

☎ 07 / pop 1500

Childers is an attractive town, littered with heritage buildings, that still thrives off the surrounding orchards. It's best known as a sure thing to earn some dosh through fruit-picking work, but a fire at the Palace Backpackers Hostel in 2000, in which 15 backpackers died, marked the town indelibly. Childers is blessed with a remarkably tight and supportive community though, a quality that has been particularly highlighted since that tragedy. There is a moving memorial at the **Childers Palace Memorial Art Gallery & Information Centre** (☎ 4126 3886; 9am-5pm Mon-Fri, to noon Sat & Sun), where you'll also find a good gallery and the visitors centre.

Interesting old buildings along Churchill St include the **Federal Hotel**, on the corner of North St, and the historic, wooden **National Bank**, built in 1895.

Isis Historical Complex (Taylor St; adult/child $2/free; 9am-noon Mon-Fri, 9am-3pm Sun) is a mock historical town, with several cottages, a general store and a post office. There's also a museum that houses Aboriginal artefacts and photos.

Sleeping

Avocado Motor Inn (☎ 4126 1608; avocadomotorinn@bigpond.com; Bruce Hwy; r $56-65;) Ignore the 1970s décor and grab one of the comfortable rooms down the back, where the views over the valley are priceless.

Sugarbowl Caravan Park (☎ /fax 4126 1521; 4660 Bruce Hwy; tent sites $15, cabins with/without bathroom $60/50;) This caravan park has plenty of space and a good scattering of foliage between sites. The en-suite cabins are a cut above, and the owners can help backpackers find work and provide transport to the farms.

McKenzie, **Jennings**, **Birrabeen** and **Boomanjin Lakes**. Lake McKenzie is spectacularly clear and is ringed by sand beaches, making it a great place to swim, but Lake Birrabeen sees fewer tour and backpacker groups.

About 4km north of Eurong along the beach is a signposted walking trail, which leads across sandblows (enormous dunes created by wind-blown sand) to the beautiful **Lake Wabby**, the most accessible of Fraser's lakes. An easier route is from the lookout on the inland track. Lake Wabby is surrounded on three sides by eucalypt forest, while the fourth side is a massive sandblow that encroaches on the lake at about 3m a year. The lake is deceptively shallow and diving is very dangerous.

As you drive up the beach you may have to detour inland to avoid Poyungan and Yidney Rocks during high tide before you reach **Happy Valley**, with places to stay, a shop and bistro. About 10km north is **Eli Creek**, a fast-moving, crystal-clear waterway that will carry you effortlessly downstream. About 2km from Eli Creek is the rotting hulk of the **Maheno**, a former passenger liner blown ashore by a cyclone in 1935 as it was being towed to a Japanese scrapyard.

Roughly 5km north of the *Maheno* you'll find the **Pinnacles** – an eroded section of coloured sand cliffs – and, about 10km beyond, **Dundubara**, with a ranger station and excellent camping ground. Then there's a 20km stretch of beach before you come to the rock outcrop of **Indian Head**. Sharks, manta rays, dolphins and, during the migration season, whales can often be seen from the top of this headland.

Between Indian Head and Waddy Point the trail branches inland, passing **Champagne Pools**, which offer the only safe saltwater swimming on the island. There are good camping areas at **Waddy Point** and **Orchid Beach**, the last settlement on the island.

Many tracks north of this are closed, for environmental protection.

On the island scenic flights are available from **MI Helicopters** (☎ 1800 600 345; 10/25/60min flight per person from $70/145/310), which is based at Fraser Island Wilderness Retreat, or with **Air Fraser** (☎ 1800 600 345; 10min flights per person from $60).

Sleeping & Eating

Sailfish on Fraser (☎ 4127 9494; www.sailfishonfraser.com.au; Happy Valley; d from $200;) Any notions of roughing it will be quickly forgotten at this plush retreat. All 10 apartments are cavernous and classy, with wall-to-wall glass doors, spas, mod cons, modern furnishings and an alluring pool. Bookings are recommended.

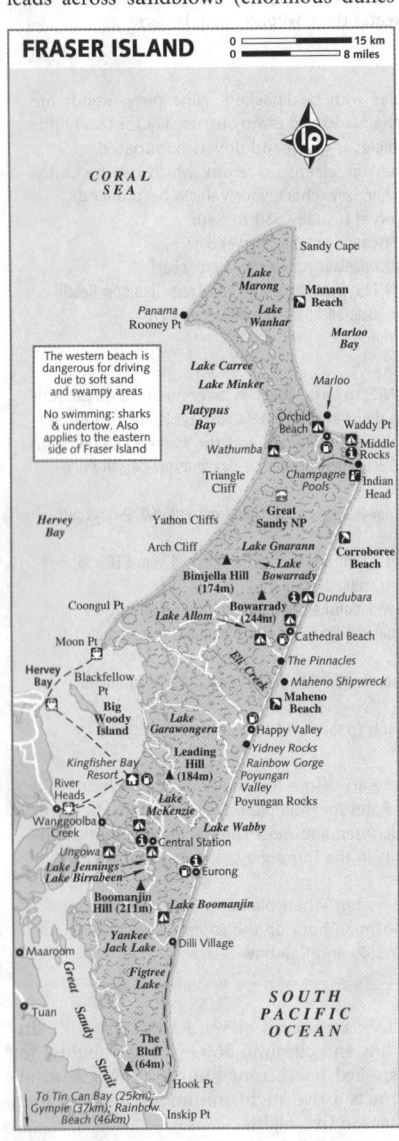

FRASER ISLAND

CORAL SEA

SOUTH PACIFIC OCEAN

SAND SAFARIS

There's a sci-fi otherworldliness to Fraser Island, as 4WDs with towering wheel bases and chunky tyres all pull in to refuel against an idyllic beach backdrop of white sand and waving palm trees. The surfeit of sand and the lack of paved roads mean that only 4WD vehicles can negotiate the island. If you're a committed hiker, you can cover some attractions, perhaps with the help of the **Fraser Island Taxi Service** (☎ 4127 9188), but for most travellers transport comes down to the following three options. Please bear in mind, when choosing, that the greater the number of individual vehicles driving on the island, the greater the environmental damage.

Self-drive Tours

Unbeatable on price, these are incredibly popular with backpackers. Nine new friends are assigned to a vehicle to drive their own convoy to the island and camp out, usually for two nights and three days. Instruction about driving 4WD vehicles is given and drivers nominated.

We've heard complaints about dodgy vehicle damage claims on return, which can be costly; booking through a local hostel reduces this risk. Either way, check your vehicle beforehand.

Rates hover around $140 and exclude food and fuel (usually $30 to $40).

A1 Fraser Roving (☎ 4125 6386, 1800 989 811; www.fraserroving.com.au; Hervey Bay)
Colonial Log Cabins (☎ 4125 1844, 1800 818 280; www.coloniallogcabins.com; Hervey Bay)
Dingo's Backpacker's Resort (☎ 5486 8200, 1800 111 126; www.dingosatrainbow.com; Rainbow Beach)
Koala Beach Resort (☎ 4125 3601, 1800 354 535; www.koala-backpackers.com; Hervey Bay)

Tours

There are plenty of tours in anything from private 4WDs to large coaches carrying up to 40 passengers. Most include accommodation (for two or more days) and all meals, and typically visit rainforests, Eli Creek, Lakes Mackenzie and Wabby, the coloured Pinnacles and the *Maheno* shipwreck.

Fraser Experience (☎ 4124 4244, 1800 689 819; www.fraserexperience.com; 2-day tours per person $195) Small groups and flexible itinerary.
Fraser Island Company (☎ 4125 3933, 1800 063 933; day tours per adult/child from $105/60, 2-day tours from $195/140) Range of tours, from small groups to coaches.
Fraser Venture (☎ 4125 4444, 1800 249 122; www.fraser-is.com; day tours per adult/child from $105/55, 2-/3-day tours per person from $215/305) Sizable coaches on strict schedules.
Kingfisher Bay Tours (☎ 4120 3353, 1800 072 555; www.kingfisherbay.com; day tours per adult/child $125/65, 2-/3-day tours per person from $230/305) Ranger-guided day tours in 4WDs. Multiday tours targeted at 18 to 35 year olds.
Sand Island Safaris (☎ 1800 246 911; 3-day tours per person from $315) Well-regarded small-group tours.

Tours to Fraser Island also leave from Rainbow Beach (p350) and Noosa (p338).

4WD Vehicle Hire

Hervey Bay has loads of rental companies, but there are also a few in Rainbow Beach and the ferry from there is quicker and cheaper (see p362). Rates for multiple-day rentals start at around $120 per day for a Suzuki Sierra to $180 for a Landcruiser, and most companies also rent camping gear. All companies require a hefty bond, usually in the form of a credit card imprint, which you *will* lose if you drive in salt water.

A driving instruction video will usually be shown, but when planning your trip, reckon on covering 20km an hour on the inland tracks and 50km an hour on the eastern beach.

Rental companies are listed under Hervey Bay (p357) and Rainbow Beach (p351).

Fraser Island Beachhouses (☎ 4127 9205, 1800 626 230; www.fraserislandbeachhouses.com.au; Eurong Second Valley; d per 2 nights $250-350; 🖳) This luxurious complex contains sunny, self-contained units kitted out with polished wood, cable TVs and ocean views. Rates start with studios and climb to $600 (for two nights) for six-bed beachfront houses. Low season attracts a two-night minimum stay and high season five nights.

Fraser Island Wilderness Retreat (☎ 4127 9144; www.fraserislandco.com.au; Happy Valley; d & tr $125-160; mains $10-20; breakfast, lunch & dinner; 🖳) This small resort has a series of self-contained timber lodges cascading down a gentle slope amid plenty of tropical foliage. The lodges are a good comfortable option with a rustic edge to them. There's also a restaurant and shop.

Kingfisher Bay Resort (☎ 4120 3333, 1800 072 555; www.kingfisherbay.com; Kingfisher Bay; r from $270; 🍴 🖳) This elegant ecoresort has smart hotel rooms with private balconies and sophisticated two- and three-bedroom timber villas (three-night minimum from $820), which are elevated to limit their environmental impact. The latter are utterly gorgeous and some have spas on their private decks. There are also restaurants, bars and shops.

Eurong Beach Resort (☎ 4127 9122; www.fraser-is.com; Eurong; r $100-170; mains $15-30; breakfast, lunch & dinner; 🍴 🖳) This bright and cheerful place is the main resort on the east coast and the most accessible for all budgets: from simple motel rooms and units to apartments and A-frame chalets. On site is a cavernous restaurant and the popular Beach Bar.

CAMPING

If you're camping or self-catering come well equipped, as supplies on the island are limited and costly. Be prepared for mosquitoes and March flies.

The most developed **QPWS camp grounds** (per person/family $4/16), with coin-operated hot showers, toilets and barbecues, are at Waddy Point, Dundubara and Central Station. Campers with vehicles can also use the smaller camp grounds with fewer facilities at Lake Boomanjin, Lake Allom and, on the western coast, Ungowa and Wathumba. There is also a camp ground for hikers only at Lake McKenzie. Camping is permitted on designated stretches of the eastern beach but no facilities are provided. Fires are prohibited except in communal fire rings at Waddy Point and Dundabara, and to utilise these you'll need to bring your own firewood in the form of untreated, milled timber.

Frasers at Cathedral Beach (☎ 4127 9177; www.fraserislandco.com.au; Cathedral Beach; tent/caravan sites $18/28, cabins from $110) This spacious park with its abundant flat, grassy sites is a fave with families. Excellent facilities include large barbecue areas and spotless amenities. The quaint and comfortable cabins come with private picnic tables.

Dilli Village Recreation Camp (☎ 4127 9130; Dilli Village; tent sites $20, dm/cabins $20/100) Dilli Village offers good camp sites on softly sloping ground. The facilities are neat as a pin and the cabins are ageing but accommodating.

Getting There & Away

AIR
Air Fraser Island (☎ 4125 3600, 1800 247 992) charges $60 for a return flight (20 minutes each way) to the island's east-coast beach, departing Hervey Bay airport.

ELIZA FRASER'S LEGENDARY PHRASES

In 1836 the pregnant Eliza Fraser and her husband Captain James Fraser escaped the *Stirling Castle* shipwreck. During their six weeks adrift on the South Pacific Ocean, Eliza gave birth – the baby survived only a few hours. A week without food and water further forced them ashore. They landed on the island known to Aboriginals as Thoorgine, later named Fraser Island after Eliza.

Eliza's version of the events that followed went on to make her a legend. She was feted for battling through being 'captured' by so-called 'savages', 'stripped naked' and forced into 'slavery' in the bush. Aboriginal accounts of the same events tell how Eliza was 'rescued' and 'nurtured' by the local women (who, incidentally, wore few clothes and collected fruits and foliage in the bush for food).

After a number of months a search party located Eliza (Captain James had died) and escorted her back to Moreton Bay. She penned a lurid account of her ordeal, which became a bestseller and gave rise to the legend that later inspired poets, painters, filmmakers and authors.

After such a dramatic and high-profile life, Eliza slipped into obscurity. Years later accidentally run over and killed in Melbourne.

Eating

Laurel Tree Cottage (☎ 4126 2911; 89 Churchill St; dishes
$10-14; ☺ breakfast & lunch) The interior of this
café is very tea shoppe but the gourmet sandwiches, burgers and breakfasts are definitely
from this century. Outside, Childers' cosmopolitan set rack up lattes and savour smoked
salmon on the appealing timber deck.

Grand Hotel (☎ 4126 1763; Churchill St; mains
$10-16; ☺ lunch & dinner) The Grand Hotel's
menu is about as diverse as things get. And
whether you're ordering the crumbed calamari, T-bone steak or Cajun chicken salad
expect quantity and taste.

Tropicana Cafe (☎ 4126 1871; 102 Churchill St; snacks
$3-7; ☺ breakfast, lunch & dinner) This is probably
the best of the takeaways on the main road.

There are good bakeries on Churchill St
where you can pick up fresh pies or rolls.

Getting There & Away

Greyhound (☎ 13 14 99; www.greyhound.com.au) and
Premier (☎ 13 34 10; www.premierms.com.au) stop just
north of town at the Shell service station and
have daily services to/from Brisbane ($60,
eight hours), Hervey Bay ($15, one hour) and
Bundaberg ($15, 1¾ hours).

BURRUM COAST NATIONAL PARK

The Burrum Coast National Park covers two
sections of coastline, on either side of the little holiday community of Woodgate, 37km
east of Childers. The Woodgate section of
the park begins at the southern end of The
Esplanade; it has attractive beaches, abundant fishing and a **QPWS camping ground** (per
person $4) at Burrum Point, reached by a 4WD-

only track. Several walking tracks start at the
camping ground or Acacia St in Woodgate.
There are more isolated bush-camping areas
in the Kinkuna section of the park, a few kilometres north of Woodgate, but you'll need a
4WD to reach them. Contact the **park rangers**
(☎ 4126 8810) to book camping permits.

Barkala Caravan Park (☎ 4126 8802; barkala@isisol
.com.au; 88 The Esplanade, Woodgate; tent sites $15.50, cara-
van sites $18-21, cabins $40-65; ☒) is a tidy park close
to the national park with spacious sites and
cabins. The **Woodgate Beach Hotel-Motel** (☎ 4126
8988; fax 4126 8793; 195 The Esplanade, Woodgate; d $80-90),
at the northern end of The Esplanade, has a
block of motel units across from the beach
and dishes up decent pub grub.

BUNDABERG AREA

BUNDABERG

☎ 07 / pop 44,550

From Bundaberg to the coral-fringed coast
you'll see fields of sugarcane. It's the source
of the famous Bundy rum, and the income
for some of the local 'cockies' (farmers).

Not much has changed in this typical Australian town. The main strip, with wide streets
and towering palms, is positively gracious
and the extensive suburban development is
still dominated by stoic old Queenslanders.

'Bundy', as it's popularly known, attracts
large numbers of working backpackers who
come here to pick fruit and vegetables on
the surrounding farms and orchards. But
the town and its surrounds offer good distractions for travellers. There are spectacular
gardens, scuba diving and the chance to see
unbearably cute turtles born at Mon Repos
Beach. It's also a good jumping-off point for
Lady Elliot and Lady Musgrave Islands.

Information

Bundaberg Email Centre (☎ 4154 3417; 200 Bourbong St; per hr $4; ☺ 9am-10pm Mon-Fri, 10am-7pm
Sat, 10am-10pm Sun) Internet access.

Bundaberg visitors centre (☎ 1800 308 888; www
.bundabergregion.info; 271 Bourbong St ☎ 4153 8888; 271
Bourbong St; ☺ 9am-5pm; 186 Bourbong St ☎ 4153 9289;
186 Bourbong St; ☺ 9am-5pm Mon-Fri, to noon Sat & Sun)

Cosy Corner Internet Cafe (☎ 4153 5999; Barolin St;
per hr $4; ☺ 8am-7pm Mon-Fri, 9am-5pm Sat, 11am-
5pm Sun) Internet access.

Post office (☎ 4151 6708; cnr Bourbong & Barolin Sts)

QPWS (☎ 4131 1600; 46 Quay St) Permits for Fraser Island

FRASER C

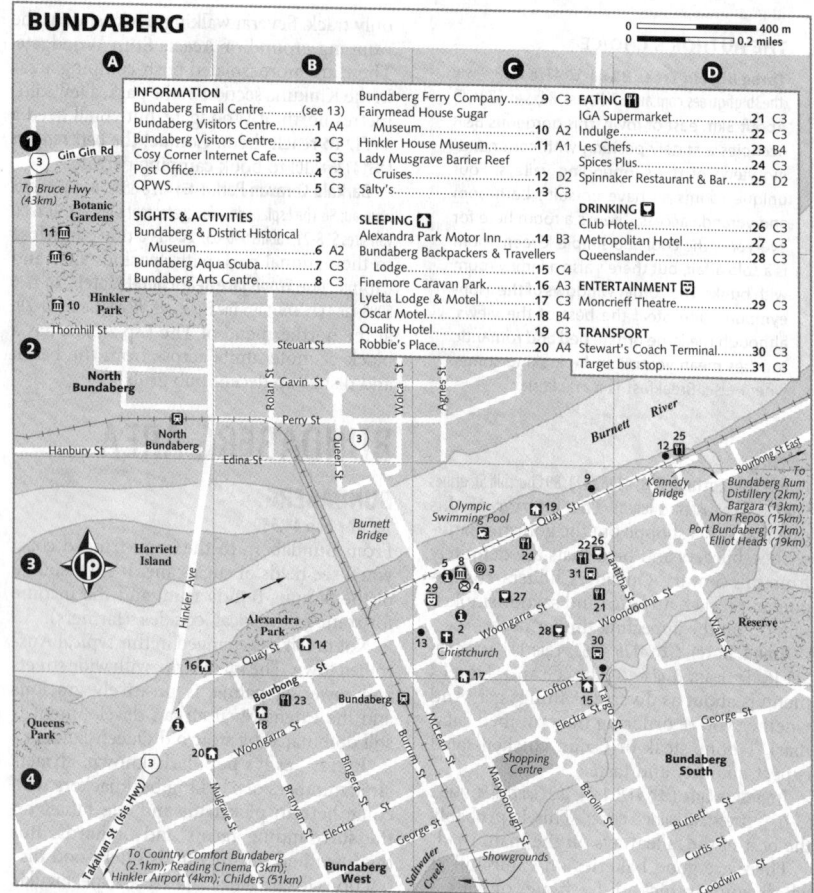

BUNDABERG

INFORMATION	
Bundaberg Email Centre	(see 13)
Bundaberg Visitors Centre	1 A4
Bundaberg Visitors Centre	2 C3
Cosy Corner Internet Cafe	3 C3
Post Office	4 C3
QPWS	5 C3

SIGHTS & ACTIVITIES	
Bundaberg & District Historical Museum	6 A2
Bundaberg Aqua Scuba	7 C3
Bundaberg Arts Centre	8 C3

Bundaberg Ferry Company	9 C3
Fairymead House Sugar Museum	10 A2
Hinkler House Museum	11 A1
Lady Musgrave Barrier Reef Cruises	12 D2
Salty's	13 C3

SLEEPING	
Alexandra Park Motor Inn	14 B3
Bundaberg Backpackers & Travellers Lodge	15 C4
Finemore Caravan Park	16 A3
Lyelta Lodge & Motel	17 C3
Oscar Motel	18 B4
Quality Hotel	19 C3
Robbie's Place	20 A4

EATING	
IGA Supermarket	21 C3
Indulge	22 C3
Les Chefs	23 B4
Spices Plus	24 C3
Spinnaker Restaurant & Bar	25 D2

DRINKING	
Club Hotel	26 C3
Metropolitan Hotel	27 C3
Queenslander	28 C3

ENTERTAINMENT	
Moncrieff Theatre	29 C3

TRANSPORT	
Stewart's Coach Terminal	30 C3
Target bus stop	31 C3

Sights

Bundaberg's splendid **Botanic Gardens** (Mt Perry Rd; ☀ 5.30am-6.45pm Sep-Apr, 6am-6.30pm May-Aug) display a network of lakes and small islands, and there are enough picnic positions to service a small country. Within the reserve are three museums. The **Hinkler House Museum** (☎ 4152 0222; adult/child $5/2.50; ☀ 10am-4pm) is set inside the house of Bundaberg's favourite son, the aviator Bert Hinkler, who made the first solo flight between England and Australia in 1928. The collection includes letters detailing his life and times. Nearby, the **Bundaberg & District Historical Museum** (☎ 4152 0101; adult/child $4/2; ☀ 10am-4pm) contains the quaint (quilts handmade by locals in the 1920s) and quirky (a series of

albums showcasing every wedding in Bundaberg since 1974). At the southern end of the park, the **Fairymead House Sugar Museum** (☎ 4153 6786; adult/child $4/2; ☀ 10am-4pm) has displays about the sugar industry.

The **Bundaberg Arts Centre** (☎ 4152 3700; www.bundaberg.qld.gov.au/arts; cnr Barolin & Quay Sts; admission free; ☀ 10am-5pm Tue-Fri, 11am-3pm Sat & Sun) is Bundaberg's premier platform for visual arts, showing temporary exhibits of Australian art.

Bundaberg's biggest claim to fame in Australia is the iconic Bundaberg rum. Enthusiasts can see vats of the sugary gold at the **Bundaberg Rum Distillery** (☎ 4131 2999; www.bundabergrum.com.au; Whittred St; adult/child $9.90/4.40; ☀ 1hr tours 10am-3pm Mon-Fri, 10am-2pm Sat & Sun), 2km east of town. Tours follow the rum's production from start to finish and include a tasting.

The **Bundaberg Ferry Company** (☎ 4152 9188; Quay St; 2½hr tours adult/child $20/13; ☺ 9.30am & 1.30pm) operates the *Bundy Belle*, an old-fashioned ferry that chugs pleasantly to the mouth of the Burnett River twice a day.

Activities

DIVING

The small beach hamlet of Bargara, about 16km east of Bundaberg, attracts divers and snorkellers with its dazzling bank of coral around Barolin Rocks and in the Woongarra Marine Park. This is one of the cheapest places in the southern hemisphere to learn how to dive. **Salty's** (☎ 4151 6422, 1800 625 476; www.saltys.net; 208 Bourbong St) and **Bundaberg Aqua Scuba** (☎ 4153 5761; Shop 1, 66 Targo St) both offer four-day PADI open-water diving courses for $170, but this only includes shore dives. Advanced open-water dive courses cost from $245.

Salty's also offers an extremely popular three-day, three-night diving package to Lady Musgrave and other islands on the Great Barrier Reef for $500. The price includes all meals and accommodation aboard their boat and up to 10 ocean dives.

Tours

Bundaberg Coach Tours (☎ 4153 1037, 1800 815 714) offers a variety of tours to local sights, including a day trip to Town of 1770, with sandboarding, lunch and an amphibious-vehicle ride (adult/child $75/50).

Sleeping

BUDGET

Bundaberg Backpackers & Travellers Lodge (☎ 4152 2080; fax 4151 3355; cnr Targo & Crofton Sts; dm per night/week $20/110; ✖ ▣) There's a cheerful buzz to this hostel, which accommodates a constant flow of working travellers. Little extras like dressers in the dorms and oodles of couches create a homely environment.

Lyelta Lodge & Motel (☎ 4151 3344; 8 Maryborough St; s/d without bathroom $35/47, with bathroom $50/55) This basic lodge seems to have changed little since the 1950s. It's welcoming, fairly central and the price is impressive.

Finemore Caravan Park (☎ 4151 3663; www .bundabergcity.qld.gov.au; 33 Quay St; tent/caravan sites from $10/12.50, cabins from $45; ✖ ▣) This neat park is on the banks of the Burnett River.

Quite a few long-termers pitch here and it's probably due for a wee makeover, but the facilities and rates are more than fair.

MIDRANGE

Robbie's Place (☎ 4152 7511; www.babs.com.au/robbies place; 109 Woongarra St; d $100; ✖ ▣) This excellent B&B features mock-period bedrooms with plump beds sidling up to a new kitchen and lounge room with stereo and cable TV. There's also a large balcony with private barbecue, and rates include breakfast.

Country Comfort Bundaberg (☎ 4151 2365; www .countrycomforthotels.com; 73 Takalvan St; d $95; ✖ ▣) Bundaberg's most comfortable motel has enough space to make you feel like the only sardine in the tin. Dated décor detracts little from the light-filled rooms, and the bathrooms glisten. It's just over 2km southwest of the town centre.

Quality Hotel (☎ 4155 8777; www.flagchoice.com.au; 7 Quay St; s/d $110/140; ✖ ▣) This pitstop is popular with business folk, but the facilities and décor-from-the-new-millennium set it apart: the rooms are stylish and there's a gym, sauna, laundry service and wheelchair facilities. Bookings recommended.

Oscar Motel (☎ 4152 3666; oscarmotel@hotmail .com; 252 Bourbong St; d $71-85; ✖ ▣) The Oscar offers a range of rooms; smaller digs are functional and warm and the larger rooms can be utterly cavernous. All have cable TV and tea and coffee facilities.

Alexandra Park Motor Inn (☎ 4152 7255, 1800 803 419; alex.parkmotorinn@bigpond.com; 66 Quay St; d $85-95; ✖ ▣) A gracious timber exterior, complete with sweeping balcony, greets visitors to this quiet motel off the main road into town. The downstairs rooms are cosy and the more expensive rooms upstairs are large and contain kitchenettes.

Eating

Les Chefs (☎ 4153 1770; 238 Bourbong St; mains $20; ☺ lunch Mon-Fri, dinner daily) This upscale and intimate restaurant goes global, treating diners to duck, veal, seafood, chicken and beef dishes à la Nepal, Mexico, France, India and more. Dinner bookings are recommended.

Spices Plus (☎ 4154 3320; 1 Targo St; dishes $8-14; ☺ dinner) The authentic Indian food served inside the beautiful old Union Bank building will have your taste buds dancing to the tune of *jalfrezi*, *marsala*, vindaloo and tandoori, as well as a host of vegie dishes.

FRASER COAST

Spinnaker Restaurant & Bar (☎ 4152 8033; 1A Quay St; dishes $17-30; ☺ lunch Mon-Fri, dinner Mon-Sat) Bundaberg's classiest restaurant woos diners with a picturesque perch above the Burnett River and fine food. Aside from perfectly cooked fish you can also savour Moreton Bay bugs and macadamia-crumbed calamari. A few fancy poultry dishes also grace the menu.

Indulge (☎ 4154 2344; 80 Bourbong St; dishes $8-14; ☺ breakfast & lunch) This sophisticated café offers fancy brekkies and lunches, but the highlight is all things sweet. Homemade cakes, slices and muffins show off from behind the glass counter and it all goes down well with a fresh coffee.

Self-caterers can stock up at the **IGA Supermarket** (Woongarra St).

Drinking

Metropolitan Hotel (☎ 4151 3154; 166 Bourbong St) Locals flock to the Metro's public bar, filling the place with genuine and lively chatter and charm.

Club Hotel (☎ 4151 3262; cnr Tantitha & Bourbong Sts) The bar at this big corner pub is friendly enough but the best spot for a coldie is in the sheltered beer garden attached to the bistro.

Queenslander (☎ 4152 4691; 61 Targo St) This old corner pub painted in a collage of all things Bundaberg has sadly suffered from a pokies infestation, but the beer garden out the back is a great spot for a drink.

Entertainment

The Queenslander (see previous section) has frequent live gigs, with either rock or DJs every Friday and Saturday night, plus sporadic week nights. When the weather is fine the gigs move into the beer garden.

Moncrieff Theatre (☎ 4153 1985; 177 Bourbong St) Bundaberg's lovely old cinema; it may not have a huge selection at any one time but there's something special about catching a flick here; you almost expect an intermission.

Reading Cinema (☎ 4152 1233; Takalvan St) A big, modern complex that screens commercial blockbusters; it's on the way to the airport .

Getting There & Around

AIR

Bundaberg's **Hinkler Airport** (Takalvan St) is about 4km southwest of the centre. **QantasLink** (☎ 13 13 13; www.qantas.com.au) has several flights daily between Bundaberg and Brisbane ($133, one hour).

BUS

The main bus stop is **Stewart's Coach Terminal** (☎ 4153 2646; 66 Targo St). **Greyhound** (☎ 13 14 99; www.greyhound.com.au) and **Premier** (☎ 13 34 10; www.premierms.com.au) have daily services connecting Bundaberg with Brisbane ($65, seven hours), Hervey Bay ($25, 1½ hours), Rockhampton ($55, four hours) and Gladstone ($45, 2½ hours).

Local bus services are handled by **Duffy's Coaches** (☎ 4151 4226). It has four services every weekday to Bargara ($5, 35 minutes) and Port Bundaberg ($5, 35 minutes); buses depart from the Target bus stop on Woongarra St (in front of the Target store).

TRAIN

Queensland Rail (☎ 1300 1131 722; www.traveltrain .com.au) operates *Sunlander* ($60, seven hours, four weekly) and the *Tilt Train* ($60, five hours, Sunday to Friday), which travel from Brisbane to Bundaberg on their respective route to Cairns and Rockhampton.

AROUND BUNDABERG

In many people's eyes, the beach hamlets around Bundaberg are more attractive than the town itself. Some 25km north of the centre is **Moore Park**, with wide, flat beaches. Locals and visitors also flock to **Mon Repos Beach** to see baby turtles hatching from November to March (see the boxed text, opposite).

Some 16km east of Bundaberg lies the cruisy beach village of **Bargara**. This picturesque little spot is drawing increasing numbers. Families find Bargara attractive for both the turtle-shaped playground on its main foreshore and for the sheltered swimming areas for kids at Kellys Beach. Local buses run to these places from the Target bus stop in Bundaberg; see above.

Bargara Beach Dive (☎ 4159 2663; www.bargara dive.com; Shop 4, 16 See St, Bargara) operates open-water dive courses with small classes for $300; you can also hire equipment. **Bargara Shoreline Apartments** (☎ 4159 1180; www.shore lineapartments.com.au; 104 Miller St, Bargara; d $75-90; ☒ ☒) has excellent accommodation 500m or so from the beach. The motel rooms are clean and simple and the bright and breezy one- and two-bedroom apartments ($100/140) are fully self-contained.

Turtle Sands Caravan Park (☎ 4159 2340; www .turtlesands.com.au; Mon Repos Beach; tent sites from $16.50, on-site vans from $27.50, cabins from $45; ☒) is a pretty park with good facilities and a great location right on the beachfront.

The fabulous **Kacy's Restaurant & Bar** (☎ 4130 1100; cnr See & Bauer Sts, Bargara; mains $10-25; ☖ lunch & dinner), at the Bargara Beach Hotel, is like a South Pacific oasis. Sitting on the capacious deck you can choose New Orleans gumbo, Thai curry prawns and bugs done any way you please from the huge menu.

LADY MUSGRAVE & LADY ELLIOT ISLANDS

The Capricornia section of the Great Barrier Reef, which includes the Southern Reef Islands of Lady Elliot and Lady Musgrave, begins 80km northeast of Bundaberg around Lady Elliot Island. The coral reefs and cays in this group dot the ocean for about 140km up to Tryon Island, east of Rockhampton. See p376 for more information on Southern Reef Islands accessed from Gladstone, including Heron Island.

Lady Musgrave Island

Lady Musgrave Island is an uninhabited national park about 100km northeast of Bundaberg. The island sits at the western end of a huge lagoon, which is one of the few places along the Great Barrier Reef where ships can safely enter. Lady Musgrave Island offers some excellent snorkelling and diving opportunities, and the day-trip boats can supply you with gear.

The island has a dense canopy of pisonia forest, which is brimming with terns, shearwaters and white-capped noddies during nesting. The birds nest from October to April, and green turtles nest from November to February.

You can walk around the island in 30 minutes, and there is a trail across the middle to the **QPWS camping ground** (☎ 4131 1600; www.epa.qld.gov.au; per person $4) on the western side. Its only facilities are bush toilets, and campers – a maximum of 40 – must be totally self-sufficient. Bring your own drinking water and a gas or fuel stove.

Lady Musgrave Barrier Reef Cruises (Map p364; ☎ 4159 4519, 1800 072 110; www.lmcruises.com.au; adult/child $140/72) operates day trips from Port Bundaberg marina at 8am Monday, Thursday, Saturday and Sunday, returning at 5.45pm. The tour includes lunch, snorkelling gear and a glass-bottom boat ride. The trip takes

---

TURTLE TOTS

Mon Repos beach, 15km northeast of Bundaberg, is Australia's most accessible turtle rookery. From November to late March, when marine turtles drag themselves up the beach to lay their eggs and the young then emerge, the **EPA visitors centre** (☎ 4159 1652; ☖ 7.30am-4pm Mon-Fri) organises ranger-guided tours nightly (adult/child $5.50/3, 7pm to midnight). Bookings are mandatory and can be made through the Bundaberg visitors centres (p363). Alternatively, you can take a turtle-watching tour with the highly recommended **Footprints Adventures** (☎ 4152 3659; www.footprintsadventures.com.au; adult/child incl transfers $50/25). Either way, take warm clothing, rain protection and insect repellent.

2¼ hours and you have about four hours on the island. You can also use this service for camping drop offs ($260 return).

There are also day trips from Town of 1770 (see p371).

Lady Elliot Island

About 80km northeast of Bundaberg, Lady Elliot is a 40-hectare vegetated coral cay at the southern end of the Great Barrier Reef. The island has a resort and its own airstrip. It is popular with divers and snorkellers, and has superb diving straight off the beach, as well as numerous shipwrecks, coral gardens, bommies (isolated patches of reef) and blowholes to explore.

Lady Elliot Island is not a national park, and camping is not allowed.

The tariff at **Lady Elliot Island Resort** (☎ 1800 072 200; www.ladyelliot.com.au; tent s/d $220/290, s/d from $250/390) includes breakfast and dinner, snorkelling gear and some guided tours. The resort is a no-frills kind of place, with basic tent cabins, simple motel-style units and more expensive self-contained suites with two bedrooms. Most people are here for the spectacular diving and not the resort lifestyle.

Scenic Air (book through the resort) flies guests to the resort from Bundaberg and Hervey Bay for $175/88 per adult/child return. From Bundaberg or Hervey Bay, you can pay $279/139 for a day trip, which includes the flight, lunch and snorkelling gear.

Capricorn Coast

Astride the tropic of Capricorn, this section of coast includes the mega port of Gladstone and the brash beef capital of Australia, Rockhampton. This region's premier attractions are offshore, and include the popular resort Great Keppel Island, and Heron Island, one of Australia's leading diving locations. Away from the two regional cities and the Coral Sea islands, there's a beautiful coastline of secluded seaside havens, national parks and lonely beaches.

One of the most accessible coastal areas is south of Gladstone around the small holiday towns Agnes Water and Town of 1770 on the Discovery Coast. Here you can learn to surf, access the Great Barrier Reef or relax in style. Along with nearby Gladstone, one of Queensland's major industrial and shipping centres, Town of 1770 offers access to the southernmost part of the Great Barrier Reef. These superb coral cays offer some of the best diving and snorkelling on the entire Great Barrier Reef. Lady Elliot and Heron Islands both have resorts geared for underwater activity. For an adventure to an isolated coral cay, you can take an unforgettable Barrier Reef day trip or camp overnight on uninhabited Lady Musgrave Island.

Rockhampton is Australia's cattle capital, raging rodeo bulls are ridden by locals, and steak is on the menu just about everywhere. Just north of town you can visit a bat cave, the beach at Yeppoon or catch a boat to popular Great Keppel Island. Further north is the ruggedly beautiful Byfield National Park and several back-to-nature bush retreats.

HIGHLIGHTS

- Surfing the breaks, or at least learning how to, at **Agnes Water** (p370), Queensland's most northerly surf beach

- Snorkelling among the coral gardens and unbelievably clear waters of Fitzroy Reef Lagoon on the **Great Barrier Reef** (p371)

- Claiming a tropical beach for the day on **Great Keppel Island** (p382)

- Diving the clear, warm and coral-crammed waters surrounding **Heron Island** (p376)

- Watching the action at a rodeo, riding a mechanical bull and tucking into a juicy steak at Australia's beef capital, **Rockhampton** (p376)

- Viewing the works of Australia's best artists at the excellent **Rockhampton City Art Gallery** (p378)

- Cooling off in a crystal-clear stream while getting back to nature in remote **Byfield National Park** (p384)

★ Byfield National Park

★ Great Keppel Island

★ Rockhampton

Heron Island ★

Great ★ Barrier Reef

Agnes ★ Water

- TELEPHONE CODE: 07
- www.capricorncoast.com.au

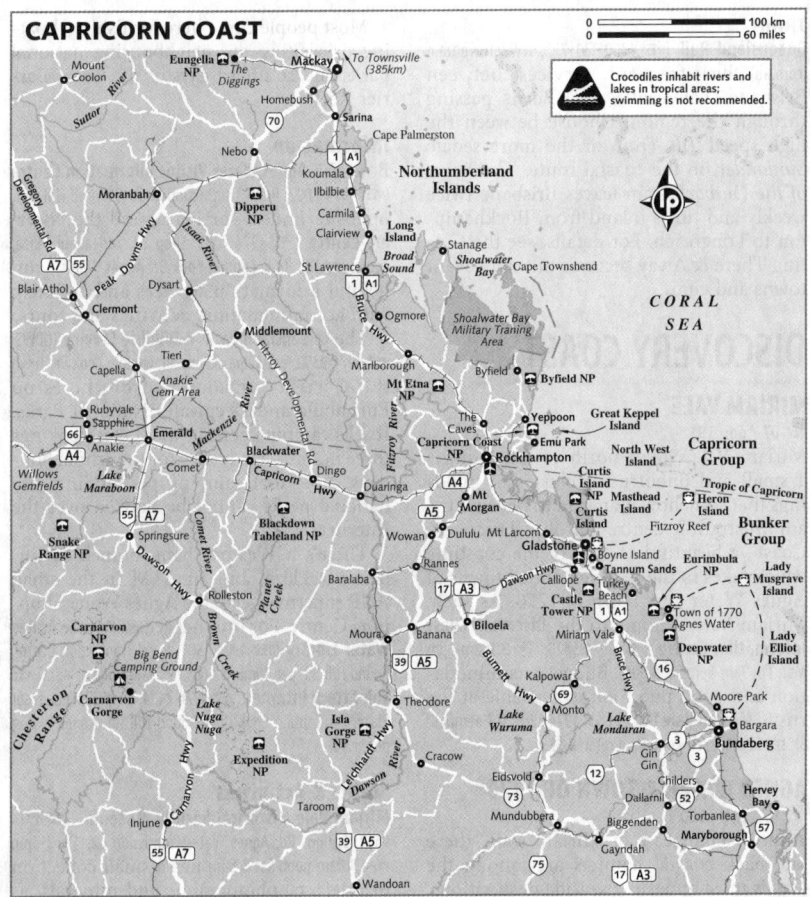

CAPRICORN COAST

Crocodiles inhabit rivers and lakes in tropical areas; swimming is not recommended.

CORAL SEA

Tropic of Capricorn

Getting There & away

AIR
Rockhampton and Gladstone both have major domestic airports. **Jetstar** (☎ 13 15 38; www.jetstar.com.au) connects Rockhampton with Brisbane and Sydney. **Qantas** (☎ 13 13 13; www.qantas.com.au) connects Rockhampton with Mackay, Gladstone, Brisbane and Sydney, and Gladstone with Brisbane. **Virgin Blue** (☎ 13 67 89; www.virginblue.com.au) has a daily flight between Rockhampton and Brisbane.

BUS
Greyhound (☎ 13 14 99; www.greyhound.com.au) and **Premier** (☎ 13 34 10; www.premierms.com.au) have regular coach services along the Bruce Hwy.

Greyhound offers regular services to/from Rockhampton, Gladstone and Agnes Water, while Premier operates a Brisbane to Cairns service, stopping at Miriam Vale and Rockhampton.

CAR & MOTORCYCLE
The Bruce Hwy runs all the way up the Capricorn Coast; however, it goes a fair way inland and it's only possible to get glimpses of the coast at Clairview. The Burnett Hwy, which starts at Rockhampton and heads all the way south through the old gold-mining town of Mt Morgan (see the boxed text, p375) is an interesting and worthwhile alternative inland route between Brisbane and Rockhampton.

TRAIN

Queensland Rail (☎ 1300 131 722; www.traveltrain .com.au) has frequent services between Brisbane, Townsville and Cairns passing through the region. Choose between the high speed *Tilt Train* or the more sedate *Sunlander* on the coastal route. The *Spirit of the Outback* train leaves Brisbane twice weekly and turns inland from Rockhampton to Longreach. For details, see the Getting There & Away sections of the relevant towns and cities.

DISCOVERY COAST

MIRIAM VALE

☎ 07 / pop 391

Miriam Vale, 96km north of Gin Gin, is a small and unobtrusive cluster of buildings that somehow managed to become the administration centre for the 'Discovery Coast', a beautiful section of the coastline which takes in the seaside holiday towns of Agnes Water and Town of 1770. As such, Miriam Vale is home to the **Discovery Coast Information Centre** (☎ 4974 5428; ☷ 8.30am-5pm Mon-Fri, 9am-5pm Sat & Sun). Budget accommodation and good pub food is available at the rustic **Miriam Vale Hotel** (☎ 4974 5209; 9 Bloomfield St; s/d $22/30, self-contained cabin d $55).

AGNES WATER & TOWN OF 1770

☎ 07 / pop 2000

Almost 60km east of Miriam Vale, these laid-back coastal hamlets are among the state's most appealing seaside destinations. Although experiencing a boom in popularity, the two towns, which are surrounded by national parks, beaches and the ocean, are far enough off the beaten track to retain their natural beauty and small-town charm.

Agnes Water is senior sibling in this partnership, boasting plenty of accommodation, shopping centres, information and a pretty beach that is Queensland's most northerly surf beach. Town of 1770, 5km further down the track, is a little more laid-back. Originally gazetted as Round Hill, Town of 1770 was renamed in 1936 in honour of James Cook's landing here on Bustard Beach on 24 May 1770 – the second place he landed in Australia, and the first in what is now Queensland.

Most people come here for fishing, boating or visiting the neighbouring national parks and southern cays of the Great Barrier Reef.

Information

Both the **Agnes Water Visitor Information Centre** (☎ 4974 7002; Rural Transaction Centre, Round Hill Rd), opposite Endeavour Plaza, and the **Discovery Centre** (☎ 4974 7002; Shop 12, Endeavour Plaza, cnr Round Hill Rd & Captain Cook Dr, Agnes Water), run helpful information services and can help with accommodation, activities and tours.

The **Queensland Parks & Wildlife Service** (QPWS; ☎ 4974 9350; www.epa.qld.gov.au; Captain Cook Dr, Town of 1770) has information and brochures on Eurimbula and Deepwater National Parks. It sells camping permits and takes bookings three months in advance for the school holidays. Note that camping permits in these national parks cannot be booked over the Internet.

There's a Westpac bank branch in Endeavour Plaza, and an ATM in the small AUR supermarket in the Agnes Water Shopping Centre. For Internet access try the **Agnes Water Library** (☎ 4902 1501; Rural Transaction Centre, Round Hill Rd; per 30min $2.60; ☷ 9am-noon, 1-4pm) or **Yok Attack Internet** (☎ 4974 7454, Shop 22, Endeavour Plaza, cnr Captain Cook Dr & Round Hill Rd, Agnes Water; per hr $4).

Sights & Activities

Miriam Vale Historical Society Museum (☎ 4974 9511; Springs Rd, Agnes Water; admission $2; ☷ 1-3pm Wed, 10am-noon Sat & Sun) has a small collection of artefacts, photographs and minerals, as well as extracts from Cook's journal.

Agnes Water is Queensland's northernmost **surf beach**. A Surf Life Saving Club patrols the main beach and there are often good breaks along the coast. Learn to surf on the gentle breaks of the main beach with **Reef 2 Beach Surf School** (☎ 4974 9072; 1/10 Round Hill Rd, Agnes Water).

Dive 1770 (☎ 4974 9359) offers dive courses and Great Barrier Reef dives aboard the *Spirit of 1770* (see the next section). Two dives plus gear costs $65 plus your boat ticket.

Round Hill Creek at Town of 1770 provides a calm anchorage for boats. There's good fishing and mudcrabbing upstream, and **1770 Marine Services** (☎ 4974 9227) hires out aluminium dinghies for exploring Round Hill Creek at $80/50 for a day/half-day. There

STINGERS

The potentially deadly Chironex box jellyfish and Irukandji jellyfish, also known as sea wasps or marine stingers, occur in Queensland's coastal waters north of Agnes Water (occasionally further south) from around October to April, and swimming is definitely not advisable during these times. These potentially lethal jellyfish are usually found close to the coast, especially around river mouths. Fortunately, swimming and snorkelling is usually safe around the reef islands throughout the year; however, the rare and tiny (1cm to 2cm across) Irukandji has been recorded on the outer reef and islands.

The large (up to 30cm across) Chironex box jellyfish's stinging tentacles spread several metres from its body; by the time victims see the jellyfish, they've already been stung. Treatment is similar for both species: urgently douse the stings with vinegar (available on many beaches or from nearby houses), and call for an ambulance (if there's a first-aider present, they may have to apply CPR until the ambulance arrives). Do *not* attempt to remove the tentacles.

Some coastal resorts erect 'stinger nets' that provide small areas for safe swimming, but elsewhere, stay out of the sea or wear a protective stinger suit when the stingers are around.

are also **catamarans** (☎ 4974 9539) at $15 for 30 minutes; a **houseboat** (☎ 4974 9643) from $100; and **canoes** (☎ 4974 9470) at $30 per half-day.

There are charter boats available for fishing, surfing, snorkelling and diving trips to the Great Barrier Reef. The **MV James Cook** (☎ 1800 177 011) sleeps 10 people for tours up to seven days duration, and **Sport Fish 1770** (☎ 4974 9686) offers sport-, game-, reef- and fly-fishing tours of the Great Barrier Reef at $600/380 per adult/child.

Tours

1770 Holidays (☎ 4974 9422; 1800 177 011; www.1770 holidays.com; 535 Captain Cook Dr; adult/child incl environment tax $130/70, diving optional extra $65) operates the *Fitzroy Reef Jet* from the Town of 1770 marina. This high-speed boat whisks passengers out to pristine Fitzroy Reef Lagoon on the Great Barrier Reef for a day's snorkelling. The tour departs at 8am and returns around 5pm; lunch and morning/afternoon teas are provided.

1770 Holidays also run enjoyable full-day tours in its amphibious vehicles – *Sir Joseph Banks* and *Dr DC Solander*. The **tours** (adult/child, incl lunch $95/65) take in Middle Island, Bustard Head and Eurimbula National Park, and operate on Monday, Wednesday and Saturday. There are also daily one-hour **sunset cruises** (adult/child $22/12).

1770 Great Barrier Reef Cruises (☎ 4974 9077; Captain Cook Dr; adult/child incl environment tax $135/70) has excellent day trips to Lady Musgrave Island on board the *Spirit of 1770*. It takes 75 minutes to get there and six hours is spent at the island and its acclaimed la-

goon. Lunch, snorkelling and fishing gear are provided on the cruises, which depart the Town of 1770 marina on Tuesday, Wednesday, Thursday, Saturday and Sunday (more often during holiday periods). Island camping transfers are also available for $225 per person ($245 in school holidays), which include lunch and reef fishing on the return journey.

Discovery Coast Detours (☎ 4974 9794; half-/full-day tour per person $28/51) Offers 4WD tours of Deepwater and Eurimbula National Parks featuring wildlife and seldom-visited coastline.

Extreme Adrenaline Ocean Runners (☎ 1300 661 770; www.oceanrunners.com.au; per person $75) Zooms adrenaline junkies around Bustard Bay in a very fast boat.

Jetski 1770 (☎ 4974 7765; per 30min from $60) Conducts jet-ski tours.

Sleeping

AGNES WATER

Accommodation ranges from a salubrious B&B to excellent budget backpackers.

Hideaway (☎ /fax 4974 9144; thehideawaybb@ bigpond.com; 2510 Round Hill Rd; d $130; 🖳) This B&B is an idyllic rural treat in a bush setting just 4km west of Agnes Water. The colonial-style homestead has three luxurious double bedrooms with en suites, a lounge room, outdoor dining area and barbecue area. For an extra $35 you can get dinner, and you can stay seven nights for the price of five.

Mango Tree Motel (☎ /fax 4974 9132; 7 Agnes St; s/d from $80/90; 🖳) Only 100m from the beach, this motel offers large self-contained rooms (sleeping up to six per room) with the option of a continental breakfast. There's also a licensed restaurant.

Cool Bannanas (☎ 1800 227 660; www.coolbananas .net.au; 2 Springs Rd; dm $23; 🖳) This purpose-built backpackers has roomy dorms with eight beds, as well as comfortable communal areas, tropical gardens and friendly staff. Call to be picked up from Bundaberg.

Agnes Water Caravan Park (☎ 4974 9193; 51 Jeffrey Ct; tent/caravan sites $18/25, cabins $55-80) With absolute beach frontage and a variety of cabins, this park is a great budget choice.

TOWN OF 1770
In 1770 you can stay in luxury 'shacks' or camp beside the beach.

Beach Shacks (☎ /fax 4974 9463; beachshack@1770 .net; 578 Captain Cook Dr; d from $148) These attractive self-contained 'shacks' are decorated in timber, cane and bamboo. They offer grand views and magnificent, private accommodation just a minute's walk from the water.

Sovereign Lodge (☎ 4974 9257; mickeyd73@bigpond .com; 1 Elliot St; d $85-220; 🖳 🖳) As well as a range of immaculate self-contained rooms, some with excellent views, there is a Balinese 'Body Temple' where, among other offerings, you can be massaged, wrapped in clay, rubbed with hot rocks and scrubbed with salt.

1770 Camping Grounds (☎ 4974 9286; fax 4974 9583; campground1770@bigpond.com; Captain Cook Dr; tent/caravan sites $18/21) This small and peaceful park has camp sites right by the beach and plenty of shady trees.

Eating
Saltwater Café 1770 (☎ 4974 9599; Captain Cook Dr, Town of 1770; mains $10-26; ☽ lunch & dinner) This cosy salt-encrusted waterfront diner has plenty of charm and a small bar. The fare is simple and fresh, ranging from humble but delicious fish and chips to sublime local mud crab. Pizza is the speciality on Tuesday night, and Wednesday is curry night.

Yok Attack (☎ 4974 7454; Shop 22, Endeavour Plaza, cnr Captain Cook Dr & Round Hill Rd, Agnes Water; mains $13-19; ☽ lunch & dinner) Here you can check your email while dining on authentic home-style dishes. This restaurant, run by a friendly Thai family, comes highly recommended by readers.

Aggies Restaurant (☎ 4974 9469; Agnes Water Tavern, 1 Tavern Rd, Agnes Water; mains $22-26; ☽ lunch & dinner) This restaurant offers delicious sea-

food, excellent steaks and a shaded outdoor dining area, though cheaper pub grub is available in the bar.

Getting There & Away
Only one of several daily **Greyhound** (☎ 13 14 99; www.greyhound.com.au) buses detours from the Bruce Hwy to Agnes Water. Others are met at Fingerboard Rd by a local **shuttle service** (☎ 4974 7540; $17); ask for Macca, who can also book Greyhound tickets. The direct bus leaves Bundaberg at 4.35pm and arrives at Agnes Water (opposite Cool Bananas) at 6pm. In the other direction the bus leaves Agnes Water at 6.45am and arrives in Bundaberg at 8.15am.

EURIMBULA & DEEPWATER NATIONAL PARKS
For information or to book camp sites (per person/family $4/16) contact the **QPWS** (www .epa.qld.gov.au; Bundaberg ☎ 4131 1600; 46 Quay St; Town of 1770 ☎ 4974 9350; Captain Cook Dr). Alternatively, the parks have self-registration stands. Note that you cannot use the website to book sites at these camping grounds.

The 78-sq-km **Eurimbula National Park**, on the northern side of Round Hill Creek, has a landscape of dunes, mangroves and eucalypt forest. There are two basic camping grounds, one at **Bustard Beach** with toilets and (unreliable) rainwater and the other at **Middle Creek** (no facilities). The main access road to the park is about 10km southwest of Agnes Water. It's 15km of gravel road to Bustard Beach and on the way you should check out the signposted **Ganoonga Noonga Lookout**. The lookout is at the end of a short, steep track and gives fabulous views of the coast, swamps, dunes and heath.

Deepwater National Park is south of Agnes Water. This park has an unspoiled coastal landscape with long sandy beaches, freshwater creeks, good fishing spots and two camping grounds. It's also a major breeding ground for **loggerhead turtles**, which dig nests and lay eggs on the beaches between November and February. You can watch the turtles laying and see hatchlings emerging at night between January and April, but you need to observe various precautions outlined in the QPWS park brochure (available from the office in Town of 1770).

The northern park entrance is 8km south of Agnes Water and is only accessible by

4WD vehicles. It's another 5km to the basic camp site at Middle Rock (no facilities) and a further 2km to the Wreck Rock camping ground and picnic area with both rain- and bore water and composting toilets. Wreck Point can also be accessed from the south by conventional vehicle via Baffle Creek.

MIRIAM VALE TO GLADSTONE
About 25km north of Miriam Vale is the turn-off to **Turkey Beach**, a tiny coastal village 24km down a dirt road, which has some of the best fishing in the region. Another 20km up the highway is the turn-off for **Tannum Sands**, a far more developed place with a nice park on the Esplanade and a good beach. At low tide you can walk across to **Wild Cattle Island National Park**, a wilderness park with no facilities.

Back on the highway, Benaraby is the turn-off to **Lake Awoonga**, created by the construction of the Awoonga Dam in 1984. Backed by the rugged **Castle Tower National Park**, it's a popular boating and fishing area and is stocked with barramundi. There's also picnic areas, a kiosk-restaurant, barbecues, walking trails, birdlife and the fairly basic **Lake Awoonga Caravan Park** (☎ 4975 0155; Awoonga Dam Rd; tent/caravan sites $18/23, cabins from $67).

A further 5km past Benaraby is the **Cedar Galleries Artists Retreat** (☎ 4975 0444; Lot 100 Bruce Hwy; admission $2; ☺ 9am-4pm Thu-Sun), which has a small café and several slab-hut studios where visitors can watch artists at work.

A short drive takes you to Calliope, just off the highway, where you can see a depiction of the area's pioneer days at the **Calliope River Historical Village** (☎ 4975 7428; Dawson Hwy; admission $2; ☺ 8am-4pm), with restored period buildings including an old pub, a church and a schoolhouse. From Calliope the Dawson Hwy takes you 20km into Gladstone.

GLADSTONE
☎ 07 / pop 27,400
About 20km off the Bruce Hwy, Gladstone is one of the busiest ports in Australia, handling agricultural, mineral and coal exports from central Queensland. That Gladstone is an industrial town can't be missed: there's the huge port with coal- and bauxite-loading terminals and oil tanks; the world's largest alumina refinery; and a power station, to name a few of the town's big industries. When the working clothes come off, Gladstone is well placed for exploring some beautiful coral cays and lagoons on the southern Great Barrier Reef. Gladstone's marina is the main departure point for boats to the superb coral cay islands of Heron, Masthead and Wilson.

Orientation & Information
Most of the shops, pubs and restaurants are on the main drag, Goondoon St. Across Auckland Inlet, via Marine Pde, is the marina where boats depart for Heron Island.
Gladstone City Library (☎ 4976 6400; 39 Goondoon St; ☺ 9.30am-5.45pm Mon-Fri, 9am-4.30pm Sat) Has free Internet access but you must book in advance.
QPWS (☎ 4971 6500; 3rd fl, 136 Goondoon St; ☺ 8.30am-5pm Mon-Fri) Provides information on all the southern Great Barrier Reef islands, as well as the area's mainland parks.
Visitor Information Centre (☎ 4972 9000; Bryan Jordan Dr; ☺ 8.30am-5pm Mon-Fri, 9am-5pm Sat & Sun) Located at the marina.

Sights
In the old town hall, the **Gladstone Regional Art Gallery & Museum** (☎ 4976 6766; cnr Goondoon & Bramston Sts; admission free; ☺ 10am-5pm Mon-Fri, 10am-4pm Sat) displays a rolling programme of local and national exhibitions.

The **Auckland Point Lookout**, off Flinders Pde, has good views over the harbour, port facilities and shipping terminals. A brass tablet on the lookout maps the harbour and its many islands.

The beautiful and elaborate **Tondoon Botanic Gardens** (☎ 4979 3326; Glenlyon Rd; admission free; ☺ 9am-6pm Oct-Mar, 8.30am-5.30pm Apr-Sep), about 7km south of the town centre, is an 83-hectare area of rainforest and Australian native plants, with extensive walking trails. It's a beautiful garden with a visitors centre, free guided tours (10am every Tuesday between April and September) and extensive wheelchair access.

Activities
Gladstone Dive Centre (☎ 4972 9185; 16 Goondoon St) offers PADI (Professional Association of Diving Instructors) dive courses and day trips to the reef. All gear is available for hire.

The picturesque **Gecko Valley Winery** (☎ 4979 0400; Bailiff Rd; ☺ 11am-4pm) welcomes visitors and wine buffs to taste its unique subtropical wines. It's in a bush setting adjacent to the botanic gardens.

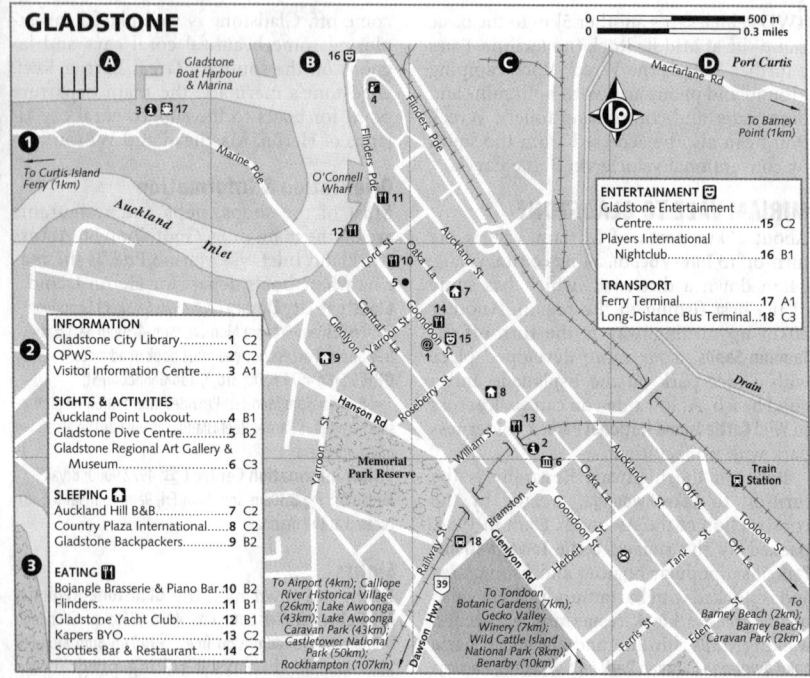

GLADSTONE

Tours

Gladstone's various industries, including the power station and port authority, open their doors for free tours. The one- or 1½-hour tours start at different times on different days of the week depending on the industry. Book at the visitor information centre.

Sleeping

Auckland Hill B&B (☎ 4972 4907; www.ahbb.com.au; 15 Yarroon St; s/d $99/125; ✷ ✷) This sprawling, comfortable Queenslander has six spacious rooms, all with king-sized beds. Each is individually decorated, and there is a luxury spa suite, and one with wheelchair access and disabled facilities. Breakfasts are hearty and the mood is relaxed.

Country Plaza International (☎ 1800 244 904; 100 Goondoon St; d $109-124; ✷ ✷) The Country Plaza is a 4½-star high-rise that has spacious rooms with balconies and views, and a restaurant and bar. Catering primarily to business travellers, the rooms are well appointed and substantially discounted on the weekend.

Barney Beach Caravan Park (☎ 4972 1366; fax 4972 7549; Friend St; tent/caravan sites $18/20, cabins $42-56, self-contained villas $80; ✷) About 2km east of the city centre, and not far from the foreshore, this is the most central of the caravan parks. It's large and tidy, with a good camp kitchen and excellent self-contained accommodation. Complimentary transfers to the marina are available to guests visiting Heron Island.

Gladstone Backpackers (☎ 4972 5744; 12 Rollo St; dm/d $22/48) This fairly central hostel (with three- and four-bed dorms) is friendly if a little scruffy, with a good kitchen and adequate bathrooms. There's free use of bicycles and pick-ups from marina, bus and train.

Eating

Flinders (☎ 4972 8322; 2 Oaka Lane; mains $30-40; ⏰ lunch & dinner Mon-Sat) This cosy restaurant specialises in seafood and does it well. Chilli mud crab is just one of the four mouth-watering ways this tasty local crustacean is presented. Although the quality, prices and ambience draw visiting suits and romantic couples most evenings, there is also a good-value lunch menu (eg $11 Barra Burger) and kids' menu ($15) keeping it casual during the day.

Scotties Bar & Restaurant (☎ /fax 4972 9999; 46 Goondoon St; mains $21-27; ☽ from 6pm Mon-Sat, from noon Fri) Thai, Mediterranean, steak, seafood and pasta: this popular restaurant with the decidedly blue theme has an eclectic and always changing menu that includes a couple of vegetarian options.

Bojangle Brasserie & Piano Bar (☎ 4972 2847; 6 Goondoon St; mains $17-20; ☽ dinner Wed-Sat) The 'Piano Man' pulls out all the Billy and Elton favourites while you sip your cocktail on one of the plentiful comfy lounges. There are pool tables, outdoor tables and the menu includes scrumptious wood-fired pizzas ($10 to $20).

Kapers BYO (☎ 4972 7902; 124B Goondoon St; mains $26-30; ☽ dinner Mon-Sat) A bright, breezy, offbeat place with hand-painted tables and an imaginative and varied menu. There's always a friendly reception and several excellent vegetarian dishes are available.

Gladstone Yacht Club (Yachties Bistro; ☎ 4972 8611; 1 Goondoon St; mains $10-19; ☽ lunch & dinner) The yacht club is a popular place to wine and dine on a budget. The steak, chicken, pasta and seafood are tasty and generous, there are daily buffet specials ($8) and you can eat on the deck overlooking the water.

Entertainment

Gladstone Entertainment Centre (☎ 4972 2822; 58 Goondoon St; ☽ box office 8.30am-5.30pm Mon-Fri, 9am-12.30pm Sat) Showcases various visiting live acts.

Gladstone Cinemas (☎ 4979 0755; 1 Hixon St) Just off the Gladstone–Benaraby Rd; screens new release movies.

Players International Nightclub (☎ 4972 6333; Flinders Pde; ☽ 10pm-late)

Getting There & Away
AIR
QantasLink (☎ 13 13 13; www.qantas.com.au) has several daily flights between Brisbane and Gladstone and one flight a day between Rockhampton and Gladstone. The airport is 7km from the centre and about $15 by taxi.

BUS
Greyhound (☎ 13 14 99; www.greyhound.com.au) has several coach services along the Bruce Hwy each day, about half of which stop in Gladstone. The terminal for long-distance buses is at the Mobil 24 Hour Roadhouse, on the Dawson Hwy about 200m southwest of the centre.

TRAIN
Queensland Rail (☎ 1300 131 722; www.traveltrain .com.au) has frequent services between Brisbane and Rockhampton, and Cairns and

---

DETOUR: MT MORGAN

There's very little to divert you on the 104km of road from Gladstone to Rockhampton, which hugs the railway line through some attractive mountain scenery. Just south of Rockhampton, however, is the turn-off to the historic gold- and copper-mining town of Mt Morgan, 27km away, where ore was extracted from 1880 until 1981.

Mt Morgan has a well-preserved collection of late-19th-century buildings, and is registered as a heritage town. **Mt Morgan Historical Museum** (☎ 4938 2122; 87 Morgan St; adult/child $5/1; ☽ 10am-4pm) has an extensive collection of artefacts, including a 1921 black Buick hearse, old mining equipment and photographs tracing the mine's history. Mt Morgan's lovely **train station** is a focal point for the town. It houses the **tourist information centre** (☎ 4938 2312; Railway Pde; ☽ 8am-4pm), and is the departure point for mine tours and the historic **steam train rides** (adult/child/family $15/12/42) to Cattle Creek and back.

Mt Morgan Tours (☎ 4938 2312), also based in the old train station, runs several value-packed tours that take in the town's sights, the open-cut mine and a large cave with dinosaur footprints on the roof. The one-hour tours of the mine and cave depart at 2.30pm and cost $25/20/70 per adult/child/family. The two-hour tour comprises town, mine and cave; it departs at 11.30am and costs $35/30/100 including a lunch voucher. All tours depart from the train station.

There are a few places to stay, including a caravan park and a motel, but the comfortable self-contained cabins at **Ferns' Miners Rest** (☎ 4938 2350; 44 Coronation Dr; cabins $50; ☷) sleep a family of four and are exceptionally good value.

Longreach, that stop at Gladstone. Fares and departure times vary greatly, so check the website or a timetable to find the most convenient train.

Getting Around

Buslink Queensland (☎ 4972 1670) runs local bus services on weekdays only, including a service along Goondoon St to Barney Point and the beach, which stops out the front of the caravan park. To book a taxi, call **Blue & White Taxis** (☎ 4972 1800).

SOUTHERN REEF ISLANDS

The Capricornia section of the Great Barrier Reef includes the southern Reef Islands and begins 80km northeast of Bundaberg around Lady Elliot Island (p367). Several cays in this part of the reef are excellent for snorkelling, diving and just getting back to nature – though reaching them is generally more expensive than reaching islands nearer the coast. Some of the islands are important breeding grounds for turtles and seabirds, and visitors should be aware of the necessary precautions outlined in the relevant QPWS information sheets.

Camping is allowed on **Lady Musgrave**, **Masthead** and **North West Islands**, and campers must be totally self-sufficient and abide by National Park rules and restrictions. Numbers are limited, so it's advisable to apply well ahead for a camping permit (per person/family $4/16). You can book up to 11 months ahead for these islands instead of the usual six to 12 weeks for other Queensland national parks. Contact the Gladstone **QPWS/EPA** (Environmental Protection Agency; ☎ 4971 6500).

See p367 for details on tours to Lady Elliot Island and Lady Musgrave Islands that depart from Bundaberg or Hervey Bay. The best way to get to Lady Musgrave Island, however, is a day trip from Town of 1770, which gives you more time on the island for the same price; see p371. Other access points are Gladstone and Rosslyn Bay near Yeppoon.

HERON ISLAND

Only 1km long and 0.17 sq km in area, Heron Island is 72km east of Gladstone and has long

been a favourite destination for divers: the beautiful Heron Island bommie (isolated patch of reef) area has appeared in almost every underwater documentary shot on the Great Barrier Reef. It's a true coral cay, densely vegetated with pisonia trees and surrounded by 24 sq km of reef. There's a resort and a research station on the northeastern third of the island: the rest is national park, but there's no camping and no day trips.

Heron Island Resort (☎ 4972 9055, 1800 737 678; www.heronisland.com; s/d from $350/480) has several levels of comfortable accommodation suited to families and couples; the Point Suites have the best views. All meals are included in the tariff, but guests pay $180/90 per adult/child return launch transfer from Gladstone. The helicopter option, also from Gladstone, costs $495/248. Stand-by rates can be as low as $185 per person.

ROCKHAMPTON & GREAT KEPPEL ISLAND

ROCKHAMPTON

☎ 07 / pop 64,000

Queensland's largest river, the Fitzroy, flows through the heart of Rockhampton, which also sits astride the tropic of Capricorn. Established as a river trading port in 1853, Rockhampton's fortunes grew with a minor gold rush at Canoona in 1858, and surged with the discovery of rich gold and copper deposits at Mt Morgan in 1882. Rockhampton quickly developed into the major trading centre for the surrounding region, and its early-20th-century prosperity is evident in its many fine Victorian-era buildings.

Today Rockhampton is Queensland's Beef Capital, with more than two million of the beasts to be found within a 250km radius of the city. Even if you didn't know this, the statues of bulls at the city's gates, and the number of men on the streets wearing cowboy hats, give the game away. Needless to say, you can get an outstanding steak here.

'Rocky' (as it's known) has several tourist attractions of its own, including the best art gallery north of Brisbane, an enlightening Aboriginal cultural centre and some excellent gardens and parklands. In addition it is the gateway to Yeppoon and Great Keppel Island.

EXPERIENCING THE GREAT BARRIER REEF

The Great Barrier Reef is one of Australia's World Heritage Areas and one of the seven wonders of the natural world. Stretching 2000km from just south of the tropic of Capricorn (near Gladstone) to Torres Strait (just south of New Guinea), it is the most extensive reef system in the world.

The southern and fragmented end of the reef spreads itself as far as 300km from the mainland, but at the northern end the reef sits close to the coast in continuous stretches up to 80km wide. The lagoon between the outer reef and the mainland is dotted with smaller reefs, cays and islands. It's said you could dive here every day of your life and still not see the entire Great Barrier Reef. Consequently, selecting where to get wet can be quite bewildering. Some of the most popular ports providing good access to the reef are detailed here.

Agnes Water & Town of 1770

Tours (p370) head to **Fitzroy Reef Lagoon**, one of the most pristine sections of the reef, and idyllic **Lady Musgrave Island**, for excellent snorkelling and diving.

Gladstone

Gladstone (p373) is the closest access point to the southern, or Capricorn, reef islands and innumerable cays. Among these is Lady Elliot Island (p367).

Airlie Beach

The big attraction at Airlie Beach (p400) is spending two or more days aboard a boat and seeing some of the fringing coral reefs amid the **Whitsunday Islands**. There are, however, several fast cats that zoom out to pontoons moored on spectacular **Knuckle** and **Hardy Reefs**, which provide outstanding snorkelling and diving.

Townsville

Near Townsville (p413), **Kelso Reef** and the **Yongala shipwreck** in particular are teeming with marine life. As well as overnight tours for divers, there are one- or two- day-trip options in glass-bottomed boats. The **Reef HQ Aquarium**, which is the Great Barrier Reef in a nutshell, is also here.

Mission Beach

Closer to the reef than any other gateway destination, Mission Beach (p430) is small and quiet and has a few boat- and diving tours to the outer reef. Although the choice isn't big, neither are the crowds.

Cairns

Undeniably the main launching pad for Great Barrier Reef tours: from Cairns (p441) you can do anything from relatively inexpensive day trips on huge, crowded boats to intimate five-day luxury charters. Some operators go as far north as **Lizard Island** for spectacular night diving and the famous Cod Hole.

Port Douglas

This swanky resort town (p454) is the gateway to the **Low Isles** and the **Agincourt Reef**, an outer ribbon reef with crystal-clear water and particularly stunning coral. Diving, snorkelling and cruising trips tend to be classier, pricier and less crowded than in Cairns.

Cooktown

Cooktown's (p464) lure is its close proximity to **Lizard Island**. A handful of tour operators promise unrushed experiences, but operations pretty much shut down between November and May.

CAPRICORN COAST

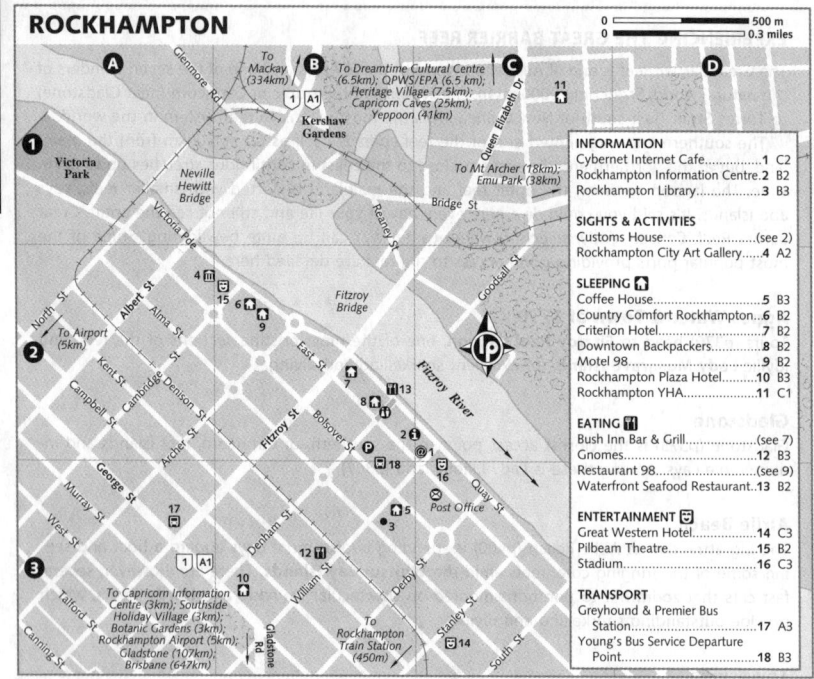

ROCKHAMPTON

0 — 500 m
0 — 0.3 miles

INFORMATION
Cybernet Internet Cafe...............1 C2
Rockhampton Information Centre.2 B2
Rockhampton Library.................3 B3

SIGHTS & ACTIVITIES
Customs House.........................(see 2)
Rockhampton City Art Gallery.....4 A2

SLEEPING
Coffee House...............................5 B3
Country Comfort Rockhampton...6 B2
Criterion Hotel............................7 B2
Downtown Backpackers................8 B2
Motel 98....................................9 B2
Rockhampton Plaza Hotel...........10 B3
Rockhampton YHA......................11 C1

EATING
Bush Inn Bar & Grill..................(see 7)
Gnomes....................................12 B3
Restaurant 98...........................(see 9)
Waterfront Seafood Restaurant..13 B2

ENTERTAINMENT
Great Western Hotel..................14 C3
Pilbeam Theatre.......................15 B2
Stadium...................................16 C3

TRANSPORT
Greyhound & Premier Bus
  Station.................................17 A3
Young's Bus Service Departure
  Point....................................18 B3

Orientation

Rockhampton is about 40km from the coast. The Fitzroy River flows through the heart of the city, with the small commercial centre, the oldest part of Rocky, on the southern bank. The long Fitzroy Bridge connects the city centre with the northern suburbs.

Information

Capricorn Information Centre (☎ 4927 2055; Gladstone Rd; ◔ 8am-5pm) Helpful centre on the highway beside the tropic of Capricorn marker, 3km south of the centre.
Cybernet Internet Cafe (☎ 4927 3633; 12 William St; ◔ 10am-5.30pm; per hr $5)
QPWS/EPA (☎ 4936 0511; 61 Yeppoon Rd, North Rockhampton) About 7km northwest of central Rockhampton.
Rockhampton Information Centre (☎ /fax 4922 5339; 208 Quay St; ◔ 8.30am-4.30pm Mon-Fri, 9am-4pm Sat & Sun) Very helpful central office in the former Customs House.
Rockhampton library (☎ 4936 8265; 69 William St; ◔ from 9.15am-5.30pm Mon-Sat, except 1-8pm Wed) Free Internet access, but you need to book.

Sights

Rockhampton is blessed with some fine old buildings, mostly dating from the city's halcyon mining days. Most can be found on Quay St and East St, including the extravagant neoclassic **Customs House** (1901), the ornate and multitiered **Heritage Tavern** (1898) and the imposing Victorian **Walter Reid Apartments** (1894). Pick up the excellent *Rockhampton's Heritage* pamphlet from the information centre and have a wander.

The **Rockhampton City Art Gallery** (☎ 4936 8248; 62 Victoria Pde; admission free; ◔ 10am-4pm Tue-Fri, 11am-4pm Sat & Sun) is a splendid gallery with good examples of many of Australia's major 20th-century painters, including Jeffrey Smart, Grace Cossington Smith, Sidney Nolan and Fred Williams. What's more, the gallery has room enough to keep its fine collection on permanent display, along with a rolling series of exhibitions.

About 7km north of the centre, the **Dreamtime Cultural Centre** (☎ 4936 1655; Bruce Hwy; adult/child $13/6; ◔ 10am-3.30pm Mon-Fri, tours 10.30am & 1pm) is an engaging exploration of regional Indigenous heritage and includes an art gallery, a sporting hall of fame, interpretive walking trails and excellent 90-minute tours.

South of the centre are the wonderful **Botanic Gardens** (☎ 4922 1654; Spencer St; admission free; ☽ 6am-6pm, zoo feeding 2.30-3.30pm). Established in 1869, the 6 hectares of gardens are beautifully landscaped, and include a formal Japanese garden, a fernery, lagoons and more than 200 species of palms and cycads. There is also a kiosk, plenty of lawns and a small zoo with a koala enclosure and walk-through aviary.

Just north of the Fitzroy River, **Kershaw Gardens** (☎ 4936 8254; via Charles St; admission free; ☽ 6am-6pm) is a botanical park devoted to Australian native plants. It features a waterfall, scented gardens and heritage architecture.

Mt Archer rises 604m out of the landscape northeast of Rockhampton, offering stunning views of the city and hinterland from the summit, especially at night. It's an environmental park with walking trails weaving through eucalypts and rainforest abundant in wildlife. A good brochure is available from the information centre.

Rockhampton's **Heritage Village** (☎ 4936 1026; Bruce Hwy; adult/child/family $6.50/2/15; ☽ 9am-3pm Mon-Fri, 10am-4pm Sat & Sun), 10km north of the city centre, is an interactive museum of replica historic buildings with townspeople at work in period garb.

Tours
Beef n Reef Adventures (☎ 1800 753 786; www .beefnreef.com) promises both the real Australia and the unexpected. Capricorn Dave takes punters on a whirlwind tour around Rocky's hidden bush gems and also runs visits to Koorana Croc farm or Capricorn Caves. The (very) full-day tour costs $85 and includes lunch. Overnight options can include the tidal bore on the Styx River, a ghost town and Great Keppel Island adventures.

Sleeping
BUDGET
Criterion Hotel (☎ 4922 1225; fax 4922 1226; 150 Quay St; s $40-45, d $60; ☒) Right on the Fitzroy River, this is a magnificent old-style pub with dozens of rooms in its top two storeys, some of which overlook the river, plus a range of bars and restaurants below.

Rockhampton YHA (☎ 4927 5288; peter.karen@ yhaqld.org; 60 MacFarlane St; dm members/nonmembers $19/23, d $50-59) This place is inconveniently

sited well north of the river, but it has welltended rooms, a very good kitchen and a large lounge and dining area. It does courtesy pick-ups and takes bookings for the Great Keppel Island YHA.

Downtown Backpackers (☎ 4922 1837; fax 4922 1050; Oxford Hotel, 91 East St; dm $19.50) Offers basic, clean budget accommodation right in the centre of town, but the bar downstairs can get boisterous.

Southside Holiday Village (☎ 4927 3013, 1800 075 911; fax 4927 7750; Lower Dawson Rd; tent/caravan sites $15/23, cabins $45-65) Roughly 3km south of town, this is one of the city's best caravan parks. It has neat, self-contained cabins with elevated decking, large grassed camp sites, a courtesy coach and a camp kitchen with microwave and fridge.

MIDRANGE
Coffee House (☎ 4927 5722; www.coffeehouse.com.au; 51 William St; d from $99; ☒ ☒) Has gorgeous selfcontained apartments and is popular with visiting professionals. It also has a restaurant (see the boxed text, p380), wine bar and a café with Rocky's best coffee and cakes.

Motel 98 (☎ 4927 5322; www.motel98.com.au; 98 Victoria Pde; d $109; ☒ ☐ ☒) The smart Motel 98 has well-appointed, spacious rooms around the inviting pool. The elegant dining room, Restaurant 98, has a terrace overlooking the river.

Country Comfort Rockhampton (☎ 4927 9933; fax 4927 1615; 86 Victoria Pde; d $105-180; ☒ ☐ ☒) The Country Comfort boasts big rooms with views and excellent service. Luxurious penthouses and family rooms are available, and downstairs you'll find a stylish restaurant and bar.

Rockhampton Plaza Hotel (☎ 4927 5855, 1800 001 800; 161-67 George St; d $99-109; ☒ ☐ ☒) The Plaza has typical well-appointed four-star hotel rooms that overlook a park. There's a bar and restaurant and it's located a short stroll southwest of the centre close to the train station.

Eating
Waterfront Seafood Restaurant (☎ 4922 0855; 179 Quay St; mains $25-50; ☽ lunch & dinner Mon-Sat, lunch Sun) Despite the name, you'll find more than seafood on the pricey but excellent Asian/Mediterranean-influenced menu. The location, in a riverside building with a balcony over the river, is terrific.

Restaurant 98 (☎ 4927 5322; 98 Victoria Pde; mains $22-34; ☽ lunch & dinner) This elegant licensed dining room features modern Australian versions of kangaroo, steak, lamb and seafood. Sit inside or out on the terrace overlooking the Fitzroy River.

Bush Inn Bar & Grill (☎ 4922 1225; Criterion Hotel, 150 Quay St; dishes $10-20; ☽ lunch & dinner) The Bush Inn serves some of the best pub food in town and is very popular. There are huge steaks, slabs of barra, chicken dishes and pizzas on the menu.

Gnomes (☎ 4927 4713; 106 William St; mains $13-19; ☽ lunch & dinner Tue-Sat) If you're looking for excellent seafood and vegetarian dishes in a casual BYO setting where you can dine in a charming courtyard, then look no further.

Entertainment

Great Western Hotel (☎ 4922 1862; 39 Stanley St; admission $7.70) Owned by country musician Lee Kernaghan, this pub looks like a spaghetti western film set. On Friday night there's a DJ and occasional live acts, but the real action takes place out the back in the bullring. Each Wednesday night you can watch poor brave fools being thrown from real bucking bulls and broncos. Professional rodeos are also held here throughout the year.

Stadium (☎ 4927 9988; 234 Quay St; admission after 10pm $5; ☽ until late Wed-Sun) The place most partygoers head to after the pub. It's a large, flashy club with a sporty theme, a central bar and pool tables.

Pilbeam Theatre (☎ 4927 4111; Victoria Pde) A plush 967-seat theatre located in the Rockhampton Performing Arts Complex that hosts a range of national and international acts.

THE AUTHOR'S CHOICE

Coffee House (☎ 4927 5722; 51 William St; mains $20-30; ☽ breakfast, lunch & dinner) The stylish Coffee House is a popular though relaxed café/restaurant/wine bar that delivers excellent meals and service throughout the day. The big breakfasts and superb coffee (the best in Rocky) help kick-start your day, while the extensive wine menu and the Modern Australian menu, showcasing local seafood and beef, provide an excellent way to wind down in the evening.

Getting There & Away

AIR

Jetstar (☎ 13 15 38; www.jetstar.com.au) Connects Rockhampton with Brisbane and Sydney.

Qantas (☎ 13 13 13; www.qantas.com.au) Connects Rockhampton with Mackay, Gladstone, Brisbane and Sydney.

Virgin Blue (☎ 13 67 89; www.virginblue.com.au) Has a daily flight between Rockhampton and Brisbane.

BUS

Greyhound (☎ 13 14 99; www.greyhound.com.au) and **Premier** (☎ 13 34 10; www.premierms.com.au) have regular coach services along the Bruce Hwy, and the Rocky station for both carriers is at the Mobil roadhouse (91 George St). Greyhound has regular services from Rockhampton to Mackay ($50, four hours), Brisbane ($85, 11 hours) and Cairns ($130, 16 hours).

Young's Bus Service (☎ 4922 3813) operates several services to Yeppoon including a loop via Rosslyn Bay and Emu Park. Young's also has buses to Mt Morgan from Monday to Friday. Buses depart the Kern Arcade in Bolsover St.

Rothery's Coaches (☎ 4922 4320) does three runs a day from Rockhampton airport (one way/return $15/30), or Rockhampton accommodation ($8.25/16.50) by arrangement, to Rosslyn Bay; the ferry terminal for Great Keppel Island.

TRAIN

Queensland Rail (☎ 1300 131 722; www.traveltrain.com.au) has frequent services between Brisbane, Cairns and Longreach that stop at Rockhampton. Choose between the speedy *Tilt Train* or the *Sunlander* and *Spirit of the Outback*. You can book tickets at the **Queensland Rail Travel Centre** (☎ 4932 0453) at the train station, 1km southeast of the centre.

Getting Around

Rockhampton airport is 5km south of the centre. A taxi – **Rocky Cabs** (☎ 13 10 08) – costs about $12. There's a reasonably comprehensive city bus network operating all day Monday to Friday, and Saturday morning. All services terminate in Bolsover St, between William and Denham Sts.

ROCKHAMPTON TO YEPPOON

On the way to Emu Park is **Koorana Crocodile Farm** (☎ 4934 4749; Coowonga Rd; adult/child $15/7; ☽ 10am-3pm, tours 10.30am & 1pm), a simple place, well signposted off the main road, where you can see crocs and buy croc-related products.

Emu Park is a sleepy holiday town on a lovely beach. At the top of Churchill's Lookout by the beach is the **Singing Ship memorial** – erected in 1970 for the 200th anniversary of Cook's visit to Australia – which has tubes and pipes that whistle and moan in the breeze. The **Emu Park Museum** (☎ 4939 6080; 17 Hill St; admission free; 🕑 9am-1pm Mon-Fri, 10am-2pm Sun) has a small collection of photographs and memorabilia, and local tourist information.

For accommodation in Emu Park, the **Endeavour Inn** (☎ 4939 6777; fax 4939 6733; 18-20 Hill St; s/d from $60/70) has smallish but nicely appointed units, plus a passable Chinese restaurant. On the beachfront, **Bell Park Caravan Park** (☎ 4939 6202; Pattinson St; tent/caravan sites $15/18; cabins $72) has spacious sites, clean amenities and comfortable cabins a stone's throw from the beach.

There are beaches dotted all along the 19km coast running north from Emu Park to Yeppoon. Along the way are three fine headlands with good views – Pinnacle Point, Bluff Point and Double Head – which collectively make up the **Capricorn Coast National Park**. About 7km south of Yeppoon, **Rosslyn Bay Harbour** is the departure point for trips to Great Keppel and other Keppel Bay islands. A great place to stay is the **Rosslyn Bay Inn** (☎ 4933 6333; www.rosslynbayinn .com.au; Vin. E. Jones Dr; s/d from $79/99; 🛇 🖭), which offers comfortable studio rooms and one- and two-bedroom units, as well as a bar and restaurant.

YEPPOON

☎ 07 / pop 8810

Yeppoon is a bustling and attractive seaside town 43km northeast of Rockhampton. Although Great Keppel Island is the area's main attraction, Yeppoon is a popular holiday town with a broad stretch of beach and a rugged hinterland worth exploring. Boats to Great Keppel leave from Rosslyn Bay, 7km south of town.

Information

Capricorn Coast Information Centre (☎ 4939 4888, 1800 675 785; www.capricorncoast.com.au; Scenic Hwy; 🕑 9am-5pm) Beside the Ross Creek roundabout at the entrance to the town; has plenty of information on the Capricorn Coast and Great Keppel Island.

Click On Central (☎ 4939 5300; cnr Mary & James Sts) Has Internet access.

Yeppoon library (☎ 4939 3433; 78 John St) Also with Internet access.

Sleeping

As well as those listed here, there's a string of budget motels and holiday units facing the beach along Anzac Pde.

Driftwood Motel & Holiday Units (☎ 4939 2446; fax 4939 1231; 7 Todd Ave; s/d $75/85; 🛇 🖭) Huge self-contained units at motel prices with absolute beach frontage make Driftwood a great bargain. There are good family units with separate bedrooms and there's a children's playground.

While Away B&B (☎ 4939 5719; www.whileaway bandb.com.au; 44 Todd Ave; d from $105; 🛇) With four good-sized rooms and an immaculately clean house with wheelchair access, this B&B is a perfect quiet getaway for the child-free traveller. There are complimentary nibbles, tea, coffee, port and sherry as well as generous breakfasts.

Rydges Capricorn Resort (☎ 4925 2525, 1800 075 902; www.capricornresort.com; Farnborough Rd; d $250-320; 🛇 🖭) This lavish resort about 8km north of Yeppoon is geared to golfers. Its accommodation ranges from standard hotel rooms to plush self-contained apartments, and there's a huge pool, a gym and several bars and restaurants. The resort's two immaculate golf courses are open to the public at $69 for 18 holes, which includes a motorised buggy.

Bayview Tower Motel (☎ 4939 4500; www.bayview tower.com.au; 4 Adelaide St; d $88-105; 🛇 🖭) On the beachfront, the eight-storey Bayview Tower looks luxurious, but is reasonably priced and, once inside, most rooms are fairly standard. The best feature is the balconies with views of the ocean and Keppel islands. Rates increase the higher up you go.

Beachside Caravan Park (☎ 4939 3738; Farnborough Rd; tent/caravan sites $15/18) This basic but neat little camping park north of the town centre boasts an absolute beachfront location. It has good amenities and grassed sites with some shade but no cabins or on-site vans.

Yeppoon Backpackers (☎ 4939 4702, 1800 636 828; 30 Queen St; dm/d $20/42; 🖭) This is a friendly and homey backpackers in a rambling old timber house on the hill overlooking the town and beach. It has a big backyard, clean facilities, OK rooms, and does free pick-ups from Rockhampton twice daily.

Eating

Maggy's Café-Bistro (☎ 4939 4566; cnr James & Mary Sts; mains $8-22; ✆ breakfast & lunch, dinner Fri & Sat) Maggy's is a casual but gourmet BYO café by day as well as being a great place for breakfast and lunch. It raises its profile on Friday and Saturday nights: Friday is curry night and on Saturday night there is a small à la carte selection.

Lure (☎ 4939 4666; 14 Anzac Pde; mains $17-28; ✆ dinner) A modish bar and café with extra-friendly staff who serve up excellent soup, pasta, steak, fish of the day and nightly specials with a minimum of fuss.

Thai Take-Away (☎ 4939 3920; shop 1, 24 Anzac Pde; mains $15-20; ✆ dinner) This is a deservedly popular Thai BYO restaurant where you can choose to sit outside on the sidewalk and catch a sea breeze while satisfying those basil, chilli and coconut cravings. There's a large selection of seafood dishes and snappy service.

Strand Hotel (☎ 4939 1301; 2 Normanby St, cnr Anzac Pde; mains $10-18) The Strand has plans for major refurbishment, but it's still a good place for a beer, a counter meal and live music. Bands play on Friday, Saturday and Sunday night in the open dining section.

Keppel Bay Sailing Club (☎ 4939 9537; Anzac Pde; mains $8-25; ✆ lunch & dinner) Choose between the beachfront clubhouse and deck with good steak and seafood, such as mouth-watering crumbed coral trout, or cross the road for a cheap buffet meal and the din of countless pokies at Spinnakers.

Getting There & Away

If you're heading for Great Keppel or the reef, some ferry operators will transport you from your accommodation to Rosslyn Bay Harbour. Otherwise, **Young's Bus Service** (☎ 4922 3813) runs buses from Rockhampton to Yeppoon ($7.70 one way, daily). **Rothery's Coaches** (☎ 4922 4320) does three runs a day from Rockhampton airport ($15/30 one way/return), or by arrangement from Rockhampton accommodation ($8.25/16.50) to Rosslyn Bay.

If you're driving to Rosslyn Bay there's a free daytime car park at the harbour, and, associated with the Rosslyn Bay Inn Resort, is the **Great Keppel Island Security Car Park** (☎ 4933 6670; per day $8), which is the closest lock-up car park.

GREAT KEPPEL ISLAND

One of the most accessible and down-to-earth of Queensland's island resorts, Great Keppel has almost all of the attractions you'll find in the more exclusive resorts, even though it's only 13km offshore. Because it's not on the Great Barrier Reef, you won't see truly spectacular coral life, but the beaches are superb, the water is warm and crystal clear, the marine life is plentiful and there are heaps of activities. It's also large (14 sq km), and mostly natural bushland, so you can happily spend a few days exploring its forests and white-sand beaches. What's more, there's plenty of budget and midrange accommodation on offer, meaning a tropical holiday is within the reach of pretty well everyone.

Great Keppel is also a popular destination for day trips; the main resort has a separate section for day-trippers, with a small pool, bar, outdoor tables and umbrellas, a restaurant, café and all sorts of water-sports gear for hire.

Sights

Great Keppel's beaches are simply gorgeous, and there are 18km of them to explore, guaranteeing privacy if you're willing to hike far enough away. There is some reasonable coral and excellent fish life around the island, especially between Great Keppel and Humpy Island to the south. A 30-minute walk around the headland south of the resort brings you to **Monkey Beach**, where there's also good snorkelling. The same trail continues another several hundred metres to **Long Beach**, perhaps the best of the island's beaches.

There are several bushwalking tracks from **Fisherman's Beach**, the main beach. The longest leads to the 2.5m 'lighthouse' near **Bald Rock Point** on the far side of the island (three hours return). Walking tracks also connect the resort area to **Second Beach**, **Svendsons Beach**, **Big Sandhills Beach** and **Wreck Beach**.

There's an **underwater observatory** by Middle Island, near Great Keppel. A confiscated Taiwanese fishing junk was sunk next to the observatory to provide a haven for fish.

Activities

The **Beach Shed** (☎ 4925 0624; Putney Beach) and the resort's **Watersports Hut** (Fisherman's Beach) both hire out sailboards, catamarans, motorboats, fishing tackle and snorkelling gear, and the staff can also take you parasailing or water-skiing. The **Great Keppel Island Dive Centre** (☎ 4939 5022; Putney Beach) offers introductory dives with all gear supplied for $100, or two boat dives for qualified divers for $130.

Tours

Freedom Fast Cats (☎ 4933 6244, 1800 336 244; Rosslyn Bay Marina; adult/child $51/28) operates a coral cruise to the best location of the day (depending on tides and weather), which includes viewing through a glass-bottomed boat and fish feeding. The cruise leaves Rosslyn Bay Marina at 9am.

Keppel Tourist Services (☎ 4933 6744; Rosslyn Bay Marina) has a 'ferry plus one cruise' deal from Rosslyn Bay and Fisherman's Beach. The morning tour includes a commentary cruise of Great Keppel Island, a visit to Middle Island Underwater Observatory and coral-viewing on a glass-bottomed boat. It departs Rosslyn Bay at 9.15am and Fisherman's Beach at 10am, and costs $52/26 per adult/child. The two-hour afternoon cruise leaves Fisherman's Beach at 2.15pm, and includes boom netting and snorkelling. The full-day cruise incorporates all the above ($77/44 with lunch).

Sleeping

BUDGET

Great Keppel Island Holiday Village (☎ 4939 8655; www.gkiholidayvillage.com.au; s/d tents $40/60, dm $27, s/d in cabin with bathroom $90/100) This YHA-affiliated resort is a collection of good budget accommodation (including four- and six-bed dorms and cabins that sleep four). It's a friendly, relaxed place, with shared bathroom facilities and a good communal kitchen and barbecue area. If you stay for seven nights you need only pay for six.

Keppel Haven (Keppel Tourist Services; ☎ 4933 6744; fax 4933 6429; Rosslyn Bay Marina; s/d tent $28/40, d bunkhouse $80, cabins from $120) This place squeezes a variety of accommodation in rather too small an area. It's a pleasant enough place to stay, however, with simple, permanent tents (with beds and lighting) and comfortable bunkhouses nestled in an established tropical greenery. It has a bar and bistro serving breakfast, lunch and dinner, and offers discount packages that include ferry transfers.

MIDRANGE & TOP END

Keppel Lodge (☎ 4939 4251; info@keppelllodge.com.au; s/d $90/110, each additional person $40) Keppel Lodge is a pleasant open-plan house with four good-sized bedrooms with en suites branching from a large communal lounge and kitchen. The house is available in its entirety – ideal for a group booking – or as individual motel-type suites.

Mercure Resort Great Keppel Island (☎ 1800 245 658; www.greatkeppelresort.com.au; r from $142 per night; ❄ 🖳 🏊) This popular resort went through a transformation in early 2005. No longer is it the 18 to 30-something party venue. With a new Kids Club and conference facilities, the resort is now aiming for families, couples and mature-age travellers. The resort boasts four room styles – rooms with two queen beds, a queen and two single beds, a queen and single bed, and three single beds. It offers facilities including bars, restaurants and a nightclub. There are tennis and squash courts, a golf course and water sports from snorkelling to skiing. More than 40 of the activities are free to guests. The resort offers a range of package deals to make longer stays cheaper, and two meals are included in the tariff.

Eating

If you want to cook, it's best to bring supplies with you, although the kiosks at Keppel Haven and the adjacent Great Keppel Island Holiday Village have a few basics like soup and noodles.

Island Pizza (☎ 4939 4699; The Esplanade; dishes $6-30; ❄ dinner Tue-Sun, lunch Sat & Sun) This friendly place prides itself on its uniquely healthy pizza recipe that has plenty of toppings. The pizzas are rather pricey but still tempting. Hot dogs and pastas are also available.

Keppel Haven Bar & Bistro (☎ 4933 6744; dishes $7-25; ❄ breakfast, lunch & dinner) This pleasant, airy eatery is conveniently located for backpackers and budget travellers. Moderately pricey, it does have some good-value specials that include a glass of beer.

Reef (Mercure Resort, Great Keppel Island; mains $7-20) In the day-trippers' area; offers pretty average light lunches and hot food, including wraps, pizzas, burgers and the ever-present chips.

Micro Market (Mercure Resort, Great Keppel Island; ❄ 10am-5pm) Also in the day-trippers' area; offers pretty ordinary espresso coffee as well as snacks and limited groceries. Internet access and newspapers are also available.

Entertainment

Splash is the bar in the day-trippers' area and is the place to party, with pool tables, a dance floor and live music.

Resort guests can party into the night at **Salt** (admission $5; ☑ Mon-Sat till late).

Getting There & Away

Ferries for Great Keppel leave from Rosslyn Bay Harbour, about 7km south of Yeppoon. If you have booked accommodation, check that someone will meet you on the beach to help with your luggage.

Keppel Tourist Services (☎ 4933 6744) operates daily ferries to the island, departing at 7.30am, 9.15am, 11.30am and 3.30pm, and leaving on the return trip at 8.15am, 2pm and 4.30pm. The cost is $32/16/80 per adult/child/family return. Keppel Tourist Services and **Rothery's Coaches** (☎ 4922 4320) run a daily bus service from Rockhampton to Rosslyn Bay, picking up from the airport ($30 return) and accommodation in Rocky ($16.50 return).

Freedom Fast Cats (☎ 4833 6244, 1800 336 244) departs the Keppel Bay Marina in Rosslyn Bay at 9am, 11.30am and 3pm, and leaves Great Keppel at 10am, 2pm and 4pm. The fare is $32/16/78 per adult/child/family return.

OTHER KEPPEL BAY ISLANDS

Great Keppel is the biggest of 18 continental islands dotted around Keppel Bay, all of which are within 20km of the coast. You can pay a visit to **Middle Island**, with its underwater observatory, or to **Halfway** and **Humpy Islands** if you're staying on Great Keppel.

Some of the islands are national parks where you can take the opportunity to maroon yourself for a few days of self-sufficient camping. Most have clean, white beaches and several, notably Halfway Island, have good fringing coral reefs, excellent for snorkelling or diving.

If you wish to camp on a national park island, you need to take all your own supplies, including water. Camper numbers on each island are restricted. You can get information and permits from the **QPWS/EPA** (www.epa.qld.gov.au; Rockhampton ☎ 4936 0511; Rosslyn Bay ☎ 4933 6608). **Funtastic Cruises** (☎ 0438 909 502) can take you from Rosslyn Bay to the islands to camp.

NORTH OF YEPPOON

YEPPOON TO BYFIELD

The hinterland north of Yeppoon is largely undeveloped state forest and national park bordering the large Shoalwater Bay Military Training Area. The best access to the coast is at the Sandy Point section of the **Byfield National Park**, about 25km north of Yeppoon via the Rydges Resort. It's an important breeding area for endangered little terns; there's good boating and fishing in Corio Bay (although no camping); and the eastern stretch of the peninsula has a long and little-visited beach. The last 10km of the access road is gravel, but it's OK for conventional vehicles.

Just south of Byfield are turn-offs to **Nob Creek Pottery** (☎ 4935 1161; 216 Arnolds Rd; admission free; ☑ 9am-5pm), where you can visit the workshop and gallery, and to the **Waterpark Creek Camping Ground** (☎ 13 13 04; sites per adult/family $4/16) which should be prebooked. It's 2km east from the main road to the creek crossing, beyond which is an attractive picnic area with toilets, tables and gas barbecues. From here, a 4WD-only dirt road continues through the pine plantations to the northern section of Byfield National Park, notable for its massive dunes in the south and granite peaks in the north. If you have a 4WD, you can continue to Five Rocks and Nine Mile Beach, which are popular with anglers.

Byfield consists of a general store and café, a school, a handful of houses and a private gallery which was closed at the time of research. There is no bottle shop in Byfield – so come prepared.

Just north of Byfield is **Ferns Hideaway Resort** (☎ /fax 4935 1235; www.fernshideaway.com.au; 76 Cahills Rd; tent site $24, d $130-150; ☒ ☒), a beautiful, secluded retreat popular with families. The main timber homestead has an à la carte **restaurant** (mains $13-25; ☑ lunch Sat & Sun, dinner Sat), while nestled among the trees are five cosy, rustic self-contained cabins with wood fires. There are also tennis courts, canoes, a pool and rainforest trails to explore.

Waterpark Cabins (☎ /fax 4935 1241; Yaxley Rd; d $110-130) is another secluded bush retreat perfect for couples. It has four superbly finished log cabins surrounded by bush, offering rustic comfort, along with a log fire, spa and wood-fired barbecue.

All other routes require a 4WD.

NORTH OF ROCKHAMPTON

From Rockhampton to Mackay is a long, lonely 329km ribbon of road, punctuated by only a few small townships. Around 17km north of Rockhampton is the tiny village of the **Caves**, where the **Caves Country Pub** (☎ 4934 2769; mains $7-15; ☽ noon-2pm, 6-8pm), an atmospheric old timber place, serves good counter meals.

Almost 3km east of the Caves is **Capricorn Caverns** (☎ 4934 2883; www.capricorncaves.com.au; Caves Rd; ☽ 9am-4pm), a dry cave system with easy guided walks ($16/8 per adult/child; one hour) leaving on the hour. More adventurous caving options are available, and each year the caverns celebrate the **Summer Solstice Light Spectacular**: from 1 December to 14 January, when the sun is directly overhead at midday, sunlight beams into the caves via fissures in the rock, creating an incredible spectacle. To see the light, take the 11am Cathedral Tour.

Nearby, **Mt Etna National Park** (☎ 4936 0511; adult/child $7.50/3.70; ☽ tours 5.30pm Mon, Wed, Fri & Sat Dec-Feb) is one of only five recorded maternity sites of the little bent-wing bat. There are no facilities and access is restricted. The park rangers run night tours of the bat caves (bookings essential) from the Caves township. Book using the number for Mt Etna National Park.

At **Clairview** you get a glimpse of the coast from the highway. The town is just a single row of houses jammed between the railway line and the beach. Much of the surrounding area is mud and mangroves, and the area is famed for its outstanding crabbing and fishing. There's only one place to stay: **Clairview Beach Holiday Park** (☎ 4956 0190; 1 Colonial Dr; tent/caravan sites $13/18, on-site vans from $32, d cabins from $46), a superfriendly place on the beach with a great open-air longhouse for communal cooking, a small bar (guests only), a useful little shop and evening meals ($10).

The last 100km into Sarina is broken up by just three tiny settlements: Carmila, Ilbilbie and Koumala. See the Whitsunday Coast chapter for details of Sarina (p388) and Mackay (p389).

WHITSUNDAY COAST

Whitsunday Coast

The Whitsunday Islands are rightly the focus of this part of the coast; the islands boast sublime palm-fringed beaches, holiday resorts and wilderness camping, sailing, diving and snorkelling. The coral gardens and the surrounding water host sea turtles, dolphins, whales and a myriad of tropical fish. Much of this 74-island archipelago belongs to the Great Barrier Reef Marine Park, ensuring that this marine wonderland stays pristine; a notable benefit is that its delights are accessible to all budgets. There's a range of resorts, and bush and beach camping grounds for those who want to get away from it all.

This chapter also covers the coastal strip from Sarina to Hydeaway Bay, and includes some hinterland excursions. Mackay is this sugar-cane-growing region's major city. It is a bustling port and handy base for Eungalla National Park and the Cumberland Group, including the Brampton Island resort. At Eungalla National Park you are virtually guaranteed to see wild platypuses and other native animals. Here you can enjoy rainforest walks and excellent camp-sites and other accommodation options at the Broken River or Finch Hatton Gorge sections of this outstanding park. The experience continues at Cape Hillsborough National Park, where you can meet kangaroos, discover the region's Indigenous history and comb the beach.

Airlie Beach is the lively gateway to the Whitsunday Islands. Every conceivable tour, activity and category of accommodation can be found here. Every night is party night, and there are numerous restaurants, bars and clubs to get you into the holiday spirit.

HIGHLIGHTS

- Sail a leisurely course through the turquoise passages of the magnificent **Whitsunday Islands** (p396)

- Stroll and swimming along the brilliant white arc of **Whitehaven Beach** (p410) on Whitsunday Island

- Take a high-speed trip to the outer **Great Barrier Reef** (p398) for superb snorkelling and diving.

- Glide your sea kayak over coral gardens before finding a bush camp on idyllic **Hook Island** (p407)

- Hike through the rainforest and spot playful platypuses at **Eungella National Park** (p394)

- Lap up the luxury on a well-earned break at **Hamilton Island** (p408)

- Party hard, graze in a restaurant or just recuperate at **Airlie Beach** (p400), gateway to the islands, reef, sun and fun

- Rejuvenate the spirit and get back to nature at serene **Cape Hillsborough National Park** (p396)

★ Hook Island ★ Great Barrier Reef
Airlie ★ ★ Whitehaven Beach
Beach ★ Hamilton Island
Whitsunday Islands
Cape Hillsborough
★ National Park
★ Eungella National Park

- TELEPHONE CODE: 07
- www.whitsundaytourism.com

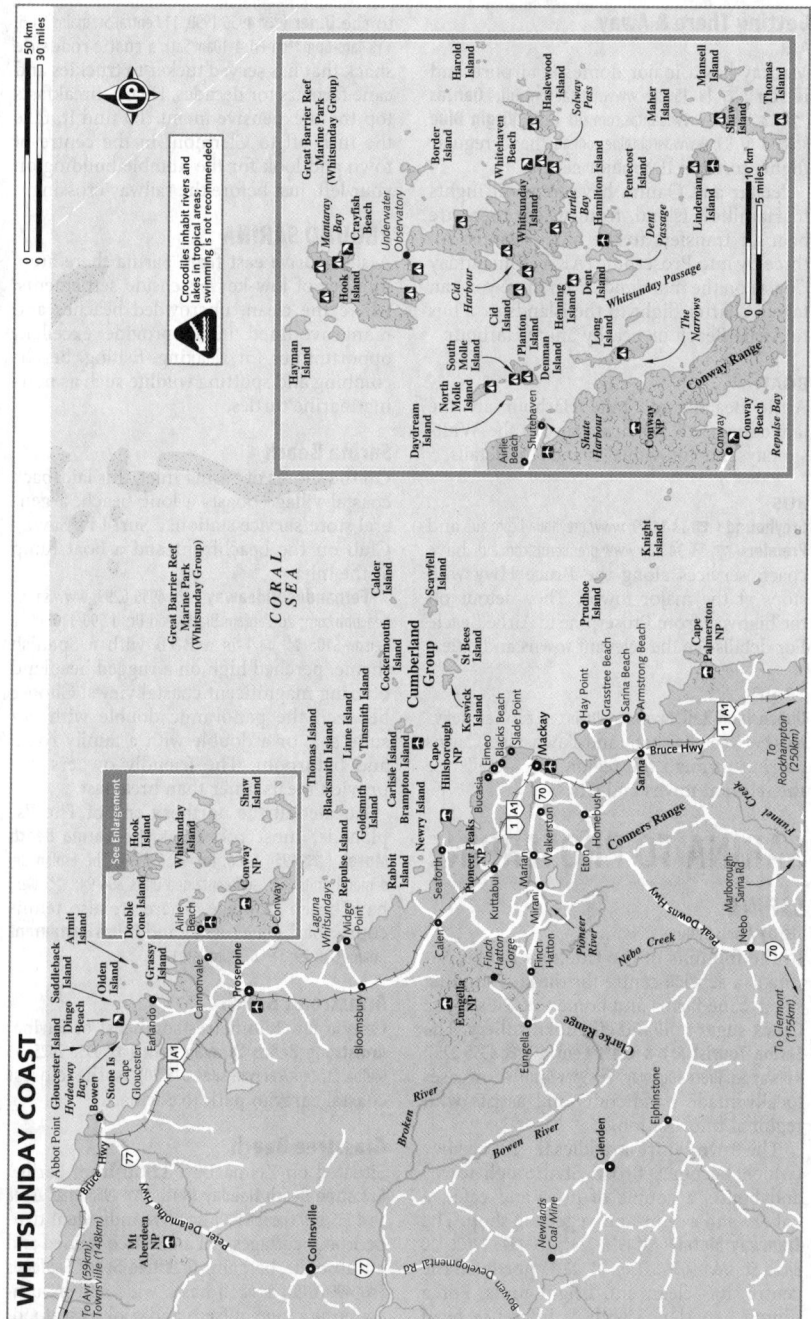

WHITSUNDAY COAST

Crocodiles inhabit rivers and lakes in tropical areas; swimming is not recommended.

Getting There & Away

AIR

Mackay has a major domestic airport, and **Jetstar** (☎ 13 15 38; www.jetstar.com.au), **Qantas** (☎ 13 13 13; www.qantas.com.au) and **Virgin Blue** (☎ 13 67 89; www.virginblue.com.au) have regular flights to/from the major centres.

Jetstar and Qantas have frequent flights to Hamilton Island, from where there are boat/air transfers to the other islands. All three fly into Proserpine (AKA Whitsunday Coast) on the mainland; from there you can take a charter flight to the islands or a bus to Airlie Beach or nearby Shute Harbour.

BOAT

Airlie Beach and Shute Harbour are the launching pads for boat trips to the Whitsundays; see individual islands for details.

BUS

Greyhound (☎ 13 14 99; www.greyhound.com.au) and **Premier** (☎ 13 34 10; www.premierms.com.au) have coach services along the Bruce Hwy with stops at the major towns. They detour off the highway from Proserpine to Airlie Beach. For details see the relevant towns and cities.

TRAIN

Queensland Rail (www.traveltrain.com.au) has services between Brisbane and Townsville/Cairns passing through the region. For details see the relevant towns and cities.

SARINA TO PROSERPINE

SARINA

☎ 07 / pop 3200

In the foothills of the Connors Range, Sarina is a service centre for the surrounding sugar-cane farms and home to CSR's Plane Creek sugar mill and ethanol distillery. The **Sarina Tourist Art & Craft Centre** (☎ 4956 2251; Railway Sq, Bruce Highway; ☯9am-5pm) showcases locally made handicrafts and assists with regional information.

The town centre straddles the Bruce Hwy (which becomes Broad St through town) and boasts a couple of pubs and cafés, a bakery and a fruit-and-vegetable shop. The **Tramway Motel** (☎ 4956 2244; fax 4943 1262; 110 Broad St; s/d/f $65/75/130; ✖ ♨), north of the centre, has clean and bright units. For a dining experience with a difference head

to the **Diner** (☎ 4956 1990; 11 Central St; mains $4-6; ☯4am-6pm Mon-Fri, 4-10am Sat), a rustic roadside shack that has served tucker to truckies and cane farmers for decades. Hearty breakfasts top the inexpensive menu. To find it, take the turn-off to Clermont in the centre of town and look for the humble building on your left, just before the railway crossing.

AROUND SARINA

A short drive east from Sarina there are a number of low-key beachside settlements, where the clean, uncrowded beaches and mangrove-lined inlets provide excellent opportunities for relaxing, fishing, beach-combing and spotting wildlife such as nesting marine turtles.

Sarina Beach

On the shores of Sarina Inlet, this laid-back coastal village boasts a long beach, a general store/service station, a Surf Life Saving Club on the beachfront and a boat ramp at the inlet.

Fernandos Hideaway (☎ 4956 6299; www.sarina beachbb.com; 26 Captain Blackwood Dr; d $90-110, extra person $10; ✖ ♨) is a B&B with a Spanish theme, perched high on a rugged headland offering magnificent coastal views. Choose between the panoramic double with en-suite spa, or a double with a family room and bathroom. The friendly owners can provide meals other than breakfast.

Located at the northern end of The Esplanade, most rooms at the **Sarina Beach Motel** (☎ 4956 6266; fax 4956 6197; The Esplanade; d motel units $75, self-contained units $64-94; ✖ ♨) have beach frontage. There are also tennis courts, barbeques, a bar and **Palms Restaurant** (mains $16-29; ☯6.30pm-late).

Armstrong Beach

Only a few kilometres southeast of Sarina, **Armstrong Beach Caravan Park** (☎ 4956 2425; 66 Melba St; tent/caravan sites $18/20) is the closest coastal caravan park to Sarina.

Grasstree Beach

Situated on Zelma Bay, 12km from Sarina, **Grasstree Beach Holiday Units** (☎ 4956 6180; Zelma St; d $65, extra person $10) has five individual two-bedroom cottages. All are self-contained and an absolute bargain. **Grasstree Beach Seafoods** (☎ 4956 6151; Zelma St) has a wide and mouth-watering range of fresh and cooked seafood.

MACKAY

☎ 07 / pop 73,000

Mackay is a vibrant regional city powered by agriculture, mining and tourism, and boasts one of the world's largest sugar-loading terminals. One of Mackay's best features is its attractive centre with heritage buildings and plenty of bird-filled shady trees. The surrounding coastal plains and hinterland are carpeted in sugar cane and there are good beaches a short bus ride away.

Mackay is an excellent base for visiting Eungella National Park with its famous platypuses and wild Finch Hatton Gorge, and for exploring the pretty Pioneer Valley. It is also the access point for ruggedly beautiful Cape Hillsborough National Park to the north, and several tropical islands including the popular Brampton Island.

Orientation

Mackay's city centre is compact, with the main streets laid out in a grid south of the broad Pioneer River. Victoria, Wood and Sydney Sts are the places to go for restaurants, bars and pubs. The train station, airport, botanic gardens and visitor information centre are about 3km south of the city centre.

Sydney St takes you across Forgan Bridge to North Mackay, the city's newer suburbs and the northern beaches. Mackay Harbour, 6km northeast of the centre, is dominated

WHITSUNDAY COAST

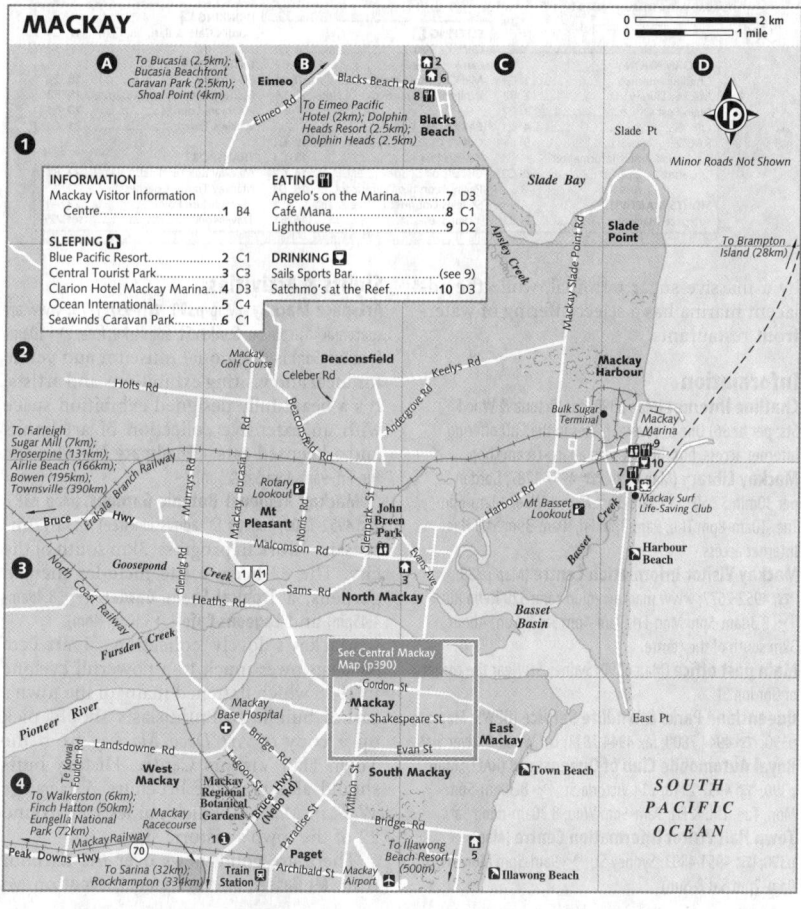

MACKAY

| 0 | 2 km |
| 0 | 1 mile |

INFORMATION
Mackay Visitor Information
Centre.....................................**1** B4

SLEEPING 🛏
Blue Pacific Resort.....................**2** C1
Central Tourist Park...................**3** C3
Clarion Hotel Mackay Marina.....**4** D3
Ocean International....................**5** C4
Seawinds Caravan Park.............**6** C1

EATING 🍴
Angelo's on the Marina...............**7** D3
Café Mana.................................**8** C1
Lighthouse................................**9** D2

DRINKING 🍷
Sails Sports Bar......................(see 9)
Satchmo's at the Reef..............**10** D3

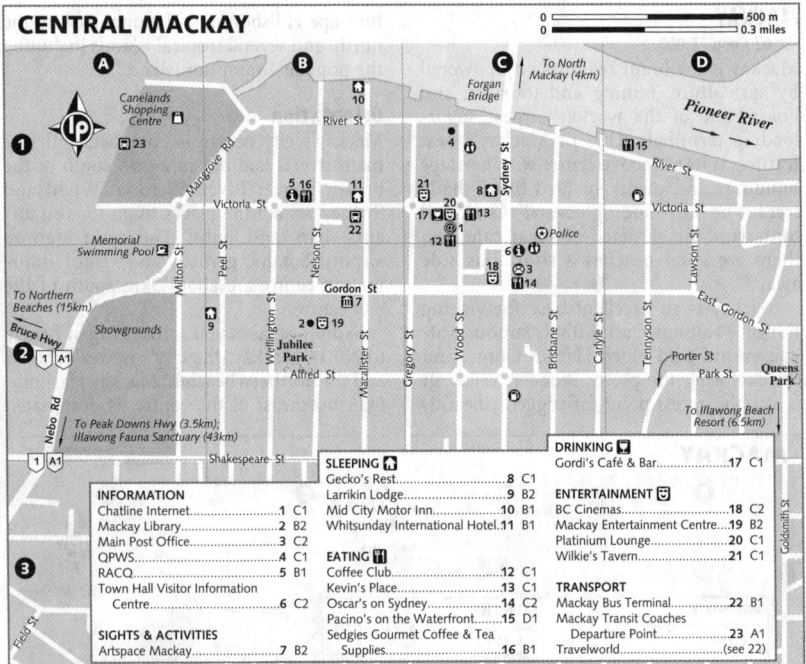

by a massive sugar terminal, while the adjacent marina has a select offering of waterfront restaurants.

Information

Chatline Internet (Map p390; cnr Victoria & Wood Sts; per hr $6) One of several places in the CBD offering Internet access, but this one is in an ice-cream shop.

Mackay Library (Map p390; ☎ 4957 1787; Gordon St; per 30min $2.50; ☷ 9am-5pm Mon & Wed, 10am-6pm Tue, 10am-8pm Thu, 9am-3pm Fri, 10am-3pm Sat) Has Internet access.

Mackay Visitor Information Centre (Map p389; ☎ 4952 2677; www.mackayregion.com; 320 Nebo Rd; ☷ 8.30am-5pm Mon-Fri, 9am-4pm Sat & Sun) About 3km south of the centre.

Main post office (Map p390; Sydney St) Near the corner of Gordon St.

Queensland Parks & Wildlife Service (QPWS; Map p390; ☎ 4944 7800; fax 4944 7811; cnr Wood & River Sts)

Royal Automobile Club of Queensland (RACQ; Map p390; ☎ 4957 2918; 214 Victoria St; ☷ 8.30am-5pm Mon, Tue, Thu & Fri, 9am-5pm Wed, 8.30am-noon Sat)

Town Hall Visitor Information Centre (Map p390; ☎ 4951 4803; Sydney St; ☷ 9am-5pm Mon-Fri, 9am-2pm Sat & Sun)

Sights & Activities

Artspace Mackay (Map p390; ☎ 4957 1775; www.art spacemackay.com.au; Gordon St; admission free; ☷ 10am-5pm Tue-Sun) is a regional museum and venue for local and visiting exhibitions and artists. It's a beautifully designed exhibition space with an extensive collection of art books and a licensed café – **Foodspace** (☷ 10am-4pm Tue-Fri, 9am-4pm Sat & Sun).

Mackay Regional Botanic Gardens (Map p389; ☎ 4952 7300; Lagoon St; admission free) is an impressive 'work in progress' 3km south of the city. The 33-hectare site includes themed gardens, a **Tropical Shade Garden** (☷ 8.45am-4.45pm) and **Lagoons Café** (☷ 10am-4pm).

Mackay's lovely collection of **Art Deco buildings** owes much to a powerful cyclone in 1918 which flattened many of the town's earlier buildings. Enthusiasts should pick up a copy of *Art Deco Mackay* from the Town Hall Visitors Centre. History buffs should also grab the brochure *A Heritage Walk in Mackay*, which guides you around 22 of the town's historic sites.

There are good views over the harbour from **Mt Basset**, and at **Rotary Lookout** on Mt

WHITSUNDAY COAST

Oscar in North Mackay. **Mackay Marina** is a pleasant place to wine and dine with a waterfront view, or to simply picnic in the park and stroll along the breakwater.

Mackay has plenty of beaches, although not all of them are ideal for swimming. The best ones are about 16km north of Mackay at Blacks Beach, Eimeo and Bucasia (see p393 for details).

The best option near town is **Harbour Beach**, 6km north of the centre and just south of the Mackay Marina. The beach here is patrolled and there's a foreshore reserve with picnic tables and barbecues.

Tours

Farleigh Sugar Mill (☎ 4963 2700; admin@skillsstm .com.au; adult/child/family $17/10/40; ⊙ 2hr tour, 1pm Mon-Fri Jun-Nov) In the cane-crushing season you can visit this mill and see how the sweet crystals are made. Learn about the history, production and technology; but dress for a working mill, which means long sleeves, long pants and closed shoes. The mill is 10km northwest of Mackay.

Jungle Johno Tours (☎ 4951 3728; larrikin@mackay .net.au;adult/YHA member/child $75/68/40) These Platypus Safaris, which include Finch Hatton Gorge and the Broken River platypuses, operate out of Larrikin Lodge, and are a good way to see the best bits of Eungella and surrounds in one day. The tour includes pick-up, morning tea and lunch. Overnight camping is also available.

Mackay Water Taxi & Adventures (☎ 0417 073 969, 4942 7372; tjpic@mcs.net.au) Runs fishing charters (from $165 per person), day trips to Keswick and St Bee's Islands (from $135), and snorkelling and diving trips to the Great Barrier Reef, the Whitsunday and Cumberland Islands.

Reeforest Adventure Tours (☎ 1800 500 353; www .reeforest.com) Offers a day-long Platypus & Rainforest Ecosafari (adult/child/family $75/64/225) which explores Finch Hatton Gorge and visits the platypuses of Broken River. It also includes lunch at a secluded bush retreat. Among other tours is a day tour to Cape Hillsborough for $90/64/265, featuring Aboriginal middens, stone fish-traps and a bush-tucker trail.

Sleeping

BUDGET

There are plenty of motels strung along busy Nebo Rd, south of the centre. The budget options (around $50 for a double) post their prices out front and tend to suffer from road noise.

Larrikin Lodge (Map p390; ☎ 4951 3728; fax 4957 2978; 32 Peel St; dm/tw/f $19/44/69; ⊙ reception 7am-2pm & 5-8.30pm) This is a clean and quiet YHA-associated hostel in an airy timber house.

The friendly owners also operate Jungle Johno tours out to Eungella National Park (see left), and will pick you up from the bus if you ring during office hours.

Gecko's Rest (Map p390; ☎ 4944 1230; info@geckos rest.com.au; 34 Sydney St; dm/s/d $20/30/46; 🏵 🖵) This centrally located backpackers has well-presented quads and triples, though some lack windows. There's a large kitchen, comfortable lounge and games area, and there should be a roof deck for alfresco lounging by the time you read this.

Central Tourist Park (Map p389; ☎ 4957 6141; Malcomson St, North Mackay; tent/caravan sites $13/18, cabins $28-40; 🏵) Not overflowing with character, but the cabins here are serviceable and it's an inexpensive option, relatively close to the city and accessible by bus 5/6.

MIDRANGE

Ocean International (Map p389; ☎ 4957 2044, 1800 635 104; www.ocean-international.com.au; 1 Bridge Rd, Illawong Beach; d $130-219; 🏵 🖵 🏊) On the beach, close to the airport and only 3km south of the centre, this four-star, four-storey complex overlooks the Coral Sea. There's an excellent restaurant and cocktail bar, a spa and sauna, business centre, and harbour or airport transfer service.

Mid City Motor Inn (Map p390; ☎ 4951 1666; fax 4951 1968; 2 Macalister St; s/d $70/75; 🏵 🏊) On the banks of the river in a quiet locale, yet handy to the city centre, this spick-and-span motel has the best of both worlds.

Illawong Beach Resort (Map p389; ☎ 4957 8427; fax 4957 8460; 73 Illawong Drive, Illawong Beach; d $120-140, extra person $15.50; 🏵 🏊) This manicured beachside resort has 37 two-bedroom, fully self-contained villas ideal for families. As well as the pool there's tennis, a children's games room and a small lake for fishing.

Whitsunday International Hotel (Map p390; ☎ 4957 2811; fax 4951 1785; 176 Victoria St; d $66-99; 🏵) This large, centrally located hotel has well-maintained motel-style and self-contained rooms. There are a couple of bars, a restaurant and a nightclub on the ground floor but there's very little noise disturbance in the rooms.

TOP END

Clarion Hotel Mackay Marina (Map p389; ☎ 4955 9400, 1800 386 386; www.mackaymarinahotel.com; Mulherin Dr, Mackay Harbour; d $165-275; 🏵 🖵 🏊) Part of the rapidly developing Marina precinct, the Marina International was just about ready for business when we visited. Every room boasts ocean views, and there's also the option of standard or deluxe studios as well as spa or family suites. There's a bar and restaurant on site, while beaches, parks and waterfront restaurants are all just a hop away.

Eating

RESTAURANTS

Angelo's on the Marina (Map p389; ☎ 4955 5600; Mulherin Dr, Mackay Marina; mains $15-33; ☿ 8am-late) A large, lively restaurant in a delightful marina setting, with an extensive range of pasta and a mouth-watering Mediterranean menu. It's fully licensed and there's a free courtesy bus for parties of six or more people, so join a group and enjoy. *Alla tua salute!*

Kevin's Place (Map p390; ☎ 4953 5835; cnr Victoria & Wood Sts; mains $18-25; ☿ 11.30am-2.30pm & 6pm-late Mon-Sat) Sizzling, spicy Singaporean dishes and efficient, revved-up staff combine with the building's colonial ambience and tropical climes to create a Rafflesque dining experience.

Pacino's on the Waterfront (Map p390; ☎ 4957 8131; Mulherin Dr, Mackay Harbour; mains $15-35) Set among the warehouses, Pacino's is a romantic Mediterranean restaurant and bar with a breezy alfresco deck overlooking the water. The speciality is seafood, though there's pasta and pizza as well.

Lighthouse (Map p389; ☎ 4955 5022; Mulherin Dr, Mackay Harbour; mains $22-29; ☿ 6am-late) A very popular seafood restaurant in a nautical setting that doubles as a **takeaway** (☎ 4955 5699). Its forte is fresh seafood, but the specials board usually has steak, chicken and lamb options.

CAFÉS

Sedgies Gourmet Coffee & Tea Supplies (Map p390; ☎ 4957 4845; cnr Nelson & Victoria Sts; breakfast $5-11, lunch $5-11; ☿ 8am-3pm Mon-Fri, 8am-noon Sat) A deservedly popular place for breakfast or to just sip a coffee. Sedgies offers a huge range of teas and coffees. Breakfast is served from 8am to 10.30am and the lunchtime sandwiches and salads are excellent.

Oscar's on Sydney (Map p390; ☎ 4944 0173; cnr Sydney & Gordon Sts; mains $10-23; ☿ 7am-10pm Tue-Sat, to 9.30pm Sun & Mon) Pancakes for breakfast, pizzas and grills for lunch, more sophisticated mains in the evening; there's something for all tastes at this licensed café. Try the delicious *poffertjes* (authentic Dutch pancakes with traditional toppings; $5) – yum!

Coffee Club (Map p390; ☎ 4957 8294; 48 Wood St; breakfast $6-14, mains $11-22) This big, relaxed meeting place offers a range of meals and a licensed bar in addition to the excellent espresso and cakes. Try the tapas before heading around the corner to see a movie.

Drinking

Sails Sports Bar (Map p389; ☎ 4955 5022; Mulherin Dr, Mackay Harbour) This outdoors bar adjacent to the Lighthouse Seafood Restaurant usually hums with a good crowd on the weekends.

Gordi's Café & Bar (Map p390; ☎ 4951 2611; 85 Victoria St; mains $14-20) Cruisy café with lunchtime specials, such as noodles and curries for $6 to $8, by day and a good bar atmosphere in the evening.

Satchmo's at the Reef (Map p389; ☎ 4955 6055; Mulherin Dr, Mackay Harbour; ☿ 11am-late) A classy wine and tapas bar full of boaties and featuring live music on Sunday afternoon.

Entertainment

Wilkie's Tavern (Map p390; ☎ 4957 2241; cnr Victoria & Gregory Sts) Karaoke seems to be taking over many of the pub venues, but this place usually has someone strumming a guitar on Thursday, Friday and Saturday nights.

Platinum Lounge (Map p390; ☎ 4957 2220; 83 Victoria St; ☿ 7pm-late Wed, Thu & Sat, 5pm-late Fri & Sun) On the 1st floor above the corner of Victoria and Wood Sts, this is a good place to unwind and converse without shouting. Wednesday and Thursday nights are karaoke nights here.

Cinema and theatre options:

BC Cinemas (Map p390; ☎ 4957 3515; 30 Gordon St; adult/child $13.50/9.50) This complex screens all the latest flicks.

Mackay Entertainment Centre (Map p390; ☎ 4957 2255; Gordon St) The city's main venue for live performances.

Getting There & Away

Located at the long-distance bus station, **Travelworld** (Map p389; ☎ 4944 2144; roseh@mkytworld.com.au; cnr Victoria & Macalister Sts; ☿ 7am-6pm Mon-Fri, 7am-4pm Sat) handles air, bus and train tickets and can help with transport connections. On Sunday, bus tickets can be purchased at the nearby café.

Great Keppel Island (p382), Queensland

Blue star fish, Lady Elliot Island (p367), Queensland

Train station, Maryborough (p351), Queensland

Great Sandy National Park (p342), Fraser Island, Queensland

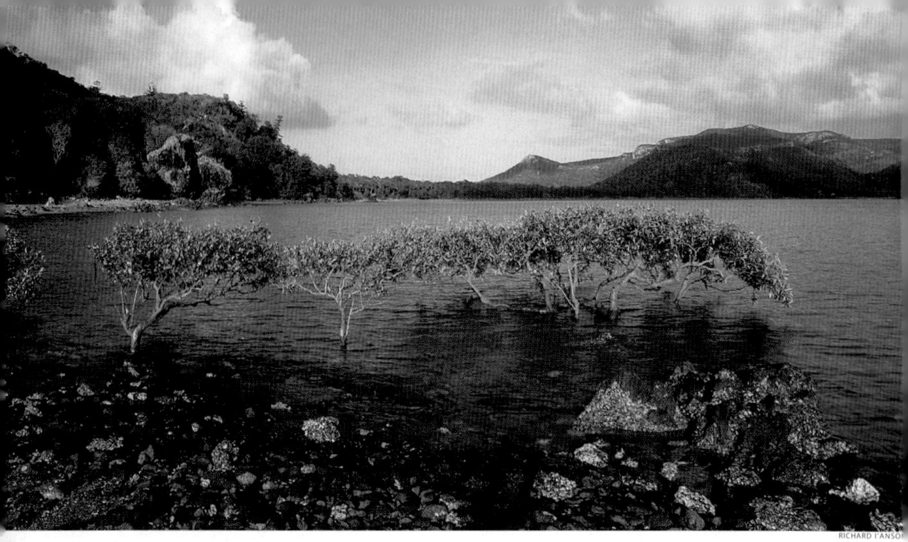
RICHARD I'ANSON
Mangroves in Cape Hillsborough National Park (p396), Queensland

Hamilton Island (p408), Queensland
RICHARD I'ANSON

MANFRED GOTTSCHALK
Whitehaven Beach (p410), Queensland

A kookaburra in Eungella National Park (p394), Queensland
JOHN NOBLE

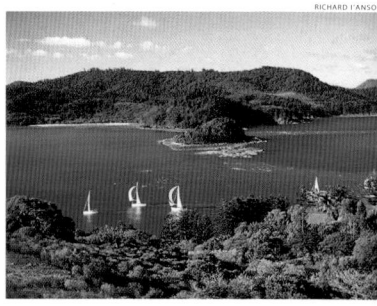

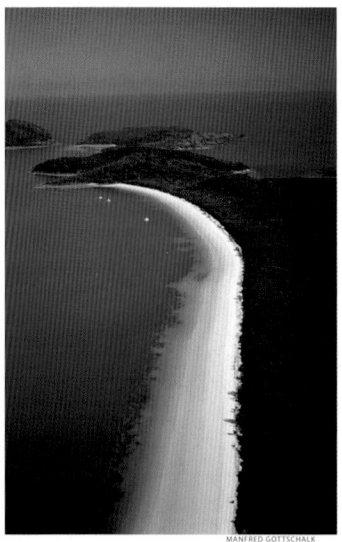

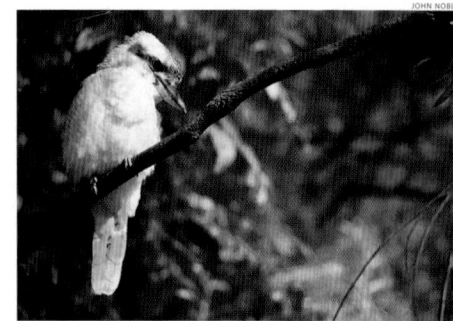

AIR

The airport is about 3km south of the centre of Mackay.

Jetstar (☎ 13 15 38; www.jetstar.com.au) Flights to/from Brisbane (from $89 one way) and Sydney (from $189).

Qantas (☎ 13 13 13; www.qantas.com.au) Direct flights most days between Mackay and Brisbane (from $110), Sydney ($467), Rockhampton ($89) and Townsville ($88).

VirginBlue (☎ 13 67 89; www.virginblue.com.au) Two flights a day to/from Brisbane (from $125 one way) with flights connecting with services to several major centres.

BUS

Buses stop at Travelworld, where tickets can also be booked.

Con-X-ion (☎ 1300 308 718; www.con-x-ion.com) Connects Mackay airport and Mackay bus terminal with Airlie Beach twice a day. Adult/child one-way fares are $44/22.

Greyhound (☎ 13 14 99; www.greyhound.com.au) Travels up and down the coast. Sample one-way adult fares and journey times are: Airlie Beach ($26, two hours), Townsville ($64, six hours), Cairns ($110, 12 hours), Rockhampton ($47, four hours), Hervey Bay ($101, 11 hours) and Brisbane ($130, 15 hours).

Premier (☎ 13 34 10; www.premierms.com.au) Cheaper but not as many services as Greyhound. Sample fares are: Airlie Beach ($20), Cairns ($98), Rockhampton ($35) and Brisbane ($114).

TRAIN

Queensland Rail (www.traveltrain.com.au) has several services that stop at Mackay on their way between Brisbane and Townsville/Cairns. The speedy *Tilt Train* has departures on Monday, Wednesday and Friday heading to Cairns ($162, 12 hours) via Townsville ($92, 5½ hours), and on Sunday, Wednesday and Friday heading to Brisbane ($207, 13 hours). Fares shown are adult business-class.

The *Sunlander* train service departs at 1.55am heading to Townsville on Tuesday and Saturday, and to Cairns on Sunday and Thursday. It departs Mackay for Brisbane at 10.44pm on Monday, Tuesday, Thursday and Saturday. Adult fares to/from Brisbane (17 hours) are $138/190/571 in sitting economy berth/Queenslander; to/from Townsville (6½ hours) it's $62/114/443; and to/from Cairns (12½ hours) it's $108/161/528.

The train station is at Paget, about 3km south of the centre. Bookings can be made at any travel agency, such as Travelworld.

Getting Around

Avis (☎ 4951 1266), **Budget** (☎ 4951 1400) and **Hertz** (☎ 4951 3334) have counters at the airport. **Mackay Transit Coaches** (☎ 4957 3330) has several services around the city and connects the city with the harbour and the northern beaches; pick up a timetable from the visitor centres. Routes begin from Canelands Shopping Centre and there are many signposted bus stops, but you can hail a bus anywhere along the route as long as there is room for the bus to pull over. For a taxi, call **Mackay Taxis** (☎ 13 13 08). Count on about $15 for a taxi from either the train station or the airport to the city centre.

AROUND MACKAY
Mackay's Northern Beaches

The coastline north of Mackay is made up of a series of headlands and bays sheltering small residential communities with holiday accommodation. There are some reasonably good beaches for swimming and fishing along here and the prevailing winds keep the kite surfers happy.

At **Blacks Beach** the beach extends for 6km, so stretch those legs and claim a piece of Coral Sea coast for a day. If you are just passing through you can grab breakfast, lunch or a coffee at **Café Mana** (Map p389; ☎ 4954 9480; Turtle Shores Shopping Centre, Blacks Beach; �־ 6am-4pm Tue-Fri, 8am-5pm Sat & Sun) and enjoy the local art. For accommodation try **Blue Pacific Resort** (Map p389; ☎ 4954 9090, 1800 808 386; www.bluepacificresort.com.au; 26 Bourke St, Blacks Beach; d $92-145; 🖳 🖾), where all the units are self-contained and set in an immaculate garden. A good budget option is the **Seawinds Caravan Park** (Map p389; ☎ 4954 9334; 16 Bourke St, Blacks Beach; tent/caravan sites $18/19, caravans $32, cabins $44; 🖾), with lots of shade for camping, but the cabins are pretty average.

At the northern end of Blacks Beach is **Dolphin Heads**, where you can stay at the four-star **Dolphin Heads Resort** (Map p389; ☎ 4954 9666, 1800 075 088; www.dolphinheadsresort.com.au; Beach Rd, Dolphin Heads; d $110-160; 🖳 🖾). The 80 comfortable motel-style units overlook an attractive rocky inlet.

North of Dolphin Heads is **Eimeo**, where the **Eimeo Pacific Hotel** (Map p389; ☎ 4954 6105; Mango Ave; mains $13-21) crowns a headland commanding magnificent Coral Sea views. It's open every day, and is a great place for a beer.

WHITSUNDAY COAST

Bucasia is across Sunset Bay from Eimeo and Dolphin Heads, but you have to head all the way back to the main road to get up there. **Bucasia Beachfront Caravan Resort** (Map p389; ☎ 4954 6375; bucasia@bigpond.com; 2 The Esplanade; tent/caravan sites $15/20, cabins $43-70; ☒) has en-suite cabins right on the beach.

Pioneer Valley

The route to Eungella National Park, the Mackay–Eungella Rd, branches off the Peak Downs Hwy about 10km west of Mackay and follows the Pioneer River through a long valley carpeted with fields of cane broken only by the occasional small town, steam-belching sugar mill and the odd local attraction.

Just beyond the town of **Mirani** is the **Illawong Fauna Sanctuary** (☎ 4959 1777; fax 4959 1888; adult/child $12/6; ☒ 8am-6.30pm), where you can witness crocodile feeding (daily at 2.30pm) and koalas feeding (5.15pm). There's also the option of dinner, bed and breakfast at the sanctuary's **homestay** (per person $50; ☒).

About 27km west of Mirani is the turnoff for Finch Hatton Gorge, part of Eungella National Park, and 1.5km past the turn-off is the pretty township of **Finch Hatton**. The historic **train station** (☒ 10am-3pm) doesn't see trains anymore but it has an interesting display on local history, and has Internet access ($2 per half-hour). The friendly **Criterion Hotel** (☎ 4958 3252; 9 Eungella Rd; s/d $15/30; mains $5-16) has spotless hotel rooms atop the spiral staircase, and good, inexpensive meals, while the **Finch Hatton Caravan Park** (☎ 4958 3222; Zahmel St; tent/caravan sites $14/17, onsite vans from $30) has plenty of shade.

From Finch Hatton, it's another 18km to Eungella, a quaint mountain village overlooking the valley. The last section of this road climbs suddenly and steeply, with several incredibly sharp corners – towing a large caravan up here is not recommended.

Eungella

Perched at the head of the Pioneer Valley is the lovely village of Eungella (*young*-gulla, meaning Land of Clouds). There's a **General Store** (☎ 4958 4520) with snacks, groceries and fuel, and a couple of accommodation and eating options.

The old-fashioned **Eungella Chalet** (☎ 4958 4509; fax 4958 4503; s/d with shared bathroom $38/50, d with en suite $72, 1-/2-bedroom cabins $88/109; mains $5-25; ☒)

perches on the mountain's edge and commands magnificent views. Its once-grand atmosphere is friendly but slightly musty. Upstairs rooms are clean and simple, while behind the chalet are modern timber cabins. There's a small bar downstairs, and the dining room serves breakfast, lunch and dinner.

Eungalla Holiday Park (☎ 4958 4590; tent/caravan sites $16/20, cabins $75-110) is a small park located just north of the township, right on the edge of the escarpment. The owner is happy to shuttle guests to bushwalks in the national park and there's a kiosk with groceries, snacks and an ATM.

The charming Suzanne welcomes visitors to her balconied café/gallery **Hideaway Cafe** (☎ 4958 4533; Broken River Rd; light meals $4-8; ☒ 9am-4pm Mon-Sun) overlooking the township. Be tempted by wonderful homecooked pasties, apple strudel and several excellent vegetarian options from the European menu.

EUNGELLA NATIONAL PARK

The beautiful Eungella National Park, 84km west of Mackay, is renowned for its platypus population. It's probably the most reliable place in Queensland to see these shy creatures. This mountainous national park covers nearly 500 sq km of the Clarke Range, and while much of it is inaccessible there are several terrific walking trails and great accommodation options around Broken River and Finch Hatton Gorge, making it an ideal overnight excursion from the coast.

Getting There & Away

There are no buses to Eungella or Finch Hatton, but Reeforest Adventure Tours and Jungle Johno Tours both run day trips from Mackay and will drop off and pick up those who want to linger (see p391).

Broken River

There's a **QPWS information office** (☎ 4958 4552; ☒ 8am-4pm), picnic area and **kiosk** (☒ 10am-5pm) near the bridge over Broken River, 5km south of Eungella. A **platypus-viewing platform** has been built near the bridge, and the best viewing times are the hours immediately after dawn and before dark. There are some excellent walking trails between the Broken River picnic ground and Eungella; maps are available from the information office and kiosk.

You have the choice of camping or cabins at Broken River.

Fern Flat Camping Ground (☎ 4958 4552; fax 4958 4501; sites per person/family $4/16) is a lovely place, with shady sites adjacent to the river where the platypuses play, and with the most amazing bird chorus in the morning. The camping ground is about 500m past the information centre and kiosk, and can probably claim to have the coldest showers in Queensland. You need to claim a site and self-register so it's best to arrive in the morning.

If you forgot the tent, **Broken River Mountain Retreat** (☎ 4958 4528; fax 4958 4564; d $80-125; ❁ ❁) is a comfortable alternative. Accommodation comprises cedar cabins ranging from small motel-style rooms to large self-contained units sleeping up to six. There's a large guests' lounge with an open fire and the friendly **Platypus Lodge Restaurant & Bar** (mains $18-25) with a good selection of steak, seafood and chicken dishes and a moderately priced wine list. The retreat organises several (mostly free) activities for its guests, including spotlighting, canoeing and guided walks.

Finch Hatton Gorge

About 27km west of Mirani, just before the town of Finch Hatton, is the turn-off to Finch Hatton Gorge. The last couple of kilometres of the 10km drive from the main road are on unsealed roads with several creek crossings that can become impassable after heavy rain. At the gorge car park, there's a picnic area with barbecues. A 1.6km walking trail leads from the picnic area to **Araluen Falls**, with its tumbling waterfalls and swimming holes, and a further 1km hike takes you to the **Wheel of Fire Falls**, another cascade with a deep swimming hole.

A fun and informative way to explore the rainforest here is to glide through the canopy on a cable with **Forest Flying** (☎ 4958 3359; www.forestflying.com; $45). Prior booking is essential.

These places are signposted on the road to the gorge.

The comfortable self-contained cabins at **Finch Hatton Gorge Cabins** (☎ 4958 3281; camp site per person $8, dm/d $15/77, extra person $5.50; ❁) sleep up to five; perfect if you're travelling with young kids. Linen is provided in the cabins and the bunkhouse and there's a well-equipped camp kitchen. There's a large grassed area and the creek runs close by.

THE AUTHOR'S CHOICE

Platypus Bush Camp (☎ 4958 3204; www .bushcamp.net; Finch Hatton Gorge; camp site per person $8, dm/d $20/60) A true bush retreat, this back-to-nature camp is nestled in a beautiful forest setting, just a couple of kilometres from the Finch Hatton Gorge. A creek with platypuses and great swimming holes runs alongside the camp, and accommodation is in slab-timber huts (basically roofed-over sleeping platforms with open sides and canvas flaps). The communal kitchen and eating area is the heart of the camp and a great place to listen to yarns. There are wonderful hot showers with a green forest wall and a very cosy stone hot tub. Bring your own food and linen. Booking ahead is strongly advised. Transport to/from Mackay can be arranged by the owner with prior notice.

The friendly **Gorge Kiosk** (☎ 4958 3321) serves ice cream (delicious mango plus other flavours), pies and lemonade – all homemade and excellent. Picnic and barbecue packs are available to take up the road to the national park picnic ground.

CUMBERLAND ISLANDS
Brampton Island

About 32km northeast of Mackay, mountainous Brampton Island has a top-end resort that's popular with honeymooners and others looking for a quiet time amid natural beauty. Most of the island is national park and features beautiful beaches, lush forests, pleasant walking trails and coral reefs.

Brampton Island Resort (☎ 4951 4499, 1300 134 044; www.brampton-island.com; s $345-485, d $460-740; ❁ ❁ ❁) has four grades of rooms depending on the view and facilities. All meals are served in the Blue Water Restaurant; breakfast and lunch are buffet style, while dinner is more formal. As with many resorts, discounted stand-by rates and packages are often available, so it's worth checking.

The resort has two swimming pools, tennis courts and a small golf course, as well as snorkelling gear, catamarans, windsurfers and paddle skis. The main beach at Sandy Point is very pleasant, and there's good snorkelling over the coral in the channel between Brampton and Carlisle Islands.

Island transfers by either helicopter or launch from Mackay are organised through the resort when booking accommodation.

Other Cumberland Islands

If you have your own boat, or can afford to charter a boat or seaplane, most other islands in the Cumberland Group and the Sir James Smith Group to the north are also beautiful national parks.

Camp-site availability, bookings and permits for **Carlisle**, **Scawfell** and **Goldsmith Islands** and others can be made online at www.epa.qld.gov.au or at the Mackay **QPWS** (☎ 4944 7800; cnr River & Wood Sts; per person/family $4/16).

Carlisle Island can be reached from Brampton Island via the sandspit at low tide or by chartering a boat at Brampton resort. Scawfel and Goldsmith Islands are reached by charter boat, which can be organised through the **Mackay Visitor Information Centre** (☎ 4952 2677; www.mackayregion.com; 320 Nebo Rd).

MACKAY TO PROSERPINE

There's little to distract you on the main road to Proserpine, but there are several small holiday towns along the coast, and a particularly worthwhile detour to Cape Hillsborough National Park. The Seaforth Yakapari Rd leaves the highway 19km out of Mackay, skirting the Pioneer Peaks National Park on its 23km journey to Seaforth. About 3km before Seaforth is the turn-off to Cape Hillsborough. From Seaforth, the Mt Ossa Rd takes you back to the highway.

Further up the coast, the seaside town of Midge Point and the exclusive golfing resort of Laguna Whitsundays are the only places of note before you reach Proserpine and the road to Airlie Beach.

CAPE HILLSBOROUGH NATIONAL PARK

This small coastal park covers a rocky promontory and the nearby Andrews Point and Wedge Island. The scenery ranges from rocky coastal cliffs to a broad sandy beach, and from sand dunes to rainforest. Kangaroos, wallabies, sugar gliders and turtles are quite common in the park, and there are remains of Aboriginal middens and stone fish-traps to be seen which can be accessed by good walking tracks.

There's a range of cabin and motel accommodation at the idyllic, low-key **Cape**

Hillsborough Nature Resort (☎ 4959 0152; www.capehillsboroughresort.com.au; MS 895 Mackay; tent/caravan sites $13/18; d $39-74; mains $12-19; ☐ ☒). Camp sites are nicely terraced into the forest and wildlife abounds. Facilities include a bar and restaurant .

Smalleys Beach Campground (sites per person/family $4/16) is a small, pretty, grassed camping ground hugging the foreshore and jumping with kangaroos. Self-register/pay at the camping ground.

WHITSUNDAYS AREA

The 74 beautiful islands in the Whitsunday Group are the best known of Queensland's holiday islands and attract hordes of visitors year-round. Most of the islands and the surrounding waters are protected as national park. Only seven islands have resorts and, apart from Hamilton and Daydream, the development takes up only a tiny proportion of the land, leaving plenty of room for some back-to-nature serenity, beach camping and bushwalking.

Apart from the islands themselves, the Whitsundays region takes in the gateway town of Airlie Beach and nearby Shute Harbour (where you catch the island ferries), and the large Conway National Park on the promontory south of Shute Harbour.

Orientation & Information

Airlie Beach is the mainland centre for the Whitsundays, with plenty of accommodation options, travel agents and tour operators. Shute Harbour, about 10km east of Airlie, is the port for most day-trip cruises and island ferries, while most of the yachts berth at Abel Point Marina at Airlie Beach.

The Whitsunday district office of the **QPWS** (☎ 4946 7022; fax 4946 7023; cnr Shute Harbour & Mandalay Rds; ☺ 9am-5pm Mon-Fri) is 3km past Airlie Beach on the road to Shute Harbour. This office deals with camping permits for the islands, and its staff are very helpful and a good source of information on a wide range of topics. This should be your first place to visit if you are interested in exploring the islands independently.

The official **Tourism Whitsundays Information Centre** (☎ 4945 3711, 1800 801 252; www.whitsundaytourism.com) is on the Bruce Hwy at the southern entry to Proserpine.

MAPS & BOOKS

100 Magic Miles of the Great Barrier Reef – The Whitsunday Islands by David Colfelt is sometimes referred to as the bible to the Whitsundays. It contains an exhaustive collection of charts with descriptions of all boat anchorages around the islands as well as articles on the islands and resorts, and features on diving, sailing, fishing, camping and natural history.

Two of the best maps to this region are the Travelog *Great Barrier Reef* map, which has a *Whitsunday Passage* map on the reverse side, and Sunmap's *Australia's Whitsundays*.

Activities

SAILING

The Whitsundays are a paradise of protected waters and numerous safe and picturesque anchorages. Here you can learn to sail, join an overnight tour on a racing maxi or a graceful tall ship, or charter a yacht and skipper it yourself. Read the Sailing the Whitsundays boxed text (below) before checking out what the following companies have on offer.

There are a number of bareboat charter companies around Airlie Beach, including the following:

Charter Yachts Australia (☎ 1800 639 520; www.cya .com.au; Abel Point Marina)

SAILING THE WHITSUNDAYS

Bareboat Charters

These have become enormously popular in the Whitsundays. 'Bareboat' doesn't refer to what you wear on board; it simply means you rent the boat without skipper, crew or provisions. While you don't require formal qualifications to hire a yacht, you will need to prove to the company that at least one person in your group is fully competent in operating the vessel. On the first day you should receive around four hours of briefing and familiarisation with the yacht, during which time your own abilities will be assessed. If necessary you may be required to pay for additional tutoring for around $200 per day, or it may be necessary for you to hire a skipper for an hourly rate. If you lack experience, it's a good idea to hire an experienced skipper at least for the first day.

The operators usually require a booking deposit of $500 to $750 and a security bond of between $1000 and $2000 (depending on the kind of boat), payable on arrival and refunded after the boat is returned undamaged. Bedding is usually supplied and provisions can also be provided if you wish. Most companies have a minimum hire period of five days.

There's a wide range of yachts and cruisers available. You'll pay $500 to $800 a day in the high season (September, October, December and January) for a yacht that will comfortably sleep four to six passengers. It's worth asking if the company you choose belongs to the Whitsunday Bareboat Operators Association, a self-regulatory body that guarantees certain standards. Also check that the latest edition of David Colfelt's *100 Magic Miles* is stowed on board, and pick up a copy of the *Public Moorings and Anchoring* leaflet from QPWS.

Sailing Tours

These tours, which supply professional crew and catering, are all the rage in Airlie Beach. It can be hard work sorting through the glossy brochures, the stand-by rates and the word of mouth. Price can be a very good indication; we get stacks of letters complaining about the cheaper companies, everything from lengthy delays, boats breaking down, unsanitary conditions, even serious safety concerns. Look out for the tick of approval from the WCBIA (Whitsunday Charter Boat Industry Association) on the brochure. The usual package is three days and two nights, but longer cruises are possible, as are day tours, sailing courses and even ocean racing.

Crewing

A third option is to crew a private vessel by responding to 'Crew Wanted' notices pasted up in backpackers or at the marina and yacht club. Just like hitching a ride in a car, the experience could be life affirming or life threatening. Think about yourself stuck with someone you don't know on 10m of boat, several kilometres from shore, before you actually find yourself there. Be sure to let others know where you are going, with whom and when you expect to return.

WHITSUNDAY COAST

Cumberland Charter Yachts (☎ 1800 075 101; www
.ccy.com.au; Abel Point Marina)

Queensland Yacht Charters (☎ 1800 075 013; www
.yachtcharters.com.au; Abel Point Marina)

Sail Whitsunday (☎ 1800 075 045; www.sailwhitsun
day.com.au; Abel Point Marina)

Whitsunday Escape (☎ 4946 5222, 1800 075 145;
www.whitsundayescape.com; Abel Point Marina)

Whitsunday Rent A Yacht (☎ 1800 075 111; www
.rentayacht.com.au; Trinity Jetty, Shute Harbour)

The following are some of the numerous
sailing tours that have been recommended
by readers:

Aussie Adventure Sailing (☎ 1800 359 554; www.aussie
sailing.com.au) This company has a range of vessels on its
books, including three tall ships, four racers and four sail and
dive boats. There's also a sailing school if you catch the bug.
Three-day, two-night packages start from $420 per person.

Maxi Ragamuffin (☎ 1800 454 777; www.maxiaction
.com.au) *Ragamuffin* has two day trips. On Monday,
Wednesday and Saturday she visits Hayman Island's beautiful Blue Pearl Bay for snorkelling. On Tuesday, Thursday
and Sunday she heads for Whitehaven Beach. Cruises
depart Shute Harbour at 8.45am and return about 4.30pm
(adult/child/family $89/50/248). There is also a Two Cruise
Special (ie two separate days).

ProSail (Map p401; ☎ 1800 810 116; www.prosail.com
.au; cnr Waterson Rd & Begley St, Airlie Beach) Prosail runs
a range of vessels including racing yachts and a traditionally rigged schooner. There's also a sailing school and
cruises geared for diving enthusiasts. Three-day, two-night
packages start at $430 per person. The popular America's
Cup challenge is a hands-on, three-hour challenge (two
races) on board either *Australia* or *Steak'n Kidney*, 12m
America's Cup contenders ($79/59 adult/child).

Southern Cross Sailing Adventures (Map p401;
☎ 1800 675 790; www.soxsail.com.au; 4 The Esplanade,
Airlie Beach) Southern Cross runs adventure sailing cruises on
racing yachts such as *Siska* and *Southern Cross*, as well as more
sedate cruises aboard the magnificent tall ship *Solway Lass*.
Or you can combine the racing-yacht and tall-ship experience.
Three-day, two-night packages start at $409 per person.

The Whitsundays is also one of the best
and most popular places to learn how to
sail. Should this be your calling, the following are a selection of Airlie Beach sailing
schools, each with several courses:

Prosail (☎ 1800 810 116; www.prosail.com.au; cnr
Waterson Rd & Begley St, Airlie Beach)

Whitsunday Marine Academy (Aussie Adventure
Sailing; ☎ 4948 2350; www.whitsundaysailtraining.com;
277 Shute Harbour Rd)

Whitsunday Sailing Club (☎ 4946 6138; Airlie Point)

DIVING

The ultimate diving experience to be had
here is on the actual Great Barrier Reef, at
places such as Black, Knuckle and Elizabeth Reefs. Dive boats should leave in the
evening so that you wake up at your dive
site. The dive companies listed below offer
a good range of diving trips for certified
divers, which combine the reef with the
islands. These companies also offer dive
courses; open-water courses with several
ocean dives start at around $500.

Oceania Dive (Map p401; ☎ 4946 6032, 1800 075
035; www.oceaniadive.com; 257 Shute Harbour Rd, Airlie
Beach)

Pro-Dive (Map p401; ☎ 4948 1888, 1800 075 035;
www.prodivewhitsundays.com.au; 344 Shute Harbour Rd,
Airlie Beach)

Reef Dive (☎ 4946 6508, 1800 075 120; www.reefdive
.com.au; 16 Commerce Close, Cannonvale)

Apart from these companies, most of the island resorts also have their own dive schools
and free snorkelling gear.

KAYAKING

Paddling serenely in search of an island
with dolphins and turtles as company is
one of the best ways to experience the Whitsundays. **Salty Dog Sea Kayaking** (☎ 4946 1388;
www.saltydog.com.au) offers guided tours and
kayak rental. Half-/full-day tours from
Shute Harbour cost $50/90, and it's also
possible to arrange extended island camping trips.

Tours
ISLAND & REEF CRUISES

There are several ways to tour the islands
and the Great Barrier Reef. For information about overnight sailing packages see
p397. If sailing isn't your cup of tea and
you want to visit the islands, the famous
beaches, do a bit of snorkelling or even
try out some of the resorts, then it's just a
matter of hunting down the tour that will
suit you.

Most day trips will include activities like
snorkelling or boom netting, with scuba
diving as an optional extra. Following are
some (by no means all) of the day trips on
offer and bookings can be made at any of
the tour agents in Airlie Beach.

Cruise Whitsundays (☎ 4946 4662; www.cruisewhit
sundays.com; Shingley Dr, Abel Point Marina, Airlie Beach)

A huge wave-piercing catamaran speeds out to a pontoon moored at Knuckle Reef Lagoon on the Great Barrier Reef for spectacular snorkelling. There's an underwater observatory, water slide and children's swimming enclosure, and optional extras such as diving and sea walking. Lunch is included in the price (adult/child/family $166/90/405) and there's an expensive but thrilling option of flying in or out by helicopter.

Fantasea/Blue Ferries (☎ 4946 5111; www.fanta sea.com.au; 11 Shute Harbour Rd, Jubilee Pocket) The largest tour operator in Airlie Beach and operator of the island ferries; offers a number of options. A high-speed catamaran cruises to Hardy Reef on the Great Barrier Reef, where you transfer to a large pontoon for snorkelling, lunch and coral viewing in a semisubmersable (adult/child/family $152/81/355). The Yellow Sub tour includes Whitehaven Beach, snorkelling and semisubmersible coral-viewing on Bali Hai Island ($89/59/257). There are several options for spending a day at one of the island resorts, as well as a Three Island Discover Cruise that visits Long, Daydream and Hamilton Islands ($59/40/158).

Mantaray Charters (☎ 1800 816 365; www.mantaray charters.com; departures from Shute Harbour; adult/child/family $99/55/295) This tour allows you to spend the most time on Whitehaven Beach, followed by a visit to Mantaray Bay; includes snorkelling and lunch.

Voyager 3 Island Cruise (☎ 4946 5255; departures from Shute Harbour; adult/child $74/37) A good-value day cruise that includes snorkelling at Hook Island, beachcombing and swimming at Whitehaven Beach, and checking out Club Croc on Long Island. Onboard lunch (adult/child $11/6) and introductory scuba dive ($60) are optional extras.

Most of the cruise operators who operate from Shute Harbour do coach pick-ups from Airlie Beach and Cannonvale. You can take a bus to Shute Harbour, or you can leave your car in the Shute Harbour car park for $8 for 24 hours; or there's **Shute Harbour Secured Parking** (☎ 4946 9666) costing $6/11 per day/overnight.

SCENIC FLIGHTS

Air Whitsunday Seaplanes (☎ 4946 9111) Flying is the only way to do day trips to exclusive Hayman Island and the cost is $175/155 an adult/child. Other tours include a three-hour Reef Adventure ($265/165) and a four-hour Panorama ($295/195).

Island Air/Helireef (☎ 4946 9102) This company has a range of seaplane and helicopter tours including a Whitehaven Beach Picnic (per person $289) and a 10-minute Whitsunday Highlight for $79. There is also a Hayman Island day trip ($379).

Sleeping

RESORTS

There are resorts on seven of the Whitsunday Islands. Each resort is quite different from the next, ranging from Hayman's five-star luxury to the basic cabins on Hook, and from the high-rise development of Hamilton to the beachfront huts of ecofriendly South Long Island Wilderness Lodge.

The rates quoted in this chapter are the standard rates, but hardly anyone pays these. Most travel agents can put together a range of discounted package deals that combine air fares, transfers, accommodation and meals.

It's also worth noting that, unless they're full, almost all resorts offer heavily discounted stand-by rates when you book less than five days in advance. All the agents in Airlie Beach can provide information on the resorts.

CAMPING

QPWS (www.epa.qld.gov.au) manages national park camping grounds on several islands for both independent campers as well as groups on commercial trips. Camping permits are available over the Internet and from the Whitsunday QPWS office and cost $4 per person ($16 per family) per night. If you book online don't forget to pick up your permit/tag from the office.

There's a national parks leaflet, *Island Camping in the Whitsundays*, which describes the various sites, and provides detailed information on what to take and do. You must be self-sufficient, and are advised to take 5L of water per person per day, plus three days' extra supply in case you get stuck. You should also have a fuel stove; wood fires are banned on all islands.

Get to your island by Blue Ferry or a day-cruise boat; the booking agencies in Airlie Beach will be able to assist. Or use an island-camping specialist such as **Island Camping Connections** (☎ 4946 5255), who can drop you at North or South Molle, Planton or Denman Islands for $45 return; Whitsunday Island or Henning Island for $109; and Hook Island for $150. All prices are return (minimum of two people). **Camping Whitsunday Islands** (☎ 4946 9330) have similar prices, and both operations can help with provisions and snorkelling gear.

WHITSUNDAY COAST

Getting There & Around

AIR

The two main airports for the Whitsundays are at Hamilton Island (see p409) and Proserpine (see below). The Whitsunday airport, near Airlie Beach, has regular flights from the mainland to the islands by light plane, seaplane and helicopter; see p404 for details. Lindeman Island also has its own airstrip.

BOAT

Blue Ferries (☎ 4946 5111) provide ferry transfers to the islands from Shute Harbour; see the individual islands for transfer details.

BUS

Greyhound (☎ 13 14 99; www.greyhound.com.au) and **Premier** (☎ 13 34 10; www.premierms.com.au) buses detour off the Bruce Hwy to Airlie Beach. **Whitsunday Transit** (☎ 4946 1800) connects Proserpine, Cannonvale, Abel Point, Airlie Beach and Shute Harbour. Get a schedule from any travel agency.

PROSERPINE

☎ 07 / pop 3250

The turn-off point for Airlie Beach and the Whitsundays, Proserpine is a busy sugar-mill town and industrial centre for the region. Although it can't be mistaken for a tourist town, it is the home of the comprehensive **Whitsunday Information Centre** (☎ 1800 801 252; www.whitsundaytourism.com.au; ☺ 10am-6pm), on the Bruce Hwy south of town.

Proserpine Airport is 14km south of town and is serviced from Brisbane as well as some other capitals by **Jetstar** (☎ 13 15 38; www.jetstar.com.au), **Qantas** (☎ 13 13 13; www.qantas.com.au) and **VirginBlue** (☎ 13 67 89; www.virginblue.com.au).

In addition to meeting all planes and trains, **Whitsunday Transit** (☎ 4946 1800) has six scheduled bus services running daily from Proserpine to Airlie Beach; tickets from the airport/train station cost $16/8.

AIRLIE BEACH

☎ 07 / pop 4000

Airlie Beach, 25km northwest of Proserpine, is the lively gateway to the Whitsunday Islands. The whole town revolves around tourism, and attracts a bustling and diverse bunch of boaties, divers, backpackers and families. Airlie has a huge range of accommodation, cafés and restaurants, a lively nightlife and an attractive man-made swimming lagoon on the foreshore.

Airlie is a great base for sampling the island resorts and all the sun-soaked possibilities that the Whitsundays have to offer. The town has a reputation as a centre for sailing and scuba diving, with beginners' courses and countless tours available. There's also whale-watching between July and September, and horse riding and hiking in the hinterland. Airlie is also a great place to stop travelling and start partying.

Orientation

Nearly everything lies along Shute Harbour Rd, a short busy strip packed with tour agents, cafés, restaurants and backpackers. The town faces Airlie Bay, with a couple of small beaches east and west of Airlie Creek, but the man-made lagoon is the best place to swim year-round. The large recreation reserve between the shore and The Esplanade at the east end of town hosts a Saturday morning market and a dusty car park where the long-distance buses pull in. Shute Harbour, where the island ferries depart from, is about 12km east, and Abel Point Marina, home to many of the cruising yachts, is about 1.5km west.

Information

The main drag is stacked with privately run tour agencies, all able to answer queries on island transport, and book tours and accommodation. Check out their notice boards for stand-by rates on sailing tours and resort accommodation. Internet access is widely available; many of the hostels have terminals and there are several dedicated Internet cafés.

Airlie Beach Newsagency (☎ 4946 6410; 354 Shute Harbour Rd) Stocks interstate and overseas newspapers.

Airlie Beach Tourist Information Centre (☎ 4946 6665; 277 Shute Harbour Rd)

Book Nook (☎ 4946 6410; 388 Shute Harbour Rd) A large selection of holiday reading, travel guides and books on the Whitsundays.

Destination Whitsundays (☎ 4946 6846; 295 Shute Harbour Rd) Tourist information.

Internet Centre (346 Shute Harbour Rd; per hr $2.50) The cheapest we found.

Post office (372 Shute Harbour Rd; ☺ 9am-5pm Mon-Fri, 9am-12.30pm Sat)

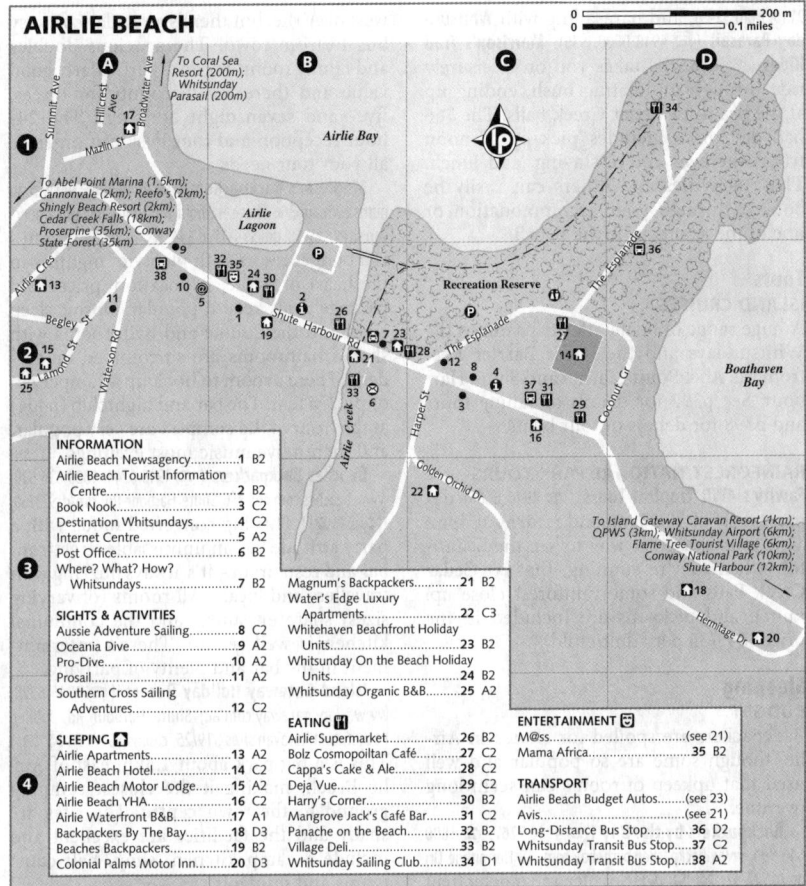

AIRLIE BEACH

0   200 m
0   0.1 miles

WHITSUNDAY COAST

INFORMATION		
Airlie Beach Newsagency	**1**	B2
Airlie Beach Tourist Information		
Centre	**2**	B2
Book Nook	**3**	C2
Destination Whitsundays	**4**	C2
Internet Centre	**5**	A2
Post Office	**6**	B2
Where? What? How?		
Whitsundays	**7**	B2

SIGHTS & ACTIVITIES		
Aussie Adventure Sailing	**8**	C2
Oceania Dive	**9**	A2
Pro-Dive	**10**	A2
Prosail	**11**	A2
Southern Cross Sailing		
Adventures	**12**	C2

SLEEPING		
Airlie Apartments	**13**	A2
Airlie Beach Hotel	**14**	C2
Airlie Beach Motor Lodge	**15**	A2
Airlie Beach YHA	**16**	C2
Airlie Waterfront B&B	**17**	A1
Backpackers By The Bay	**18**	D3
Beaches Backpackers	**19**	B2
Colonial Palms Motor Inn	**20**	D3

Magnum's Backpackers	**21**	B2
Water's Edge Luxury		
Apartments	**22**	C3
Whitehaven Beachfront Holiday		
Units	**23**	B2
Whitsunday On the Beach Holiday		
Units	**24**	B2
Whitsunday Organic B&B	**25**	A2

EATING		
Airlie Supermarket	**26**	B2
Bolz Cosmopoiltan Café	**27**	C2
Cappa's Cake & Ale	**28**	C2
Deja Vue	**29**	C2
Harry's Corner	**30**	B2
Mangrove Jack's Café Bar	**31**	C2
Panache on the Beach	**32**	B2
Village Deli	**33**	B2
Whitsunday Sailing Club	**34**	D1

ENTERTAINMENT		
M@ss	(see 21)	
Mama Africa	**35**	B2

TRANSPORT		
Airlie Beach Budget Autos	(see 23)	
Avis	(see 21)	
Long-Distance Bus Stop	**36**	D2
Whitsunday Transit Bus Stop	**37**	C2
Whitsunday Transit Bus Stop	**38**	A2

Where? What? How? Whitsundays (☎ 4946 5255;
283 Shute Harbour Rd) Tourist information.

Activities
For details on sailing, diving and kayaking
around the islands, see p397.

SWIMMING & WATER SPORTS
The lagoon on Airlie's foreshore provides
safe swimming. The beaches at Airlie Beach
and Cannonvale are OK for swimming,
but the presence of marine stingers means
swimming in the sea isn't advisable between
October and May. There are (seasonal) water-
sports equipment operators in front of the
Airlie Beach Hotel that hire out jet skis, catamarans, windsurfers and paddle skis.

BUSHWALKS
The Conway Range behind Airlie Beach is
part national park (see p405) and part state
forest, and provides for some great walking in coastal rainforest. With information
supplied at the tracks you can learn about
the forest ecology and the traditional life
of Indigenous people. Try the 2.4km climb
up Mt Rooper for great views, or the short
Coral Beach Track at Shute Harbour, or
the three-day Whitsunday Great Walk. For
advice and track notes on these and other
walks visit the QPWS (see p396).

OTHER ACTIVITIES
Other active pursuits include tandem skydiving with **Tandem Skydive Airlie Beach** (☎ 4946

9115; from $249), and parasailing with **Whitsunday Parasail** (☎ 4948 0000; $55). **Morrison's Trail Rides** (☎ 4946 5299) takes you on a leisurely ride through undulating bush, ending up at the beautiful Cedar Creek Falls. The $66 half-day price includes pick-up at noon from wherever you're staying, and lunch. These activities and others can easily be booked through your accommodation or one of the agents in Airlie Beach.

Tours

ISLAND CRUISES

A huge range of boats offer trips out to the Whitsundays and the Great Barrier Reef from the Abel Point Marina and Shute Harbour. See p397 for details of sailing tours and p398 for details of tour boats.

RAINFOREST/NATIONAL PARK TOURS

Fawlty's 4WD Tropical Tours (☎ 4946 6665) departs daily at 10.30am, and returns at 4pm. This tour is a great way to see the beautiful (when they're running, that is) Cedar Creek Falls and some rainforest close up. Lunch and pick-ups are included in the price ($49/35 per adult/child).

Sleeping

BUDGET

Backpackers are spoiled for choice in Airlie, though some are so popular and well used that upkeep of rooms can seem long overdue.

Backpackers by the Bay (☎ 4946 7267, ☎ 1800 646 994; www.backpackersbythebay.com; 12 Hermitage Dr; dm/d $22/52; ❄ ⌨ ⌷) Smaller and quieter than some of the other hostels, this relaxed place is a five- to 10-minute walk from the centre. The atmosphere is friendly, the dorms have four beds and the double rooms are some of the best around (air-conditioning costs an extra $0.50 per person).

Airlie Beach YHA (☎ 4946 6312, 1800 247 251; airliebeach@yhaqld.org; 394 Shute Harbour Rd; dm $25, d from $59; ❄ ⌨ ⌷) This friendly hostel is in a converted motel at the end of the main drag. The rooms are spotless and most have an en suite. Although it was once a motel, parking is now severely limited.

Reefo's (Reef Oceania Village; ☎ 4946 6137, 1800 800 795; www.reeforesort.com; 147 Shute Harbour Rd, Cannonvale; dm $12-18, d $55; ❄ ⌨ ⌷) This big, comfortable backpackers resort with bar, restaurant and a huge pool is about 3km

west of Airlie, but there's a regular courtesy bus to/from town. The spacious doubles and family rooms here are particularly good value and there are discounts for three-, five- and seven-night bookings. The 24-hour reception and tour desk can organise all your tour needs.

Magnum's Backpackers (☎ 4946 6266; www.magnums.com.au; 366 Shute Harbour Rd; tent/caravan/campervan sites $15-18, dm $14-17, d $44; ❄ ⌷) Magnum's is a budget resort with plenty of nightlife in the heart of Airlie; its location, prices and package deals keep it popular. Dorms sleep eight and the double and twin rooms with shared bathrooms are surrounded by gardens. There's room to hook up a campervan or pitch a tent. The bar and nightclub (p404) at the front of the complex are very popular, and there's live music most evenings.

Beaches Backpackers (☎ 4946 6244, 1800 636 630; www.beaches.com.au; 356 Shute Harbour Rd; dm/d $23/60; ❄ ⌨ ⌷) This big converted motel with a party attitude has an unmissable streetfront bar and restaurant – it's always buzzing with travellers and locals. All rooms (of varying sizes) share en suites, and the communal kitchen is well set up. There's entertainment in the bar and plenty of partying.

Island Gateway Holiday Resort (☎ 4946 6228; www.islandgateway.com.au; Shute Harbour Rd, Jubilee Pocket; tent/caravan sites $19/25, cabins $50-95; ❄ ⌷) This is a big park about 1.5km east of Airlie Beach, making it the closest camping ground to the town centre. The sites are shady and the facilities are excellent and include a camp kitchen, shop, half-court tennis and minigolf.

Flame Tree Tourist Village (☎ 4946 9388; www.flametreevillage.com.au; Shute Harbour Rd; tent/caravan sites $17/21, cabins from $62; ❄ ⌷) Not as glitzy as the other big parks, but the spacious sites are scattered through lovely bird-filled gardens and there's a good camp kitchen and barbecue area. The park is 6km west of Airlie, about midway to Shute Harbour.

MIDRANGE

Whitsunday Organic B&B (☎ 4946 7161; www.whitsundaybb.com.au; 8 Lamond St; s/d $90/120) A very stylish ecofriendly designed B&B, with well-appointed rooms and wholesome organic breakfasts. Dinners are also available, as are wonderfully relaxing massages and help with organising tours. There are discounts for longer stays, and stand-by rates.

Airlie Beach Hotel (☎ 4964 1999, 1800 466 233; www.airliebeachhotel.com.au; cnr The Esplanade & Coconut Grove; s $89-159, d $99-169; ☒ ☒) With one of the best locations downtown, this slick hotel is hard to beat. There are comfortable motel-style rooms surrounding the pool, and spacious hotel rooms and suites with great views. There are also facilities for disabled guests and a couple of excellent restaurants at street level.

Airlie Beach Motor Lodge (☎ 4946 6418, 1800 810 925; www.airliebeachmotorlodge.com.au; 6 Lamond St; d from $105; ☒ ☒) Tucked away in a residential area of Airlie, this quiet motel is just a short walk from Shute Harbour Rd action and the lagoon. As well as neat motel rooms there are self-contained units and a purpose-built facility for disabled guests.

Colonial Palms Motor Inn (☎ 4946 9500; fax 4946 9469; cnr Shute Harbour Rd & Hermitage Dr; d from $105; ☒ ☒) This motel is in a great location – central but quiet – and has spacious rooms, some self-contained, and a large restaurant. Plus there's a 10% discount if you belong to a motoring club.

There are quite a few blocks of older-style holiday apartments as well as more modern resorts in and around Airlie that can be good value, especially for a group or a family. Many have discounts for stays of three nights or more, and minimum stays of two nights.

Airlie Apartments (☎ 4946 6222; www.airlieapartments.com; 22-24 Airlie Cres; d $84-116; ☒ ☒) A good-value option ideal for families. The one-, two- and three-bedroom apartments are fully self-contained, with views over Abel Point and the action on Shute Harbour Rd is not far away.

Shingly Beach Resort (☎ 4948 8300; www.shingley beachresort.com; 1 Shingley Dr; d $115-220; ☒ ☒) These midrange, self-contained holiday apartments are close to Abel Point Marina and feature good views. There are four different room configurations, a bar and restaurant, a massage and yoga studio, and a seriously deep pool.

Whitehaven Beachfront Holiday Units (☎ 4946 5710; fax 4946 5711; 285 Shute Harbour Rd; s/d $85/95; ☒) Smack in the centre of Airlie Beach, these six well-presented though older-style apartments all have balconies overlooking the foreshore park. As they're set back from the main road, noise is not a problem.

Whitsunday on the Beach Holiday Units (☎ 4946 6359; fax 4946 7995; 269 Shute Harbour Rd; d $95-100; ☒) In the centre of Airlie with the magnificent lagoon at your doorstep, this block of airy, spacious, self-contained units is convenient to everything.

TOP END

Airlie Waterfront B&B (☎ 4946 7631; www.airlie waterfrontbnb.com.au; cnr Broadwater Ave & Mazlin St; d from $169; ☒) Beautifully presented and sumptuously furnished with antiques, this is a lovely relaxing option which is still convenient to the action. Two double rooms have their own private spa.

Most of the resorts here have package deals and stand-by rates that are much cheaper than their regular rates.

Coral Sea Resort (☎ 4946 6458, 1800 075 061; www.coralsearesort.com; 25 Ocean View Ave; d $195-335, 1-/2-bedroom apt $285/295; ☒ ☒) At the end of a low headland overlooking the water, Coral Sea Resort has one of the best positions in the area. There's a huge range of well-appointed rooms – both motel style and self-contained, many with stunning views. The excellent swimming pool is large and flanked by ocean on one side and a bar/restaurant on the other. Parasailing and ocean rafting launch from the resort's private jetty.

Waters Edge Luxury Apartments (☎ 4948 2655; fax 4948 2755; www.watersedgewhitsundays.com.au; 4 Golden Orchid Dr; d from $190; ☒ ☒) The Southeast Asian theme, cool stone architecture, wet-edge pools and attentive service all convey luxury and the rooms don't disappoint. One-, two- or three-bedroom apartments boast large lounges, are fully self-contained and some have spas. The views are superb, the resort offers a poolside restaurant and gym, and it's only a short stroll to the shops and the lagoon.

Eating
RESTAURANTS
Shute Harbour Rd abounds with restaurants; though also consider some of the resorts if you are after a quiet restaurant with a view.

Deja Vue (☎ 4946 5700; 301 Shute Harbour Rd; mains $21-30; ☼ dinner Tue-Sat) Tucked away in a small courtyard at the eastern end of the main drag is an unpretentious BYO restaurant with a menu promising modern interpretations of Thai, Mediterranean, Indian and others, and their execution and presentation is faultless. The ambience is relaxed – elegant but still Airlie.

Bolz Cosmopolitan Café (☎ 4946 7755; 7 Beach Plaza, The Esplanade; mains $10-25; ☷ breakfast, lunch & dinner) Sit on zebra-skin booths or the terrace in this classy pizza and pasta restaurant and watch the passing parade. The service can be a little erratic, but the individual pizzas, such as mango and prawn, are a delight.

Panache on the Beach (☎ 4946 5541; Mango Tce; 263 Shute Harbour Rd; mains $19-27; ☷ lunch & dinner) With a lovely position overlooking the lagoon and foreshore, Panache offers Mediterranean cuisine, with both brasserie-style meals (until 6pm) and a more formal menu reflecting the chef's French origins.

Mangrove Jack's Café Bar (☎ 4964 1888; 297 Shute Harbour Rd; mains $19-26; ☷ lunch & dinner) A breezy, open-air, streetfront restaurant that offers Asian and continental mains, but it's the imaginative and individual wood-fired pizzas that keep people coming back.

Airlie Thai (☎ /fax 4946 4683; 1st fl, Beach Plaza, The Esplanade; mains $16-26; ☷ lunch & dinner) This pleasant licensed restaurant is upstairs in the Beach Plaza complex; sit out on the veranda and tuck in to the delicious *pad thai*, among other traditional dishes.

Whitsunday Sailing Club (☎ 4946 7894; 261 Shute Harbour Rd; mains $14-32; ☷ lunch & dinner) The Sailing Club terrace is a great place for a meal and a drink. Choose from the usual steak and schnitzel off the inexpensive bistro blackboard, or select from the more upmarket Commodore's Table menu.

CAFES & QUICK EATS

If you're looking for a quick coffee, breakfast or light lunch, Airlie has plenty of places to go.

Village Deli (☎ 4964 1121; 351 Shute Harbour Rd; mains $10-15; ☷ 8am-5.30pm) This casual, funky café/deli serves tasty light meals – and they know how to make coffee. The mixed salad plate is great value, and big, healthy breakfasts, gelati and juices are on the go all day. Takeaway provisions and picnic boxes are a speciality.

Harry's Corner (☎ 4946 7459; 273 Shute Harbour Rd; mains $8-12; ☷ 7am-4pm) This small, popular café cooks up huge tasty breakfasts, and delivers coffee, cakes and snacks until closing. A great meeting place.

Cappa's Cake & Ale (☎ 4946 5033; Pavilion Arcade; mains $6-15; ☷ 8am-8pm) In a small arcade off the main drag near The Esplanade, this busy café serves up breakfasts, burgers, pizzas and more. If it can be wrapped, sandwiched, toasted or grilled you'll find it here with good coffee, smoothies and juices to wash it down.

SELF-CATERING

If you're preparing your own food, there's the small **Airlie Supermarket** (277 Shute Harbour Rd) in the centre of town and a larger one in Cannonvale, about 2km west of town.

Entertainment

Airlie Beach has a reputation for partying hard. The bars at Magnum's and Beaches, the two big backpackers in the centre of town, are usually crowded, and are good places to meet travellers. Drinks tend to be cheaper and there's usually live music or some other form of entertainment every night.

M@ss (☎ 4946 6266; Magnum's Backpackers, 366 Shute Harbour Rd; ☷ 10pm-5am) The gothic inspired nightclub at Magnum's plays crowd favourites and hosts foam parties.

Mamma Africa (☎ 4948 0438; 263 Shute Harbour Rd; ☷ 10pm-5am) Tribal cool and dance favourites keep this place rockin' all night.

Getting There & Away

AIR

The closest major airports are Proserpine (p400) and Hamilton Island (see p409).

Whitsunday airport (☎ 4946 9933), a small airfield 6km east of Airlie Beach, is midway between Airlie Beach and Shute Harbour. Half a dozen different operators are based here, and you can take a helicopter, light plane or seaplane out to the islands or the reef. **Island Air Taxis** (☎ 4946 9933) flies to Hamilton and Lindeman Islands for $60. **Air Whitsunday Seaplanes** (☎ 4946 9111) flies to Hayman, Daydream, Long, and South Molle Islands for $450 per flight, carrying a maximum of six passengers. **Helireef** (☎ 4946 9102), Air Whitsunday Seaplanes and Island Air Taxis all offer joy flights out over the reef.

BOAT

Blue Ferries (☎ 4946 5111) provide ferry transfers to/from the islands; see Getting There & Away under the individual islands for details.

BUS

Greyhound (☎ 13 14 99; www.greyhound.com.au) and **Premier** (☎ 13 34 10; www.premierms.com.au) run services between Airlie Beach and all the major centres along the coast, including Brisbane ($148, 18 hours), Mackay ($26, 2½ hours) and Cairns ($92, 11 hours). Long-distance buses stop on The Esplanade, between the Sailing Club and the Airlie Beach Hotel. Any of the booking agencies along Shute Harbour Rd can sell bus tickets.

Con-X-ion (☎ 1300 308 718; www.con-x-ion.com) connects Mackay airport and Mackay bus terminal with Airlie Beach twice a day. Adult/child one-way fares are $44/22.

Whitsunday Transit (☎ 4946 1800) connects Proserpine (Whitsunday Coast airport), Cannonvale, Abel Point, Airlie Beach and Shute Harbour. Buses operate from 6am to 10.30pm daily and stop outside Mangrove Jack's and just up from Pro-Dive. Schedules are readily available from any tour agency.

Getting Around

Airlie Beach is small enough to cover by foot, and all of the cruise boats have courtesy buses that will pick you up from wherever you're staying and take you to either Shute Harbour or the Abel Point Marina. To book a taxi, call **Whitsunday Taxis** (☎ 13 10 08); there's a taxi rank on Shute Harbour Rd, opposite Magnum's.

Several car-rental agencies operate locally including:

Avis (☎ 4946 6318; 366 Shute Harbour Rd) Next to Magnums.

Airlie Beach Budget Autos (☎ 4948 0300; 285 Shute Harbour Rd) In courtyard of Whitehaven Holiday Units.

CONWAY NATIONAL PARK

The mountains of this national park and the Whitsunday Islands are part of the same coastal mountain range. Rising sea levels following the last ice age flooded the lower valleys leaving only the highest peaks as islands, now cut off from the mainland.

Most of the park is composed of rugged ranges and valleys covered in rainforest, although there are also areas of mangroves and open forest. Only a small area of the park is accessible by road.

The road from Airlie Beach to Shute Harbour passes through the northern section of the park. Several walking trails start from near the picnic and day-use area.

About 1km past the day-use area, there's a 2.4km walk up to the Mt Rooper lookout, which provides good views of the Whitsunday Passage and islands. Further along the main road, towards Coral Point (before Shute Harbour), there's a 1km track leading down to Coral Beach and The Beak lookout. This track was created with the assistance of the Giru Dala, the traditional custodians of the Whitsunday area; a brochure available at the start of the trail explains how the local Aborigines used plants growing in the area.

Cedar Creek Falls

To reach the beautiful Cedar Creek Falls, turn off the Proserpine to Airlie Beach road on to Conway Rd, 8km north of Proserpine. It's then about 15km to the falls; the roads are well signposted. This is a popular picnic and swimming spot – when there's enough water, that is!

LONG ISLAND

The closest of the resort islands to the coast, Long Island is mostly national park, with three resorts on offer. The island is about 11km long but not much more than 1.5km wide, and a channel only 500m wide separates it from the mainland.

Activities

The beaches on Long Island are among the best in the Whitsundays and there are 13km of walking tracks with some fine lookouts. Day-trippers to the island can use the facilities at Club Croc or Peppers Palm Bay resorts. **Long Island Dive & Snorkel** (☎ 0417 161 998) has a range of courses, gear for hire and trips for certified divers.

Sea kayaking is a featured activity at the South Long Island Wilderness Lodge (see the following section) on the southern side of the island (guests only).

Sleeping & Eating

Long Island has one large mainstream resort and two smaller, quieter resorts.

Peppers Palm Bay (☎ 4946 9233, 1800 095 025; www.peppers.com.au/palmbay; d $380-680; ❑ ❑ ❑) Peppers is a boutique resort of 21 cabins which house a maximum of 42 guests in comfort. The cabins, complete with swinging double hammock but no TV or telephone, sit around the pretty, sandy sweep of

WHITSUNDAY COAST

DETOUR: DINGO BEACH & CAPE GLOUCESTER

To get to Dingo Beach or Cape Gloucester, head east out of Airlie Beach and take the Cannon Valley Rd north after about 10km, and then follow the signs. The turn-off to Cape Gloucester (and Hydeaway Bay) is about 1km before Dingo Beach. True, nothing much happens here outside the odd 'one that got away' yarn, but it's a popular spot with families, the fishing and sailing fraternities, and those in the know.

Dingo Beach is a quiet little retreat set on a long sandy bay backed by low forested mountains. The only facilities are the Dingo Beach General Store, which sells fuel, booze, takeaway meals and a small range of groceries, and the **Dingo Beach Hotel & Units** (☎ 4945 7153; 1 Deicke Crescent; d $80), a modest block of spacious two-bedroom, self-contained units. **Dingo Beach Escape** (☎ /fax 4945 7215) offers day trips from Airlie Beach ($80), which include lunch and water sports. They also provide transfers to **Gloucester** and **Saddleback Islands** for around $40 return, and rent out dinghies for $15 per hour ($75 per day) including fuel.

At secluded **Hydeaway Bay**, the friendly **Hydeaway Bay Caravan Park** (☎ 4945 7170; tent/caravan sites $15/18, on-site van $40) has plenty of exposed sites, and a small kiosk. Further down the track, however, are a couple of real surprises. **Cape Gloucester Eco-Resort** (☎ 4945 7242; www.capegloucester.com; d $120-150) is a very modern, very well-executed ecoresort with spacious self-contained units and motel-style rooms facing a picture-perfect sandy beach. A huge pool fronts the relaxing restaurant, **The Oar** (mains $21-24; ☺ breakfast, lunch & dinner), where guests and visiting yachties enjoy excellent seafood, pasta and Thai dishes.

Also along the rough dirt track out to Cape Gloucester is an older, more understated resort. **Montes Reef Resort** (☎ 4945 7177; d $120-130; mains $14-18) is the sort of place where outback graziers have been bringing the family for their annual seaside holiday for eons. Montes has discovered that the secret to achieving ecostyle is to keep things simple and let a couple of decades of modern trends pass by. The spacious bungalows are designed to catch the breeze and are literally a few steps from the beach. The licensed restaurant is almost austere, but simplicity is the name of the game here.

Palm Bay. At the heart of the resort is a pool and a large comfortable building that serves as the main dining area, bar and lounge.

South Long Island Wilderness Lodge (☎ 3839 7799; www.southlongisland.com; 5-night packages per person $2990) This secluded lodge on Paradise Bay consists of spacious waterfront cabins; there's no phone, no TV and no air-conditioning, but the cabins are positioned to make the most of the sea breezes. The lodge is staffed by a friendly crew of just three and the maximum number of guests is just 12. All meals are included in the tariff and are served buffet style. There's a five-night minimum stay, no day visitors or children, and no motorised water sports, so you're guaranteed peace and tranquillity. The tariff includes helicopter transfer from Hamilton Island. Nature lovers will enjoy the guided kayaking tours into the mangrove estuaries of Conway National Park.

Club Croc (☎ 4946 9400, 1800 075 125; www.clubcroc .com.au; d $240-368; ☒ ☒) Sitting on Happy Bay in the north of the island, Club Croc is a midrange, well-used resort with three levels of accommodation. It's popular with families and couples, and there are plenty of activities to keep all age groups busy. The basic Lodge units are small and bathroom facilities are shared; the Beachfront or Garden rooms are well worth the extra expense. The resort has two swimming pools, tennis courts, a gym and minigolf; guests also have free use of all the nonpowered water-sports gear. Four- to 14-year-olds can be kept busy in the free kids' club. All meals are included in the tariff.

There's a secluded National Park camping ground at Sandy Bay, midway along the western side of the island. For details see p399.

Getting There & Around

Blue Ferries (☎ 4946 5111) connects Long Island (Club Croc) to Shute Harbour by frequent daily services. The direct trip takes about 15 minutes and costs $18/12 per adult/child.

It's 2km between the Club Croc and Peppers Palm Bay resorts and you can walk between them in about 25 minutes.

HOOK ISLAND

The second largest of the Whitsundays, 53-sq-km Hook Island is predominantly national park and rises to 450m at Hook Peak. There are several good beaches dotted around the island, and Hook boasts some of the best kayaking, diving and snorkelling locations in the Whitsundays. There is an old underwater observatory where a spiral staircase leads you down to the reef floor where you can peer through tiny windows – but don't expect to see a vibrant wonderland of reef creatures! There's also a small, low-key resort at the southern end as well as several excellent camping grounds.

Hook Island Wilderness Resort (☎ 4946 9380; www.hookislandresort.com; camp sites per person $25, dm $35/20, d $90, d with en suite $130; mains $14-18; ⌗ ⌑) While it's basic, this is also the cheapest resort in the Whitsundays, and its other advantage is that there's great snorkelling just offshore. The simple adjoining units each sleep up to six or eight people. The en-suite bathrooms are *tiny*, and rates include linen but not towels. Tea and coffee facilities are supplied and there's a camp kitchen for campers only, plus a couple of barbecues. The simple restaurant serves seafood, steak and pasta, and there's usually a vegetarian option at night, while snacks are available the rest of the day; there's also a small bar.

There are some wonderful national park camping grounds at Maureen Cove, Steen's Beach, Bloodhorn Beach, Curlew Beach and Crayfish Beach. For details see p399.

Transfers to the resort are organised when you book your accommodation. Return transfer is by regular tour boat. The **Voyager** (☎ 4946 5255) does a daily three-island cruise (see p398) as well as return transfer to Hook for $40/20 for an adult/child. **Island Camping Connections** (☎ 4946 5255) or **Camping Whitsunday Islands** (☎ 4946 9330) can organise drop offs to the camping grounds for around $150.

SOUTH MOLLE ISLAND

Largest of the Molle group of islands at 4 sq km, South Molle is virtually joined to Mid Molle and North Molle Islands – indeed you can walk across a causeway to Mid Molle. The island is crisscrossed by 15km of walking tracks, and has some superb lookout points. The highest point is Mt Jeffreys (198m), but the climb up Spion Kop is also worthwhile.

The island is known for its prolific bird life. The most noticeable birds are the dozens of tame, colourful lorikeets, black currawongs and the rather intimidating stone curlews. The resort, which is decidedly nonglitzy, also has a nine-hole golf course, a gym, and tennis and squash courts. There is also a wide range of water-sports gear available for day-trippers to hire.

South Molle Island Resort (☎ 4946 9433, 1800 075 080; www.southmolleisland.com.au; d without meals from $240, d with full board from $350; ⌗ ⌑) Full-board tariffs include three buffet meals a day, and all tariffs include use of the golf course, tennis courts, nonmotorised water-sports equipment and nightly entertainment. South Molle is a popular resort with families, as children are well catered for.

Breakfast and lunch buffets are served in the main **Island Restaurant** (mains $20-30); bistro-style dinners are also served here. The Discover Bar has nightly entertainment and there's a coffee shop for drinks and snacks.

There are two national park camping grounds: one at Sandy Bay, in the south, and one at Paddle Bay, near the resort. For details see p399.

Blue Ferries frequently stop off en route between Hamilton, Daydream and Long Islands and Shute Harbour. In addition, there are direct connections with Shute Harbour ($18/12 per adult/child). South Molle can also be visited as part of the **Fantasea** (☎ 4946 5111; www.fantasea.com.au; adult/child $59/40) three-island day trip.

DAYDREAM ISLAND

Daydream, the closest of the resort islands to Shute Harbour, is just over 1km long and only a couple of hundred metres across at its widest point. It's a popular day-trip destination, with a wide range of water-sports gear available for hire.

A steep and rocky path, taking about 20 minutes to walk, links the southern and northern ends of the island. There's another short walk to the tiny but lovely Sunlovers Beach, and a concreted path leads around the eastern side of the island. And once you've done these walks, you've just about covered Daydream Island from head to foot.

Surrounded by beautifully landscaped tropical gardens, the large (296 rooms) **Daydream Island Resort & Spa** (☎ 4948 8488, 1800 075 040; www.daydream.net.au; 6-night packages per person

$670; ☒ ☒) has tennis courts, a gym, catamarans, windsurfers and three swimming pools, all of which are included in the tariff. There are five grades of accommodation and most, but not all, package deals include a buffet breakfast. There's also a club with constant activities to keep children occupied. This is a large resort on a small island, so it's not the place to head if you're seeking isolation.

Breakfast is served buffet style at the Waterfall Restaurant, which stays open all day, serving snacks, lunch and dinner (buffet $39, vegetarian $29). More formal is **Mermaids** (mains $24-35), on the beachfront, or there's the Boathouse bakery, which will provide coffee, sandwiches and other lunchtime snacks. The casual **Fishbowl Tavern** (mains $15-30; ☒ Mon, Wed & Fri) provides meals on the nights that the outdoor cinema is screening movies.

Blue Ferries connect Daydream Island to Shute Harbour by frequent daily services for $18/12 per adult/child. Daydream can be visited as part of the **Fantasea** (☎ 4946 5111; www.fantasea.com.au; adult/child $59/40) three-island day trip.

HAMILTON ISLAND

☎ 07 / pop 1837

The most heavily developed island in the Whitsundays, Hamilton is more like a town than a resort, with its own airport, a 200-boat marina, shops, restaurants, bars and accommodation for more than 2000 guests.

The sheer size of this resort means there are plenty of entertainment possibilities, many of which are available to day-trippers. The resort has tennis courts, squash courts, a gym, a golf-driving range and a minigolf course. From **Catseye Beach**, in front of the resort, you can hire windsurfers, catamarans, jet skis and other equipment, and go parasailing or water-skiing. Among the other options are helicopter joyrides, game fishing and paintball skirmish. A dive shop by the harbour organises dives and certificate courses; you can take a variety of cruises to other islands and the outer reef.

There are a few **walking trails** on the island, the best being from Catseye Bay up to 230m Passage Peak on the northeastern corner of the island. Hamilton also has day care and a free Clownfish Club. Kids up to 14 years old can stay and play free of charge.

Sleeping

Hamilton Island Resort (☎ 4946 9999, 1800 075 110; www.hamiltonisland.com.au; d $250-1500; ☒ ☐ ☒) has a huge range of accommodation, from basic bungalows and hotel rooms to serviced apartments, self-contained villas and luxury penthouses.

Eating

RESORTSIDE

The following restaurants are found within the resort.

Beach House (☎ 4946 8580; mains $22-42; ☒ lunch & dinner) Modern Australian cuisine forms the basis of the menu at Beach House, Hamilton's signature restaurant. Dishes include tuna, eye fillet and spatchcock.

Toucan Tango Cafe & Bar (☎ 4946 8562; mains $14-26; ☒ breakfast, lunch & dinner) This large, casual eatery has a large à la carte menu except on Friday and Saturday nights, when there's a seafood buffet.

HARBOURSIDE

There are plenty of restaurants strung along the harbour waterfront in what is known as Marina Village (or simply Harbourside).

Mariners Seafood Restaurant (☎ 4946 8628; mains $26-38; ☒ dinner Mon-Sat) In a big enclosed veranda overlooking the harbour, Mariners is both licensed and BYO. While the emphasis is on seafood, grills are also available; it's a stylish restaurant with a menu to match.

Romano's (☎ 4946 8212; mains $30-37; ☒ dinner Thu-Tue) This is a relaxed Italian restaurant with a large enclosed deck built right out over the water. The Italian menu includes pasta entrées and wicked deserts, and kids are well catered for ($13).

Manta Ray Cafe (☎ 4946 8213; mains $15-28; ☒ breakfast, lunch & dinner) If you come to Hamilton on a day trip that includes lunch, this café is one of the choices you have. Late breakfasts are popular here and so are the gourmet pizzas.

There's also a bakery, ice-cream shop and a supermarket/general store for those preparing their own meals.

Entertainment

The bars in the resort and Harbourside offer nightly entertainment. Toucan Tango has live entertainment most nights, or you can head to Harbourside's **Boheme's Night-Club** (☒ 9pm-late).

Getting There & Away

AIR

The Hamilton Island airport is the main arrival centre for the Whitsundays.

Jetstar (☎ 13 15 38; www.jetstar.com.au) Has flights to/from Brisbane, Sydney and Melbourne.

QantasLink (☎ 13 13 13; www.qantas.com.au) Has flights to/from Townsville and Cairns.

Island Air Taxis (☎ 4946 9933) and **Hamilton Island Aviation** (☎ 4946 8249) connect Hamilton with Mackay ($135), Airlie Beach ($60) and Lindeman Island ($60). Helicopter transfers from Hamilton are available to several of the other resort islands and Airlie Beach ($210).

BOAT

Blue Ferries (☎ 4946 5111) connects Hamilton Island to Shute Harbour by frequent daily services for $24/12 per adult/child, and the trip takes about 30 minutes. Hamilton can be visited as part of the **Fantasea** (☎ 4946 5111; www.fantasea.com.au; adult/child $59/40) three-island day trip package.

With regular daily flights to and from the major capital cities, Hamilton is also the main arrival point for Long, South Molle, Daydream, Hayman and Lindeman Islands. Blue Ferries meet all incoming and outgoing flights, and connect Hamilton to the other islands. Transfers to South Molle and Long Islands cost $18/12 per adult/child one way. Transfers to Lindeman are usually included in accommodation packages.

Getting Around

On arrival and departure there's a free bus service for guests between the airport or marina and the resort. There is a shuttle service between the airport, harbour and resort which costs $2.50 per trip, but is complimentary between 5pm and 10pm, and is usually included in guest transfers. You can also hire a golf buggy ($35 per hour or $60 for a full day) from the office near the resort's reception or the ferry terminal.

HAYMAN ISLAND

The most northerly island in the Whitsunday Group, Hayman is a mountainous 4-sq-km island with forested hills, valleys and beaches, plus a wide, shallow reef that emerges from the water at low tide. It boasts excellent bushwalking, diving and snorkelling, and is home to one of Australia's most luxurious resorts.

The private **Hayman Great Barrier Reef** (☎ 4940 1234, 1800 075 175; www.hayman.com.au; d $620-4400; ❌ ▢ ▣) resort is a member of the exclusive 'Leading Hotels of the World' group, and is the most luxurious resort on the Great Barrier Reef. It has 214 rooms, six restaurants, five bars, a hectare of swimming pools, landscaped gardens, an impressive collection of antiques and art, and exclusive boutiques.

Guests have free use of catamarans, windsurfers and paddle skis, but they must pay for just about everything else, including tennis and squash. For golfers there's a driving range and a putting green; there's also a gym, a dive shop, organised trips to the Barrier Reef and seaplane tours.

Guests flying in to Hamilton Island are met by Hayman staff and escorted to one of the resort's fleet of luxury cruisers ($205/103 per adult/child, one way) for a pampered transfer to the resort. **Air Whitsunday Seaplanes** (☎ 4946 9111) provides a seaplane service from Hamilton Island for $675 per plane.

Flying is the only way to do day trips to Hayman. Check out **Air Whitsunday Seaplanes** (☎ 4946 9111; adult/child $175/155) and **Island Air/ Helireef** (☎ 4946 9102; per person$379).

LINDEMAN ISLAND

Lindeman covers 8 sq km, most of which is national park, and has more than 20km of walking trails and numerous beaches and secluded bays.

Club Med Resort (☎ 4946 9333, 1800 258 2633; www.clubmed.com; packages per person per night $215-310; ❌ ▣) The famous Club Med style is evident here, with plenty of activities, nightly entertainment and young, friendly staff to help you get the most out of your stay. The main resort complex, with its pool, dining and entertainment areas, is flanked by three-storey accommodation blocks looking out over the water; all the motel-style rooms have their own balcony.

Rates include all meals and most activities. There are also five-night packages available from major cities, which include airfares and transfers; and special deals from Mackay and Airlie Beach. Contact the resort for details.

There is a national park camping ground at Boat Port, in the north of the island. For details see p399.

Island Air Taxis (☎ 4946 9933) has flights from Airlie Beach to Lindeman (one way/return $60/120) and Mackay ($135/270). Club Med also has its own launch that connects with flights from the airport at Hamilton Island.

WHITSUNDAY ISLAND

The largest of the Whitsunday group, this island covers 109 sq km and rises to 438m at Whitsunday Peak. There's no resort, but it has some fine bushwalking, and the 6km-long **Whitehaven Beach** on the southeastern coast is the longest and best beach in the group (some say in the country), with good snorkelling off its southern end. Many of the day-trip boats visit Whitehaven. The pure-white silicon sand can be dazzling on a sunny day, so make sure you have sunglasses!

There are national park camping grounds at Dugong, Sawmill, Nari's and Joe's Beaches in the west; at Turtle Bay and Chance Bay in the south; at the southern end of White-haven Beach; and Peter Bay in the north. For details see p399.

OTHER WHITSUNDAY ISLANDS

The northern islands of the Whitsundays group are undeveloped and seldom visited by cruise boats or water taxis. Several of these – Gloucester, Saddleback, Olden and Armit Islands – have national park camping grounds; see p399 for details. The **QPWS office** (☎ 4946 7022; www.epa.qld.gov.au), 3km south of Airlie Beach, can issue camping permits and advise you on which islands to visit and how to get there.

North Queensland Coast

Queensland's north coast is a smorgasbord of national parks and islands. Natural-history buffs will be in heaven, with a range of wildlife, from cassowaries, crocodiles, turtles and rock wallabies to mahogany gliders, bowerbirds and kingfishers. If you want to bushwalk, there are dozens of trails, including the granddaddy of them all: the Thorsborne Trail on Hinchinbrook Island.

It may be the largest city in the north, but Townsville presents a fresh, neighbourly face. Its sunny demeanour comes through in the many eating and sleeping options on offer. Not only does it have a beach in walking distance of the city, it has an island just offshore. Magnetic Island has substantial bush tracks, a tangible military history and beautiful sandy bays.

The waters around Magnetic Island and Townsville are home to hundreds of varieties of fish and coral that form part of the Great Barrier Reef. The eerie wreck of the *Yongala* lies just offshore, and attracts its fair share of divers. Little islands line this stretch of coast like crumbs from the mainland. Those seeking a laid-back retreat should head over to Magnetic Island, while those looking for the resort experience should go for Dunk, Bedarra or Orpheus Islands, which are among the finest on the entire coast.

There's something for everyone in north Queensland. It's the gateway to some wonderful sections of the Great Barrier Reef. If you've come from the south – with its pace, development and crowds – this is where the payoff really begins.

HIGHLIGHTS

- Ferrying out to the bush-covered hills and secluded bays at **Magnetic Island** (p420)
- Stopping in at cheerful **Townsville** (p413), the hub of the north, with stellar services
- Lolling on a patch of sand at **Mission Beach** (p430) and wondering whether it's time to have lunch, stroll in the nearby rainforest or just turn over
- Understanding why they call the Barrier Reef 'Great' by snorkelling or diving from **Mission Beach** (p431) or **Townsville** (p416)
- Gaining some quiet time in the cool, leafy surrounds of **Paluma** (p425)
- Getting back to nature on **Hinchinbrook Island** (p429), where she struts her splendid stuff
- Frolicking in the turquoise waters that surround quaint **Dunk Island** (p434)

Mission Beach ★ ★ Dunk Island
Hinchinbrook ★ ★ Great Barrier Reef
Island
Paluma ★ Magnetic ★ Island
Townsville ★

- TELEPHONE CODE: 07
- www.gbrmpa.gov.au

Dangers & Annoyances

Swimming in coastal waters is inadvisable from October to April due to the possible presence of marine stingers; see the boxed text, p371.

Saltwater crocodiles inhabit the mangroves, estuaries and open water in parts of north Queensland. Warning signs are posted around waterways where crocs may be present.

BOWEN TO TOWNSVILLE

BOWEN

☎ 07 / pop 8000

Bowen sprawls out along a model stretch of coast: its beaches sandwiched between rustling palms and turquoise water. Its most popular beaches are at Horseshoe and Rose Bays, just north of town. The town has rendered its colourful history on many public buildings, with murals depicting notable events such as the re-emergence of James Morrill after disappearing in a shipwreck 17 years prior, the salt harvest and scenes from Aboriginal life.

Information

Apart from the usual trove of information, the **Bowen visitors centre** (☎ 4786 4222; www.bowentourism.com.au; Bruce Hwy; ⌚ 8.30am-5pm) also has a giant mango – in case you were wondering what that huge orange blob was. It marks the area's vibrant fruit- and vegetable-growing industry.

Sleeping & Eating

Murrays Bay Resort (☎ 4786 2402; fax 4786 3388; Murray Bay; d $77; ▩) This humble low-rise place offers 11 self-contained units with loads of space. There's an excellent palmshaded foreshore leading down to the private beach with first-rate swimming and snorkelling.

Rose Bay Resort (☎ 4786 1064; www.rosebayresortvillas.com; Pandanus St; d $125-155; Ⓟ ▨ ▩) Offers a range of comfy resort-style accommodation, from studio to penthouse. Each option is self-contained and fronts a secluded beach; all have balconies with views.

Bowen Backpackers (☎ 4786 3433; bowenbackpackers@bigpond.com.au; beach end Herbert St; dm/d

$21/50; ⌚ closed Dec-early Mar) Bowen's backpackers accommodation specialise in housing semipermanent fruit pickers. You could try this place.

Horseshoe Bay Cafe (☎ 4786 3280; Horseshoe Bay; mains $18-29; ⌚ breakfast, lunch & dinner) A cosy café right on Horseshoe Bay, with outdoor seating overlooking the palms and water. There's plenty on the menu, which covers the three main meals of the day.

Getting There & Away

The long-distance bus stop is outside **Bowen Travel** (☎ 4786 2835; Williams St), between Herbert and Gregory Sts. **Greyhound** (☎ 13 14 99; www.greyhound.com.au) and **Premier** (☎ 13 34 10; www.premierms.com.au) have a number of daily bus services along the coast stopping at destinations including Airlie Beach ($20, one hour) and Townsville ($32, three hours).

Queensland Rail (☎ 1300 131 722; www.traveltrain.com.au) operates the *Sunlander*, which runs four times a week between Brisbane and Cairns. It stops at Bootooloo Siding, 3km south of the centre.

AYR

☎ 07 / pop 8515

Ayr is on the delta of one of the biggest rivers in Queensland, the Burdekin, and is the major commercial centre for the rich farmlands of the Burdekin Valley. The towns and territory are devoted to the production and harvesting of sugarcane, melons and mangos.

The **Burdekin visitors centre** (☎ 4783 5988; www.burdekintourism.com.au; Bruce Hwy) is to be found in Plantation Park, on the southern side of town.

FESTIVALS & EVENTS

Italian-Australian Festival Ingham turns on the charm with three days of celebrations in May honouring the town's substantial Italian population. Try your hand at the greasy-pole climb or tuck into the spaghetti-eating challenge.

Capsicum Festival Gumlu (60km north of Bowen) crowns the champion capsicum grower with toilet races (!), music and food stalls. In June.

Palmer St Jazz Festival (www.palmerstreetjazzfestival.nq.com.au) Townsville hosts this three-day event in August.

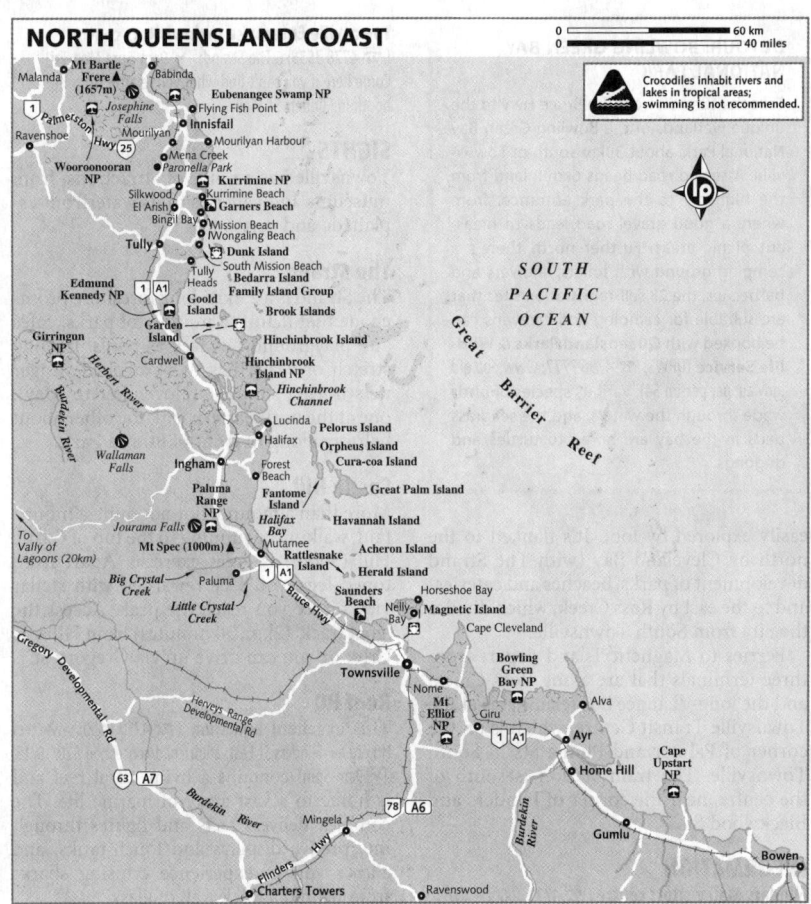

NORTH QUEENSLAND COAST

Crocodiles inhabit rivers and lakes in tropical areas; swimming is not recommended.

The **Billabong Sanctuary** (☎ 4778 8344; www .billabongsanctuary.com.au; Bruce Hwy; adult/child $24/13; ☺ 8am-5pm), 17km south of Townsville, is a 10-hectare wildlife park with Australian native animals and birds. There are barbecue areas, a swimming pool and a kiosk in the park, and various shows (eg hold a koala/ wombat/python) throughout the day.

TOWNSVILLE

☎ 07 / pop 150,000

Townsville's faultless blue skies, long beachfront esplanade and neat centre provide for a wholesale sunny demeanour. The third-largest city in Queensland, it is endowed with a grand coastal position, parklands, purpose-built attractions, a lively café-and-restaurant scene, and lofty Castle Hill, from whose peak you can survey the lot. Offshore is endearing Magnetic Island, and the splendid Great Barrier Reef is just a few hours out by fast catamaran. It's also home to a major armed-forces base and James Cook University, giving it a significant population of young adults and a better-than-average nightlife. The hub of the north, Townsville has come a long way from its genesis in 1864 as a boiling-down works for animal carcasses.

ORIENTATION

Townsville's suburban sprawl is extensive, but the city centre is fairly compact and

DETOUR: BOWLING GREEN BAY NATIONAL PARK

Take the turn-off from the Bruce Hwy to the unique wetlands of the Bowling Green Bay National Park, about 30km south of Townsville. A sealed road heads 6km inland from the highway to the park entrance, from where a good gravel road leads to pleasant picnic areas. Further north there's a camping ground with toilets, showers and barbecues; the 23 self-registration sites that are suitable for camping and caravans can be booked with **Queensland Parks & Wildlife Service** (QPWS; ☎ 4796 7777; www.epa.qld .gov.au; per person $4). Various species of birds wade through the waters, and the seagrass beds in the bay are home to turtles and dugongs.

easily explored by foot. It's flanked to the north by Cleveland Bay (with The Strand development of parks, beaches and eateries) and to the east by Ross Creek, which divides the city from South Townsville.

Ferries to Magnetic Island depart from three terminals that are along Ross Creek, and the long-distance bus terminal is at the Townsville Transit Centre, which is on the corner of Palmer and Plume Sts in South Townsville. The train station is south of the centre, near the corner of Flinders and Blackwood Sts.

INFORMATION

Flinders Mall visitors centre (☎ 4721 3660; www .townsvilleonline.com.au; Flinders St Mall, btwn Stokes & Denham Sts; ◷ 9am-5pm Mon-Fri, 9am-12.30pm Sat & Sun) Two sections: one has general information, the other specialises in diving and reef tours (www.divecruisetravel .com).

Internet Den (☎ 4721 4500; 265 Flinders St Mall; per hr $5; ◷ 9am-9pm Mon-Fri, 10am-8pm Sat & Sun) Also has chessboards.

Jim's Book Exchange (☎ 4771 6020; Shaw's Arcade) Off Flinders St Mall; a variety of secondhand books.

Main post office (☎ 13 13 18; Post Office Plaza, Sturt St) Has a poste-restante window.

Mary Who Bookshop (☎ 4771 3824; 414 Flinders St Mall) A range of books and music.

Townsville City Library (☎ 4727 9666; 272-78 Flinders St Mall; ◷ 9.30am-5pm Mon-Fri, 9am-noon Sat & Sun) Free Internet access, but you'll need to book hours in advance.

Townsville Enterprise main visitors centre (☎ 4778 3555; 6 The Strand; ◷ 9am-5pm Mon-Fri) Come here if you can't find what you're after from the booth in Flinders St Mall.

SIGHTS

Townsville has a range of attractions, from museums and galleries to its waterfront esplanade and gardens.

The Strand

The Strand is a 2.2km-long foreshore promenade that flaunts a number of parks, cafés and playgrounds, as well as pools. Its long stretch of beach has two patrolled stinger nets during summer (November to May): one at the northeastern end, the other about halfway along in front of Strand Park.

Castle Hill

More than a mound, but not quite a mountain, walking or running to the top of Castle Hill (300m) is great exercise. Apart from toned legs, you'll be rewarded with stellar views once you reach the peak. Access the 'goat track' (2km, 30 minutes) from Hillside Cres; or you can drive up via Gregory St.

Reef HQ

This excellent **aquarium** (☎ 4750 0800; www.reef HQ.org.au; Flinders St East; adult/child/concession $20/10/15; ◷ 9am-5pm) contains a living coral reef and is home to a vast array of marine life. The complex delivers facts and figures through interpretive displays and touch-tanks, and allows you to experience cruising sharks from behind a thick wall of glass.

There's an IMAX cinema next door; for further details, see p419.

Museum of Tropical Queensland

The focus of this terrific **museum** (☎ 4726 0606; www.mtq.qld.gov.au; 70-102 Flinders St East; adult/ child/student $9/5/7; ◷ 9.30am-5pm) is the *Pandora*, wrecked in the Torres Strait in 1791. There's a reconstruction of the bow, plus relics and videos associated with the story. There's also a kid-friendly science centre, displays on natural history and an exhibition of Aboriginal and Torres Strait artefacts and culture.

Perc Tucker Regional Gallery

This contemporary **art gallery** (☎ 4727 9011; ptrg@townsville.qld.gov.au; cnr Denham St & Flinders St Mall; admission free; ◷ 10am-5pm Mon-Fri, 10am-2pm

TOWNSVILLE

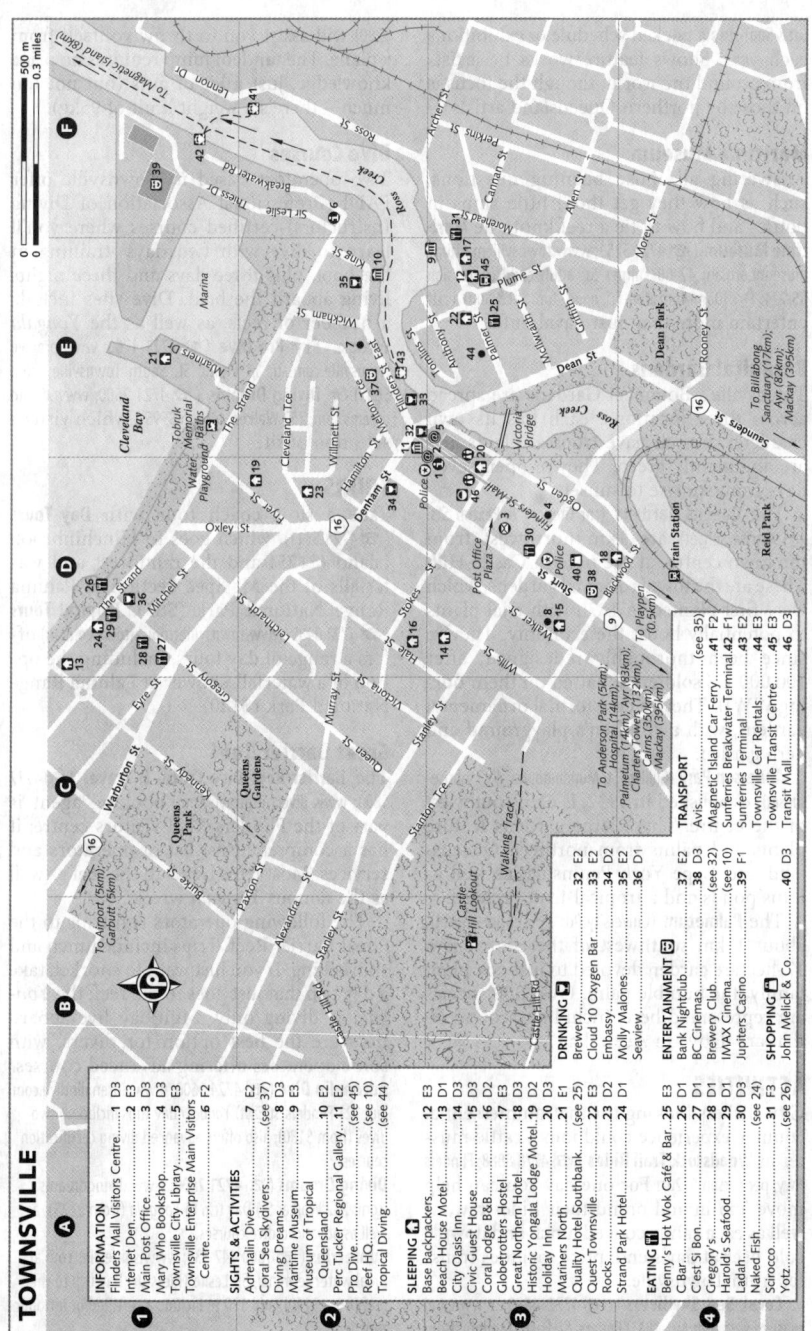

INFORMATION

Flinders Mall Visitors Centre.....1	D3
Internet Den.........................2	E3
Main Post Office....................3	D3
Mary Who Bookshop.................4	E3
Townsville City Library.............5	E3
Townsville Enterprise Main Visitors	
Centre..............................6	F2

SIGHTS & ACTIVITIES

Adrenalin Dive....................7	E2
Coral Sea Skydivers.........(see 37)	
Diving Dreams......................8	E3
Maritime Museum..................9	E3
Museum of Tropical	
Queensland.....................10	E2
Perc Tucker Regional Gallery...11	E2
Pro Dive.....................(see 45)	
Reef HQ.......................(see 10)	
Tropical Diving..............(see 44)	

SLEEPING

Base Backpackers.................12	E3
Beach House Motel................13	D1
City Oasis Inn......................14	D3
Civic Guest House.................15	D3
Coral Lodge B&B..................16	D2
Globetrotters Hostel...............17	E3
Great Northern Hotel..............18	D3
Historic Yongala Lodge Motel...19	D2
Holiday Inn........................20	D3
Mariners North...................21	E1
Quality Hotel Southbank......(see 25)	
Quest Townsville.................22	E3
Rocks.............................23	D2
Strand Park Hotel.................24	D1

EATING

Benny's Hot Wok Café & Bar..25	E3
C Bar.............................26	D1
C'est Si Bon......................27	D1
Gregory's.........................28	D1
Harold's Seafood.................29	D1
Ladah.............................30	D3
Naked Fish.................(see 24)	
Scirocco.........................31	F3
Yotz.........................(see 26)	

DRINKING

Brewery...........................32	E2
Cloud 10 Oxygen Bar.............33	E2
Embassy..........................34	D2
Molly Malones....................35	E2
Seaview...........................36	D1

ENTERTAINMENT

Bank Nightclub...................37	E2
BC Cinemas......................38	D3
Brewery Club...............(see 32)	
IMAX Cinema.................(see 10)	
Jupiters Casino...................39	F1

SHOPPING

John Melick & Co................40	D3

TRANSPORT

Avis..........................(see 35)	
Magnetic Island Car Ferry......41	F2
Sunferries Breakwater Terminal..42	F1
Sunferries Terminal..............43	E2
Townsville Car Rentals..........44	E3
Townsville Transit Centre........45	E3
Transit Mall.....................46	D3

Sat & Sun) has a packed schedule of exhibitions each year. Shows feature works by artists from around the world, though the focus is on those by northern Queensland artists.

Maritime Museum

Answering all those burning questions, such as how they get those little ships in bottles and how to tie a reef knot, the **Maritime Museum** (☎ 4721 5251; www.townsvillemaritime museum.org.au; 42-68 Palmer St; adult/child/concession $5/2/4; ☺ 10am-4pm Mon-Fri, noon-4pm Sat & Sun) will entertain more than just naval buffs.

Botanical Gardens

Townsville's Botanical Gardens are spread across three locations: each has its own character, but all have tropical plants and are abundantly green. They're open seven days from sunrise to sunset.

The **Queens Gardens** (cnr Gregory & Paxton Sts; ☺ sunrise-sunset) are 1km northwest from the town centre, at the base of Castle Hill. These are the town's original gardens, which were first planted in 1870 with trial plants to potentially boost the economy. They've since been thoroughly redesigned, after 100,000 US soldiers squatted on them during WWII. They're now formal ornamental gardens, with a children's playground and herb garden.

Anderson Park (Gulliver St, Mundingburra; ☺ sunrise-sunset), established in 1932, is 6km southwest of the centre. These large gardens feature plants and palms from northern Queensland and Cape York Peninsula, as well as lotus ponds and a tropical-fruit orchard.

The **Palmetum** (University Rd; ☺ sunrise-sunset), about 15km southwest of the centre, is a 17-hectare garden devoted to just one plant family, the humble palm. Over 300 species are represented here, including around 60 that are native to Australia.

ACTIVITIES

City slickers looking for that quintessential country experience could join a cattle muster at **Woodstock Trail Rides** (☎ 4778 8888; Flinders Hwy; per person $120). For one day you can help move 'em in and brand their hides raw, as well as eat a camp-cooked lunch and down a cold beer at day's end; price includes transfer from Townsville.

Coral Sea Skydivers (☎ 4772 4889; www.coral seaskydivers.com.au; 181 Flinders St East; tandem from $290) will assist you to throw yourself from a plane. The tandem jump requires no prior knowledge, just a lot of guts (but not too much – there's a weight limit of 95kg).

Dive Courses

Two operators based in Townsville offer PADI (Professional Association of Diving Instructors)-certified courses where you'll learn to dive with two days' training in the pool, plus three days and three nights living aboard the boat. Dive sites include a number of reefs, as well as the *Yongala* wreck. Try **Pro Dive** (☎ 4721 1760; www.prodive townsville.com.au; 14 Plume St, South Townsville; from $645) or **Diving Dreams** (☎ 4721 2500; www.diving dreams.com; 252 Walker St; from $595), which visits a selection of sites.

TOURS

Take a slow coach tour with **Day Tours** (☎ 4728 5311), which goes to Hinchinbrook Island ($125) and the rainforest and waterfalls of the Mt Spec Section of Paluma Range National Park ($85). **Tropical Tours** (☎ 4721 6489; www.townsvilletropicaltours.com.au) offers a range of day tours, including the option of a waterfall-shower at Paluma Range National Park ($120).

Great Barrier Reef

The **Barrier Reef Dive Cruise & Travel** (☎ 4772 5800; www.divecruisetravel.com) booking agent is part of the Flinders Mall visitors centre; it has a comprehensive list of operators and services. Most trips travel to the reef as well as the famous *Yongala* wreck.

The following operators run trips to the Great Barrier Reef. Trips include lunch and snorkelling. If you just want to snorkel, take a day trip that just goes to the reef; the *Yongala* is diving only. Multiday live-aboard trips are the best option for divers, with some operators offering advanced courses.

Adrenalin Dive (☎ 4724 0600; www.adrenalindive .au; 121 Flinders St East) *Yongala* day trips including two dives (from $180); also offers advanced diving certification courses.

Diving Dreams (☎ 4721 2500; www.divingdreams .com; 252 Walker St) Day trip to *Yongala* (from $175), as well as advanced dive courses.

Sunferries (☎ 1800 447 333; www.sunferries.com.au; Breakwater Terminal, Sir Leslie Thiess Dr) Day trip to the reef (from $140); add $70 to include a certified or introductory dive.

Tropical Diving (☎ 1800 776 150; www.tropicaldiving .com.au; 14 Palmer St) Day trips to the reef (from $130), certified or introductory dive $60.

SLEEPING
Budget
Great Northern Hotel (☎ 4771 6191; fax 4771 6190; 496 Flinders St West; s/d $35/45; P ⊠) The faded vinyl floor tiles and heavy bedhead-cum-storage units that are fixed to the wall imbue a holiday-house frivolity to this place. All rooms have bathrooms; ask for a room that opens out to the broad veranda. Downstairs in the pub, there are nightly bistro specials ($6). Come for the Aussie pub culture, not just 'cause it's cheap.

Civic Guest House (☎ 4771 5381, 1800 646 619; www.backpackersinn.com.au; 262 Walker St; dm $20, s $39-43, d & tw $42-48, with bathroom $60; ⊠ ⊠) Easygoing and sedate, this hostel hosts a free barbecue for guests on Friday night, and offers deals with the dive school next door. The pricier rooms have air-con, and dorms sleep four to six.

Coral Lodge B&B (☎ 4771 5512, 1800 614 613; www.corallodge.com.au; 32 Hale St; s/d $60/70, unit s/d $65/75; ⊠) This quaint old Queenslander has two self-contained units upstairs and eight guestrooms downstairs that share a bathroom and nifty communal kitchen. It's a quiet good-value place with lots of lace and floral flourishes.

Globetrotters Hostel (☎ 4771 3242, 1800 008 533; globetrotters@austranet.com.au; 45 Palmer St; dm $20-21, r with/without bathroom $60/50; ⊠ ⊡ ⊠) This comfortable hostel offers rooms in an old house, as well as in a newer building behind. Rooms are functional, with coin-operated air-con, and the dorms sleep six. Globetrotters is a quieter option without boozy backpacker nights.

Base Backpackers (☎ 4721 2322, 1800 628 836; www.basebackpackers.com; 21 Plume St; dm/d $21/60; ⊠ ⊡) Base has pretty basic rooms and facilities, but includes that all-important one – the in-house bar. After sipping on a bright alcoholic fizzy drink, you could get lost in the maze of corridors here. Base is above the transit centre and convenient for bus departures and ferry terminals.

Midrange
Rocks (☎ 4771 5700; www.therocksguesthouse.com; 20 Cleveland Tce; s/d $100/120; ⊠ ⊡) This boutique B&B balances personal service with profes-sionalism, plus a dash of theatrics. Antique furnishings and period pieces set the stage in the drawing room, where you can take your six-o'clock sherry. This historic home features lavish furnishings, an outdoor spa, and a huge balcony from where you can gaze out to Magnetic Island. There is wheelchair access, and rates include breakfast.

Beach House Motel (☎ 4721 1333; www.beach housemotel.com.au; 66 The Strand; s/d $86/96; P ⊠ ⊠) Louvred windows usher in the seabreeze from Cleveland Bay, which is just out the front of these modern motel rooms. Big bathrooms, spacious sleeping quarters and cheerful décor are features here. Rooms are well equipped with all the modern conveniences, such as a minifridge, phone and TV, as well as a few more traditional ones, such as a bedside Bible.

Historic Yongala Lodge Motel (☎ 4772 4633; www.historicyongala.com.au; 11 Fryer St; r $100-110, units from $115; P ⊠ ⊠) Most of the rooms here have heritage-style décor and fittings. Self-contained motel-style units are available out the back, and there's a restaurant on the premises that's licensed and open for breakfast and dinner.

Holiday Inn (☎ 4772 2477; www.townsville.holiday -inn.com; 334 Flinders St Mall; r $116-128; P ⊠ ⊠) Scanning Townsville's skyline, you can't miss the 'sugar shaker', a 20-storey circular building in the city's mall housing 197 rooms. Guests have free use of a gym, can order room service, and wake up to a free newspaper slipped under the door. You can also pay a premium for a room with a view.

Strand Park Hotel (☎ 4750 7888; www.strandpark hotel.com.au; 59-60 The Strand; r $115-145; P ⊠ ⊠) This waterfront complex houses 30 self-contained units. Standard rooms are situated on the ground floor, moving up, literally, to the superior and deluxe rooms with ocean views, balconies and perhaps a spa. The hotel also has a decent restaurant, Naked Fish.

Quest Townsville (☎ 4772 6477; www.quest apartments.com.au; 30-34 Palmer St; apt from $130; P ⊠ ⊠) This high-rise apartment complex houses hundreds of happy holiday-makers in its studio apartments. Rooms are serviced daily and are fully self-contained. Families are also catered for with one- and two-bedroom apartments, and a baby-sitting service.

Quality Hotel Southbank (☎ 4726 5265; www.south bankhotel.com.au; 23 Palmer St; r from $105; P ⊠ ☐ ⊠) This multilevel hotel has rooms with practical, unfussy interiors. Those in Townsville for business or a break from business will love the opulent executive rooms with lounge and ocean views.

Top End

Mariners North (☎ 4722 0777; www.marinersnorth .com.au; 7 Mariners Dr; apt from $165; P ⊠ ⊠) This soaring apartment complex, in the breakwater of the marina, provides spectacular views of the boat traffic out in Cleveland Bay. The two-bedroom and two-bathroom apartments have fully equipped kitchens and laundries. Guests have free rein in the use of the complex's tennis court and barbecue facilities.

City Oasis Inn (☎ 4771 6048, 1800 809 515; www.city oasis.com.au; 143 Wills St; r $170-200; P ⊠ ⊠) You'll have to allow time for your eyes to adjust to all the sparkling white surfaces here. The fabulous loft apartments have an upstairs bedroom separate from the downstairs kitchen, or you can opt for even more space by going for the two-bedroom apartments. There's a restaurant, children's playground and laundry facilities on the premises.

EATING

For an honest meal in casual surrounds head to one of Townsville's pubs. Wherever you go, the seafood is usually sublime.

Restaurants

C Bar (☎ 4724 0333; Gregory St Headland; meals $12-16; ☺ breakfast, lunch & dinner) Everything tastes better with views like this. From the broad outdoor deck on the waterfront, sausages and mash become 'gourmet sausages and mash'. Drag yourself inside to order and pay at the counter at this good-looking licensed restaurant.

Naked Fish (☎ 4724 4623; 60 The Strand, Strand Park Hotel; mains $18-24; ☺ dinner Mon-Sat) The ocean inspiration in the menu at Naked Fish spills over into the décor, with cool green-blue walls and a starry ceiling. Apart from seafood, the extensive menu includes Cajun and Moroccan dishes, tempura and risotto. Naked Fish has some outdoor seating beneath the giant strangled fig, and is licensed.

Benny's Hot Wok Café & Bar (☎ 4724 3243; 17-21 Palmer St; mains $15-20; ☺ lunch Thu-Fri & Sun, dinner Tue-Sun) Benny's exudes funky Asian ambience and offers a fusion of Japanese, Thai and Chinese cuisine. You might try the sizzling honey-pepper steak or the salt-and-pepper calamari. Benny's is licensed with a good range of wines and beers.

Scirocco (☎ 4724 4508; 61 Palmer St; mains $16-21; ☺ breakfast & lunch Tue-Sun, dinner Tue-Sat) Scirocco's high ceilings and motif-painted walls present an understated sophistication that's also evident in the service and food. You might try the pickled beetroot and goat's cheese risotto. A good selection of wine is available by the glass.

Yotz (☎ 4724 5488; Gregory St Headland, The Strand; mains $23-26; ☺ lunch & dinner) There's a frisky ambience at this bar and grill. From its outside area you can smoke Cuban cigars ($5 to $25), or just look at the views of the harbour and Magnetic Island. The menu includes double-baked sandcrab soufflé, and mushroom angel-hair noodles, as well as a range of Australian wines.

Cafés & Quick Eats

Ladah (☎ 4724 0402; cnr Sturt & Stanley Sts; dishes $7-10; ☺ breakfast & lunch Mon-Fri & Sun) This is a fabulous casual city café. Come for breakfast: perhaps rice porridge or raisin toast with smashed banana and brown sugar. The coffee is good, and there's a range of muffins, cakes and tarts ($3.50 to $4).

C'est Si Bon (☎ 4772 5828; 48 Gregory St; meals $8-15; ☺ breakfast & lunch) Order your quiche, bagel or breakfast at the counter, then find a seat along the communal table that runs the length of this large licensed café. The sleek ambience here is warmed by jazzy tunes that drift out of the speakers.

Harold's Seafood (☎ 4724 1322; cnr The Strand & Gregory St; fish boxes $6.50; ☺ lunch & dinner) Frying up all your favourites, this is a superb fish-and-chip joint. It has a window full of prawns that are ready to go: wait for a side of chips then scurry over to the waterfront to tear off their heads and legs…mmm.

Gregory's (☎ 4772 0553; 48 Gregory St; dishes $5-9; ☺ breakfast & lunch) This perky café has solid, healthy fare, and there's outdoor seating. After you've ordered at the counter, find a seat and the friendly staff will find you; it's hard to miss you sitting there with a pineapple on a stick – which is what you're given instead of a number – or an eggplant, kiwi fruit…

DRINKING

Many of Townsville's multitalented pubs and bars also serve food. Much of the action is along Flinders St and winds down around 1am.

Brewery (☎ 4724 9999; 242 Flinders St Mall; 🕙 lunch & dinner) This handsome all-in-one venue contains a sports bar, a nightclub, bistro and brewery. An after-work crew crowd the outdoor deck, with hearty bistro meals ($11 to $15) available between drinks. You might try one of the Brewery's own: Ned's Red Ale or Lager Lout. The sports bar down the back caters to armchair sportspeople, with 17 TVs and an assortment of sporty paraphernalia.

Embassy (☎ 4724 5000; 13 Sturt St) Dress smart and come for the tantalising meals ($24 to $27) on offer, or stride in later for the DJ spinning funk and house vinyl. Embassy's downstairs location, split-level interior, subdued lighting and effortless chic imbue it with an in-the-know ambience.

Molly Malones (☎ 4771 3428; 87 Flinders St East) This good-looking Irish pub serves wrist-snapping plates of food (meals $7 to $10; lunch Monday to Friday, dinner nightly). You could consume the equivalent of a week's worth of required iron in the steak accompanied by a Guinness. Molly's has a discreet gaming area, stages live music most nights and a nightclub out the back called Mantaz (open Friday and Saturday night).

Cloud 10 Oxygen Bar (☎ 4724 0202; Shop C, 194 Flinders St East; 5min & 3 flavours $7.50) 'Death by chocolate' and 'fuzzy navel' are all oxygen 'cocktails'. While it's not strictly drinking, people hit this oxygen bar before they hit the other bars – hoping that the promise of inhaling pure oxygen will offset their pending hangover.

Seaview (☎ 4771 5005; cnr The Strand & Gregory St) It seems the entire population jams into the huge concrete courtyard at the Seaview on a Sunday, when there's live music and entertainment.

ENTERTAINMENT
Cinemas & Casinos

BC Cinemas (☎ 4771 4101; cnr Sturt & Blackwood Sts) If you fancy a flick, this place screens mainstream films.

IMAX cinema (☎ 4721 1481; Flinders St East; adult/child/concession $14/8/12; 🕙 10.30am-4.30pm) You can see it all larger than life at the 18m-high domed screen next door to Reef HQ.

Jupiters Casino (☎ 4722 2333; Sir Leslie Thiess Dr) For a flutter head to this casino, which signals for attention by flashing its neon faux fireworks.

Nightclubs

Licensed until 5am, Townsville's clubs pick up from where the bars left off.

Bank Niteclub (☎ 4771 6148; 169 Flinders St East; admission $5; 🕙 closed Sun) House and dance beats; slinky surrounds.

Playpen (☎ 4721 5555; cnr Flinders St West & Knapp St; admission after 10pm $6) Multilevel place with dancing downstairs, plus pool tables. It's 500m southwest of the centre.

Brewery Club (☎ 4724 2999; 242 Flinders St East; 🕙 Fri & Sat) Resident DJ spins dance and progressive house, as well as beats and breaks.

SHOPPING

Cotters Market (Flinders St Mall; 🕙 8.30am-1pm Sun) Has about 200 craft and food stalls, as well as live entertainment; it's wheelchair accessible. There's also a night market along The Strand on the first Friday of the month from May to December.

John Melick & Co (☎ 4771 2292; 481 Flinders St West) The place to go for a good range of camping and bushwalking gear, and Aussie workwear.

GETTING THERE & AWAY
Air

Virgin Blue (☎ 13 67 89; www.virginblue.com.au) and **Qantas** (☎ 13 13 13; www.qantas.com.au) – and its subsidiaries – fly from Townsville to all the major cities, at least daily. Following are ballpark fares for flights from Townsville to: Brisbane ($130, 1¾ hours), Sydney (via Brisbane, $170, three hours), Melbourne ($240, 1¾ hours), Perth ($290, 5¾ hours), Adelaide ($260, 4½ hours), Canberra (via Brisbane, $250, 2¼ hours) and Hobart (via Brisbane, $250, three hours).

Bus

The long-distance bus station is at the **Townsville Transit Centre** (☎ 4721 3082; transittsv@bigpond .com.au; 21 Plume St). You'll find agents for the major bus companies, including **Transit Centre Backpackers** (☎ 4721 2322), which is the agent for Premier Motor Service.

Also in the Transit Centre is **Greyhound** (☎ 13 14 99; www.greyhound.com.au), with services running at least daily to Brisbane ($175,

23 hours), Rockhampton ($100, 11 hours), Airlie Beach ($55, four hours), Mission Beach ($50, four hours) and Cairns ($55, six hours).

Car

The larger car-rental agencies are all represented in Townsville.

Avis (☎ 4721 2688, 1300 137 498; www.avis.com.au; 81 Flinders St East) Also has an airport counter.

Europcar (☎ 4762 7050, 1300 131 390; www.deltaeuroopcar.com.au; 305 Ingham Rd, Garbutt) Also has an airport counter and 4WDs.

Thrifty (☎ 4725 4600; thriftytsv@thriftytsv.com.au; 289 Ingham Rd, Garbutt)

Train

The train station and **Queensland Rail Travel Centre** (☎ 1300 131 722; www.traveltrain.com.au; 502 Flinders St West; ◷ 8.30am-5pm Mon-Fri) are about 1km south of the centre. The Brisbane–Cairns *Sunlander* travels through Townsville four times a week.

GETTING AROUND
To/From the Airport

Townsville airport is 5km northwest of the city centre at Garbutt. A taxi to the centre costs about $20. **Abacus Tours** (☎ 4775 5544) operates a shuttle servicing all Qantas and Virgin arrivals and departures; if you arrive after 11pm you'll need to book. The cost one way/return is $8/14, and it will drop off and pick up anywhere within the central business district.

Bus

Sunbus (☎ 4725 8482; www.sunbus.com.au) runs local bus services around Townsville. Route maps and timetables are available at the visitors centre in Flinders Mall and at the newsagent in the Transit Mall.

Car & Motorcycle

Townsville Car Rentals (☎ 4772 1093; 12 Palmer St, South Townsville) hires small cars, bikes and scooters.

Taxis congregate outside the Transit Mall, or call **Townsville Taxis** (☎ 13 10 08, 4778 9555).

MAGNETIC ISLAND
☎ 07 / pop 2500

Magnetic Island's interior landscape ripples with bushland that peters down to the coastline, which has a number of peace-ful bays and beaches. The four tiny villages on the island consist of clusters of accommodation and laid-back tourist services. Only 8km off the coast 'Maggie' is almost a suburb of Townsville; it has a suburban atmosphere, but with a better-than-average backyard.

It's an unpretentious place: families splash about in and among the island's many bays and you can wear thongs (flip-flops) to dinner if you like. The island is steadily being commercialised, with an enormous marina and housing development under way at Nelly Bay and a waterfront face-lift at Picnic Bay due for completion by the time you read this.

About 70% of the island is national park, and the surrounding waters are part of the precious Great Barrier Reef World Heritage Area.

Orientation & Information

The main road runs up the eastern side of the island, linking Picnic Bay in the south to Horseshoe Bay in the north. There's also a rough track up the west coast leading from Picnic Bay to a secluded beach.

Some backpacker operators have Internet access. There's an ATM at **Arkies** (☎ 4778 5177, 1800 663 666; 7 Marine Pde, Arcadia) and most places have Eftpos and credit facilities.

Passenger ferries dock at Nelly Bay, where a visitors centre is planned; until then pop into the Townsville visitors centre (p414). There's an office for **Queensland Parks & Wildlife Service** (QPWS; ☎ 4778 5378; Hurst St; ◷ 7.30am-4pm) at Picnic Bay.

Sights & Activities
PICNIC BAY

Perhaps it's the twinkling night views of Townsville that draw families to Picnic Bay. Or it could be the handful of eateries along the mall, the jetty or the stinger-free enclosure on the beach.

To the west of town is Cockle Bay, with the wreck of HMS *City of Adelaide* languishing on the ocean floor. Heading east round the coast is Rocky Bay, where there's a short, steep walk down to its beautiful sheltered beach. The popular Picnic Bay golf course at the **Magnetic Island Country Club** (☎ 4778 5188; Hurst St, Picnic Bay; 9/18 holes $14/20; ◷ dawn-dusk) is open to the public and rents clubs and all equipment.

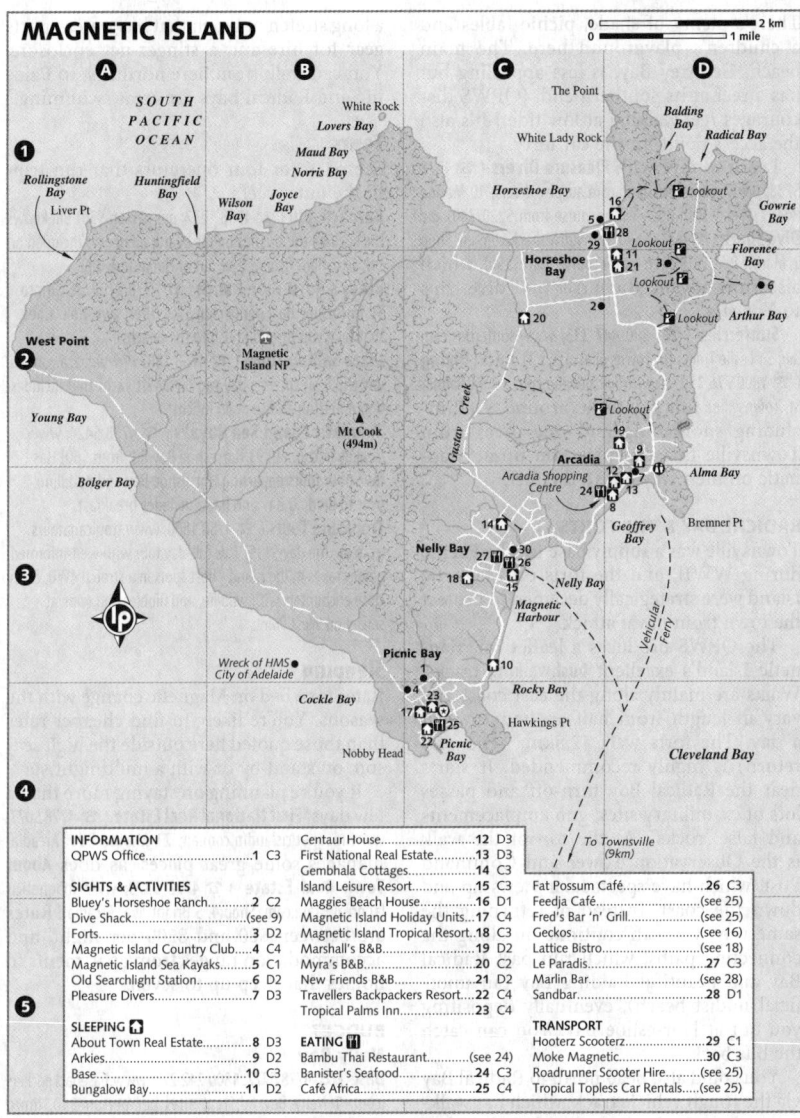

MAGNETIC ISLAND

| 0 | | 2 km |
| 0 | | 1 mile |

SOUTH
PACIFIC
OCEAN

White Rock
Lovers Bay
Maud Bay
Norris Bay

Rollingstone
Bay
Liver Pt

Huntingfield
Bay

Wilson
Bay

Joyce
Bay

The Point

Balding
Bay

Radical Bay

White Lady Rock

Horseshoe Bay

Lookout

Gowrie
Bay

Horseshoe
Bay

Lookout

Florence
Bay

Lookout

Arthur Bay

West Point

Magnetic
Island NP

Young Bay

Mt Cook
(494m)

Lookout

Bolger Bay

Arcadia

Alma Bay

Arcadia Shopping
Centre

Bremner Pt

Nelly Bay

Geoffrey
Bay

Wreck of HMS
City of Adelaide

Nelly Bay

Magnetic
Harbour

Vehicular Ferry

Picnic Bay

Cockle Bay

Rocky Bay

Hawkings Pt

Nobby Head

Picnic
Bay

Cleveland Bay

To Townsville
(9km)

**NORTH COAST
QUEENSLAND**

INFORMATION		
QPWS Office	1	C3
SIGHTS & ACTIVITIES		
Bluey's Horseshoe Ranch	2	C2
Dive Shack	(see 9)	
Forts	3	D2
Magnetic Island Country Club	4	C4
Magnetic Island Sea Kayaks	5	C1
Old Searchlight Station	6	D2
Pleasure Divers	7	D3
SLEEPING		
About Town Real Estate	8	D3
Arkies	9	D2
Base	10	C3
Bungalow Bay	11	D2

Centaur House	12	D3
First National Real Estate	13	D3
Gembhala Cottages	14	C3
Island Leisure Resort	15	C3
Maggies Beach House	16	D1
Magnetic Island Holiday Units	17	C4
Magnetic Island Tropical Resort	18	C3
Marshall's B&B	19	D2
Myra's B&B	20	D2
New Friends B&B	21	D2
Travellers Backpackers Resort	22	C4
Tropical Palms Inn	23	C4
EATING		
Bambu Thai Restaurant	(see 24)	
Banister's Seafood	24	C3
Café Africa	25	C4

Fat Possum Café	26	C3
Feedja Café	(see 25)	
Fred's Bar 'n' Grill	(see 25)	
Geckos	(see 16)	
Lattice Bistro	(see 18)	
Le Paradis	27	C3
Marlin Bar	(see 28)	
Sandbar	28	D1
TRANSPORT		
Hooterz Scooterz	29	C1
Moke Magnetic	30	C3
Roadrunner Scooter Hire	(see 25)	
Tropical Topless Car Rentals	(see 25)	

NELLY BAY

Sunferries disgorges passengers at Nelly Bay, all of whom have opportunities to shop and gawk at the marina as the enormous Magnetic Harbour commercial and residential development takes shape. The first stages opened in 2005, calling for businesses to lease new shopfronts, with the marina, boat ramp and private homes opening in stages over the following years. Magnetic Harbour is set to transform Nelly into a hub for the island – to the dismay of concerned locals.

ARCADIA

Arcadia village has pretty Alma Bay cove, with a grassy hill and sheltered beach.

There's plenty of shade, picnic tables and a children's playground here. The main beach, Geoffrey Bay, is less appealing but has a reef at its southern end. (QPWS discourages reef walking at low tide.) It's also the access point for the car ferry.

Learn to dive with **Pleasure Divers** (☎ 4778 5788; www.magnetic-island.com.au/plsr-divers; 10 Marine Pde; 3-/4-day PADI open-water course from $220/340) or **Dive Shack** (☎ 4778 5690; www.diveshack.com.au; Shop 2, Marine Pde; PADI open-water course from $250), which also runs advanced courses and dive trips to *Yongala*.

Sunferries (☎ 1800 447 333; www.sunferries.com .au; Sir Leslie Thiess Dr, Townsville) and **Tropical Diving** (☎ 1800 776 150; www.tropicaldiving.com.au; 14 Palmer St, Townsville) run day trips (around $200 including snorkelling and one dive) from Townsville that can pick you up at Magnetic on their way out to the reef.

RADICAL BAY & THE FORTS
Townsville was a supply base for the Pacific during WWII, and the forts on Magnetic Island were strategically designed to protect the town from naval attack.

The QPWS produces a leaflet for Magnetic Island's excellent **bushwalking** tracks. Walks are mainly along the east coast and vary in length from half an hour to half a day. The forts walk (2.8km, 1½ hours return) is highly recommended. It starts near the Radical Bay turn-off and passes lots of ex-military sites, gun emplacements and false 'rocks'. At the top of the walk is the Observation Tower and Command Post, which have spectacular views up and down the coast. Instead of returning the same way, you can continue on along the connecting paths, which run past Radical Bay and beautiful Balding Bay (an unofficial nudist beach), eventually depositing you out at Horseshoe Bay. You can catch the bus back.

You could also head north to Radical Bay via the rough vehicle track, which has walking paths off it leading to secluded Arthur and Florence Bays (great for snorkelling) and the old searchlight station on the headland between the two.

HORSESHOE BAY
On the north coast of the island, Horseshoe Bay attracts a younger crowd. It has a few shops, a good range of accommodation and a long stretch of beach that has water-sports gear for hire and a stinger-net enclosure. You can walk from here northeast to Balding and Radical Bays for great swimming.

Tours
See p416 for tour operators that run trips to the outer reef.

Barnacle Bill (☎ 4758 1237; per person $50) Bill knows the sea like the bristles on his beard; all gear is included on this two-hour fishing tour out of Horseshoe Bay.

Bluey's Horseshoe Ranch (☎ 4778 5109; 38 Gifford St, Horseshoe Bay; per person $70) Offers two-hour rides that take you through bush to the beach.

Jazza Sailing Tours (☎ 4758 1887; www.jazza.com.au; day trip $95) Offers a day trip on a 42ft yacht that includes boom netting and seafood lunch.

Magnetic Island Sea Kayaks (☎ 4778 5424; www .seakayak.com.au; 93 Horseshoe Bay Rd; from $60) Has four-hour tours departing Horseshoe Bay and paddling over to Balding Bay and back; includes breakfast.

Tropicana Tours (☎ 4758 1800; www.tropicanatours .com.au; full day $135) This full-day tour with well-informed guides takes in the island's best spots in a stretch 4WD. Enjoy close encounters with wildlife, and nibbles and wine at sunset on West Point.

Sleeping
Rates for a bed on Magnetic change with the seasons. You're likely to find cheaper rates than those quoted here outside the high season, on stand-by or with a multinight stay.

If you're planning on staying more than a few days, **First National Real Estate** (☎ 4778 5077; www.magneticislandfn.com.au; 21 Marine Pde, Arcadia) manages some great places, as does **About Town Real Estate** (☎ 4778 5570; www.magneticis landrealestate.com; Shop 4, 5 Bright Ave, Arcadia). Rates are between $80 and $200 per night, and accommodation ranges from apartments to homes that sleep up to seven.

BUDGET
Nelly Bay
Base (☎ 4778 5777, 1800 242 273; www.basebackpackers .com; 1 Nelly Bay Rd; tent sites per person $10, dm/d $20/70; 🖳 🖭) Even if you're not into full-moon parties and the backpacker scene, you should consider staying here. Ask for a beachfront A-frame, where the Coral Sea laps at your doorstep. The large decking and dining area is also absolute beachfront and absolutely gorgeous. Base will pick you up from Nelly Bay ferry terminal, and there is a dive school on site.

Arcadia

Centaur House (☎ 4778 5668, 1800 655 680; www.bpf
.com.au; 27 Marine Pde; dm/s/d $18/35/42) Mosquito
netting hangs from high painted ceilings
over your bed here. Add to that the gentle
whir of an overhead fan and a beachfront
location and you'll be swooning. This little
hostel's rooms are all upstairs, with a sham-
bolic shared undercroft area downstairs.

Arkies (☎ 4778 5177, 1800 663 666; www.arkiesonmag
netic.com; 7 Marine Pde; dm $15-20, d $49.50; ☒ ☐ ☒)
Arkies is a large backpackers complex that's
short on charm but big on the party vibe.
The complex has a bistro and bar with loads
of entertainment, including toad racing and
trivia nights. At the time of writing, the big
daggy rooms were set to be refurbished.

Horseshoe Bay

Bungalow Bay (☎ 4778 5577, 1800 285 577; www
.bungalowbay.com.au; 40 Horseshoe Bay Rd; tent/caravan
sites per person $10/25, dm/d $21.50/57; ☐ ☒) Cedar
A-frames prop on expansive natural land
here. The good facilities include an excellent pool, low-key bar and restaurant, as
well as a communal kitchen and bike hire.
The eight-bed dorm cabins have their own
bathroom, but the four-bed dorms don't.

Maggies Beach House (☎ 4778 5144; www.maggies
beachhouse.com.au; Pacific Dr; dm $21-26, d $52-75;
☒ ☐ ☒) Maggies has a fabulous loca-
tion right on the beachfront, and some
dorms have balconies with views. The
functional rooms are colourfully painted;
prices increase according to whether you
have a bathroom and/or view. Also on the
premises is a bar and Geckos restaurant.

MIDRANGE
Picnic Bay

Magnetic Island Holiday Units (☎ 4778 5246; 16 Yule
St; d $94; ☒ ☒) These homely self-contained
units are tightly spaced, set amid a leafy garden and manicured lawn. Apart from the
one-bedroom units, two-bedders are also
available for $110; any more than two people
costs $10 extra per person per night.

Travellers Backpackers Resort (☎ 4778 5166,
1800 000 290; travellers@getonit.net.au; 1 The Esplanade;
dm $12-20, r with/without bathroom $55/46; ☒ ☐ ☒)
This enormous complex has basic rooms
across several buildings; dorms sleep from
four to six. A pub and bistro are part of
the complex, as well as a concrete outdoor
courtyard and crocodile…uh huh!

Tropical Palms Inn (☎ 4778 5076, 1800 777 076;
tropicalpalmsinn@hotmail.com; 34 Picnic St; s/d $85/92;
☒ ☒) The bright rooms here could be described as motel-style, althouhg the drive-
to-your-door facility is missing. All rooms
have a sink, microwave and TV to keep you
semi-self-contained.

Nelly Bay

Gembhala Cottages (☎ 4778 5435; 28 Mango Parkway; d from $90; ☒ ☒) These Balinese-inspired
cottages are set in a lantern-lit tropical garden that's trafficked by butterflies. Inside,
louvre windows filter the light, and bright
bed linen, carved wood features and open-
air bathrooms complete the unique design.
Thumbs up.

Magnetic Island Tropical Resort (☎ 4778 5955,
1800 069 122; www.magnetictropicalresort.com; 56 Yates St;
d $130; ☒ ☒) A-frame cabins encircle large
bird-filled gardens here. This secluded resort
often plays host to a wedding party, so if this
is your first taste of Magnetic, don't think
that taffeta and tuxes are the island's dress
code. The resort features lawn tennis courts
and a seafood-and-steak restaurant (also
open to nonguests), called Lattice Bistro.

Island Leisure Resort (☎ 4778 5000; www.island
leisure.com.au; 4 Kelly St; d $145, extra person $10; ☒ ☒)
A block back from the bay and with palms
leaping from every patch of surrounding
dirt, Island Leisure Resort is well situated.
The self-contained rooms are spacious, so
suitable for families – though there may be
fights over the TV remote. There is a communal laundry, tennis court, and games
room on the premises.

Arcadia

Marshall's B&B (☎ 4778 5112; 3-5 Endeavour Rd; s/d
$50/70) Marshall's friendly hosts have four
basic rooms in their humble home. You're
welcome to use the lounge room and pleasant bird-filled garden with outdoor seating.

Horseshoe Bay

Myra's B&B (☎ 4758 1277; 101 Swenson St; s/d $50/70;
☒) The little cabin at the back of this property is sublime: set in rambling bush that
you'll share with possums and birds. The
cabin has its own bathroom, and there's a
room in the main house that shares the bathroom. Myra's is a bit out of the way, but great
value; there's free use of bikes and the owners will shuttle you to and from the ferry.

New Friends B&B (☎ 4758 1220; 48B Horseshoe Bay Rd; s/d $70/90; ⚡) Lovely modern rooms with their own bathrooms are nestled in the main house, which makes for some friendly communal living. There's a fabulous garden inlaid with a swimming pool, and backed by jungle palms. A large breakfast spread welcomes in the day.

Eating

Each of Magnetic's villages has its dining hub; of them, Horseshoe Bay would be the most fruitful and diverse.

PICNIC BAY

Fred's Bar 'n' Grill (☎ 4778 5911; Picnic Bay Mall; mains $15-20; ⏱ lunch & dinner Tue-Sat) This unpretentious place offers bistro favourites, such as well-prepared steaks and pastas, as well as daily specials. It has a big corner location, with seats inside and out.

Café Africa (☎ 4758 1119; Picnic Bay Mall; dishes $5-9; ⏱ breakfast & lunch) Specialising in all-day breakfast and sweet and savoury crepes; a good place to linger.

Feedja Café (☎ 4778 5833; Picnic Bay Mall; $6-10; ⏱ breakfast & lunch) Also a good place to linger, this neohippy café has soy products aplenty, plus juices and wraps.

NELLY BAY

Le Paradis (☎ 4778 5044; cnr Mandalay & Sooning Sts; mains $14-20; ⏱ breakfast Sun, lunch & dinner Tue-Sun) This polished BYO restaurant offers a range of Med-inspired dishes on its extensive menu. Large angular sails shelter the outdoor seating and the tables are smartly dressed in linen.

Lattice Bistro (☎ 4778 5955; 56 Yates St, Magnetic Island Tropical Resort; dishes $15-25; ⏱ dinner Thu-Tue) The Tropical Resort's restaurant is also open to nonguests who fancy a hearty steak or seafood meal. There is usually a vegie option and a kid-friendly meal or two. The open-sided restaurant is licensed and you may be serenaded with live music on Thursday and Friday nights in high season.

Fat Possum Café (☎ 4778 5409; 55 Spooning St; dishes $5-10; ⏱ breakfast, lunch & dinner) This nofuss café cheerily dishes up just-assembled sandwiches, gourmet pies and sushi from its daytime menu. Coffee is a popular adjunct, with a shady roadside courtyard in which to drink it. Night-time is BYO and bowls of noodles.

ARCADIA

Bambu Thai Restaurant (☎ 4778 5645; Bright Ave; mains $16-20; ⏱ dinner Thu-Tue) This intimate little restaurant serves Thai in its little backyard. It's BYO and takeaway is also available. Its gallery is open 10.30am to 5.30pm for coffee and cake.

Banister's Seafood (☎ 4778 5700; 22 McCabe Cres; mains $5-22; ⏱ lunch & dinner) For finger-lickin' fish and chips; a good takeaway, with a casual BYO dining area out the front.

HORSESHOE BAY

In addition to the places listed here, Horseshoe Bay's waterfront Pacific Dr is a bustling little strip, with a number of takeaway places and shops.

Sandbar (☎ 4778 5477; Pacific Dr; mains $15-20; ⏱ breakfast & lunch daily, dinner Wed-Sun) This licensed café-restaurant brandishes a confident menu with dishes made up of fresh ingredients and sassy flavours. The lunch and dinner menus favour seafood, and breakfasts are big plates of all your favourites.

Marlin Bar (☎ 4758 1588; 3 Pacific Dr; mains $10-20; ⏱ lunch daily, dinner Tue-Sat) This lively waterfront pub does decent vegie dishes and pasta. The range of mains takes in the entire farm, with veal, chicken, beef and pork dishes. Salads are obviously hard to come by, with a basic Greek salad costing as much as a steak ($20).

Geckos (☎ 4778 5144; Pacific Dr; mains $10-18; ⏱ breakfast, lunch & dinner) The restaurant at Maggie's Beach House is open to nonguests, and serves bistro-style meals all day. It's a superrelaxed, order-at-the-bar type of affair, with outdoor seating at white plastic settings. The bar here occasionally stages live music.

Getting There & Away

Sunferries (☎ 4771 3855; www.sunferries.com.au; ⏱ 6.45am-7pm Mon-Fri, 7am-5.30pm Sat & Sun) operates a frequent passenger ferry service between Townsville and Magnetic Island (return $20, about 20 minutes). Ferries depart from the terminal on Flinders St East in Townsville, also stopping at the breakwater terminal on Sir Leslie Thiess Dr. There is car parking here ($4 per day).

The **Magnetic Island Car Ferry** (☎ 4772 5422; Ross St, South Townsville; ⏱ 7.15am-5.30pm, closes 3.45pm Sat) does the crossing six times daily from the south side of Ross Creek. It costs $127 (return) for a car and three passen-

The peace of Paluma may inspire you to stay a night or two.

The candy-pink self-contained units at **Misthaven** (☎ 4771 5964; d $60; P) are fabulously kitsch. Each of the one-bedroom units is large and fully fitted with cutlery, a fridge and microwave. They're set on a neat patch of grass and have flowering pot plants around the entrance. (Card-payment facilities aren't available.) Otherwise **Paluma Rainforest Cottages** (☎ 4770 8520; www.palumarainforest.com.au; d $75-90; P) manages a number of self-contained properties in the area that sleep up to five people and include all linen and laundry facilities.

Unless you plan to subsist on scones and tea, bring supplies. If you *do* fancy Devonshire tea, stop by **Ivy Cottage** (☎ 4770 8533; teas $6; ⏰ 9am-4pm).

About 11km beyond Paluma is **Lake Paluma**, a drinking-water storage dam, with a dedicated foreshore area for swimming and picnicking. You can camp with permission from **NQ Water** (☎ 4770 8526; www.nqwater.com.au), or stay in out-of-the-way log cabins at **Hidden Valley Cabins** (☎ 4770 8088; www.hiddenvalleycabins.com.au; backpaker s/d $30/40, s/d $55/75; P), which has regular rooms as well as motel-style backpacker rooms and a licensed restaurant.

Jourama Falls Section
Jourama Falls and a further series of cascades and rapids tumble along Waterview

Creek, which is enclosed by palms and umbrella trees. It's a small area that's well developed, with a few lookouts, picnic areas and a **QPWS camping ground** (☎ 13 13 04; www.epa.qld.gov.au; per person $4) with drinking water, toilets and showers.

Access to this part of the park is via a 6km dirt road 90km north of Townsville or 25km south of Ingham. Access may be restricted during the wet summer months.

INGHAM
☎ 07 / pop 5000
No one's in a hurry in charming Ingham, with frequent cane trains clattering across the main street during harvest, and small clusters of locals on the pavement who've stopped for a natter. Ingham has banks, supermarkets and civic-service outlets at the centre of a substantial sugar-cane district. The first crops were established in the 1880s, and the town has a significant Italian population who originally came to work the cane fields.

Information
Ingham Library (☎ 4776 4683; 25 Lannercost St; ⏰ 9.30am-5pm Mon, 8.30am-5pm Tue-Fri, 9am-noon Sat)
QPWS office (☎ 4776 1700; www.epa.qld.gov.au; 49 Cassady St; ⏰ 9am-5pm Mon-Fri) Can handle permits for camping in the area.
Visitors centre (☎ 4776 5211; www.hinchinbrooknq.com.au; 21 Lannercost St; ⏰ 8.45am-5pm Mon-Fri, 9am-2pm Sat & Sun) Superhelpful and well-stocked.

PUB WITHOUT BEER
Probably Ingham's best-known local is Dan Sheahan (1882–1977), a canecutter, horseman and poet. Dan's poems carried on the Australian literary tradition, set by Banjo Paterson and Henry Lawson, of investigating Australian bush identity through verse. Sheahan focused on examining the Australian identity during WWII. The Ingham Library stocks a few of his collected works. Though Sheahan enjoyed mild success from his poetry, one of his poems was to become wildly popular – albeit as a song.

Sheahan penned 'Pub Without Beer' (over a glass of wine) at Ingham's Day Dawn Hotel after arriving to find that US troops had just been through his local and drained it dry of beer. (The Day Dawn was demolished in 1960, Lees Hotel now stands in its place.) The weekly *North Queensland Register* published the poem in 1944.

But it wasn't until 1956 that Gordon Parsons used Sheahan's poem as inspiration to compose the song 'Pub with No Beer' (over whisky) at a pub in Taylors Arms, New South Wales. The song was then immortalised by the late Australian country-music icon Slim Dusty, who went on to record *Duncan* ('...love to have a beer with...') in 1980, and whose album *Beer Drinking Songs* (1986) went gold within three weeks of its release.

Which all goes a fair way to proving that the humble beer is an integral part of the Australian identity.

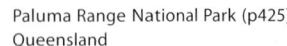

Townsville (p413), Queensland, with Castle Hill in the background

ROSS BARNETT

Mission Beach (p430), Queensland

WAYNE WALTON

Paluma Range National Park (p425), Queensland

MARTIN COHEN

Sights

The Ingham **cemetery**, about 3km out of town via Forrest Beach Rd, is unique for its sprawl of ornate Italianate mausoleums. In death as in life; these dwellings are adorned with flamboyant statuary, tiled, and shuttered with Venetian blinds.

Under an hour's drive west from Ingham (about 50km) are the dazzling heights of **Wallaman Falls** – the longest single-drop waterfall in Australia. The falls plunge around 300m off Seaview Range in the Girringun National Park, and have much more oomph in the wet season, after rains. There's a walking track to the base of the falls (return two hours, 4km) or a shorter track to rock pools (return 30 minutes, 1.2km) that leaves from the camping ground. You can swim both at the base of the falls and in the rock pools if the water level is not too high.

Sleeping & Eating

Station Hotel (☎ 4776 2076; 91 Cartwright St; s/d $20/40) This is the kind of place where you can have a room key if you want, but it's not necessary. Its bar is where you'll be privy to such local wisdom as the steel bar-fridge doors frosting over signalling that it's going to rain. It's full of fabulous '50s furniture, has an encircling veranda and generally rosy demeanour.

Herbert Valley Motel (☎ 4776 1777; fax 4776 3646; 37 Townsville Rd; s/d $55/70; P ⊠ ⊠) There are 30 identical motel rooms set back from the main approach into Ingham. The forgettable rooms have bathrooms, kettles and what you've really come for, a comfy bed.

Lees Hotel (☎ 4776 1577; leeshotel@ozemail.com .au; 58 Lannercost St; s/d $50/60; ⊠) The moulded horseman on the roof and talking dog out the front make it hard to miss Lees. On the same site as the Day Dawn Hotel, of 'Pub Without Beer' fame (see the boxed text, opposite), Lees has decent rooms upstairs (rates include breakfast). Lunch and dinner are available in the downstairs bistro (Monday to Saturday).

Elda's (☎ 4776 2039; 78 Lannercost St; sandwiches $4-5; ⊠ breakfast daily, lunch Mon-Fri) What looks like a humble fruit shop and deli is also the provider of truly spectacular sandwiches. Past the imported Italian dry goods and fresh fruit and veg is where John deftly assembles ingredients from the deli, including those he has lovingly marinated – think aniseed and sweet chilli.

Victory Café (☎ 4776 2108; 92 Cartwright St; meals $5-12; ⊠ lunch & dinner Tue-Sun) You won't need to wear your good shirt to dinner here, but this BYO diner-style café has a varied menu with hearty helpings of food. You might try a pizza, steak or burger, but the homemade lasagne comes highly recommended. Takeaway also available.

Getting There & Away

Greyhound (☎ 13 14 99; www.greyhound.com.au) buses run between Townsville and Ingham ($27, 1¼ hours); they stop in the centre of town on Townsville Rd, close to the corner of Lannercost St (and the information centre). Ingham is also on the **Queensland Rail** (☎ 1300 131 722; www.traveltrain.com.au; ⊠ 6am-9pm) Brisbane–Cairns line, which also stops in Townsville.

LUCINDA

☎ 07 / pop 783

Most people come to the seaside town of Lucinda to fish or gawk at its extraordinarily long jetty (6km). The world's longest bulk sugar–loading jetty, it allows enormous carrier ships to dock. About 25km northeast of Ingham, Lucinda is at the southern end of the Hinchinbrook Channel, a protected waterway that contains streams supporting mangroves, barramundi and crocs. Lucinda is also the closest mainland connection to stunning Hinchinbrook Island (p429).

Hinchinbrook Wilderness Safaris (☎ 4777 8307; www.hinchinbrookwildernesssafaris.com.au; 12 Bruce Pde) runs fishing tours ($150, four hours) between March and November, tours along the channel (per person $30, 2½ hours) and transfers to Hinchinbrook (from $46).

If the fish are biting, think about staying at **Wanderer's Holiday Village** (☎ 4777 8213; www .wanderers-lucinda.com.au; Bruce Pde; tent/caravan sites $16/20, d $70; P ⊠ ⊠). It's extremely well equipped, with barbecues, children's play area, laundry and activities room, and the cabins are self-contained (linen hire $6 per bed, includes towels).

Lucinda Point Hotel-Motel (☎ 4777 8103; cmusso@ bigpond.com.au; cnr Halifax & Dungeness Rds; r $75-95; P ⊠ ⊠) has self-contained rooms, and you'll have to contain yourself in the plush executive rooms that include bathrobes, biscuits and Egyptian cotton towels. You can tell the story of the one that got away over a bistro meal (lunch and dinner) and a beer in the main hotel.

ORPHEUS ISLAND

Only 11km long and about 1km wide, Orpheus is the second largest of the Palm Islands Group. There are 10 other islands in the group; apart from Orpheus and nearby council-run Pelorus, the islands are in the hands of Aboriginal communities and have restricted access.

The secluded Orpheus Island lies about 25km off the coast of Ingham. It's mostly national park, but it's the magnificent fringing reef (a reef that fringes the coast) that is the main attraction here.

Large coral bommies (isolated patches of reef) can be found in Little Pioneer Bay, Cattle Bay and around the Yank's Jetty area. The snorkelling is best around the island's northeast tip. The beaches at Mangrove Bay, Yanks Bay and Pioneer Bay are simply beautiful, but shallow at low tide.

Apart from the national park, with three camping grounds, the island has two leases: one an exclusive resort, the other a marine research station.

Orpheus Island Resort (☎ 4777 7377, 1800 077 167; www.orpheus.com.au; d from $725; ✍ ✉) This long-established luxury resort trades on its isolation: no day-trippers, no phones, no TVs. Everything is included: meals, snacks, snorkelling and tennis. The resort also runs diving trips and courses for guests; people under 15 years of age aren't welcome.

There are bush camping sites at Yank's Jetty, South Beach and Pioneer Bay. You'll need to bring drinking water and a fuel stove. Permits can be obtained from **QPWS** (☎ 13 13 04; www.epa.qld.gov.au; per person $4).

There are no public ferry services to Orpheus; access is by private charter. **Lucinda Reef & Island Charters** (☎ 4777 8220; per person $120) taxis to Orpheus on demand, as does **Orpheus Island Diving** (☎ 0407 378 968, 4777 9062; www.orpheusislanddiving.com.au; per person $130), which includes drinking water and mobile phone access.

CARDWELL

☎ 07 / pop 1420

Cardwell is a quiet, uncomplicated place sprawled along a 3km length of the Bruce Hwy, and is best known as the gateway to Hinchinbrook Island. It's also a popular fishing spot and has a smattering of sights in its vicinity.

The QPWS **Reef & Rainforest Centre** (☎ 4066 8601; www.epa.qld.gov.au; Bruce Hwy; ☽ 8am-4.40pm), beside the main jetty, has a rainforest interactive display, and information on Hinchinbrook Island and the nearby state and national parks.

The **Cardwell Forest Drive** starts from the centre of town and is a scenic 26km round trip, with excellent lookouts, walking tracks and picnic areas signposted along the way. There are super swimming opportunities at Attie and Dead Horse Creek, as well as Spa Pool.

Tours

Cardwell Charters (☎ 4066 846; www.oz-e.com.au /cardair) offers a scenic flight around local attractions ($50, 20 minutes) or the grand tour ($180, 1¼ hours) over the reef and islands, inland falls and Hinchinbrook Channel.

Hinchinbrook Explorer (☎ 4088 6154; www.h explorer.com.au; per person $130) offers fishing tours in the Hinchinbrook Channel, and tours of the Girringun and Edmund Kennedy National Parks.

Sleeping & Eating

Mudbrick Manor (☎ 4066 2299; www.mudbrickmanor .com.au; Lot 13, Stony Creek Rd; d $100-125; ℗ ✍ ✉) This outstanding hand-built mudbrick home has a casual country finesse. The huge indoor lounge area has activities aplenty or you could simply occupy yourself poking around all the decorative pieces. Ask about the three-course dinners – you may stay another night. Rates include breakfast.

Kookaburra Holiday Park (☎ 4066 8648; www .kookaburraholidaypark.com.au; 175 Bruce Hwy; tent/ caravan sites $18/20, d $35-90; ℗ ✍ ✉) This enormous holiday village almost outsizes Cardwell itself. Set in attractive tropical grounds, there's an accommodation option to suit all tastes and budgets, from on-site vans to two-bedroom villas.

Hinchinbrook YHA (☎ 4066 8648; tent site s/d $11/18, dm/s/d $18/35/40) Out the back of the Kookaburra Holiday Park is this bright backpackers with access to all of the park's fabulous facilities.

Port Hinchinbrook Resort Hotel (☎ 4066 2000; www.porthinchinbrook.com.au; Bruce Hwy; d from $155; mains around $20; ☽ breakfast, lunch & dinner; ℗ ✍ ✉) The comfortable, modern cabins here are compact, yet well equipped. As a resort, the complex has big plans but a long way to go, generally lacking in any ambience.

Its Portside Café, open to nonguests, is a slightly upscale pub menu serving reef 'n' beef, parmagiana and pastas.

Latitudz (☎ 4066 8907; Victoria St; mains $17-20; ☽ lunch & dinner Wed-Mon) The string of takeaway joints along the main drag is interrupted by this smart-looking café serving barramundi, oysters and other seafood.

Getting There & Away

Greyhound (☎ 13 14 99; www.greyhound.com.au) goes from Townsville to Cairns, stopping at Cardwell; from Townsville the trip costs $32 (two hours), from Cairns $31 (three hours).

Cardwell is also on the Brisbane–Cairns train line; contact **Queensland Rail** (☎ 1300 131 722; www.traveltrain.com.au) for details.

HINCHINBROOK ISLAND

Lucky you, if you have time to explore this superb unspoilt island. All 400 sq km of the island is national park, and rugged Mt Bowen (1121m) is its highest peak. It's alive with animal life, including the pretty-faced wallaby and Ulysses butterfly; there are also bush rats, crocodiles and sandflies.

Walking opportunities here are excellent; however, some trails may close between November and March due to adverse weather. The highlight is the **Thorsborne Trail**, a 32km coastal track from Ramsay Bay to Zoe Bay (with its beautiful waterfall) and on to George Point at the southern tip. It's recommended that you spend three nights to complete the trail. Return walks of individual sections are also possible. You'll need to wear a layer of insect repellent, protect your food from ravenous rats, draw water from creeks as you go and be alert to the possibility of crocs being present. The trail is ungraded and at times rough, including challenging creek crossings; you should carry a map, drinking water, fuel stove and trowel.

Apart from the Thorsborne Trail, camping and short walks are available at **Macushla** (5km to 8km, 1½ to two hours), and the **Haven circuit** (1km, 15 minutes).

In general, beach fishing is allowed, but be mindful of marine stingers (see the boxed text, p371) that are present in the sea and waterways from October to April.

Bookings for the Thorsborne Trail need to be made in advance: for a place during the high season, **QPWS** (☎ 13 13 04; www.epa .qld.gov.au; per person $4) recommends booking a year ahead (six months ahead for other dates). Its **Reef & Rainforest Centre** (☎ 4066 8270; Bruce Hwy; ☽ 8am-4.40pm) in Cardwell stocks the imperative 'Thorsborne Trail' brochure and screens the 15-minute *Without a Trace* video, which walkers are required to view. Cancellations for places on the Thorsborne Trail are not unheard of, so it's worth asking about the possibility of a place at the centre if you've arrived without a booking.

Hinchinbrook Island Ferries (below) runs day tours ($85 per person) to Hinchinbrook Island, departing from Cardwell's Hinchinbrook Marina. The tour includes exploration of the mangroves, visiting the long stretch of beach at Ramsay Bay and the option of walking through the rainforest at Macushla.

Sleeping

Hinchinbrook Island Resort (☎ 4066 8270; www.hin chinbrookresort.com.au; beach cabins $165, tree houses $300; ☒) You'll find these tree houses with floor-to-ceiling windows, a balcony, minikitchen and bathroom in the island's north. The beachfront cabins are self-contained, and the price is for up to four people. Guests are free to use the resort's canoes, surf-skis and snorkelling gear. All meals are available from the licensed restaurant (only available to guests) and are not included in the accommodation rates; full-board packages are also available. Transfers with Hinchinbrook Island Ferries are an additional cost also, see the following section.

There are six **QPWS camping grounds** (☎ 13 13 40; www.epa.qld.gov.au; per person $4) along the Thorsborne Trail, plus the two at Macushla Bay and the Haven in the north.

Getting There & Away

Hinchinbrook Island Ferries (☎ 4066 8270; www .hinchinbrookferries.com.au) has a daily service from May to October and three services a week from November to April; services are suspended in February during the wet season. Boats depart from Cardwell's Port Hinchinbrook Marina and dock at the Hinchinbrook Resort. The journey takes about 50 minutes and costs from $100 return. If you're walking the Thorsborne Trail a one-way transfer costs $60. Walkers usually pick up the **Hinchinbrook Wilderness Safaris'** (☎ 4777 8307; www.hinchinbrookwildernesssafaris.com.au; one way/return $47/57) service at the southern end.

GOOLD & GARDEN ISLANDS

These uninhabited islands provide the perfect setting for you to play castaway: both are national parks and are off the everyday-tourist radar, so you could find you have the islands to yourself. **Goold Island**, just 17km northeast of Cardwell, supports open forest, mangroves and a sandy beach on both the west and south sides. There's a **QPWS camping ground** (☎ 13 13 04; www.epa.qld.gov.au; per person $4) on the island's west, with toilets, picnic tables and a gas barbecue. Bring drinking water, a book and frayed-leg pants.

Just south of Goold Island is tiny **Garden Island**, with a recreation reserve controlled by the local council. Permits to camp are required and available from the **Cardwell Newsagency** (☎ 4066 8622; 83 Victoria St; per person $3.85). The island has a good sandy beach but no fresh water; no children under six years permitted.

Hinchinbrook Island Ferries (☎ 4066 8270; www.hinchinbrookferries.com.au; return $85) can ferry campers on request.

TULLY

☎ 07 / pop 2800

Tiny Tully carries the reputation as the wettest place in Australia. It holds the record for the highest annual rainfall in a populated area of Australia – which it 'won' in 1950 when it received 7.9m. (It's no coincidence that the giant gumboot at the entrance to town is also 7.9m tall.) The banana plantations around Tully provide seasonal employment that attracts droves of young backpackers on working holidays. As most of the accommodation is geared to this market, most travellers stay at nearby Mission Beach. The rapids in the rivers close by provide hours of frothy excitement for white-water rafters. Commercial trips on the Tully River are timed to coincide with when the hydroelectricity company opens the floodgates.

The Tully **visitors centre** (☎ 4068 2288; www.tropicalaustralia.com.au; Bruce Hwy; ☼ 8.30am-4.45pm Mon-Fri, 9am-2.30pm Sat & Sun) is on the highway just south of the Tully turn-off. Book here for **Tully Sugar Mill tours** (adult/child $10/6.50; ☼ tours 10am, 11am & 1.30pm Mon-Fri, 11am Sat & Sun Jun-Nov). During the crushing season the mill operates 24/7 processing about two million tonnes of cane. The 1½-hour tours must be booked at least half an hour before departure; wear closed shoes and a shirt with sleeves. There is

good walking in the **Tully State Forests**, located 40km from Tully along Cardstone Rd. **Tully Gorge** has picnic facilities, as well as river access for swimming, though you may be converged upon by pumped and paddle-wielding kayakers, and the gentle burble of the Tully River can turn suddenly into a rapid when the hydroelectricity company opens its floodgates. A number of disused logging roads in the area have been revitalised into walking trails; the visitors centre in Tully has a map, as does www.mistymountains.com.au.

Day trips with **Raging Thunder Adventures** (☎ 4030 7990; www.ragingthunder.com.au/rafting.asp) or **R'n'R White Water Rafting** (☎ 4051 7777; www.raft.com.au) cost about $150 and include barbecue lunch and transfers from Mission Beach, Cairns or Port Douglas.

Greyhound (☎ 13 14 99; www.greyhound.com.au) runs from Townsville to Tully ($36, 3¼ hours). Tully is also on the Brisbane–Cairns train line; contact **Queensland Rail** (☎ 1300 131 722; www.traveltrain.com.au) for details.

MISSION BEACH

☎ 07 / pop 1090

There is little to distract you from long, lazy days on the stunning beach here, except for the lush World Heritage–listed rainforest just inland and, off-shore, the extraordinary coral and marine life of the Great Barrier Reef – oh…and the tropical-island playground of Dunk Island.

Mission Beach consists of five contented settlements made up of low-key places to stay and eat: Wongaling Beach and South Mission Beach are to the south, Mission Beach is in the middle, and Bingil Bay and beautiful Garners Beach are in the north.

There are opportunities for gentle walks, snorkelling and diving, as well as 'woo-hoo'-inducing activities such as skydiving and white-water rafting. Sophisticated restaurants and boutique B&Bs mix in with modest cafés and casual backpackers, keeping holiday-makers happy.

The area is named after the Aboriginal mission that had only been established for four years before it was destroyed in 1918 by one of the state's worst cyclones.

Information

Mission Beach village has comprehensive services: Internet access is available at a number of places on the main strip, ATMs

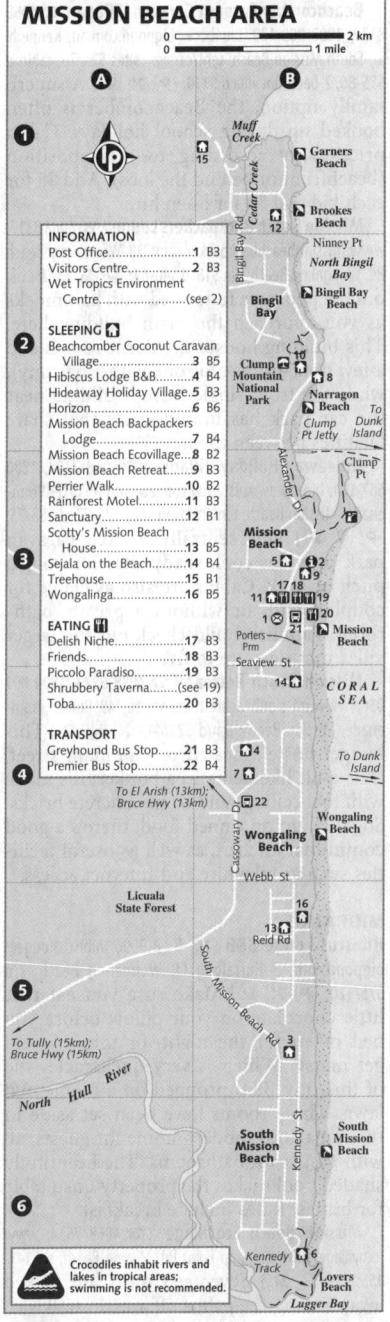

MISSION BEACH AREA

0   2 km
0   1 mile

INFORMATION
Post Office..........................1 B3
Visitors Centre..................2 B3
Wet Tropics Environment
  Centre..........................(see 2)

SLEEPING
Beachcomber Coconut Caravan
  Village..........................3 B5
Hibiscus Lodge B&B..........4 B4
Hideaway Holiday Village.5 B3
Horizon.............................6 B6
Mission Beach Backpackers
  Lodge.............................7 B4
Mission Beach Ecovillage...8 B2
Mission Beach Retreat......9 B3
Perrier Walk.....................10 B2
Rainforest Motel..............11 B3
Sanctuary.........................12 B1
Scotty's Mission Beach
  House............................13 B5
Sejala on the Beach.........14 B4
Treehouse.......................15 B1
Wongalinga......................16 B5

EATING
Delish Niche.....................17 B3
Friends..............................18 B3
Piccolo Paradiso...............19 B3
Shrubbery Taverna........(see 19)
Toba.................................20 B3

TRANSPORT
Greyhound Bus Stop.......21 B3
Premier Bus Stop.............22 B4

Crocodiles inhabit rivers and
lakes in tropical areas;
swimming is not recommended.

are located in the newsagent and supermarket, and you'll find the post office in the main group of shops.

The Mission Beach **visitors centre** (☎ 4068 7099; www.missionbeachtourism.com; Porters Promenade; ☺ 9am-5pm) has a wall of pamphlets (in a number of languages). It shares the premises with the **Wet Tropics Environment Centre** (☎ 4068 7179; www.wettropics.gov.au), with rainforest and cassowary conservation displays. It's staffed by a group of volunteers from the **Community for Cassowary & Coastal Conservation** (C4; www.cassowaryconservation.asn.au). Proceeds from purchases of some items at the centre go towards buying cassowary habitat, which is being depleted by development, and threatens the survival of the species; see the boxed text, p462.

Sights & Activities

Dunk Island (p434) is a popular day trip from Mission Beach. The Great Barrier Reef is around an hour away, and rainforest walks can get quite exciting if you come across a cassowary.

DIVING & SNORKELLING

All boats depart from thriving little Clump Point jetty.

Day cruises to the outer reef with **Quick Cat** (☎ 4068 7289; www.quickcatscuba.com) include a 45-minute stop at Dunk Island, snorkelling, lunch and glass-bottom boat jaunt for $140; add $80 for an introductory dive or $60 for a certified dive. A return ferry to Dunk Island is also available ($34). *Quick Cat* has a capacity of 100, though averages half that.

Experienced divers should try **Calypso Dive** (☎ 4068 8432; www.calypsodive.com), which runs cruises to the *Lady Bowen* wreck (from $160) on Friday. Day cruises include snorkelling and lunch ($100), with the option of an introductory dive ($60) and certified dive ($40).

WALKING

Walkers should pick up a free walking guide from the visitors centre that details the many trails in the area. Among them is the superb coastal Kennedy Track (7km, three hours return), which leads past secluded Lovers Beach and the lookout at Lugger Bay. The inland walks through interior rainforest are where you're most likely to see a cassowary. Licuala State Forest has a number of rainforest walks.

NORTH COAST QUEENSLAND

OTHER ACTIVITIES

R'n'R (☎ 1800 079 039; www.raft.com.au) and **Raging Thunder** (☎ 4030 7990; www.ragingthunder.com.au/rafting.asp) charge $140 from Mission Beach for day trips on the Tully River, with lunch.

Paddle over to Dunk Island for the day with **Coral Sea Kayaking** (☎ 4068 9154; www.coralseakayaking.com; half-/full day $60/95), or bob around the coastline for half a day; trips depart South Mission Beach.

Jump the Beach (☎ 4031 1822; www.jumpthebeach.com; tandem from $295) uses the sand of Mission Beach to cushion your landing.

Tours

River Rat Eco Cruises (☎ 4068 8018; www.riverratcruises.com; adult/child $50/25) and **Hinchinbrook Explorer** (☎ 4088 6154; www.hexplorer.com.au; adult/child $50/25) run informed wildlife-spotting tours along the Hull River that last for around four hours and include a light meal.

Clump Mountain (☎ 4068 7408; clumpmountain@dodo.com.au; half-day $40) offers a guided walk that heads through the Clump Mountain rainforest with a local, learning about bush tucker, bush medicine and the Dreamtime.

Sleeping

Mission Beach is less affected than areas like Cairns and Port Douglas, and so prices remain pretty stable year-round; there might be a slight dip during the wet season. Most of the action is clustered around Mission Beach, and Wongaling Beach to a lesser extent.

BUDGET

Treehouse (☎ 4068 7137; www.yha.com.au; Bingil Bay Rd, Bingil Bay; tent sites $12, dm/d $20/50; P ⊠) The timber building here merges effortlessly with the surrounding rainforest. The generous balcony space is dotted with heavy wooden tables that are strewn with board games, international newspapers and books. It all makes for a remarkably restful and affable stay. Treehouse is a YHA-affiliated hostel.

Scotty's Mission Beach House (☎ 4068 8676, 1800 665 567; scottysbeachhouse@bigpond.com; 167 Reid Rd, Wongaling Beach; dm $19-23, d $55; ⊠ ⬛ ⊠) Behind the white picket fence of Scotty's Bar & Grill is a secluded pocket of accommodation with beautiful grounds and stellar facilities. The bright dorm rooms, sleeping four to 12, are a beachy shade of blue, and the basic doubles have their own bathroom. Friendly staff will welcome you to the fold.

Beachcomber Coconut Caravan Village (☎ 4068 8129, 1800 008 129; big4bccv@bigpond.com.au; Kennedy St, South Mission Beach; tent/caravan sites $24/28, cabin d $55-80, 2-bedroom villa d $110; P ⊠ ⊠) A superb family option, the Beachcomber is often booked up during school holidays. Cabin prices vary according to their position (beachfront or behind the loos). Add $8 for each kid and $8 for linen hire.

Mission Beach Backpackers Lodge (☎ 4068 8317; www.missionbeachbackpacker.com; 28 Wongaling Beach Rd, Wongaling Beach; dm $18, d $40-44; ⬛ ⊠) Check out the pool area festooned with hammocks as you approach the main building here. This building houses the dorm rooms and a few doubles (ask for one with a balcony), while the front single-storey building near the car park has four doubles that share facilities between them.

Hideaway Holiday Village (☎ 4068 7104, 1800 687 104; hideaway@austarnet.com.au; 58-60 Porter Promenade, Mission Beach; tent/caravan sites $23/27, d $58-75; P ⬛ ⊠) This centrally located caravan park provides cool, shady sites for you to pitch or park. Cabins are also available for couples, with or without a private bathroom. Families could check out the larger villas that sleep up to five.

Mission Beach Retreat (☎ 4088 6229, 1800 001 056; www.missionbeachretreat.com.au; 49 Porter Promenade, Mission Beach; dm/d $21/44; ⊠ ⬛ ⊠) This budget hostel, located on the main street, feels a bit like being in a bunker: it's made with low ceilings and from concrete bricks. So stock up on tinned food; there's a good communal kitchen, as well as useful facilities such as bike hire and Internet access.

MIDRANGE

Hibiscus Lodge B&B (☎ 4068 9096; hibiscuslodge@bigpond.com; 5 Kurrajong Cl, Wongaling Beach; s/d $75/120; P ⊠ ⊠) Make sure you eat that little chocolate on your pillow before you bed down for the night, or things could get messy. Which is very uncharacteristic of this tidy B&B propped on a manicured lawn. Three rooms have been set aside in this capacious modern home for guests, all with their own bathrooms. The beautifully shaded pool makes the property unsuitable for littlies. Rates include breakfast.

Mission Beach Ecovillage (☎ 4068 7534; www.ecovillage.com.au; Clump Point Rd, Mission Beach; d $141-155; P ⊠ ⊠) Seventeen units are tucked away among the palms off a main walkway.

Each unassuming unit has a kitchen and dining area, big beds and, if you go for the deluxe room, a spa. The freeform pool is a stunner, and you can see the beach from the bar.

Rainforest Motel (☎ 4068 7556; www.mission beachrainforestmotel.com; 9 Endeavour Ave, Mission Beach; d $80; P ✗ ♨) A few tidy rooms enclose the faux rainforest in the courtyard. Each of the good-sized rooms has a little fridge, a kettle and microwave, and its own bathroom. A path leads out the back of the motel through to the shops on the main street.

Sanctuary (☎ 4088 6067, 1800 777 012; www.sanc tuaryatmission.com; 72 Holt Rd, Bingil Bay; dm $33, hut s/d $60/61, cabin s/d $130/150; P ▢ ♨) These minimalist huts are designed to make you feel at one with the surrounding nature. The Om ambience is not so hardline as to disallow a few indulgences, however: its restaurant serves such treats as vodka-and-lime chicken, and perhaps *affogato* for dessert. Sanctuary hosts regular yoga retreats and classes, and is unsuitable for anyone under 11 years.

TOP END

Horizon (☎ 4068 8154; www.thehorizon.com.au; Explorer Dr, South Mission Beach; r $220-420; P ✗ ♨) This resort is tucked in the rainforest above Luggers Beach, with views out to Dunk Island and beyond. If you go for the best they've got, you could appreciate that view from your king-sized bed. There's a tour-booking desk and restaurant, which is open to nonguests.

Wongalinga (☎ 4068 8221; www.wongalinga.com .au; 64 Reid Rd, Wongaling Beach; 1-/2-/3-bedroom apt $180/210/250; P ✗ ♨) Grab a friend or two and live very comfortably here for the duration of your stay in Mission Beach. Prices for these fully self-contained contemporary pads are for two people in the one-bedroom apartment, four people in the two-bedroom and six people in the three-bedder. Each apartment has an outdoor- and indoor-entertainment area.

Sejala on the Beach (☎ 4088 6699; http://mission beachholidays.com.au/sejala; 1 Pacific St, Mission Beach; d $175-195; P ✗ ♨) These fancy beach huts are screened to allow sea breezes through. The open-plan interior, with kitchen and bathroom, makes a comfortable retreat for couples. There are three huts of varying sizes, each painted a saucy solid colour.

Eating

Mission Beach has a medley of places to eat, from main-street cafés with familiar menus

---

THE AUTHOR'S CHOICE

Perrier Walk (☎ 4068 7141; www.perrierwalk .nq.nu; Alexander Dr; s/d $125/150; P ✗ ♨) What do you get when you cross a landscape designer with a chef? A choice B&B with extraordinary gardens and a very classy breakfast. Expect to have permanently water-crinkled skin as you flit between the stone bath and tree shower in the jungle bathroom, and the swimming pool down the back of this large property. Three huge pet barramundi live in the little lake and your colourfully rendered Mexican-style room (no doors) is enveloped by giant exotic flowering plants. Real coffee and homemade bread can be served in the lounge area, or perhaps around the lily ponds?

---

of sandwiches and light lunches to stylish restaurants with attentive service.

Friends (☎ 4068 7107; Porter Promenade, Mission Beach; mains $17-25; ☾ dinner Tue-Sun) This cosy restaurant has dutiful staff cruising around low-key surrounds with plates of old favourites, such as roast chicken and laksa. There's a small selection of specials, and a specially good wine list; Friends is licensed and BYO.

Toba (☎ 4068 7852; 37 Porter Promenade, Mission Beach; mains $21-25; ☾ dinner Wed-Sun) Toba dishes up polite portions of Asian-inspired meals, such as Thai green curry. The courtyard is the main attraction, especially the platform hut with floor-cushion seating. Well-spaced tables and formal service make Toba's popular with small groups and couples.

Shrubbery Taverna (☎ 4068 7803; David St, Mission Beach; main $17-20; ☾ lunch Sat & Sun, dinner daily) Locals like the laid-back service and courtyard dining here at the Shrubbery. Balmy nights and the sound of waves washing the beach do wonders for the Mediterranean/Greek menu. And there's a happy hour-and-a-half between 4.30pm and 6pm.

Delish Niche (☎ 4088 6004; Porter Promenade, Mission Beach; dishes $6-10; ☾ breakfast & lunch) This homestyle café can whip up a fine cooked breakfast and light lunches such as quiche or a sandwich. Sit inside, among the curious collection of crafty gift items, or preferably under a big umbrella on the street.

Piccolo Paradiso (☎ 4068 7008; David St, Mission Beach; ☾ breakfast, lunch & dinner) This casual place is always busy, which may account for the sometimes-perfunctory service. The dinner menu is predominantly pizza and pasta, with a selection of specials such as barramundi. By day it's also an Internet café, serving breakfast till 10.30am.

There are supermarkets for self-caterers at Mission Beach and Wongaling Beach.

Getting There & Away

Greyhound (☎ 13 14 99; www.greyhound.com.au) does a detour from the Bruce Hwy, stopping on Porters Promenade in the village of Mission Beach. **Premier** (☎ 13 34 10; www.premierms.com.au) buses stop in Wongaling Beach. The average bus fare from Cairns is $25 (two hours) and from Townsville $45 (3¾ hours).

The **Trans North** (☎ 4068 7400; from $3; ☺ Mon-Sat) local bus runs almost every hour between Bingil Bay and South Mission Beach; the visitors centre has timetables.

DUNK ISLAND

Part national park, part resort, Dunk Island (one of the Family Island Group) is about 4km (20 minutes) off the coast and is an easy day trip from Mission Beach. Once there you can take a walk in the park, swim, snorkel or partake in the range of watersports on offer.

The island is known for its abundant species of birds (over 100), butterflies, coral gardens and marine life. You can visit **Bruce Arthur's Gallery** (admission $4; ☺ 10am-1pm Mon & Thu), at the southern end of Pallon Beach, which exhibits pottery, jewellery and paintings by resident artists.

You can almost circumnavigate the island using the park's well-marked **walking trails** (three hours, 9km). Otherwise, a walk to the top of Mt Kootaloo (271m; return 1½ hours, 5.6km) allows you to look back at the mainland and see the Hinchinbrook Channel fanning out before you. There's good **snorkelling** over bommies at Muggy Muggy and great **swimming** at Coconut Beach.

Otherwise daytrippers can utilise a limited number of the resort's facilities by purchasing a Resort Experience Pass (adult/child $40/20), available from the Watersports Centre just south of the jetty. This entitles you to lunch at one of the resort's cafés and an hour's use of a paddle ski.

Sleeping & Eating

Options here are limited to the resort's offerings or camping.

Dunk Island Resort (☎ 4068 8199, reservations 1800 737 678; www.dunk-island.com; s $365-520, d $500-800; ☒ ☒) Rates include breakfast and dinner, plus unlimited use of nonmotorised watersports equipment. Handsome rooms range from great to sublime, especially if you choose to stay in a beachfront suite. Think split-level accommodation, a huge bed, personal access to the beach, and views over Brammo Bay.

The **QPWS camping ground** (☎ 4068 8199; www.epa.qld.gov.au; per person $4) has nine sites on a gravel patch just back from the jetty; there are toilets and showers.

Day-trippers can buy food and beverages from the licensed café south of the jetty.

Getting There & Away

Macair (☎ 13 13 13; www.macair.com.au) has regular flights to and from Cairns for around $190 (40 minutes).

Mission Beach Dunk Island Connections (☎ 4059 2709; www.missionbeachdunkconnections.com.au) does combination bus and boat transfers to Dunk from Cairns ($50, 2½ hours) and Port Douglas ($75, 3¾ hours).

Return ferry trips (including snorkelling) over to Dunk Island from Mission Beach cost about $22 with **Dunk Island Express Water Taxi** (☎ 4068 8310; Banfield Pde, Wongalling) and **Dunk Island Ferry & Cruises** (☎ 4068 7211; www.dunkferry .com.au; Clump Point), which also does a cruise to Bedarra Island.

Quick Cat (p431) also does transfers, or you can paddle over with Coral Sea Kayaking (see p432).

BEDARRA ISLAND

Part of the Family Island Group, Bedarra is cloaked in rainforest and fringed with sandy beaches. It's famed for its exclusive resort; what began as a small tourist resort in 1979 blossomed into the exclusive Bedarra Resort variously owned and renovated by Qantas, P&O and most recently Voyager.

Each of the 16 split-level villas at **Bedarra Island Resort** (☎ 4068 8233; www.bedarraisland.com; s $1240-1850, d $1980-3200; ☒ ☐ ☒) has its own plunge pool and outdoor area with a day bed, where a bucket of ice and plate of canapés is delivered daily. It's open-bar 24/7 and all meals are included; choose from the daily changing menu. Order a gourmet picnic hamper before you shoot off in the dinghy to explore other parts of the island. See the website for more details.

Far North Queensland Coast

An extraordinary combination of reefs, rivers and rainforests comprise the bulging pocket of biodiversity that is far north Queensland (FNQ). Though geographically small, this region is big on its variety of ecological systems: rainforest spills out on to stretches of sandy beach, mangroves crowd riverbanks, and coral gardens bloom out on the reefs. It all makes for one of Australia's most popular holiday destinations.

From Innisfail in the south to the offbeat outpost of Cooktown in the north, the region is brimming with attractions. The bustling tourist hub of Cairns and elegant simmering centre of Port Douglas are the best places to access the outer reef. Dozens of operators depart the bustling city of Cairns, and cut a swathe through the water to the outlying wonders of the Great Barrier Reef. There's a less hectic scene operating from Port Douglas. Cairns is also the springboard to the upland rainforest and waterfalls of the Atherton Tableland, while Port Douglas is the gateway to the wilderness of the Daintree River area. The coastal rainforest of the Daintree National Park reaches down to the long beaches around Cape Tribulation and is famously stunning; there are some fantastic places to stay nestled in the rainforest here. Further north is the frontier town of Cooktown and exquisite Lizard Island.

The area's human landscape is equally diverse: Aboriginal communities, farmers and conservationists all live here, contributing boundless character and depth to this spectacular region.

HIGHLIGHTS

- Doing nothing along one of **Cairns' northern beaches** (p450)
- Snorkelling over a bommie (isolated patch of reef) on the Great Barrier Reef out of boutique **Port Douglas** (p454) or seething **Cairns** (p443)
- Having a dip among the ancient boulders at **Mossman Gorge** (p458)
- Trudging through rainforest that tumbles out on to pristine beach at **Cape Tribulation** (p459)
- Visiting the isolated outpost and stunning surrounds of **Cooktown** (p464)
- Visiting the pretty rainforest hub of **Kuranda** (p452), high on the Tablelands
- Being a self-imposed castaway on the **Frankland Islands** (p450)

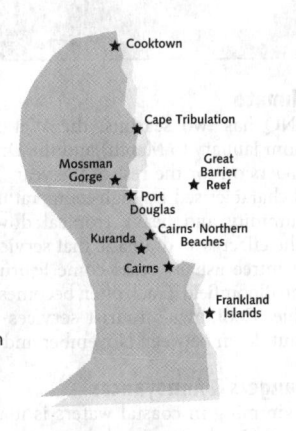

- ★ Cooktown
- ★ Cape Tribulation
- Mossman Gorge ★
- ★ Great Barrier Reef
- ★ Port Douglas
- Kuranda ★
- ★ Cairns' Northern Beaches
- Cairns ★
- ★ Frankland Islands

- TELEPHONE CODE: 07
- www.dctta.asn.au

FAR NORTH COAST QUEENSLAND

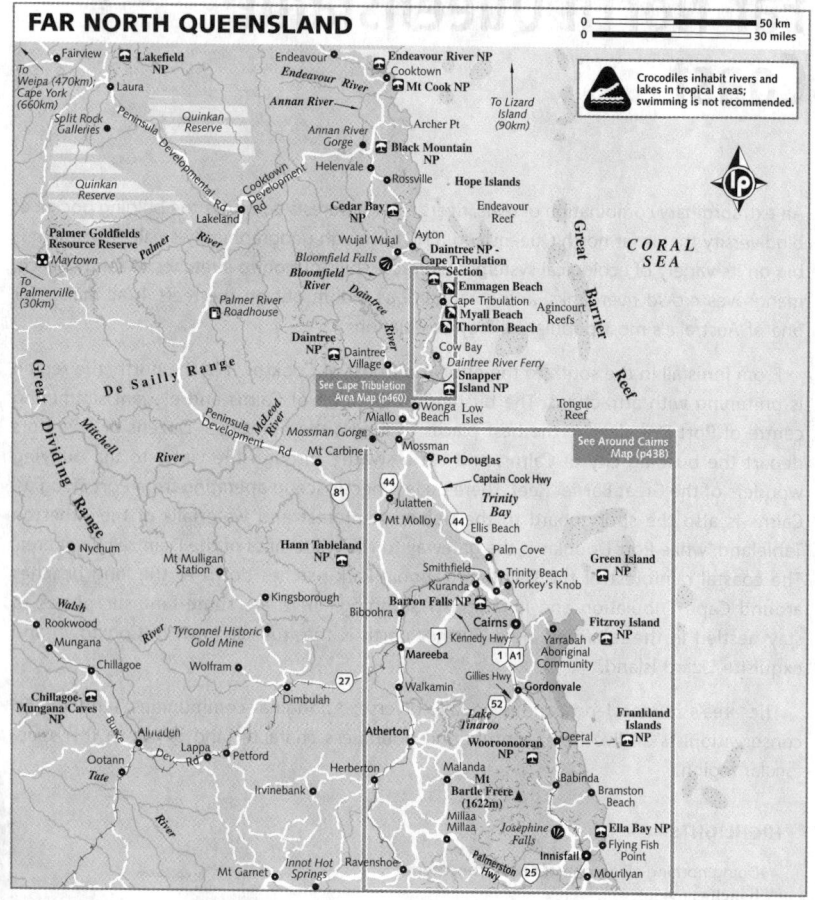

FAR NORTH QUEENSLAND

Crocodiles inhabit rivers and lakes in tropical areas; swimming is not recommended.

CORAL SEA

Great Barrier Reef

Climate

FNQ has two seasons: the Wet (roughly from January to March) and the Dry, which lingers on for the rest of the year. The Wet is characterised by high temperatures, high humidity and heavy tropical downpours. The effect is so dramatic that services in the Daintree usually cease come February, and the Bloomfield Track often becomes impassable. Cooktown's tourist services virtually shut down between November and March.

Dangers & Annoyances

Swimming in coastal waters is inadvisable from October to April due to the possible presence of marine stingers; see the boxed text, p371.

Saltwater crocodiles inhabit the mangroves, estuaries and open water of FNQ. Look out for the warning signs, which are posted around waterways where crocs may be present.

FESTIVALS & EVENTS

Re-enactment of the 1888 landing of Captain James Cook Cooktown in June.
Great Pyramid Race Gordonvale hosts this race, where enthusiasts dash up to Walshs Pyramid and back; in August.
Festival Cairns (www.festivalcairns.com.au) Cairns turns on the charm for two weeks in September for this regional festival.

MISSION BEACH TO GORDONVALE

From Mission Beach in north Queensland (see p430), the Bruce Hwy stays 20km or so inland of the coast, leading through a corridor of national parks, with burbling swimming holes and tranquil walking trails.

MISSION BEACH TO INNISFAIL

The road north from Mission Beach rejoins the Bruce Hwy at the tiny township of El Arish (about 17km north of Tully).

Continue straight along the Bruce Hwy to Mourilyan, 7km south of Innisfail, for the **Australian Sugar Industry Museum** (☎ 4063 2306; www.sugarmuseum.org.au; cnr Bruce Hwy & Peregrine St; adult/child $8/6; ◷ 9am-5pm Mon-Sat, to 3pm Sun May-Oct; 9am-5pm Mon-Fri, to 3pm Sat, to noon Sun Nov-Apr), which has a collection of old machinery and displays depicting the sugar-production process, as well as a small gallery with contemporary visual art exhibits.

Alternatively, take the scenic route along the Old Bruce Hwy (also called Japoonvale Rd), which leaves the highway 8km north of El Arish, meeting up with the main highway again at the southern outskirts of Innisfail. Among the banana plantations and cane fields are the eccentric and wildly romantic ruins of **Paronella Park** (☎ 4065 3225; www .paronellapark.com.au; Japoonvale Rd; adult/child $20/10; ◷ 9am-9.30pm), just south of Mena Creek. The rambling mossy Spanish castle, Lovers Tunnel and stunning gardens are testament to a couple's quest to bring a whimsical entertainment centre to the area's hard-working folk. Take one of the excellent tours included in your admission price to hear the full fascinating story.

INNISFAIL

☎ 07 / pop 8530

Innisfail's Art Deco architecture and riverside position have it sitting pretty in the eye of the tourist storm. Despite its size, it retains a sedate quality, and essentially services the area's banana and sugar cane industries. Innisfail's cosmopolitan past credits Chinese settlers with establishing the area's banana plantations, and Italian immigrants arrived in the early 20th century to work the cane fields (during the 1930s there was even a local branch of the Mafia, called the Black Hand). The influence of these two cultures is still evident in the town's population and architecture.

The **visitors centre** (☎ 4061 7422; Bruce Hwy; ◷ 9am-5pm Mon-Fri, 10am-3pm Sat & Sun) is about 3km south of town. Among the tourist literature it distributes is a town walk brochure, which outlines significant buildings. The **Queensland Parks & Wildlife Service** (QPWS; ☎ 4061 5900; www.epa.qld.gov.au; Flying Fish Point Rd) has an office in town.

The **Local History Museum** (☎ 4061 2731; 11 Edith St; admission $3; ◷ 10am-noon & 1-3pm Mon-Fri) has an eclectic collection of items.

A reminder of FNQ's once-extensive Chinese diaspora is the **Lit Zing Khuong** (Temple of the Universal God; Owen St; admission by donation).

Sleeping & Eating

Barrier Reef Motel (☎ 4061 4988; www.barrierreefmotel .com.au; Bruce Hwy; s/d $75/85; P ✖ 🖳 🖵) You could make a pit stop at this two-storey complex. Standard rooms have bathroom and TVs with enough channels to wear out the remote. There are laundry facilities, as well as a licensed restaurant on the premises.

The town's hostels cater mainly to semipermanent tenants working on the surrounding banana plantations.

Codge Lodge (☎ 4061 8055; 63 Rankin St; dm $20; ✖ 🖳 🖵) A terrific option with large verandas and a lofty aspect overlooking the river.

Walkabout Motel & Backpacker (☎ 4061 2311; motelwalkabout@bigpond.com; 20-24 Gowan Dr; dm/d $20/60; P ✖) Has dowdy backpacker units and motel rooms, plus a communal kitchen and laundry.

Mango Tree Van Park (☎ 4061 1656; mangotree park@bigpond.com; tent sites $15, d $70; P ✖) Just off the Bruce Hwy, about 3.5km south of town. It has two great cabins and camping sites along the banks of the South Johnstone River.

Oliveri's Continental Deli (☎ 4061 3354; 41 Edith St; sandwiches from $6; ◷ 8.30am-5.30pm Mon-Fri, to 1pm Sat) This place, which has been serving up salamis and cheeses for almost 80 years, makes a mean *panini*.

Also recommended are the following:

Rivers Rainforest Cafe (☎ 4061 9490; 2 Edith St; mains $10-13; ◷ breakfast & lunch Mon-Sat) A licensed place with outdoor tables and a varied menu.

Roscoe's Piazza (☎ 4061 6888; 3B Ernest St; mains $10-14; ◷ lunch & dinner) For pizza and pasta.

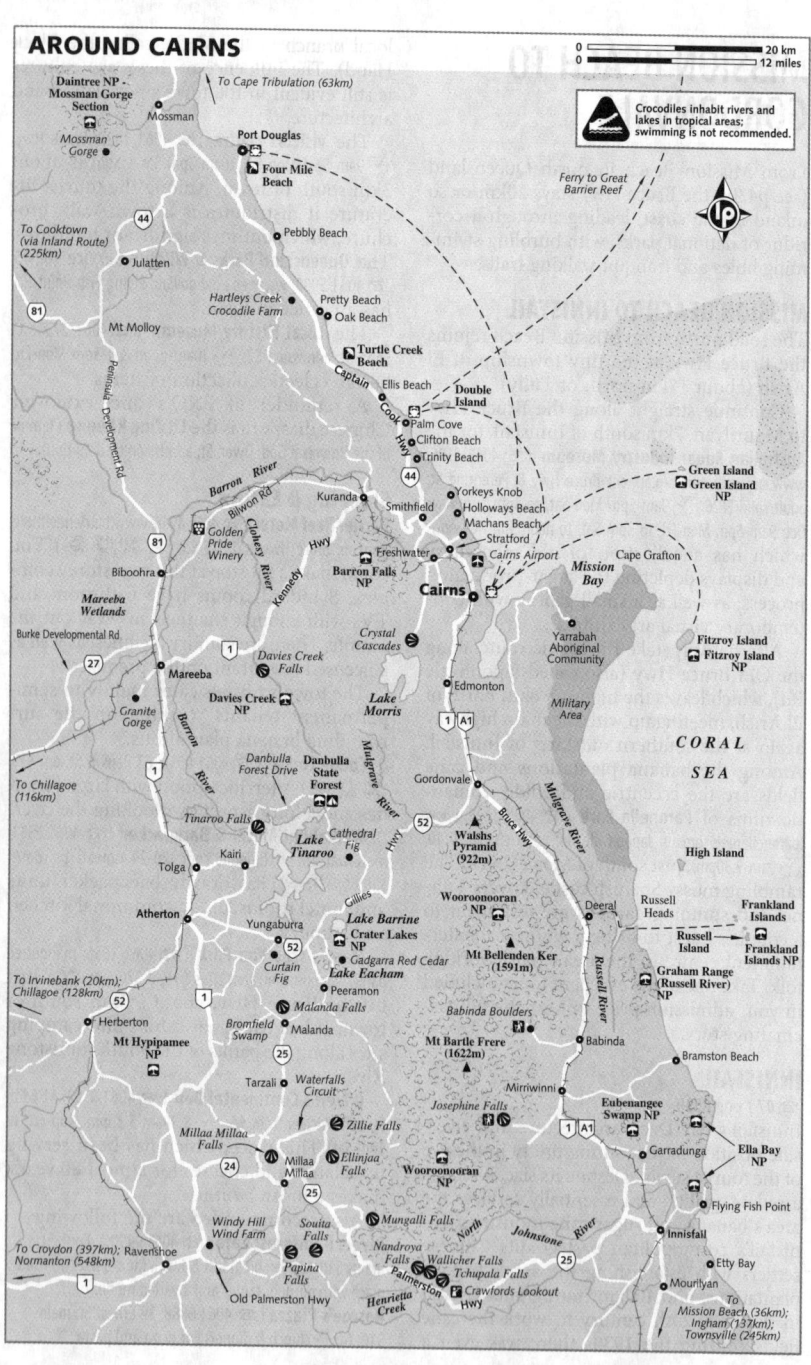

AROUND CAIRNS

0 — 20 km
0 — 12 miles

Crocodiles inhabit rivers and lakes in tropical areas; swimming is not recommended.

FAR NORTH COAST QUEENSLAND

Getting There & Around

Bus services operate at least daily from Innisfail to Townsville ($48, four hours) and Cairns ($22, 1¼ hours) with **Premier** (☎ 13 34 10; www.premierms.com.au) and **Greyhound Australia** (☎ 13 14 99; www.greyhound.com.au), departing from the bus centre opposite King George Sq on Edith St.

WOOROONOORAN NATIONAL PARK: JOSEPHINE FALLS SECTION

Fed by rain that collects around Queensland's highest mountain, Mt Bartle Frere (1622m), the **Josephine Falls** are a series of stepped clear-water pools fringed by giant tree roots. The turn-off is about 20km north of Innisfail and the falls are 8km inland from the highway. It's on the eastern fringe of Wooroonooran National Park, an enormous reserve of tropical rainforest. Access is via a gentle 800m track that has viewing platforms over the upper reaches of the river. The lower swimming hole is a great place for a dip; be careful after rain, as flash flooding can occur.

Josephine Falls also marks the start of the demanding **Mt Bartle Frere Summit Track**, a two-day return trip for fit, experienced and well-equipped walkers only. The trail rises 1500m in 7.5km; cloud can close in suddenly and you're almost certain to experience rain. The track also branches to **Broken Nose** (962m; 10km return). Get advice on conditions and a copy of the *Mt Bartle Frere Trail Guide* from **QPWS** (☎ 13 13 04; www.epa.qld .gov.au) before you head off. You'll also need a camping permit ($4 per person), and you can self-register at the start of the walk.

BABINDA

☎ 07 / pop 1230

In the rush north to Cairns, few people stop by bitty Babinda, hidden behind a huge sugar mill on the Bruce Hwy. Babinda's veranda-fronted buildings and old timber pubs are backed by the Bellenden Ker Range and neighboured by fertile forest.

The **Babinda visitors centre** (☎ 4067 1008; cnr Munro St & Bruce Hwy; ☽ 9am-4pm) is wallpapered with information brochures about the area.

Try to see a movie at the endearing **Munro Theatre** (☎ 4067 1032; Munro St; ☽ sessions 7.30pm Fri & Sat), which dates from the 1950s. Recline in a hessian-slung seat and check out the canvas-covered ceiling (for the best acoustics).

Remarkably, the **Babinda State Hotel** (☎ 4067 1202; 73 Munro St) was built by the Queensland state government in 1917 (the only state-owned pub), which controlled the sale of alcohol within the Babinda Sugar Works Area until 1930.

About 7km west of Babinda, in the Wooroonooran National Park, the **Babinda Boulders** is a stretch of massive granite boulders that have been sculpted by the fast-running creek. At the lower end is a grassy picnic area with a gentle clear-water swimming hole, while walking trails lead upstream to **Devil's Pool Lookout** (470m) and the **Boulders Gorge Lookout** (600m). Note that swimming has been banned in the upper reaches after several drownings. If you cross the suspension bridge there's an 850m loop through a beautiful section of rainforest.

INNISFAIL TO GORDONVALE VIA THE ATHERTON TABLELAND

The Atherton Tableland is a lush region, with lakes and waterfalls set in rainforest, dotted with quaint villages. The tableland's altitude tempers the tropical heat, and the abundant rainfall and rich volcanic soil combine to make this one of the greenest places in Queensland. A popular weekend escape for Cairns' residents, the tableland has some outstanding B&Bs; ask at any visitors centre for accommodation recommendations.

Our route takes the Palmerston Hwy (which leaves the Bruce Hwy 5km northwest of Innisfail) to the waterfalls of Millaa Millaa then north along minor roads to the Crater Lakes National Park, before descending to Gordonvale, just south of Cairns.

Wooroonooran National Park: Palmerston Section

There are more than 500 tree types, waterfalls and walks in this area – all very good reasons to visit this section of Wooroonooran, which is home to some of the oldest continually surviving rainforest in Australia. Its fertile soil and superwet climate (3500mm rainfall annually) make it one of the richest biological regions in the country.

The park features several walking tracks through dense rainforest to beautiful water falls and swimming holes; these can be accessed from various points en route.

Just inside the park boundary is **Crawfords Lookout**, with fine views of the coast; a 5km

(2½-hour) walking track links it with the twin cascades of **Tchupala Falls**. The highlight of the area is a 7.5km loop walk (three to four hours) through superb high-canopied rainforest to the spectacular **Nandroya Falls**, which crash into a beautiful, deep swimming hole.

There are picnic areas throughout the park and a good self-registration **QPWS camping ground** (☎ 13 13 04; www.epa.qld.gov.au; per person $4) at Henrietta Creek, with toilets and coin-operated barbecues. Water is available from the creek.

Millaa Millaa

☎ 07 / pop 320

On the beautiful 'waterfalls circuit', Millaa Millaa is a little clutch of houses that was once a town supporting the thriving local dairy industry. The workers – black-and-white Friesian cows – still dot the surrounding green pastures.

At **Mungalli Creek Dairy** (☎ 4097 2232; www.mill aa.com/Mungalli/directions.htm; 254 Brooks Rd; 🕙 10am-4pm) you can sample boutique biodynamic yoghurt and cheese.

The **Falls Teahouse** (☎ 4097 2237; www.fallstea house.com.au; Palmerston Hwy; s $65-95, d $95-140; meals $8-14; 🕙 10am-5pm), overlooking the rolling Tableland hills, is a charming B&B. It's just out of the township, on the turn-off to Millaa Millaa Falls. It also does substantial meals.

The **waterfalls circuit**, about 3km before Millaa Millaa, is a 16km loop that takes in three of the most picturesque falls on the Tableland – take your bathers.

PRICKLY PLANTS

There are a few rainforest plants that may grab your attention in a less-than-pleasant manner. The *gimpi gimpi*, also known as the stinging tree, can cause severe and long-lasting pain if you brush against it, which is easy to do given that it grows best along cleared walking trails where there's plenty of sunlight. It has large, hairy heart-shaped leaves with serrated edges and can grow up to 6m high.

Another is the lawyer vine, a fish-barbed climbing palm that trails from rainforest ferns. Once you're hooked, you'll have to patiently unhook – hence the plant's other nickname of 'wait-a-while'.

Malanda

☎ 07 / pop 860

Surrounded by some lovely patches of rainforest, Malanda is a small town with a big character and several top-notch B&Bs. The town has had a long association with milk, ever since 500 bedraggled cattle made the overland journey from NSW (taking 16 months) in 1908.

The **Malanda Falls visitors centre** (☎ 4096 6957; Atherton Rd; 🕙 9am-4.30pm) has plenty of information. It also arranges guided rainforest walks ($10) led by members of the Ngadjonji community; advance bookings are required.

On the outskirts of town, beside the North Johnstone River crossing, **Malanda Falls** drop into a big concreted pool, surrounded by lawns and forest. It's a popular swimming spot, and a 1km **walking trail** passes through the forest nearby, but you can never quite escape the traffic noise.

A couple of kilometres west of Malanda is **Bromfield Swamp**, an important waterbird sanctuary. There's a viewing platform beside the road that overlooks an eroded volcanic crater.

Crater Lakes National Park

Part of the Wet Tropics World Heritage Area, the two volcanic lakes of Lake Barrine and Lake Eacham offer great swimming, walking and picnicking possibilities.

Lake Eacham, on Lakes Dr between Peeramon and the Gillies Hwy, is the nicer and less developed of the two. An almost perfect circle, the lake is deep, deliciously cold and full of fish and turtles. You can walk its 4km circumference or there's an interpretive 700m walk to the rangers station.

If you continue up Lakes Dr you'll pass a turn-off to the breathtaking **Gadgarra Red Cedar**, which is within Gadgarra State Forest. This behemoth is the largest red cedar remaining in FNQ.

Turning east on to the Gillies Hwy takes you to the larger **Lake Barrine**, which also has a circumference walk (6km), though reeds and noisy tour boats make it inappropriate for swimming. Nearby are two magnificent 1000-year-old **kauri pines**.

From here, it's a slow, steep and winding 35km drive down to Gordonvale, where you rejoin the Bruce Hwy to head north to Cairns.

DETOUR: YUNGABURRA

Before heading back down to the highway, you should check out the pretty National Trust–registered village of Yungaburra, 3km west of Lake Eacham. It's famous for its markets, held on the fourth Saturday of every month. The town is utterly mad on those days, but at other times it's simply gorgeous, with a lovely old pub, a few fine eateries and plenty of good accommodation options too. Call in to the **visitors centre** (☎ 4095 2416; www.yungaburra.com; Cedar St; ◷ 9am-6pm) for details.

GORDONVALE & YARRABAH
☎ 07 / pop 5670

Gordonvale is a delightfully old-fashioned town featuring a disproportionate number of timber pubs set around a central park, plus an enormous sugar mill. It's all backed by the looming presence of Walshs Pyramid. Gordonvale has the dubious honour of being the first place where cane toads were released in 1935.

Between Gordonvale and Edmonton is a turn-off to the Yarrabah Aboriginal community. It's a scenic 37km drive through cane fields and mountains to Yarrabah, set on Mission Bay, a pretty cove backed by palm trees. You can visit the **Yarrabah Menmuny Museum** (☎ 4056 9154; http://cwpp.slq.qld.gov .au/Yarrabah; Back Beach Rd; adult/child $6/4; ◷ 8am-4pm Mon-Fri), which has a collection of Aboriginal artefacts and cultural exhibits. The museum also has spear-throwing demonstrations and a guided boardwalk tour (adult/child $14/10, including museum admission). To reach the museum turn right at the police station. It's down the road opposite the high school.

CAIRNS

☎ 07 / pop 98,981

What Cairns lacks in soul, it makes up for in services. Anything is possible in this purpose-built tourist town, where an armada of operators awaits to whisk you away to the magnificent Great Barrier Reef and to ancient rainforest.

Cairns has arguably Australia's most intense and complete tourist infrastructure, including comprehensive transport links.

Hotels, restaurants and souvenir shops abound, as do grinning tour operators who'll have you white-water rafting or scuba diving in no time.

Before the '80s, Cairns was just another sugar town sustained by its rail terminus and port. It gained momentum in the '80s with the upgrade of the airport – when the tourist floodgates opened.

ORIENTATION
Central Cairns is mostly contained to the area between The Esplanade and Sheridan St, and bordered by Wharf and Aplin Sts. Reef Fleet Terminal is the main departure point for reef trips. Further south along Wharf St is Trinity Wharf, with a cruise-liner dock and transit centre for the arrival and departure of long-distance buses. The train station is inside Cairns Central Shopping Centre on McLeod St. The airport is about 7km north of the city centre.

Maps
Royal Automobile Club of Queensland (RACQ; ☎ 4033 6711, road conditions 1300 130 595; www.racq .com.au; 520 Mulgrave St, Earlville) can supply maps.

INFORMATION
Bookshops
Angus & Robertson (☎ 4041 0591; Shop 141, Cairns Central Shopping Centre, McLeod St) Carries most mainstream titles from a range of genres.
Exchange Bookshop (☎ 4051 1443; 78 Grafton St) New and secondhand books.

Emergency
Emergency services (☎ 000; ◷ 24hr) Ambulance, fire brigade and police are all available on the one number.

Internet Access
Abbott St is the Internet café hub; most places charge between $2 and $5 per hour and are open from around 8.30am to 11pm.
Call Station (☎ 4052 1572; 123 Abbott St)
Global Gossip (☎ 4031 6411; 125 Abbott St)

Medical Services
Cairns Base Hospital (☎ 4050 6333; The Esplanade) Has a casualty ward.
Cairns City 24 Hour Medical Centre (☎ 4052 1119; cnr Florence & Grafton Sts)
Cairns Travel Clinic (☎ 4041 1699; ctlmed@iig.com .au; 15 Lake St)

CENTRAL CAIRNS

0 ——— 300 m
0 ——— 0.2 miles

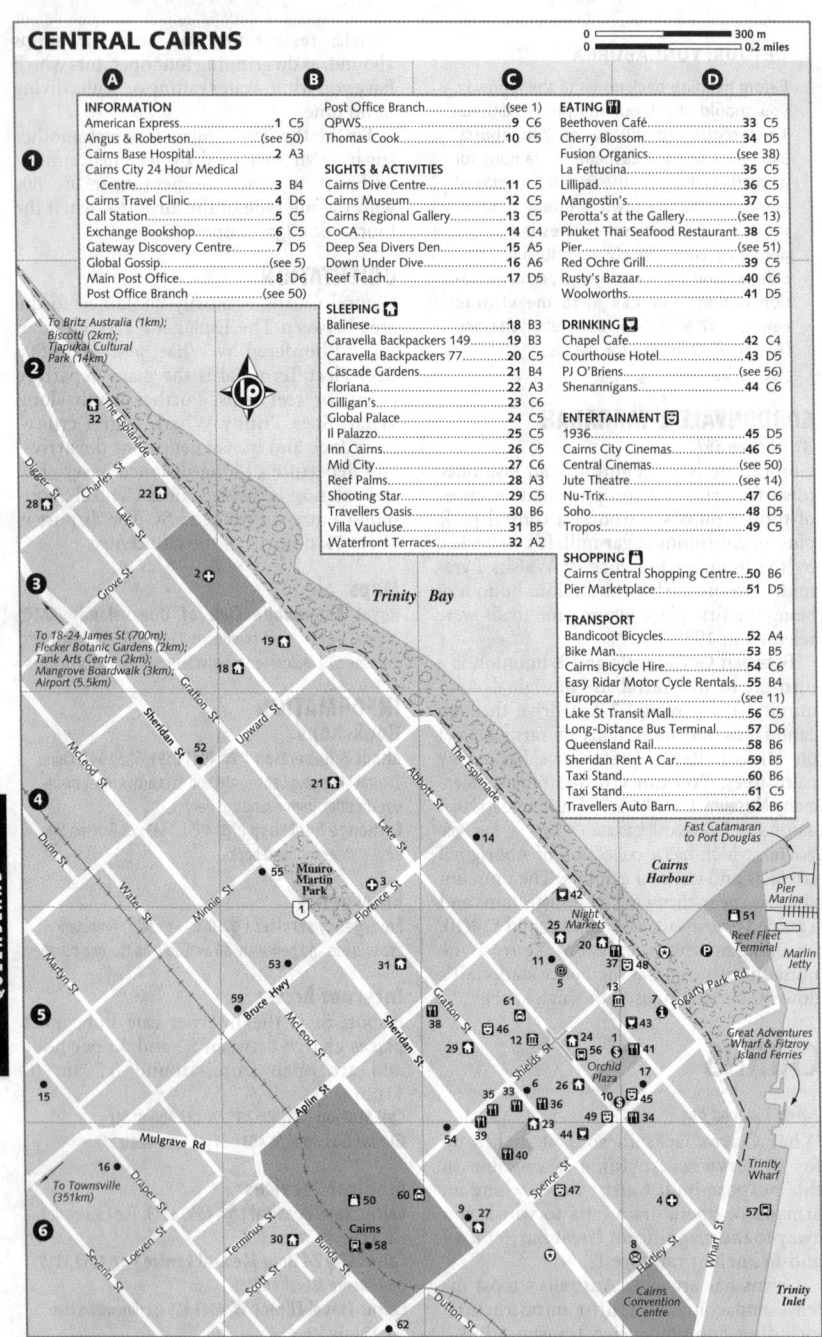

INFORMATION
American Express	**1** C5
Angus & Robertson	(see 50)
Cairns Base Hospital	**2** A3
Cairns City 24 Hour Medical Centre	**3** B4
Cairns Travel Clinic	**4** D6
Call Station	**5** C5
Exchange Bookshop	**6** C5
Gateway Discovery Centre	**7** D5
Global Gossip	(see 5)
Main Post Office	**8** D6
Post Office Branch	(see 50)
Post Office Branch	(see 1)
QPWS	**9** C6
Thomas Cook	**10** C5

SIGHTS & ACTIVITIES
Cairns Dive Centre	**11** C5
Cairns Museum	**12** C5
Cairns Regional Gallery	**13** C5
CoCA	**14** C4
Deep Sea Divers Den	**15** A5
Down Under Dive	**16** A6
Reef Teach	**17** D5

SLEEPING
Balinese	**18** B3
Caravella Backpackers 149	**19** B3
Caravella Backpackers 77	**20** C5
Cascade Gardens	**21** B4
Floriana	**22** A3
Gilligan's	**23** C6
Global Palace	**24** C5
Il Palazzo	**25** C5
Inn Cairns	**26** C5
Mid City	**27** C6
Reef Palms	**28** A3
Shooting Star	**29** C5
Travellers Oasis	**30** B6
Villa Vaucluse	**31** B5
Waterfront Terraces	**32** A2

EATING
Beethoven Café	**33** C5
Cherry Blossom	**34** D5
Fusion Organics	(see 38)
La Fettucina	**35** C5
Lillipad	**36** C5
Mangostin's	**37** C5
Perotta's at the Gallery	(see 13)
Phuket Thai Seafood Restaurant	**38** C5
Pier	(see 51)
Red Ochre Grill	**39** C5
Rusty's Bazaar	**40** C6
Woolworths	**41** D5

DRINKING
Chapel Cafe	**42** C4
Courthouse Hotel	**43** D5
PJ O'Briens	(see 56)
Shenannigans	**44** C6

ENTERTAINMENT
1936	**45** D5
Cairns City Cinemas	**46** C5
Central Cinemas	(see 50)
Jute Theatre	(see 14)
Nu-Trix	**47** C6
Soho	**48** D5
Tropos	**49** C5

SHOPPING
Cairns Central Shopping Centre	**50** B6
Pier Marketplace	**51** D5

TRANSPORT
Bandicoot Bicycles	**52** A4
Bike Man	**53** B6
Cairns Bicycle Hire	**54** C6
Easy Ridar Motor Cycle Rentals	**55** B4
Europcar	(see 11)
Lake St Transit Mall	**56** C5
Long-Distance Bus Terminal	**57** D6
Queensland Rail	**58** B6
Sheridan R A Car	**59** B6
Taxi Stand	**60** B6
Taxi Stand	**61** C5
Travellers Auto Barn	**62** B6

To Britz Australia (1km); Biscotti (2km); Tjapukai Cultural Park (14km)

The Esplanade

Digger St

Charles St

Lake St

Grove St

Trinity Bay

To 18-24 James St (700m); Flecker Botanic Gardens (2km); Tank Arts Centre (2km); Mangrove Boardwalk (3km); Airport (5.5km)

Sheridan St

Upward St

Grafton St

Lake St

The Esplanade

Abbott St

McLeod St

Sheridan St

Dunn St

Water St

Minnie St

Munro Martin Park

Florence St

Fast Catamaran to Port Douglas

Cairns Harbour

Pier Marina

Reef Fleet Terminal

Marlin Jetty

Night Markets

Marlyn St

Bruce Hwy

McLeod St

Sheridan St

Grafton St

Shields St

Orchid Plaza

Great Adventures Wharf & Fitzroy Island Ferries

Aplin St

Mulgrave Rd

To Townsville (351km)

Draper St

Spence St

Trinity Wharf

Cairns

Terminus St

Scott St

Bunda St

Dutton St

Hartley St

Wharf St

Cairns Convention Centre

Trinity Inlet

Money

All of the major banks have branches with ATMs throughout central Cairns. Most banks change foreign currency, as do the following:

American Express (☎ 4051 8811; Orchid Plaza, Abbott St)
Thomas Cook (☎ 4031 3040; 13 Spence St)

Post

Main post office (☎ 13 13 18; 13 Grafton St) Handles poste restante. There are also branches in Orchid Plaza on Lake St and in Cairns Central Shopping Centre.

Tourist Information

There are dozens of privately run 'information centres' in Cairns (basically tour-booking agencies), and most places to stay also have tour-booking desks.

Gateway Discovery Centre (☎ 4051 3588; www .tropicalaustralia.com.au; 51 The Esplanade; ☼ 8.30am-6.30pm) This government-run visitors centre offers impartial advice, books tours and houses an interpretive centre.

QPWS (☎ 4046 6602; www.epa.qld.gov.au; 2-4 McLeod St; ☼ 9am-4.30pm Mon-Fri) Information on the host of national parks around Cairns, including camping permits.

SIGHTS

The foreshore is Cairns' main attraction, with a 3km-long pedestrian promenade that is punctuated with bird-watching platforms over the mangroves, and a giant saltwater swimming lagoon.

The **Cairns Regional Gallery** (☎ 4031 6865; www.cairnsregionalgallery.com.au; cnr Abbott & Shields Sts; adult/child under 10 $4/free; ☼ 10am-5pm Mon-Sat, 1-5pm Sun) has an impressive permanent collection, including works by several notable Aboriginal artists. The gallery also has a café, Perotta's at the Gallery (p447). For contemporary works, visit the superb **Centre of Contemporary Arts** (CoCA; ☎ 4050 9401; www.coca .org.au; 96 Abbott St; ☼ 11am-5pm Tue-Sun).

Cairns Museum (☎ 4051 5582; www.cairnsmuseum .org.au; cnr Lake & Shields Sts; adult/child $5/2; ☼ 10am-4pm Mon-Sat) has displays on topics that have influenced FNQ, including Aboriginal artefacts and the contents of a now-demolished Chinese temple. It also has an excellent collection of local books for sale downstairs.

A trip over to the **Flecker Botanic Gardens** (☎ 4044 3398; www.cairns.qld.gov.au; Collins Ave, Edge Hill; ☼ 7.30am-5.30pm Mon-Fri, 8.30am-5.30pm Sat & Sun), just 4km northwest of the centre, is an excellent idea. Once here, there are a number of other distractions. Not only do you get to wander around these lush tropical gardens or take a guided walk (adult/child under 14 $10/free), but over the road, a boardwalk leads through a patch of rainforest to **Saltwater Creek** and **Centenary Lakes**, which showcase FNQ's saltwater and freshwater ecosystems. Next door is the stylish community **Tanks Arts Centre** (☎ 4032 2349; 46 Collins Ave, Edge Hill; ☼ 11am-4pm Mon-Fri), where giant circular cement and iron WWII naval supply tanks have been transformed into an exhibition and performance space.

Near the gardens is the entrance to the **Mt Whitfield Conservation Park**, the last remnant of Cairns rainforest, with a few walks: the **Red Arrow Trail** (one hour) and the **Blue Arrow Trail** (3½ hours), offering good views over the city and coast.

On Airport Ave, 200m before the airport, is a **mangrove boardwalk**, with signs explaining the ecological complexities of mangrove forests, plus a small observation platform.

About 15km north of the centre, **Tjapu-kai Cultural Park** (☎ 4042 9999; www.tjapukai.com .au; Kamerunga Rd, Carevonica; adult/child $29/14.50, incl transfers from Cairns & Palm Cove $48.50/24.25; ☼ 9am-5pm) is an extravaganza, combining Indigenous culture with show biz. It includes the Creation Theatre, which tells the story of creation using actors and giant holograms; there's also a Dance Theatre, and boomerang- and spear-throwing demonstrations.

ACTIVITIES

Diving

Many of the 1.4 million dives on the Great Barrier Reef each year are arranged from Cairns, making it one of the most popular diving destinations in the world. It's also a popular place to gain the PADI (Professional Association of Diving Instructors) open-water classification. Advanced courses are also available for certified divers.

For newbies to the sport, options range from budget four-day courses combining pool training and reef dives (from $320) to five-day courses (from $550) that include a few days' pool theory and three days living aboard a boat out on the reef.

A selection of reputable dive schools in Cairns:

Cairns Dive Centre (☎ 4051 0294; www.cairnsdive .com.au; 121 Abbott St; ☼ 8am-7pm)
Deep Sea Divers Den (☎ 4046 7333; www.diversden .com.au; 319 Draper St; ☼ 6am-6pm)

FAR NORTH COAST QUEENSLAND

Down Under Dive (☎ 4052 8300; www.downunder dive.com.au; 287 Draper St; ⏰ 7am-7pm)

To deepen your knowledge of the reef, visit **Reef Teach** (☎ 4031 7794; www.reefteach.com.au; 14 Spence St; ⏰ 10am-9pm Mon-Sat), which runs an informative and entertaining lecture at 6.15pm Monday to Saturday ($13).

Quite a few operators offer live-aboard trips for certified divers who want to maximise their dive time, and perhaps take an advanced course. These trips typically range from three to seven days ($1200 to $2400) and head to the outer reefs (including the renowned Cod Hole and Lizard Island). They include:

Explorer Ventures (☎ 4031 5566; www.explorer ventures.com)

Mike Ball Dive Expeditions (☎ 4031 5484; www.mike ball.com)

White-Water Rafting

There's excellent white-water rafting down the Tully, Russell and Barron Rivers. The Tully River is probably the best of them; a day trip costs around $150. However, it's 140km from Cairns, so if you're heading to Mission Beach, it's cheaper to do the tour from there.

The main operators are **Raging Thunder** (☎ 4030 7990; www.ragingthunder.com.au), **Foaming Fury** (☎ 4032 3460; www.foamingfury.com.au) and **R'n'R** (☎ 4051 4777; www.raft.com.au).

Other Activities

AJ Hackett Bungee & Minjin (☎ 4057 7188; www .ajhackett.com.au; bungee $110-140, minjin swing $80) The minjin swings thrill-seekers in a harness high above the forest canopy.

Hot Air Ballooning (☎ 4039 2900; www.hotair.com .au; adult/child $180/125)

Skydive Cairns (☎ 4031 5466; www.skydivecairns.com .au; tandem jump from $250)

Springmount Station Horse Riding (☎ 4093 4493; www.springmountstation.com; half-/full day $90/110)

TOURS

There's a bewildering variety of tours on offer from Cairns, but the market's so tight that they're generally good value and have seasoned and entertaining guides.

Great Barrier Reef & Islands

Most of the innumerable tours to the reef include lunch and snorkelling gear. Gener-

ally you'll pay around $150 for the day with dives an optional extra (about $70). Trips vary according to which part of the reef they visit and the quality of the extras. The outer reefs generally provide better diving. All of the dive-course operators also run day trips.

Coral Princess (☎ 4040 9999; www.coralprincess .au; from $1350) Four-day cruises between Cairns and Townsville; no diving offered, just snorkelling.

Great Adventures (☎ 4044 9944, 1800 079 080; www.greatadventures.com.au; adult/child $165/85) This large operator offers a wide range of combination cruises, including a day trip stopping at Green Island.

Sunlover (☎ 4050 1333, 1800 810 512; www.sunlover .com.au; adult/child $150/75) Tours sail to Arlington Reef, and include a ride in a semisubmersible, and a glass bottomed–boat tour.

Atherton Tableland

Bandicoot Bicycle Tours (☎ 4055 0155; 59 Sheridan St; full day $100; ⏰ tours Mon, Wed & Fri) Bike tours of the Tableland.

On the Wallaby (☎ 4050 0650; www.onthewallaby .com; day tour $85) Lively activity-based tours that include wildlife-spotting and canoeing.

Uncle Brian's Tours (☎ 4050 0615; day tour $85) Popular tours to the area around Babinda, Josephine Falls and Lake Eacham.

Daintree & Cape Tribulation

After the Great Barrier Reef, the Daintree River and Cape Tribulation area are the next most popular for day trips, and there is a regular onslaught of vehicles that head there daily. Most operators use 4WD vehicles to give more of a 'safari feel' to the whole experience, but the road is sealed all the way to the Bloomfield Track. Operators include:

Billy Tea Bush Safaris (☎ 4032 0077; www.billytea .com.au; adult/child $130/90)

Cape Trib Connections (☎ 4041 7447; www.capetrib connections.com; day trip $110)

Trek North Safaris (☎ 4051 4328; www.treknorth .com.au; adult/child $140/95)

Cooktown

Wilderness Challenge (☎ 4055 4488; www.wilder ness-challenge.com.au; 2-day tour from $360; ⏰ tours Mon, Wed & Fri) travels to Cooktown via the inland route and returns via the Bloomfield Track. Or fly there with **Daintree Air Services** (☎ 4034 9300, 1800 246 206; www.daintreeair.com.au; day tour $880; ⏰ tours Wed Apr-Oct).

SLEEPING

The accommodation business is extremely competitive and prices go up and down with the seasons. Lower weekly rates are par for the course, as are stand-by rates for midrange and top-end options. Prices quoted here are peak-season prices (1 June to 31 October).

Budget

Global Palace (☎ 4031 7921; www.globalpalace.com.au; City Place, cnr Lake & Shields Sts; dm/d $23/52; 🗙 🖳 🐱) This tidy hostel has a great central location, with a broad veranda overlooking the street. There are no bunks in the dorms (three to five beds). There's a small rooftop pool and spacious communal areas that make a welcome contrast to the compact rooms.

Floriana (☎ 4051 7886; flori@cairnsinfo.com; 183 The Esplanade; s $40, d & tw $65; 🗙 🐱) This charismatic guesthouse boasts personalised rooms with polished boards and original Deco fittings. Right on The Esplanade; some rooms here have balconies, a sink, microwave and TV. Floriana is about 1km from the centre of town.

Gilligan's (☎ 4041 6566; www.gilligansbackpackers.com.au; 57-89 Grafton St; dm $24-28, r $80; 🗙 🖳 🐱) Most travellers come here for the whole package, with sleeping and socialising potential. This enormous high-rise offers elemental dorm accommodation (four to six bunk beds) and hotel-style rooms. Its Internet café doubles as a pizzeria, the 1000-capacity beer hall does meals and the gaming room and swimming pool are also licensed.

Caravella Backpackers 149 (☎ 4031 5680; 149 The Esplanade; www.caravella.com.au; dm $18-20, d $45-48; 🗙 🖳 🐱) One of the old stagers in Cairns, Caravella has two locations along The Esplanade, and 149 is the more appealing of the two. The more expensive dorms have fewer beds, air-con and en-suite bathroom.

Caravella Backpackers 77 (☎ 4051 2159; 77 The Esplanade; www.caravella.com.au; dm $18-20, d $45-48; 🗙 🖳 🐱) The other half of the Caravella duo, number 77 is smaller and more central than 149.

Travellers Oasis (☎ 4052 1377; www.travoasis.com.au; 8 Scott St; dm/s/d $20/30/45; 🗙 🖳 🐱) This laid-back place eschews the party vibe, keeping things low-key and limited, with a maximum of 50 guests. All rooms have a ceiling fan, and you'll pay extra for air-conditioning. It has all the usual facilities – kitchen and laundry – painted primary cartoon colours.

Midrange

Shooting Star (☎ 4047 7200; www.shootingstarapartments.com.au; 117 Grafton St; apt $90; 🅿 🗙 🖳 🐱) This blue-and-white complex resembles a cluster of oversized beach boxes, and houses a surprisingly large number of neat, tiled studio-style apartments. Each has a kitchen, lounge and bed all in the one area, and are a great deal for couples and families. There are also specially fitted wheelchair-accessible rooms.

Balinese (☎ 4051 9922; www.balinese.com.au; 215 Lake St; s $85, d & tw $95; 🅿 🗙 🖳 🐱) This small-scale low-rise resort brings a smidgen of Bali to Cairns. Stylish carved wooden furnishings and ceramic pieces in each room provide that languorous tropical flavour. The room rate includes a basic breakfast of cereal, and there's access to the communal kitchen should you fancy a fry-up.

Cascade Gardens (☎ 4047 6300, 1800 817 902; cascadegardens@harveyworld.com.au; 175 Lake St; apt $120-140; 🅿 🗙 🐱) The cane furniture and floral drapes in these rooms won't feature in any interior-design magazine, but the rooms are spacious, well equipped and super-comfy. Each has a self-contained kitchen, lounge area, balcony and bathroom, and some have their own washing machine and dryer. Apartments are spread over three levels – mobility-impaired visitors (and slackers) will note that there is no lift.

Inn Cairns (☎ 4041 2350; www.inncairns.com.au; 71 Lake St; apt $160; 🗙 🐱) Live in an inner city apartment while you're on holiday, making a habit of catching the lift to the rooftop each day to watch the champagne level in your flute and the sun go down simultaneously. These elegant self-contained apartments feature modern furnishings and fittings. There's also a licensed bistro on the premises.

Mid City (☎ 4051 5050; www.midcity.com.au; 6 McLeod St; 1-bed apt $150; 🅿 🗙 🖳 🐱) You just might forget you're not at home after a night here. Each apartment is fitted with a superb kitchen, washing machine and dryer. The functional rooms, with wrought-iron furnishings and terracotta-tiled floors, are serviced daily; that means fresh towels and new little soaps. Each room also has its own balcony, but some of the views are inglorious – unless you enjoy gazing out to department stores.

18-24 James (☎ 4051 4644, 1800 621 824; www.18-24james.com.au; 18-24 James St; s $110, d & tw $140; P 🞩 ⌨ 🞩) This gay-friendly accommodation is mostly for male guests. The pool area is clothing-optional and the resort's gym is apparently clothing-minimal. The handsome rooms, inclusive of airport transfer and breakfast, could just represent a pot of gold at the end of that big rainbow.

Villa Vaucluse (☎ 4051 8566, 1800 623 263; www.villavaucluse.com.au; 141-143 Grafton St; 1-bed apt $140; P 🞩 🞩) These sturdy modern pads are private and sumptuously fitted. The Vaucluse has only been open for a few years, so the apartments are still fresh and trim. The separate kitchen is fully equipped and the bathroom has a bath. There's a dash of Mediterranean in the décor, a tropical central atrium and secluded swimming pool.

Reef Palms (☎ 4051 2599, 1800 815 421; www.reefpalms.com.au; 41-47 Digger St; apt $85-125; P 🞩 🞩) The crisp white interiors of Reef Palms' apartments will have you wearing your sunglasses inside. All rooms have cooking facilities, and increase in price commensurate with the increased space, including a lounge area and a spa. If you don't mind sharing, there's a communal outdoor spa and a miniwaterfall at the edge of the pool.

Top End

Il Palazzo (☎ 4041 2155; www.ilpalazzo.com.au; 62 Abbott St; r from $180; P 🞩 🞩) This charming boutique high-rise hotel is quietly stylish, in a soft-focus, terracotta-urns and water-feature kind of way. The welcome and service are remarkable; you can flit between the attached beauty parlour and your opulent apartment. Right in the centre of town, it features a balcony, laundry and full kitchen – although room service is always an option.

Waterfront Terraces (☎ 4031 8333; www.cairnsluxury.com; 233 The Esplanade; 1-/2-bedroom apt $170/205; P 🞩 🞩) This low-rise Queenslander-style building is set in neat and trim tropical grounds just across the road from the waterfront. Handsomely furnished apartments have a separate tiled lounge and kitchen area.

THE AUTHOR'S CHOICE

Pier (☎ 4031 4677; Pier Marketplace, Pier Point Rd; mains around $18; 🕑 lunch & dinner Mon-Sun) On the marina and waterfront, punters come off the boat deck straight to this broad table-lined deck with views and breezes. There's a handful of mains, such as salmon on papaya salad, a few pastas, starters and nibbles. Wood-fired pizzas are available until late, as well as for dessert: hazelnut-chocolate spread, marshmallows and coffee ice-cream pizza anyone?

EATING

Cairns' eateries offer a huge range of national cuisines, from Indian to Italian, and a combination of styles and ingredients. Restaurants and cafés are spread throughout town, though many cluster together along The Esplanade to take advantage of the waterfront (you'll pay extra for the wafts of sea air).

Restaurants

Cairns has dozens of restaurant choices packed into the city centre. Most pubs also serve meals (see opposite).

La Fettuccina (☎ 4031 5959; 43 Shields St; mains $20-24; 🕑 dinner) Be prepared to stain the white linen tablecloths as you slurp saucy homemade pastas. This small, atmospheric Italian restaurant offers the gamut of pastas and sauces. It's licensed and BYO, with a suave décor that'll transport you to Rome – especially after a few grappas.

Cherry Blossom (☎ 4052 1050; cnr Spence & Lake Sts; mains $14-24; 🕑 lunch Wed-Fri, dinner Mon-Sat) This upstairs Japanese restaurant is reminiscent of an *Iron Chef* cook-off; two chefs work at opposite ends of the restaurant floor. A lobster head provides the finishing touch to the sushi chef's inspired dish, answered by the conjured steam cloud and incumbent hiss from the *teppanyaki* chef across the floor. A range of Japanese beers is available, and in among the authentic dishes such as tempura and *yakitori* you'll find item No 17: 'Aussie Animals – crocodile, kangaroo and emu in a cheese basket'.

Phuket Thai Seafood Restaurant (☎ 4031 0777; 3/135 Grafton St; dishes $13-17; 🕑 lunch Mon-Fri, dinner Mon-Sun) We're all familiar with Thai food: the creeping chilli kick partnered with ginger and basil, perhaps tempered by coconut milk;

well this is a cut above and may surpass your expectations. Phuket Thai is licensed, with a modest, clean-cut interior and courtyard dining – and nary a gilt buddha in sight.

Mangostin's (☎ 4031 9888; 65 The Esplanade; mains around $25; ☺ lunch & dinner) This formal two-storey restaurant sits proudly in its prime location on The Esplanade. There are separate lunch and dinner menus, both leaning towards the Mod Oz category, and relying on rich meats (veal, 'roo and duck), as well as seafood. You might try steamed north Queensland mud crab with a chilli and kaffir-lime sauce. Mangostin's has a can't-go-wrong winelist, with stellar Australian wines, as well as champagne (French of course).

Red Ochre Grill (☎ 4051 0100; 43 Shields St; mains $26-30; ☺ lunch Mon-Fri, dinner Mon-Sun) Red Ochre's inventive menu utilises native Australian ingredients and locally produced products, artfully prepared to pioneer its own culinary genre. There are the animals (croc, 'roo and emu) but Aussie flora also appears on the menu. You might want to try the wattleseed pavlova with plum sorbet and macadamia toast. A good selection of wine and beer is also on offer in slick, sophisticated surrounds.

Cafés & Quick Eats

Fusion Organics (☎ 4051 1388; cnr Grafton & Aplin Sts; dishes $5-10; ☺ breakfast & lunch Mon-Sat) Pluck a word for the day from the bowl next to the cash register: 'enthusiasm', 'patience'? Fusion is inspiring to the core. Its sublime coffee and juice brews will rouse even the weariest of bodies. And stellar quiches, frittata and filled breads stir the senses. Its interior features local art, or you can settle in the spacious undercover courtyard.

Perrotta's at the Gallery (☎ 4031 5899; Cairns Regional Gallery, 38 Abbott St; mains around $25; ☺ breakfast, lunch & dinner) The long black-aproned staff swish about the deck delivering a superb range of food and beverages. Come for the coffee alone (excellent) or break your fast with ricotta hotcakes basking in honeycomb butter and banana. The dinner menu has more than a hint of a Mediterranean influence, and the choice wine list favours boutique producers.

Beethoven Cafe (☎ 4051 0292; 105 Grafton St; dishes $5-7; ☺ breakfast Mon-Sat, lunch Mon-Fri) This excellent European-style café makes the best sandwiches and rolls in town. Choose from the combinations suggested – like Buendnerfleisch (air-dried beef, Swiss cheese and gherkin) – or get creative and invent your own. Try to save room for a slab of poppyseed cake or cheesecake.

Biscotti (☎ 4032 0222; 3/139 Collins Ave, Edge Hill; dishes $5-9; ☺ breakfast & lunch) Near the Botanic Gardens, this sleek café has a hard-edged interior softened by warm service and comfort food. Black banquette seating faces glass-fronted cabinets: one keeps a selection of savoury quiches, filo pastries and gourmet rolls made off the premises. A second cabinet displays handmade chocolates and other little sweet things such as fig-filled shortbread biscuits.

Lillipad (☎ 4051 9565; 72 Grafton St; dishes $5-7; ☺ breakfast & lunch Mon-Sat) Walk down the long, narrow seating area of Lillipad and meet the maker of your fabulously big breakfast, who toils in the kitchen just behind the service counter. There's love in your Full Monty fry-up, your panini and your salad. Vegetarians are spoilt for choice here, and there's a range of cakes available until 4pm.

Self-Catering

Woolworths (Sheridan St) There's a Woolworth's the size of a small city in town, stocking everything you can think of, and you'll find at least two supermarkets in **Cairns Central Shopping Centre** (McLeod St).

Rusty's Bazaar (Grafton St, btwn Sheilds & Spence Sts; ☺ Fri & Sat) If you prefer a little ambience with your shopping head to this bazaar; it has fresh fruit and vegies, herbs and honey.

DRINKING

Many travellers start or finish their Australian odyssey in Cairns, so the pubs and clubs have enthusiastic revellers. Most places are multipurpose, offering food, alcohol and some form of entertainment. Bars and pubs are generally licensed until 1am. Local street rag **Barfly** (www.thefly.com.au) publishes listings and reviews of music gigs, pubs and clubs; pick it up in cafés and venues.

Gilligan's (☎ 4041 6566; www.gilligansbackpackers .com.au; 57-89 Grafton St) You're guaranteed a crowd here, as the 400-odd backpackers staying in this resort complex work up a thirst; it's also popular with locals. Gilligan's is a respectable venue that features regular club nights, as well as special live-music events – no naff cover bands here.

Courthouse Hotel (☎ 4031 4166; 38 Abbott St; meals $6-19) You should stay for at least one drink to do this old courthouse justice. A spacious courtyard encircles the main room, with a well-stocked bar at its centre. A mixed crew – generally suave and clean-cut – gathers at the Courthouse, which also serves Mediterranean fare.

Shenannigans (☎ 4051 2490; 48 Spence St; meals $8-15) This Irish-themed pub has a public bar decked out in dark timber. There's also a huge beer garden and outdoor bistro. From Thursday to Saturday night, a band plays before a DJ moves in for the late shift. There's also a gaming lounge, and karaoke on Monday nights.

PJ O'Briens (☎ 4031 5333; 87 Lake St) This is a popular pub with an Irish theme; there are 'Thank Guinness it's Friday' nights (when the dark ale's cheap), and Wednesday's entertainment is dancing girls – not that there's anything particularly Irish about girls in bikinis dancing on the bar.

Chapel Cafe (☎ 4041 4222; Level 1, 91 The Esplanade; meals $18-26) Large groups drink and dine in stylish surrounds of green booths lit by low-slung, low-wattage bulbs. There's a large balcony overlooking The Esplanade, which makes a stellar place for a drink. Acoustic music plays live most nights.

ENTERTAINMENT
Nightclubs

Move things up a gear at one of Cairns in-numerable clubs. Most open around 10pm and close between 5am and 6am. That said, entry is generally refused after 3am, so get to where you're going by then. Cover charges vary from $5 to $10.

1936 (28 Spence St; ☽ Wed-Sun) At its new two-level premises, 1936 is a thumping hard venue featuring respected local and touring DJs. A second room plays funk and hip-hop. Freakquency on Friday is always popular.

Soho (☎ 4051 2666; cnr The Esplanade & Shields St; ☽ Wed-Sun) This funky spot features resident DJs, as well as touring local and national turntableists. Fall into the leather lounge, or prop up one of the bars.

Tropos (☎ 4031 2530; cnr Spence & Lake Sts; ☽ from 8pm) Wear something short, tight and white. This young, high-energy crowd drinks cocktails with names like 'attitude improvement' on the enormous balcony furnished with pool tables.

Nu-Trix (☎ 4051 8223; 53 Spence St; ☽ Wed-Sun) Drag shows are a feature at this gay venue. The shiny metal-clad exterior acts as armour against the morning sun, keeping things dark and doofing until late.

Theatre & Cinemas

Jute Theatre (☎ 4050 9444; www.jute.com.au; CoCA, 96 Abbott St; admission $22-30) Stages a variety of contemporary Australian works; check out what's currently playing at the Just Us Theatre Ensemble's sexy new venue, in the Centre of Contemporary Arts.

Cairns City Cinemas (☎ 4031 1077; 108 Grafton St) and **Central Cinemas** (☎ 4052 1166; Cairns Central Shopping Centre) screen mainstream new-release flicks. Tickets cost from $8 to $13.

SHOPPING

Head to the **Night Markets** (The Esplanade; ☽ 4.30pm-midnight) and **Mud Markets** (Pier Marketplace; ☽ Sat morning from sunrise) if your supply of 'Cairns Australia' T-shirts is running low, or you need your name on a grain of rice.

Cairns has two multilevel shopping centres where you can peruse a vast array of shops in one climate-controlled bubble: **Pier Marketplace** (Pier Point Rd) and **Cairns Central Shopping Centre** (McLeod St).

For food-related shopping, see p447.

GETTING THERE & AWAY
Air

Departures for international cities leave Cairns frequently with **Australian Airlines** (www.australianairlines.com.au) heading to four Japanese cities, Hong Kong and Singapore; **Cathay Pacific** (www.cathaypacific.com) to Hong Kong; and **Air New Zealand** (www.airnewzealand.com) to Auckland.

For domestic connections between Cairns and Brisbane ($140, two hours), Sydney ($190, four hours) and Melbourne ($210, 5½ hours) try **Virgin Blue** (☎ 13 67 89; www.virginblue.com.au) or **Qantas** (☎ 13 13 13, 4050 4000; www.qantas.com.au; cnr Shields & Lake Sts) and its subsidiary **Jetstar** (☎ 13 15 38; www.jetstar.com.au), with around four departures daily. Qantas and Virgin also fly at least daily to other capital cities, including Darwin via Alice Springs ($250, seven hours), Hobart ($250, 6½ hours), Perth ($300, 9½ hours) and Adelaide ($280, 9½ hours).

Macair (☎ 13 13 13; www.macair.com.au) flies to Lizard Island ($300, one hour) and Dunk

Island ($180, 45 minutes). Rates can drop by as much as 20% if you purchase your ticket three days in advance.

Skytrans (☎ 4046 2462, 1800 818 405; www.sky trans.com.au) flies twice a day between Cairns and Cooktown (adult/child $107/54, 45 minutes).

Boat

Quicksilver (☎ 4031 4299; www.quicksilver-cruises .com; one way/return $26/39) departs from the Pier Marina in Cairns at 8am for Port Douglas, and returns at 5.15pm; the journey takes 1½ hours.

Bus

Greyhound (☎ 13 14 99; www.greyhound.com.au) has daily services departing Cairns' coach terminal at Trinity Wharf for Brisbane ($200, 29 hours), Rockhampton ($140, 17 hours) and Townsville ($53, six hours). You can stop over at any point along the way, as long you hop back on within six days.

Premier (☎ 13 34 10; www.premierms.com.au) runs a daily service from Cairns to Innisfail ($15, 1½ hours), Mission Beach ($15, two hours), Tully ($22, 2½ hours), Cardwell ($26, three hours), Ingham ($29, 3¼ hours) and Townsville ($48, 5½ hours).

Sun Palm Transport (☎ 4032 4999; www.sunpalm transport.com) runs a daily service from Cairns (Trinity Wharf) to Port Douglas ($25, 1½ hours), Mossman ($31, 1¾ hours) and Cape Tribulation ($45, 3¼ hours). It travels to Cooktown ($70, 5¼ hours) on the inland route Wednesday, Friday and Sunday, and via the coast road (7½ hours) Tuesday, Thursday and Saturday.

Coral Reef Coaches (☎ 4098 2600; www.coralreef coaches.com.au) also runs a daily service from Cairns to Cape Tribulation ($40, four hours), stopping in Port Douglas ($20, 1¼ hours), Mossman ($25, two hours) and Cow Bay ($37, 2½ hours).

John's Kuranda Bus (☎ 0418 772 953; $2) operates a service from Cairns to Kuranda at least twice a day, up to seven times Wednesday to Friday. Buses depart from Cairns' Lake St Transit Mall. **Kuranda Shuttle** (☎ 0402 032 085; $2) departs Cairns' Transit Mall every two hours from 9am to 3pm, and Kuranda (Therwine St) at 10am, 12.15pm and 2pm. **Whitecar Coaches** (☎ 4091 1855; $4) has five departures from 46 Spence St, outside Shenannigans. The trip takes about half an hour.

Car & Motorcycle

Hiring a car or motorcycle is a good way to travel from Cairns to the far north; it costs from around $50 per day. Most companies restrict conventional vehicles to sealed roads; if you want to travel to Cooktown via the Bloomfield Track (or coastal route), hire a 4WD. A number of rental companies are located on Lake St, between Aplin and Florence Sts. You might try one of the following:
Britz Australia (☎ 4032 2611; www.britz.com.au; 411 Sheridan St) Campervans.
Easy Rider Motor Cycles (☎ 4052 1188; www.easy ridermotorcyclehire.com.au; 144 Sheridan St)
Europcar (☎ 4051 4600; www.deltaeuropcar.com.au; 135 Abbott St) Also has an airport desk.
Sheridan Rent a Car (☎ 4051 3942; owers@top.net .au; 36 Water St)
Thrifty (☎ 1300 367 277; www.thrifty.com.au; Cairns International Airport)
Travellers Auto Barn (☎ 4041 3722; www.travellers -autobarn.com.au; 123 Bunda St) Campervans.

If you're in for the long haul, consider buying a vehicle; **Cairns Cars Online** (www.cairnscars .com) buys and sells mostly budget cars.

Train

Queensland Rail (☎ 1300 131 722; www.traveltrain .com.au; Cairns Central Shopping Centre, McLeod St) has at least four trains per week between Cairns and Brisbane (from $190). It also operates the Scenic Railway to Kuranda (see p453).

GETTING AROUND
To/From the Airport

The airport is about 7km from central Cairns. **Australia Coach** (☎ 4048 8355; adult/child $8/4) meets all incoming flights and runs a shuttle bus to the CBD. **Black & White Taxis** (☎ 4048 8444) charges around $15.

Bicycle

You can hire bicycles from any of the following:
Bandicoot Bicycles (☎ 4041; 153 Sheridan St; per day $18)
Bike Man (☎ 4041 5566; www.bikeman.com.au; 30 Florence St; per week $40)
Cairns Bicycle Hire (☎ 4031 3444; 47 Shields St; per day/week $10/40) Groovy bikes and scooters.

Bus

Sunbus (☎ 4057 7411; www.sunbus.com.au) runs regular services in and around Cairns that leave from Lake Street Transit Mall where schedules for most routes are posted. Buses run from early morning to late evening.

Taxi

Black & White Taxis (☎ 4048 8333) has a rank near the corner of Lake and Shields Sts, and one on McLeod St, outside Cairns Central Shopping Centre.

ISLANDS OFF CAIRNS

You *could* entertain romantic notions of a deserted tropical-island jaunt at Green or Fitzroy Islands – if you ignored the boat-loads of other travellers trying to do the same. A short distance off the coast from Cairns, these islands attract hordes of happy day-trippers. The Frankland Islands further south also make an excellent day trip.

Green Island

Tiny Green Island, 45 minutes from Cairns, provides just enough rainforest to break up hours of loafing on stunning beaches and snorkelling offshore. Although national park, the island also supports a plush resort, part of which is open to day-trippers. Facilities include a pool, a bar, several eateries and water-sports gear for hire.

The luxurious **Green Island Resort** (☎ 4031 330; www.greenislandresort.com.au; r $480-570; 🅿 🖭) has stylish split-level rooms, each with its own private balcony. Two styles of room are available: the larger room sleeps up to four; or you can have one all to yourself and shuffle around in your complimentary slippers and bathrobe.

Regular services to Green Island are run by **Great Adventures** (☎ 4051 0455; www.greatad ventures.com.au; return from $56); snorkelling and use of the resort's pool are included in the price. **Big Cat** (☎ 4051 0444; www.bigcat-cruises.com .au; return from $58) offers cruises that include snorkelling gear.

Fitzroy Island

A steep mountaintop peeping from the sea, Fitzroy Island National Park has beaches covered in coral, woodlands and walking trails, as well as a budget resort – all within the day-trip radar. Day-trippers can hire water-sports equipment from the resort, or join dive courses or sea-kayak tours.

There are a number of places to snorkel; the most popular is around the rocks at

Nudey Beach. Walking tracks include the 2km **Secret Garden Walk** and the steep 4km **Lighthouse & Summit Trail**. The budget **Fitzroy Island Resort** (☎ 4051 9588; www.fitzroyisland.com .au; dm/d/cabins $31/58/220; mains $12-20; 🅿 🖭) has a kiosk, bar and waterfront restaurant that opens at 5pm for guests only. All rooms except villa units share facilities (kitchen, bathroom and laundry). Saturday night is Party Night, when the resort shuttles revellers over from Cairns ($15) at 4pm and 7pm.

Transfers are operated by **Fitzroy Island Ferries** (☎ 4030 7907; adult/child return $38/18) three times a day, and **Sunlover Cruises** (☎ 1800 810 512; www.sunlover.com.au; adult/child $40/20) once a day.

Frankland Islands

No resorts and few facilities make these uninhabited islands a *very* attractive option. Drag your feet along the sandy beaches and frolic in the surrounding reefs. The five islands in the group include High Island to the north and four smaller islands to the south: Normanby, Mabel, Round and Russell.

Campers can be dropped at High or Russell Islands, both of which feature rainforest areas. Obtain a permit from **QPWS** (☎ 4046 6602; www .epa.qld.gov.au; 2-4 McLeod St; per person $4) and come prepared with water, a stove and food.

Frankland Islands Cruise & Dive (☎ 4031 6300; www.franklandislands.com; adult/child $150/90) runs a day tour from Cairns and will drop off campers ($145 return).

CAIRNS' NORTHERN BEACHES

These attractive beach communities are de facto city suburbs of Cairns linked by a busy highway. The exception is the ostentatious little resort town of Palm Cove, which has been transformed by massive development. All the beaches, which have stinger nets, make super day trips from Cairns, although there are excellent sleeping options if you think you can handle a number of days of beach inaction. **Machans Beach** (a bit of a misnomer, as it has no beach) is the first suburb north. Its shallow sandflats keep it stinger-net-free and development-free, with locals enjoying angling at the mouth of the Barron River, one block back from the esplanade.

Holloways Beach

The Coral Sea meets a rough ribbon of sand at a suitable depth for swimming at Holloways Beach. It's a mostly residential area, with beachside homes making way for a few tourist developments.

Strait on the Beach (☎ 4055 9616; 100 Oleandar St; meals $6-16; ☒ breakfast & lunch), overlooking the shallows, offers decent café fare. Or pop next door to **Coolum's on the Beach** (☎ 4055 9200; cnr Hibiscus & Oleandar Sts; mains $15-27; ☒ breakfast & lunch Sun, dinner daily). With its Mod Oz menu it is especially popular on a Sunday afternoon when live jazz sessions have people spilling out of the bar on to the beach.

Yorkeys Knob

Yorkeys Knob is a sprawling low-key settlement along a white-sand, windswept beach. The 'knob' refers to the rocky headland that cradles the bay to the north, allowing the wind to whip the water south.

Yorkey's makes a pleasant place to overnight. You could try **Yorkeys Beach Bungalows** (☎ 4055 7755; www.yorkeysbeachbungalows.com; 23 Sims Esplanade; d $80; P ☒), a cluster of basic self-contained bungalows made from timber and mesh wire; the sparse interior lends a rustic feel. Or for something a little more conventional, **York Beachfront Apartments** (☎ 4055 8733; www.yorkapartments.com.au; 61-63 Sims Esplanade; apt $120; P ☒ ☒) offers apartments with a fully equipped kitchen and laundry, and a separate bedroom.

Yorkeys Knob Boating Club (☎ 4055 7711; 25 Buckley St; mains $12-18; ☒ breakfast Sun, lunch & dinner daily) serves grills, pastas and burgers, and has sea views. You can also stop in for a quiet brew: quiet if you position yourself away from the pokie machines.

Trinity Beach

A long stretch of sheltered white sand helps make Trinity Beach one of the prettiest of Cairns' northern beaches. High-rise holiday units detract from its castaway ambience; however, holiday-makers love it.

Amaroo (☎ 4055 6066; www.amarooresort.com; 92 Moore St; apt $170; P ☒ ☒) has tasteful self-contained apartments with views of the beach below. It has its own steps leading down to the beach, and a tennis court.

The one- or two-bedroom apartments at the **Roydon** (☎ 4057 6512; www.roydon.com.au; 83-87 Vasey Esplanade; apt $120-150; P ☒ ☒), just back from the beach, are good value. Each has its own spacious balcony, living area and full kitchen. The snazzy white décor is fresh and modern.

L'unico Trattoria (☎ 4057 8855; 75 Vasey Esplanade; mains $18-23; ☒ breakfast, lunch & dinner) is a stylish Italian restaurant with professional service and a stellar corner beachfront location. You can BYO or choose from L'unico's own drinks list, which includes a solid choice of wines. The menu features risottos, pizzas, pastas and mains, and there's a separate menu for *bambinis*.

Clifton Beach

Local and leisurely, Clifton Beach is a good balance of residential and resort accommodation and services.

The freestanding single-storey apartments at **Clifton Palms** (☎ 4055 3839; www.clifton palms.com.au; 35-41 Upolu Esplanade; cabins/units $70/110; P ☒ ☒) are backed by a curtain of green hills. There's a huge range of accommodation options to suit any budget, and standby and low-season rates are jaw-droppingly good. The huge poolside barbecue area will win you over.

Paradise Gardens Caravan Resort (☎ 4055 3712; cnr Captain Cook Hwy & Clifton Rd; tent/caravan sites $15/22.50, cabins $52-77; P ☒) has well-tended grassy grounds. The same grey nomads flock back here each year for their three-monthly stay before heading north for the winter.

Clifton Capers Bar & Grill (☎ 4055 3355, 14 Clifton Rd; mains around $17.50; ☒ dinner Tue-Sun) is a licensed restaurant that does a range of international dishes and pizzas, and has a selection of nightly specials. Casual service befits the pleasant, relaxed setting.

Palm Cove

Palm Cove's beachfront is jammed with boutique hotels and expensive eateries, which encourage idleness and indulgence.

There is an ATM, post office and Internet café in the Paradise Village complex on Williams Esplanade. Quicksilver and Sunlover stop at the jetty for pick-ups on the way out to the reef.

Beach strolls and leisurely swims will be your chief activities, but if you need more stimulus, head to **Cairns Tropical Zoo** (☎ 4055 3669; www.wildworld.com.au; Captain Cook Hwy; adult/child $25/12.50; ☒ 8.30am-5pm), a 'cuddly animal' zoo set up for busloads of tourists.

SLEEPING

Angsana Resort & Spa (☎ 4055 3000; www.angsana .com; 1 Veivers Rd; r from $455; mains $17-24; ☒ breakfast, lunch & dinner; ⓟ ⓧ ⓛ ⓦ) Folding louvered doors open out to your own balcony, and design touches such as contrasting fabrics and feature walls make for stylish décor here. Resort facilities include three swimming pools, a chapel wedding service, spa treatments (with practitioners trained in Thailand), plus two bars and a fine restaurant, Far Horizons.

Outrigger (☎ 4059 9200; www.outrigger.com; 123-127 Williams Esplanade; r from $295; ⓟ ⓧ ⓦ) Outrigger outdoes many of the international resorts in Palm Cove, both in size and opulence. It starts with the bathrobes in your room, continues to the swimming pools – one with waterfall, one with sand edges – and doesn't end at the spa treatments – like the 45-minute 'rainbar': alternating warm and cold jets directed at your exfoliated body. Did we mention the resort's two *Gourmet Traveller*–listed restaurants, Nu Nu and Tamara?

Silvester Palms (☎ 4055 3831; www.silvesterpalms .com; 32 Veivers Rd; d from $100; ⓟ ⓧ ⓦ) These self-contained apartments in a small block are a refreshing alternative to the area's city-sized resorts. The communal barbecue area and fenced swimming pool make Silvesters a great option for families.

Palm Cove Accommodation (☎ 4055 3797; 19 Veivers Rd; s/d $65/80) This is the only budget option in Palm Cove. Next door to the beautician, this small complex offers a limited number of rooms, which are all bright and airy.

EATING

Blue (☎ 4055 3999; cnr Williams Esplanade & Veivers Rd; mains around $30; ❍ lunch & dinner) This hotel restaurant does delicate dishes with flair; try the steamed salmon with black mussels and caviar in a champagne sauce. If that doesn't dazzle you, the wood-fired pizzas might. Service is attentive and the décor is sparse and modern.

Cocky's at the Cove (☎ 4059 1691; Veivers Rd; dishes $5-10; ❍ breakfast & lunch) For casual all-day breakfasts or an honest sandwich for lunch, Cocky's is a solid choice.

Apres Beach Bar & Grill (☎ 4055 3300; 119-121 Williams Esplanade; dishes $8-28; ❍ breakfast, lunch & dinner) The large outdoor seating area is often full of people either having a drink or partaking in the food menu. There's something for everyone, with vegie dishes, steak dishes, seafood, pasta and servings for children.

Ellis Beach

The highway meets the coast at stunning little Ellis Beach. It has a beautiful, sheltered white-sand beach, complete with a stinger net and lifeguard in summer. Just past Ellis Beach is **Hartley's Creek Crocodile Farm** (☎ 4055 3576; www.crocodileadventures.com; adult/child $25/12.50; ❍ 8.30am-5pm). Free tours of the farm run at 10am and there are crocodile-feeding demonstrations at 11am and 3pm. You can have your photo taken with a koala at 3.45pm (for an additional cost).

The tidy **Ellis Beach Oceanfront Bungalows** (☎ 4055 3538, 1800 637 036; www.ellisbeachbungalows .com; Captain Cook Hwy; tent sites $26, caravan sites $28-32, cabins $75, bungalows $140-175; ⓟ ⓧ) have camping and cabins.

CAIRNS TO COOKTOWN

There are two routes to Cooktown from the south: the first is north to Cape Tribulation along the Captain Cook Hwy, then continuing up the 4WD Bloomfield Track (known as the 'coast road') from Cape Tribulation. Alternatively you can turn inland off the Captain Cook Hwy near Smithfield and take the Kennedy Hwy to the Peninsula Development and Cooktown Development Rds (known as the 'inland route').

The inland route passes by the mountain village of Kuranda in the Atherton Tableland, which also makes a popular detour from the coastal route (and day trip from Cairns). Taking the coastal route north, the highway hugs the coastline until the turn-off to Port Douglas. This stretch of road is one of the most picturesque on the Queensland coast. Mossman is a pleasant little town that's the gateway to the magnificent forests of the Daintree and Cape Tribulation. The Bloomfield Track continues to Cooktown.

KURANDA

☎ 07 / pop 670

A steep winding road climbs through rainforest before reaching the mountain village of Kuranda. Between 10am and 4pm it's a flurry of daytrippers; big-ticket tours, purpose-built attractions and loads of B-grade merchandise make the town feel more like a theme park. After 4pm, however, Kuranda reveals a mellower side: a mixed community living in beautiful rainforest surrounds. In

Kuranda, it's as much about the journey – getting here by cableway or by scenic railway is half of its appeal.

The **Kuranda visitors centre** (☎ 4093 9311; www .kuranda.org; 🕙 10am-5pm) is located in Centenary Park.

Sights & Activities

The original **Kuranda Markets** (☎ 4093 8772; 7 Therwine St; 🕙 9am-3pm Wed-Fri & Sun) are gradually being supplanted by the **Heritage Markets** (☎ 4093 8060; www.kurandaline.com.au/market; Rob Vievers Dr; 🕙 9am-3pm). Between them you'll find souvenirs such as ceramics, emu oil, jewellery and figurines made from pistachio nuts. Genuine crafts made by professional artists are for sale at the **Kuranda Arts Co-op** (☎ 4093 9026; www.artskuranda.asn.au; Kuranda Settlement Village, 12 Rob Vievers Dr; 🕙 10am-4pm).

The real stars in Kuranda's show are the walks through nearby rainforests – with their plentiful birds, frogs and fruit bats – and the booming **waterfalls** in **Barron Gorge National Park**, which are something to behold after rain. There are several signposted walks in and around the town, plus a short walk through **Jumrum Creek Environmental Park**, off the Barron Falls Rd, 700m from the bottom of Thongon St.

Further down, the Barron Falls Rd divides: the left fork takes you to a **lookout** over the falls, while a further 1.5km along the right fork brings you to **Wrights Lookout**, where you can see back down the Barron Gorge National Park to Cairns.

Sleeping

Sleeping over in Kuranda allows you to experience it without the innumerable daytrippers, and perhaps appreciate how it became so popular in the first place.

Kuranda Rainforest Park (☎ 4093 7316; www .kurandarainforestpark.com.au; Kuranda Heights Rd; tent/ caravan sites $17/20, s/d $30/50, units from $100; P 🐾) You'll wake in the morning to birds trilling in the surrounding rainforest here. A range of accommodation suits families, solo travellers and couples. Budget rooms share a kitchen and bathroom, while units are self-contained with poolside or garden views. The park is a 10-minute walk from town.

Kuranda Backpackers Hostel (☎ 4093 7355; www .kurandabackpackershostel.com; cnr Arara & Barang Sts; dm/d $18/42; P 🐾) This agreeably rambling double-storey home is surrounded by a large garden. There are loads of communal spaces over two levels to hang about in, which promotes a low-key chummy environment; show off in the large kitchen or retreat to the reading room.

Eating

Annabel's Pantry (☎ 4093 7605; Therwine St; pies $4-6; 🕙 breakfast & lunch) Offering more varieties of pie than there are letters in the alphabet, Annabel's has come up with some creative fillings, such as with the Matilda ('roo filled). A few flimsy outdoor settings are available.

Monkey's Cafe (☎ 4093 7451; 1 Therwine St; mains $12-16; 🕙 lunch) The fabulous garden surrounds here at Monkey's might inspire you to swing from the trees. Specialising in big gourmet sandwiches, this licensed café is a welcome place to retreat and linger.

Veg Out Cafe (☎ 4093 8483; Shop 5, 24 Coondoo St; meals $5-10; 🕙 lunch) You'll be lulled by Hare Krishna chanting as you tuck into your wholesome vegetarian dish here; wheat- and sugar-free meals are also on offer. Veg Out is located in the Red House mall.

There's a small supermarket on Coondoo St for self-caterers.

Getting There & Away

Kuranda Scenic Railway (☎ 4036 9288; www.travel train.com.au; adult/child/concession $35/17.50/27) winds 34km from Cairns train station to Kuranda through picturesque mountains and 15 tunnels. The trip takes 1¾ hours and trains depart Cairns at 8.30am and 9.30am Sunday to Friday (8.30am Saturday), returning from pretty Kuranda station at 2pm and 3.30pm Sunday to Friday (3.30pm Saturday).

At 7.5km-long, **Skyrail Rainforest Cableway** (☎ 4038 1555; www.skyrail.com.au; adult/child $35/17.50; 🕙 8.15am-5.15pm) is one of the world's longest gondola cableways. It runs from the corner of Kemerunga Rd and the Cook Hwy in Smithfield to Kuranda (Arara St), taking 90 minutes. It includes two stops along the way where you can disembark and enjoy the boardwalks and interpretive panels that are a feature of each stop. One of the stops features a walk below the burly Barron Falls, which are reduced to a trickle in the dry season. The last departure from Cairns and Kuranda is at 3.30pm; transfers to/ from the terminal (15 minutes' drive north of Cairns) and combination (scenic railway and cableway) deals are also available.

John's Kuranda Bus (☎ 0418 772 953; $2) operates a service between Cairns and Kuranda at least twice a day, up to seven times Wednesday to Friday. Buses depart from Cairns' Lake St Transit Mall. **Kuranda Shuttle** (☎ 0402 032 085; $2) departs Cairns' City Mall every two hours between 9am and 3pm, and Kuranda (Therwine St) at 10am, 12.15pm and 2pm. **White-car Coaches** (☎ 4091 1855; $4) has five departures from 46 Spence St, outside Shenannigans. The trip takes around half an hour.

PORT DOUGLAS
☎ 07 / pop 5867

Port Douglas' resort accommodation, swish eateries, boutique clothing stores and uninterrupted beach have successfully wooed the top-end tourist market – and all in the best possible taste. Careful planning has kept Port Douglas (known locally as 'Port') a low-rise settlement with an endearing character and down-to-earth locals. And it's all within air-conditioned reach of the far north's signature attractions, such as rugged Cape Tribulation and the Great Barrier Reef.

Orientation
From the Captain Cook Hwy it's 6km along a low spit of land to Port Douglas. The main entry road, Davidson St, ends in a T-intersection with Macrossan St. To the left is the town centre, with most of the shops and restaurants; the beach is to the right. The Marina Mirage is the departure point for most of the reef trips.

Information
All the major banks have branches with ATMs along Macrossan St.
Main post office (Owen St)
Pages Bookshop (☎ 4099 5094; Shop 3, 35 Macrossan St; ☺ 9am-6pm) Has a range of fiction and nonfiction titles.
Uptown (☎ 4099 5568; www.uptown.com.au; 48 Macrossan St; per 30min $5) Internet access.
Visitors centre (☎ 4099 5599; 23 Macrossan St; ☺ 8am-6.30pm) Has maps and can provide full accommodation lists and general information, as well as book tours.

Sights
There's a good chance you'll put in at least a few hours on the gorgeous **Four Mile Beach**, a band of palm-lined sand that is patrolled and has a stinger net in summer.

The **Rainforest Habitat** (☎ 4099 3235; www.rainforesthabitat.com.au; Port Douglas Rd; adult/child $28/14; ☺ 8am-5.30pm), about 4km south of the town centre, is an artificial rainforest environment that keeps koalas, kangaroos, crocs and a staggering amount of bird life. Come early for **Breakfast with the Birds** (adult/child incl admission $40/20; ☺ 8-10.30am).

Port's popular **Sunday Markets** (Anzac Park; ☺ 8.30am-1.30pm) always attract a good crowd. There are dozens of stalls selling fresh tropical fruits and ice creams, fresh coconut juice, vegies and crafts. Also in Anzac Park, **St Mary's by the Sea** is a teeny white timber chapel built in 1911, and restored and relocated to its present site in 1989.

Activities
Port has a host of activities to keep you occupied. From a hut on Four Mile Beach you can go **parasailing** (☎ 4099 3175; xtraactionwater@optusnet.com.au; from $65). Or you can glide between holes in your electric golf buggy at the esteemed **Links Golf Course** (☎ 4099 5888; www.thelinks.com.au; 18-holes $105), part of the Mirage resort. The **Port Douglas Yacht Club** (☎ 4099 4386; www.portdouglasyachtclub.com.au; Wharf St) offers free sailing every Wednesday at 4pm.

Several companies offer PADI open-water certification, as well as advanced dive certificates. **Discover Dive School** (☎ 4099 6800; www.discoverdiveschool.com; Shop 6, Grant St; 4-day course $580) and **Tech Dive Academy** (☎ 4099 6880; www.tech-dive-academy.com; 1/18 Macrossan St; 4-day course $575) provide instruction with limited numbers per class (four to six). **Quicksilver Dive School** (☎ 4099 5050; www.quicksilverdive.com.au; Marina Mirage; 4-day course $550) holds two days of its training course in Palm Cove; transfers from Port Douglas are included.

Tours
The overwhelming number of tour options here almost rivals that of Cairns.

GREAT BARRIER REEF
All reef trips provide a buffet lunch and free snorkelling equipment, with most also having optional introductory or certified dives. Trips leave daily from the Marina Mirage at around 8.30am.

Unlike towns further south, Port has a great many small boats that head out to the reef, providing a much more enjoyable experience than 100- to 300-seat behemoths. Expect to pay around $150 for a trip to the outer reef, depending on the distance

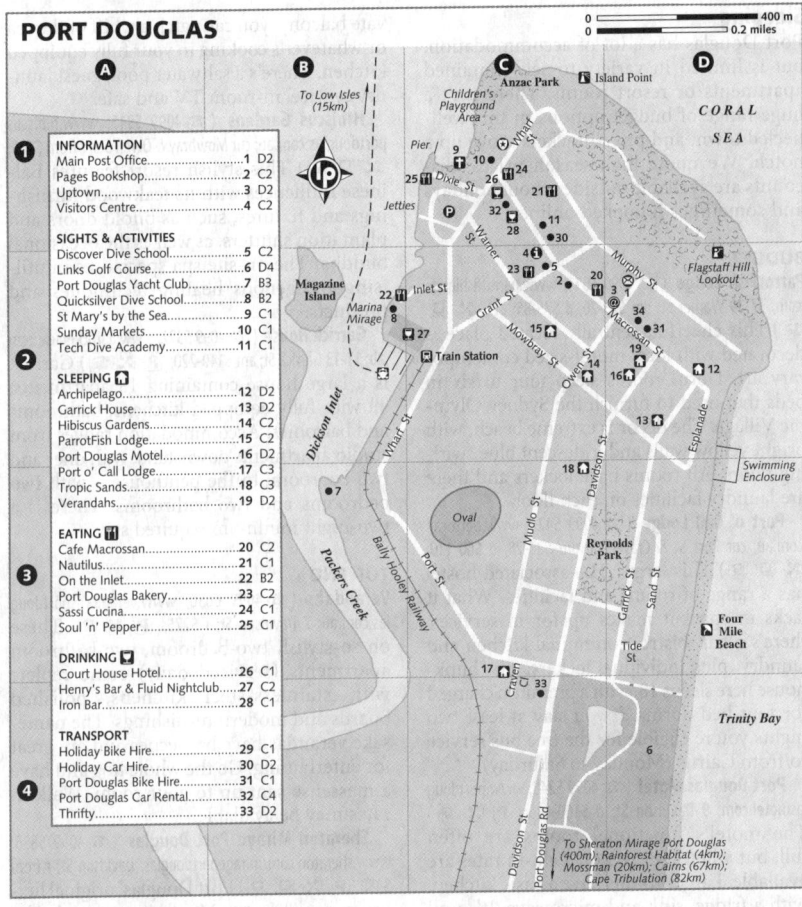

PORT DOUGLAS

0   400 m
0   0.2 miles

INFORMATION	
Main Post Office	1 D2
Pages Bookshop	2 C2
Uptown	3 D2
Visitors Centre	4 C2

SIGHTS & ACTIVITIES	
Discover Dive School	5 C2
Links Golf Course	6 D4
Port Douglas Yacht Club	7 B3
Quicksilver Dive School	8 B2
St Mary's by the Sea	9 C1
Sunday Markets	10 C1
Tech Dive Academy	11 C1

SLEEPING 🏠	
Archipelago	12 D2
Garrick House	13 D2
Hibiscus Gardens	14 C2
ParrotFish Lodge	15 C2
Port Douglas Motel	16 D2
Port o' Call Lodge	17 C3
Tropic Sands	18 C3
Verandahs	19 D2

EATING 🍴	
Cafe Macrossan	20 C2
Nautilus	21 C1
On the Inlet	22 B2
Port Douglas Bakery	23 C1
Sassi Cucina	24 C1
Soul 'n' Pepper	25 C1

DRINKING 🍷	
Court House Hotel	26 C1
Henry's Bar & Fluid Nightclub	27 C2
Iron Bar	28 C1

TRANSPORT	
Holiday Bike Hire	29 C1
Holiday Car Hire	30 D2
Port Douglas Bike Hire	31 C1
Port Douglas Car Rental	32 C4
Thrifty	33 D2

To Low Isles (15km)

Children's Playground Area

Anzac Park

Island Point

CORAL SEA

Pier

Jetties

Magazine Island

Marina Mirage

Train Station

Dickson Inlet

Packers Creek

Bally Hooley Railway

Oval

Flagstaff Hill Lookout

Swimming Enclosure

Reynolds Park

Four Mile Beach

Tide St

Trinity Bay

To Sheraton Mirage Port Douglas (400m); Rainforest Habitat (4km); Mossman (20km); Cairns (67km); Cape Tribulation (82km)

FAR NORTH COAST QUEENSLAND

and number of passengers. Good operators include the following:

Calypso (☎ 4099 3377; www.calypsocharters.com.au; adult/child $145/105)

Haba (☎ 4099 5254; www.habadive.com.au; adult/child $140/90)

Poseidon (☎ 4099 4772; www.poseidon-cruises.com .au; adult/child $150/115)

LOW ISLES

This coral cay 15km offshore is surrounded by a lagoon and topped by an old lighthouse. Tours usually include lunch and snorkelling, and are good for families. Operators include:

Sailaway (☎ 4099 4772; www.sailawayportdouglas.com; adult/child $125/75)

Shaolin (☎ 4099 1231; http://home.austarnet.com. au/shaolin; adult/child $135/65) A refitted Chinese junk.

OTHER TOURS

There are numerous operators offering day trips to Cape Tribulation, some via Mossman Gorge. Many of the tours out of Cairns also do pick-ups from Port Douglas.

Reef & Rainforest Connections (☎ 4099 5333; www.reefandrainforest.com.au) offers a huge range of day tours, including a trip to Kuranda using the Skyrail and Scenic Railway (adult/ child $105/55), and to Cape Tribulation (adult/child $165/125).

Fine Feather Tours (☎ 4094 1199; www.finefeather tours.com.au; half-/full day $145/205) is great for amateur and serious wildlife-spotters.

Sleeping

Port Douglas has a lot of accommodation, but is limited in variety to self-contained apartments or resort rooms. There isn't a huge range of budget options in this well-heeled town, and price brackets move up a notch. We quote high-season prices; discounts are available outside school holidays and sometimes if booked online.

BUDGET

ParrotFish Lodge (☎ 4099 5011; www.parrotfishlodge .com; 37-39 Warner St; dm $23-26, d $75-85; P ⊠ 🖳 🖲) This cheerful, centrally located place is decorated with local mural-sized contemporary art. Dorm rooms sleep four to six in beds that used to furnish the Sydney Olympic Village. The décor is extreme beach, with bright yellow walls and iridescent blue swirling floors. All rooms have lockers and there are laundry facilities on each floor.

Port o' Call Lodge (☎ 4099 5422; www.portocall .com.au; cnr Port St & Craven Cl; dm $23-28, d $60-110; ⊠ 🖳 🖲) This large YHA-associated hostel has a range of rooms and facilities. What it lacks in spirit it makes up for in services: there's a bar, bistro, communal kitchen and laundry, plus individual lockers. The bunkhouse here sleeps 18, with a premium charged for four-bed dorms. If you stay at least two nights you're eligible for the free bus service to/from Cairns (Monday to Saturday).

Port Douglas Motel (☎ 4099 5248; www.portdoug lasmotel.com; 9 Davidson St; d $100-115; P ⊠ 🖲) The motel's functional rooms are often full, but when they're not, walk-in rates are available. Larger rooms have a basic kitchen, with a fridge, sink and microwave. It's well situated, near both the beach and main street, but rooms are crammed together – definitely without views.

MIDRANGE

Archipelago (☎ 4099 5387; www.archipelago.com.au; 72 Macrossan St; d from $130; P ⊠ 🖲) This complex is very near the beach, with 12 self-contained rooms spread over three levels. The upper rooms have 'filtered' views to the beach (through trees and other properties). Rooms are neat and functional, with a writing desk, balcony and cane interior furniture.

Tropic Sands (☎ 4099 4533; www.tropicsands.com .au; 21 Davidson St; r $160; P ⊠ 🖳 🖲) The handsome open-plan rooms are in a beautiful white colonial-style building. From your pri-

vate balcony, you can catch a whiff of the sea or whatever's cooking in your fully equipped kitchen. There's a saltwater pool, guest laundry service, in-room TV and safe.

Hibiscus Gardens (☎ 4099 5315; www.hibiscus portdouglas.com.au; cnr Mowbray & Owen Sts; r from $165; ⊠ 🖳 🖲) This stylish resort features Balinese influences with its teakwood furnishings and fixtures, such as bifold doors and plantation shutters, as well as the occasional buddha. The on-site spa specialises in utilising Indigenous healing techniques and products.

Garrick House (☎ 4099 5322; www.garrickhouse.com .au; 11-13 Garrick St; apt $140-220; P ⊠ 🖲) Garrick is a large house containing 18 apartments, all with fully equipped kitchens, bathrooms and balconies. Accommodation ranges from studio apartments downstairs, with one- and two-bedroom, to the penthouse – with two bedrooms and two bathrooms. There is a two-night minimum required stay.

TOP END

Verandahs (☎ 4099 6650; www.verandahsportdoug las.com.au; 7 Davidson St; r $275; P ⊠ 🖲) These oh-so-stylish two-bedroom, two-bathroom apartments (serviced daily) come replete with stainless-steel kitchens, polished boards and modern furnishings. The namesake verandas have barbecues and are great for entertaining. Go the whole hog and have a masseuse sent up to your room. Walk-in rates may be available.

Sheraton Mirage Port Douglas (☎ 4099 5888; www.sheraton.com/mirageportdouglas; Davidson St; r from $480; P ⊠ 🖳 🖲) Port Douglas' original luxury resort, Sheraton Mirage is surrounded by two hectares of swimmable lagoons, has five eating establishments (open to nonguests), a golf course, childcare facilities and a florist. The resort has its own beachfront, shuttle service into town, tennis courts and gym. It's just south of the town centre.

Eating

You're spoilt with quality choices here, and the Port's pubs also do decent grub; see opposite.

RESTAURANTS

On the Inlet (☎ 4099 5255; 3 Inlet St; mains around $25; �られ lunch & dinner) Make the most of the early-dinner deal here, when between 3.30pm and 5.30pm $16.50 gets you a bucket of prawns and a drink. Otherwise settle for any number of this excellent restaurant's seafood dishes.

Sassi Cucina (☎ 4099 6100; cnr Wharf & Macrossan Sts; mains $28-38; ☻ breakfast, lunch & dinner) This Italian eatery serves authentic fare, where the pastas and risottos are pared back to just a few perfectly balanced ingredients. Of course the coffee is deftly prepared, and there's a range of inspired desserts. Italian Sassi goes Japanese with a fine sushi bar next door.

Nautilus (☎ 4099 5330; 17 Murphy St; mains $38-40; ☻ dinner) Nautilus has been a dining institution in Port Douglas for more than 50 years. Tables in two lush outdoor settings are dressed in white linen. Dining is taken seriously; children under eight aren't welcome.

CAFÉS & QUICK EATS
Soul 'n' Pepper (☎ 4099 4499; 2 Dixie St; meals $9-18; ☻ breakfast & dinner daily, lunch Mon-Sat) This laid-back outdoor café, opposite the pier, is a welcoming place – excitable young children excepted. Soul 'n' Pepper promotes an easy pace, playing soul music and offering casual service and surrounds.

Cafe Macrossan (☎ 4099 4372; Shop 1, 42 Macrossan St; mains $13-20; ☻ breakfast, lunch & dinner) This reliable licensed café opens out to the street and is often full – despite the sometimes-prickly service. Breakfast might include muesli with tropical fruits and minted honey yoghurt. You can also have eggs (any way) and there's decent coffee.

Port Douglas Bakery (3 Grant St; pastries & sandwiches $4-9; ☻ breakfast & lunch) Bless the bakery, because even in swanky Port Douglas there'll come a time when you just want a pie with sauce, or an egg sandwich followed by a lamington or doughnut. The bakery has a few outside tables, and, of course, sells fresh baked loaves and rolls.

Drinking
Iron Bar (☎ 4099 4776; 5 Macrossan St; mains $18-27; ☻ lunch & dinner) The meaty meals on offer at Port Douglas' favourite pub must be good, as nobody seems to notice the fridge suspended from the ceiling and nobody minds that the place is made up to look like a country woolshed. After polishing off your T-bone or reef 'n' beef, you can have a flutter on the cane-toad races, which feature every Tuesday, Thursday and Sunday night.

Court House Hotel (☎ 4099 5181; cnr Macrossan & Wharf Sts; meals $15-21; ☻ lunch & dinner) Command-

ing a corner location, this hotel often has a queue of dads waiting to order bistro meals snaking its way through the pleasant open-air courtyard. After the families have eaten, the low-key drinkers move in, entertained by cover bands (on weekends), pokies in the gaming room, and their friends hopefully.

Henry's Bar & Fluid Nightclub (☎ 4099 5200; Shop 54, Marina Mirage; ☻ till 5am) What begins downstairs at Henry's moves upstairs later in the night to Fluid. Open until 5am every night, Fluid reiterates the notion that punters in Port Douglas are not operating within a nine-to-five schedule. Tuesday night is backpacker night, and there are occasional touring bands and DJs.

Getting There & Away
For information on getting to/from Cairns, see p448.

Sun Palm (☎ 4084 2626; www.sunpalmtransport.com) runs a daily (except Monday) service from Port Douglas to Cairns ($25, 1½ hours), Mossman ($8, 20 minutes), Mossman Gorge ($12, 30 minutes), Cape Tribulation ($45, three hours) and Cooktown ($69, six hours). Its return fares are better value.

Coral Reef Coaches (☎ 4098 2600; www.coralreefcoaches.com.au) runs from Port Douglas to Mossman ($5, 20 minutes), Cow Bay ($22, two hours), Daintree Village (on request, two hours) and Cape Tribulation ($30, 2½ hours). It also connects with Cairns ($20, 1¼ hours).

Quicksilver (☎ 4031 4299; www.quicksilver-cruises.com; one way/return $26/39) has a fast catamaran service that departs Port Douglas at 5.15pm, arriving in Cairns at around 6.45pm.

Getting Around
TO/FROM THE AIRPORT
Airport Connections (☎ 4099 5950; www.tnqshuttle.com; ☻ 3.30am-4.30pm) runs a shuttle-bus service to/from Cairns airport ($23, hourly), as does **Sun Palm** (☎ 4084 2626; www.sunpalmtransport.com; $25), though less frequently.

BICYCLE
Cycling around Port Douglas is a sensible method of transport. The following hire mountain bikes.

Holiday Bike Hire (☎ 4099 6144; 6/42 Macrossan St; per day $17-21; ☻ 9am-5pm)

Port Douglas Bike Hire (☎ 4099 5799; 40 Macrossan St; per day from $15)

BUS

Sun Palm (☎ 4084 2626; www.sunpalmtransport.com; tickets $1.50-4; ☷ 7am-midnight) runs in a continuous loop every half-hour from the Rainforest Habitat (near the Captain Cook Hwy turn-off) to the Marina, stopping regularly. Flag the driver down at the marked bus stops.

CAR & TAXI

If you're planning to continue north up the Bloomfield Track to Cooktown, Port Douglas is the last place you can hire a 4WD vehicle for the job. These cost upwards of about $50 per day.

Holiday Car Hire (☎ 4099 4999; 54 Macrossan St; ☷ 8am-5.30pm Mon-Fri, to noon Sat & Sun)

Port Douglas Car Rental (☎ 4099 4988; www.port carrental.com.au; 81 Davidson St; ☷ 6.30am-8.30pm Mon-Fri, to 1.30pm Sat & Sun)

Thrifty (☎ 4099 5555; www.thrifty.com.au; 50 Macrossan St; ☷ 9am-4pm Mon-Fri, to noon Sat & Sun)

A 24-hour taxi service is offered by **Port Douglas Taxis** (☎ 4099 5345).

MOSSMAN

☎ 07 / pop 1941

Of the millions of holiday-makers who zoom through Mossman on their way up to Cape Tribulation, few slow down enough to notice this small town's charming architecture. Shadowed by Mt Demi, Mossman is at the centre of Queensland's most northerly sugar-growing district. The main attraction is the boulder-strewn river valley of Mossman Gorge, in the southern section of Daintree National Park.

The **Mossman QPWS** (☎ 4098 2188; www.epa.qld .gov.au; Demi View Plaza, 1 Front St; ☷ 10am-4pm Mon-Fri) has information on the Daintree.

Sparkling water washing over ancient rocks creates a stunning natural swimming hole at **Mossman Gorge**, 5km west of Mossman. Beyond the swimming hole, a suspension bridge takes you across the river to a 2.4km loop walking trail through superb lowland rainforest. Interpretive signs explain the traditional uses of the plants.

The area forms part of the traditional lands of the Kuku Yalanji Aboriginal people. Aboriginal-guided walks are run by **Kuku-Yalanji Dreamtime Walks** (☎ 4098 2595; www.yalanji .com.au; adult/child $17/8.50; ☷ walks 10am, noon & 2pm Mon-Fri).

Discover the intricate details of the process of turning a giant tropical grass into sugar at **Mossman Mill** (☎ 4030 4190; Mill St; adult/child $20/10; ☷ tours 2pm Mon, 10am & 2pm Tue-Fri Jun-Nov); wear closed shoes.

For fresh juices, wraps and sandwiches try **Tropical Boost** (☎ 4098 1089; 10 Front St; dishes $7-9; ☷ breakfast & lunch Mon-Sat), or **Goodies Cafe** (☎ 4098 1118; 33 Front St; mains around $10; ☷ lunch) for healthy meals homemade from organic produce.

Coral Reef Coaches (☎ 4098 2800; www.coralreef coaches.com.au) stops in Mossman on its way from Cairns ($25, two hours) and from Port Douglas ($5, 20 minutes)

Sun Palm (☎ 4084 2626; www.sunpalmtransport .com) runs regular bus services between Mossman and Cairns ($31, two hours), and Port Douglas ($8, 20 minutes).

DAINTREE VILLAGE

☎ 07 / pop 200

Daintree Village is a quiet little town on the Daintree River about 35km north from Mossman. It's the staging point for a host of river cruises. It was established as a logging town, with timber cutters concentrating on the prized red cedars that were once common in this area.

A common misconception among travellers is that Daintree Village is at the centre of the famous Daintree rainforests. In fact, most of the land around Daintree Village is cleared farmland, and you need to cross the river and head further north towards Cape Tribulation to access the Daintree National Park.

Tours

About a dozen operators offer river trips on the Daintree from various points between the ferry crossing and Daintree Village. Most trade on wildlife sightings, particularly crocs.

Chris Dahlberg's River Tours (☎ 4098 7997; www .daintreerivertours.info; Daintree Village; 2hr tour $45; ☷ tours 6.30am Apr-Oct, 6am Nov-Jan) Excellent birdwatching tours for early birds.

Crocodile Express (☎ 4098 6120; Daintree Village; 1½hr cruise adult/child $22/10; ☷ tours hourly 9.30am-3.30pm, plus 4pm) River cruises.

Electric Boat Cruises (☎ 1800 686 103; 1hr cruise adult/child $18/9; ☷ tours hourly 10.30am-2.30pm & 4pm & 5pm Mar-Jan, closed Feb) Takes groups of 12 in quiet, ecofriendly electric-powered boats.

Sleeping & Eating

There are several excellent B&Bs in the village and in the surrounding farmland, and a number of eateries.

Red Mill House (☎ 4098 6233; www.redmillhouse .com.au; Stewart St; d $105; P ✂ 🖳 🐾) This excellent B&B plays host to more than just paying guests, with a range of birds and frogs regularly stopping by. Rooms are well appointed, with bathrooms, and there's a large communal lounge area stacked with nature books.

River Home Cottages (☎ 4098 6225; www.river homecottages.com.au; Upper Daintree Rd; d $150; P ✂) Drive 5km down an unsealed road to reach these secluded self-contained cottages. Each is perched on a rise overlooking lush pasture filtered by the surrounding trees. Rates include breakfast. Barney, the owner, can show you to a secluded waterfall and swimming hole at the back of the property, or you can use the spa fitted in each cabin.

Foodwise, there are a number of options along the village's main street.

Papaya (☎ 4098 6173; Stewart St; mains $12-18; 🕑 lunch & dinner Wed-Sun) A snappy bar and bistro serving a range of standard favourites, such as fish and chips and beef pies, as well as tourist-teasers like crocodile wontons.

Blingkumu Restaurant (☎ 4098 6100; 20 Daintree Rd; mains $18-23; 🕑 breakfast, lunch & dinner) For a treat head to this restaurant, part of the Daintree Eco Lodge & Spa, where dishes are prepared using local produce incorporating indigenous berries, nuts, leaves and flowers – gourmet bush tucker.

Getting There & Away

Public transport is limited to **Coral Reef Coaches** (☎ 4098 2800; www.coralreefcoaches.com.au), which runs from Cairns and Port Douglas to Cape Tribulation, and will stop in Daintree Village on request; from Cairns it's $37 (2½ hours).

CAPE TRIBULATION AREA

About 10km before Daintree Village is the turn-off to the Daintree River ferry that takes you into the Cape Tribulation area. The Indigenous Kuku Yalanji people called the area Kulki, but Captain Cook called it Cape Tribulation after his ship ran aground on an outlying reef.

The region from the Daintree River north to Cape Tribulation is famed for its superb scenery, with long, sandy beaches and a backdrop of the rugged, forest-covered mountains of Thornton Peak (1375m) and Mt Sorrow (770m). It's an incredibly beautiful stretch of coast, and one of the few places in Australia (and the world) where tropical rainforest reaches down to the sea. These rainforests, dry woodlands and coastal mangroves are home to a host of unique plants and animals.

In recognition of this unique environment, much of it is protected by the Daintree National Park and the Wet Tropics World Heritage Area. Cow Bay and Cape Tribulation are loosely termed villages, and the whole Cape Tribulation Rd is scattered with places to stay and eat. Cape Trib is one of the most popular day trips from Port Douglas and Cairns, and accommodation is often booked solid during peak periods.

Information

There are no banks, though most places have card-payment facilities. And while there isn't an official visitors centre, the Bat House is a good source of information, as is Mason's Store (p461).

Sights & Activities

About 3km past the Daintree River crossing, Cape Kimberley Rd turns off the main road and heads down to **Cape Kimberley Beach**, near the estuary of the Daintree River. Just offshore is **Snapper Island**, which you can sea kayak to with nearby Crocodylus Village hostel.

About 9km from the ferry, you climb to the **Walu Wugirriga (Alexandra Range) Lookout**, with panoramic views over the Daintree River estuary and the national park, before dropping again to the **Daintree Discovery Centre** (☎ 4098 9171; www.daintree-rec.com.au; Cape Tribulation Rd; adult/child $20/7.50; 🕑 8.30am-5pm). This rainforest interpretive centre features aerial walkways, a small theatre and a 23m tower that stretches up into the jungle canopy. The **Jindalba Boardwalk** is a 700m circuit that snakes through the rainforest behind the centre.

About 12km from the ferry you reach Buchanan Creek Rd, which is the turn-off for picturesque **Cow Bay** (5.5km).

After crossing Hutchinson Creek the road swings sharply inland before striking the shore again at **Thornton Beach**. The **Daintree Entomological Museum** (☎ 4098 9045; www.daintreemuseum.com.au; Turpentine Rd; adult/child $12/6; 🕑 10.30am-4pm) displays a large private

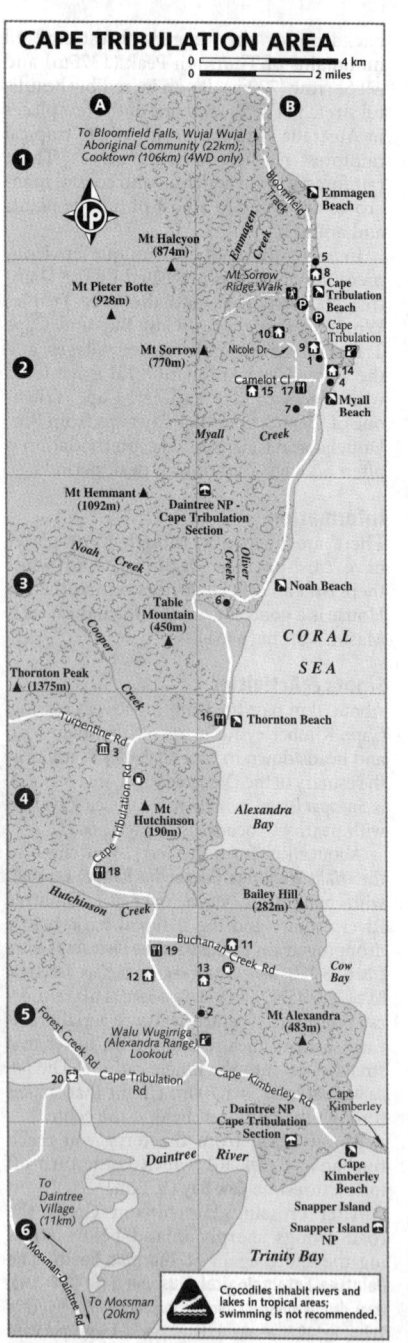

CAPE TRIBULATION AREA

0 |————| 4 km
0 |————| 2 miles

To Bloomfield Falls, Wujal Wujal
Aboriginal Community (22km);
Cooktown (106km) (4WD only)

Emmagen Beach

Mt Halcyon
(874m)

Mt Pieter Botte
(928m)

Mt Sorrow
Ridge Walk

Cape
Tribulation
Beach

Cape
Tribulation

Mt Sorrow
(770m)

Nicole Dr

Camelot Cl

Myall
Beach

Myall Creek

Mt Hemmant
(1092m)

Daintree NP -
Cape Tribulation
Section

Noah Creek

Table
Mountain
(450m)

Noah Beach

CORAL
SEA

Thornton Peak
(1375m)

Thornton Beach

Mt
Hutchinson
(190m)

Alexandra
Bay

Bailey Hill
(282m)

Buchanan
Creek Rd

Cow
Bay

Hutchinson Creek

Mt Alexandra
(483m)

Walu Wugirriga
(Alexandra Range)
Lookout

Cape Tribulation
Rd

Cape Kimberley Rd

Cape
Kimberley

Daintree NP
Cape Tribulation
Section

Daintree River

Cape
Kimberley
Beach

Snapper Island

To
Daintree
Village
(11km)

Snapper Island
NP

Trinity Bay

To Mossman
(20km)

Crocodiles inhabit rivers and
lakes in tropical areas;
swimming is not recommended.

collection of bugs, butterflies and spiders found locally and all over the world. Apart from the delicately pinned specimens, there are also live exhibits of giant cockroaches. Further north the **Marrdja Botanical Walk** follows Noah Creek through rainforest and mangroves for 800m.

In Cape Tribulation, the **Bat House** (☎ 4098 0063; www.austrop.org.au; Cape Tribulation Rd; admission by donation; ⏲ 10.30am-3.30pm Tue-Sun) is an information and education centre. Volunteers from Austrop, a local conservation organisation, run the centre. As the name suggests, it's also a nursery for fruit bats, and there's usually one hanging around (sorry) for you to meet.

The **Dubuji Boardwalk** is a 1.8km circuit walk down to superb Myall Beach through rainforest and mangroves. Further north is the 400m **Kulki Boardwalk**, which leads to a platform overlooking the beach. To get to Myall Beach from here, walk over the saddle west of the headland.

Serious walkers should lace up early for the **Mt Sorrow Ridge Walk** (return six hours, 3.5km), which climbs steeply to a lookout with awesome views across the windswept vegetation over the cape. The trail is about 150m north of the Kulki Boardwalk.

Tours

Guided night walks are offered by **Jungle Adventures** (☎ 4098 0090; www.junglesurfingcanopy tours.com; $25-28); it also does 'jungle surfing' tours, where you can ride in a harness over

---

DAINTREE: LOVING IT TO DEATH?

The Daintree area comprises a small part of the Wet Tropics World Heritage Area, which stretches from Townsville to Cooktown. Its 3000km boundary covers only 0.01% of Australia's surface area, but has 36% of its mammal species, 50% of its bird species, around 60% of its butterfly species and 65% of its fern species.

The Daintree first grabbed the world's attention in the '80s when conservationists and the state government locked horns over the cutting of the Bloomfield Track – the detrimental affects of traffic leading through such a delicate environment being the focus of the debate. Blockades indirectly led to the Federal Government's moves to nominate the area for World Heritage listing, to which it was added in 1988.

More recently, the traditional rivals of developers and conservationists have joined forces to curb a new threat – mass tourism. Both recognise the importance of the area and endeavour to preserve its essence, its biodiversity and beauty from the thousands of holiday-makers who collectively strain resources.

The area remains controversial, however: while World Heritage listing prohibits logging, the area around Cow Bay is largely privately owned, and is unaffected by the World Heritage listing. A submission by 26 leading international scientists stating that any further development would impact on the ecosystem led to a moratorium on building. Outraged landowners have appealed to the UN for the area to be removed from World Heritage listing, arguing that it comprises only a tiny percentage of the total area.

---

the rainforest canopy ($70). **Mason's Store** (☎ 4098 0070; www.masonstours.com.au; Cape Tribulation Rd) has interesting walks for a few hours (adult/child $30/23) or a half-day ($36/28), as well as extended 4WD tours.

Two operators run trips to the Great Barrier Reef that include snorkelling, and offer certified and introductory diving opportunities. The sailing catamaran **Rum Runner** (☎ 1300 556 332; www.rumrunner.com.au; $116; ☺ Apr-Feb) is a local outfit, with a maximum of 40 passengers. **Odyssey** (☎ 1300 134 044; www.voyages.com.au; $136), operated by the Voyages resort company, uses a motorised boat.

Book ahead for a **Cooper Creek Wilderness guided walk** (☎ 4098 9126; www.ccwild.com; adult $30).

Sleeping

Electricity is powered by generators; few places have air-con and not everywhere has 24-hour power. Many places are in a rainforest setting, which keeps things naturally cool.

DAINTREE RIVER TO CAPE TRIB

This is where you'll find the cheaper mid-range options.

Epiphyte B&B (☎ 4098 9039; www.rainforestbb .com; 22 Silkwood Rd; s/d/tr $45/65/80; P) This spectacularly laid-back B&B has rooms that are

individually styled – and some are bigger than others. The encircling veranda is festooned with hammocks, from where you're able to catch views of imposing Thornton's Peak. If you arrive unannounced, a blackboard indicates whether there's a vacancy. Go ahead and let yourself in and head to the beach, which is where you'll probably find the manager.

Crocodylus Village (☎ 4098 9166; www.crocody luscapetrib.com; Lot 5, Buchanan Creek Rd; dm/d $20/75; P 🖳 🖳 🖳) A number of green canvas safari-style huts merge with the surrounding trees at this YHA-associated hostel. Dorm rooms contain 16 to 20 beds and have all the ambience of school camp. There's a restaurant and bar, as well as a range of activities. Crocodylus runs excellent two-day sea-kayaking tours to Snapper Island ($180) that leave early in the morning, so you'll need to overnight in Cow Bay. Guided walks ($20, three hours) are also available in the morning and afternoon.

Daintree Rainforest Retreat Motel (☎ 4098 9101; www.daintreeretreat.com.au; 336 Cape Tribulation Rd; r $100-120; P 🖳) The beds are as comfy as clouds in these modern motel rooms. All rooms have their own bathroom, TV and kettle. Breakfast is included and is at whatever time you nominate, and the quiet setting is ruffled only when someone is splashing about in the pool.

CASSOWARIES' PRECIOUS POO

The cassowary commands respect. Apart from being as tall as a grown man, having three toes, a blue-and-purple head, red wattles and a helmet-like horn, the flightless cassowary is considered to be largely responsible for the appearance of the rainforest.

The cassowary is the only animal capable of dispersing the seeds of more than 70 species of trees whose fruit is too large for other rainforest animals to digest and pass. Cassowaries swallow fruit whole and excrete the fruit's seed intact in large piles of dung, which acts as fertiliser encouraging growth of the seed.

An endangered species, the cassowary's greatest threat is the loss of the very thing it helps to create – rainforest habitat. Cassowaries can also become aggressive; if you feel threatened, don't run, and try to have a tree between you and it.

CAPE TRIB

Rainforest Hideaway (☎ 4098 0108; www.rainforest hideaway.com; 19 Camelot Cl; r $85-115) This beautifully rambling accommodation was virtually single-handedly built by the owner. Walk through the densely forested back yard to the self-contained rustic haven with an outdoor shower. Or there's a small cabin at the front of the house, plus a two-level room inside the house suitable for families.

Cape Trib Beach House (☎ 4098 0030; www.capetrib beach.com.au; Cape Tribulation Rd; dm $25-32, r $70-135; P ✗ ☐ ☐) Most of the rooms (including dorms) in these A-frame rainforest huts have air-con, and the great facilities include a restaurant-bar (mains $15 to $20; open breakfast, lunch and dinner) and small communal kitchen, as well as private beach access.

PK's Jungle Village (☎ 4098 0197; www.pksjungle village.com; Cape Tribulation Rd; tent sites per person $15, dm $25, d $88-110; ✗ ☐ ☐) PK's has the works, from postal facilities through to salsa dance classes in its lively bar. Dorms have eight beds, and air-conditioned rooms with en-suite bathrooms are available. There's also a restaurant (mains $15 to $20; open breakfast, lunch and dinner) and communal kitchen.

Cape Tribulation Retreat (☎ 4098 0028; www .capetribretreat.com.au; 19 Nicole Dr; d $150; P) This gorgeous B&B has a creek running alongside it, and rainforest in the back yard. All rooms are in a modern timber home, and have en-suite bathrooms; rates include breakfast. The unfenced creek makes this place unsuitable for small children.

Cape Trib Farmstay (☎ 4098 0042; www.capetrib farmstay.com; Cape Tribulation Rd; d $100; P) This tropical fruit orchard has neat and private timber cottages with joyous views of Mt Sorrow. One of the eight cabins – all with en-suite bathroom – has wheelchair access.

There's a communal kitchen and open grass areas between fruit trees.

Eating

Most of the accommodation complexes have restaurants, plus there are a few options dotted along Cape Tribulation Rd. Self-caterers should stock up in Mossman.

Dragonfly Gallery Cafe (☎ 4098 0121; Lot 9, Camelot Cl, Cape Tribulation; mains $15-20; ⏱ lunch & dinner) A licensed café in a timber pole-house with beautiful garden views. You can use the Internet upstairs in the loft, or just peruse local art displayed around the interior.

Le Bistrot (☎ 4098 9016; Cape Tribulation Rd, Cow Bay; mains $19-30; ⏱ lunch) This boutique place serves formal savoury and sweet dishes in thatched huts dotted around the grounds. Also on the premises is the tiny Floravilla gallery, displaying the owners', Bill and Betty Hinton, photographs and plants.

Fan Palm Boardwalk Cafe (☎ 4098 9119; Cape Tribulation Rd, Cow Bay; mains $8-16; ⏱ breakfast, lunch & dinner) This open-air licensed café serves perky wraps and sandwiches, as well as more substantial fare, such as fish and chips and rib-eye steak. There's a wheelchair-accessible deck leading through giant palms (noneaters $2).

Cafe on Sea (☎ 4098 9718; Thornton Beach; mains $10-15; ⏱ breakfast & lunch) A towel-length from the beach, with excellent meals such as Thai fish burgers, and decent espresso.

Getting There & Away

Daintree River cable ferry (car/motorcycle/bicycle & pedestrian $16/8/3; ⏱ 6am-midnight) runs every 15 minutes or so, and takes about four minutes to cross.

Sun Palm (☎ 4084 2626; www.sunpalmtransport .com) runs a daily (except Monday) service from Cape Tribulation to Cairns ($45, three hours). It also travels up the coastal road to Cooktown ($100, 3¼ hours) every second day. **Coral Reef Coaches** (☎ 4098 2800; www .coralreefcoaches.com.au) runs a daily bus service from Cape Tribulation to Cairns ($40, four hours).

CAPE TRIBULATION TO COOKTOWN: THE COAST ROAD

The Bloomfield Track carves its way through mountains and dense rainforest for almost 80km before linking up with the Cooktown Development Rd, 28km south of Cooktown. During the wet season this road can be closed; ask locally at **Mason's Store** (☎ 4098 0070; Cape Tribulation Rd; ☺ 7am-7pm) about current conditions.

The track was built in 1983, when the Douglas Shire Council decided to bulldoze a gravel road through the forest from just north of Cape Tribulation to the Bloomfield River, and Cape Trib became the scene of a classic greenies-versus-bulldozers blockade. The debate over the track continues today, with the majority of locals seeking its staged closure over the next 10 to 15 years.

Cape Tribulation to the Bloomfield River

It's 5km from Cape Tribulation to Emmagen Creek, the official start of the Bloomfield Track. Just before you reach Emmagen Creek, the road passes a huge strangler fig, where there's a path to a pretty crescent-shaped **Emmagen Beach**. A little way beyond this crossing, the road begins to climb and descend a series of extremely steep hills – this is the most challenging (and enjoyable) section of the drive and is over all too soon.

The road then follows the broad Bloomfield River, before crossing it on a causeway 30km north of Cape Trib. On the northern bank of the river is the **Wujal Wujal** Aboriginal community (population 293). Turning left takes you to the powerful and attractive **Bloomfield Falls** – for looking only, as crocs live here.

The road condition improves the further north you go. On the way you pass through the tiny hamlets of Rossville and Helenvale.

The **Lion's Den Hotel** (☎ 4060 3911; www.lions denhotel.com.au; Helenvale; tent sites $7.50, dm/d $25/50;

☐ ☒) is slap-bang in the middle of nowhere. Its corrugated, graffiti-covered tin walls and slab-timber bar attract a steady stream of travellers and local characters. It has a restaurant that serves up excellent budget meals.

Around 4km further on, the road meets the Cooktown Development Rd.

A short distance further on, you'll come to the oddly stunning peaks of the **Black Mountain National Park**, which are covered in boulders. Known to the Kuku Yalanji people as Kalcajagga (Place of the Spears), the mountains were formed 260 million years ago by magma extrusions. The rocks (which are coloured black by algae) are home to three unique species, including a frog, a gecko and a skink. From here, it's another 28km to Cooktown.

CAIRNS TO COOKTOWN: THE INLAND ROUTE

The main route between Cairns and Cooktown remains stoically arid whatever the season. It's 332km long (4½ to five hours' drive) and sweeps inland from Cairns, mainly following the Peninsula Development Rd before joining the Cooktown Development Rd at Lakeland. From here it's another 80km to Cooktown, with just 30km left to seal, due for completion by the time you read this.

After heading north out of Cairns, take the turn-off to Kuranda and climb over the Atherton Tableland. At Mareeba you meet the Peninsula Development Rd, which takes you north through the small township of Mt Molloy and the former wolfram (tungsten)-mining town of **Mt Carbine** before the road climbs through the De Sailly Range, where there are panoramic views over the savanna.

Palmer River Roadhouse (☎ 4060 2020; tent & caravan sites $12.50; ☺ 7am-late) has food and high-priced fuel; it's just past the Palmer River crossing, 85km northwest of Mt Carbine.

It's another 30km from the Palmer River to **Lakeland**, a hamlet at the junction of the Peninsula Development Rd and the Cooktown Development Rd. Further still down the road is the turn-off to the Coast Rd and the Black Mountain National Park. Straight ahead is Cooktown, which is another 30km away.

COOKTOWN

☎ 07 / pop 1410

Peak hour in Cooktown is early evening, when the fish are biting and the beer is flowing. About a dozen 4WDs gather at either end of town: half park at the pier, the other half outside the pub. Years of isolation and hard living have imbued the locals with a matter-of-fact, laconic character and a great sense of humour. They're not afraid of hard work, and equally not shy of a smoko – say from October to June…

The Wet has traditionally cut Cooktown off from the south to all but those with 4WDs and gutsy determination. Its isolation has kept it shielded from the burgeoning tourist industry that is creeping north. As such, unlike its southern sibling towns, Cooktown exists despite tourism. It remains unadorned and unfussed by the attention it receives. There's increasing recognition for the area's Indigenous community and unspoilt natural environment. It has diverse habitats of wetlands, mangroves, rainforest and long, lonely beaches.

Traditionally, it has been Cooktown's history of European contact that has drawn travellers. It can claim to be Australia's first non-Indigenous settlement – albeit for 48 days. From June to August 1770, Captain James Cook beached his barque *Endeavour* here, during which time the chief naturalist, Joseph Banks, collected 186 Australian plant species from along the banks of the Endeavour River and wrote the first European description of a kangaroo.

Orientation

Cooktown's main street, Charlotte St, runs south from the wharf. Overlooking the town from the northern end of the headland is Grassy Hill, and east of the town centre are Cherry Tree and Finch Bays, the Botanic Gardens and Mt Cook National Park. The airfield is 10km west of the town centre along McIvor Rd.

Information

Cooktown Library (☎ 4069 5009; Helen St) Internet access.

Cooktown QPWS (☎ 4069 5777; Webber Esplanade; ☯ 8am-3pm Mon-Fri) Closes for lunch.

Cooktown Travel Centre (☎ 4069 5446; cooktowntravel@bigpond.com; Charlotte St; ☯ 8.30am-5pm Mon-Fri, to noon Sat) Tourist information.

Nature's Powerhouse (☎ 4069 6004; www.nature spowerhouse.info; Walker St; ☯ 9am-5pm) Information centre.

Sights & Activities

Cooktown hibernates during the wet season (locals call it the dead season) and reduced hours or closure may apply to the town's museums and cruises.

The delightful **James Cook Historical Museum** (☎ 4069 5386; cnr Helen & Furneaux Sts; adult/child $7/2.50; ☯ 9.30am-4pm), in a handsome 1880s convent, has displays relating to all aspects of Cooktown's past, including the Palmer River gold rush, the Chinese community and Aboriginal oral-history accounts of Cook's first landing.

You'll get more than plants at Cooktown's **Botanic Gardens**: it also houses **Nature's Powerhouse** (☎ 4069 6004; www.naturespowerhouse .info; Walker St; galleries adult/child $2/free; ☯ 9am-5pm), an information centre with a café and two galleries. The Charlie Tanner Gallery is dedicated to Cooktown's 'snakeman' and only-on-the-cape wildlife. The Vera Scarth-Johnson Gallery is a collection of delicate botanical illustrations. Nature's Powerhouse distributes the 'Cooktown Heritage & Scenic Rim' flyer, which details the gamut of Cooktown's excellent walks.

Charlotte St has a number of interesting **monuments** (really), including the **Milbi Wall** (Story Wall; built by the Gungarde Aboriginal community), a snaking mosaic-tiled wall that tells the story of European settlement from an Aboriginal perspective.

The **Grassy Hill Lookout** has sensational 360-degree views of the town, river and ocean. Captain Cook apparently climbed this hill looking for a passage out through the reefs. At the top sits a compact 19th-century corrugated-iron lighthouse. A walking trail (1½km, 45 minutes) leads from the summit down to the beach at Cherry Tree Bay.

Tours

Limited tours operate from November to at least April.

Barts Bush Adventures (☎ 4069 6229; bartbush@ tpg.com.au; tours adult/child $165/85) Runs a variety of tours, including the Bush & Beach that goes to Coloured Sands and Elim Beach.

Cooktown Tours (☎ 4069 5125; www.cooktowntours .com) Offers 1½-hour town tours (adult/child $20/12) and

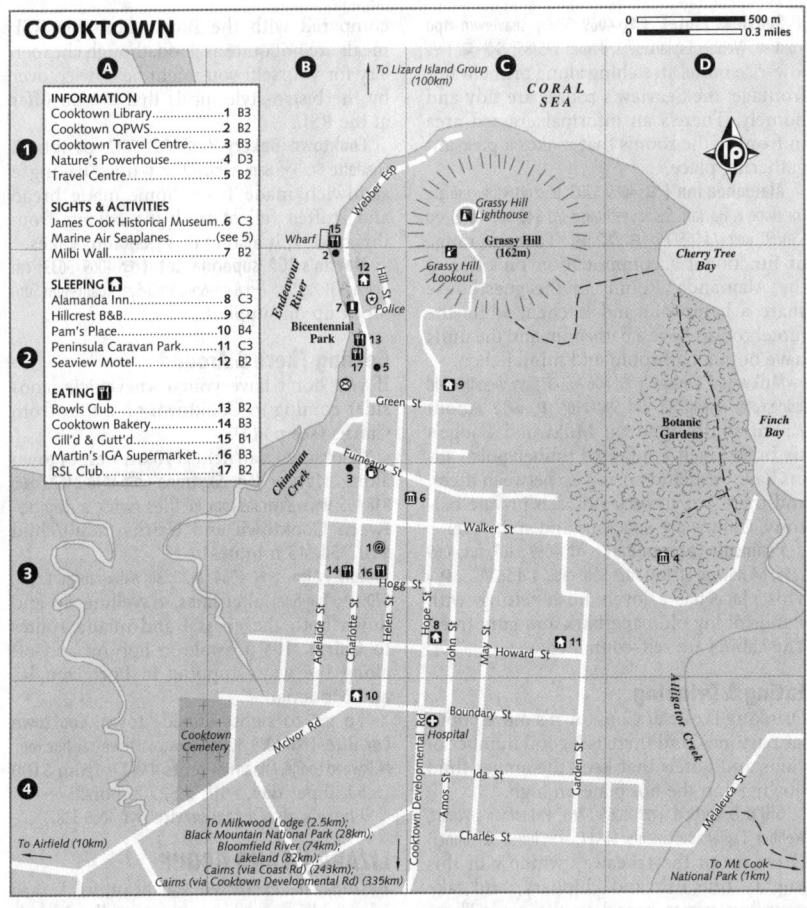

COOKTOWN

0 — 500 m
0 — 0.3 miles

INFORMATION
Cooktown Library.................1 B3
Cooktown QPWS................2 B2
Cooktown Travel Centre........3 B3
Nature's Powerhouse.............4 D3
Travel Centre........................5 B2

SIGHTS & ACTIVITIES
James Cook Historical Museum..6 C3
Marine Air Seaplanes.............(see 5)
Milbi Wall...............................7 B2

SLEEPING
Alamanda Inn.........................8 C3
Hillcrest B&B...........................9 C2
Pam's Place.............................10 B4
Peninsula Caravan Park.........11 C3
Seaview Motel.........................12 B2

EATING
Bowls Club.............................13 B2
Cooktown Bakery....................14 B3
Gill'd & Gutt'd.........................15 B1
Martin's IGA Supermarket......16 B3
RSL Club.................................17 B2

To Lizard Island Group (100km)

CORAL SEA

Grassy Hill Lighthouse
Grassy Hill (162m)
Grassy Hill Lookout

Cherry Tree Bay

Wharf
Endeavour River
Hope St
Police
Bicentennial Park

Botanic Gardens

Finch Bay

Green St

Chinamun Creek
Furneaux St

Walker St

Hogg St
Adelaide St
Charlotte St
Helen St
Hope St
John St
May St
Howard St

Boundary St
Hospital
Ida St
Amos St
Garden St

Charles St

Cooktown Cemetery
McIvor Rd
Cooktown Developmental Rd

Alligator Creek
Maleleuca St

To Mt Cook National Park (1km)

To Airfield (10km)

To Milkwood Lodge (2.5km);
Black Mountain National Park (28km);
Bloomfield River (74km);
Lakeland (82km);
Cairns (via Coast Rd) (243km);
Cairns (via Cooktown Developmental Rd) (335km)

half-day trips to Black Mountain and the Lion's Den Hotel (adult/child $55/23); both depart daily at 9am.

Guurrbi Tours (☎ 4069 5166; williegordon@fni.aunz .com; 2/4hr tour $80/105, self-drive $55/70) Willie, a Nugal-warra elder, runs a unique tour that uses the physical landscape to describe the emotional landscape. The tour includes bottled drinking water and perhaps a snack of green ants, and takes you to a number of rock-art sites. Book at Pam's Place (hostel).

Marine Air Seaplanes (☎ 4069 5915; www.marineair .com.au) Offers scenic reef flights ($125 to $175) and an extraordinary Lizard Island tour ($330), which lands in Watson's Bay by seaplane.

Paradise Blue (☎ 0408 183 261; www.paradise-blue .com; snorkelling tour $110) Don't expect to battle other tour boats on the Great Barrier Reef from here. Sailing tours to the reef or river, including fishing.

Sleeping

Pam's Place (☎ 4069 5166; www.cooktownhostel.com; cnr Charlotte & Boundary Sts; dm/s/d $20/40/50; P 🅿) This comfortable YHA-associate hostel has a leafy garden and an assortment of neurotic parrots. There are also four new self-contained units (two people $80). All facilities are top-notch, and management can provide loads of useful information about the area.

Hillcrest B&B (☎ 4069 5305; www.hillcrestb-b.com; 130 Hope St; guesthouse s/d/tr $40/50/70, unit s/d $60/70;) Backed by a garden concealed beneath greenhouse awnings, this charming old-style guesthouse has basic rooms with shared bathroom, and units with air-con and private bathroom. Breakfast is $5 extra, and there's an outdoor area in which to eat it.

Seaview Motel (☎ 4069 5377; seaviewm@tpg .com.au; Webber Esplanade; s/d from $75/85; 🕑 🛎) A low-rise motel stretching along prime water frontage, the Seaview's rooms are tidy and homely. There's an informal grassed area in front of the rooms that makes a pleasant gathering place.

Alamanda Inn (☎ 4069 5203; phscott@tpg.com.au; cnr Hope & Howard Sts; guesthouse s/d $40/50, motel s/d $50/60, unit s/d $65/75; 🅿 🕑 🛎) There's a range of functional accommodation on offer at the Alamanda. Rooms in the guesthouse share a bathroom and kitchen, while the motel rooms have a bathroom and the units have both a bathroom and minikitchen.

Milkwood Lodge (☎ 4069 5007; www.milkwood lodge.com; Annan Rd; s/d $90/110; 🅿 🛎) About 2.5km south of town, Milkwood Lodge's six breezy, self-contained timber-pole cabins have bushland oozing up between them, and there are views from each private balcony. Cabins are spacious and split-level.

Peninsula Caravan Park (☎ 4069 5107; fax 4069 5255; 64 Howard St; tent sites $18, cabin s/d $60/65; 🅿) This place has a lovely bush setting, with stands of big old paperbark and gum trees. The cabins are self-contained.

Eating & Drinking

Drinking is one of Cooktown's more popular pastimes, and there is a good number of clubs and hotels that keep the amber fluid flowing and the hot plate on high.

Gill'd & Gutt'd (☎ 4069 5863; Fisherman's Wharf, Webber Esplanade; meals $8-17; 🕑 lunch & dinner) Drive up to the takeaway window of this mighty fine fish and chippery, and take your hot paper parcel to the pier. These are fancy fish and chips, with your choice of barramundi or Spanish mackerel. Alternatively you can walk around to the riverside and dine in. The restaurant is licensed, with highly sought after waterfront tables (though the ambience is flat).

Bowls Club (☎ 4069 6173; Charlotte St; mains $12-20; 🕑 dinner) Sign yourself in at the door, and join the club for the night. Apart from enormous, wholesome mains (such as fish or steak) you're able to visit the salad bar as often as you like, though you'd struggle to go for seconds. The club fills up on weekends, when you might just win yourself a meat tray in the raffle.

RSL Club (☎ 4069 5780; Charlotte St; mains 10-16; 🕑 dinner) The word on Charlotte St is that compared with the Bowls Club the RSL meals are not quite as good, though cheaper. Try for yourself: you might be bowled over by the bistro-style meals that are on offer at the RSL.

Cooktown Bakery (☎ 4069 5612; cnr Helen & Charlotte St; 🕑 8am-4pm) Don't miss having a sandwich made from home-made bread and stuffed full of fresh ingredients from this bakery; it also makes delicious cakes.

Martin's IGA supermarket (☎ 4069 5633; cnr Helen & Hogg Sts; 🕑 8am-6pm Mon-Sat, 10am-3pm Sun) Stock up on supplies.

Getting There & Around

If you don't have your own vehicle, consider coming to Cooktown on a tour from Cairns (see p444).

Cooktown's airfield is 10km west of town along McIvor Rd. **Skytrans** (☎ 4046 2462, 1800 818 405; www.skytrans.com.au) flies twice a day between Cooktown and Cairns (adult/child $107/54, 45 minutes).

Sun Palm (☎ 4084 2626; sunpalmtransport.com; $70; 🕑 Tue-Sun) alternates, travelling up and down both the coastal and inland routes to Cairns. It's possible to hop on and off along the way, stopping in Port Douglas and Mossman.

To get to sights outside town, **Cooktown Car Hire** (☎ 4069 5007; www.cooktown-car-hire.com; Milkwood Lodge, Annan Rd) rents 4WDs from $100 to $150 per day, with a $2200 bond.

There's also a **taxi service** (☎ 4069 5387).

LIZARD ISLAND GROUP

Besides the exclusive and beautiful Lizard Island, there are four other smaller islands in the Lizard Group. **Osprey Island**, with its nesting birds, is right in front of the Lizard Island Resort and can be waded to. Around the edge of Blue Lagoon, south of the main island, are **Palfrey Island**, with an automatic lighthouse, **South Island** and **Seabird Islet**.

Lizard Island

Lizard Island, the furthest north of the Barrier Reef resort islands, is about 100km from Cooktown. It has 20-odd superb beaches for swimming, and relatively untouched fringing reef (a reef that fringes the coast) for snorkelling and diving. Bushwalking is another possibility, with great views from Cook's Look (360m), the highest point on the island. Apart from the ground where the luxury resort stands, the entire island is national park, which means it's open to anyone who makes the effort to get here.

Captain Cook and his crew were the first non-Indigenous people to visit the island. Having patched up the *Endeavour* in Cooktown, they sailed north and stopped on Lizard Island, where Cook and Banks climbed to the top of Cook's Look to search for a way through the Barrier Reef. Banks named the island after its large lizards, which are from the same family as Indonesia's Komodo dragons.

Jigurru (Lizard Island) has long been a sacred place for the Dingaal Aboriginal people, and worlds collided in 1881 when a group of Dingaal people attacked Mary Watson, the wife of a man who ran a trepang (sea cucumber) harvesting operation on the island. A Chinese worker Ah Sam was killed, and Mary fled the island in a trepang boiling pot with her child and another worker Ah Leong. The three eventually died of thirst on a barren island to the north; Mary left a diary of their last days that can be viewed in Brisbane's Queensland Museum.

SLEEPING

Accommodation is only available on Lizard Island, and the choice is extreme – camping or five-star luxury.

Lizard Island Resort (☎ 4060 3999, 1800 737 678; www.lizardisland.com.au; Anchor Bay; s/d from $1025/1530; 🟦 🟦 🟦) With a maximum of 80 guests in 40 villas, a menu that changes daily and spa treatments that are inspired by the sea, this is a genuine island retreat. Rooms have designer décor, a private deck, books for all those hours on the beach, and bathrobes. Rates include all meals and a range of activities.

The camping ground is at the northern end of Watson's Bay; contact **QPWS** (☎ 4069 5446; www.epa.qld.gov.au; per person $4) in Cooktown or go online to obtain a permit. There are toilets, gas barbecues, tables and benches, and fresh water is available from a pump about 250m from the site.

GETTING THERE & AWAY

Macair (☎ 13 15 28; www.macair.com.au) flies to Lizard Island from Cairns ($260, one hour). From Cooktown **Marine Air Seaplanes** (Map p465; ☎ 4069 5915; Charlotte St) has tours to Lizard Island ($330), flying into Watson's Bay and walking to the top of Cook's Look. The tour includes lunch and snorkelling gear; camping drop-off can also be arranged.

The fishing and boat-hire places in Cooktown also offer personalised charters and may be able to take you over; ask at the **Travel Centre** (Map p465; ☎ 4069 5446; Charlotte St).

Directory

CONTENTS

PRACTICALITIES

- Plugs have angled pins; voltage is 220V to 240V, 50Hz.

- Broadsheet dailies include the *Sydney Morning Herald*, Melbourne's *Age* and the national *Australian*.

- The metric system is used for weights and measures.

- Free-to-air TV is provided by the government-sponsored Australian Broadcasting Corporation (ABC) and multicultural SBS, and three commercial stations, namely Seven, Nine and Ten.

- Videos use the PAL system.

ACCOMMODATION

The East Coast is a well-trodden route with plenty of accommodation options to suit all budgets. Endowed with Australia's largest cities and most famous holiday resorts, the coast boasts abundant motels, guesthouses, B&Bs, hostels, pubs and caravan parks with camp sites. There are also lots of less-conventional possibilities such as farmstays, houseboats and yachts.

The listings in this guidebook are ordered from budget to midrange to top end, with the best options within each category listed first. Where a Sleeping section does not carry subheadings, listings are given in order of author preference. Any place that charges up to $40 per single or $80 per double has been categorised as budget accommodation. Midrange prices are from $80 to $150 per double, while the top-end tag is applied to places charging more than $150 per double. Inevitably, for the more expensive cities such as Sydney and Melbourne, our price ranges differ slightly, with budget stretching to $100 a double and midrange places going as high as $170 a double.

In many regions prices don't vary dramatically from season to season, and we have simply listed the prices that are charged for the majority of the year. In other areas there are dramatic seasonal price variations; in these cases we have listed high-season prices but not the short peak season around Christmas, when many coastal resorts have a short-lived price spike in the middle of the high season. Along the southeastern coast, the summer months are high season, particularly the school holidays that begin just before Christmas. The southern winter coincides with the mild northern dry season and the northern migration (particularly during school holidays) keeps prices high.

B&Bs

In country areas, guesthouses and B&Bs are the fastest-growing segment of the accommodation market. New places are opening all the time, and the options include everything from a room in a restored Victorian-era mansion or rambling Queenslander to a contemporary purpose-built cottage.

Tariffs cover a wide price range. They're typically in the $80 to $150 (per double) bracket, but can be much higher in areas that attract weekend getaways and romantic escapes from the cities.

Local tourist offices usually have a list of places but for some online searching try the B&B sites at www.babs.com.au or www.innaustralia.com.au.

Camping

If you want to explore the East Coast on a shoestring then camping is the way to go. Camping in national parks can cost from $4 per person – nights spent around a campfire under the stars are unforgettable. Tent sites at private camping and caravan parks cost around $12 to $20 per couple per night, a few dollars more with power.

When it comes to urban camping, remember that most city caravan parks are a long way from the centre of town. Most caravan parks are good value, with almost all of them equipped with hot showers, toilets and laundry facilities, and usually a pool. Many have on-site cabins. The size and facilities offered in these cabins varies but expect to pay $50 to $80 for two people in a cabin with a kitchenette – about the same as a cheap motel. If you intend to do a lot of caravanning or camping, it's not a bad idea to join one of the major chains such as **Big 4 Holiday Parks** (☎ 03-9421 0100, 1800 632 444; www.big4.com.au). It gives you discounts on accommodation at member parks as well as various other tourist discounts.

Note that all camping and cabin rates quoted throughout this guide are for two people.

Farmstays

Many coastal and hinterland farms offer a bed for a night and the chance to see rural Australia at work. At some you sit back and watch other people raise a sweat, while others like to get you involved in day-to-day activities. Check out the options on the website for **Australian Farmhost Holidays** (www.australiafarmhost.com). For travellers who don't mind getting their hands dirty, there's **Willing Workers on Organic Farms** (WWOOF; ☎ 03-5155 0218; www.wwoof.com.au). Regional and town tourist offices should also be able to tell you what's available in their area.

Hostels

Hostels or 'backpackers' are a highly social, low-cost fixture of the East Coast accommodation scene. There is a staggering number, ranging from family-run places in converted houses to huge, custom-built resorts replete with bars, nightclubs and a party attitude. Standards range from outstanding to awful, and management from friendly to scary.

Dorm beds typically cost $20 to $25, with singles hovering around $45 and doubles costing $60 to $80.

Useful organisations:

Nomads Backpackers (☎ 02-9264 5533, 1800 819 883; www.nomadsworld.com) Membership ($39 for 12 months) entitles you to numerous discounts.

VIP Backpacker Resorts (☎ 07-3395 6052; www.vipbackpackers.com) Membership ($41 for 12 months) entitles you to a $1 discount on accommodation and a 5% to 15% discount on other products such as air and bus transport, tours and activities.

YHA (☎ 07-3236 1680; www.yha.com.au) Membership ($39 for 12 months) entitles you to discounts at YHA and many independent hostels.

A warning for Australian and Kiwi travellers: some hostels will only admit overseas backpackers, mainly because they've had problems with locals sleeping over and bothering the backpackers. Fortunately it's only a rowdy minority that makes trouble, and often hostels will only ask for identification in order to deter potential troublemakers.

Hotels & Motels

Hotels in cities or places visited by lots of tourists are generally of the business or luxury variety where you get a comfortable, anonymous and mod con–filled room. These places tend to have a pool, restaurant/café, room service and other facilities. We quote 'rack rates' (official advertised rates) throughout this book, but often hotels will offer regular discounts and special deals.

For comfortable midrange accommodation, motels (or motor inns) are a reliable option. Almost every country town has at least one, and the larger towns have dozens to choose from. Prices vary, and there's rarely a cheaper rate for singles, so they tend to be better for couples. Most motels have similar features (tea- and coffee-making facilities, fridge, TV, air-con, bathroom) but the price will indicate the standard. You'll mostly pay between $50 and $120 for a room.

Pubs

For the budget traveller, rooms in pubs (more formally known as public houses) AKA hotels AKA 'the local' can be a good option. In the cities they are less attractive, and the rooms are either noisy or run down or both. In the country, however, pubs usually make for a convenient and often interesting choice. In tourist areas some of these pubs have been restored as they are in outstanding heritage buildings, but generally the rooms remain small and old-fashioned, with a long amble down the hall to the bathroom. Never book a room above the bar if you're a light sleeper.

Pubs usually have single/double/twin rooms with shared facilities for around $35/60/60, obviously more if you want a private bathroom. The website www.pubstay.com.au lists an array of the better places.

Rental Accommodation

Rental accommodation is found in the form of holiday flats (in tourist areas) and serviced apartments (in cities). A holiday flat is much like a motel unit but has a serviceable kitchen. Holiday flats are often rented on a weekly basis; expect to pay anywhere from $80 to $120 per night for a one-bedroom flat. Ask a local real-estate agent about holiday rentals.

If you want to stay for a longer period, the first place to look for a shared flat or a room in the cities is the classified advertisements sections of daily newspapers. Wednesday and Saturday are the best days for these ads. Notice boards at universities, hostels and cafés are also good places to look for flats and houses to share or rooms to rent.

Or try the following websites:

Australian Flatmates Directory (www.flatmates.com.au)
domain.com.au (www.domain.com.au)
Gumtree (www.gumtree.com.au)
Sleeping with the Enemy (www.sleepingwiththeenemy.com)

Keep in mind that some long-term lodgings require deposits (or bonds) and don't come furnished.

ACTIVITIES

See the East Coast Australia Outdoors chapter on p47.

BUSINESS HOURS

Most shops and businesses open at 9am and close at 5pm or 5.30pm weekdays, and at either noon or 5pm on Saturday. Sunday trading is becoming increasingly common, but it's mostly limited to the larger cities. In most towns there are usually one or two late shopping nights each week, when the doors stay open until 9pm or 9.30pm. Usually it's Thursday and/or Friday night. Supermarkets are generally open till at least 8pm and sometimes 24 hours. You'll also find milk bars (general stores) and convenience stores that open late. In tourist resort areas (eg Cairns and the Gold Coast) shops may stay open later and all day on Sunday.

Banks are generally open from 9.30am to 4pm Monday to Thursday, and until 5pm on Friday. Post offices open from 9am to 5pm Monday to Friday.

Restaurants typically open at noon for lunch and 6pm for dinner. Restaurants stay open until at least 9pm, but tend to serve food much later on Friday and Saturday nights. Cafés tend to be all-day affairs, opening at 7am and closing around 5pm, unless they simply continue their business into the night. Pubs usually serve food from noon to 2pm and from 6pm to 8pm. Pubs and bars often open at lunchtime and continue well into the evening, particularly from Thursday to Saturday.

CHILDREN
Practicalities

All cities and most major towns have centrally located public rooms where parents can go to nurse their baby or change its nappy; check with the local tourist office or city council for details. While many Australians have a relaxed attitude about breast-feeding or nappy changing in public, others frown upon it.

Most motels and better-equipped caravan parks supply cots and baby's baths; many also have playgrounds, swimming pools and in-house videos for children, as well as child-minding services. Many B&Bs, on the other hand, market themselves as sanctuaries from all things child-related.

If you want to leave Junior behind for a few hours, numerous licensed childcare agencies have places set aside for casual care, or many of the larger hotels have facilities. Licensed centres are subject to government regulation and usually have a high standard; to be on the safe side avoid unlicensed ones.

Child concessions (and family rates) often apply for such things as accommodation, tours, admission fees, and air, bus and train transport, with some discounts as high as 50% of the adult rate. However, the definition of 'child' can vary from under 12 to under 18 years.

Medical services and facilities in Australia are of a high standard, and items such as baby food formula and disposable nappies are widely available in urban centres. Major hire-car companies will supply and fit booster seats for you.

Lonely Planet's *Travel with Children* contains plenty of additional information that you may find useful.

Sights & Activities

There's plenty to keep kids occupied along the East Coast. Theme parks such as Sea World and Movie World on the Gold Coast are popular, but there are many cheaper and free options as well. In Sydney look for a copy of *Sydney's Child*, a free monthly paper listing businesses and activities that are geared to ankle biters. Websites www .sydneyschild.com.au and www.melbournes child.com.au have useful information.

CLIMATE

Australia's size means there's a lot of climatic variation along the entire East Coast, but without severe extremes. From Melbourne to Sydney the coast has cold (though generally not freezing), wet winters (June to August). Summers (December to February) are pleasant and warm, sometimes quite hot and usually dry. Violent electrical storms and sudden downpours are likely culminations to a period of hot summer weather on the coast. Spring (September to November) and autumn (March to May) are transition months, much the same as in Europe and North America.

As you head north of Sydney and into the subtropics, seasonal variation becomes less dramatic. In far north Queensland, however, you enter the monsoon belt of the tropics where there are two seasons: hot and very wet (ie the wet season), and hot and dry (the dry season).

See p15 for more information on Australia's East Coast seasons.

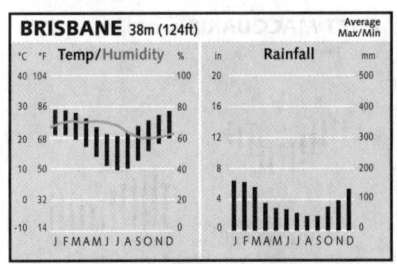

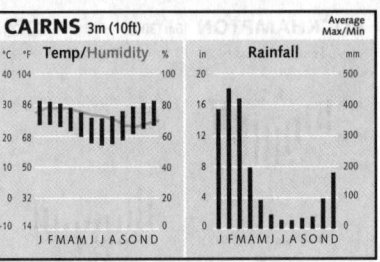

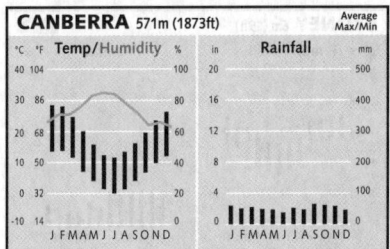

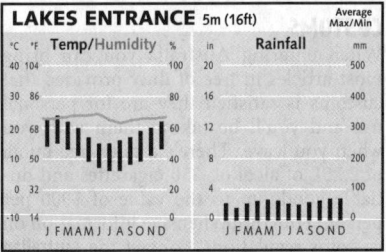

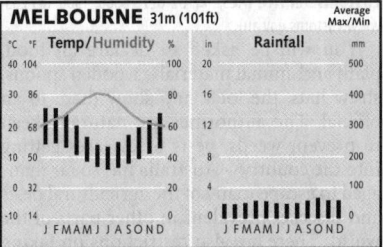

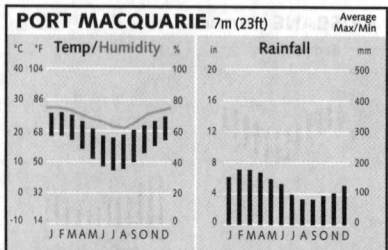

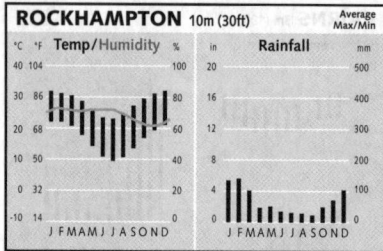

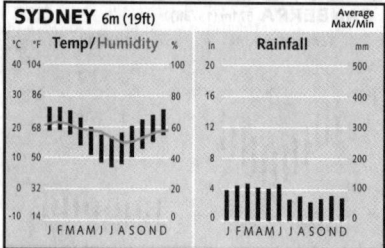

CUSTOMS

When entering Australia you can bring most articles in free of duty provided that customs is satisfied they are for personal use and you'll be taking them with you when you leave. There's a duty-free quota of 2.25L of alcohol, 250 cigarettes and dutiable goods up to the value of $900 per person. For comprehensive information on customs regulations, contact the **Australian Customs Service** (ACS; ☎ 02-6275 6666, 1300 363 263; www.customs.gov.au).

You will be asked to declare all food, plant and animal material – wooden spoons, straw hats, the lot – and show them to an official. The authorities are naturally keen to prevent weeds, pests or diseases getting into the country – Australia has so far managed to escape many of the agricultural pests and diseases prevalent in other parts of the world. There are also restrictions on taking fruit and vegetables between states (see the boxed text, p492). If you have any doubts about what you can bring into Australia, ring the closest Australian embassy or check the government's customs information see the ACS website listed above. For further information on quarantine regulations contact the **Australian Quarantine & Inspection Service** (AQIS; www.aqis.gov.au).

DANGERS & ANNOYANCES
Animal Hazards

Australia is often marvelled at for its profusion of dangerous creatures. Nothing strikes fear into the hearts of visiting campers and hikers more than stories of spiders in sleeping bags and snakes on walking trails. Australia has also had its share of shark and crocodile attacks. Of course, unless you go looking for these things, you'll probably never see one, let alone be attacked by one. Hospitals have antivenin on hand for all common snake and spider bites, but it helps to know what it was that bit you.

MARINE STINGERS

The Chironex box and the Irukandji jellyfish, also known as sea wasps or 'stingers', are found north of Agnes Water on Queensland's coast. For information on these potentially fatal hazards see the boxed text, p371.

CROCODILES

Commonly known as 'salties', saltwater (or estuarine) crocodiles are a real danger up north – they have been known to sample humans. As well as living around the coast they are found in estuaries, creeks and rivers, sometimes a long way inland. Observe safety signs or ask locals whether an inviting waterhole or river is croc-free before plunging in.

INSECTS

For four to six months of the year you'll have to cope with those two banes of the Australian outdoors – the fly and the mosquito (mozzie).

In the cities the flies aren't too bad; it's in the bush they start getting out of hand. The humble fly net, which fits on a hat, is very effective even if it looks ridiculous. Repellents may help to deter the little bastards but don't count on it.

Mozzies can be a problem in summer, especially near wetlands in tropical areas – some species are carriers of viral infections (see p500). You need to keep arms and legs covered as soon as the sun goes down and make liberal use of insect repellent.

SNAKES

There are many venomous snakes but few are aggressive – unless you're interfering with one, or have the misfortune to stand on one, it's unlikely that you'll be bitten. The most common venomous snakes in Australia are the brown and tiger snakes. The golden rule is 'if you see a snake leave it alone'. Don't try to catch or kill it. See p499 for information on treating snake bites.

SPIDERS

Nasty spiders include the funnel-web, the redback and the white-tailed spider. The deadly funnel-web spider is found in NSW (including Sydney) and its bite is treated in the same way as snake bite. The redback spider is black with a distinctive red stripe on its body; for bites, apply ice and seek medical attention. The white-tailed is a long, thin black spider with, you guessed it, a white tail, and has a nasty bite that can lead to local inflammation and ulceration. The large and frightening huntsman spider, which often enters homes, is harmless.

Bushfires & Blizzards

Bushfires happen every year along the East Coast. In hot, dry and windy weather, be extremely careful with any flame – cigarette butts thrown out of the windows of cars have started many a fire. On a total fire ban day it is forbidden even to use a camping stove. The locals won't be amused if they catch you; they'll happily dob you in, and the penalties are severe.

Take local advice before setting out on a bushwalk. On a day of total fire ban, don't go; delay your trip until the weather has changed. If you're out in the bush and you see smoke, even a long way away, take it seriously. Go to the nearest open space, downhill if possible. A forested ridge is the most dangerous place to be. Bushfires move very quickly and change direction with the wind.

Still, more bushwalkers die of cold than in bushfires. Even in summer, temperatures can drop below freezing at night in the mountains

and the weather can change very quickly. Exposure in even moderately cool temperatures can sometimes result in hypothermia; for more information on hypothermia and how to minimise its risk, see p500.

Driving

Australian drivers are generally fairly courteous, but there are some particular dangers on the open road in rural areas. See p491 for more information.

Swimming

Be aware that many surf beaches can be dangerous places to swim if you are not used to the conditions. Undertows (or rips) are the main problem, but a number of people are paralysed each year by diving into waves in shallow water and hitting a sand bar – check first.

Many beaches are patrolled by surf lifesavers, and patrolled areas are marked off by flags. If you swim between the flags, help should arrive quickly if you get into trouble; raise your arm (and yell) if you need help. Outside the flags and on unpatrolled beaches you are more or less on your own.

If you find yourself being carried out by a rip, the important thing to do is just keep afloat; don't panic or try to swim against the rip. In most cases the current stops within a couple of hundred metres of the shore; swim parallel to the shore for a short way to get out of the rip and then make your way back.

Theft

The East Coast is a relatively safe place to visit but you should still take the usual precautions. Don't leave hotel rooms or cars unlocked. Most hotels have lockers or at least a safe at reception where you can leave your valuables. Don't leave money, wallets, purses or cameras unattended or in full view through car windows, and don't leave valuables on the beach unattended. If you are unlucky enough to have something stolen, immediately report all details to the nearest police station.

DISABLED TRAVELLERS

Disability awareness in Australia is reasonably high. Legislation requires that new accommodation must meet accessibility standards and tourist operators must not discriminate.

Reliable information is the key ingredient for travellers with a disability, and the best place to start is the **National Information Communication & Awareness Network** (Nican; ☎ / TTY 02-6285 3713, TTY 1800 806 769; www.nican.com.au; 4/2 Phipps Cl, Deakin, ACT 2600). It's an Australia-wide directory providing information on access, accommodation, sporting and recreational activities, transport and specialist tour operators.

The website of the **Australian Tourist Commission** (ATC; www.australia.com) publishes detailed, downloadable information for people with disabilities, including travel and transport tips and contact addresses of organisations in each state. For more on the commission, see Tourist Information (p481). It publishes *Travel in Australia for People with Disabilities*, which has travel tips and contact addresses of useful organisations. Look out for *Accessing Sydney*, *Accessing Melbourne* and *Access Brisbane*, which provide a directory of accessible activities, accommodation and events.

Easy Access Australia is a publication that provides details on easily accessible transport, accommodation and attraction options. You can order it from the website www.easyaccessaustralia.com.au.

Getting Around

All of Australia's major airports have dedicated disabled parking spaces, wheelchair access to terminals, accessible toilets and facilities to convey passengers onto planes. **Qantas** (☎ 13 13 13, 1800 652 660) accepts Carers Concession Cards, which entitle disabled persons and carers travelling with them to a 50% discount on the full economy fare; call Nican for eligibility and an application form.

The international wheelchair symbol (blue on a white background) for parking in allocated bays is recognised. Maps of central business districts showing accessible routes, toilets etc are available from major city councils, some regional councils and at information centres.

Most of the taxi companies in major cities and towns have modified vehicles to accommodate wheelchairs. Avis and Hertz offer hire cars with hand controls at no extra charge for pick up at capital cities and the major airports, but advance notice is required.

DISCOUNT CARDS
Senior Cards

Australian senior travellers with some form of identification are often eligible for concession prices. Overseas pensioners are entitled to discounts of at least 10% on most express bus fares and bus passes with Greyhound. Travellers over 60 years of age (both Australian residents and visitors) will simply need to present current age-proving identification to be eligible for discounts off regular air fares.

Student & Youth Cards

Carrying a student card entitles you to a wide variety of discounts throughout Australia. The most common card is the International Student Identity Card (ISIC), which is issued to full-time students aged 12 years and over, and gives the bearer discounts on accommodation, transport and admission to some attractions. It's available from student unions, hostelling organisations and some travel agencies; for more information, see the website of the **International Student Travel Confederation** (ISTC; www.istc.org).

The ISTC is also the body behind the International Youth Travel Card (IYTC or Go25), which is issued to people who are between 12 and 26 years of age and not full-time students, and gives equivalent benefits to the ISIC. A similar ISTC brainchild is the International Teacher Identity Card (ITIC), available to teaching professionals.

EMBASSIES & CONSULATES
Australian Embassies & Consulates

The **Department of Foreign Affairs & Trade** (www.dfat.gov.au) lists all Australian diplomatic missions overseas. They include:

Canada (☎ 613-236 0841; www.ahc-ottawa.org; Suite 710, 7th fl, 50 O'Connor St, Ottawa, Ontario K1P 6L2) Also in Vancouver and Toronto.

France (☎ 01 40 59 33 00; www.france.embassy.gov.au; 4 Rue Jean Rey, 75724 Paris Cedex 15)

Germany (☎ 030-880 08 80; www.australian-embassy .de; Wallstrasse 76-79, Berlin 10179) Also in Frankfurt.

Ireland (☎ 01-664 5300; www.australianembassy.ie; 7th fl, Fitzwilton House, Wilton Terrace, Dublin 2)

Japan (☎ 03-5232 4111; www.australia.or.jp; 2-1-14 Mita, Minato-Ku, Tokyo 108-8361) Also in Osaka, Nagoya and Fukuoka City.

Netherlands (☎ 070-310 82 00; www.australian-embassy.nl; Carnegielaan 4, The Hague 2517 KH)

New Zealand Auckland (☎ 09-921 8800; Level 7, Price Waterhouse Coopers Bldg, 186-194 Quay St, Auckland);

Wellington (☎ 04-473 6411; www.aust
ralia.org.nz; 72-76 Hobson St, Thorndon, Wellington)
Singapore (☎ 6836 4100; www.singapore.embassy
.gov.au; 25 Napier Rd, Singapore 258507)
South Africa (☎ 27 12 342 3781; www.australia.co.za;
292 Orient Street, Arcadia, Pretoria 0083)
UK (☎ 020-7379 4334; www.australia.org.uk; Australia
House, The Strand, London WC2B 4LA) Also in Edinburgh
and Manchester.
USA (☎ 202-797 3000; www.austemb.org; 1601 Mas-
sachusetts Ave NW, Washington DC 20036) Also in Los
Angeles, New York and other major cities.

Embassies & Consulates in Australia

The principal diplomatic representations to
Australia are in Canberra; there are also
representatives of some countries in Brisbane, Melbourne and Sydney; look in the
Yellow Pages for a complete listing.
Canada Canberra (☎ 02-6270 4000; www.dfait-maeci
.gc.ca/australia; Commonwealth Ave, Canberra, ACT 2600);
Melbourne (☎ 03-9653 9674; Level 50, 101 Collins St,
Melbourne, Vic 3000); Sydney (☎ 02-9364 3000; Level 5,
111 Harrington St, Sydney, NSW 2000)
France Brisbane (☎ 07-3229 8201; Level 10, AXA Bldg,
144 Edward St, Brisbane, Qld, 4000); Canberra (☎ 02-6216
0100; www.ambafrance-au.org; 6 Perth Ave, Yarralumla,
ACT 2600); Melbourne (☎ 03-9602 5024; Suite 805, Level
8, 150 Queen Street, Melbourne, Vic 3000); Sydney (☎ 02-
9261 5779; www.consulfrance-sydney.org; Level 26, St
Martins Tower, 31 Market St, Sydney, NSW 2000)
Germany Brisbane (☎ 07-3221 7819; 10 Eagle St,
Brisbane, Qld 4000); Canberra (☎ 02-6270 1911; www
.germanembassy.org.au; 119 Empire Circuit, Yarralumla,
ACT 2600); Melbourne (☎ 03-9864 6888; 480 Punt Rd,
South Yarra, Vic 3141); Sydney (☎ 02-9328 7733;
13 Trelawney St, Woollahra, NSW 2025)
Ireland Canberra (☎ 02-6273 3022; irishemb@cyberone
.com.au; 20 Arkana St, Yarralumla, ACT 2600); Sydney
(☎ 02-9231 6999; Level 30, 400 George St, Sydney, NSW
2000)
Japan Canberra (☎ 02-6273 3244; www.japan.org.au;
112 Empire Circuit, Yarralumla, ACT 2600); Sydney (☎ 02-
9231 3455; Level 34, Colonial Centre, 52 Martin Pl, Sydney,
NSW 2000)
Netherlands Canberra (☎ 02-6220 9400; www.nether
lands.org.au; 120 Empire Circuit, Yarralumla, ACT
2600); Melbourne (☎ 03-9670 5573; melbourne.
consulate@netherlands.org.au; Level 4, 118 Queen St,
Melbourne Vic 3000); Sydney (☎ 02-9387 6644; Level 23,
Plaza Tower II, 500 Oxford St, Bondi Junction, NSW 2022)
New Zealand Canberra (☎ 02-6270 4211;
nzhccba@austarmetro.com.au; Commonwealth Ave, Canberra, ACT 2600); Sydney (☎ 02-8256 2000; nzcgsydney@
bigpond.com; Level 10, 55 Hunter St, Sydney, NSW 2000)

Singapore Canberra (☎ 02-6273 3944; 17 Forster Cres,
Yarralumla, ACT 2600)
South Africa Canberra (☎ 02-6273 2424; www.rsa
.emb.gov.au; cnr Rhodes Place & State Circle, Yarralumla,
ACT 2600)
UK Brisbane (☎ 07-3223 3200; Level 26, 1 Eagle St,
Brisbane, Qld 4000); Canberra (☎ 02-6270 6666; www
.uk.emb.gov.au; Commonwealth Ave, Yarralumla, ACT
2600); Melbourne (☎ 03-9652 1600; 17th fl, 90 Collins St,
Melbourne, Vic 3000); Sydney (☎ 02-9247 7521; 16th fl,
1 Macquarie Pl, Sydney Cove, NSW 2000)
USA Canberra (☎ 02-6214 5600; http://usembassy-
australia.state.gov/index.html; 21 Moonah Pl, Yarralumla,
ACT 2600); Melbourne (☎ 03-9526 5900; 553 St Kilda Rd,
Melbourne, Vic 3004); Sydney (☎ 02-9373 9200; Level 59,
19-29 Martin Pl, Sydney, NSW 2000)

FESTIVALS & EVENTS

Some of the most enjoyable festivals are also
the most typically Australian, like surf life-
saving competitions on beaches during summer. There are also some big city-based street
festivals, sporting events, and arts festivals
that showcase comedy, music and dance.

The following is a snapshot of some of the
many festivals and special events held along
the East Coast during the year. Tourist offices should be able to give precise dates.

January

Big Day Out (www.bigdayout.com) This huge open-air
music concert tours Sydney, Melbourne and the Gold Coast
(as well as Adelaide and Perth), stopping over for one day
in each city. It attracts big-name international acts and
dozens of local bands.
Midsumma (www.midsumma.org.au) Melbourne's gay,
lesbian and transgender festival runs through January and
February, starts with a street party, includes the famous
Red Raw dance party and ends with the Midsumma
Carnival in early February.

February

Sydney Gay & Lesbian Mardi Gras (www.mardigras
.org.au) One of Australia's biggest and wildest festivals,
the month-long Mardi Gras has an amazing street parade
down Oxford St and a riotous Mardi Gras party.

March/April

East Coast Blues and Roots Festival (www.bluesfest
.com.au) There's an explosion of music over the Easter long
weekend when artists from all over the world set up camp
in lovely Byron Bay.
Melbourne International Comedy Festival (www
.comedyfestival.com.au) Just over three weeks of laughs can
be had at one of the largest comedy festivals in the world.

May

Nimbin Mardi Grass The alternative community of Nimbin swells for this mother-of-all-hippy-festivals – pitch a tent and chill out, man.

Wintermoon Festival (www.wintermoonfestival.com) Held 70km north of Mackay each year around May/June, this festival is a great opportunity to hear local and interstate musicians strut their stuff.

June

Cooktown Endeavour Festival Commemorating Captain Cook's landing in 1770, this knees-up is held over the Queen's Birthday weekend.

July

Brisbane Festival of Music Held biennially (odd-numbered years), this festival features Australian and international musicians and styles: jazz, rock, indigenous, classical and world music.

Melbourne International Film Festival (www .melbournefilmfestival.com.au) Australia's oldest international film event presents the best in contemporary world cinema.

August

Hervey Bay Whale Festival Held over a fortnight, this festival celebrates the return of these magnificent creatures.

September

AFL Grand Final (www.afl.com.au) The football season culminates with one of Australia's biggest sporting events: the AFL Grand Final at the MCG in Melbourne on the last Saturday in September.

October

IndyCar (www.indy.com.au) Rev your engine for the IndyCar race and the parties that follow in its tailwind. Surfers Paradise is manic at the best of times but during this three-day celebration it really goes off.

Melbourne Festival (www.melbournefestival.com.au) This annual festival offers some of the best of opera, theatre, dance and the visual arts from around Australia and the world. It starts in early October and runs to early November.

November

Melbourne Cup (www.melbournecup.com.au) Australia's premier horse race is in Melbourne, but the whole country shuts down while the race is run. Many country towns schedule race meetings to coincide with it; people take the afternoon off work and wear posh hats at the pub.

December

Sydney to Hobart Yacht Race Sydney Harbour is a sight to behold on Boxing Day (26 December), when boats of all shapes and sizes crowd its waters to farewell the yachts competing in this gruelling race.

Woodford Folk Festival Held between Christmas and New Year, this five-day festival in Queensland is Australia's largest folk festival.

FOOD

There's an impressive range and quality of food in major cities of the East Coast, largely thanks to the immigrants who flooded into Australia in the late 20th century, bringing their cuisines with them. The eating recommendations provided in this book are grouped into restaurants, cafés, quick eats, and self-catering. Within these groups we endeavour to cover the whole gamut of price levels and cuisines with a critical eye on quality, value and ambience.

Quality restaurants charge from $18 to $40 for a main course. The best value can be found in ethnic restaurants and modern cafés, where a good meal in casual surroundings costs less than $20 and a cooked breakfast will set you back about $10. A number of inner-city pubs offer upmarket restaurant-style fare, but most serve standard (often large-portion) bistro meals, usually in the $10 to $19 range. Bar (or counter) meals, which are eaten in the public bar, usually cost between $6 and $10. Generally, opening hours for breakfast are between 6am and 11am, lunch is served from around noon to 3pm and dinner usually starts after 6pm.

See also p56.

GAY & LESBIAN TRAVELLERS

The East Coast of Australia – Sydney especially – is a popular destination for gay and lesbian travellers. Certain areas are the focus of the gay and lesbian communities: Cairns and Noosa in Queensland; Sydney's Oxford St and Kings Cross; the Blue Mountains, Hunter Valley and the NSW north-coast hinterland; and the Melbourne suburbs of Prahran, St Kilda and Collingwood are all popular areas. As well as Sydney's Mardi Gras in February to early March, there's Melbourne's Midsumma Festival in January and February.

In general Australians are open-minded about homosexuality, but the further out of the big towns and cities you get, the more likely you are to run into homophobia. Homosexual acts are legal in all states but the age of consent between males varies. In the Australian Capital

Territory, Victoria and NSW it is 16 years, and in Queensland it is 18.

Australia's gay community produces a wide range of publications including *DNA*, *Lesbians on the Loose* and the art magazine *Blue*.

Useful websites:

Gay & Lesbian Tourism Australia (Galta; www.galta .com.au)

Gay Australia (www.gayaustraliaguide.bigstep.com)

Pink Board (www.pinkboard.com.au)

HOLIDAYS
Public Holidays

Public holidays vary quite a bit from state to state. The following is a list of the main national and state public holidays; for precise dates (which vary from year to year), check locally (* indicates holidays are only observed locally).

NATIONAL
New Year's Day 1 January
Australia Day 26 January
Easter (Good Friday to Easter Monday inclusive) March/April
Anzac Day 25 April
Queen's Birthday Second Monday in June
Christmas Day 25 December
Boxing Day 26 December

NEW SOUTH WALES
Bank Holiday First Monday in August
Labour Day First Monday in October

QUEENSLAND
Labour Day First Monday in May
RNA Show Day (Brisbane) August *

VICTORIA
Labour Day Second Monday in March
Melbourne Cup Day First Tuesday in November*

School Holidays

The Christmas holiday season, from mid-December to late January, is part of the summer school vacation; it's the time you are most likely to find accommodation booked out and long queues at tourist attractions. There are three shorter school holiday periods during the year, but they vary by a week or two from state to state. They fall from early to mid-April, late June to mid-July, and late September to early October.

INSURANCE

Don't underestimate the importance of a good travel-insurance policy that covers theft, loss and medical problems. Most policies offer lower and higher medical-expense options; the higher ones are chiefly for countries that have extremely high medical costs, such as the USA. There is a wide variety of policies available, so compare the small print.

Some policies specifically exclude designated 'dangerous activities' such as scuba diving, parasailing, bungee jumping, motorcycling, skiing and even bushwalking. If you plan on doing any of these things, make sure the policy you choose fully covers you for your activity of choice.

See p496 for information on health insurance and p490 for information on insurance related to car travel and rental.

INTERNET ACCESS

Email and Internet addicts will find it fairly easy to get connected throughout East Coast Australia. Connection speeds and prices vary from one place to the next, but they all offer straightforward access to the Internet. All public libraries have limited access, or there are loads of Internet cafés with super-fast connections. Access charges range from $4 to $9 an hour. The average is about $6 an hour, usually with a minimum of 10 minutes access. Most youth hostels and backpacker places can hook you up, as can many hotels and caravan parks.

If you're bringing your own palmtop or notebook computer, check with your Internet Service Provider (ISP) to find out if there are access numbers you can dial into. Be aware that your modem may not work once you leave your home country. The safest option is to buy a reputable 'global' modem before you leave home, or buy a local PC-card modem if you're spending an extended time in any one country. For more information on travelling with a portable computer, see www.teleadapt .com.

Australia primarily uses the RJ-45 telephone plugs, although you may see Telstra EXI-160 four-pin plugs; electronics shops such as Tandy and Dick Smith should be able to help. Most motel and hotel rooms have phone/modem sockets.

Also see p17 for Internet Resources.

LEGAL MATTERS

Most travellers will have no contact with the Australian police or any other part of the legal system. Those that do are likely to experience it while driving. The country's roads have a significant police presence, with the power to stop your car and ask to see your licence (you're required to carry it), check your vehicle for roadworthiness, and also to insist that you take a breath test to check your blood-alcohol level – needless to say, drink-driving offences are taken very seriously here.

First offenders who are caught with small amounts of illegal drugs are likely to get a fine rather than go to jail, but nonetheless the recording of a conviction against you may affect your visa status.

If you are arrested, it's your right to telephone a friend, relative or lawyer before any formal questioning begins. Legal Aid is available only in serious cases and only to the truly needy (for links to Legal Aid offices see www.nla.aust.net.au). However, many solicitors do not charge for an initial consultation.

MAPS

You'll find plenty of maps available when you arrive in Australia. Tourist offices usually have good, free maps of the region; these are usually all you will need. Automobile associations (p489) are a good source of reliable road maps.

Lonely Planet publishes handy foldout city maps of Melbourne, Sydney, and Brisbane and the Gold Coast, and also publishes the *Australia Road Atlas*, a comprehensive, easy-to-use book covering the entire country. City street directories such as those produced by Ausway and UBD are very useful

but they're expensive, bulky and usually only worth getting if you intend to do a lot of city driving.

For bushwalking and other outdoor activities for which large-scale maps are essential, browse the topographic sheets put out by **Geoscience Australia** (☎ 02-6201 4201, 1800 800 173; www.ga.gov.au; Scrivener Bldg, Dunlop Ct, Fern Hill Park, Bruce, ACT 2617). Many of the more popular sheets are usually available over the counter at outdoor-equipment shops.

MONEY

In this book, unless otherwise stated, all prices given in dollars refer to Australian dollars. Exchange rates are listed on the front cover flap. For an idea of the money required to travel in East Coast Australia, see p15.

ATMs & Eftpos

ANZ, Commonwealth, National and Westpac bank branches are found nationwide and most have 24-hour ATMs attached. Of course, you won't find ATMs everywhere – not off the beaten track or in very small towns – so make sure you've got cash if you're heading well away from population centres on a weekend. Most ATMs now accept cards from other banks and are linked to international networks.

Eftpos (Electronic Funds Transfer at Point of Sale) is a very convenient service that many Australian businesses have embraced. It means you can use your bank card to pay for services or purchases direct, and often withdraw cash as well. Eftpos is available practically everywhere these days, but many places demand a minimum purchase of about $10.

Cash

Australia's currency is the Australian dollar, made up of 100 cents. There are 5¢, 10¢, 20¢, 50¢, $1 and $2 coins, and $5, $10, $20, $50 and $100 notes. Although the smallest coin in circulation is 5¢, prices are often still marked in single cents, and then rounded to the nearest 5¢ when you come to pay.

Credit Cards

Credit cards (Visa and MasterCard) are accepted widely along the East Coast. Charge cards such as Diners Club and Amex are not as widely accepted. Credit cards can

---

HOW OLD?

- You can drive when you're 17.

- The legal age for voting is 18.

- The heterosexual age of consent is 16 (Victoria and NSW) or 17 (Queensland). The age of consent between males is 16 in the ACT, Victoria and NSW, and 18 in Queensland.

- The legal drinking age is 18.

also be used to get cash advances over the counter at banks and from many ATMs, depending on the card. Fees for using your debit card at a foreign bank or ATM vary depending on your home bank; ask before you leave.

The most flexible option is to carry both a credit and a debit card; some banking institutions link the two to one card.

Moneychangers
Changing travellers cheques or foreign currency usually isn't a problem at banks in the region. Licensed moneychangers such as American Express will only be found in major cities; most large hotels will change currency or travellers cheques for guests, but the rates are generally poor.

Tipping
In Australia, tipping is not seen as the essential part of society it is in the USA. As in the UK and most of continental Europe, it's customary to tip in restaurants and also in upmarket cafés. This applies more in the cities, particularly Melbourne and Sydney. Out in the sticks, a tip might be received with a level of surprise. Tip if you think the service warrants it; 5% to 10% of the bill is usually enough. Taxi drivers don't expect tips as such but many of them do expect you to round up to the nearest dollar and may fuss over the handing out of change if you don't offer.

Travellers Cheques
Amex, Thomas Cook and other well-known international brands of travellers cheques are easily exchanged. You need to present your passport for identification when cashing them.

Increasingly, international travellers simply withdraw cash from ATMs, enjoying the convenience and the usually good exchange rates.

POST
Australia's postal services are efficient and reasonably cheap. It costs 50¢ to send a standard letter or postcard within the country. **Australia Post** (www.auspost.com.au) has divided international destinations into two regions: Asia-Pacific and Rest of the World. Airmail letters up to 50g cost $1.10 and $1.65 respectively. The cost of a postcard (up to 20g) is $1 and an aerogram to any country is 85¢. There

are five international parcel zones and rates vary by distance and class of service.

All post offices will hold mail for visitors, and some city GPOs (main or general post offices) have very busy poste restante sections. You need to provide some form of identification (such as a passport) to collect mail. Post office opening hours are generally 9am to 5pm Monday to Friday.

SOLO TRAVELLERS
People travelling alone along the East Coast face the unpredictability that is an inherent part of making contact with entire communities of strangers: sometimes you'll be completely ignored, and other times you'll be greeted with such enthusiasm it's as if you've been spontaneously adopted. Suffice to say that the latter moments will likely become highlights of your trip.

Solo travellers are a common sight in Australia and there is certainly no stigma attached to lone visitors. In some places you may find there's an expectation that solo visitors should engage in some way with the locals, particularly in rural pubs where keeping to yourself can prove harder than it sounds. Women travelling on their own should exercise caution when in less-populated areas, and will find that guys can get annoyingly attentive in drinking establishments.

TELEPHONE
There are several providers offering services. The two main players are the mostly government-owned **Telstra** (www.telstra.com.au)

and the fully private **Optus** (www.optus.com.au). Both are also major players in the mobile (cell) market.

Domestic & International Calls

INFORMATION & TOLL-FREE CALLS

Numbers starting with ☎ 190 are usually recorded information services, charged at anything from 35¢ to $5 or more per minute (more from mobiles and payphones). To make a reverse-charge (collect) call from any public or private phone, just dial ☎ 1800-REVERSE (738 3773) or ☎ 12 550.

Toll-free numbers (prefix ☎ 1800) can be called free of charge from anywhere in Australia, though they may not be accessible from interstate or from mobile phones. Calls to numbers beginning with ☎ 13 or ☎ 1300 are charged at the rate of a local call. Telephone numbers beginning with ☎ 1800, ☎ 13 or ☎ 1300 cannot be dialled from outside Australia.

INTERNATIONAL CALLS

If dialling from overseas, the country code is ☎ 61 and you need to drop the 0 (zero) in the area codes.

Most payphones allow ISD (International Subscriber Dialling) calls; the cost and international dialling code will vary depending on which provider you're using. International calls from Australia are very cheap and subject to specials that reduce the rates even more, so it's worth shopping around.

The **Country Direct service** (☎ 1800 801 800) connects callers in Australia with operators in nearly 60 countries to make reverse-charge or credit-card calls.

When calling overseas you need to dial the international access code from Australia (☎ 0011 or ☎ 0018).

LOCAL CALLS

Calls from private phones cost 15¢ to 25¢ while local calls from public phones cost 40¢; both involve unlimited talk time. Calls to mobile phones attract higher rates and are timed. Blue phones or gold phones that you sometimes find in hotel lobbies or other businesses usually cost a minimum of 50¢ for a local call.

LONG DISTANCE CALLS & AREA CODES

For long-distance calls, East Coast Australia uses four Subscriber Trunk Dialling (STD) area codes. STD calls can be made from virtually any public phone and are cheaper during off-peak hours, generally between 7pm and 7am. Long-distance calls (ie more than about 50km away) within these areas are charged at long-distance rates, even though they have the same area code. The following are the area codes in East Coast Australia:

State/Territory	Area code
Australian Capital Territory	☎ 02
New South Wales	☎ 02
Queensland	☎ 07
Victoria	☎ 03

Mobile Phones

Local numbers with the prefixes ☎ 04xx or ☎ 04xxx belong to mobile phones. Australia's mobile networks – digital GSM and digital CDMA – service more than 90% of the population, but vast tracts of Australia's interior are uncovered. The East Coast gets good reception, but away from the major towns it can be haphazard or nonexistent.

Australia's digital network is compatible with GSM 900 and 1800 (used in Europe), but generally not with the systems used in the USA or Japan. It's easy and cheap enough to get connected short-term, though, as the main service providers all have prepaid mobile systems. Just buy a starter kit, which may include a phone or, if you have your own phone, a SIM card (around $15) and a prepaid charge card. The calls tend to be a bit more expensive than with standard contracts, but there are no connection fees or line-rental charges and you can buy the recharge cards at convenience stores and newsagents. Don't forget to shop around between the various carriers (such as Optus, Telstra, Vodaphone and 3) as their products differ.

Phonecards

A wide range of phonecards is available; they can be bought at newsagents and post offices for a fixed dollar value (usually $10, $20, $30 etc) and can be used with any public or private phone by dialling a toll-free access number and then the PIN number on the card. Once again, it's well worth shopping around. Some public phones also accept credit cards.

TIME

Victoria, NSW and Queensland keep Eastern Standard Time, which is 10 hours ahead of Greenwich Mean Time (UTC). When it's noon in Sydney, the time in London is 3am (April to October) or 1am (November to March); 5pm/7pm the previous day in Los Angeles, 8pm/10pm the previous day in New York and 2pm in Auckland.

Daylight saving – for which clocks are put forward an hour – operates in Victoria and NSW from the last Sunday in October to the last Sunday in March. Queensland doesn't have daylight saving.

TOURIST INFORMATION

Tourist information is provided in Australia by various regional and local offices, details of which are given in the relevant city and town sections throughout this book. Each state has a government-run tourist organisation ready to inundate you with information. Check out the following:

Tourism New South Wales (☎ 13 20 77; www.tourism .nsw.gov.au)

Tourism Queensland (☎ 13 18 01; www.tq.com.au)

Tourism Victoria (☎ 13 28 42; www.visitvictoria.com.au)

The **Australian Tourism Commission** (ATC; ☎ 02-9360 1111, 1300 361 650; www.australia.com; 4th fl, 80 William St, Woolloomooloo, NSW 2011) is the government body charged with improving foreign tourist relations and has a website with information in nine languages (including French and German). For ATC branches in other countries visit www.tour ism.australia.com.

TOURS

There are all sorts of tours along the East Coast for all budgets: camping tours, adventure tours and 4WD safaris are just a start. You can also walk, ski, boat, raft, canoe, ride a horse or camel, or take to the air in a balloon, helicopter, microlight or other plane. To go into detail here would be impossible, but we list some of the better or more interesting operators throughout this book. For comprehensive listings contact the various state tourism organisations (see the previous section). If you're travelling between Melbourne, Sydney, Brisbane and even further north and want to visit the highlights along the way, there are some interesting hop-on hop-off bus tour alternatives (see p488 for details).

VISAS

All visitors to Australia need a visa. Only New Zealand nationals are exempt, and even they receive a 'special category' visa on arrival.

Visa application forms are available from Australian diplomatic missions overseas, travel agents and the website of the **Department of Immigration & Multicultural & Indigenous Affairs** (☎ 13 18 81; www.immi.gov.au). There are several types of visa, as explained in the following sections.

Electronic Travel Authority

Many visitors can get an Electronic Travel Authority (ETA) through International Air Transport Association (IATA) registered travel agents or overseas airline. They make the application direct when you buy a ticket and issue the ETA, which replaces the usual visa stamped in your passport; it's common practice for travel agents to charge a fee for issuing an ETA (usually US$15). This system is available to passport holders of some 33 countries, including the UK, the USA and Canada, most European and Scandinavian countries, Malaysia, Singapore, Japan and Korea. You can also make an online ETA application at www.eta.immi.gov.au, where no fees apply.

Tourist Visas

Short-term tourist visas have largely been replaced by the free ETA. However, if you are from a country not covered by the ETA, or you want to stay longer than three months, you'll need to apply for a visa. Standard visas (which cost $65) allow one (or in some cases multiple) entry and stays of up to three months, and are valid for use within 12 months of issue. A long-stay tourist visa (also $65) can allow a visit of up to a year.

Visa Extensions

Visitors are allowed a maximum stay of 12 months, including extensions. Visa extensions are made through the Department of Immigration & Multicultural & Indigenous Affairs and it's best to apply at least two or three weeks before your visa expires. The application fee is $160 – it's nonrefundable, even if your application is rejected.

Working Holiday Makers Visas

Young, single visitors from Canada, Cyprus, Denmark, Finland, Germany, Hong Kong, Ireland, Japan, Korea, Malta, the Netherlands, Norway, Sweden and the UK are eligible for a Working Holiday Makers (WHM) visa, which allows you to visit for up to two years and gain casual employment. 'Young' is defined as between 18 and 30 years of age, and visa holders are only supposed to work for any one employer for a maximum of three months. There is an application fee of $160, and visas must be applied for only at Australian diplomatic missions abroad. For more information on the WHM, see www.immi.gov.au/e_visa /visit.htm.

WORK

New Zealanders can work in Australia without having to apply for a special visa or permit, but other short-term visitors can only work in Australia if they have a Working Holiday (WH) visa. Major tourist centres like the resort towns along the Queensland coast and the ski fields of Victoria and NSW are all good prospects for casual work during peak seasons.

Seasonal fruit-picking (harvesting) relies on casual labour, and there is something to be picked, pruned or farmed somewhere in Australia all year round. It's hard work that involves early morning starts, and you're usually paid by how much you pick (per bin/bucket); expect to earn A$50 to A$60 a day to start with, more when you get quicker at it. Some work, such as pruning or sorting, is paid by the hour. **Harvest Hotline** (☎ 1300 720 126) can connect you with the relevant fruit-picking regions.

Other options for casual employment include factory work, labouring, bar work and waiting on tables. People with computer, secretarial, nursing and teaching skills can find work temping in the major cities by registering with a relevant agency.

Resources

Australian Job Search (www.jobsearch.gov.au) is a Commonwealth government agency with plenty of jobs on offer, including a 'Harvest Trail' for backpackers to follow around

the country. **My Career** (www.mycareer.com.au) is one of the country's busiest employment websites.

Backpacker accommodation, magazines and newspapers are good resources for local work opportunities. **Workabout Australia** (www .workaboutaustralia.com.au), a book by Barry Brebner, details seasonal work opportunities.

Tax & Superannuation

If you have a WH visa, you should apply for a Tax File Number (TFN). Without it, tax will be deducted from any wages you receive at the maximum rate (around 47%). Apply for a TFN online via the **Australian Taxation Office** (ATO; ☎ 13 28 61; www.ato.gov.au); it takes about four weeks to issue.

Even with a TFN, nonresidents (including WH visa holders) pay a higher rate of tax than Australian residents, especially those on a low income. There's no tax-free threshold for nonresidents, so you pay tax on every dollar you earn, starting at 29% on an annual income of up to A$21,600 (A$415 per week).

If tax is deducted as you earn, it's unlikely you'll be entitled to a tax refund when you leave Australia. However, if you have had tax deducted at 47% because you didn't submit a TFN, you will be entitled to a partial refund of tax paid. To get the refund you must lodge a tax return with the ATO.

To lodge a tax return you must first obtain a TFN and have a copy of your Group Certificate (an official summary of your earnings and tax payments) provided by your employer; give them written advice at least 14 days in advance that you want the certificate on your last day at work, otherwise you may have to wait until the end of the financial year (30 June).

As part of the government's compulsory superannuation scheme, if you're earning more than A$450 per calendar month your employer must make contributions on your behalf to a retirement or superannuation (super) fund. These contributions are at the rate of 9% of your wage, and the money must remain in the fund until you reach 'preservation age', currently 60 years. Find out the latest from the ATO and the relevant super fund.

Transport

CONTENTS

GETTING THERE & AWAY

This section covers how to get to/from major cities along the East Coast for visitors to Australia. For information about travelling along the East Coast see p486.

ENTERING THE COUNTRY

Disembarkation in Australia is generally a straightforward affair, with only the usual customs declarations (p472) and the race to the luggage carousel to endure. If you're flying in with Qantas, Air New Zealand, British Airways, Cathay Pacific, Japan Airlines or Singapore Airlines, ask the carrier about the 'Express' passenger card, which will speed your way through customs.

Recent global instability, thanks (or rather, no thanks) to terrorism and war-fever have resulted in conspicuously increased security in Australian airports, both in domestic and international terminals, and you may find that customs procedures are now more time-consuming.

Passport

There are no restrictions when it comes to foreign citizens entering Australia. If you have a visa (p481) you should be fine.

THINGS CHANGE...

The information in this chapter is particularly vulnerable to change. You should check directly with the airline or a travel agent to make sure you understand how a fare (and ticket you may buy) works and be aware of the security requirements for international travel. Shop carefully. The details given in this chapter should be regarded as pointers and are not a substitute for your own careful, up-to-date research.

AIR – DOMESTIC

The domestic airline industry has undergone some major upheavals in recent years, with intense competition among airlines. Few people pay full fare as the airlines continue to offer a wide range of discounts. These come and go and there are regular special fares, so keep your eyes open.

Airlines

Jetstar (☎ 13 15 38; www.jetstar.com.au) Flies to Adelaide, Brisbane, Cairns, Gold Coast, Hamilton Island, Hobart, Launceston, Mackay, Melbourne, Newcastle, Rockhampton, Sydney, Sunshine Coast and Whitsunday Coast (Proserpine).

Qantas (☎ 13 13 13; www.qantas.com.au) Flies to all capital cities and numerous regional centres.

QantasLink (☎ 13 13 13; www.qantas.com.au) Qantas affiliate that covers some regional routes.

Regional Express (Rex; ☎ 13 17 13; www.regional express.com.au) Flies to Sydney, Melbourne, Adelaide, Canberra, Devonport, as well as 12 other destinations in New South Wales, Victoria, South Australia and Tasmania.

Virgin Blue (☎ 13 67 89; www.virginblue.com.au) Flies to Adelaide, Alice Springs, Ballina, Brisbane, Broome, Cairns, Coffs Harbour, Darwin, Gold Coast, Hobart, Launceston, Mackay, Melbourne, Rockhampton, Sunshine Coast, Sydney, Townsville and Whitsunday Coast (Proserpine).

There are also special deals available only to foreign visitors (in possession of an outbound ticket). If booked in Australia, these fares offer a 40% discount off a full-fare economy ticket. They can also be booked from overseas (which usually works out a bit cheaper). All airports and domestic flights are nonsmoking.

AIR – INTERNATIONAL

Australia is a long way from just about everywhere, and getting there usually means a long, bleary-eyed flight punctuated by too many in-flight meals. Any time of year is busy for flying in or out of the country: the festive or 'silly' season sees many more punters take to the air, so book well ahead for travel over Christmas and Easter. Similarly, popular routes such as Hong Kong, Bangkok or Singapore to Sydney or Melbourne quickly fill up. In other words, always book well ahead. Most fares quoted in this section are for flights into Sydney, and all include the various taxes. For information about domestic airlines and routes, see p486.

Airlines

Sydney and Melbourne (Australia's busiest international gateways), and Brisbane and Cairns are on the East Coast route. Other cities in Australia not covered in this book but regularly serviced by international flights include Perth (which gets many flights from Asia and Europe and has direct flights to New Zealand) and Adelaide.

Australia's main carrier is **Qantas** (☎ 13 13 13; www.qantas.com.au), which flies international and domestic routes.

Air Canada (☎ 1300 655 767; www.aircanada.ca) Flies to Sydney.

Air New Zealand (☎ 13 24 76; www.airnz.com.au) Flies to Brisbane, Cairns, Melbourne and Sydney.

Air Paradise International (☎ 1300 799 066; www .airparadise.co.id) Flies to Brisbane, Melbourne and Sydney.

American Airlines (☎ 1300 650 747; www.aa.com) Flies to Brisbane, Cairns, Melbourne and Sydney.

Australian Airlines (☎ 1300 799 798; http://australian airlines.com.au) Flies to Coolangatta and Cairns, Melbourne and Sydney.

Austrian Airlines (☎ 02 9251 6155, 1800 642 438; www.aua.com/au/eng) Flies to Melbourne and Sydney.

British Airways (☎ 1300 767 177; www.britishairways .com.au) Flies to all major Australian cities, including Brisbane and Cairns.

Cathay Pacific (☎ 13 17 47; www.cathaypacific.com) Flies to Brisbane, Cairns, Melbourne and Sydney.

Emirates (☎ 1300 303 777; www.emirates.com) Flies to Brisbane, Melbourne and Sydney.

Freedom Air (☎ 1800 122 000; www.freedomair.com) Flies to Brisbane, Coolangatta, Melbourne and Sydney.

Garuda Indonesia (☎ 1300 365 330; www.garuda -indonesia.com) Flies to Brisbane, Melbourne and Sydney.

Gulf Air (☎ 02-9244 2199; www.gulfairco.com) Flies to Sydney.

Japan Airlines (☎ 02-9272 1111; www.au.jal.com) Flies to Brisbane, Cairns, Melbourne and Sydney.

KLM (☎ 3407 7282; www.klm.com.au) Flies to Brisbane, Melbourne and Sydney.

Malaysian Airlines (☎ 13 26 27; www.malaysiaair lines.com.au) Flies to Brisbane, Melbourne and Sydney.

Qantas (☎ 13 13 13; www.qantas.com.au) Flies to all major Australian cities, including Brisbane and Cairns.

Royal Brunei Airlines (☎ 1300 721 271; www.royal bruneiairlines.com.au) Flies to Brisbane and Sydney.

Singapore Airlines (☎ 13 10 11; www.singaporeair .com.au) Flies to Brisbane, Melbourne and Sydney.

South African Airways (☎ 1800 221 699; www.flysaa .com) Flies to Perth and Sydney.

Thai Airways International (☎ 1300 651 960; www .thaiairways.com.au) Flies to Brisbane, Melbourne and Sydney.

United Airlines (☎ 13 17 77; www.unitedairlines.com .au) Flies to Melbourne and Sydney.

Tickets

Be sure you research the options carefully to make sure you get the best deal. The Internet is a useful resource for checking airline prices.

Automated online ticket sales work well if you're doing a simple one-way or return trip on specified dates, but are no substitute for a travel agent with the lowdown on special deals, strategies for avoiding stopovers and other useful advice.

Paying by credit card offers some protection if you unwittingly end up dealing with a rogue fly-by-night agency in your search for the cheapest fare, as most card issuers provide refunds if you can prove you didn't get what you paid for. Alternatively, buy a ticket from a bonded agent, such as one covered by the **Air Travel Organiser's Licence** (ATOL; www.atol.org.uk) scheme in the UK. If you have doubts about the service provider, at the very least call the airline and confirm that your booking has been made.

Round-the-world tickets can be a good option for getting to Australia.

For online bookings, start with the following websites:

Airbrokers (www.airbrokers.com) US company specialising in cheap tickets.

Cheap Flights (www.cheapflights.com) Informative site with specials, airline information and flight searches from the USA and other regions.

Cheapest Flights (www.cheapestflights.co.uk) Cheap worldwide flights from the UK; get in early for the bargains.

Expedia (www.expedia.msn.com) Mainly US-related travel site.

TRANSPORT

Flight Centre International (www.flightcentre.com) Respected operator handling direct flights, with sites for Australia, Canada, New Zealand, UK and USA.

Opodo (www.opodo.com) Reliable company with French, German and UK sites.

Orbitz (www.orbitz.com) Excellent site for Web-only fares for US airlines.

STA (www.statravel.com) Prominent in international student travel, but you don't have to be a student; site linked to worldwide STA sites.

Travel Online (www.travelonline.co.nz) Good place to check worldwide flights from New Zealand.

Travel.com (www.travel.com.au) Good Australian site; look up fares and flights into and out of the country.

Travelocity (www.travelocity.com) US site that allows you to search fares (in US dollars) to/from practically anywhere.

Roundtheworld.com (www.roundtheworldflights.com) This excellent site allows you to build your own trip from the UK with up to six stops.

Zuji (www.zuji.com.au) Good Asia Pacific–based site.

Asia

Most Asian countries offer fairly competitive air-fare deals; with Bangkok, Singapore and Hong Kong being the best places to shop for discount tickets.

Flights between Hong Kong and Australia are notorious for being heavily booked. Flights to/from Bangkok and Singapore are often just one part of the longer Europe-to-Australia route, so they are also sometimes full. The moral of the story is that you need to plan your preferred itinerary well in advance.

Typical return fares to Brisbane (in Australian dollars) from Bangkok, Singapore, Kuala Lumpur and Hong Kong in high season are $1200 to $1600, and in low season $1000 to $1200.

There are several good local agents in Asia:

Hong Kong Student Travel Bureau (☎ 2730 3269)

Phoenix Services (☎ 2722 7378)

STA Travel Bangkok (☎ 02 236 0262; www.statravel .co.th); Singapore (☎ 65 6737 7188; www.statravel.com .sg); Tokyo (☎ 03 5391 3205; www.statravel.co.jp)

DEPARTURE TAX

There is a $40 departure tax when leaving Australia, but this is incorporated into the price of your air ticket so you don't have to produce any money at the airport.

From Bangkok, Singapore and Kuala Lumpur one-way fares to Sydney start at US$350. From Tokyo, fares start at US$650.

From East Coast Australia, return fares to Bangkok, Singapore and Kuala Lumpur range from $1100 to $1600; and to Hong Kong from $950 to $1900, depending on the airline and when you're travelling.

Canada

The air routes from Canada are similar to those from mainland USA; most Toronto and Vancouver flights stopping in one US city such as Los Angeles or Honolulu before heading to Australia. Air Canada flies from Vancouver to Sydney via Honolulu and from Toronto to Melbourne via Honolulu.

Canadian discount air ticket sellers are known as consolidators and their air fares tend to be about 10% higher than those in the USA. **Travel Cuts** (☎ 1866 246 9762; www .travelcuts.com) is Canada's national student travel agency and has offices in major cities.

Fares from Vancouver to Sydney or Melbourne (in Australian dollars) cost from $1800/2300 in the low/high season. From Toronto, fares go from around $1950/2400.

Continental Europe

From the major destinations in Europe, most flights travel via one of the Asian capitals. Some flights are also routed through London before arriving in Australia via Singapore, Bangkok, Hong Kong or Kuala Lumpur.

Fares from Paris in low/high season cost around €1000/1200.

Some agents in Paris include:

Nouvelles Frontiéres (☎ 08 25 00 07 47; www .nouvelles-frontieres.fr) Also has branches outside Paris.

OTU Voyages (☎ 01 40 29 12 12; www.otu.fr) Student/ youth oriented, with offices in many cities.

Usit Connect Voyages (☎ 01 43 29 69 50; www.usit connections.fr) Student/youth specialists, with offices in many cities.

Voyageurs du Monde (☎ 01 42 86 16 00; www.vdm .com/vdm) Has branches throughout France.

A good option in the Dutch travel industry is **Holland International** (☎ 070 307 6307; www.hol landinternational.nl). From Amsterdam, return fares start at around €1500.

In Germany, good travel agencies include the Berlin branch of **STA Travel** (☎ 030 311 0950; www.statravel.de). Fares start at around €900/1000 in the low/high season.

TRANSPORT

New Zealand

Competition on the trans-Tasman route is intense, with several airlines in the market offering cheap flights. Air New Zealand, Qantas, Emirates and Virgin Blue all offer cheap fares between Sydney, Melbourne or Brisbane and New Zealand cities such as Auckland, Wellington or Christchurch. At the time of writing, discounted return fares were available for around NZ$300.

To get good advice on up-to-date trans-Tasman options, contact the following:

Flight Centre (☎ 0800 243 544; www.flightcentre .co.nz) Has a large central office in Auckland and many branches throughout the country.

STA Travel (☎ 0508 782 872; www.statravel.co.nz) Has offices in various cities.

South Africa

South African Airways and Qantas both fly from Johannesburg to Perth and Sydney, with connections to Melbourne and Brisbane. One-way/return fares from Johannesburg to Australia cost around $1400/2100. Some good South African–based travel agents:

Flight Centre (☎ 0860 400 727; www.flightcentre .co.za) South African wing of this international company, with offices throughout the country.

Rennies Travel (www.renniestravel.co.za) Reliable South African–based travel agent.

UK & Ireland

There are two routes from the UK: the western route via the USA and the Pacific, and the eastern route via the Middle East and Asia. Flights are cheaper and more frequent on the latter. Some of the best deals are with Emirates, Gulf Air, Malaysian Airlines, Japan Airlines and Thai Airways International. Unless there are special deals on offer, British Airways, Singapore Airlines and Qantas are more expensive but are more direct.

A popular agent is the ubiquitous **STA Travel** (☎ 0870-160 0599; www.statravel.co.uk).

Typical direct fares from London to Sydney are UK£400/650 one way/return during the low season (March to June). In September and mid-December fares go up by as much as 30%, while the rest of the year they're somewhere in between.

From Australia you can expect to pay around $900/1650 one way/return in the low season to London and other European capitals (with stops in Asia on the way) and $1100/2050 in the high season.

USA

Airlines flying directly from Australia to Los Angeles or San Francisco include Qantas, Air New Zealand and United Airlines. There are also numerous airlines offering flights via Asia, with stopover possibilities including Tokyo, Kuala Lumpur, Bangkok, Hong Kong and Singapore; and via the Pacific with stopover possibilities like Nadi (Fiji), Rarotonga (Cook Islands), Tahiti (French Polynesia) and Auckland (NZ).

As in Canada, discount travel agents in the USA are known as consolidators. San Francisco is the ticket consolidator capital of America, although some good deals can be found in Los Angeles, New York and other big cities.

STA Travel (☎ 800-781 4040; www.statravel.com) has offices around the country, and can assist with tickets.

Typically you can get a return ticket to Melbourne or Sydney from the west coast for US$1300/1700 in the low/high season, or from the east coast for US$1600/1900. From Australia, return low/high-season fares to the US west coast cost up to $1750/1850, and to New York $1800/1950.

SEA

It's possible to make your way to/from countries such as New Zealand, Papua New Guinea and Indonesia by hitching or crewing on yachts. Usually you have to contribute something towards food. Ask around at harbours, marinas and yacht- and sailing clubs in Cairns – anywhere boats call in. Good places on the East Coast include Coffs Harbour, Great Keppel Island, Airlie Beach and the Whitsundays. Darwin is a good place to hitch a lift to Indonesia. A lot of boats move north to escape the winter, so April is a good time to look for a berth in the Sydney area.

Passenger liners don't operate to/from Australia any more, and finding a berth on a cargo ship isn't particularly easy or cheap.

GETTING AROUND

AIR

East Coast Australia is well serviced by airlines, many of which are subsidiaries of Qantas. The following regional carriers access locations along the coast from East Coast cities:

The state organisations have reciprocal arrangements with other states and with similar organisations overseas. So, if you're a member of the National Roads and Motorists Association (NRMA) in NSW, you can use the Royal Automobile Club of Victoria's (RACV) facilities in Victoria. Similarly, if you're a member of the AAA in the USA, or the RAC or AA in the UK, you can use any of the Australian state organisations' facilities. Bring proof of membership with you.

The main state association contact details are:

New South Wales & ACT NRMA (☎ 13 21 32; www.nrma.com.au)

Queensland RACQ (☎ 13 19 05; www.racq.com.au)

Victoria RACV (☎ 13 19 55; www.racv.com.au)

Driving Licence

You can use your home country's driving licence in Victoria, NSW and Queensland, as long as it is written in English (if it's in another language, a certified translation must be carried) and carries your photograph for identification.

Insurance

In Australia, third-party personal injury insurance is always included in the vehicle registration cost. This ensures that every registered vehicle carries at least minimum insurance. You'd be wise to extend that minimum to at least third-party property insurance as well – minor collisions with other vehicles can be amazingly expensive.

When it comes to hire cars, know exactly what your liability is in the event of an accident. Rather than risk paying out thousands of dollars if you do have an accident, you can take out your own comprehensive insurance on the car, or (the usual option) pay an additional daily amount to the rental company for an 'insurance excess reduction' policy. This brings the amount of excess you must pay in the event of an accident down from between $2000 and $5000 to a few hundred dollars.

Be aware that if you are travelling on dirt roads you will not be covered by insurance unless you have a 4WD – in other words, if you have an accident you'll be liable for all the costs involved. Also most companies' insurance won't cover the cost of damage to glass (including the windscreen) or tyres. Always read the small print.

Purchase

If you're planning a stay of several months with plenty of driving, buying is much cheaper than renting. But remember that reliability is all-important. You'll probably get any car cheaper by buying privately through newspaper classifieds rather than through a car dealer. Buying through a dealer does have the advantage of some sort of guarantee, but this might not be much use if you plan to take the car to another state.

There's plenty of debate among travellers about where the best place is to buy and sell used cars. Sydney is a particularly good place to buy cars from backpackers who have finished their trips. These vehicles will have done plenty of kilometres but they often come complete with camping gear, Eskies, water containers, tools and road maps. The best place to look is on hostel noticeboards or at car markets. Sydney is also well set up for travellers to sell vehicles, see p205 for more information.

When you come to buy or sell a car, every state has its own regulations, particularly with registration (rego). In Victoria, for example, a car has to have a compulsory safety check (Road Worthy Certificate – RWC) before it can be registered in the new owner's name. In NSW safety checks are compulsory every year when you come to renew the registration.

Note that it's much easier to sell a car in the same state that it's registered in, otherwise you (or the buyer) must re-register it in the new state, and that's a hassle.

Before you buy any vehicle, regardless of who the seller is, we strongly recommend that you have it thoroughly checked by a competent mechanic. The state automobile associations have contact with reputable mechanics.

The **Register of Encumbered Vehicles** (REVS; ☎ 02-9633 6333; www.revs.nsw.gov.au) is a government organisation that can check to ensure the car you're buying is fully paid-up and owned by the seller.

BUY-BACK DEALS

One way of getting around the hassles of buying and selling a vehicle privately is to enter into a buy-back arrangement with a car or motorcycle dealer; make sure you read the small print and don't accept any verbal guarantees – get it in writing. However, some

Australian Airlines (☎ 13 13 13; www.australianairlines.com.au) Flies between Cairns and the Gold Coast.

Jetstar (☎ 13 15 38; www.jetstar.com.au) Flies between Brisbane, Hamilton Island, Melbourne, Sydney and Whitsunday Coast (Proserpine).

Macair (☎ 13 13 13; www.macair.com.au) Flies to Cairns, Dunk Island, Toowoomba and Townsville plus many Queensland outback locations.

Qantas (☎ 13 13 13; www.qantas.com.au) Flies to Brisbane, Cairns, Melbourne, Sydney and Townsville.

QantasLink (☎ 13 13 13; www.qantas.com.au) Qantas affiliate that covers some regional routes.

Skytrans (☎ 1800 818 405, 07-4046 2462; www.skytrans.com.au) Flies between Cairns and Cooktown.

Regional Express (Rex; ☎ 13 17 13; www.regionalexpress.com.au) Flies to Canberra, Melbourne, and Sydney as well as other destinations in New South Wales and Victoria.

Sunshine Express (☎ 13 13 13; www.sunshineexpress.com.au) Flies to Armidale, Brisbane, Coffs Harbour, Hervey Bay and Tamworth.

Virgin Blue (☎ 13 67 89; www.virginblue.com.au) Flies between Cairns, Brisbane, Gold Coast, Mackay, Hervey Bay, Rockhampton, Sunshine Coast, Townsville and Whitsunday Coast.

BICYCLE

Whether you're hiring a bike to ride around a city or wearing out your chain wheels on a long-distance haul, the East Coast is a great place for cycling. There are bike paths in most major cities, and in the country you'll find thousands of kilometres of good roads. In many areas along the coast the countryside is flat or composed of gently rolling hills.

It can be surprisingly difficult to find places that hire out bikes for longer than a day or two, so if you're coming specifically to tour, it makes sense to bring your own – check with your airline for costs and the degree of dismantling and packing required. If you want to buy, **Bicycling Australia** (www.bicyclingaustralia.com), which is a commercial organisation with publications and events, is a good place to start looking for secondhand bikes.

Within Australia you can load your bike on to a bus or train to skip the boring bits. Bus companies require you to dismantle your bike, and some don't guarantee that it will travel on the same bus as you. Trains can be easier, but supervise the loading and if possible tie your bike upright. Check conditions ahead of travel: the fast XPT service between Melbourne, Sydney and Brisbane will only carry three boxed bikes per service; Victoria's newer 'sprinter' intercity trains only have room for two bikes.

Much of eastern Australia was settled on the principle of not having more than a day's horse ride between pubs, so it's possible to plan even ultra-long routes and still get a shower at the end of each day. Most cyclists carry camping equipment but it's feasible to travel from town to town staying in hostels, hotels or caravan parks.

You can get by with standard road maps but, as you'll probably want to avoid both the highways and the low-grade unsealed roads, the government series by **National Mapping – Geoscience Australia** (☎ 1800 800 173, 02-6201 4201; www.ga.gov.au) is best. They are widely available in speciality map shops.

No matter how fit you are, water is vital. Dehydration is no joke and heatstroke can be life threatening (see p500). It can get very hot in summer, and you should take things easy, wear a helmet with a peak (or a cap under your helmet) and plenty of sunscreen, avoid cycling in the middle of the day and drink lots of water. Remember that it can get very cold in the mountains, so pack appropriately. In the south, be aware of the blistering hot 'northerlies' that can make a north-bound cyclist's life hell in summer. Bicycle helmets are compulsory, as are white front lights and red rear lights for riding at night. It's rare to find a good-sized town that doesn't have a shop stocking at least basic bike parts.

For more information see p50, and Lonely Planet's *Cycling Australia*. It includes a 31-day East Coast Explorer tour which may be exactly what you're after.

The national cycling body is the **Bicycle Federation of Australia** (www.bfa.asn.au; GPO Box 3222, ACT 2601). Each state has a touring organisation that can help with information, tell you about tour operators and bike hirers, and put you in touch with touring clubs:

Bicycle New South Wales (☎ 02-9283 5200; www.bicyclensw.org.au; 209 Castlereagh St, Sydney, NSW 2000)

Bicycle Queensland (☎ /fax 07-3844 1144, www.bq.org.au; PO Box 8321, Woolloongabba, Brisbane, Queensland 4102)

Bicycle Victoria (☎ 03-8636 8888, www.bv.com.au; 446 Collins St, Melbourne, Victoria 3001)

Purchase

If you arrive in Australia without a set of wheels and want to buy a new road cycle or mountain bike that won't leave a trail of worn-out or busted metal parts once it leaves the city limits, your starting point (and we mean your absolute bottom-level starting point) is $400 to $500. To set yourself up with a new bike, plus all the requisite on-the-road equipment such as panniers, helmet etc, your starting point becomes $1500 to $2000. Second-hand bikes are worth checking out in the cities, as are the post-Christmas sales and mid-year stocktakes, when newish cycles may be heavily discounted.

Your best bet for reselling your bike is the **Trading Post** (☎ 1300 138 016; www.tradingpost .com.au), which is distributed in newspaper form in urban centres around Australia, and which also has a busy online trading site.

Rental

The rates charged by most outfits for renting road or mountain bikes (not including the discounted fees offered by budget accommodation places to their guests) are anywhere from $10 to $15 per hour and $20 to $40 per day. Security deposits can range from $50 to $200, depending on the rental period.

BUS

Other than hitching or driving your own car, bus travel is generally the cheapest way to get around and it gives you the greatest coverage. But it can be a tedious form of transport and requires a bit of planning if you intend to do more than straightforward city-to-city trips. Travelling by bus also means you miss out on seeing off-the-beaten-track highlights of the coast.

There's only one national bus network, **Greyhound Australia** (☎ 13 14 99; www.greyhound .com.au). The next biggest player on the East Coast is **Premier Motor Service** (☎ 13 34 10; www .premierms.com.au). Premier is the main competitor to Greyhound on the East Coast route; it has fewer services per day but costs a few dollars less on most routes.

There are also many smaller bus companies either operating locally or specialising in one or two main intercity routes. These often offer the best deals – **Firefly Express** (☎ 1800 631 164; www.fireflyexpress.com.au) charges $60 for a Sydney to Melbourne express (via the Hume Hwy) for example. In Victoria, **V/Line** (☎ 13 61 96; www.vlinepassenger.com.au) op-

erates bus services to places trains no longer go and in NSW **Countrylink** (☎ 13 22 32; www .countrylink.nsw.gov.au) does the same.

In most towns up the East Coast there is just one bus terminal, and in very small towns there might not even be a terminal – just a drop-off/pick-up point. Big city terminals are usually well equipped with toilets, showers and other facilities.

Backpacker Buses

Several companies offer transport options for budget travellers along the East Coast. While most of these are pretty much organised tours, they do also get you from A to B (sometimes with hop-on, hop-off services), so can be a good alternative to the big bus companies.

Autopia Tours (☎ 03-9326 5536, 1800 000 507; www.autopiatours.com.au) operates a busy 3½-day Melbourne to Sydney tour via the Snowy Mountains, Canberra and the Blue Mountains for $195. Accommodation and meals are extra.

Oz Experience (☎ 02-8356 1766, 1300 300 028; www.ozexperience.com) is one of those hop-on hop-off buses you'll either love or hate. It's the biggest backpacker bus network in the country and we get mixed reports on the service. Some travellers complain they can't get a seat on the bus of their choice and are left on stand-by lists for days because services are oversubscribed, but lots of backpackers rave about it and have a great time meeting other travellers.

Wildlife Tours (☎ 03-9534 8868; www.wildlife tours.com.au) offers a number of trips from Melbourne to Sydney visiting the Snowy Mountains and Canberra along the way (with possible side trips to the Blue Mountains or Phillip Island). Expect to pay from $145 to $210.

Bus Passes

Bus passes are a good option if you plan plenty of stopovers. You should book/phone at least a day ahead to reserve a seat if you're using any of the following passes.

Greyhound (☎ 13 14 99; www.greyhound.com.au) offers many passes and it's worth checking its website or brochures available at travel agents and Greyhound offices for full details. There's a 10% discount for members of YHA, VIP, Nomads and other approved organisations, as well as card-carrying students.

The Aussie Kilometre Pass is the simplest and gives you a specified amount of travel, starting at 2000km ($328) and going up in increments of 1000km to a maximum of 20,000km ($2310). The pass is valid for 12 months; you can travel where and in what direction you like, and stop as many times as you like. A 2000km pass will get you from Brisbane to Cairns, or 4000km ($558) will get you from Melbourne to Cairns.

Greyhound also has 23 Aussie Explorer Passes, with 10 of them covering much of the East Coast. With these passes you don't get the go-anywhere flexibility of the Aussie Kilometre Pass (you can't backtrack), but if you can find a route that suits you it generally works out cheaper. An option worth looking into is the Sunseeker Pass, which allows travel between Melbourne and Cairns for 183 days ($415).

Premier (☎ 13 34 10; www.premierms.com.au) offers several passes for travel along the East Coast. The Ocean Pass ($85) allows one stopover between Sydney and Brisbane, the Byron Bay Getaway Pass ($260) and the Eastcoaster Pass ($365) allows unlimited stopovers between Byron Bay and Cairns and between Melbourne and Cairns, respectively. Passes are valid for three months and there are 10% discounts for members of YHA, VIP, Nomads and other approved organisations, as well as card-carrying students.

Classes

There are no separate classes on buses, and the vehicles of the different companies all look pretty similar and are equipped with air-con, toilets and videos. Smoking isn't permitted on Australian buses.

Costs

Following are average, non-discounted, adult, one-way bus fares on some well-travelled Australian routes.

Melbourne to Canberra (adult/child/concession $70/55/65)

Melbourne to Sydney (adult/child/concession $60/50/55)

Sydney to Byron Bay (adult/child/concession $85/75/80)

Sydney to Brisbane (adult/child/concession $95/80/85)

Brisbane to Airlie Beach (adult/child/concession $140/120/125)

Brisbane to Cairns (adult/child/concession $190/160/170)

Reservations

Over summer, school holidays and public holidays, you should book well ahead, especially on the inter-city services. At other times you should have few problems getting on to your preferred service. But if your long-term travel plans rely on catching a particular bus, book at least a day or two ahead.

You should make a reservation at least a day in advance if you're using a travel pass.

CAR & MOTORCYCLE

The best way to see the East Coast is by car – it's certainly the only way to get to those interesting out-of-the-way places without taking a tour.

Super, diesel and unleaded fuel is available from service stations. LPG (gas) is also available in the populated areas but not always at more remote service stations – if you're on gas it's safer to have dual fuel capacity. Prices vary according to place and time. Unleaded petrol (used in most new cars) is around 90¢ to $1 a litre in the cities. On main highways there's usually a small town or petrol station roughly every 50km to 100km or so.

Motorcycles are very popular, as the climate is just about ideal for bikes for much of the year. Bringing your own motorcycle into Australia will entail an expensive shipping exercise, valid registration in the country of origin and a *Carnet De Passages en Douanes*. This is an internationally recognised customs document that allows you to import your vehicle without paying customs duty or taxes. To get one, apply to a motoring organisation/ association in your home country. You'll also need a rider's licence and a helmet. A fuel range of 350km will easily cover fuel stops up the East Coast and, for that matter, around the continent. The long, open roads are really made for large-capacity machines above 750cc, which Australians prefer once they outgrow their 250cc learner restrictions.

Automobile Associations

The national **Australian Automobile Association** (www.aaa.asn.au) is an umbrella organisation for the various state associations and maintains links with similar bodies throughout the world. Day-to-day operations are handled by the state organisations, which provide emergency breakdown services, literature, excellent touring maps and detailed guides to accommodation and camp sites.

dealers may find ways of knocking down the price when you return the vehicle, even if it was agreed to in writing – sometimes by pointing out expensive repairs that allegedly will be required to gain the dreaded RWC needed to transfer the registration.

A company that specialises in buy-back on cars and campervans is **Travellers Autobarn** (☎ 02-9360 1500, 1800 674 374; www.travellers-autobarn .com.au). It has offices in Brisbane and Cairns and Sydney, and offers a range of vehicles. The buy-back arrangement is guaranteed in writing before you depart and the basic deal is 50% of the purchase price if you have the vehicle for eight weeks, 40% for up to six months, or 30% for up to 12 months.

Another option, for cars and motor-cycles, is **Car Connection Australia** (☎ 03-5473 4469; www.carconnection.com.au). Rather than re-quiring you to outlay the full amount and then sell it back, it offers a fixed price of about one-third of the full cost of the vehi-cle. For example, a 4WD campervan costs $9350 and a Ford Falcon station wagon or Yamaha XT600 trail bike costs $2150 – these rates are valid for up to six months.

Better Bikes (☎ 02-9718 6668; www.betterbikes .com.au; 605 Canterbury Rd, Belmore) is a Sydney dealer that offers buy-back deals on motor-cycles. Elizabeth St in Melbourne is also a good hunting ground for this kind of deal.

Rental

There are plenty of car-rental companies ready and willing to put you behind the wheel. Between a group, car hire can be reasonably economical. The main thing to remember is distance – if you want to travel far, you need unlimited kilometres.

Major companies include **Budget** (☎ 1300 362 8484; www.budget.com.au), **Hertz** (☎ 13 30 39; www.hertz.com.au), **Avis** (☎ 13 63 33; www.avis .com.au) and **Thrifty** (☎ 13 61 39; www.thrifty.com .au), which often has the best rates of the lot. These companies have offices or agents in most major towns. There is a vast number of local firms. These are almost always cheaper than the big operators – sometimes half the price – but cheap car hire often comes with serious restrictions.

The big firms sometimes offer one-way rentals – pick up a car in Melbourne and leave it in Sydney, for example. There are, however, a variety of restrictions on this and sometimes there's a substantial drop-off fee.

The major companies offer a choice of deals, either unlimited kilometres or 100km or so a day free plus so many cents per kilo-metre over this. Daily rates are typically about $60 a day for a small car, from $75 to $80 a day for a medium car, or $85 to $100 a day for a big car, not including insurance. You must be at least 21 years old to hire from most firms – if you're under 25 you may only be able to hire a small car or pay a surcharge. It gets cheaper if you rent for a week or more and there are often low-season and weekend discounts. Credit cards are the usual payment method.

4WD & CAMPERVAN

Having a 4WD enables you to get right off the beaten track and out to some of the natural wonders that most travellers miss. Check the insurance conditions carefully, especially the excess, as they can be on-erous. Even for a 4WD, the insurance of-fered by most companies does not cover damage caused when travelling 'off-road', which basically means anything that is not a maintained bitumen or dirt road.

Hertz, Budget and Avis have 4WD rentals. **Britz Rentals** (☎ 1800 331 454; www.britz.com) hires fully equipped 4WDs fitted out as camper-vans. Several other companies rent out campervans, including **Backpacker Campervans** (☎ 1800 670 232; www.backpackercampervans.com).

Road Conditions & Hazards

Australia has few multilane highways, al-though there are stretches of divided road (four or six lanes) in some particularly busy areas, including along most of the Pacific Hwy from Sydney to Brisbane, and the Hume Hwy in NSW and Victoria. Elsewhere the major roads are sealed with two lanes.

You don't have to get far off the beaten track to find yourself on dirt roads. In fact, anybody who sets out to see the countryside in reasonable detail should expect some dirt-road travelling. The problem here is that if you have a hire car, the company's insurance won't cover you unless you've hired an expensive 4WD.

ANIMAL HAZARDS

Kangaroos are common hazards on coun-try roads. If you're travelling at any sort of speed, hitting one can make a real mess of your car, not to mention the kangaroo.

TRANSPORT

They are most active at dawn and dusk, and often travel in groups. Many Australians avoid travelling altogether after dark because of the hazards posed by animals.

If you are travelling at night and a large animal appears in front of you, hit the brakes (if there isn't a car right behind you), dip your lights (so you don't continue to dazzle and confuse it) and only swerve if it's safe to do so. Numerous travellers have been killed in accidents caused by swerving to miss animals. It's better to damage your car and perhaps kill the animal than cause the death of yourself and your passengers and other motorists on the road.

Road Rules

Driving in Australia holds few surprises, other than the odd animal caught in your headlights. Australians drive on the left-hand side of the road and all cars are right-hand drive. An important road rule is 'give way to the right' – if an intersection is unmarked (unusual), you must give way to vehicles entering the intersection from your right.

The general speed limit in built-up areas is 60km/h, although this has been reduced to 50km/h on many residential streets. Near schools, the limit is 40km/h in the morning and afternoon. On the open highway it's usually 100km/h or 110km/h. Keep an eye out for signs. The police have speed radar guns and cameras, and are very fond of using them in strategically concealed locations.

All new cars in Australia have seat belts back and front and it's the law to wear yours – you're likely to get a fine if you don't. Small children must be belted into an approved safety seat.

DRINK-DRIVING

Along the East Coast, drink driving is a real problem, especially in country areas. Serious attempts are being made to reduce the road toll, and random breath tests are not uncommon in built-up areas. If you're caught with a blood-alcohol level of more than 0.05% be prepared for a hefty fine and the loss of your licence. In Victoria you must be *under* 0.05%.

PARKING

One of the big problems with driving around big cities like Sydney and Melbourne (or popular tourist towns like Byron Bay) is finding somewhere to park. Even if you do find a spot there's likely to be a time restriction, meter (or ticket machine) or both. Parking officers in Australia are like parking officers the world over – they'd put a ticket on a fire hydrant if it had wheels. Parking fines range from about $50 to $120 and if you park in a clearway your car will be towed away or clamped – look for signs. In the cities there are large multistorey car parks where you can park all day for $15 to $25.

HITCHING

Hitching is never entirely safe in any country in the world, and we don't recommend it. Travellers who decide to hitch should understand that they are taking a small but potentially serious risk. People who do choose to hitch will be safer if they travel in pairs and let someone know where they are planning to go.

In Australia, the hitching signal can be a thumbs up, but a downward-pointed finger is more widely understood.

INTERSTATE QUARANTINE

When travelling in Australia, whether by land or air, you'll come across signs (mainly in airports, interstate train stations and at state borders) warning of the possible dangers of carrying fruit, plants and vegetables (which may be infected with a disease or pest) from one area to another. Certain pests and diseases – such as fruit fly, cucurbit thrips, grape phylloxera and potato cyst nematodes, to name a few – are prevalent in some areas but not in others, and for obvious reasons authorities would like to limit them spreading.

There are quarantine inspection posts on some state borders and occasionally elsewhere. While quarantine control often relies on honesty, many posts are staffed and the officers are entitled to search your car for undeclared items. Generally they'll confiscate all fresh fruit and vegetables, so it's best to leave shopping for these items until the first town past the inspection point.

SYDNEY TO MELBOURNE VIA THE PRINCES HWY

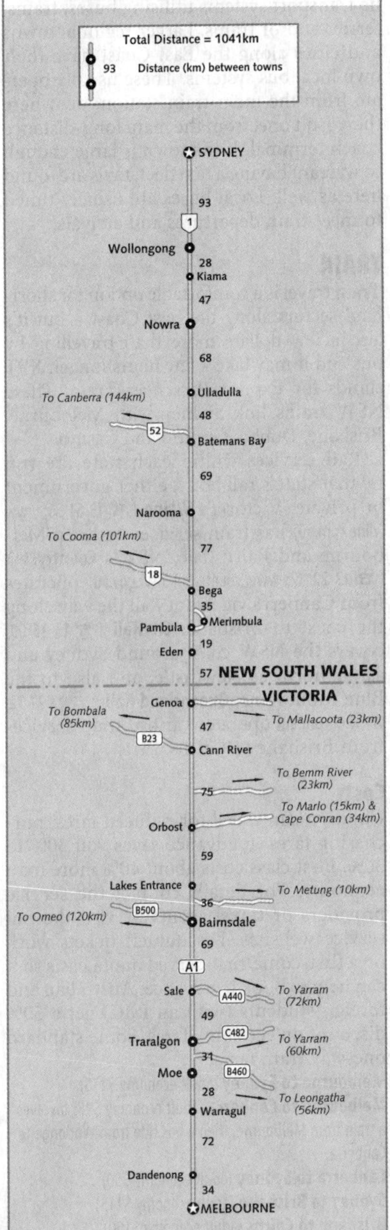

Total Distance = 1041km

93 Distance (km) between towns

⊗ SYDNEY

93

①
Wollongong ●
28
● Kiama
47

Nowra ●

68

● Ulladulla
To Canberra (144km)   48

[52]
● Batemans Bay

69

Narooma ●
To Cooma (101km)   77
[18]
● Bega
35
● Merimbula
Pambula ●
19
Eden ●
57 **NEW SOUTH WALES**
VICTORIA
Genoa ●
To Bombala   → To Mallacoota (23km)
(85km)   47
[B23]
● Cann River
→ To Bemm River
75   (23km)
→ To Marlo (15km) &
Orbost ●   Cape Conran (34km)

59

Lakes Entrance ●   → To Metung (10km)
36
To Omeo (120km) [B500]
● Bairnsdale

69

[A1]
Sale ●   → To Yarram
[A440]   (72km)
49
Traralgon ● [C482]   → To Yarram
31   (60km)
Moe ● [B460]
28   → To Leongatha
Warragul ●   (56km)

72

Dandenong ●
34
⊗ MELBOURNE

SYDNEY TO BRISBANE VIA THE PACIFIC HWY

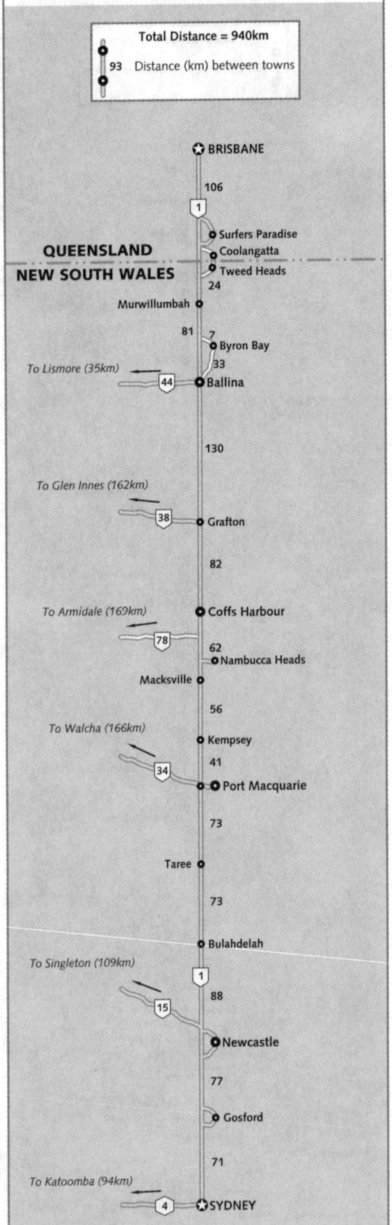

Total Distance = 940km

93 Distance (km) between towns

⊗ BRISBANE

106

①
● Surfers Paradise
QUEENSLAND   ● Coolangatta
NEW SOUTH WALES   ● Tweed Heads
Murwillumbah ●   24
81   7
● Byron Bay
To Lismore (35km)   33
[44] ● Ballina

130

To Glen Innes (162km)
[38]
● Grafton

82

To Armidale (169km) ● Coffs Harbour
[78] 62
● Nambucca Heads
Macksville ●
56

To Walcha (166km)   ● Kempsey
[34] 41
● Port Macquarie

73

Taree ●

73

● Bulahdelah
To Singleton (109km)
①
[15] 88

● Newcastle

77

● Gosford

71

To Katoomba (94km)
[4] ⊗ SYDNEY

BRISBANE TO CAIRNS VIA THE BRUCE HWY

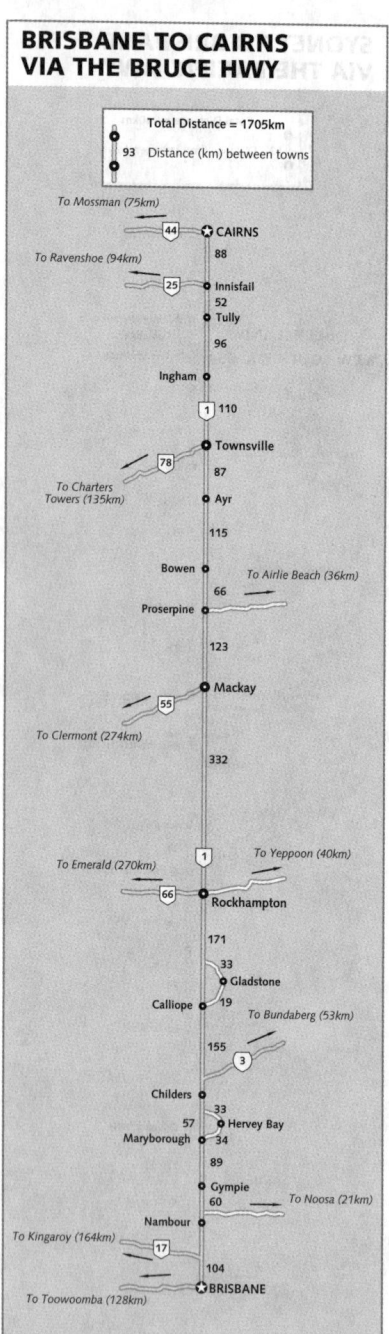

Total Distance = 1705km

93 Distance (km) between towns

To Mossman (75km)

44 ✪ CAIRNS
88
To Ravenshoe (94km)
25 ● Innisfail
52
● Tully
96
Ingham ●
1 110
● Townsville
78 87
To Charters
Towers (135km)
● Ayr
115
Bowen ●   To Airlie Beach (36km)
66
Proserpine ●
123
55 ● Mackay
To Clermont (274km)
332
To Emerald (270km) To Yeppoon (40km)
1
66 ● Rockhampton
171
33
● Gladstone
Calliope ● 19
To Bundaberg (53km)
155
3
Childers ●
33
57 ● Hervey Bay
Maryborough ● 34
89
● Gympie
60 To Noosa (21km)
Nambour ●
To Kingaroy (164km)
17
104
✪ BRISBANE
To Toowoomba (128km)

LOCAL TRANSPORT

Brisbane, Melbourne and Sydney have public transport systems utilising buses, trains, ferries and/or trams. Larger regional towns and cities along the East Coast have their own local bus systems. These usually operate from the main train station, or, where there isn't one, from the main long-distance coach terminal. If the town is large enough to warrant having a taxi fleet, taxis are found here as well. Local buses are usually timed to meet train departures and arrivals.

TRAIN

Train travel is a comfortable option for short-haul sectors along the East Coast – but it's also a few dollars more than travelling by bus and it may take a few hours longer. XPT stands for Express Passenger Train. These NSW trains link Sydney with Melbourne, Brisbane, Dubbo, Grafton and Casino.

Rail services within each state are run by that state's rail body, either government or private. Victoria's **V/Line** (☎ 13 61 96; www .vline.com.au) has train services between Melbourne and Bairnsdale; NSW's **CountryLink** (☎ 13 22 32; www.countrylink.nsw.gov.au) operates from Canberra via Sydney all the way along the coast to Brisbane; **CityRail** (☎ 13 15 00) covers the NSW coast around Sydney and as far north as Newcastle, and also to the Blue Mountains; **Queensland Rail** (☎ 13 22 32; www.qr.com.au) operates various train services from Brisbane to Cairns.

Costs

Children can travel for reduced fares; purchasing fares in advance saves you 30% to 50%. First class costs about 40% more than economy. For details contact the service providers or travel agents or visit the rail service websites. Discounted tickets work on a first-come/first-served quota basis so it can help to book in advance. Australian and foreign students (with an ISIC) get a 50% discount on economy fares. Some standard one-way train fares:

Melbourne to Sydney (adult economy $115)

Melbourne to Canberra (adult economy $95) Involves a train from Melbourne, then a bus ride from Wodonga to Canberra.

Canberra to Sydney (adult economy $50)

Sydney to Brisbane (adult economy $115)

Brisbane to Cairns (adult economy $190)

Reservations

As the railway booking system is computerised, any station (other than those on metropolitan lines) can make a booking for any journey throughout the country. For reservations telephone ☎ 13 22 32 during office hours; this will connect you to the nearest main-line station.

Discounted tickets work on a first-come first-served quota basis, so it may help to book in advance.

Train Passes

Rail Australia (www.railaustralia.com.au) provides information on train passes available from **CountryLink** (☎ 13 22 32; www.countrylink.nsw.gov.au) and also from **Queensland Rail** (☎ 13 22 32; www .qr.com.au).

The Austrail Flexipass allows a set number of economy-class travelling days within a six-month period. The cost is $600 for eight days of travel, $865 for 15 days, $1210 for 22 days and $1570 for 29 days.

CountryLink offers two types of passes to foreign nationals with valid passports. The East Coast Discovery Pass allows one-way economy travel between Melbourne and Cairns (in either direction) with unlimited stopovers, and is valid for six months. The full trip costs $395, Brisbane to Cairns is $225 and Sydney to Cairns is $315. The Backtracker Rail Pass allows travel on the entire CountryLink network and comes in four versions: a 14-day/1-/3-/6-month pass costs $220/250/275/385, respectively.

TRANSPORT

Health Dr David Millar

CONTENTS

East Coast Australia is a remarkably healthy region in which to travel, considering that such a large portion of it lies in the tropics. Tropical diseases such as malaria and yellow fever are unknown, diseases of insanitation such as cholera and typhoid are unheard of. Thanks to Australia's isolation and quarantine standards, even some animal diseases such as rabies and foot-and-mouth disease have yet to be recorded.

Few travellers to this area will experience anything worse than an upset stomach or a bad hangover, and if you do fall ill the standard of hospitals and health care is high.

BEFORE YOU GO

Since most vaccines don't produce immunity until at least two weeks after they're given, visit a physician four to eight weeks before departure. Ask your doctor for an International Certificate of Vaccination (otherwise known as 'the yellow booklet'), which will list all the vaccinations you've received. This is mandatory for countries that require proof of yellow fever vaccination upon entry (sometimes required in Australia, see opposite), but it's a good idea to carry a record of all your vaccinations wherever you travel.

Bring medications in their original, clearly labelled containers. A signed and dated letter from your physician describing your medical conditions and medications, including generic names, is also a good idea. If carrying syringes or needles, be sure to have a physician's letter documenting their medical necessity.

If your health insurance doesn't cover you for medical expenses abroad, consider extra insurance; check www.lonelyplanet.com for more information. Find out in advance if your insurance will make payments directly to providers or reimburse you later for overseas health expenditures. In Australia, as in many countries, doctors expect payment at the time of consultation. Make sure you get a receipt detailing the service and keep the contact details of the health provider. See below for details of health care in Australia.

INSURANCE

Health insurance is essential for all travellers. While health care in Australia is of a high standard and is not overly expensive by international standards, considerable costs can build up and repatriation is extremely expensive. Make sure your existing health insurance will cover you; if not, organise extra insurance.

MEDICAL CHECKLIST

- antibiotics
- antidiarrhoeal drugs (eg loperamide)
- acetaminophen/paracetamol or aspirin
- anti-inflammatory drugs (eg ibuprofen)
- antihistamines (for hay fever and allergic reactions)
- antibacterial ointment in case of cuts
- steroid cream or cortisone (for poison ivy and other allergic rashes)
- bandages, gauze, gauze rolls
- adhesive or paper tape
- scissors, safety pins, tweezers
- thermometer
- pocketknife
- DEET-containing insect repellent
- permethrin-containing insect spray for clothing, tents and bed nets
- sunblock
- oral rehydration salts
- iodine tablets or water filter (for water purification)

REQUIRED & RECOMMENDED VACCINATIONS

Proof of yellow fever vaccination is required only from travellers entering Australia within six days of having stayed overnight or longer in a yellow fever–infected country. For a full list of these countries visit the World Health Organization website (www.who.int/wer/) or the Centers for Disease Control and Prevention website (www.cdc.gov/travel/blusheet.htm).

If you're really worried about health when travelling, there are a few vaccinations you could consider. The World Health Organization recommends that all travellers should be covered for diphtheria, tetanus, measles, mumps, rubella, chickenpox and polio, as well as hepatitis B, regardless of their destination. When you're planning to travel it's a great time to ensure that all routine vaccination cover is complete. The consequences of these diseases can be severe and while Australia has high levels of childhood vaccination coverage, outbreaks of these diseases do occur.

INTERNET RESOURCES

There is a wealth of travel health advice to be found on the Internet. For further information, the Lonely Planet website (www.lonelyplanet.com) is a good place to start. The **World Health Organization** (www.who.int/ith) publishes a superb book called *International Travel and Health*, which is revised annually and is available online at no cost. Another website of general interest is **MD Travel Health** (www.mdtravelhealth.com), which provides complete travel health recommendations for every country and is updated daily.

FURTHER READING

Lonely Planet's *Healthy Travel Australia, New Zealand & The Pacific* is a handy, pocket-sized guide packed with useful information including pretrip planning, emergency first aid, immunisation and disease information and what to do if you get sick on the road. *Travel with Children* from Lonely Planet includes advice on travel health for younger children. Other recommended references include *Traveller's Health* by Dr Richard Dawood (Oxford University Press) and *International Travel Health Guide* by Stuart R Rose, MD (Travel Medicine Inc).

TRAVEL HEALTH WEBSITES

It's usually a good idea to consult your government's travel health website before departure, if one is available.

Australia (www.dfat.gov.au/travel)
Canada (www.travelhealth.gc.ca)
UK (www.doh.gov.uk/traveladvice)
USA (www.cdc.gov/travel)

IN TRANSIT

DEEP VEIN THROMBOSIS

Blood clots may form in the legs (deep vein thrombosis) during plane flights, chiefly because of prolonged immobility. The longer the flight, the greater the risk. Though most blood clots are reabsorbed uneventfully, some may break off and travel through the blood vessels to the lungs, where they could cause life-threatening complications.

The chief symptom of deep vein thrombosis is swelling or pain of the foot, ankle or calf, usually – but not always – on just one side. When a blood clot travels to the lungs, it may cause chest pain and breathing difficulties. Travellers with any of these symptoms should immediately seek medical attention.

To prevent the development of deep vein thrombosis on long flights, you should walk about the cabin, perform isometric contractions of the leg muscles (ie flex the leg muscles while sitting), drink plenty of fluids and avoid alcohol and tobacco.

JET LAG & MOTION SICKNESS

Jet lag is common when crossing more than five time zones, resulting in fatigue, malaise, insomnia or nausea. To avoid jet lag drink plenty of (nonalcoholic) fluids and eat light meals. Upon arrival, expose yourself to sunlight and readjust your schedule (for meals, sleep etc) as soon as possible.

Antihistamines such as dimenhydrinate and meclizine are usually the first choice for treating motion sickness. Their main side effect is drowsiness. A herbal alternative is ginger, which works like a charm for some people.

HEALTH

ON THE EAST COAST OF AUSTRALIA

AVAILABILITY & COST OF HEALTH CARE

Australia has an excellent health-care system. It's a mixture of privately run medical clinics and hospitals alongside a system of public hospitals funded by the government. The Medicare system covers Australian residents for some health-care costs. Visitors from countries with which Australia has a reciprocal health-care agreement are eligible for benefits specified under the Medicare programme. Agreements are currently in place with New Zealand, the UK, the Netherlands, Sweden, Finland, Italy, Malta and Ireland; check the details before departing these countries. In general, agreements provide for any ill-health that requires prompt medical attention. For further details visit www.health.gov.au/pubs/mbs/mbs3/medicare.htm.

There are excellent, specialised public-health facilities for women and children in Australia's major centres.

Self-care

In Australia's remote locations it is possible there'll be a significant delay in emergency services reaching you in the event of serious accident or illness. Don't underestimate the distance between towns; an increased level of self-reliance and preparation is essential.

Consider taking a wilderness first-aid course, such as those offered at the **Wilderness Medicine Institute** (www.wmi.net.au); take a comprehensive first-aid kit that is appropriate for the activities planned; and ensure that you have adequate means of communication. Australia has extensive mobile-phone coverage but additional radio communication is important for remote areas. The **Royal Flying Doctor Service** (www.rfds.org.au) provides an important backup for remote communities.

Pharmaceutical Supplies

Over-the-counter medications are widely available at chemists throughout Australia. These include painkillers, antihistamines for allergies and skin-care products.

You may find that medications readily available over the counter in some countries are only available in Australia by prescription. These include the oral contraceptive pill, most medications for asthma and all antibiotics. If you take medication on a regular basis, bring an adequate supply and ensure you have details of the generic name as brand names may differ between countries.

INFECTIOUS DISEASES

Bat lyssavirus Related to rabies; some deaths have occurred after bites. The risk is greatest for animal handlers and vets. Rabies vaccine is effective, but the risk to travellers is low.

Dengue fever Occurs in northern Queensland, particularly during the wet season (November to April). Also known as 'breakbone fever', because of the severe muscular pains that accompany it, this viral disease is spread by a species of mosquito that feeds primarily during the day. Most people recover in a few days but more severe forms of the disease can occur, particularly in residents who are exposed to another strain of the virus (there are four types) in a subsequent season.

Giardiasis Widespread in the waterways around Australia. Drinking untreated water from streams and lakes is not recommended. Water filters and boiling or treating water with iodine are effective in preventing the disease. Symptoms consist of bad-smelling diarrhoea, abdominal bloating and wind. Treatment is available (tinidazole or metronidazole).

Hepatitis C A growing problem among intravenous drug users. Blood transfusion services screen all blood before use.

HIV Rates in Australia have stabilised and levels are similar to other Western countries. Clean needles and syringes are widely available through all chemists.

Malaria Not an ongoing problem in the region although isolated cases have occurred in northern Queensland. The risk to travellers is low.

Meningococcal disease Occurs worldwide and is a risk with prolonged dormitory-style accommodation. A vaccine exists for some types (meningococcal A, C, Y and W). No vaccine is presently available for the viral type of meningitis.

Ross River fever Widespread throughout Australia. The virus is spread by mosquitoes living in marshy areas. In addition to fever it causes headache, joint and muscular pains and a rash, and resolves after five to seven days.

Sexually transmitted diseases Occur at rates similar to most other Western countries. The most common symptoms are pain while passing urine and a discharge. Infection can also be present without symptoms. Throughout the country, you'll find sexual health clinics in all of the major hospitals. Always use a condom with any new sexual partner. Condoms are readily available in chemists and through vending machines in many public places including toilets.

Tick typhus Cases have been reported through Australia, but predominantly in Queensland and New South Wales. A week or so after being bitten, a dark area forms around the bite, followed by a rash and possible fever, headache and inflamed lymph nodes. The disease is treatable with antibiotics (doxycycline). See a doctor if you suspect you have been bitten.

Viral encephalitis (Murray Valley encephalitis virus) Spread by mosquitoes and is most common in northern Australia, especially during the wet season (October to March). This potentially serious disease is normally accompanied by headache, muscle pains and light insensitivity. Residual neurological damage can occur and no specific treatment is available. However, the risk to most travellers is low.

TRAVELLER'S DIARRHOEA

Tap water is universally safe in Australia. All water other than tap water should be boiled, filtered or chemically disinfected (with iodine tablets) to prevent traveller's diarrhoea and giardia.

If you develop diarrhoea, drink plenty of fluids, preferably an oral rehydration solution containing lots of salt and sugar. A few loose stools don't require treatment but if you have more than four or five stools a day, you should take an antibiotic (usually a quinolone drug) and an antidiarrhoeal agent (such as loperamide). If diarrhoea is bloody, persists for more than 72 hours or is accompanied by fever, shaking chills or severe abdominal pain you should seek medical attention.

ENVIRONMENTAL HAZARDS
Animal Bites & Stings
MARINE ANIMALS

Marine spikes, such as those found on sea urchins, stonefish, scorpion fish, catfish and stingrays, can cause severe local pain. If this occurs, immediately immerse the affected area in hot water (as high a temperature as can be tolerated). Keep topping up with hot water until the pain subsides and medical care can be reached. The stonefish is found only in tropical Australia, including northern Queensland. Antivenin is available.

Marine stings from jellyfish such as Chironex box and Irukandji also occur in Australia's tropical waters, particularly during the wet season (November to April). The box jelly has an incredibly potent sting and has been known to cause fatalities. Warning signs exist at affected beaches and stinger nets are in place at the more popular beaches. Never dive into water unless you have checked it's safe with local beach lifesavers. 'Stinger suits' (full-body Lycra swimsuits) prevent stinging, as do wetsuits. If you are stung, first aid consists of washing the skin with vinegar to prevent further discharge of remaining stinging cells, followed by rapid transfer to a hospital; antivenin is widely available.

SHARKS & CROCODILES

The risk of shark attack in Australian waters is no greater than in other countries with extensive coastlines. There's also low risk of an attack by tropical sharks on scuba divers in northern Australian waters. Great white sharks are now few in number in the temperate southern waters. Check with surf-lifesaving groups about local risks.

The risk of crocodile attack in tropical northern Australia is real but predictable and largely preventable. Discuss the local risk with police or tourist agencies before swimming in rivers, water holes and in the sea.

SNAKES

Australian snakes have a fearful reputation that is justified in terms of the potency of their venom, but unjustified in terms of the actual risk to travellers and locals. Snakes are usually quite timid and in most instances will move away if disturbed. They have small fangs, making it easy to prevent bites to the lower limbs (where 80% of bites occur) by wearing protective clothing (such as gaiters) when bushwalking. The bite marks are very small and may even go unnoticed.

In all confirmed or suspected bites, prevent the spread of venom by applying pressure to the wound and immobilising the area with a splint or sling before seeking medical attention. Firmly wrap an elastic bandage (you can improvise with a T-shirt) around the entire limb, but not so tight as to cut off the circulation. Along with immobilisation, this is a life-saving first-aid measure.

SPIDERS

Australia has a number of poisonous spiders. The Sydney funnel-web spider causes severe local pain, as well as generalised symptoms (vomiting, abdominal pain and sweating). Antivenin exists, so apply pressure to the wound and immobilise the area before transferring to a hospital.

Red-back spiders are found throughout the country. Bites cause pain at the site followed by profuse sweating and generalised symptoms (including muscular weakness, sweating at the site of the bite and nausea). First aid includes application of ice or cold packs to the bite, then transfer to hospital.

White-tailed spider bites may cause an ulcer that is difficult to heal. Clean the wound thoroughly and seek medical assistance.

HEALTH

Heatstroke

There's very hot weather all year round in northern Queensland and during the summer months for most of the country. When arriving from a temperate or cold climate, it takes two weeks for acclimatisation to occur. Before the body is acclimatised an excessive amount of salt is lost in perspiration, so increasing the salt in your diet is essential.

Heat exhaustion occurs when fluid intake does not keep up with fluid loss. Symptoms include dizziness, fainting, fatigue, nausea or vomiting. On observation the skin is usually pale, cool and clammy. Treatment consists of rest in a cool, shady place and fluid replacement with water or diluted sports drinks.

Heatstroke is a severe form of heat illness that occurs after fluid depletion or extreme heat challenge from heavy exercise. This is a medical emergency, with heating of the brain leading to disorientation, hallucinations and seizures. Heatstroke is prevented by maintaining an adequate fluid intake to ensure the continued passage of clear and copious urine, especially during physical exertion.

A number of unprepared travellers die from dehydration each year in outback Australia. This can be prevented by following these simple rules:

- Carry sufficient water for any trip including extra in case of breakdown.
- Always let someone, such as the local police, know where you are going and when you expect to arrive.
- Carry communications equipment of some form.
- Stay with the vehicle rather than walking for help.

Hypothermia

Hypothermia is a significant risk, especially during the winter months in southern parts of Australia. Despite the absence of high mountain ranges, strong winds produce a high chill factor that can result in hypothermia even in moderately cool temperatures. Early signs include the inability to perform fine movements (such as doing up buttons), shivering and a bad case of the 'umbles' (fumbles, mumbles, grumbles, stumbles). The key elements of treatment include moving out of the cold, changing out of wet clothing into dry clothes with wind- and water-proof layers, adding insulation and providing fuel (water and carbohydrate) to allow shivering, which builds the internal temperature. In severe hypothermia, shivering actually stops; this is a medical emergency requiring rapid evacuation in addition to the above measures.

Insect-Borne Illness

Various insects can be a source of irritation and, in Australia, may be the source of specific diseases (dengue fever, Ross River fever). Protection from mosquitoes, sandflies, ticks and leeches can be achieved by a combination of the following strategies:

- wear loose-fitting long-sleeved clothing
- apply 30% DEET on all exposed skin and repeating every three to four hours
- impregnate clothing with permethrin (an insecticide that kills insects but is completely safe to humans).

Surf Beaches & Drowning

The East Coast has exceptional surf, but beaches vary in their conditions: the slope offshore can result in changeable and often powerful surf. Check with local surf-lifesaving organisations and be aware of your expertise and limitations before entering the water.

Ultraviolet Light Exposure

Australia has one of the highest rates of skin cancer in the world. Monitor your exposure to sunlight closely. UV is strongest between 10am and 4pm so avoid skin exposure during these times. Always use 30+ sunscreen, apply 30 minutes before going into the sun and repeat regularly to minimise damage.

Water-Borne Illness

Tap water is universally safe in the region. Increasing numbers of lakes, streams and rivers, however, are contaminated by bugs that cause diarrhoea, making water purification essential. The simplest way for you to purify water is to boil it thoroughly.

Consider purchasing a water filter. It's very important to read the specifications, so that you know exactly what it removes from the water and what it doesn't. Filtering will not remove all dangerous organisms, so if you can't boil water it should be treated chemically. Chlorine tablets will kill many pathogens, but not some parasites like giardia and amoebic cysts. Iodine is more effective in purifying water and is available in tablet form. Follow the directions carefully and remember that too much iodine can be harmful.

Glossary

ACT – Australian Capital Territory
ALP – Australian Labor Party
Anzac – Australian and New Zealand Army Corps
award wage – minimum pay rate

bastard – form of address which can mean many things, from high praise or respect ('He's the bravest bastard I know') to dire insult ('You rotten bastard!'). Avoid using if unsure!
BBQ – barbecue
bêche-de-mer – sea cucumber
bevan – mildly abusive Queensland term for an unsophisticated youth
bogan – mildly abusive term for an unsophisticated youth
boogie board – half-sized surfboard
billabong – ox-bow bend in a river cut off by changed watercourse (a water hole)
billy – tin container used to boil tea in the *bush*
bitumen – surfaced road
bombora – isolate patch of offshore reef ('bommie')
boom netting – riding through the surf on nets in the front or rear of a travelling boat
boomerang – curved, flat, wooden implement traditionally used by Aboriginal people for hunting
booner – mildly abusive *ACT* term for an unsophisticated youth
bora ring – circular area ringed with banked earth used for Aboriginal ceremonial purposes, created mainly in *NSW* and southeastern Queensland
bottleshop – liquor store, off-licence
box jellyfish – species of deadly jellyfish; also known as sea wasp, box jelly, sea jelly, stinger
brekkie – breakfast
bug – Moreton Bay/Balmain bug, a small edible crustacean
bunyip – mythical *bush* animal or spirit
bush tucker – native foods, usually in the *outback*
bush, the – countryside, usually covered with trees or shrubs; anywhere away from the city
bushranger – Australia's equivalent to the outlaws of the Wild West (some goodies, some baddies)
BYO – bring your own; a restaurant licence that permits customers to drink alcohol they have purchased elsewhere

camp-o-tel – semi-permanent tent with beds and lights
chook – chicken
counter meal – pub meal, usually eaten at the bar
cuppa – 'cup of' tea, coffee etc

dag – dirty lump of wool at back end of a sheep; affectionate or mildly abusive term for an unfashionable or socially inept person

damper – bush loaf made from flour and water and cooked in a fire or camp oven
DEET – N, N diethyl-*m*-toluamide (a broad-spectrum insect repellent)
didjeridu, didj – cylindrical wooden musical instrument traditionally played by Aboriginal men
donga – sugar-cane cutter's cabin (archaic); prefabricated transportable cabin
Dreamtime, the – concept that forms the basis of Aboriginal spirituality, incorporating the creation of the world and spiritual energies around us
Dry, the – dry season in northern Australia
dunny – outdoor lavatory

Eftpos – electronic funds transfer at point of sale (method of paying for goods or services, or withdrawing cash)
EPA – Environmental Protection Agency (Queensland government department that runs the *QPWS*)

flake – shark meat, often served in fish and chip shops
freshie – freshwater crocodile
4WD – four wheel drive vehicle

galah – noisy cockatoo; noisy idiot
grog – general term for alcoholic drinks
gum tree – eucalyptus tree

jackeroo – young male trainee on a *station*
jillaroo – young female trainee on a *station*
jumper – sweater; pullover

Koorie – collective term used to identify Aboriginal people from southeastern Australia

lamington – square of sponge cake covered in chocolate icing and coconut
larrikin – someone who is playfully mischievous
lay-by – a deposit on an article so the shop will hold it for you
live-aboard – cruise or dive boat offering accommodation

mal – Malibu surfboard
mangrove – coastal tree that grows in salt water
middy – 285ml glass of beer, NSW; see *pot*
milk bar – general store
Mod Oz – modern Australian cuisine, influenced by a wide range of foreign cuisines, but with a definite local flavour
mozzies – mosquitoes
Murri – collective term used to identify Aboriginal people from northeastern Australia

GLOSSARY

NRMA – National Roads and Motorists Association (*NSW* automobile club)
NSW – New South Wales
outback – remote part of the *bush*

paddock – fenced area of land, usually intended for livestock
PADI – Professional Association of Diving Instructors, an international diving organisation that provides scuba training
pokies – poker machines
pot – 285ml glass of beer, Vic and Queensland; see *middy*

QPWS – Queensland Parks & Wildlife Service (parks division of the *EPA*)
Queenslander – traditional raised timber dwelling; resident of Queensland

RACQ – Royal Automobile Club of Queensland
RACV – Royal Automobile Club of Victoria
rashie – 'rash-vest', UV-resistant skin-tight surfing top
road train – a truck pulling a number of linked trailers (semitrailer-trailer-trailer)
RSL – Returned Servicemen's League, or community venue operated by same
saltie – saltwater or estuarine crocodile
scarr tree – a tree from which bark has been removed and treated to make canoes, dishes, shields or other items
scrub – *bush*; trees, shrubs and other plants growing in an arid area
sea wasp – deadly *box jellyfish*

sealed road – hard-surfaced or bitumen-covered road
shout – buy a round of drinks (as in 'It's your shout')
SLSC – Surf Life Saving Club, a branch of the *Surf Life Saving Association*, or community venue operated by same
station – large farm
stinger – deadly *box jellyfish*
Stolen Generations – generations of Indigenous children forcibly removed from their parents
stubby – 375ml bottle of beer
Surf Life Saving Association – a water safety and rescue authority primarily staffed by volunteers
swag – canvas-covered bed-roll used in the *outback*; a large quantity
swagman – (archaic) vagabond; itinerant labourer

terra nullius – legal concept that Australia was uninhabited at the time of British colonisation
thongs – flip-flops (footwear)
tinny – 375ml can of beer; small, aluminium fishing dinghy
tucker – food

vegie – vegetable; vegetarian

walkabout – lengthy walk away from it all
wattle – Australian acacia species with furry, yellow flowers
Wet, the – wet season in northern Australia

yabbie – freshwater crayfish
yum cha – classic southern Chinese dumpling feast

Behind the Scenes

This Book

Lonely Planet's *East Coast Australia* was first published in 2002, the brainchild of Greg Alford and Jane Thompson, delivered through the hard work of authors Verity Campbell, Pete Cruttenden, Kate Daly and Chris Rowthorn (and a slew of in-housers). This second edition was coordinated by Lindsay Brown, who also wrote half the Queensland chapters. Simone Egger assisted in Queensland, while NSW was written by Sandra Bao, Ryan Ver Berkmoes and Simon Sellars. Simon also wrote a considerable proportion of the front matter, including Destination East Coast Australia, Snapshot and The Culture. Cathy Lanigan wrote the two Victoria chapters. Michael Cathcart wrote the History chapter, Tim Flannery wrote the Environment chapter and Matthew Evans covered Food & Drink.

As well as the authors above, we acknowledge the tireless research efforts of Justine Vaisutis (Queensland), Paul Smitz (Canberra), Sally O'Brien (Melbourne) and Nina Rousseau (Around Melbourne).

THANKS from the Authors

Lindsay Brown A big thanks to the always helpful staff patrolling the information centres on the Capricorn and Whitsunday coasts. Thanks to Stefanie, Marg, Errol and Corinne at Lonely Planet for coordinating my East Coast wanderings and special thanks to Jenny, Patrick and Sinead for their patience, support and love.

Sandra Bao Sydney is full of gracious and very helpful folks whose contributions greatly aided my work during the research of this book. I met them everywhere I went, and their friendliness made this Lonely Planet gig one of my best ever. But I'd like to thank one person especially for his help and companionship – my friend Dilip Varma. A quick nod also to Sydney's very helpful tourist staff and to fellow authors Ryan Ver Berkmoes and Paul Smitz. And as always thanks to Mom, Dad and Daniel, for behind-the-scenes support. Last but not least, my husband Ben's help made this project possible. I couldn't have done it nearly as well without you by my side, sweetie – even when you were back home!

Ryan Ver Berkmoes Huge thanks go to Errol Hunt, Stefanie Di Trocchio, Corie Waddell and many others in the Lonely Planet Melbourne office. These amazing people worked miracles (at no small cost to their own sanity) so I could divert my energies from this book to the tragedies of the Indian Ocean tsunami. I am also indebted to the many fine folks up and down the coast of NSW who helped me understand the multitude of pleasures possible.

Simone Egger Thanks to Justine Vaisutis, Marg Toohey and Errol Hunt from Lonely Planet, and all those vigilant readers who actually get around to writing in. Huge thanks to Warren Egger, Leahey, Simon King, Ruthie Davis and mum.

Cath Lanigan Thanks to Parks Victoria staff, particularly Graeme Baxter, Andrew Schulze, and Peter Kershaw for nitty gritty details on national parks; Rhonda James at East Gippsland Shire Council for

---

THE LONELY PLANET STORY

The story begins with a classic travel adventure: Tony and Maureen Wheeler's 1972 journey across Europe and Asia to Australia. There was no useful information about the overland trail then, so Tony and Maureen published the first Lonely Planet guidebook to meet a growing need.

From a kitchen table, Lonely Planet has grown to become the largest independent travel publisher in the world, with offices in Melbourne (Australia), Oakland (USA) and London (UK). Today Lonely Planet guidebooks cover the globe. There is an ever-growing list of books and information in a variety of media. Some things haven't changed. The main aim is still to make it possible for adventurous travellers to get out there – to explore and better understand the world.

At Lonely Planet we believe travellers can make a positive contribution to the countries they visit – if they respect their host communities and spend their money wisely. Every year 5% of company profit is donated to charities around the world.

information on local transport innovations; Andrea Hall, Jenny Doran, Eva Schain, Kirstie Pearce, Barb Young, Jack Travis, Deb Morgan, Hilary Rigg, Jenny Hurley, Pauline Crunden, Rachel Hughes and Helen Wilson for Gippsland eating recommendations; Noel and Fiona Maud in South Gippsland for local recommendations and inspiration; and a huge thanks to my partner John for doing all the driving, helping with the maps and providing constant support, and big, big thanks to Zoe for researching all of Gippsland's playgrounds. Thanks to Marg and Stef for all their in-house support.

Simon Sellars Thanks to Daniel New for braving the coast with me. And to Rachel Thorpe for everything else. At Lonely Planet, thanks to Stefanie Di Trocchio, Errol Hunt, Lucy Monie, Csanad Csutoros, Hunor Csutoros and Michael Day for invaluable insider trading.

Credits

Commissioning Editors Stefanie Di Trocchio, Errol Hunt, Marg Toohey
Coordinating Editor Lucy Monie
Coordinating Cartographer Anthony Phelan
Coordinating Layout Designer Laura Jane
Managing Editors Brigitte Ellemor, Jennifer Garrett, Stephanie Pearson
Managing Cartographer Corie Waddell
Assisting Editors Charlotte Orr, Kyla Gillzan, Trent Holden
Assisting Cartographers Jolyon Philcox, Helen Rowley, Malisa Plesa, Valentina Kremenchutskaya, Sarah Sloane
Assisting Layout Designer Indra Kilfoyle
Cover Designer Gerilyn Atteberry
Project Manager Ray Thomson
Thanks to Fiona Siseman for permissions work; Jen Mundy-Nordin for readers' letters; Vivek Wagle. Thanks also to the authors for coping with what was a monumental and sometimes bamboozling task. Special thanks to Lindsay and Simon, who agreed at short notice to radically extend the scope of their involvement with this book.

THANKS from Lonely Planet

Many thanks to the following travellers who used the last edition and wrote to us with helpful hints, useful advice and interesting anecdotes.

A Tina Abbey, Juliet Allan, Ruth Ann, Stephanie B Arnold, Neal Ashcroft **B** MA Beevers, Marcus & Astrid Beitelhoff, James Bell, Sarianna & Pierre-Yves Benain, Anne Bennett, Gerry Bieker, Silvia & Egbert Boertien, John & Karen Bolton, Mark Boon, Roy Bossons, Michael Bratvold, Michael Broderick, Steve Brookwell, James Brown, Donna Bush **C** Lisa Cardus, MR Carter, Sharon Chandler, Jean Chapple, Matthew Charles, Arthur Chiang, Dawna Chow, Eleanor & Peter Christensen, Lynn Clark, Todd Clark, Lynn Clarke, Alex Cohen, Melissa Cole, Rebecca Curtis **D** Marion Dale Lage, Elke Dausch,

Trina Davies, David Dawson, Erik de Ryk, M Deibert, Emmanuel Demanez, Helen Dempsey, Sylvia DeNardi, Jen Diamond, Heribert Dieter, Gabrielle Dijon, Matthias Dnrbeck, Julie Douglas, Beth Dowle **E** Susann Elmquist Bentsen, Wolfram Engelhardt, Alexander Etterich, Chris P Evans **F** Tara Farley, Tony Feeney, Jesse Ferris, Russell Fowlie, Richard Fox Prof, Samantha Fraser, Andreas Friman, Nadine Funke **G** Barb Garii, Joao Girao, Peter Granquist, T Gray Shaw, Alenka Grealish, Roger Griffiths **H** Mark Halle, Christine & John Hamilton, Rob Haub, Al Herbert, Pia Hesse Kovstrup, Pettina Hodgson, Matt Holden, Chris & Jan Hopkins, Mark Huard, Rebeca & Kim Humphreys, A Hutchinson, A & C Hutchinson **I** Jo Ilbury, Kas Io **J** Isa Johansson, Karen Johnson, Tony Johnson, Volkmar Junge **K** Barbara A Kelly, Linda Kibak, Tanja Klagge, Angela Knuchel, K Kreider, Joni Kyle **L** Stuart Lacey, Susanna Lackner, M Lage, Lindy Laing, Susan Lang, Lisa Leef, Kurt Lehmann, Julie Lemieux, Gina Lempa, Gina & Leonard Lempa, Rain Lily, Sari Lindvall, Heather Linson Lindberg, Geoff & Judith Lomas, Debbie Lord, Susan Lorette, Nancy Lowell, Prema & Raj Lucas **M** Karen Mancey-Barratt, Harry Manzinger, Julia Margetson, Christian Martin, Miquel Martin, Wendy Matthews, Wolfgang Mayr, Malcolm & Denise McDonaugh, Paul McGuinness, Jens Meincke, Sandra Menzel, Glen Menzies, Anne Miller, David S Miller, Lynn Miller, Alison Mills, Ian Morphett, Carl Mott **N** AR Newton, M Nichols, Mannela Noack **O** Mariko Obokata, Simone Ortmann **P** Jo Patel, Lary Peevey, GB Poppelwell **R** David Reeder, Pauline Reeves, John Reid, Sarah Reid, Gail Rendle, Margitta Retz, Gail Revesz, Charles Robb, Becky Robinson, Jo Robinson, Andrea Rogge, Susanne Runde, Johnnie H Russell **S** Udo J Sabock, Bill Sanders, Volker Sauer, Andi Scheef, Gunther Schaefer, Jonathan Sheridan-

BEHIND THE SCENES

Jones, Paul Simonite, Renu Singh, M Skadsen, Annemarie Skerrett, Rilke Slatt, Tara Smale, Barry Smiler, Glenys Spence, Michaela Spettmann, Jay Stewart, Jan Stieber, Niels Stoffers, Magnus Stomfelt, Akos Szent-Istvany **T** Bob & Halcyon Thomas, Gerald Thompson, Connie Toews, Judy Trombly, Gregory Tuck **U** Stephen M Usery **V** Diederik Vanderburg, Karen Vaughan, Claus Viref, Rene Volchansky **W** Alun Wall, Chris Walsh, Mercedes Warner, Janine Watson, Erich Weigele, Knut Werner, Sarah & Paul Westcar, Nicola Whiteoak, Daniel Whui, Martin Wielecki, Allen Wilbourne, Carol Wilson, Cindy Wilson, Jean-Philippe Wispelaere, Martin Wood, Keith Worby, Rolk Wrelf, Chandi Wyant **Y** Charles Yap, Robert Youker **Z** Natalie Zacek, Bernhard Zeimetz

ACKNOWLEDGMENTS

Many thanks to the following for the use of their content:
CityRail's Sydney Suburban Network Map © 2005 CityRail; Sydney Ferries Corporation Network Map © 2004 Sydney Ferries Corporation; Melbourne Train Network Map © 2005 Metlink

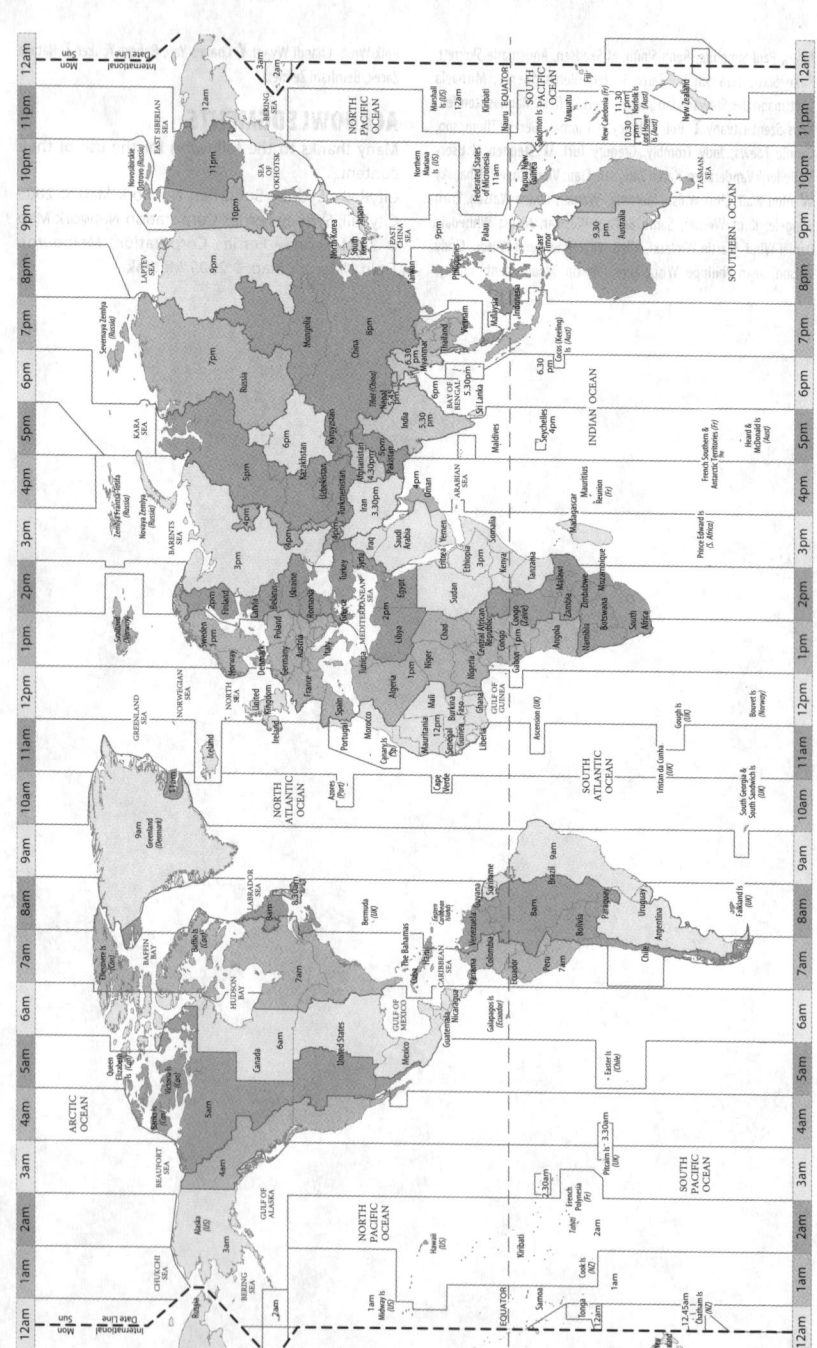

Index

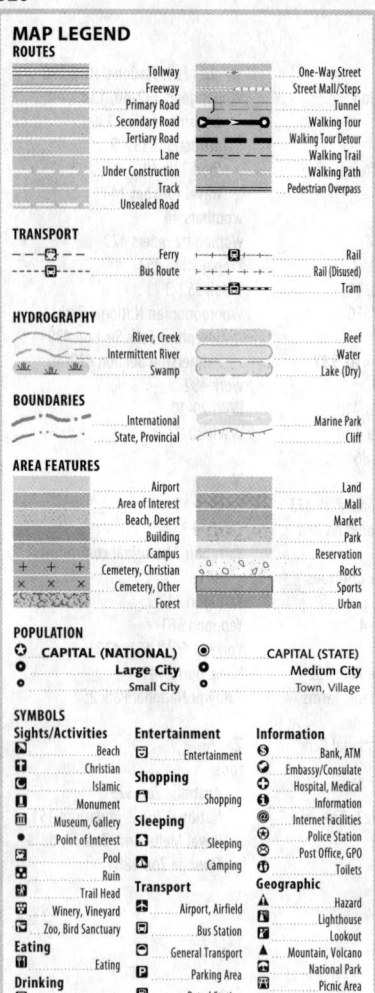

MAP LEGEND

ROUTES

Tollway	One-Way Street
Freeway	Street Mall/Steps
Primary Road	Tunnel
Secondary Road	Walking Tour
Tertiary Road	Walking Tour Detour
Lane	Walking Trail
Under Construction	Walking Path
Track	Pedestrian Overpass
Unsealed Road	

TRANSPORT

Ferry	Rail
Bus Route	Rail (Disused)
	Tram

HYDROGRAPHY

River, Creek	Reef
Intermittent River	Water
Swamp	Lake (Dry)

BOUNDARIES

International	Marine Park
State, Provincial	Cliff

AREA FEATURES

Airport	Land
Area of Interest	Mall
Beach, Desert	Market
Building	Park
Campus	Reservation
Cemetery, Christian	Rocks
Cemetery, Other	Sports
Forest	Urban

POPULATION

✪ CAPITAL (NATIONAL)	◉ CAPITAL (STATE)
● Large City	● Medium City
○ Small City	○ Town, Village

SYMBOLS

Sights/Activities
- Beach
- Christian
- Islamic
- Monument
- Museum, Gallery
- Point of Interest
- Pool
- Ruin
- Trail Head
- Winery, Vineyard
- Zoo, Bird Sanctuary

Eating
- Eating

Drinking
- Drinking
- Café

Entertainment
- Entertainment

Shopping
- Shopping

Sleeping
- Sleeping
- Camping

Transport
- Airport, Airfield
- Bus Station
- General Transport
- Parking Area
- Petrol Station
- Taxi Rank

Information
- Bank, ATM
- Embassy/Consulate
- Hospital, Medical
- Information
- Internet Facilities
- Police Station
- Post Office, GPO
- Toilets

Geographic
- Hazard
- Lighthouse
- Lookout
- Mountain, Volcano
- National Park
- Picnic Area
- River Flow
- Waterfall

LONELY PLANET OFFICES

Australia
Head Office
Locked Bag 1, Footscray, Victoria 3011
☎ 03 8379 8000, fax 03 8379 8111
talk2us@lonelyplanet.com.au

USA
150 Linden St, Oakland, CA 94607
☎ 510 893 8555, toll free 800 275 8555
fax 510 893 8572, info@lonelyplanet.com

UK
72-82 Rosebery Ave,
Clerkenwell, London EC1R 4RW
☎ 020 7841 9000, fax 020 7841 9001
go@lonelyplanet.co.uk

Published by Lonely Planet Publications Pty Ltd
ABN 36 005 607 983

2nd Edition – Oct 2005

First Published – Oct 2002